Presented to

**Kingwood Branch Library**

By

**Donated by the National Charity**
**League – Kingwood Chapter**

Harris County
Public Library

*your pathway to knowledge*

# Gale Contextual Encyclopedia of American Literature

# Gale Contextual Encyclopedia of American Literature

VOLUME 1

**A–E**

GALE
CENGAGE Learning

Detroit • New York • San Francisco • New Haven, Conn • Waterville, Maine • London

**Gale Contextual Encyclopedia
of American Literature**

Project Editors: Anne Marie Hacht and Dwayne
   D. Hayes

Editorial: Ira Mark Milne

Rights Acquisition and Management: Kelly Quin,
   Robyn Young, and Tracie Richardson

Composition: Evi Abou-El-Seoud

Manufacturing: Wendy Blurton

Imaging: John Watkins

Product Design: Jennifer Wahi and Pam Galbreath

© 2009 Gale, a part of Cengage Learning

For product information and technology assistance, contact us at
**Gale Customer Support, 1-800-877-4253.**
For permission to use material from this text or product,
submit all requests online at **www.cengage.com/permissions.**
Further permissions questions can be emailed to
**permissionrequest@cengage.com**

Cover photographs reproduced by permission. Steinbeck, John, photograph. The
Library of Congress; Angelou, Maya, photograph. AP Images; Fitzgerald, F. Scott,
photograph. The Library of Congress; Twain, Mark, photograph. The Library of Congress;
Poe, Edgar Allan, public domain; London, Jack, photograph. The Library of Congress;
Hughes, Langston, 1943, photo by Gordon Parks. The Library of Congress; Dickinson, Emily.
The Library of Congress; Hemingway, Ernest, photograph. AP Images; Hemingway, Ernest,
photograph. AP Images; Lee, Harper, photograph. AP Images; Tan, Amy, 1993, photograph.
AP Images; Walker, Alice, photograph. AP Images.

While every effort has been made to ensure the reliability of the information presented
in this publication, Gale, a part of Cengage Learning, does not guarantee the accuracy of the
data contained herein. Gale accepts no payment for listing; and inclusion in the publication
of any organization, agency, institution, publication, service, or individual does not imply
endorsement of the editors or publisher. Errors brought to the attention of the publisher
and verified to the satisfaction of the publisher will be corrected in future editions.

Editorial Data Privacy Policy. Does this publication contain information about you as
an individual? If so, for more information about our editorial data privacy policies,
please see our Privacy Statement at www.gale.com.

**Library of Congress Cataloging-in-Publication Data**

Gale contextual encyclopedia of American literature / editorial, Anne Marie
Hacht, Dwayne D. Hayes.
    p. cm.
    Includes bibliographical references and index.
    ISBN 978-1-4144-3130-7 (set) -- ISBN 978-1-4144-3131-4 (v. 1) --
ISBN 978-1-4144-3132-1 (v. 2) -- ISBN 978-1-4144-3133-8 (v. 3) --
ISBN 978-1-4144-3134-5 (v. 4) -- ISBN  978-1-4144-3139-0 (e-book)
    1. American literature--Encyclopedias. 2.  American literature--Bio-bibliography.
3. Authors, American--Biography--Dictionaries. 4.  American literature--History and
criticism--Encyclopedias.  I. Hacht, Anne Marie. II. Hayes, Dwayne D.

PS21.G36 2009
810'.9--dc22                                                                    2008051753

978-1-4144-3130-7 (set)              1-4144-3130-9 (set)
978-1-4144-3131-4 (vol. 1)           1-4144-3131-7 (vol. 1)
978-1-4144-3132-1 (vol. 2)           1-4144-3132-5 (vol. 2)
978-1-4144-3133-8 (vol. 3)           1-4144-3133-3 (vol. 3)
978-1-4144-3134-5 (vol. 4)           1-4144-3134-1 (vol. 4)

This title is also available as an e-book.
ISBN-13: 978-1-4144-3139-0 ISBN-10: 1-4144-3139-2
Contact your Gale, a part of Cengage Learning sales representative for ordering information.

Printed in the United States of America
1 2 3 4 5 6 7 13 12 11 10 09

# Contents

## VOLUME 2

### F-G

# H

GALE CONTEXTUAL ENCYCLOPEDIA OF AMERICAN LITERATURE

## VOLUME 3

## L

## N-Q

# VOLUME 4

## R

## S

# Introduction

## How to Use This Book

The *Gale Contextual Encyclopedia of American Literature* is a resource for students who seek information beyond the simple biographical details of an author's life or a brief overview of the author's major works. This book is designed to offer a comprehensive view of how an author's work fits within the context of the author's life, historical events, and the literary world. This allows for a greater understanding of both the author's work and the cultural and historical environment in which it was created.

The *Gale Contextual Encyclopedia of American Literature* is divided into entries, each focused on a particular writer who has made significant contributions to literature. In some cases, these individuals may be known primarily for actions and contributions outside the realm of literature. John F. Kennedy and Martin Luther King Jr., for example, are two figures famous for their political activism; Rachel Carson is known primarily as a biologist and ecologist; Cotton Mather is remembered for his connection to the infamous Salem Witch Trials. However, all of these figures have, aside from their other accomplishments and activities, created significant works of literature that have stood the test of time and affected readers beyond the borders of their own cultures.

This book is best used not just to locate the facts of a writer's life and work, but as a way to understand the social, literary, and historical environment in which the writer lived and created. By understanding the context of the writer's work, you are more likely to recognize key themes and stylistic traits as elements of larger trends in the literary world, as well as understand the impact of historical events from a new and unique perspective.

### Sections Found within Each Entry in This Book

Each entry in this book is divided into three main parts: Works in Biographical and Historical Context; Works in Literary Context; and Works in Critical Context. These sections are discussed below.

In addition, each entry includes: a Key Facts section, containing birth/death date information as well as a list of major works; a Responses to Literature section, containing discussion and writing activities related to the author in question; a

Further Reading section that includes bibliographic citations as well as reputable sources of additional material about the author in the form of books, periodicals, or Web sites; a Literary and Historical Contemporaries sidebar, listing several famous contemporaries of the author; and a Common Human Experience sidebar, offering examples of other literary or artistic works that share themes or techniques with those of the subject of the entry.

***Works in Biographical and Historical Context*** In this section, you will find information about how events and concerns in the author's life helped to shape the author's work. For example, Kurt Vonnegut's experiences in a German prison camp in Dresden during the Allied bombing of that city in 1945 led him to write *Slaughterhouse-Five* (1969), while events surrounding Watergate (the political scandal that brought about the resignation of President Richard Nixon) led him to write *Jailbird* (1979). This section also includes information on historical events or trends that had an effect on the author. For example, the scientific and technological advancements of the late twentieth century greatly influenced the subject matter of the popular fiction of Michael Crichton, which often centered on the theme of modern technology run amok.

***Works in Literary Context*** In this section, you will find information about how the author's work fits within the context of literature in general. This may include a description of a stylistic trait exhibited in the author's writing; for example, Mark Twain is known for his brilliant use of colloquial speech, and information on this technique—as well as examples of how the author used it—can be found in his entry. This section may also include a discussion of the writer's work as it exists within a specific genre, such as Southern Gothic fiction or modernist poetry. Finally, the Works in Literary Context section may contain discussion of specific themes commonly found in the author's work. The writings of James Baldwin, for example, frequently address the theme of race relations.

***Works in Critical Context*** In this section, you will find a survey of critical and popular opinion related to the author and the author's most important works. The emphasis is on contemporary opinions, or those formed by readers and critics at the time the author's work was first published. In some cases, critical or popular opinion from the time of publication may not be available; this may be due simply to the passage of time, or due to the writer's lack of fame during his or her own lifetime. This section also includes information on how critical or popular opinion of an author has changed over time. Herman Melville's masterwork *Moby-Dick* (1851) met with a tepid reception upon publication, but is now considered one of the finest achievements in American literature. Kate Chopin's novella *The Awakening* (1899) earned her critical scorn and ruined her career, but the work is now considered a breakthrough in women's literature. Conversely, some works that enjoyed widespread acclaim initially are less well regarded or even forgotten today. Joel Chandler Harris's *Uncle Remus* books (published between 1880 and 1905) based on African American folk tales were popular with white and black readers in the North and South at the time; today, many critics accuse Harris (a white journalist) of misappropriating elements of African American culture, and his work has fallen out of favor. Likewise, James Branch Cabell was one of the most celebrated writers of the 1920s, made internationally famous because of the scandal stirred up by the obscenity charges attached to his 1919 novel *Jurgen*; today, his work is rarely read.

## Other Information Contained in This Book

In addition to the entries for individual authors, this book also contains a chronology that indicates some major historical events related to the development of American literature. At the end of the book, you will find a glossary of terms—primarily literary and historical in nature—that are used in various entries throughout the book, along with a brief explanation of each term, a general index, and a nationality/ethnicity index.

# Advisory Board

**Alicia Baker Elley**

*taught undergraduate and high school literature, composition, and technical writing classes for over ten years. She is currently district librarian for the Harmony Independent School District in Texas.*

**Maureen Reed**

*has taught literature, history, and American Studies courses at Minnesota State University Moorhead, Lewis and Clark College, and Portland State University. She earned a Ph.D. in American Studies from the University of Texas at Austin and held a Fulbright Lectureship in American Studies at the University of Regensburg in Germany.*

**Roger K. Smith**

*has been a teacher of English, writing, and other humanities courses at such institutions as Ithaca College, Rutgers University, and Edward R. Murrow High School (Brooklyn). He holds a BA from Swarthmore College and an MA from New York University.*

**Patrick Walsh**

*holds a Ph.D. in history from the University of Texas at Austin. He has taught English and Multidisciplinary Studies at Concordia College and Minnesota State University, in Moorhead, Minnesota. A Fulbright Lecturer in American Studies at the University of Passau in Germany, he now teaches at the Catlin Gabel School in Portland, Oregon.*

# Chronology

This chronology contains a brief overview of some of the major events in the history of American literature. This includes the development of technologies and tools that advanced the writing and publishing process, as well as some significant historical events that had an impact on the development of literature.

## 1500–1700

*1576*   English explorers begin searching for the Northwest Passage, a hoped-for water route around North America to Asia.

*1607*   Jamestown settlement established in Virginia.

*1620*   The Pilgrims traveling from England aboard *The Mayflower* reach Cape Cod and form a settlement at Plymouth, Massachusetts.

*1624*   The Dutch establish a city called New Amsterdam on the island of Manhattan. The city later became known as New York City, a major center of American commerce and publishing.

*1630*   Massachusetts Bay Colony Governor John Winthrop begins keeping his journal of life in New England. William Bradford, governor of Plymouth, begins his own book, later titled *History of Plymouth Plantation*.

*1650*   Anne Bradstreet publishes her first volume of poetry.

*1689*   Enlightenment thinker John Locke anonymously publishes *Two Treatises of Government*, a work that attacks the idea of the "divine right" of kings and argues for a government that operates with the consent of the governed. The work exerts a strong influence over eighteenth-century French philosophers and America's founding fathers.

*1692–1693*
          The Salem Witch Trials are conducted. One hundred fifty people are arrested and accused of witchcraft, twenty-nine are convicted, and eighteen are executed.

## 1700–1800

*1702*   Cotton Mather publishes *Magnalia Christi Americana*, described as an ecclesiastical history of New England. It is one of the first works that attempts to define the American experience.

*1718*   The city of New Orleans, Louisiana, is founded by French and Canadian settlers.

*1732*   Benjamin Franklin begins writing *Poor Richard's Almanac*.

*1740*   Religious leader Jonathan Edwards begins writing his *Personal Narrative*.

*1754–1763*
          The French and Indian War is fought between France and Great Britain and their respective Native American allies. The conflict is part of a broader power struggle between France and Great Britain that is waged in Europe (the Seven Years War).

*1762*   Jean-Jacques Rousseau publishes *The Social Contract*, a landmark work of political philosophy.

1767  Daniel Boone explores territory west of the Appalachian Mountains.

1770  British soldiers fire into a crowd of rowdy, protesting colonists in Boston, killing five. The event, which helps spark the American Revolution, becomes known as the Boston Massacre.

1773  The British Parliament enacts the Tea Act; in protest, a group of men dressed as Native Americans dump a shipment of tea from Great Britain into Boston Harbor, an event called the Boston Tea Party.

1774  The British Parliament passes measures collectively known as the Intolerable Acts in an effort to punish Massachusetts for the Boston Tea Party.

1775  Patrick Henry gives his famous "Give me liberty, or give me death" speech; Paul Revere goes on his "midnight ride" to warn colonists to take arms against approaching British soldiers; Minutemen fight the British in Lexington and Concord, the first battles of the American Revolution.

1776  Thomas Paine publishes *Common Sense*; Thomas Jefferson writes, and Congress adopts, the Declaration of Independence.

1781  British general Charles Cornwallis surrenders to American General George Washington at Yorktown, ending the American Revolution.

1789  A mob storms the Bastille prison in Paris, France, setting off the French Revolution.

1794  Thomas Paine publishes *The Age of Reason*.

## 1800–1900

1800  John Chapman, also known as "Johnny Appleseed," travels through the Ohio Valley region giving settlers apple seeds.

1803  President Thomas Jefferson negotiates with France to purchase the Louisiana Territory for $15 million; Jefferson sets Meriwether Lewis and William Clark off on an expedition of the newly acquired territory and the lands west of it for the purpose of determining whether a water route existed between the Missouri River and the Pacific Ocean.

1812–1815
      Great Britain and the United States fight the War of 1812.

1819  Washington Irving publishes *The Sketch Book* containing such well-known short stories as "The Legend of Sleepy Hollow" and "Rip Van Winkle."

1820  Congress passes the Missouri Compromise, by which slavery is prohibited in the northern Louisiana territory, Maine is admitted to the Union as a free state, and Missouri is admitted as a slave state. The delicate balance between the interests of slave and free states is preserved for the next three decades.

1821  Sequoyah develops a Native American alphabet and uses it to help Cherokees read and write their own language.

1831  Nat Turner leads a slave rebellion in Virginia in which fifty-five white people are killed; Turner is captured and executed; several eastern Native American tribes are removed from their homelands and forced to march to Oklahoma Territory, a harsh, deadly journey dubbed "the trail of tears."

1832  Samuel Morse invents the telegraph.

1836  Texas declares its independence after revolting against Mexico; Ralph Waldo Emerson publishes *Nature*.

1841  Brook Farm, a utopian cooperative, is established in West Roxbury, Massachusetts, by Unitarian minister George Ripley.

1845  The United States annexes Texas.

1846–1847
      Mexican-American War waged; the United States wins the short war, and gains much of what is now the western United States, including present-day California, Arizona, Nevada, Utah, New Mexico, Colorado, and Wyoming.

1848  Women's Rights Convention held in Seneca Falls, New York.

1849  After gold is discovered in California in 1848, a rush of prospectors—known as forty-niners—flood into California in hopes of striking it rich.

1850  Nathaniel Hawthorne publishes *The Scarlet Letter*; after much bitter debate, Congress passes the Compromise of 1850, which includes multiple provisions designed to maintain a balance between the relative power of slave and free states in Congress.

1851  Herman Melville publishes *Moby-Dick*.

1852  Harriet Beecher Stowe publishes *Uncle Tom's Cabin*.

1854  Henry David Thoreau publishes *Walden*.

1855  Walt Whitman publishes his first version of the poetry collection *Leaves of Grass*.

1859  Abolitionist John Brown attacks the U.S. arsenal at Harper's Ferry, West Virginia, in an attempt to gain weapons to start a slave insurrection; he is captured, tried, and hanged.

1861–1865
      United States Civil War fought between the Union and the pro-slavery Confederate States of America. The war is effectively ended with the surrender of Confederate general Robert E. Lee to Union general Ulysses S. Grant, in Appomattox, Virginia, in 1865; President Abraham Lincoln is assassinated in 1865.

1869  The Fifteenth Amendment to the Constitution grants African Americans the right to vote.

1876  Alexander Graham Bell invents the telephone.

1879  Thomas Edison invents the electric light bulb.

1884  Mark Twain publishes *Adventures of Huckleberry Finn*.

1890  *The Poems of Emily Dickinson* is published posthumously, by the poet's sister.

1895  Stephen Crane publishes *The Red Badge of Courage*.

1898  The United States and Spain fight the Spanish-American War. The United States quickly wins the war, and gains Puerto Rico, Guam, and the Philippines. The war establishes the United States as a major world power.

## 1900–Now

1901  A major oil strike is made at Spindletop, Texas.

1903  Orville and Wilbur Wright launch the first successful manned airplane flight in Kitty Hawk, North Carolina; Henry Ford founds the Ford Motor Company.

1909  The National Association for the Advancement of Colored People (NAACP) is formed.

1914  World War I begins in Europe.

1917  The United States enters World War I on the side of the Entente Powers.

1918  Germany and its allies are defeated, and World War I ends.

1920  The Nineteenth Amendment to the Constitution grants women the right to vote.

1925  F. Scott Fitzgerald publishes *The Great Gatsby*.

1926  Ernest Hemingway publishes *The Sun Also Rises*; the Radio Corporation of America (RCA) organizes the National Broadcasting Company (NBC): the first radio network set up for public entertainment and information.

1927  American pilot Charles Lindbergh flies solo across the Atlantic Ocean from New York to France.

1929  The U.S. stock market crashes, causing financial panic; William Faulkner publishes *The Sound and the Fury*.

1929–1939
      The Great Depression, a global economic downturn, causes widespread unemployment and deflation.

1932  Amelia Earhart becomes first woman to fly solo across the Atlantic Ocean.

1936  Eugene O'Neill wins Nobel Prize in Literature.

1938  Thorton Wilder publishes the play *Our Town*; Pearl S. Buck wins Nobel Prize in Literature.

1939  World War II begins in Europe with the German invasion of Poland.

1940  Richard Wright publishes *Native Son*; Carson McCullers publishes *The Heart Is a Lonely Hunter*.

1941  Japanese fighter pilots attack the United States naval base at Pearl Harbor, Hawaii. The United States declares war on Japan and, subsequently, on Japanese ally Germany, effecting U.S. entry into World War II; the U.S. begins the Manhattan Project, a secret program to develop an atomic bomb.

1942  President Franklin Roosevelt signs an executive order authorizing the forced relocation of Japanese Americans to internment camps for the duration of the war.

1945  The United States drops atomic bombs on the Japanese cities of Hiroshima and Nagasaki, killing more than 100,000 people. Japan surrenders. Germany surrenders.

1947  Jackie Robinson becomes the first African American major-league baseball player; Tennessee Williams publishes the play *A Streetcar Named Desire*.

1948    Congress approves the Marshall Plan for the reconstruction and assistance of Europe; Jewish state of Israel proclaimed; first television broadcast of *Texaco Star Theater*, hosted by Milton Berle—the first major television program in America.

1949    William Faulkner wins Nobel Prize in Literature.

1950    Senator Joseph McCarthy claims that the United States State Department has been infiltrated by communists; President Harry Truman sends U.S. troops to Korea after communist North Korea invades pro-Western South Korea; Isaac Asimov publishes *I, Robot*.

1951    J. D. Salinger publishes *The Catcher in the Rye*.

1953    Senator Joseph McCarthy becomes chairman of the Senate Committee on Government Operations and launches his notorious investigations into purported communist activity in the United States.

1954    The Supreme Court case *Brown v. the Board of Education of Topeka* declares segregation in public schools unconstitutional; Ernest Hemingway wins Nobel Prize in Literature.

1955    Dr. Martin Luther King Jr. leads the Montgomery Bus Boycott.

1957    Jack Kerouac publishes *On the Road*; Theodore Seuss Geisel (Dr. Seuss) publishes *The Cat in the Hat*; the Soviet Union launches *Sputnik 1*, sparking the U.S./Soviet space race.

1959    Lorraine Hansberry publishes the play *A Raisin in the Sun*.

1960    Harper Lee publishes *To Kill a Mockingbird*; birth control pills are made available to the public.

1962    Cuban Missile Crisis occurs: a tense standoff between nuclear superpowers the United States and the Soviet Union; John Steinbeck wins Nobel Prize in Literature.

1963    President John F. Kennedy assassinated in Dallas, Texas.

1964    Congress passes the Civil Rights Act, prohibiting racial discrimination in public places.

1965    President Lyndon Johnson escalates hostilities against North Vietnam, ordering bombing raids; Dr. Martin Luther King Jr. leads a civil rights march from Selma to Montgomery, Alabama; African American rights activist Malcolm X assassinated; Voting Rights Act passed by Congress.

1968    Martin Luther King Jr. assassinated; presidential candidate Robert Kennedy assassinated.

1969    Kurt Vonnegut publishes *Slaughterhouse-Five*; astronaut Neil Armstrong becomes first human to set foot on the moon.

1974    President Richard Nixon resigns in the wake of the Watergate scandal.

1975    Vietnam War ends.

1976    Saul Bellow wins Nobel Prize in Literature.

1978    Isaac Bashevis Singer wins Nobel Prize in Literature.

1979    Radical Islamists storm the American embassy in Iran and take fifty-two hostages, most of whom are held for 444 days.

1981    The IBM personal computer first becomes available.

1984    Sandra Cisneros publishes *The House on Mango Street*.

1986    Cormac McCarthy publishes *Blood Meridian*.

1989    The Berlin Wall is torn down.

1990    First commercial dial-up access to the Internet becomes available; the Soviet Union collapses, and independent nations are formed of its former territory.

1993    Toni Morrison wins Nobel Prize in Literature.

1998    President Bill Clinton impeached by the U.S. House of Representatives.

2001    In a coordinated suicide mission, radical Islamists associated with terrorist organization al-Qaeda hijack commercial airliners and crash them into the World Trade Center in New York City and the Pentagon building in Virginia, killing nearly 3,000 people; Jonathan Franzen publishes *The Corrections*.

2003    The United States invades Iraq and topples the regime of Saddam Hussein.

2009    Barack Obama sworn in as president of the United States, the first African American ever elected to that office.

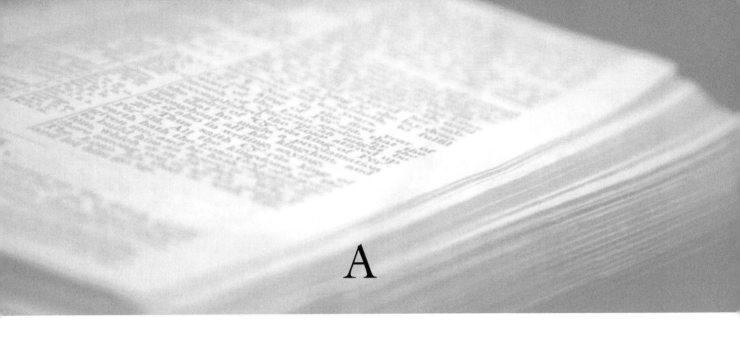

# A

# Abigail Adams

BORN: *1744, Weymouth, Massachusetts*

DIED: *1818, Quincy, Massachusetts*

NATIONALITY: *American*

GENRE: *Nonfiction*

MAJOR WORKS:

*Letters of Mrs. Adams, The Wife of John Adams* (1840)

*The Familiar Letters of John Adams and His Wife Abigail During the Revolution* (1875)

*New Letters of Abigail Adams, 1788–1801* (1947)

*The Book of Abigail and John; Selected Letters of the Adams Family, 1762–1784* (1975)

*My Dearest Friend: Letters of Abigail and John Adams* (2007)

## Overview

In a literary context, Abigail Adams is best known for the thousands of letters she wrote from the 1760s until her death in 1818. The wife of John Adams, the second president of the United States, and the mother of John Quincy Adams, the sixth president, Abigail Adams's correspondence reflected a woman's experience during this key era in American history. Adams's letters to her husband and others include information on her domestic life as well as her commentary on the political, social, and cultural events of her time. Thousands of her letters survived and have been published in several collections beginning in the mid-nineteenth century.

## Works in Biographical and Historical Context

***Traditional Puritan Family*** Adams was born Abigail Smith in Weymouth, Massachusetts, on November 11, 1744, the daughter of Reverend William Smith and his wife, Elizabeth Quincy Smith. Her father was a Congregational minister, while her mother was descended from a line of distinguished New England clergymen and Puritan leaders of Massachusetts. The Congregational Church was the established church of the Puritan religious group that began settling in New England in the early 1600s.

Adams was raised in a traditional Puritan household in Weymouth and received a thorough education at home. Her father had an extensive library, and Adams was an avid reader of the books. From an early age, the outspoken Adams wrote letters to various family members. She met her future husband, the Harvard-educated lawyer John Adams, when she was fifteen years old. During the course of their five-year courtship, they exchanged many letters as John Adams lived five miles away in Braintree, Massachusetts (later known as Quincy, Massachusetts).

***Marriage to John Adams*** In October 1764, Abigail Adams married John Adams. She gave birth to six children over the next thirteen years, but only four would survive to adulthood. The family lived in Braintree, where John Adams also owned a farm. Between 1765 and 1770, Abigail continued to have an extensive correspondence with family and friends. In 1773, she began a correspondence with Mercy Otis Warren, an American writer and future revolutionary.

In her letters of this period, Adams wrote primarily about her family but also touched on political issues of the day, especially with Warren. The women wrote about increasing legal rights for women, including the right of married women to own property, which was not legal at that time, and the need for a republican form of government.

***Political Wife*** In the early 1770s, John Adams began his political career, first as a local selectman and then as a member of the Massachusetts legislature. He was considered the best lawyer in Massachusetts, and both he and his wife greatly supported the burgeoning American Revolution. The revolution was caused by the increasingly

Abigail Adams   *Hulton Archives / Stock Montage / Getty Images*

strained relationship between the American colonies and Great Britain in the eighteenth century. While the colonies had been essentially self-governing for much of their existence, Great Britain tried to increase control, add trade restrictions and more taxation, and deny the colonies a representative voice in the British government. Because Great Britain was unwilling to change its methods of governance, the resistant colonies declared their independence. From 1775 to 1783, American and British troops fought for control of North America.

During the last quarter of the eighteenth century, John Adams spent a significant amount of time away from his wife and family as his increasingly important role in American politics demanded he travel and, sometimes live, in distant places in North America and Europe. For the most part, Abigail Adams remained in Braintree, where she ran the farm and supported her family through small business ventures such as buying and selling property in John Adams's name, speculating in currency, and selling items her husband sent from Europe.

***Influential Correspondence*** Because of the physical separation, Adams began writing many letters to her husband as he traveled as well as to other family members (such as her sisters Elizabeth Smith Shaw and Mary Smith Cranch) and friends (such as Thomas Jefferson and Warren). In her letters, she expressed no resentment for

taking on additional responsibilities at home while her husband was gone. Indeed, she regarded it as her patriotic duty in a time of war. While John Adams was away on diplomatic missions, he came to depend on his wife's letters for information on politics and the activities of Congress as well as the revolutionary battles she witnessed.

Adams sometimes tried to influence her husband in her letters. In one famous letter written on March 31, 1776, she urged her husband to remember women and women's rights as he and his colleagues wrote the Declaration of Independence, the formal document in which the colonies broke with Great Britain. In the same letter, she also suggested that slavery should not be allowed to continue. Other letters from Adams to her husband later in the summer urged him to improve education for women.

***A Leading Lady of the United States*** After the end of the Revolutionary War in 1783, John Adams was asked to remain in France to negotiate trade agreements with European countries. Abigail Adams joined him in Paris in 1784. The couple then moved to London in 1785 when John Adams became the first U.S. minister to Great Britain. In her letters of this time period, she shared her impressions of Europe in letters to her family and friends.

After the couple returned to the United States, John Adams was elected vice president in 1789. He retained the role for two terms, and then was elected president in 1796. In her letters of this time period, Abigail Adams described the events, spirit, and consciousness of the era informed by her public role at the early capitals of the United States: New York City, Philadelphia, and Washington.

***Life at Home in Quincy*** When John Adams left office in 1801, the family returned to their home in Quincy. In her letters of this time period, Adams described her life and beliefs as she continued to run the family farm and finances, gardened, attended church services, remained informed about political events of the day, and engaged in social activities.

Adams died on October 24, 1818, in Quincy, Massachusetts. Sources vary on the cause of her death (stroke, typhoid fever, and typhus are all listed as causes), although all agree she was ill for a time at the end of her life. Her letters were never intended for publication, and she often asked her husband to burn them. Instead, John Adams held onto them, and they were regularly collected for publication in the centuries after her death.

## Works in Literary Context

Adams wrote eloquent, insightful letters that provide a detailed social history of her and her life with John Adams. While many creative outlets were considered unsuitable for women to pursue in eighteenth century America, letter writing was a socially sanctioned literary art for women. Abigail Adams felt compelled to write and was prolific in the medium, although she stayed within the prescribed social roles for women of her day. Her letters featured her frank opinions on a variety of subject matters from manners to morals, feelings, and ideas. They were regularly newsy, and they underscored her sense of humor. The correspondence also related the happiness and heartache of early American families and almost always included a discussion of the politics of the day.

*Women's Rights* In some of the best known of Adams's letters, she touches on issues related to women's rights and is regarded as an early proponent of them. Writing to her husband in 1776 as the new United States was being legally defined, she asked John Adams to establish such legal rights as guaranteeing women protection from physical abuse and allowing property ownership in their own names. She also expressed her belief that women, like men, had a right to independence.

Adams also advocated equal education for women within the context of her perception of women's traditional domestic roles. She strongly believed that education was as important for women as it was for men. Adams held that because women taught the sons who were destined to become leaders, women had an important role in maintaining the existence of an informed citizenry capable of supporting a republican government. To teach their sons successfully, women required equal education, which Adams hoped would be supported by law.

*Impressions of Europe and American Superiority* Although many of Adams's letters focused on domestic concerns, some of her letters were written while living abroad in the 1780s as John Adams represented the United States in France and Great Britain. In her letters home from Europe, she shared her opinions on French manners and morals and her observations on French culture. Coming from a frugal background, she was amazed by the number of servants that upper-class Europeans needed to maintain a large house and the time and money spent on looking fashionable. She disapproved of the behavior of the wealthy French people, telling her friends that they mainly pursued luxury and pleasure. She also dismissed Paris as one of the dirtiest cities she had ever seen.

Adams's letters from Great Britain were similarly full of descriptions of her adventures in and impressions of that country. In one letter, she described a holdup of her coach in Blackheath, a forest notorious for its roving bands of robbers. Adams admitted that she sympathized with one bandit, a young, desperate man. Adams was also appalled at the conditions in which rural people, most of them poor, lived. She often compared conditions in the Old World with those at home. While noting the differences appreciatively, she most often concluded that things, including people, food, customs, and church architecture, were better in America.

## Works in Critical Context

Adams's letters were not published during her lifetime but in various collections starting several decades after her death. The earliest collections were put together by her grandson, Charles Francis Adams, who edited *Letters of*

---

## LITERARY AND HISTORICAL CONTEMPORARIES

Adams's famous contemporaries include:

**Thomas Jefferson** (1743–1826): This American politician, scientist, lawyer, farmer, and philosopher helped the American colonies achieve their independence. The author of the Declaration of Independence, Jefferson also served as the third president of the United States.

**Catharine Macaulay** (1731–1791): This British author was the first female British historian and also corresponded with Abigail Adams. Her works included *History of England from the Accession of James I to the Elevation of the House of Hanover* (1763–1783).

**Jean Paul Marat** (1743–1793): This Swiss politician, journalist, and physician was an influential advocate of revolutionary views and measures during the French Revolution. He expressed his ideas in such books as *The Chains of Slavery* (1744).

**George Washington** (1732–1799): This hero of the American Revolutionary War became the first president of the United States in 1789.

**Thomas Paine** (1737–1809): This American philosopher and writer helped the cause of the American Revolution through his works. Among the best known of his writings is the pamphlet *Common Sense* (1776).

---

*Mrs. Adams, The Wife of John Adams* (1840) and *The Familiar Letters of John Adams and His Wife Abigail During the Revolution* (1875). Collections of Adams's letters have been published regularly since then, allowing readers to learn about the customs, habits, and manners of the Adams family daily life as well as the details about the American Revolution. The initial enthusiasm for the letters was rooted in the way the John and Abigail Adams epitomized the values of independence, sacrifice, and fortitude associated with revolutionary America.

Over time, critics continued to praise the letters in such collections for insights into politically significant men like John Adams and Thomas Jefferson. Critics also agree that the letters have historical and literary value of their own, reflecting on the great political and social developments of the early American nation as well as on the personal and domestic concerns of people of the age. Adams's letters provided an invaluable view of the concerns of eighteenth century women and their participation in a literary sphere that existed independently of the world of print but was nonetheless culturally significant.

*My Dearest Friend: Letters of Abigail and John Adams* As with many collections of the letters of Adams and her husband, critics writing about the 2007 volume *My Dearest Friend: Letters of Abigail and John*

## COMMON HUMAN EXPERIENCE

Personal letters can provide a view of the writer's own experiences, opinions, and environment in a direct way that other literature seldom does. Here are some other collections of letters which provide insights into their authors:

*The Letters of Noël Coward* (2007), by Noël Coward and edited by Barry Day. This collection of correspondence by the British playwright, actor, and songwriter emphasizes his wit and charm while providing insight into the world of the theater in the twentieth century.

*The Mitfords: Letters Between Six Sisters* (2007), edited by Charlotte Mosley. These six aristocratic daughters of the Baron Redesdale wrote approximately 12,000 letters to each other over the course of the twentieth century. This collection includes only a few hundred of their letters but illustrates their turbulent lives.

*Letters to Sam: A Grandfather's Lessons on Love, Loss, and the Gift of Life* (2006), by Daniel Gottlieb. Upon the birth of his grandson Sam, the author began writing letters about life to him fearing that he would not live long enough to see his grandchild reach adulthood. His grandson was diagnosed with a significant disability as an infant, changing the tone and content of the letters over time.

*Letters to Malcolm: Chiefly on Prayer* (1964), by C. S. Lewis. In this collection of essays extracted from a correspondence with a close friend, Lewis shows a more relaxed side as he deliberates on matters of faith and prayer.

2. In a group of three or four students, have each student read a correspondence between Adams and a different person, including perhaps her husband, her sisters, Thomas Jefferson, and such literary figures as Mercy Otis Warren. Discuss the differences in tone and content as well as what the letters reflect about each relationship.

3. Create a presentation focusing on Adams's letters written over the course of her travels in Europe. In your presentation, illustrate the political, social, and cultural observations of Adams's letters with further information about the events and countries she is experiencing. Include your opinions of Adams's insights.

4. Research another political marriage, such as that of George and Martha Washington or Bill and Hillary Clinton. In an essay, compare and contrast the relationship of John and Abigail Adams as expressed in her letters with the other political couple. How do Adams's letters add to such insights?

BIBLIOGRAPHY

**Books**

Gelles, Edith B. *Abigail Adams: A Writing Life.* New York: Routledge, 2002.

**Periodicals**

Achorn, Edward. "Epistolary Marriage: An Intimate Glimpse of the Adams Household." *Weekly Standard* (June 2, 2008).

Leber, Michele. Review of *My Dearest Friend: Letters of Abigail and John Adams. Booklist* (September 15, 2007): 20.

*Adams* found the correspondence illuminating of their relationship as well as of the era in which the couple lived. In the *Weekly Standard*, Edward Achorn wrote of the letters, "The crude stuff of life is here, illuminated with the lightning flashes of history. The letters remind us that these were two people who were groping in the darkness, unsure what would become of their lives and their new country. The loneliness and boredom, particularly in Abigail's life, seem palpable." Writing in *Booklist*, Michele Leber noted positively that "This is a treasure, for general readers and scholars alike."

### Responses to Literature

1. Read Adams's famous letter of March 31, 1776, which asks her husband to "Remember the ladies." After doing research on the era in which the letter was written, write an essay in which you compare Adams's desires with the social mores of the times and laws that were put in place in the new United States.

# ✹ Henry Adams

BORN: *1838, Boston, Massachusetts*

DIED: *1918, Washington, District of Columbia*

NATIONALITY: *American*

GENRE: *Nonfiction, fiction*

MAJOR WORKS:

*Democracy: An American Novel* (1880)

*History of the United States of America During the Administration of Thomas Jefferson and James Madison* (1889–1891)

*Mont-Saint-Michel and Chartres* (1904)

*The Education of Henry Adams* (1907)

## Overview

Henry Adams is considered to be the foremost American historian of the nineteenth century. In addition, he wrote one of the most well known autobiographies, *The Education of Henry Adams* (1907). A scion of a leading

Henry Adams   *Bettmann / Corbis*

and began his efforts in journalism. In 1860, Adams returned to the United States, where he became employed as his father's private secretary in Washington, D.C.

***Exposure to Civil Service***  When Charles Francis Adams was appointed the ambassador to Great Britain in 1861, his son went with him and continued to act as his secretary. At the time of his appointment, the Civil War had just broken out. After years of compromises over such issues as slavery, many people in the South felt their way of life was threatened. Southern regions of the United States began withdrawing from the union. The newly elected president, Abraham Lincoln, fought to preserve the country, leading to war. Lincoln selected Charles Francis Adams to serve as ambassador to counteract Southern attempts to gain recognition and support from the British. While working for his father, Adams continued writing for American periodicals.

In 1868, Adams returned to Washington, D.C., and began working as a journalist, publishing essays in such publications as *North American Review* and *The Nation*. He was appalled by the corruption and incompetence of the administration of President Ulysses S. Grant. As the United States continued Reconstruction (where the country was put back together and the South was rebuilt after the end of the Civil War) Adams called for civil service reform (wanting civil servants to be given their jobs based on qualifications and not as a reward for personal loyalty), retention of the gold standard as a basis for currency, and warned against economic monopolies, especially within the railways.

***Taught at Harvard***  Unable to affect political reform in Washington through his articles and actions, Adams returned to Harvard after two years and, in 1870, began his academic career. As an assistant professor of medieval history, Adams taught both medieval and American history while researching and writing his first nonfiction books. He resigned in 1877 and moved to Washington, D.C., where he focused all of his attention on writing.

***An Expert on History and Politics***  In 1879, Adams published his first major book, *The Life of Albert Gallatin*, a biography of Thomas Jefferson's secretary of the treasury. He then published one of his two novels, *Democracy: An American Novel* (1880), an exploration of the culture of Washington and its powerbrokers through the eyes of an everyday, Midwestern woman. The novel was informed by the author's own knowledge of and experience with American politics, and although the main political figures in the work were fictional, their similarities to actual figures may have been the reason Adams published the work anonymously. Although he was not credited as the author until after his death, the book became very popular at the time of its publication, even without his name attached. Adams's next book was another biography, *John Randolph* (1882). He then

American family, Adams incorporated the theme of power in various forms in many of his works. Adams's importance is primarily as a privileged man of broad learning and cultural experience who fully applied his intelligence in dealing with perennial and modern issues in history, literature, and philosophy.

## Works in Biographical and Historical Context

***Privileged Childhood***  Born Henry Brooks Adams in Massachusetts in 1838, he was the son of Charles Francis Adams, a congressman and diplomat, and his wife, Abigail Brown Brooks Adams. Henry Adams was part of a distinguished family: both his great-grandfather (John Adams) and grandfather (John Quincy Adams) served as presidents of the United States. His mother's family had made a fortune in the mercantile trade. Although he was raised in one of the wealthiest families in Boston, his childhood instilled in him a belief in the virtues of public duty and political service.

While attending Harvard College, Adams claimed he learned nothing but still graduated in 1858. After completing his degree, he traveled in Europe for two years

## LITERARY AND HISTORICAL CONTEMPORARIES

Adams's famous contemporaries include:

**Oliver Wendell Holmes** (1809–1894): This American poet and essayist was also a renowned physician who became the first dean at Harvard Medical School. His famous poems include "Old Ironsides" (1836) and "The Chambered Nautilus" (1858).

**John Hay** (1838–1905): This American politician served as secretary of state from 1898 to 1905 under both President William McKinley and Theodore Roosevelt. During his administration, he promulgated the Open Door policy towards China, ended the dispute over Alaska's boundary, and helped to acquire the Panama Canal Zone.

**Henry Cabot Lodge** (1850–1924): This American politician served as both a U.S. representative and senator from Massachusetts. During his long, distinguished career, he supported civil service reform, the protective tariff, and territorial acquisition.

**Mark Twain** (1835–1910): This American author, born Samuel Langhorne Clemens, is best known for such novels as *The Adventures of Tom Sawyer* (1876) and *The Prince and the Pauper* (1881).

**John Pierpont Morgan** (1837–1913): This American businessman built a fortune in banking, railroad finance, and government securities. In 1892, he managed the formation of General Electric, and went on to perform similar functions for other businesses.

focused on his monumental nine-volume *History of the United States During the Administrations of Thomas Jefferson and James Madison* (1889–1891).

Adams faced personal tragedy while writing *History of the United States During the Administrations of Thomas Jefferson and James Madison*, which slightly delayed its completion and publication. He had married Marian "Clover" Hooper in 1872. She committed suicide in 1885, compelling Adams to stop writing for a time. Instead, he focused on restless travel, and he withdrew from public life. *History of the United States During the Administrations of Thomas Jefferson and James Madison* became a classic of American historical writing and won the 1894 Loubat Prize from Columbia University.

***Published Masterworks*** In the early 1900s, Adams published two more major works, which were initially privately published for family and friends and not intended for a commercial audience. In *Mont-Saint-Michel and Chartres* (1904), Adams offered a mediation on these two wonders of medieval French architecture in the form of a travel guidebook to his nieces. He emphasized how

the titular cathedral and monastery emphasized a desirable image of unity in a society that triumphed over hardship to create enduring art. Adams saw that American society of this time period was much more divided.

Adams continued the musings he began in *Mont-Saint-Michel and Chartres* when he published what became his masterwork, *The Education of Henry Adams* (1907). In this highly regarded autobiography, which has been compared to St. Augustine's *Confessions* (c. 1397), he documented his struggles to come to terms with the changing political and cultural character of mid-nineteenth-century to early-twentieth-century America.

Adams suffered a stroke in 1912 and was partially paralyzed until his death. As Adams neared the end of his life, he was troubled by World War I. The so-called "Great War" was raging, dividing the European continent through entangling alliances and changing societies. As the war neared its end, Adams died on March 27, 1918, in Washington, D.C. A year after his death, he received the Pulitzer Prize for autobiography for the commercial publication of *The Education of Henry Adams*.

### Works in Literary Context

As a historian, Adams is considered one of the greatest produced by the United States; as a writer, he crossed literary boundaries to present fresh, challenging ideas and works. Adams helped fashion and define the school of "scientific" history with *History of the United States of America During the Administrations of Thomas Jefferson and James Madison*. In the essays in *Mont-Saint-Michel and Chartres* and his autobiography *The Education of Henry Adams*, he combined philosophical dissertation, memoir, and intellectual ideas. Descended from a family of prominent politicians and statesmen, as well as greatly influenced by his experiences and knowledge of such people, Adams emphasized the theme of power in many of his works. Among Adams's influences included Edward Gibbon, Edward A. Freeman, Henry Sumner Maine, and Jules Michelet.

***"Scientific" Historiography*** Adams's *History of the United States of America During the Administrations of Thomas Jefferson and James Madison* was an early model of scientific historiography. Rather than telling an entertaining narrative, Adams arranged the facts of the two presidential administrations in sequence and invited his readers to form their own conclusions about them. Accordingly, the series is voluminously detailed, reflecting the author's heavy use of documents and papers from the era. The objectivity of such a method was not absolute, and Adams's history portrays Jefferson and Madison's efforts as an admirable experiment in popular democracy that failed because of the incompatibility of its ideals with America's geographic immensity and its fragmentation of culture and identity into sectionalism. *History of the United States of America During the Administrations of Thomas Jefferson and James Madison* ends with questions that Adams saw his generation struggling to answer about the direction of the country, its goals, and how society will be united.

*Theme of Power*  In a number of his works, Adams explored the concept of power—religious power, scientific power, and political power. In *Mont-Saint-Michel and Chartres*, power takes the form of religious belief and focus as a means of creating the two structures he talks about in depth. The metaphor for Adams's incomprehension of the twentieth century in *The Education of Henry Adams* is the dynamo (an industrial electric generator which makes a direct current), which Adams had seen at the Chicago World's Fair. Adams saw that power in the twentieth century was coming from what he considered the alarming growth of science and technology, and he believed that the world was less stable and coherent than it once was.

Most of Adams's output focused on political power in some form. From *The Life of Albert Gallatin* to the *History of the United States of America During the Administrations of Thomas Jefferson and James Madison*, he emphasized how politics and issues of power shaped America and its leaders. Even *John Randolph* looks at power through the story of the Virginia politician and advocate for states' rights who opposed Thomas Jefferson's efforts to build a strong federal government. In Adams's fiction, the corruption of power emerges as a major theme. In *Democracy: An American Novel* (1880), an ordinary woman, Mrs. Lightfoot Lee, moves from ignorance to knowledge to disillusionment as she encounters the corruption Adams considered endemic in late nineteenth-century American democracy.

## Works in Critical Context

Today, Adams's works are read primarily as reflecting the philosophical and social concerns of his generation and class at a time when American cultural and political authority was passing from the colonial-era patricians of New England and Virginia to the capitalists and party-machine newcomers of the Gilded Age. Since the mid-twentieth century, *Mont-Saint-Michel and Chartres* and *The Education of Henry Adams* have come to be regarded as his most important and influential works. Adams's longest work, the *History of the United States of America During the Administrations of Thomas Jefferson and James Madison*, is also considered his most significant work of history.

*The Education of Henry Adams*  Privately printed in 1907, *The Education of Henry Adams* was first known only to a small audience. When the book was published commercially in 1918 after Adams's death, it attracted widespread attention. Critics have praised it as an original and intriguing self-portrait, an achievement that by itself contradicts the author's claim to failure. George Hochfield wrote in *Henry Adams: An Introduction*, "In the brilliance and intellectual daring of the quest itself, Adams

---

## COMMON HUMAN EXPERIENCE

In *The Education of Henry Adams*, Adams indicted Gilded Age politics. Other books that explore this tumultuous time in American history, which spanned the 1870s and 1880s, include:

*The Gilded Age: A Tale of To-Day* (1873), a novel by Mark Twain and Charles Dudley Warner. This satiric story coined the phrase that defined the era.

*Age of Betrayal: The Triumph of Money in America, 1865–1900* (2007), a nonfiction book by Jack Beatty. In this work of history, Beatty argues that corporations, not the people, controlled the United States during the Gilded Age.

*An American Politician* (1884), a novel by Francis Marion Crawford. This political novel looks at the disputed election of Rutherford B. Hayes and includes a tale of romance.

*Sex Wars: A Novel of Gilded Age New York* (2006), a novel by Marge Piercy. This novel uses such real-life figures as Victoria Woodhull (the first woman to run for U.S. president), suffragette Elizabeth Cady Stanton, and industrialist Cornelius Vanderbilt to explore power and gender wars in this era.

*The Age of Innocence* (1993), a film by Martin Scorsese. Set in New York City in the 1870s and focused on a man torn by love for two different women, *The Age of Innocence* is based on a 1920 novel by Edith Wharton.

---

converts failure into heroism.... *The Education of Henry Adams* is ... an enduring and invigorating work of art."

*History of the United States of America During the Administrations of Thomas Jefferson and James Madison*  The *History of the United States of America During the Administrations of Thomas Jefferson and James Madison* was initially met with apathy by critics. Some early reviewers also felt that Adams was too harsh in his treatment of the nation. In a review for *Dial*, Henry W. Thurston praised Adams's abundant use of primary sources but commented that "one may well question whether or not another, having had access to the same sources, would have found so little of which to approve."

*History of the United States of America During the Administrations of Thomas Jefferson and James Madison* eventually became regarded as a historical work of the highest order. Praised for its broad scope and accuracy of detail, this work came to be credited with providing historical analysis with new possibilities and perspectives through Adams's questioning of dogmatic philosophical assumptions of the period. In the *Atlantic Monthly*, a reviewer commented, "The period may be discussed with different predilections; it will never be discussed more keenly and more profoundly. In a word, the book is one of marked ability and very great value."

## Responses to Literature

1. Read *The Education of Henry Adams*. Then write your own brief autobiographical essay in similar fashion, focusing on a single learning experience from your life. What was the lasting impact of that experience?

2. Research Adams's illustrious family. Create a presentation in which you explore the roles the Adams family has had in shaping American history. Is the Adams family's history still relevant in the twenty-first century? Why or why not?

3. Have each member of a small group read the essays in *Mont-Saint-Michel and Chartres*. Using Adams's ideas, discuss your own experiences with a specific work of art. This can include paintings, books, television shows, movies, or even video games. Share your ideas with the group.

4. One concept that interested Adams was power. Using his theories about political power in the nineteenth and early twentieth centuries, write a paper in which you apply them to modern times. Do you think his ideas about power are still applicable today? Why or why not?

BIBLIOGRAPHY

**Books**

Hochfield, George. *Henry Adams: An Introduction and Interpretation*. New York: Barnes & Noble, 1962.

**Periodicals**

Review of *History of the United States of America During the Administrations of Thomas Jefferson and James Madison*. Atlantic Monthly (February 1891).

Thurston, Henry W. Review of *History of the United States of America During the Administrations of Thomas Jefferson and James Madison*. Dial (February 1890).

## ✱ Arnold Adoff

BORN: *1935, New York, New York*

NATIONALITY: *American*

GENRE: *Poetry, fiction*

MAJOR WORKS:
*Malcolm X* (1970)
*MA nDA LA* (1971)
*Black Is Brown Is Tan* (1973)
*Love Letters* (1997)
*Daring Dog and Captain Cat* (2001)

Arnold Adoff    *Adoff, Arnold with his Love Letters book, photograph by Virginia Hamilton Adoff. Reproduced by permission of Arnold Adoff.*

## Overview

American poet and editor Arnold Adoff has written numerous collections of poetry for children that celebrate a sense of family, diversity, and the importance of children's imagination. His poems range in tone and mood from the festive to the meditative, with a common element of a sense of gentle warmth. Adoff also published at least one prose work, a biography of Malcolm X entitled *Malcolm X* (1970), intended for a younger audience. In addition to his own writing, Adoff compiled a number of highly regarded anthologies of African-American authors.

## Works in Biographical and Historical Context

*Early Love of Music* Adoff was born in 1935 in the East Bronx section of New York City to Aaron Jacob and Rebecca (Stein) Adoff. His parents were Russian Jewish immigrants, and his father worked as a pharmacist. Raised in multi-racial South Bronx, Adoff's parents instilled in him a respect for his Jewish heritage as well as a deep concern for social justice. His home life was full of heated discussion about current issues. Music was an important part of his family life. His mother and aunt both performed and music was often played on the radio. Books and being well read were also encouraged. By his teen years, Adoff was a confirmed jazz fan and began writing poetry, but he planned on becoming a doctor.

While attending Columbia University, Adoff realized that he did not want a medical career. He transferred to the City College of New York, majored in history and literature, and graduated in 1956. Adoff continued his education with graduate studies in American history at Columbia University, which he attended from 1956 to 1958, and later the New School for Social Research, from 1965 to 1967. During the 1950s, Adoff became active in the increasingly tumultuous Civil Rights Movement as his parents were before him. By the 1950s, African Americans in the United States were calling for an end to legal segregation, especially in the South where many blacks were denied basic civil rights and faced daily reminders of their lesser status. Civil Rights activists in the 1950s and 1960s worked to change this situation through civil disobedience as well as legal action. Such laws as the Civil Rights Act of 1957 and the Civil Rights Acts of the 1960s led to changes, though it took decades for changes to be fully implemented.

*Mingus Manager and Teacher*   In the late 1950s, Adoff was employed as the manager of jazz bassist and composer Charles Mingus while working as a teacher in New York City, first in a yeshiva in Brooklyn then as a substitute teacher in public schools. Through Mingus, Adoff met Virginia Hamilton, an African-American writer in 1958. The couple married in 1960, and later had two children, Leigh and Jaime Levi. At the time, interracial marriage was uncommon and, in fact, illegal in a number of states in the United States. Such anti-miscegenation laws were declared unconstitutional by the Supreme Court in 1967. At the beginning of the marriage between Adoff and Hamilton, they lived in Spain and France, though they returned to the United States to continue their activities in the Civil Rights Movement. Adoff continued his career as an educator upon his return. He taught in public schools in Harlem and the Upper West Side of New York City through 1969. Most of his students were African Americans, yet there was little literature by African Americans available in schools.

To benefit his students, he collected the works of African American poets to use in the classroom, including works that were uplifting and contained themes of hope, survival, and triumph. By the late 1960s, he was compiling and editing anthologies of such poets beginning with *I Am the Darker Brother: An Anthology of Modern Poems by Negro Americans* (1968). Over the years, Adoff published at least eight more anthologies, which included poetry, fiction, and commentaries of black writers.

*Launched Writing Career*   Adoff published his first original book in 1970, an illustrated biography of Malcolm X entitled *Malcolm X*. Adoff's book is a forthright account of the major events of the civil rights leaders' life and overviews his mission. Still a jazz fan and inspired by

the poets he anthologized, Adoff began publishing his own original poetry in the early 1970s. His poetry featured lively rhythms, creating what he dubbed "singing poems." Adoff's first poetry collection was *MA nDA LA* (1971), which only uses words that contain the sound "ah."

After this point, Adoff regularly published poetry collections for children focusing on varying themes. In collections like *Black Is Brown Is Tan* (1973) and *All the Colors of the Race* (1982), he drew on his own experiences as the father of mixed-race children to write about the lives of children from mixed-race marriages. *Black Is Brown Is Tan* was one of the first children's books to touch on this subject. Family is also at the center of collections like *Big Sister Tells Me That I'm Black* (1976), which features a small boy who offers a rousing cheer for himself and all who are like him.

*Became Literary Agent*   After spending several years focusing exclusively on writing, Adoff moved to Yellow Springs, Ohio, where he developed a secondary career as a literary agent with the founding of the Arnold Adoff Agency. He also continued to write his own poetry for children. By the late 1970s and early 1980s, Adoff's poetry for children expanded its thematic concerns. The 1979 collection *Eats* celebrates good food and the joys of eating. In *The Cabbages Are Chasing the Rabbits* (1985), Adoff energetically looks at cabbages who turn the tables on the rabbits who have been nibbling on them. The result is a wild and crazy pursuit. The thirty-seven poems that make up *Sports Pages* (1986) explore the thrill of victory and the agony of defeat for young athletes in lyrical blank verse.

Though Adoff continued to make his primary home in Ohio, he returned to New York City on occasion. From 1986 to 1987, he served as a visiting professor at Queens College in Flushing. The poetry collections he published in the late 1980s continued to reflect a variety of themes and ideas. In *Greens* (1988), Adoff offers imaginative observations on things that are green, from grasshoppers to pea soup. In contrast, *Flamboyan* (1988) is a rhythmic mélange of poetry and prose that describes the day and dreams of a young Puerto Rican girl whose hair is the color of the Flamboyan tree blossoms.

*Continued Literary Output*   Adoff continued to publish innovative collections in the 1990s and early 2000s. In 1995, he published *Street Music: City Poems*, a collection of jazzy poems in free verse that celebrate the vibrancy of city life. That same year, he put out *Slow Dance Heart Break Blues*, a collection about the thoughts and experiences of adolescence intended for readers in their early teens. Still writing for younger readers as well, he published valentines for elementary-aged students in *Love Letters* (1997). Again targeting young readers, *Daring Dog and Captain Cat* (2001) explores two pets who become superheroes when their owners are asleep.

Adoff received numerous accolades over the course of his career including the 1988 National Council of Teachers of English Award for Excellence in Poetry for Children. His wife, Virginia Hamilton, also became a highly regarded children's author in her own right. After she died of cancer in 2002, Adoff continued to write and read his poetry while teaching poetry and creative writing as a lecturer and instructor at various colleges throughout the country. Adoff continues to live in Yellow Springs, Ohio, where he still operates his literary agency.

## Works in Literary Context

As an author, Adoff was greatly influenced by his own lifelong love of jazz as well as the many African American authors he included in the anthologies he edited. He also found inspiration in William Shakespeare, John Steinbeck, James Joyce, Gertrude Stein, Dylan Thomas, E. E. Cummings, Rainer Maria Rilke, Marianne Moore, Gwendolyn Brooks, Robert Hayden, and Jose Garcia Villa. In his own poetry, Adoff uses free verse, vivid images, and unusual structures and sounds to create warm, affectionate family portraits. His poetry also includes the intimate thoughts and feelings of children, and he employs a variety of moods and tones. His poetry is noted for its invention and innovation.

*"Shaped Speech" Poetry*   Adoff favors what he calls the "Shaped Speech" style of poetry. He believes that the way the words are arranged on the page contributes to the poem's meaning. His poetry also features an idiosyncratic use of capitalization and punctuation, elements the poet believes have a strong effect on the movement and rhythm of these poems. Adoff seeks to visually represent the meaning of the words of his poetry by including

variations of line length, type size, and letter arrangement. In such shaped speech poems, Adoff uses punctuation and rhyme sparingly, and the words are often run together or broken up to add to the dramatic effect. Such poems can be found in *Daring Dog and Captain Cat*.

*Musicality*   The rhythms of jazz influence Adoff's use of lively rhythms in his original poetry. His so-called "singing poems" reflect this sense of musicality. This quality is best appreciated when Adoff's poems are read aloud. Unusual word, phrase, and sentence configurations, which may appear arbitrary on the page, take on a rhythmic logic when spoken. For example, in *MA nDA La*, a cycle of African family life in a small village, this story poem uses sounds which when spoken aloud evoke a sense of celebration.

*Family and Diversity*   As the editor of a number of anthologies of African-American writers and the father of mixed race children, Adoff often celebrates diversity and family with affection in his poetry. This tenderness is most clearly evident in his affectionate family portraits. For example, *Black Is Brown Is Tan* describes the everyday experiences of an interracial family. The collection begins by focusing on the wide spectrum of colors apparent in family members, then expresses delight in every hue, and concludes by focusing beyond color to encompass a family's delight in each other.

Other poetry collections include this theme. The interrelated poems in *All the Colors of the Race* center on an individual, interracial child's thoughts as she explores her sense of identity through her family's background. The poems contain a variety of emotions as the young girl expresses pride in her varied ancestry and a sense of affiliation with all the colors, religions, and cultures that have contributed to her unique self. She is also aware of potential prejudice as she goes on a family outing, but enjoys the outing nonetheless.

## Works in Critical Context

Praised for the depth and range of subjects of his poetry, as well as for its sensitivity, insight, musicality, structure, and control, Adoff is perceived by critics as a poet whose skill with language and unexpected variances of meaning and rhythm help make his works especially distinctive. Adoff is also recognized as one of the first and finest champions of multiculturalism in American juvenile literature. Several of his books—most notably the anthologies *I Am the Darker Brother* (1968) and *City in All Directions: An Anthology of Modern Poems* (1969), the biography *Malcolm X*, and the original poetry collection *Black Is Brown Is Tan*—are acknowledged as groundbreaking titles in their respective genres. Critics have lauded Adoff's work for its constant, imaginative expression of faith in people and their spirit, noting that each poem, in its own way, salutes the human condition and its ability to triumph.

*Black Is Brown Is Tan*   *Black Is Brown Is Tan*, a landmark collection of original poetry, was widely praised when it was originally published. Writing in the *School Library Journal*, Marilyn Singer comments, "*Black Is Brown Is Tan* is warm is love is a beautiful picture of a family." Singer also notes that "This book is a first in that it is about an interracial family," she concludes that "more important, however, is that it is an artistic achievement. Arnold Adoff's spare free verse combines familiar images in a startling original way." Another critic, Anne Wheeler notes, in *Children's Book Review Service*, "it deals fairly with the subject [interracial families] and serves as an important beginning in the field of easy books for children about different kinds of families." *Black Is Brown Is Tan* was published again in 2002 with new illustrations, and remained a critical favorite with Dorothy N. Bowen in the *School Library Journal* calling it "A beautiful picture of an interracial home in which there is fun, security, and plenty of love."

***Daring Dog and Captain Cat*** Adoff's *Daring Dog and Captain Cat* was also highly praised. The *Publishers Weekly* reviewer noted "Free verse, frozen into solid blocks of text, enriches this story of double lives." The review concludes, "Youngsters will appreciate the covert proceedings: while the images tell a breezy tale of carousing, the experimental poetry implies that ordinary pets harbor hidden personas." Similarly, Nina Lindsay in *School Library Journal* praised, "Adoff's free verse dashes and leaps across the page and tongue, much like animals chasing shadows through a house at night."

## Responses to Literature

1. Research the Civil Rights Movement in the United States and find a related work in one of Adoff's anthologies. Write a paper in which you link the movement and the work. How did the Civil Rights Movement affect the writings of African Americans?

2. In a group, read aloud the poems in *MA nDA LA*. Discuss how the musicality of the poems enhances the words of the page. Also, debate your interpretations and opinions of the poems.

3. Read *Daring Dog and Captain Cat*. Write your own poem or short story about your own pet or inanimate object, and what your chosen topic does while you are asleep.

4. Until recently, there has been limited literature about multiracial children and families. Research the books that exist on the topic, then create a presentation about the changing face of literature focusing on multiracial children.

BIBLIOGRAPHY

**Books**

Copeland, Jeffrey S. *Speaking of Poets: Interviews with Poets Who Write for Children and Young Adults* Urbana, Ill.: National Council of Teachers of English, 1993.

---

## COMMON HUMAN EXPERIENCE

Adoff put together a number of anthologies of works by African-American poets and was greatly influenced by them. Here are some other books of poetry by African-American authors:

*Selected Poems of Langston Hughes* (1959), a poetry collection by Langston Hughes. These poems capture the everyday qualities of African-American life.

*Spin a Soft Black Song* (1971), a poetry collection by Nikki Giovanni. These poems focus on simple African-American childhood experiences such as making friends, taking a bath, and bragging.

*It's a New Day* (1971), a poetry collection by Sonia Sanchez. These poems for children are an honest, but angry, affirmation of African-American pride.

*Nathaniel Talking* (1988), a poetry collection by Eloise Greenfield. These verse poems relate the feelings and experiences of a young black boy.

**Periodicals**

Adoff, Arnold. "Politics, Poetry, and Teaching Children: A Personal Journey." *The Lion and the Unicorn: A Critical Journal of Children's Literature* 10 (1986): 9–14.

Bowen, Dorothy N. Review of *Black Is Brown Is Tan*. *School Library Journal* (July 2002): 76.

Lindsay, Nina. Review of *Daring Dog and Captain Cat*. *School Library Journal* (September 2001): 182.

Singer, Marilyn. Review of *Black Is Brown Is Tan*. *School Library Journal* (September 1973): 54.

Thomas, Joseph T., Jr. "Mel Glenn and Arnold Adoff: The Poetics of Power in the Adolescent Voice-Lyric." *Style* (Fall 2001): 486.

Wheeler, Anne. Review of *Black Is Brown Is Tan*. *Children's Book Review Service* (October 1973): 9.

**Web sites**

Adoff, Arnold. *Arnold Adoff*. Retrieved September 14, 2008, from http://www.arnoldadoff.com.

# ✸ James Agee

BORN: *1909, Knoxville, Tennessee*

DIED: *1955, New York, New York*

NATIONALITY: *American*

GENRE: *Poetry, fiction, screenplays, criticism*

MAJOR WORKS:

*Permit Me Voyage* (1934)

*Let Us Now Praise Famous Men* (1941)

James Agee   *The Library of Congress.*

*The Morning Watch* (1951)

*A Death in the Family* (1957)

*Agee on Film: Reviews and Comments* (1958)

## Overview

Perhaps best known for *Let Us Now Praise Famous Men* (1941), which is Agee's documentary book about share-croppers, James Agee was also a gifted man of letters who wrote poetry, novels, screenplays, criticism, and articles for magazines. Agee drew on his own life, experiences, and background for many of his works. Agee's status was cemented by an Academy Award nomination for his script for *The African Queen* (1951) and a posthumous Pulitzer Prize for his novel *A Death in the Family* (1957) after his premature death at the age of 45.

## Works in Biographical and Historical Context

*Early Tragedy, Sharp Intellect*   Agee was born November 27, 1909, in Knoxville, Tennessee, the son of Hugh James and Laura (Tyler) Agee. His father worked for a small construction company founded by his father-in-law, while his pious mother enjoyed writing poetry, an art her son would soon come to love. Agee's father died in a car accident when Agee was six years old and his death greatly impacted Agee's life.

After Hugh Agee's death, the family moved to the mountains of south central Tennessee, where Agee received his early education at Saint Andrews, a private school run by members of the Order of the Holy Cross. There, Agee became close with Father James Harold Flye, a member of the order with whom he shared many intellectual interests and a life-long correspondence. In 1925, Agee began attending a prestigious college prep school, Phillips Exeter Academy, in New Hampshire.

*Focused on Writing Career*   By this time, Agee's interest had focused on literature and writing. He became the editor of the school magazine, the *Monthly*, and president of the literary club, the Lantern, in 1927. Agee was also writing poetry, and his burgeoning talent was recognized by such famous poets as Robert Frost.

Agee then entered Harvard University, where his determination to become a writer intensified. However, he was also often sidetracked by uncertainty, and his spirits would plummet so low that he sometimes considered suicide. The next day, his mood would often greatly improve. Such emotional extremes continued throughout his life. Despite this internal conflict, he wrote for, then became president of, the Harvard *Advocate*.

*Joined Fortune*   After graduating from Harvard in 1932, Agee was hired by *Fortune* magazine to work as a reporter. By this time, the United States was deep in the Great Depression. The Great Depression was the worst economic crisis in the history of the United States and soon spread worldwide. It officially began with the stock market crashing on October 29, 1929, and lasted nearly a decade. All major economic indexes fell, and the unemployment rate became extremely high. At the peak of the Great Depression in 1933, more than one out of every four people in the labor force were without jobs.

For *Fortune*, Agee wrote about various businesses as well as the Tennessee Valley Authority, the massive New Deal project which brought jobs and electricity to the Southeast. The New Deal was the name given to the many programs launched during the administration of President Franklin D. Roosevelt, intended to help the United States recover from the Great Depression.

*Published First Books*   While writing for *Fortune*, Agee published the only volume of poetry collected during his lifetime, *Permit Me to Voyage* (1934). The poems in the collection were highly personal and included poems written while he was a student at Exeter. Agee would continue to write poetry throughout his life, and the poems were published after his death in *The Collected Poems of James Agee* (1968).

In 1936, *Fortune* sent Agee to Alabama to study the Southern farm economy and write a documentary series about the daily life of a sharecropping family. Sharecroppers were tenant farmers who were supplied with land

and tools by the landowners in exchange for a share of the crops. During the Great Depression, most sharecroppers earned no more than a few hundred dollars for their crops and were often left destitute after paying their bills.

Agee chose to write about three families and emphasize their human dignity instead of the viewpoint that they were "social problems." The passionate articles created by Agee, as well as the accompanying photographs taken by Walker Evans, were rejected by *Fortune*, but Agee did not let the project die. Instead, Agee and Evans created a book, *Let Us Now Praise Famous Men*, which was published by Houghton Mifflin in 1941. Initially a failure, the book was reprinted in 1960 and became one of the most significant literary documents produced during the Great Depression.

### Wrote About and For Films

By the time *Let Us Now Praise Famous Men* was originally published, Agee was working at *Time* magazine. He joined the magazine in 1939 as a book reviewer, then became its movie critic in 1941. Agee wrote highly regarded film reviews for the magazine until 1948. At the same time, he also composed a well-known movie column, which included film reviews, for the *Nation* from 1942 to 1948. In his reviews for *Time* and the *Nation*, he was the first to raise the level of weekly reviewing to that of prose art. In 1949 and 1950, Agee also contributed several long film essays to *Life* magazine.

A life-long film buff, Agee also wrote original movie scripts, though none were ever produced. He did write screenplays based on the novels of other authors, including such films as *The African Queen* (1951) and *The Night of the Hunter* (1955). While Agee was writing such high-profile films, he was also writing several lauded novels that were published in the 1950s. Among the best known was the short novel, *The Morning Watch* (1951), about a twelve-year-old boy attending an Episcopal school. In the autobiographical novel, Agee explores how a child experiences a spiritual crisis yet comes to an appreciation and sense of real self.

### Early Death

After decades of using and abusing tobacco and alcohol, as well as suffering several heart attacks, Agee died of heart failure on May 16, 1955, in New York City. After his death, his literary career continued. One of his best known novels, *A Death in the Family*, was published in 1957 and won the 1958 Pulitzer Prize for fiction. Also autobiographical, the novel is a period evocation of Southern Americana, as well as an aching memoir of parents, children, and the negotiation of loss after a father dies in a car accident when the protagonist is a child. Agee also received notice for his collected film reviews, *Agee on Film: Reviews and Comments* (1958), the reprint of *Let Us Now Praise Famous Men*, and collections of his poetry and prose published in 1968.

## Works in Literary Context

Agee's literary themes were strongly influenced by his childhood experiences: growing up in a Christian family in Tennessee; suffering the loss of his father as a small

---

## LITERARY AND HISTORICAL CONTEMPORARIES

Agee's famous contemporaries include:

**Robert Frost** (1874–1963): This American poet was perhaps the most beloved poet of the twentieth century. He often focused on simply nature lyrics, and his works include *North of Boston* (1914).

**Franklin D. Roosevelt** (1882–1945): This American politician was elected to the presidency a record four times (a Constitutional amendment now limits presidents to two terms in office). He led the United States during the darkest days of the Great Depression through much of World War II until his death from lung cancer while still in office.

**John Huston** (1906–1987): This American filmmaker left an indelible mark on American cinema as a director, writer, and actor. Among his films were *The Maltese Falcon* (1941), *The Treasure of the Sierra Madre* (1948), and *The African Queen* (1951).

**Joan Didion** (1934–): This American novelist and essayist is considered a leading example of personal journalism. Her works include the novel *Run River* (1963) and the nonfiction *Slouching Towards Bethlehem* (1968).

**Tennessee Williams** (1911–1983): This American playwright is considered among the greatest dramatists of the mid-twentieth century. His plays were greatly influenced by the emotional currents of his life, including *The Glass Menagerie* (1944).

---

child; and attending an Episcopalian grammar school, where he was taught various social and religious philosophies. His work as a reporter and film critic also informed his writing, though his personal point of view often showed through even in his journalistic works. His best-known book, *Let Us Now Praise Famous Men*, was an example of a new journalistic movement: personal journalism. Among the writers who influenced Agee were William Shakespeare, Walt Whitman, and William Blake.

### Autobiographical Inspiration

Much of Agee's writings, including his poetry and two novels, draws from personal experience and is autobiographical in nature. In fictional works that are autobiographical, authors incorporate elements from their own lives into their writings. In both *The Morning Watch* and *A Death in the Family*, Agee draws on two elemental facts from his childhood which deeply influenced his life and affected his outlook: the death of his father when Agee was six years old, and the religious piety of his mother, a piety with which he would constantly struggle. *The Morning Watch*, for example, is the story of a young student at a religious school who grows away from orthodoxy and toward self-awareness, and, eventually

## COMMON HUMAN EXPERIENCE

*Let Us Now Praise Famous Men* is considered an early example of personal journalism. Here are some other works of journalism in which the author puts himself or herself into the story:

> *Black Like Me* (1961), a nonfiction work by John Howard Griffin. In this book, the white author, a native of Texas, describes his six weeks of travel through racially segregated Southern states while posing as an African American.
> *NewJack: Guarding Sing Sing* (2000), a nonfiction work by Ted Conover. In this work, Conover relates his experiences working as a correctional officer for a year in the New York state correctional system to better understand it.
> *Nickel and Dimed: On (Not) Getting By in America* (2001), a nonfiction work by Barbara Ehrenreich. In this book, Ehrenreich writes from the perspective of an undercover journalist to look at the impact of the welfare reforms enacted in 1996 on the working poor in the United States.
> *In Cold Blood* (1965), a nonfiction novel by Truman Capote. In this work, Capote investigates the brutal murder of Kansas farmer Herbert W. Clutter and his family by two men for apparently little profit. He presents the work in novelistic form.

alienation. In *A Death in the Family*, the young protagonist's father has been killed in an automobile accident—just like Agee's father—leaving the boy and his family to cope with his absence, just as Agee's family had to do.

**Personal Journalism**   *Let Us Now Praise Famous Men* is one of the first examples of personal journalism. This book challenged the traditional conventions of reporting and literature which demanded objectivity. Instead, Agee inserted himself and his personal beliefs into the story in a variety of ways. Occasionally self-indulgent, his language is often breathtaking in its intellectual passion, moral force, and near holographic reproduction of the physical reality of the sharecroppers' lives. Agee's prose is also turbulent, extravagant, and self-reflexive. Part anatomy of the impoverished conditions surrounding a tenant farmer's life, part poetic and metaphysical inquiry into the mysteries of existence, part intimate confession of Agee's search for his aesthetic identity and family roots, *Let Us Now Praise Famous Men* was a highly original work. By using such personal journalism techniques, Agee comes to a realization and understanding of the humanity within himself and in others. The genre of personal journalism became more common in the 1960s, influenced in part by the reprint of this book in 1961.

## Works in Critical Context

While most Agee's works are highly praised, many critics believed that he failed to reach the artistic achievement for which he seemed destined. Instead of settling on one particular genre and doing it well, he chose instead to try it all during his lifetime and never focused long enough to achieve sustained greatness, though such novels as *A Morning Watch* were highly regarded. Agee's premature death also meant that his greatest fame came after his death. Such was the case with what many critics consider his most important contribution to literature, *Let Us Now Praise Famous Men*.

**The Morning Watch**   The autobiographical novel *The Morning Watch* has been praised by critics for its subtle rendering of the protagonist's development from immature idealism to a mature awareness of life's complexity. At the same time, commentators have frequently criticized the work for sacrificing substance to technique, particularly in its overly rhetorical style and excessive reliance on symbolism. As Victor A. Kramer noted in *Renascence*, "Throughout *The Morning Watch*, Agee is most concerned with evoking the complex emotions of particular imagined moments." Commenting on the symbolism, John S. Phillipson in the *Western Humanities Review* commented "In the one hundred and twenty pages of James Agee's *The Morning Watch*, the symbols and motifs act, interact, and interrelate complexly. In their ordered complexity they contrast with the disorder and confusion within the mind of the book's protagonist...."

**Let Us Now Praise Famous Men**   Upon publication in 1941, a few critics noted that *Let Us Now Praise Famous Men* featured Agee's technically ambitious prose along with Evans' harshly realistic photographs. However, the book failed to engage an American public increasingly preoccupied with World War II. After his publisher put out a reprint of the book in 1961, the critical and popular response to *Let Us Now Praise Famous Men* changed. The book was lauded for creating a stirring portrait of sharecroppers' lives as well as an incisive expression of the artist's dilemma in fashioning that portrait.

For example, William Stott, in his book *Documentary Expression and Thirties America*, noted that "*Let Us Now Praise Famous Men* is confessional in a way no documentary had been" and that "Agee's extraordinary participation in the narrative ... set the book apart from other documentary writing of the thirties." An expanded edition of *Let Us Now Praise Famous Men* was published in 2000, and continued to receive positive notices. A reviewer in *Creative Review* commented, "Stylistically, Agee veers from the compact sections describing with minute fascination the physical environment and the waking, sleeping, eating, working social lives of his hosts to long, meandering almost stream-of-consciousness passages, expressing his personal response to the situation of the sharecroppers."

## Responses to Literature

1. Read several poems by Agee included in *Permit Me Voyage* or in a collection published after his death. In a paper, relate the poem(s) to Agee's life.

2. In 1960, a theatrical adaptation of *A Death in the Family* was a hit on Broadway and won a Pulitzer Prize. In an essay, compare and contrast the novel and the play. Also explore critical and popular reaction to both works.

3. Read John Steinbeck's classic novel about the Great Depression, *The Grapes of Wrath* (1939). This novel is often studied along with *Let Us Now Praise Famous Men*. Create a presentation in which you compare and contrast the books, their themes, depiction of poverty, and related issues.

4. Working in a small group, watch a film that Agee reviewed. Using his review, discuss his interpretation of the film with your own reading of the film. Each member of the group can also compose their own review.

BIBLIOGRAPHY

**Books**

Bergeen, Laurence. *James Agee: A Life*. New York: Dutton, 1984.

Lofaro, Michael A., ed. *James Agee: Reconsiderations*. Knoxville: University of Tennessee Press, 1992.

Lowe, James. *The Creative Process of James Agee*. Baton Rouge: Louisiana State University Press, 1994.

Scott, William. *Documentary Expresion and Thirties America*. New York: Oxford University Press, 1973.

**Periodicals**

Garner, Dwight. "Grievous Angel: The Unruly James Agee." *Harper's Magazine* (November 2005): 91.

"Let Us Praise a Famous Book." *Creative Review* (July 2001): 68.

Kramer, Victor A. Review of *The Morning Watch*. *Renascence* (Summer 1975): 221–230.

Valinuas, Algis. "What James Agee Achieved." *Commentary* (February 2006): 49.

## ⊛ Conrad Aiken

BORN: *1889, Savannah, Georgia*

DIED: *1973, Savannah, Georgia*

NATIONALITY: *American*

GENRE: *Poetry, fiction, nonfiction*

MAJOR WORKS:

*Senlin: A Biography* (1918)

*Punch: The Immortal Liar, Documents in His History* (1921)

*Selected Poems* (1929)

Conrad Aiken  *The Library of Congress.*

*"Silent Snow, Secret Snow"* (1934)

*Ushant: An Essay* (1952)

## Overview

Conrad Aiken was principally successful as a poet. He is generally considered to have significantly influenced the development of modern poetry, though his short stories, novels, and criticism were also highly regarded. A modernist, Aiken was greatly influenced by psychoanalytic thought and the theories of Sigmund Freud and George Santayana. In his writings, Aiken blended spiritual, philosophical, and psychological elements to explore facets of modern existence and the evolution of human consciousness. He was interested in conscious and unconscious reality and explored these themes in his works using physical details and psychological drama. The result was complex works of literature that are significant on several levels.

## Works in Biographical and Historical Context

*Early Tragedy*  Aiken was born on August 5, 1889, in Savannah, Georgia, the son of William Ford and Anna Aiken Potter. His wealthy parents were cousins of well-respected

Puritan stock. They had moved to Georgia from New England. His father became a highly respected physician and surgeon. As a boy growing up in Savannah, Aiken enjoyed reading the horror stories of Edgar Allan Poe at a former burial ground, Colonial Park.

Aiken's young life was radically changed in February 1901 when his father became mentally unbalanced and killed his wife, and then himself. Not only did the young Aiken suffer the trauma of losing both parents at the age of eleven; he actually heard the gunshots and was the one who discovered their bodies. The violent deaths of his parents overshadowed the rest of his life and writings. From that point forward, he feared he would one day go insane like his father.

**Educated in New England**   After his parents' death, Aiken was sent to live with an aunt in New Bedford, Massachusetts, where he spent the rest of his childhood. After graduating from the Middlesex School—where he edited the school paper—he entered Harvard University in 1907. There, he studied literature and wrote for the Harvard *Advocate*. Aiken also studied with and was deeply influenced by Santayana, a renowned philosopher and poet. Aiken also made a lifelong friend in classmate T. S. Eliot, who would become a major poet in his own right.

**A Burgeoning Poet**   By the time he graduated from Harvard in 1912, Aiken was already working as a freelance writer and spending much time writing his own prose. He published his first book in 1914, *Earth Triumphant and Other Tales in Verse*. In his early poetry—which he wrote while living in Cambridge, Massachusetts, and during travels abroad—Aiken experimented with adapting musical forms to poetry and using common individuals as central characters in his poems.

His interest in combining music and poetry peaked with a unified series of six long poems written between 1915 and 1920. He dubbed these poems "symphonies". These poems expressed a theme of personal identity and struggle to understand one's self. The most successful of Aiken's symphonies was *Senlin: A Biography* (1918).

**Writing Through World War I**   Aiken wrote these works—as well as his important narrative poem *Punch: The Immortal Liar, Documents in His History* (1921)—as World War I raged. World War I began in 1914 after Archduke Franz Ferdinand, the heir to the Austro-Hungarian throne, was assassinated, setting off a conflict between Austria-Hungary and Serbia. Because of entangled alliances, the whole of Europe was soon engulfed in the conflict. After being provoked by Germany in 1917, the United States joined the war on the side of France, Great Britain, and Russia. Aiken was granted an exemption from service because of his claim that he was in an "essential industry" as a poet.

In 1921, several years after the war ended, Aiken moved his family to England. (He had married Jessie McDonald in 1912, and had three children with her.)

They first lived in London before settling in Rye, Sussex. There, Aiken began to contribute reviews and commentaries on contemporary poetry to such periodicals as the *London Athenaeum*, while branching out into fiction. Among his first experiments with fiction was *Priapus and the Pool* (1922). Aiken also published significant collections of short stories, such as *Bring! Bring! and Other Stories* (1925) and *Costumes by Eros* (1928), as well as his first semi-autobiographical novel, *Blue Voyage* (1927).

**Personal Turmoil, Literary Triumph**   In the late 1920s and early 1930s, Aiken experienced a period of intense personal suffering that coincided with an extraordinarily productive literary phase in which he produced some of his most significant work. In 1930, Aiken both divorced his first wife and married Clarice Lorenz. He then attempted suicide in 1932. Amidst all this turmoil, he won a Pulitzer Prize in 1930 for his poetry compilation *Selected Poems* (1929), and published his novel *Great Circle* (1933), which the founder of psychoanalysis, Sigmund Freud, considered a masterpiece.

Aiken also began to publish verse that examined the self in relation to the greater world. Such books included *Time in the Rock: Preludes to Definition* (1936), which explored themes like the nature of love and betrayal as well as the attainment of understanding and transcendence. From 1934 to 1936, Aiken also continued his journalistic career by serving as a London correspondent for the *New Yorker* under the pseudonym Samuel Jeake Jr. His personal life continued to be tumultuous; he divorced his second wife in 1937, and married his third, the painter Mary Augusta Hoover, that same year.

**More War, More Poems**   Aiken returned to Massachusetts in 1939 as World War II was beginning in Europe. The war began when Nazi Germany, led by Adolf Hitler, invaded Poland in September 1939. England and France declared war on Germany, but Germany's powerful army soon controlled much of the European continent. The United States entered the war in 1941 after its Hawaiian naval base was bombed by Japan. The war was fought in a number of theaters in Europe, Asia, Africa, and the South Pacific, involving 61 countries and leaving 55 million people dead. But in Massachusetts, Aiken was far from the violence and bloodshed, and his poetry throughout the 1940s focused instead on his experiences in New England. Such collections as *Brownstone Eclogues and Other Poems* (1942) and *The Soldier* (1944) feature various stanzaic, rhythmic, and rhyme patterns, and concentrated Aiken's interest in cultural and ancestral heritage. Aiken's novels of this period were also New England-centered, including *A Heart for the Gods of Mexico* (1939) and *Conversation; or, Pilgrims' Progress* (1940).

From 1950 to 1952, Aiken served as a consultant in poetry to the Library of Congress. In 1952, he published his autobiographical novel, *Ushant: An Essay*, in which he wrote candidly about his marriages and affairs, his suicide attempt, and friendships with accomplished writers like Eliot and Ezra Pound. Aiken continued to publish challenging poetry, though at a slower pace than earlier in his life. Among these collections were *Sheepfold Hill: Fifteen Poems* (1958) and *Thee* (1967). In the early 1960s, Aiken returned to his native city, Savannah, Georgia, and remained there for the rest of his life. In 1973 he was appointed the Poet Laureate of Georgia, and died in Savannah on August 17 of that year.

## Works in Literary Context

*A Range of Influences* As a writer, Aiken was greatly influenced by his Harvard mentor, George Santayana. In Santayana's view, the world exists as a tactile and luminescent reality, full of beauty that serves as the framework of all vital, self-conscious existence. This aesthetic reaction to the world is found in Aiken's own poetry and fiction. However, because of the great pain and loss he personally experienced, Aiken did not view life naively or optimistically. Indeed, the murder-suicide of his parents also greatly informed his works and contributed to his interest in psychoanalytic thought. Aiken was further influenced by such authors as John Masefield, Edgar Allen Poe, Walt Whitman, Henry James, William James, Edgar Lee Masters, the Symbolists, and English Romanticists, as well as the composer Richard Strauss. For Aiken, music and poetry were undeniably linked, as he made clear in his poetic symphonies.

Aiken readily admitted that the influence of Sigmund Freud could be found throughout his work. In both his poetry and fiction, Aiken tried to expose motivations buried in the subconscious. He believed that if such motivations were left there, unspoken and unacknowledged, they could have as disastrous an effect as they had on his own father's life. In the novel *Great Circle* (1933), for example, the central character has to learn to accept his past—with the help of a psychoanalyst. *Blue Voyage* (1927) is ostensibly about a voyage to England, but the real voyage in this stream-of-consciousness novel is in the mind. Finally, the highly regarded short story "Silent Snow, Secret Snow" (1934) is a psychoanalytic portrait of a disturbed boy.

*Symphonies* Between 1915 and 1920, Aiken composed a unified sequence of six poems that he called "symphonies". This set included *The Jig of Forslin: A Symphony* (1916) and *The Pilgrimage of Festus* (1923). The six long pieces strived to achieve the contrapuntal effects of music by juxtaposing patterns of narrative repetition and variation. In the poems, words are regularly repeated. The opening and closing sections of *The House of Dust: A Symphony* (1920) feature the repetition of whole lines. Words and phrases are also repeated or echoed in multiple or varied situations, such as in the opening passages of parts one and two of *The House of Dust*. Though there is verbal repetition, situations are varied, such as in the morning, noon, and evening songs of

## LITERARY AND HISTORICAL CONTEMPORARIES

Conrad Aiken's famous contemporaries include:

**T. S. Eliot** (1888–1965): A Harvard classmate of Aiken's, this American-born poet and dramatist is considered by some critics to be the most important English-language poet of the twentieth century. He is best known for his poem *The Waste Land* (1922).

**Ezra Pound** (1885–1972): This modern American poet founded a poetic movement called Imagism, which linked techniques derived from the Symbolist movement with Asian poetry, like haiku. Pound's most famous poem is *Hugh Selwyn Mauberley* (1920).

**William Carlos Williams** (1883–1963): This American poet was also a medical doctor who had his own practice in Rutherford, New Jersey. Much of his work reflected the themes and speech patterns of ordinary life he observed in his medical practice. His works include *The Tempers* (1913).

**Sigmund Freud** (1856–1939): The Austrian founder of psychoanalysis, Freud launched the field of modern psychology by providing what he considered the first systematic explanation of the mental phenomena that determine human behavior. His publications include *The Interpretation of Dreams* (1901).

**James Whistler** (1834–1903): This American painter championed "art for art's sake" and introduced a subtle style of painting in which atmosphere and mood predominated. Literary critics have said that Whistler's paintings are reminiscent of Aiken's poetry. Among Whistler's best known works is "Arrangement in Grey and Black, the Artist's Mother" (1872).

*Senlin*. Interestingly, while the origins of the symphonies came from Aiken's passion for Richard Strauss, Aiken favored a more modern symphonic tradition. Aiken's poems feature abrupt transitions and elements of cacophony similar to the works of composer Igor Stravinsky.

## Works in Critical Context

Aiken received many prestigious literary awards, including the Pulitzer Prize, and he earned the critical acclaim of some of the most respected writers and critics of his time. However, he was never truly popular among critics and readers. The central problem for many critics is that his poetry seems to lack intensity. It conveys feelings of indefiniteness, and emotion seems dispersed or passive. Other critics feel that Aiken fails to speak with the intensity and precision of other poets because his poems dealt with aspects of man's psychology that are, by their very nature, indefinite, and indefinable in any precise way. Aiken was also praised for his ability to suggest through

# COMMON HUMAN EXPERIENCE

Aiken was influenced by the English Romantic poets. Significant poems written by these poets include:

*Lyrical Ballads, with a Few Other Poems* (1798), a poetry collection by William Wordsworth and Samuel Taylor Coleridge. This collection is considered the beginning of the English Romantic movement, and includes the famous Coleridge poem "The Rime of the Ancient Mariner."

"Queen Mab; A Philosophical Poem; With Notes" (1813), a poem by Percy Bysshe Shelley. This first large poetic work by Shelley outlines his theory of revolution.

*Don Juan* (1819–1824), a narrative poem by Lord Byron. This satiric poem is based on the legend of Don Juan, but portrays the notorious womanizer as a man easily seduced by women.

"Endymion" (1818), a poem by John Keats. This epic poem is based on the Greek myth of Endymion and is written in rhyming couplets in iambic pentameter.

sound, image, and rhythm the things that would otherwise remain unknown to readers. Many critics concluded that his fiction was merely a prosaic version of his poetry.

*Punch: The Immortal Liar, Documents In His History*   Of Aiken's earlier works, the narrative poem *Punch: The Immortal Liar, Documents In His History* was one of the best critically received of the time. Based on the figure from the Punch and Judy puppet shows, Aiken's protagonist is presented from several points of view that alternatively depict life as mysterious, ironic, and deterministic. Critics embraced this book more readily than Aiken's other works, with critics like Maxwell Anderson calling the second part of *Punch* "one of the most poignant lyrics ever written." In the *New Republic*, Amy Lowell commented that *Punch* was "one of the most significant books of the poetry renaissance."

*"Silent Snow, Secret Snow"*   "Silent Snow, Secret Snow" is another highly regarded piece by Aiken. Published in 1934, this short story focuses on a boy who is losing contact with reality and becoming schizophrenic. Aiken once admitted this story was an exploration of his own tendency towards insanity. Many critics regarded it as a Poe-like horror story in that it explored the tapping of unconscious fears. Critics praised how Aiken explored psyches, with Jesse G. Swan noting in a commentary on both the story and *Senlin: A Biography* in *The Southern Literary Journal* that, "In both pieces, the central figures experience something to which no one else seems to be sensitive. As this experience is uncommon, it demands uncommon material. Aiken succeeds in presenting these nebulous experiences by carefully casting silences into his work."

## Responses to Literature

1. Some critics regard Aiken's verse as very musical, reminiscent of the composer Claude Debussy. Listen to a few works by Debussy, and also find musical criticism about them. Then, write a paper in which you compare Aiken's verse, particularly his symphony poems, to what you hear in and read about Debussy.

2. Look at several paintings by James Whistler, particularly his atmospheric paintings from the early 1870s that he called the "nocturnes." Create a presentation in which you compare Aiken's verse to Whistler's paintings, as some critics believe that Whistler's paintings of this period are reminiscent of Aiken's poetry.

3. In a small group, research the New York School of poetry, with which Aiken is sometimes linked because of his experiments with poetic music. Compare Aiken's poetry with the works of other poets in the group, especially John Ashbery.

4. Research the theories of Sigmund Freud or George Santayana. Write an essay in which you apply a theory or philosophical idea to a work of Aiken's, perhaps a poem or short story, or one of his novels.

BIBLIOGRAPHY

**Books**

Butscher, Edward. *Conrad Aiken: Poet of White Horse Vale*. Athens, Ga.: University of Georgia Press, 1988.

Denney, Reuel. *Conrad Aiken*. Minneapolis, Minn.: University of Minnesota Press, 1964.

Killorin, Joseph, ed. *Selected Letters of Conrad Aiken*. New Haven, Conn.: Yale University Press, 1978.

Martin, Jay. *Conrad Aiken, A Life of His Art*. Princeton, N.J.: Princeton University Press, 1962.

Spivey, Ted Ray. *Time's Stop in Savannah: Conrad Aiken's Inner Journey*. Macon, Ga.: Mercer University Press, 1997.

**Periodicals**

Anderson, Maxwell. Review of *Punch: The Immortal Liar, Documents In His History*. *Measure* (May 1921).

Lowell, Amy. Review of *Punch: The Immortal Liar, Documents In His History*. *New Republic* (September 1921).

Swan, Jesse G. "At the Edge of Sound and Silence: Conrad Aiken's *Senlin: A Biography* and 'Silent Snow, Secret Snow'." *Southern Literary Journal* (Fall 1989): 41–49.

# ✸ Edward Albee

BORN: *1928, Virginia*

NATIONALITY: *American*

GENRE: *Drama*

MAJOR WORKS:

*The Zoo Story* (1959)

*Who's Afraid of Virginia Woolf?* (1962)

*A Delicate Balance* (1966)

*Three Tall Women* (1994)

*The Goat, or Who Is Sylvia?* (2002)

## Overview

Best known for his first full-length drama, *Who's Afraid of Virginia Woolf?* (1962), Edward Albee is among the United States' most acclaimed contemporary playwrights. A multiple Pulitzer Prize-winner, Albee's peak came in the 1960s when his controversial dramas were both celebrated for their intensity and reviled for their graphic nature. Albee has continued to write plays over subse-quent decades, finding success into the twenty-first century with the Tony Award-winning *The Goat, or Who Is Sylvia?* (2002).

## Works in Biographical and Historical Context

*A Rich But Lonely Life* Albee was born Edward Harvey on March 12, 1928, most likely in the state of Virginia. He was adopted at birth by Reed Albee and Frances Cotter, who renamed him Edward Franklin Albee III. Albee's adoptive father was heir to the Keith-Albee chain of vaudeville theaters. This theater circuit controlled many playhouses across the country, at which vaudeville acts, plays, and movies were shown.

The Albees were wealthy and as a child, young Edward was spoiled and pampered. Yet despite his indulgent childhood, Albee's early years were generally unhappy. His domineering mother took every opportunity to remind him that he was adopted, especially when she was angry with him. He had a similarly troubled relationship with his father. As a result, Albee was a bit

Edward Albee    © *Jerry Bauer. Reproduced by permission.*

of a loner, and took up writing poetry at the age of six. He found solace in parental surrogates, including a beloved governess and his maternal grandmother.

***A Blossoming Playwright*** Albee was exposed to theater at an early age. The family chauffeur would regularly drive him and his nanny to New York City where they would catch matinees of Broadway shows. When he was twelve years old, Albee wrote his first play, a three-act sexual comedy called *Aliqueen*. It was perhaps his early exploration of sex through writing that helped Albee realize he was homosexual by the age of thirteen.

By this time, Albee was being educated at private boarding and military schools as his parents traveled to the South each winter. After being expelled from two schools for his sometimes rambunctious behavior, Albee completed his education at Choate, an elite, private, boarding school in Wallingford, Connecticut. There, he blossomed intellectually. At Choate he wrote his first novel, *The Flesh of Unbelievers*, and became a prolific poet. In fact, Albee published his first poem in a professional publication, the *Kalediograph*, while still attending the school.

After graduating from Choate in 1946, Albee attended Trinity College, where he spent three semesters. However, he was an unenthusiastic student, and was expelled in 1947 for skipping classes and other behavior. Albee returned to his parents' home for a time, then moved to New York City, living off a small trust fund he inherited upon the death of his paternal grandmother in 1949. Albee cut off communication with his parents at this point. He made his home in Greenwich Village, but traveled to Italy, where he wrote a novel. When he was not writing or traveling, Albee held various odd jobs, such as a messenger for Western Union. It was also during this time that he befriended other authors, including poet W.H. Auden and playwright Thornton Wilder. It was these relationships and his love of writing that helped him decide to pursue writing as a career.

As Albee's thirtieth birthday approached, he felt intensely dissatisfied. While he had written many plays during the 1950s, most were never published or produced. In a blitz of inspiration, in February 1958 he quit his Western Union job and wrote what became his first hit play, a one-act called *The Zoo Story*, in just three weeks. The play was a darkly humorous exchange between a disturbed outcast and a conventional, middle-class man. Unable to find a U.S. producer for *The Zoo Story*, Albee premiered the work in Berlin in 1959. The play debuted in the U.S. in 1960, when American theater was beginning to examine a seamier and more graphic side of life.

***New York Star*** In 1960 and 1961, Albee wrote four more one-act plays which met with great success Off-Broadway. These included *The Sandbox* (1960) and *The American Dream* (1961). In 1962, Albee's first full-length play, *Who's Afraid of Virginia Woolf?*, was produced on Broadway. The play focuses on two couples—one of whom verbally abuse each other in front of the other—who come together in a harrowing, drunken, late-night journey into truth and illusion. Audiences both laughed and gasped at the play's passion and maliciousness. *Who's Afraid of Virginia Woolf?* won the Tony Award for Best Play in 1963, and cemented Albee's success as a playwright.

Despite his professional triumphs, in the 1960s, Albee—along with playwrights William Inge and Tennessee Williams—became the victim of several vicious homophobic attacks from the press, particularly the *New York Times*. Critics accused him and his gay colleagues of sullying American theater with homosexual influences. Despite such accusations, *Virginia Woolf* was embraced by homosexuals as an important part of gay culture.

***Triumphs and Flops*** After two adaptations of other author's works which were relative failures (*The Ballad of the Sad Café*, 1963; *Malcolm*, 1966); and the problematic original play *Tiny Alice* (1964), Albee won his first Pulitzer Prize with the well-received *A Delicate Balance* (1966). He rounded out the decade with an adaptation of *Everything in the Garden* (1967) and two inter-related abstract works, *Box* (1968) and *Quotations from Chairman Mao Tse-Tung* (1968).

Albee continued to write for the next five decades, though critics did not always embrace him or his plays. While he won his second Pulitzer Prize for the 1975 play *Seascape*, other plays, such as *The Lady from Dubuque* (1978) and *The Man Who Had Three Arms* (1982), became legendary Broadway disasters. Perhaps Albee's most ill-fated work during this time was his adaptation of the novel *Lolita* (1981), originally by Vladimir Nabokov. Albee's play was rejected by audiences and critics alike.

***The Dropout Returns to University*** By the 1980s, Albee became involved in teaching, an ironic turn for a college dropout. He taught at several universities, including the University of California at Irvine from 1983 to 1985. He also formed a long-term relationship with the University of Houston beginning in 1984, and served as the chairman of the theater department at Fordham University for a time. Albee's creative writing during this period did not abate, however, and he honed his skills on a series of short plays. He returned to writing full-length dramas in the early 1990s, at which point he won his third Pulitzer Prize for *Three Tall Women* (1994). This play was as intensely autobiographical as any of his other works, but stylistically experimental. *Three Tall Women* featured an ineffectual father and a monstrous mother who spends a significant portion of the play attacking her gay son. The characters clearly reflected the troubled relationship Albee had with his own parents. Interestingly, his mother died in 1990, just before the play was written.

Albee wrote at least two more full-length plays in the early twenty-first century as he continued to teach at the university level. *The Play About the Baby* was produced in London and Off-Broadway in 2001, and *The Goat, or Who is Sylvia?* (2000) garnered him another Tony Award in 2002. Albee continues to live and write in New York City.

## Works in Literary Context

Albee usually combines elements from the American tradition of social criticism established by such playwrights as Arthur Miller, Tennessee Williams (a primary influence), and Eugene O'Neill with aspects of the Theater of the Absurd, a style of writing practiced by Samuel Beckett and Eugène Ionesco, which views the human condition as meaningless and inexplicable. However, while Albee often portrays alienated individuals who suffer as a result of unjust social, moral, or religious strictures, he usually offers solutions to conflicts rather than conveying an absurdist sense of inescapable determinism. In many of Albee's plays, especially the quasi-autobiographical ones, he writes about his troubled relationship with his adoptive parents, a source of inspiration for much of his work.

*Albee and Absurdism*   In absurdism or the "Theater of the Absurd," writers address the absurdity of modern life. Such writers believe the world is full of evil and view life as a malevolent condition that cannot be explained by traditional standards of morality. Since there can be no certainty that God exists, individuals find themselves forced to live without hope in a chaotic world filled with irrationality and certain death. Albee wrote at least four plays considered by critics and scholars to be absurdist. The characters in these plays struggle with moral issues and have to learn the lesson that truth is what an individual thinks it is.

The Death of Bessie Smith (1960), for example, commented on the absurdity of race relations in the United States at that time. The story focuses on the demise of an African-American singer who bled to death after a car accident because she was denied care at an all-white hospital. Through his characters, Albee criticized the American values and social institutions that would allow such a death to occur. Albee took the opportunity to comment further on American society in *The Zoo Story*, (1958) which focused on the material comfort, hypocrisy, and optimism that pervaded American culture in the 1950s. The play reflects his disillusioned cynicism as well his rebellion against a world filled with conformity.

*Dysfunctional, Cruel Families*   As a result of his own negative childhood and difficult relationship with his parents, especially his mother, Albee often depicts family life in the United States as complacent and cruel. Plays such as *The American Dream* and *The Sandbox* reflect the playwright's concern with the lack of true family values. In *The American Dream*, for example, an adopted son is punished to death by his middle-class parents for misbehaving and failing to meet their expectations. After he dies, his long-lost twin appears as a young man and is adopted by the same family, but the twin carries the emotional scars of his deceased brother's abuse. Albee portrays a similarly dysfunctional family in *Who's Afraid of Virginia Woolf?* via the relationship of George and Martha, who are verbally abusive to one another. Albee

---

## LITERARY AND HISTORICAL CONTEMPORARIES

Edward Albee's famous contemporaries include:

**W.H. Auden** (1907–1973): This modernist poet was born and raised in England, but immigrated to the United States and became an American citizen. His books include *Another Time* (1940).

**Thornton Wilder** (1897–1975): This American playwright is considered one of the best in American history. A professor of poetry at Harvard, his plays included the Pulitzer Prize-winning *Our Town* (1938).

**Mike Nichols** (1931–): This Academy Award-winning filmmaker directed the film version of *Who's Afraid of Virginia Woolf?*, released in 1966.

**William Inge** (1913–1973): This American playwright and screenwriter often focused on Midwestern, small town America in his works. His plays include *Picnic* (1953) and *Bus Stop* (1955).

**Eugène Ionesco** (1912–1994): This Romanian-born French dramatist is considered one of the leading absurdist playwrights, a style of dramatism embraced by Albee. His plays include *The Chairs* (1952).

---

returns to more specifically autobiographical matters in *Three Tall Women*. The primary character was inspired by his own mother, and the play by their troubled relationship. His mother was a bigoted, insensitive woman who pushed her homosexual son out of her life, as does the woman in the play.

## Works in Critical Context

In his best works, critics believe that Albee successfully combined the experimentation of modern British and continental playwrights, such as Jean Genet, with the American fascination with the family. Yet Albee's detractors criticize the chilly, intellectual quality of his work. Thus, his position in the history of American drama is difficult to assess. He has ardent admirers who laud his dialogue and technical skills, while others lament his popular and critical success as disproportionate to his talent. He is generally congratulated, however, for being willing to experiment (even if he sometimes failed) with blending the surreal, the poetic, and hermetic into a naturalistic tradition, all while committing himself to the serious articulation of the existential questions of our time.

*The American Dream*   When *The American Dream* debuted in 1961, it received mixed reviews. While some critics praised the play for its insight into the contemporary mindset, John Gassner in *Dramatic Soundings:*

## COMMON HUMAN EXPERIENCE

Some of the most highly acclaimed plays of Albee's career were identified with the "Theater of the Absurd." Here are some other absurdist plays:

*The New Tenant* (1957), a play by Eugène Ionesco. This play centers on a protagonist whose apartment becomes progressively filled with furniture.

*The Dumb Waiter* (1959), a play by Harold Pinter. The play focuses on two working class British lads who spend a morning in a basement bedroom in Birmingham, England, awaiting instructions from the organization for which they work. One is eventually ordered to kill the other.

*Waiting for Godot* (1953), a play by Samuel Beckett. This avant-garde tragicomic play has at its center two tramps who are awaiting the arrival of a mysterious Mr. Godot.

*Deathwatch* (1949), a play by Jean Genet. This play focuses on the ritualistic efforts of a petty criminal, trapped in a cell with two killers, to achieve the saintly designation of murderer. Because he has not killed without reason or motive, as his cellmates have, he is ridiculed for his immoral inferiority.

*Evaluations and Retractions Culled from 30 Years of Drama Criticism* wrote, "The trouble with Albee's acutely original play, *The American Dream*, is that its bizarre Ionesco details don't add up to an experience." Other critics initially characterized *The American Dream* as defeatist and nihilistic. Yet the play was also commended for its savage parody of traditional American values. More recent critics appreciate the play's breakdown in conventional dramatic language. In *American Playwrights Since 1945: A Guide to Scholarship, Criticism, and Performance*, Matthew Roudane writes "In both text and performance, Albee's technical virtuosity emanates from an ability to capture the values, personal politics, and perceptions of his characters through language."

### Who's Afraid of Virginia Woolf?

*Who's Afraid of Virginia Woolf?* was Albee's most acclaimed drama when produced on Broadway in 1961. Since its original production, it has generated popular and critical notoriety for its controversial depiction of marital strife. Yet *Virginia Woolf* was also faulted as morbid and self-indulgent by early critics. Over the years, many scholars have offered different interpretations of the drama. Some see it as a problem play in the tradition of August Strindberg, a Scandinavian author who experimented with Naturalism and Expressionism. Others view it as a campy parody, while still others interpret it as a latent homosexual critique of conventional relationships.

Since the 1960s, *Virginia Woolf* has also been assessed as a classic American drama for its tight control of form and command of both colloquial and abstruse dialogue. Of the play, Robert Corrigon in *The Theater in Search of a Fix* observed, "Great drama has always shown man at the limits of possibility.... In *Virginia Woolf* Albee has stretched them some, and in doing so he has given, not only the American theatre, but the theatre of the whole world, a sense of new possiblity."

## Responses to Literature

1. While some critics have identified Albee's early one-act plays with the "Theater of the Absurd," the playwright does not believe his plays fall under this category. Read one of these plays. Based on your reading of the play and your understanding of the "Theater of the Absurd," argue whether or not you think Albee is, in fact, an absurdist.

2. Create a presentation in which you compare and contrast a play of Eugene O'Neill's with Albee's *Who's Afraid of Virginia Woolf?* Why do you think critics see Albee as O'Neill's heir? How are the playwrights and their plays similar and different?

3. Read *Three Tall Women* aloud in a small group. Have each person in the group take the point of view of a character. Then, debate the nature of the drama and how it relates to Albee's life.

4. Watch the film version of *Who's Afraid of Virginia Woolf?* (1966), directed by Mike Nichols. In an essay, compare and contrast the play with the film. What creative choices make the film different from the play? What elements of Albee's work are preserved and which ones are altered?

BIBLIOGRAPHY

**Books**

Corrigan, Robert. *The Theater in Search of a Fix* New York; Delacorte, 1973.

Gassner, John. "Edward Albee: An American Dream?" In *Dramatic Soundings: Evaluations and Retractions Culled from 30 Years of Drama Criticism.* New York: Crown, 1968, pp, 591–592.

Gussow, Mel. *Edward Albee: A Singular Journey.* New York: Simon and Schuster, 1999.

Roudane, Matthew. "Edward Albee [28 March 1928–]." In *American Playwrights Since 1945: A Guide to Scholarship, Criticism, and Performance.* New York: Greenwood Press, 1989.

**Periodicals**

Carter, Steven. "Albee's *Who's Afraid of Virginia Woolf?*" *Explicator* (Summer 1998): 215–218.

Kuhn, John. "Getting Albee's Goat: 'Notes Toward a Definition of Tragedy'." *American Drama* (Summer 2004): 1–32.

Pero, Allan. "The Crux of Melancholy: Edward Albee's *A Delicate Balance.*" *Modern Drama* (Summer 2006): 174–184.

MacFarquhar, Larissa "Passion Plays: The Making of Edward Albee." *New Yorker* (April 4, 2005): 69–77.

Rocamora, Carol. "Albee Sizes Up the Dark Vast: Older, Wiser, and as Prolific as Ever, the Much-honored Playwright Still Chooses his Words with Immaculate Care." *American Theatre* (January 2008): 30.

# ✸ Mitch Albom

BORN: *1958, Passaic, New Jersey*

NATIONALITY: *American*

GENRE: *Nonfiction, fiction*

MAJOR WORKS:

*Tuesdays with Morrie: An Old Man, A Young Man, and Life's Greatest Lesson* (1997)

*The Five People You Meet in Heaven* (2003)

*For One More Day* (2006)

## Overview

An award-winning sports reporter, Mitch Albom earned national attention for his sports columns which were distinguished by his insight, humor, and empathy. These qualities led to a secondary career as an internationally acclaimed nonfiction author, and later novelist. Albom became a phenomenon in the late 1990s with publication of his memoir *Tuesdays with Morrie: An Old Man, a Young Man, and Life's Greatest Lesson* (1997), about the time he spent with his former professor as he was dying of amyotrophic lateral sclerosis (ALS), also known as Lou Gehrig's disease.

## Works in Biographical and Historical Context

***Studied with Morrie Schwartz*** Mitchell David Albom was born May 23, 1958, in Passaic, New Jersey, the second of three children of Ira and Rhoda Albom. His father worked as a corporate executive while his mother was an interior designer. Albom earned his BA in sociology from Brandeis University in 1979. While a student at Brandeis, he was particularly influenced by one professor, Morrie Schwartz, who urged his students to disdain high-paying careers and follow their hearts instead. Though Schwartz urged him to stay in touch after graduation, Albom did not contact him for over sixteen years. Instead, Albom moved to New York City, and while briefly working on a music career as a piano player, he enrolled at Columbia University, where he earned a masters of journalism in 1981 and an MBA in 1982.

By this time, Albom had begun his newspaper career as an editor at the *Queens Tribune* from 1981 to 1982. He then moved on to contributing-writer positions at

Mitch Albom    *Albom, Mitch, photograph. AP Images.*

several different East Coast newspapers. In 1985, Albom joined the *Detroit Free Press* as a sports columnist and soon became a star writer.

***Award-Winning Sports Writer*** Writing for the *Free Press*, Albom dismissed the negative stereotypes about Detroit and spent several decades writing about what he considered one of the leading sports cities in the United States. At the time, Detroit, like much of Michigan, was still recovering from the economic recession of the early 1980s which deeply affected the auto industry—the state's dominant employer. This recovery would last throughout the late 1980s, though Detroit, and Michigan as a whole, would continue to rely on the automotive industry to its economic detriment for many years to come.

As a sports writer, Albom reflected the concerns of his readers in this environment. He disdained the questionable ethical conduct, drug problems, and overinflated egos often found in the sports world. Instead, he emphasized honesty and accountability. Albom highlighted instances of athletic courage and determination while providing factual commentary on an individual or team's performance. His ability to sympathize with fans, as well

## LITERARY AND HISTORICAL CONTEMPORARIES

Albom's famous contemporaries include:

**Amy Tan** (1952–): This Asian American novelist began writing fiction as a distraction from her job as a technical writer. Her best-selling books include *The Joy Luck Club* (1989).

**Dave Barry** (1947–): This American humorist was a long-time columnist for the *Miami Herald*. His humor books include *The Taming of the Screw: Several Million Homeowners' Problems* (1983).

**Stephen King** (1947–): This American author is one of the best-selling writers of all time. Best known for his horror novels, King's works include *Carrie* (1973) and *Insomnia* (1994).

**Bill Clinton** (1946–): This two-term American president oversaw strong economic growth through much of the 1990s. Clinton previously served as the governor of Arkansas.

**Lee Iacocca** (1924–): An American businessman, he was the president and chairman of the Chrysler Corporation, an automotive manufacturer, from 1979 to 1992.

as their teams, earned him a loyal following and a reputation as a writer with a blue-collar perspective.

The quality of Albom's sports writing has led to numerous awards. He was named the number-one sports columnist in the United States by the Associated Press Sports editors every year between 1987 and 1998. His success in print has also carried over into the broadcast media. Albom had also branched into writing books. In addition to the first compilation of his sports columns, *The Live Albom: The Best of Detroit Free Press Sports Columnist Mitch Albom* (1988), he also helped legendary University of Michigan football coach Bo Schembechler write his autobiography, *Bo: The Bo Schembechler Story* (1988). In this book, Albom underscored how the seemingly churlish coach was a really a sincere family man whose surly demeanor was a deliberate act.

***Success with Tuesdays with Morrie***   Albom continued to write sports-related books in the early 1990s. Watching *Nightline* one night in 1995, Albom saw his former professor Morrie Schwartz discussing his battles with ALS while remaining cheerful, pragmatic, and writing a book about the final stages of life. ALS is a neurodegenerative disease in which specific nerve cells—motor neurons that control movement—are damaged or killed. The cause of the disease is unknown. It is always fatal.

Soon thereafter, Albom went to visit Schwartz at his home in Massachusetts on a Tuesday, and returned on the same day of the week for the next fourteen weeks, till

Schwartz died. Albom wrote a book based on their conversations to help defray the family's medical expenses, and to share his revelation that his dying professor was a happier, more peaceful person than he was, though Albom was younger, healthier, and more successful. The book became the best-selling nonfiction book in the United States in 1998, spent at least four years on the best-seller list, and was later made into a popular television movie.

***Published Two More Novels***   Because of the popularity of *Tuesdays with Morrie*, Albom's career expanded as he began writing more often about non-sports topics and became a sought-after public speaker. Continuing to challenge himself, Albom published his first novel in 2003, *Five People You Meet in Heaven*. The stories are based on stories his uncle told him as a child, and concern a grizzled old man named Eddie who does not learn his true worth as a person until after his death. *Five People You Meet in Heaven* was also a best-seller for Albom, with at least eight million copies in print.

After writing his first produced stage play—the comedy *Duck Hunter Shoots Angel* was staged at the Purple Rose Theater in Chelsea, Michigan, in 2004—Albom returned to novels with *One More Day* (2006). In this book, a washed-up athlete, Charles "Chick" Benetto, fails in a suicide attempt. Yet, while he is injured, he is somehow transported to his childhood home and gains self-knowledge from the ghost of his deceased mother.

Albom continues to live in Detroit, where he writes about sports and other topics for the *Free Press*, hosts his syndicated radio program, *The Mitch Albom Show*, and produces popular literature.

## Works in Literary Context

Albom has written several best-selling, non-sports books that emphasize the importance of self-awareness, the idea that life matters, and the value of having convictions and ideals. Often using the power of death as a springboard to a better understanding of self and how to live, his works are intended to inspire readers to change their lives for the better instead of focusing on such pursuits as fame and fortune. Albom also emphasizes that time is not endless. As an author, Albom was greatly influenced by his college mentor, Schwartz, who was the focus of *Tuesdays with Morrie*.

***Importance of Living with Ideals***   In his non-sports books, Albom often underscores the importance of living a life that is reflective, appreciative, and, in some ways, idealistic. In *Tuesdays with Morrie* for example, Albom relates how, without realizing it, he had slowly abandoned his youthful ideals, and become cynical, spiritually shallow, and materialistic. Working around the clock to maintain his career had left him with little time for reflection. Schwartz, Albom noted, helped his former student to refocus his life, and the pair discussed such weighty topics as fear, aging, greed, family, and forgiveness. A similar message is imparted in Albom's novel *For One More Day*. In that work, the main character comes to understand how he should live his life.

**Death and the Value of Life**   In his popular writing, Albom often uses the concept of death to highlight the importance of life. In *Tuesdays with Morrie*, the dying Schwartz encourages Albom to slow down and appreciate the life he has been given. In Albom's novels, this idea is explored more deeply. At the center of *The Five People You Meet in Heaven* is Eddie, an older, unappreciated veteran who works as a maintenance man at an amusement park and dies while trying to save the life of a little girl. It is not until his death that the value of his life becomes clear to him and the reader. In heaven, Eddie meets five people who help him gain understanding about life's meaning and his own value. Similarly, in *For One More Day*, Chick tries to kill himself after the death of his mother, Pauline. Only injured, he finds himself transported to his boyhood home. There, Pauline's ghost returns to life for one more day to present him with basic truths about himself and their shared past.

## Works in Critical Context

While Albom is highly regarded as a sports writer, many critics are dismissive of his non-sports books as sentimental and overly simplistic in how they address major themes and ideas. *Tuesdays with Morrie* may have been wildly popular with readers, but a number of reviewers found fault with the book as well as Albom's two novels. They have often cited these works' schmaltzy language and predictable plots.

**Tuesdays with Morrie**   Critics were divided over *Tuesdays with Morrie*; many found the book generally facile, but others contended that its message was indeed inspiring. In the *New York Times*, Alain de Botton was critical of Schwartz's words of wisdom. Botton wrote that "One gets whiffs of Jesus, the Buddha, Epicurus, Montaigne and Erik Erikson" from his discourses. Botton admits that Schwartz gave "true and sometimes touching pieces of advice" but that such words "don't add up to a very wise book." In contrast, an anonymous reviewer in *Publishers Weekly* concluded that *Tuesday with Morrie* was "an emotionally rich book and a deeply affecting memorial to a wise mentor." *People* contributor William Plummer responded positively to the book, noting

> the reader hears Morrie advise Mitch to slow down and savor the moment . . . to give up striving for bigger toys and, above all, to invest himself in love. Familiar pronouncements, of course, but what makes them fresh is Morrie's eloquence, his lack of self-pity . . . and his transcendent humor, even in the face of death.

**The Five People You Meet in Heaven**   As with *Tuesdays with Morrie*, critics were divided over the way

## COMMON HUMAN EXPERIENCE

*The Five People You Meet in Heaven* is set in heaven. Here are some other books which are set in heaven or in which heaven plays a prominent role:

*The Lovely Bones* (2002), a novel by Alice Sebold. Told from the perspective of a young murder victim in heaven, the novel also explores the effect her absence has on her family and community.

*Divine Comedy* (c. 1308–1321), an epic poem by Dante. In each of its three sections (Inferno, Purgatory, and Paradise), Dante the poet recounts the travels and spiritual awakening of his alter ego, the Pilgrim.

*Can't Wait to Get to Heaven: A Novel* (2006), a novel by Fannie Flagg. In this book, the aged Elner Shimfissle falls out of a tree, seems to die, and believes she visits heaven.

*The Great Divorce* (1945), a novel by C. S. Lewis. In this work, the narrator accompanies a busload of souls from hell on a trip to the outskirts of heaven. Each chapter is an episode in which a soul has to wrestle with its sin and decide either to repent and win heaven or to refuse and return to hell.

Albom delivered his message in *The Five People You Meet in Heaven*. Writing in *Book*, reviewer Don McLeese noted that "Eddie's story mainly serves as an excuse for a string of quasi-platitudes, warmed-over wisdom." More positively, an anonymous reviewer in *Publishers Weekly* commented, "One by one, these mostly unexpected characters remind [Eddie] that we all live in a vast web of interconnection . . . and that loyalty and love matter to a degree that we can never fathom." And *Booklist* contributor Brad Hooper called the novel "A sweet book that makes you smile but is not gooey with overwrought sentiment."

## Responses to Literature

1. Using *Tuesdays with Morrie* as a model, write a short story about an individual who changes someone's life.

2. Some critics have compared *The Five People You Meet in Heaven* to the classic Charles Dickens novel *A Christmas Carol*. Write an essay in which you compare and contrast the two works.

3. Watch the television movie version of *Tuesdays with Morrie* (1999), starring Hank Azaria as Albom and Jack Lemmon as Schwartz. Create a presentation in which you compare and contrast the book and movie versions. In what ways are the two different? Which do you think offers a more compelling experience, and why?

4. Have each member of a small group read Albom's two novels. In a group setting, discuss how Albom depicts the afterlife in each book. Which novel is more effective in underscoring its message?

BIBLIOGRAPHY

**Periodicals**

De Botton, Alain. Review of *Tuesdays with Morrie*. *New York Times* (November 23, 1997): 20.

Hooper, Brad. Review of *Five People You Meet in Heaven*. *Booklist* (September 1, 2003): 5.

McLeese, Don. Review of *Five People You Meet in Heaven*. *Book* (September 1, 2003): 5.

Plummer, William. "Memento Morrie: Morrie Schwartz, While Dying, Teaches Writer Mitch Albom the Secrets of Living." *People* (January 12, 1998): 141.

Review of *Five People You Meet in Heaven*. *Publishers Weekly* (July 28, 2003): 18.

Review of *Tuesdays with Morrie*. *Publishers Weekly* (June 30, 1997): 60.

# ✸ Louisa May Alcott

BORN: *1832, Germantown, Pennsylvania*

DIED: *1888, Boston, Massachusetts*

NATIONALITY: *American*

GENRE: *Fiction*

MAJOR WORKS:

*Little Women, or Meg, Jo, Beth, and Amy* (1868–69)

*Little Men: Life at Plumfield with Jo's Boys* (1871)

*Work: A Story of Experience* (1873)

*Under the Lilacs* (1878)

*Jo's Boys, and How They Turned Out: A Sequel to "Little Men"* (1886)

## Overview

Louisa May Alcott is best known for her sentimental yet realistic depictions of nineteenth-century domestic life. Her "Little Women" series attracted young and old readers alike and remains popular today. Alcott's continuing popular appeal is generally attributed to her believable characterizations and simple, charming writing style, reflected in her adage: "Never use a long word when a short one will do as well." In the late-twentieth century, scholars gave increased attention to Alcott's works, with literary critics noting her prevalent feminist and psychosexual themes. Alcott scholar Madeleine B. Stern noted that "today...[Alcott] is viewed as an experimenting, complex writer, and her work has become fertile ground for the exploration both of literary historians and psychohistorians."

Louisa May Alcott   *AP Images*

## Works in Biographical and Historical Context

***Daughter of a Famous New England Family***
Louisa May Alcott, the second of four daughters, was born in Germantown, Pennsylvania, and raised in Boston and Concord, Massachusetts. Her father, Amos Bronson Alcott, was a noted New England transcendentalist philosopher and educator who worked only sporadically throughout Louisa May's life. Her mother, Abigail May Alcott, was descended from Judge Samuel Sewall (a former chief justice of Massachusetts infamous for his role in the Salem witch trials of 1692) and the noted abolitionist Colonel Joseph May. Although her family was poor, Alcott's childhood was apparently happy. Taught by her father, Alcott was deeply influenced by his transcendentalist thought and experimental educational philosophies. Ralph Waldo Emerson's personal library of classics and philosophy was available for use to the young Alcott. Also influential on Alcott was Henry David Thoreau, whose cabin she visited and who taught her botany. Margaret Fuller, Nathaniel Hawthorne, and Julia Ward Howe were only a few of the Alcott family's intellectually influential neighbors and friends.

Bronson Alcott founded several schools based on his controversial educational methods, but all of them failed, forcing Abigail and her daughters to undertake the financial support of the family. Later, Alcott often remarked that her entire career was inspired by her desire to compensate for her family's early discomfort. Alcott taught school, took in sewing, and worked briefly as a domestic servant. At age sixteen she began writing, convinced that she could eventually earn enough money to alleviate the family's poverty. In 1851, her first poem was published under the pseudonym Flora Fairfield, bringing Alcott little money but a great deal of confidence. It was during the ensuing years that Alcott published, as A. M. Barnard, a number of sensational serial stories in low-price magazines; the works were both popular and lucrative.

*Civil War Nursing Experience*  In 1862, Alcott traveled to Washington, D.C., to serve as a nurse to soldiers wounded in the U.S. Civil War. The Civil War remains the costliest war ever fought by the United States in terms of lives lost. More than 600,000 soldiers died in the conflict. Women played a major role in the care of wounded soldiers, and their volunteer work in hospitals during the war paved the way for women seeking to enter the nursing profession in future generations. Alcott's time as a nurse was a short-lived experience, however, for she contracted typhoid within a month and nearly died. Her good health, undermined by the long illness and by mercury poisoning from her medication, was never fully recovered. Alcott later recounted her experiences as a nurse in her popular *Hospital Sketches* (1863). Her first novel, the ambitious *Moods* (1864), was pronounced immoral by critics, yet sold well, and its success encouraged Alcott to continue writing. In 1865, Alcott traveled through Europe as a companion to a wealthy invalid and wrote for periodicals. While abroad, she was offered the editorship of *Merry's Museum*, an American journal featuring juvenile literature. She accepted the position and became the journal's chief contributor.

*Finding Fame in Family Stories*  The turning point in Alcott's career came with the publication of *Little Women; or, Meg, Jo, Beth, and Amy*, the first part of which appeared in 1868. The project was initiated after Alcott's editor suggested she pen a book for girls, a project for which Alcott expressed little interest. Without other inspiration, Alcott produced an idealized, autobiographical account of nineteenth-century family life, recasting the youth of herself and her sisters. The work was an immediate success and established Alcott as a major American author. She published four sequels to *Little Women*, entitled *Good Wives* (volume two of *Little Women*), *Little Men: Life at Plumfield with Jo's Boys* (1871), *Aunt Jo's Scrap Bag* (1872–82), and *Jo's Boys and How They Turned Out* (1886). Alcott was regarded as a celebrity and was easily able to support her family with her earnings.

*Life After Little Women*  Although she had become a well-known and beloved author, Alcott continued liv-

ing with her parents, never marrying, and churning out a string of successful novels. She apparently wrote a chapter a day as she hurried to finish the second part of *Little Women* and biographers speculate that her health suffered greatly from such periods of intense productivity. From 1875 onward, as her health deteriorated, Alcott primarily produced popular juvenile literature. Most of her later works, particularly *Work: A Story of Experience* (1873) and *Rose in Bloom* (1876), depict heroines who have acquired inner strength through personal hardship and achieved personal satisfaction through careers and without marriage. In general, these works, often autobiographical, provoked mixed reviews. Working until she could no longer hold a pen, Alcott died in March 1888, just two days after the death of her father.

# COMMON HUMAN EXPERIENCE

Alcott's most enduring works concern the adventures of American families as they struggle to remain devout and moral while respecting the lives to which family members, especially young women, are called. Often, her characters find their desire to be true to themselves clashes with conventional social roles for women. Other works which focus on these issues include the following:

*Pride and Prejudice* (1813), a novel by Jane Austen. This British novel traces the fortunes of the Bennet family and the plight of each daughter as the family seeks to find them good husbands. The story focuses on the playful and intelligent Elizabeth Bennet and her relationship with the mysterious Mr. Darcy.

*The Morgesons* (1862), a novel by Elizabeth Stoddard. Written by a lesser-known contemporary of Alcott, this novel tells the tale of Cassandra Morgenson, a woman who seeks to live life by her own rules within the restrictive culture of nineteenth-century New England.

*The Bell Jar* (1963), a novel by Sylvia Plath. An enduringly popular novel that helped spark the second feminist movement of the 1960s. The story follows the brilliant but troubled Esther Greenwood as she tries to choose between a career and motherhood in the United States of the 1950s.

*Bend it Like Beckham* (2002), a film directed by Gurinder Chadha. This British film uses humor to consider the difficult choices often faced by immigrant women. Jesminder is a daughter of Punjabi Sikh immigrants to London. She finds herself dreaming of life as a professional soccer player rather than as a traditional Punjabi mother and homemaker.

## Works in Literary Context

**Sentimental Fiction** Many of Alcott's contemporary popular women novelists have fallen out of print but she wrote in a widely-used fashion clearly identifiable to her readers. Often called sentimental or domestic fiction, novels such as *Little Women* centered on the spiritual and moral progress of young women toward adulthood and marriage and constituted perhaps the most popular genre of the era. Such works were usually overt in their Christian imagery and message: often the heroine was compelled to make difficult choices that challenged her moral purity. Other stories concerned the plight of women who sought to use their innate goodness to influence men, who held all social, economic, and political power. Popular and important examples of this tradition include Susan Warner's *The Wide, Wide, World* (1850) and Harriet Beecher Stowe's *Uncle Tom's Cabin* (1851).

Although clearly writing in this tradition, Alcott often produced more complex narratives than many of her contemporaries because of her interest in the psychological and economic independence of many of her heroines. Thus, Alcott's work at times simultaneously championed and challenged dominant nineteenth-century beliefs about the proper behavior and social role of American women. For example, Jo March, the central character of *Little Women*, is heroic because of her determination to support herself as a writer despite the fact that popular portrayals of working women during the era often pictured them as socially deviant or lacking in the necessary qualities for motherhood. Many of Alcott's most important characters, on the other hand, also seek to find happiness as wives, mothers, and working women. This complexity is likely a partial cause of her immediate popularity and a chief factor as to why Alcott remains in print while so many of her contemporaries have not.

## Works in Critical Context

**Little Women** Alcott's critical reputation has waxed and waned dramatically over the past century and a half. Her most famous novel, *Little Women*, was initially greeted widely as a welcome, moral tale for young readers. Early critics ignored the more subversive messages in the novel regarding women and work. By the early twentieth century, however, the rise of male-dominated American modernist literature, like that of Ernest Hemingway and William Faulkner, relegated Alcott to the realm of children's stories, seemingly unworthy of serious study. With the advent of the second feminist movement, Alcott's works were revisited and since the 1960s, critics since have been divided over whether her writing represents an early call for women's self-determination or whether her writing, especially in the character of Jo March, signals a capitulation to dominant ideas about womanhood. In 2006, for example, Susan Cheever wrote that *Little Women*, "transformed the lives of women into something worthy of literature." Others, including Angela M. Estes and Kathleen Margaret Lant, find the conclusion of *Little Women* powerfully disappointing, as Alcott marries off the rebellious, ambitious Jo and has her open a school for boys. Estes and Lant call this decision to turn Jo away from independence a "tragedy" and accuse Alcott of sacrificing her for a "sufficiently traditional or comfortable narrative pattern."

**Short Fiction** In recent years, critics have also rediscovered and become much more interested in the short works Alcott produced for sensational magazines prior to the publication of *Little Women*. This interest is often biographical in nature, often focusing on feminist plotlines or the fact that such lurid stories revealed emotions repressed in her later works, rather than on the originality or quality of the hurriedly written stories themselves. That said, critic Gail K. Smith obliquely connects these sensational stories to themes apparent in Alcott's better-known books, noting that, "Nowhere is Alcott's skillful reworking of gender and identity more apparent than in her [sensational] stories in which women gain trust and devotion of their willing victims in order to outwit them and gain what they desire."

## Responses to Literature

1. Watch one of the film versions of *Little Women*, and compare it to Alcott's novel. In what ways is it significantly different then the novel? Why do you suppose the changes to the story or characters were made?

2. Alcott's tales are set in mid-nineteenth century America. The country has been completely transformed by technological and social revolutions since that time. Why, then, do the novels of the Little Women series continue to be so popular with readers?

3. Alcott wrote scores of stories, novels, and articles, yet *Little Women* continues to be the text for which she is best known. Read two other works by Alcott: the late novel *Work* and one of her early, sensational stories. How do the underlying themes of the stories compare? Is there a style or theme that you see running through all of Alcott's output?

4. Using your library and the Internet, find out more about the roles women played in supplying medical care to wounded soldiers during the U.S. Civil War. Write a paper summarizing your findings.

BIBLIOGRAPHY

**Books**

Cheever, Susan. *American Bloomsbury: Louisa May Alcott, Ralph Waldo Emerson, Margaret Fuller, Nathaniel Hawthorne, and Henry David Thoreau: Their Lives, Their Loves, Their Work*. New York: Simon and Schuster, 2006.

Stern, Madeleine B., Myerson, Joel, and Daniel Shealy, eds. *A Double Life: Newly Discovered Thrillers by Louisa May Alcott*. Boston: Little, Brown, and Company, 1988.

**Periodicals**

Estes, Angela M. and Kathleen Margaret Lant. "Dismembering the Text: The Horror of Louisa May Alcott's *Little Women*." *Children's Literature* (1989).

## ✸ Sherman Alexie

BORN: *1966, Wellpinit, Washington*

NATIONALITY: *American*

GENRE: *Poetry, fiction, screenplays*

MAJOR WORKS:

*The Lone Ranger and Tonto Fistfight in Heaven* (1993)

*Reservation Blues* (1995)

Sherman Alexie   *Ulf Andersen / Getty Images*

*Indian Killer* (1996)

*The Absolutely True Diary of a Part-Time Indian* (2007)

## Overview

Sherman Alexie, a Native American whose ancestry includes both the Spokane and Coeur d'Alene tribes, emerged in the 1990s as one of the most prominent American Indian writers of his generation. In his critically acclaimed poetry, short stories, and novels, he writes about the hardships and joys of life on contemporary reservations. Alexie's works are celebrated for their detailed descriptions of the psychology and environment of the reservation. The author does not shy away from exploring the ravages of alcohol abuse that is often part of life on the reservation, but he includes a broad, universal message of hope and perseverance in his works.

## Works in Biographical and Historical Context

***Raised on a Reservation***   Alexie was born in 1966 on the Spokane Indian Reservation located in Wellpinit,

Washington. He was the son of Sherman Joseph and Lillian Agnes (Cox) Alexie. His father was a Coeur d'Alene Indian and an alcoholic who was often absent from the home, while his Spokane Indian mother helped support the family by selling her hand-sewn quilts and working at the Wellpinit Trading Post. She later became a social worker. Though Alexie was raised in an environment often characterized by depression, poverty, and alcohol abuse, he was an exemplary student from elementary school forward. An avid reader from an early age, he read every book in his elementary-school library as well as most in his local public library.

During Alexie's childhood, Native Americans were demanding greater civil and property rights, and were inspired in some ways by the African American civil rights movement of the 1950s and 1960s. From 1969 to 1971, a group of Indians of various tribes claimed Alcatraz Island, where the famous penitentiary was still located, by right of discovery and offered to pay for the land. In 1972, there was a famous march on Washington, D.C., by American Indians. Three years later, a shoot-out between the FBI and members of the American Indian Movement (AIM) took place at the Pine Ridge Reservation. AIM had been founded in 1968 to demand legal reforms to benefit Native Americans.

***Encouraged to Become a Writer***   After graduating from Reardan High School, Alexie was admitted to Gonzaga University in 1985. There, under intense pressure to succeed, he became dependent on alcohol. Two years later, Alexie transferred to Washington State University in Pullman, where he majored in American Studies and began writing poetry and short fiction with the encouragement of his creative writing teacher Alex Kuo. A selection of Alexie's work was published in the magazine *Hanging Loose* in 1990, and more poems were soon published in other periodicals. This early success provided Alexie with the will and incentive to quit drinking and to devote himself to building a career as a writer.

In 1991, Alexie earned his BA summa cum laude from Washington State, then won a Washington State Arts Commission poetry fellowship. The following year, he was awarded a poetry fellowship from the National Endowment of the Arts. Also in 1992, Alexie published his first poetry collection, the award-winning chapbook *I Would Steal Horses*, and a collection of short stories and poetry entitled *The Business of Fancydancing*. The latter collection grew out of the first writing workshop he attended at Washington State and received critical raves as soon as it hit print. Focusing on what he termed "Crazy Horse Dreams"—a metaphor for aspirations, either farfetched or close-at-hand, that succeed or fail without any apparent logic—*The Business of Fancydancing* introduced a broad range of characters, many of whom repeatedly appeared in his works.

***An Important Anniversary***   Alexie entered the literary world at a time when the reading public wanted to hear from Native American writers. The publication of his first

books coincided with the five hundredth anniversary of explorer Christopher Columbus's arrival in North America. While many American history books claimed Columbus "discovered" the Americas, many Native American writers have pointed out that a land with people on it does not need to be discovered and that Columbus and his men murdered and enslaved the native populations they met while searching for gold. This anniversary sparked controversy about the way European-based culture has remembered the history of the Americas. Alexie's writings helped to express the anger many people felt about the quincentennial.

Continuing to be prolific, Alexie published three books in 1993, including two collections of poetry as well as the highly acclaimed short story collection, *The Lone Ranger and Tonto Fistfight in Heaven*. The stories in *Lone Ranger* were often autobiographical in nature, primarily set on the reservation and in Spokane, and focus on survival and forgiveness as major themes.

***Novels and Screenplays***   In the mid-1990s, Alexie continued to regularly put out poetry collections but also turned to novels. He published *Reservation Blues* in 1995, then *Indian Killer* in 1996. The former focuses on the trials and tribulations of an all-Native American rock band while the latter is a thriller which features a killer who scalps his victims. Later in the decade, Alexie returned to a focus on poetry, turning out three collections, including *The Man Who Loves Salmon* (1998) and *One Stick Song* (1999).

Alexie branched out into a new writing form in the late 1990s with a screenplay entitled *Smoke Signals* (1998), based on stories found in *Lone Ranger*. It was the first film to be produced, directed, and acted by Native Americans. While filmmaking continued to be an interest for Alexie, who made his directorial debut in 2003 with *The Business of Fancydancing*, he still focused much of his time on writing. Alexie published more lauded collections of short stories, including *The Toughest Indian in the World* (2000), which featured heartbreaking tales of hope and love amidst pain and chaos, and *Ten Little Indians: Stories* (2003), which focused on the Native American-white conflict with a darkly comic tone.

Continuing to challenge himself, Alexie published his first book for young adult readers, *The Absolutely True Diary of a Part-Time Indian* (2007), which won a 2007 National Book Award for young people's literature. Alexie lives in Seattle, Washington, gives hundreds of readings of his work every year, and continues to write.

## Works in Literary Context

As a writer, Alexie draws on the oral, religious, and spiritual traditions of his Spokane/Coeur d'Alene Indian heritage, as well as bits and pieces of his own life. His works repeatedly underscore the importance of retaining tribal connections and the wandering story lines of his novels often employ non-mainstream organizational structures, shifting time settings, and multi-leveled connections between people.

As in oral tradition, Alexie's narratives aim for sudden brief insights as connections that initially elude readers gradually take meaningful shape over time. He often employs dark humor in his stories, and one of his goals is to debunk what he sees as political and cultural myths. In addition to drawing on his Native American background, Alexie, a prolific reader, has found inspiration in a number of authors, including Stephen King.

***Shifting Time and the Web of Life*** Greatly influenced by his Native American heritage as a writer, Alexie's story lines—particularly in his novels, but also in many short stories—reflect organizational structures, approaches, and attitudes as they shift time settings (mythical, historical, and modern), place, and person to gradually reveal tribal, family, and personal connections in keeping with the Native American philosophical framework: the web of life. The interconnected nature of his narrative writings can be seen in such stories as "Distances" in *The Lone Ranger and Tonto Fistfight in Heaven.* The story typifies the crossover vision of intersecting times as Alexie's modern characters successfully reenact the failed nineteenth-century Plains Indian Ghost Dance. Alexie's dystopian vision captures the futility of yearning for a return to the past, asking if modern technology and anyone with white blood were willed away, as the Ghost Dance promised, who and what would be left on the reservation?

***Native American Life on the Reservation*** Many of Alexie's stories and novels are set on the reservation—primarily the Spokane Indian Reservation in which he grew up—and they explore the harshness of life for Native Americans. Beginning with the collection *The Business of Fancydancing,* Alexie introduced many recurring characters who evoke the despair, poverty, and alcoholism that often pervades the lives of Native Americans on reservations. The novel *Reservation Blues* extends Alexie's literary use of the locale and inhabitants of the Spokane reservation, reiterating his focus on the conditions of life on the reservation and the hardships faced by many Native Americans.

While Alexie's poetry collections are not always specifically set on the reservation, such books as *I Would Steal Horses* and *Old Shirts & New Skins* unblinkingly explore Native American life. Alexie's poetry evokes sadness and indignation by showing Native Americans struggling to survive the constant battering of their minds, bodies, and spirits by white American society as well as their own sense of self-hatred and powerlessness. While Alexie does not shy away from depicting involvement with crime, alcohol, and drugs, his poems also evoke a sense of respect and compassion for characters who are in seemingly hopeless situations.

## Works in Critical Context

Critics have generally responded positively to Alexie and his writings, regarding him as a major literary voice who is especially praised for his keen insights into the plight of

---

## LITERARY AND HISTORICAL CONTEMPORARIES

Alexie's famous contemporaries include:

**Russell Means** (1940–): This Native American activist organized numerous protests against the American government's treatment of American Indians. He was a major figure in AIM and later headed the American Indian Anti-Defamation League.

**Hank Adams** (1944–): This Native American activist became politically active in the 1960s and eventually became the director of the Survival of American Indians Association, a group dedicated to the Indian treaty-fishing rights battle.

**N. Scott Momaday** (1934–): This Native American writer, poet, and educator won a Pulitzer Prize for his novel *The House Made of Dawn* (1968).

**Leslie Marmon Silko** (1948–): This Native American author received the Pushcart Prize for Poetry in 1977. Her works include *Ceremony* (1977).

**Adam Beach** (1972–): This Canadian actor from the Saluteaux tribe had a starring role in *Smoke Signals*. He was nominated for a Golden Globe Award in 2008 for *Bury My Heart At Wounded Knee* (2007).

---

Native Americans living on reservations. Reviewers have noted that his characters are not clichéd, stone-faced people who accept their lot in life, and that Alexie draws on the rich sense of humor that Indians commonly use to deal with their problems. In addition, critics have praised the energy and emotion he brings to his work in all genres as well as his ability to help non-Native Americans recognize the issues that Indians face and dispel old notions of who Indians are.

***Reservation Blues*** Alexie's first novel, *Reservation Blues,* focuses on a group of native Americans who form a rock band after coming into possession of legendary blues musician Robert Johnson's magical guitar. Critics generally praised the book and its ability to appeal to both American Indian and white readers. In the *Los Angeles Times Book Review,* Verlyn Klinkenberg concludes that although Alexie makes a point of educating his readers about particulars of Native American life, he "never sounds didactic. His timing is too good for that. *Reservation Blues* never misses a beat, never sounds a false note." Similarly, Abigail Davis in *The Bloomsbury Review* states, "The reader closes the book feeling troubled, hurt, hopeful, profoundly thoughtful, and somehow exhausted, as if the quest of the characters had been a personal experience."

***The Toughest Indian in the World*** The nine short stories contained in Alexie's *The Toughest Indian in the*

*World* were also praised by critics. In *Seattle Weekly*, Emily White commented that the collection "proves once again that [Alexie] is the real deal: a master stylist, a born storyteller as well as a writer of inspired formal innovations and experiments." *Denver Post* contributor Ron Franscell found two stories—"Dear John Wayne" and "South by Southwest"—particularly inspiring, writing that he was impressed by the way Alexie "puts himself inside the heads and hearts of non-Indians. The result is tender, touching and erotic." Describing an aspect of the appeal of *The Toughest Indian*, Ken Foster of the *San Francisco Chronicle* concludes that Alexie "doesn't feel the need to instruct his readers in the details of contemporary American Indian culture, and why should he? The lives he portrays are so finely detailed...that even the most culturally sheltered reader is transported."

### Responses to Literature

1. Alexie often refers to his writing as "fancydancing," a name given to the changes Native American dancers made to their traditional dances. Research this concept and relate it to a short story or poem by Alexie.

2. Research the Ghost Dance movement among Plains Indians in the nineteenth-century, then read Alexie's short story "Distances" or the novel *Indian Killer*. Write a paper in which you compare the reality of the original Ghost Dance with the way Alexie employs it in modern times in one of his works.

3. In a group, discuss this quote by Alexie: "Good art doesn't come out of assimilation—it comes out of tribalism." How does this philosophy relate to his books?

4. Create a presentation about a poem in one of Alexie's early collections. It has been noted that the poems in these books mainly focus on the fight to maintain self-respect in the face of obstacles such as racism, alcohol, and drugs, and a sense of powerlessness. How do these ideas relate to the poem you have chosen?

BIBLIOGRAPHY

**Books**

Grassian, Daniel. *Understanding Sherman Alexie.* Columbia, S.C.: University of South Carolina Press, 2005.

James, Meredith K. *Literary and Cinematic Reservation in Selected Works of Native American Author Sherman Alexie.* Lewiston, N.Y.: Edwin Mellen Press, 2005.

**Periodicals**

Coulombe, Joseph. "The Approximate Size of His Favorite Humor: Sherman Alexie's Comic Connections and Disconnections in *The Lone Ranger and Tonto Fistfight in Heaven*." *The American Indian Quarterly* (Winter 2002): 94.

Davis, Abigail. Review of *Reservation Blues. Bloomsbury Review* (July/August 1995).

Franscell, Ron. "Alexie's Tribal Perspective Universal in Its Appeal." *Denver Post* (May 21, 2000).

Foster, Ken. Review of *The Toughest Indian in the World. San Francisco Chronicle* (May 21, 2000).

Klinkenberg, Verlyn. Review of *Reservation Blues. Los Angeles Times Books Review* (June 18, 1995): 2.

White, Emily. Review of *The Toughest Indian in the World. Seattle Weekly* (May 11–17, 2000).

# Horatio Alger, Jr.

BORN: *1832, Chelsea, Massachusetts*

DIED: *1899, South Natick, Massachusetts*

NATIONALITY: *American*

GENRE: *Fiction, poetry*

MAJOR WORKS:

*Ragged Dick; or, Street Life in New York With the Boot-Blacks* (1868)

*Rough and Ready; or, Life Among the New York Newsboys* (1870)

*Tattered Tom; or, The Story of a Young Street Arab* (1871)

Horatio Alger, Jr.   *AP Images*

## Overview

Horatio Alger, Jr. was a prolific late nineteenth-century American writer of more than one hundred books for children, most of which feature young orphaned heroes and heroines who are born penniless and must face harsh urban living and working conditions. His enormously popular "rags to riches" stories are closely identified with the American Dream: through shrewdness and hard work his protagonists avoid poverty and crime and become wealthy and respectable middle-class citizens. He is also remembered as a child labor activist; in both his life and work, he advocated for improved conditions for children living in urban slums.

## Works in Biographical and Historical Context

***Early Illness and Home Schooling*** Horatio Alger, Jr., was born on January 13, 1832, in Chelsea, Massachusetts. His father was a Unitarian minister and a noted writer of biblical commentary, and his mother was the daughter of a well-known and prosperous businessman of Chelsea. Alger was the eldest of five children.

Alger was a sickly child and therefore did not receive formal schooling until the age of ten. During his early education at home, he enjoyed reading and became acquainted with a wide variety of books.

***Economic Hardship and Further Schooling*** In the late 1830s Horatio Alger, Sr. fell into debt, and in April 1844 his lands were assigned to Carpenter Staniels, who perhaps was the prototype of the hardhearted squire who forecloses the mortgage in so many of Alger's novels. The family moved in December 1844 to Marlborough, Massachusetts. Marlborough was a pleasant town, which the younger Alger was to remember with affection and use as a model for many country towns in his books. Although primarily an agricultural center, it also was noted for the manufacture of shoes in small, unmechanized factories. In later years, many of Alger's protagonists worked either on farms or in cobbler shops such as he had seen in his boyhood. Alger attended school in Marlborough for two years and entered Harvard College in 1848, when he was sixteen.

***Harvard and First Publication*** During his college career, Alger was already evincing an interest in writing. While in college, he wrote to novelist James Fenimore Cooper, praising his work and requesting his autograph. Cooper's influence can be seen in some of Alger's books, especially his later works set in the West. Alger also called upon Henry Wadsworth Longfellow while in college, an event that he later indicated influenced his writing of poetry.

Alger entered Harvard Divinity School in 1853 with the intent of becoming a minister, but he withdrew after a few months to become assistant editor of the *Boston Daily Advertiser*. For the next four years, Alger taught in various preparatory schools and wrote for multiple newspapers. His first book *Bertha's Christmas Vision: An Autumn Sheaf* (1856) was published by Brown, Bazin and Company. In 1857, Alger again entered the Divinity School at Cambridge.

***Success with Children's Literature*** Alger graduated from Divinity School in 1860. In September of that year, he traveled to Europe with two other men, visiting the British Isles, Belgium, the Netherlands, Germany, Switzerland, Italy, and France, and wrote several travelogues based on his experiences.

After returning to the United States in April 1861, Alger preached in Dover, Massachusetts, tutored in Cambridge, and taught in schools in Nahant, Massachusetts. As the United States descended into civil war between Union and Confederate forces, he was drafted by the Union Army in 1863, but was exempted because of his small stature and poor eyesight.

In 1864 Alger published his first juvenile novel, *Frank's Campaign*. He found that it was easier to achieve

## LITERARY AND HISTORICAL CONTEMPORARIES

Alger's famous contemporaries include:

**James A. Garfield** (1831–1881): Garfield, the twentieth president of the United States, would serve only six months in office before being assassinated in 1881. He was the subject of three biographies by Alger.

**Jacob Riis** (1849–1914): a Danish-American journalist, photographer, and social reformer. Riis's monumental photo-essay *How the Other Half Lives: Studies Among the Tenements of New York* (1890) spurred labor reform and the late nineteenth-century movement to improve living conditions in New York slums.

**Elizabeth Cady Stanton** (1850–1902): an American women's rights activist, abolitionist, and social reformer. Stanton advocated women's parental and custody rights, property rights, employment and income rights, divorce laws, and birth control.

**Charles Dickens** (1812–1870): Perhaps the most prolific author of the Victorian period in Britain, Dickens was known as a social reformer with a particular advocacy for the rights of children. His famous novel *Oliver Twist* (1838) features orphaned boys corrupted by criminals in the London underworld.

a reputation with children's literature than with adult literature because there were fewer juvenile authors. He also found that his juvenile novel was better received and better paid than its predecessors. Alger decided to dedicate himself to succeeding in a new genre.

*A Writing Life in the City* Alger's Campaign series proved popular enough for him to write two more volumes. These books show the early development of the author's trademark complexity of plot, touches of humor, and leisurely pace. The New York setting and the liberal use of coincidence to advance the plot are all typical of Alger. The books are also the first juvenile example of one of Alger's chief themes: the poor boy who makes good. The protagonists rise "from rags to respectability."

In 1868, the Loring Company began publication of Alger's six book Ragged Dick series, the most famous of which being *Ragged Dick; or, Street Life in New York With the Boot-Blacks* (1868), *Fame and Fortune; or, The Progress of Richard Hunter* (1868), and *Rough and Ready; or, Life Among the New York Newsboys* (1869). These stories, both in serialized and book form, were enormously popular, and remain the most well-known of Alger's work.

Although there are stock characters in Alger's books, many of the boys in these books were drawn from real life, including Rough and Ready, whom Alger met at the Newsboys' Lodging House. Minor characters in the

Ragged Dick series, such as Johnny Nolan, the unambitious bootblack, and Micky Maguire, the street tough, were also modeled on real street boys. Alger supported Brace's Children's Aid Society and sought to help the boys that he encountered through his volunteer work at the Newsboys' Lodging House. Many of the New York City novels mention the Lodging House, and Mark, the Match Boy, gives a detailed explanation of how it was run. Alger was interested in moral reform movements and was active in charitable missions among the street boys of New York.

*Further Child Advocacy and Changes in Content*
In 1872, Alger made a personal contribution to the child welfare movement. His interest was aroused by a particular group of street boys, whom he described as "young Italian musicians, who wander about our streets with harps, violins, or tambourines, playing wherever they can secure an audience." These boys were victims of the *padrone* system. The *padrone* bought the services of poor Italian peasant boys from their parents, taught them basic musical skills, and brought them to America. They were expected to wander the city streets, collecting money for their owners through their performances. Alger gathered information about the system and wrote *Phil, the Fiddler; or, The Story of a Young Street Musician*. Alger's intention in writing the book was to expose the *padrone* system and to show, as he put it in the preface, "the inhumane treatment which [the boys] receive from the speculators who buy them from their parents in Italy."

In 1874, Alger published a second Tattered Tom series, which expressed Alger's continued interest in the work of the Children's Aid Society. The group provided a relocation program that helped street boys find positions in the West, where there were plenty of jobs available for young men. Several of the books written during this period draw on Alger's teaching experience for episodes that gently satirize the educational process.

Alger's Brave and Bold series also made its debut in 1874. In all four books, Alger continued his turn away from stories of street life. As his sales slipped, the books became more disjointed and melodramatic. In an effort to bolster sagging sales, Alger began to travel to gather material about settings other than New York and the Northeast. His book sales did not increase, however, and Alger turned to writing moderately successful biographies of James A. Garfield, Daniel Webster, and Abraham Lincoln.

During the last two decades of his life, Alger practiced what he had preached in so many books; he became a patron for three poor boys whom he educated and set up in a trade. He found it more difficult to do his charitable works as sales of his books continued to dwindle and his income decreased. In 1896, Alger suffered a nervous breakdown; he wrote very little thereafter. He retired to South Natick, Massachusetts, where he lived with his sister, Olive Augusta Cheney, and her husband, until his death in 1899.

## Works in Literary Context

***The American Dream*** Alger wrote during a period when America was viewed as a promised land for individuals who believed success and wealth could be won by hard work. The expansion of the labor force and the rise of mechanized industry, however, resulted in low wages, squalid working conditions, and the construction of grim and unsound tenement buildings that housed the urban poor. Characters such as Ragged Dick and Phil the Fiddler, finding success and wealth in the streets of New York, represent the concept of the American Dream in a positive light, yet are often attacked by critics as misrepresenting the realities of nineteenth-century urban America.

***The Spirit of Social Reform*** Alger sought to explore the effects of modernity and mechanization on children specifically, and gathered much of his information from the social reformers and journalists of his day. While other American writers, such as the humorist Mark Twain, had used children as fictional protagonists, few had placed these protagonists in modern urban settings. Alger's unique choice of character and setting would influence later American realist writers such as Theodore Dreiser and Upton Sinclair, who exposed social inequalities within cities and large industries.

***Lone Orphan in a Hostile World*** His characters Ragged Dick and Tattered Tom emerge from a long literary tradition of individualism, and this theme is perhaps most influenced by the works of Charles Dickens. In books like *Oliver Twist* and *Bleak House*, Dickens featured orphans who are left to the mercy of corrupt social or legal systems, and whose only defenses against these injustices are to remain pure in mind and action. As in many of Alger's books, these heroes or heroines find (after a series of trials and temptations) that they are actually of noble rather than "low" birth, leaving the reader to question whether the author is making a correlation between morality and class.

## Works in Critical Context

Because Alger's books feature redundant characters, plots, and themes, his works are most often discussed by critics in a historical or cultural rather than literary context. Scholars also face the problem of the sheer volume of works Alger produced; it is nearly impossible to cite all of his books, and thus critics usually compress their discussions of Alger to broad themes or settings. As Quentin Reynolds says in *The Fiction Factory* (1955), "Alger, according to his biographer, Herbert R. Mayes, wrote 119 books. Actually, he wrote one book and rewrote it 118 times."

During Alger's lifetime critics paid scant attention to his work; not only were the books considered pulp potboilers, but the fact that they were written for children at a time when children were not considered sophisticated readers prohibited serious attention. Still, his works

---

### COMMON HUMAN EXPERIENCE

Almost all of Alger's stories feature a young child, usually an orphan, who must face a harsh world populated by danger and criminals. Other works that feature similar young heroes and heroines include:

*Oliver Twist* (1838), a novel by Charles Dickens. Dickens wrote this story of a lost London orphan as a protest against harsh British Poor Laws and the squalid conditions of the workhouses they legislated. Both Oliver Twist and his pick-pocketing friends, The Artful Dodger and Charley Bates, became models for Horatio Alger, Jr.'s protagonists.

*The Life of Mr. Jonathan Wild the Great* (1743), a novel by Henry Fielding. Fielding's novel—both a black comedy and a scathing political satire—traces the life of one of the most famous members of the eighteenth-century London underworld. Fielding's tale follows the "great" Wild from birth to the gallows.

*A Star Called Henry* (1999), a novel by Roddy Doyle. Doyle's fictional Henry Smart is born into the squalid streets of Dublin, quickly orphaned, and must live by his wits. Through this protagonist Doyle traces the history of Ireland: Smart partakes in the 1916 Easter Uprising, the Dublin Labor Movement, and the Anglo-Irish Civil War.

*Annie!* (1976), a musical written by Charles Strouse and Martin Charnin. This popular musical features a street-smart red-headed orphan living in a New York orphanage during the Great Depression. In 1982 the play was adapted to a successful film starring Aileen Quinn and Carol Burnett.

---

received occasional reviews in various publications. An unsigned reviewer for *Putnam's Magazine* in 1868 praised *Ragged Dick* as "a well-told story of street-life in New York, that will, we should judge, be well received by the boy-readers, for whom it is intended." However, a reviewer for *The Nation* in 1869 found the author's *Rough and Ready* lacking in realism, noting that "whoever bases his notions of the newsboy's character on a belief in the truthfulness of Mr. Alger's romance will get false notions of the character of the average newsboy." S. S. Green, in an 1879 essay for the *Library Journal* discussing the books of Alger and William T. Adams, states of these works, "They are poor books. Poor as they are, however, they have a work to do in the world. Many persons need them. They have been written by men who mean well."

According to Frank Luther Mott's estimate in *Golden Multitudes* (1947), Alger's greatest popularity came after his death. His sales reached their zenith during the first two decades of the twentieth century, when his books were published in cheap editions and when the temper of the country favored their message. As mechanization increased at the turn of the century, readers prized the plucky protagonists put forward by Alger.

Critics generally agree that Alger's Ragged Dick and Tattered Tom series constitute his finest work. Alger's extensive knowledge of New York City and the Northeast, combined with the firsthand experience of the streets which he gained from his mission work, result in credible accounts of street boys' lives in the nineteenth century.

## Responses to Literature

1. Although Alger published a number of books for adults, he is remembered primarily as a writer of children's literature. What aspects of his writing style make his stories appropriate or accessible to children rather than adults? Consider his choices of setting, dialog, and character. Explain why these aspects of his writing appeal to juvenile readers.

2. Critics often argue that Alger's fame rests on his ability to equate his "rags to riches" characters (such as Ragged Dick) to the American dream. Do you think Alger's model of American success resonates with young readers in America today? In a small group, brainstorm what traits a modern Ragged Dick character would need to possess in today's American society. Can you think of any characters similar to Ragged Dick that you have come across in your own reading?

3. Many critics argue that Alger's books equate money with success, while others argue that Alger's heroes and heroines seek respectability, not just material gain. Considering books such as *Rough and Ready* and *Phil, the Fiddler*, try to define Alger's views on money and its importance. Is money the crucial element in Alger's depiction of success? How do his views of money develop his idea of the American Dream?

4. Go to your school library and locate a copy of Jacob Riis's *How the Other Half Lives: Studies Among the Tenements of New York* (1890), which provides pictures of New York's Lower East Side in the late nineteenth century. How do these realistic portrayals compare with the descriptions provided by Alger's books? Should Alger be criticized for romanticizing the lives of the poor, or praised for bringing attention to the grim realities of children living in urban poverty?

BIBLIOGRAPHY

**Books**

Gardner, Ralph D. *Horatio Alger, or The American Hero Era*. Mendota, Ill.: Wayside Press, 1964.

"Horatio Alger, Jr. (1832–1899)." *Nineteenth-Century Literature Criticism*. Edited by Laurie Lanzen Harris and Emily B. Tennyson. Vol. 8. Detroit: Gale Research, 1985, pp.13–49.

Hoyt, Edwin P. *Horatio's Boys: The Life and Works of Horatio Alger, Jr*. Radnor, Pa.: Chilton Book Company, 1974.

Mayes, Herbert R. *Alger: A Biography Without a Hero*. New York: Macy-Masius, 1928.

Mott, Frank Luther. *Golden Multitudes: The Story of Best Sellers in the United States*. New York: R. R. Bowker, 1947.

Reynolds, Quentin. *The Fiction Factory, or From Pulp Row to Quality Street*. New York: Random House, 1955.

Scharnhorst, Gary and Jack Bales. *The Lost Life of Horatio Alger, Jr.*. Bloomington, Ind.: Indiana University Press, 1985.

Tebbel, John. *From Rags to Riches: Horatio Alger, Jr., and The American Dream*. New York: Macmillan, 1963.

**Periodicals**

Bales, Jack. "Herbert R. Mayes and Horatio Alger, Jr.; or The Story of a Unique Literary Hoax." *Journal of Popular Culture* 8 (Fall 1974): 317–319.

# ✹ Paula Gunn Allen

BORN: *1939, Cubero, New Mexico*

DIED: *2008, Fort Bragg, California*

NATIONALITY: *American*

GENRE: *Poetry, fiction, nonfiction*

MAJOR WORKS:

*The Woman Who Owned the Shadows* (1983)

*The Sacred Hoop: Recovering the Feminine in American Indian Traditions* (1986)

## Overview

A renowned literary figure, an eminent scholar, and a dedicated feminist, Paula Gunn Allen attempted to educate mainstream audiences about Native American themes, issues, and concerns. Throughout her life, she promoted Native American literature as a viable and rich source of study. Her fiction and poetry frequently refer to her identity as a mixed blood and, like her critical essays and the numerous anthologies she edited, emphasize the status of American Indian women in various native cultures.

## Works in Biographical and Historical Context

*The Influence of a Mixed Ancestry* A registered member of the Laguna Pueblo tribe, Paula Gunn Allen was born in 1939 in Cubero, New Mexico, a rural land grant situated next to the Laguna Pueblo reservation, the

Paula Gunn Allen    *Allen, Paula Gunn, 1993, photograph. AP Images.*

Acoma reservation, and Cibola National Forest. Her mother was of Laguna Pueblo, Sioux, and Scottish descent, and her father, who grew up on a Mexican land grant in the American Southwest and once served as lieutenant-governor of New Mexico, was of Lebanese ancestry. Allen credits these mixed origins as a major influence on her writing as well as a source of inspiration: "I think in some respects the whole world is a multicultural event, and it's possible, if it's possible for me to stay alive, then it's possible for the whole world to stay alive. If I can communicate, then all the different people in the world can communicate with one another."

Although Allen had a diverse ethnic heritage, it was her American Indian roots that informed and directed her work. In an interview with Robin Pogrebin of the *New York Times Book Review*, Allen characterized Native Americans as "something other than victims—mostly what we are is unrecognized."

***Reconciling Multiple Perspectives***   After spending her early years in Cubero, Allen was sent to a Catholic boarding school in Albuquerque at age six. The influence of her religious education often surfaces in the symbolism and themes of her works, but Allen would not be considered a strictly religious writer. According to Kathy

J. Whitson in the book *Native American Literatures*, Allen noted: "Sometimes I get in a dialogue between what the Church taught me, what the nuns taught me, what my mother taught me, what my experience growing up where I grew up taught me. Often you can't reconcile them. I can't reconcile them."

An avid reader, Allen encountered the works of Gertrude Stein in high school, and she noted that her early attempts at writing were highly influenced by the American novelist and poet. Allen also cited American poet Robert Creeley, under whose direction she once studied writing, and Kiowa novelist N. Scott Momaday as individuals who had a strong impact on her work. Initially intending to become an actress, Allen attended various schools before earning a BA in English in 1966. Allen married while in college and had two children before divorcing. After the divorce, she went back to school and studied writing, receiving an MFA in creative writing in 1968 from the University of Oregon. She received her PhD in American Studies and American Indian Studies from the University of New Mexico in 1975. Afterward she taught at the University of California, Berkeley; the University of California, Los Angeles; and San Francisco State University.

## LITERARY AND HISTORICAL CONTEMPORARIES

Allen's famous contemporaries include:

**N. Scott Momaday** (1934–): Momaday, a Native American (Kiowa) writer, is credited with having brought mainstream attention to Native American literature with the publication of his Pulitzer Prize-winning work *House Made of Dawn* (1968).

**Robert Creeley** (1926–2005): An American poet and author who is credited with beginning the Black Mountain School of Poetry.

**Margaret Atwood** (1939–): Canadian poet, novelist, literary critic, and feminist who is best known for *The Handmaid's Tale* (1985) and the Booker Prize-winning *The Blind Assassin* (2000).

**Henry Louis Gates, Jr.** (1950–): An African American academic, writer, literary critic, and activist.

Throughout her teaching career Allen published poetry, novels, and academic novels, as well as editing numerous anthologies of Native American writing. The subject matter of her poems and stories—domestic spaces and the experiences of the modern woman artist—led to her involvement with feminist causes and the women's movement of the 1970s. In addition, her publication *The Sacred Hoop: Recovering the Feminine in American Indian Traditions* (1986) established her as a leader of the Native American Renaissance in literature, which followed the success of the works of writer N. Scott Momaday. In 1990 she received a National Endowment for the Arts Fellowship and was awarded the Before Columbus Foundation American Book Award for *Spider Woman's Granddaughters* (1989), a collection by various Native American writers. Allen died in May 2008 after a long struggle with lung cancer.

### Works in Literary Context

*The Search for Cultural and Gender Identity*
Like the mixed-blood characters of her novels, Allen's literary lineage is difficult to categorize. While her work certainly is influenced by Native American writers, such as N. Scott Momaday, she also cites feminist and lesbian poets, such as Adrienne Rich, as a source of inspiration. In almost all her work, Allen seeks to blend racial and gender identities, exploring their meanings and boundaries. Focusing on the themes of assimilation, self-identity, and remembrance, she frequently examines the quest for spiritual wholeness. For example, her poetry collections, which include *The Blind Lion* (1974), *Shadow Country* (1982), and *Skins and Bones* (1988), often emphasize the female journey to spiritual transcendence. The search for

self-actualization and an integrated self are also central to her 1983 novel, *The Woman Who Owned the Shadows*, in which the protagonist, a lesbian half-blood, eventually learns to accept her sexual orientation and cultural identity rather than conform to social stereotypes. This work, which is dedicated to the Native American deity Thought Woman, additionally emphasizes the importance of storytelling in Native American culture, incorporating such diverse narrative modes as folk tales, letters, legends, dreams, and Pueblo "thought singing." Allen's scholarly works, including her popular essay collection *The Sacred Hoop: Recovering the Feminine in American Indian Traditions*, deal with women's issues, the oral tradition, lesbianism, and female deities. In *Spider Woman's Granddaughters*, an anthology of tales by Leslie Marmon Silko, Linda Hogan, Louise Erdrich, Anna Lee Waters, Pretty Shield, and other Native American women, Allen attempts to introduce "tribal women's literature" to non-Native American readers.

### Works in Critical Context

Allen's works have generally received positive acclaim. Her poetry is recognized for its musical qualities and her novel, though faulted at times for its broad focus, has been praised for its examination of racism and sexism. While occasionally criticized for their lack of documentation, her nonfiction works have been lauded as attempts to preserve Native American culture for all individuals regardless of their ethnic heritage. Elizabeth I. Hanson has asserted: "Allen creates her own myths; she reinvokes primordial sacred time with a contemporary profane time in order to recover and remake her self. That restored, renewed self suggests in symbolic terms a revival within Native American experience as a whole."

*The Woman Who Owned the Shadows* Allen's 1983 novel *The Woman Who Owned the Shadows* received a favorable review from Alice Hoffman in the *New York Times Book Review*. "In those sections where the author forsakes the artifice of her style," declared the critic, "an absorbing, often fascinating world is created." The novel's heroine, Ephanie, is emotionally wounded as a young girl and struggles to mend her fractured core "guided," according to Hoffman, "by the traditional tales of spirit women."

*The Woman Who Owned the Shadows* uses a variety of narrative elements, including Native American folklore, letters, dreams, and therapy transcripts to tell Ephanie's story. While some critics, like Hoffman, found this compilation to be forced, others believed it to be effective and enjoyable. "Allen continues her cultural traditional in her novel by using it in the same way in which the traditional arts have always functioned for the Laguna Pueblo," noted Annette Van Dyke in *Lesbian Texts and Contexts: Radical Revisions*, describing the work as "a form of curing ceremony for her readers."

*Spider Woman's Granddaughters: Traditional Tales and Contemporary Writing by Native American Women* In 1989 Allen edited *Spider Woman's Granddaughters*, which Karvar called "a companion in spirit" to the author's book of essays *The Sacred Hoop*. In *Spider Woman's Granddaughters*, Allen gives space not only to contemporary authors such as Vickie L. Sears, but also to legends of old deities such as the Pueblos' mother goddess of corn. She also includes the words of Pretty Shield, a Crow native who told her life story to ethnographer Frank B. Linderman early in the twentieth century. In the *New York Times Book Review*, Ursula K. Le Guin praised the organization of the book, noting that Allen has arranged the pieces "so that they interact to form larger patterns, giving the book an esthetic wholeness rare in anthologies."

In equal parts reviewers have indicated that Allen succeeds at both entertaining and educating her audience. In *Paula Gunn Allen*, Elizabeth I. Hanson asserted that Allen combines the sacredness of the past with the reality of the present as a means of self-renewal. "Like Allen's own vision of self," said Hanson, "contemporary Native Americans exist not in a romantic past but instead in a community which extends throughout the whole of American experience."

## Responses to Literature

1. Allen uses various methods of storytelling in her book *The Woman Who Owned Shadows*, some traditional and some modern. Which of these methods do you find most effective? How does the combination of these storytelling methods affect the way you read the novel?

2. Writers such as N. Scott Momaday, Paula Gunn Allen, and Leslie Marmon Silko have maintained that they would like to bring Native American literature to a mainstream contemporary audience. What elements of the Native American experience seem most important in their works? In a small group, write down the stereotypes of Native Americans that you were aware of before you read their works. How does the literature change your way of thinking about these stereotypes?

3. Allen identified herself as a feminist and a lesbian as well as a Native American. Does her identification with any one of these minority groups inform her experience of another? Pinpoint sections of her work where these experiences intersect, and discuss the implications of the passage.

BIBLIOGRAPHY

**Books**

Bataille, Gretchen M. and Kathleen M. Sands, eds. *American Indian Women: Telling Their Lives*. Lincoln, Neb.: University of Nebraska Press, 1984.

Bruchac, Joseph. *Survival This Way: Interviews with American Indian Poets*. Tucson, Ariz: University of Arizona Press, 1987.

## COMMON HUMAN EXPERIENCE

Allen's work focuses on the personal and cultural difficulties entailed in being a person of mixed race and identity. Other works that explore this theme include:

*We Wish to Inform You that Tomorrow We Will Be Killed with Our Families* (1998), a nonfiction book by Philip Gourevitch. This work focuses on the 1994 genocide in Rwanda, during which mixed tribe Tutsi and Hutu citizens of the country were the primary targets of violence.

*Brick Lane* (2003), a novel by Monica Ali. This work tells the story of Nanzeen, a Bangladeshi girl who moves to London at the age of eighteen, and who must learn a new language and a new way of life.

*On Beauty* (2005), a novel by Zadie Smith. This book follows the lives of a mixed race British and American family, exploring both their political and personal differences.

Coltelli, Laura, ed. *Winged Words: American Indian Writers Speak*. Lincoln: University of Nebraska Press, 1990.

Crawford, C. F., John F. William Balassi, and Annie O. Ersturox. *This about Vision: Interviews with Southwestern Writers*. Albuquerque, N.M.: University of New Mexico Press, 1990.

Hanson, Elizabeth J. *Paula Gunn Allen*. Boise, Idaho: Boise State University, 1990.

Keating, Ana Louise. *Women Reading Women Writing: Self-Invention in Paula Gunn Allen, Gloria Anzaldua, and Audre Lorde*. Philadelphia: Temple University Press, 1996.

# Dorothy Allison

BORN: *1949, Greenville, South Carolina*

NATIONALITY: *American*

GENRE: *Fiction, poetry*

MAJOR WORKS:

*Bastard Out of Carolina* (1992)

*Two or Three Things I Know for Sure* (1995)

*Cavedweller* (1998)

## Overview

Dorothy E. Allison became a recognized poet and short story writer in the 1980s with her collections *The Women Who Hate Me* (1983) and *Trash* (1988). Allison is best known for *Bastard Out of Carolina* (1992), a novel about a young girl growing up in rural South Carolina during

Dorothy Allison   *Lara Jo Regan / Liaison / Getty Images.*

the 1960s. The book has garnered widespread praise for its realism, vivid characterization, and conversational, idiomatic prose. Allison has secured her reputation as a writer who deals frankly and boldly with issues of gender, class, and sexual orientation. In an essay published in the *New York Times Book Review*, Allison commented on the importance of literature that deals honestly with such themes: "We are the ones they make fiction of—we gay and disenfranchised and female—and we have the right to demand our full, nasty, complicated lives."

## Works in Biographical and Historical Context

### The Healing Powers of Feminism and Literature

Allison was born in 1949 in Greenville, South Carolina, to a poor, unmarried fifteen-year-old girl. When Allison was five, her stepfather—her mother having since married—began sexually abusing her. The abuse lasted for several years before Allison was finally able to tell a relative; the relative informed Allison's mother, who put a stop to the abuse. Nonetheless, the family stayed together. The conditions of Allison's upbringing, specifically her experience of poverty, Southern culture, and sexual abuse, would figure largely in the characters and content of her most

highly-praised works, *Bastard Out of Carolina* and *Cavedweller* (1998).

When she was eighteen, Allison left home to attend college in Florida. Allison attended college during the Civil Rights Movement in the late 1960s, a period when young Americans, particularly university students, often staged political protests aimed at gaining social and political equality for women and minorities. These political protests were especially widespread in the American South, where a younger generation sought to repeal racist policies and social practices that had been in place since the end of the American Civil War.

While Allison attended college, she was also introduced to feminism, which she embraced and that, as she noted in a *New York Times Book Review* essay, "gave me a vision of the world totally different from everything I had ever assumed or hoped. The concept of a feminist literature offered the possibility of pride in my sexuality." Later, she attended graduate school in New York City and became involved in the gay and lesbian pride movements that followed in the wake of the Civil Rights Movement of the late 1960s. However, it was not until the early 1980s that she began writing seriously. She published poetry and short story collections and began work on *Bastard Out of Carolina*. Allison is frequently referred to as a "third-wave feminist." Third-wave feminism, which emerged in the early 1980s, sought not just legal reform, but also reform of culturally or socially constructed ideas of womanhood. Enlarging upon previous feminists' credo that "the personal is the political," third-wave feminists aligned the women's movement with minority and gay rights activists.

*Autobiographical Fiction: Bastard Out of Carolina*  Drawn heavily from Allison's own experiences of incest and abuse, *Bastard Out of Carolina* is a fictional portrayal of a young girl's life in a poor Southern family. Ruth Anne Boatwright, the protagonist, relates how she earned her nickname of "Bone," when she was prematurely born "the size of a knucklebone" after her mother was in a car accident. Allison admitted in an interview with Lynn Karpen in the *New York Times Book Review* that these introductory details are largely autobiographical. The author further commented, "A lot of the novel is based on real experience, but not the entire thing. The characters are modeled on members of my family and on stories I heard when I was growing up."

*Further Works and Public Outreach*  Allison followed *Bastard Out of Carolina* with a collection of essays, *Skin: Talking about Sex, Class, and Literature* (1994), and a memoir, *Two or Three Things I Know for Sure* (1995). Reviewers reacted positively to both works, again praising the author's spare, straightforward writing style and expressing admiration for her hard-won and individual voice. Commenting on *Skin: Talking about Sex, Class, and Literature* in the *Los Angeles Times Book Review*, Carla Tomaso noted, "one marvels at the incredible achievement this is for someone born poor and despised in the South."

Allison's literary success has brought her widespread media attention and made her a popular draw on the lecture circuit. In an interview with Alexis Jetter for the *New York Times Magazine*, she spoke about the importance of storytelling in her life. "I believe that storytelling can be a strategy to help you make sense of your life," she told Jetter. "It's what I've done."

## Works in Literary Context

As both a writer and an activist, Dorothy Allison has made an enormous impact in the reception of women's fiction. Avoiding the cold intellectualism of postmodern novels, Allison provides her readers with unadorned—and often shocking—graphic details of real-life situations and abuse.

*Fiction and Feminism*  Allison's *Bastard Out of Carolina* is considered an iconic text within the third-wave feminist movement; not only does it provide a personalized and semi-autobiographical story, but it also addresses the issue of forging a female and lesbian identity in a misogynistic, homophobic culture. Bone typifies a third-wave feminist heroine; not only does she face misogyny and violence, which is ignored or hidden by her family and

culture, but she must also face the prospect of establishing a new identity as a survivor and lesbian. Allison's autobiographical descriptions of sexual abuse, as well as her identification as a lesbian and a Southerner, have made her a valuable spokesperson for the movement. Other writers associated with third-wave feminism include Erica Jong, Jeanette Winterson, Toni Morrison, Audre Lord, and Grace Paley.

*Southern Roots, Southern Gothic*  Critics have often noted that Allison's works innovate the tradition of the Southern Gothic novel. The Southern Gothic literary tradition, associated with such writers as Tennessee Williams, Carson McCullers, and William Faulkner, uses unusual or ironic situations to advance plot and features deeply flawed, often hypocritical characters (such as Daddy Glenn in *Bastard Out of Carolina*). These characters, intriguing yet often grotesque, reveal truths about social issues pertaining to the South and allow the reader insight into its culture. Allison's combination of dark content and wry humor have encouraged reviewers to compare her novels to those of Flannery O'Connor; she has also been compared to contemporary Southern Gothic authors such as Lee Smith. Allison is frequently praised for her ability to infuse humor into her works without mocking the South or Southern characters. In *Publishers Weekly*, for example, a reviewer stated that Allison "doesn't condescend to her 'white trash' characters; she portrays them with understanding and love."

## Works in Critical Context

Though Allison's earlier collections were favorably reviewed when they appeared, her debut novel, *Bastard Out of Carolina*, triggered a critical crescendo when it appeared in 1992. Allison followed this work with a collection

# COMMON HUMAN EXPERIENCE

Allison's novels feature small-town women and girls who must persevere through prejudice, economic hardship, and abuse in order to achieve success and self-respect. Works which feature similar protagonists and situations include:

*Raney* (1985), a novel by Clyde Edgerton. Written in Southern idiom, *Raney* tells the story of a small-town Southern Baptist and her marriage to Charles, a seemingly more educated and sophisticated individual than his wife. With humor and wit, Edgerton demystifies stereotypes often assigned to women of the South.

*Memoirs of an Ex-Prom Queen* (1972), a novel by Alix Kates Shulman. Often considered one of the landmark novels to emerge from the women's liberation movement, this novel tells the story of former prom-queen Sasha Davis and explores her adolescent experiences of sexuality, date rape, and abortion.

*Fair and Tender Ladies* (1988), a novel by Lee Smith. This epistolary novel, written in dialect, tells the story of Ivy Rowe, an intelligent and passionate girl who is raised in the Virginia Appalachia region. On the eve of leaving for a formal education in the Northeast, Rowe is "ruint" by an unwanted pregnancy and must reconstruct her life as an outcast in a small farming community.

*I Know Why the Caged Bird Sings* (1969), a memoir by Maya Angelou. This early autobiographical work focuses on Pulitzer Prize nominee Angelou's childhood in a small, racially divided town in Arkansas, where she has been sent to live with her grandmother.

of essays, *Skin: Talking about Sex, Class, and Literature*, and a memoir, *Two or Three Things I Know for Sure*. Susie Bright, reviewing *Skin: Talking about Sex, Class, and Literature* in the *New York Times Book Review*, wrote that "the tautness of Ms. Allison's storytelling comes from her ability to describe cruelty and desperate measures with such grace that it leaves a sensual impression unmistakable to the literary touch."

**Bastard Out of Carolina** When *Bastard Out of Carolina* was published, reviewers commended Allison for her realistic, unsentimental, and often humorous portrayal of her eccentric characters, and the novel was nominated for a National Book award. Allison's descriptions of Bone's sexual abuse and feelings of betrayal garnered the most attention. Vince Aletti observed: "Allison casts a savage, unblinking eye...describing the terrible knot of violence and eroticism without ever slipping into softcore voyeurism or shocked prudery." A *Washington Post Book World* contributor complained that *Bastard out of Carolina* "has a tendency to bog down in its own heat,

speech and atmosphere," but also acknowledged that "Allison has a superb ear for the specific dialogue of her characters." George Garrett, writing in the *New York Times Book Review* declared that Allison's "technical skill in both large things and details, so gracefully executed as to be always at the service of the story and its characters and thus almost invisible, is simply stunning."

**Cavedweller** Allison also received high praise for her 1998 novel *Cavedweller*. The book tells the story of Delia Byrd, a singer with a rock and roll band, who returns to her Georgia hometown with Cissy, her daughter by a rock-star lover who had been killed in a motorcycle accident, and works to earn the town's respect. A *Christian Century* contributor wrote that the theme of Allison's *Cavedweller* is redemption, "the need for it, the courage it requires, and the time and effort that may be necessary to achieve it." *Advocate* writer Carol Anshaw said it "is a woman's book through and through, filled with women's suffering, women's strength, women's survival."

## Responses to Literature

1. In *Bastard Out of Carolina* Bone considers both her mother and her Aunt Raylene as role models. What does she learn—or reject—from these two women?

2. Allison has admitted in multiple interviews that her novels are heavily autobiographical. How does this knowledge affect you as you read them? Would you read the novels differently if they were entirely fictional?

3. As a feminist, Dorothy Allison makes correlations between her identity as a woman and her identity as "poor white trash" from the South. What are the similarities and differences between these two identities? Why does Allison make this connection? What power, if any, does it add to her narrative?

BIBLIOGRAPHY

**Periodicals**

Giles, Jeff. "Return of the Rebel Belle: A New Novel from Dorothy Allison, Author of *Bastard Out of Carolina*." *Newsweek* (March 30, 1998), p.66.

Horvitz, Deborah. "'Sadism Demands a Story': Oedipus, Feminism, and Sexuality in Gayl Jones's Corregidora and Dorothy Allison's *Bastard Out of Carolina*." *Contemporary Literature* (Summer 1998), p. 238.

Irving, Katrina. "'Writing It down So That It Would Be Real': Narrative Strategies in Dorothy Allison's *Bastard Out of Carolina*." *College Literature* (Spring 1998), p. 94.

King, Vincent. "Hopeful Grief: The Prospect of a Postmodernist Feminism in Allison's *Bastard Out of Carolina*." *Southern Literary Journal* (Fall 2000), p.120.

# ⊛ Julia Alvarez

BORN: *1950, New York, New York*

NATIONALITY: *American*

GENRE: *Fiction, poetry*

MAJOR WORKS:

*How the García Girls Lost Their Accents* (1991)
*In the Time of the Butterflies* (1994)

## Overview

Best known for her first novel, *How the García Girls Lost Their Accents* (1991), Julia Alvarez is noted for portrayals of familial relationships, the Hispanic immigrant experience, and for insights into such issues as acculturation, alienation, and prejudice. Alvarez frequently blurs the lines between poetry and fiction and uses circular rather than chronological narrative structures. Writing about *How the García Girls Lost Their Accents*, Jason Zappe has stated that "Alvarez speaks for many families and brings to light the challenges faced by many immigrants. She shows how the tensions of successes and failures don't have to tear families apart."

## Works in Biographical and Historical Context

***Escape to New York*** Born in New York City, Julia Altagracia Alvarez grew up in the Dominican Republic until the age of ten, when in 1960 her father and the rest of the family escaped the country after supporting a rebel faction trying to oust dictator Rafael Trujillo. Trujillo had come into power in 1930 in an election overrun with fraud, but his efforts to secure control of the Dominican government resulted in thirty years of tyrannical rule by him and his carefully chosen surrogates. He was infamous for his use of violence against those who disagreed with his policies and also against his country's Haitian neighbors. It was this deadly regime, and her family's escape from it, that inspired much of Alvarez's most successful works. Alvarez's father (who often recited poems to Alvarez) established a medical practice in the Bronx while her mother, born Julia Tavares, attended to their four daughters.

***Balancing Personal and Professional Life*** Alvarez attended Connecticut College for two years, graduated summa cum laude from Middlebury College in 1971, and earned her MA in Creative Writing at Syracuse

Julia Alvarez *AP Images*

# LITERARY AND HISTORICAL CONTEMPORARIES

Alvarez's famous contemporaries include:

**Rafael Trujillo** (1891–1961): Trujillo was dictator of the Dominican Republic from 1930 until his assassination in 1961. He ruled the country with violence and absolute power. Alvarez describes this period of the Dominican Republic's history in her novel *In the Time of Butterflies*.

**Gabriel García Márquez** (1927–): A Nobel Prize winner who is considered one of the most important writers of the twentieth and twenty-first centuries, Márquez specializes in fictional recreations of his native Colombian family stories and folk tales. Through the literary techniques of magic realism, he uses supernatural elements to explain real experiences.

**Jamaica Kincaid** (1949–): Born in Antigua, Jamaica Kincaid moved to New York City at the age of sixteen and launched a successful career as a journalist and novelist. Like Julia Alvarez, her works often focus on domestic spaces such as the kitchen and garden.

**Sammy Sosa** (1968–): Sosa, who was born in the Dominican Republic, is the all-time home run leader among foreign-born major league baseball players. He is one of five players to have hit six hundred career home runs.

**Freddie Prinze** (1954–1977): Prinze, an actor and stand-up comedian of combined Puerto Rican and Hungarian descent, is best remembered for his role on the hit television series *Chico and the Man*.

University in 1975. Alvarez wrote her first book, the full-length poetry collection *Homecoming* (1984), while teaching at the University of Vermont. Much of the book was composed when she was thirty-three, about eight years after she earned her master's degree. As she explains in *Something to Declare* (1998), she married and divorced twice before turning thirty, setting aside her writing each time, believing, as she had been told by the women in her family, that she could (and should) write later. The second divorce had the unexpected effect, however, of freeing her to do as she wished. Having failed traditional expectations, she enrolled in a fiction workshop and accepted a temporary teaching position that afforded her time to write.

### The García Girls and Continued Success

In the years between publishing *Homecoming* and *The Other Side: El Otro Lado* (1995), Alvarez found an agent who won her a contract with Algonquin Books for her first novel, *How the García Girls Lost Their Accents*. The novel received almost instant critical praise. Exhibiting Alvarez's innovation in narrative form, the book is a series of fifteen short stories interwoven to tell one tale in reverse chronological order. Spanning the years from 1956 to 1989, this work chronicles the lives of the Garcia sisters—Carla, Sandra, Yolonda, and Sophia—from their upbringing in the Dominican Republic to their escape to the United States. Largely autobiographical, the work explores such issues as acculturation, coming of age, and social status.

Alvarez's next novel, *In the Time of the Butterflies* (1994), is set in the Dominican Republic and relates in fictional form the true story of the four Mirabal sisters, also known as the Butterflies, or Las Mariposas. As active opponents of Trujillo, three of the four sisters were murdered by the government in 1960. In arguing for the importance of the part they played in Dominican history and consciousness, Alvarez also explores more universal themes of history, tyranny, freedom, and survival. *In the Time of the Butterflies* was also well-received, and during this period Alvarez earned numerous awards and grants for excellence in multicultural literature.

While writing her novels, Alvarez put an end to her itinerancy by accepting a teaching post at Middlebury College in 1988 and marrying Bill Eichner, an ophthalmologist and author of *The New Family Cookbook* (2000), with whom she built a house on eleven country acres in Vermont. She earned tenure in 1991 and was promoted to full professor in 1996. While she considers receiving praise after so many years of work wonderful, Alvarez has mentioned in interviews and autobiographical essays how difficult it was for her to field questions that assumed her life exactly mirrored that of her characters. Alvarez, in order to spend more time on her writing, gave up her full-time post in 1998, yet maintained her relationship with Middlebury College as a writer-in-residence. Since producing her second collection of poems, the prolific Alvarez has published additional novels, a collection of autobiographical essays, and children's books.

## Works in Literary Context

### A Multicultural Woman's Perspective

Like her contemporaries Amy Tan and Jamaica Kincaid, Alvarez explores multicultural experiences by focusing on domestic spaces and featuring the voices of women. Thus, for example, *How the García Girls Lost Their Accents* tackles issues of acculturation through family stories, and *In the Time of the Butterflies*, while focusing on the Mirabal sisters, provides readers with a historical account of the bloodthirsty rule of the Dominican Republic's dictator Rafael Trujillo. In both her novels and her poems, domestic spaces and family relationships provide safety from tyranny, misunderstanding, and prejudice.

### The Caribbean and Post-Colonialism

In both her poetry and prose, Alvarez tackles issues that pertain specifically to countries (such as the Dominican Republic) that have experienced colonial occupation and ensuing chaotic—and often violent—social conditions. The characters from Alvarez's works often confront hardship, uncertainty, prejudice, and fear. In addition, as in the case of the García sisters, they must also face the difficulties of immigration, becoming acculturated to new American surroundings, and homesickness. Joining the ranks of Haitian-American writer Edwidge Danticat and West Indies poet Derek Walcott, Alvarez seeks to expose both the advantages and difficulties of forging a new Caribbean-American identity in the post-colonial period.

***The Influence of Poets and Poetry***   Though Alvarez is perhaps best known for her novels, critics have noted that her work is heavily influenced by nineteenth- and twentieth-century poets. Scholar Kathrine Varnes, for example, has noted similarities in tone and style between Alvarez's poems and those of Elizabeth Bishop and W. H. Auden. Even while writing prose, Alvarez shows her love of poetry, often as an important part of a character's life, whether in Yoyo's discovery of Walt Whitman in *How the García Girls Lost Their Accents*, or in Minerva's love of poetry in *In the Time of the Butterflies*, or in the narrative of *In the Name of Salomé* (2000), in which the main character Camila mourns the loss of her mother, Salomé Urena, a poet whom Alvarez describes as the Emily Dickinson of the Dominican Republic.

## Works in Critical Context

The critical reaction to Alvarez's works has been generally positive, with most critics praising her sympathetic and personal portraits of families and the immigrant experience. While Alvarez is praised for her poetry in literary circles, it was the 1991 publication of *How the García Girls Lost Their Accents* that secured her place as one of the most important of contemporary Caribbean-American writers. Alvarez received continued popular acclaim for her second novel, *In the Time of the Butterflies.*

***How the García Girls Lost Their Accents***   The novel became an international bestseller and won her a PEN Oakland Award and a notable book designation with the American Library Association and *The New York Times*. Most praise from commentators has been aimed at her ability to effectively portray the immigrant experience. As Donna Rifkind wrote of the author in the *New York Times Book Review*, "She has, to her great credit, beautifully captured the threshold experience of the new immigrant, where the past is not yet a memory and the future remains an anxious dream." However, Rifkind was less enamored with other elements: "The García girls may have indeed lost their accents, but in her first work of fiction Julia Alvarez has not yet quite found a voice." Similarly, Ilan Stavans has stated of the work: "Alvarez has an acute eye for the secret complexities that permeate family life. Although once in a while she sets into melodrama, her descriptions are full of pathos." Jason Zappe, writing for *The Americas Review*, noted that Alvarez "displays a talent for portraying the immigrant experience with sensitivity and light-heartedness."

> ## COMMON HUMAN EXPERIENCE
>
> Alvarez's works focus on sisterhood and the centering power of domestic spaces, such as the kitchen and the garden. Other works that explore this theme include:
>
> *The Book of Salt* (2003), a novel by Monique Truong. This novel recreates the life and experiences of Binh, the Vietnamese exile who served as the cook for Gertrude Stein and Alice Toklas in their Paris home in the 1930s.
>
> *The Color Purple* (1983), a novel by Alice Walker. Walker's novel explores the inequality of African American women living in the South in the 1930s. After suffering years of terror and humiliation from her abusive husband, the novel's protagonist, Celie, leaves to establish her own home and business and is eventually reunited with her long-lost sister.
>
> *One Hundred Years of Solitude* (1967), a novel by Gabriel García Márquez. García Márquez's highly-praised novel tells the story of several generations of the Buendía family, who live in one of the largest houses in the fictional village of Macondo.
>
> *The Joy Luck Club* (1993), a film by Wayne Wang. Based on the 1989 novel by Amy Tan, the film focuses on the relationships between generations of Chinese-American women living in San Francisco.

***In the Time of the Butterflies***   In her second novel, *In the Time of the Butterflies*, Alvarez recalls a grim incident in Dominican history: the untimely deaths in 1960 of three sisters—the Mirabals—who had denounced Rafael Trujillo's dictatorship. Alvarez chooses to portray these events from a subjective fictional perspective rather than as historical biography. According to Roberto Gonzalez Echevarria, writing in the *New York Times Book Review*, "by dealing with real historical figures in this novel, Ms. Alvarez has been much more ambitious than she was in her first, as if she needed to have her American self learn what it was really like in her native land." *Nation* contributor Ilan Stavans stated that, although Alvarez's subject matter is not unique, "her pen lends it an authenticity and sense of urgency seldom found elsewhere." Stavans went on to state that *In the Time of the Butterflies* is "full of pathos and passion, with beautifully crafted anecdotes interstitched to create a patchwork quilt of meaning and ideology."

## Responses to Literature

1. Write a paper in which you compare the presentations of violence in Julia Alvarez's *In the Time of the Butterflies* and Edwidge Danticat's *The Dew Breaker* (2003). How does the atmosphere of violence affect

the two households described by Alvarez and Danticat?

2. Many critics have argued that Alvarez's *How the García Girls Lost Their Accents* should not be considered a novel but a collection of short stories. What do you think are the advantages of Alvarez's unconventional storytelling method in the book? How do the interrelated stories and reverse chronology affect your understanding of the stories and their meaning?

3. Throughout Alvarez's work, the author explores the complications of differing female roles: wife, mother, daughter, divorcee, homemaker, female author. Choose one of these identifications and explore Alvarez's exploration of it in her poetry. How is it affected by her identity as a Caribbean or an immigrant?

BIBLIOGRAPHY

**Books**

Narins, Brigham, Deborah A. Stanley and George H. Blair, eds. "Julia Alvarez (1950–)" *in Contemporary Literary Criticism*, vol. 93. Detroit: Gale Research, 1996, pp. 1–20.

Sirias, Silvio. *Julia Alvarez: A Critical Companion.* Westport, Conn.: Greenwood Press, 2001.

**Periodicals**

Stavans, Ilan. Review of *In the Time of the Butterflies. Nation.* November 7, 1994, pp. 552–556.

Tabor, Maria Garcia. "The Truth According to Your Characters: Interview with Julia Alvarez." *Prairie Schooner* 74, Summer 2000, pp. 151–56.

Varnes, Kathrine. "'Practicing for the Real Me': Form and Authenticity in the Poetry of Julia Alvarez." *Antipodas* 10, 1998.

Vela, Richard. "Daughter of Invention: The Poetry of Julia Alvarez." *Postscript: Publication of the Philological Association of the Carolinas* 16, 1999, pp. 33–42.

# ⊛ Rudolfo Anaya

BORN: *October 30, 1937, Pastura, New Mexico*

NATIONALITY: *American*

GENRE: *Fiction, drama*

MAJOR WORKS:

*Bless Me, Ultima* (1972)

*Alburquerque* (1992)

## Overview

One of the most influential authors in Chicano literature, Rudolfo Anaya is acclaimed for his skillful mingling of realism, fantasy, and myth in novels exploring the experiences of Hispanics in the American Southwest. Stem-

Rudolfo Anaya  *Anaya, Rudolfo, photograph by Cynthia Farah. Reproduced by permission.*

ming from his fascination with the mystical nature of Spanish-American oral folk tales, Anaya's works often address his loss of religious faith. As Anaya has explained, his education caused him to question his religious beliefs, and that, in turn, led him to write poetry and prose. "I lost faith in my God," Anaya has stated, "and if there was no God there was no meaning, no secure road to salvation.... The depth of loss one feels is linked to one's salvation. That may be why I write. It is easier to ascribe those times and their bittersweet emotions to my characters."

## Works in Biographical and Historical Context

***Introduction to the Oral Tradition***   Rudolfo Anaya was born in 1937 in the village of Pastura, New Mexico. There, and later in nearby Santa Rosa, where Anaya spent the majority of his childhood, people gathered to hear and tell stories, anecdotes, and riddles. Anaya has commented:

> I was always in a milieu of words, whether they were printed or in the oral tradition. And I think

that's important to stimulate the writer's imagination; to respond to what is going on around him, to incorporate the materials and then rehash them and make fiction—to start at a point of reference which is close to one's being and then to transcend it—that's important.

The author was profoundly affected by the old storytellers, the myths of his Mexican-Indian ancestors, and the land itself. The plains in which he was raised provide the setting for most of his novels and short stories.

*Early Influences and Well-received Novels*  In 1955 Anaya graduated from Albuquerque High School. He then attended Browning Business School for two years before entering the University of New Mexico, where he received his master's degree in English in 1968. Anaya wrote that he "really fell in love with reading when I was a student at the University of New Mexico. I read everything in those days when a liberal education meant preparing the student in world literature—multicultural literature." At the university Anaya studied such novelists as Thomas Wolfe, William Faulkner, Ernest Hemingway, and John Steinbeck; aspiring to become a writer himself, he attempted to imitate their style and technique but was unsuccessful. "I made a simple discovery," Anaya has related. "I found I needed to write in my voice about my characters, using my indigenous symbols."

Thus, he began writing *Bless Me, Ultima* (1972), a novel about a boy growing up in New Mexico shortly after World War II. Anaya spent nearly seven years writing and rewriting this first novel. Completed in 1972, *Bless Me, Ultima* was a resounding success, earning Anaya the second annual Premio Quinto Sol prize for literature. His two subsequent novels, *Heart of Aztlan* (1976) and *Tortuga* (1979), consolidated Anaya's reputation as an important American author of fiction. In addition to writing novels, Anaya has taught courses in creative writing and Chicano literature at the University of New Mexico, edited several books on Chicano literature, experimented in drama and script-writing, published a collection of short stories, and contributed many articles to literary periodicals. He also received the 1993 PEN Fiction award for his novel *Alburquerque* (1992).

*Coming of Age Trilogy*  Centering around the dilemmas of young Spanish-Americans, *Bless Me, Ultima, Heart of Aztlan,* and *Tortuga* form a loose trilogy, embedded in myth and bound by common themes that focus on the deterioration of traditional Hispanic ways of life, social injustice and oppression, disillusionment and loss of faith, and the regenerative power of love. Anaya drew heavily from his own background in the writings of these works; as the son of a sheepherder, he was well-acquainted with the hardships of agricultural work, and as a young child he struggled with the strict Catholicism practiced by his mother's family. *Bless Me, Ultima* features a young boy named Antonio whose maturation is linked to his struggle with religious faith and his difficulty in choosing between

## LITERARY AND HISTORICAL CONTEMPORARIES

Anaya's famous contemporaries include:

**Sandra Cisneros** (1954–): Cisneros is a Latina novelist and poet best known for her book *The House on Mango Street* (1984).

**Gary Soto** (1952–): Soto is a Latino poet from California who focuses his work on the working class Mexican-American experience.

**Luis Echeverría Álvarez** (1922–): Echeverría served as president of Mexico from 1970 to 1976. During his time in office, he implemented various populist social and economic reforms, including nationalizing industries and seizing private lands to be redistributed to peasants.

the nomadic life of his father's family, and the agricultural lifestyle of his mother's. *Heart of Aztlan* relates the story of a Chicano worker who, due to financial difficulties, is forced to move his family from their rural home to the city, where he has obtained employment in the railroad factories. A sociopolitical work, the novel examines life in a Chicano ghetto, addressing the exploitation of poverty-ridden laborers by corrupt elements in religion and industry. In this work Anaya also drew from personal experience; his family moved from the rural plains of New Mexico to Albuquerque in 1952, and there Anaya first perceived the racism and prejudice faced by Latino immigrants in urban post-war America. In Albuquerque, at the age of sixteen, Anaya suffered a fall, broke two vertebrae in his neck, and suffered through a long and painful convalescence—an experience which would serve as the basis for *Tortuga*. The plight of the title character—a young boy suffering from paralysis—dramatically emphasizes the need for healing in what Anaya has described as "a society that was crushing and mutilating" people. Tortuga's recovery, hastened by the emotional well-being that results from his love for a nurse's aide, exemplifies the healing power of love and the inextricable link between emotional, spiritual, and physical health.

## Works in Literary Context

*Influence of Modernism*  Anaya has stated in interviews that his writing has been profoundly influenced by Modernist writers, particularly Southern writers, such as William Faulkner and Thomas Wolfe. Modernist writers, working largely in the period between World Wars I and II, addressed the alienation the individual feels in an ever-expanding, mechanized world. American Modernist writers, including T. S. Eliot, Ezra Pound, and Ernest Hemingway, spent much of their time as expatriates living

## COMMON HUMAN EXPERIENCE

*Bless Me, Ultima* and *Tortuga* feature young Mexican-American characters that move from feeling marginalized and alienated from society to feeling proud of their heritage and at peace with their surroundings. Other books which focus on similar characters include:

*The House on Mango Street* (1984), a novella by Sandra Cisneros. Cisneros's novella is the coming-of-age story of a young girl living in a Chicago Chicano ghetto.

*Autobiography of a Brown Buffalo* (1972), a novel by Oscar Zeta Acosta. Acosta, known as "Dr. Gonzo" in Hunter S. Thompson's *Fear and Loathing in Las Vegas*, wrote this fictionalized autobiography of a Mexican-American lawyer who gives up drugs, alcohol, and a low self-image in favor of Chicano activism.

*So Far From God* (1993), a novel by Ana Castillo. Using magic realism, Castillo tells the story of a Latina mother struggling to raise her four daughters in a small town in New Mexico.

and writing in Europe, and tried to forge their American identities with the literary traditions of Britain and France. Similarly, Anaya, in works such as *Bless Me, Ultima* and *Tortuga* attempts to explore the individual's experience of the boundaries between Mexican and American culture.

***Spirituality Versus Organized Religion*** Modernist writers are also known for their rejection of established institutions, particularly the church. Often, however, the protagonists of Modernist novels (such as, for example, Quentin Compson of Faulkner's *Absalom, Absalom!*) seek a sense of spirituality based on their own experiences in the world rather than the dogma provided by social or cultural establishments. Much like Antonio in *Bless Me, Ultima*, these protagonists seek to heal their disillusionment with the world by finding an individual code of ethics.

***The Bi-racial American Experience*** Anaya's *Bless Me, Ultima* is often cited as a landmark of multicultural American literature; it was the first novel written about the Mexican-American experience to reach a widespread audience. Furthermore, the book followed in the wake of the "counter-cultural" revolution of the 1960s. During this period, America witnessed radical political protests and drastic social reforms, most of which were centered on issues of racial equality and integration. While the social reforms of the 1960s dealt primarily with the African American experience, Anaya's work helped to bring to light the need to reevaluate the living and working conditions of all minorities in America.

## Works in Critical Context

Anaya's novels have been studied and analyzed with an intensity accorded to few other Hispanic writers. Praised for their universal appeal, his works have been translated into a number of languages. Of Anaya's international success, Antonio Marquez has written, "It is befitting for Anaya to receive the honor and the task of leading Chicano literature into the canons of world literature. He is the most acclaimed and the most popular and universal Chicano writer, and one of the most influential voices in contemporary Chicano literature."

***Bless Me, Ultima*** *Bless Me, Ultima* has generated more critical review, analysis, and interpretation than any other novel in contemporary Chicano literature. Critics of this work have found Anaya's story unique, his narrative technique compelling, and his prose both meticulous and lyrical. *America* reviewer Scott Wood called the book "unique" and "remarkable," and stated, "Living apart from the mainstream, a young New Mexican Chicano has offered in this, his first novel, a rich and powerful synthesis for some of life's sharpest oppositions." Ron Arias, writing for *The American Book Review*, states, "As entertainment, the novel *moves*, as a work written for reflection, it provokes . . ." Raymond J. Rodrigues, in a review for *English Journal*, calls the book "an important contribution to literature in a pluralistic United States."

***Heart of Aztlan*** The reception of *Heart of Aztlan*, however, has been less enthusiastic. Although many critics have approved of the novel's mythic substructure, some commentators have found Anaya's intermingling of myth and politics confusing. Juan Bruce-Novoa has noted that "*Ultima* produced expectations that *Heart of Aztlan* did not satisfy. . . . [I]t is a matter of the craftsmanship, not of the themes, and Heart, for whatever reason, is less polished, less accomplished." Marvin A. Lewis observed in *Revista Chicano-Requena* that

on the surface, the outcome [of Heart of Aztlan] is a shallow, romantic, adolescent novel which nearly overshadows the treatment of adult problems. The novel [has] redeeming qualities, however, in its treatment of the urban experience and the problems with racism inherent therein, as well as in its attempt to define the mythic dimension of the Chicano experience.

Similarly, *World Literature Today* critic Charles R. Larson felt that *Heart of Aztlan*, along with *Bless Me, Ultima*, "provide[s] us with a vivid sense of Chicano Life since World War II."

***Tortuga*** *Tortuga* has also prompted a mixed critical response. Some commentators, such as Antonio Marquez in *The Magic of Words*, praised the novel's structural complexity and innovative depiction of Chicano life, and have proclaimed *Tortuga* "Anaya's best work"; others, however, have denigrated the novel as melodramatic and unrealistic. For instance, Cordelia Candelaria has asserted that the characters presented in *Tortuga* are "lacking in human vitality and motivation" and "perform like mechanical metaphors."

## Responses to Literature

1. Anaya has often cited Modernist American writers such as Ernest Hemingway, William Faulkner, and Thomas Wolfe as his literary influences. Research both the lives of these writers and the themes which they incorporated in their works. Why do you think Anaya found inspiration in these writers and their works? How do these writers' experiences and books correspond to his own?

2. Anaya's *Bless Me, Ultima* is considered a landmark in the genre of coming-of-age books which tackle the issue of race in America. Can you think of recent books, movies, or films which address similar themes? For example, you may want to consider John Singleton's *Boyz N the Hood* or Sandra Cisneros's *The House on Mango Street*. How is the multi-cultural experience of America different now than it was when *Bless Me, Ultima* was published in 1972?

3. In interviews, Anaya has stated that he has always been fascinated by oral traditions, and has incorporated many of the techniques of traditional Hispanic storytelling into his novels. Can you identify some modern forms of oral storytelling (i.e., hip-hop, poetry slams, documentary movies)? What is the advantage of oral versus written storytelling? Do you find one more powerful than the other?

BIBLIOGRAPHY

**Books**

Baeza, Abelardo. *Keep Blessing Us, Ultima: A Teaching Guide for Bless Me, Ultima by Rudolfo Anaya*. Austin, Tex.: Easkin Press, 1997.

"Bless Me, Ultima by Rudolfo Anaya." *Children's Literature Review*. Edited by Tom Burns. Vol. 129. Detroit: Thomson Gale, 2008, pp. 1–68.

Bruce-Novoa, Juan D., *Chicano Authors: Inquiry by Interview* Austin: University of Texas Press, 1980.

Chavez, John R. *The Lost Land, The Chicano Image of the Southwest*. Albuquerque: University of New Mexico Press, 1984.

Dick, Bruce and Silvio Sirias. *Conversations with Rudolfo Anaya*. Jackson: University Press of Mississippi, 1998.

Fabre, Genviere. *European Perspectives on Hispanic Literature of the United States*. Houston, Tex.: Arte Publico Press, 1988.

Vassallo, Paul and Antonio Marquez. *Magic of Words: Rudolfo A. Anaya and His Writings*. Albuquerque: University of New Mexico Press, 1982.

## ✸ Jack Anderson

BORN: *1922, Long Beach, California*

DIED: *2005, Bethesda, Maryland*

NATIONALITY: *American*

GENRE: *Nonfiction, journalism, fiction*

MAJOR WORKS:

*McCarthy: The Man, the Senator, the "ism"* (1952)

*The Anderson Papers* (1973)

*Peace, War, and Politics: An Eyewitness Account* (1999)

### Overview

Jack Anderson was one of the most well-known pioneers of American investigative journalism and is best known for his Pulitzer Prize-winning syndicated column "Washington Merry-Go-Round." Anderson belonged to the tradition of "muckraking" journalists who exposed scandal, particularly in the arena of politics. During Anderson's long career he covered such high-profile topics as

Jack Anderson   *Cynthia Johnson / Time Life Pictures / Getty Images*

## LITERARY AND HISTORICAL CONTEMPORARIES

Anderson's famous contemporaries include:

**Drew Pearson** (1879–1969): This muckraking American journalist was Anderson's collaborator on the syndicated column "Washington Merry-Go-Round." He was an outspoken opponent of Cold War McCarthyism.

**Richard Nixon** (1913–1994): The thirty-seventh president of the United States. Nixon resigned from office after the Watergate scandal.

**J. Edgar Hoover** (1895–1972): Hoover was the first director of the Federal Bureau of Investigation, a post he would hold for nearly forty years. Hoover was often accused of using illegal means to gather intelligence, and was exposed by Jack Anderson for having ties to the Mafia and the Watergate scandal.

**Walter Cronkite** (1916–): Cronkite was a television journalist from 1950 until 1981 and was renowned for his coverage of historical events, such as the assassination of President John F. Kennedy and the Apollo 11 moon landing.

J. Edgar Hoover's ties to the Mafia, the CIA's plots to assassinate Cuban dictator Fidel Castro, the Watergate scandal, and Iran-Contra affair.

## Works in Biographical and Historical Context

### Mormon Upbringing and War Correspondence

The influential journalist Jackson Northman Anderson was born in Long Beach, California, on October 19, 1922, to a large family of the Mormon faith. When Anderson was two years old, the family moved to Utah, the stronghold of the Mormon church. Critics have often linked Anderson's journalistic writing style, which incorporated an often moralistic tone and a desire to enlighten readers of hidden corruption, to his upbringing in a religious faith that prized sexual abstinence, purity of mind and body, and the value of mission work. Anderson himself would serve as a Mormon missionary for two years, in between reporting jobs with local newspapers and attendance at the University of Utah. Afterwards, Anderson served in World War II, where he gained valuable journalistic experience as a war correspondent in China. Accompanying Chinese soldiers in harrowing conditions and difficult missions, Anderson developed the dogged style of pursuing news for which he was later celebrated.

### Breaking Ground in Washington

After returning from service in World War II, Anderson took a job with the high-profile journalist Drew Pearson. Pearson had already established himself as a "muckraker," a journalist dedicated to exposing corruption in government and business, who would use any means necessary to get the next scoop. The ambitious Anderson became an invaluable collaborator on Pearson's "Washington Merry-Go-Round" column. For ten years Anderson labored in virtual anonymity, lacking a byline even though he provided most of the information for which the column received attention. In 1957, however, Anderson threatened to quit unless Pearson publicly recognized his contribution to the success of their "Washington Merry-Go-Round" feature. The elder journalist then agreed to give Anderson more bylines and promised him that he would one day inherit the column.

Upon Pearson's death, Anderson became the sole author of "Washington Merry-Go-Round," though he was assisted by several other reporters and investigators (whose contributions he was quick to acknowledge). The column then developed a reputation for being "a more scrupulous, if somewhat less passionate institution," wrote Joe Klein for the *New York Times Book Review*. Anderson, for example, tried to avoid the more blatant propagandizing that was common during Pearson's heyday, and he insisted that his reporters go after the "spare, hard exposé" regardless of the wrongdoer's political affiliation.

### Tips, Informants, and Whistle-blowing

Anderson launched his career in Washington under the political climate of McCarthyism—so called for the influence of Joseph McCarthy and the House of Un-American Activities, which was given power by Congress to investigate the presence of Communist activity in America. During the Cold War period when America reached a stand-off with Soviet Russia and its allies, many politicians feared that America's post-war enemies (namely Russia) would infiltrate the country with spies and informants. The investigations of McCarthy and his colleagues began a "Red Scare" in which high-profile politicians, artists, and public figures were often unjustly accused of Communist sympathies. Though Anderson initially supported McCarthy and his cronies, he soon surmised that their accusations took on the air of a witch-hunt, and in his column he asserted himself to criticizing the House of Un-American Activities' abuses of power and to clearing the names of the accused. Anderson's reporting on the McCarthy hearings influenced several other works on the subject, for example, Richard Condon's novel *The Manchurian Candidate* (1959) and Arthur Miller's dramatic adaptation *The Crucible* (1953).

As the height of the Red Scare receded, Anderson expanded his attention to other areas of politics and government where he sensed injustice or corruption. In one of his most widely-read columns, he exposed the Central Intelligence Agency's plot to kill Cuban Communist dictator Fidel Castro. This earned him the life-long antagonism of the powerful director of the Federal Bureau of Investigation, J. Edgar Hoover, who famously referred to

Anderson as "lower than the regurgitated filth of vultures." Throughout the 1960s and 1970s, Anderson doggedly pursued high-level government and business scandal and corruption, though his methods of gaining information were often questioned by those exposed for wrongdoing; Anderson was accused of eavesdropping, bribing, and rifling through garbage, among other accusations.

In 1972 Anderson reported on America's secret support of Pakistan during the Bangledeshi war for independence and also linked the Justice Department's settlement of an antitrust suit against the ITT Corporation to the company's $400,000 pledge to President Richard Nixon's re-election campaign fund. For these efforts Anderson won the Pulitzer Prize and went on to play a vital role in the coverage of the 1974 Watergate scanda, which would eventually cause President Richard Nixon to resign. During the administration of Ronald Reagan, Anderson would reveal the Reagan administration's efforts to sell arms illegally to Iran and funnel the proceeds to anti-Communist forces in Central America.

In later life, the journalist published several novels and an autobiography based on his experiences in politics. Anderson died of Parkinson's disease in 2005, at the age of eighty-three.

## Works in Literary Context

*The Muckraking Tradition*   Anderson's journalistic style has often been associated with a group of writers called "muckrakers"—a term generally applied to journalists of the late nineteenth and early twentieth centuries who exposed poor working and living conditions in slums, hospitals, sweatshops, mines, prisons, and schools. They often wrote in a controversial, sensational tabloid style, and were frequently accused of socialist or communist leanings.

*Exposure of Political Corruption*   During his long career as a journalist, Anderson covered such disparate topics as the McCarthy trials, Watergate, and the savings and loan and Iran arms scandals. The common theme is the exposure of wrongdoing at the highest levels of government and other offices of power. *New York Times Book Review* critic Al Marlens asserted

> Mr. Anderson is paying the bills we all owe for the continuing health of the First Amendment. It is too often forgotten, as Mr. Anderson observes, that power in our democracy lies ultimately with the citizens, and that government secrecy disarms them.

## Works in Critical Context

Throughout his long career, Anderson has met with mixed reviews for his investigative journalism. *Washington Post* writer Tony Kornheiser related that "Washington Merry-Go-Round," Anderson's column, "has been called everything from 'gold' to 'garbage.' Sometimes on the

## COMMON HUMAN EXPERIENCE

Anderson focused his famous column "Washington Merry-Go-Round" on exposing corruption and scandal at the highest levels of government. Other works that have explored the investigative journalist's ability to check the abuse of power include:

> *All The President's Men* (1974), a nonfiction book by Bob Woodward and Carl Bernstein. This exposé documents Woodward and Bernstein's famed investigation of the Watergate scandal, focusing on their interaction with the informant known only as "Deep Throat."
> *All the King's Men* (1946), a novel by Robert Penn Warren. This Pulitzer Prize-winning novel is a fictional recreation of the life of Huey Long, a governor of Louisiana known for corruption and abuse of power. The story is narrated by Jack Burden, a political reporter who is recruited to work as the governor's assistant.
> *Public Opinion* (1922), a nonfiction book by Walter Lippman. In this political tract, influential journalist Walter Lippman argues that public awareness of politics had decreased in the modern age and that investigative journalists have a responsibility to enlighten readers about corruption at the highest levels of government.

same day. Sometimes in the same sentence." Some critics, however, have lauded Anderson's integrity; they argue that he was not the muckraker his predecessors were and find that in spite of his faults, Anderson performed an invaluable service. "He plays a unique role in American journalism," proclaimed Peter Osnos in the *Washington Post Book World*, "tackling sensitive subjects head on with a permanent sense of indignation at wrongdoing and a determination to get the news that officials might prefer to keep quiet."

## Responses to Literature

1. One of the largest scandals of recent memory involved the Enron Corporation and the indictment of its highest-level executives. Using the Internet, research the investigative reporting that surrounded the Enron scandal. What part did journalists play in the downfall of Enron? How did newspaper articles influence public opinion about the company and its CEOs? Can you trace the influence of Anderson in these reports?

2. According to traditional journalistic ethos, reporters are supposed to uphold an objective viewpoint, and document "just the facts." Anderson, however, was often criticized for asserting a moralistic tone and writing in a theatrical, sensationalist style. Do you think these accusations are credible? Use actual texts

(either Anderson's books or news reports) to back up your claims.

3. Consider the condition of news reporting today. Most Americans receive their news from television or the Internet as opposed to newspapers or magazines. How have these new media influenced the reporting of news? What are the positive and negative points surrounding these new technologies?

BIBLIOGRAPHY

**Books**

Anderson, Douglas A. *A "Washington Merry-go-round" of Libel Actions.* Chicago: Nelson-Hall, 1980.

Anderson, Jack. *Confessions of a Muckraker: The Inside Story of Life in Washington during the Truman, Eisenhower, Kennedy and Johnson Years.* New York: Random House, 1979.

Hume, Brit. *Inside Story.* Garden City, N.Y.: Doubleday, 1974.

**Periodicals**

Corn, David. "Mellowing of a Muckraker." *Nation* (November 14, 1987).

Kornheiser, Tony. "Jack Anderson & His Crusading Crew." *Washington Post* (August 7), 1983, p. 1.

Sherrill, Robert. Review of *Confessions of a Muckraker. Chicago Tribune Book World* (May 6), 1979, p. 1.

# ❀ Laurie Halse Anderson

BORN: *1961, Potsdam, New York*

NATIONALITY: *American*

GENRE: *Fiction*

MAJOR WORKS:

*Speak* (1999)

*Fever 1793* (2000)

## Overview

Laurie Halse Anderson writes books for children and young adults. She is noted for the wide range of her writings. Some are lighthearted folktales, such as *Ndito Runs* (1996) and the morality tales in her "Wild at Heart" series, while books such as *Speak* (1999) address issues of child abuse, rape, and violence. Her works typically feature female adolescent protagonists.

## Works in Biographical and Historical Context

***Combining Religion and Adventure*** Laurie Halse Anderson was born in 1961 in Potsdam, New York, and was the daughter of a Methodist minister. Her early religious background, as well as her later conversion to Quakerism, a faith that emphasizes social and political pacifism, are often cited as moral influences on her works.

Anderson knew she wanted to be an author from a young age. As she once explained, after her second grade teacher introduced her to writing poetry, she "spent hours and hours and hours reading every book in my school library. The books took me everywhere—ripping through time barriers, across cultures, experiencing all the magic an elementary school library can hold." She traveled across cultures in her first published picture book, *Ndito Runs* (1996). The book follows a young Kenyan girl as she makes her lighthearted and cheerful journey from her home to her school. Ndito leaves her village and enters the countryside, imagining herself to be any number of animals and birds indigenous to the African savanna. As Hazel Rochman commented in a *Booklist* review of *Ndito Runs*, Anderson's "simple, poetic words...express Ndito's exhilaration and her connection with nature and with people."

After the success of *Ndito Runs*, Anderson published the humorous picture books *Turkey Pox* (1996) and *No Time for Mother's Day* (1999). In *The Big Cheese of Third Street* (2002), Anderson explores the issue of body image by telling a story from the perspective of Benny Antonelli, a very small child in a neighborhood filled with tremendously large men, women, and older kids.

***Shift in Audience*** Moving to older readers in 1999, Anderson published her first young adult novel, *Speak*, and was nominated for two prestigious literary awards. The narrator of *Speak* is a high-school freshman named Melinda who has become nearly mute after being ostracized by her fellow students for calling 911 during a drinking party the previous summer. Although she can hardly bring herself to speak to her peers or teachers, Melinda's written narrative is bursting with language that is angry, sardonic, frightened, sad, and sometimes even funny. A popular novel, *Speak* was also adapted as a television movie.

Following the success of *Speak*, Anderson developed an interest in historical settings for her novels, particularly her adopted hometown of Philadelphia. Her 2000 publication *Fever 1793*, also geared for teens, is a historical novel set during a yellow-fever epidemic that swept through Philadelphia during the period when it was still the capital of the United States. The disease is estimated to have killed approximately five thousand people, or one out of every ten Philadelphians, making it the worst yellow-fever epidemic to ever strike the United States. Like *Speak*, *Fever 1793* features a first-person narrative of a fourteen-year-old girl living through a trauma. Here, Matilda reports with growing horror on her life running a coffeehouse with her widowed mother and grandfather as her community is struck by yellow fever, which kills thousands in a matter of a few months.

***Recent and Current Works*** Since the publications of *Speak* and *Fever 1793*, Anderson has published several novels lighter in tone. *Prom* (2005), for example, describes an ordinary teen named Ashley as she becomes drawn into her best friend's plan to save their school's senior prom. In *Twisted* (2007), nerdy Tyler goes from social outcast to local legend when he is caught spraying graffiti at school. Anderson has also published a "Wild at Heart" series for elementary school readers.

Anderson, however, has not abandoned the historical novel nor her narratives of female protagonists who face trauma. Anderson once explained: "Despite evidence to the contrary, I believe the world has an abundance of goodness. Not all children get to see this, sadly. I would like to think my books serve up some goodness—with hot fudge, whipped cream, and a cherry on top."

## Works in Literary Context

*Mothers and Daughters*    The majority of Anderson's novels feature female protagonists, and often these protagonists explore their often conflicted relationships with their mothers. For example, Charity, in *No Time for Mother's Day*, is puzzled by what to give her tremendously busy mother for Mother's Day. Ultimately, it dawns on the girl that the best gift of all would be to turn off all the clocks and machines in the house, because these timekeepers seem to be the cause of her mom's stress. Similarly, *Catalyst* (2002), a book directed toward a slightly older reader, follows the consequences of eighteen-year-old Kate's decision to only apply to the college attended by her late mother. When she is rejected by the school, she must confront issues regarding her identity as an independent young woman.

*The Importance of Women in History*    Anderson often adopts historical settings for her novels; frequently she uses these past time periods to show that young women, though often overlooked in the formal historical record, played a large role in America's formation. The picture book *Thank You, Sarah: The Woman Who Saved Thanksgiving* (2002), for example, describes young Sarah Hale's efforts to turn Thanksgiving into a national holiday, and her appeals to President Abraham Lincoln. A *Kirkus Reviews* contributor wrote of the book that "Anderson offers readers both an indomitable role model and a memorable, often hilarious glimpse into the historical development of this country's common culture." Even more recently, Anderson has tried to revise eighteenth-century American history; her *Independent Dames: What You Never Knew About the Women and Girls in the American Revolution* (2008) tells the stories of women and girls who acted as spies, organized boycotts, even disguised themselves as men to enlist in the Revolution.

## Works in Critical Context

Criticism of both Anderson's children's and young adult novels have been consistently positive, with reviewers frequently commenting on Anderson's versatility of style. Noting the variety of genres in which Anderson works, critic Cynthia Leitich Smith wrote that the author is "always taking chances—writing books that are very different from one another—and still hitting it out of the

---

## LITERARY AND HISTORICAL CONTEMPORARIES

Anderson's famous contemporaries include:

**J. K. Rowling** (1965–): Rowling is the author of the internationally bestselling *Harry Potter* series of fantasy books, which concern a wizard in training and his schoolmates.
**Yann Martel** (1963–): Martel is a Canadian author best known for his Booker Prize-winning novel *Life of Pi* (2001).
**Matthew Tobin Anderson** (1968–): Anderson is an award-winning young adult novelist best known for his novels *Feed* (2002) and *The Astonishing Life of Octavian Nothing* (2006).

---

## COMMON HUMAN EXPERIENCE

Although Anderson has written many young adult novels with humor and levity, critics most praise her novels that address such issues as child abuse and the sexual mistreatment of minors. Other young-adult novels that tackle similar sensitive issues include:

*Sold* (2006), a novel by Patricia McCormick. *Sold* tells the story of thirteen-year-old Lakshmi, a Nepalese girl who is sold into the slave trade by her stepfather and must struggle to find a way out of the brothel she is kept in.
*Beasts of No Nation* (2005), a novel by Uzodinma Iweala. This book tells the story of Agu, a boy who is recruited as a child soldier by a guerilla group after civil war engulfs his country in Western Africa.
*The Astonishing Life of Octavian Nothing* (2006), a novel by Matthew Tobin Anderson. Anderson's novel tells the story of an African boy adopted as a specimen of study by a scientific college. Once he runs away and joins the colonial army, he learns the harsh realities of racial inequalities and cruelty.

---

literary ballpark." Anderson seems to garner the highest praise, however, when she addresses issues of trauma or executes a revision of women's roles in American history.

*Speak (1999)*    *Speak*, a first-person narrative written in the voice of a young rape victim, was a Michael L. Printz Award Honor Book the first year the prize was awarded. "An uncannily funny book even as it plumbs the darkness, *Speak* will hold readers from first word to last," wrote a *Horn Book* contributor. Other reviewers focused on Anderson's realistic depiction of adolescent life.

According to a *Publishers Weekly* reviewer, the author "uses keen observations and vivid imagery to pull readers into the head of an isolated teenager."

## Responses to Literature

1. Anderson's *Fever 1793* attempts to recreate the life of a young girl living in a past period of social upheaval. Choose a time period other than the American Revolution, and outline a story that chronicles the experiences of a young female protagonist during this period. Use historical research to add detail to your story.

2. Imagine Anderson is visiting your classroom to get ideas for her next book. With your classmates, brainstorm pertinent young adult topics that are often overlooked in young adult novels. What issues would you like to see raised in her next novel?

3. Anderson has written books that are classified as both children's literature and young adult novels. Compare two examples of these genres. What are the differences in theme and language? Do you have suggestions for how difficult subject topics should be approached, depending on the age of the audience?

BIBLIOGRAPHY

**Periodicals**

Burkam, Anita L. Review of *Fever 1793*. *Horn Book* September 2000.

Bradburn, Frances. Review of *Fever 1793*. *Booklist*, October 1, 2000.

Rochman, Hazel. Review of *Ndito Runs*. *Booklist*, March 15, 1996.

Review of *Speak*. *Horn Book*, September 1999.

Review of *Speak*. *Publishers Weekly*, September 13, 1999.

Review of *Thank You, Sarah*. *Kirkus Reviews*, October 1, 2002.

**Web sites**

Smith, Cynthia Leitich. *Review of* Prom. Retrieved September 18, 2008, from http://cynthialeitich smith.blogspot.com/2005/01/prom-by-laurie-halse-anderson.html.

## ❂ Sherwood Anderson

BORN: *1876, Camden, Ohio*

DIED: *1941, Cristobal, Panama*

NATIONALITY: *American*

GENRE: *Fiction, poetry, nonfiction*

MAJOR WORKS:

*Winesburg, Ohio: A Group of Tales of Ohio Small Town Life* (1919)

*Dark Laughter* (1927)

*Death in the Woods* (1933)

Sherwood Anderson    *Sherwood Anderson, 1984, photograph by Alfred Stieglitz. The Library of Congress.*

## Overview

Sherwood Anderson was among the first American authors to explore the influence of the unconscious upon human behavior. A writer of brooding, introspective works, his "hunger to see beneath the surface of lives" was best expressed in the bittersweet stories which form the classic *Winesburg, Ohio: A Group of Tales of Ohio Small Town Life* (1919). This, his most important book, exhibits the author's characteristically simple prose style and his personal vision, which combines a sense of wonder at the potential beauty of life with despair over its tragic aspects.

## Works in Biographical and Historical Context

*Living and Observing Everyday Life in Ohio*
Born in 1876 in Ohio to an out-of-work harness maker and a washerwoman, Sherwood Anderson was raised in the small town of Clyde, which later served as the model for Winesburg in his celebrated short story collection *Winesburg, Ohio: A Group of Tales of Ohio Small Town Life*. In Clyde, while coming to hate the self-sacrificing drudgery to which his mother was reduced and the irresponsibility of his alcoholic father, Anderson first learned the art of telling stories while listening to his father tell

the entertaining anecdotes for which he was known. Attending school infrequently, Anderson took a number of temporary jobs to help his impoverished family, working as a newsboy, a housepainter, a field worker, and a "swipe," or stablehand. These experiences, along with the awkward sexual initiation described in his *Memoirs* (1942), later provided thematic and incidental material for his fiction.

*From Businessman to Artist* After a brief stint in the U.S. Army during the Spanish-American War, Anderson married, became an advertising copywriter in Chicago, and then went on to manage his own paint factory, the Anderson Manufacturing Company, in Elyria, Ohio. His commercial success, however, did not satisfy his awakening artistic aspirations, and he spent his spare time—and a fair amount of company time—writing fiction.

Scholars have noted that the year 1912 marked a watershed in Anderson's artistic and professional life. In November of that year, overworked and beset by various worries, Anderson suffered a mental breakdown; as best as can be determined from the conflicting accounts in his writings, he suddenly walked out of his office in the midst of dictating a letter and was discovered four days later many miles away, babbling incoherently. Shortly afterward his marriage and business failed, and he returned to Chicago to resume work in advertising. There he met such writers of the Chicago Renaissance as Floyd Dell, Carl Sandburg, Theodore Dreiser, Ben Hecht, and Burton Rascoe, who read his early fiction and encouraged him. Most of his early stories were printed in *Masses*, *Little Review*, *Seven Arts*, and other "little" magazines.

Anderson attained recognition as an important new voice in American literature with the appearance of *Winesburg, Ohio* in 1919. Published the same year that World War I concluded, the book exhibits many of the bleak aspects of modern life that concerned writers after a prolonged period of strife and sorrow. For example, reacting perhaps to the return of shell-shocked soldiers from the trenches of modern warfare (and the renewed interest in psychology they caused), Anderson focuses on individuals rather than on groups, and regards these individuals as isolated and alone. Some critics denounced the book as morbid, depressing, and overly concerned with sex; others, however, praised it for its honesty and depth, comparing Anderson's accomplishment with that of Anton Chekhov and Fyodor Dostoyevsky in its concern with the buried life of the soul. Commentators noted that Anderson achieved a fusion of simply stated fiction and brooding psychological analysis—"half tale and half psychological anatomizing" was famed critic H. L. Mencken's description—which reveals the essential loneliness and beauty of ordinary people living out their lives during the twilight days of agrarian America in a fading Ohio town.

*Outside Influences and Changes in Style* Anderson's style was shaped during the 1920s by the works of Gertrude Stein, particularly her *Three Lives*, while his

## LITERARY AND HISTORICAL CONTEMPORARIES

Sherwood Anderson's famous contemporaries include:

**Charles W. Chesnutt** (1858–1932): Chesnutt was an influential African American novelist, essayist, and activist who is remembered for his regionalist short stories set in the rural South.

**Gertrude Stein** (1874–1946): A writer known for her terse, spare writing style, Stein became a leader of the avant-garde art movement of the 1920s.

**H. L. Mencken** (1880–1956): Literary critic, essayist, and satirist H. L. Mencken wrote *The American Language*, a groundbreaking study of the dialect and slang of America.

personal philosophy reflected that of D. H. Lawrence. In such stories as "Unused" and "The New Englander," he attempted to write with the simple, repetitive verbiage and rhythms of Stein and to develop Lawrence's beliefs concerning the psychologically crippling effects of sexual repression. Exploring the psychological undercurrents of life in industrialized America, Anderson wrote some of his strongest works in the 1920s, though he was compelled to continue working in advertising until 1922. That year he received *Dial* magazine's first annual Dial Award for his accomplishment in *The Triumph of the Egg* and the cash award enabled Anderson to leave advertising and to devote himself full-time to writing.

In 1927, with the earnings from his novel *Dark Laughter*—the only commercially successful work of his lifetime—Anderson settled in the town of Marion, Virginia, where he bought two weekly newspapers which he wrote for and edited. He spent much of the rest of his life in rural southwestern Virginia among the small-town people with whom he had always felt a warm kinship, occasionally publishing collections of his newspaper columns and essays on American life. His final collection of short fiction, *Death in the Woods*, appeared in 1933 during the Great Depression and sold poorly. He wrote little during the last few years of his life, declaring that writing was a dead art in America and that the future for artistic achievement lay in motion pictures. While on a cruise to South America in 1941, Anderson died of peritonitis after accidentally swallowing part of a wooden toothpick at a shipboard banquet. He is buried just outside Marion, with his chosen epitaph inscribed upon his gravestone: "Life, not death, is the great adventure."

## Works in Literary Context

*Writing In Between Literary Movements* Though writing in a period of industrialization and urbanization

# COMMON HUMAN EXPERIENCE

Sherwood Anderson's famed short story collection *Winesburg, Ohio* has been noted as one of twentieth-century American literature's finest examples of dialect writing and regionalism. Other works from this time period that make extensive use of local color include:

*A White Heron* (1886), a collection of short stories by Sarah Orne Jewett. Jewett was famous for recreating the dialogue of the small Maine fishing village of South Berwick.

*The Conjure Woman* (1899), a collection of short stories by Charles W. Chesnutt. In this collection, African American writer and political activist Charles W. Chesnutt uses dialect to tell stories set in rural North Carolina.

*The Adventures of Tom Sawyer* (1833), a novel by Mark Twain. Twain's humorous tale of a young scamp's boyhood in rural Missouri has long been considered one of the landmarks of local color.

at the beginning of the twentieth century, Sherwood Anderson avoided the Naturalistic style of writing, popularized by writers such as Theodore Dreiser and Upton Sinclair. While Naturalists focused on urban settings and viewed the world as a hostile, dangerous place, Anderson chose small towns as his settings, and focused on the individualized experiences of lone characters. Thus, Anderson's style is more akin to the Modernists—who focused on the individual rather than the crowd—that followed him. The style and outlook of *Winesburg, Ohio* and of Anderson's three other short story collections— *The Triumph of the Egg* (1921), *Horses and Men* (1923), and *Death in the Woods, and Other Stories* (1933)—were influential in shaping the writings of Ernest Hemingway, William Faulkner, Thomas Wolfe, John Steinbeck, and many other American authors.

Two important ramifications of his aesthetic stance are his views of plot and characterization. He bitterly attacked the stories of O. Henry and others for their 'poison plots'—stories that sacrificed characterization and fidelity to life for the sake of striking turns of event. Anderson expected a writer to have utter loyalty to the characters in his imagination. His typical stories, then—both unique and typically modern in eschewing strict plots—offered a compelling model for other writers.

*Local Color*   Anderson wrote his *Winesburg, Ohio* during a time period marked by increased industrialization, and the vast migration of workers from small towns to large cities. Due to this depersonalizing mechanization and the wide-scale experience of anonymity in urban life, both writers and readers became interested in narratives of small town or rural communities and their idiosyncratic characters. Many writers—such as Anderson, Sarah Orne Jewett, Bret Harte, and James Lane Allen—sought to preserve the manners and customs, or "local color," of the regions in which they were raised or lived.

Anderson's stories are set in a small town in Ohio during the late nineteenth century, in the interim period between the end of the American Civil War and the rise of industrialism. The stories themselves feature characters in isolation, yet taken as a whole, these characters produce the character and identity of the town. In "Hands," for example, the secrets of the town's ostracized schoolmaster are revealed; in "Respectability" the ugliest man in Winesburg explains that his hatred of women came from his manipulative mother-in-law. As Professor David D. Anderson reflected:

> Winesburg is refuge, it is nurturer, it is prison, it is point of departure; it provides, sometimes simultaneously, psychological support and spiritual torment as it plays its active part in the lives of its people, providing at once the walls that isolate them, the values that alienate them, and the ideals that liberate them.

## Works in Critical Context

Critics agree that Anderson's short stories best convey his vision of life, which is often despairing but tempered by his folksy, poignant tone and sense of wonder. "In Anderson, when all is said and done," wrote Henry Miller, "it is the strong human quality which draws one to him and leads one to prefer him sometimes to those who are undeniably superior to him as artists."

Anderson was long called a leader in "the revolt from the village" in American literature, an often-quoted appellation given him by Carl Van Doren in a 1921 essay. But while he examined the troubled, darker aspects of provincial life, he saw the small town as an essential and admirable part of America, and he attacked Sinclair Lewis and Mencken for their incessant satirical gibes at village vulgarity. Hostile reviewers of his works called him 'Sherwood Lawrence' (a reference to the controversial writer D. H. Lawrence) and tended to portray him as a writer obsessed with sex, though the next generation of American writers made his treatment of sexual relations seem tame by comparison. And some critics and readers who had early enjoyed Anderson's books found them, in later years, stylistically and thematically adolescent and repetitive: reviewing *Death in the Woods* for *New Republic* in 1933, T. S. Matthews spoke for many critics when he wrote that he was "so used to Anderson now, to his puzzled confidences, his groping repetitions, his occasional stumblings into real inspiration that perhaps we tend to underrate him as an American phenomenon. Or perhaps we no longer overrate him." However, Theodore Dreiser spoke for many of Anderson's readers when in 1941 he wrote:

Anderson, his life and his writings, epitomize for me the pilgrimage of a poet and dreamer across this limited stage called Life, whose reactions to the mystery of our beings and doings here . . . involved tenderness, love and beauty, delight in the strangeness of our will-less reactions as well as pity, sympathy and love for all things both great and small.

***Winesburg, Ohio*** *Winesburg, Ohio* is one of the most critically discussed books within the American short story tradition. It has been interpreted in a variety of ways: as commentary on social and sexual mores in small town rural America; as an allegory of the sociopolitical changes occurring at the turn of the twentieth century; and, by feminists, as a glimpse of the determined gender roles that stifled women before the Industrial Revolution. In general, however, critics agree that the great strength of the work lies in its use of local color and subtle characterization. Writing in 1927, critic Cleveland B. Chase commented that the novel's really effective episodes are rarely those that bear directly on the main story; much more often they are detached vignettes, sketches of minor characters, "colorful" episodes inserted to describe a desired atmosphere.

## Responses to Literature

1. Sherwood Anderson's stories are praised for their use of local color and dialect. Consider the community in which you currently live. What constitutes the "local color" of your surroundings? Write a short story in which you describe these elements, using language common to your environment.

2. Research the themes commonly associated with works of American Naturalism and Modernism, paying particular attention to the role of the individual in society. Anderson, falling in between these two literary movements, shares elements of both. Identify which thematic elements of Naturalism Anderson accepted or rejected, and discuss his possible influence on later Modernist writers.

3. Late in his life Sherwood Anderson essentially abandoned fiction writing, stating that the future of expressive art in America lay in motion pictures. Take Anderson at his word, and envision how you would adapt the stories of *Winesburg, Ohio* to the screen. Who would you cast for the main characters? What would the set look like? What music would you use for the score?

BIBLIOGRAPHY

**Books**

Anderson, David D., ed. *Critical Essays on Sherwood Anderson*. Boston: G. K. Hall, 1981.
Burbank, Rex. *Sherwood Anderson*. London: Twayne, 1964.
Chase, Cleveland B. "Anderson's Writings." In *Sherwood Anderson*. New York: Robert M. McBride, 1927.
Rideout, Walter B., ed. *Sherwood Anderson: A Collection of Critical Essays*. New York: Prentice-Hall, 1974.
Small, Judy Jo. *A Reader's Guide to the Short Stories of Sherwood Anderson*. Boston: G. K. Hall, 1994.

# ✺ Maya Angelou

BORN: *1928, St. Louis, Missouri*

NATIONALITY: *American*

GENRE: *Memoir, poetry, fiction*

MAJOR WORKS:

*I Know Why the Caged Bird Sings* (1970)

*Just Give Me a Cool Drink of Water 'fore I Diiie* (1971)

*All God's Children Need Traveling Shoes* (1986)

## Overview

Hailed as one of the great voices of contemporary African-American literature, Maya Angelou is best known for *I Know Why the Caged Bird Sings* (1970), the first of her series of autobiographical works. Her autobiography and

Maya Angelou  *AP Images.*

poetry have generated great interest because they reflect her tenacity in overcoming social obstacles and her struggle for self-acceptance. Critics particularly praise her dynamic prose style, poignant satire, and her universal messages relevant to the human condition. Angelou herself explained: "I speak to the black experience but I am always talking about the human condition—about what we can endure, dream, fail at and still survive."

## Works in Biographical and Historical Context

*Social and Economic Hardship* Maya Angelou was born in 1928 in St. Louis, Missouri. She was raised, therefore, during the Great Depression, a period of widespread economic disparity in America marked by pervasive poverty and unemployment. Her memoirs capture the effects of this difficult time period and reflect its particular influence on African-American families that would battle poverty as well as racial prejudice. As Angelou relates in *I Know Why the Caged Bird Sings*, she was just three years old when her parents divorced. Divorce, during this time period, was uncommon, and her family faced ostracism within their community. After the divorce, her father sent Angelou and her four-year-old brother alone by train to the home of his mother in Stamps, Arkansas. In Stamps, a segregated town, "Momma" (as Angelou and her brother Bailey called their grandmother) took care of the children and ran a lunch business and a store. The children were expected to stay clean and sinless and to do well in school. Although she followed the example of her independent and strong-willed grandmother, Angelou felt ugly and unloved. When she was seven years old, Maya and her brother were sent back to St. Louis to live with their mother.

*Recovering from Trauma* Life in St. Louis was different from that in Stamps; Angelou was unprepared for the rushing noises of city life and the Saturday night parties thrown by her socialite mother. Soon after arriving, Angelou would face an act of violence that would change the course of her life and become the central scene of her autobiographical works. In one of the most evocative (and controversial) moments in *I Know Why the Caged Bird Sings*, Angelou describes how she was first lovingly cuddled, then raped by her mother's boyfriend. When the man was murdered by her uncles for his crime, Angelou felt responsible, and she stopped talking. She and her brother were sent back to Stamps. Angelou remained mute for five years, but she developed a love for language and the spoken word. She read and memorized books, including the works of black authors and poets Langston Hughes, W. E. B. Du Bois, and Paul Lawrence Dunbar. Even though she and Bailey were discouraged from reading the works of white writers at home, Angelou read and fell in love with the works of William Shakespeare, Charles Dickens, and Edgar Allan Poe. When Angelou was twelve,

Mrs. Flowers, an educated black woman, finally got her to speak again. Mrs. Flowers, as Angelou recalled in *Mrs. Flowers: A Moment of Friendship*, emphasized the importance of the spoken word, explained the nature of and importance of education, and instilled in Angelou a love of poetry.

When race relations made Stamps a dangerous place for Angelou and her brother, "Momma" took the children to San Francisco, where Angelou's mother was working as a professional gambler. World War II was raging, and while San Franciscans prepared for air raids that never came, Angelou prepared for the rest of her life by attending George Washington High School and by taking lessons in dance and drama on a scholarship at the California Labor School. When Angelou, just seventeen, graduated from high school and gave birth to a son, she began to work as well. She worked as the first female and black street car conductor in San Francisco.

As a young black woman growing up in the South, and later in wartime San Francisco, Angelou faced racism from whites and poor treatment from many men. She found that, in this position, few things in life came easily to her. Instead of letting forces beyond her control overcome her, Angelou began to forge art from her early experiences and to change the world as she had once known it. She became a singer, dancer, actress, composer, and Hollywood's first female black director. She became a writer, editor, essayist, playwright, poet, and screenwriter.

*Involvement in the Civil Rights Movement* Angelou married a white ex-sailor, Tosh Angelos, in 1950. The pair did not have much in common, and Angelou began to take note of the reaction of people—especially African Americans—to their union, a subject she would discuss at length in her memoirs. After they separated, Angelou continued her study of dance in New York City. Then, with the encouragement of writer John Killens, she joined the Harlem Writers Guild and met James Baldwin and other important writers. It was during this time that Angelou had the opportunity to hear Dr. Martin Luther King, Jr. speak. Inspired by his message, she decided to become an active participant in the Civil Rights Movement, which aimed for social and racial equality in the years following World War II. So, with comedian Godfrey Cambridge, she wrote, produced, directed, and starred in *Cabaret for Freedom* in 1960, a benefit for Dr. King's Southern Christian Leadership Conference (SCLC). Given the organizational abilities she demonstrated as she worked for the benefit, she was offered a position as the northern coordinator for Dr. King's SCLC.

During this period Angelou began to live with Vusumzi Make, a South African freedom fighter. With Angelou's son Guy, they relocated to Cairo, Egypt. There, Angelou found work as an associate editor at the *Arab Observer*. As she recalled in *The Heart of a Woman*, she learned a great deal about writing there, but Vusumzi could not tolerate the fact that she was working. After her relationship with him ended, Angelou went on to Ghana, in West Africa, in 1962. She worked at the University of Ghana's School of Music and Drama as an assistant administrator.

*Autobiography and a New Literary Career* Angelou returned to the United States in the mid-1960s and found a position as a lecturer at the University of California in Los Angeles in 1966. In this period, she was encouraged by author James Baldwin and Random House publishers to write an autobiography. Initially, Angelou declined offers but eventually changed her mind and wrote *I Know Why the Caged Bird Sings*. The book, which chronicles Angelou's childhood and ends with the birth of her son Guy, bears what Selwyn R. Cudjoe in *Black Women Writers* calls a burden "to demonstrate the manner in which the Black female is violated . . . in her tender years and to demonstrate the 'unnecessary insult' of Southern girlhood in her movement to adolescence." *I Know Why the Caged Bird Sings* won immediate success and a nomination for a National Book Award.

Although Angelou did not write *I Know Why the Caged Bird Sings* with the intention of writing other autobiographies, she eventually wrote four more, so it may be read as the first in a series. Most critics have judged the subsequent autobiographies in light of the first, and *I Know Why the Caged Bird Sings* remains the most highly praised. *Gather Together in My Name* (1974) begins when Angelou is seventeen and a new mother; it describes a destructive love affair, Angelou's work as a prostitute, her rejection of drug addiction, and the kidnapping of her son. The next volumes of Angelou's autobiography, which include *Singin' and Swingin' and Gettin' Merry like Christmas* (1976), *The Heart of a Woman* (1981), and *All God's Children Need Traveling Shoes* (1986)—continue to trace the author's psychological, spiritual, and political odyssey. As she emerges from a disturbing and oppressive childhood to become a prominent figure in contemporary American literature, Angelou's quest for self-identity and emotional fulfillment results in extraordinary experiences, such as encounters with Malcolm X and Dr. Martin Luther King, Jr. Angelou's personal involvement with the civil rights and feminist movements both in the United States and in Africa, her developing relationship with her son, and her knowledge of the hardships associated with the lower class of American society are recurrent themes throughout the series.

While writing her memoirs, Angelou also published poems and was recognized for her 1971 collection *Just Give Me a Cool Drink of Water 'fore I Diiie*. One of the most important sources of Angelou's fame in the early 1990s was President Bill Clinton's invitation to write and read the first inaugural poem in decades. "On the Pulse of Morning" calls for peace, racial and religious harmony, and social justice for people of different origins, incomes, genders, and sexual orientations. It recalls the Civil Rights Movement and Dr. Martin Luther King, Jr.'s

## LITERARY AND HISTORICAL CONTEMPORARIES

Angelou's famous contemporaries include:

**Toni Morrison** (1931–): Morrison, author of *Beloved* (1988) and *Song of Solomon* (1977), was the first African American woman to win a Nobel Prize.

**Oprah Winfrey** (1954–): A talk-show host, actress, and philanthropist, Winfrey has promoted the popularity of women's African American writing through her "Oprah's Book Club."

**Bill Clinton** (1946–): Clinton, the forty-second president of the United States, is known for advocating policies aimed toward racial equality. Upon his induction to office he selected Maya Angelou to compose an inaugural poem.

**Martin Luther King, Jr.** (1929–1968): King was a leader of the American Civil Rights Movement, best known for his 1963 "I Have a Dream" speech, which Angelou would use as inspiration for her 1993 inaugural poem.

**James Baldwin** (1924–1987): An African American novelist and activist, Baldwin is best known for his treatment of racial and sexual prejudice in *Go Tell It on the Mountain* (1953). He was a mentor and friend to Angelou, and he encouraged her to write her memoirs.

famous "I Have a Dream" speech as it urges America to "Give birth again / To the Dream" of equality. Angelou challenged the new administration and all Americans to work together for progress. Angelou continues her work as a writer and activist and is a professor at Wake Forest University in Winston-Salem, North Carolina.

## Works in Literary Context

*The Female African-American Voice and the Civil Rights Movement* Angelou has been a social activist since the early days of the Civil Rights Movement, which sought equal rights for all races and ethnicities. She also has been a spokeswoman for the feminist movement, which functioned in the 1960s under the credo "the personal is the political." Her autobiographies in particular embody this belief; not only does *I Know Why the Cage Bird Sings* emphasize the impact sexual abuse had on Angelou's life, but her later works document her personal involvement with political activists such as Martin Luther King, Jr. and Malcolm X. Her works are often compared to similarly feminist African American writers such as Toni Morrison and Alice Walker.

*The Tradition of the Memoir* Angelou's autobiographical works have an important place in the African-American tradition of personal narrative, and they continue

# COMMON HUMAN EXPERIENCE

Angelou is best known for her autobiographies, which capture the experience of growing up as an African American in a place and time period marked by racial prejudice. Other autobiographies which have described such experiences include:

*Narrative of the Life of Frederick Douglass, an American Slave* (1845), a book by Frederick Douglass. Douglass, one of the best-known abolitionists and orators of nineteenth-century America, wrote this autobiography to educate the public about the humiliation of slave life. The book became an international bestseller, bringing worldwide attention to the abolitionists' cause in America.

*Incidents in the Life of a Slave Girl* (1861), a book by Harriet Jacobs. In this narrative Jacobs describes the experiences and humiliations suffered by female slaves in the South prior to the Civil War. The book has come to be a core component in the genres of African-American and feminist literatures.

*The Autobiography of Malcolm X* (1965), a book by Malcolm X and Alex Haley. Haley, author of the celebrated novel *Roots*, based this work on a series of interviews he conducted with Malcolm X just before the activist's death in 1965. In 1992 the book was adapted into an award-winning film by Spike Lee.

to garner praise for their honesty and moving sense of dignity. Although an accomplished poet and dramatist, Angelou is most dedicated to the art of autobiography, and her memoirs have been compared in importance to such works as Frederick Douglass's *Narrative of the Life of Frederick Douglass, an American Slave* (1845), and Harriet Jacobs's *Incidents in the Life of a Slave Girl* (1861). Angelou acknowledges herself as part of this tradition, and explains that she is

> not afraid of the ties [between past and present]. I cherish them, rather. It's the vulnerability... it's allowing oneself to be hypnotized. That's frightening because we have no defenses, nothing. We've slipped down the well and every side is slippery. And how on earth are you going to come out? That's scary. But I've chosen it, and I've chosen this mode as my mode.

## Works in Critical Context

*I Know Why the Caged Bird Sings* Angelou wrote this first volume of her autobiography after friends, among them such notable writers as James Baldwin and Jules Feiffer, suggested she write about her childhood spent between rural, segregated Stamps, Arkansas, where

her pious grandmother owned a general store, and St. Louis, Missouri, where her worldly, glamorous mother lived. *I Know Why the Caged Bird Sings* gained instant international acclaim, and was nominated for a National Book Award. In addition to being a trenchant account of a black girl's coming of age, this work affords insights into the social and political tensions of the 1930s. Sidonie Ann Smith echoed many critics when she wrote: "Angelou's genius as a writer is her ability to recapture the texture of the way of life in the texture of its idioms, its idiosyncratic vocabulary and especially in its process of image-making."

*Additional Autobiographies* Angelou's four subsequent memoirs are generally considered inferior to *I Know Why the Caged Bird Sings*; critics cite lack of moral complexity and failure to generate empathy or universal appeal. Lynn Z. Bloom believes that perhaps the decreasing popularity of subsequent volumes resulted because Angelou appeared a "less admirable" character as her autobiography progressed. In *Gather Together in My Name*, for example, Angelou barely escapes a life of prostitution and drug addiction; in the process, Bloom maintains, Angelou "abandons or jeopardizes the maturity, honesty, and intuitive good judgment toward which she had been moving in *I Know Why the Caged Bird Sings*." Nevertheless, critics continue to praise Angelou's narrative skills and her impassioned responses to the challenges in her life.

*Poetry* Angelou's poetry, which is collected in such volumes as *Just Give Me a Cool Drink of Water 'fore I Diiie* (1971) and *And Still I Rise* (1976), is fashioned almost entirely of short lyrics and jazzy rhythms. Although her poetry has contributed to her reputation and is especially popular among young people, most commentators reserve their highest praise for her prose. Angelou's dependence on alliteration, her heavy use of short lines, and her conventional vocabulary has led several critics to declare her poetry superficial and devoid of her celebrated humor. Other reviewers, however, praise her poetic style as refreshing and graceful. They also laud Angelou for addressing social and political issues relevant to African Americans and for challenging the validity of traditional American values and myths.

## Responses to Literature

1. Angelou's series of autobiographies span an enormous range of cultural history: they describe the experiences of living through the Great Depression, World War II, the Vietnam War, the Civil Rights Movement, and the Women's Liberation Movement. Imagine that you have been asked to write your own memoirs. What events in contemporary history would influence your writing? How have recent political or cultural events influenced your personal experience of the world?

2. Angelou is often grouped with other African-American writers such as Alice Walker and Toni Morrison. Read a book by one of these authors—such as Walker's *The Color Purple* or Morrison's *Beloved*—and compare their writing styles with Angelou's. How are they alike or different? How does the fact that Angelou writes autobiography instead of fiction affect your reception of her work?

3. Using the Internet, find a clip of Maya Angelou reading "On the Pulse of the Morning" at Bill Clinton's presidential inauguration. What are your impressions of her performance of the poem? Write an essay in which you analyze how Angelou shaped both the content and the style of the poem to the public nature of the event.

BIBLIOGRAPHY

**Books**

Bloom, Harold, ed. *Maya Angelou's I Know Why the Caged Bird Sings.* New York, N.Y.: Chelsea House Publishers, 1995.

Braxton, Joanne M., ed. *Maya Angelou's I Know Why the Caged Bird Sings: A Casebook.* New York, N.Y.: Oxford University Press, 1999.

King, Sarah E. *Maya Angelou: Greeting the Morning.* Brookfield, Conn.: Millbrook Press, 1994.

**Periodicals**

Angaza, Maitefa. "Maya: A Precious Prism." *Black Issues Book Review*, March, 2001: p. 30.

Angelou, Maya and George Plimpton. "The Art of Fiction CXIX: Maya Angelou," *Paris Review*, Fall 1990: pp. 145–167.

Lupton, Mary Jane. "Singing the Black Mother: Maya Angelou and Autobiographical Continuity." *Black American Literature Forum*, Summer 1990: pp. 257–276.

# ✳ Piers Anthony

BORN: *1934, Oxford, England*

NATIONALITY: *American*

GENRE: *Science fiction*

MAJOR WORKS:

*Chthon* (1967)

*Macroscope* (1969)

*A Spell for Chameleon* (1977)

## Overview

Piers Anthony writes science fiction and fantasy novels for young adults and is the creator of the best-selling *Xanth* fantasy series. Using puns and wordplay, literary allusions, mythical characters, and whimsical satire, he creates works of light entertainment that include a madcap sense of wondrous discovery. Anthony has been praised for his imagination and his inventive brand of philosophical logic that tends toward the humorous.

## Works in Biographical and Historical Context

*Pacifism at an Early Age*  Piers Anthony is the pen name of Piers Anthony Dillingham Jacob, an Englishman who became an American citizen in 1958. "My major motivation as a writer," he observes, "has been my inability to quit writing, and my dissatisfaction with all other modes of employment." Because of this focusing of energies, Anthony has authored or coauthored twenty-four novels since 1967. Born in Oxford, England, Anthony was brought to the United States as a child. He was raised in the Quaker faith, and the pacifist beliefs of his religion figure largely in his works, which generally condemn unnecessary warfare and aggression. Anthony spent much of his childhood in isolation; he was frequently ill, often bullied at school, and suffered from a learning disability that went unrecognized and caused adults to treat him as if he were below average intelligence. In addition, his parents divorced when he was eighteen, creating much discord within the extended family. Despite these setbacks, Anthony was a dedicated reader and developed an early love of books, particularly the genre of science fiction.

*Full-time Writer*  In 1956 Anthony earned his BA from Goddard College, submitting as his creative writing thesis his first science-fiction novel. He married Carol Marble on June 23, 1956, and later served in the U.S. Army from 1957 to 1959. Anthony's moral convictions made military service difficult for him, and, as he says, he "barely made it through basic [training]," being a "pacifistically inclined vegetarian." After eight years of working odd jobs and submitting stories to magazines, Anthony sold his first piece, "Possible to Rue," to *Fantastic* magazine in 1962. In the next several years he worked variously as a freelance writer and English teacher, but finally decided to devote all of his time to writing. His first published novel, *Chthon*, came out in 1967. It received numerous award nominations and caught the attention of both critics and readers in the science-fiction genre. During this same year Anthony's *Sos the Rope*, a revised segment of his BA thesis, won a $5000 prize that allowed Anthony to continue writing on a full-time basis.

Publication became easier at this point in Anthony's career, and *Sos the Rope* was only one of three books he published in 1968. Anthony followed the success of his *Chthon* and *Battle Circle* series with the well-received *Omnivore* trilogy, which provided a forum for Anthony to further his exploration of the dangers humankind continues to inflict upon itself. It also introduced his support of vegetarianism. Anthony, writing during the Vietnam War and the Cold War—a period marked by

## LITERARY AND HISTORICAL CONTEMPORARIES

Anthony's famous contemporaries include:

**Carl Sagan** (1934–1996): Sagan was an American astronomer famous for his popular 1980 television series *Cosmos*.

**Connie Willis** (1945–): Willis is the author of acclaimed science fiction works *The Doomsday Book* (1993) and *To Say Nothing of the Dog* (1999), which focus on a group of time-traveling history students at the University of Oxford.

**Michael Moorcock** (1939–): Moorcock is a British science fiction and fantasy author best known for his *Elric* series and the Nebula Award-winning novella *Behold, the Man* (1966), in which a man travels back in time to meet Jesus.

**Neil Armstrong** (1930–): As the mission commander for the 1969 *Apollo 11* space flight, Armstrong became the first human being to walk on the Moon.

**Ursula K. Le Guin** (1929–): Best known for her *Earthsea* trilogy, Ursula K. Le Guin has written science fiction and fantasy fiction, poetry, and essays for over thirty years. She is often lauded by critics for her signature treatment of feminist and ecological issues within her works.

the proliferation of nuclear weapons in the United States and the Soviet Union—used his alternative universes as allegories for the state of man and the dangers of technology. The *Battle Circle* series, for example, speculates on the possible state of the world in the aftermath of a nuclear holocaust.

Anthony's next novel, considered his best by many readers, was *Macroscope* (1969). The mechanical invention of the title is a device that permits man to see the entire continuum of space and time. The novel focuses on the effect such a machine could have on a humanity that finds itself diminished in relation to the vastness of the universe; in doing so, it becomes an allegory on the fate of the individual diminished and possibly destroyed by mass society.

*The Universe of Xanth*   Throughout the 1970s Anthony continued to write science fiction novels. In 1977, however, he published his first fantasy novel, *A Spell for Chameleon*. The novel marked the beginning of Anthony's immensely popular *Xanth* series, which would include over twenty books written over two decades. The novels in the series are generally less complex and easier to read than Anthony's earlier works, and they appeal to younger readers as well as adults. The land of Xanth closely resembles Anthony's longtime home state of Florida in size and shape, and its place names are often wittily twisted versions of Floridian ones. In Xanth, everyone and everything has a magical talent, except its protagonist, Bink. *A Spell for Chameleon* follows Bink on his quest to discover his

talent or face exile to the boring, powerless land of Mundania. In the process, Bink gains not only knowledge of his talent but emotional maturity as well.

Anthony continues to write and publish novels and is known for his loyal readership among adults and adolescents alike. Recently, he has put aside fantasy and returned to science fiction in his *Cluster* and *Tarot* trilogies. These series, however, carry the same message of pacifism as do his earlier writings and exhibit a similar linguistic style. Writing in *Twentieth-Century Young Adult Writers*, Lesa Dill concluded: "While entertaining his readers with his inventive word play, numerous literary allusions, apt symbolism, humorous satire, and wild adventures, Anthony effectively conveys his personal convictions about man's responsibilities in and to the universe."

## Works in Literary Context

*The Cold War and the Threat of Nuclear Holocaust*   Anthony began his writing career in the aftermath of the Vietnam War, and his works exhibit an anxiety over the Cold War between the United States and the Soviet Union. As rival superpowers, the United States and the USSR stockpiled enough nuclear weapons in the 1970s to destroy civilization, should war break out. The two nations also engaged in a space race, competing with the most advanced technologies that would allow them to claim and colonize outer space. Anthony is most clearly influenced by the Cold War in his *Battle Circle* trilogy. Set in America in the wake of a nuclear holocaust, the novels contrast a tribe of nomadic barbarians named for the weapons they use with a group of technologically oriented humans. To avoid another holocaust, the "techies" maintain the warlike nomads as an outlet for human aggression. Anthony thus illustrates the need to acknowledge aggression as a part of human nature. The novels also speak against the dangers of centralized civilization and overpopulation.

*Pacifism*   Many critics have pointed out that Anthony's pacifism may be linked to his Quaker upbringing and his experiences of growing up during the Cold War, when human aggression reached the capacity—through nuclear weapons—to destroy the planet. Throughout his works, Anthony deals carefully with the theme of pacifism, intimating that the balance between aggression and passivity requires the ultimate honesty in an individual. In *The Ring*, for example, he questions the aggression of a youthful hero in quest of justice and vengeance, this time on an Earth ruled by the morally questionable "Ultra Conscience." The enslaving Ring of the novel's title introduces an important moral question in Anthony's fiction, for the Ring "makes a man a pacifist when the world is a battlefield." For Anthony, the will to moral activism is one of the distinctive marks of being human, and pacifism can be a negative quality when it is used as a facade for moral complacency, be it in speculative fiction or international politics. In Anthony's best fiction, questions of man's place in the ecology of the natural universe blend with considerations of the individual's role in providing satisfactory and humane answers.

*Vegetarianism* The thematic concerns of Anthony's fiction are often reflections of his own ardent vegetarianism. His story entitled "In the Barn," for example, features female humans on an alien planet who are kept as animals, as "cows" for giving milk. By exploring the relationship between man and alien, Anthony collapses the distance between human and nonhuman and provides an allegory through which readers can reevaluate their own relationships to animals.

Likewise the *Omnivore* trilogy deals with the ethics of animal-eating. Critic Michael Collings observed, "*Omnivore* deals with control—specifically, with controlling the most dangerous omnivore of all, man." Within the series three interplanetary explorers, the herbivorous Veg, carnivorous Cal, and omnivorous Aquilon, play out Anthony's views. The three journey to the planet Nacre, and must report and justify their actions to a far-away scribe.

## Works in Critical Context

*The Xanth Series* Critics generally agree that Anthony's *Xanth* series represents his most accomplished work. Richard Mathews contends that the Xanth series "ranks with the best of American and classic fantasy literature." Among the most revered novels in the series are *The Source of Magic* (1979), *Centaur Aisle* (1982), and *Dragon on a Pedestal* (1983). Critics have lauded the books' attention to environmental concerns, and they have also pointed out that the puns and language tricks of the novels heighten the reader's entertainment. Writing in a fairy-tale tone, Anthony portrays a world populated by such creatures as ogres, magicians, and zombies. "In Xanth," Michael Collings noted, Anthony "incorporates much of this interest in language in furthering the plot and in establishing the essence of his fantasy universe."

*Macroscope* *Macroscope*, described by Michael Collings as "one of Anthony's most ambitious and complex novels," seeks to place humanity in its proper context within the galaxy. The publication of *Macroscope* was a milestone in Anthony's career. In a *Luna Monthly* review, Samuel Mines observed, "*Macroscope* recaptures the tremendous glamour and excitement of science fiction, pounding the reader into submission with the sheer weight of its ideas which seem to pour out in an inexhaustible flood."

## Responses to Literature

1. Pinpoint a passage in the *Omnivore* series where Anthony discusses the dietary habits of the characters Veg, Cal, and Aquilon. Do you agree with Anthony's advocacy of vegetarianism? Identify how Anthony makes his argument, and try to make arguments both for and against his point of view.

---

# COMMON HUMAN EXPERIENCE

Anthony's works often deal with the fall of a civilization (through nuclear holocaust, alien invasion, or ecological disaster) and the survivors's attempts to rebuild society. Other science fiction works that explore apocalypse and its aftermath include:

*The Stand* (1978), a novel by Stephen King. This epic novel follows the survivors of an epidemic of a human-made virus that has wiped out the majority of the population of North America. The survivors travel across America for a final battle between good and evil.

*Planet of the Apes* (1968), a film directed by Franklin J. Schaffner and starring Charlton Heston. This film, based loosely on the 1963 book by Pierre Boulle, features time travelers who land on a future earth which has been virtually destroyed but repopulated by a primitive ape society that enslaves humans.

*The War of the Worlds* (1898), a novel by H. G. Wells. This novel, which describes a violent alien invasion of Earth, was produced in a famous radio version by Orson Welles in 1938. The broadcast was so realistic many believed a Martian invasion of Earth was in progress, and mass hysteria ensued.

*A Canticle for Leibowitz* (1960), a novel by Walter M. Miller, Jr. This novel, considered a classic of science fiction, explores the rebuilding of society from the perspective of Roman Catholic monks living in a post-nuclear world.

---

2. In recent years, Hollywood has produced a number of "disaster films" which have brought the idea of the apocalypse to the big screen. Some examples include *Independence Day*, *I am Legend*, *The War of the Worlds*, and *Wall-E*. Choose one of these modern apocalyptic films and compare it to the *Battle Circle* novels by Piers Anthony. What are the similarities and differences?

3. Critics often praise Piers Anthony for his ability to create fantastical worlds that parallel Earth in ways that reflect contemporary issues. Pretend that you are assigned to create a world similar to those used in Anthony's novels. What would your world look like, and what kind of characters would live in it? In small groups, discuss which current political issues you would like to see reflected in your world.

BIBLIOGRAPHY

**Books**

Anthony, Piers. *Bio of an Ogre.* New York: Ace Books, 1988.

Collings, Michael R. *Piers Anthony*. Mercer Island, Wash.: Starmont House, 1983.

Dill, Lesa. *Twentieth-Century Young Adult Writers*. Detroit, Mich.: St. James Press, 1994.

Platt, Charles. *Dream Makers Volume II: The Uncommon Men and Women Who Write Science Fiction*. New York: Berkley Publishing, 1983.

Searles, Baird, Beth Meacham, and Michael Franklin. *A Reader's Guide to Fantasy*. New York: Avon, 1982.

Searles, Baird, Martin Last, Beth Meacham, and Michael Franklin. *A Reader's Guide to Science Fiction*. New York: Avon, 1979.

**Periodicals**

Mines, Samuel. Review of *Macroscope*. *Luna Monthly*, September 1970: p. 22.

Atkins, Holly. "Fantasy Flourishes in Florida Forests." *St. Petersburg Times* (St. Petersburg, Fla.), March 11, 2002, p. D4.

# ✸ Mary Antin

BORN: *1881, Polotzk, Russia*

DIED: *1949, Suffern, New York*

NATIONALITY: *American*

GENRE: *Nonfiction, fiction*

MAJOR WORKS:

*From Plotzk to Boston* (1899)

*The Promised Land* (1912)

## Overview

Mary Antin is known for her autobiographical accounts of her family's immigration to the United States. Her work provides a revealing look at the journey made by millions of Jews between 1891 and 1914. Praising her adopted home and the merits of open immigration, Antin traveled the country to spread her belief that America needed its immigrants as much as the immigrants needed America.

## Works in Biographical and Historical Context

*From Prosperity to Poverty*  Born June 13, 1881, to a Jewish family in Polotzk, Russia, Mary Antin grew up in the wake of Czar Alexander III's infamous May Laws of 1882, anti-Jewish policies that led to the expulsion of Jews from certain areas of Russia. Because her mother had inherited a prosperous family business, Antin lived well in the early years of her life and was privileged enough to be tutored in Hebrew, Russian, German, and arithmetic. Unfortunately, illness struck the family, leaving Antin's mother bedridden for two years. Mounting medical bills eventually led to financial ruin. The Antin family's struggles with debt, combined with the anti-

Mary Antin  *Bettmann / Corbis*

Semitic policies that prevailed in Russia at the time, ultimately compelled Israel, Antin's father, to join a mass migration of Eastern European Jews headed to America at the end of the nineteenth century.

*A Noble Desire to Learn*  After arriving in the United States in 1891, Israel worked while his family remained in Polotzk; three years later, a Jewish benevolent society sponsored the journey of his wife and four children. The Antins lived in a series of immigrant slums in Boston, Massachusetts, where Israel enrolled three of his children in school, believing free public education to be, according to Antin in her memoir *The Promised Land*, "the essence of American opportunity, the treasure that no thief could touch." To extend Antin's formal education in America, Israel told school officials that his daughter was eleven, not thirteen, a claim that was never challenged. Later, Antin fictionalized this event in "The Lie" (1913), a story that emphasizes the importance of education to immigrants, as well as the necessity of American teachers to recognize the nobility of the immigrant in his desire to learn.

Although she had never been formally educated before, Antin excelled in school. She quickly learned English and completed the first five grades of school in only six months. When a teacher helped her publish one of her early essays in a primary school journal, Antin was so excited to see her work in print that she decided to become a writer. At her grammar-school graduation in 1897, Antin was presented as a model of how the American system of public education could benefit immigrants.

*Important Social Contacts* Antin attracted the attention of prominent Jewish leaders in Boston, including the Hecht family, philanthropists and social reformers who encouraged the girl's writing, and Josephine Lazarus, sister of Emma Lazarus, an American poet whose poem "The New Colossus" (1883) is inscribed on the pedestal of the Statue of Liberty. Through the Hechts, Antin met other people willing to promote her literary career, including Rabbi Solomon Schindler, who helped her translate the letters that she had written at age thirteen to her uncle in Russia from the original Yiddish. These letters form the basis for Antin's book *From Plotzk to Boston* (1899). ("Plotzk" is an older, alternative spelling of "Polotzk".) At the time of the book's publication, many Americans were opposed to immigration; Antin's book encourages Americans to identify with immigrants and view them in positive ways.

Considering the limited possibilities of public education for most Americans at the turn of the century, Antin's education was exceptional. During high school, Antin attended the Boston Latin Grammar School for Girls, the public preparatory school for Radcliffe University. Even when they combined their earnings, the members of the Antin family continued to live in virtual poverty. However, they were determined to provide their promising daughter with an education, even if the family suffered a little. As a result, Antin found herself caught between two social classes: the students and teachers at the Boston Latin Grammar School and the immigrant tenement districts.

Through the Natural History Club at Hale House, Antin met Amadeus Grabau, a German American graduate student at Harvard University. The two were married in Boston in 1901. When her husband took a post at Columbia University in New York, Antin enrolled at Barnard University before joining a national lecture circuit to discuss her writings. Her friendship with Josephine Lazarus deepened, and it was Lazarus who encouraged Antin to write her autobiography. When Antin gave birth to her only child in 1907, she named her Josephine Esther, after Josephine Lazarus and Esther Weltman Antin, guiding figures in Antin's life.

*Promise at the Gates* Following Lazarus's death in 1910, Antin began the autobiography her friend had been urging her to write. Serialized in the *Atlantic Monthly* in 1911–1912 and published in book form in 1912, *The Promised Land* was dedicated to Lazarus. The

## LITERARY AND HISTORICAL CONTEMPORARIES

Mary Antin's famous contemporaries include:

**Israel Joshua Singer** (1893–1944): Born in Poland before becoming a U.S. citizen in 1939, this Yiddish author is a master of the family novel in which an entire society or epoch is portrayed.

**Isaac Rosenberg** (1890–1918): Rosenberg was a Jewish World War I poet who recognized early on that the pastoral mode of Georgian poetics would be inadequate in poetry dealing with the war.

**Leon Trotsky** (1879–1940): Along with Vladimir Lenin, Trotsky was a communist leader of the Bolshevik party, the Russian revolutionary party that seized power in October 1917.

**Eleanor Roosevelt** (1884–1962): Wife of President Franklin D. Roosevelt, Eleanor became chairman of the Commission on Human Rights of the United Nations Economic and Social Council after her husband's death.

**Herman Wouk** (1915–): Many of Wouk's novels deal with Jewish families and the importance of religious roots to American Jews.

book, which champions settlement houses, public education, and libraries as resources immigrants can use to succeed in their new environment, brought her instant fame.

When former United States President Theodore Roosevelt recruited Antin to lecture for the Progressive Party, she used her position to her advantage. In such venues as Carnegie Hall and the Tuskegee Institute, she explained what she believed to be America's responsibilities concerning immigration. In 1914, Antin published *They Who Knock at Our Gates: A Complete Gospel of Immigration*, a treatise on immigration policy that argues for open immigration and reveals the ways in which immigrants were victimized.

*A Search for Spirituality* By 1918, Antin was a passionate Zionist and supported the creation of a new nation for Jews in the Middle East. Her Zionist ideology led to her separation from Grabau in 1919. Antin developed an interest in philosophy and spirituality when a physical breakdown forced her to retire from the lecture circuit. During her recovery, she met William and Agnes Gould, founders of the Gould Farm in the Adirondack Mountains, a psychiatric institute based on the belief that love can lead to spiritual wholeness. As she collected material for a book about William Gould, she studied Christianity because she thought it would help her

# COMMON HUMAN EXPERIENCE

Throughout the years, many immigrant groups in the United States have been represented by migration narratives. Antin herself compares the immigrant experience to being reborn. Other works that capture the immigrant experience—one not always as positive as Antin's—include the following:

> *House of Sand and Fog* (1999), a novel by Andre Dubus III. When the American Dream becomes an obsession for a former colonel in the Iranian military, a small house becomes the scene of a brutal tragedy in this work.
>
> *Golden Country* (2006), a novel by Jennifer Gilmore. Capturing the excitement of the promise of the American Dream, this novel also exposes the dark aspects of that dream as the narrative follows the lives of three Jewish immigrant families.
>
> *America Is in the Heart* (1946), a memoir by Carlos Bulosan. *America Is in the Heart* documents Bulosan's search for the ideal United States he had learned about in school, as opposed to its harsh realities he discovered as an immigrant.

discuss Gould's work more thoroughly. Nevertheless, she completed only one chapter of the book.

Her last publications include "The Soundless Trumpet" (1937), an *Atlantic Monthly* essay exploring mystical experiences, and "House of One Father" (1941), an essay addressing the complexity of her own identity as a Jew and as an American. Once again, Antin praises her adopted homeland, a place where doors of opportunity open. She links Judaism to democracy, arguing that the Hebrew and American philosophical systems are essentially one. After battling cancer for the last few years of her life, Antin died in a Suffern, New York, nursing home on May 15, 1949.

## Works in Literary Context

The factor that had the greatest impact on Antin's success as a writer was her education. Had her family remained in Polotzk, Antin would have been denied a formal education, as neither Orthodox Jews nor women in Eastern Europe were permitted an education beyond learning to read the Psalms in Hebrew. In America, however, she was encouraged by her father to identify with her teachers and the school system, which dominated—but did not erase—her Jewish knowledge and practices. Because she embraced her opportunities in her new homeland, Antin experienced a nationalistic pride and patriotism previously unknown to her. As a result, her influence on immigration issues and attitudes in America was vast.

*Americanization as a Theme* Written in the pre-World War I period of mass immigration and Americanization, Antin's *From Plotzk to Boston* and *The Promised Land* came to represent not only the story of a Russian Jewish immigrant girl, but also the experience of Americanization itself. Certainly, her autobiographies capture much of the mythologized Americanization experience that is described by Philip Gleason in *The Harvard Encyclopedia of American Ethnic Groups* (1980) as "cosmopolitan nationalism." When Antin was a child in Russia, the idea of nationalism represented tyranny, exclusion, and oppression. By contrast, Americanization signaled a promise of freedom and inclusion in a democracy. To Antin, becoming an American meant sharing ideals and identity with such historic Americans as George Washington and Abraham Lincoln, and even in the face of strong protests against immigration, she did indeed view her adopted home as a land of promise.

## Works in Critical Context

Admired for her mastery of English and her descriptive, engaging style, Antin's work was well received in both the literary and political worlds, earning the author high praise for its significance. Scholar Israel Zangwell contends that Antin's message is a "human document of considerable value," for it gives a vision of the "inner feelings of the people themselves" and the "magic vision of free America" that lures immigrants to the United States. Likewise, Albert E. Stone writes that Antin's work "dramatizes the historical experience of Americanization in frankly mythic terms." Stone concludes that Antin "represents herself as the prototypical immigrant transformed into a new self." Most recently, interdisciplinary scholarship has focused on issues of gender and ethnicity, leading to a renewed interest in Antin and a reassessment of her life and work.

*The Promised Land* *The Promised Land* was an immediate literary success when it was published in 1912. Drawn to Antin's sense of nationalism for her adopted homeland, readers have compared it to the autobiographies of social reformer and immigrant Jacop Riis, patriot Benjamin Franklin, and educator Booker T. Washington. Reviewer Percy F. Bicknell, for instance, observed that Antin's "Americanism is as thoroughgoing as any true patriot could wish, and her enthusiasm in espousing the cause of both the immigrant and the new land to which he is hastening, is contagious." Deeming the work "a unique contribution to our modern literature and to our modern history," Scholar James Craig Holte agrees that "Mary Antin provides an example of Americanization at its best." Because it has been so widely read and received, *The Promised Land* is considered to be a classic in immigrant fiction.

## Responses to Literature

1. Compare the immigration experiences of Antin to those of Carlos Bulosan. What do you think

contributed to the differences in their lives in America? How might Antin's life have been different if she had entered the United States on the West Coast instead of the East Coast?

2. Do you believe that a non-native American can truly be called a patriot? To become an American president, a person must have been born in the United States. Explain why you think our country has such a requirement. Why does it not apply to other government offices? Do other countries have the same constraint on elected officials?

3. Read *Streets of Gold*, a children's picture book by Rosemary Wells. Based on what you know about Antin's *The Promised Land*, how well do you believe Wells captures the spirit of Antin's work? Do the illustrations in *Streets of Gold* truly capture the meaning of Antin's life?

4. Research the May Laws of 1882. Why did Tsar Alexander III enforce these rulings? In what specific ways did they contribute to the waves of Jewish immigrants to America? What do you think Antin's life would have been like if the May Laws had not been created?

BIBLIOGRAPHY

**Books**

Dearborn, Mary V. *Pocahontas's Daughters: Gender and Ethnicity in American Culture*. New York: Oxford University Press, 1986.

Holt, James Craig. *The Ethnic I: A Sourcebook for Ethnic-American Autobiography*. New York: Greenwood Press, 1988.

Nadell, Pamela A. Introduction to *From Plotzk to Boston*. New York: Marcus Wiener, 1986, pp. v–xxi.

Stone, Albert E., ed. *The American Autobiography: A Collection of Critical Essays*. Englewood Cliffs, N.J.: Prentice-Hall, 1981.

Sollors, Werner. Introduction to *The Promised Land*. New York: Penguin, 1997, pp. xi–1.

Themstrom, Stephan, Ann Orlov, and Oscar Handlin, eds. *Harvard Encyclopedia of American Ethnic Groups*. Boston: Belknap Press, 1980.

Warner, Sam Bass. *Province of Reason*. Cambridge, Mass.: Harvard University Press, 1984.

Zangwill, Israel. Foreword to *From Plotzk to Boston*. Boston: Clarke, 1899, pp. 7–9.

**Periodicals**

Bicknell, Percy F. "How One Immigrant Girl Discovered America." *The Dial: A Semi-Monthly Journal of Literary Criticism, Discussion, and Information* (June 1, 1914): vol. 56, no. 671, pp. 348–350.

Sedgwick, Ellery. "Mary Antin." *American Magazine* 77 (March 1914): 64–65.

# ❊ John Ashbery

BORN: *1927, Rochester, New York*

NATIONALITY: *American*

GENRE: *Poetry*

MAJOR WORKS:
*Some Trees* (1956)
*The Tennis Court Oath* (1962)
*Self-Portrait in a Convex Mirror* (1975)
*Flow Chart* (1991)

## Overview

John Ashbery is considered one of the most influential and controversial contemporary American poets. Much of his verse features long, conversational passages in which he experiments with syntactical structure and perspective, producing poems that seem accessible yet resist interpretation. Critic Roberta Berke once commented: "In Ashbery's poems there are constant echoes of other secret dimensions, like chambers resounding behind hollow panels of an old mansion rumored to contain secret passages (which our guide emphatically denies exist)." Although some critics fault Ashbery's works for obscurity and lack of thematic depth, many regard him as an innovator whose works incorporate randomness, invention, and improvisation to explore the complex and elusive relationships between existence, time, and perception.

John Ashbery  *John Jonas Gruen / Hulton Archive / Getty Images*

## LITERARY AND HISTORICAL CONTEMPORARIES

Ashbery's famous contemporaries include:

**Frank O'Hara** (1926–1966): A leader of the New York School of Poetry best known for his volume entitled *Lunch Poems* (1964).

**Jackson Pollock** (1912–1956): Pollock was an American abstract expressionist painter famous for his singular method of dripping liquid paint on large canvasses laid on his studio floor.

**Billie Holiday** (1915–1959): Holiday, one of the most popular female jazz vocalists of the 1950s, is best remembered for songs "God Bless the Child" and "Lady Sing the Blues." Her death was immortalized in one of the most famous of the New York School poems, Frank O'Hara's "The Day Lady Died."

**Edward Gorey** (1925–2000): Gorey, who worked in New York advertising in the 1950s along with John Ashbery and Frank O'Hara, was a writer and illustrator popular for combining a gothic imagination and Victorian and Edwardian settings in such books as *The Object Lesson*.

**Robert Venturi Jr.** (1925–): Venturi is an award-winning American architect considered a leading figure in postmodern architecture.

## Works in Biographical and Historical Context

*New Media for a New Poetry* Poet John Ashbery was born July 28, 1927, in Rochester, New York, the son of a farmer and a high school biology teacher. An avid reader as a child, Ashbery was sent by his parents to Deerfield Academy. Later, as a student at Harvard University. Ashbery became interested in writing, and after receiving his bachelor's degree moved to New York to work in the publishing industry. There he also became involved with the "New York School of Poets" who wrote poems influenced by the explosion of media and technology that followed in the wake of World War II. Drawing inspiration from such modes of communication as advertising, modern art, jazz, film, and television, these poets sought to write poetry in a conversational style heavily influenced by visual images. The poems of the New York School are often noted for their surrealism and abstract impressionism. Ashbery himself worked as an advertising copywriter and art critic in New York in the 1950s while pursuing graduate work at Columbia and New York Universities, and many critics have pointed to these experiences, as well as his involvement in the New York School of Poets, as the primary influences on his early works.

*France and the Influence of Modern Art* In the mid-1950s, Ashbery won a scholarship to study in France. He lived there for ten years, studying and supporting himself by working as a poet and translator and by writing art criticism for the Paris edition of *The New York Herald Tribune*. Painting, which first attracted Ashbery when he was in his teens, has had a lasting influence on his approach to writing poetry. He once stated: "I attempt to use words abstractly, as an artist uses paint."

During the period Ashbery lived in Paris, the art world of France was dominated by the abstract expressionist movement, which stressed nonrepresentational methods of picturing reality. Abstract expressionism, which built upon the expressionism of the New York School of Poets, would be an especially important presence in Ashbery's work.

Ashbery's experience as an art critic in France and America strengthened his ties to abstract expressionism and instilled in his poetry a sensitivity to the interrelatedness of artistic media. His poetry is open-ended and multiplex because life itself is, he told Bryan Appleyard in the *London Times*: "My poetry imitates or reproduces the way knowledge or awareness come to me, which is by fits and starts and by indirection. I don't think poetry arranged in neat patterns would reflect that situation."

*Publication and Praise* Ashbery received immediate critical recognition with the publication of his first volume *Some Trees* in 1956. Although many critics rejected the experimental nature of Ashbery's works during the 1960s, his *Self-Portrait in a Convex Mirror*, published in 1975, won the Pulitzer Prize, the National Book Award, and the National Book Critics Circle Prize, and is widely regarded as a masterpiece in the realm of contemporary poetry. The volume established Ashbery as a highly original poet whose works subvert traditional concepts of structure, content, and theme. Ashbery's recent works, including *April Galleons* and his book-length poem *Flow Chart*, have continued to demonstrate his sense of humor and his penchant for bizarre juxtapositions of words and phrases and experimentation with poetic form.

Since the publication of *Some Trees*, Ashbery has been a prolific writer not just of books of poetry but of art criticism as well. He is generally considered one of the most important of contemporary living poets. In addition to his writing, he has taught at Brooklyn College and Harvard University. Currently he is a faculty member at Bard College.

## Works in Literary Context

*Modern Art and Surrealism* Ashbery is often cited as being influenced by early twentieth-century writers such as T. S. Eliot, whose works relied heavily on symbols (often drawn from popular culture) and emphasized the uncertainty of modern life. Ashbery, the New York School of Poets, and the abstract expressionist painters of the 1950s would extend these ideas of uncertainty into surrealist images and poems.

The New York School's poetic style is noted for its painterly emphasis on setting, luxurious detailing, and leisurely meditative argument. This group closely identified itself with abstract expressionist painters and with the Museum of Modern Art; some of these poets wrote for the popular journal *Art News*. Ashbery was directly connected with all three spheres, and from the painters learned a curious collage-like style of poetry made of bits and pieces of lyric phrasing. This mode of speech, lacking transition between leaps of thought and reflection, marked Ashbery's early writing as difficult, if not impenetrable. Ashbery's first publication *Some Trees* is generally regarded as his volume most influenced by the New York School and abstract expressionism.

***Prose Poetry*** Unlike many of his contemporaries in the New York School of Poetry, Ashbery favors lengthy, seemingly narrative poems over shorter verses. Beginning with *Rivers and Mountains* (1966), Ashbery introduced his specialty, the long discursive meditation running to many pages in which the effort is made to piece together the fragments of experience into a sensible whole; a single poem, "The Skaters," makes up half of the book. The meditative style is pursued most fully in *Three Poems* (1972), prose poems that are linked and in which the speaker loses himself in the metaphysical and spiritual ambiguities of his existence. Much of the poetry of these books is suffused with a restrained melancholy.

***Discarding the Desire for Meaning*** Many critics have commented on the manner in which Ashbery's fluid style has helped to convey a major concern in his poetry: the refusal to impose an arbitrary order on a world of flux and chaos. In his verse, Ashbery attempts to mirror the stream of perceptions of which human consciousness is composed. His poems move, often without continuity, from one image to the next, prompting some critics to praise his expressionist technique and others to accuse him of producing art that is unintelligible, or even meaningless.

Ashbery's poetry challenges its readers to discard all presumptions about traditional themes and styles of verse in favor of a literature that reflects upon the limits of language and the randomness of thought. In the *New Criterion*, critic William Logan noted: "Few poets have so cleverly manipulated, or just plain tortured, our soiled desire for meaning." Raymond Carney likewise contended that Ashbery's work "is a continuous criticism of all the ways in which literature would tidy up experience and make the world safe for poetry."

---

## COMMON HUMAN EXPERIENCE

Ashbery's poem "Self-Portrait in a Convex Mirror" is a long meditation inspired by a painting by the Renaissance artist Francesco Parmigianino. Other famous poems which have been inspired by paintings include:

"My Last Duchess" (1842), a poem by Robert Browning. In this poem, written as a dramatic monologue, the speaker explains to a guest the unfortunate fate of his late wife by discussing a painting of her hanging on his wall.

"Musée des Beaux Arts" (1940), a poem by W. H. Auden. In this poem the narrator meditates upon the "Older Master"'s treatments of human suffering, particularly in the painting *Landscape with the Fall of Icarus*, generally credited to Pieter Brueghel the Elder.

"Why I am Not a Painter" (1971), a poem by Frank O'Hara. O'Hara compares his own artistic poetical process to that of his friend, the painter Mike Goldberg.

---

## Works in Critical Context

Ashbery's poetic style, once considered avant-garde, has since become "so influential that its imitators are legion," Helen Vendler observed in the *New Yorker*. Although even his strongest supporters admit that his poetry is often difficult to read and difficult to understand, Ashbery has become, as James Atlas noted in the *New York Times Sunday Magazine*, "the most widely honored poet of his generation."

***The Tennis Court Oath*** Beginning with the publication of *The Tennis Court Oath* Ashbery's verbal expressionism has attracted mixed critical response. James Schevill, in a *Saturday Review* article on *The Tennis Court Oath*, wrote: "The trouble with Ashbery's work is that he is influenced by modern painting to the point where he tries to apply words to the page as if they were abstract.... Consequently, his work loses coherence." In the *New York Times Book Review*, X. J. Kennedy praised the same title: "If the reader can shut off that portion of the brain which insists words be related logically, he may dive with pleasure into Ashbery's stream of consciousness." Critic Bryan Appleyard argued for the invigorating effect of the volume, asserting that "however initially baffling his poetry may seem, it is impossible to deny the extraordinary beauty of its surface, its calm and haunting evocation of a world of fragmentary knowledge."

***Self-Portrait in a Convex Mirror*** Ashbery's position in American letters is confirmed by his unprecedented sweep of the literary "triple crown" in 1976, when *Self-Portrait in a Convex Mirror* won the Pulitzer

Prize, the National Book Award, and the National Book Critics Circle Prize.

In a review of *Self-Portrait in a Convex Mirror* for *Harper's,* writer Paul Auster contended that

> few poets today have such an uncanny ability to undermine our certainties, to articulate so fully the ambiguous zones of our consciousness. We are constantly thrown off guard as we read his poems. The ordinary becomes strange, and things that a moment ago seemed clear are cast into doubt.

In their reviews of the poem, critics often emphasize Ashbery's continuing interest in the complex relationships between perception, reality, and the process of creating art.

***Recent Writings*** Since the publication of *Self-Portrait in a Convex Mirror,* Ashbery has been considered one of the most influential figures in the mainstream of American poetry and is among the most highly honored poets of his generation. Although his poetry is occasionally faulted for obscurity, many critics argue that traditional critical approaches often lead to misinterpretations of Ashbery's works, which are concerned with the process of creating art rather than the final product. He continues to publish poems that emphasize the uncertainty of modern life and the flux of the artistic process. His 1991 work *Flow Chart,* for example, is a book-length poem that encompasses an expansive range of subject matter in a ruminating, trance-like style. Many reviewers have asserted that *Flow Chart* addresses the complexity of human experience and reveals Ashbery's concern with contemporary moral consciousness despite its characteristically farcical tone. Writing in *Poetry,* Alfred Corn suggested that though the book is Ashbery's most dense work, "the reach of *Flow Chart* suggests that it is Ashbery's most important book, and certainly his most human."

## Responses to Literature

1. Ashbery's "Self-Portrait in a Convex Mirror" is a poem inspired by a Renaissance painting of the same name. Choose a painting—old or modern—and write a poem about how it affects you. How does writing the poem change the way you react to the piece of art?

2. Ashbery, Frank O'Hara, and other members of the New York School of Poets worked in the advertising industry in New York in the 1950s, and their language is both affected by and often mocks the language and images used in advertisements. Think about the advertisements you see today, in magazines, on television, and on the Internet. How do you think the language and images of advertising affects the books, music, and films you encounter today?

3. Ashbery's literary career has spanned nearly five decades, and he is considered as representative of the condition of uncertainty in modern society. Take one of Ashbery's earliest poems (from the 1950s) and compare it to one of his recent works. What differences do you see in style and subject matter? How do you think these differences are influenced by the historical events Ashbery has witnessed?

BIBLIOGRAPHY
**Books**

Bloom, Harold. *John Ashbery.* New York: Chelsea House, 1985.
Herd, David. *John Ashbery and American Poetry: Fit to Cope with Our Occasions.* New York: St. Martin's Press, 2001.
Lehman, David, ed. *John Ashbery.* Ithaca, N.Y.: Cornell University Press, 1979.

**Periodicals**

Atlas, James. Review of *Self-Portrait in a Convex Mirror. The New York Times Sunday Magazine* (May 23, 1976).
Auster, Paul. Review of *Self-Portrait in a Convex Mirror. Harper's* (November 1975), p. 106.
Corn, Alfred. Review of *Flow Chart. Poetry* (December 1991), p. 169.
Kennedy, X. J. Review of *The Tennis Court Oath. The New York Times Book Review* (July 15, 1962).
Logan, William. "Soiled Desires." *New Criterion* (June 1998), p. 61.

# ⊛ Isaac Asimov

BORN: *1920, Petrovichi, U.S.S.R.*

DIED: *1992, New York, New York*

NATIONALITY: *American, Russian*

GENRE: *Science fiction, nonfiction*

MAJOR WORKS:
*I, Robot* (1950)
*Foundation* (1951)
*The Caves of Steel* (1954)

## Overview

Isaac Asimov was "the world's most prolific science writer," according to David N. Samuelson in *Twentieth-Century Science-Fiction Writers,* and he "has written some of the best-known science fiction ever published." Writing over five hundred books of science fiction and fact over five decades, Asimov remained throughout his life a potent force in the genre. Stories such as "Nightfall" and "The Bicentennial Man," and novels such as *The Gods Themselves* and *Foundation,* which cover scientific topics as diverse as nuclear fusion to the theory of numbers, have received numerous honors and are recognized as among the best science fiction ever written.

Isaac Asimov    *Asimov, Isaac, photograph. AP Images.*

## Works in Biographical and Historical Context

***Early Interest in Popular Culture and Science***
Isaac Asimov was born in 1920 to middle-class Jewish parents in Petrovichi, Russia, then part of the Smolensk district in the Soviet Union. His family immigrated to the United States in 1923, settling in Brooklyn, New York, where they owned and operated a candy store. As a child, Asimov read both nonfiction and literary classics, but he was most intrigued by the glossy adventure story magazines sold on the racks in his parents' store. By the age of eleven, Asimov was already writing stories that mixed the popular magazines' plot formulas with characters and settings that featured outer space and robots.

In 1934, while attending Boys High School of Brooklyn, Asimov published his first story, "Little Brothers," in the school newspaper. A year later, he entered Columbia University, where he studied biology and chemistry—two fields that, despite his extensive writings about the future of scientific discovery, would not feature prominently in his fiction. Asimov himself has noted that while thorough knowledge of the sciences is necessary to create durable science fiction, extensive technical knowledge of a particular branch of science may hinder a writer's ability to make the imaginative—and often unscientific—leaps often necessary when crafting compelling futuristic

worlds. During the next two years, Asimov's interest in history grew, and he read numerous books on the subject. Many of these—particularly Edward Gibbon's *Decline and Fall of the Roman Empire*—would inform his creation of the "future history" settings of the *Foundation* trilogy. During his college years, Asimov also read science fiction magazines and wrote stories. His first professionally published story, "Marooned off Vesta," appeared in *Astounding Stories* in 1939.

***Spearheading the Genre***    The publication of "Marooned off Vesta" began Isaac Asimov's long and substantial relationship with editor John W. Campbell, who was to influence the work of some of the most prominent authors of modern science fiction, including Arthur C. Clarke, Robert Heinlein, Poul Anderson, L. Sprague de Camp, and Theodore Sturgeon. Because Campbell was also one of the best-known science fiction writers of the 1930s and *Astounding* one of the most prestigious publications in its field at the time, Asimov was quickly catapulted to fame within the science fiction genre. Campbell guided Asimov through his formative beginnings as a science fiction writer and would continue to be his mentor throughout his career, introducing him to other prominent writers within the genre.

***Prolific Experiences and Writings***    While continuing to write stories for Campbell, Asimov graduated from Columbia University with a B.S. in chemistry in 1939, and later earned an M.A. and Ph.D., and worked as a professor of biochemistry at Boston University School of Medicine. Between 1942 and 1945, he worked as a civilian chemist at the U.S. Air Experimental Station, where he enhanced his knowledge of new technologies in the fields of aerospace engineering and robotics. In 1945–1946, he served in the United States Army during World War II. Many critics have traced Asimov's preoccupation with the dangers of high-tech weapons to his reaction to the U.S. military's dropping of atomic bombs on the Japanese cities of Hiroshima and Nagasaki during the war.

After returning from military service, Asimov dedicated himself to full-time writing, becoming one of the most prolific writers of all time. He became the leader of the "humanist" movement (which championed practical, rational, yet peaceful politics) and became an outspoken opponent of the nuclear arms race between the United States and the U.S.S.R. that began after the conclusion of World War II. He is perhaps best remembered for his novels *I, Robot*, *The Gods Themselves*, and the "future-history" stories of the *Foundation* series. Yet he also produced multiple works of nonfiction and juvenile literature. Toward the end of his career, Asimov was concerned with a variety of subjects that went far beyond the scientific, and wrote on such diverse topics as the Bible, mythology, William Shakespeare, ecology, and American history. In addition, Asimov wrote several volumes of autobiography before his death in 1992.

## LITERARY AND HISTORICAL CONTEMPORARIES

Asimov's famous contemporaries include:

**Robert Heinlein** (1907–1988): Heinlein, a science fiction writer noted for treating themes related to militarism and politics, was as prolific a writer as Asimov and is known for works such as *Starship Troopers* (1959) and *Stranger in a Strange Land* (1961).

**Mikhail Gorbachev** (1931–): Gorbachev was leader of the Soviet Union from 1985–1991 and is credited for attempts to end the Cold War during summits with American President Ronald Reagan.

**George Devol** (1912–): Devol is commonly considered the inventor of the first industrial robot (in 1956) and was the co-founder of America's first robotics company.

**Stanley Kubrick** (1928–1999): Film director Stanley Kubrick is perhaps best known for his 1968 collaboration with Arthur C. Clarke, *2001: A Space Odyssey*.

## COMMON HUMAN EXPERIENCE

Many of Isaac Asimov's works—most notably *I, Robot*—explore the issue of artificial life and question whether or not robots and humans can peacefully coexist. Other works which explore the role of robots in society include:

*Blade Runner* (1982), a film directed by Ridley Scott, based on the novel *Do Androids Dream of Electric Sheep?* (1968) by Philip K. Dick. This film is set in a future Los Angeles, where robotic "replicants" have staged a revolution, and are being hunted down and killed by humans.

*2001: A Space Odyssey* (1968), a novel by Arthur C. Clarke. This pinnacle science fiction work features the famous robot HAL, who becomes a dangerous enemy of humans as he discovers both emotion and power.

*WALL-E* (2008), a computer-animated film directed by Andrew Stanton. This film features the last robot left on a polluted and deserted Earth. He travels to a space station, where he convinces humans to return and repopulate the planet.

## Works in Literary Context

*Robotics* Isaac Asimov has been credited with the introduction of several innovative concepts into the science fiction genre, including the formulation of the "Three Laws of Robotics." According to Asimov, the successful integration of robots into society would require the following three laws:

> 1. A robot may not injure a human being or, through inaction, allow a human being to come to harm. 2. A robot must obey the orders given it by human beings except where such orders would conflict with the First Law. 3. A robot must protect its own existence as long as such protection does not conflict with the First or Second Laws.

Asimov used these precepts as the basis for dozens of fictional works, and he felt that he was "probably more famous for them than for anything else I have written." The three laws gained general acceptance among readers and among other science-fiction writers; Asimov, in his autobiography, wrote that they "revolutionized" science fiction and that "no writer could write a stupid robot story if he used the Three Laws. The story might be bad on other counts, but it wouldn't be stupid." The laws became so popular, and seemed so logical, that many people believed real robots would eventually be designed according to Asimov's basic principles.

*Future Histories* The novels of Isaac Asimov's *Foundation* series were written as "future histories," or stories being told in a society of the distant future which relates events of that society's history. The concept was not invented by Asimov, but there can be little doubt that he became a master of the technique. In his autobiographies, Asimov stated that his concept for the future history formula arose out of his love of reading histories of past civilizations and empires. *Foundation* (1951), *Foundation and Empire* (1952), and *Second Foundation* (1953) have achieved special standing among science-fiction enthusiasts. In 1966, the World Science Fiction Convention honored them with a special Hugo Award as the best all-time science-fiction series.

*Melding Genres* Throughout his long career, Asimov was known for his innovation in mixing science fiction with other popular genres, thus widening the appeal of the often marginalized literary subset. His books about robots—most notably *I, Robot*, *The Caves of Steel*, and *The Naked Sun*—did much to legitimize science fiction by augmenting the genre's traditional material with the narrative structures of such established genres as mystery and detective stories, while displaying a thematic concern for technological progress and its implications for humanity.

### Works in Critical Context

Many critics, scientists, and educators believe Asimov's greatest talent was for popularizing or, as he called it, "translating" science for the lay reader. His many fiction and nonfiction books on atomic theory, chemistry, astronomy, and physics have been recognized for their extraordinary clarity, and Asimov has been praised for his ability to synthesize complex data into readable, unthreatening prose. An editorial in *The Washington Post* concluded that he redefined the rule "as to how many things a person is allowed to be an expert on" and that his "extraordinary capabilities aside, [his] breadth of interest deserves more admiration than it gets."

*I, Robot*  In *I, Robot*—a collection of nine short stories linked by key characters and themes—Asimov describes a future society in which human beings and nearly sentient robots coexist. Critics consider it a pivotal work in the development of realistic science fiction literature, mainly for its elaboration of Asimov's "Three Laws of Robotics" as a viable ethical and moral code. *I, Robot* is also significant for its espousal of the benefits of technology—a rather rare position in the history of science fiction and fantastic literature, which traditionally viewed technology and science as threats to human existence.

The critical reception of *I, Robot* has been generally favorable. Most commentators applaud Asimov's Three Laws of Robotics, arguing that they give the stories a sense of realism and moral depth. Others note his ability to tell an engaging story and his facility for combining elements of the mystery and detective genres with the conventions of science fiction. Although many critics fault Asimov's predictable characterizations and "naïve" sentimentality, most credit his realistic, ethical portrayal of futuristic society in *I, Robot* as revolutionary in the science fiction genre, changing the way fantastic literature could be conceived and written.

## Responses to Literature

1. Review the "Three Laws of Robotics" from Isaac Asimov's *I, Robot*. Then, compare Asimov's views on robots to those of more modern works that feature robots, such as the movie *WALL-E*. How do the representations of artificial intelligence differ?

2. Asimov is often cited as a writer who anticipated and explored many of the political and ecological issues which are primary concerns in modern society. Find three specific examples from his work of futuristic predictions that seem to mirror the problems of modern society. Was Asimov ahead of his time, and how accurate were his predictions? If you were writing a similar series today, what problems would you anticipate for a future society?

3. Arthur C. Clarke's famous science fiction novel *2001: A Space Odyssey* explores the role of robots in society, but with a much less optimistic view than that presented in Asimov's *I, Robot*. Choose a robot from *I, Robot* and compare it to HAL from *2001*. What are the differences between the two robots and their relationships to humans? Can the robots be considered ethical or unethical beings?

BIBLIOGRAPHY
**Books**

Boerst, William J. *Isaac Asimov: Writer of the Future.* Greensboro, N.C.: Morgan Reynolds, 1998.

Carter, Paul A. *The Creation of Tomorrow: Fifty Years of Magazine Science Fiction.* New York: Columbia University Press, 1977.

Knight, Damon. *The Futurians.* New York: John Day, 1977.

Miller, Marjorie. *Isaac Asimov: A Checklist.* Kent, Ohio: Kent State University Press, 1972.

Olander, Joseph D., and Martin Harry Greenberg, eds. *Isaac Asimov.* New York: Taplinger, 1977.

Patrouch, Joseph F. *The Science Fiction of Isaac Asimov.* Garden City, N.J.: Doubleday, 1974.

Samuelson, David N. *Twentieth-Century Science-Fiction Writers, 2nd edition.* Detroit, Mich.: St. James Press, 1986.

Slusser, George E. *Isaac Asimov: The Foundations of His Science Fiction.* San Bernardino, Calif.: Borgo Press, 1979.

# ❀ Jean Auel

BORN: *1936, Chicago, Illinois*

NATIONALITY: *American*

GENRE: *Fiction*

MAJOR WORKS:
*The Clan of the Cave Bear* (1980)
*The Valley of Horses* (1982)
*The Mammoth Hunters* (1985)

## Overview

Jean Auel catapulted from obscurity to the bestseller lists with the publication of her first novel, *The Clan of the Cave Bear* (1980), the story of an adventurous and resilient young Cro-Magnon heroine, Ayla. Feminist themes are prevalent throughout the book, as well as issues of racial and gender prejudice and xenophobia. The success of the book spawned several sequels, including *The Valley of the Horses* (1982) and *The Mammoth Hunters* (1985), which along with *The Clan of the Cave Bear* are known collectively as the "Earth's Children" series.

## Works in Biographical and Historical Context

*Research on Prehistory*  Jean Auel was born in 1936 in Chicago, Illinois, to Neil S. Untinene, a painter and decorator, and Martha (Wirtanen) Untinene. As a child she was an avid reader of both fiction and nonfiction and developed an interest in prehistory. She attended

Jean Auel    *Auel, Jean, photograph. © Jerry Bauer. Reproduced by permission.*

Portland State University and throughout her undergraduate education worked as a credit manager and technical writer in order to support herself. She married her business manager, Ray B. Auel, in 1954, and the couple eventually had five children.

Though busy with work and the running of a household, Auel continued to pursue her love of prehistoric times, and she followed the works and discoveries of such biological anthropologists as Dr. Jean Clottes, Pierre Teilhard de Chardin, Tim White, Maurice Taieb, and Raymond Dart. Auel also conducted an intensive personal study of the Ice Age and researched hominid ancestors of modern human beings—australopithecines, Neanderthals, and Cro-Magnons. Her interest was particularly encouraged by the 1974 discovery of the "Lucy" skeleton in Ethiopia. This landmark discovery of a three-million-year-old-female australopithecine (Lucy was, at the time of her discovery, the oldest hominid specimen found) proved that humankind's australopithecine ancestors were more human than apelike. By examining the skeleton of Lucy, scientists determined that australopithecines walked upright and had brain sizes closer to those of modern humans than previously believed. The discovery of Lucy sparked violent debate between creationists (who contended that man was created by God a few thousand years ago, in the form of Adam and Eve) and scientists who believed that man descended, through the process of natural selection, from the same primate ancestor as that of apes. Auel followed this debate closely and corresponded with many of the leading anthropologists involved with the study of prehistoric man.

***Combining Feminism and Ancient History***   Though continuing to work, raise children, and to study for an MBA (which she ultimately received from the University of Portland in 1976), Auel pursued her interest in the scientific discoveries and debates concerning ancient hominids. Influenced perhaps by the concurrent American Civil Rights Movement as well as the fact that the australopithecine skeleton found in Ethiopia was a female, Auel began to outline a historical novel that imagined a woman protagonist living in Paleolithic times. In her spare time, Auel began writing the story that would eventually be published in 1980 as *The Clan of the Cave Bear*. The story's heroine, Ayla, is a Cro-Magnon woman adopted early in life by a tribe of Neanderthals after her own people had perished in an earthquake. An outcast because of her unusual appearance (Ayla resembled modern humans more than her adopted family did) the young protagonist ultimately uses her creativity and inventiveness to overcome the obstacles of her world. The innovative Ayla perfects the sling as a weapon, uses a sewing needle, makes fire with flint and iron pyrite, domesticates animals, and practices medicine.

This first volume of the "Earth's Children" series was an overwhelming hit among readers; it had a lengthy stay on the bestseller lists and won an American Book Award nomination for best first novel. What makes the success of the series even more notable, as critics have pointed out, is its genre. "Caveman" fiction had heretofore not been considered a prime prospect for blockbuster books. But Auel's novels appeared at a time when longstanding notions of prehistoric life were being reassessed. As *Newsweek* writer Sharon Begley related, the real-life "Earth's Children" of some 17,000–35,000 years ago were far from the brutish, unintelligent creatures of stereotype. On the contrary, their era, ripe with art and invention, was actually the "cradle of human culture."

Equally popular to *The Clan of the Cave Bear* was its 1982 sequel *The Valley of Horses*. The third book of the series, *The Mammoth Hunters*, shattered existing publishing records with a first printing of 1.1 million copies. The fourth book in the series, *The Plains of Passage* (1990), debuted as number one on the *New York Times* bestseller list and sold one hundred thousand copies the first two days it was on sale. Auel kept many fans anxiously waiting by letting twelve years pass before publishing the fifth book in the series, *The Shelters of Stone* (2002). She continues to write and has received honorary degrees from the University of Portland, the University of Maine, Mount Vernon College, and Pacific University.

## Works in Literary Context

*Feminist Views in a Prehistoric Setting* Auel's novels were written during the period of "third-wave feminism" in America. Unlike the second-wave feminists of the 1970s who advocated the credo "the personal is the political" and focused on liberating women from oppression in domestic spaces, such third-wave feminists as Susan Sontag and Dorothy Allison focused on achieving equality for women in the legal and political sphere. Auel's works reflect both these movements by describing the heroine Alya's domestic life, but also by outlining the differences in attitudes toward women held by Neanderthal and Cro-Magnon cultures. Linda S. Bergmann, writing for *Twentieth-Century Romance and Historical Writers*, believed that Auel's novels "can perhaps best be described as feminist prehistorical romances. Drawing on feminist theories of matriarchal prehistory and fertility-based religion . . . Auel uses the conventions of historical romance to create prehistoric feminist utopias." Bergmann further noted that "although this series is set in the Stone Age, it raises contemporary feminist concerns about gender roles, and is as much about our own time as about prehistory."

*Clash of Cultures* Throughout Auel's works, the protagonist Ayla, a Cro-Magnon woman who is orphaned after a natural disaster kills every other member of her tribe, must adapt to a Neanderthal culture that is not as evolutionarily advanced as her own. Thus Ayla, who is ostracized from her adopted culture due to her dissimilar appearance and penchant for innovation, must learn to exist in a culture where women are oppressed and advanced technology is treated with skepticism. The strong-willed Ayla threatens the status quo by refusing to be blindly obedient to chauvinist customs and by introducing such practices as sewing clothing, domesticating animals, and curing illness with medicine. She and her lover Jondalar, whom Auel described as "the early equivalent of today's technical genius, the engineer, the computer nut," revolutionize Cro-Magnon culture through advanced ideas and technologies that change daily life and the roles of women as well as social traditions and methods of warfare.

## Works in Critical Context

Though sometimes citing technical imperfections of plot and dialogue, many reviewers agree with Auel's thousands of fans that her "Earth's Children" books have merit as both adventures and as keys to understanding the lives of early humans. Ellen Emery Heltzel commented in *Book* that "Auel's love for the natural sciences, along with her attention to minutiae, is much of what captivates readers." In general, critics were more pleased with Auel's strong, believable characters, their intriguing conflicts, and her meticulous historical research than with her resolution of conflict and lack of dialogue. Her knowledge of this era of history was so complete, some

---

## LITERARY AND HISTORICAL CONTEMPORARIES

Auel's literary and historical contemporaries include:

**Diane Fossey** (1932–1985): An American primatologist who devoted her career to studying the gorillas of Rwanda and speaking out against the poachers who illegally kill the gorillas. She was found murdered in her cabin in Rwanda in 1985. The murder is unsolved, but it is suspected she was killed by poachers who wished to silence her.

**Margaret Atwood** (1939–): Canadian poet, novelist, literary critic, and feminist who is best known for *The Handmaid's Tale* (1985) and the Booker Prize-winning *The Blind Assassin* (2000).

**Jared Diamond** (1937–): Diamond is an American evolutionary biologist and writer of popular scientific nonfiction. His Pulitzer-Prize-winning *Guns, Germs, and Steel* (1998) traces the effects of violence and disease on human history.

**James A. Michener** (1907–1997): A prolific author of epic novels, Michener was known for the extensive historical research he put into such well-regarded books as *Texas* (1985) and *Alaska* (1988).

**Donald Johansen** (1943–): Johansen is a biological anthropologist best known for his discovery, with his colleagues Maurice Taieb and Tim White, of the Lucy skeleton in Ethiopia in 1974.

---

claimed, that her protracted explanations and details of tribal life contributed to a sometimes plodding pace.

*The Clan of the Cave Bear* Writing about *The Clan of the Cave Bear* in a *Los Angeles Times Book Review* article, Willard Simms remarked that "painstaking and meticulous research went into this book. There's an authenticity about the life styles and survival techniques of these cavemen that's deeply moving." John Pfeiffer praised Auel's insight in the *New York Times Book Review*: "There was a great and subtle gap between the Neanderthals and their successors, people like ourselves, and [Auel] has caught its essence beautifully. [In *The Clan of the Cave Bear*,] she has written an exciting, imaginative and intuitively solid book." The relationship between Neanderthals and Cro-Magnons also attracted the attention of Ken Ringle. Ringle pointed out in a *Washington Post* article that anthropologists

have puzzled for decades over why Neanderthal man died out. Auel, while generally scrupulous to the known facts about Neanderthals, decided to endow them with a dominant racial memory that wedded them to the past, while Cro-Magnon man's ability to learn and adapt better equipped him for the future. This melding of known fact with imagination may be Auel's greatest achievement.

## COMMON HUMAN EXPERIENCE

Though Auel was one of the first writers to use the Stone Age as a setting to advance feminist ideas, many female writers have set their novels in past time periods in order to explore issues of gender and equality. Examples of works which explore feminist concerns through historical fiction include:

*The Blind Assassin* (2000), a novel by Margaret Atwood. This Booker Prize-winning novel traces the life of Ira Chase in a fictional Ontario town in the 1930s and 40s. Canadian politics and history serve as a backdrop to the story of the domestic lives of Ira and her sister.

*Orlando* (1928), a novel by Virginia Woolf. In writing this novel, Woolf adapted the fictionalized life of her friend Vita Sackville-West to an Elizabethan setting. The novel's protagonist decides to change genders, and the book is remembered as one of the first novels of the twentieth century to openly address lesbianism.

*In America* (1999), a novel by Susan Sontag. This novel, set in the nineteenth century, recreates the life of Polish actress Helena Modjeska and explores feminist concerns as well as issues of immigration.

*The Other Boleyn Girl* (2001), a novel by Philippa Gregory. This novel imagines the life of Ann Boleyn's sister, Mary Boleyn. Ann Boleyn was the second wife of King Henry VIII in sixteenth-century Tudor England.

**The Valley of Horses and The Mammoth Hunters**
The sequels to *The Clan of the Cave Bear* received critical attention as well, though they were not universally praised as highly as Auel's first novel. In a *Washington Post* review of *The Valley of Horses*, Octavia E. Butler, who said she enjoyed *The Clan of the Cave Bear* and believed that the author "can create strong, believable characters and give them enough trouble, enough sustained, compelling conflict to keep a story moving and hold a reader's interest," nevertheless faulted Auel's second volume for the tendency to show "troubles, large or small, [being] all quickly resolved . . . just in time." *Detroit News* critic John R. Alden, however, continued to see a timeless quality in Auel's stories. Writing about *The Mammoth Hunters*, Alden said that the book "is successful because it presents prehistoric people as human beings, with the same kinds of emotional conflicts we contemporary earthlings have today." As for the adventure aspect, Alden added, "If hunting a herd of mammoth at the base of a mile-high wall of ice doesn't provoke your imagination, I don't know what will."

### Responses to Literature

1. Research the issues involved with human evolution, beginning with the works of Charles Darwin. In small groups, outline the viewpoints held by both sides of the "evolution debate." Why do such discoveries as Lucy continue to inspire debate? How does the theory of natural selection affect mankind's view of itself?

2. Choose a work by another feminist author that, like *The Clan of the Cave Bear*, explores the roles of women in a past historical period. Does the author choose to focus on the same elements of civilization and society as does Auel? Why did the author choose the time period she did? What aspects of the setting are analogous to the modern day?

3. *The Clan of the Cave Bear* was adapted to film in 1986, directed by Michael Chapman and starring Darryl Hannah. Watch the film and discuss the elements of the movie in relation to the book. Does the movie take liberties with the text, and if so, why? How is prehistory portrayed? If you were adapting the movie today, what choices in terms of set and casting would you make?

BIBLIOGRAPHY

**Books**

Bergman, Linda S. *Twentieth-Century Romance and Historical Writers*, 3rd. ed. Detroit.: St. James Press, 1994.

**Periodicals**

Alden, John R. Review of *The Mammoth Hunters*. *Detroit News* (December 8, 1985).

Butler, Octavia E. Review of *The Valley of Horses*. *Washington Post* (September 13, 1982).

Heltzel, Ellen Emery. "The Return of Jean Auel." *Book* (May–June 2002): 40–44.

Pfeiffer, John. Review of *The Clan of the Cave Bear*. *New York Times Book Review* (August 31, 1980).

Simms, Willard. Review of *The Clan of the Cave Bear*. *Los Angeles Times Book Review* (November 2, 1980).

# ❂ Paul Auster

BORN: *1947, Newark, New Jersey*

NATIONALITY: *American*

GENRE: *Fiction, poetry*

MAJOR WORKS:
*City of Glass* (1985)
*Ghosts* (1986)
*The Locked Room* (1987)

## Overview

A provocative experimental novelist whose work represents an amalgam of several genres, Paul Auster is best known for his New York Trilogy, which consists of *City of Glass* (1985), *Ghosts* (1986), and *The Locked Room*

Paul Auster    *Auster, Paul, photograph. AP Images.*

read such authors as Ralph Waldo Emerson, Nathaniel Hawthorne, and Henry David Thoreau, and would later model many of his characters on those from their works. During this period, Auster also became involved with the Civil Rights Movement, which emphasized racial and gender equality, and encouraged young people to break with traditional thinking. Auster adopted these ideas, and began experimenting with literary forms that veered away from accepted models of plot and dialogue. While still in college, he wrote both poetry and prose and participated in campus protests against the Vietnam War.

***The Influence of French Philosophy***    After receiving his degrees from Columbia University, Auster worked as a merchant seaman for several months to fund a move to France, where he remained for four years and worked a variety of odd jobs to make ends meet. In France, Auster was heavily influenced by philosophers and psychoanalysts such as Jacques Derrida and Jacques Lacan, who argued that man's whole universe is created and maintained through language, and because each individual is trapped in this network of language man experiences the frustration of never being able to obtain truth and meaning. Language, itself largely arbitrary, keeps the individual from finding their true identity. Derrida and Lacan, who applied psychoanalysis to literary criticism, spearheaded the school of thought known as Post-structuralism. The ideas put forward by these French thinkers would encourage Auster to experiment with different varieties of language and voices, and to examine the role of chance and accident throughout his works.

***Experiments in Poetry and Prose***    Auster returned to New York, and continued to support himself by translating French poets into English. In 1974, he married writer and translator Lydia Davis, with whom he shares a son. They divorced in 1979 and Auster married Siri Hustvedt in 1981. After returning to New York, Auster published his first two books—the poetry collections *Unearth* (1974) and *Wall Writing* (1976). The books were well-received and Auster gained a name for himself as a new "post-modern" writer. Postmodern writers, influenced by post-structuralist philosophy, were known for their experimentation, wordplay, self-awareness, irony, and sense of the absurd.

Following the favorable reviews of his first two books of poetry, Auster was awarded Ingram Merrill Foundation grants in 1975 and 1982, as well as National Endowment of the Arts fellowships in 1979 and 1985. He continued to labor in relative obscurity as a poet, essayist, and translator of French literature until the publication of his first novel, *City of Glass*. That work, which had been rejected by seventeen other publishers, was finally issued by Sun & Moon Press in 1985. The novel, which fused postmodern techniques with the traditional detective novel, received high critical acclaim, and was nominated for an Edgar Award for best mystery novel in 1986. Auster followed this novel with *Ghosts*, which also

(1986). In these novels and others he combines elements of hard-boiled detective fiction, film noir, dystopian fantasy, and postmodern narratives to address the nature of knowledge, human redemption, and the function of language. His ambitious work is distinguished for challenging the limits of the novel form and tackling difficult philosophical concepts.

## Works in Biographical and Historical Context

***New York in the 1960s***    Born on the outskirts of New York City, in Newark, New Jersey, Paul Auster was raised in a middle-class Jewish family by his parents, Samuel, a landlord, and Queenie. His early experiences and observations of life in the city and its suburbs would later figure largely in his famed New York Trilogy. The teenaged Auster became an avid reader and soon resolved to become a writer. Upon graduating from high school, he attended Columbia University, where he earned a BA in English in 1969 and an MA in 1970. Auster developed an interest in the American Transcendental writers of the nineteenth century, who emphasized individualism, universal human rights, and harmony with nature. Auster

# LITERARY AND HISTORICAL CONTEMPORARIES

Auster's famous contemporaries include:

**Philip Roth** (1933–): Like Auster, Philip Roth is a writer born to a Jewish family in Newark, New Jersey, and often adopts New York City as the setting for his novels. He is known for such bestselling books as *Portnoy's Complaint* (1969) and *American Pastoral* (1997).

**A. B. Byatt** (1936–): Postmodern British writer renowned for such works as *Possession* (1990), a Booker Prize–winning novel.

**Julian Barnes** (1946–): Barnes, an experimental postmodern writer, is best known for his novels *Flaubert's Parrot* (1984) and *England, England* (1998). Like Auster, Barnes often experiments with the genre of the detective novel.

**Jacques Lacan** (1901–1981): The French philosopher and linguist Jacques Lacan is known for fusing psychoanalytic theories to literary criticism. Throughout the 1960s and 1970s he wrote and lectured on literature with an emphasis on the limitations of language and the presence of unconscious drives of both writers and their characters.

received favorable criticism. The third volume of his New York Trilogy, *The Locked Room*, was nominated for several awards and is considered by critics as the strongest work of the trilogy. After the success of his trilogy, Auster continued to investigate philosophical concepts of knowledge and language in such novels as *In the Country of Last Things* (1987), *The Music of Chance* (1990), and *Leviathan* (1992). Auster taught creative writing at Princeton University from 1986 to 1990. In 1994 he collaborated with director Wayne Wang on the films *Smoke* and *Blue in the Face*, which he co-directed. Auster was awarded the prestigious Chevalier de l'Ordre des Arts et des Lettres in 1993.

Auster has continued his success as a novelist, publishing *Travels in the Scriptorium* in 2007 and *Man in the Dark* in 2008.

## Works in Literary Context

"Paul Auster's books are dominated by the twin themes of chance and mortality and revolve around writers, even drawing on himself," London *Guardian* contributor James Campbell noted. "Writing is a potent strength in the world created by Auster. His characters constantly stress the force of the word set free."

**The Mystery Genre** Though Auster is generally considered a postmodern experimental writer rather than a genre writer, he often adopts certain genres such as the

detective novel to underscore the ambiguous nature of language and identity. While instances of confused or mistaken identity are common in the mystery genre, Auster adapts this stock device into a metaphor for contemporary urban life in his New York Trilogy, deliberately blurring the distinction between author and text. For example, *City of Glass*, a grim and intellectually puzzling story, superficially resembles a mystery novel that exploits the conventions of the detective genre. "The real mystery, however, is one of confused character identity," suggested *New York Times Book Review* contributor Toby Olson, "the descent of a writer into a labyrinth in which fact and fiction become increasingly difficult to separate." The protagonist, Quinn, is a pseudonymous mystery novelist who assumes the identity of a real detective, named Paul Auster, after receiving a phone call intended for Auster. In *Ghosts*, the second volume of the trilogy, Auster continues his investigation into lost identity with increasing abstraction, including characters identified only as Blue, White, and Black. The novel's coy tone and austere plot—a detective named Blue is contracted by a client named White to pursue a man named Black—places the action in a theoretical context disconnected from reality, forcing the reader to solve the "mystery" of Auster's narrative technique.

**Postmodern Experimentation** Auster pursues his philosophical interest in the nature of language and reality not just through the content of his novels, but in the forms of their narratives. Thus, Auster's novels frequently shift speakers and points of view, address the reader directly, and sometimes, as in *City of Glass*, incorporate Auster himself as a character. Thus, the reader is forced to evaluate his or her own role in the reading of the novel, as well as Auster's role in the writing of it.

**Chance and Accident** Throughout his works, Auster has pursued the theme of chance, encouraging the reader to regard life itself to be as arbitrary as the language with which we describe and experience it. Auster, therefore, often uses irony to explore the idea of an individual having a set destiny. Auster's novel, *The Music of Chance*, for example, is the story of personal journey, bringing to mind such fictional characters as Mark Twain's Huck Finn, John Updike's Rabbit Angstrom, and Jack Kerouac's Dean Moriarty. Protagonist Jim Nashe hits the road in search of self-knowledge after his wife leaves him and he receives an inheritance from his deceased father. Soon, however, he falls in with gamblers, loses his money, and must adapt to conditions that affect him in an arbitrary manner. He does not learn any concrete truth about himself, but instead learns to respond to the ever-changing world around him.

## Works in Critical Context

Though generally regarded as a postmodern writer because of his narrative experimentation and ironic posturing, reviewers repeatedly note that Paul Auster's idiosyncratic work resists simple categorization. His critical reputation rests largely upon his New York Trilogy, which was enthusiastically received by reviewers, and which won him respect as a formidable new literary talent during the mid-1980s. *The Locked Room* is widely judged to be the richest and by far the most compelling book of the trilogy, yet all three volumes have been commended for their facile appropriation—and dismantling—of conventional detective motifs to expose contradictory aspects of reality, literary artifice, and self-perception. Though some commentators have dismissed Auster's intellectual game-playing as unconvincing and gratuitous, most critics praise his sophisticated narrative structures, lucid prose, and daring forays into the philosophical paradoxes surrounding issues of linguistic self-invention and spiritual doubt. His innovative work is appreciated by many critics for reclaiming the vitality of contemporary experimental literature.

**City of Glass** Critical response to *City of Glass* was highly enthusiastic. *Los Angeles Times Book Review* critic Carolyn See described the book's main themes as "the degeneration of language, the shiftings of identity, the struggle to remain human in a great metropolis, when the city itself is cranking on its own falling-apart mechanical life that completely overrides any and every individual." She deemed the book "an experimental novel that wanders and digresses and loses its own narrative thread, but with all that...thoughtfully and cleverly draws our attention to these questions of self." The way the novel subtly shifts from a standard mystery story to an existential quest for identity also captured Toby Olson's attention in the *New York Times Book Review*: "Each detail, each small revelation must be attended to as significant. And such attention brings ambiguity, confusion, and paranoia." Despite its challenges, Olson believed that "the book is a pleasure to read, full of suspense and action."

**Ghosts** In *Ghosts*, the second volume of the trilogy, Auster continues his investigation of lost identity on a more abstract plane. "A client named White hires a detective named Blue to follow a man named Black," Dennis Drabelle explained in *Washington Post Book World*. "Gradually Blue realizes he's been ruined. All he can do is stare at Black, eternally writing a book in the rented room across the street, and draw a weekly paycheck." Auster's choice of names for his protagonists coupled with his coy and knowing tone throughout the book suggest that he is playing mind games with the reader. The real mystery, he implies, is not within the story but "on some higher level," as Rebecca Goldstein observed in the *New York Times Book Review*, acknowledging that *Ghosts* solves the internal mystery, but leaves the larger questions unanswered. Nonetheless, she judged the work "nearly perfect."

**The Locked Room** The trilogy's concluding volume, *The Locked Room*, was widely judged to be the richest and

## COMMON HUMAN EXPERIENCE

Because of his use of wordplay, experimental narrative technique, and ironic distance from the reader, Paul Auster is often categorized as a postmodern writer. Other works which are considered postmodern include:

*Gravity's Rainbow* (1973), a novel by Thomas Pynchon. This epic novel, set in Europe during World War II, is generally considered by critics to be one of the most important postmodern novels of the twentieth century.

*The French Lieutenant's Woman* (1969), a novel by John Fowles. In this novel postmodern writer John Fowles explores the social ethics of the Victorian period. The book is noted for its narrative experimentation; Fowles offers his reader three different choices for the ending of the story.

*Flaubert's Parrot* (1984), a novel by Julian Barnes. This novel describes the experiences of a retired widower who visits France to research the life of the writer Gustave Flaubert; interspersed within his story, however, are chapters which provide the reader with fictionalized (and often contradictory) accounts of Flaubert's life.

by far the most compelling volume in the trilogy. Less abstract and more accessible than the previous books, this story features flesh-and-blood characters with whom readers can easily identify. Several reviewers suggested that Auster's use of a first-person narrator enhances the book. "When Auster finally allows himself the luxury of character, what a delicious treat he serves up for the reader!" Carolyn See wrote in the *Los Angeles Times*. Though *The Locked Room* is a mystery like the first two installments, this novel is narrated by "a genuine character who feels love and pain and envy." Because of the first-person narration, "Mr. Auster's philosophical asides now sound heartfelt instead of stentorian and his descents into semiological Angst feel genuinely anguished and near," Steven Schiff suggested in the *New York Times Book Review*. He and other critics hypothesized that the nameless narrator represents Auster himself.

## Responses to Literature

1. Critics have often praised Auster's *The Locked Room* as the most meaningful and accessible of his New York Trilogy, largely because the use of the first person point of view makes the text easier for the reader. Compare the viewpoint in *The Locked Room* to those of *City of Glass* and *Ghosts*. Who is speaking, and how do the viewpoints affect the experience of reading the book? Do you agree with the critics, or

do you think the first-person point of view limits the scope of the book?

2. Paul Auster was heavily influenced by French psychoanalysts, philosophers, and poststructuralist literary critics at work in the 1960s and 1970s. Choose one of these critics—for example Jacques Derrida, Jacques Lacan, or Roland Barthe—and research his ideas about the nature of language. Outline his arguments using simple language and present your findings to the class. How can you see the influence of this thinker in the works of Auster?

3. In the New York Trilogy, Auster uses the genre of the mystery story to present the reader with philosophical questions regarding language and identity. Imagine that you have been assigned a similar project. Pick a genre—such as science fiction or horror or the comic book—and list the larger questions you could address through it. Outline a story that uses the standard conventions of a genre to ask questions about personal identity.

BIBLIOGRAPHY

**Books**

Handler, Nina. *Drawn into the Circle of Its Repetitions: Paul Auster's New York Trilogy.* San Bernardino, Calif.: Borgo Press, 1996.

Holzapfel, Anne M. *The New York Trilogy: Whodunit?: Tracking the Structure of Paul Auster's Anti-Detective Novels.* New York: Peter Lang, 1996.

**Periodicals**

Drabelle, Dennis. Review of *The Locked Room.* *Washington Post Book World* (March 29, 1987): 3.

Goldstein, Rebecca. Review of *Ghosts.* *New York Times Book Review* (June 29, 1986): 13.

Olson, Toby. Review of *City of Glass.* *New York Times Book Review* (November 3, 1985): 31.

Schiff, Steven. Review of *The Locked Room.* *New York Times Book Review* (January 4, 1987): 14.

See, Carolyn. Review of *City of Glass.* *Los Angeles Times Book Review* (November 17, 1985): 3.

———. Review of *The Locked Room.* *Los Angeles Times* (March 2, 1987): V4.

# ✸ Mary Hunter Austin

BORN: *1868, Carlinville, Illinois*

DIED: *1934, Santa Fe, New Mexico*

NATIONALITY: *American*

GENRE: *Fiction, nonfiction*

MAJOR WORKS:
*The Land of Little Rain* (1903)
*A Woman of Genius* (1912)
*Earth Horizon: An Autobiography* (1932)

Mary Hunter Austin   *The Library of Congress*

## Overview

Mary Hunter Austin challenged American ideas about nature, gender, and culture in the early twentieth century. Her best known works are about the desert environment and native peoples she encountered as a young woman in southern California. She also wrote extensively about the frustrating experience of being an unconventional woman in a family and a society that prized traditional femininity. Because she advocated feminist ideals and environmental awareness, Austin offers readers today the voice of a woman who was ahead of her time.

## Works in Biographical and Historical Context

*Early Life in Illinois*   Mary Hunter Austin was born Mary Hunter in 1868 to a father who loved to read and a mother whose religious convictions made her suspicious of her daughter's imagination. Austin's father died when she was ten; her beloved little sister died soon after. Her mother raised Austin and her two brothers sternly, prioritizing her sons' needs over her daughter's. As Austin later wrote in her autobiography, *Earth Horizon*, when Austin became very ill after a year at a teacher's preparation college, her mother agreed with the family doctor that this was likely due to the "natural incapacity of the female mind for intellectual achievement."

Austin's mother believed women should restrict themselves to family-related activities. This included church, and like other women of her era, this led to involvement in the temperance movement, which focused on ending the sale and use of alcohol in the United States. The temperance movement began gathering steam in the United States in the early nineteenth century. Most of its participants were women, and by the second half of the nineteenth century, they had amassed significant political power. By 1919, the temperance movement could take credit for a constitutional amendment that banned the manufacture, sale, or transport of alcohol in the United States (the amendment was repealed in 1933). Witnessing the power of the temperance movement inspired Austin and many women of her generation to become involved politically and to speak out for what they believed in, though in Austin's case the causes she espoused differed from those prized by her mother.

***Move to California*** Just after Austin graduated from Blackburn College in 1882, her family moved to the southern California desert, where her older brother filed a homestead claim. The writing for which Austin is most famous, about the California landscape, had its start with this move. Settling near Bakersfield, the Hunter family proved unprepared for farming on unirrigated land. Austin, who believed she could thrive only in a city among culture and books, found herself withering in the isolation imposed by this harsh environment.

However, Austin later experienced a spiritual awakening in the desert. Adapting to it and meeting Native Americans (specifically, Paiutes) and other settlers who had made peace with the environment, became for her, a process of discovery, and writing about this process would eventually grant her both inspiration and fame. As America became a more modern, industrial place, readers wanted to know more about this exotic environment and its inhabitants. Austin would eventually use her writing to criticize the choices Americans made with their lives, in particular that of conquering the land rather than making peace with it. For example, Austin expressed disappointment when, in 1908, the city of Los Angeles began building an aqueduct that completely drained the desert regions north of the city of the water that had once allowed for sustainable farming in the fragile environment.

***Marriage and a Writing Career*** Austin set out to earn a living for herself, and while teaching, she met Stafford Wallace Austin, whom she married in 1891. The couple would move often, settling in several southern California towns. Her husband's efforts to earn a fortune through land speculation and farming never paid off, however, and Austin continued to work to support the family even after the birth of her daughter, Ruth, a developmentally disabled child born in 1892. Bearing such disappointments did not come easily; rather than

supporting her, Austin's mother referred to Ruth's disability as a "judgement" from God. While she perceived empathy and understanding from the Paiute community, the Anglo community found Austin unconventional. She was dismissed from a Methodist church for her nontraditional religious views, and found little support when she tried to speak out against the rape of two Native American schoolgirls.

Like other early feminists who sought greater recognition for women's needs and accomplishments in the public sphere, Austin had to fight against public opinion to establish herself as a writer, a lifelong ambition she began to pursue in earnest. Her husband's lack of support led her to leave him, and her daughter's needs eventually led her to place the child in an institution. These were not easy decisions for Austin. But they did allow her the chance for intellectual freedom and growth, which she found when she spent time in places where other California writers had gathered, specifically Los Angeles and the emerging writer's colony in Carmel, California. While her first book, *The Land of Little Rain* was a publishing success, she eventually felt that she would need to leave the region that had inspired her, in order to gain a greater audience.

***Time Away from the Desert*** While Austin would often return to the home she had built in Carmel, she spent much of the two decades after the publication of *The Land of Little Rain* traveling, with extended stays in London and New York. In these years she worked to establish her reputation as a writer who dealt with concerns more universal than the regional inspiration of the desert. In particular, women's concerns of the era framed her work. In both Europe and the U.S., suffragists fought for the right to vote; American women's right to head to the polls was finally established by the Nineteenth Amendment in 1920. New York was also the center of a debate about birth control, sparked when Margaret Sanger tried to open a women's health clinic there in 1916, only to have it closed on grounds of "obscenity". Austin worked for both of these causes, but her literary efforts focused more on the spiritual and artistic needs of women's lives. *A Woman of Genius*, published in 1912, portrayed a woman who, like Austin, struggled to achieve both marital happiness and a creative career.

Austin found that even when she lived and traveled elsewhere, her heart lay in the Southwest. She continued to campaign on behalf of water issues and Native American rights. In 1922, for example, she joined other writers and artists in raising opposition to legislation known as the Bursum Bill, that would deprive Native Americans in New Mexico of their land. This campaign was part of a larger cultural interest called primitivism, in which Americans' interest in the artistic traditions of Native Americans led them to question federal policies regarding education, land, and assimilation. One of Austin's New York friends, writer and arts patron Mabel Dodge Luhan,

# LITERARY AND HISTORICAL CONTEMPORARIES

Austin's famous contemporaries include:

**Gertrude Bonnin** (1876–1938): Bonnin, also known as Zitkala-Sa, was a Sioux woman who published essays about her struggles to balance her Native American identity and upbringing with the education she acquired in assimilation-oriented schools. She became one of the leaders of the "Pan-Indian" Movement of the 1920s and 1930s, lobbying on behalf of the concerns of Native American women.

**Ernest Hemingway** (1899–1961) After a conventional Midwestern upbringing, Hemingway witnessed the horrors unleashed by World War I. Trained as a journalist, he became a novelist known for his stark prose and bleak fiction, often profiling characters who sought refuge from modern life in wilderness or exotic cultures.

**Mabel Dodge Luhan** (1879–1962): Raised in a wealthy family, Luhan abandoned her conventional New York society life in the interest of pursuing a modern one. After living in Italy and Greenwich Village, Luhan moved to Taos, New Mexico, where she married her fourth husband, Antonio Lujan. Inspired by Native American culture, she wrote memoirs describing her efforts to lure other writers and artists to the Southwest.

**John Muir** (1838–1914): Born in Scotland, Muir immigrated to the United States as a small child. Raised in the Midwest, he was struck by the grandeur of California's Yosemite Valley when he first visited it as a young man. He became one of the nation's leading conservationists, founding the Sierra Club in 1892.

**Frances Willard** (1839–1898): Trained as a teacher, Willard rose to national prominence as the head of the Woman's Christian Temperance Union, an organization she led from 1879 until her death. Under her leadership, the organization expanded its efforts at reform from temperance to suffrage.

invited Austin to experience New Mexican culture for herself at the home Luhan had built near Taos.

*A New Home in New Mexico* Austin eventually decided to move to New Mexico herself. Like Luhan, she felt the multicultural desert environment she found there could be a new center for American culture. They took part in a movement that emerged from larger trends in American modernism, a desire to rethink culture and art by casting off European traditions and by seeking inspiration in cultures that had once been considered less advanced. Austin continued the work she had begun in the California desert, that of not only trying to interest Americans in the Southwest but changing their attitudes about culture and art in the process. Painter Georgia

O'Keeffe, another member of this circle, was also drawn to the possibilities of this environment, where she also eventually settled.

Austin began building a house in Santa Fe in 1924, naming it *Casa Querida* (Beloved House). From this home she continued her advocacy of causes ranging from speaking on behalf of feminism to preserving Spanish colonial arts. She also continued to write and publish. Her autobiography, *Earth Horizon*, published in 1932, won critical praise as well as readers, in part because Austin's long and eventful life had put her in touch with so many notable people and trends. Living from the 1860s to the 1930s meant that her life spanned an era of great change in American history. America had become a leading nation, dominated by industry and cities swelling with the population gained by the immigration surges of the 1890s. Austin, who died in 1934 of a brain hemorrhage, challenged readers to keep up with modernity by asking them to rethink how they thought about land and culture.

## Works in Literary Context

While not typically considered a modernist, Austin does fit into a generation of writers whose works broke new, modern ground by questioning the ideals of the nineteenth century. Though she would write about how her style had been influenced by American Indian art forms, for the most part, her style of writing remained fairly conventional. Where she did break from the past was in the way she wrote about biological and cultural aspects of the environment simultaneously, as well as in the way she expressed women's concerns of her era. It is for these reasons that she is considered important by contemporary readers.

*Regionalism* Austin's writings about life in the desert show the influence of earlier nineteenth-century writers like Henry David Thoreau, who documented his life at Walden Pond, and Sarah Orne Jewett, who wrote about the Maine woods. Austin shifted readers' attention to the Southwestern desert, showing them in both prose and fiction how an environment some in the East might consider lifeless actually played host not only to amazing natural processes, but also a distinct and multicultural history of settlers. She challenged readers to re-think how they thought about the environment by crafting intimate portraits of the people, especially Native Americans, who made the desert home.

*Feminism* Austin grew up in the kind of world described in women's literary texts like Louisa May Alcott's *Little Women*, which advocated the message that women best served society through moral influence and submissive family roles. However, like Jo, the main character in that novel, Austin grew up wanting something different for herself, and her writing shows the impact of her own struggle to break away from conventional femininity. Like Charlotte Perkins Gilman, one of her contemporaries, Austin wrote fiction in which women struggled to assert themselves as individuals and artists in a world that still prized them most as wives and mothers.

## Works in Critical Context

Austin, though popular with her contemporaries and of interest to recent literary scholars, nevertheless has had a mixed critical reputation. In part, this unevenness results from her large output. Austin wrote at a fast pace about many different topics, and no matter the subject, she considered herself an expert. When reviewing the thus-far published works of Mary Austin in 1923, literary critic Carl Van Doren wrote that "it may be that what Mrs. Austin lacks is the ability to focus her diffused powers and interests, however great, within a necessarily narrow field."

*Desert Culture*   The desert and its culture emerged as one of the most successful themes, in critics' eyes, of Austin's work. For this reason, her first book continues to be considered by many as her best. *The Land of Little Rain* modernized the spiritual outlook on nature held in previous years by popular Transcendentalist writers such as Ralph Waldo Emerson and Henry David Thoreau, riveting attention on the many layers of life sustained by the desert. "What makes it more than a California classic, truly an American classic, is its fidelity to the landscape and lore of its region," wrote critic Lawrence Clark Powell in 1971. "Here we see a perfect conjunction of life, landscape, and literature."

Austin's autobiography, *Earth Horizon*, published near the end of her life, also ranks among her most critically successful. Her telling of her life story shows how place and identity wove together in her own life, with a particular emphasis on how moving to the Southwest enhanced her desire to redefine womanhood. As Vera Norwood wrote in 1982, Austin defined the desert as unconventionally feminine, defined by "self-sufficiency and an unwillingness to be molded by the needs of men, rather than, to mold men to her needs." This theme also emerges strongly in *A Woman of Genius*, but that book's Eastern setting struck critics less forcefully than Austin's own story.

Critics remain divided about how all of Austin's books characterize her relationship to Native Americans: while her sympathy and admiration for indigenous traditions emerges strongly, what remains unclear is whether her efforts presume to know more about other cultures than is ethically acceptable to readers today. "Whether or not she is successful in accurately portraying their experiences," critic Jennie Camp wrote, in 2005 of Austin's efforts to re-tell Indian stories, her efforts made it possible "for varied cultures to come together" because of Austin's desire to achieve "multicultural empathy."

## Responses to Literature

1. Write a paper in which you compare Austin's portrayal of the desert wilderness to an earlier portrayal

---

## COMMON HUMAN EXPERIENCE

Both when she was first published as well as today, readers turned to Austin's writing because both the author's own story and the ones she told dealt with an enduring and appealing theme: women's search for identity in environments of physical and spiritual wilderness.

*The Sovereignty & Goodness of God* (1682), a captivity narrative by Mary Rowlandson. The first American best-seller, Rowlandson's captivity narrative told the harrowing tale of her time in captivity during King Philip's War, when Native Americans resisted British colonists' encroachments upon their land. Rowlandson describes how the traumatic experience and her eventual release affirmed her Christian faith.

*O Pioneers!* (1913), a novel by Willa Cather. Alexandra Bergson, the heroine of this novel, is the daughter of Swedish immigrants who transforms a bleak Midwestern homestead into a thriving, prosperous farm after her father's death. Her brothers' resentment and her difficulty in finding romance testify to the costs ambitious women faced in the era.

*The Bean Trees* (1988), a novel by Barbara Kingsolver. The bestselling author's first novel narrates the adventures of Taylor Greer, an unconventional heroine who makes her way from Kentucky to Arizona in search of a better life. Though she wants to be independent, becoming a foster mother to a Cherokee child and a friend to Guatemalan refugees ultimately deepens her sense of community responsibility.

*The Road from Coorain* (1989), a memoir by Jill Ker Conway. This autobiography describes Conway's 1930s and 1940s childhood on a remote Australian sheep ranch. Conway pursued an education that would eventually lead her to a Ph.D. in History from Harvard University and a job as the first woman president of Smith College.

---

of nature written by a Puritan writer (such as Mary Rowlandson) or a Transcendentalist (such as Thoreau), or a later one written by a contemporary nature writer (such as Annie Dillard, Terry Tempest Williams, or Wendell Berry). How does Austin's approach both resemble and differ from these earlier and later efforts to represent nature?

2. One of the reasons Austin moved to New Mexico was that she felt that Spanish and Native American traditions remained so strong in the area, and she wanted to help preserve them. Tourism grew rapidly in the area during the era and continues to be an important industry in New Mexico. After reading

---

some of Mary Austin's writings about her adopted home state, use your library or the Internet to see how travel articles depict the state today. How do you think Austin would feel about tourism in New Mexico?

3. Two of the most famous novels published about New Mexico since Austin's era are by Native American writers. N. Scott Momaday published *House Made of Dawn* in 1968, and Leslie Marmon Silko published *Ceremony* in 1977. Read one of these novels and consider how their portrayal of the lives of twentieth-century Native Americans differs from Austin's work.

4. How much has changed in American women's lives since the passage of the Nineteenth Amendment in 1920? Do the obstacles that Austin described still affect women's efforts to combine careers with family life? Interview women from different generations to see how they perceive their lives in this respect.

BIBLIOGRAPHY

**Books**

Fink, Augusta. *I-Mary: A Biography of Mary Austin.* Tucson: University of Arizona Press, 1983.

Graulich, Melody and Elizabeth Klimasmith, eds. *Exploring Lost Borders: Critical Essays on Mary Austin.* Reno: University of Nevada Press, 1999.

Lanigan, Esther. *Mary Austin: Song of a Maverick.* New Haven: Yale University Press, 1989.

Norwood, Vera. *Made from This Earth: American Women and Nature.* Chapel Hill: University of North Carolina Press, 1993.

Powell, Lawrence Clark. "Mary Austin: The Land of Little Rain." In *California Classics: The Creative Literature of the Golden State.* 1971. Reprint by Capra Press, 1982. 44–52.

Reed, Maureen. *A Woman's Place: Women Writing New Mexico.* Albuquerque: University of New Mexico Press, 2005.

**Periodicals**

Jennie, Camp A. Review of *One-Smoke Stories. The Rocky Mountain Review of Language and Literature* 59.1 (Spring 2005): 71–4.

Langlois, Karen S. "A Fresh Voice from the West: Mary Austin, California, and American Literary Magazines, 1892-1910." *California History* 64 (Spring 1990): 22–35.

Norwood, Vera. "The Photographer and the Naturalist: Laura Gilpin and Mary Austin in the Southwest." *Journal of American Culture* 5.2 (Summer 1982): 1–28.

Van Doren, Carl. "Mary Austin: Discoverer and Prophet." *The Century.* 7.1 (Nov. 1923): 151–156.

# Avi

BORN: *1937, New York, New York*

NATIONALITY: *American*

GENRE: *Fiction*

MAJOR WORKS:

*The True Confessions of Charlotte Doyle* (1990)

*Nothing but the Truth* (1991)

*Crispin: The Cross of Lead* (2002)

## Overview

Edward Wortis is well known to critics, teachers, parents, and particularly to young readers by his pen name "Avi." His many award-winning books, which include *The True Confessions of Charlotte Doyle*, *Nothing but the Truth*, and the Newbery Award–winning *Crispin: The Cross of Lead*, consist of a wide variety of genres, including mysteries, adventure yarns, historical fiction, supernatural tales, coming-of-age novels, and comic stories.

## Works in Biographical and Historical Context

***Hurdles to Learning*** Born in New York City in 1937 and raised in Boston, Avi grew up in an artistic environment.

Avi Wortis    *AP Images.*

His great-grandparents and a grandmother were writers, two uncles were painters, and both parents wrote. His family was also politically active, its members aligning themselves with the civil rights movement—1950s and 1960s reforms to end racial discrimination against African Americans—and other radical movements. Politics and art led to abundant intellectual stimulation and lively family discussion in Avi's home. The author once explained that his extended family comprised "a very strong art community and...there was always a kind of uproarious sense of debate. It was all a very affectionate sharing of ideas—arguing, but not arguing in anger, arguing about ideas."

This early stimulation at home may have prepared Avi for challenges to come in his education. Although he was an avid reader as a child, difficulties in writing eventually caused him to flunk out of one school. He later learned that he has a dysfunction known as dysgraphia, a marginal impairment in his writing abilities that causes him to reverse letters or misspell words. "One of my aunts said I could spell a four letter word wrong five ways," he once commented. "In a school environment, I was perceived as being sloppy and erratic, and not paying attention." Despite constant criticism at school, Avi kept writing and he credits his family's emphasis on the arts for his perseverance.

The first step on Avi's course to writing professionally was reading: everything from comic books and science magazines to histories, plays, and novels. Despite the skepticism of his teachers, he decided to make a career of writing while still in high school. Between his junior and senior years, his parents hired a tutor to work with him on his writing skills. According to Avi, "That summer I met every day with a wonderful teacher who not only taught me writing basics, but also instilled in me the conviction that I wanted to be a writer myself."

***University Prose*** Attending Antioch University, Avi enrolled in playwriting rather than English courses. Following graduation from the University of Wisconsin–Madison, he worked at a variety of jobs and in 1963 was briefly married to a weaver, Joan Gabriner. Avi continued his graduate education at Columbia University where he studied library science and graduated in 1964. He took a job in the theater collection of the New York Public library. This began his twenty-four-year career as a librarian. Avi's determination to be a writer never flagged during this time. He married Coppelia Kahn, a professor of English with whom he had two sons. After he had written nearly eight hundred pages of his "great American novel," an odd series of events turned his attention toward children's literature. It all began with telling stories to his two sons. "My oldest would tell me what the story should be about—he would invent stuff, a story about a glass of water and so forth. It became a game."

***Getting Published*** Along with telling stories, Avi was a doodler, and drew pictures for fun. A friend who was writing a children's book, having seen his drawings,

wanted Avi to provide illustrations. When the friend took the book with Avi's illustrations to a publisher, the book was rejected, but Avi was asked to illustrate other children's books. Arguing with the publisher that he was a writer and not an artist, he submitted several stories that were turned down. But, seven publishers later, Doubleday accepted his first work for publication. *Things That Sometimes Happen: Very Short Stories for Very Young Readers*, was published—although without Avi's artwork—in 1970.

***Popular Plots*** Avi achieved great success with historical novels aimed at young readers. These works include *Captain Grey* (1977), *Night Journeys* (1979), and *Encounter at Easton* (1980). Avi even won the Scott O'Dell Historical Fiction Award for children for his novel *The Fighting Ground* (1984). He continued writing successful stories based on historical events, including the Newbery Award–winning *Crispin: The Cross of Lead*, or on real historical figures, as in *The Man Who Was Poe* (1989).

Though very successful with his historical novels, Avi continued publication of contemporary stories with narratives mixing comic adventures with more serious examinations "of the darker layers of imaginative experience." Avi once commented on his 1992 Newbery Honor novel *Nothing but the Truth* that he got the idea for the structure of this contemporary novel from a form of theater that arose in the 1930s called "Living Newspapers"—

## COMMON HUMAN EXPERIENCE

Avi's fiction chronicles life and characters adventuring among the historical, contemporary and the creature worlds. Some other works of historical adventure are:

*The Call of the Wild* (1903), a novel by Jack London. This classic tale is told from the perspective of a domesticated dog whose primordial instincts return when he has the misfortune to become a sled dog in the Yukon during the Alaska Gold Rush of the late 1800s.

*The Last Silk Dress* (1971), a historical novel by Ann Rinaldi. Set during the American Civil War, this work follows the adventures of Susan as she finds a way to help the Confederate Army and uncovers a series of mysterious family secrets.

*Chain of Fire* (1990), a novel by Beverly Naidoo. This is the story of the inhabitants of a black South African town who resist the white government's plan for their relocation.

*Treasure Island* (1883), a novel by Robert Louis Stevenson. This is a classic tale of adventure with pirates, treasure maps, and a treacherous quest for buried gold, silver and weapons.

*Dinosaurs Before Dark* (1992), a children's novel by Mary Pope Osborne. The first in the Magic Tree House series, which chronicles the time travel adventures of a brother and sister.

dramatizations of issues and problems confronting American society presented through a "hodge podge" of document readings and dialogues.

***Quirky and Fun*** In *Publishers Weekly* a contributor describes *The Mayor of Central Park* (2003) as "an over-the-top romp" and added that Avi's "tough-talking prose would do an old gangster movie proud." Avi's captivating and oft-described "quirky" stories have continued unabated with *The Book Without Words: A Fable of Medieval Magic* (2005), *Crispin: At the Edge of the World* (2006), *The Traitors' Gate* (2007), *Iron Thunder* (2007), and *The Seer of Shadows* (2008). In his book *A Beginning, a Muddle and an End* (2008), Avi engages in every manner of wordplay. In this escapade the protagonists learn, as Avi's prolific writing has exemplified, that creating and imagining your own adventures is much more fun and more rewarding than searching for adventure.

### Works in Literary Context

Avi's fiction is acclaimed by critics for its uniqueness and wit. Critic Claire Rosser lauds Avi as "the master of a good story that takes young readers into another historical era." Avi's works encompass historical narratives as well as contemporary stories written in his characteristic quirky style that abounds with puns, wit and charming protagonists. While his prose largely has a traditional structure, there are occasions where he experiments with point of view and other style elements. For example, in *Hard Gold: The Colorado Gold Rush of 1859* (2008), the chapters follow diary entries that narrate a wagon-train adventure and "add much to the understanding of an earlier way of life," according to Debra Banna of *School Library Journal.*

***Historical Novels*** Avi has written many different forms of the novel. Several of his early works, including *Captain Grey*, *Night Journeys*, and *Encounter at Easton*, are set in colonial America. He quickly earned a reputation as a historical novelist and *The Fighting Ground* won the Scott O'Dell Historical Fiction Award for children.

*The Man Who Was Poe* is Avi's fictionalized portrait of nineteenth-century writer Edgar Allan Poe that intertwines fiction and history on several levels. In another unique twist on the convention of historical novels, *The True Confessions of Charlotte Doyle* presents the unlikely story of a very proper thirteen-year-old girl who, as the sole passenger and only female on a trans-Atlantic ship in 1832, becomes involved in a mutiny at sea. Another of Avi's highly lauded historical novels, the Newbery Award–winning *Crispin: The Cross of Lead*, is set in England during the fourteenth century, as poverty, a greedy aristocracy, and the Black Plague ravage the country.

"The historical novel is a curious construction," Avi once commented. "It represents history but it's not truly accurate. It's a style." He elaborates in an interview with Jim Roginski in *Behind the Covers*: "Somewhere along the line, I can't explain where, I developed an understanding of history not as fact but as story." And Avi's historical tales are fascinating stories of riveting events and people enlivened by his "keen sense of time and place," as his writing is described in *School Library Journal.*

***Writing from Various Points of View*** In *Nothing but the Truth*, Avi offers an unusual perspective as the story is without a narrator; rather, its tale is related through bits of evidence such as school memos, diaries and newspaper articles. Another book, *Poppy* (1995), which received a Boston Globe-Horn Book Award in 1996, tells a story from the point of view of two deer mice, Ragweed and Poppy, who are about to marry when the self-proclaimed king of Dimwood Forest—an owl named Mr. Ocax—eats Ragweed, supposedly as punishment for neglecting to seek his permission to marry. Similarly, *The Good Dog* (2001), a tale for younger readers, is told from the point of view of a malamute named McKinley.

### Works in Critical Context

Avi's writing has been applauded for its storyteller's ease with blending his themes of self-discovery, honesty and courage into drama, history, and mystery in a unique and sincere way. Critics and readers alike admire the unique vision that Avi brings to his reading audience. Publication of *The True Confessions of Charlotte Doyle* won Avi his first Newbery honor in 1991. Avi won additional Newbery honors in 1992 and 2003, and his books continue to be popular with young readers. Anita Moss states of his writing, "Avi deserves credit for his sensitivity and humorous portrayals of adolescent characters, his willingness to question received values and the ability to recreate the ambience of historical periods."

***The True Confessions of Charlotte Doyle*** *School Library Journal* terms this historical novel "a crackling good yarn." Bloom and Mercier, in their book on Avi, conclude that this story "posits yet a more sophisticated understanding of the adolescent's journey toward the home of self." According to *Publishers Weekly*, "[A]wash with shipboard activity, intense feelings, and a keen sense of time and place, the story is a throwback to good old-fashioned adventure yarns on the high seas."

***Crispin: The Cross of Lead*** Avi's *Crispin: The Cross of Lead* (2002) "introduces some of his most unforgettable characters," according to *Booklist* contributor Ilene Cooper. Critic Hazel Rochman declares that the author "builds an impressive backdrop for his arresting characters." "Avi's plot is engineered for maximum thrills, with twists, turns and treachery aplenty," notes a *Publishers Weekly* contributor, adding that the "compellingly drawn" friendship between the boy and the old juggler gives the book its emotional heart.

## Responses to Literature

1. In *Nothing but the Truth*, we follow the story of the media frenzy surrounding Philip and his teacher. Give three examples from the story that demonstrate conflicting points of view. What are the sources used by the author to express these perspectives? What is the impact of telling a story through a variety of sources?

2. Read *The True Confessions of Charlotte Doyle*. How does Charlotte's life change when she leaves the boarding school to go aboard the ship? What are some of the gender restrictions that limit her? How is she freed from those?

3. Avi's *Crispin: The Cross of Lead* is a story of a young boy finding his place in the world amid the backdrop

of England's peasant revolt of 1381. In what ways does this book chronicle social classes? Relate specific examples from the book of how peasants are treated. Where might these biases toward social classes exist in contemporary society?

### BIBLIOGRAPHY

**Books**

Avi. *The Fighting Ground*. Philadelphia.: Lippincott, 1984.

Bloom, Susan P., Mercier, Cathryn M. *Presenting Avi.* New York: Simon & Schuster Macmillan, 1997.

Chevalier, Tracy, Ed. *Twentieth-Century Children's Writers* Detroit: St. James's Press, 1986, pp. 45–46.

Lynch-Brown, Carol and Carl Tomlinson. *Essentials of Young Adult Literature*. Boston: Pearson, 2005, pp. 25, 27, 85–93.

Lynn, Ruth Nadelman. *Fantasy Literature for Children and Young Adults*. New Providence, N.J.: Bowker, 1995, p. 615.

Sutherland, Zena. *Children and Books*. Glenview, Ill.: Scott Foresman, 1986, p. 403.

Roginski, Jim. *Behind the Covers: Interviews with Authors and Illustrators of Books for Children and Young Adults*. Westport, Conn.: Libraries Unlimited, 1985, pp. 33–41.

**Periodicals**

Cooper, Ilene. Review of *Crispin: The Cross of Lead*. *Booklist* (May 15, 2002): 1604.

Engberg, Gillian. Review of "Things That Sometimes Happen." *Booklist* (October 1, 2002): 332.

Miles, Betty. "School Visits: The Author's Viewpoint." *School Library Journal* (October 1987): 124.

Review of *Nothing but the Truth. Publishers Weekly* (September 6, 1991): 105.

Review of *Crispin. Publishers Weekly* (June 3, 2002): 88.

Review of *Things That Sometimes Happen. Publishers Weekly* (September 30, 2002): 70.

Rochman, Hazel. "A Conversation with Avi." *Booklist* (January 15, 1992): 930.

Rosser, Claire. "Hard gold; the Colorado Gold Rush of 1859." *Kliatt* 42.5 (September 2008): 6–7.

**Web Sites**

*Avi.* Retrieved November 27, 2008, from www.avi-writer.com/.

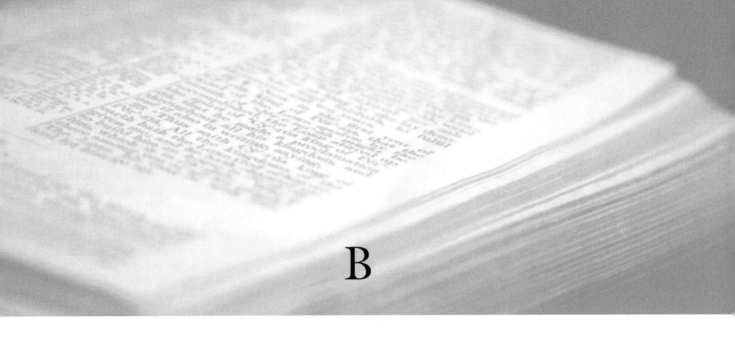

# B

## Jimmy Santiago Baca

BORN: *1952, New Mexico*

NATIONALITY: *American*

GENRE: *Poetry, nonfiction*

MAJOR WORKS:

*Immigrants in Our Own Land: Poems* (1979)

*Martin and Meditations on the South Valley*
   (1987)

### Overview

Jimmy Santiago Baca is recognized as a leading figure in contemporary Hispanic literature and has been praised for the rich imagery and lyricism of his poetry. An ex-convict who taught himself to read while in prison, he writes of spiritual rebirth and triumph over tragedy—unlike many "prison writers" whose works teem with rage and desolation. Baca's poetry has garnered praise for the insight it offers into the experience of Hispanic and Amerindian peoples.

### Works in Biographical and Historical Context

*Life on the Street and in Prison* A Mestizo—or mixed-race descendant—of Chicano and Apache descent, Jimmy Santiago Baca was born to a poor family in New Mexico in 1952. Baca was abandoned by his parents at the age of two and, after a brief stay with a grandparent, was placed in a New Mexico orphanage. He fled the orphanage at age eleven and spent most of his teen years on the streets of Albuquerque. In 1972 Baca was convicted on a narcotics charge and sentenced to five years in an Arizona maximum-security prison.

Baca's experience in federal prison was marked by a succession of lockdowns, humiliations, confrontations with racist inmates, and beatings by prison guards, all of which would push him to the lowest point of his life. Recalcitrant behavior earned him additional time on his sentence, as well as electric shock treatments and nearly four years in solitary confinement. The humiliations he lived through in prison—as well as the personal spiritual transformation that followed them—would later become the primary subject of his poetry. Of these experiences, he says, "Nothing was being nourished to discover and create, and I finally destroyed myself in this huge cemetery called the prisons of America. When I went to prison I no longer existed. I was a non-entity." During the latter half of his prison sentence, however, Baca changed his approach toward his confinement: instead of cultivating anger, he focused on healing the hurt he had experienced as a child and young adult. Baca began a prolonged process of self-discovery and education, that showed him that language could become a vehicle for bringing order to the chaos that surrounded him. In prison Baca became fully literate in both Spanish and English, immersing himself in the world of books.

Initially drawn to poetry, Baca began to read the work of diverse poets. While teaching himself Spanish, he read the works of Pablo Neruda, Juan Ramón Jiménez, and Federico García Lorca; in English he read William Wordsworth, Mary Baker, Lawrence Ferlinghetti, Robert Frost, Ezra Pound, Walt Whitman, Denise Levertov, and Allen Ginsberg. He has explained: "I was tired of being treated like an animal. I wanted to learn how to read and to write and to understand. . . . The only way of transcending was through language and understanding." Baca began writing his own poetry and, encouraged by a fellow inmate, sent a sample of his work to *Mother Jones* magazine. Not only were these poems accepted for publication, but the journal's poetry editor, Denise Levertov, assisted Baca in finding a publisher for his first collection of poetry, *Immigrants in Our Own Land* (1979). *Immigrants* was followed by two more collections, *Swords of Darkness* (1981) and *What's Happening* (1982).

*Transition* After leaving prison in the late 1980s, Baca spent some time in North Carolina before returning to New Mexico, where he then spent some years living in

Jimmy Santiago Baca    *Baca, Jimmy Santiago, photograph. AP Images.*

Albuquerque working odd jobs as a night watchman, janitor, and laborer, and redirected his life through what was to be a sustained period of bittersweet events. During these years Baca fought and eventually overcame bouts of drug addiction and alcoholism. He would eventually view marriage and family as vital and central in providing meaning to his life. Indeed he attributes much of his success to the love and support of his wife, Beatrice, and his children. After a period of severe spiritual crisis, Baca once again found solace in the writing of poetry. Baca's fourth book, *Martin and Meditations on the South Valley* (1987), a semiautobiographical work that critics termed a novel in verse, won the prestigious American Book Award from the Before Columbus Foundation in 1988. The subject matter of the collection reflects the long period of transition and uncertainty Baca experienced during the eight-year hiatus between the publication of *Immigrants* and that of *Martin and Meditations on the South Valley*. These years were filled with restless, unresolved dilemmas and ongoing struggles in his personal life. Baca explains that, although he continued to publish minor works, he had all but abandoned poetry and writing:

> I was trying to figure out whether I was going to live in prison forever or whether I could live in this world. I wanted to go back to prison, 'cause I couldn't live in this world and I was bored and I couldn't deal with the world out here.

***Further Success and Activism***    After the success of *Martin and Meditations on the South Valley*, Baca began writing prolifically. In 1988 he published *Black Mesa Poems*, for which he earned the Wallace Stevens Poetry Award and the National Hispanic Heritage Award. He has also published a collection of autobiographical essays titled *Working in the Dark: Reflections of a Poet in the Barrio* (1992). Baca has been poet in residence at both Yale University and the University of California at Berkeley, but he has rejected many further offers to lecture and

teach, remaining primarily on his farm in Albuquerque with his wife and children.

While Baca continues to write poetry and teach and lecture at colleges, he also works with people in the inner city who face the same persecution he faced as an abandoned teenager. He is the founder of a nonprofit grassroots cooperative for inner-city youth called Black Mesa Enterprises. He runs a creative writing workshop with steelworkers, and the product of that class is an anthology called *The Heat*. When Barbara Stahura of the *Progressive* asked him if the reason he works with gang members, convicts, and illiterate adults is because of his own empowerment through language, he responded,

> Damn right. Right into the barrios and the projects and the poor white areas. They have such a reverence for language. They can't believe the language can carry so much power, and once they get hold of that, they begin to unteach what they were taught about who they are. If they were taught to be racist or violent, language has this amazing ability to unteach all that, and make them question it. It gives them back their power toward regaining their humanity. That's why I do it.

## Works in Literary Context

***Racial and Cultural Heritage***    Baca's poetry identifies and explores the Chicano Mestizo experience in the American Southwest, fusing issues of cultural heritage to the more universal theme of an individual's painful search for identity and meaning. The bold poetic images for which he is noted are not the collected perceptions of a large ethnic group but the sharp vision of a single Mestizo struggling to find himself. Critic Scott Slovic has written that "to read Jimmy Santiago Baca's poetry is to tramp across the uneven terrain of human experience, sometimes lulled by the everydayness of work or relationships, and then dazzled by a flood of emotion or vibrant observation." In *Immigrants in Our Own Land*, Baca vividly conveys the physical and mental barriers of prison life and identifies how racial prejudice influences the individual's sense of isolation; in the poems comprising the later *What's Happening*, he relates his struggle to reenter a world and culture that has brought him much pain and suffering. Within these accounts, however, there resonate the broader elements of Baca's Mestizo heritage. *Martin and Meditations*, for example, explicitly links the success of the hero's self-exploration with the discovery of his ancestry. "I wanted Martin to be a real human being and let him live in this world and have a mythology that was his as well as the people's," Baca has written.

***Spiritual Transformation***    Critic A. Gabriel Melendez has cited that "Baca's poetry is to a large degree infused with elements drawn from his experiences, and ... recurrent themes of transformation, metamorphosis, and self-actualization that have accompanied the poet's own trajectory as an individual and a writer." Attuned to real-life circumstances, each of Baca's books represents a concrete step in the process of rebuilding his life from the point of nonexistence that he associates with the years spent in prison. Thus each book in turn marks a step in Baca's determination to move his personal and poetic endeavor toward full realization. Baca's chief concern in *Immigrants in Our Own Land*, for example, is regaining a sense of self, which is obscured by the prison system's ability to strip the individual of dignity and self-worth.

*Family and Community*   Baca's efforts to reconstruct his own psyche and sense of identity immediately move him to reflect upon his connection to family and community. In *Immigrants*, for example, Baca seeks a connection to the collective meaning and past of his ancestors. His search for personal meaning emerges in *Immigrants* as an ever-widening series of connections that lead him to an individual and collective examination of his incarceration. In *Martin*, Baca points toward the love and support of family as an invaluable component of an individual's spiritual transformation.

## Works in Critical Context

According to critic A. Gabriel Melendez, Jimmy Santiago Baca "has come to the forefront as one of the most widely read and recognized Chicano poets working today." Melendez also notes that one of Baca's most important accomplishments was "to widen the critical attention directed by mainstream critics and publishers toward his own work and that of other Chicano writers."

*Immigrants in Our Own Land*   Baca's first major collection, *Immigrants in Our Own Land* appeared in 1979. The poems, highlighting the splendor of human existence amid the desolate surroundings of prison life, met with rave reviews. Critics have repeatedly applauded Baca's forthright style and the passion he generates in his poetry. Marion Taylor called Baca's poems "astonishingly beautiful" for their "celebration of the human spirit in extreme situations." Denise Levertov found that "his work is rich in image and music, full of abundant energy and love of life even when describing the brutal and tragic." Writing in the *American Book Review*, renowned Hispanic writer Ron Arias commends the poet's skill and versatility: "At times [Baca] can be terse, narrowly focused, directly to the point. . . . Other times he can resemble an exuberant Walt Whitman in the long-lined rhythm and sweep of his emotions—expansive, wordy, even conversational." He concludes that Baca "is a freshly aggressive poet of many abilities. . . . His is a gifted, young vision, and judging from this collection, I get the feeling he is just warming up. I look forward to more." Melendez observed that the publication of *Immigrants in Our Own Land* "established Baca's potential as a serious and prolific new voice on the poetry scene."

## LITERARY AND HISTORICAL CONTEMPORARIES

Jimmy Santiago Baca's famous contemporaries include:

**Michel Foucault** (1924–1984): French philosopher and historian Michel Foucault became an activist for the prison reform movement and was the author of *Discipline and Punish* (1975), which examined the balance of power in prison systems.
**Sandra Cisneros** (1954–): Cisneros is a Latina novelist and poet best known for her book *The House on Mango Street* (1984).
**Gary Soto** (1952–): Soto is a Latino poet from California who focuses his work on the working-class Mexican American experience.
**Luis Echeverría Álvarez** (1922–): Echeverría served as president of Mexico from 1970 to 1976. During his time in office he implemented various populist social and economic reforms, including nationalizing industries and seizing private lands to be redistributed to peasants.
**N. Scott Momaday** (1934–): Momaday, a Native American (Kiowa) writer, is credited with having brought mainstream attention to Native American literature with the publication of his Pulitzer Prize–winning work *House Made of Dawn* (1968).

*Martin and Meditations on the South Valley*   Baca's next work, *Martin and Meditations on the South Valley*, met with outstanding success, earning Baca the American Book Award for poetry. A semiautobiographical work that critics termed a novel in verse, the book chronicles the life of Martin, an orphaned "detribalized" Apache who sojourns across the United States in search of permanence and meaning in his life. Intended to convey the sometimes traumatic Chicano experience in America, *Martin and Meditations* details the protagonist's sense of abandonment and displacement. "With *Martin and Meditations on the South Valley*," A. Gabriel Melendez suggests, "Baca brings to closure that phase of his poetry that deals with loss, dejection, a searching for identity, and a sense of belonging. . . . Absent are the self-destructive tendencies that typified Baca's earlier years of searching and wandering."

Critics found much to praise in *Martin and Meditations on the South Valley*. While several recognized the work as a forceful sociological and cultural document, Liam Rector in the *Hudson Review* also deems the poetry volume "a book of great complicity, maturity, and finally responsibility. . . . It is a contemporary hero tale." Ron Arias has expressed admiration for Baca's impassioned writings, comparing his inventiveness to that of a jazz musician: "Whether or not the melody or train of images

## COMMON HUMAN EXPERIENCE

In almost all his books, Jimmy Santiago Baca draws upon his experiences in prison as an inspiration for his poetry. Other works that seek to capture and explore both the physical and spiritual conditions of prison inmates include:

*The Autobiography of Malcolm X* (1965), a book by Malcolm X and Alex Haley. Haley, author of the celebrated novel *Roots*, based this work on a series of interviews he conducted with Malcolm X just before the activist's death in 1965. In 1992 the book was adapted into an award-winning film by Spike Lee.

*The Gulag Archipelago* (1973), a book by Aleksandr Solzhenitsyn. This massive work of nonfiction details the history of Soviet labor camps as well as the author's experience as a prisoner of the state; it was not officially published in the Soviet Union until sixteen years after it had been published elsewhere.

*In the Belly of the Beast* (1981), a collection of letters written by Jack Henry Abbott to Norman Mailer. This volume became a popular best seller and raised public awareness about prison conditions.

*The Bridge on the River Kwai* (1957), a film directed by David Lean, starring Alec Guinness and William Holden. This film dramatizes the interactions between Japanese military officials and their British captives in a prisoner-of-war camp during World War II.

works as a unified piece with a clear theme is of secondary importance to the journey itself, a journey of discovery unbound by prison walls and fences."

### Responses to Literature

1. Although Baca's works describe the conditions of the prison system, his poems tend to emphasize personal spiritual transformation rather than calling for the reform of the prison system. Compare Baca's works to others that examine life in prison, for example the book *In the Belly of the Beast*. How do the themes and subject matter of Baca's poems compare to other works in the prison writing genre? What similarities and differences do you note?

2. Race plays a crucial role in the poems of Jimmy Santiago Baca, both in terms of the speaker's identity and in his treatment within the prison system. Review the poems in *Immigrants in Our Own Land* and *Martin and Meditations on the South Valley*. How does race and racial heritage affect the experience of the speaker and those around him? Outline the author's relationship to his racial identity, paying particular attention to how it changes over time.

3. Baca has stated that while in prison he read and was influenced by nineteenth-century American writers such as Ralph Waldo Emerson and Henry David Thoreau. Research these writers, particularly their relationships to the concepts of self-reliance and civil disobedience. Construct an essay in which you explore their influence on Baca's poems.

BIBLIOGRAPHY

**Books**

Levertov, Denise. Afterword to Baca's *What's Happening*. Willimantic, Conn.: Curbstone, 1982.
————. Introduction to Baca's *Martin and Meditations on the South Valley*. New York: New Directions, 1987.

**Periodicals**

Arias, Ron. Review of *Immigrants in Our Own Land: Poems. American Book Review* (January 1982): 11–12.
Krier, Beth Ann. "Baca: A Poet Emerges from Prison of His Past." *Los Angeles Times*, February 15, 1989.
Rector, Liam. Review of *Martin and Meditations on the South Valley. Hudson Review* (Summer 1989): 393–400.

# ✺ Russell Baker

BORN: *1925, Loudoun, Virginia*

NATIONALITY: *American*

GENRE: *Journalism, nonfiction*

MAJOR WORKS:

The "Observer" newspaper column (1962–)
*Growing Up* (1982)
*The Good Times* (1989)

## Overview

Russell Baker is a highly regarded Pulitzer Prize–winning newspaper columnist and humorist. While serving on the Washington bureau of the *New York Times* during the mid-1950s and early 1960s, Baker earned recognition for his wry commentaries on federal bureaucracy. Since 1962, Baker has written the "Observer" column in the *Times*. The essays in this column satirize such issues as politics, the economy, and popular culture. He has also published several highly popular memoirs. Baker is especially praised for his insight into the human condition, particularly the daily problems of ordinary people.

## Works in Biographical and Historical Context

*Growing Up During the Great Depression* American humorist Russell Baker was born in 1925 in Loudoun, Virginia. His father, a blue-collar laborer fond of

Russell Baker    *Dirck Halstead / Time & Life Pictures / Getty Images*

alcohol, died in an acute diabetic coma when Baker was five. Almost simultaneously, the American stock market crashed, beginning the Great Depression that would leave millions of families—including Baker's—in desperate economic need. Baker's mother, Lucy Elizabeth, suddenly widowed and impoverished, accepted her brother's offer to live with his family in New Jersey. Before moving, Lucy left her youngest daughter, Audrey, in the care of wealthier relatives who could provide the infant with a more comfortable existence than she could. In his memoir *Growing Up* (1982), Baker bore witness to his mother's pain over this decision: "It was the only deed of her entire life for which I ever heard her express guilt." Nevertheless, throughout his life and work, Baker would express admiration for his mother's courage during the Depression, often equating her will to survive difficult times with the quintessential American spirit.

Baker's family lived off the kindness of relatives for years, finally settling in Baltimore, where Lucy eventually remarried. Baker got his first taste of journalistic life at a young age when, at his mother's insistence, he began selling copies of the *Saturday Evening Post*. Lucy exerted a strong influence over Baker's life, serving as "goad, critic, and inspiration to her son," in the words of *New York Times Book Review* critic Ward Just. Baker's mother, haunted by her life of poverty, became obsessed with the idea that her son would achieve success. "I would make something of myself," Baker wrote in *Growing Up*, "and if I lacked the grit to do it, well then she would make me make something of myself."

***Learning about Life in London***    Baker pursued this success by attending Johns Hopkins University, where he received his BA in 1947. Although he was a member of the U.S. Naval Reserve from 1943 to 1945, he did not see active duty during World War II. Hired in 1947 as a writer for the *Baltimore Sun*, Baker developed a reputation as a fast, accurate reporter and eventually earned a promotion to the post of London bureau chief. Here he witnessed the residents of London rebuild after the multiple blitzes and bombings that destroyed whole areas of the city during the war, and he chronicled the new Europe emerging in the wake of Hitler. Though Baker enjoyed London and would later cite his time there as a period during which he matured both personally and professionally, he moved on to become the *Sun*'s White House correspondent, a decision he soon regretted. Once in Washington, Baker found the work boring, the atmosphere stifling, and his writing style unappreciated. Writing in *The Good Times*, Baker acknowledged:

> I had swapped the freedom to roam one of the world's great cities and report whatever struck my fancy. And what had I got in return? A glamorous job which entitled me to sit in a confined space, listening to my colleagues breathe.

***Americana and Column-writing***    Frustrated at the *Sun*, Baker jumped at an offer to write for the *New York Times* Washington bureau, although he insisted on covering the Senate, hoping to capture the human side of the country's leaders. But in time even Congress, with its fawning politicians and controlled press briefings, proved disappointing. Recalling his dissatisfaction with the work, Baker told *Time*, "I began to wonder why, at the age of thirty-seven, I was wearing out my hams waiting for somebody to come out and lie to me." When the *Sun* attempted to regain Baker's services with the promise of a column, the *Times* promptly countered the offer with its own column, a proposal that convinced Baker to stay.

Thus, in 1962 Baker began to write the "Observer" column for which he is best known. Combining insider knowledge of politics and celebrity with modest and humorous commentary on American life, the column was instantly popular with his audience, and soon syndicated. Baker's personable portrayals of political heavyweights like John Kennedy, Lyndon Johnson, Barry Goldwater, and Richard Nixon intrigued readers; he also offered reflections on American public figures such as William Randolph Hearst, Joe DiMaggio, Marilyn Monroe, and Martin Luther King Jr. Baker also profiled some of his fellow journalists, saving his harshest criticisms for those reporters who compromised their professional

# LITERARY AND HISTORICAL CONTEMPORARIES

Russell Baker's famous contemporaries include:

**Walter Cronkite** (1916–): Cronkite was a television journalist from 1950 until 1981 and was renowned for his coverage of historical events such as the assassination of President John F. Kennedy and the Apollo 11 moon landing.

**Jack Anderson** (1922–2005): Anderson was a famous muckraking journalist best known for his "Washington Merry-Go-Round" column, which exposed scandal in government and big business.

**Richard Nixon** (1913–1994): The thirty-seventh president of the United States, Nixon resigned from office after the Watergate scandal, in which he was implicated in the cover-up of a theft from the headquarters of the National Democratic Party.

**Joe DiMaggio** (1914–1999): DiMaggio, one of the most celebrated home run hitters in major league baseball history, was the longtime star of the New York Yankees and made even more headlines by marrying movie star Marilyn Monroe in 1954.

**Barry Goldwater** (1909–1998): Goldwater was a conservative politician who would serve nearly forty years in Congress and would lose the presidential election to Democrat Lyndon B. Johnson in 1964.

integrity by letting themselves become seduced by savvy politicians.

Throughout his career, which has spanned over forty years, Baker has witnessed such political upheavals as the American civil rights movement, which sought to achieve social and legal equality for women and minorities in the 1960s and 1970s; the Vietnam War; the Watergate scandal, which would force the resignation of President Richard Nixon; and the threat of nuclear warfare in the modern age. Baker wrote often about these topics, frequently satirizing the government and its legal, economic, and military tactics. Though a great number of Baker's columns concern themselves with the dealings of pompous politicians and the muddled antics of bureaucrats, not all of the author's essays are political in nature. All manner of human excesses, fads, and trendy behavior have come under Baker's scrutiny. Among the topics he has satirized are Super Bowl Sunday, the Miss America pageant, and television commercials. Other selections have touched on the author's anger over the physical and moral decay of urban America.

***Further Writings*** Many of Baker's columns have been published in collections, such as *No Cause for Panic* (1969), *Poor Russell's Almanac* (1972), and *So This Is*

*Depravity* (1980). In 1979 Baker was awarded the Pulitzer Prize for distinguished commentary for his columns. He was the first humorist to win the award in that category since its inception in 1970. In 1982 Baker published the enormously popular autobiography *Growing Up*, which earned him another Pulitzer Prize. He followed the success of *Growing Up* with a sequel, *The Good Times*, in 1984. This book was also well received by critics. Baker continues to write his syndicated column and publish books on various subjects pertaining to American popular and political culture.

## Works in Literary Context

Throughout his career, Russell Baker has been praised for writing about both the large and small events of American life in a humorous and modest tone. This tone makes his works accessible to a wide variety of readers, perhaps accounting for his column's wide syndication and long-standing popularity with audiences across the country.

***Emphasizing the Personal*** Throughout Baker's career as both a journalist and a memoir writer, readers and reviewers have praised his ability to add a common human dimension to seemingly larger-than-life public figures. Also, many critics have lauded Baker's ability to translate his personal memories into works of universal experience. Critic Jonathan Yardley, for example, affirmed that Baker finds "shape and meaning in his own life" and "make[s] it interesting and pertinent to the reader." In Baker's autobiography *Growing Up*, Yardley asserts that he tells "a story that is deeply in the American grain, one in which countless readers will find echoes of their own."

***The Great Depression and Local Color*** Baker's autobiography *Growing Up* recounts his childhood and family life during the Great Depression and chronicles the personal and economic hardships Baker and his family withstood during the difficult era of America in the 1930s. The quiet humor and the lack of melodrama in his portrayal of that era prompted critics such as Mary Lee Settle to compare *Growing Up* to the works of Mark Twain. In a style that is understated yet powerful, Baker describes personal hardships with subtle emotion. Also, he details with humor and humanity both the places and the people that populated his childhood. Reviewers such as *New Statesman* critic Brian Martin admired the author's "sharp eye for the details of ordinary life," and praised his ability to add this "local color" to his works.

## Works in Critical Context

Regarded by *Washington Post Book World* critic Robert Sherrill as "the supreme satirist" of the late twentieth century, Baker has been credited with taking newspaper humor and turning it into "literature—funny, but full of the pain and absurdity of the age," according to John Skow of *Time* magazine.

**The "Observer" Column**  Armed with a sense of humor described by *Washington Post* writer Jim Naughton as "quick, dry, and accessibly cerebral," Baker has taken aim at a wide range of targets in his "Observer" column, including the presidency, the national economy, and the military, as well as everyday American home life and such disparate areas of popular culture as beauty pageants and the Super Bowl. Though Baker is certainly esteemed for his political commentary, critics generally reserve their highest praise for his writings on family and everyday society. *Spectator* critic Joe Mysak, for example, applauded this type of essay, judging its significance to be "closer to the grain of American life" than Baker's politically tinged writings, and columns of this sort moved Sherrill to write that "when it comes to satire of a controlled but effervescent ferocity, nobody can touch Baker."

**Growing Up**  Described by Mary Lee Settle in the *Los Angeles Times Book Review* as "a wondrous book, funny, sad, and strong," *Growing Up* explores the often difficult circumstances of Baker's childhood with a mix of humor and sadness. *Spectator* critic Peter Paterson saw the work as "a tribute" to the women in Baker's life, first and foremost to his mother, "who dominates the book as she dominated her son's existence."

Many critics of the book found it to be a moving testimony of the realities of life during the 1930s and the Great Depression. In a review for *Washington Post Book World*, writer Jonathan Yardley writes that Baker "passed through rites that for our culture are now only memories, though cherished ones, from first exposure to the miracle of indoor plumbing to trying on his first pair of long pants," and Settle found Baker's descriptions of such scenes "as funny and as touching as Mark Twain's."

**The Good Times**  Many critics viewed *The Good Times* favorably, including *New York Times Book Review* critic Ward Just, who in his review calls the book "a superb autobiography, wonderfully told, often hilarious, always intelligent and unsparing." Some reviewers, however, felt that Baker's trademark sense of modesty is used to excess in the book. Jim Naughton of the *Washington Post*, for example, was critical of Baker's style, asserting that "his humility weakens the book." Other reviewers observed that, because of its subject matter, *The Good Times* necessarily evokes different feelings from its predecessor, *Growing Up*. "Some readers may find that this sequel lacks the emotional tug of the original," Robert Shogan states in the *Los Angeles Times Book Review*, noting that "what *The Good Times* offers instead is an insider's view of modern American journalism that illuminates both the author and his trade." Baker received much positive criticism for his depictions of iconic figures from the latter half of the twentieth century. Complimenting Baker on his balanced characterizations, Ward Just reports that the author's "level gaze is on full display here in the deft, edged portraits" of his congressional contacts, while William

## COMMON HUMAN EXPERIENCE

Russell Baker is perhaps best known for his widely syndicated newspaper columns, which have informed and entertained readers for over forty years and which have become a central component of American popular culture. Other important syndicated works from the same time period include:

   "At Wit's End" (1965–1996), a newspaper column written by Erma Bombeck. Bombeck's enormously popular column described and commented on life in middle-class American homes, often taking a humorous look at gender roles in the suburbs.

   "On Language" (1979–), a weekly column published in the *New York Times Magazine* by William Safire. This column, written by a seasoned journalist, speechwriter, and etymologist, focuses on the current state of grammar, usage, and vocabulary in the English language.

   *All the President's Men* (1974), a nonfiction book by Bob Woodward and Carl Bernstein, which collects their columns written in the *Washington Post* between 1972 and 1973. This exposé documents Woodward and Bernstein's famed investigation of the Watergate scandal, focusing on their interaction with the informant known only as "Deep Throat."

   "Washington Merry-Go-Round" (1946–2006), a newspaper column by Jack Anderson. Anderson, a muckraking journalist who sought to expose scandal in both government and big business, used his column to comment upon such people and events as J. Edgar Hoover, Joseph McCarthy, the Watergate scandal, and the cold war.

   *At the Movies* (1986–1999), a syndicated television program starring Roger Ebert and Gene Siskel. Siskel and Ebert, Chicago-based newspaper columnists known for their movie reviews, joined in 1986 to host an enormously popular talk show dedicated to film criticism.

French of the *Toronto Globe and Mail* states that "Baker's thumbnail sketches of the Washington movers and shakers of his time are vivid."

## Responses to Literature

1. Russell Baker was well known for adding "local color" to his newspaper columns and memoirs. Take the most recent edition of your local paper and peruse the articles. Pick an article that reports on a recent local event in a straightforward manner, and then attempt to write about that event in the form of a column written in Baker's style. How can you add your own personal style and humor to your discussion of the event? What dimension does this add to the portrayal of the event?

2. Baker is often praised for his writings on new technologies and trends in American popular culture. Read a variety of these columns, both older and more recent. What do you think is the role of satire in Baker's discussions of television, computers, or celebrity culture? Is he showing disapproval for these aspects of culture? Write an essay in which you form your arguments by using specific passages from his columns.

3. Many critics have pointed out that Baker's autobiography *Growing Up* shows the author's high esteem for women who, like his mother, persevered through the difficult times of the Great Depression. Look through Baker's columns and find several instances where he discusses women, either as public or private figures. What do you find, overall, are his attitudes toward women? How might these attitudes have changed over time? What historical events may have influenced his attitudes?

BIBLIOGRAPHY

**Periodicals**

French, William. Review of *The Good Times. Toronto Globe and Mail* (June 24, 1989).

Just, Ward. Review of *The Good Times. New York Times Book Review* (May 28, 1989).

Naughton, Jim. Review of *The Good Times. Washington Post* (July 25, 1989).

Paterson, Peter. Review of *Growing Up. Spectator* (February 1984).

Settle, Mary Lee. Review of *Growing Up. Los Angeles Times Book Review* (October 10, 1982).

Shogan, Robert. Review of *The Good Times. Los Angeles Times Book Review* (June 11, 1989).

Yardley, Jonathan. Review of *Growing Up. Washington Post Book World* (October 3, 1982).

# ✸ James Baldwin

BORN: *1924, New York, New York*

DIED: *1987, St. Paul de Vence, France*

NATIONALITY: *American*

GENRE: *Fiction, nonfiction, drama, poetry*

MAJOR WORKS:

*Go Tell It on the Mountain* (1953)

*The Amen Corner* (1955)

*Giovanni's Room* (1956)

*The Fire Next Time* (1963)

*Blues for Mister Charlie* (1964)

## Overview

James Baldwin is recognized as one of the most important writers in post–World War II American literature. In

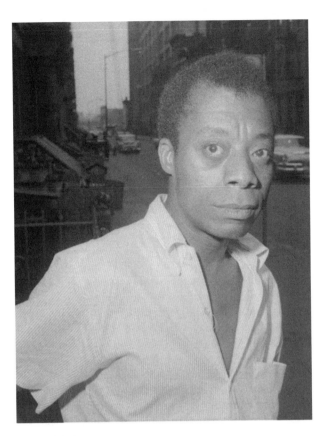

James Baldwin  *AP Images*

his works he exposed racial and sexual polarization in American society and challenged readers to confront and resolve these differences. Baldwin's influence and popularity reached their peak during the 1960s, when he was regarded by many as the leading literary spokesman of the civil rights movement. His novels, essays, and other writings attest to his premise that the black American, as an object of suffering and abuse, represents a universal symbol of human conflict.

## Works in Biographical and Historical Context

*Difficult Childhood* Much of Baldwin's work is based on his unhappy childhood and adolescence. He was born and raised in Harlem under very trying circumstances. His stepfather, an evangelical preacher, struggled to support a large family and demanded the most rigorous religious behavior from his nine children. According to John W. Roberts, "Baldwin's ambivalent relationship with his stepfather served as a constant source of tension during his formative years and informs some of his best mature writings. . . . The demands of caring for younger siblings and his stepfather's religious convictions in large part shielded the boy from the harsh realities of Harlem street life during the 1930s." As a youth Baldwin read constantly and even tried his hand at writing. He once noted, "For me writing was an act of love. It was an attempt—not to get the world's attention—it was an attempt to be loved. It seemed a way to save myself and to save my family. It came out of despair. And it seemed the only way to another world." During the summer of his fourteenth birthday he underwent a dramatic religious conversion, partly in response to his emerging sexuality and partly as a further buffer against the omnipresent temptations of drugs and crime. Baldwin served as a junior minister for three years at the Fireside Pentecostal Assembly, but gradually he lost his desire to preach as he began to question blacks' acceptance of Christian tenets that had, in essence, been used to enslave them.

Shortly after his conversion, Baldwin was accepted at De Witt Clinton High School, a predominantly white, Jewish school in the Bronx. This new environment was also a cause of Baldwin's reassessment and eventual rejection of his religious stance. Soon after he graduated in 1942, Baldwin was compelled to find work in order to help support his brothers and sisters. He took a job in the defense industry in Belle Meade, New Jersey, and there, not for the first time, he was confronted with racism, discrimination, and the debilitating regulations of segregation. Baldwin's disagreeable experiences in New Jersey were closely followed by his stepfather's death, after which Baldwin determined to make writing his sole profession. He moved to Greenwich Village and began to write a novel, and supported himself by performing a variety of odd jobs. In 1944 he met African-American author Richard Wright, who helped him obtain the 1945 Eugene F. Saxton fellowship. Despite the financial freedom the fellowship provided, Baldwin was unable to complete his novel that year. Moreover, he found the social and cultural tenor of the United States increasingly stifling. Eventually, in 1948, he moved to Paris, using funds from a Rosenwald Foundation fellowship to pay his passage. Most critics believe that this journey abroad was fundamental to Baldwin's development as a writer.

*Life and Work Abroad* "Once I found myself on the other side of the ocean," Baldwin told the *New York Times*, "I could see where I came from very clearly, and I could see that I carried myself, which is my home, with me. You can never escape that. I am the grandson of a slave, and I am a writer. I must deal with both." Through some difficult financial and emotional periods, the young author undertook a process of self-realization that included both an acceptance of his heritage and an admittance of his homosexuality. Robert A. Bone noted that Europe gave Baldwin many things: "It gave him a world perspective from which to approach the question of his own identity. It gave him a tender love affair which would dominate the pages of his later fiction. But above all, Europe gave him back himself. The immediate fruit of self-recovery was a great creative outburst. First came two [works] of reconciliation with his racial heritage. *Go Tell It on the Mountain* and *The Amen Corner* represent a

search for roots, a surrender to tradition, an acceptance of the Negro past. Then came a series of essays which probe, deeper than anyone has dared, the psychic history of this nation. They are a moving record of a man's struggle to define the forces that have shaped him, in order that he may accept himself."

Baldwin's fiction of the late 1960s and early 1970s was primarily influenced by his involvement in the civil rights movement. *Tell Me How Long the Train's Been Gone* (1968) centers on two brothers and their different attempts to escape the ghetto; one finds success in the entertainment industry, while the other is nearly destroyed by racism and violence. *If Beale Street Could Talk* (1974) further examined blacks living in a hostile environment. In *Just above My Head* (1979), Baldwin returned to his earlier themes of religion and sexuality in a complex story of a homosexual gospel singer. Although these works were best-sellers, they signaled for most critics a decline in Baldwin's creative talents due to his reliance on didacticism. In a 1985 interview, Baldwin discussed his erratic literary position: "The rise and fall of one's reputation. What can you do about it? I think that comes with the territory. … Any real artist will never be judged in the time of his time; whatever judgment is delivered in the time of his time cannot be trusted."

*Nonfiction and Drama* Although Baldwin is best known as a novelist, his nonfiction works have also received substantial critical acclaim. The essay "Everybody's Protest Novel," published in 1949, introduced him to the New York intelligentsia and generated controversy for its attack on authors of protest fiction, including Richard Wright, who, Baldwin maintained, perpetuated rather than condemned negative racial stereotypes. While Baldwin viewed this piece as an exploration of the thematic options that black writers could follow, Wright considered it a personal affront and subsequently terminated his professional alliance with Baldwin. Nevertheless, critics praised Baldwin for his perceptive analysis of protest literature and for his lucid prose.

At the time of his death from stomach cancer late in 1987, Baldwin was still working on two projects—a play, *The Welcome Table*, and a biography of Martin Luther King, Jr. Although he lived primarily in France, he had never relinquished his United States citizenship and preferred to think of himself as a "commuter" rather than as an expatriate.

## Works in Literary Context

Baldwin's fiction was highly autobiographical, drawing upon his own experiences growing up with a difficult and domineering father, and his experiences with racism and homosexuality as an adult.

*Father-Son Relationships* Baldwin was hailed by critics as a major novelist and a worthy successor to Ralph Ellison and Richard Wright following the publication of his semi-autobiographical novel *Go Tell It on the*

# LITERARY AND HISTORICAL CONTEMPORARIES

Baldwin's famous contemporaries include:

**Ralph Ellison** (1914–1994): An African-American writer most noted for his novel *Invisible Man* (1952), about the experiences of a black man in New York City in the 1940s. The novel won the National Book Award in 1953.

**W. E. B. Du Bois** (1868–1963): Du Bois was the leading African-American intellectual during the first half of the twentieth century. Writer, editor, scholar, and civil rights activist, his most influential work was *The Souls of Black Folk* (1903).

**Christine Jorgensen** (1926–1989): Born George Jorgensen Jr., Christine Jorgensen made international headlines in the 1950s when she became the first well-known person to undergo sex reassignment surgery through a combination of surgical procedures and hormone therapy. She used her fame to speak out on behalf of transsexual and transgender issues.

**Jonas Salk** (1914–1995): The son of Russian Jewish immigrants, Salk secured his name in the history books with the development of a vaccine for the polio virus, putting an end to one of the most dreaded diseases of the twentieth century. Towards the end of his life he turned his attentions towards the quest for an HIV vaccine.

**W. H. Auden** (1907–1973): One of the most acclaimed poets of the twentieth century, Auden was English by birth but emigrated to America in 1939. His poems have continued to enjoy widespread popularity long after his death.

*Mountain.* The book dramatizes the events leading to the religious confirmation of John Grimes, a sensitive Harlem youth struggling to come to terms with his confusion over his sexuality and his religious upbringing. At the core of the novel is a family's legacy of brutality and hate, augmented by the destructive relationship between John and his stepfather, a fundamentalist preacher whose insecurities over his own religious commitment result in his abusive treatment of John and his emotional neglect of the family. Baldwin earned unanimous praise for his skillful evocation of his characters' squalid lives and for his powerful language, which some critics likened to a fire-and-brimstone oratory.

*Homosexuality*   While most critics regarded *Go Tell It on the Mountain* as a cathartic novel in which Baldwin attempted to resolve the emotional anguish of his adolescence, others viewed his next work, *Giovanni's Room*, as the one in which he openly confronted his homosexuality. The novel was controversial, because Baldwin was one of the first black writers to openly discuss homo-

sexuality in his fiction. *Giovanni's Room*, which is set in Paris, is the story of an ill-fated love affair between a white American student and an Italian bartender. Many critics were outraged by Baldwin's blunt language and his polemic topic, though some reviewers echoed David Littlejohn's assessment that the work is "certainly one of the most subtle novels of the homosexual world." Baldwin continued his investigation of sexual politics in the novel *Another Country* (1962), which provoked even more debate. Although it received largely negative reviews due to Baldwin's candid depiction of sexual relations, some commentators considered *Another Country* superior to *Giovanni's Room* in terms of thematic scope and descriptive quality.

*Race Relations*   In the essays collected in *Notes of a Native Son* (1955) and *Nobody Knows My Name: More Notes of a Native Son* (1961). Baldwin optimistically examined the condition of race relations in the United States and abroad. The essays that range from poignant autobiographical remembrances to scholarly literary and social criticism. He also used personal experience to address the problems artists face when drawn to political activism. His next nonfiction work, *The Fire Next Time* was a passionate plea for reconciliation between the races and a manifesto for black liberation. As racial tensions escalated in the mid-1960s, Baldwin's vision of America turned increasingly bitter and his prose more inflammatory. After the publication of *No Name in the Street* (1972), Baldwin was faulted for abandoning his deft powers of persuasion in favor of rhetoric and was accused by some of racism.

## Works in Critical Context

Critics have accorded Baldwin high praise for both his style and his themes. "Baldwin has carved a literary niche through his exploration of 'the mystery of the human being' in his art," observed Louis H. Pratt in *James Baldwin. Saturday Review* correspondent Benjamin De Mott concluded that Baldwin "retains a place in an extremely select group: That composed of the few genuinely indispensable American writers."

However, his work was also controversial in some quarters. Because Baldwin sought to inform and confront whites, and because his fiction contains interracial love affairs, he came under attack from writers of the Black Arts Movement, who called for a literature exclusively by and for blacks. Baldwin refused to align himself with the movement; he continued to call himself an "American writer" as opposed to a "black writer" and continued to confront the issues facing a multi-racial society. Eldridge Cleaver, in his book *Soul on Ice* (1968), accused Baldwin of a hatred of black people and a "shameful, fanatical fawning" love of whites. What Cleaver saw as complicity with whites, Baldwin saw rather as an attempt to alter the real daily environment with which black Americans have been faced all their lives.

The publication of his collected essays, *The Price of the Ticket: Collected Nonfiction, 1948–1985* (1985), and his subsequent death sparked reassessments of his career and commentary on the quality of his lasting legacy. "Mr. Baldwin has become a kind of prophet, a man who has been able to give a public issue all its deeper moral, historical, and personal significance," remarked Robert F. Sayre. Perhaps the most telling demonstration of the results of Baldwin's achievement comes from other black writers. Orde Coombs, for instance, concluded that "[because] he existed we felt that the racial miasma that swirled around us would not consume us, and it is not too much to say that this man saved our lives, or at least, gave us the necessary ammunition to face what we knew would continue to be a hostile and condescending world." Playwright and poet Amiri Baraka offered similar thoughts in his eulogy to Baldwin. "This man traveled the earth like its history and its biographer," Baraka said. In a posthumous tribute for the *Washington Post*, Juan Williams wrote: "The success of Baldwin's effort as the witness is evidenced time and again by the people, black and white, gay and straight, famous and anonymous, whose humanity he unveiled in his writings."

*Giovanni's Room*   Baldwin had a difficult time getting *Giovanni's Room* published in the United States, largely because of the explicit depiction of homosexual relationships. Critical responses have been mixed to this endeavor to treat the physical and psychological aspects of male love: Anthony West acknowledged the solemnity of the story but advocated that it "described a *passade*, a riffle in the surface of life, that completely lacks the validity of actual experience"; on the other hand, David Karp insisted that Baldwin had taken "a very special theme" and treated it with "great artistry and restraint," and Stanley Macebuh praised the work as "one of the few novels in America in which the homosexual sensibility is treated with some measure of creative seriousness."

The varied critical response to the novel was Baldwin's introduction to the racialized literary world. Many reviewers, such as Leslie Fiedler, seemed disturbed that a novel by an African-American writer did not feature any African-American characters. In February 1957 James Ivy reviewed *Giovanni's Room* for *The Crisis*, the publication of the National Association for the Advancement of Colored People, under the title "Faerie Queens." He lamented the fact that Baldwin, already known as an advocate for African-Americans, wasted his talent writing about a homosexual affair involving white men.

*The Fire Next Time*   Many critics view Baldwin's essays as his most significant contribution to American literature. Works such as *The Fire Next Time* "serve to illuminate the condition of the black man in twentieth-century America," according to Louis H. Pratt. Highly personal and analytical, the essays probe deeper than the mere provincial problems of white versus black to uncover the essential issues of self-determination, identity, and reality. *South Atlantic Quarterly* contributor Fred L. Standley asserted that this quest for personal

---

## COMMON HUMAN EXPERIENCE

James Baldwin was the first of several authors who have chronicled the experiences of the homosexual in the repressive atmosphere of 1950s America. Other, more recent works to touch on the subject include:

*Stuck Rubber Baby* (1995), a novel by by Howard Cruse. A comic take on a young gay man's coming of age in a fictional Southern town, and his involvement in the civil rights movement even as he attempts to come to terms with his own issues.

*Father of Frankenstein* (1995), a novel by Christopher Bram. A fictionalized retelling of the life of James Whale, a famed Hollywood director who was a homosexual.

*Sex-Crime Panic: A Journey to the Paranoid Heart of the 1950s* (2002), a nonfiction work by Neil Miller. A study of a public panic that broke out in an Iowa town after the murder of two children led to the arrest of twenty so-called sexual psychopaths, mostly homosexuals, who were subsequently committed to a mental asylum.

---

identity "is indispensable in Baldwin's opinion and the failure to experience such is indicative of a fatal weakness in human life." C. W. E. Bigsby elaborated in *The Fifties: Fiction, Poetry, Drama*: "Baldwin's central theme is the need to accept reality as a necessary foundation for individual identity and thus a logical prerequisite for the kind of saving love in which he places his whole faith." Ultimately, *The Fire Next Time* very likely helped "in restoring the personal essay to its place as a form of creative literature," as John Henrik Clarke has asserted.

## Responses to Literature

1. In *Go Tell It on the Mountain*, the adult characters have relocated from the rural South to urban New York. This reflects a pattern of migration that was occurring in the African-American community during the first half of the twentieth century. Research the reasons behind this migration. Choose a major city such as New York, Chicago, or Los Angeles and research why African-Americans chose to move there and how that city's society, politics, and population were changed by black migration.

2. Analyze two of Baldwin's essays on racism, one from early in his career, and one from later on. Compare how the tone changes. Do you think Baldwin becomes less thoughtful, more strident in his analysis and arguments, as some critics have claimed? Which essay do you think makes a more persuasive argument?

3. Baldwin had a complicated relationship with religion, first embracing it, then rejecting it as a lingering instrument of white oppression. Research the history of Christian belief in the black community. What role has it played in African-American life and communities over the years?

4. Read *Giovanni's Room*, a novel that, because of its homosexual theme, shocked readers when it was first published. Are readers today likely to be shocked by this novel? How have society's attitudes to homosexuality changed in the fifty years since the novel was published? Draw up a timeline showing some of the major events and issues in gay rights during this period.

BIBLIOGRAPHY

**Books**

Champion, Ernest A. *Mr. Baldwin, I Presume: James Baldwin—Chinua Achebe, A Meeting of the Minds.* Lanham: Md.: University Press of America, 1995.

Eckman, Fern Marja. *The Furious Passage of James Baldwin.* New York: M. Evans, 1966.

Gottfried, Ted. *James Baldwin: Voice from Harlem.* New York: F. Watts, 1997.

Kenan, Randall. *James Baldwin.* New York: Chelsea House, 1994.

King, Malcolm. *Baldwin: Three Interviews* Middletown, Conn.: Wesleyan University Press, 1985.

Kinnamon, Kenneth, ed. *James Baldwin: A Collection of Critical Essays.* Englewood Cliffs, N.J.: Prentice-Hall, 1974.

O'Daniel, Therman B. *James Baldwin: A Critical Evaluation.* Washington, D.C.: Howard University Press, 1977.

Standley, Fred, and Nancy Standley. *James Baldwin: A Reference Guide.* Boston: G. K. Hall, 1980.

# ☸ Toni Cade Bambara

BORN: *1939, New York, New York*

DIED: *1995, Philadelphia, Pennsylvania*

NATIONALITY: *American*

GENRE: *Fiction*

MAJOR WORKS:

*Gorilla, My Love* (1972)

*The Sea Birds Are Still Alive* (1977)

*The Salt Eaters* (1980)

## Overview

A writer and social activist, T. C. (short for Toni Cade) Bambara is "one of the best representatives of the group of African American writers who, during the 1960s, became directly involved in the cultural and sociopolitical activities in urban communities across the country," according to Alice A. Deck. Bambara, who initially gained recognition as a short story writer, branched out into other genres and media over the course of her career. All of her work is marked by a focus on issues of racial awareness and feminism.

## Works in Biographical and Historical Context

Born Miltona Mirkin Cade in New York City, she later acquired the name "Bambara" after discovering it as part of a signature on a sketchbook in her great-grandmother's trunk. Bambara was generally silent about her childhood, but she did reveal a few details from her youth. In an interview with Beverly Guy-Sheftall in *Sturdy Black Bridges: Visions of Black Women in Literature*, Bambara discussed some women who influenced her work:

> For example, in every neighborhood I lived in there were always two types of women that somehow pulled me and sort of got their wagons in a circle around me. I call them Miss Naomi and Miss Gladys, although I'm sure they came under various names. The Miss Naomi types ... would give me advice like, "When you meet a man, have a birthday, demand a present that's hockable, and be careful." ... The Miss Gladyses were usually the type that hung out the window in Apartment 1-A leaning on the pillow giving single-action advice on numbers or giving you advice about how to get your homework done or telling you to stay away from those cruising cars that moved through the neighborhood patrolling little girls.

After attending Queens College in New York City and several European institutions, Bambara worked as a freelance writer and lecturer, social investigator for the New York State department of welfare, and director of recreation in the psychiatry department at Metropolitan Hospital in New York City. As she told Guy-Sheftall, writing at that time seemed to her "rather frivolous ... something you did because you didn't feel like doing any work. But ... I've come to appreciate that it is a perfectly legitimate way to participate in a struggle."

Bambara received a bachelor's degree in theater arts and English from Queens College in 1959. In the following decade she served as a social worker and director of neighborhood programs in Harlem and Brooklyn, published short stories in periodicals, earned a master's degree in 1964, and spent a year at the Commedia dell'Arte in Milan, Italy. She also directed a theater program and various publications funded by the City College Seek program. This wide variety of experience inevitably found its way into her fiction and influenced her political sensibility as well.

Bambara's interest in black liberation and women's movements led her to edit and publish an anthology titled *The Black Woman* in 1970. The work is a collection of poetry, short stories, and essays by such celebrated writers as Nikki Giovanni, Audre Lorde, Alice Walker, and Paule Marshall. *The Black Woman* also contained short stories by Bambara, who was at that time still writing under the name of Cade. According to Deck, Bambara saw the work as "a response to all the male 'experts' both black and white who had been publishing articles and conducting sociological studies on black women." Another anthology, *Tales and Stories for Black Folks*, followed in 1971. Bambara explained in the introduction to this short story collection that the work's aim is to instruct young blacks about "Our Great Kitchen Tradition," Bambara's term for the black tradition of storytelling. In the first part of *Tales and Stories*, Bambara included works by writers Langston Hughes, Alice Walker, and Ernest Gaines—stories she wished she had read while growing up. The second part of the collection contains stories by students in a first-year composition class Bambara was teaching at Livingston College, Rutgers University.

### Writing Career Begins in Earnest

Most of Bambara's early writings—short stories written between 1959 and 1970 under the name Toni Cade—were collected in her next work, *Gorilla, My Love* (1972). Bambara told Claudia Tate in an interview published in *Black Women Writers at Work* that when her agent suggested she assemble some old stories for a book, she thought, "Aha, I'll get the old kid stuff out and see if I can't clear some space to get into something else." Nevertheless, *Gorilla, My Love* remains her most widely read collection. Deck noted that after the publication of her first collection, "major events took place in Toni Cade Bambara's life which were to have an effect on her writing." Bambara traveled to Cuba in 1973 and Vietnam in 1975, meeting with both the Federation of Cuban Women and the Women's Union in Vietnam. She was impressed with both groups, particularly with the ability of the Cuban women to surpass class and color conflicts and with the Vietnamese women's resistance to their traditional place in society. Furthermore, upon returning to the United States, Bambara moved to the South, where she became a founding member of the Southern Collective of African American Writers. Her travels and her involvement with community groups like the collective influenced the themes and settings of *The Sea Birds Are Still Alive* (1977), her second collection of short stories. These stories take place in diverse geographical areas and center chiefly around communities instead of individuals. With both collections, critics noted Bambara's skill in the genre, and many praised the musical nature of language and dialogue in her stories, which she herself likened to "riffs" and "be-bop."

Although Bambara admittedly favored the short story genre, her next work, *The Salt Eaters* (1980), was a novel. She explained in *Black Women Writers*:

> Of all the writing forms, I've always been partial to the short story. ... But the major publishing indus-

try, the academic establishment, reviewers, and critics favor the novel. ... Career. Economics. Critical Attention. A major motive behind the production of Salt.

The novel, which focuses on the recovery of community organizer Velma Henry from an attempted suicide, consists of a "fugue-like interweaving of voices," Bambara's specialty. *The Salt Eaters* succeeded in gaining more critical attention for Bambara.

### Move into Screenwriting

After the publication of *The Salt Eaters* in 1980, Bambara devoted herself to another medium: film. She told Tate in *Black Women Writers at Work*:

> Quite frankly, I've always considered myself a film person. ... There's not too much more I want to experiment with in terms of writing. It gives me pleasure, insight, keeps me centered, sane. But, oh, to get my hands on some movie equipment.

Bambara nevertheless remained committed to working within black communities and she continued to address issues of black awareness and feminism in her art. One of her best-known projects for film, *The Bombing of Osage*, explores a notorious incident in which the Philadelphia authorities used lethal force against a group of militant black citizens. The author did continue to write books; her more recent projects include two other adult novels, *Those Bones Are Not My Child* (published posthumously in 1999), and a juvenile work, *Raymond's Run* (1971), about a pair of siblings who like to run foot races.

Toni Cade Bambara died of colon cancer in 1995.

## Works in Literary Context

### Civil Rights and African American Culture

In many ways Bambara was one of the best representatives of the group of African American writers who, during the 1960s, became directly involved in the cultural and sociopolitical activities in urban communities across the country. Like James Baldwin, Imamu Amiri Baraka, Nikki Giovanni, June Jordan, Sonia Sanchez, and Alice Walker, she immersed herself in civil rights issues by lecturing and helping to organize rallies within the black community, while at the same time using these experiences as the nucleus for her essays and creative writing. Like others of that era, Bambara wrote from a stance of near defiance—pushing the cultural assumptions of the larger American society aside to show her audience what she believed to be the distinguishing characteristics of African American culture. Her fiction reflected the African American idiomatic expressions, habits of interpersonal relationships, and, most important, its myths, music, and history. While some who rode the tide of enormous popularity during the 1960s passed on to virtual obscurity in the 1970s, Bambara was one of the few who continued to work within the black urban communities (filming, lecturing, organizing, and reading from her works at rallies and

# LITERARY AND HISTORICAL CONTEMPORARIES

Bambara's famous contemporaries include:

**Angela Davis** (1944–): The defendant in a sensational murder trial and a controversial figure in the Black Power movement of the 1960s and 1970s, Angela Davis has continued to teach and lobby for revolutionary and feminist causes since her acquittal.

**Francis Ford Coppola** (1939–): Movie producer, director, and screenwriter, Coppola was one of the leading figures of the "New Hollywood" cinema of the 1970s. Several of his movies, in particular the first two *Godfather* films (1972 and 1974) and *Apocalypse Now* (1979), are considered by most critics to be among the best films ever made.

**George Wallace** (1919–1998): Four-time governor of Alabama and one-time presidential candidate, George Wallace was the prototypical Southern Democrat of the 1960s, vocally and notoriously opposed to segregation, the champion of white blue-collar workers. During his 1972 presidential bid, he was the target of an assassination attempt that left him paralyzed from the waist down.

**Andrei Sakharov** (1921–1989): Awarded the Nobel Peace Prize in 1972, Sakharov, a Soviet physicist, was a vocal campaigner for human rights reforms and nuclear nonproliferation.

**Richard Pryor** (1940–2005): A comedian, actor, and writer, Pryor was perhaps best known for his uncompromisingly bold takes on African American life and racism in society, as well as his use of vulgarity and profanity in his stand-up routines. Fellow comedians have lauded him as perhaps the most influential stand-up performer of the last quarter century.

conferences), producing imaginative reenactments of these experiences in her fiction.

The hallmark of Toni Cade Bambara's fiction was her keen ear and ability to transcribe the African American dialect accurately. She wrote as one who has had a long personal relationship with the black working class and said that she was very much interested in continuing to write all of her fiction in this idiom. Writing and teaching others to write effectively became a tool, a means of working within the community.

***The Short Story***   In several interviews and in an essay ("What It Is I Think I'm Doing Anyhow"), Bambara emphasized her preference for the short story as both a convenient tool for use in the classroom and in lecture engagements (she referred to them as "portable") and as an easier art form to produce than the novel. The brevity, and its "modest appeal for attention," is what she finds

most effective about the short story, but in Bambara's own figurative style of explaining it, she says, "Temperamentally, I move toward the short story because I'm a sprinter rather than a long-distance runner."

Bambara could also be a harsh critic of her own work. She commented to an interviewer that she felt that the stories in *The Sea Birds Are Still Alive* were too long:

> To my mind, the six-page story is the gem. If it takes more than six pages to say it, something is the matter. So I'm not too pleased with the new collection *The Sea Birds Are Still Alive*. Most of these stories are too sprawling and hairy for my taste, although I'm very pleased, feel perfectly fine about them as pieces. But as stories they're too damn long and dense.

## Works in Critical Context

Bambara's short stories and her novel have frequently been praised for her realistic portrayal of the lives of African Americans, including her ability to capture colloquial African American speech. For example, Susan Lardner remarks in the *New Yorker* that Bambara's short stories

> describing the lives of black people in the North and the South, could be more exactly typed as vignettes and significant anecdotes, although a few of them are fairly long. ... All are notable for their purposefulness, a more or less explicit inspirational angle, and a distinctive motion of the prose, which swings from colloquial narrative to precarious metaphorical heights and over to street talk, at which Bambara is unbeatable.

***The Sea Birds Are Still Alive***   A critic writing in *Newsweek* describes Bambara's second collection of short stories, *The Sea Birds Are Still Alive*, in this manner: "Bambara directs her vigorous sense and sensibility to black neighborhoods in big cities, with occasional trips to small Southern towns. ... The stories start and stop like rapid-fire conversations conducted in a rhythmic, black-inflected, sweet-and-sour language." In fact, according to Anne Tyler in the *Washington Post Book World*, Bambara's particular style of narration is one of the most distinctive qualities of her writing. "What pulls us along is the language of [her] characters, which is startlingly beautiful without once striking a false note," declares Tyler. "Everything these people say, you feel, ordinary, real-life people are saying right now on any street corner. It's only that the rest of us didn't realize it was sheer poetry they were speaking."

***The Salt Eaters***   In 1980 Bambara published her first novel, a generally well-received work titled *The Salt Eaters*. Written in an almost dreamlike style, *The Salt Eaters* explores the relationship between two women with totally different backgrounds and lifestyles brought together by a suicide attempt by one of the women. John

Leonard, who describes the book as "extraordinary," writes in the *New York Times* that *The Salt Eaters*

> is almost an incantation, poem-drunk, myth-happy, mud-caked, jazz-ridden, prodigal in meanings, a kite and a mask. It astonishes because Toni Cade Bambara is so adept at switching from politics to legend, from particularities of character to prehistorical song, from LaSalle Street to voodoo. It is as if she jived the very stones to groan.

In a *Times Literary Supplement* review, Carol Rumens states that *The Salt Eaters* "is a hymn to individual courage, a sombre message of hope that has confronted the late twentieth-century pathology of racist violence and is still able to articulate its faith in 'the dream.'" And John Wideman notes in the *New York Times Book Review*:

> In her highly acclaimed fiction and in lectures, [Bambara] emphasizes the necessity for black people to maintain their best traditions, to remain healthy and whole as they struggle for political power. *The Salt Eaters*, her first novel, eloquently summarizes and extends the abiding concerns of her previous work.

In addition to this praise from reviewers, there was considerable criticism of the structure, the dialogue, and the general expansiveness of *The Salt Eaters*. The numerous breaks in the story line required to accommodate the various narrative strains became the sticking point for most who reviewed the novel. As one critic said in *First World*, "the very act of reading *The Salt Eaters* through requires transformative agility." Reviewing the novel for the *Washington Post*, Anne Tyler commented that "too many people swarm by too quickly. Too much is described too elliptically, as if cutting through to the heart of the matter might be considered crude, lacking in gracefulness, not sufficiently artistic." Judith Wilson, in another review, noted that while the novel contained much food for thought on all of the sociopolitical issues raised by the characters, "Bambara's facility for dialogue sometimes leads her astray. Too many snatches of conversation, though clever and convincing, repeat previously stated themes or offer trivial observations that disrupt the narrative."

## Responses to Literature

1. How central is the subject of race in the short story "Gorilla, My Love"? How would Hazel's story differ if she found herself in different circumstances, such as another place or time?

2. What age group of readers do you think Bambara's stories are generally aimed at? Explain how you came to your conclusion.

3. In an interview, Bambara has said that "An awful lot of my stories ... were written, I suspect, with performance in mind." Take one of Bambara's stories and adapt it as a play, including staging notes. How

---

# COMMON HUMAN EXPERIENCE

Bambara was one of several prominent female African American authors who used her work to communicate the experience of being black in America. Other works by female African Americans to touch upon this theme include:

*The Color Purple* (1983), a novel by Alice Walker. Winner of the Pulitzer Prize and National Book Award, and later adapted into a successful film and musical, this novel focuses on female African American life in rural Georgia during the 1930s.

*Their Eyes Were Watching God* (1937), a novel by Zora Neale Hurston. Although largely regarded today as a landmark of African American literature, this novel met with controversy in the black community upon its initial publication because of its use of phonetically written dialogue meant to replicate Southern black dialects (a technique that anticipated Bambara's mastery of "street" dialogue). There were even charges that Hurston was trying to pander to white audiences.

*The Bluest Eye* (1970), a novel by Toni Morrison. Controversial for its discussions of incest and molestation, Morrison's first novel tells the tale of a young black girl during the Great Depression, the corruption of society and her family, and racist attitudes about appearance— the book's title is a reference to the main character's wish that her eyes would turn blue.

*I Know Why the Caged Bird Sings* (1969), an autobiographical novel by Maya Angelou. An autobiography in novel form, this was the first of a six-part narrative of poet Angelou's life, describing how she grew up in a racist and segregated society and the personal triumphs that emerged from dire circumstances.

---

does this process contribute to your understanding and appreciation of the work?

4. Compare and contrast Bambara's portrayal of her young female protagonists, such as Hazel Parker, with the portrayal of similar characters in other works of literature such as in Toni Morrison's *The Bluest Eye* or in Alice Walker's short story "Everyday Use."

BIBLIOGRAPHY

**Books**

Bell, Roseann P., Bettye J. Parker, and Beverly Guy-Sheftall, eds. *Sturdy Black Bridges: Visions of Black Women in Literature*. Garden City, N.Y.: Doubleday, 1979.

Butler-Evans, Elliott. *Race, Gender, and Desire: Narrative Strategies in the Fiction of Toni Cade Bambara, Toni Morrison, and Alice Walker*. Philadelphia, Pa.: Temple University Press, 1989.

Franko, Carol. "Toni Cade Bambara." In *A Reader's Companion to the Short Story in English*, edited by Erin Fallon, R. C. Feddersen, James Kurtzleben, Maurice A. Lee, and Susan Rochette-Crawley. Westport, Conn.: Greenwood, 2001, pp. 38–47.

Hull, Akasha (Gloria). "What It Is I Think She's Doing Anyhow: A Reading of Toni Cade Bambara's *The Salt Eaters*." In *Home Girls: A Black Feminist Anthology*, edited by Barbara Smith. New Brunswick, N.J.: Rutgers University Press, 2000, pp. 124–142.

Milne, Ira Mark, ed. "Gorilla, My Love." In *Short Stories for Students*. Vol. 21. Detroit, Mich.: Gale, 2005.

Nelson, Emmanuel S., ed. *Contemporary African American Novelists*. Westport, Conn.: Greenwood Press, 1999.

Tate, Claudia, ed. *Black Women Writers at Work*. New York: Continuum, 1983.

Wilentz, Gay. *Healing Narratives: Women Writers Curing Cultural Disease*. New Brunswick, N.J.: Rutgers University Press, 2000.

**Periodicals**

Barrett, Lindon. "Identities and Identity Studies: Reading Toni Cade Bambara's 'The Hammer Man.'" *Cultural Critique* 39 (1998): 5–29.

Muther, Elizabeth. "Bambara's Feisty Girls: Resistance Narratives in *Gorilla, My Love*." *African American Review* 36, no. 3 (2002): 447–459.

Taylor, Carole Anne. "Postmodern Disconnection and the Archive of Bones: Toni Cade Bambara's Last Work." *Novel: A Forum on Fiction* 35, nos. 2–3 (2002): 258–280.

# ✸ Mary Jo Bang

BORN: *1946, Waynesville, Missouri*

NATIONALITY: *American*

GENRE: *Poetry*

MAJOR WORKS:

*Apology for Want* (1997)

*Elegy* (2007)

## Overview

Mary Jo Bang is a Missouri-based poet who has come to critical and popular attention over the course of the last decade with a series of acclaimed poetry collections. She has the reputation of being a distinctly intellectual poet who asks major philosophical questions about art and existence, but her lively poetry has popular appeal as well.

## Works in Biographical and Historical Context

*Obscurity, Critical Acclaim* Mary Jo Bang (née Ward) was born in central Missouri, in the town of Way-

Mary Jo Bang   *AP Images*

nesville, and grew up in St. Louis. She attended Northwestern University, where she earned both a bachelor's and a master's degree in sociology, graduating summa cum laude. Bang also earned a bachelor's in photography from the University of Westminster, U.K. and a master's in creative writing at Columbia University. She had one son from an early marriage; he died at age thirty-seven from an overdose of prescription pills.

Bang has made a career of editing and teaching poetry, serving as poetry co-editor for the *Boston Review* from 1995 to 2005 and, in her home town of St. Louis, teaching as Professor of English and Director of the Creative Writing Program at Washington University.

Bang would not publish her first collection of poetry, *Apology for Want*, until 1997. The book garnered immediate attention and critical praise, winning several awards, including the Bakeless Prize. She has three times been selected for inclusion in the *Best American Poetry* series and has won a Pushcart Prize and Guggenheim fellowship.

In all, she has published five books: *Apology for Want, Louise in Love, The Downstream Extremity of the Isle of the Swans* (both 2001), *The Eye Like a Strange Balloon* (2004), and *Elegy* (2007). Her latest book, *Elegy* (2007), was written in the aftermath of the death of her son and dwells on the theme of grief, pain, and loss in the wake of death. Although she did not write the poems with an eye towards publishing them, when her editors asked for new material, these works were, at that time, all she had to show them. Their success surprised her, as she told *Newsweek*:

What does it mean, they "loved the poem"? I was talking about wanting to kill myself. What made these poems acceptable? T. S. Eliot taught us you can write about your nervous breakdown, but call it "The Waste Land" and make it big and crazy enough to hide behind. I'm not hiding behind much here.

## Works in Literary Context

Bang's poetry is characterized by a light, playful rhythm and tone that is simultaneously subtle and intellectual. Her themes tend to be ambitiously philosophical. As an example of her depth, Bang makes frequent use of irony in her poetry, using language to imply the opposite of an apparent literal meaning. She often uses her irony to tease the reader as much as her subject, challenging expectations and interpretations.

*Ekphrasis*  Bang has demonstrated a repeated interest in a poetic technique known as ekphrasis, a term used to refer to poetry that expresses visual elements, particularly as expressed through paintings. Bang's entire collection *The Eye like a Strange Balloon* is based on ekphrasis—each poem takes a different work of art as its subject. Bang's use of ekphrasis is typically not merely concerned with analyzing a work of art, such as the 1820 poem "Ode on a Grecian Urn" by John Keats, but rather uses the work of art as a jumping-off point to explore deeper, tangential themes.

## Works in Critical Context

Bang first gained widespread, largely positive critical attention after the publication of *Apology for Want* in 1997. Since then, she has continued to enjoy support and praise from the critical community, with each of her collections receiving positive reviews.

### *Apology for Want*

In *Ploughshares*, Susan Conley wrote of *Apology for Want* that "[t]here is a quiet anarchy in the spare poems" about modern American culture, "one of shopping malls and consumption. . . . But the voice is subversive and unsettling, the syntax wholly unique and invented for the dark ephemeral region of longing this book inhabits." Frank Allen, writing in the *American Book Review*, said that Bang's poems "are a route to a new way of looking at what we've grown into, 'the longing' that restores us to what we once 'hoped' to be." *Publishers Weekly* picked out for special praise the "nice tension between the clarity of form and the open-endedness of Bang's articulated emotion."

Writing in *Library Journal*, Ellen Kaufman found the poems "difficult, [and] allusive" but "interesting, with occasional flashes of brilliance." Conley agreed with this sentiment, saying that the effect of the poems is to leave one "slightly stunned each time by their impact and exactitude—daring to ask the very largest of questions."

## LITERARY AND HISTORICAL CONTEMPORARIES

Bang's famous contemporaries include:

**Hillary Rodham Clinton** (1947–): U.S. Senator and wife of former President Bill Clinton, Hillary Clinton was one of the most polarizing First Ladies in the history of the American presidency, because of the active role she assumed early on in her husband's presidency. After leaving the White House, Hillary Clinton became a Senator from New York and mounted a very strong but ultimately unsuccessful run for the Democratic presidential nomination in 2008.

**Khaled Hosseini** (1965–): Originally a doctor from Afghanistan, Hosseini rocketed to international fame with his debut novel, *The Kite Runner* (2003), a fictionalized account of a child's coming of age in war-ravaged Afghanistan.

**Boris Yeltsin** (1931–2007): A Soviet politician, Yeltsin rode a wave of enthusiasm in Russia after the collapse of the Soviet Union in 1991, becoming his country's first democratically-elected leader. Expectations were soon dashed, however, in the wake of a decade of economic and political turmoil as Russia adjusted to its new democratic, free-market system.

**Robert Pinsky** (1940–): An American poet and literary critic, Pinsky is a leading figure in the world of poetry. Author of over fifteen books, Pinsky is noted for both his criticism and the technically-precise, "musical" quality of his own poetry.

**Johnny Depp** (1963–): Over the course of a long career, American actor Depp has managed to become both a reliable box-office draw and earn a reputation as an "actor's actor," often taking on challenging or unusual roles in everything from summer blockbusters to low-budget art house films.

## Responses to Literature

1. Bang refers to the ancient Greek myth of Prometheus in "Allegory." Why do you think the mythology about him has been influential over Western literature? Why do you think Bang refers to him in her poem, and how do you think this reference affects the poem?

2. The convention of ekphrasis stretches all of the way back to ancient Greece and Rome, and it was particularly popular in the romantic period. Discuss the relationship between words and images today. When and why does literature become highly visual? What does this say about the work of literature? What are some of the ways a contemporary writer would go

## COMMON HUMAN EXPERIENCE

Bang's work in ekphrasis comes from a much longer tradition that stretches back to the classical world. Ekphrasis was particularly popular among romantic poets, in part because poetry of the romantic era was interested in visionary glimpses of nature and art.

"Ode on a Grecian Urn" (1820), a poem by John Keats. Perhaps the best-known work of ekphrasis by one of the leading Romantic poets, this ode contemplates the ageless beauty of an ancient Greek vase, and the imagery frozen in time upon its fragile surface.

"Archaic Torso of Apollo" (1907), a poem by Rainer Maria Rilke. A meditation on an ancient Greek statue missing its limbs and head, which, the poem argues, makes the statue more powerful than if it were whole, for we, the viewers, are left to "fill in the blanks" in our own minds.

"Self-Portrait in a Convex Mirror" (1974), a poem by John Ashbery. A poem written about a painting of the same name, this is perhaps the most influential modern ekphrastic poem, a touchstone event upon its publication.

"The Shield of Achilles" (1953), a book by W. H. Auden. The earliest example of ekphrasis comes from Homer's epic *Iliad*, in which he describes the god Hephaestus forging Achilles's shield. Auden's take reimagines the process, but with the facets of modern war, such as barbed wire and atrocities, rather than bronze, gold, and iron, as the raw materials.

about describing artwork, and why would he or she choose to do so?

3. Bang based the poems in *Elegy* on the emotions she was feeling around the death of her son. How can poetry be used to deal with intense emotions? Think of a time in your life when you were feeling particularly intense emotions, whether happiness, grief, anger, etc. Write a poem about your feelings and/or the events surrounding those feelings.

4. An allegory is a work in which each the story and characters are meant to symbolize something beyond the straightforward story. Think of a lesson you would like to teach and then create an allegory for it. Brainstorm until you find the right story and situation to bring across your message. Then tell your allegory to a group of friends or classmates and ask them to describe its message. How did their response compare with your original idea?

BIBLIOGRAPHY

**Books**

"Allegory." *Poetry for Students*. Ed. Anne Marie Hacht. Vol. 23. Detroit: Gale, 2006.

Keaton, Rebekah. "Bang, Mary Jo." *Contemporary Poets*. Ed. Thomas Riggs. 7th ed. Detroit: St. James Press, 2001.

**Periodicals**

Adler, Jerry. "The Poetry Of Pain." *Newsweek* 151.22 (June 2, 2008): 49.

**Web sites**

"Mary Jo Bang (1946–)." *Poetry Foundation*. Retrieved October 4, 2008, from http://www.poetry foundation.org/archive/poet.html?id=81903.

"Mary Jo Bang." *Poets.org*. Retrieved October 4, 2008, from http://www.poets.org/poet.php/prmPID/548.

# Amiri Baraka

BORN: *1934, Newark, New Jersey*

NATIONALITY: *American*

GENRE: *Fiction, drama, poetry*

MAJOR WORKS:

*Blues People: Negro Music in White America* (1963)

*Dutchman* (1964)

*The System of Dante's Hell* (1965)

*Slave Ship: A Historical Pageant* (1967)

## Overview

A controversial writer who rose to prominence in the late 1950s and early 1960s, Amiri Baraka is considered a seminal figure in the development of contemporary black literature. According to some scholars, he succeeds W. E. B. Du Bois and Richard Wright as one of the most prolific and persistent critics of twentieth-century America. His works, which cover a variety of literary genres, concern the oppression of blacks in white society. He received worldwide acclaim for his first professional play production, *Dutchman* (1964), and his subsequent work for the theater has provoked both praise and controversy. Having rejected white values and white society, Baraka strives to create art with a firm didactic purpose: to forge an African American literature that reflects the values of the black community.

## Works in Biographical and Historical Context

Born Everett LeRoy Jones in New Jersey in 1934, Baraka spent his early childhood creating comic strips and writing science fiction stories. He was a descendant of preachers, and he dreamed of becoming a minister because, as he recalled, at that time ministers were the most

Amiri Baraka    *AP Images*

respected leaders in the black community. At school Baraka excelled in his studies, graduating from high school at the age of fifteen. About his school experience, he recalled: "When I was in high school, I used to drink a lot of wine, throw bottles around, walk down the street in women's clothes just because I couldn't find anything to do to satisfy myself." Perhaps hoping to satisfy himself in college, he enrolled at Howard University in 1952. Shortly before his first year at the university, he began spelling his name *LeRoi*; scholar William J. Harris suggests that Baraka may have been trying to create a new identity for himself by altering his name. At Howard he studied with famous black scholars E. Franklin Frazier, Nathan A. Scott Jr., and Sterling A. Brown. Despite these exceptional teachers, Baraka found Howard stifling and flunked out of school in 1954. Shortly thereafter, he joined the United States Air Force. Of his experience in the service, he told interviewer Judy Stone that

> the Howard thing let me understand the Negro sickness. They teach you how to pretend to be white. But the Air Force made me understand the white sickness. It shocked me into realizing what was happening to me and others.

In 1957, after being dishonorably discharged, he moved to New York's Greenwich Village. There he became a part of the Beat movement and associated with members Allen Ginsberg, Frank O'Hara, and Charles Olson. During the next few years he established a reputation as a music critic, writing jazz criticism for magazines *Downbeat*, *Metronome*, and the *Jazz Review*. Along with Hettie Roberta Cohen—a white Jewish woman whom he later married in 1958—he also founded *Yugen*, a magazine forum for the poetry of Beat writers. By the late 1950s, his own poetry began attracting critical atten-

tion; his first volume of poetry, *Preface to a Twenty Volume Suicide Note* ... (1961), met with general approval for its unconventional style and language. Critics would later observe that this is the only work of Baraka's that is "free from ethnic torment."

In 1960, after reading Baraka's poem "January 1, 1959: Fidel Castro," the New York chapter of the Fair Play for Cuba Committee offered Baraka an invitation to visit Cuba. In *The Autobiography of LeRoi Jones* (1984), he referred to this visit as "a turning point in my life," noting, "Cuba split me open." While there he met Third World political artists and intellectuals who forced him to reconsider his art and his apolitical stance. They attacked him for being an American and labeled him a "cowardly bourgeois individualist." He tried to defend himself in "Cuba Libre" (1961), an essay reprinted in *Home: Social Essays* (1966), by writing: "Look, why jump on me?... I'm in complete agreement with you. I'm a poet ... what can I do? I write, that's all, I'm not even interested in politics." Mexican poet Jaime Shelley answered him: "You want to cultivate your soul? In that ugliness you live in, you want to cultivate your soul? Well, we've got millions of starving people to feed, and that moves me enough to make poems out of." Finally, Baraka came to realize the futility of his unpolitical art and began forsaking his life as a literary bohemian to embrace black nationalism. During this transitional period he produced some of his best-known works, including an analysis of contemporary black music, *Blues People: Negro Music in White America* (1963), and a second volume of poetry, *The Dead Lecturer: Poems* (1964).

### Success as a Dramatist

Although Baraka wrote a number of plays during this period, *Dutchman* is widely considered his masterpiece. The play received an Obie Award for best Off-Broadway play and rocketed Baraka into the public eye. *Dutchman* centers on a volatile encounter involving Lula, an attractive, flirtatious white woman, and Clay, a young, quiet, well-dressed black intellectual. While on a New York subway, Lula mocks and taunts Clay mercilessly, using harsh language and racial epithets, for trying to act white. Clay, in a fit of rage, explodes: "I sit here in this buttoned-up suit to keep myself from cutting all your throats. If I'm a middle-class fake white man—let me be. The only thing that would cure my neurosis would be your murder." Feeling justified, Lula stabs Clay to death, and as the play ends, she calmly turns to another black man who has just entered the subway.

Baraka followed up *Dutchman* with two plays in 1964, *The Toilet* and *The Slave*. "The Slave," Baraka remarked,

> was really the last play where I tried to balance and talk to blacks and whites. ... [I] began to focus on my own identity about that time and came to the conclusion that it was the black community I must direct myself to—we've tried talking to the white society and it's useless.

In 1965 Baraka divorced his white wife, deserted the white literary colony of Greenwich Village, and moved to

Harlem. Completely dissociating himself from the white race, Baraka dedicated himself to creating works that were inspired by and spoke to the black community. With increasingly violent overtones, his writings called for blacks to unite and establish their own nation. Experimenting with ritual forms in his drama, he wrote *Slave Ship: A Historical Pageant* (1967), a re-creation of the passage of slaves into America. Other works written during his black nationalist period are *The System of Dante's Hell* (1965), his only novel, and *Tales* (1967), a collection of short stories. Around this time Baraka also became more vocal about his hatred of whites; when a white woman approached him one day and asked what whites could do to help blacks, he retorted, "You can help by dying. You are a cancer." Although some people, especially his white friends, were shocked and upset over his violent outbursts, he continued to denounce all things "white." Hoping to withdraw even further, he approved of his name change in 1968 to Imamu Amiri Baraka, meaning "blessed spiritual leader." According to critic Floyd Gaffney, Baraka's marriage to black woman Sylvia Robinson in 1966 also signaled his "complete commitment to the black cause." Baraka's complex, symbolic plays *Great Goodness of Life (A Coon Show)* (1967), *Madheart: A Morality Play* (1967), and *Police* (1968), Gaffney continued, are further examples of Baraka's new "sociopolitical consciousness."

### From Black Nationalism to Marxism
By 1974 Baraka dropped the spiritual title "Imamu," and in a dramatic reversal of his earlier nationalist stance, declared himself an adherent of Marxist-Leninist thought. Categorically rejecting black nationalism, he now advocated socialism, stating: "It is a narrow nationalism that says the white man is the enemy. ... The black liberation movement in essence is a struggle for socialism." Explaining his decision to change philosophies, he told an interviewer in 1980: "I came to my Marxist view as a result of having struggled as a Nationalist and found certain dead ends theoretically and ideologically, as far as Nationalism was concerned, and had to reach out for a communist ideology." During his socialist period he wrote *Hard Facts: Excerpts* (1975), a volume of poetry, and produced the plays *S-1* (1978), *The Motion of History* (1978), and *The Sidnee Poet Heroical: In 29 Scenes* (1979). In the fall of 1979, he joined the Africana Studies Department at State University of New York at Stony Brook as a teacher of creative writing. In the same year, as cited by William J. Harris, "[Baraka] was arrested after two policemen allegedly attempted to intercede in a dispute between him and his wife over the price of children's shoes." While serving his sentence at a Harlem halfway house, he wrote *The Autobiography of LeRoi Jones* (1984). Other works he wrote in the 1980s include "Why's/Wise" (1985), an epic poem; *The Music: Reflection on Jazz and Blues* (1987) with his wife Amina Baraka; and "Reflections" (1988), a poem published in the periodical *Black Scholar*.

Notable publications during the 1990s include *Transbluesency, The Selected Poems of Amiri Bakara/LeRoi Jones* (1995), and *Funk Lore: New Poems* (1996).

In his introduction to *The Motion of History and Other Plays* (1978) Baraka defended his work by stating that his shift in political philosophy represented the direction toward which he had been moving since the very beginning of his career. He emphasized not *change* but *growth*. Nonetheless, his literary reputation has been declining over the last two decades. However, even if Baraka were to write no more plays, he would still hold a permanent place in the history of American theater. His work with the Black Arts Repertory Theatre/School helped to revolutionize black theater in America by providing a model for workshop/participation and street theater that has served aspiring drama groups throughout the United States. His understanding of the relationship between the theories of the function of culture and art has made an obvious impact on African American playwright Ed Bullins and others. Even more significant is the fact that with his plays in the mid-1960s he drew into vivid perspective the conditions and difficulties of blacks who sought to forge their own identities.

## Works in Literary Context

### Black Arts Movement
Baraka was a leading writer in the Black Arts movement (BAM), sometimes called the Black Aesthetics movement, which was the first major African American artistic movement since the Harlem Renaissance. Beginning in the early 1960s, BAM lasted through the mid-1970s. It flourished alongside the civil rights marches and the call for the independence of the African American community. African American writers set out to define what it meant to be a black writer in a white culture. While writers of the Harlem Renaissance seemed to investigate their identity within, writers of the Black Arts movement desired to define themselves and their era before being defined by others.

For the most part, participants in the Black Arts movement were, like Baraka, supportive of separatist politics and a black nationalist ideology. Larry Neal wrote in an essay "The Black Arts Movement" (1968) that the movement was the "aesthetic and spiritual sister of the Black Power concept." Rebelling against the mainstream society by being essentially anti-white, anti-American, and anti-middle class, these artists moved from the Renaissance view of art for art's sake into a philosophy of art for politics' sake.

The Black Arts movement attempted to produce works of art that would be meaningful to the African American masses. To this end, Baraka founded the Black Arts Repertory Theatre/School to make theater more accessible by "taking it to the streets." The objective was to promote interaction between the artists and the audience. Popular African American music of the day, including

John Coltrane's jazz and James Brown's soul, as well as street talk, were some of the other inspirational forces for the movement. In fact, much of the language used in these works, as in Baraka's plays, was aggressive, profane, and shocking—this was often a conscious attempt to show the vitality and power of African American activists. These writers tended to be revolutionaries, supporting both radical and peaceful protests for change as promoted by Malcolm X and Martin Luther King Jr. In addition, they believed that artists were required to do more than create: artists also had to be political activists in order to achieve nationalist goals. In addition to Baraka, some of the award-winning playwrights of the BAM were Ed Bullins, Richard Wesley, Sonia Sanchez, and Adrienne Kennedy.

## Works in Critical Context

Critical opinion has been sharply divided between those who feel, with *Dissent* contributor Stanley Kaufman, that Baraka's race and political moment account for his fame, and those who feel that Baraka stands among the most important writers of the age. In *American Book Review*, Arnold Rampersad counts Baraka with Phyllis Wheatley, Frederick Douglass, Paul Laurence Dunbar, Langston Hughes, Zora Neale Hurston, Richard Wright, and Ralph Ellison "as one of the eight figures ... who have significantly affected the course of African-American literary culture."

In his 1985 retrospective study of Baraka and his work, William J. Harris observed that assessment of Baraka has fallen into two general camps:

> The white response ... has been either silence or anger—and, in a few cases, sadness. ... One general complaint is that Baraka has forsaken art for politics. ... Another common accusation holds that Baraka used to be a good poet before he became a virulent racist. The reaction to Baraka in most of the black world has been very different from that in the white. In the black world Baraka is a famous artist. He is regarded as a father by the younger generation of poets; he is quoted in the streets—a fame almost never claimed by an American poet.

Whatever the reaction to Baraka, no one is left unaffected by his works. People bristle at his depictions of "white America," critics assert, because he mirrors the ugly and hideous facets of American society.

Called by one critic the "Malcolm X of Literature," Baraka's most important contributions may be his influence on other black writers and his "championing" of black people.

*Dutchman* *Dutchman* has long been regarded as Baraka's finest play. Norman Mailer, for example, acknowledged it as "the best play in America." In the view of James A. Miller, the play "merges private themes, mythical allusion, surrealistic techniques, and social statement into a play of astonishing power and resonance." However, the play did not receive a unanimously positive reception. While some critics praised it for its "power,"

"freshness," and "deadly wit," others were outraged by its language, its perpetuation of interracial hostility, and its portrayal of whites. Baraka countered:

> Lula ... is not meant to represent white people—as some critics have thought—but America itself ... the spirit of America. ... The play is about the difficulty of becoming and remaining a man in America. ... Manhood—black or white—is not wanted here.

While some critics may have had their reservations, *Dutchman* appears to be surviving the test of time. Years after the play's debut, Darryl Pinckley wrote in the *New York Times Book Review*:

> [Baraka] is a highly gifted dramatist. Much of the black protest literature of the 60s now seems diminished in power, even sentimental. But *Dutchman* immediately seizes the imagination. It is radically economical in structure, striking in the vivacity of its language and rapid shifts of mood.

# COMMON HUMAN EXPERIENCE

Baraka's abiding concern is with racial oppression and the need for a literature that embodies African American values. Here are some other famous works that explore similar themes:

*Roots: The Saga of an American Family* (1976), a novel by Alex Haley. Inspired by oral histories passed down through several generations of his family, Haley set about researching his family's past, going all the way back to his forbear Kunta Kinte, an African who was taken and sold into slavery in late-eighteenth-century America. The book then traces the story of Kunta's descendents down to the mid-twentieth century. The book was made into a massively successful TV miniseries.

*Soul on Ice* (1968), a collection of essays by Eldridge Cleaver. Written by the leader of the Black Panther party, this is a collection of essays that outline the black revolutionary cause and worldview at the time.

*The Autobiography of Malcolm X* (1965), an autobiography by Malcolm X as told to Alex Haley. After interviewing the controversial civil rights leader for *Playboy* magazine, Haley began transcribing Malcolm X's life story, which traced his rise from crime and poverty in Michigan to his prison conversion to Islam and his membership in the Nation of Islam.

*Radical Chic and Mau Mauing the Flak Catchers* (1970), a collection of essays by Tom Wolfe. This is a book containing two essays discussing radicalism, politics, and race relations in the 1960s.

## Responses to Literature

1. Critics have commented on Baraka's use of profanity in his dramas, particularly in *The Baptism*. Read this play, and examine how you feel about the use of harsh or profane language in drama and film. How necessary is it, and why?

2. Read Baraka's play, *Dutchman*. What challenge does Clay face in his life, and how does he go about meeting it? Write an essay in which you examine Baraka's comment that the play is about "the difficulty of becoming ... a man in America." Is this still true today or have things changed since the play was written in 1964?

3. Research the state of African American theater and arts today. How has it changed from the time Baraka founded the Black Arts Repertory Theatre/School? What principles of the Black Arts movement are still embraced today? In what ways have contemporary African American playwrights changed or moved away from the Black Arts movement?

4. Research black nationalism and Islam, particularly as it is practiced in the African American community. Who were some important figures in the black nationalist movement? What is your opinion of the movement and philosophy?

BIBLIOGRAPHY

**Books**

Bernotas, Bob. *Amiri Baraka*. New York: Chelsea House, 1991.

Benston, Kimberly A., ed. *Baraka: The Renegade and the Mask*. New Haven, Conn.: Yale University Press, 1976.

———, ed. *Imamu Amiri Baraka (Leroi Jones): a Collection of Critical Essays*. Englewood Cliffs, N.J.: Prentice-Hall, 1978.

Elam, Harry Justin. *Taking It to the Streets: The Social Protest Theater of Luis Valdez and Amiri Baraka*. Ann Arbor: University of Michigan Press, 1997.

Galens, David M. "Dutchman." In *Drama for Students*. Vol. 3. Detroit, Mich.: Gale, 1998.

———, ed. "The Baptism." In *Drama for Students*. Vol. 16. Detroit, Mich.: Gale, 2003.

Gwynne, James B., ed. *Amiri Baraka: The Kaleidoscopic Torch*. New York: Steppingstones Press, 1985.

Harris, William J. *The Poetry and Poetics of Amiri Baraka: The Jazz Aesthetic*. Columbia: University of Missouri Press, 1985.

Hudson, Theodore R. *From LeRoi Jones to Amiri Baraka: the Literary Works*. Durham, N.C.: Duke University Press, 1973.

Lacey, Henry C. *To Raise, Destroy, and Create: The Poetry, Drama, and Fiction of Imamu Amiri Baraka (LeRoi Jones)*. Troy, N.Y.: Whitson Publishing Company, 1981.

Milne, Ira Mark. "In Memory of Radio." In *Poetry for Students*. Vol. 9. Detroit, Mich.: Gale Group, 2000.

Sollors, Werner. *Amiri Baraka/LeRoi Jones: The Quest for a "Populist Modernism"*. New York: Columbia University Press, 1978.

Thomason, Elizabeth, ed. "Slave Ship." In *Drama for Students*. Vol. 11. Detroit, Mich.: Gale, 2001.

# ✿ Djuna Barnes

BORN: *1892, Cornwall-on-Hudson, New York*

DIED: *1982, New York, New York*

NATIONALITY: *American*

GENRE: *Fiction, poetry*

MAJOR WORKS:

*The Book of Repulsive Women: 8 Rhythms and 5 Drawings* (1915)

*Nightwood* (1936)

*Spillway* (1962)

Djuna Barnes    *Barnes, Djuna, 1959, photograph.* © Bettmann / Corbis.

## Overview

An experimental writer associated with the early modernists, Djuna Barnes combined elements of Surrealism, Gothicism, black humor, and poetry to depict the hopelessness of modern life. Barnes, who often described herself as "the most famous unknown in the world," was in fact a well-known writer in the bohemian communities of Greenwich Village and Paris from 1910 to 1930. Barnes was recognized for her sharp wit and quirky journalism, as well as her strange, dark fiction, plays, and poetry. She was also an illustrator, drawing ink or charcoal portraits of such illustrious models as James Joyce and Gertrude Stein. Many of her colleagues deemed her writing the product of genius, but the general reading public failed to embrace her.

## Works in Biographical and Historical Context

### An Unusual Upbringing and Early Notoriety
Barnes was born in Corrnwall-on-Hudson, New York, to an English mother and an idealistic, domineering father who mistrusted society and eventually moved the family to a self-supporting farm on Long Island. Educated at home by her father and her paternal grandmother, an author and suffragist (an advocate of a woman's right to vote, at a time when it was not yet allowed), Barnes was infused as a young girl with a knowledge of art, music, and

literature. She studied formally only briefly at the Pratt Institute and the Art Students' League in New York City, and by age twenty-one had gained a job writing and illustrating features and interviews for the *Brooklyn Eagle*.

Her first poems were accepted by *Harpers Weekly* in 1913. During the next two decades she published stories, poems, and plays in newspapers as well as such popular and artistic magazines as *Vanity Fair*. She became involved in theater as an actor and reviewer, and three of her one-act plays were performed by Eugene O'Neill's Provincetown Players during the 1919–1920 season. Barnes also played a leading role among the untraditional, antiauthoritarian bohemian art scene thriving at the time in Greenwich Village, where she became notorious for her mordant humor, inspired conversation, and striking appearance. Her first published volume, *The Book of Repulsive Women* (1915), was self-illustrated with sinuous pen-and-ink drawings, and for many years Barnes was known as much for her artwork as for her writing.

### Move to Paris, Life-Changing Relationships
Like her grandmother before her, Barnes's success as a journalist in New York led to her assignment in Europe in 1921 for *McCall's*. She stayed for over a decade. Her Paris years were some of her most important, personally as well as professionally. Soon after arriving in Paris, and following a brief stint in Berlin, Barnes met Thelma Wood, a sculptor and silverpoint artist from St. Louis, whose previous lovers included Edna St. Vincent Millay and the photographer Berenice Abbott. The difficult relationship and cohabitation that ensued between Barnes and Wood lasted nearly a decade and was the impetus behind *Nightwood* (1936).

Barnes lived and wrote as part of the expatriate literary enclave in Paris's fashionable Left Bank, where she became acquainted with celebrated figures Ezra Pound, Gertrude Stein, and James Joyce, whose stream-of-consciousness technique influenced her prose style, notably in her novel *Ryder* (1928). Barnes was a regular visitor at the salon of Natalie Clifford Barney, whose lesbian circle she caricatured in drawings and Elizabethan verse in her *Ladies' Almanac* (1928), offering subtle and sly high praise to a fictional saint based on Barney.

*Nightwood* was published by Faber and Faber in 1936, after several years of difficult revision by Barnes and rejections from several different publishing companies. The novel had its supporters, including T. S. Eliot, who endorsed publication of the novel after Barnes's friend Emily Coleman persuaded him to read it. Harcourt and Brace published the American edition in 1937. At the center of the tragedy is the broken relationship between Nora and Robin. Doctor Matthew O'Connor, a grand gay transvestite character who philosophizes in witty monologues, counsels and consoles Nora in the painful reality of her betrayal by a woman who is "a beast turning human" and who "lives in two worlds—meet of

# LITERARY AND HISTORICAL CONTEMPORARIES

Barnes's famous contemporaries include:

**Emperor Hirohito** (1901–1989): The 124th Emperor of Japan, Emperor Hirohito reigned longer than any other Japanese monarch. During his reign, Japan underwent massive changes, going from a semi-industrialized country to an economic powerhouse.

**Sergei Prokofiev** (1891–1953): One of the greatest twentieth-century Russian composers, Prokofiev wrote the famous musical children's story *Peter and the Wolf*, in which different instruments represent different animals.

**Margaret Mitchell** (1900–1949): An Atlanta-based reporter and columnist, Mitchell wrote the massive historical potboiler *Gone With the Wind* (1936) while recuperating from a broken ankle. Initially written for her own amusement, Mitchell only reluctantly submitted it to a publisher years later. It was an overnight blockbuster and went on to become the second best-selling book, after The Bible.

**Joe Louis** (1914–1981): Considered one of the greatest boxers of all time, "The Brown Bomber" held the American heavyweight championship for eleven straight years, a feat that has never been equaled.

**John Dos Passos** (1896–1970): Called one of the writers of the "Lost Generation" (along with Ernest Hemingway and F. Scott Fitzgerald), Dos Passos's novels are marked by experimental elements, such as stream-of-consciousness writing, nonlinear plots, and incorporation of autobiographical and factual elements (including newspaper clippings) into otherwise fictional stories.

child and desperado." Nora's love cannot tame Robin, and Robin leaves her for another woman.

Thelma Wood's reaction to *Nightwood* was not favorable. She was angered by Barnes's portrayal of her as the selfish, nearly inhuman Robin. Barnes knew the risks involved in this public indictment of Wood's betrayal. While writing the novel she wrote to Coleman: "Had a letter from Thelma, possibly the last in my life if the book does get printed ... She will hate me so. It's awful—God almighty what a price one pays for 200 pages." But, as Cheryl Plumb asserted in her article "Revising *Nightwood*": "a kind of glee of despair for Barnes 's writing is the recompense, the resurrection." Plumb quoted from a letter from Barnes to Coleman, dated July 22, 1936: "I come to love my invention more—so I am able—perhaps only so able—to put Thelma aside—because now she is not Robin."

***The Life of a Recluse*** The next several years after the publication of *Nightwood* were difficult for Barnes, who battled depression, alcoholism, and illness. Relations with her surviving family members were also strained, especially when her brothers and mother conspired to send her to a sanitarium. In general, her family did not appreciate her creative work and pressured her to get a steady job.

After moving throughout Europe during the 1930s, Barnes returned to New York before the outbreak of World War II. Apart from *The Antiphon* (1958), a Jacobean-styled family tragedy, she published little, eschewing the interviews and literary memoirs that kept many of her contemporaries in the public eye. She lived her last forty years in a small flat in Greenwich Village as a self-described recluse, visited by her friends T. S. Eliot, Henry Miller, Dag Hammarskjold, and E. E. Cummings. As observers often note, Barnes has become something of a legend because of her association with many of the century's greatest artists and her insistence on personal and artistic freedom.

## Works in Literary Context

In a 1971 interview with James B. Scott, Barnes admitted that "every writer writes out of his life." At the same time, however, Barnes was intensely private, resisting or refusing most attempts at interview or biography. She also resisted being classified in either her work or her personal life, which may account for her conflict with critics, scholars, and admirers who embraced her as a lesbian writer.

***The Halt Position of the Damned*** Barnes's full-length and short stories alike are marked by black humor, decadent and sometimes obscure characters, a keen sense of the absurdity of existence, and a Gothic tone of menace and foreboding. Commentators note Barnes's use of doll and animal images to depict modern man and woman as less-than-human creatures trapped midway between salvation and damnation. In "A Night among the Horses," for example, a wealthy woman with "a battery for a heart and the body of a toy" attempts to possess her unwilling stableman. The stableman perceives that the woman wants to transform him into "a thing, half standing, half crouching, like those figures under the roofs of historic buildings, the halt position of the damned." By the story's end, he has become a grotesque creature who can live neither in society nor in a natural, animal state; during an attempt to escape from the woman's mechanistic world, he is trampled to death by his beloved horses.

"The halt position of the damned" is a phrase critics often cite in describing Barnes's alienated, depersonalized characters. In addition to qualities of bestiality and mechanization, commentators point to decadence as a mark of damnation among her protagonists, a condition exemplified by Madame Erling von Bartmann, the central figure of "Aller et retour." Traveling to visit her daughter in the south of France, Madame is engulfed by images of sex, religion, and death: gaudy postcards of bathing beauties displayed near tawdry funeral wreaths, a prostitute plucking a robin, and foul odors, which "neither pleased nor displeased" her. She later urges her meek daughter to delve fully into the horrors and beauties of life, but the girl becomes engaged to a dull, secure man. "Ah, how unnecessary," Madame von Bartmann remarks at the end of the story as she heads back toward Paris, resuming, critics note, the meaningless cycle of comings and goings suggested by the story's title.

## Works in Critical Context

Although Barnes's short fiction is faulted by some critics as mannered, obscure, and melodramatic, others assert that it is superior to her longer works in its economy of language and form. Commentators generally agree that while *Nightwood* has become Barnes's best-known work, her short stories occupy a significant place in a distinctive body of work. Kenneth Rexroth wrote:

> Djuna Barnes may be considered a late born voice of the fin de siècle literary Decadence, but she is also an early born prophet of the black comedy, theater of cruelty, and literature of total alienation of the later years of the century, the period of decadence and disintegration of Western Civilization, the time of permanent Apocalypse.

Fourteen of Barnes's earliest short stories, all originally published in New York newspapers and previously uncollected, appeared in 1982 in *Smoke, and Other Early Stories*. Critics note that these pieces diverge from Barnes's later short fiction in their reportorial tone and journalistic style of exposition, their flat, stereotyped, urban characters, and their surprise, twist endings. The publication of this volume is indicative of the heightened interest in Barnes that emerged during the 1970s and 1980s, when she attracted readers not only for her innovative talent, but for her inherent feminist sensibility. In addition to *Smoke, and Other Early Stories*, a biography of Barnes as well as the first extensive critical studies of her works were published during these decades.

### Nightwood

Barnes's literary reputation rests largely on *Nightwood*, a novel of sexual and spiritual alienation that T. S. Eliot praised for its "quality of horror and doom very nearly related to that of Elizabethan tragedy." The novel is so astonishing that even today, nearly fifty years after its publication, it prompts division among knowledgeable critics. Melvin Friedman's comment, for example, that *Nightwood* may "usurp the enviable position shared by Proust and Joyce" does not square with Leslie Fiedler's dismissal in *Love and Death in the American Novel* (1962) of its "dislocated lyricism, hallucinated vision and oddly skewed language."

Although *Nightwood* has a tragic and even nightmarish side, it is also a humorous novel. Elizabeth Pochoda,

---

## COMMON HUMAN EXPERIENCE

Barnes was a pioneer of black humor, or finding comic entertainment in normally grim or upsetting circumstances. Here are other authors whose works were known for black humor.

*"Résumé"* (1925), a poem by Dorothy Parker. Perhaps the most famously caustic wit of the 1920s-era bohemian scene, Parker was not above even making light of her own repeated suicide attempts, which she enumerates in this short poem.

*Dr. Strangelove; or, How I Learned to Stop Worrying and Love the Bomb* (1963), a film directed by Stanley Kubrick. Perhaps the definitive cinematic treatment of black humor, *Dr. Strangelove* pokes fun at just about everyone involved with the military and political structures that held Earth's fate in the balance during the nuclear standoff of the Cold War.

*The Magic Christian* (1959), a novel by Terry Southern. Southern coauthored the script for *Dr. Strangelove*, having previously honed his dark comedic chops with this dark satire about a billionaire who plays elaborate practical jokes, proving that "everyone has their price."

---

commenting in *Twentieth Century Literature*, called *Nightwood* "a tremendously funny book in a desperately surgical sort of way." The novel's humor lies in its wit and its use of paradox and hoax, Pochoda argued, and all actions in the novel "are reduced to their initial hoax. Only then is sympathy allowable. The apparently touching love story of Robin and Nora is also a kind of hoaxing." Donald J. Greiner, writing in *Critique: Studies in Modern Fiction*, saw the paradoxical combination of humor and sadness as fundamental to all black humor. Barnes's "sense of humor is evident from the beginning," Greiner wrote, "and her use of funny elements with a depressing theme reflects the perplexing mixture so vital to black humor." *Nightwood*, Greiner concluded, "remains the most successful early example of the American black humor novel."

## Responses to Literature

1. Barnes made it a point to live a varied life and then processed the events of that remarkable life through her writing. Do you like to read about lives similar to your own, or do you prefer to read about places and people you have never encountered before? Do you think it is more difficult to write about ordinary places and events, or to write about extraordinary places and events?

2. Can Barnes's works be taken seriously, given the fact she wrote from such a personal place? Do you think

that all writers create from a personal or subjective place? Would it be possible to write anything without thinking about your own views about the topic first?

3. How can traumatic personal events be an inspiring resource for writing? Is writing a good way to vent feelings that might be too intense to talk about? If you wrote about your family history would you include events that might not portray your family in the best light?

4. Barnes wrote satirical pieces about the people she knew and had relationships with. Write and illustrate a satirical mini-booklet about your close circle of friends and your daily lives, making it as accurate as possible to your own perceptions of them and yourself.

BIBLIOGRAPHY

**Books**

Allen, Carolyn. *Following Djuna: Women Lovers and the Erotics of Loss.* Bloomington, Ind.: Indiana University Press, 1996.

Broe, Mary Lynn, editor. *Silence and Power: A Reevaluation of Djuna Barnes.* Carbondale, Ill.: Southern Illinois University Press, 1991.

Burke, Kenneth. "Version, Con-, Per-, and In-(Thoughts on Djuna Barnes' Novel Nightwood)," in his *Language as Symbolic Action: Essays on Life, Literature, and Method.* Berkeley, Calif.: University of California Press, 1968, pp. 240–253.

Curry, Lynda C. "The Second Metamorphosis: A Study of the Development of The Antiphon by Djuna Barnes." PhD dissertation. Miami: Miami University, 1978.

Field, Andrew. *Djuna: The Life and Times of Djuna Barnes.* New York: Putnam's, 1983.

Frank, Joseph. "Spatial Form in Modern Literature," in his *The Widening Gyre: Crisis and Mastery in Modern Literature.* New Brunswick, N.J.: Rutgers University Press, 1963, pp. 3–62.

Herring, Philip. *Djuna: The Life and Work of Djuna Barnes.* New York: Viking Press, 1995.

O'Neal, Hank. *"Life Is Painful, Nasty, and Short—in My Case It Has Only Been Painful and Nasty": Djuna Barnes, 1978–1981: An Informal Memoir.* New York: Paragon House, 1990.

Kannenstine, Louis F. *The Art of Djuna Barnes: Duality and Damnation.* New York: New York University Press, 1977.

Messerli, Douglas. *Djuna Barnes: A Bibliography.* Rhinebeck, N.Y.: David Lewis, 1975.

Nemerov, Howard. "A Response to The Antiphon," in his *Reflections on Poetry & Poetics.* New Brunswick, N.J.: Rutgers University Press, 1972, pp. 66–70.

Plumb, Cheryl. *Fancy's Craft: Art and Identity in the Early Works of Djuna Barnes.* Selinsgrove, Pa.: Susquehanna University Press, 1987.

Scott, James B. *Djuna Barnes.* Boston: Twayne, 1976.

Spencer, Sharon. *Space, Time and Structure in the Modern Novel.* New York: New York University Press, 1971, pp. 39–43.

# John Barth

BORN: *1930, Cambridge, Maryland*

NATIONALITY: *American*

GENRE: *Fiction*

MAJOR WORKS:

*The Sot-Weed Factor* (1960)

*Giles Goat-Boy; or, The Revised New Syllabus* (1966)

*Lost in the Funhouse: Fiction for Print, Tape, Live Voice* (1968)

*Chimera* (1973)

## Overview

An eminent practitioner and theoretician of postmodernist fiction, John Barth often defines himself as a "concocter of comic novels," an inventor of universes who is, above all, a lover of storytelling. For more than forty

John Barth    *Barth, John, photograph. AP Images.*

years, the Maryland-born author has experimented with a variety of fictional forms, drawing upon his vast experience with Western literary tradition. His short stories, novellas, and novels concern themselves with the interaction of reader and text as well as the more fundamental questions of personal identity and the innate absurdity of human existence.

## Works in Biographical and Historical Context

*An Inauspicious Beginning*  John Simmons Barth Jr. was born, with his twin sister Jill, on May 27, 1930, in Cambridge, Maryland, to John Jacob Barth and Georgia Simmons. The Barth family was deeply rooted in this rural southern corner of the Old Line State. Barth's grandfather, a stone carver by trade, also dealt in real estate, selling marshland to his fellow German immigrants. The boy's father, known as "Whitey," was the proprietor of a combination candy store and restaurant. In addition, he was chief judge of the Orphan's Court in Cambridge, a small port on the Choptank River.

Barth's childhood and adolescence in Cambridge were quiet and uneventful. John Jacob Barth saw no early evidence of literary genius in his son: "This talent must have come later," he commented in 1966, "I didn't notice it when he was younger." Barth's twin sister had similar recollections; she remembered her brother as "more serious than outgoing" and recalled that "he got a lot of things without trying very hard at school." Barth's older brother, William, echoed his father and sister: "Looking back I'd never expected him to be a writer."

*From Music to Writing*  As a young man intent on pursuing music as a career, Barth went to the Juilliard School of Music in New York to become a jazz arranger. Instead, he found himself a talented amateur among professionals, and "went home to think of some other way to become distinguished." As an undergraduate at Johns Hopkins University, he filed books in the Classics Department and the stacks of the Oriental Seminary, and became enchanted with the tenth-century Sanskrit *Ocean of Story* and Richard Burton's annotated *Arabian Nights*—both of which inspired him throughout his career.

*An Educator and Rearranger*  Barth graduated with a commitment to become a writer and meanwhile earn a living by teaching. Barth's subsequent career as an English professor also plays an important role in his fiction; many of his books are set in universities and contain allusions to works of literature. He has taught at Pennsylvania State University, the State University of New York at Buffalo, and at his alma mater, Johns Hopkins University. Partly due to these affiliations, Barth has been called an academic writer. Though he resisted this label at first, by mid-life he recognized, as he says in "Getting Oriented," that all of his novels are about education—or rather, "imperfect or misfired education." However, perhaps because of his musical background, Barth remains an arranger at heart. As he states in *The Friday Book*, his "chief pleasure is to take a received melody—an old narrative poem, a classical myth, a shopworn literary convention ...—and, improvising like a jazzman within its constraints, reorchestrating it to its present purpose."

In the fall of 1954, Barth chanced upon a photograph of *The Floating Theater*, an old showboat that had entertained in the Tidewater area during the author's childhood. Barth remembered that he saw the boat "when I was about seven. ... I thought it would be a good idea to write a philosophical minstrel show ... only it was going to be a work of literature." This "philosophical minstrel show" became Barth's first published novel, *The Floating Opera* (1956). Although Barth's early novels were not commercially successful, they garnered him an elite readership of scholars and college students.

*Sucess with Goat-Boy*  In 1958 Barth completed research on a historical novel which he had begun two years earlier. This novel, according to Barth, would have a plot fancier and more contrived than that of *Tom Jones* (1749), British novelist Henry Fielding's sprawling comedy. Barth finished this novel, *The Sot-Weed Factor*, in March 1959, and Doubleday published the mammoth 806-page book in August 1960. Like its forerunners, *The Sot-Weed Factor* (the title means tobacco merchant) was a commercial failure, selling only 5,000 copies.

From 1959 to 1965 Barth worked on the novel that would be his first financial success. Before it was finished, he commented that "What I really wanted to write after *The Sot-Weed Factor* was a new Old Testament, a comic Old Testament. I guess that's what the new novel *Giles Goat-Boy* is going to be. A souped-up Bible." In April 1959 Barth had begun a novel called "The Seeker," but in June 1960 he put this project aside and started work on *Giles Goat-Boy*. He completed this "souped-up Bible" in 1965, having worked on it exclusively except for a six-month period from January to June of 1963 when he and his family toured Europe.

After publication of *The Sot-Weed Factor*, several critics suggested that Barth had relied on Lord Raglan's twenty-two points of the hero, a systematic progression of heroic moments or archetypes that often figure in mythological tales. Barth had not read Raglan's treatise, but he decided to investigate the subject thoroughly. He took notes for two years on the hero myth and related notions, especially from Raglan's *The Hero*, Joseph Campbell's *The Hero with a Thousand Faces*, and Otto Rank's *The Myth of the Birth of the Hero*. Barth also reread Homer, Virgil, and the Gospels before beginning actual composition in 1962. Doubleday published the 710-page *Giles Goat-Boy* in August 1966. Sales reached 50,000, four times the combined sales of Barth's first three novels. *Giles Goat-Boy* even appeared briefly on the best-seller lists. Barth released *Lost in the Funhouse* in 1968, a collection of what many critics consider the finest examples of postmodern short stories.

# LITERARY AND HISTORICAL CONTEMPORARIES

John Barth's famous contemporaries include:

**Joseph Campbell** (1904–1987): A Sarah Lawrence College professor of mythology, Campbell wrote the highly influential *Hero With A Thousand Faces* (1949), which analyzed myths from around the world in a search for universal themes.

**August Derleth** (1909–1971): A prolific author in his own right, Derleth is perhaps best remembered today for his efforts to keep the works of horror author H. P. Lovecraft in print.

**Elvis Presley** (1935–1977): One of the towering cultural icons of the twentieth century, Presley is generally credited with popularizing rock and roll into a national phenomenon, making him one of the best-selling and most successful performers of all time.

**Theodor Geisel** (1904–1991): Known and beloved by his millions of fans as Dr. Seuss, Geisel wrote and illustrated children's books such as *The Cat in the Hat*, *Green Eggs and Ham*, and *How the Grinch Stole Christmas*.

**Barry Goldwater** (1909–1998): A U.S. Senator from Arizona, Goldwater is widely credited with re-energizing right wing American politics in the wake of the New Deal and President Eisenhower's more centrist conservatism.

Following the success of *Giles Goat-Boy*, Barth held a series of professorships at prestigious northeastern universities, finishing his academic career at Johns Hopkins University, where he retired from teaching in 1995.

After years of exploring shorter-form storytelling, Barth switched to the challenge of creating "book-end" works when he published *Once Upon a Time: A Floating Opera* in 1994. Purported to be the final work of a fictional character named John Barth, the novel is a meditation on autobiography, memoir, and narrative. In 2008, Barth published *The Development*, a novel set in a retirement community.

## Works in Literary Context

*Postmodernism* Barth is an eminent practitioner and theoretician of postmodernist fiction, a movement in which literary works are often interpreted as studies of how fiction is created and how reader and text interact. Barth's approach to writing derives from his belief that the narrative possibilities of the traditional novel have been exhausted. In "The Literature of Exhaustion," an essay first published in the *Atlantic Monthly* in 1967, he describes the contemporary experimental writer, who "confronts an intellectual dead end and employs it

against itself to accomplish new human work." Rather than attempt to convey the experience of reality, Barth investigates authorial imagination in "novels which imitate the form of the Novel, by an author who imitates the role of the Author." Recurring features of Barth's work include black humor, bawdy wordplay, vivid imagery, labyrinthine plots, blurring of past and present, and the often farcical use of mythical and historical characters. Throughout his fiction, Barth is primarily concerned with the question of whether individuals can transcend the innate absurdity of human existence.

*Metafiction* Metafiction is a literary style characterized by the author calling the reader's attention to the fact that the story is a fictional creation existing in its own fabricated reality. This fabricated reality is often reflected back at our own reality, or vice versa. A common metafictional technique is to tell a "story within a story," in which the fictional characters are writing their own made-up tales, thereby creating multiple levels of reality: the reality of the reader, the characters in the novel, and the characters within the story created by the character in the novel. There might also be supposedly real sources, such as newspaper articles or interviews with real people, that are in fact made up, created to serve the story. Another common metafictional technique is to have the main character address the author and/or reader, often commenting on the course of the story or directly foreshadowing certain turns of the plot.

Although novels had in the past occasionally employed a self-reflexive technique in which the author would directly address the reader, metafiction added a postmodern element that took the story's own awareness of itself to a new level, in effect assuming that reality itself was an artificial construct and parodying various literary techniques, as Barth did in *Lost in the Funhouse* (1968).

Barth is often credited as the father of metafiction, in no small part thanks to his essay "The Literature of Exhaustion," published in 1967. The title refers to the genesis of metafiction, which arose from the commonly-held belief among intellectuals around the middle of the twentieth century that the novel, as a story-telling medium, was exhausted and dead. Everything that could be done, stylistically, had been done, some thought, and there were few directions left in which push the envelope of the novelistic form. Thus metafiction, which openly acknowledged the many different forms and techniques of novel-writing, played with and deconstructed them, and became a new technique in its own right.

Eventually, the experimentation of metafiction proved to be its own creative dead end. By the mid-1970s readers were growing tired of literary experimentation for its own sake, and seemed to acknowledge that although there was little uncharted territory left in the novelistic form, that did not necessarily render it obsolete. Although metafiction remains a viable literary subgenre today, its relevance and dominance are much reduced from its heyday of the 1960s.

## Works in Critical Context

Barth's complex and demanding fiction has been the subject of numerous scholarly studies, but general readers often find that "in his fascinated commitment to the art—and to the criticism—of storytelling, he has no rival," declares William Pritchard in the *New York Times Book Review*. *John Barth* author E. P. Walkiewicz names the subject of his study a "writer who throughout his career has exhibited great versatility, technical virtuosity, learning, and wit."

The unpredictable author's encyclopedic fictions have baffled some critics, yet many reviewers claim to recognize his genius even when pronouncing his novels unreadable or tedious. A review in the *Times Literary Supplement* rates *The Sot-Weed Factor*, *Giles Goat-Boy*, and *Chimera* "easily the best worst in modern fiction." Their author, critics have found, is just as difficult to assess. Efforts to place Barth in a literary category are futile, Walkiewicz explains, due to "the formal complexity, verbal richness, and eclectic content" of his books.

*The Sot-Weed Factor* A complex, epic work with several subplots, *The Sot-Weed Factor* (1960) secured Barth's reputation among literary critics and scholars and elicited favorable comparisons to such works as Henry Fielding's *Tom Jones*, Voltaire's *Candide*, and Miguel de Cervantes's *Don Quixote*. Leslie Fiedler deemed *The Sot-Weed Factor* "closer to the 'Great American Novel' than any other book of the last decade," and Richard Kostelanetz praised it as "one of the greatest works of fiction of our time."

In *Forum-Service*, Leslie Fiedler notes that although the book is a parody, it is nonetheless "utterly serious, the farce and melodrama evoke terror and pity, and the flagrant mockery of a happy ending constricts the heart. And all the while one laughs, at a pitch somewhere between hysteria and sheer delight." "The notion of any serious historical inquiry is undermined" in *The Sot-Weed Factor*, Tanner maintains. The book reminds us that American history is the result of "storytelling," one of "our attempts to name and control the world around us," McConnell concurs. For Heide Ziegler, *The Sot-Weed Factor* is "a, or even the, decisive landmark in the development of postmodern fiction."

## Responses to Literature

1. Do you think the traditional novel has been exhausted creatively? Why or why not? Speculate on new ways that people might tell each other stories if the novel is no longer used as a medium.

2. Research the defining elements of postmodern literature. Who are some other postmodernist authors? How does Barth's work fit within the strictures of postmodernism?

---

### COMMON HUMAN EXPERIENCE

Much of Barth's work can be classified as metafiction—a type of fiction that is conscious of itself, either in pointing out its fictional nature to the reader or otherwise playing around with the normal conceits of literary fiction.

*Breakfast of Champions* (1973), a novel by Kurt Vonnegut. This novel features appearances from Vonnegut himself, who proceeds to have discussions with his own characters; the climax of the story is Vonnegut's conversation with his own alter-ego, Kilgore Trout.

*If on a Winter's Night a Traveler* (1979), a novel by Italo Calvino. A book that is about reading, or rather attempting to read, a book called *If on a Winter's Night a Traveler*, every other chapter is the "book" itself, the other chapters being second-person descriptions of the reader preparing to read the following chapter.

*The Princess Bride* (1973), a novel by William Goldman. As the original cover put it, this was an "abridged" version of "the good parts" of "S. Morgenstern's classic." Goldman goes on to provide a running commentary through the entirety of this post-modern take on classic fairy tales.

---

3. *Giles Goat-Boy* is set entirely within the confines of a university campus, which represents the known world. Imagine your own school is the universe; how would you divide it up? What real-life factions would the faculty and the student body represent? What would a map of the campus look like if each building represented a country?

4. Do you think Barth's literary experiments have merit as art, or are they merely a waste of time as some critics have asserted? Present arguments for both interpretations.

BIBLIOGRAPHY

**Books**

Bowen, Zack R. *A Reader's Guide to John Barth*. Westport, Conn.: Greenwood Press, 1994.

Fogel, Stanley. *Understanding John Barth*. Columbia, S.C.: University of South Carolina Press, 1990.

Lindsay, Alan. *Death in the Funhouse: John Barth and Poststructural Aesthetics*. Bern, Switzerland: Peter Lang, 1995.

Vine, Richard Allan. *John Barth: An Annotated Bibliography*. Metuchen, N.J.: Scarecrow, 1977.

# ✸ Donald Barthelme

BORN: *1931, Philadelphia, Pennsylvania*

DIED: *1989, Houston, Texas*

NATIONALITY: *American*

GENRE: *Fiction*

MAJOR WORKS:
*Come Back, Dr. Caligari* (1964)
*Unspeakable Practices, Unnatural Acts* (1968)
*City Life* (1971)
*The Dead Father* (1975)

## Overview

A preeminent writer of experimental fiction, Donald Barthelme created humorous and often unsettling stories by juxtaposing incongruous elements of contemporary language and culture. Barthelme's writing is characterized by the absence of traditional plot and character development, disjointed syntax and dialogue, parodies of jargon and cliché, and a humor, according to Thomas M. Leitch, that arises "from a contract between outrageous premises and deadpan presentation." Although some critics perceive a destructive impulse to subvert language and culture in

Donald Barthelme    *Barthelme, Donald, photograph. © Jerry Bauer. Reproduced by permission.*

much of his fiction, Barthelme has enjoyed widespread critical acclaim and is particularly praised as a stylist who offers vital and regenerative qualities to literature.

## Works in Biographical and Historical Context

***Never a Native, Always an Observer*** Barthelme was slightly dislocated throughout his life, never quite a native of any particular place, however much he may have loved his adopted home in New York City. He was born on April 7, 1931, in Philadelphia, where his father, Donald Sr., had met his wife-to-be, Helen Bechtold, at the University of Pennsylvania. The family moved to Houston when Donald Jr. was two years old. There his father worked both as a practicing architect and as a professor of architecture at the University of Houston. Helen, a former English major, helped her husband create a stimulating oasis of scholarly interests in the midst of what seemed to their son an intellectually barren culture in Texas.

He was reading and writing imitations of James Joyce and T. S. Eliot in his teens, and he began publishing while editing his high-school newspaper, *The Eagle*. His juvenile work brought him several awards. At the University of Houston, Barthelme contributed both fiction and nonfiction pieces to *The Cougar*, the student newspaper. In his mature work in the 1960s, his lasting interest in both kinds of writing was demonstrated in his contributions to the "Comments" column in *The New Yorker*, where he published short pieces combining objective reportage and subjective impressionism in his own Barthelmesque form of New Journalism.

Barthelme indulged in both his writing ambitions and his interests in the visual arts, which was inherited from his parents, while working as a reporter on cultural events for the *Houston Post*, where he was hired after dropping out of his junior year of college in 1951. Even after he was drafted into active service during the Korean War two years later, he was fortunate enough to be assigned editorial work on the army newspaper. Arriving in Korea on the same day a truce was signed afforded him a non-threatening opportunity to observe military life. His observations of the absurdities of military bureaucracy resurface in his later stories.

***An Unusual Literary Style Emerges*** Barthelme's first stories appeared in literary periodicals during the early 1960s. In these works, many of which were first published in the *New Yorker* and subsequently collected in book form, Barthelme incorporated advertising slogans, comic-book captions, catalog descriptions, and jacket blurbs from records and books into a style that features verbal puns, non sequiturs, and fractured dialogue and narrative. These volumes contain some of his best-known and most highly praised stories.

Barthelme's first novel, *Snow White* (1976), is a darkly comic and erotic parody of the popular fairy tale.

Composed largely of fragmented episodes in which indistinguishable characters attempt to express themselves in often nonsensical speech, *Snow White* has commonly been interpreted as an examination of the failure of language and the inability of literature to transcend or transform contemporary reality. *The Dead Father* (1975) is often considered one of Barthelme's most sustained and cohesive narrative works, but even then his developing prose style created a novel that was based upon an unusual and multi-layered technique. In this novel, a surrealistic, mock-epic account of the Dead Father's journey to his grave and his burial by his son and a cast of disreputable characters, Barthelme weaves mythological, biblical, and literary allusions. In his third novel, *Paradise* (1986), Barthelme's literary experiments continue, as he uses spare, formalistic prose marked by both a sense of playfulness and sorrow.

In addition to the critical acclaim accorded his adult works, Barthelme's children's book *The Slightly Irregular Fire Engine; or, The Hithering Thithering Djinn* (1971), received the National Book Award for children's literature. *Sixty Stories* (1981) contains a selection of his short fiction as well as miscellaneous prose pieces and an excerpt from *The Dead Father*. Barthelme has also adapted his novel *Snow White* and seven stories from *Great Days* for the stage.

## Works in Literary Context

*Postmodernism*  Critics have applied a variety of labels to Barthelme in an attempt to place him accurately in the context of contemporary fiction. Alfred Kazin calls him an "antinovelist"; Frederick R. Karl a "minimalist"; and Jack Hicks a "metafictionist." Charles Molesworth, dubbing him "perhaps the final post-Enlightenment writer," locates him on the frontier between modernism and postmodernism. In general, Barthelme's worked is considered part of the broad category of postmodernist fiction. Modernist art and fiction were a reaction to World War I and revealed a loss of faith in nineteenth-century power structures, such as the European monarchies and organized religion, along with a simultaneous excitement over and fear of advances in science and technology. Postmodernism sprang from the further disillusionment of Western society after World War II. Postmodernist literature often reflects an extremely relativistic, amoral outlook; a breakdown of the traditional categories of high and low culture; and a general feeling that life is absurd or just impossible to interpret.

*Collage Stories*  Barthelme's fiction produces its effects by combining materials calling for different responses, a process called juxtaposition. Barthelme has called this structural procedure "the principle of collage ... the central principle of all art in the twentieth century in all media," and explained:

> New York City is or can be regarded as a collage, as opposed to, say, a tribal village in which all the

huts ... are the same hut, duplicated. The point of collage is that unlike things are stuck together to make, in the best case, a new reality. This new reality, in the best case, may be or imply a comment on the other reality from which it came, and may be also much else. It's an *itself*, if it's successful: [an] ... "anxious object," which does not know whether it's a work of art or a pile of junk.

*Tragic Humor*  Barthelme's idiosyncratic humor is perhaps the one constant in his work, which coheres around his comic view of a tragically fractured cosmos. Much of that humor grows out of his topical references to recognizable developments on the newspaper front page and style sections: his weirdly warped echoes of currently fashionable ideas and consumer products, his surrealistically skewed sketches of familiar urban locales or banal current events, and his gleeful, albeit revisionary, deployment of current slang.

For example, in his short story "The Indian Uprising," Barthelme uses the familiar trope of Native Americans fighting against the U.S. Cavalry during the Indian Wars of the nineteenth century in a way that evokes the televised horrors of the Vietnam War, the first mass-media war, that was ongoing at the time the story was written. The story also features an intersecting flashback to the narrator's girlfriend and female teacher, both of whom end up betraying him, that seems to paint "the

## COMMON HUMAN EXPERIENCE

Barthelme's re-imagining of *Snow White* is one of several such post-modern re-imaginings of classic tales.

*Briar Rose* (1997), a novel by Robert Coover. A retelling of the Sleeping Beauty fairy tale, this time told from the Princess's perspective, all the while experimenting with language and story structure.

*Beauty and the Beast* (1987–1990), a television series created by Ron Koslow. This series placed the classic tale of a woman's love for a cursed man-beast into modern New York City, adding a utopian society of bestial outcasts to the story.

*The Rose and the Beast: Fairy Tales Retold* (2007), a short story collection by Francesca Lia Block. A collection of distinctly dark retellings of nine of the most popular fairy tales, including Bluebeard, Cinderella, and Little Red Riding Hood.

"Snow, Glass, Apples" (1994), a short story by Neil Gaiman. Another take on the Snow White tale, which adds a postmodern spin by casting the "evil" queen as the narrator, and Snow White as a monstrous abomination.

battle of sexes" in the same light as the cavalry versus the Indians.

### Works in Critical Context

Two years after Donald Barthelme's death, his friend Robert Coover observed that his name had achieved a new currency as an adjective: the term "Barthelmesque," Coover wrote, refers not only to a style—"precise, urbane, ironic, rivetingly succinct, and accumulative in its comical and often surreal juxtapositions"—but also to a perspective familiar to Barthelme's readers, a world-view "bleakly comic, paradoxical, and grounded in the beautiful absurdities of language." John Barth, another friend, noted that Barthelme's view changed only slightly over the course of his career as editor, journalist, novelist, and short-story master, that he seemed as an artist "to have been born full-grown." In comments included in the Summer 1991 issue of *Review of Contemporary Fiction*, Barth speaks for most of Barthelme's critics in noting further that his immediately recognizable voice found its most influential forum in the rigorously confined genre of short fiction: "His natural narrative space was the short story, if *story* is the right word for those often plotless marvels of which he published some seven volumes over twenty years."

Critic Mark C. Krupnick responded to Barthelme's work with charges of "self-congratulatory narcissism." Other critics, however, hold that missing the occasional erudite allusion does not invalidate the pleasure of reading Barthelme's work. Because of his reliance upon language to carry the theme of his stories, Barthelme has incurred the wrath of such traditional critics as Alfred Kazin and Nathan Scott. With Barthelme we have been "sentenced to the sentence," Kazin writes in *Bright Book of Life* (1973) and further complains that "he operates by countermeasures only, and the system that is his own joy to attack permits him what an authoritarian system always permits its lonely dissenters: the sense of their own weakness." Several of Barthelme's most severe critics base their objections on moral grounds. Pearl K. Bell numbered Barthelme among "those celebrants of unreason, chaos, and inexorable decay ... a horde of mini-Jeremiahs crying havoc in the Western world." Nathan Scott complained that Barthelme's reinvention of the world "offers us an effective release from the bullying of all the vexations of history," but that such an aesthetic was too facile, the opting-out chosen "by the hordes of those young long-haired, jean-clad, pot-smoking bohemians who have entered the world of psychedelia."

By 1970 the *New York Times Book Review* began to give Barthelme longer and deeper reviews, probing the nature of his linguistic games and imaginative reinventions of social life, robbing negative critics of their strongest support. Still, Barthelme expected and duly received critical censure for his stylistic risk-taking, and he sometimes returned the sentiment. In one of his ahistorical revisions of literary history, "Conversations with Goethe," he makes Johann Wolfgang von Goethe himself intone against reviewers: "Critics, Goethe said, are the cracked mirror in the grand ballroom of the creative spirit."

*Paradise* As Barthelme continued his prose experiments well into his late career, critical reaction remained mixed. Michiko Kakutani found that in *Paradise* (1986) "wit and intellectual one-upmanship dwindle into fun and games; detachment into mechanism; narrative fragmentation into mere absurdity for absurdity's sake." According to Kakutani, the novel's structure is "predictably idiosyncratic" and that it "has little of the vitality or inventiveness of the author's earlier work and none of its provocative intelligence."

Yet, Elizabeth Jolley, writing in *The New York Times Book Review*, found *Paradise* a "shock and revelation." "It is a very funny novel; I laughed aloud, a rare thing while reading contemporary fiction," said Jolley. "It is also a sad book," she concludes, "a disturbing book because it is a fantasy of freedom in a world where there is none."

### Responses to Literature

1. Barthelme was noted for his inventive, genre-bending fiction. Take a well-known folktale or myth and reinterpret it in a postmodern way—try playing around with the setting and time period, or try telling the story from the perspective of someone other than the traditional "hero."

2. How does Barthelme's work compare to that of his fellow American postmodernist Thomas Pynchon? How do their styles differ? Do you feel they are alike enough to both be called postmodernists? Why or why not?

3. Read Barthelme's essay "Not Knowing." How does Barthelme frame the interaction between language and the world? Examine how you use language in your everyday conversation with friends and family. Does language ever get in the way of what you're trying to communicate?

4. How does Barthelme's writing correspond with movements in the art world in the 1950s and 1960s? Research Abstract Expressionism, minimalism, constructivism, and pop art. Do you feel Barthelme was influenced by the philosophies underlying these movements? If so, how? If not, why not?

BIBLIOGRAPHY

**Books**

Couturier, Maurice and Regis Durand. *Donald Barthelme*. New York: Methuen, 1982.

Gordon, Lois. *Donald Barthelme*, New York: Twayne, 1981.

Klinkowitz, Jerome et al. eds. *Donald Barthelme: A Comprehensive Bibliography and Annotated Secondary Checklist*, Hamden, Conn.: Shoe String, 1977.

Molesworth, Charles. *Donald Barthelme's Fiction: The Ironist Saved from Drowning*, Columbia, Mo.: University of Missouri Press, 1982.

Patteson, Richard F., ed. *Critical Essays on Donald Barthelme*, New York: G. K. Hall, 1992.

Roe, Barbara L. *Donald Barthelme: A Study of the Short Fiction*, New York: Twayne, 1992.

Stengel, Wayne B. *The Shape of Art in the Short Stories of Donald Barthelme*, Baton Rouge, La.: Louisiana State University Press, 1985.

Trachtenberg, Stanley. *Understanding Donald Barthelme*, Columbia, S.C.: University of South Carolina Press, 1990.

## ✳ L. Frank Baum

BORN: *1856, Chittenango, New York*

DIED: *1919, Hollywood, California*

NATIONALITY: *American*

GENRE: *Fiction*

MAJOR WORKS:

*Mother Goose in Prose* (1897)

*The Wonderful Wizard of Oz* (1900)

L. Frank Baum    *Dana Hall / LOC / Writer Pictures*

## Overview

In creating the Land of Oz in *The Wonderful Wizard of Oz* (1900), L. Frank Baum earned a special place in the history of juvenile literature. Children's books have just not been the same since Dorothy first went to the Emerald City. Indeed, Oz has a reality not even its creator could have imagined. The Scarecrow, the Tin Woodman, and the Cowardly Lion have entered the collective consciousness of childhood. Even those boys and girls who have never heard of L. Frank Baum know Dorothy and her odd companions. Although Baum wrote much more than *The Wonderful Wizard of Oz*, it is as the Royal Historian of Oz that he has been most affectionately remembered.

## Works in Biographical and Historical Context

L. Frank Baum seemed to have been born with the proverbial silver spoon in his mouth. Frank (as he was known to his friends) was born into the wealthy family of Benjamin Ward Baum, a barrel maker and sawyer who had made a fortune in the Pennsylvania oil fields during the Civil War. Since the young Baum suffered from a weak heart—a defect that forced him to lead a sheltered childhood—he was tutored at home, on the family estate of Roselawn outside the city of Syracuse, New York. An attempt to have him schooled at Peekskill Military

Academy failed; young Baum had a seizure that was diagnosed as a heart attack, and the trauma left him with a lifelong distaste for educators and the military in general.

### Searching for Success

Frank Baum's life exhibited a "boom and bust" cycle, a pattern that began in his youth and lasted for the rest of his life. When he acquired a small printing press in 1870, he showed immediate enthusiasm, producing a small newspaper, *The Rose Lawn Home Journal*, and several other periodicals publishing news on subjects ranging from postage stamps to fancy chicken breeding. Still later, he displayed a passion for the stage, acted for a while with a Shakespearean troupe, and then wrote a five-act Irish melodrama titled "The Maid of Arran." The drama was financed in part by his father, and Baum took it on the road in 1882, even performing it with moderate success in New York City. While still acting in his play he married Maud Gage, the youngest daughter of the noted women's rights campaigner Matilda Joslyn Gage.

The Baums left the theater in 1883, and Baum opened an oil store and helped found Baum's Castorine Company. It was at this point that bad fortune struck. As a playwright, he proved unable to repeat the success of "The Maid of Arran." The company that manufactured his family's lubricant, "Baum's Castorine," suffered financial hardships in the late 1880s. Baum moved west to be near his wife's family, but the store he opened in Aberdeen, South Dakota, closed after only a year (partly because of his liberal credit policies), and the newspaper he edited, the *Aberdeen Saturday Pioneer*, folded early in 1891. He then moved his family from South Dakota to Chicago, where he took a job as a newspaper editor, a job that lasted less than a month. In the mid-1890s he proved moderately successful as a traveling crockery salesman.

### Mother and Father Goose

The one occupation in which Baum seemed to excel was storytelling. In the evenings at home, Baum was in the habit of relating original stories based on Mother Goose rhymes in order to amuse his sons, and his mother-in-law eventually suggested that he should try to sell them. In 1897 the firm of Way & Williams published *Mother Goose in Prose*, Baum's first book for children. The volume sold reasonably well, although the author later admitted that the illustrations by Maxfield Parrish—who became one of America's most popular artists—were more attractive than the text.

"Baum had spent many years feeling his way uncertainly," reported David L. Greene and Dick Martin in *The Oz Scrapbook*. "Now, in his early forties, he had a certain sense of his own future; he would earn his living as a writer." In November of 1897 he started *The Show Window*, a magazine for window dressers that proved very successful and provided Baum with a steady income, as well as allowing him time to write other children's books. Working with W. W. Denslow, an artist acquaintance, Baum produced a volume of children's verses with poster-like illustrations, which he called *Father Goose: His Book* (1899). The book met with much acclaim—although, according to Michael Patrick Hearn in *The Annotated Wizard of Oz*, Baum once again attributed its popularity to the pictures rather than the verses—and it quickly became the best-selling juvenile picture book of 1899.

The success of *Father Goose* led Baum to complete another story, which he called variously *The Emerald City, From Kansas to Fairyland* and finally *The Wonderful Wizard of Oz*. It tells of Dorothy Gale's journey from her Kansas prairie home to the land of Oz, the strange friends she makes there, and the adventures they have while trying to send Dorothy home. Published by the George M. Hill Company, a small Chicago press, in September 1900, the book earned Baum "a special place in the history of children's literature," wrote Hearn in the *Dictionary of Literary Biography*, for its decor as well as its story. "Even today," Hearn continued, "the first edition of *The Wonderful Wizard of Oz* is an impressive piece of bookmaking"; like *Father Goose*, it was lavishly illustrated by Denslow, sporting two dozen color plates and over a hundred textual illustrations.

### Success Found in the Land of Oz

*The Wonderful Wizard of Oz* was greeted with the same enthusiasm that met *Father Goose*; according to Hearn in *The Annotated Wizard of Oz*, the first printing of ten thousand copies ran out about two weeks after publication, and by January of 1901 the Hill company advertised that it had published around ninety thousand copies of *The Wonderful Wizard of Oz*.

Although *The Wonderful Wizard of Oz* proved very popular, it was not as financially successful as *Father Goose* had been. However, in 1902 Baum helped adapt the book into a stage musical, which was a smash hit and ran on Broadway for a record 293 performances. The production was graced with many attractive sets and astonishing (for the time) special effects. In order to conform with theatrical tastes of the period, however, Baum and his collaborators had to make some drastic changes in the plot: Dorothy became a teenager, and she was provided with a lover, a poet named Sir Dashemoff Daily, and a pantomime cow named Imogene instead of her little dog Toto. Gag writers turned the comedy team of Fred Stone and David Montgomery—as the Scarecrow and Tin Woodman—into the stars of the show. The prosperity of the stage "Wizard" encouraged many imitations; among the most successful was Victor Herbert's "Babes in Toyland." Herbert went on to feature Montgomery and Stone in his operetta "The Red Mill."

### Work in Stage and Film

The stage *Wizard* had considerable influence on Baum's future writings as well as the American musical theater. Although the production proved lucrative, Greene and Martin reported that "expenses and continued financial bad luck offset his income from books and from the play of *The Wizard* to such an extent that in 1903 ... Baum was insolvent." In

1904, after many requests by children for more adventures of the Scarecrow and Tin Woodman, Baum produced *The Marvelous Land of Oz*. Hoping that the new book could be turned into a musical as successful as the *Wizard*, Baum introduced many elements from contemporary theater into his plot, including an army of pretty girls in tight uniforms, another pair of comic grotesques in the form of Jack Pumpkinhead and the Woggle-Bug, and changing the leading boy into a girl at the story's end. The book was very successful; however, when a stage version was produced under the title *The Woggle-Bug*, it failed. Baum was never able to repeat the dramatic success of *The Wizard*, although he continued to put theatrical elements in many of his later Oz books.

Popular demand and financial difficulties forced Baum to return to Oz again and again. In 1908 he had invested in the "Fairylogue and Radio Plays," a combination slide and motion picture presentation about Oz, which, although popular, left him with large debts. In an attempt to save money, the Baums moved to Hollywood, California, in 1910. Baum tried to end the Oz series that year with the publication of *The Emerald City of Oz*, but circumstances intervened; in June 1911, the author declared bankruptcy. In 1913 Baum published *The Patchwork Girl of Oz* and, taking the title of "Royal Historian of Oz," resigned himself to producing a new Oz book each year.

Living in Hollywood, Baum soon became involved in the nascent motion picture industry. With some friends, he formed the Oz Film Manufacturing Company and produced several films based on his Oz books and some of his other novels. Although marked by very good special effects, most of the films were not commercially successful, and the company failed in 1915; fortunately, Baum had not invested his own money in the venture and escaped the collapse without financial damage. His failing heath, however, curtailed these activities. An operation left him bedridden for the last year of his life, without strength to do much more than answer letters from children. "When the Royal Historian of Oz died on May 6, 1919," declared Allen Eyles in *The World of Oz*, "he was the most celebrated children's author of his time." "The Royal Historian," Eyles concluded, "was going home."

## Works in Literary Context

*Children's Literature*   At the end of the nineteenth century there was a rise in literature written for children in Britain and the United States. In 1872, for example, Scottish writer George MacDonald (1824–1904) published *The Princess and the Goblin* (1872), a children's fantasy novel, and many other fantasies and fairy tales, including *The Wise Woman: A Parable* (1875). E. Nesbit (1858–1924) wrote over sixty books for children, many of them fantasy tales, including *The Story of the Treasure Seekers* (1898). In the United States, Howard Pyle

---

## LITERARY AND HISTORICAL CONTEMPORARIES

Baum's famous contemporaries include:

**William McKinley** (1843–1901): The twenty-fifth president of the United States, and the third president to be assassinated. His two terms marked a time of increasing American prosperity, as well as the expansion of U.S. overseas possessions in the wake of the Spanish-American War. He was assassinated by an anarchist, Leon Czolgosz, and was succeeded by Theodore Roosevelt.

**Carrie Nation** (1846–1911): A radical advocate of temperance, the opposition to alcohol as a recreational drink, Nation was notorious for her practice of walking into bars, often accompanied by a gang of followers singing hymns, and smashing bottles with a hatchet. Between 1900 and 1910 she was arrested over two dozen times and became a national celebrity, giving lectures and selling souvenir hatchets.

**Colette** (1873–1954): The pen name of Sidonie-Gabrielle Colette, author, sophisticate, singer-actress, notorious in her own time for her many open lesbian relationships. Her best-known work, thanks to its adaptation into a musical and movie, is the novel *Gigi* (1944).

**Max Planck** (1858–1947): Considered one of the great physicists of the twentieth century, arguably second only to Albert Einstein, German scientist Planck is today perhaps most notable for his foundational work in quantum theory.

**H. G. Wells** (1866–1946): British science-fiction author and futurist, Wells was rivaled in his time by perhaps only Jules Verne for his imaginative visions of times to come, future technologies and scientific advancements, and popularity. His tales, such as *War of the Worlds* (1898) continue to be adapted today, over a hundred years after their publication.

---

(1853–1911) was well known for his many books for children, including *The Merry Adventures of Robin Hood* (1883). A few years after the publication of *The Wonderful Wizard of Oz*, J. M. Barrie created the character of Peter Pan, the boy who would never grow up, resulting in a stage play and two novels, *Peter Pan in Kensington Gardens* (1906) and *Peter and Wendy* (1911). The literary ground at the turn of the century was thus fertile for children's fantasy literature. Baum had his own ideas about what would best entertain the children of his time. He wrote the following in an introduction to his best-known book:

> The old-time fairy tale, having served for generations, may now be classed as "historical" in the children's library; for the time has come for a series of newer "wonder tales" in which the stereotyped

# COMMON HUMAN EXPERIENCE

The concept of a young protagonist passing through an invisible barrier to visit a magical realm is an enduring and popular theme in children's literature. Here are some other books that feature this theme:

*Alice's Adventures in Wonderland* (1865), a novel by Lewis Carroll. This book and its sequel, *Through the Looking Glass* (1872), were based on nonsense tales Carroll would tell his young niece—the world that Alice adventures through is almost dreamlike in its surreal weirdness.

*Peter Pan* (1904), a play by J. M. Barrie. This is the tale of a boy who never grew up, thanks to living in the realm of Never-Never-Land. When he comes to fetch the Darling children—Wendy, John, and Michael—they must decide whether to return to the real world and grow up or remain children forever.

*Bridge to Terabithia* (1977), a novel by Katherine Patterson. This is a story about a fantasy world created in the shared imaginations of two friends, who use it to cope with the everyday challenges of their lives—and the grief that comes when one of them dies tragically.

*The Golden Compass* (1995), a novel by Philip Pullman. The first novel in the "His Dark Materials" trilogy, the story is set in an alternate version of Earth in which people are accompanied by "demons," manifestations of the person's soul that take the shape of animals.

genie, dwarf, and fairy are eliminated, together with all the horrible and blood-curdling incident devised by their authors to point a fearsome moral to each tale. Modern education includes morality; therefore the modern child seeks only entertainment in its wonder-tales and gladly dispenses with all disagreeable incident. Having this thought in mind, the story of *The Wonderful Wizard of Oz* was written solely to pleasure children of today. It aspires to being a modernized fairy tale, in which the wonderment and joy are retained and the heart-aches and nightmares are left out.

Although *The Wonderful Wizard* does use some traditional fairy-tale trappings—witches, wizards, and magic—the novel is more remarkable for the changes it introduced into the genre. "Most fairy tales are universal because they occur in distant times and places," Greene and Martin explained. "Baum achieved universality by combining the folk tale with elements familiar to every child—cornfields, things made of tin, circus balloons." Edward Wagenknecht wrote in *Utopia Americana*,

Baum taught American children to look for wonder in the life around them, to realize even smoke and machinery may be transformed into fairy lore if only we have sufficient energy and vision to pene-

trate to their significance and transform them to our use.

Baum's book broke new ground in other ways as well. "*The Wonderful Wizard of Oz*," Hearn explained in the *Dictionary of Literary Biography*, "pooh-poohed the old Puritan belief that literature must teach; Baum's book was revolutionary in that it was written 'solely to pleasure children of today.' But . . . the principal reason *The Wonderful Wizard of Oz* survives is that it is an exceptional story." The book, Greene and Martin explained,

was published during a time of populists and progressives and Utopian schemes based on an optimistic view of man that, after two world wars, is attractive today precisely because it is so hard to accept. In Oz, good motives, ingenuity and trust in oneself always win, although the way to victory is often rough. Oz is a proving ground in which Dorothy and the other child heroes and heroines develop these quintessentially American ideals.

## Works in Critical Context

"L. Frank Baum is dead," the *New York Times* stated in an editorial after the author's death in 1919,

and the children, if they knew it, would mourn. The endless procession of "Oz" books, coming out just before Christmas, is to cease. . . . there will never be any more of them, and the children have suffered a loss they do not know.

This was more tribute than Baum had been used to in his day, when his books, although read by children, were shunned by librarians and neglected by scholars of children's literature. However, over the course of the twentieth century, scholarly interest in Baum's work increased, and the Oz books have recently received a healthy burst of critical attention. Nearly every current critical trend, from populist to Marxist, psychoanalytic to feminist, has been applied to Baum's famous children's stories. Indeed, perhaps more is being written today on Baum's work than on that of any other classic American writer of books for boys and girls.

*The Wonderful Wizard of Oz* The traditional view of *The Wonderful Wizard of Oz* as merely an entertaining fantasy for children changed in the 1960s, when high school teacher Henry M. Littlefield published an essay in *American Quarterly* claiming that Baum's charming tale concealed a clever allegory on the populist movement, the agrarian revolt that swept across the Midwest in the 1890s. In an ingenuous act of imaginative scholarship, Littlefield linked the characters and the storyline of the Oz tale to the political landscape of the Mauve Decade. The discovery was little less than astonishing: Baum's children's story was in fact a full-blown "parable on populism," a "vibrant and ironic portrait" of America on the eve of the new century.

The reaction to Littlefield was, predictably, mixed. Scholars and teachers, who saw the allegorical reading (as Littlefield himself had) as a useful "teaching mechanism," tended to be enthusiastic. Many among the Oz faithful, however, were not impressed, including Baum's great-grandson, who curtly dismissed the parable thesis as "insane" (Moyer 1998, 46). Although neither side produced much evidence, Littlefield's interpretation gained widespread currency in academic circles, and by the 1980s it had assumed the proportions of an "urban legend," as history textbooks and scholarly works on populism paid homage to the Oz allegory.

Other critical perspectives include the notion that Baum explores in *The Wonderful Wizard of Oz* political and philosophical concerns debated since the founding of the United States: the conflict between personal rights and freedoms and the good of the community. Baum creates Oz, an idyllic community that favors cultural pluralism. Cooperation extends to human beings, minorities, inanimate, mechanical beings, and flora and fauna.

## Responses to Literature

1. Compare the book version of *The Wonderful Wizard of Oz* with the 1939 film version starring Judy Garland. How do you think Baum would have felt about the changes made for the adaptation to cinema? Do you think he would have approved? Why or why not?

2. How crucial do you think the illustrations of W. W. Denslow were to the success of the Oz books? How do you personally feel about the artwork? Does it still hold appeal today, a century later? Could you make a case for or against including the illustrations in future editions of the book? How would you make your argument?

3. Thanks to its mythical structure and imagery, *The Wonderful Wizard of Oz* has been the subject of all manner of critical interpretations, including political, economic, feminist, and psychological. Choose a particular discipline or viewpoint and write your own analysis of the story, or part of the story, from that standpoint with an eye toward developing a new interpretation of certain aspects of the book.

4. Why do you think Baum continually tried to move beyond the Oz books once they became successful? How would you react if you found success as an artist but were only expected to produce a single type of art? Would you welcome the success or reject it?

BIBLIOGRAPHY

**Books**

"The Wonderful Wizard of Oz." *Novels for Students*, Vol. 13, edited by Elizabeth Thomason. Detroit, Mich.: Gale, 2002.

Baum, Frank J., and Russell P. MacFall. *To Please a Child: A Biography of L. Frank Baum, Royal Historian of Oz*. Chicago: Reilly & Lee, 1961.

Carpenter, Angelica Shirley, and Jean Shirley. *L. Frank Baum: Royal Historian of Oz*. Minneapolis: Lerner Publications Co., 1992.

Earle, Neil. *The Wonderful Wizard of Oz in American Popular Culture: Uneasy in Eden*. Lewiston, N.Y.: Edwin Mellen Press, 1993.

Greene, Douglas G., et al. *Bibliographia Oziana: A Concise Bibliographical Checklist of the Oz Books by L. Frank Baum and His Successors*. Revised and expanded ed. Kinderhook, Ill.: International Wizard of Oz Club, 1988.

Hearn, Michael Patrick. *W. W. Denslow: The Other Wizard of Oz*. Chadds Ford, Pa.: Brandywine River Museum, 1996.

Rahn, Suzanne. *The Wizard of Oz: Shaping an Imaginary World*. New York: Twayne, 1998.

Riley, Michael O'Neal, *Oz and Beyond: The Fantasy World of L. Frank Baum*. Lawrence: University Press of Kansas, 1997.

Wheeler, Jill C. *L. Frank Baum*. Edina, Minn.: Abdo & Daughters, 1997.

**Periodicals**

*American Book Collector* (December 1962).

## ⚛ Ann Beattie

BORN: *1947, Washington, D.C.*

NATIONALITY: *American*

GENRE: *Fiction*

MAJOR WORKS:
*Distortions* (1976)
*Chilly Scenes of Winter* (1976)

### Overview

A noted crafter of keenly observed, minimalist short stories and novels, Ann Beattie, by her own admission, "fell into" writing, rising to overnight celebrity with the simultaneous publication of her first novel and short story collection in 1976. Hailed as a voice of the Baby Boomer generation, growing older and increasingly more bitter in the post-counterculture 1970s, Beattie herself largely rejected any such labels. Although she has continued to write regularly, she has also distanced herself more and more from the celebrity and attention she feels was thrust upon her.

### Works in Biographical and Historical Context

*Falling Into Writing* Anne Beattie was born into a typical American middle-class family in the national capital. Although her childhood was largely unremarkable, by her teenage years she began to run into trouble. By

Anne Beattie   *William F. Campbell / Time Life Pictures / Getty Images*

dashed off in the space of a few hours. Finally, in 1973, she submitted a story ("Victor Blue") to *The Atlantic Monthly* that met with editorial approval; Beattie's publishing career was underway. Her first story in *The New Yorker* ("A Platonic Relationship") appeared the next year. It would mark the beginning of Beattie as a regular contributor to the magazine.

In 1976, Beattie saw the publication of both her first novel, *Chilly Scenes of Winter* (written in three weeks), and her first collection of short stories, *Distortions*. Beattie drew instant praise and comparisons to such authors as John Updike and J. D. Salinger. Her dry, witty, observational prose also struck a chord with the reading public, many of whom could identify as well with the characters in Beattie's stories—former 1960s counterculture revolutionaries now cast adrift in the post-Woodstock doldrums of the 1970s, aimlessly chasing after cheap thrills and "the next big thing."

***A Retreat from Stardom***   Beattie was uncomfortable both with her sudden notoriety and the label being applied to her as the voice of her generation. One critic went so far as to call Beattie "the Annie Hall of American letters," invoking Diane Keaton's famously sardonic and bemused character from the Woody Allen movie of the same name. Although she continued to write, producing eight novels under contract with her publisher, she largely withdrew from the public eye. Although she taught classes at such universities as Harvard and University of Virginia, she has largely supported herself through her writing, a career path that she clearly feels increasingly ambivalent about. As she states on *About Ann Beattie: A Profile*:

> Any notion that this gets easier, or that people treat me nicer—it's exactly the opposite of what really is the case. ... The ground rules are always changed by those in control, the people who own the publishing houses. ... I was thinking that really I had to admit to myself that there was no other skill I had, and that I couldn't just get into a snit and change careers, because it just wasn't going to happen. I mean, you just hope that there's mercy.

## Works in Literary Context

When Beattie began writing, "short story writer" was not generally perceived as a legitimate aspiration for aspiring authors. Beattie is credited by many critics with, along with Raymond Carver, reviving the short-story form in the 1970s. Beattie also received critical praise for her spare, witty craftsmanship and mastery of characterization. Beattie's work is characterized by her ruminations on her aging generation, and by her distinctive style, which has been included with the minimalist school of literature.

***Minimalism***   Literary minimalism is a specific style of writing that has reappeared at different periods of time, though the characteristics are broadly the same. As the

her senior year, according to Beattie, she had a D minus average because of an awful high school experience that included indifferent teachers and uninspired lessons. After barely graduating, her father was able to call in some favors and get his daughter admitted to American University.

Once in college, Beattie chose journalism as a major, though she was not terribly interested in the subject. As she progressed through college, a boyfriend convinced her to abandon journalism, which he referred to as a hopelessly middle-class profession, to focus on artistic pursuits. Beattie switched to an English major and took up writing as a hobby. After graduating with her English degree, Beattie decided on a career in academia and began pursuing a PhD in literature, still writing short stories for her own amusement but with no intention of getting them published.

***Overnight Success***   It was through professor J. D. O'Hara that Beattie first began to look into publishing her stories. O'Hara had heard of Beattie's writing through a shared friend, and he offered to critique her writing. Beattie dropped off her stories in O'Hara's inbox at work, and he returned them to her the next day, full of marginal notes. Beattie credits O'Hara with helping her polish and hone her writing skills—"He really became my official editor. He taught me more about writing than I could have imagined learning elsewhere"—and with getting her to submit her stories to magazines, most notably *The New Yorker*.

Although Beattie sent in twenty-two stories to *The New Yorker*, it was no hardship; most of her stories were name suggests, minimalist stories are marked by a certain starkness, in everything from the author's descriptions to the dialogue to the scope of the story. Minimalist stories rely on hinted suggestions rather than overt proclamations, and generally feature a narrow focus, often involving rather unexceptional "everyman" characters.

Ernest Hemingway was one of the first authors to explore minimalist style in his prose, drawing instant attention for his clipped, spare dialogue and understated descriptions. Crime writers of the 1940s and 1950s such as Mickey Spillane would carry forward Hemingway's prose style into a more commercialized format. Yet the minimalist school that Beattie belonged to arose out of a different set of influences, reacting against the "new novels" of the 1950s and 1960s, in which writers like John Barth and Kurt Vonnegut explored a style of self-referential, irony-laced fiction known as metafiction. Minimalist writers rejected the postmodern, reflective qualities of metafiction in favor of a cooler, more detached perspective. Beattie's style is typical of this approach, often eschewing direct descriptions of characters in favor of intricate examinations of their surroundings, from the food they eat to the music they listen to. Beattie has said that by examining what a person surrounds themselves with, we can form our own mental picture of what they might look like.

## Works in Critical Context

Critical reaction to Beattie's work has been decidedly mixed. These extreme reactions seem to rest largely on Beattie's minimalist approach: while some critics enjoy the spare, stripped-down fiction; others find it bland and uninteresting. Joshua Gilder, writing in the *New Criterion*, famously attacked minimalist writers like Beattie, claiming that their writing was not a case of "less is more," but rather "less is less." But for readers like Margaret Atwood, who is herself a much-admired novelist, poet, and playwright, and is on record as an admirer of Beattie's, the level of involvement minimalism demands of its readers is precisely the appeal.

*Distortions* J. D. O'Hara, Beattie's mentor when she was in college, wrote a glowing review of her first novel, *Distortions*: "Beattie is a writer for all audiences . . . She combines a remarkable array of technical skills with material of wide popular appeal." In particular, O'Hara singled out Beattie's command of character, saying that, "[h]er characters inhabit our drab contemporary worlds and brood like us about their lovers, politicians and lives . . . They compose a wide-screen panorama of Life in These United States."

Anatole Broyard, writing in *The New York Times*, was a bit harsher, saying her "stories are rather like a high-fashioned model: All the humanity is dieted away in the attempt to achieve beauty and drama . . . After reading *Distortions*, I felt like a psychiatrist at the end of a hard day." Broyard summed up his thoughts by saying, "I am convinced that Beattie is, potentially, a good writer. In

## LITERARY AND HISTORICAL CONTEMPORARIES

Beattie's famous contemporaries include:

**Gerald Ford** (1913–2006): A Republican congressman, Gerald Ford was appointed to the vice presidency in 1973 following the resignation of Spiro Agnew. The following year, he became the thirty-eighth president of the United States when Richard Nixon resigned in the wake of the Watergate scandal. Ford's single term in office was marked by economic woes, political controversy—particularly his pardon of Nixon—and an assassination attempt. Ford lost the 1976 election to Jimmy Carter, making him the only President to have never won a national election.

**Rubin "Hurricane" Carter** (1937–): A successful middleweight boxer in the 1960s, Carter gained national attention when he was convicted for a 1967 triple murder. The circumstances of his trial led many to believe he'd been wrongly convicted, and he became the centerpiece of a Bob Dylan protest song. After twenty years in prison, Carter's conviction was overturned and he was released.

**Osamu Tezuka** (1928–1989): Called "the Father of Anime," Tezuka pioneered Japanese animation with such works as *Astro Boy* (1963) and *Kimba the White Lion* (1965), both based on comics he created. His distinctive "big eye, small mouth" style of drawing, itself heavily influenced by his idol Walt Disney, set the look for Japanese cartoons and comic books for decades to come.

**Patty Hearst** (1954–): Granddaughter of newspaper tycoon William Randolph Hearst, Patricia Hearst became famous overnight after she was first kidnapped by a radical group calling itself the Symbionese Liberation Army (SLA), then claimed she had willingly joined the group and participated in bank robberies with SLA members. After her arrest, she avoided jail time for the robbery by arguing that she had been brainwashed and physically and mentally abused during her time with the SLA.

**Saul Bellow** (1915–2005): Born in Canada, Bellow came of age in Chicago, and it is there that much of his fiction—noted for its blend of intellectualism and street smarts—is set. Bellow won the Nobel Prize in Literature in 1976.

spite of a style that virtually eliminates personality, she still manages to haunt the reader with her work."

## Responses to Literature

1. Do you feel that Beattie's work will hold up to the test of time, given that it examines a very specific cultural generation at a specific point in time? Can universal themes in literature be found in such

## COMMON HUMAN EXPERIENCE

Beattie earned critical and commercial adulation for her stories which chronicled the place of the Baby Boomer generation. Other artists, from writers to directors to musicians, have also taken a critical look at the state of their own generation.

*Parenthood* (1989), a film directed by Ron Howard. This film is a comedic look at the state of middle-aged Baby Boomers and their children, represented in a large extended family that includes a father who worries about raising children "right," an intellectual, Yuppie couple, a single mom and her troubled teen kids, and an aimless, aging hipster.

*The Bonfire of the Vanities* (1987), a novel by Tom Wolfe. Getting his start in the 1960s, Wolfe was a noted journalist and social critic. In this, his first novel, Wolfe paints a picture of excess and racial division among greed-driven Manhattan Baby Boomers.

*Born in the U.S.A.* (1984), an album by Bruce Springsteen. In this, his most commercially successful album, Springsteen's message—notably in the title track and "Glory Days," which looks at middle-aged Baby Boomers caught in terminal nostalgia for days of youth gone by—is couched in some of his most accessible, radio-friendly tunes.

generationally-specific material? Find an example of a literary work considered to be a classic that is focused on a specific time and place.

2. Beattie has been called "the Annie Hall of American letters." Watch the Woody Allen film of the same name and give your opinion on what this might mean specifically.

3. Write about your own generation: what are some of its defining characteristics? Where do you think your generation will be in thirty years?

4. Read some of Beattie's short stories, paying particular attention to her dry, minimalist writing style. What defines minimalist writing? Do you agree with the idea that "less is more" when it comes to writing style? Write a short story of your own that utilizes minimalist writing techniques.

BIBLIOGRAPHY

**Books**

"Ann Beattie." *The Columbia Electronic Encyclopedia, Sixth Edition.* New York: Columbia University Press, 2003.

"Ann Beattie." *The Chronology of American Literature.* New York: Houghton Mifflin Company, 2004.

"Janus." *Short Stories for Students.* Vol. 9. Detroit: Thomson Gale, 2000.

**Periodicals**

Maynard, Joyce. "Visiting Anne Beattie." *The New York Times* (May 11, 1980).

**Web sites**

Lee, Don. *About Ann Beattie: A Profile.* Retrieved September 28, 2008, from http://www.pshares. org/issues/article.cfm?prmArticleID=3901

Garner, Dwight. *Anne Beattie at 60.* Retrieved September 30, 2008, from http://papercuts. blogs.nytimes.com/2007/09/07/anne-beattie-at-60/

# ✹ Edward Bellamy

BORN: *1850, Chicopee Falls, Massachusetts*

DIED: *1898, Chicopee Falls, Massachusetts*

NATIONALITY: *American*

GENRE: *Fiction*

MAJOR WORKS:
*Looking Backward* (1888)

## Overview

Edward Bellamy owes his entire literary reputation to a single work, *Looking Backward* (1888), one of the relatively few American books to have an indisputable effect on society and politics. The purpose of the book was to offer a blueprint of what Bellamy considered to be an ideal society. Along with *Uncle Tom's Cabin* (1852) and *Ben-Hur* (1880), *Looking Backward* was one of the best-selling books of the nineteenth century, selling over one million copies after its initial publication.

## Works in Biographical and Historical Context

*Unexceptional Origins* Although it might be possible to discover hints of some of Bellamy's mature thought in published and unpublished writings of his earlier years, there is little in either Bellamy's life or work prior to 1888 to suggest his sudden emergence as an important social thinker. Bellamy was born in Chicopee Falls, Massachusetts, the son of a Baptist minister, Rufus King Bellamy, and Maria Putnam Bellamy. He was a descendant, on both sides of his family, from generations of solid, earnest, but otherwise unexceptional New England clergymen, educators, and merchants. Edward inherited the family tradition of rectitude and responsibility, and more specifically, his father's optimistic and benevolent view of mankind. However, there is nothing in his family background to suggest his eventual social and economic ideas.

*In Search of an Identity* In 1867, after failing the physical examination for the U.S. Military Academy at West Point, Bellamy entered Union College. However,

Edward Bellamy    *Kean Collection / Hulton Archive / Getty Images*

his career there was cut short when his parents urged him to join his brother Packer in Europe. Bellamy spent about a year (1868–1869) in Germany and was moved by his observation of industrial conditions there. When he returned to America, he undertook the study of law with a Springfield, Massachusetts, attorney. After accepting a single case as a lawyer, Bellamy abandoned that profession in favor of journalism. He worked briefly on the *New York Evening Post* and for five years with the *Springfield Union* as an editorialist and book reviewer. Ill health caused him to give up that position in 1877, and in 1880, in partnership with his brother Charles, he began what became the *Springfield Daily News*. However, after less than a year as a publisher, Bellamy left newspaper journalism for good and devoted himself to the writing that would culminate in *Looking Backward*.

During his newspaper days Bellamy wrote a number of short stories (many of them later collected in *The Blindman's World*, 1898) and four novels. For the most part these early fictions are significant only as they anticipate ideas developed more importantly in *Looking Backward*.

### A Half-formed Manifesto
In 1888, Bellamy finished his sweeping futuristic view of Utopia, *Looking Backward*. To make his presentation of Utopia more palatable to the general reader, he encased it in a romantic plot: A young Bostonian after a hypnotic sleep of 113 years awakens in the year 2000 to discover a totally transformed social and economic order. Falling in love with a girl descended from his fiancée of 1887, he learns from her father, a physician, the details of the state socialism

that has replaced the unregulated capitalism that was in effect before his long sleep. Under the new order all commerce, industry, and other economic and professional activities have been nationalized into one vast interlocking enterprise. All men and women between the ages of twenty-one and forty-five are required to engage in work suitable to their abilities and, when possible, to their tastes; and all, no matter what occupation they may be in, receive the same wages. Superior ability and productivity are rewarded by social recognition and by assignment to positions of leadership. After the age of forty-five all are retired and are free to do what they wish.

Although that nostalgic vision probably accounts for the otherwise surprising popular acceptance of the book, the prescription for economic and political reform understandably provoked a more fully articulated response. However, while his outline of an egalitarian society had excited great public interest, Bellamy had in fact only sketchily developed his reformist ideas in *Looking Backward*. As those ideas became part of the currency of contemporary political debate, Bellamy felt the need to fill in the programmatic chinks of *Looking Backward* and to answer his critics. In the preface to the follow-up volume entitled *Equality* he explains

> *Looking Backward* was a small book, and I was not able to get into all I wished to say on the subject. Since it was published what was left out of it has loomed up as so much more important than what it contained that I have been constrained to write another book.

As such a statement suggests, the resultant book, *Equality* (1897), makes little pretense to being a novel, opting instead to attempt a message of economic education. Chapter titles such as "Private Capital Stolen from the Social Fund," "Economic Suicide of the Profit System," and "Inequality of Wealth Destroys Liberty" suggest the more or less orthodox socialism espoused in *Equality*. Whereas *Looking Backward* had promised that through painless evolution technological progress would end in the recovery of idyllically pastoral culture, *Equality*, by contrast, seems only a relatively charming but essentially predictable recipe for a socialist economy. The sales of Equality were insignificant in comparison to those of *Looking Backward*, and while the book does clarify many of Bellamy's ideas, it had little discoverable public impact.

### Nationalism
The excitement generated by *Looking Backward* translated itself into the formation of clubs dedicated to the discussion and advancement of the book's ideas. The first such Nationalist Club was founded in Boston in December 1888. Within a year there were enough clubs nationwide to justify speaking of a Nationalist movement. The primary goal of Nationalism was the transfer of corporate property—in the beginning utilities and other quasi monopolies—to public ownership. For Bellamy and his followers, Nationalism meant what would now be called nationalization; it had no overtones

# LITERARY AND HISTORICAL CONTEMPORARIES

Bellamy's famous contemporaries include:

**Rudyard Kipling** (1865–1935): One of the most popular English-language writers at the turn of the twentieth century, Kipling drew upon his background growing up in British-ruled India to write such classics as *The Jungle Book* (1894) and *Kim* (1901).

**H. Rider Haggard** (1856–1925): A writer of popular adventure tales, Haggard invented the Lost World genre of adventure stories, and his Alan Quartermain character established the archetype of the scholar-adventurer.

**Pyotr Ilyich Tchaikovsky** (1840–1893): A Russian composer identified with the Romantic movement, Tchaikovsky's most famous composition remains *The Nutcracker*.

**George Eastman** (1854–1932): The founder of the Eastman Kodak company, Eastman invented the roll of film, enabling the construction of smaller, more portable cameras, making photography a technology available to the mass consumer market for the first time.

**Friedrich Engels** (1820–1895): Along with Karl Marx, German philosopher Engels developed the theory of communism, co-authoring *The Communist Manifesto* (1848).

of devotion to a single state, and as it was concerned with world politics was distinctly internationalist. Nationalist ideas strongly influenced the Populist platform of 1892, and Bellamy himself became increasingly involved in political activism and in 1891 started his own magazine, the *New Nation*. As Nationalism became more and more identified with and influenced by other reform movements, it seemed to Bellamy to drift farther from what he considered the spiritual and religious foundations of his ideas. Inevitably the movement became fragmented, and Bellamy's became increasingly a solitary voice. Nationalism as a political force had all but disappeared by 1895; in 1896 Bellamy abandoned the *New Nation* and devoted his dwindling energies to writing *Equality*. Bellamy had never been particularly robust. Since the 1870s he had suffered from recurrent pulmonary and digestive disorders; by the early 1890s he had contracted tuberculosis. He died in Chicopee Falls on May 22, 1898.

## Works in Literary Context

Probably more directly than any other American novel, except perhaps *Uncle Tom's Cabin*, *Looking Backward* rendered in comprehensible terms its readers' deepest social anxieties. Bellamy's analysis of the dislocations of an increasingly industrialized America and his mixture of

cultural and technological solutions to the most disturbing social problems, at once confirmed and resolved doubts his generation had begun to express about the moral and material future of the nation. Bellamy clubs and publications advocating Bellamy's reformism sprang up throughout the United States, and his ideas were translated into legislative acts and party platforms. *Looking Backward* inspired a host of utopian and dystopian novels, and within a few years of its publication was the most widely familiar "socialist" work of its time. It influenced a generation of American and European reformers, and its place as the most important American depiction of utopia remains secure and unchallenged.

*Socialist Utopia Looking Backward*, like many descriptions of utopias (including Sir Thomas More's), ironically seeks through its futurism the recovery of a lost golden age—in Bellamy's case one characterized by the myth of pastoral America and the dream of romantic selfhood. *Looking Backward* appeared at the end of two decades of rapid, unsettling change in American life. Industrialization, urbanization, immigration, the opening of the trans-Missouri West, the apparently uncontrollable power of trusts and political machines had radically altered society. Business panic followed expansionist boom in an ever-quickening cycle. Surrounded by what appeared to be social chaos, many Americans of Bellamy's age and class sensed, sometimes vaguely, that while they had won a great Civil War to preserve their nation, they had somehow in the process been cheated and dispossessed of the America that was properly their heritage. Both the serious and popular literature of the period is suffused with nostalgic idealization of the pre-Civil War village.

At the same time, the middle-class Americans who felt deprived of their birthright were often participants in and beneficiaries of the very progress responsible for the cultural upheaval. In the flood of reformist writing of the period, *Looking Backward* is distinguished by its promise to restore the idealized culture of village America while retaining all the more attractive fruits of industrialization, technology, and economic centralization. It is probably that double, not to say contradictory, character of the book which accounted for both its vast popularity and its considerable influence upon the reform movement.

The double focus of *Looking Backward* makes it in a sense two books. More familiarly it appears to be a blueprint for a more or less socialist utopia; but that blueprint is framed in a narrative of nineteenth-century cultural unrest. Bellamy often spoke of the latter aspect of the book, which is the personal story of his hero, Julian West, as a "sugar-coating" for his utopian message. Julian's story conveys the cultural reassurance that is ultimately the justification for Bellamy's social and economic reforms.

## Works in Critical Context

Almost none of Bellamy's fiction before *Looking Backward* has much intrinsic appeal or value. He seldom created compelling or even convincing actions. His characters lack dimension or, except for the ideas put into their mouths, interest. His style is at best serviceable, and in the more specifically romantic novels that William Dean Howells admired somewhat, it is not always appropriate to Bellamy's "spiritual" subjects. In all of the earlier novels, as in *Looking Backward*, ideological dialogue or debates predominate over plot and character development. Nevertheless, several of his novels, among them *Dr. Heidenhoff's Process* and *Miss Ludington's Sister*, received favorable notice in their day; his *The Duke of Stockbridge* has been called, perhaps extravagantly, "one of the greatest historical novels."

*Looking Backward* *Looking Backward* was never considered seriously as literature; its appeal lay in its message. *The Nation*, writing in 1897, was typical of the critical reaction the book:

> *Looking Backward* was a clever piece of literary work, which had some of the interest of a novel, besides the fascination of all ingenious speculation about the future of the world. ... [In] reality, although a great deal is said about work, we find, in the end, that there is little or none [accomplished in Bellamy's proposed society], and that, strange as it may seem, after all, what our Utopian guide has had in mind all along, though he has cleverly concealed it, is the old dream of a paradise of sloth and ease.

## Responses to Literature

1. Make a list of the predictions that Bellamy laid out for the future. Which of those predictions have come to pass? Which did not, and why?

2. Compare Bellamy's utopian economic and political system to communism. How are they similar? How are they different? Are there any governmental systems in the world today that come close to Bellamy's vision?

3. What changes have been made since Bellamy's day to protect the worker? What was the labor situation in the late nineteenth century? How has the average worker's lot improved since then?

4. Why do you think Bellamy chose to use the format of a novel to lay out his political beliefs? What other methods could he have used? Do you think any of those methods would have been more effective?

BIBLIOGRAPHY

**Books**

Bowman, Sylvia E. *The Year 2000: A Critical Biography of Edward Bellamy*. New York: Bookman Associates, 1958.

Morgan, Arthur. *Edward Bellamy*. New York: Columbia University Press, 1944.

Roemer, Kenneth. *The Obsolete Necessity: America in Utopian Writings*. Kent, Ohio: Kent State University Press, 1976.

**Periodicals**

Becker, George. "Edward Bellamy: Utopia, American Plan." *Antioch Review* 14 (June 1954): 181–194.

Bleich, David. "Eros and Bellamy." *American Quarterly* 16 (Fall 1964): 445–459.

Sanford, Charles. "Classics of American Reform Literature." *American Quarterly* 10 (Fall 1958): 295–311.

Towers, Tom H. "The Insomnia of Julian West." *American Literature* 47 (March 1975): 52–63.

## COMMON HUMAN EXPERIENCE

Bellamy was just one of many authors who have speculated on utopian societies and what it would take to create them.

*Utopia* (1516), a philosophical work by Sir Thomas More. Despite modern connotations of the word, More did not set out to describe his Utopia (a word he invented meaning "no-place land") as an ideal society, but rather as the antithesis of the chaotic, war-torn society around him. In so doing, he hoped to promote discussion and action towards changing European society in the present, as opposed to working towards some ideal future goal.

*For Us, The Living* (2004), a novel by Robert Heinlein. An unpublished novel written in 1938 and recently discovered among the science-fiction master's papers, this tale mirror's Bellamy's, in that it concerns a man who is propelled into the next century, into a vastly different society. Heinlein's utopia revolves around granting economic freedom to potential workers, who are then free to pursue whatever type of work they feel best suits them, regardless of pay.

*The Shape of Things to Come* (1933), a fictional chronology by H. G. Wells. Another book to employ Bellamy's plot device of a modern "sleeper" cast forward into a future society, although in this case the "sleeper" is just that: a professor who catches glimpses of a future society through dream visions. Wells envisions society destroying itself through war, then the ascension of a "benevolent dictatorship" that paves the way for the emergence of a Utopian society.

*Sleeper* (1973), a film by Woody Allen. A comedic take on Bellamy's theme of a modern man awakening in a future society, this film presents instead a repressive dictatorship masquerading as a utopia.

# ✸ Saul Bellow

BORN: *1915, Lachine, Quebec, Canada*

DIED: *2005, Brookline, Massachusetts*

NATIONALITY: *American*

GENRE: *Fiction, drama*

MAJOR WORKS:

*The Adventures of Augie March* (1953)

*Herzog* (1964)

*Humboldt's Gift* (1975)

## Overview

Pulitzer Prize and Nobel Prize-winning novelist Saul Bellow has taken a place among the leading figures in twentieth-century American literature. In his writing and teaching, Bellow championed human and moral possibilities in the face of personal and social struggle. In a *Times Literary Supplement* article, Julian Symons compared Bellow to two British "other-sayers," George Orwell and Wyndham Lewis. "In the United States," writes Symons,

Saul Bellow  *Michael Mauney / Time Life Pictures / Getty Images*

"Saul Bellow has, for the past twenty years and more, been saying unpopular things about American culture in general, and about the relationship between the society and its literature in particular."

## Works in Biographical and Historical Context

***Canadian Childhood, Escape to America***  The son of Russian-born parents living in a slum in Lachine, Quebec, Bellow was confined to a hospital for a year during his childhood; he passed the time reading. At seventeen, as the Great Depression was ravaging the Canadian economy, he and friend Sydney J. Harris (later a noted newspaper columnist) ran away to New York to sell their first novels, unfortunately without success. Eventually, Bellow enrolled at the University of Chicago. In 1937 he graduated from Northwestern University, where he founded a socialists' club, with honors in sociology and anthropology. He found employment writing biographical sketches of Midwestern writers.

***Beginning of a Literary Career***  Later, with the outbreak of the Second World War, Bellow tried to join the Canadian Army, an active British ally, but he was turned down for medical reasons. This experience provided the germ for his first published novel, *Dangling Man* (1944). Using his own life events to inspire his fiction would prove a lifelong habit. A persistent criticism of Bellow is that he merges with his protagonists. Bellow has said, "I would have to suffer from dissociation of personality to be all these people in the books," but he confessed, "I lend a character, out of pure friendship, whatever he needs." He lent Joseph of *Dangling Man* his Canadian birth and Chicago upbringing. In 1943, he worked on Mortimer Adler's "Great Books" project for the *Encyclopedia Britannica*. He then returned to New York and did freelance work before taking a teaching job at the University of Minnesota in 1946. He published his second novel, *The Victim*, in 1947 (with that work's character Asa Leventhal he shared the editing experience he got at the *Encyclopedia Britannica*) and traveled to France in 1948. He taught at various universities and traveled extensively. In 1963, he accepted a permanent position on the Committee on Social Thought at the University of Chicago.

***The Adventures of Saul Bellow***  Bellow's best-known protagonist, Augie March, starts out in Bellow's own 1920s Chicago and ends up, after his merchant-marine stint, in France, where Bellow, after some merchant-marine service of his own, started writing *The Adventures of Augie March* (1953). The vexed and effortful hero of Bellow's next novel, *Herzog* (1964), got Bellow's Chicago and Canadian roots, his bootlegging immigrant father, and his two ex-wives.

Frequently Bellow shares with his protagonists his station in life, intellectual inclination, and cultural background. There is, moreover, a correspondence between Bellow's conception of the artist and his conception of his protagonists. Just as the artist must demonstrate his trust in intuitions radically deeper than his conscious knowledge, so the characters Henderson, Herzog, Sammler, and Citrine hold themselves accountable for the utterance of what they know unaccountably. These protagonists reflect Bellow's own struggle to "express a variety of things I knew intimately," according to the author.

## Works in Literary Context

In his works, Bellow addresses the question of what it is to be human in an increasingly impersonal and mechanistic world. Writing in a humorous, anecdotal style that combines exalted meditation and modern vernacular, Bellow often depicts introspective individuals who suffer a conflict between Old World and New World values while trying to understand their personal anxieties and aspirations.

Throughout his career, Saul Bellow showed himself to be a stylist equally at ease with the comic and tragic voices. As a writer who often explored the most sensitive and difficult public and private aspects of contemporary life, he won the respect of critics but has also suffered the approbation of feminist critics for perceived sexist and misogynist portraits of female characters and of leftist critics for alleged conservative political and cultural values.

*The Holocaust and Anti-Semitism*   Bellow was among the first American writers to treat anti-Semitism (prejudice against those of Jewish descent and/or belief) and the Holocaust in fiction. He addressed cultural anti-Semitism in *The Victim* (1947); religious anti-Semitism in *The Adventures of Augie March* (1953); economic and social anti–Semitism in "The Old System" (1967); and violent anti-Semitism in *Herzog* (1964), "Mosby's Memoirs" (1968), and the National Book Award winner *Mr. Sammler's Planet* (1970). The Holocaust is rarely at the thematic center of Bellow's novels, yet it is an ever-present element in characters haunted by its specter. In *Humboldt's Gift* (1975), for example, Humboldt Fleisher declines an invitation to present a lecture series in Berlin because a year in Germany would be a constant reminder of "the destruction of the death camps, the earth soaked in blood, and the fumes of cremation still in the air of Europe."

*The "Bellow Hero"*   In their many books and essays on Bellow's works, critics often concentrate on two aspects of Bellow's fiction: his skillfully crafted protagonists, who collectively exemplify the "Bellow hero," and his expansive prose style. Bellow's typical protagonist, who is generally a male, urbanite Jewish intellectual, was described by the Nobel Committee as a man "who keeps trying to find a foothold during his wanderings in our tottering world, one who can never relinquish his faith that the value of life depends on its dignity, not its

## LITERARY AND HISTORICAL CONTEMPORARIES

Bellow's famous contemporaries include:

**Arthur Miller** (1915–2005): Miller was an American playwright, whose many plays, such as *The Crucible* (1953) and *Death of a Salesman* (1949), continue to be studied and performed regularly.

**Dag Hammarskjold** (1905–1961): Called by John Kennedy "the greatest statesman of our time," Hammarskjold was the second Secretary-General of the United Nations, a post he held for nearly a decade before dying in a plane crash while traveling to negotiate a cease-fire in Africa. He was awarded the Nobel Peace Prize the same year, becoming the only recipient to win the award posthumously.

**Aldous Huxley** (1894–1963): Huxley was a successful novelist and essayist who explored such themes as the future of humanity, pacifism, mysticism, and the use of psychedelic drugs.

**Edmund Hillary** (1919–2008): A New Zealand mountaineer who in 1953 became, along with Sherpa mountaineer Tenzig Norgay, the first to reach the summit of Mount Everest.

**Fidel Castro** (1926–): Cuban revolutionary leader Fidel Castro directed the overthrow of the U.S.-backed Batista regime in 1959. He led Cuba from 1959 until his retirement in 2008, forming a Communist government that was closely allied to the Soviet Union and supported various revolutionary causes in other Third World nations.

success." In developing his characters Bellow emphasizes dialogue and interior monologue, and his prose style features sudden flashes of wit and philosophical epigrams. As his protagonists speak to themselves and to others, the reader is drawn into their struggles with self and society. Bellow's earliest novels, *Dangling Man* and *The Victim*, are written in a disciplined, realistic style that he later rejected as constraining. During the 1950s, Bellow developed a lively prose style that could accommodate comic misadventures and philosophical digression. He began to write picaresque narratives that employ larger-than-life protagonists and various rhetorical elements. *The Adventures of Augie March* (1953), for example, features an extroverted, exuberant character who believes that a "man's character is his fate." With *Herzog*, Bellow successfully fused the formal realism of his early works with the vitality of his picaresque novels of the 1950s.

## Works in Critical Context

The recipient of the 1976 Nobel Prize in Literature, Bellow is among the most celebrated authors of the

# COMMON HUMAN EXPERIENCE

*The Adventures of Augie March* is an example of a classic "coming of age" story, in which the protagonist matures over the course of the narrative, often with the guidance of a mentor and by passing through a series of tests. Other such tales include:

*Bless Me, Ultima* (1972), a novel by Rudolfo Anaya. Set in rural New Mexico just after the Second World War, this novel traces the story of a young boy as he learns about life, death, and nature with the help of a healer ("curandera") named Ultima.

*The Last Unicorn* (1968), a film by Arthur Rankin, Jr. and Jules Bass. Based on a 1968 novel by Peter S. Beagle, this animated tale is an unusual take on the typical coming of age story: its protagonist is a young unicorn who, freed from a carnival by the bumbling wizard Schmendrick, sets off to find out if she is indeed the last of her kind.

*Little Women* (1868), a novel by Louisa May Alcott. This is a classic tale of four sisters each coming to terms with growing up and overcoming their character flaws during and after the American Civil War.

*Daughter of Fortune* (1999), a novel by Isabel Allende. Beginning in mid-nineteenth century Chile with the adoption of an abandoned baby, this story then follows the girl as she grows from hapless victim of circumstance to independent woman living in the California gold fields.

twentieth century. He has received three National Book Awards, a Pulitzer Prize, and the 1976 Nobel Prize in Literature. According to Irving Howe, Bellow evolved "the first major new style in American prose fiction since those of Hemingway and Faulkner."

**The Adventures of Augie March**  Despite being his third novel, *The Adventures of Augie March* (1953) was Bellow's first major success. Charles J. Rolo, in his review for the *Atlantic Monthly*, states that "Mr. Bellow's novel is a notable achievement, and it should be one of the year's outstanding successes." Rolo's one criticism, however, is that the author "has not tried to take us more deeply inside his hero." Some other critics were less impressed. In a review for *Commonweal*, T. E. Cassidy notes that while the author "has some fine things in this book," the novel ultimately fails because "there is no depth and no great theme." However, Robert Penn Warren, in a review for *New Republic*, disagrees with this assessment, stating that it is a "rich, various, fascinating, and important book, and from now on any discussion of fiction in America in our time will have to take account of it."

**Herzog**  *Herzog* (1964) is notable for the the split it caused among critics. Bellow's second National Book Award-winner, it was both praised and highly criticized. Alfred Kazin called it Bellow's "most brilliant" novel while Brendan Gill termed it "faultless." Other critics worried that Herzog pondered only himself, making the novel concerned only with the self. Critics divide largely into those who forgive this disorganization (since it reflects Herzog's mind) and those who do not.

## Responses to Literature

1. Research one of the historical recipients of a letter in *Herzog*. Write a response to the letter addressed to that person as you feel they would have responded.

2. Compare and contrast the protagonists of *Seize the Day* and *Leaving the Yellow House*. How do the two environments of the characters—urban for the former and rural for the latter—influence their lives and differentiate them? How are they similar?

3. Based on Bellow's depiction of his female characters, particularly in *Herzog*, how would you characterize the author's view of women? Provide examples from the text that support your view.

4. What role does Bellow's Jewish background play in his fiction? Is understanding the viewpoint of the urban, Jewish intellectual critical to understanding Bellow's stories?

BIBLIOGRAPHY

**Books**

"The Adventures of Augie March by Saul Bellow." *Contemporary Literary Criticism.* Edited by Tom Burns and Jeffrey W. Hunter. Vol. 190. Detroit: Thomson Gale, 2004, pp. 1–76.

Bigler, Walter. *Figures of Madness in Saul Bellow's Longer Fiction.* New York: Peter Lang, 1998.

Cohen, Sarah Blacher. *Saul Bellow's Enigmatic Laughter.* Champaign, Ill.: University of Illinois Press, 1974.

"Herzog." *Novels for Students.* Edited by Jennifer Smith. Vol. 14. Detroit: Gale, 2002.

Kramer, Michael P., editor. *New Essays on Seize the Day.* Cambridge, Mass.: Cambridge University Press, 1998.

McCadden, Joseph F. *The Flight from Women in the Fiction of Saul Bellow.* Lanham, Md.: University Press of America, 1980.

"Leaving the Yellow House." *Short Stories for Students.* Edited by Jennifer Smith. Vol. 12. Detroit: Gale Group, 2001.

"Seize the Day." *Novels for Students.* Edited by Marie Rose Napierkowski. Vol. 4. Detroit: Gale, 1998.

Wasserman, Harriet. *Handsome Is: Adventures with Saul Bellow, A Memoir.* New York: Fromm International, 1997.

# ✳ Aimee Bender

BORN: *1969, Los Angeles, California*

NATIONALITY: *American*

GENRE: *Fiction*

MAJOR WORKS:

*The Girl in the Flammable Skirt* (1998)

*An Invisible Sign of My Own* (2000)

*Willful Creatures* (2005)

## Overview

Aimee Bender is a critically-acclaimed novelist and short story author noted for her surrealist fiction. Her use of magic realism in her stories keeps alive a literary tradition stretching back over half a century. She has used her stories to explore both the hilarious and grotesque aspects of everyday life.

## Works in Biographical and Historical Context

*Early Influences* Born on June 28, 1969, in Los Angeles, California, Aimee Bender was the youngest of three daughters. She grew up idolizing her older sisters and holding her psychologist father and choreographer mother in high regard. Bender, in an interview with *pif* magazine, said,

> My dad, through psychiatry, is dealing with the unconscious.... and my mom is delving into her own unconscious to make up dances. ... And I'm sort of the combo platter, in that psychiatry is so essentially verbal ... and also I am like [my mother] in that it's all about creating from this inexplicable mysterious place.

Bender's first literary influence, encountered when Bender was a teenager, was *Transformations*, a book of comically twisted fairy tales by the poet Anne Sexton. As Bender noted, "Only later, in rereading it, did I see how hugely it had influenced my own stuff," said Bender in a 2006 interview with the *Yalabusha Review*.

*Publishing Fiction* After taking her undergraduate degree at the University of California, San Diego, Bender joined the master of fine arts in Creative Writing program at University of California, Irvine. There she studied with Judith Grossman and Geoffrey Wolff and met and befriended a classmate named Alice Sebold, who would also go on to enjoy her own literary success.

After graduating with her MFA, Bender began to get her stories published in such literary reviews as *Three-penny Review*, *Granta*, and *Story*. In 1998, her previously published short stories were collected together into her first book, *The Girl in the Flammable Skirt*. Chosen as a *New York Times* Notable Book for that year, it also spent several weeks on *The Los Angeles Times* bestseller list.

Aimee Bender    © *Jerry Bauer. Reproduced by permission.*

Bender followed up her success with a full-length novel in 2000, *An Invisible Sign of My Own*. This book earned praise, too, being selected by the *Los Angeles Times* as one of the Best Books of 2000. It also continued Bender's explorations into the realm of magical realism and surrealism, which she had begun in her short stories. The novel involves a young math teacher who, caring for her ailing father, retreats into a dreamlike world of numbers and formula. After her novel was published, Bender continued to write short stories, still in the magical-realism vein, which were put out in a second collection, *Willful Creatures* (2005). The book was nominated by the literary magazine *The Believer* as one of the best books of the year.

In addition to pursuing her writing career, Bender has taught creative writing at several universities. She currently teaches the subject at the University of Southern California. She has continued to publish short stories in such magazines as *GQ*, *Harper's*, *McSweeney's*, and the *Paris Review*, and has twice been awarded the Pushcart Prize.

## Works in Literary Context

Bender's stories employ well-worn themes. They teem with the cheerful anguish of family life, aging parents, teen alienation and the still-forming sexuality of young

# LITERARY AND HISTORICAL CONTEMPORARIES

Bender's famous contemporaries include:

**J. K. Rowling** (1965–): Rowling herself became a modern "rags to riches" story when the first book of her Harry Potter series, a modern fantasy saga of young boy who attends a school for wizards, launched a worldwide phenomenon.

**Bill Gates** (1955–): One of the richest people in the world, Gates built up his company Microsoft (co-founded with Paul Allen) through aggressive marketing of software and operating systems, including Windows and Internet Explorer.

**Bill Clinton** (1946–): The forty-second president of the United States, Clinton served two terms, from 1993 to 2001. He ended his presidency with the highest approval rating of any President since World War II.

**Michael Ondaatje** (1943–): A Sri Lankan-Canadian novelist and poet, perhaps best known for his book *The English Patient* (1992), which was adapted into an Oscar-winning movie.

**Khaled Hosseini** (1965–): Hosseini is an American author (born in Afghanistan) famous for such novels as *The Kite Runner* (2003) and *A Thousand Splendid Suns* (2007).

adulthood. In the story "The Rememberer," a young woman watches as her boyfriend regresses through evolution. "I don't know how it happened," the narrator deadpans, "only that one day he was my lover and the next he was some kind of ape. It's been a month and now he's a sea turtle." But Bender ultimately resists heavy psychological symbolism.

In an interview with *pif* magazine, Bender outlined the themes she deals with in her fiction:

> [the] desire for connection, isolation from others, burden of caretaking, the ways loss gets expressed, suppression of passion, acting out of desires in a painful way, self-mutilation, deformity as a way to show loss or change, the connectedness of everyone, sex as an expression of loss, rage, obliteration, connection, or freedom, hmmmm, man vs. man, man vs. nature, man vs. himself—ha. ... Hmmm. Kind of a weighty list. Plus I know I'm missing tons of them. But there's a start.

*Magical Realism* Bender's writing style is usually categorized as magical realism. This genre was first recognized as an emerging literary genre during the Latin American literary "Boom" of the 1950s and 1960s. Magical realism refers to the practice of placing bizarre, surreal events in a realistic context, and treating the unrealistic events as real—those involved in the story rarely if ever seem to notice or comment upon the seemingly strange elements occurring around them. It is as if they are operating in an entirely different, internally consistent reality, much like the logic that defines dreams.

It is this blending of the surreal unconsciousness with the firm, internally logical conscious reality that, by forcing the reader/outsider to "decode" the magical reality, allows magical realist authors like Bender to explore the condition of human psychology, perceptions, myth, subconscious desires, and culture.

## Works in Critical Context

"Once in a while, a writer comes along who makes you grateful for the very existence of language," wrote Carol Lloyd in the *San Francisco Chronicle*. "It's not a gratitude sparked by awe-inspiring virtuosity, but one that issues from the infectious, if inexplicable, pleasure that radiates from the pages themselves." An unnamed reviewer for *Publisher's Weekly* commented that "as Bender explores a spectrum of human relationships, her perfectly pitched, shapely writing blurs the lines between prose and poetry." In *The New York Times Book Review*, Lisa Zeidner wrote that Bender's stories "are powered by voice— by the pleasure of the electric simile." Writes Lloyd, "[e]ven when Bender dances on the edge of goofier-than-thou poetry, these near-magical stories are more than whimsical field trips into the unconscious."

Some reviewers did fault Bender's debut collection, however, noting that while it was overall an impressive work, the author's relative inexperience as a writer sometimes showed. Margot Mifflin wrote, "Some of Bender's forays into magical realism feel like collegiate exercises," and Lisa Zeidner of the *New York Times Book Review* agreed: "The weakest [stories] juxtapose multiple plot lines—a standard creative-writing workshop ploy— without much more point than to showcase the skill of the juggler." Both Mifflin's and Zeidner's overall reviews of the collection, however, were positive.

*An Invisible Sign of My Own* After her precocious beginning with *The Girl in the Flammable Skirt*, critics were curious to see if Bender could sustain her surreal storytelling over the course of a full-length novel. Reviewing this work for *Booklist*, Michelle Kaske noted that the book is a "wonderful ... treatment of anxiety, depression, and compulsion." Writing in the *San Francisco Chronicle*, Gina Nahai summarized the book in the following way: "In the end, *An Invisible Sign of My Own* achieves what all good fiction strives for: It gives a face to human suffering but sprinkles it with just enough magic to make reality tolerable."

## Responses to Literature

1. In 1971 Anne Sexton, a noted poet, wrote a collection of twisted fairy tales entitled *Transformations*. Amy Bender has cited this book as a major influence on her own writing. What is the connection between magical realism and fairy tales? Try rewriting a traditional fairy tale in a modern setting, giving it a dark or comical twist if possible.

2. Bender has written about transformation from human to animal in her short story "The Rememberer". Research the short story "The Metamorphosis" by Franz Kafka. How do the two stories compare? How do they differ?

3. Research and define magical realism. How does Bender's work compare to the standard you've set? What elements of her work mark her fiction as belonging to the magical realism genre? How does her work differ from the genre conventions?

4. Write your own magical-realism story. Take a normal, seemingly mundane situation (perhaps a regular day at school) and introduce surreal, off-the-wall elements to the narrative.

BIBLIOGRAPHY

**Books**

"Bender, Aimee." *Contemporary Authors, New Revision Series.* Vol. 153. Detroit: Gale, 2007.

"The Rememberer." *Short Stories for Students.* Ed. Ira Mark Milne. Vol. 25. Detroit: Gale, 2007.

**Periodicals**

Burkhardt, Joanna M. "The Girl in the Flammable Skirt." *Library Journal* (June 15, 1998): 109.

Anderson, Beth E. "An Invisible Sign of My Own." *Library Journal* (May 15, 2000): 123.

**Web sites**

Aimee Bender's Website. "Biography." Retrieved September 22, 2008, from http://www.flammable skirt.com/biography.html.

Boudinot, Ryan. *Amy [sic] Bender.* Retrieved September 22, 2008, from http://www.pifmagazine.com/SID/498/.

Hobart. "An Interview with Aimee Bender." Retrieved September 22, 2008, from http://hobartpulp.com/interviews/bender.html.

Kelby, N. M. *A Plastic Buddha.* Retrieved September 22, 2008, from http://webdelsol.com/Literary_Dialogues/interview-wds-bender.htm.

Welch, Dave. *Aimee Bender's Cabinet of Wonder.* Retrieved September 22, 2008, from http://www.powells.com/interviews/bender.html.

# ✸ Stephen Vincent Benét

BORN: *1898, Bethlehem, Pennsylvania*

DIED: *1943, New York, New York*

NATIONALITY: *American*

GENRE: *Drama, poetry*

MAJOR WORKS:

*John Brown's Body* (1928)

"The Devil and Daniel Webster" (1937)

"By the Waters of Babylon" (1937)

## COMMON HUMAN EXPERIENCE

Bender's work is often associated with magical realism, a literary genre that began in the years following World War II in which magical or illogical scenarios are presented in an otherwise normal, mundane setting.

*Midnight's Children* (1981), a novel by Salman Rushdie. Using the conceit that children born during the hour after India became independent (midnight on August 15, 1947) were granted special powers, Rushdie examines the issues that faced India during its early statehood.

*The Bloody Chamber* (1979), a collection of short stories by Angela Carter. Many of Carter's short stories contained in this volume are magical realist re-tellings of classic fairy tales, including a personal favorite of Bender's: "The Company of Wolves," a different take on Little Red Riding Hood.

*The House of the Spirits* (1982), a novel by Isabel Allende. A book begun as a letter to Allende's grandfather, the story follows four generations of a Latin American family and the upheavals of the country they live in; interwoven throughout the narrative are a variety of magical realist elements.

*Like Water for Chocolate* (1989), a novel by Laura Esquivel. With each chapter of the book starting with a recipe, the magical power of food is the focus of this story of a woman who infuses her cooking with her repressed emotions.

## Overview

Stephen Vincent Benét occupies a curiously uncertain position in American letters. One of America's best known and rewarded poets and storytellers (his "The Devil and Daniel Webster" became an instant classic upon its publication), he has at the same time been virtually ignored in academic discussions of major twentieth-century writers and is seldom anthologized. In light of the greater critical success enjoyed by his student friends at Yale—Thornton Wilder, Archibald MacLeish, and Philip Barry—Benét's reputation seems thin indeed.

## Works in Biographical and Historical Context

*A Serious Upbringing* Born in Bethlehem, Pennsylvania, Stephen Vincent Benét was the son of James Walker Benét, a career military officer, and his wife, Frances Neill Rose Benét. The travels of the family during Benét's early life nurtured a broad and resilient sense of his country that is the basis of much of his most important work. His parents also fostered a strong interest in

Stephen Vincent Benet    *photograph by Pirie MacDonald. The Library of Congress.*

history and encouraged the open-minded exploration of books and ideas, but against a background of firm professionalism. Thus, it hardly seems surprising that from an early age Benét took his writing very seriously and published his first book at the age of seventeen, in the same year that he entered Yale University.

At Yale he made contacts who put him in touch with the New York literary world, and henceforth (except for fellowships from Yale and from the Guggenheim Foundation) he earned his livelihood as a professional writer. According to his biographer, Charles A. Fenton, Benét "wrote short stories for money and poetry for love" throughout his career. Such production meant, of course, a perpetual struggle to meet the specifications of the mass-circulation magazines, which focused almost exclusively on simple-minded, saccharine romance. Benét spent the early 1920s wrestling with the formula and became predictably frustrated with the conflict among his own literary standards, the popular taste, and editorial prejudice, until he began to develop the kind of historical materials that would secure his reputation not only in fiction but in poetry.

***Commercial Americana*** In 1926 he published "The Sobbin' Women" (collected in *Thirteen O'Clock*, 1937), a farfetched but engaging tale of seven frontier brothers who literally kidnap wives for themselves. Notwithstanding the echo of the legend of the Sabine women, the characters, tone, and setting of the story are thoroughly American, and Benét introduces here the "Oldest Inhabitant" narrator upon whom he would call repeatedly throughout his career. The story was the first of a series of historical tales written at the same time he was working on *John Brown's Body* (1928), which won the Pulitzer Prize for Poetry in 1929. *John Brown's Body* was inspired by the American Civil War. The title refers to John Brown, an anti-slavery activist who raided Harpers Ferry Armory in Virginia in 1859, in a failed attempt to start a slave uprising, an event cited by many historians as a key precursor to the Civil War.

Benét continued work in a similar vein for the remainder of his literary career, penning stories of the American spirit, or folksy Americana, until the advent of World War II, upon which he turned his talents towards writing war propaganda. Benét died of a heart attack in 1943, as America was still locked in struggle against the Germans and the Japanese.

## Works in Literary Context

***Americana*** Benét's writing exhibits an unbounded, nineteenth-century faith in the promises of American democracy and an expansive love for what seemed the nation's special attributes: diversity; amplitude; self-sufficiency; frankness; and innocence. He praised New York as the communal achievement of the spirit of man and America because there every man could most freely become what God meant him to be. "Out of your fever and your moving on," he said in the "Prelude" to *Western Star*, "Americans, Americans, Americans … I make my song."

Both in sentiment and in style, Benét's work attempts to embody the very democratic virtues found in its subject matter. Like Carl Sandburg, Hart Crane, and Vachel Lindsay, he uses the zesty tempos, conversational rhythms, and laconic everyday speech to capture the spirit of greatness in the strength and simplicity of the nation's common people. In his book *A Book of Americans*, which contains fifty-six verses about famous American men and women, great and small, Benét says of the greatest and humblest of American native sons: "Lincoln was a long man / He liked the out of doors. / He liked the wind blowing / And the talk in country stores."

***Good, Evil, and National Identity*** The human reality of both good and evil is at the core of the story "The Devil and Daniel Webster," in which the legendary orator pleads successfully for the soul of a Yankee farmer in a court full of sinister renegades and reprobates from national history. At one level the power of the story derives from its folksy narrator and national hero. Old Scratch, the Devil, is described as having tiny, winged souls he carries casually wrapped in his handkerchief; the orator/hero is gifted with a homespun, blustering wit and is humanized by a twinkle of manly mischief: "[T]here's a jug on the table and a case in hand. And I never left a jug or a case half-finished in my life," he says.

With the climax of the story, Benét changes direction technically and also reveals another, more important level of meaning. Webster's presentation for the defense is not given directly, but summarized in little more than a page. Recognizing "his own anger and horror" as being shared by the jury made up of the damned, he eschews the bombast of the politician or lawyer and instead talks quietly "about the things that make a country a country, and a man a man." He wins his case by allowing the jurors to see that they and the defendant are all part of "the story and the failures and the endless journey of mankind."

The theme that surfaces here is foreshadowed earlier when the Devil points out that he was there "When the first wrong was done to the first Indian. . . . When the first slaver put out for the Congo." The same point is made by the American identity of the villainous jurors: that the nation, like the individual, like humanity itself, embodies both good and evil, and that "everybody has played a part . . . even the traitors." Thus, Webster draws the jurors into an identification with his client, and Benét draws his readers into an identification with the nation and with the human family.

## Works in Critical Context

Despite the warmth, genuineness, and impish charm with which Benét celebrates the country's democratic potential, his failure to win wider critical respectability may be attributable to the fact that his breadth of sympathy and deep-rooted patriotism seem parochial and old-fashioned to many modern scholars, and that even his best work, viewed alongside the more realistic and richly inventive fiction of such contemporaries as Stephen Crane, James Joyce, Marcel Proust, and T. S. Eliot, appears lacking in depth, subtlety, and originality. The pastoral rebellion of the earth against machines, against the "Age of Steam," which pervades so many of his poems, and his use of conventional verse forms and technical devices that have made him dear to school teachers, seem, in the words of one critic, "all too clear and all too facile." It is significant that Benét's writing has been praised more for its lively evocation of American history than for its aesthetic value.

*John Brown's Body* *John Brown's Body* was acclaimed as a long-awaited American epic. For a work of poetry it gained an unusually wide readership, and Benét was awarded a Pulitzer Prize in 1929. Though criticized for a variety of faults in both style and sentiment, Benét's more important achievement still finds admirers among those who share his affection for America's past.

Allen Tate, puzzling over the lack of aesthetic unity in *John Brown's Body*, once asked: "Is it possible that Mr. Benét supposed the poem to be about the Civil War, rather than about his own mind?" Critics have both

## LITERARY AND HISTORICAL CONTEMPORARIES

Stephen Vincent Benét's famous contemporaries include:

**Georges Prosper Remi** (1907–1983): Better known by his pen name of Hergé, Remi was internationally famous for his "Tintin" comic books, printed in large-format, full color installments. His artistic style, featuring precisely rendered backgrounds and simply-drawn cartoon figures, would prove highly influential on later generations of artists, particularly European illustrators and Japanese *manga* cartoonists.

**Leon Trotsky** (1879–1940): Lenin's second-in-command during the October Revolution that toppled Russia's tsarist monarchy in 1917, Trotsky was instrumental in consolidating and solidifying the nascent Soviet Union, playing a key role as a military commander during the Russian Civil War.

**Al Capone** (1899–1947): Nicknamed "Scarface," Capone was perhaps the most infamous gangster of Prohibition-era organized crime. He built a criminal empire running bootleg liquor in Chicago, famously flaunting the law in the process through a combination of bribery, blackmail, and creative bookkeeping.

**D. H. Lawrence** (1885–1930): A highly controversial English writer criticized as a pornographer during his lifetime, Lawrence has since his death achieved the status as one of the great writers of the twentieth century.

**Erich Maria Remarque** (1898–1970): After serving in the German army during World War I, Remarque wrote about his experiences and the horror of war in the classic novel *All Quiet on the Western Front* (1929).

praised and denigrated Benét's poem as a work in the epic genre. His characterizations of such historic figures as President Lincoln and Robert E. Lee have received particularly mixed criticism; some commentators dismiss the characterizations as shallow and inept, while others applaud them as insightful and faithful to their originals. Most frequently attacked in *John Brown's Body* are what Allen Tate calls its "hair-raising defects" of banal phrasing, unpoetic rhythms, and flawed diction. Benét's use of a wide range of poetic meters resulted in stylistic looseness and fragmentation, leaving his best work to be discovered in individual sections, especially the ballads, rather than the poem as a whole.

## Responses to Literature

1. Benét's writing was inspired by historical events unfolding in the mid-1800s. Has there been a recent historical event that has changed the way you

# COMMON HUMAN EXPERIENCE

Benét attempted, through his poetry and prose alike, to epically evoke a sense of America's fundamental spirit. Other works have explored the same themes.

*Leaves of Grass* (1855), a poetry collection by Walt Whitman. Many critics consider Whitman the quintessential American poet, with some going so far as to call him the quintessential *American*. This collection, revised many times over Whitman's life, contains some of his best known and most distinctively American poems.

*The Song of Hiawatha* (1855), a poem by Henry Wadsworth Longfellow. Intentionally written as an epic in the style of the ancient verses of Scandinavia and Finland, Longfellow's massive poem about a fictional Native American princess was intended to help create a new American mythology.

*The Adventures of Huckleberry Finn* (1884), a novel by Mark Twain. Begun as a follow-up to his more light-hearted *The Adventures of Tom Sawyer* (1876), this seminal work eventually became a novel of much deeper import. It was one of the first major publications to feature dialogue written in regional dialect, giving the language a distinctly American feel. It is also simultaneously a careful document and a vicious satire of aspects of American society, particularly racism.

perceive the world around you? What is your reaction to this particular event?

2. According to Benét, what does it actually mean to be an American? If one can commit wrongdoings and still be embraced as American, what does that say about American culture?

3. Parables are stories that offer a specific message or lesson to the reader. Are parables an effective way to talk about current issues? Take a current event and formulate a parable that talks about the various sides of the issues being debated.

4. Benét chose famous orator Daniel Webster as his defense attorney to go up against the Devil. Who would you choose to defend your soul? What arguments do you think would be most effective in persuading a jury to take your side of the argument?

BIBLIOGRAPHY

**Books**

"An End to Dreams." *Short Stories for Students*. Ed. Ira Mark Milne. Vol. 22. Detroit: Gale, 2006.

Benét, Laura. *When William Rose, Stephen Vincent, and I Were Young*. New York: Dodd, Mead, 1976.

Benét, William Rose. *The Dust Which Is God*. New York: Dodd, Mead, 1941.

Fenton, Charles A. *Stephen Vincent Benét: The Life and Times of a Man of Letters, 1893–1943*. New Haven, Conn.: Yale University Press, 1958.

———, ed. *Selected Letters of Stephen Vincent Benét*. New Haven, Conn.: Yale University Press, 1960.

Izzo, David Garrett. *The American World of Stephen Vincent Benét*. Orem, Utah: Encore Publishing, 1999.

Stroud, Parry Edmond. *Stephen Vincent Benét*. New York: Twayne, 1962.

**Periodicals**

Maddocks, Gladys Louise. "Stephen Vincent Benét: A Bibliography." *Bulletin of Bibliography* 20 (September 1951): 142–146; (April 1952): 158–160.

# ⊛ Wendell Berry

BORN: *1934, Henry County, Kentucky*

NATIONALITY: *American*

GENRE: *Fiction, nonfiction, poetry*

MAJOR WORKS:

*The Unsettling of America: Culture and Agriculture* (1977)

*Collected Poems, 1957–1982* (1985)

*The Wild Birds: Six Stories of the Port William Membership* (1986)

## Overview

Wendell Berry is a poet, novelist, and essayist whose steady literary achievement has earned him wide recognition both as an artist and as a spokesman for contemporary environmental concerns. Since the publication of his first novel, *Nathan Coulter* (1960), Berry has earned a place as an important American thinker and artist whose philosophy and aesthetics are grounded in a regional, environmentally sound, agrarian approach to community. Berry's fiction, as well as his essays and poetry, are closely tied to the farming community of Port Royal, a small town near the confluence of the Kentucky and Ohio Rivers.

## Works in Biographical and Historical Context

***Back to the Land*** Berry was born in Henry County, Kentucky. After receiving his BA and MA degrees from the University of Kentucky in 1956 and 1957, he held a Wallace Stegner Writing Fellowship at Stanford University in 1958–1959. He remained at Stanford for one year as a lecturer in creative writing and, later, taught briefly at New York University before accepting an appointment as a professor of English at the University of Kentucky in 1964. "A Native Hill," one of the essays in Berry's *The*

*Long-Legged House* (1969), contains a section in which the writer examines his decision to leave New York City and "the literary world" and return to Kentucky. Berry writes that he

> never doubted that the world was more important to me than the literary world; and the world would always be most fully and clearly present to me in the place I was fated by birth to know better than any other.

Berry operates his Henry County farm organically, returning to the soil all organic matter and cultivating the land with a team of horses. He says that his education as a poet helped him to become an organic farmer: "Learning to write poetry helped me to see farming as a way of life, not merely as a 'scientific' manipulation of techniques and quantities." He sees a farm and a poem as similar; both are living structures "of interdependent, interconnected parts that mutually clarify and sustain one another."

*Community-Inspired Writing*   Having chosen to return to Port Royal, Berry chose as well the constant subject of his poetry and fiction—his native community. Within his close circle of family and friends, Berry writes that he learned the "two halves of a whole relationship to the earth." Particularly from his grandfather and father came the sense of continuity with and responsibility for the land; and from Nick, a patron black farm worker, a sense of intimacy, the pleasure of "*being* there." Old Nick and Aunt Georgie are the focus of *The Hidden Wound* (1970), a study of the impact of slavery on his native culture and of the contemporary attitudes toward working the land that it has fostered. Berry writes that his memory of these two respected members of the farm has been "one of the persistent forces" in his intellectual growth.

Berry's formative education—as is his art—was drawn from the historical unity of past, present, and future. Linked by this inseparable thread of descent, the resulting body of work is unusually coherent, unified, and consistent. At its core lies a primary humility before the mystery of the world, a belief in the dignity of physical work, and an inevitable, personal responsibility for one's actions in the world.

## Works in Literary Context

In his poetry and prose, Berry documents the rural lifestyle of his native Kentucky. He often draws upon his experiences as a farmer to evidence the dangers of disrupting the natural life cycle and to lament the passing of provincial American traditions. The thematic unity evident throughout Berry's writings has prompted many critics to praise his control of several diverse genres. Like Henry David Thoreau, with whom he has been compared, Berry is also admired for his pragmatic and even-tempered approach to environmental and ecological issues.

## LITERARY AND HISTORICAL CONTEMPORARIES

Berry's famous contemporaries include:

**John Glenn** (1921–): A decorated Marine pilot, Glenn joined NASA's Mercury space program in the late 1950s. In 1962 he became the first American to orbit the Earth, and later served in the U.S. Senate for twenty-five years.

**Margaret Chase Smith** (1897–1995): The first woman to be elected to both the United States House of Representatives and Senate, Smith also became the first woman to have her name placed in nomination for the Presidency by a major party, at the 1964 Republican convention.

**Henry Miller** (1891–1980): An American writer and painter, Miller pioneered a new form of fiction that mixed autobiographical elements with philosophy, mysticism, and free association.

**Nelson Mandela** (1918–): When he became the first democratically elected president of South Africa, Mandela was already a global representative of the struggle for human rights, thanks to his activism against the South African policy of apartheid, the legally-sanctioned suppression of the nation's black majority by a white minority.

**Michael Moorcock** (1939–): An English writer best known for his science-fiction and fantasy novels, Moorcock was one of a breed of writers in the 1960s dubbed the "new wave" sci-fi authors, who approached the genre with a literary seriousness and devotion to plausibility and social relevance.

*Autobiographical Essays*   Books like *The Long-Legged House* combine his strongest qualities as a writer. Like *The Memory of Old Jack*, this nonfiction work is autobiographical and allows Berry to draw on the particular circumstances of his life that give substance to his arguments. Never does he present himself as an abstract philosopher; what wisdom he dispenses comes from a specific awareness of his life in a particular world.

For Berry, autobiography does not mean confession, self-indulgence, or self-service. The essays in *The Long-Legged House*, whether concerned with the war in Vietnam or a sportsman's misuse of the Kentucky River, assume the voice of the Kentucky farmer-artist-philosopher. His arguments are rarely speculative or theoretical; they are the commonsense deliberations of a person looking at the realities of his world. To fragment Berry and treat books like *The Long-Legged House* as separate from his poetry would do him, and the work, a disservice, for the particularity of perceived detail and the inventive metaphors raise portions of *The Long-Legged House* to the intensity of poetry. For instance, "A Native Hill,"

## COMMON HUMAN EXPERIENCE

Berry's work has often been categorized with other influential books about the importance of sustainable living and respect for the environment. These books were critical in the development of the conservation movement, as well as the popular "back to the land" movement of the 1960s and 1970s.

   *A Sand County Almanac* (1949), a nonfiction book by Aldo Leopold. This work is a collection of essays that outline Leopold's vision for a new "land ethic" that argued against economic exploitation of the environment.
   *Silent Spring* (1962), a nonfiction book by Rachel Carson. The first book to criticize the unregulated use of pesticides, this widely read work led directly to the banning of dangerous chemicals such as DDT and is widely credited with launching the modern environmental movement.
   *Animal, Vegetable, Miracle: A Year of Food Life* (2007), a nonfiction book by Barbara Kingsolver. A chronicle of popular author Kingsolver's attempt to live for a year eating only locally-grown foods or foods grown by her family on their newly purchased farm.

the concluding essay, achieves a rich resolution when the writer lies down in the woods and suddenly "apprehends the dark proposal of the earth."

Although he recognizes the comprehensiveness of his form in *The Unsettling of America*, Berry insists that an argument "is always tentative," "always a little dry, airy, detached even from the truth it is trying to defend." In short, "You can learn a lot from a good argument and its form. But an argument cannot make you happy."

***The Fictional Locus***   In the tradition of Faulkner and others, Berry creates a mythic landscape from his historical place. Port William, the author's fictional equivalent of Port Royal, is the home of seven generations of farming families whose lineage reaches back to the early 1800s. The major narratives, however, occur sometime within the early decades of the twentieth century and up to the early 1950s. This represents the final days of America's traditional farm communities prior to the period when they began to break apart under the influence of technological and economic forces at the end of World War II. Berry's characters, who are three distantly related families being the Coulters, the Feltners, and the Beechums, farm the rolling hills and bottomlands west of the Appalachians in the lower part of the Kentucky River watershed. Farming there requires special care and attention if it is to remain productive. From this necessity grows his major unifying theme of stewardship, often

symbolized as interlocking marriages between a man and his family, his community, and the land.

Berry's interest in preserving the character and identity of his native culture generates a rich mixture in his fiction of autobiography and imaginative history. While incidents and dialogue in the novels are often recognizable from his autobiographical essays in *The Long-Legged House* and *The Hidden Wound*, the larger history of Port William is the product of an enduring oral tradition, and Berry writes largely from its collective memory. His fiction then is both an exploration and a discovery of the meaning of his own place in his native land and a reconstruction of the collective identity of a community kept alive in the consciousness of its inheritors. Finding this effort in some ways satisfying, and in others limiting, Berry has described his novels as a record of what he considers to be only a partially successful attempt to find, in the words of Edwin Muir, a "pure image of temporal life."

### Works in Critical Context

Considering Berry's body of work, Charles Hudson marvels at the author's versatility and praises him for his appreciation of the plain things in life. "In an age when many writers have committed themselves to their 'specialty'—even though doing so can lead to commercialism, preciousness, self-indulgence, social irresponsibility, or even nihilism—Berry has refused to specialize," Hudson writes in the *Georgia Review*. "He is a novelist, a poet, an essayist, a naturalist, *and* a small farmer. He has embraced the commonplace and has ennobled it." Pondering Berry's message of responsibility to the land, Larry Woiwode states in the *Washington Post Book Review*: "If one were to distill the thrust of his thought, it might be, [a]ll land is a gift, and all of it is good, if we only had the eyes to see that." Berry, Woiwode continues, is "speaking with calm and sanity out of the wilderness. We would do well to hear him."

It was as a poet that Berry first gained literary recognition. In volumes such as *The Broken Ground*, *Openings: Poems*, *Farming: A Handbook*, and *The Country of Marriage*, he wrote of the countryside, the turning of the seasons, the routines of the farm, and the life of the family. Reviewing *Collected Poems, 1957–1982*, *New York Times Book Review* contributor David Ray calls Berry's style "resonant" and "authentic," and claims that Berry

can be said to have returned American poetry to a Wordsworthian clarity of purpose. . . . There are times when we might think he is returning us to the simplicities of John Clare or the crustiness of Robert Frost. . . . But, as with every major poet, passages in which style threatens to become a voice of its own suddenly give way, like the sound of chopping in a murmurous forest, to lines of power and memorable resonance. Many of Mr. Berry's short poems are as fine as any written in our time.

Critics generally have found favor with Berry's fiction as well, both for the quality of his prose and for the way he brings his concerns for farming and community to life in his narratives. As Gregory L. Morris states in *Prairie Schooner*: "Berry's stories are constructed of humor, of elegy, of prose that carries within it the cadences of the hymn." Although Berry's writing appeals to a variety of readers, criticism and scholarship have inadequately taken him into account, possibly because his work often appears in what scholars may regard as out-of-the-way places. When Robert Rodale publishes Berry's poems in *Organic Gardening*, he does so with full knowledge that many of his readers do not normally look at poems.

***The Unsettling of America***  It was Berry's essays that brought him to a much broader readership. In one of his most popular early collections, *The Unsettling of America: Culture and Agriculture*, Berry argues that agriculture is the foundation of our greater culture. He makes a strong case against the U.S. government's agricultural policy, which promotes practices leading to overproduction, pollution, and soil erosion. *Dictionary of Literary Biography* contributor Leon V. Driskell calls *The Unsettling of America* "an apocalyptic book that places in bold relief the ecological and environmental problems of the American nation." Charles Hudson, writing in the *Georgia Review*, notes that "like Thoreau, in his quest for principles Berry has chosen to simplify his life, and much of what he writes about is what has attended this simplification." David Rains Wallace declares in the *San Francisco Review of Books*: "There's no living essayist better than Wendell Berry. ... It's like master cabinetry or Shaker furniture, drawing elegance from precision and grace from simplicity." Wallace allows that at times, "Berry may overestimate agriculture's ability to assure order and stability," yet he maintains that the author's "attempts to integrate ecological and agricultural thinking remain of the first importance."

## Responses to Literature

1. Berry's discussion and activism about local farming and food production are perfectly suited to the recent trends in social awareness about the ecological ramifications of food production in the U.S. What are some of Berry's ideas concerning support of local farms? How would supporting these farms help the community they are based in and the entire country as a whole?

2. What are the values of agrarianism? How would such practices help individuals and communities? Is this type of social movement possible with increased urbanization of open spaces?

3. Where does technology fit into the ideas that Berry promotes? Can there ever be a marriage of nature and technology that can benefit people and their communities? Are genetically modified foods a good example of this type of marriage?

4. Can you think of another media example of using a fictional place as a backdrop to explore themes that interest the writer? How does the creation of a fictional place help to expand upon philosophical ideas? If you were to create a fictional backdrop to explore your personal value system, what would it look like?

### BIBLIOGRAPHY

**Books**

Angyal, Andrew J. *Wendell Berry*. Boston: Twayne, 1995.
Goodrich, Janet. *The Unforeseen Self in the Works of Wendell Berry*. Columbia, Mo.: University of Missouri Press, 2001.
Merchant, Paul, editor. *Wendell Berry*. Lewiston, Idaho: Confluence, 1991.

**Periodicals**

Basney, Lionel. "A Conversation with Wendell Berry." *Image: A Journal of the Arts and Religion*, 26 (Spring 2000): 45–56.
Gamble, David E. "Wendell Berry: The Mad Farmer and Wilderness." *Kentucky Review*, 2 (1988): 40–52.
Knott, John R. "Into the Woods with Wendell Berry." *Essays in Literature*, 23, no. 1 (Spring 1996): 124–140.
Lang, John. "'Close Mystery': Wendell Berry's Poetry of Incarnation." *Renascence*, 35 (1982): 258–268.
McKibben, Bill. "Prophet in Kentucky." *New York Review of Books*, June 14, 1990, pp. 30–34.
Snell, Marilyn Berlin. "The Art of Place: An Interview with Wendell Berry." *New Perspectives Quarterly*, 9, no. 2 (1992): 29–34.
Whited, Stephen. "On Devotion to the 'Communal Order': Wendell Berry's Record of Fidelity, Interdependence, and Love." *Studies in the Literary Imagination*, 27 (Fall 1994): 9–28.

# ✹ John Berryman

BORN: *1914, McAlester, Oklahoma*
DIED: *1972, Minneapolis, Minnesota*
NATIONALITY: *American*
GENRE: *Fiction, poetry*
MAJOR WORKS:
*77 Dream Songs* (1964)
*His Toy, His Dream, His Rest* (1968)

## Overview

John Berryman is best known as the author of *The Dream Songs*, an unconventional, innovative poem sequence often compared to Walt Whitman's *Leaves of Grass* for its magnitude and uniquely American voice. His poetry,

John Berryman   *Mark Kauffman / Time Life Pictures / Getty Images*

often chaotic and idiosyncratic, reflected his life and relationships. A major figure in American post-war poetry, Berryman is often credited as one of the founders of Confessional poetry.

## Works in Biographical and Historical Context

*A Tortured Artist*   Berryman's experiences played a crucial role in determining the subject and form of his poetry. He was born John Smith in McAlester, Oklahoma, and was twelve years old when his father committed suicide. His mother quickly remarried, and his surname changed from Smith to Berryman. As an adolescent, Berryman attended a private school in Connecticut where he was bullied by fellow students and unsuccessfully attempted suicide. At Columbia University in New York, Berryman studied poetry under Mark Van Doren, whom he considered his mentor. He received an academic fellowship to Cambridge University in England, where he studied Shakespeare and met W. H. Auden,

Dylan Thomas, and the elderly William Butler Yeats. Berryman taught at various universities throughout his adult life, including Harvard, Princeton, and, from 1958 until his death, at the University of Minnesota. He was renowned as a charismatic and formidably intelligent teacher. Berryman's public demeanor contrasted greatly with the insecure and sometimes morbid personality found in much of his work. Like his friend Dylan Thomas, Berryman was given to outrageous public behavior, including drunkenness and inappropriate sexual conduct. Berryman was married three times, and, during the final two decades of his life, he struggled to overcome an alcohol and pill addiction. In 1972, he took his own life. Many literary historians believe that the death of his biological father heavily influenced both Berryman's poetry and his life.

*Growth as a Poet*   Much of the poetry Berryman produced in the 1940s is imitative of the highly allusive, impersonal verse favored by critics and academics at the time. Berryman's first collection, simply titled *Poems*

(1942), is characterized by well-crafted verse often focusing on other works of art rather than human concerns. Although noting the poems were products of an obviously educated and sensitive mind, critics generally found the pieces in *Poems* too studied and rhetorical to be moving. Berryman's second volume, *The Dispossessed* (1948), was also faulted for these reasons. While critics generally agree that Berryman had yet to master the distinctive voices he emulated, "The Nervous Songs" from *The Dispossessed* are considered exceptional. Utilizing a flexible, though regular form, and taking the poet himself for its subject, "The Nervous Songs" are often seen as forerunners of *The Dream Songs*.

In 1947, Berryman began an adulterous affair with the wife of a Princeton graduate student. The intense feelings of guilt, joy, and pain he felt throughout this period inspired a frenzied outpouring of verse, which, when it was published twenty years later, became *Berryman's Sonnets*. Republished in the posthumous *Collected Poems 1937–1971* as *Sonnets to Chris*, these verses chronicle the ongoing affair in broken and twisted syntax mixed with archaic phrases within the form of the Petrarchan sonnet. Berryman's name for his lover in the sonnets, "Lise," was changed to "Chris," the real name of the woman who had been his lover, in the posthumous collection. "Lise" is considered an anagram after the Elizabethan fashion for "lies." Although it was published after *Homage to Mistress Bradstreet* (1956) and *77 Dream Songs* (1964), *Berryman's Sonnets* is the poet's first successful incorporation of the events of his life into his art.

*Homage to Mistress Bradstreet*, Berryman's next published volume, is often viewed as a sublimation of his adultery and consequent guilt and remorse. This long poem blends historical facts regarding Anne Bradstreet's life with creative embellishments, as Bradstreet, the first American poet, is summoned by the speaker, who falls in love with her. Berryman's personal obsessions, including adulterous longings, loss, creative difficulties, God, and the poet's relation to his society, are thematic elements in *Homage to Mistress Bradstreet*. Some critics accused Berryman of creating an elaborate mirror for his personal concerns, yet the poem is generally considered a successful work of art in which structure and theme cohere on a number of metaphorical levels. Gary Q. Arpin remarked: "*Homage to Mistress Bradstreet* is in many ways Berryman's central work, the breakthrough that fulfills earlier promises of genius and makes new promises for the future."

**Dream Songs and Final Works**   The Dream Songs is Berryman's most celebrated accomplishment. First published in two parts as *77 Dream Songs* and *His Toy, His Dream, His Rest*, several hundred dream songs have been published, including those collected in a posthumous volume, *Henry's Fate and Other Poems: 1967–1972*. Each song is comprised of three six-line stanzas of irregular rhyme and meter. The persona, variously called Henry House, Henry Pussycat, and Mr. Bones, shares similar life

circumstances, experiences, and friends with Berryman, and is usually considered interchangeable with him. *The Dream Songs* is an ambitious amalgam of obscure allusions, twisted and fragmented syntax, and minstrel-show language. The tone of these songs ranges from comedy to pathos, and the series of elegies for Theodore Roethke, Delmore Schwartz, Randall Jarrell, and Sylvia Plath are considered among the best in the dream song mode. Topical issues are also a concern in some of the songs, including the deaths of such prominent figures as President John F. Kennedy and Reverend Martin Luther King. Death, particularly the suicide of Berryman's father, is considered to overshadow this extended poem sequence. Unlike Walt Whitman's *Song of Myself*, one of Berryman's models, *The Dream Songs*, does not contain a philosophy, but rather an extended character study of a multi-faceted, troubled, American persona.

*Love and Fame* and *Delusions, Etc.* are the last collections of Berryman's work published under his own direction. Extremely personal in subject matter, the majority of these poems are memoirs in verse regarding such unusual poetic matters as money and Berryman's grades in school. His "Eleven Addresses to the Lord," which conclude *Love and Fame*, are considered among the most moving and subtle religious poems in contemporary American literature.

As an unnamed critic for the *Times Literary Supplement* wrote in 1973, "The last books have an intense but narrowly documentary appeal," and represent "the brave valediction of a man who chose his own way to die." In 1971, Berryman won a Senior Fellowship from the National Endowment for the Humanities in order to complete a critical biography of Shakespeare, but he would not live to do so. He committed suicide by jumping from the Washington Avenue Bridge in Minneapolis on January 7, 1972.

## Works in Literary Context

*The "Middle Generation" and Confessionalism* Credited as an early practitioner of such postmodern techniques as unreliable narration, multiple viewpoints, and pastiche, Berryman created fragmentary verses that reflect his view of the chaotic nature of existence— although at times he worried his pieces were *too* fragmentary. In a 1962 letter to Robert Lowell, Berryman worried that his dream songs "are partly independent but only if . . . the reader is familiar with Henry's tone, personality, friend, activities; otherwise, in small numbers, they seem simply crazy . . ." but many good critics have demonstrated not only the folly of accusing the poem of confessional self-indulgence and disorder, but also that what Berryman thought a weakness was actually a strength.

This confessional aspect of his poetry is what has associated Berryman with both the "Middle Generation" of poets, those who came to maturity between the World Wars, as well as with such Confessional poets as Sylvia Plath and Robert Lowell, who wrote intense lyrics reflecting their volatile emotional states. Berryman's distinctive verse encompasses a broad range of subject matter, occasional use of strict, traditional forms, and a skillful mixture of pathos, farce, and sentimentality. Influenced by W. B. Yeats, Gerard Manley Hopkins, and W. H. Auden, Berryman's poetry has been described as nervous, humorous, and difficult.

*Meditations on Pain and Death* Berryman believed that feelings might be imaginatively controlled through art, and hoped that *The Dream Songs* might be as useful to the reader as to himself. *The Dream Songs*, which Berryman called an epic, is a poem as ambitious as Walt Whitman's *Song of Myself*, William Carlos Williams's *Paterson*, or Hart Crane's *The Bridge*, but unlike *Song of Myself*, for instance, it proposes no system. It is, above all, a pragmatic poem, essaying ideas and emotions, love, lust, lament, and grief. Topical issues are also a concern in some of the songs, including the deaths of such prominent figures as President John F. Kennedy and Rev. Martin Luther King. Death, particularly the suicide of Berryman's father, is considered to overshadow this extended poem sequence.

Several of the finest poems are elegies for fellow poets— Delmore Schwartz, Randall Jarrell, Theodore Roethke, Sylvia Plath—and certain key songs encompass Berryman's ambivalent feelings for his dead father.

"Always," Kenneth Connelly has written, "Henry stands above his 'father's grave with rage,' resentful, compassionate, jealous, accusing, finally gaining the courage to spit upon it." Through the persona of Henry, Berryman, as Wasserstrom, expresses it, "synthesizes all fragments of the self [and] helps the self to mediate [and] accommodate" destructive emotions. The desire to transcend his undefined existence wears down into defeat in later sections of this sequence, until "Henry hates the world. What the world to Henry did will not bear thought." The despair deepens into rejection: "This world is gradually becoming a place / where I do not care to be any more." He broods upon death in all its forms and nightmare possibilities, including the frequent lamentations for other poets who have died recently, and who seem to share his dark view of the world.

Berryman's Henry shares Whitman's infinite expansiveness and inclusiveness, but while the ability to accept everything and not bring things to an end is a source of much power for Whitman's poetic vision, it is another source of Henry's anguish: he is in pain because the past will not let him go, because he cannot ignore what is happening and what has happened to him, and because he cannot forget. Whitman's expansiveness led to a new poetic line, a new kind of singing, free from the restrictions of traditional prosody. Henry, on the other hand, can transform his hell into song only by electing a formal and altogether arbitrary verse pattern. If his songs were to expand with the grand, arching lines of Whitman's verse, the pain would expand unbearably with them. It is only by keeping the poetic form constrained and tight that Henry is able to hold in his pain, survive it, and transform it into redemptive song. *The Dream Songs*, begun exactly a hundred years after the first edition of *Leaves of Grass*, is Berryman's dark inversion of Whitman's *Song of Myself*.

## Works in Critical Context

Edwin Morgan stated of Berryman that "no one conveys better the sheer *mess* of life, the failures and disappointments, betrayals and jealousies, lust and drunkenness, the endless nagging disjunction between ambition and reality." Much of the critical attention Berryman's work received in the 1980s focused on the literary and biographical sources of *The Dream Songs*, as well as its themes and motifs.

*The Dream Songs* It is worth emphasizing the word *heroic* in Robert Lowell's claim that *The Dream Songs* is "the single most heroic work in English poetry since the War, since Ezra Pound's Pisan Cantos." In fact, Berryman purposely emulated the form of ancient epic poetry, and the sections of his songs that come closest to mirroring that form have consistently been singled out for the highest critical praise. Book 4, the opus posthumous sequence which occupies the middle section of the poem, is considered by many critics to be among the finest of the songs; Robert Lowell told Berryman he considered Book 4 "the crown of your wonderful work, witty, heart-breaking, all of a piece ... one of the lovely things in our literature."

A number of critics have objected to Berryman's "abuse" of syntax, the whirligig of his demotic and literary diction—Robert Lowell found himself "rattled" by "mannerisms"—and what Denis Donoghue has called his "hotspur materials." The writing of the songs was a mammoth undertaking, and constructed largely without thought for an overarching narrative, which has rubbed some critics the wrong way. The dissociated "pieces," as Denis Donoghue has explained, go to make up the whole of the man and his work: "This is not Whitman's way. Whitman's aesthetic implies that the self is the sum of its experiences, not the sum of its dissociated fragments ..." The highly individualistic nature of the fragmented pieces has also been singled out as a strength, as when Adrienne Rich noted "the power of that identity to define its surroundings so accurately.... a truly original work, in the sense in which Berryman has made one, is superior in inner necessity and by the force of a unique human character."

### Responses to Literature

1. Write a "confessional" poem of your own—choose an event or strongly held belief or emotion from your life and express it through poetry. You can also try writing the poem through the perspective of an alter-ego, like Berryman's "Henry."

2. The suicide of Berryman's father stood out as a central event of the poet's life. How do you perceive the suicide as influencing Berryman's poetry? Provide examples from his work to support your view.

3. Do you think Berryman's poetry suffered or prospered from his chaotic life and dramatic failures? Would he have reached even greater heights without the demons of alcoholism and depression, or did those provide a necessary grist for his poetic mill?

4. Analyze a set of Berryman's Dream Poems. Why do you think he chose the precise arrangement of verses and stanzas? What purpose does this arrangement ultimately serve?

BIBLIOGRAPHY

**Books**

Kelly, R. J. *John Berryman: A Checklist.* Lanham, Md.: Scarecrow, 1972.

Kelly, Richard J. *John Berryman's Personal Library: A Catalogue.* New York: Peter Lang, 1998.

Mariani, Paul L. *Dream Song: The Life of John Berryman.* Amherst, Mass.: University of Massachusetts Press, 1996.

Vendler, Helen Hennessy. *The Given and the Made: Strategies of Poetic Redefinition.* Cambridge, Mass.: Harvard University Press, 1995.

## Ambrose Bierce

BORN: *1842, Horse Cave Creek, Ohio*

DIED: *1914, Mexico*

NATIONALITY: *American*

GENRE: *Fiction, poetry*

MAJOR WORKS:

"An Occurrence at Owl Creek Bridge" (1890)

"The Damned Thing" (1894)

*The Devil's Dictionary* (1906)

### Overview

Ambrose Bierce's literary reputation is based primarily on his short stories about the Civil War and the supernatural—a body of work that makes up a relatively small part of his total output. Often compared to the tales of Edgar

Ambrose Bierce   *Bierce, Ambrosee, photograph. Mary Evans Picture Library / Alamy.*

In such units as the Ninth Indiana Infantry Regiment and Buell's Army of the Ohio, he fought bravely in numerous military engagements, including the battles of Shiloh and Chickamauga and in Sherman's March to the Sea. After the war, Bierce traveled with a military expedition to San Francisco, where he left the army and prepared himself for a literary career.

### Channeling Horror and Cynicism into Success

Bierce's early poetry and prose appeared in the *Californian*. In 1868 he became the editor of *The News Letter*, for which he wrote his famous "Town Crier" column. Bierce became something of a noted figure in California literary society, forming friendships with Mark Twain, Bret Harte, and Joaquin Miller. In 1872 Bierce and his wife moved to England, where during a three-year stay he wrote for *Fun* and *Figaro* magazines and acquired the nickname "Bitter Bierce." When the English climate aggravated Bierce's asthma, he returned to San Francisco. In 1887 he began writing for William Randolph Hearst's *San Francisco Examiner*, continuing the "Prattler" column he had done for *The Argonaut* and *The Wasp*. This provided him with a regular outlet for his essays, epigrams, and short stories.

Bierce's major fiction was collected in *Tales of Soldiers and Civilians* (1891) and *Can Such Things Be?* (1893). Many of these stories are realistic depictions of the author's experiences in the Civil War. His most striking fictional effects depend on an adept manipulation of the reader's viewpoint: a bloody battlefield seen through the eyes of a deaf child in "Chickamauga"; the deceptive escape dreamed by a man about to be hanged in "An Occurrence at Owl Creek Bridge" the shifting perspectives of "The Death of Halpin Frayser."

### An Often-Hated Genius

Along with his tales of terror, Bierce's most acclaimed work is *The Devil's Dictionary* (1906), a lexicon of its author's wit and animosity. His definition for the word ghost, "the outward and visible sign of an inward fear," clarifies his fundamentally psychological approach to the supernatural. In *The Devil's Dictionary* Bierce vented much of his contempt for politics, religion, society, and conventional human values. A committed opponent of hypocrisy, prejudice, and corruption, Bierce acquired the public persona of an admired but often hated genius, a man of contradiction and mystery. In 1914, he informed some of his correspondents that he intended to enter Mexico and join Pancho Villa's forces as an observer during that country's civil war, a chaotic conflict that arose over issues of rampant poverty and the need for sweeping social, political, and economic reform. Bierce's interest, judging from letters to friends and family, seems to have arisen from a desire for one last great adventure. Despite the numerous fanciful accounts of what happened thereafter, the present consensus among scholars is that Ambrose Bierce was probably killed in the battle of Ojinaga on January 11, 1914.

Allan Poe, these stories share an attraction to death in its more bizarre forms, featuring depictions of mental deterioration and uncanny, other worldly manifestations and expressing the horror of existence in a meaningless universe. Like Poe, Bierce professed to be mainly concerned with the artistry of his work, yet critics find him more intent on conveying his misanthropy and pessimism. In his lifetime Bierce was famous as a California journalist dedicated to exposing the truth as he understood it, regardless of whose reputations were harmed by his attacks. For his sardonic wit and damning observations on the personalities and events of the day, he became known as "the wickedest man in San Francisco."

## Works in Biographical and Historical Context

### Forged by War

Bierce was born in Meigs County, Ohio. His parents were farmers and he was the tenth of thirteen children, all of whom were given names beginning with "A" at their father's insistence. The family moved to Indiana, where Bierce went to high school; he later attended the Kentucky Military Institute. At the outbreak of the Civil War, he enlisted in the Union army.

## Works in Literary Context

Like Edgar Allan Poe, Bierce believed that poems must be short, for otherwise the poetic quality cannot be sustained, and that a novel was only "a short story padded." His style, even in his fiction, has something of the baldness and directness of journalism, but he combines this with a military or aristocratic formality and reserve. The eighteenth-century "serenity, fortitude and reasonableness" he professed to admire shows not in his subject matter, which is often highly sensational, but only in his passion for correctness and his emotional reserve. The last book published during his lifetime was a literary manual called *Write It Right* (1909). Like Aristotle and James Branch Cabell, he wanted a writer to "represent life, not as it is, but as it might be; character, not as he finds it, but as he wants it to be." In his own stories there is little character, with the whole emphasis being upon situation. Slang for Bierce was "the grunt of the human hog." This viewpoint separated Bierce from many other writers of the period, such as Stephen Crane and Mark Twain, who used such techniques to enhance the realism in their works.

*Horror and Fear* The principal themes of Bierce's short stories are war, death, horror, madness, ghosts, fear, and bitter irony. Thus, "One of the Missing" is an almost sadistic study of a trapped, immobilized soldier, frightened to death by his own rifle pointed at his head, although the gun is not loaded. In "One Officer, One Man," Captain Graffenreid falls upon his own sword when "the strain upon his nervous organism" grows "insupportable." Such terrors are not confined to the battlefield. In "The Man and the Snake," Harker Brayton, spending the night in a herpetologist's house, is frightened to death by a stuffed reptile in his bedroom.

*Chilling Depictions of War* Historically, Bierce ranks with J. W. DeForest and Stephen Crane as having pioneered in the realistic portrayal of war in fiction. To him a soldier is an assassin for his country, a "hardened and impenitent man-killer." In his pages son kills father and troops fire on their own men and shell their own homes. In "One Kind of Officer," he offers a bleak picture of the mindlessness of military discipline. Yet, he has none of the moral revulsion against war that characterized the war novels published after World War I. Although he is free of "patriotics," one often finds it difficult to decide whether his emphasis upon war's horrors has been inspired by what he calls its "criminal insanity" or by his love of sensation.

*Literary Impressionism* Ambrose Bierce is far more than a regional, or western, writer. He has come to be recognized as an outstanding exemplar of literary impressionism, a counterweight to the emphasis on realism and naturalism embodied in the work of most of his important contemporaries at the end of the nineteenth century. Bierce's writing shows the dependence of external reality

on the shifting awareness of a perceiver. He often manipulates space and time and builds to an individual's sudden flash of insight, or epiphany. Such features have led critics to cite Bierce as an early postmodernist.

With such literary techniques Bierce opposed the literary trends of his day. In both his journalism and his fiction, for example, he waged war against a simplistic notion of realism. He believed any view of life which ignored the unconscious processes of mind could not call itself realistic. Similarly, although many of his stories appear naturalistic in their bleak depiction of humans in hostile environments and in their meticulous description of violence, Bierce held humans more accountable for their actions than the naturalists. He also tended to interject his peculiar humor into the most gruesome of scenes, creating a tone more similar to Franz Kafka than to Frank Norris or Jack London.

*Aphorisms* Bierce's aphorisms or clever sayings, collected in *The Devil's Dictionary*, can be classified according to various types of ascending significance. Several entries feature wordplay in and of itself, as in his definitions of *helpmate* ("A wife, or bitter half"), *harangue* ("A speech by an opponent, who is known

## COMMON HUMAN EXPERIENCE

Bierce was hardly the only author to visit the American Civil War and the personal emotions and experiences of the soldiers fighting in that conflict. Here are some other works that deal with that war.

*The Red Badge of Courage* (1895), a novel by Stephen Crane. A novel as brief as Crane's own life, it nonetheless manages to examine deep-seated issues of bravery and cowardice in the face of mass slaughter.

*The March* (2005), a novel by E. L. Doctorow. The tale of General William T. Sherman's "march to the sea" takes several narrative viewpoints, from a young girl posing as a drummer boy all the way up to General Sherman himself. With the perspectives of both the victors and the defeated examined, Doctorow is able to show how events of nearly a century and a half ago planted the seeds of many of our modern racial and political dilemmas.

*Cold Mountain* (1997), by Charles Frazier. A story told from two perspectives, one of a Confederate deserter wending his way home through three hundred miles of mountainous wilderness, the other of his lady love, who is having to learn fend for herself in the war-torn economy.

*Gettysburg* (1993), a film by Ronald F. Maxwell. Based on the 1974 book *The Killer Angels*, by Michael Shaara, this film examines the Battle of Gettysburg through multiple perspectives on both sides of the battle, from privates to generals.

as an harangue-outang"), or *architect* ("One who drafts a plan of your house, and plans a draft of your money"). He also makes full use of comic pairings or juxtaposition within definitions or between definitions, as in the two definitions of *belladonna* ("In Italian, a beautiful lady; in English a deadly poison. A striking example of the essential identity of the two tongues").

Then there are those definitions which zero in on ideas concerning society, religion, and self by forcing readers to confront the ways they misuse language to deceive and abuse. Their cynical but truthful edge cuts deep even as the reader chuckles: the *scriptures*, for example, are "The sacred books of our holy religion, as distinguished from the false and profane writings on which all other faiths are based," and *infidel* has two contradictory meanings ("In New York, one who does not believe in the Christian religion; in Constantinople, one who does").

### Works in Critical Context

Although he stopped writing fiction by 1899 and although he produced fewer than a hundred short stories, Bierce was an influential writer. Stephen Crane said of

Bierce's "An Occurrence at Owl Creek Bridge," "Nothing better exists—the story has everything," and, as has been well documented, Crane consciously modeled his own impressionist tales of war on Bierce's. H. L. Mencken, Carey McWilliams, and other writers of the post-World War I era appreciated Bierce's scathing journalism and his sardonic tall tales. In fact, Bierce was almost a folk hero of the Roaring Twenties, as indicated by the fact that one year, 1929, saw the publication of no fewer than four popular biographies of the author.

***Tales of Soldiers and Civilians***   The decade of the 1890s saw the publication of Bierce's first books since 1874, beginning with the collection *Tales of Soldiers and Civilians*. These collections of war, supernatural, and frontier stories engendered much favorable reaction on both sides of the Atlantic, with especially significant praise coming from such American reviewers as Walter Blackburn Harte, Percival Pollard, Brander Matthews, and William Dean Howells. Not all were enthusiastic about his work, however. An unnamed reviewer for *The Critic* notes that the author "has caught the modern knack of telling a story about nothing and telling it well," and adds that "he sometimes commits the fault of telling about something, and not telling it well but theatrically." He further notes that the stories "lack variety, in fact are tiresomely alike." A *Bookman* reviewer of an 1898 collection of the same and additional stories offered much greater praise: "Nowhere can the art of how and when to end a story be more perfectly exemplified than in some of these remarkable tales."

While Bierce's short stories are widely anthologized, they have received relatively little critical attention. Yet, in the past two decades this situation has begun to change. His surrealistic literary techniques and rhetorical presentations of subjective and objective time strike a contemporary note. Such modern masters of fiction as Jorge Luis Borges, Julio Cortázar, and Carlos Fuentes have been influenced by Bierce's stories, particularly by his juxtaposition of multiple points of view and often contradictory perspectives, and by his expositions of the deceptions that the mind plays upon itself. Increasingly, Bierce is recognized as one of the masters of the short-story form.

### Responses to Literature

1. Research American literature in the schools of Realism, Romanticism, and Naturalism. How does Bierce's "An Occurrence at Owl Creek Bridge" fit into each school?

2. Explain how Bierce was influenced by and used his experience fighting for the Union in the American Civil War in his fiction.

3. Compare Bierce's ghost stories such as "The Boarded Window" to other works of the macabre by authors such as Edgar Allan Poe and H. P. Lovecraft. How do the stories differ? How are they similar?

4. It seems every generation of literary scholars "redis-covers" Bierce, claiming he is unappreciated and deserves a wider readership. Do you agree with this assessment? Why or why not?

BIBLIOGRAPHY

**Books**

"Ambrose Bierce (1842–1914?)." *Short Story Criticism.* Edited by Thomas Votteler. Vol. 9. Detroit: Gale Research, 1992, pp. 48–101.

"An Occurrence at Owl Creek Bridge." *Short Stories for Students.* Edited by Kathleen Wilson. Vol. 2. Detroit: Gale, 1997.

Barret, Gerald R. and Thomas L. Erskine, compilers. *From Fiction to Film: Ambrose Bierce's "An Occurrence at Owl Creek Bridge."* Encino, Calif.: Dickenson Publishing Company, 1973.

Davidson, Cathy N. *The Experimental Fictions of Ambrose Bierce: Structuring the Ineffable.* Lincoln, Nebr.: University of Nebraska Press, 1984.

Morris, Jr., Roy. *Ambrose Bierce: Alone in Bad Company.* New York: Crown Publishers, 1995.

Saunders, Richard. *Ambrose Bierce: The Making of a Misanthrope.* San Francisco: Chronicle Books, 1985.

# ❂ Elizabeth Bishop

BORN: *1911, Worcester, Massachusetts*

DIED: *1979, Boston, Massachusetts*

NATIONALITY: *American*

GENRE: *Poetry*

MAJOR WORKS:
*North & South* (1946)
*Questions of Travel* (1965)

## Overview

Elizabeth Bishop's reputation as an accomplished poet rests on a small but significant body of highly crafted poems that have been praised for their precise observa-tions and understated, descriptive quality. Honored in her lifetime with numerous literary awards by both critics and poets, Bishop is now gaining the attention of literary historians for the imagination and intensity of her poems.

## Works in Biographical and Historical Context

*Rootlessness in Youth* Bishop was born in 1911, in Worcester, Massachusetts. Eight months later, Bishop's father died and her mother suffered a nervous breakdown from which she never recovered. During her childhood, Bishop lived first with her mother until the latter was institutionalized and then with her maternal grandparents in Great Village, Nova Scotia. She later moved to the

Elizabeth Bishop    *photograph by J.L. Castel. The Library of Congress.*

home of her father's parents in Worcester and then to her aunt's in Boston, Massachusetts. The memories of these early years are expressed in much of Bishop's poetry through the theme of rootlessness. As a child, Bishop suffered from a variety of illnesses and thus spent a great deal of time alone, acquiring an early interest in reading and writing poetry.

A lonely child in Great Village and Worcester, Bishop found "a much more congenial and sympathetic world for herself in books," according to biographer Anne Stevenson. In a 1966 *Shenandoah* interview with Ashley Brown, Bishop recollected that while her relatives were not literary, they did own many books, that she started reading poetry when she was eight years old, and that she was also "crazy about fairy tales—Andersen, Grimm, and so on." In "Influences," a memoir published in the *American Poetry Review*, she remembered how old English ballads, nursery rhymes, fairy tales, and riddles affected her as a child and later as a poet. Bishop told Brown during the 1966 interview that when she was thirteen she discovered Walt Whitman; at about the same time, she encountered Emily Dickinson, H. D. (Hilda Doolittle), Joseph Conrad, and Henry James. Soon after, she first read some of Gerard Manley Hopkins's poetry, which captivated her.

### From Vassar to the Library of Congress

In 1930, she entered Vassar College, where she distinguished herself as a member of the intellectual circle that included future authors Mary McCarthy and Eleanor Clark, with whom she co-founded the literary magazine *Con Spirito*. An admirer of Marianne Moore's poetry, Bishop met the elder poet in 1934 and the two quickly developed a lifelong friendship. Moore also became Bishop's mentor, encouraging the younger woman to write and offering editorial advice early in her career. Upon graduating from Vassar in 1934, Bishop moved to Greenwich Village in New York City, publishing her early poems in the anthology *Trial Balances* in 1935. During the next few years, she traveled extensively in North Africa and Europe, settling briefly in Paris, France. In 1939, Bishop moved to Key West, Florida, but frequently journeyed along the Eastern seaboard and to Mexico. In 1946, she published her first volume of poetry, *North & South*, for which she received the Houghton Mifflin Poetry Award. That same year Bishop met poet Robert Lowell, with whom she developed an enduring friendship based on a mutual admiration of each other's works.

In 1949, Bishop was named poetry consultant to the Library of Congress and moved to Washington, D.C. However, she admitted to both Anne Stevenson and Elizabeth Spires that she did not enjoy the year. As she told Spires,

> There were so many government buildings that looked like Moscow. There was a very nice secretary ... [who] did most of the work. I'd write something and she'd say, 'Oh, no, that isn't official,' so then she'd rewrite it in gobbledegook. We used to bet on the horses. She and I would sit there reading the Racing Form when poets came to call.

### Relocation to Brazil

In 1951, Bishop set out on a trip around the world. Her first stop was in Rio de Janeiro in order to visit Lota de Macedo Soares and Mary Morse, two women she had met in New York in 1942. Soares and Morse owned an apartment in Rio and were building a house on Soares's estate, Samambaia, near Petrópolis. Bishop spent three weeks touring the countryside in Soares's Jaguar sports car and writing in the Rio apartment. She was scheduled to rejoin her freighter on January 26. However, sometime in mid-December Bishop sampled the exotic fruit of the Brazilian cashew tree and fell violently ill with an allergic reaction: her face and hands swelled so that she could neither see nor write. Three weeks later she was still bedridden but was nonetheless astounded by the love and care shown her by Soares and Morse as well as by the household servants and their children. By mid January she had decided to stay and recuperate for at least another month. By February she admitted that the idea of continuing her trip, or

of going back to the United States, was farther and farther from her mind. For her birthday a neighbor gave her a toucan, and with her new pet she settled into Soares's half-finished house, high on a mountainside amid "fantastic" scenery. In April, Bishop, accompanied by Soares, returned to New York to arrange for the shipping of her possessions to Brazil.

During those first few months back in Brazil, Bishop continued her recovery and in the process fell in love with Lota Soares. Meanwhile, she planned to complete *A Cold Spring*. It would be three years before the book appeared, and she would be unable to finish any of the older poems she hoped to include. But, she immediately began "Arrival at Santos" and by the end of August had finished "The Shampoo." The two Brazilian poems would give *A Cold Spring* a strange, forward-looking lift at the end.

Ten years passed between the publication of *A Cold Spring* and Bishop's next book of poetry, *Questions of Travel* (1965), a period also marked by the appearance of a pictorial history, *Brazil*, which Bishop wrote with the editors of *Life*. Her perception of herself and her world changed recognizably during these years. There she found a culture that contrasted in values and priorities with the North American culture she had known. It is no wonder that the poems in *Questions of Travel* often explored previously unfelt or rediscovered emotions set vibrating by this exotic, emotional culture.

When the reviews of *Questions of Travel* began to appear in the spring of 1966, Bishop was in the United States, having taken on the first teaching job of her life. At the University of Washington in Seattle she taught poetry and creative writing. The job at first terrified her. She had never worked for a living; she had been out of the country for fifteen years, and all of the transformations of the 1960s were new to her. She found that she was able to do it, especially with the help of good friends. Early in her stay in Seattle, Bishop fell in love with a young woman, and with that relationship, her Brazilian life began to fall apart.

### Late-emerging Reputation

By 1976 Bishop, having returned to the United States, no longer treated Brazil in her poetry. The lush, colorful, and sometimes humorous dimensions that Brazil inspired in her verse therefore disappeared, and *Geography III*, which was published eleven years after *Questions of Travel*, possessed a much more subdued form, tone, and emphasis. While part of *Questions of Travel*'s thematic preoccupation had been the struggle for vision and its ensuing perceptions, *Geography III* seemed to take that vision for granted and to concentrate instead on observing the world with an unfaltering, unclouded eye.

Elizabeth Bishop started publishing poems about 1935, but her reputation as one of the best American poets has emerged rather slowly. She never rushed into print, and only in her last years did she give public readings of her work. She was honored in a number of ways. In

1976 she was the first American writer to receive the Books Abroad / Neustadt International Prize for Literature, and in the following year the poet Anthony Hecht, writing in the *London Times Literary Supplement*, said that "Hers is about the finest product our country can offer the world; we have little by other artists that can match it." Bishop died of a cerebral hemhorrage in 1979.

## Works in Literary Context

Because Bishop's poems were often difficult to place in a particular style and because nearly a decade elapsed between publications of each of her collections, several critics have suggested that the works of her contemporaries overshadowed her own. Recent criticism has viewed Bishop's poetry within a broader context, focusing on her unique imaginative vision. Considered masterpieces of descriptive verse, her works are praised for their calm, understated tone and for the ease with which she gradually shifts from observations of ordinary objects to philosophical insights. Although her poems are often personal, critics note that Bishop avoids self-pity and egoism to extend her themes from the specific to the universal.

*Travel, Loss, and the Search for Self* A fascination with travel in Bishop's own life also occupies an important place in her poetry, as in the collection *Questions of Travel*. The theme of travel imbues Bishop's poems with varied settings and images and also becomes a central metaphor, often signifying the search for self. This theme is suggested by the final line of "Arrival at Santos" in which Bishop writes that "we are driving to the interior." Dislocation, loneliness, and doubt are associated with such a search, but an acceptance of hardship prevails in these poems. In "Questions of Travel," Bishop ponders the wisdom of leaving the stability and familiarity of home to travel abroad. The poem implies that without continual risk and uncertainty there can be no spiritual growth. In addition to verse in the first section of *Questions of Travel* describing the exotic Brazilian landscape, Bishop also included works that recall her previous homes and points of travel under the heading "Elsewhere." These poems are concerned with such diverse subjects as a sandpiper, her childhood in Nova Scotia, and her observations on Ezra Pound, whom she had visited while he was a patient in St. Elizabeth's Hospital, a mental institution, in Washington, D.C. "First Death in Nova Scotia" is a highly personal poem about her childhood, a subject she had previously eschewed in her poetry. This treatment marked an increased focus on personal loss, which became significant in her later poems.

## Works in Critical Context

Perhaps because of their friendship and because Marianne Moore helped get Bishop's work published in the anthology *Trial Balances*, the introduction of which included Moore's statements appreciative of Bishop, early reviewers continually linked Bishop's poetry with Moore's. They noticed that both poets often described animals and

## LITERARY AND HISTORICAL CONTEMPORARIES

Bishop's famous contemporaries include:

**Nikita Khrushchev** (1894–1971): Following the death of Joseph Stalin, Krushchev took over leadership of the Soviet Union for eleven years. During that time he clashed repeatedly with the United States and its allies; the tension culminated in the Cuban Missile Crisis of 1962, when the two major powers came closest to outright nuclear warfare.

**Jerry Lewis** (1926–): American comedian, actor, writer, and director, Lewis got his start as part of a comedy duo, and later went on to star in a string of successful movies that emphasized his genius for physical comedy.

**Octavio Paz** (1914–1998): Mexican writer and poet Paz won the Nobel Prize in Literature in 1990, after a long career that included acclaimed works of surrealist poetry, essays on Mexican politics and identity, and plays.

**Carl Perkins** (1932–1998): A pioneer of rockabilly music, a style that fused country with rhythm and blues, Perkins was one of the godfathers of rock and roll, admired and covered by artists from Elvis Presley to The Beatles to Bob Dylan.

**P. G. Wodehouse** (1881–1975): An English comic novelist with a career spanning seven decades, Wodehouse is best remembered for his "Jeeves and Wooster" books, which skewer English aristocracy, as do many of his other works.

## COMMON HUMAN EXPERIENCE

Bishop's poetry often touched upon the themes of loss and rootlessness, reflections of recurring themes in her own life. Other poets have meditated on the same themes as well.

"Ariel" (1961), a poem by Sylvia Plath. Published posthumously, after Plath's suicide, this poem's seemingly nonsensical verse powerfully reflects the chaos and torment that was swirling in Plath's life during her final years.

"We Real Cool" (1959), a poem by Gwendolyn Brooks. Although only eight lines total, this short poem effectively evokes feelings of sadness and existential dread, as if the "we" of the poem are lost, directionless, questioning their very existence.

"Skunk Hour" (1976), a poem by Robert Lowell. A lifelong friend of Bishop's, Lowell dedicated this poem to her; the imagery evokes decay and glory days long gone, and a pervasive sense of loss.

emphasized a visual quality in their work. In a review later collected in *Poetry and the Age*, Randall Jarrell wrote of a poem in *North & South*, "you don't need to be told that the poetry of Marianne Moore was, in the beginning, an appropriately selected foundation for Miss Bishop's work." Less enthusiastically, Louise Bogan noted in a 1946 *New Yorker* review Bishop's "slight addiction to the poetic methods of Marianne Moore."

In his book *American Poetry since 1945: A Critical Survey*, Stephen Stepanchev made astute observations about *North & South* and *A Cold Spring* that apply to the rest of Bishop's canon. He declared that Bishop's "At the Fishhouses" "tells brilliantly what Miss Bishop thinks of human knowledge, which is always undermined by time, by change. It is obvious that change is the most disturbing principle of reality for her."

Elizabeth Bishop's critical reputation has grown steadily since her death in 1979. Always a respected poet honored by her peers, Bishop was not well known outside the poetry circles of New York and Boston during her lifetime. Today her poems are widely read and taught in classrooms, and a steady stream of essays and books about her life and work has followed since the publication of *The Complete Poems, 1927–1979* in 1983. One can account for this extraordinary attention in several ways: the rise of feminist scholarship and the attendant search for neglected female writers; the continuing respect for Bishop's poems shown by teachers and other poets; and most important, the simultaneous profundity and accessibility of the poems and the remarkable appeal of the distinctive and personal voice in which they are written.

***Questions of Travel*** In *The New Republic*, Frank J. Warnke noted that "*Questions of Travel* is impressively varied in its forms and modes." Warnke found "the Brazilian half of the book more exciting" but pointed out the technical achievement of "Visits to St. Elizabeth's," which recounted the poet's responses to Ezra Pound, who had been confined to a mental hospital for his pro-Mussolini broadcasts during World War II. Remarking on the revolutionary quality of Bishop's verse, Willard Spiegelman in the *Centennial Review* found a "natural hero" in Bishop's work, a hero who "occupies a privileged position which is unattainable by the super— or unnatural—exploits of masculine achievement which the poetry constantly debunks."

While critics twenty years later would see that Bishop was strongly involved with the world, most contemporary reviewers of *Questions of Travel* missed this characteristic amid the more spectacularly dramatic political movements and poetry of the time. Stepanchev, among others, felt that "public events, political issues, or socioeconomic ideology" did not inspire Bishop and that her poetry left readers unaware of Hitler and World War II: "Unlike many of her Auden-influenced contemporaries, she distrusts history, with its melodramatic blacks and whites, and prefers geography, with its subtle gradations of color."

## Responses to Literature

1. Many of Bishop's poems, such as "Filling Station," find beauty in everyday objects. Write a poem praising the aesthetic beauty of an object or place that is normally considered ordinary or utilitarian.

2. Bishop had a strong mentor relationship with poet Marianne Moore. Who has been mentor to you in terms of your interests and ambitions? If you were able to help someone younger than you to succeed in the same field as you, how would you help them? Why is it important to assist younger generations?

3. Do you believe that one has to experience an event or location in order to write about it? Write two descriptions: one of a place you have never been to and the other of a place you see every day. Have someone read both descriptions and guess which place you have actually been to.

4. Bishop considered herself an outsider no matter where she lived. How does this attitude influence her poetry? How does her recurring theme of loss relate to her other recurring theme of travel?

BIBLIOGRAPHY

**Books**

Bishop, Elizabeth and George Monteiro. *Conversations with Elizabeth Bishop.* Jackson, Miss.: University Press of Mississippi, 1996.

*Elizabeth Bishop: A Bibliography, 1927–1979*, compiled by Candace MacMahon. Charlottesville, Va.: University Press of Virginia, 1980.

Fountain, Gary and Peter Brazeau. *Remembering Elizabeth Bishop: An Oral Biography.* Amherst, Mass.: University of Massachusetts Press, 1994.

Lombardi, Marilyn May. *The Body and the Song: Elizabeth Bishop's Poetics.* Carbondale, Ill.: Southern Illinois University, 1995.

McCabe, Susan. *Elizabeth Bishop: Her Poetics of Loss.* University Park, Pa.: Pennsylvania State University Press, 1994.

Schwartz, Lloyd and Sybil P. Estess, eds. *Elizabeth Bishop and Her Art.* Ann Arbor, Mich.: University of Michigan Press, 1983.

Shigley, Sally Bishop. *Dazzling Dialectics: Elizabeth Bishop's Resonating Feminist Reality.* New York: Peter Lang, 1997.

Stevenson, Anne. *Elizabeth Bishop.* Boston: Twayne, 1966.

**Web sites**

*Elizabeth Bishop at Vassar College.* Retrieved September 20, 2008, from http://projects.vassar.edu/bishop.

# ☸ Black Elk

BORN: *1863, Little Powder River, Wyoming*

DIED: *1950, Manderson, South Dakota*

NATIONALITY: *American*

GENRE: *Nonfiction*

MAJOR WORKS:

*Black Elk Speaks: Being the Life Story of a Holy
Man of the Oglala Sioux as Told to John G.
Neihardt (Flaming Rainbow)* (1932)

*The Sacred Pipe: Black Elk's Account of the Seven
Rites of the Oglala Sioux* (1953)

## Overview

Black Elk was a Native American warrior and holy man
who witnessed some of the most dramatic events of the
final period of Indian-U.S. conflict. After the Indian Wars
came to a close at the end of the nineteenth century,
Black Elk converted to Catholicism, blending his native
beliefs with his newly-adopted faith. Towards the end of
his life, he gave two extensive series of interviews, first to
a poet, then to an anthropologist, that resulted in two
books—*Black Elk Speaks* (1932) and *The Sacred Pipe*
(1953). These works provided important perspective on
a disappearing way of life and offered inspiration to
future generations interested in the Native American
world view.

## Works in Biographical and Historical Context

***The Indian Wars*** Black Elk, whose father and
grandfather were both medicine men, was born along
the Little Powder River, probably in what is now the state
of Wyoming. While his people, the Oglala Lakota branch
of the Sioux nation, were able to maintain their traditional way of life during Black Elk's earliest years, the
westward migration of white settlers and the associated
expansion of an industrialized infrastructure—railroads,
towns, and large ranches—soon made that impossible.
During the 1870s and 1880s, the Sioux engaged in a
series of battles with the United States Army for control
of their tribal lands. These included the Battle of the
Little Bighorn—remembered by white Americans as
"Custer's Last Stand"—in which Black Elk participated
when he was thirteen. After Chief Crazy Horse, Black
Elk's cousin, was assassinated by United States soldiers
in 1877, Black Elk's tribe fled to Canada, where they
remained until 1880.

***Travels with Wild Bill*** After his tribe returned to
the United States, Black Elk acted on a vision he had
experienced when he was nine. In Sioux religious tradition such experiences are often used as guides to determine the course to be taken by individuals and entire

Black Elk    *AP Images*

tribes. In the vision Black Elk foresaw the destruction of
a "sacred hoop" representing the unity of his people, and
was instructed in the manner in which he might one day
use a sacred herb to destroy his nation's enemies and
restore unity. Following an enactment of the vision by
his tribe, in accord with Sioux custom, Black Elk began a
career as a medicine man. Compelled to take on an even
larger role, Black Elk accepted an offer to join Buffalo
Bill's Wild West Show in 1886, explaining, "I thought I
ought to go, because I might learn some secret of the
Wasichu [whites] that would help my people somehow."
After spending three years touring with the show through
Great Britain and Europe, featuring a performance at
Queen Victoria's Golden Jubilee, he returned to the
United States in 1889. While he had learned about Euro-
pean cultures and traditions, he felt that he had lost the
power of his vision while he was away.

***The Ghost Dance*** Upon returning to his tribe, which
was now living on Pine Ridge Reservation in South
Dakota, Black Elk found famine, disease, and despair
among the Sioux and learned that a religious movement
called the Dance of the Ghosts was spreading across the
reservations. The professed belief of the Ghost Dancers
was that, through dancing, the spirits of their departed
ancestors could be called back to drive away the white
encroachers and return the Native Americans to their

# LITERARY AND HISTORICAL CONTEMPORARIES

Black Elk's famous contemporaries include:

**William "Buffalo Bill" Cody** (1846–1917): American soldier, bison hunter—from which he earned his famous nickname—and entertainer, Buffalo Bill was a consummate showman whose traveling "Wild West Show" capitalized on the already mythical status of the American frontier.

**Pius X** (1835–1914): The 257th Pope of the Roman Catholic Church, Pius assumed the office in 1903. His reform-based agenda strengthened the Church in the face of attempts to integrate the rising tide of secular beliefs at the dawn of the twentieth century. He was the first pope to be canonized since Pius V in the sixteenth century.

**Beatrix Potter** (1866–1943): A sheltered child of privilege, Potter held a long-standing interest in art and nature, which she combined in drawings of plants and animals. Her twin loves eventually led her to publish a series of illustrated children's books, beginning with *The Tale of Peter Rabbit*, that featured garden animals as main characters in a whimsical country setting.

**Orville Wright** (1871–1948): Along with his brother Wilbur, Orville Wright is generally credited with inventing the first controlled, powered, heavier-than-air aircraft.

**W. E. B. DuBois** (1868–1963): Educator, writer, editor, poet, and scholar, DuBois was a central figure in the African-American civil rights movement of the twentieth century. Although his theories could arouse controversy among whites and blacks alike, DuBois more often provided an eloquent, well-spoken voice of reason during some of the grimmest years for race relations in the United States.

traditional lifestyle. Black Elk joined the Ghost Dance when he perceived significant similarities between its prophecy of a new world for Native Americans and the image of the restoration of the sacred hoop in his own vision. The incessant and frenzied dancing associated with the movement greatly alarmed officials on the reservations, who called in the United States Army to preserve order. Tension between the Native Americans and soldiers finally erupted on December 29, 1890, when the troops massacred some three hundred unarmed men, women, and children camped along Wounded Knee Creek on the Pine Ridge Reservation.

The massacre at Wounded Knee marked the end of the Native Americans' hope for preserving their land and their autonomy. Black Elk remained on the Pine Ridge Reservation after the massacre and continued to act as a

medicine man despite the expressed disapproval of Jesuit priests who had founded a mission there. In 1904, Black Elk joined the Catholic Church; it is not known why he converted after years of maintaining traditional religious practices. Whatever his motivation, attempting to reconcile the two religions would be a continuing process for Black Elk. He became a respected leader in the local Catholic community, served as a Catholic catechist, or teacher to the newly converted, and traveled to other reservations in that capacity.

***Black Elk's Story*** In 1930, Black Elk was approached by John G. Neihardt, an author seeking information about the Ghost Dance and the Wounded Knee massacre for an epic poem depicting the history of the American West. While Neihardt's interest was at first restricted to Sioux history, Black Elk announced that he felt a spiritual kinship with Neihardt and wanted to share his vision with him in order to preserve it. According to Neihardt, Black Elk told him after their first meeting,

> There is so much to teach you. What I know was given to me for men and it is true and it is beautiful. Soon I shall be under the grass and it will be lost. You were sent to save it, and you must come back so that I can teach you.

Neihardt decided that he could create a book based on Black Elk's life rather than simply incorporating the material into his poem, and he returned to Pine Ridge for a series of extensive interviews. The resulting narrative, *Black Elk Speaks*, was published in 1932. With the publication of the book, Black Elk was again in conflict with the Jesuits, who were appalled that one of their most reliable catechists had apparently re-embraced his ancestral religion. The publicity surrounding *Black Elk Speaks* also brought additional writers and scholars to Pine Ridge to interview Black Elk. Joseph Epes Brown, an anthropology student, lived with Black Elk for several months during the winter of 1947–1948 and recorded his account of Sioux religious rituals, publishing the information as *The Sacred Pipe* in 1953, three years after Black Elk's death. While *The Sacred Pipe* is considered a valuable resource in the preservation of Sioux cultural history, it is generally judged inferior to *Black Elk Speaks* as a literary work and has received little critical attention.

Neither Black Elk nor Neihardt could speak, read, or write the other's language, and the interview procedure was complex. Black Elk's spoken Lakota was translated into English by his son Ben Black Elk, restated by Neihardt, translated back to Black Elk for further clarification when necessary, and recorded in shorthand by Neihardt's daughter Enid, who later arranged her notes in chronological order and typed them. Neihardt then wrote the text of *Black Elk Speaks* from Enid's typewritten transcripts; he told Black Elk's story in the first person but also included descriptions of events and battles that Black

Elk did not experience or was too young to remember, which were provided by other Sioux who were present during some of the interviews.

Black Elk was not entirely satisfied with the final manuscript Neihardt produced. In particular, the focus on Black Elk's childhood and early adulthood angered the aging holy man, who wrote a strongly worded letter to Neihardt contradicting the book's apparent assertion that Black Elk's life effectively ended with Wounded Knee, that no good had come to him since. Black Elk insisted that his religious conversion had made him a better man, and indeed, he saw little difference between the old faith and his newly-adopted religion.

## Works in Literary Context

*Black Elk Speaks* tells the story of Black Elk from his early childhood to the Wounded Knee massacre in 1890. Widely praised for vividly portraying both the personality of Black Elk and the Native American way of life, the book has been variously examined as autobiography, ethnology, psychology, and philosophy. At the same time, critics agree that *Black Elk Speaks* is preeminently a work of literature, not scholarship, praising in particular the book's simple and forceful prose style. While some critics contend that Neihardt's success at representing qualities of the Lakota language in English is proof of his faithfulness to Black Elk's words, others argue that the highly literary nature of the prose is evidence that the words are Neihardt's and not Black Elk's. This dispute raises larger questions regarding Neihardt's role in the creation of *Black Elk Speaks* which are the focus of much of the commentary on the work.

*Oral History and Tradition*   *Black Elk Speaks*, the life story of Black Elk, is considered the most authentic literary account of the experience of the Plains Indians during the nineteenth century. In addition to garnering praise for presenting Native American religion and culture in a way that non-Indians can understand, *Black Elk Speaks* has been called the "bible" of younger generations of Native Americans seeking to learn more about their heritage. Along with *The Sacred Pipe*, which recounts the seven sacred rituals of the Sioux, *Black Elk Speaks* has played a crucial role in preserving Native American traditions and in encouraging the expression of a Native American heritage and consciousness.

Black Elk's account is centered in the oral tradition, a term used to describe the transmission of history and culture through a spoken rather than written medium. The oral tradition is the oldest human tradition of preserving and passing on knowledge, and is centered around a sort of formalized storytelling, closer to a testimonial than a personal, autobiographical story as participants in the written tradition would understand it.

Native American literature was originally passed on by word of mouth, so it consisted largely of stories and events that were easily memorized. Much of the oral

---

## COMMON HUMAN EXPERIENCE

*Black Elk Speaks* is an example of an oral tradition, incorporating both historical events and traditional belief systems, transmitted into written form. Since the discipline of anthropology developed in the nineteenth century, attempts have been made to record the oral traditions of other disappearing cultures as well.

*Kalevala* (1888), an epic poem compiled by Elias Lonnrot, translated into English by John Martin Crawford. Called the "national epic" of Finland, this massive poem, consisting of over 22,000 verses, was passed down from memory from one generation of Finnish story-teller to another until it was finally committed to paper in the nineteenth century.

*Penguin Book of American Folk Songs* (1968), a music book by Alan Lomax. Traveling through the American South in the 1930s, Lomax became the country's foremost musical folklorist, recording hours of traditional songs from Appalachia and the Deep South. His work helped preserve and bring attention to America's own oral tradition, the stories passed down in song form.

*Grimm's Fairy Tales* (1812), a book by Jacob and Wilhelm Grimm. The work that arguably kick-started the modern academic discipline of folklore studies, this famous collection of tales told by German peasants was collected by the Grimm brothers over a period of years as they systematically worked their way through villages and towns, interviewing storytellers and writing down the stories they were told.

---

literature consisted of folk tales and myths. Native American prose, even today, is often rhythmic like poetry because of the rich heritage of oral literature. Many contemporary authors deal with the ancient tales in their writings, continuing to develop stories using American Indian mythology. The late 1960s saw a Native American Renaissance, marked by modern writers' desire to draw on the oral literature of their culture.

## Works in Critical Context

While *Black Elk Speaks* received positive reviews, it was not popular among readers, and suffered several decades of neglect. In the 1950s, Carl Jung and other European psychologists and anthropologists rediscovered the book and studied Black Elk's vision as an example of the importance of cultural symbols, and their examination sparked renewed interest in the work in the United States. During the 1960s and 1970s, concern for the status of ethnic minorities and the environment focused attention on Native Americans, and *Black Elk Speaks*, considered the preeminent account of the Native American experience, became increasingly popular. While debate regarding

Neihardt's editorial role continues, the importance of *Black Elk Speaks* as both a work of literature and a source for the understanding of Native American culture has been widely acknowledged.

**Black Elk Speaks** Critics have questioned Neihardt's chosen focus for the book, noting that by ending *Black Elk Speaks* with the massacre at Wounded Knee in 1890, Neihardt omitted a forty-year period in Black Elk's life and ignored his conversion to Catholicism. Some commentators suggest that these decisions reflect Neihardt's desire to portray Black Elk's life as a symbol for the demise of the Sioux nation, the theme he was exploring in his own work. Critics have also questioned Neihardt's depiction of Black Elk's vision, noting that he eliminated some of the violent aspects of Black Elk's description, including the destructive herb. While Raymond J. DeMallie argues that Neihardt was justified in this decision because Black Elk himself rejected violence by becoming a Christian, others maintain that he unjustifiably misrepresented Black Elk's story in order to emphasize its universal aspects and to avoid alienating white readers. Commentators have also criticized Neihardt for portraying Black Elk as a tragic and pathetic figure, maintaining that the transcripts of the Black Elk interviews belie this portrait.

### Responses to Literature

1. What was the significance of Black Elk's sacred vision quest in *Black Elk Speaks*? Why do you think Black Elk placed so much importance on it?

2. Contrast Black Elk's character when he was younger with his personality and beliefs when he was older. What is the significance of his conversion to Catholicism?

3. What were the historical circumstances that led Black Elk to take up arms against the U.S. Army? Do you think his choice to fight was right? What would you do in similar circumstances?

4. Research conditions today on Pine Ridge or another Indian reservation. How do they compare to Black Elk's time? What improvements have been made? What remains to be done in order to bring reservation life up to the standard of living common throughout the rest of the country?

BIBLIOGRAPHY

**Books**

Petri, Hilda Neihardt. *Black Elk and Flaming Rainbow: Personal Memories of the Lakota Holy Man and John Neihardt*. Lincoln, Neb.: University of Nebraska Press, 1995.

Steltenkamp, Michael F. *Black Elk: Holy Man of the Oglala*. Norman, Okla.: University of Oklahoma Press, 1993.

Deloria, Vine, Jr., ed. *A Sender of Words: Essays in Memory of John G. Neihardt*. Salt Lake City, Utah: Howe Brothers, 1984.

Rice, Julian. *Black Elk's Story: Distinguishing Its Lakota Purpose*. Albuquerque, N.M.: University of New Mexico Press, 1991.

# ✹ Lee Blessing

BORN: *1949, Minneapolis, Minnesota*

NATIONALITY: *American*

GENRE: *Drama*

MAJOR WORKS:
*A Walk in the Woods* (1986)

## Overview

Lee Blessing is a Minneapolis-based playwright noted for the varied themes and topics of his plays. He has won numerous awards and praise, most notably for *A Walk in the Woods* (1986), which was nominated for the Pulitzer Prize and Tony Award.

Lee Blessing  *Daniel Acker / Bloomberg News / Landov*

## Works in Biographical and Historical Context

*An Unremarkable Upbringing* Lee Blessing was born to a typically American Midwest household. His upbringing was fairly conventional. His parents were not great lovers of the theater, and Blessing himself seemingly stumbled into play writing when, while still in high school, he chose to pen a short piece in lieu of writing a thirty-page term paper on a subject he was not particularly interested in. However, Blessing found he had a knack for writing plays, and soon had determined upon a career path as a playwright.

After graduating from high school, Blessing attended the University of Minnesota for two years before enrolling at Reed College in Portland, Oregon, where he graduated with a bachelor's degree in English in 1971. As a reward, his parents, who had become enthusiastic supporters of his writing, offered him the choice of a used car or a trip to Russia. He chose the latter, traveling to Moscow. He would return to the Russian capital nearly two decades later to stage a production of his most acclaimed play, *A Walk in the Woods*.

*Success in Local Theaters and on Broadway* After his time abroad, Blessing returned to the Midwest, attending the University of Iowa from 1974 to 1979. He spent his years there first earning a master of fine arts in English, then taking an MFA in speech and theater. He supported himself by teaching playwriting, which he also would later teach at the Playwrights' Center in Minneapolis from 1986 to 1988.

After writing and producing five plays between 1979 and 1985, Blessing began to garner critical attention with *Eleemosynary*, a tale of three generations of gifted women and their complex familial relationships. *Time* reviewer William A. Henry, III felt that "every woman, and everyone who knows and loves one, will recognize too familiar truths in the dilemmas Blessing depicts." The following year, *A Walk in the Woods* premiered at the Eugene O'Neill Theater in Waterford, Connecticut. The play would go on to runs on Broadway, in Moscow, and in London, where it would star esteemed actor Sir Alec Guinness. An adaptation of the production also aired on the Public Broadcasting System's *American Playhouse*.

Although his plays have been staged around the world and on Broadway, Blessing maintains his focus in his hometown of Minneapolis, and prefers the intimacy of small theater productions. He continues to write on a variety of themes and subjects—his 2004 play, *Whores*, for example, concerns the rape and murder of Catholic nuns in El Salvador in 1980, during a period of civil war and instability, a result of Cold War meddling by the United States and the Soviet Union, each of which backed a rival faction in the conflict.

*A Variety of Themes* Such heady political drama is no stranger to Blessing, but he also writes about more

personal subjects. Several of Blessing's works—*Cobb* (1989), *Cooperstown* (1993) and *The Winning Streak* (2002)—have incorporated his love of baseball into their storylines. He has also written plays dealing with as wide a diversity of subjects as serial killers (*Down the Road*, 1989), AIDS (*Patient A*, 1993), the clash of art and politics (*Chesapeake*, 1999), and the experience of being gay in America (*Thief River*, 2000).

## Works in Literary Context

Noted for his eclectic choice of subject matter, Blessing's plays focus on politics both private and public, and on human relationships, most notably in the family unit.

*Sports Metaphors* The combination of sports and theatrical drama has a history stretching back to the ancient Greeks. The ups and downs experienced by athletes both on and off the playing field, along with their heroic status counterbalanced by their all-too-mortal fallibilities, make for naturally gripping storytelling.

Blessing's own love of baseball has spurred him to write two plays and a teleplay, all of which examine much broader themes through the medium of sports. *Cobb* is a biographical sketch of notorious Detroit Tigers

## COMMON HUMAN EXPERIENCE

Blessing's love of baseball has led him to pen three stories incorporating the sport into broader themes. Other works that use sports to examine the human condition include:

*End Zone* (1972), a novel by Don DeLillo. An early work by noted American author DeLillo, who uses the aggression of football to mirror the threat of nuclear warfare during the Cold War.

*The Celebrant* (1983), a novel by Eric Rolfe Greenberg. Like Blessing's *Cobb*, this book uses the story of an early baseball hero, Christy Mathewson, to provide commentary and contrast on the shaping of America, in this case personified by a family of Jewish immigrants who look to baseball as their means of assimilating into their newly-adopted culture.

*Unforgivable Blackness: The Rise and Fall of Jack Johnson* (2005), a documentary by Ken Burns. Based on the 2004 nonfiction book by Geoffrey C. Ward, this two-part documentary chronicles the career of the first African American heavyweight boxing champion, particularly the hardships he faced outside the ring in an era just a few short decades removed from the American Civil War.

centerfielder Ty Cobb, sports' first millionaire and, by his own admission, "the most hated man in baseball." Blessing uses this dichotomy to examine, as *Time* reviewer William A. Henry, III put it, "... Blessing's thesis is that Cobb changed baseball in exactly the ways that the twentieth century changed America, by bringing the techniques of science and the mentality of all-out warfare to what had been a pastoral pastime."

Blessing also used sports metaphors to explore much more personal territory. Inspired by his father, who was dying of cancer but who clung to life long enough to root for a San Diego Padres winning streak, Blessing wrote *Winning Streak*, an emotionally charged work about a grown son reconnecting with a father, a baseball umpire, he never knew.

### Works in Critical Context

Blessing's works have been mostly well-received by critics. In addition to receiving Pulitzer Prize and Tony nominations for *A Walk in the Woods*, the play also won him the American Theater Critics Association award in 1987 and the Dramalogue Award in 1988; in 1989, Blessing received a Guggenheim fellowship. He was also awarded a National Endowment for the Arts grant, and received a 1997 Los Angeles Drama Critics Circle Award for Best Writing as well as the Great American Play Award, and the George and Elisabeth Marton Award, among others.

*A Walk in the Woods*  Critics singled out *A Walk in the Woods* for its sensitive and humorous treatment of a very weighty issue. Frank Rich said the play drives home the message that "all people and nations are fundamentally alike, and that all world problems could be solved if only the adversaries might build mutual trust by chatting face to face on a park bench." In a review in the *New Yorker*, Edith Oliver wrote that "one of the many pleasures the play affords is that of watching the molds crack as the characters deepen and, above all, connect." *Chicago Sun-Times* contributor Hedy Weiss described the play as "a series of riveting discussions between two men possessed of exceptional intelligence, powerful egos, and intense but carefully disguised passions."

### Responses to Literature

1. In Blessing's play *Whores*, the playwright uses sex as a means to shock the audience. Blessing himself has said, "Sexual elements still have the power to frighten, disgust, and outrage us." Why do you think sex has more power to shock in our society than violence? Do you think it is right to use sex in order to frighten, disgust, or outrage an audience?

2. Blessing's plays often address family dynamics. Analyze two of his plays that feature family relationships as a central theme, such as *Eleemosynary* and *Independence*. Compare the treatments of family dynamics in the two plays. How do they differ? How are they similar?

3. Growing up in the Midwest has left an indelible stamp on Blessing's work. Do you think it is possible for writers to completely separate themselves from the circumstances of their upbringing? If you were an author or a playwright, would the environment of your formative years influence your work later? If so, how and why?

4. Blessing has incorporated his love of baseball into several projects. What are you truly passionate about? How would you structure a play or script about your interest? Write a simple plot outline of a story that concerns your hobby or interest as a central element.

BIBLIOGRAPHY

**Books**

"Eleemosynary." *Drama for Students*. Edited by Sara Constantakis. Vol. 23. Detroit: Gale, 2006.

"Lee Blessing (1949–)." *Contemporary Literary Criticism*. Edited by Daniel G. Marowski, Roger Matuz, and Sean R. Pollock. Vol. 54. Detroit: Gale Research, 1989.

**Periodicals**

Kilian, Michael. Review of *Whores*, interview with Blessing. *Chicago Tribune* (July 24, 2003): 9.

**Web sites**

The Playwrights Database. *Lee Blessing—complete guide to the Playwright and Plays.* Retrieved September 24, 2008, from http://www.doollee.com/PlaywrightsB/blessing-lee.html

# ✸ Harold Bloom

BORN: *1930, New York, New York*

NATIONALITY: *American*

GENRE: *Fiction, literary criticism*

MAJOR WORKS:

*The Anxiety of Influence: A Theory of Poetry* (1973)

*Poetry and Repression: Revisionism from Blake to Stevens* (1976)

*The Western Canon: The Books and School of the Ages* (1994)

Harold Bloom    *Bloom, Harold, photograph. Mark Mainz / Getty Images.*

## Overview

Harold Bloom "is arguably the best-known literary critic in America, probably the most controversial and undoubtedly as idiosyncratic as they come—a description with which he would not quarrel," according to *Newsweek* writer David Lehman. Describing the influence of the past upon poetry as a relationship of conflict, Bloom's writings have consistently contradicted mainstream trends in literary theory.

## Works in Biographical and Historical Context

*A Man of Many Talents*    The son of William and Paula Lev Bloom, Harold Bloom was born in New York City and lived there until he entered Cornell University, where he earned a B.A. in 1951. Going on to Yale University for graduate study, he received his Ph.D. in 1955 and has been a member of the Yale faculty since that time. In 1958, he married Jeanne Gould; they have two sons, Daniel and David.

Even in his early years, Bloom read voraciously; it may be a true story that he read English before he spoke it. J. Hillis Miller says that poetry came to Bloom more naturally than prose, and Bloom reminisces about his reading of Hart Crane and Walt Whitman between the ages of eight and twelve. His photographic memory is legendary among his peers; stories tell of his starting to recite *Paradise Lost* and realizing that he could go on for as long as Milton had. His interests are wide, ranging from baseball to vampire movies, on which he has written an occasional essay for popular magazines.

Bloom's love of Western literature began at a young age, and formed the foundation of his later beliefs about the importance of the Western canon of literature. He wrote studies on Percy Shelley, William Blake, and Wallace Stevens prior to gaining national fame for his theories on literary criticism, after which he was seen by many as a defender of a more traditionalist Western curriculum. But perhaps his religion was as important to his later theories as the giants of Western literature were.

Raised in a traditional Jewish household, Bloom approached the books of the Old Testament with the same devotion he gave to the poets of centuries past. He would argue strongly in later writings in favor of the view that the so-called J author of some of the earliest books of the Old Testament was a female scribe, and that her writings were originally intended as ironic critiques of the rather inflexible, male-dominated religion of her time. His interest in spirituality would later manifest in what he called "Jewish gnosticism," a complex belief system that views humans as perfect souls trapped in an imperfect world. He would later introduce elements of his gnostic beliefs directly into his literary criticism.

*Career in Literary Criticism*    In 1973, a small book was published under the title *The Anxiety of Influence*. It

## LITERARY AND HISTORICAL CONTEMPORARIES

Harold Bloom's famous contemporaries include:

**Cormac McCarthy** (1933–): An American novelist and playwright sometimes compared to William Faulkner, McCarthy's ten novels have spanned a wide range of subjects and genres, from Western to Post-Apocalyptic.

**Richard Nixon** (1914–1994): Beginning his political career as a congressman from California, Nixon was elected president of the United States for two terms. Due to the scandal known as Watergate, Nixon resigned the office of president in 1973—the only president in the history of the United States to do so.

**Kurt Vonnegut** (1922–2007): After serving in World War II and famously witnessing the fire-bombing of Dresden in December 1944, Vonnegut began a prolific literary career that included the landmark work *Slaughterhouse-Five*.

**Queen Elizabeth II** (1926–): Queen of the United Kingdom and associated Commonwealth territories, Elizabeth II is one of Britain's longest-reigning monarchs.

**Hunter S. Thompson** (1937–2005): The creator of "Gonzo journalism," in which the reporter becomes the central actor in their own story, Thompson is best known for his novel *Fear and Loathing in Las Vegas*.

was to mark Harold Bloom's dramatic entrance into literary theory, and was to mark as well the theoretical discourse of our century. Since the publication of this book, it has been impossible to discuss theories of influence and tradition without reference to Bloom. Before *The Anxiety of Influence*, twentieth-century criticism had been guided by Matthew Arnold's humanistic vision of tradition, subscribed to by T. S. Eliot and sustained by the so-called New Criticism. Tradition was viewed as a gathering up, an addition without loss. In *The Anxiety of Influence* Bloom proposed a radical revision of the concepts of tradition and influence, which he termed "antithetical criticism." This criticism transformed the conventional landscape of literary history into a battleground in which each poet, coming late upon the scene, enters into what might seem to be an Oedipal struggle with his precursors.

Even before the publication of this book, Bloom was a distinguished literary critic. His works on Romanticism had helped bring about a re-evaluation of Romantic poetry and of the critical stances through which Romanticism was being read. His five books published prior to *The Anxiety of Influence* rejected the modernist and New Critical assumptions which had devalued Romantic poetry. Bloom's re-reading of this tradition, along with Geoffrey Hartman's monumental studies of Wordsworth and Paul de Man's significant work on the Romantics,

had the effect of reestablishing the fortunes of British Romanticism.

***An Academic Outcast*** Bloom is utterly iconoclastic about academic traditions, a fact which has earned him the active antipathy of a certain traditional segment of the academic establishment. In a profession that lives by its *curriculum vitae* (a sort of academic résumé), he refuses to compile one. On occasion, like Whitman, he has written a review of his own work ("The Criticism of Our Climate," *Yale Review*, October 1982) though, unlike Whitman, he has signed his name to it. He has been known to write in the middle of a party, oblivious to the crowd around him. *The Visionary Company* (1961) was written on the dinner table, with his baby son in front of him and dinner displacing the manuscript. In the age of the computer, he writes his books longhand, and they go from typist to print, since he objects forcefully to being copyedited. He quotes entirely from memory and eschews footnotes altogether. These "stances" (Bloom's term) are idiosyncrasies to the establishment, but they are rooted in Bloom's theories of poetry.

His views of Western canon, rooted firmly in Dante and Shakespeare, earned Bloom further enmity during the "culture wars" of the 1970s and 80s, which pitted the Western-centered approach favored by Bloom against a more multi-cultural program that incorporated contributions from women, non-Western sources, and traditionally marginalized groups.

He writes with some regularity for the *New York Review of Books*, the *New York Times Book Review*, and other literary magazines. The author of fourteen books, his work has been translated into many languages, including German, Italian, Spanish, Serbo-Croatian, Romanian, and Japanese. He is at present Sterling Professor of the Humanities at Yale University.

## Works in Literary Context

As important to literary criticism as he is controversial, Harold Bloom has been a major contributor to academic scholarship for over thirty-five years. His work has been influenced by a wide variety of sources, ranging from Freud and Nietzsche to Gnosticism and Judaism. Most of Bloom's books are concerned with the development of his theory of poetics, which centers on the notion that poets engage in a constant struggle with their literary forebears. This "anxiety of influence," as Bloom has termed it, has been alternately referred to as "genius" and "idiosyncratic" by his scholarly peers.

Critic Alan Rosenfeld has referred to Bloom's work as a "theory in progress," noting that as new volumes appear, new influences are brought to bear on his ideas, such as with *A Map of Misreading* (1980), in which Bloom turns to Lurianic Kabbalism (a form of Jewish mysticism) as "the ultimate model for Western revisionism from the Renaissance to the present."

***Influence and "Misreading"*** At the center of Bloom's "anxiety of influence," the focus of his theory of poetics, is the notion that modern writers wrestle with the writers of the past in an effort to create something new and original. Since the Enlightenment, Bloom contends, writers have suffered from a feeling of "belatedness." As Denis Donoghue writes: "Born too late, they find everything already said and done; they cannot be first, priority has by definition, and the indifference of fate, escaped them." The weak writer fails to find his own voice, while the strong writer challenges his precursor, willfully "misreading" him so as to clear a space for himself. In the *New York Times Book Review*, Edward Said comments, "it is the essence of Bloom's vision that every poem is the result by which another, earlier poem is deliberately misread, and hence re-written." Such a vision sets each poem in a hostile relationship with others: "No text can be complete," Said notes, "because on the one hand it is an attempt to struggle free of earlier texts impinging on it and, on the other, it is preparing itself to savage texts not yet written by authors not yet born." In subsequent books, Bloom further refines his theoretical approach, utilizing psychoanalysis (Freud), philosophy (Nietzsche and Vico), and Jewish theology (Gnosis and Kabbalah) to create an intricate theory of poetics that continues to spur critical debate.

*The "Yale School" of Literary Criticism* Bloom did not achieve this transformation of criticism in twentieth-century America single-handedly. From the 1950s on, critics who were to become known as members of the "Yale School" began to put into question the humanistic underpinnings of the English language tradition: its assumptions of meaning, the importance of literature, the separation of literature and criticism. The members of this school shared in these challenges to the old humanistic system, but each took off in his own direction: Jacques Derrida, with his rhetorical dismantling of literary and philosophical texts in what came to be called deconstruction; Paul de Man, with the concerns that arose from deconstruction as the undoing of all understanding; J. Hillis Miller, moving from phenomenology to deconstruction; and Geoffrey H. Hartman, undertaking a critique of criticism whose effect was to de-emphasize the Greek philosophical tradition and to bring into contact the "literary" and the "critical" endeavors. Bloom, like the other members of this group, attacked humanism and contemporary ideas of form and meaning; but unlike the other members of this group, he also attacked deconstruction and its reliance on philosophical models.

## Works in Critical Context

Not unlike Jacques Derrida and Michel Foucault, Harold Bloom is a literary critic who has received a great deal of critical attention of his own. His work is reviewed widely, attacked critically, and often praised. Many critics have lauded his daring, "antithetical" approach, while others have called him "willfully offensive to the profession." Bloom's reply to these praises and criticisms is, as Alvin

---

## COMMON HUMAN EXPERIENCE

Bloom is merely the latest in a long line of distinguished literary critics, all of whom have made significant contributions to the field of literary theory.

*Anatomy of Criticism* (1957), a collection of essays by Herman Northrop Frye. A highly influential theorist, this is Frye's attempt to formulate a unified approach to literary theory grounded solely in literature, exploring modes, myths, symbols, and genres over the course of four essays.

*Of Grammatology* (1967), a book by Jacques Derrida. In contrast to Frye's work, Derrida ushered in the era of deconstructivism with this work, which argues that the meaning of language exists as a series of signs, as expressed through writing; since writing is an external system imposed on the language user, their intended meaning is not fully under the user's control.

*Lives of the Most Eminent English Poets* (1781), a book by Samuel Johnson. Considered the father of English literary criticism, Johnson, among other things, edited a new and more faithful edition of Shakespeare's plays, and assembled an authoritative dictionary that was a standard reference for over one hundred years. This collection is one of the earliest works of literary criticism, encompassing the biographies and evaluations of fifty-two poets.

---

Rosenfeld states, "perhaps the most outrageous thing of all: *he writes another book*." Denis Donoghue, who holds the Henry James Chair of English and American Letters at New York University, frequently reviews Bloom's books and has ambivalent feelings regarding his work, saying in one review that he finds Bloom "quite wondrous, even when I don't believe him."

Several reviewers charge that Bloom's literary theory is excessively reductive. Writing for the *New York Times Book Review*, Christopher Ricks notes repetition in the arguments appearing in *The Anxiety of Influence, A Map of Misreading, Kabbalah and Criticism*, and *Poetry and Repression*, then declares, "Bloom had an idea; now the idea has him. . . . He now has nothing left to do but to say the same things about new contests and with more decibels." However, in a *New Republic* review of *Agon: Towards a Theory of Revisionism*, Helen Vendler writes, "Any collection of essays and addresses composed in the span of a few years by a single powerful mind will tend to return to the same questions, and to urge (even covertly) the same views."

*Omens of Millennium* *Omens of Millennium* (1996) is a more personal book in which Bloom discusses contemporary spirituality and his own Gnosticist beliefs. As

*Los Angeles Times Book Review* critic Jonathan Kirsch writes, "The whole point of Bloom's book is that the offerings of the so-called New Age—'an endless saturnalia of ill-defined longings,' as he defines it—are shallow and silly when compared to what the ancients knew." Commenting on Bloom's disclosure of his struggle with depression in his thirties, Kirsch notes that Bloom "is apparently too courtly, too cerebral and perhaps too shy to engage in much baring of the soul." Instead, as *Washington Post Book World* critic Marina Warner notes, Bloom invokes the wisdom of ancient Zoroastrianism, early Christian Gnosticism, medieval Sufism, and Kabbalism "in order to create an antidote to the New Age." Praising the "trenchancy, verve and learning" of the book, Warner writes that "*Omens of Millennium* is born of despair, but it focuses throughout on possibility, with a true teacher's refusal to give up the job of stimulating and informing, no matter how restless the class or desolate the wasteland of the schoolyard outside."

## Responses to Literature

1. Do you think it is possible to create something completely new, or must all creative work nowadays come out of something that came before? Explain your position, and cite specific examples if possible.

2. Look up the six terms Bloom uses in *The Anxiety of Influence* to define the different ways a poem can be misread. Why do you think he used ancient Greek concepts to label each ratio? Come up with your own label and definition for the six terms. Can you add any more terms to Bloom's list?

3. Bloom has said that all would-be artists must carve out a niche for themselves by looking at the great works that have come before them and misreading the original work. What do you think of this theory? Are great works universal, or can their intended meaning be lost over time as the result of later generations applying new, unintended meanings? Do you feel that this process dilutes the original work or enhances it? Can you think of any examples of works of poetry, literature, music, or art whose meaning has changed radically over time?

4. Research the theories of Freud or Nietschze, or the tenets of Kabbalah or Gnosticism. Now take a favorite poem or book of yours and apply what you've researched to interpreting the work. Can you see, for example, Freudian elements or Nietschzean philosophy in the plot, characters, or theme of the work you're evaluating?

BIBLIOGRAPHY

**Books**

Allen, Graham. *Harold Bloom: Poetics of Conflict.* New York: Harvester Wheatsheaf, 1994.

Fite, David. *Harold Bloom: The Rhetoric of Romantic Vision.* Amherst, Mass.: University of Massachusetts Press, 1985.

Scherr, Barry J. *D. H. Lawrence's Response to Plato: A Bloomian Interpretation.* New York: P. Lang, 1995.

# ✳ Judy Blume

BORN: *1938, Elizabeth, New Jersey*

NATIONALITY: *American*

GENRE: *Fiction*

MAJOR WORKS:
*Are You There God? It's Me, Margaret* (1970)
*Tales of a Fourth Grade Nothing* (1972)
*Blubber* (1974)
*Forever . . .* (1975)

## Overview

Perhaps the most popular contemporary author of works for upper elementary to junior high school readers, Judy Blume is the creator of frank, often humorous stories that

Judy Blume   *Gregory Pace / FilmMagic / Getty Images*

focus on the emotional and social concerns of suburban adolescents. She has also enjoyed success as a novelist for adults with her best-selling works *Wifey* (1978) and *Summer Sisters* (1998).

## Works in Biographical and Historical Context

*A Family Divided by Geography*   Blume was born on February 12, 1938, in Elizabeth, New Jersey, to Rudolph and Esther Sussman. Her father, a dentist, shared with her a penchant for fantasy and game-playing and provided emotional support when she was ill, unhappy, or fearful. Blume describes her mother as a traditional homemaker and a reader who spent every afternoon with books. When Blume was in the third grade, she moved with her mother and her older brother, David, to Miami Beach, where the climate would help David recuperate from an illness. Many of the incidents in her books are based on her experiences during the two years she lived in Florida during the school months while her father worked in New Jersey and saw the rest of the family only occasionally.

*An Opportunity to Write*   Blume graduated from New York University in 1961 with a degree in early childhood education. While still a student, she married John Blume, a lawyer. Blume began writing after her children entered nursery school in the mid-1960s. Though she had two short stories published in Westminster Press periodicals, she received as many as six rejection slips a week for two and a half years before Reilly and Lee accepted her first novel, *The One in the Middle Is the Green Kangaroo* (1969). *The One in the Middle Is the Green Kangaroo* established the pattern and style of other Blume books, which followed in rapid succession throughout the 1970s and early 1980s.

On the crest of the civil rights movement, Blume enrolled in a class called "Writing for Children and Teenagers." For each session, she completed a chapter of *Iggie's House*, which was published by Bradbury in 1970 after having been serialized in *Trailblazer for Juniors* in 1969. In the book, eleven-year-old Winnie spends every Saturday night with Iggie's family, from whom she absorbs an attitude of interest in and tolerance for people who are "different."

*Influences and Development*   Blume's ideas for her novels have often come from her own children's concerns. After a rash of divorces in the neighborhood, the Blume children asked whether divorce could ever happen in their family. Blume told them no, unaware that she would be married a total of three times in her life. *It's Not the End of the World* (1972) expresses the feelings of three children faced with their parents' divorce.

After Blume's first marriage ended in 1975, she explored in *Wifey* (1978), her first adult book, the paralysis of a wife in a traditional marriage. This book came

### LITERARY AND HISTORICAL CONTEMPORARIES

Blume's famous contemporaries include:

**Patricia Grace** (1937–): Grace is considered New Zealand's foremost Maori woman writer.

**Kofi Annan** (1938–): Annan is a Ghanaian diplomat who served as the secretary general of the United Nations from 1997 until 2007. He received the Nobel Peace Prize in 2001.

**Daniel Pinkwater** (1941–): Pinkwater is a popular radio commentator and children's book author known for works such as *The Snarkout Boys and the Avocado of Death* (1982).

**Peter Jennings** (1938–2005): Jennings was a Canadian-born television news journalist best known for anchoring ABC's national nightly news.

**Margaret Atwood** (1939–): Atwood is a Canadian writer who is one of the most award-winning authors of the late twentieth century and early twenty-first century.

on the heels of the women's liberation movement, which aimed to expand women's roles beyond the household and encouraged women to question traditional ideas about marriage and family. "*Wifey* was always in my head," Blume told *People* magazine. "I write out of my real life experiences, but they become fiction." Immediately following her divorce from John Blume, she married Tom Kitchens. Blume and her family lived with Kitchens in England for a period and then moved to Los Alamos, New Mexico. She divorced Kitchens in 1978 and married a third time, to George Cooper, in 1987.

During her career, Blume's writing has matured and her audience has expanded from younger children to adolescents to adults. Although she is no longer as prolific as she was during the 1970s and early 1980s, she continues to write for a dedicated audience.

## Works in Literary Context

*A Young Person's Perspective*   In less than two decades, Blume's books have sold more than thirty million copies. She deals with a wide variety of issues that are significant to adolescents. Combining intimate first-person narratives with amusing dialogue supplemented by familiar everyday details, her books reveal her East Coast upper-middle-class Jewish background while describing the anxieties of her protagonists: characteristically female preteens and teenagers who encounter problematic situations and survive them. Despite the fact that she often ends her works on a note of uncertainty, Blume consistently underscores her books with optimism about the successful adaptability of her characters.

# COMMON HUMAN EXPERIENCE

Blume deals with issues that are significant to young people, such as friction between parents and children, friendship, peer group approval, divorce, social ostracism, and emerging sexuality. Here are some other works that treat issues of peer pressure and conformity:

*Big Mouth & Ugly Girl* (2002), a novel by Joyce Carol Oates. This novel explores the pressures faced by two teenage outsiders navigating through peer pressure and parental expectations.

*The Chocolate War* (1974), a novel by Robert Cormier. This classic novel depicts the struggles of a boy fighting against conformity and mob rule at his school through the seemingly ordinary event of a fund-raising sale.

*Wringer* (1997), a novel by Jerry Spinelli. This novel explores the difficulties of facing peer pressure through the eyes of a nine-year-old bird lover who is expected to become a "wringer," one of a group of boys who breaks the necks of wounded pigeons at a local shooting event.

*Edward Scissorhands* (1990), a film by Tim Burton. This tale of a sheltered young man with both a disfigurement and a natural talent offers a unique take on the balance between maintaining individuality and fitting in.

***Controversial Subject Matter*** At the same time her books enjoy enormous popularity, they are also highly subject to censorship attempts because of their frankness in sexual content, language, and the lack of traditional moralizing and authoritarian pronouncements. Blume's books reflect a general cultural concern with feelings about self and body, interpersonal relationships, and family problems. It is her portrayal of feelings of sexuality as normal, and not rightfully subject to punishment, that revolutionized realistic fiction for children. *Are You There, God? It's Me, Margaret* (1970) depicts eleven-year-old Margaret's apprehensions about starting her period and choosing her own religion. At the time of the book's publication, Blume was praised for her warm and funny re-creation of childhood feelings and conversation but was criticized for her forthright references to the human body and its processes. The book is now considered a groundbreaking work due to the candor with which Blume presents previously taboo subjects.

Blume's refusal to prescribe solutions or advocate punishment may disturb would-be censors as much as her treatment of sexuality. Her books seldom draw distinct lines between right and wrong ways to handle a problem. Though her stories often deal with such subjects as sibling rivalry, divorce, and death, Blume resists the idea that her books are "problem books." "Life is full of problems," she responds, "Some big and some small."

## Works in Critical Context

Blume is recognized as a pioneer for her candid treatment of such topics as menstruation, masturbation, and pre-marital sex. She is also considered a controversial and provocative figure by those critics and librarians who object to the explicit nature of her works. However, Blume has won the devotion of an extensive and loyal youthful following; as critic Naomi Decter observes, "there is, indeed, scarcely a literate girl of novel-reading age who has not read one or more Blume books."

Blume has won over fifty national and international child-selected awards for her various works. Critics are strongly divided as to the success of Blume's plots, characterization, writing style, and nonjudgmental approach; some object to her uninhibited language and permissive attitude toward sexuality, and complain that her cavalier treatment of love, death, pain, and religion trivializes young people and the literature written for them. However, most commentators agree that Blume accurately captures the speech, emotions, and private thoughts of children, for whom she has made reading both easy and enjoyable.

***Are You There God? It's Me, Margaret*** Several of Blume's books have been the target of attempted censorship, including *Are You There God? It's Me, Margaret.* Although the *New York Times* named it one of the outstanding children's books of 1970, its reception by reviewers was mixed. *Education Digest* praised its "exploration of previously untouched aspects of childhood and adolescent experience." A *New Statesman* reviewer described it as "admittedly gripping stuff no doubt for those wrestling with—or curious about future—bodily changes." A critic for *Book Window* felt that "when the author rhapsodises about the wearing of a sanitary napkin. ... Suddenly a sensitive, amusing novel has been reduced to the level of some of the advertising blurbs." The reviewer for the *Times Literary Supplement* concluded, "Margaret's private talks with God are insufferably self-conscious and arch."

Attempts at censoring the book have continued throughout its lifetime; the *Newsletter on Intellectual Freedom* reports that it has been charged with "denigrating religion and parental authority" and being "sexually offensive and amoral." Nonetheless, the book has sold more than a million copies in paperback.

***Forever ...*** The censorship attempts of *Forever ...* (1975) surpassed those of all of Blume's other books, with objectors quoted in the *Newsletter on Intellectual Freedom* as saying it "demoralizes marital sex" and "titillates and stimulates children to the point they could be prematurely awakened sexually." Some literary critics have found the characters stilted and the plot a mere recounting of steps in the process of sexual intimacy. But, the book was praised by Joyce Maynard in a *New York Times Magazine* article because it "makes kids' erotic stirrings seem to them more normal." A *School Library Journal* writer stated, "*Forever* isn't really about sex at all, it's about reassurance. Like many [young adult] novels, it addresses teenagers' feelings, sexual and otherwise, to one point: don't worry, you're normal."

## Responses to Literature

1. Blume has been criticized by both parents and librarians who see her works as overly explicit and harmfully precocious. Does Blume deserve this reputation? What about her works might be harmful for readers in their early teens, and in what ways are her books useful for this audience?

2. During the 1970s and 1980s, Blume was accused of writing to adolescents in an overly mature manner. In what ways have teenagers changed since that time? Do Blume's books continue to address the kinds of issues faced by twenty-first-century adolescents?

3. Many of Blume's stories contain adolescent characters struggling with difficult problems that are faced by teenagers everywhere. Write a story centered around a teenage character facing a struggle with which you are familiar in your life today.

4. Blume's book *Letters to Judy* is based on letters she has received from readers asking for advice on a wide range of issues dealt with in her novels. Write a letter to Judy Blume about a specific problem addressed in her fiction and compose a response based on the kind of advice you think Blume might give.

BIBLIOGRAPHY

**Books**

Fisher, Emma, and Justin Wintle. *The Pied Pipers.* New York: Paddington Press, 1975.

Gleasner, Diana. *Breakthrough: Women in Writing.* New York: Walker, 1980.

Lee, Betsey. *Judy Blume's Story.* Minneapolis: Dillon, 1981.

Weidt, Maryann. *Presenting Judy Blume.* Boston: Twayne, 1989.

Wheeler, Jill C. *Judy Blume.* Edina, Minn.: Abdo & Daughters, 1996.

**Periodicals**

Maynard, Joyce. "Coming of Age with Judy Blume." *New York Times Magazine*, December 3, 1978.

Neary, John. "The 'Jacqueline Susann of Kids' Books,' Judy Blume, Grows Up with an Adult Novel." *People*, October 16, 1978.

Saunders, Paula C. "Judy Blume as Herself." *Writer's Digest*, January 1, 1980.

"A Split Decision: Judy Blume in Peoria." *Newsletter on Intellectual Freedom* (March 1985).

# ✺ Robert Bly

BORN: *1926, Madison, Minnesota*

NATIONALITY: *American*

GENRE: *Poetry*

MAJOR WORKS:

*The Light Around the Body* (1967)

*This Tree Will Be Here for a Thousand Years* (1979)

*Iron John: A Book About Men* (1990)

## Overview

Robert Bly is one of the most prominent and influential figures in contemporary American poetry. He writes visionary and imagistic verse distinguished by its unadorned language and generally subdued tone. His poems are pervaded by the landscape and atmosphere of rural Minnesota, where he has lived most of his life, and are focused on the immediate, emotional concerns of daily life.

## Works in Biographical and Historical Context

*From Minnesota to Norway and Back* Robert Bly was born in Madison, Minnesota, and grew up on a farm nearby. After two years in the navy, he enrolled in Saint Olaf College in Northfield, Minnesota, and in the fall of 1947 transferred to Harvard, from which he graduated *magna cum laude* in 1950. Returning to northern Minnesota to live, he had a chance to read and to study poetry on his own before pursuing graduate study at the University of Iowa. In 1955 he married Carolyn McLean, and the next year he received an M.A. from the University of Iowa and a Fulbright grant to visit Norway and to translate Norwegian poetry into English.

Impressed with the works of foreign poets who were neglected in the United States, Bly determined to start a magazine devoted to publishing poetry in translation. Upon his return to the United States, Bly settled on a farm near Madison, Minnesota. In 1958 he founded the *Fifties* magazine and press, which subsequently became the *Sixties*, the *Seventies*, and the *Eighties* with the changing of the decades.

Bly's first volume, *Silence in the Snowy Fields* (1962), established him as an important voice in American poetry. The serene, haiku-like poems in this book evoke the pastoral settings of the Midwest where he was raised and espouse the virtues of solitude and self-awareness. His second volume of poetry, *The Light Around the Body* (1967), received the National Book Award for Poetry in 1968.

*An Activist Poet* In the years following World War II, the country of Vietnam, which had for a time been ruled as a colony of France, became an independent nation partitioned into a region under Communist rule (North Vietnam) and a republic (South Vietnam). The

Robert Bly   *Per Breiehagen / Time Life Pictures / Getty Images*

two sides were to be united by free election, but instead they began battling in a civil war to determine the political and ideological fate of the country. The United States supported the government of South Vietnam and sent nearly three million Americans to the region over the course of the war. Many Americans, however, felt that the conflict was not one in which the United States should have been directly involved.

During the 1960s, Bly was active in protests against the Vietnam War, and his political and social convictions are prominent in the poetry he wrote during that period. Bly even co-founded a group called American Writers Against the Vietnam War. *The Light Around the Body* is noted for its overtly political content, centering on Bly's reactions to the horrors of the Vietnam War. These poems typify his attempt to merge the personal and the public, an effort, as he explains in his essay, written during the same period, "Leaping Up into Political Poetry," necessitated by the hate and injustice rampant in the world. Before donating his National Book Award prize money to an anti-draft organization, which protested the government's requirement for certain citizens to serve in the war effort, Bly delivered an acceptance speech attacking the American role in Vietnam and chastising the literary world for its silence on the issue.

Political concerns are again present in Bly's next major work, *Sleepers Joining Hands* (1973), but they are fused with the quiet tone and pastoral imagery of his first book. One of the subjects explored in *Sleepers Joining Hands* is the division within each individual of male and female consciousness, an area of considerable importance to Bly. In an essay included in this volume, "I Came Out of the Mother Naked," Bly advocates a return to the virtues of the "Mother" culture which, in opposition to the currently dominant male-based system of rationality and aggression, stresses a sensuous, spiritual awareness of self and nature. Though some critics faulted *Sleepers Joining Hands* for flatness and pretension—most notably Eliot Weinberger, who renounced Bly's talent and importance as a poet in his review—others praised the book and asserted the continuing validity of Bly's work.

***Return to the Personal***   Although Bly is still convinced that the poet must attend to public concerns as well as the private, interior world, his work has become more and more directed toward a personal exploration of natural, spiritual, and familial matters. With its emphasis on nature, solitude, and quiet contemplation, *This Tree Will Be Here for a Thousand Years* (1979) represents a return to the concerns first developed in *Silence in the Snowy Fields*. The inward-looking, personal quality of these poems is even more strongly present in *The Man in the Black Coat Turns* (1981). Many of the poems in this volume examine the dynamics of father-son relationships and male grief, focusing particularly on Bly's feelings about his own father and sons.

With the publication of his prose work *Iron John: A Book About Men* (1990), Bly helped start the Mythopoetic Men's Movement in the United States. Following on the success of this book, an international bestseller that has been translated into many languages, Bly began conducting workshops for both men alone and men and women together. Along with his second wife and other writers, he also conducts seminars on European fairy tales, which Bly feels can be used as a tool for self-exploration and personal growth.

## Works in Literary Context

Bly is often associated with "deep image" poetry, a loosely defined movement whose adherents include James Wright, Donald Hall, and Louis Simpson. These writers look to the unconscious for inspiration, as does Bly, who uses the term "leaping" to define the associative process by which images combine to create a poem. Bly's use of imagery reflects the influence of such surrealist writers as Federico García Lorca and Pablo Neruda, and he has frequently translated the work of these and other international poets.

*Connecting the Conscious and the Unconscious* Bly's poetry is a conscious rebellion against what he sees as the prevalent literary mode in the United States, poetry that is too intellectual and too rigid. Bly often attacks modern American poetry, though he praises a number of poets, such as Rainer Maria Rilke, Georg Trakl, Cèsar Vallejo, and Pablo Neruda, among others, who point the way toward a visionary poetry that, as Bly says of Neruda's verse, is capable of finding "the hidden connection between conscious and unconscious substances" without forsaking "the outer world" of reality.

The dominant direction of Bly's verse has been towards that kind of poetry and away from the pessimism and topical relevance of his Vietnam-era poems, where he overtly dealt with moral and political issues. Most of his poetry has been an exploration of duality and the unconscious begun in his first volume, *Silence in the Snowy Fields* (1962). In both *This Body Is Made of Camphor and Gopherwood* (1977), a book of prose poems written in a visionary style, and *This Tree Will Be Here for a Thousand Years* (1979), with its emphasis on nature, solitude, and quiet contemplation, Bly attempts to bridge the gap between the conscious and unconscious. In his introduction to *This Tree Will Be Here for a Thousand Years*, Bly claims that his intention is "to achieve a poem where the inner and outer merge without a seam."

*The Mythopoetic Men's Movement* After a divorce in 1979 that led to a personal spiritual crisis, Bly began an emotional journey that led him to the writing of *Iron*

---

## LITERARY AND HISTORICAL CONTEMPORARIES

Bly's famous contemporaries include:

**William De Witt Snodgrass** (1926–2009): Snodgrass, whose pen name is S. S. Gardons, is an American poet who won the Pulitzer Prize for Poetry in 1960.

**James Merrill** (1926–1995): Merrill was an American poet who won the Pulitzer Prize for Poetry in 1977.

**Alan Greenspan** (1926–): Greenspan is an American economist who served as the Chairman of the Federal Reserve from 1987 until 2006.

**Dario Fo** (1926–): Fo is a Nobel Prize-winning Italian playwright and director noted for his comedic and satirical works.

**Harper Lee** (1926–): Lee is an American writer best known for her novel *To Kill a Mockingbird* (1960).

---

*John: A Book About Men* (1990), the foundation of his work on the Mythopoetic Men's Movement. The character of Iron John, which is based on a story by the Brothers Grimm, is an archetype intended to help men discover their true masculinity, which Bly contends is based on virtues such as courage, strength, and wisdom, not the culturally-dominant vision of men as macho or aggressive. Bly's most recent poetry, as well as his personal appearances, have been oriented towards helping men explore their psyches and wrestle with the dark side of male domination and the exploitation of others that has characterized men's behavior for centuries.

## Works in Critical Context

Though his first collection, *Silence in Snowy Fields* (1962), enjoyed success, it was *The Light Around the Body* (1967), which won the National Book Award, that demonstrated his central importance to American poetry. Howard Nelson observed that *The Light Around the Body* is "an angry, uneven, powerful book, and clearly with it Bly made a major contribution to the growth of an American poetry which is truly political and truly poetry."

Although some reviewers have been more impressed with his poems of social consciousness, Bly's quiet poems of the unconscious are seen as more clearly in the mainstream of his poetic development. As Anthony Libby said in the *Iowa Review* (1973), "Bly is ... the mystic of evolution, the poet of 'the other world' always contained in present reality but now about to burst forth in a period of destruction and transformation." In the same journal three years later, Michael Atkinson praises Bly's ability to weave together "the personal and the public, the psychological and the political modes of experience in a carefully rendered volume that echoes much of Whitman." Charles

# COMMON HUMAN EXPERIENCE

Bly's work, though highly personal, is often infused with political concerns. Here are some other works with a similar mixture of the personal and political:

> "Easter, 1916" (1916), a poem by William Butler Yeats. Yeats offers an emotional assessment of the failed attempt of by a group of Irish nationalist to wrest control of the government from the British.
>
> "America" (1956), a poem by Allen Ginsberg. This poem, which first appeared in Ginsberg's collection *Howl and Other Poems* (1956), is a largely political work that touches on various aspects of American history, but it also deals with personal issues in Ginsberg's life within that history.
>
> *I Know Why the Caged Bird Sings* (1969), an autobiography by Maya Angelou. This memoir based on Angelou's childhood traces her personal struggles through the tumultuous times of the South in 1930s and 1940s.
>
> "Let America Be America Again" (2005), a poem by Langston Hughes. This poem speaks of the author's relationship to the American Dream and his hopes for the renewal of that dream.

Molesworth in the *Rocky Mountain Review of Language and Literature* (1975) summed up Bly's contribution in his first three major volumes: "Robert Bly has shaped contemporary poetry as forcefully and distinctly as any other poet now writing." Considerably less enthusiastic is Alan Helms in the *Partisan Review* (1977), who likens reading *Sleepers Joining Hands* to "slogging ... through a violent storm." Helms concludes that Bly has turned "from charting and chanting the geography of America's psychological and moral landscape, to mapping and mourning the battered terrain of his own fragmented sensibility. ... Bly's performance is sloppy and self-conscious, as if he could suddenly hear himself thinking, and out loud at that."

***Silence in the Snowy Fields***  Bly's first volume of poetry, *Silence in the Snowy Fields* (1962), established him as an important voice in American poetry and met with praise from some critics. David Ray in *Epoch* described Bly as "one of the leading figures today in a revolt against rhetoric—a rebellion that is a taking up of the Imagist revolution betrayed, a reassertion of need of the good sense Pound brought to poetry—but also a movement which has in it much that is perfectly new." Writing in the *Nation*, D. J. Hughes found Bly's first book impressive in "its purity of tone and precision of diction." And Stephen Stepanchev in *American Poetry Since 1945* (1965) stated: "It is evident that Robert Bly's theory and

practice cohere. His poetic voice is clear, quiet, and appealing, and it has the resonance that only powerful pressures at great depths can provide." Not all comments are laudatory, however. Thomas Gunn in the *Yale Review* noted a certain naiveté in the poems. He objected to the assumption that "the presentation of things is sufficient meaning in itself," and he criticizes Bly's romantic optimism that reveals "a world generally free of evil."

## Responses to Literature

1. Bly's recent works and activities have centered around the Mythopoetic Men's Movement. In what ways are the concerns of this movement an extension of Bly's earlier poetic concerns, and in what ways does this period represent a departure for him? Based on his earlier works, does this seem like a natural development for Bly? Why or why not?

2. Bly consciously revolts against dominant poetic traditions in America, claiming that the mainstream modes of poetry are too rigid, intellectualized, and distant from real life. Does Bly's own poetry survive his criticisms of these dominant modes? In what ways could he be accused of being too rigid, intellectualized, and distant from real life, and in what ways does he succeed in his rebellion?

3. Bly asserts that he often looks to the unconscious for poetic inspiration and uses and associative process to create a poem out of various images combined. Write a poem using this process of association and combination.

4. Bly has written both overtly political and intensely personal poems. While some critics feel that his political work is more impressive, others feel that his more personal and mystical poems represent his best work. Write an essay discussing these two strains in Bly's work, making an argument that his best work is either one or the other or those works that fuse the two.

BIBLIOGRAPHY

**Books**

Daniels, Kate and Richard Jones, eds. *On Solitude and Silence: Writings on Robert Bly*. Boston: Beacon Press, 1982.

Davis, William Virgil. *Robert Bly: The Poet and His Critics*. Columbia, S.C.: Camden House, 1994.

Friberg, Ingegard. *Moving Inward: A Study of Robert Bly's Poetry*. Goteborg: Acta University Gothoburgensis, 1977.

Lensing, George S. and Ronald Moran. *Four Poets and the Emotive Imagination: Robert Bly, James Wright, Louis Simpson, and William Stafford*. Baton Rouge, La.: Louisiana State University Press, 1976.

Malkoff, Karl. *Escape from the Self: A Study in Contemporary American Poetry and Poetics*. New York: Columbia University Press, 1977.

Nelson, Howard. *Robert Bly: An Introduction to the Poetry.* New York: Columbia University Press, 1984.

Smith, Thomas R., ed. *Walking Swiftly: Writings and Images on the Occasion of Robert Bly's 65th Birthday.* St. Paul, Minn.: Ally Press, 1992.

Stepanchev, Stephen. *American Poetry Since 1945: A Critical Survey.* New York: Harper & Row, 1965.

Sugg, Richard P. *Robert Bly.* Boston: Twayne, 1986.

**Periodicals**

Molesworth, Charles. "Thrashing in the Depths: The Poetry of Robert Bly." *Rocky Mountain Review of Language and Literature* (1975).

# ✸ Gertrude Bonnin

BORN: *1876, Yankton Reservation, South Dakota*

DIED: *1938, Washington, D.C.*

NATIONALITY: *American, Native American*

GENRE: *Fiction, nonfiction, drama*

MAJOR WORKS:

*Old Indian Legends, Retold by Zitkala-Sa* (1901)

*American Indian Stories* (1921)

*Oklahoma's Poor Rich Indians: An Orgy of Graft and Exploitation of the Five Civilized Tribes, Legalized Robbery* (1924)

## Overview

Gertrude Bonnin, who was also known as Zitkala-Sa (Red Bird), was a Native American writer best known for her collections of traditional tribal stories. Strongly independent, a talented writer and musician, and an activist for Native American rights, Bonnin was one of the most dynamic Native Americans of the first quarter of the twentieth century.

## Works in Biographical and Historical Context

***Between Two Worlds*** Bonnin was born at the Yankton Sioux Agency in South Dakota. She was the third child of Tate I Yohin Win (Reaches for the Wind), a full-blood Dakota, and a white man who left the family before Bonnin's birth. As a child at the Yankton Agency, Gertrude listened to the traditional stories about the various characters and animals that she would write about in her first book, *Old Indian Legends.* She lived according to traditional Yankton ways as much as was possible on the reservation.

In 1884 she took the opportunity to get an education usually offered only to white children by attending White's Manual Labor Institute in Wabash, Indiana. This began a lifelong struggle between traditional ways and modern social causes. Her mother distrusted mission-

Gertrude Bonnin   *Photographic History Collection, National Museum of American History, Smithsonian Institution, negative number 2004-57780*

aries' efforts to educate American Indian children and fiercely opposed her daughter's decision to go to the school. When Gertrude returned from White's Institute and announced her decision to again leave the reservation to continue her schooling, she and her mother grew apart. In 1888 and 1889 she attended the Santee Normal Training School in Nebraska but returned to White's before moving on to Indiana's Earlham College in 1895.

At Earlham she applied herself vigorously to studying music and became a respectable violinist. In early 1896 her speech "Side by Side" gained her second place in statewide oratory honors among students and was printed in the March issue of the *Word Corner,* the school paper at the Santee Agency. Bonnin also studied briefly in Boston at the New England Conservatory of Music. By the end of the century, she was teaching at the Carlisle Indian School in Pennsylvania, performing with the many Sioux musicians in its orchestra. After she decided to leave her position at Carlisle, she studied at the New England Conservatory during 1900 and 1901.

***Tales of Tradition and Assimilation*** Moving to Boston put her in touch with an intellectual and artistic community that supported her career as a writer and liberated her from the assimilationist demands of her teaching experience at Carlisle, which aimed to bring Native Americans into mainstream American culture even if it meant the loss of their traditional culture. Under the Lakota name Zitkala-Sa (Red Bird) she published her autobiographical stories in the first three monthly numbers of the *Atlantic Monthly* in 1900 and rapidly developed a literary reputation among readers of the magazine. Its publication of articles by Zitkala-Sa showed the influence of a popular movement that had begun in the 1880s and continued into the first decades of the twentieth century to reform U.S. policy toward Native Americans.

Despite the strained relations with her mother, Bonnin frequently returned home, wishing to stay in touch with her heritage. She dedicated herself to recalling and preserving her Sioux culture. In 1901 Ginn and Company, located in Boston, published fourteen of her stories as *Old Indian Legends*. In addition to her *Atlantic Monthly* stories, her essays and reflections were published in such periodicals as *Harper's Magazine*, *Everybody's Magazine*, and *Red Man and Helper*.

***Move to Utah*** Soon Bonnin's romance with the acclaim of the white eastern mainstream diminished: she wanted to live near her mother again and she needed to support herself. After trying unsuccessfully to secure a reservation teaching job, she became an issue clerk at the Standing Rock Reservation, where she met Raymond Talesfase Bonnin, also a Yankton Sioux. She and Bonnin were married in May 1902. Later that year they transferred to the Uintah and Ouray Reservation—homeland of the Northern Ute tribe—near Fort Duchesne, Utah, where they spent the next fourteen years. Their son, Raymond O. Bonnin, was born there early in 1903. Her move to Utah brought a hiatus in her writing career, as she found herself in a political and artistic backwater for nearly a decade. She was frustrated by the demands of motherhood and discouraged by conditions on the Ute reservation.

***Pan-Indian Activism*** Although Bonnin was not a founding member of the Society of American Indians (SAI), a self-help organization that began in 1911 at Ohio State University, she became one of its earliest supporters and active correspondents, rising eventually to positions on its staff. The organizers of the SAI, the most important of the pan-Indian groups, which was open to all tribes, wanted a forum that would reach beyond issues affecting individual tribes; they saw themselves as advocates for issues affecting many different Indian reservation and community populations.

One endeavor that Bonnin began while living in Utah was her support for both the Indian Service and the Community Center movement. The Indian Service was run by Native Americans, many of whom were educated in mission and trade schools on or off reservations, who worked on the reservations or in other American Indian communities performing the kind of support services work that Bonnin and her husband were doing. Bonnin encouraged nonpartisanship at the centers, but the movement failed as tribalism (loyalty to individual tribes rather than American Indians in general) increased and attempts to bring them together under the banner of pan-Indianism fell by the wayside.

***New Writings and Activities*** With Bonnin's role in the SAI, the Bonnins relocated in 1916 to Washington, D.C. There Bonnin continued to help Native Americans make adjustments to white society. Although she was a respected leader, she continued experiencing the distrust of reservation Indians because she was part of both the Native American and white communities.

As if to sum up one side of her activities, Bonnin gathered several of her writings for a new book, *American Indian Stories*, published by Hayworth Press in 1921 under the name Zitkala-Sa. Bonnin probably felt her early writings were still timely for their pro-Indian self-determination stance. Meanwhile, in 1924 the Indian Rights Association, which was an organization that Bonnin had supported for many years, published a small volume, *Oklahoma's Poor Rich Indians, an Orgy of Graft and Exploitation of the Five Civilized Tribes, Legalized Robbery* that Bonnin wrote with Charles H. Fabens and Matthew K. Sniffen. This study reported on American Indians being murdered and swindled out of the recently discovered oil-rich land on which they had been living since forced there from the southern states in the nineteenth century.

Pushed to a less important position among her former pan-Indian associates, Bonnin fought with new determination for Native American rights, encouraged by the Indian Citizenship Act of 1924. She helped found the National Council of American Indians (NCAI) in 1926 and became its first president; her husband was elected secretary-treasurer. The NCAI became Bonnin's platform for calling upon Indians to support rights issues, to encourage racial consciousness and pride, and to promote pan-Indianism. Despite Bonnin's efforts, educated American Indians during the period between the two world wars continued to be involved with tribal issues rather than national Indian concerns. Even the organization's lack of progress and the criticism confronting Bonnin from time to time did not lessen her interest in Indian rights.

Bonnin continued lecturing on Indian reform and Indian rights until her health began to fail. The NCAI dissolved when she died on January 26, 1938, in Washington, D.C. Later that year the Indian Confederation of America, a New York City-based group, honored her memory at its annual powwow. Her reputation as an effective writer and activist at the forefront of the struggle to gain respect for Native Americans has gained wider appreciation, thanks to the reprinting of her first two books and various scholarly articles analyzing her writing.

## Works in Literary Context

***White Oppression and the Celebration of Tradition*** Bonnin was one of the first Native American women among her contemporaries to publish a collection of traditional tribal stories. Her command of English is refined, and her works are characterized by vivid imagery. She does not mince words, and her stories are emotionally charged, often angry, sometimes strident in directing accusations against white oppression of American Indians. With her sense of her audience shaped largely by the Christian missionary schools she attended, her work expresses her discomfort in holding the status of a white-educated Indian, her love for Native American culture, and her concern for Indian self-determination. In particular, Bonnin notes the hypocrisy of Christians and specifically those Native Americans who have adopted Christianity in calling her traditional beliefs superstitious; from her viewpoint, Christianity is superstition. She also remarks upon the fear she felt upon hearing some specific details of Christianity, such as the notion of the devil.

Bonnin's spirit encouraged other prominent Native Americans of her time, such as Charles A. Eastman, Carlos Montezuma, and Arthur C. Parker. As a writer she shared her storytelling traditions with young readers; her essays and personal reflections voiced her anger at the suffering of native people caused by elements of white society. Her life serves as an example of the hardships faced by educated American Indians trying to live in both the red and the white worlds.

## Works in Critical Context

Bonnin's works have only recently begun to receive critical attention. Bonnin wrote to revise the dominant white assessment of tribal culture. Bonnin compares Sioux and white cultures and, through the comparison, shows the cruelty, ignorance, and superstition of the invading white nation. As Zitkala-Sa, Bonnin wrote with the clear purpose of re-creating in the imagination of her mostly white audience the cultural identity of the people she had left behind her. Her life and letters exemplify the condition of a Native American writer in transition between two cultures. However, her literary achievement never overshadowed the truth that the source of her inspiration was in the traditional oral culture of the Sioux.

Though little critical opinion of Bonnin's work was generated upon publication, this excerpt from a letter to the author written by Helen Keller seems to effectively express popular opinion of *Old Indian Legends* (1901):

> Your tales of birds, beast, tree and spirit can not but hold captive the hearts of all children. They will kindle in their young minds that eternal wonder which creates poetry and keeps life fresh and eager. I wish you and your little book of Indian tales all success.

## Responses to Literature

1. Bonnin's life and essays demonstrate the difficulties of living in two different cultural worlds. In what ways did Bonnin's native upbringing and experience make it difficult for her to inhabit the white world,

and in what way did that upbringing benefit her attempts to live in two worlds at once?

2. Bonnin was an advocate for the pan-Indian cause, which attempted to transcend tribal differences to create a national American Indian movement. What obstacles were faced by advocates of the pan-Indian cause, and in what ways did Bonnin attempt to deal with these obstacles to bridge tribal differences?

3. Many of Bonnin's works are based on traditional stories that she heard from her family. Write a story based on one of the tales that you have been told by someone in your family. This need not be a myth or legend, but it should be something that connects your present to your past through a family narrative.

4. Bonnin's works often show anger at the white oppression of Native Americans. Write an argumentative essay responding to Bonnin's charges, either by extending her claims or by attempting to refute them.

BIBLIOGRAPHY

**Books**

Dockstader, Frederick J. *Great North American Indians.* New York: Van NostrandReinhold, 1977.

James, Edward T., ed. *Notable American Women, 1607–1950.* Cambridge, Mass.: Belknap Press, 1971.

Medicine, Beatrice. *The Hidden Half: Studies of Plains Indian Women.* Lanham, Md.: University Press of America, 1983.

Rappaport, Doreen. *The Flight of Red Bird: The Life of Zitkala-Sa.* New York: Dial Books, 1997.

Ruoff, A. LaVonne Brown. *American Indian Literatures: An Introduction, Bibliographic Review, and Selected Bibliography.* New York: Modern Language Association, 1990.

Welch, Deborah. *American Indian Leader: The Story of Gertrude Bonnin.* PhD diss., University of Wyoming, 1985.

Wiget, Andrew, ed. *Critical Essays on American Indian Literature.* Boston: G. K. Hall, 1985.

**Periodicals**

Cutter, Martha J. "Zitkala-Sa's Autobiographical Writings: The Problems of a Canonical Search for Language and Identity." *MELUS* (Spring 1994).

Fisher, Dexter. "Zitkala-Sa: The Evolution of a Writer." *American Indian Quarterly* (August 1977).

Susag, Dorothea M. "Zitkala-Sa (Gertrude Simmons Bonnin): A Power(full) Literary Voice." *Studies in American Indian Literatures* (Winter 1993).

Willard, William. "Zitkala-Sa, A Woman Who Would Be Heard." *Wicazo Sa Review* (1985).

**Web sites**

University of Pennsylvania Digital Library. *A Celebration of Women Writers: American Indian Stories.* Edited by Mary Mark Ockerbloom. Retrieved September 15, 2008, from http://digital.library.upenn.edu/women/zitkala-sa/stories/stories.html.

# ✸ Arna Bontemps

BORN: *1902, Alexandria, Louisiana*

DIED: *1973, Nashville, Tennessee*

NATIONALITY: *American, African American*

GENRE: *Fiction, poetry*

MAJOR WORKS:

*Black Thunder* (1936)
*The Story of the Negro* (1948)
*Young Booker: Booker T. Washington's Early Days* (1972)

## Overview

Poet, critic, playwright, novelist, historian, educator, librarian, and writer of children's books, Arna Bontemps was also a voracious reader, devoted family man, pioneering Afro-American literary figure, and, above all, a champion of freedom for all people and of dignity for the individual. A

Arna Bontemps    *Bontemps, Arna, 1966, photograph. AP Images.*

writer who began to achieve prominence in the late days of the Harlem Renaissance, the multifaceted Bontemps exercised his productive genius into the 1970s, touching audiences with a wide range of works that draw from his experience of black American culture and from his own life.

## Works in Biographical and Historical Context

*A "Miseducation"* Arnaud Wendell Bontemps was born in Alexandria, Louisiana, on October 13, 1902. His parents were of Creole stock, the source for the dialect Bontemps used in some of his early writing and that he liked to employ in his correspondence with Langston Hughes. As a result of several racially motivated incidents, including one in which a group of white men threatened to beat him up, Bontemps's father moved his family to Los Angeles, California, when Arna was three. When Bontemps was twelve, his mother died, but not before she had instilled in her son a love for books. A schoolteacher until the time of her marriage, she introduced young Arna to a world beyond the skilled labor that dominated his father's life.

The older of two children, Bontemps would experience recurring conflict with his father, who wanted him to continue the brick masonry trade into a fourth generation of the family line. Bontemps's father and his Uncle Buddy, his grandmother's younger brother who had moved to California to live with the family, would prove to be significant influences upon the young Arna after his mother's death. Bontemps's father was negative toward his writing; however, Uncle Buddy exercised a most wholesome influence upon his personal and literary development. Through Buddy, Bontemps was able to embrace the folk heritage that would form the basis for many of his works, for he loved dialect stories, preacher stories, and ghost stories.

As an adolescent, Bontemps helped to support himself after his mother's death by working as a newsboy and a gardener. Between 1917 and 1920, his father sent him to San Fernando Academy, a white boarding school, with the admonition not to "go up there acting colored," which was a frequent, embarrassing memory for Bontemps. He viewed his father's decision and the subject matter as efforts to make him forget his blackness, and he suspected—as he confirmed during his college years—that he was being "miseducated." Bontemps graduated from Pacific Union College in 1923, the year before he launched his literary career with the publication of his poem "Hope" in *Crisis*, a journal that was instrumental in advancing the careers of most of the young writers associated with the Harlem Renaissance. Although Bontemps had plans to complete a Ph.D. degree in English, the Depression years, family responsibilities, and the demands of his writing contracts with publishing houses, coupled with the rigors of fulltime employment, prevented him from following that course.

*A Renaissance in Harlem* In addition to making his literary debut in 1924, Bontemps moved from Cal-

ifornia to New York to accept a teaching job at the Harlem Academy, where he taught until 1931, the year that also saw the publication of his first book, *God Sends Sunday*. At the time, the Harlem district was experiencing a flowering of art and culture that came to be known as the Harlem Renaissance. This came hand in hand with the expansion of middleclass black communities in the northern part of the country, especially in New York City. This led to the development of music, literature, dance, and art that arose from distinctly African American roots. Notable figures of the Harlem Renaissance include activist W. E. B. Du Bois, author Zora Neale Hurston, musician Duke Ellington, and singer Billie Holiday. The artistic achievements of members of the Harlem Renaissance extended far beyond their own neighborhood, shaping the development of literature and music in mainstream American culture throughout much of the twentieth century.

In 1926 and again in 1927, Bontemps won *Opportunity* magazine's Alexander Pushkin Poetry Prize. Although he did not live in Harlem for long, Bontemps met, worked with, influenced, and was influenced by several of the important figures of the Harlem Renaissance, including Langston Hughes, Jean Toomer, Claude McKay, James Weldon Johnson, and Countee Cullen.

*Reaching Out to the Children* Bontemps moved from Harlem Academy to Huntsville, Alabama, in 1931 to teach at Oakwood Junior College, where he was on the faculty until 1934. Bontemps's situation in Alabama epitomized his career: he was always short of funds and rarely found a comfortable place to work. In Huntsville, he and his family lived through almost insufferable summer heat and damp and piercing winter cold. While in Huntsville, Bontemps turned his attention to the writing of children's books, partly out of a belief that the younger audience was more reachable. His first juvenile book, *Popo and Fifina* (1932), a story of two black children in Haiti, was written in collaboration with Langston Hughes. Over the next forty years, Bontemps continued writing for children and edited more than fifteen works for children and adolescent readers.

A new teaching assignment took Bontemps from Huntsville to Chicago and Shiloh Academy, where he taught from 1935 until 1937. He then went to work for the Illinois Writer's Project, a division of the Works Progress Administration. During his Chicago years, Bontemps published *Black Thunder* (1936), his most celebrated novel, a historical novel dealing with the theme of revolt through the recounting of a slave narrative.

*Librarian, Teacher, Scholar* Bontemps ended his early teaching endeavors in 1938 to pursue more actively his possibilities as a writer. In 1943, upon the completion of his masters degree in library science, Bontemps became librarian at Fisk University in Nashville, Tennessee, a post he would hold continuously until 1965, after which time he would return intermittently to the school. As head librarian at Fisk, Bontemps enlarged the black collection by obtaining the papers of such Harlem Renaissance

# LITERARY AND HISTORICAL CONTEMPORARIES

Bontemps's famous contemporaries include:

**Langston Hughes** (1902–1967): Hughes was an African American writer best known for his literary influence during the Harlem Renaissance.

**John Steinbeck** (1902–1968): Steinbeck was an American writer known for works such as *The Grapes of Wrath* (1939) and *Of Mice and Men* (1937). He was granted the Nobel Prize in Literature in 1962.

**Odgen Nash** (1902–1971): Nash was an American poet best known for his light verse and humorous poetry.

**Karl Popper** (1902–1994): Popper was an Austrian and British philosopher widely considered one of the most influential philosophers of science during the twentieth century.

**Leni Riefenstahl** (1902–2003): Riefenstahl was a German dancer, actress, and film director known for her pioneering cinematic techniques, but controversial because of the proganda films she made for the Nazi party during the 1930s.

figures as Langston Hughes, Jean Toomer, James Weldon Johnson, Charles S. Johnson, and Countee Cullen.

Perhaps Bontemps's most lasting contribution to Afro-American literary history is the number of scholarly anthologies he compiled and edited during these years, alone and in collaboration with Hughes. These anthologies primarily appeal to secondary school students and college undergraduates, a fact that has kept them in use since they were first issued.

In 1964, Bontemps retired from his job at Fisk. In 1966, he taught courses in black history and black literature at the University of Illinois, Chicago Circle, and in 1969, he accepted a position at Yale as lecturer and curator of the James Weldon Johnson Collection, where he remained through the 1971 school term. Returning afterwards to Nashville, he began writing his autobiography, a work he never finished. He died of a heart attack in Nashville, Tennessee, on June 4, 1973.

## Works in Literary Context

A distinguished figure in the history of American literature, Bontemps published his first work during the Harlem Renaissance. His literary career spanned a fifty-year period, and his versatility is seen in his creation of books of several genres directed to all age levels. A noted educator and librarian, Bontemps progressed from high school teacher and principal to librarian at Fisk University, professor of English at the University of Illinois, and curator of the James Weldon Johnson collection at Yale University.

*Documenting the Black Experience* Bontemps's histories of the black experience, his biographies of notable black Americans, his novels and short stories, his children's fiction, his anthologies of works by black writers, and particularly his poetry explore the relationship between the past and present and its bearing on the inheritors of the black experience. In Bontemps's writings, the assassination of Martin Luther King, Jr. in 1968 is presented as a repetition of the squelching of nineteenth-century slave uprisings. The Harlem of the 1920s echoes the primitivism and freedom of African jungles. All is of a piece. Bontemps's importance as literary artist and historian hinges upon his efforts to show black Americans that their own past is rich and various, and that their yearning for freedom, both in the past and present, is an essential common bond grounded in a proud heritage. Yet, to the white reader as well, Bontemps is an important voice—both as an American writer and as a powerful spokesman for a humanistic society. His careers as literary artist, historian, editor, critic, and as head librarian and public-relations director at Fisk University were all directed toward the goal of establishing a social and intellectual environment in which the Afro-American heritage, literature, and sense of self could be nurtured.

Bontemps was one of the first black writers for children to replace stereotyping with an accurate portrayal of black life. He also pioneered the use of realistic black speech in children's books. Seeking to instill cultural esteem in young readers, he wrote biographies of notable black men and women, a critically praised black history, realistic fiction, and humorous tall tales. Whether writing for adults or children, Bontemps conveyed optimism and pride in his culture.

## Works in Critical Context

Bontemps was the winner of numerous prizes and awards during his long and diverse writing career, and he was generally viewed positively by critics and reviewers. Virtually unquestioned is his contribution to African-American studies, both because of his writing and through his efforts as a collector and anthologist. As critic Arthur P. Davis asserts, Bontemps "kept flowing that trickle of interest in Negro American literature—that trickle which is now a torrent."

*God Sends Sunday* Bontemps's first novel, *God Sends Sunday* (1931), was recognized by critics for its authentic rendering of the "Negro language," an emotion-charged economy of speech peculiar to Louisiana Creoles that imparted uniqueness to Bontemps's fiction. Not all of the reviews of *God Sends Sunday* were positive, however; in a 1931 *Crisis* article, W. E. B. Du Bois condemned the novel for its portrayal of the less complimentary side of life in black America, calling the book "a profound disappointment." A reviewer for the *Boston Transcript* asserted that the book "is less narrative than descriptive and has no great significance," but he commented that Bontemps deserved "to be encouraged." Still, most critics, led by the reviewer for *Books*, hailed Bontemps as "one of the most important writers of his race."

***Black Thunder*** *Black Thunder* (1936) is widely considered to be the best and most popular of Bontemps's novels. When it appeared, Richard Wright praised it as "the only novel dealing forthrightly with the historical and revolutionary traditions of the Negro people." A. B. Spingarn called it "the best historical novel written by an American Negro," while Hugh M. Gloster, in *Negro Voices in American Fiction* (1948), notes positively that it "is written with restraint and detachment." Dorothy Weil, in an essay for *Southern Folklore Quarterly*, refers to the book as "a superior piece of work." Arthur P. Davis, in *From the Dark Tower: Afro-American Writers 1900–1960* (1974), states that "it is perhaps the author's outstanding publication."

## Responses to Literature

1. Bontemps wrote biographies of notable African Americans in an attempt to instill cultural pride in young African American readers. What features of his biographies help him succeed in this attempt, and in what ways do his other writings perform a similar function?

2. Bontemps spent much of his early career working as a teacher while attempting to write at the same time. In what ways can the concerns of a teacher be seen in both his early and his later writings? How much influence did his teaching experience seem to exert over his literary style and choice of topics for his books?

3. Bontemps was noted for his use of authentic speech patterns in his characters' dialogue. Write a story that features characters speaking in a form of slang or dialect with which you are familiar. Attempt to render these speech patterns as accurately as possible.

4. Bontemps's father opposed his son's attempts to write literature and wanted him instead to follow him into the family trade of masonry. Write a story that features a young character engaged in a conflict of this sort; it can be based on personal experience, or drawn completely from your own imagination.

BIBLIOGRAPHY

**Books**

"Arna Bontemps (1902–1973)." *Contemporary Literary Criticism*. Edited by Sharon R. Gunton. Vol. 18. Detroit: Gale Research, 1981, pp. 62–66.

Barksdale, Richard and Keneth Kinnamon, eds. *Black Writers of America*. New York: Macmillan, 1972.

Bone, Robert A. *The Negro Novel in America*. New Haven, Conn.: Yale University Press, 1958.

Brown, Sterling. *The Negro in American Fiction*. Washington, D.C.: The Associates in Negro Folk Education, 1937.

## COMMON HUMAN EXPERIENCE

Bontemps was widely known for his histories of the black experience, particularly his biographies of notable African Americans. Here are some other important works on the African-American experience:

*Roots: The Saga of an American Family* (1976), a novel by Alex Haley. This Pulitzer Prize-winning novel was adapted into a ground-breaking television miniseries that traced the history of an African-American family from the capture of a slave in Africa through the mid-twentieth century.

*The Autobiography of Malcolm X* (1965), an autobiography documented by Alex Haley. This book traces the life of Malcolm X from his boyhood through his assassination, as told to the author by Malcolm himself.

*Black Boy* (1945), an autobiography by Richard Wright. This book depicts the difficulty of race relations in the South as experienced by a prominent African-American novelist during his childhood.

Fleming, Robert E. *James Weldon Johnson and Arna Wendell Bontemps: A Reference Guide*. Boston: G. K. Hall, 1978.

Gloster, Hugh M. *Negro Voices in American Fiction*. Chapel Hill: University of North Carolina Press, 1948.

Jones, Kirkland C. *Renaissance Man from Louisiana: A Biography of Arna Wendell Bontemps*. Westport, Conn.: Greenwood Press, 1992.

Nichols, Charles, ed. *Arna Bontemps-Langston Hughes Letters, 1925–1967*. New York: Dodd, Mead, 1980.

Page, James A. *Selected Black American Authors: An Illustrated Bio-Bibliography*. Boston: G. K. Hall, 1977.

Whitlow, Roger. *Black American Literature: A Critical History*. Totowa, N.J.: Littlefield, Adams, 1974.

Young, James D. *Black Writers in the Thirties*. Baton Rouge: Louisiana State University Press, 1973.

# ✸ T. Coraghessan Boyle

BORN: *1948, Peekskill, New York*

NATIONALITY: *American*

GENRE: *Fiction*

MAJOR WORKS:

*The Descent of Man* (1975)

*World's End* (1987)

*The Road to Wellville* (1992)

*The Tortilla Curtain* (1995)

T. Coraghessan Boyle    *Boyle, T. Coraghessan, photograph. AP Images.*

## Overview

Much of the appeal of T. Coraghessan Boyle's novels and stories is in his creation of outrageous characters, bizarre situations, and deliberately inflated comparisons. His fiction is widely praised for its black comedy, incongruous mixture of the mundane and the surreal, wildly inventive and intricate plots, manic energy, and dazzling wordplay.

## Works in Biographical and Historical Context

*"A Pretty Good Gig"*  Born Thomas John Boyle on December 2, 1948, in Peekskill, New York, the grandson of Irish immigrants, Boyle has suggested that the mad, language-obsessed part of him derives from his Irish ancestry. At seventeen he changed his middle name to Coraghessan (pronounced "kuh-RAGG-issun"), a name from his mother's side of the family. His father, a school bus driver, and his mother, a secretary, both died of complications from alcoholism before Boyle was thirty. Although his family did not have much money, Boyle was encouraged to obtain a good education. By his own report his youth was spent "hanging out" and taking a lot of drugs.

Boyle began writing in college with an absurdist one-act play about a young boy eaten by an alligator—except

for his foot, to which his family builds a shrine in the living room. When the professor and class laughed and applauded, Boyle concluded writing was "a pretty good gig." After graduating from the State University of New York at Potsdam in 1968, Boyle taught high-school English for several years to keep from being drafted into the Vietnam War. In the fall of 1972, he published "The OD & Hepatitis RR or Bust" in *The North American Review* and, primarily on the basis of that story, was admitted into the University of Iowa Workshop.

Once at the University of Iowa he began taking literature courses as well as creative-writing courses, earning his M.F.A. in 1974. He became a model student; in his words, "I grew up. Instead of cutting classes, I sat in the front row and took notes." This transformation occurred because he felt he had found what he was meant to do: for all his irreverence and outrageousness, Boyle is absolutely serious about his writing. He completed his Ph.D. in nineteenth-and early-twentieth-century British literature in 1977 but opted for a creative dissertation; the collection of short stories Boyle wrote for his dissertation was later revised and published as *Descent of Man* (1979), a collection that earned Boyle an immediate reputation for his off-beat humor and quirky characters.

*An Active and Topical Writer*  Since 1977 Boyle has been a professor at the University of Southern California, where he founded a creative writing program. He has also been a very active writer since his first publication in 1979, producing eleven novels and eight short-story collections, many of which have taken as themes some of the dominant trends or important issues of the day. Boyle lampooned the fitness craze of the 1980s in *The Road to Wellville* (1993) and satirized extremist environmental activists in *A Friend of the Earth* (2000). He tackled the question of illegal immigration, a hot topic during the 1980s, in both *East is East* (1990) and *The Tortilla Curtain* (1995). More recently, in *Talk Talk* (2006), he explored the consequences of identity theft, a major concern of the Information Age.

## Works in Literary Context

A widely praised American comic short story writer and novelist, Boyle has been compared to such varied authors as Kingsley Amis, Evelyn Waugh, Thomas Berger, Tom Robbins, Roy Blount, Thomas Pynchon, John Barth and Mark Twain. What distinguishes Boyle from other contemporary American authors, writes Michael Adams in the *Dictionary of Literary Biography Yearbook* 1986, is that no others "write about the diverse subjects he does in the way he does." Chiefly known for his irreverent and satiric humor, Boyle is often described as an energetic, clever writer who is not afraid to take risks in plot and style.

*Surrealism Set in History*  Boyle's novels are known for their surrealistic and unexpected plot twists, the use of violence and sexuality, and the inability of men and women to communicate. Many of his novels involve historical events and situations placed in history, though Boyle rarely attempts to make the reader forget he is reading a novel rather than experiencing a true reflection of history.

His first novel, *Water Music* (1981)—which intertwines the stories of a fictional rogue and Mungo Park, a Scottish explorer who led expeditions to Africa in 1795 and 1805—relies on melodramatic devices, including stupendous cliffhangers, complicated coincidences, and even miraculous resurrections, all reminiscent of similar delights in the works of eighteenth-and nineteenth-century novelists from Henry Fielding to Dickens. In an unapologetic "Apologia" Boyle announces that he has been deliberately anachronistic, inventing language and terminology and reshaping historical facts "with full and clear conscience." In addition to beginning Boyle's trend of placing novels in historical context, *Water Music* offers what became hallmarks of Boyle's works, from deliciously gory descriptions to verbal acrobatics, delivered in a mixture of polysyllabic diction and current colloquialisms.

*World's End* (1987), Boyle's most ambitious and complicated novel, traces the intertwined fates of three families living in Peterskill, a Hudson Valley community similar to Boyle's own hometown, Peekskill, New York. With similar patterns of action and emotions occurring in both the seventeenth and twentieth centuries, the novel depicts the conflicts between the families and their descendants. Boyle's 2003 novel, *Drop City*, brings together in 1970 two exemplars of the American spirit—California hippie communards and tough individualist loners trying to live off the land in Alaska. Neither completely satirical nor nostalgic, *Drop City* is a convincing evocation of a crucial period of American history and of perennial American types of dreamers.

*Satirizing Popular Culture* Boyle also uses his historical settings to engage in satire that lampoons various aspects of modern popular culture. For instance, Boyle uses *The Road to Wellville* (1993), set in 1907 and 1908, as a vehicle for an oblique attack on some dominant modern idiocies such as ridiculous self-improvement plans and quack health schemes. The novel takes place in Battle Creek, Michigan, at the Battle Creek Sanitarium, where the director, Dr. John Harvey Kellogg, a believer in colonic irrigation, vegetarian biologic living, and sexual abstinence, employs "cures" that feature a hideous diet of nut butters, grapes, milk, and mysterious unpleasant substances, plus multiple daily enemas and special baths during which an electric current moves through a patient's body while his hands and feet are placed in water.

Boyle's sixth novel, *The Tortilla Curtain* (1995), depicts the intersecting lives of two couples living in Topanga Canyon, Los Angeles: Delaney Mossbacher, a liberal nature writer and self-styled pilgrim, and his wife, Kyra, a hotshot real estate saleswoman; and Candido Rincon, an undocumented Mexican pursuing the Amer-

## LITERARY AND HISTORICAL CONTEMPORARIES

Boyle's famous contemporaries include:

**Al Gore** (1948–): Gore is the former vice president of the United States who is also widely known for his environmental activism and warnings about climate change. He was a recipient of the Nobel Peace Prize in 2007 as well as an Academy Award winner in the same year for his work on the documentary *An Inconvenient Truth* (2006).

**James Ellroy** (1948–): Ellroy is an American writer best known for his crime stories and novels.

**Mikhail Baryshnikov** (1948–): Baryshnikov is a Russian dancer widely considered one of the greatest ballet dancers of the twentieth century.

**Rick James** (1948–2004): James was an American musician who gained popularity in the 1970s and 1980s with his punk-funk style.

**David Sedaris** (1956–): Sedaris is a New York-born humorist known for his largely autobiographical essays and contributions to the radio program *This American Life*.

ican dream of a better life while living literally hand to mouth in the canyon with his young, pregnant wife, America. The Rincons live a life of hunger, intimidation, and victimization while the Mossbachers' primary social concerns are recycling and nature preservation.

## Works in Critical Context

Throughout his career, Boyle has received high praise for his energetic writing, imaginative plots, and accurate recreation of accents and speech patterns. At the same time, some critics contend his works are superficial and lack depth. In *The New York Times Book Review*, Michiko Kakutani wrote that Boyle "has emerged as one of the most inventive and verbally exuberant writers of his generation." Likewise, Jay Tolson wrote in the *Washington Post Book World* that Boyle "pulls his most implausible inventions with wit, a perfect sense of timing, and his considerable linguistic gifts. He treasures the apt word ... and his ear for cockney, brogue, pidgin English and other dialects is sure." Eva Hoffman wrote in the *New York Times* that Boyle failed to develop the characters in *Budding Prospects* and wrote as if he were "dancing on the edges of language, afraid that if he slowed down for a minute, he might fall into a vacuum." Tolson pointed to a tiresome theme that recurs in Boyle's works: "the point [Boyle] relentlessly presses is that man is a foolish creature and that everything ends with death, though some survive longer than others."

## COMMON HUMAN EXPERIENCE

Boyle's novels and stories are characterized by a clever style of humor that is often satirical and even mocking. Here are some other novels with a similar style:

*Giles Goat-Boy* (1966), a novel by John Barth. This novel satirizes campus culture in America during the early-1960s and presents a clever allegory about the politics of the time.

*The Information* (1995), a novel by Martin Amis. This novel about a literary rivalry satirizes the present-day concerns of writers and the kinds of lives they lead.

*Survivor* (1999), a novel by Chuck Palahniuk. This novel satirizes commercial culture through the story of a former religious cult member who is turned into a media star by a public-relations company.

Despite the criticism, however, most of Boyle's reviewers acknowledge that the author is a skillful humorist. Hoffman wrote, "Boyle possesses a rare and redeeming virtue—he can be consistently, effortlessly, intelligently funny." Boyle has been hailed as one of the most imaginative contemporary American novelists, and his work enjoys wide popularity. Even his harshest critics, such as Kakutani, concede that "When it comes to pitch-black humor, Grand Guignol slapstick and linguistic acrobatics, T. Coraghessan Boyle is a master of his domain."

**Water Music** Many of Boyle's works have been received with a mixture of praise and criticism. Reviews of Boyle's first novel, *Water Music* (1981), set this pattern. In the *Library Journal*, Grove Kroger commented that "Boyle's invention flags at the end, and the explorer himself remains oddly insubstantial" but he also claimed that Ned Rise was "one of contemporary fiction's most challenging creations" as a character. Alan Friedman in *The New York Times Book Review* asserted, "Hardly ever does the novel allow the reader to enter the world it creates. When ... characters suffer (and, poor dears, how they suffer!) their sufferings seem for the most part contrived to elicit crocodile tears."

**World's End** *World's End* (1987), Boyle's most ambitious and complicated novel, won the PEN/Faulkner Award for fiction in 1988. Much of the response to *World's End* was positive; for example, in *The New York Times Book Review*, Benjamin DeMott praised the novel for providing "space for moral and emotional as well as esthetic reality, producing a narrative in which passion, need and belief breathe with striking force and freedom." Not all of the critical reception to *World's End* was positive, however. In a review in *The New York Times*,

Michiko Kakutani complained that "there's something mechanical and cumbersome about Mr. Boyle's orchestration of time past and time present" and that the proliferation of characters is such "that we never really get a chance to know them as recognizable individuals."

### Responses to Literature

1. Boyle has been criticized for his failure to create fully developed, multi-dimensional characters. Does this seem like a fair charge? In what ways are Boyle's characters lacking? Does this approach to character serve a beneficial purpose in his works, or is this a literary failing on Boyle's part?

2. Boyle is often praised for his black comedy. What purposes are served by this type of comedy, as Boyle employs it, and what messages about life and the human condition are conveyed through his dark humor? Does this type of humor detract from the messages that Boyle is trying to convey? Why or why not?

3. Boyle is noted for creating stories that place outrageous characters in bizarre situations. Write a story modeled on Boyle's style that involves an unusual situation inhabited by extreme characters.

4. Some critics claim that Boyle's works are superficial and do not deserve to be considered along with the more meaningful literature being produced by his contemporaries. Write an argumentative essay either agreeing or disagreeing with this assessment. Be sure to cite specific stories or novels to support your claims.

BIBLIOGRAPHY

**Books**

Donadieu, Marc V. *American picaresque the early novels of T. Coraghessan Boyle*. Dissertation: University of Louisiana at Lafayette, 2000.

**Periodicals**

D'Haen, Theo. "The Return of History and the Minorization of New York: T. Coraghessan Boyle and Richard Russo." *Revue Française d'Etudes Americaines* (1994): 393–403.

Friend, Tad. "Rolling Boyle." *New York Times Magazine* (December 9, 1990): 50–68.

Vaid, Krishna Baldev. "Franz Kafka Writes to T. Coraghessan Boyle." *Michigan Quarterly Review* (Summer 1996): 533–547.

**Web sites**

*All About T. Coraghessan Boyle*. Accessed September 5, 2008, from http://www.tcboyle.net/sandye.html. Last updated on May 14, 2001.

# ✸ Ray Bradbury

BORN: *1920, Waukegan, Illinois*

NATIONALITY: *American*

GENRE: *Fiction*

MAJOR WORKS:

*The Martian Chronicles* (1950)

*The Illustrated Man* (1951)

*Fahrenheit 451* (1953)

*Dandellion Wine* (1957)

*Something Wicked This Way Comes* (1962)

## Overview

An important figure in the development of science fiction, Ray Bradbury was among the first authors to combine the concepts of science fiction with a sophisticated prose style. In a career that has spanned more than forty years, Bradbury has written fantasies, crime and mystery stories, supernatural tales, and mainstream literature as well as science fiction.

## Works in Biographical and Historical Context

***Childhood Fears Make Lasting Impression*** Bradbury was born on August 22, 1920, and spent most of his childhood in Waukegan, Illinois, a small community on the western shore of Lake Michigan, which was to become the "Green Town" of many later stories. Early in life Bradbury was introduced to the world of fantasy and the supernatural. Many Bradbury stories, including several in his collection *Dark Carnival* (1947), can be traced back to specific events in his childhood. Even his earliest memories would later become raw material for his

Ray Bradbury   *Bradbury, Ray, photograph. The Library of Congress.*

fiction. By the time he was six, he had seen several horror movies, notably *The Cat and the Canary* (1927) and Lon Chaney's *The Hunchback of Notre Dame* (1923) and *The Phantom of the Opera* (1925), and had developed a morbid fear of the dark. His 1955 children's book, *Switch on the Night*, was based on these memories and designed to allay the fear of darkness for his own children.

His Aunt Neva, whose name was given to a character in a few stories and who received the dedication of the 1953 collection *The Golden Apples of the Sun*, introduced him to fairy tales and to the Oz books of L. Frank Baum, whom Bradbury later counted among his chief influences. Bradbury's father, Leonard Spaulding Bradbury, worked as a lineman for the Waukegan Bureau of Power and Light. Not only did "Leonard Spaulding" later become a Bradbury pseudonym, but even his father's mundane occupation was transformed into romance in the 1948 story "Powerhouse."

Twice during his childhood, in 1926–1927 and again in 1932–1933, Bradbury lived with his family in Arizona, where his father hoped to find work after being laid off during the Great Depression. It is possible that these early impressions of the desert affected his later visions of Mars and perhaps his sensitive views of Mexican Americans as well. But both moves were abortive, and in both cases the family returned to Waukegan. The Bradburys did not move west permanently until their 1934 move to Los Angeles. Bradbury dates his career choice from about this time: at the age of fifteen, he began submitting short stories to major national magazines, hoping ultimately for a sale to the *Saturday Evening Post* but receiving no acceptance. Encouraged by sympathetic high school literature teachers, however, he became active in his school's drama classes and wrote for school publications.

In 1937 Bradbury's first real connection with the world of science fiction began when he joined the Los Angeles Science Fiction League. Here, he met Henry Kuttner, a budding professional writer whose first story was published that same year and who would become something of a mentor to the younger writer. The league's fanzine, *Imagination!*, printed Bradbury's first published short story, "Hollerbochen's Dilemma," in 1938. His increasing involvement as a science-fiction fan led him, in 1939, to begin his own mimeographed publication, *Futuria Fantasia*. That same year he attended the World Science Fiction convention in New York and visited the New York World's Fair.

### Writing for Pulp Magazines

At the age of twenty, Bradbury was still living with his family and selling newspapers for income, but by this time a career as a writer seemed a real possibility. He began his career during the 1940s as a writer for such pulp magazines as *Black Mask*, *Amazing Stories*, and *Weird Tales*. The last-named magazine served to showcase the works of such fantasy writers as H. P. Lovecraft, Clark Ashton Smith, and August Derleth. Derleth, who founded Arkham House, a publishing company specializing in fantasy literature, accepted one of Bradbury's stories for *Who Knocks?* an anthology published by his firm.

By 1944 Bradbury, exempt from the World War II draft because of his poor vision, seemed aware that style was his strong point and he became more conscious of developing it. His career clearly on the upswing, Bradbury was so confident of his own future output that on the eve of his wedding to Marguerite McClure in 1947, he claims, he burned more than a million words of his earlier writing that he felt did not meet his current standards.

### An Established Reputation

Bradbury's career seemed to be moving rapidly in several directions at once. His first book, *Dark Carnival*, published by Arkham House in 1947, would bolster his reputation as a writer of weird fiction, but that was a kind of fiction that Bradbury was coming to write less and less frequently. From *Weird Tales* he had moved into publishing in *American Mercury*, *Mademoiselle*, *Charm*, *Harper's*, and the *New Yorker*, and his fiction was beginning to appear with some regularity in such mainstream collections as *The Best American Short Stories* and *Prize Stories: O. Henry Awards*.

The publication of *The Martian Chronicles* (1950) established Bradbury's reputation as an author of sophisticated science fiction, though he himself contended that the work was fantasy, since his vision of Mars was not intended to be plausible or realistic. Another significant collection of short stories, *The Illustrated Man* (1951), appeared the following year. Even though many of his stories were fantasy and science fiction, Bradbury was gaining a reputation as a sensitive stylist who tackled the contemporary social issues of racism and illegal immigration of Mexicans.

In 1953 Bradbury published his first novel, *Fahrenheit 451*. This book had been germinating as early as 1947 when Bradbury wrote a short story, "Bright Phoenix," about a small town whose residents foil government book burnings by each memorizing one of the censored texts. In 1951 this basic premise involving government book burners was expanded to novella length as "The Fireman," which appeared in the February issue of *Galaxy*. Bradbury doubled "The Fireman" to become *Fahrenheit 451*.

Although *Fahrenheit 451* can be viewed as a passionate attack on censorship and the McCarthyism of the early 1950s, which Bradbury and others had likened to Nazi oppression and book burning, the novel can also be seen as an attack on the growing power of 1950s mass culture, particularly television, whose dynamics disallow complexity of thought and that consistently falls prey to the demands of special interest groups. Above all, the book-burning firemen of the novel are concerned that culture be made inoffensive, unthreatening, and universally accessible, all of which were concerns about the effects of television expressed by early critics of that new medium.

*Focusing on Drama* By the mid 1960s, Bradbury was devoting much of his time to drama. *The World of Ray Bradbury* opened on the stages in Los Angeles in 1964 and in New York in 1965, and *The Wonderful Ice Cream Suit* opened as a musical in 1965. During the 1970s, Bradbury continued to concentrate on drama and poetry, producing relatively little new fiction. His 1976 collection *Long after Midnight* drew heavily on his earlier stories. Its chief value may lie in the focus it places on a kind of Bradbury story that had long been characteristic but infrequently collected: the story that depicts an epiphanic discovery of love between two people.

Though Bradbury has written little science fiction for the past four decades, his is still the name that most often comes to mind when the genre is mentioned among non-aficionado readers, and he is one of a handful of writers anywhere who can command huge printings and sales for a volume of short stories.

## Works in Literary Context

Often described as economical yet poetic, Bradbury's fiction conveys a vivid sense of place in which everyday events are transformed into unusual, sometimes sinister situations. In all of his work, he emphasizes basic human values and cautions against unthinking acceptance of technological progress. His persistent optimism, evident even in his darkest work, has led some critics to label him sentimental or naive. Bradbury, however, perceives life, even at its most mundane, with a childlike wonder and awe that charges his work with a fervent affirmation of humanity.

*Mirroring American Life* Although labeled a science-fiction writer, Bradbury has also written many realistic tales, including sympathetic stories about Mexicans, Irishmen, and Chicanos. Though his subject matter is diverse, a native regionalism characterizes his work. Bradbury's Mars bears a similarity to the American Midwest, and behind Los Angeles and Dublin and all towns on Bradbury's map lies the archetypal village: "Green Town, Illinois." Bradbury shows affinities, in lighter moments, with Steinbeck's comedies of folk tenacity and in his darker moods (and these are more numerous), with the Anderson of *Winesburg, Ohio*. Scratch the surface in Bradbury and eminently native patterns emerge. The real Bradbury is a portraitist, less the chronicler of Mars than of twisted, small-town American lives.

Bradbury was often criticized for this trait by science-fiction readers, but he has repeatedly maintained that his Mars is not a projection of the future but rather a mirror of American life. Indeed the subject matter of that book is more history than science, and what technology the book features is largely technology in the service of exploring new frontiers. Bradbury does not dwell on making his machines believable any more than he dwells on making his Mars astronomically accurate; his real concerns appeared to be conducting an exploration of

some of the key issues in American life—capitalism, technology, the family, the role of imagination—in a context free of historical or political constraints.

*A Writer of Tales* Bradbury has written in all genres—stories, novels, plays, poetry—but his real mode is short fiction. His plays, like *Pillar of Fire* (1975), are all adaptations of earlier stories, and his longer prose works are all, in some way or another, derivatives of the tale. The short novel *Fahrenheit 451* expands upon an earlier story, "The Fireman," which itself was an expanded version of a previous story, "Bright Phoenix." Both *The Martian Chronicles* and *Dandelion Wine* (1957) are frame collections, cycles of sketches and tales given thematic coherence (as in their model, *Winesburg, Ohio*) through the basic fact of geographical situation, a town or a planet. In each case many of the stories worked into the frames were published earlier as separate entities.

Bradbury's career as a storyteller can be divided into three periods: early, vintage, and late. The center of his early period is the Arkham House collection, *Dark Carnival* (1947). Bradbury himself considered these stories as oddities among his works. They are pure fantasy of the "weird" sort and include some of his most striking pieces. The vintage period extends, roughly, from 1946 to 1955. Its focal points are the story collections *The Illustrated Man* (1951) and *The Golden Apples of the Sun* (1953), the frame collection *The Martian Chronicles*, and *Fahrenheit 451*.

## COMMON HUMAN EXPERIENCE

Bradbury is noted for writing science fiction that explores lasting questions of morality, particularly the ethical treatment of people who are "different." Here are some other works of science fiction that tackle similarly lasting questions about the moral treatment of others:

*I, Robot* (1950), short stories by Isaac Asimov. This collection of related short stories about robots in the twenty-first century focus on the themes of morality and humans' interactions with machines.

*Do Androids Dream of Electric Sheep?* (1968), a novel by Philip K. Dick. This novel about a bounty hunter of androids explores the issues of discrimination and persecution of minority groups.

*Kindred* (1979), a novel by Octavia E. Butler. This novel, which involves accidental time travel by an African American woman sent back to the pre–Civil War South, explores the ethical questions raised by slavery as well as broader philosophical questions such as humans' impact on history.

Three thematic landscapes dominate this period: outer space, the future, and "odd corners" of the present or past. Bradbury's late period begins with *Dandelion Wine* (1957). It evolves through the following collections: *A Medicine for Melancholy* (1959), *The Machineries of Joy* (1964), and *I Sing the Body Electric!* (1969). These titles reveal Bradbury's increasing desire to treat the light and joyous side of human existence.

### Works in Critical Context

Ray Bradbury is a widely popular writer who has suffered from critical neglect. While Bradbury's popularity is acknowledged even by his detractors, many critics find the reasons for his success difficult to pinpoint. Some believe that the tension Bradbury creates between fantasy and reality is central to his ability to convey his visions and interests to his readers. Peter Stoler asserted that Bradbury's reputation rests on his "chillingly understated stories about a familiar world where it is always a few minutes before midnight on Halloween, and where the unspeakable and unthinkable become commonplace." Mary Ross proposed that "[p]erhaps the special quality of [Bradbury's] fantasy lies in the fact that people to whom amazing things happen are often so simply, often touchingly, like ourselves."

***The Martian Chronicles*** *The Martian Chronicles* is Bradbury's undisputed masterpiece. The publication of this book was an important event in the development of science fiction's growing respectability. The book was widely reviewed by a critical community that extended well beyond the science-fiction subculture, most notably by author Christopher Isherwood, who praised it lavishly in the journal *Tomorrow*. This praise has continued decades after the book's original publication. As Morgan Harlow wrote in 2005,

> *The Martian Chronicles* represents an original and serious work of artistic invention and vision, firmly grounded in literary tradition. It remains a force to be reckoned with, a pivotal work which has influenced the course of literature and the thinking of scientists and of ordinary citizens.

Ironically, Bradbury has been criticized by science-fiction readers, who complained that the Martian colonies in *The Martian Chronicles* are little more than transplanted small towns from the American Midwest of the 1920s.

***Fahrenheit 451*** *Fahrenheit 451* was the only work of Bradbury's that would approach *The Martian Chronicles* in popularity and influence at the time of its publication. The novel was lavishly praised for its intensity, its engaging narrative, and its concise presentation. Critics, however, have faulted the novel for an overly sentimental portrayal of culture and its elitist view of the value of literature. As Jack Zipes wrote, the main conflict in the novel "is not really constituted by the individual versus the state, but the intellectual versus the masses" with the implication that "the masses have brought this upon themselves and almost deserve to be blown up so that a new breed of book-lovers may begin to populate the world." Critics tend to agree, however, that the book represents some of Bradbury's central concerns. As one commentator put it, "*Fahrenheit 451* reflects Bradbury's lifelong love of books and his defense of the imagination against the menace of technology and government manipulation."

### Responses to Literature

1. Bradbury is one of the most recognizable names in science fiction, yet many critics contend that he is miscategorized in this genre. In what ways does the label "science-fiction author" distort Bradbury's literary legacy, and in what ways does this label accurately classify him?

2. Bradbury's writings typically present an optimistic outlook on technological progress. In what ways have the passing of time and development of technology validated or undermined this optimism? If Bradbury were a young writer today, would he have a similar attitude about technology, or would the current state of technological usage be likely to produce a more pessimistic outlook?

3. Bradbury often drew on his childhood experiences and thoughts to help craft his stories. Write a short story based on a memorable childhood experience, or write an essay that discusses how a strong

impression from your childhood has shaped the person you are today.

4. Choose one of Bradbury's science-fiction stories that seems to have an outdated take on technology and rewrite it in a present-day context with the kind of technological devices common in the twenty-first century.

## BIBLIOGRAPHY

**Books**

Amis, Kingsley. *New Maps of Hell*. New York: Ballantine, 1960.

Greenberg, Martin H., and Joseph D. Olander, eds. *Ray Bradbury*, Writers of the 21st Century Series. New York: Taplinger, 1980.

Ketterer, David. *New Worlds for Old: The Apocalyptic Imagination, Science Fiction, and American Literature*. Bloomington: Indiana University Press, 1974.

Knight, Damon. *In Search of Wonder: Essays on Modern Science Fiction*. 2nd ed. Chicago: Advent, 1967.

Mogen, David. *Ray Bradbury*. Boston: Twayne, 1986.

Moskowitz, Sam. *Seekers of Tomorrow: Masters of Modern Science Fiction*. New York: Ballantine, 1967.

Slusser, George Edgar. *The Bradbury Chronicles*. San Bernardino, Calif.: Borgo Press, 1977.

Touponce, William F. *Ray Bradbury and the Poetics of Reverie: Fantasy, Science Fiction, and the Reader*. Ann Arbor, Mich.: UMI Research Press, 1984.

Zipes, Jack. "*Fahrenheit 451*." In Rabkin, Eric S., Martin H. Greenberg, and Joseph D. Olander, eds. *No Place Else: Explorations in Utopian and Dystopian Fiction*. Carbondale: Southern Illinois University Press, 1983.

**Periodicals**

Harlow, Morgan. "Martian Legacy: Ray Bradbury's *The Martian Chronicles*." War, Literature and the Arts (2005): 311–314.

Nolan, William F. "Ray Bradbury: Prose Poet in the Age of Space." *Magazine of Fantasy and Science Fiction* (May 1963): 7–22.

Reilly, Robert. "The Artistry of Ray Bradbury." *Extrapolation* (December 1971): 64–74.

Sisario, Peter. "A Study of Allusions in Bradbury's *Fahrenheit 451*." *English Journal* (February 1970): 201–205.

## ✸ William Bradford

BORN: *1590, Austerfield, Yorkshire, England*

DIED: *1657, Plymouth Colony*

NATIONALITY: *British, American*

GENRE: *Nonfiction*

MAJOR WORKS:

*Of Plymouth Plantation* (1620–1647)

William Bradford   *MPI / Hulton Archive / Getty Images*

## Overview

William Bradford was an English Puritan who came to North America aboard the *Mayflower* and served as governor of Plymouth Colony. He aided in the survival of the colony and chronicled the life of the colonists during their first three decades in the New World.

## Works in Biographical and Historical Context

*A Puritan across the Sea*   Bradford was born in Austerfield, Yorkshire, England, early in the spring of 1590. His father, William Bradford, was a substantial yeoman farmer and his mother the daughter of the village shopkeeper. Within a year of his birth, his father died, and his mother soon remarried. Bradford was raised by a grandfather and uncles. He began to read the Geneva Bible at the age of twelve and attended a Puritan church. Puritans believed that the Anglican Church—the official church of England—had become too similar to the Catholic Church in some ways and sought to create a "purer," separate brand of Christianity for themselves. Since they had disavowed the official church of the land, they were

## LITERARY AND HISTORICAL CONTEMPORARIES

Bradford's famous contemporaries include:

**Johannes Kepler** (1571–1630): Kepler was a German astronomer who formulated laws of planetary motion and influenced Newton's theory of gravitation.

**John Donne** (1572–1631): Donne was a British metaphysical poet noted for his realistic and sensual style.

**John Smith** (1580–1631): Smith was an English explorer who helped establish the Jamestown Colony, the first permanent English settlement in North America.

**William Browne** (1590–1645): Browne was an English poet who had a great influence on later, greater poets such as John Milton and John Keats.

**Anne Hutchinson** (1591–1643): Hutchinson was a Puritan minister in the British colonies who was instrumental in pushing for greater religious freedom.

---

often persecuted by government and religious officials. At the age of seventeen, in defiance of his family, Bradford joined the Separatist congregation at Scrooby. He accompanied the congregation when it moved to Amsterdam, Holland, in 1607 and thence to Leiden.

Inheriting his parents' estate in 1611, he became a weaver and property owner. In 1613 he married Dorothy May and began the wide reading in Renaissance and Protestant literature that, along with the Geneva Bible, would influence the prose of his history of the Plymouth Colony. In 1620 he played a leading role in the decision, made by part of the Separatist community in Leyden, to establish a new colony in Virginia. However, their ship, the *Mayflower*, touched land first at Cape Cod in November 1620, and after a brief exploration the leaders decided to settle at a spot they named Plymouth. Dorothy Bradford drowned at Cape Cod in December of that year. Three years later Bradford married Alice Carpenter Southworth.

***Bradford Becomes Governor*** In April 1621, upon the death of the first governor of the colony, John Carver, Bradford was elected his successor. His leadership began with a deft Indian policy, which was described by Samuel Eliot Morison as "a nice balance of kindness and firmness." Bradford obtained seed corn, cultivation skills, and advice on fishing from the natives and prevented starvation during the first year.

Bradford strongly endorsed the abandonment of common property ownership in 1623 in favor of reliance on private property rights as incentives for enterprise and discipline. In 1627 Bradford and seven other leading Pilgrims bought out the London investors who had established the colony and paid the cost of transporting the remaining Leyden Pilgrims to Plymouth in exchange

for a six-year monopoly on the Indian trade and other fishing and tax concessions. Bradford then distributed the common livestock and land of the colony among Pilgrim and non-Pilgrim settlers alike, thereby stabilizing the economy and broadening the basis of political life.

Under Bradford's guidance the colony developed a political life of its own without the benefit of explicit legal and constitutional sanction. The Pilgrims' original land grant for territory in the Chesapeake was worthless, since they had not reached their intended destination and subsequent documents from the Crown conveying land and governing authority in New England were vague and unspecific. Freemen of the colony met infrequently as a General Court, elected the governor and assistants, and generally delegated political control to the governor, a position Bradford occupied for thirty of the first thirty-five years of the life of the colony. Forty-one original freemen signed the Mayflower Compact, a wholly informal agreement to live together as a community. Twenty years later there were some two hundred and thirty freemen in an adult male population of over six hundred. Bradford bluntly explained that freemen shared in decision making "only in some weighty matters when we think good."

***A Twenty-Seven-Year Chronicle*** Between 1620 and 1647, Bradford wrote *Of Plymouth Plantation*, a narrative and documentary record of the Pilgrims from the time of their departure from England for Holland through the first quarter-century of their existence in the New World. He intended the manuscript to inspire successive generations of his family with the heroic struggles of the early Pilgrim fathers.

In the 1650s Bradford turned to versification, speaking to the younger generation without benefit of a public mask in poems such as "On the Various Heresies in Old and New England," "A Word to New Plymouth," "A Word to New England," and "Some Observations of God's Merciful Dealing with Us in This Wilderness." His seven poems display more piety and talent for rhetorical organization than they do poetic genius, but they do attest to a widespread desire in early New England to realize experience and moral truth in poetic form.

## Works in Literary Context

Bradford's literary reputation depends almost entirely on his history, and in a curious way his history has almost become his best biography—curious because of its impersonal subjection of Bradford's private hopes and trials to the account of the difficulties of the colony. Bradford was a major figure in early American historiography because his history of the Pilgrim Colony at Plymouth was a firsthand account of the entry of English settlers into the American wilderness and because he wrote about people who had deliberately separated themselves from European culture to create a distinctly American society.

***Bradford's Styles*** A major value of Bradford's history is his faithful adherence to Separatist simplicity. Bradford often juxtaposed the primitive Christianity of the Separatists with the luxuriant chaos spawned by the forces of evil. "When by bloody and barbarous persecution by the heathen emperors" the devil sought unsuccessfully to "stop and subvert the course of the gospel," which "speedily overspread with a wonderful celerity the best known parts of the world," Bradford explains, "he then began to sow errours, heresies, and wonderful dissensions amongst the professors [of Christianity] themselves." Herein was Bradford's conception of history as a dynamic interaction of simple faith and evil aggression. He employed it with restraint and analytical effectiveness. Free from rancor or egotism, he concentrated on what he took to be the working out of the will of God in human affairs.

Bradford's use of literary sources to delineate emotional categories testifies to the discrimination of his reading as a young man in Holland and his fascination with human motivation and the interior dynamics of Separatist fellowship. Bradford's cadence, diction, and syntax in these passages reveal something of the way he must have talked and thought about personalities and events, as well as his unwavering leadership and his patient, persistent approach to organizing difficult bodies of information. His prose also reveals the rich interaction of literary art and religious inspiration in Reformation culture. *Of Plymouth Plantation*, E. F. Bradford has written in an early critical study of the book, is a work of "conscious art," which painstakingly utilizes literary conventions in order to create a moving and convincing portrait of Puritan discipleship. Bradford's prose strongly echoes that of the Geneva Bible.

Equally important is Bradford's repeated and skillful use of similes, metaphors, and what E. F. Bradford calls "balance, antithesis, and alliteration, and the frequent combination of words similar or identical in meaning." Alliteration fills the book: "bloody and barbarous," "base and beggarly," "profane persons," "callings, courts, and canons," "primitive pattern"—all common devices of the day, which serve to establish a rhythm and an oral resonance to Bradford's prose.

***Changing View of Native Americans*** Bradford's view of Native Americans changed dramatically throughout his life at Plymouth. When he began his narrative, he referred to the Indians in degrading terms, describing them as savage, brutish, wild beasts, and cannibals. The original peace treaty he negotiated with Massasoit greatly favored the colonists over the Indians. But, by the middle of his account, Bradford began using the more benign term *Indian* almost exclusively. His dealings with treacherous white men on both sides of the Atlantic served to soften his initial harsh view of Native Americans.

Toward the end of the book, Bradford spoke of the need for colonists to buy land from the Indians (an idea scorned by land-hungry colonists), remarking as well

## COMMON HUMAN EXPERIENCE

Bradford's diary chronicled the history of the first thirty years of the Plymouth Colony, providing insight into the workings of a society during important years of growth and change. Here are some other works that chronicle important historical periods in diary form:

*The Diary of a Young Girl* (1947), by Anne Frank. This book is a compelling first-person account written by a Jewish girl in Amsterdam during her two years of hiding from the Nazis during World War II.

*The Diary of Henry Machyn—Citizen and Merchant-Taylor of London (1550–1563)* (1848). This book chronicles a period of rapid political and religious change in England as witnessed and recorded by a citizen of London.

*The Diary of Hamman Yaji* (1995). This diary kept by a local Muslim ruler in Nigeria under British rule provides insight into the early years of the British colonial administration in Africa.

about a local Indian chief's legal jurisdiction over felony crimes, which was a stunning admission coming from an English governor. Later, when several white men murdered an Indian, the English court sentenced them to death. When several local whites spoke out against the execution, Bradford called the dissenters "rude and ignorant," and the colony executed the killers despite their objections.

## Works in Critical Context

When William Bradford's chronicle was first published from his manuscript as *History of Plymouth Plantation* (1856), it was immediately recognized as a uniquely valuable historical record and almost as quickly seen as one of the finest examples of seventeenth-century American literature. The intervening years have not seen any lessening of its historical importance to scholars, although there have been different opinions about the ultimate validity of Bradford's view of his fellow Pilgrims. More interesting, its appreciation as a major literary work has continued to grow. Hailed by Kenneth Murdock as an "American classic" and by Peter Gay as an "authentic masterpiece," *Of Plymouth Plantation* has, by virtue of the imaginative richness and vision with which it comprehends the facts of emigration and settlement, become one of the essential texts for anyone wishing to understand the American experience.

Although Bradford's history has had many admirers who have celebrated its authenticity and respected the character and dignity of the author, in the 1960s and 1970s the book began to acquire a new stature as an intellectual monument. The rediscovery of non-Separatist Puritan intellectuality by Perry Miller in the 1930s and 1940s left Bradford outside the corpus of major Puritan writers. In one of his few references to Bradford, Miller contrasts his intensity and single-minded reliance on divine Providence with the non-Separatist sense of being on a more complex "errand into the wilderness." Then, in the early 1960s, Harvey Wish and Peter Gay sought to make of Bradford's history a prototypical Puritan document, Wish emphasizing Bradford's identification of the Pilgrims with the Old Testament children of Israel and Gay stressing the impracticality of Bradford's vision of a godly commonwealth.

## Responses to Literature

1. Bradford kept his diary to pass down to his family so that they could understand what he went through during the early years of the Plymouth Colony. Present-day diarists often turn to blogging to enable family, friends, and other readers to have real-time access to their experiences and ideas. In what ways does blogging serve a similar function as colonial-era diary writing, and in what ways has the instant access of a blog transformed the outlook of the diarist?

2. Some commentators believe that reading *Of Plymouth Plantation* is essential for understanding the American experience. Does Bradford's diary help present-day Americans make sense of their culture and attitudes? In what ways does Bradford's diary elucidate the American experience, and in what ways have the intervening centuries changed that experience so much that Bradford's words offer only historical insight, and not contemporary understanding?

3. Keep a diary for a week or more, modeling your entries after the kind of description and analysis used by Bradford, and then write an introductory essay for these diary entries. Compare these entries to those of Bradford. How has daily life changed since the beginning of the Plymouth Colony?

4. Choose one of the decisions that Bradford describes making as governor and write an essay assessing this decision from the point of view of those impacted by the decision. Be sure to consider all of those affected by the activities in the colony.

BIBLIOGRAPHY

**Books**

Bercovitch, Sacvan, ed. *Typology and Early American Literature*. Amherst, Mass.: University of Massachusetts Press, 1972.

Emerson, Everett, ed. *Major Writers in Early American Literature*. Madison: University of Wisconsin Press, 1972.

Gay, Peter. *A Loss of Mastery: Puritan Historians in Colonial America*. Berkeley: University of California Press, 1966.

Langon, George D., Jr. *Pilgrim Colony: A History of New Plymouth, 1620–1691*. New Haven, Conn.: Yale University Press, 1966.

Smith, Bradford. *Bradford of Plymouth*. Philadelphia: Lippincott, 1951.

Smith, James Morton, ed. *Seventeenth-Century America: Essays in Colonial History*. Chapel Hill: University of North Carolina Press, 1959.

Wish, Harvey. *The American Historian: A Social-Intellectual History of the Writing of the American Past*. New York: Oxford University Press, 1960.

**Periodicals**

Bradford, E. F. "Conscious Art in Bradford's *History of Plymouth Plantation*." *New England Quarterly* (1928): 133–157.

Hovey, Kenneth Alan. "The Theology of History in *Of Plymouth Plantation* and Its Predecessors." *Early American Literature* (1975): 47–66.

Howard, Alan B. "Art and History in Bradford's *Of Plymouth Plantation*." *William and Mary Quarterly*, third series (1971): 237–266.

Levin, David. "Review Essay." *History and Theory* (1968): 385–393.

# Marion Zimmer Bradley

BORN: *1930, Albany, New York*

DIED: *1999, Berkeley, California*

NATIONALITY: *American*

GENRE: *Fiction*

MAJOR WORKS:

The *Darkover* novels (1962–1997)
*The Mists of Avalon* (1982)

## Overview

Bradley was a prolific science-fiction and fantasy writer best known for her series of novels tracing the evolution of the planet Darkover and for her retelling of the King Arthur legend in *The Mists of Avalon* (1982). Her novels exhibit a diversity of plot and time period as well as similar thematic concerns, particularly an examination of sex roles and their limitations.

## Works in Biographical and Historical Context

***Early Interest in Science Fiction*** Marion Bradley was born on a farm in Albany, New York, in 1930, during the early part of the Great Depression. Her father was a carpenter, and her mother was a historian. It was through her mother that she gained an interest in history, but she

Marian Zimmer Bradley    *Bradley, Marian Zimmer, photograph. © Jerry Bauer. Reproduced by permission.*

was also an early devotee of the science-fiction movement that was burgeoning in the 1940s. From an early age, she wanted to a writer, and while still in high school, she started her own science-fiction magazine. Before pursuing that dream, she attended New York State College to train to be a teacher. She began writing science fiction stories in 1949, the same year she married her first husband, R. A. Bradley.

***Juggling Motherhood and Writing***    Although Bradley had begun writing at the same time that her marriage began, she did not begin writing professionally until the early 1960s, largely because of the birth of her son. Throughout the 1950s, Bradley juggled motherhood and writing. During this period, she wrote numerous stories and had modest success getting them printed, but she did not publish her first novel, *The Door Through Space*, until 1961.

***A Busy Decade***    After starting her publishing career at the age of thirty, Bradley was a prolific writer, publishing over thirty books by 1980 and over one hundred books both singly and in collaboration with other authors dur-

ing her forty-year career. The 1960s were a particularly productive time for Bradley. She published five books in 1962 alone, although one of these, *The Planet Savers*, had been serialized in *Amazing Science Fiction Stories* three years earlier. Published as a novel, *The Planet Savers* would become the first of Bradley's *Darkover* novels.

Bradley's writing career took off at the same time that the modern women's movement was gaining energy. The publication of *The Feminine Mystique* in 1963 was a major impetus for the development of feminism in the mid- and late-1960s and into the 1970s. Much of Bradley's writing during this period, mostly on the *Darkover* novels, contained overtly feminist themes and was driven by concerns that Bradley shared with women and mothers of the 1950s and 1960s.

The 1960s brought significant changes in Bradley's life in addition to her success as a writer. She divorced her first husband in 1963 and married for the second time the following year. In 1965 she graduated from Hardin-Simmons University and moved to Berkeley, California, to pursue graduate studies at the University of California. Her interests in history and fantasy combined in 1966, when she cofounded the Society for Creative Anachronism.

***Beyond Science Fiction Novels***    Bradley's interest in history, along with her feminist concerns, led her to write her most popular novel, *The Mists of Avalon*, a retelling of the King Arthur legend from the perspective of the women involved. This book was an instant hit and remained on the *New York Times* best seller list for sixteen weeks. This success helped Bradley broaden her readership, and for the rest of her life, her work belonged to the wider genre of fantasy and speculative fiction. She wrote another historical novel, *The Firebrand*, in 1987, and started *Marion Zimmer Bradley's Fantasy Magazine* in 1988. She also produced Gothic fictions, such as *The Inheritor* (1984), *Ghostlight* (1995), and its sequels, *Witchlight* (1996) and *Gravelight* (1997).

During the last decade of her life, she remained active as an editor, working on her magazine as well as editing the annual *Sword and Sorcery*, but her production of novels decreased steadily, largely because of failing health. She died from a heart attack in 1999.

## Works in Literary Context

Two major themes may be identified in Bradley's works. The first is the reconciliation of conflicting or opposing forces, whether such forces are represented by different cultures or by different facets of a single personality. The second, closely related to the first, is alienation or exile from a dominant group. These features are readily seen in Bradley's *Darkover* novels, a loosely connected series dealing with the perpetual opposition between the citizens of the Terran Empire and those of the planet Darkover.

***The Clash of Opposing Forces***    The *Darkover* novels comprise a diversity of plots and time periods, yet they

## LITERARY AND HISTORICAL CONTEMPORARIES

Bradley's famous contemporaries include:

**Frank Herbert** (1920–1986): Herbert was an American science-fiction writer best known for his best-selling novels in the *Dune* saga.

**Ted Hughes** (1930–1998): Hughes was the British poet laureate from 1984 until his death in 1998.

**Cherry Wilder** (1930–2002): Wilder was a New Zealand-born science-fiction and fantasy writer.

**Harlan Ellison** (1934–): Ellison is an American fiction and television writer best known for his work on *Star Trek* and *Outer Limits*.

## COMMON HUMAN EXPERIENCE

Many of Bradley's novels explore the themes of alienation and exile. Here are some other works centered around similar themes:

*Zubaida's Window* (2008), a novel by Iqbal Al-Qazwini. This novel explores the inner struggles of a woman who fled Iraq and lives in self-imposed exile in Germany.

*The Heart of Darkness* (1902), a novella by Joseph Conrad. This work explores the growing sense of alienation experienced by a ferry boat captain on assignment on a river in the depths of Africa.

*Ignorance* (2000), a novel by Milan Kundera. This novel examines the feelings experienced by a Czech expatriate who returns to her homeland after a twenty-year absence.

share a common setting and similar thematic concerns. Although all Darkovans are descendants of explorers from Earth, two different cultures have evolved. The Terrans rely on communal support and advanced technology, while the Darkovans are self-reliant and antitechnological. Bradley does not openly favor either one; her work often explores the conflicts that arise from opposing forces, and the *Darkover* novels, like her other works, usually end in reconciliation. Lester del Rey calls Darkover "one of the most fully realized of the worlds of science fiction."

Among the serious issues addressed in the *Darkover* novels are the importance and the problems of communication between individuals. The first *Darkover* novel, *The Sword of Aldones* (1962), centers on Lew Alton and his acute sense of isolation, which stems from both his

physical deformities and his dual heritage: Darkovan and Terran. In *The Forbidden Tower* (1977), however, Bradley employs the Darkovans' telepathic powers in order to explore the extreme emotional and physical closeness of the four protagonists.

***Feminism*** An undercurrent of feminism runs throughout the *Darkover* series. Bradley frequently examines sex roles and the limitations they place on the individual. One of the most notable examples of this idea occurs in *The Shattered Chain* (1976). Revolving around the struggles of three women for independence and self-realization, this novel explores both the necessity of choice and the inevitable pain and hardship that result from the freedom to choose. Critics have praised Bradley's ability to incorporate feminist and utopian ideals into the harsh realism of Darkover without diminishing the credibility of the characters or their society.

Bradley's feminist interests are also evident in *The Mists of Avalon*. This novel, which retells the Arthurian legend from the viewpoint of the women involved, has received considerable critical attention. Critics on the whole are impressed with Bradley's accurate and detailed evocation of the times and consider *The Mists of Avalon* an important addition to the chronicles of Arthur.

### Works in Critical Context

Critics in general praise Bradley's literate writing, intricate characterizations, and logical plots. Although most of her works are favorably received by critics, the origin of her popular appeal lies in the *Darkover* series. From the beginning, her works were reviewed, usually with favor, by the speculative fiction press, but it was not until the 1970s that she began to receive attention from outside that narrow critical sphere. Since then she has been widely recognized as a capable and imaginative writer. With the publication of *The Mists of Avalon* in 1982, Bradley greatly expanded her readership beyond traditional speculative fiction audiences.

***The Darkover Series*** The *Darkover* series consists of over twenty books that span many years of that world's history. Critics have noted that Bradley uses this broad canvas to explore several important themes. As Rosemarie Arbur writes in *Twentieth-Century Science Fiction Writers*, "the Darkover novels test various attitudes about the importance of technology, and more important, they study the very nature of human intimacy." One notable feature of the *Darkover* novels, often pointed out by critics, is that each volume is both unique and able to stand alone as a novel. Dan Miller notes in his *Booklist* review for *The Shattered Chain*, "As with others in the series, no knowledge of the previous books is required for enjoyment." Lester del Rey, in a retrospective review of the two earliest books for *Analog Science Fiction/Science Fact*, contends, "Bradley refused to be bound by consistency—wisely, I think, since Darkover has evolved and improved. But even the early stories have the wonderful allure of this strange world.”

***The Mists of Avalon*** The publication of Bradley's first mainstream best seller, *The Mists of Avalon*, drew praise from a wide variety of critics. Some critics praised the book for its ambitious feminist retelling of the Arthurian legend, though as Charlotte Spivack wrote in *Merlin's Daughters: Contemporary Women Writers of Fantasy*, it "is much more than a retelling. ... [It] is a profound revisioning." Spivack contends that the book "offers a brilliant reinterpretation of the traditional material from the point of view of the major female characters." Maureen Quilligan of the *New York Times Book Review* writes, "*The Mists of Avalon* rewrites Arthur's story so that we realize it has always also been the story of his sister, the Fairy Queen." Spivack also notes that Bradley not only presents the story from a woman's perspective, she roots it "in the religious struggle between matriarchal worship of the goddess and the patriarchal institution of Christianity." According to Carrol L. Fry in the *Journal of Popular Culture*, Bradley "reverses the traditional Arthurian lore to criticize institutional Christianity. She levels much of that criticism at her perception ... of the church's misogyny."

Despite critical praise for Bradley's fresh approach to Arthurian legend, some critics were unimpressed with the book. Maude McDaniel of the *Washington Post* complained that "It all seems strangely static ... set pieces the reader watches rather than enters. ... [F]inally we are left with more bawling than brawling." Darrell Schweitzer of *Science Fiction Review* faulted the novel for making changes in the story that are "all in the direction of the mundane, the ordinary" because, as he argues, "the interesting parts happen offstage" since the women in the legend "aren't present at the crucial moments." However, most critics agreed that the novel will, as Beverly Deweese put it in a *Science Fiction Review* article, "attract and please many readers" with an Arthurian world that is "intriguingly different."

## Responses to Literature

1. Bradley's *Darkover* novels concern the relations between two very different cultures occupying the same planet. What kinds of cultural clashes on Earth today can be likened to the clashes that Bradley explores in her novels? In what ways do her novels provide us with guidance for handling our present-day cultural clashes?

2. Bradley incorporated feminist ideas in her *Darkover* novels, as well as other works. In what ways do her feminist concerns tie in with the other themes she pursues in the *Darkover* series? Do these concerns seem forced or do they flow naturally from the other issues she addresses?

3. Write an essay discussing the thematic connections between one of Bradley's *Darkover* novels and one of her other novels. Be sure to cover the ways that she explores similar themes in different settings.

4. Create a world characterized by deep cultural and individual clashes. Write an outline of this world's history and a description of its cultural and political make-up. How did this fictional clash of cultures come to be? What is the outcome of the conflict?

BIBLIOGRAPHY

**Books**

Alpers, H. J., ed. *Marion Zimmer Bradley's Darkover*. Meitingen, Germany: Corian, 1983.

Arbur, Rosemarie. *Marion Zimmer Bradley*. Mercer Island, Wash.: Starmont House, 1985.

Breen, Walter. *The Gemini Problem: A Study in Darkover*. Baltimore: T-K Graphics, 1976.

Lane, Daryl, ed. *The Sound of Wonder*. Vol. 2. Phoenix, Ariz.: Oryx, 1985.

Magill, Frank, ed. *Survey of Modern Fantasy Literature*. Vol. 1. Englewood Cliffs, NJ: Salem Press, 1983.

"Marion Zimmer Bradley (1930–)." *Contemporary Literary Criticism*. Edited by Jean C. Stine and Daniel G. Marowski. Vol. 30. Detroit: Gale Research, 1984, pp. 26–32.

Roberson, Jennifer. *Return to Avalon*. New York: DAW Books, 1996.

Spivack, Charlotte. *Merlin's Daughters: Contemporary Women Writers of Fantasy*. New York: Greenwood Press, 1987.

Staicar, Tom, ed. *The Feminine Eye: Science Fiction and the Women Who Write It*. New York: Ungar, 1982.

Wise, S. *The Darkover Dilemma: Problems of the Darkover Series*. Baltimore: T-K Graphics, 1976.

**Periodicals**

Leith, Linda. "Marion Zimmer Bradley and Darkover." *Science-Fiction Studies* (March 1980).

# ✹ Anne Bradstreet

BORN: *1612, Northampton, England*

DIED: *1672, Andover, Massachusetts*

NATIONALITY: *American*

GENRE: *Poetry*

MAJOR WORKS:

*The Tenth Muse Lately Sprung Up in America* (1650)

*The Works of Bradstreet in Prose and Verse* (1867)

## Overview

Bradstreet was America's first published poet and the first woman to produce an eduring volume of poetry in the

## LITERARY AND HISTORICAL CONTEMPORARIES

Bradstreet's famous contemporaries include:

**Rembrandt van Rijn** (1606–1669): Rembrandt was a Dutch painter widely considered one of the greatest painters of all time.

**William Bradford** (1590–1657): Bradford served as governor of the Plymouth Colony for most of its first three decades, during which he wrote the first chronicle of American life, *Of Plymouth Plantation*.

**Molière** (1622–1673): Molière was a French playwright who was one of the most celebrated authors of the seventeenth century and is widely considered one of the greatest comedy writers of all time.

**John Dryden** (1631–1700): Dryden was an English author and critic who was highly influential in the dominant literary circles of his time.

**John Locke** (1632–1704): Locke was an English philosopher whose ideas about government and natural rights influenced the American founding fathers.

English language. Although quite popular during her lifetime, she was largely ignored by subsequent generations of critics. Only in recent decades have scholars returned to her work to reexamine its worth as literature and not just for its historical significance.

### Works in Biographical and Historical Context

*Raised amid Aristrocracy* Anne Bradstreet was born in England to a Puritan family. Her father, Thomas Dudley, was steward to the Earl of Lincoln, a leading nonconformist in the religious strife of England. Puritans believed that the Anglican Church—the official church of England—had become too similar to the Catholic Church in some ways, and sought to create a "purer," separate brand of Christianity for themselves. Since they had disavowed the official church of the land, they were often persecuted by government and religious officials.

Because of Dudley's high position, his daughter received an education befitting aristocracy. The availability of the Earl's extensive library provided her the opportunity to read the works of Plutarch, Edmund Spenser, Guillaume de Salluste du Bartas, Francis Quarles, and Sir Philip Sidney, with whom her father claimed kinship.

*Move to the New World* In 1630 Bradstreet moved with her parents and husband, Simon Bradstreet, to the Massachusetts Bay Colony, where her husband and father served as governors of the struggling settlement. As a New England colonist, Bradstreet encountered a life of

hardship to which she was unaccustomed. Bradstreet had eight children between the years 1633 and 1652, which meant that her domestic responsibilities were extremely demanding. Still, she wrote poetry in spite of frequent illness and the difficulties of raising a family in the American wilderness.

The Bradstreets shared a house in Salem for many months with another family and lived in spartan style. In the winter the two families were confined to the one room in which there was a fireplace. The situation was tense as well as uncomfortable, and Bradstreet and her family moved several times in an effort to improve their worldly estates. From Salem they moved to Charlestown, then to Newtown (later called Cambridge), then to Ipswich, and finally to Andover in 1645.

Throughout her life in the New World, Bradstreet was concerned with the issues of sin and redemption, physical and emotional frailty, death and immortality. Much of her work indicates that she had a difficult time resolving the conflict she experienced between the pleasures of sensory and familial experience and the promises of heaven. As a Puritan, she struggled to subdue her attachment to the world, but as a woman she sometimes felt more strongly connected to her husband, children, and community than to God.

*The Tenth Muse and Beyond* When her brother-in-law, John Woodbridge, returned to England in 1647, he took with him the manuscript of Bradstreet's poems. Without her knowledge, he published them, entitling the collection *The Tenth Muse Lately Sprung Up in America* (1650). The volume met with immediate success as one of the "most vendable" books in London. Bradstreet was pleasantly surprised by the reception of *The Tenth Muse*, but she was dissatisfied with its unpolished state. In subsequent years, she undertook to revise the poems, though some of these alterations were lost when her home burned in 1666.

Six years after her death the revisions, along with a number of new verses, were published under the title *Several Poems*; this volume includes Bradstreet's most celebrated poem, "Contemplations." Not included were some prose meditations and reminiscences that, along with some later poems, were not printed until 1867, when John Harvard Ellis published Bradstreet's complete works, including materials from both editions of *The Tenth Muse* as well as "Religious Experiences and Occasional Pieces" and "Meditations Divine and Morall."

### Works in Literary Context

Bradstreet's first poems were published in London under the title *The Tenth Muse Lately Sprung Up in America* and created great curiosity as the first significant literature to emerge from New England. Of even greater interest to Bradstreet's contemporaries was the fact that *The Tenth Muse* was the work of a woman, authorship being a most disreputable occupation for women of the time. Yet,

Bradstreet apparently was not subjected to personal disparagement because of her compositions in *The Tenth Muse*, which are long, formal pieces deriving from well-worn poetic stock of the Renaissance. Admired as a successful example of standard poetic fare, the poetry of *The Tenth Muse* was probably composed by the time Bradstreet was thirty years old. Her later poems, however, departed from convention, displaying a sensitivity and love of beauty not usually associated with New England Puritans.

***From Convention to Introspection*** There is, in the words of Ann Stanford, "a great rift that all critics have noted" in Bradstreet's work. The early poetry is characterized by convention and imitation, the later by introspection and personal expression. The early work consists primarily of the Quaternions: four long poems of four parts each, which treat the humours, elements, seasons, and ages of man. They are cast in the form of argument, with each humor, element, season, and age personified as a sister who argues her case for preeminence.

Bradstreet's later work is quite different. It has been suggested that *The Tenth Muse* would be of only superficial historical significance if not for the lasting quality of Bradstreet's later poetry. Here, Bradstreet turned to a more personal style of expression. Thoughts on her illnesses, the death of loved ones, the raising of her children, and anxiety for her husband away on business are expressed in poems written over a period of thirty years. While she had begun poetizing her reflections on personal subjects before the publication of *The Tenth Muse*, it was not until its publication that this type of expression came to dominate her work. Bradstreet also began to write prose works in this later period: autobiographical reminiscences intended for the benefit of her children, and her "Meditations Divine and Morall," often considered among the finest aphorisms on the human condition predating those of Benjamin Franklin.

Both the reminiscences and the "Meditations" offer a valuable personal perspective on Bradstreet's life and poetry. Exemplifying her personal reflections is the poem "Contemplations," now considered her masterpiece, which records the poet's thoughts on a walk along a river. Observing nature with sensitivity and humility, she considers the transience of human existence. Some critics have seen in "Contemplations" a foreshadowing of the Romantics, for it expresses tenderness, a celebration of beauty, and honest emotion. To many commentators, these characteristics markedly differ from common perceptions of Puritan severity and insensitivity to feeling. Others see "Contemplations" as a warm and graceful view of life by a devout Puritan.

## Works in Critical Context

The publication of *The Tenth Muse* created an immediate sensation in London. Bradstreet was praised in her own time for the formal, courtly aspect of her poetry. In a

---

# COMMON HUMAN EXPERIENCE

Bradstreet's poetry reflects the tensions of a woman who wished to express her individuality in a culture that was hostile to personal autonomy. Here are some other works by women that express similar tensions:

*Poems* (1786), poems by Helen Maria Williams. This collection of poetry by the controversial British author touches on topics ranging from religion to colonial practices.

*Midaregami* (*Tangled Hair*) (1901), poems by Akiko Yosano. This collection of poems brought a passionate individualism to traditional Japanese poetry.

*What's O'Clock* (1926), poems by Amy Lowell. This collection of poetry, published just after the author's death, touches on a wide variety of themes pursued by this controversial poet and critic.

---

statement of extravagant praise Cotton Mather (1663–1728) concluded that her poems have "afforded a grateful Entertainment unto the Ingenious, and a Monument for her Memory beyond the stateliest *Marbles*." Eight years after *The Tenth Muse* appeared, it was listed by William London in his *Catalogue of the Most Vendible Books in England*, and George III is reported to have had the volume in his library.

What was most noteworthy to her contemporaries, however, was that this sophisticated poetry was produced in the wilds of America by a woman. Subsequently, she appears to have been all but ignored by critics until the late nineteenth century, when she was criticized for a "lack of taste" and for following the example of such "fantastic" poets as Richard Crashaw, John Donne, George Herbert, and Francis Quarles. Considered but a relic of America's earliest literature, her poetry was seen as a slight exception to what the nineteenth-century reader perceived as the artless, repressive nature of Puritanism.

***Feminist Resurgence*** With the rise of the feminist movement in the middle of the twentieth century, there was a surge of interest in the study of Bradstreet's work. Her formal poetry, while drawing the least comment, sparks the most disagreement. Many critics consider it forgettable; others praise it for technical, if not imaginative, skill. More attention has been paid the later lyric poems and with far more critical agreement; though differing in degree, admiration is the common response to Bradstreet's later work. Yet, much of the critical study exhibits a greater interest in Bradstreet herself, her feelings and personal growth, than in her writing. Seeing in her a figure of inspiration, many feminist critics have focused on her womanhood and her place in the history of female authors, looking upon her production of poetry under conditions of illness, pioneering, and mothering as a Herculean effort.

They perceive in her a spirit of uncommon independence within a man's world; numerous critics, feminist and otherwise, have seen in Bradstreet's poems evidence of personal rebellion against God, against a male-dominated society, or against Puritan social strictures in general. Others have noted that modern readers still labor under the nineteenth-century prejudice against Puritanism and claim that what is expressed in Bradstreet's poetry is a humble avowal of Puritan belief, rather than rebellion. These critics stress that there was probably more depth and variety to Puritanism than one previously comprehended and that a better understanding is necessary if one is to accurately appraise Bradstreet's writings.

What is certain is that Bradstreet's work has endured. Her poetry has continued to receive a positive response for more than three centuries, and she is still considered to be one of the most important early American poets and one of the most important American women poets of all time.

## Responses to Literature

1. Bradstreet's first publication was greeted with amazement that such sophisticated poetry could be written by a woman facing the harsh colonial conditions that Bradstreet endured. Do you think this amazement was justified? Do you think readers would be equally surprised if the verses were written by a man? Why or why not?

2. Some feminists view Bradstreet as a heroic example because of the difficult conditions in which she wrote. In what ways did the difficulties of colonial life hinder Bradstreet's efforts, and in what ways did these difficulties contribute to her poetic output? Do you think you would have been able to concentrate on writing if faced with the same conditions as Bradstreet? Why or why not?

3. Bradstreet's later poetry is driven by an introspective approach combined with a sensitivity to nature. Write a poem modeled after Bradsteet's later work in which you observe and speculate on some aspect of nature that surrounds you in your daily life.

4. Commentators have noted a distinct difference between Bradstreet's earlier and later works, pointing to her movement from conventional to more personal poetry. Write an essay that explores the connections between Bradstreet's earlier and later work, noting places where the style and subject matter of her early poems pre-figure the concerns of her later poems.

BIBLIOGRAPHY

**Books**

Campbell, Helen. *Anne Bradstreet and Her Time.* Boston: Lothrop, 1891.

Gilber, Sandra and Susan Gubar, eds. *Shakespeare's Sisters.* Bloomington, Ind.: Indiana University Press, 1979.

Martin, Wendy. *The Lives and Work of Anne Bradstreet, Emily Dickinson, and Adrienne Rich.* Chapel Hill, N.C.: University of North Carolina Press, 1983.

Piercy, Josephine K. *Anne Bradstreet.* New York: Twayne, 1965.

Stanford, Ann. *Anne Bradstreet: The Worldly Puritan.* New York: Burt Franklin, 1974.

White, Elizabeth Wade. *Anne Bradstreet.* New York: Oxford University Press, 1971.

**Periodicals**

Eberwein, Jane Donahue. "The 'Unrefined Ore' of Anne Bradstreet's Quaternions." *Early American Literature* 9 (1974): 19–24.

Hildebrand, Anne. "Anne Bradstreet's Quaternions and 'Contemplations.'" *Early American Literature* 8 (1973): 117–125.

Laughlin, Rosemary M. "Anne Bradstreet: Poet in Search of Form." *American Literature* 42 (1970): 1–17.

Requa, Kenneth A. "Anne Bradstreet's Poetic Voices." *Early American Literature* 9 (1974): 3–18.

Richardson, Robert. "The Puritan Poetry of Anne Bradstreet." *Texas Studies in Literature and Language* 9 (1967): 317–331.

Rosenfeld, Alvin H. "Anne Bradstreet's 'Contemplations': Patterns of Form and Meaning." *New England Quarterly* 43 (1970): 79–96.

# ✺ Richard Brautigan

BORN: *1935, Spokane, Washington*

DIED: *1984, Bolinas, California*

NATIONALITY: *American*

GENRE: *Fiction, poetry*

MAJOR WORKS:

*Trout Fishing in America* (1967)

*The Pill versus the Springhill Mine Disaster* (1968)

*In Watermelon Sugar* (1968)

*Revenge of the Lawn* (1971)

## Overview

Richard Brautigan, a San Francisco-based poet and a popular experimental novelist in the 1960s, left an uncertain critical legacy when he died, apparently by his own hand, at the age of forty-nine. Commentators have variously attempted to categorize him as "the last Beat," a Zen Buddhist, a hippie icon, an American humorist, a

Richard Brautigan  *Vernon Merritt III / Time Life Pictures / Getty Images*

modern Henry David Thoreau, and a pioneer of post-modern fiction.

## Works in Biographical and Historical Context

*A Troubled Upbringing*  Richard Brautigan was born on January 30, 1935, in Tacoma, Washington. Brautigan seldom spoke about his upbringing, but all indications are that his childhood was an unhappy one. He apparently never met his biological father, and according to Brautigan's younger sister, Barbara, their mother seldom showed affection or concern for her children. Brautigan recalled his mother's having once abandoned him and his younger sister for several days at a hotel in Great Falls, Montana.

Brautigan began writing stories in his adolescence, which was marked by a tendency toward antisocial behavior. While in high school he was arrested for throwing a rock through a police-station window and, following his arrest, was diagnosed as a paranoid schizophrenic and was committed to the Oregon State Hospital. According to his sister, he was treated there with electroshock therapy, a treatment that she believed led him to "shut down" emotionally.

Shortly after his release from the hospital, Brautigan left home for good, moving to San Francisco, where, in 1956, he frequented North Beach coffeehouses and attended Beat poetry readings. The Beat poets were critical of mainstream American values, and they advocated experimentation with nonconformist practices, both of which were themes evident in Brautigan's earliest writings. During this time, Brautigan befriended such influential Beat writers as Michael McClure and Lawrence Ferlinghetti. He married Virginia Dionne Adler in 1957; their daughter, Ianthe, was born in 1960. The family lived on a meager income while Brautigan published his small-press poetry in the late 1950s and began writing fiction seriously in the early 1960s.

*From Obscurity to Popularity*  Brautigan dedicated himself to writing fiction in the early 1960s, producing the manuscripts for several novels. Although *A Confederate General from Big Sur* (1964) was his second novel written, it was first to be published. Grove Press promoted the novel nationally, but it garnered lackluster reviews and abysmal initial sales. Reviewers, particularly East Coast reviewers, associated the novel with the fading Beat scene in San Francisco.

As a result of the poor initial showing of Brautigan's first published novel, Grove Press sold the publication

# LITERARY AND HISTORICAL CONTEMPORARIES

Brautigan's famous contemporaries include:

**Wole Soyinka** (1934–): Soyinka is a Nigerian writer considered by many to be Africa's best playwright. In 1986, he became the first African to win the Nobel Prize in Literature.

**Harlan Ellison** (1934–): Ellison is an American fiction and television writer best known for his work on *Star Trek* and *Outer Limits*.

**Elvis Presley** (1935–1977): Presley was an American musician who has become a pop-culture icon often referred to as "The King."

**Kenzaburo Oe** (1935–): Oe is a Japanese writer who is widely considered one of the foremost figures in contemporary Japanese literature; he was awarded the Nobel Prize in Literature in 1994.

**Václav Havel** (1936–): Havel is a Czech writer and politician who served as the last President of Czechoslovakia (1989–1992) and the first President of the Czech Republic (1993–2003)

**Don DeLillo** (1936–): DeLillo is an American novelist prominent as one of the pioneers of post-modern fiction.

rights of Brautigan's second novel, *Trout Fishing in America* (1967). However, the book quickly found a local following, fueled by the flourishing of the counterculture in San Francisco. Although Brautigan wrote his novel a few years before flower children, diggers, and hippies arrived en masse upon the scene, his dropout characters, gentle, unassuming narrative voice, and experimental prose style appealed to the youth movement. By the end of the decade, the author had passed from regional obscurity to the status of minor pop-culture icon. Not only did he gain a national following for *Trout Fishing in America*, but Brautigan also achieved a favorable reception among critics, many of whom admired his innovative, eclectic style and gentle humor.

*A Decade of Decline*   In 1970, Brautigan divorced his first wife after a long separation. At the same time, his writing career began going into a slump from which it would recover only briefly when, in the late 1970s, Brautigan discovered a receptive new audience in Japan. In 1977, he married a young Japanese woman named Akiko, who had sought him out because she felt the worldview of his fiction was uniquely Asian. Their marriage, which ended in divorce in 1980, served in part as the inspiration for *The Tokyo-Montana Express* (1980). Personal rejection and feelings of social isolation, either on the ranch or in Japan, mark several of the chapters,

making *The Tokyo-Montana Express* a transitional portrait of Brautigan's growing disillusionment and insecurity.

Brautigan's last novel, *So the Wind Won't Blow It All Away* (1982), failed to improve his literary reputation or sales. He faced mounting financial difficulties brought on by his decline in popularity and may have become increasingly despondent about his fading influence as a writer. These pressures and disappointments, perhaps combined with a personal life marked by heavy drinking, two divorces, and many breakups, may have led him to decide to end his life in the autumn of 1984. Brautigan's body was discovered on October 25 in his Bolinas, California home beside a .44 caliber Smith & Wesson he had borrowed weeks earlier from an acquaintance.

## Works in Literary Context

Some commentators maintain that Brautigan is an unclassifiable writer most closely allied with Kurt Vonnegut, Jr.; however, he has also been associated with such American authors as Henry David Thoreau, Walt Whitman, Herman Melville, and Ernest Hemingway. He shares with these authors an interest in the myths of rural American life, a respect for nature and solitude, and a propensity for unadorned language. Brautigan, however, does not share these writers' beliefs in the authenticity or value of rural lifestyles.

*A Tone at Odds with Serious Themes*   In his early novels, which are regarded as his most important works, Brautigan employs a poetic style of prose along with simple syntax and a whimsical tone while simultaneously exploring such serious themes as death, sex, violence, betrayal, loss of innocence, and the power of imagination to transform reality. In these works, Brautigan discards such traditional features of the novel as plot, characterization, and setting in favor of a more innovative approach that includes a carefree style that is intentionally at odds with the somber nature of his concerns. For example, *Trout Fishing in America* is considered a tragedy, which is written in a whimsical style that is purposefully inappropriate to the seriousness of Brautigan's subject matter. As Terrence Malley stated: "Ultimately, Brautigan is not writing a pastoral novel in *Trout Fishing in America*. Instead, he is writing an analysis of why the old pastoral myth of an America of freedom and tranquility is no longer viable." While some critics contend that the many brief sketches included in Brautigan's novels are only fragments unconnected in either theme or style, others find them to be humorous vignettes that interweave his central concerns without succumbing to the straightforward direction of traditional narratives.

*Linking Beat Poetry and Postmodernism*   Brautigan employed a uniquely Western American literary voice that combined an avant-garde rejection of convention with the playfulness of popular culture. His narrative style pioneered the kind of challenges to traditional prose writing that would later inform postmodern literature, where generic patterns, fixed meanings, and the undisputed authority of the narrator were all rejected. Brautigan is also considered a link between the Beat movement of the 1950s and the counterculture movement of the 1960s. *Trout Fishing in America* (1967), which is widely regarded as the most important of Brautigan's novels, exhibits many thematic and stylistic ties to Beat literature and anticipates the disillusionment experienced years later by the youth counterculture, a disillusionment that directly fed into the development of postmodern literature.

Brautigan, however, did not seem to develop along with the literary trends he initially influenced. In his novels of the 1970s, including *The Abortion: An Historical Romance, 1966* (1971), *The Hawkline Monster: A Gothic Western* (1974), and *Dreaming of Babylon: A Private Eye Novel, 1942* (1977), Brautigan parodies various genres of popular fiction, but in so doing, he became more conventional in his use of plot and characterization. While these works generated some serious critical attention, they were generally considered thematically and stylistically less significant than his early novels.

## Works in Critical Context

Although Brautigan enjoyed a generally favorable critical and commercial response to his experimental fiction in the 1960s, reviewers often panned his work as formally simplistic and conceptually light. Many critics dismissed his later fiction and poetry as self-absorbed, empty productions of a flower child whose moment had passed. While some critics found a subtle complexity and artistic purpose in Brautigan's seemingly plotless, monotone narrative fiction and his uniformly self-referential poetry, critical consensus at the time of his death cast Brautigan as a minor writer and a faddish literary icon whose significance had faded along with the counterculture out of which he emerged. While still perhaps a majority opinion, this view has begun to change slightly.

*Decline in Reputation* The late 1960s were the high point of Brautigan's critical influence and productivity, and thereafter his critical reputation as a serious writer steadily declined. As the tumultuous decade drifted into cultural memory, critics tended to categorize him as either a scene writer or a flash in the pan. Fairly or not, many reviewers characterized Brautigan's post-1960s fiction as the lesser work of an aging hippie struggling to recapture the charm and promise of his heyday. So while Brautigan's first three novels and his collected poems had at the outset of the 1970s earned him a substantial readership and some critical recognition, reviews of his subsequent literary productions often drew unfavorable comparisons with the Brautigan of *Trout Fishing in America*. By the late 1970s, interest in Brautigan's writing had waned considerably in the United States, and reviews of his last novel, *So the Wind Won't Blow It All Away* (1982), were frequently uncomplimentary.

# COMMON HUMAN EXPERIENCE

Brautigan's later novels were parodies of different popular genres. Here are some other works that parody popular styles of art:

*The History of Rasselas, Prince of Abissinia* (1759), a novella by Samuel Johnson. This novel parodies the philosophical romance that was popular in the eighteenth century.

*The Complete Works of William Shakespeare (Abridged)* (1987), plays by the Reduced Shakespeare Company. This collection of plays parodies the plays of William Shakespeare by reducing them to shortened versions capable of being presented by only three actors.

*This is Spinal Tap* (1984), a film by Rob Reiner. This film, presented in documentary form, both satirizes popular musicians and parodies the band documentary.

## Responses to Literature

1. Brautigan's later work was often criticized for being no more than parodies of various popular literary genres. Do you think parodies can qualify as having literary merit, or are such works limited by their mocking style? Provide examples to support your opinion.

2. Brautigan's works, particularly his earliest ones, were noted for employing an experimental prose style that anticipated the styles of later postmodern authors. What aspects of his style still seem experimental from a present-day perspective? In what ways do contemporary writers working in such new forms such as the blog demonstrate similar prose styles?

3. Some commentators attribute Brautigan's success in the late 1960s to the ways that his style and themes appealed to the youth movement of the time. Write an essay exploring the connections between the themes in one or more of Brautigan's first three novels with the concerns of the 1960s counterculture movement.

4. Commentators have noted that much of Brautigan's success lay in his writings being in the right place at the right time, namely the West Coast during the late 1960s. In order to explore how fair such charges are, write a review of one of Brautigan's novels as though it were published this year. Be sure to note whether or not Brautigan is in touch with the concerns of contemporary culture.

BIBLIOGRAPHY

**Books**

Abbott, Keith. *Downstream from Trout Fishing in America*. Santa Barbara, Calif.: Capra, 1989.

Boyer, Jay. *Richard Brautigan.* Boise, Idaho: Boise State University Press, 1987.

Chenetier, Marc. *Richard Brautigan.* London: Methuen, 1983.

Halsey, Edward Foster. *Richard Brautigan.* Boston: Twayne, 1983.

Kinkowitz, Jerome. *The American 1960s: Imaginative Acts in a Decade of Change.* Ames: Iowa State University Press, 1980.

Malley, Terence. *Richard Brautigan: Writers for the Seventies.* New York: Warner Paperback Library, 1972.

Tanner, Tony. *City of Words: American Fiction 1950–1970.* New York: Harper & Row, 1971.

**Periodicals**

Clayton, John. "Richard Brautigan: The Politics of Woodstock." *New American Review* 11 (1971): 56–68.

Horvath, Brooke. "Richard Brautigan's Search for Control Over Death." *American Literature* 57, no. 3 (1985): 434–455.

Schmitz, Neil. "Richard Brautigan and the Modern Pastoral." *Modern Fiction Studies* 19 (Spring 1973): 109–125.

Stevick, Philip. "Sheherazade Runs Out of Plots, Goes on Talking; the King, Puzzled, Listens: an Essay on New Fiction." *Tri-Quarterly* 26 (Winter 1973): 332–362.

Vanderwerken, David L. "*Trout Fishing in America* and the American Tradition." *Critique* 16, 1 (1974): 32–40.

# ✸ Gwendolyn Brooks

BORN: *1917, Topeka, Kansas*

DIED: *2000, Chicago, Illinois*

NATIONALITY: *American, African American*

GENRE: *Fiction, poetry*

MAJOR WORKS:

*Annie Allen* (1950)

"We Real Cool" (1960)

*Malcolm X* (1968)

## Overview

Gwendolyn Brooks, the first African American writer to win a Pulitzer Prize, was a major poet of the second half of the twentieth century. Brooks is best known for her sensitive portraits of urban blacks who encounter racism and poverty in their daily lives.

## Works in Biographical and Historical Context

***Early Notice*** Brooks was raised in Chicago, the eldest child of a schoolteacher and a janitor who, because he lacked the funds to finish school, did not achieve his dream of becoming a doctor. According to George Kent,

Gwendolyn Brooks    *Brooks, Gwendolyn, photograph. The Library of Congress.*

as a child Brooks "was spurned by members of her own race because she lacked social or athletic abilities, a light skin, and good grade hair." Brooks was hurt by such rejection, and she found solace in her writing. Impressed by her early poems, her mother predicted she would become "the lady Paul Laurence Dunbar"—one of the earliest and most famous African American poets.

Brooks received compliments on her poems and encouragement from James Weldon Johnson and Langston Hughes, prominent writers with whom she initiated correspondence and whose readings she attended in Chicago. By the age of sixteen, Brooks had compiled a substantial portfolio, including about seventy-five published poems. After graduating from Wilson Junior College in 1936, she worked briefly as a cleaning woman and then as a secretary to a "spiritual advisor" who sold potions and charms to residents of the Mecca, a Chicago tenement building. During this time she participated in poetry workshops at Chicago's South Side Community Art Center, producing verse that would appear in her first published volume, *A Street in Bronzeville* (1945).

*Growing Political Awareness* Brooks experienced a change in political consciousness and artistic direction after witnessing the combative spirit of several young black authors at the Second Black Writers' Conference at Fisk University in 1967. Around the same time, Brooks began her association with the Blackstone Rangers, a large gang of teenaged blacks in Chicago. In the late 1960s she held a poetry workshop for the Rangers. Here she began a continuing intense interest in fostering the talents of young black poets. As a result, her poetry underwent a major transformation, and she began to express a deep concern for the the black nationalist movement and racial solidarity. During that time, the Civil Rights Movement was making great strides in reducing institutionalized racial discrimination, but at the same time, radicalized leaders in the Black Power Movement were calling for more drastic measures to combat continued white domination. Her work with black artists and activists led Brooks to write poetry that more clearly advocated embracing a black identity and transforming black activism into a powerful political force.

During the 1970s, though, she began expressing disenchantment with the divisions that had emerged within and between the Black Power and Civil Rights movements. Although she did not change her political orientation, she came more and more to focus on encouraging and assisting young African American artists and supporting black businesses, particularly publishing companies. She left Harper & Row and began publishing her poetry through Dudley Randall's Broadside Press, a company that published a number of important African American writers. She has also published some of her works through Third World Press, a company run by one of the young poets she had met in the 1960s.

*Awards and Service* In addition to writing, Brooks was also dedicated to teaching, and she was a source of encouragement for younger poets. Beginning in 1963, she taught at various institutions, and in 1969 she established the Illinois Poet Laureate Award to encourage younger writers. Brooks was named poet laureate of the state of Illinois in 1978, and by the 1980s, Brooks was a widely respected and much-awarded author. In 1980, she read her works at the White House, and from 1985 to 1986, she served as Consultant in Poetry to the Library of Congress. In 1987 Brooks became the first black woman to be elected an honorary fellow of the Modern Language Association.

## Works in Literary Context

Gwendolyn Brooks holds a unique position in American letters. Not only has she combined a strong commitment to racial identity and equality with a mastery of poetic techniques, but she also has managed to bridge the gap between the academic poets of her generation in the 1940s and the young black militant writers of the 1960s.

## LITERARY AND HISTORICAL CONTEMPORARIES

Gwendolyn Brooks's famous contemporaries include:

**John F. Kennedy** (1917–1963): Kennedy was an American politician who was president of the United States from 1961 until his assassination in 1963; Kennedy also won a Pulitzer Prize for his 1957 biographical work *Profiles in Courage.*

**Carson McCullers** (1917–1967): McCullers was an American writer whose works explored themes of isolation and disenchantment in the South.

**Robert Lowell** (1917–1977): Lowell was an American poet whose confessional style earned him the Pulitzer Prize in poetry twice, in 1947 and again in 1974.

**Anthony Burgess** (1917–1993): Burgess was an English writer widely known for the film adaptation of his novel *A Clockwork Orange* (1962).

**Dizzy Gillespie** (1917–1993): Gillespie was an American musician who was one of the most influential figures in the development of bebop and modern jazz.

**Arthur C. Clarke** (1917–2008): Clark was a British writer who not only became a best-selling science fiction author with works like *2001: A Space Odyssey* (1968), but was also instrumental in developing the first geostationary communications satellites.

*Documenting the Black Experience* During her prolific career, Brooks used her writing to explore the poetic dimensions of the lives of black people. In her many forums, she listened to the voices of the kitchenette dwellers, the gang members, the woman pregnant with an unwanted child; she remained attentive to the sounds and sights of the larger world, as well. Brooks was a public poet, a democratic poet, and a word activist who had a passionate and ongoing commitment to working with young people. Whether they be college students, elementary-school students, or members of the Blackstone Rangers gang, Brooks believed that poetry has the ability to transform people's lives.

*Changing Perspectives on Discrimination* In her early work, Brooks avoided overt statements about the plight of many blacks in America, prompting critics to define the appeal of her poetry as "universal." Although Brooks's first collection of poems, *A Street in Bronzeville* (1945), focused on her experiences as a black American, it introduced broad thematic issues that would feature prominently in her works during the next two decades: family life, war, the quest for contentment and honor, and the hardships caused by racism and poverty. Her second collection of poetry, *Annie Allen* (1949), focused

# COMMON HUMAN EXPERIENCE

During the late 1960s and early 1970s, Brooks's works explored some of the most noteworthy social upheavals of the time, particularly those involving race and race relations. Here are some other works that explore race relations during that time period:

*Radical Chic & Mau-Mauing the Flak Catchers* (1970), a nonfiction work by Tom Wolfe. This book, which consists of two essays, explores the themes of black rage and white guilt during the late 1960s.

*Guess Who's Coming to Dinner* (1967), a film by Stanley Kramer. This Academy Award-winning film explores the tensions surrounding a mixed-race couple.

*Soul on Ice* (1970), an essay collection by Eldridge Cleaver. The letters and essays in this book explore a wide range of social issues, including racism, prison life, and the attitudes of members of the Nation of Islam, a prominent black nationalist organization that Cleaver had once supported.

on the growth of the title character from childhood to adulthood in an environment replete with indigence and discrimination.

During the late 1960s, however, her writing underwent a radical change in style and subject matter. Inspired by the black power movement and the militancy of such poets as Amiri Baraka (LeRoi Jones) and Haki R. Madhubuti (Don L. Lee), Brooks began to explore the marginality of black life through vivid imagery and forceful language and to recognize rage and despair among black people as her own. The verse in *Selected Poems* (1963) evidenced Brooks's growing interest in social issues and the influence of the early years of the Civil Rights Movement. It was not until *Riot* (1969) and *Family Pictures* (1970) that Brooks began examining the social upheavals of the late 1960s by exploring the revolutionary legacy of such slain black activists as Medgar Evers, Malcolm X, and Martin Luther King, Jr.

While her concern for the black nationalist movement and racial solidarity continued to dominate her verse in the early 1970s, the energy and optimism of *Riot* and *Family Pictures* were replaced with disenchantment resulting from the divisions that had appeared among civil rights and black nationalist groups. Although the increasing political schisms within the African American community as well as white reaction against gains made in the 1960s did not change Brooks's political beliefs, they did influence the tone of her poetry, pushing to explore the problems of bitterness and vengeance. Despite this shift in thematic concern, she continued to be noted for the objectivity of her poetry and her unsen-

timental take on humanity. However, as the 1970s wore on, Brooks' poetry became more overtly political than in the past. In *Beckonings* (1975) and *To Disembark* (1981), Brooks urged blacks to break free from the repression of white American society, and the clear political content of these poems led some critics to accuse her of celebrating and advocating violence.

## Works in Critical Context

Critics generally praised Brooks for her subtle humor and irony, her skillful handling of conventional poetic forms, and her invention of the sonnet-ballad, a verse structure integrating colloquial speech and formal diction. However, the literary quality of her later poetry has been debated by critics. Some commentators have faulted her for sacrificing formal complexity and subtlety for political polemic. According to D. H. Melhem, however, Brooks "enriches both black and white cultures by revealing essential life, its universal identities, and the challenge it poses to a society beset with corruption and decay."

***Annie Allen*** Brooks's second book of poems, *Annie Allen* (1949), began the movement of Brooks's poetry toward social issues, though it remained firmly grounded in real people. As Langston Hughes put it in a complimentary review of the collection, "The people and poems in Gwendolyn Brooks's book are alive, reaching, and very much of today." Despite some reservations, *Annie Allen* was well received in the mainstream press. In the *New York Times Book Review*, Phyllis McGinley found "The Anniad" outstanding and felt that when Brooks forgot "her social conscience and her Guggenheim scholarship" she created "unbearable excitement." Other reviewers mixed praise with complaints of obscurity and emerging propaganda. However, there was widespread agreement that Brooks presented a unique and compelling poetic voice. As the *Reference Guide to American Literature* put it, "Brooks writes both powerfully and universally out of the black American milieu, exploring the nature of racism, sexism, and classism in the United States in a distinctive poetic style." *Annie Allen* won the Pulitzer Prize in 1950, the first time that the award had been presented to a black honoree.

***In the Mecca*** The publication of *In the Mecca* in 1968 heralded a new political and aesthetic sensibility derived from the changing consciousness in the black community in the 1960s. To reviewers, *In the Mecca* was often a somewhat startling work, although most acknowledged that it was powerful. M. L. Rosenthal, writing in the *New York Times*, felt that the title poem was "overwrought with effects" and that the poet seemed to back away from her "overpowering subject." But he concluded that the poem "had the power of its materials and holds the imagination fixed on the horrid predicament of real Americans whose everyday world haunts the nation's conscience intolerably." William Stafford of *Poetry* magazine felt that Brooks achieved a "special kind of complexity" and that, although the poems were sometimes confusingly local in reference, "portions of the book come through strong." James N. Johnson in *Ramparts* magazine judged it Brooks's best work since *A Street in Bronzeville.*

## Responses to Literature

1. Brooks's early work tended to avoid overt statements about racism, while her later work was more directly inspired by the black power movement. In your opinion, is her message better communicated through the universal themes of her earlier poetry, or through the more direct and impassioned statements of her later work? Why? Do you see any disadvantages to the style you chose?

2. Some of Brooks's poetry, particularly from the late 1960s through the 1970s, was criticized for being more like propaganda. Find a definition for propaganda and compare it to one or more of Brooks's works from this period. Do you think the criticism is valid? Why or why not?

3. Brooks believed that poetry could change people's lives, and she dedicated much of her career to teaching creative writing and fostering the talents of young African American writers. Write an essay exploring the ways in which poetry can change people's lives, or write an argumentative essay either supporting or disputing Brooks's view.

4. Brooks's first collection of poems explored the problems of family life, war, the quest for happiness, and the difficulties of living life amid poverty and racism. These problems remained important themes for Brooks throughout much of her career, even as her poetry changed in other ways. Write an essay comparing Brooks's treatment of one or more of these themes in an early and later work.

BIBLIOGRAPHY

**Books**

Baker, Houston A., Jr. *Singers of Daybreak: Studies in Black American Literature*. Washington, D.C.: Howartt University Press, 1974.

Berry, S. L. *Gwendolyn Brooks*. Mankato, Minn.: Creative Education, 1993.

Brown, Patricia Scott, Don L. Lee, and Francis Ward, eds. *To Gwen with Love: An Anthology Dedicated to Gwendolyn Brooks*. Chicago: Johnson Publishing, 1971.

Erkkila, Betsy. *The Wicked Sisters: Women Poets, Literary History & Discord*. New York: Oxford University Press, 1993.

Evans, Mar, ed. *Black Women Writers (1950–1980): A Critical Evaluation*. Garden City, N.Y.: Anchor/ Doubleday, 1984.

Kamp, Jim, ed. *Reference Guide to American Literature*, 3rd ed. Chicago: St. James Press, 1994.

Kent, George E. *A Life of Gwendolyn Brooks*. Lexington, Ky.: University Press of Kentucky, 1990.

Melhem, D. H. *Gwendolyn Brooks: Poetry and the Heroic Voice*. Lexington, Ky.: University Press of Kentucky, 1987.

Miller, R. Baxter. *Langston Hughes and Gwendolyn Brooks: A Reference Guide*. Ann Arbor, Mich.: University of Michigan Press, 1966.

Mootry, Maria K. and Gary Smith, eds. *A Life Distilled: Gwendolyn Brooks, Her Poetry and Fiction*. Urbana, Ill.: University of Illinois Press, 1987.

Redmond, Eugene B. *Drumvoices: the Mission of Afro-American Poetry*. New York: Doubleday, 1976.

Wright, Stephen Caldwell. *On Gwendolyn Brooks: reliant contemplation*. Ann Arbor, Mich.: University of Michigan Press, 1996.

**Periodicals**

Hughes, Langston. "Name, Race, and Gift in Common." *Voices* (Winter 1950): 54–56.

# ✹ Charles Brockden Brown

BORN: *1771, Philadelphia, Pennsylvania*

DIED: *1810, Philadelphia, Pennsylvania*

NATIONALITY: *American*

GENRE: *Fiction*

MAJOR WORKS:

*Wieland* (1798)

*Ormond; Or the Secret Witness* (1799)

*Arthur Mervyn; Or, Memoirs of the Year 1793* (1799, 1800)

*Jane Talbot* (1801)

## Overview

Charles Brockden Brown was America's first professional man of letters, a novelist, publisher, and editor whose morally earnest Gothic tales attracted the attention of John Keats and Percy Shelley abroad and, among others, Edgar Allan Poe and Nathaniel Hawthorne at home. His career as a novelist was brief, intense, and brilliant, but he helped prepare for the more luxuriant flowering of American letters that was to come.

## Works in Biographical and Historical Context

*From Law to Writing* Charles Brockden Brown was born to a Quaker family in Philadelphia on January 17, 1771. His father was a merchant, descended from a family whose Quaker roots can be traced to the seventeenth century. His maternal ancestors, the Armitts, shared a similar heritage. The family business failed, although Brown's father managed to support his large family, probably through establishing new business activities in real estate.

From about the age of eleven to sixteen, Brown studied under the tutelage of Robert Proud at the Friends

Charles Brockden Brown    *Brown, Charles Brockden (body facing front), print.*

Latin School in Philadelphia, and after leaving it he went to work in the Philadelphia law office of Alexander Wilcocks without having attended college. The legal profession seems to have held little attraction for Brown, but he formed deep friendships at this time, particularly with William Wood Wilkins and Joseph Bringhurst, both of whom shared Brown's literary interests. The three of them were active in the Belles Lettres Club of Philadelphia, which was formed in 1786 and lasted until 1793. When Wilkins, who had gone on to complete his legal education, died in 1795, Brown lost his closest tie to the profession of law. By then Brown had already declined to complete his own education as a lawyer.

Brown had begun experimenting with the writing of literature even while he studied law. In 1789, a series of his essays, known as "The Rhapsodist," was published in *Columbian Magazine* in Philadelphia, and, after abandoning the law a few years later, he dabbled in poetry and fiction. In 1797, he finished a novel called "Sky-Walk," though he never published it and the manuscript has been lost. In 1798, he began having his work published at a remarkable pace. During this year, he brought out a portion of *Arthur Mervyn* in the *Weekly Magazine* as well as two complete works, *Wieland* and *Alcuin.*

***Experience with the Plague***   At around this time, several regions of the United States were afflicted with outbreaks of yellow fever, a potentially lethal viral disease transmitted by mosquitoes. Many victims of yellow fever developed a jaundiced appearance, which led to the disease's colorful name. There was no cure for yellow fever, and in severe cases the victim could bleed internally, which often resulted in death. The most severe American outbreak was in Philadelphia in 1793, where the disease is estimated to have killed approximately five thousand people, or one out of every ten Philadelphians. Another outbreak several years later had a profound impact on Brown's life and work.

The year in which Brown published *Wieland*, one of his best-known works, he had gone to live in New York. He shared his living accommodations with Elihu Hubbard Smith, a doctor whom he had met in 1792 and who may have been his closest friend, and another friend named William Johnson. Smith, through an altruistic impulse, had brought to their home an ailing Italian physician who soon died from yellow fever. Shortly afterward, Smith contracted the disease and died, and Brown was stricken as well. Thus, Brown was a close witness to the horrors of yellow fever, and his temptation to escape the city was obvious. However, he chose to remain in the midst of the plague, perhaps underestimating its threat.

In Philadelphia, early in 1798, he began his serial publication in the Weekly Magazine of "The Man at Home," a story drawing on the plague. It is certainly possible, however, that his experience in New York accounted for some of the contents of his published fiction in 1799. That year he had published *Ormond* and part one of *Arthur Mervyn,* both of which make use of the horrors of plague that Brown knew so well.

***Magazine Publishing***   In 1799, in addition to publishing *Edgar Huntly,* Brown began publication of a magazine, the *Monthly Magazine and American Review.* Although the magazine only survived until the end of 1800, during that time Brown doggedly pursued the task of searching out suitable contributions for the journal; he also contributed heavily from his own writing. He left New York in 1800, headed to Philadelphia, and looked for other means to earn money. He soon joined his family in the importing business. Brown seems to have maintained a connection with the family business until 1806, although his primary energies remained directed toward literary enterprises.

Toward the end of 1807, Brown introduced a new periodical, the *American Register, or General Repository of History, Politics, and Science.* Brown edited five volumes. Although the pages of this journal included literary topics, such as poetry (including Brown's own) and reviews of British and American literature, the main emphasis now reflected Brown's political and historical interests. Essentially, the *Register* was what its name implied. It kept a record of laws and state papers, but it also gave written accounts of contemporary events, such as a report on the gun duel between Alexander Hamilton, one of America's founding fathers, and Vice President Aaron Burr. During this time, Brown, who was never a very healthy individual, began to become more and more sickly. As was customary in his day, he took trips in hopes of restoring his health, but he succumbed to tuberculosis—a highly infectious and deadly disease usually characterized by bleeding in the lungs—in 1810, before turning forty.

## Works in Literary Context

*An American Perspective* Beginning in the years immediately after America gained its independence from England, America's artistic intellectuals called for a literature that would reflect well on the creative capacities of the new nation, a literature that could earn the respect of England even as it treated indigenous themes. In Charles Brockden Brown, a handful of critics on both sides of the Atlantic found a writer who appeared to meet these requirements. While many scholars have tended to see Brown as a derivative writer, one who drew heavily on the political ideas of William Godwin and on the Gothic tradition in literature, those contemporaries of his who admired him saw in his works the beginning of an original American literature of which the new country could be proud. For some of Brown's appeal lay in his depictions of American scenes, whether in writings about plagues in Philadelphia or in those about battles with Indians in the wilderness.

*Americanized Gothic Literature* Brown's four major novels have all attracted modern critical attention and have appeared in twentieth-century editions, largely because of Brown's use of Gothic conventions to explore psychological themes. For example, in *Wieland*, the theme is religious fanaticism that leads to madness and murder; in *Ormond* and *Arthur Mervyn*, vivid scenes of the plague in Philadelphia create an atmosphere of terror and mystery; and in *Edgar Huntly* wilderness settings and Indian wars become Gothic trappings for another tale of madness and murder, told by a sleepwalker. In these works, Brown adapted native materials to the conventions of Gothic romance, thus Americanizing Old World literary modes.

The elements and themes that predominate in Brown's fiction, however, are less Gothic than moral, social, and intellectual. All events that first appear mysterious, supernatural, or irrational in the works are eventually explained scientifically and rationally. For example, the disembodied voices in *Wieland* are the work of a ventriloquist, Ormond's extraordinary range of knowledge is due to his artful eavesdropping, and Edgar Huntly's inexplicable adventures result from his sleepwalking. However much Brown is torn between his fascination with the irrational and his interest in testing the strengths of rationally

---

## LITERARY AND HISTORICAL CONTEMPORARIES

Brown's famous contemporaries include:

**Napoleon Bonaparte** (1769–1821): Napoleon was a French general and political leader who ruled France following the French Revolution.

**Ludwig van Beethoven** (1770–1827): Beethoven was a German composer who is considered one of the greatest musical minds of all time.

**Georg Wilhelm Friedrich Hegel** (1770–1831): Hegel was a German philosopher whose writings influenced a wide range of subsequent thinkers, from Karl Marx to Jean-Paul Sartre.

**William Wordsworth** (1770–1850): Wordsworth was an English poet who is considered one of the primary founders of the Romantic Age in English literature.

**Sir Walter Scott** (1771–1832): Scott was a Scottish writer best known for his historical novels, particularly *Ivanhoe* (1820).

---

educated individuals, the key recurring moral point in his fiction seems to be a reaffirmation of basic Christianity. His flawed do-gooders all pointedly lack orthodox Christian training. His last published novel, *Jane Talbot* (1801), demonstrates his belief in the value of basic Christian principles against radical idealism. The social-moral philosophy of his fiction, thus, seems to arrive at a fairly conservative reaffirmation of the plain morality of his parents' Quakerism.

## Works in Critical Context

One of the great ironies of Brown's literary career was that he strove so hard to foster and participate in the development of a native American literature, yet his greatest recognition, mostly positive, came from English critics. That Americans paid inadequate attention to him was the subject of numerous essays in America that appeared over the years, but the calls for broader recognition notwithstanding, Brown remained an obscure writer in his native land, appreciated by only a handful of people.

In recent years, scholarly interest in Brown has increased significantly, and some critics have begun to make claims for him which indicate that he may have been ahead of his time. For example, Edwin Sill Fussell posited that *Wieland* was actually about Brown's struggle to break with dominant literary conventions, and that "in *Wieland* Charles Brockden Brown was writing about writing ... about that American literature not yet in existence but coming into existence as he confronted and incorporated the stiffest resistance imaginable, his own impossibility." Warren Barton Blake wrote in 1910 that "Brown

## COMMON HUMAN EXPERIENCE

Brown's writing was considered uniquely American because of his vivid depictions of scenes in American life. Here are some other works that feature memorable depictions of such uniquely American scenes:

*The Adventures of Tom Sawyer* (1876), a novel by Mark Twain. The action in this novel takes place along the Mississippi River and features numerous scenes of life in that region.

*The Grapes of Wrath* (1939), a novel by John Steinbeck. This novel tracks the progress of a family of sharecroppers driven from their home in the Midwest to seek a better life in California.

*The Last of the Mohicans* (1826), a novel by James Fenimore Cooper. This novel, which takes place during the French and Indian War, depicts the conditions in the American interior during the period prior to the American Revolution.

was, above all, a transitional figure" and that his works, "if they seem to us the crude expression of youth, are the expression of a literature's youth no less than an author's." Yet, oddly enough, whether seeing in his writing something to be condemned or praised, Brown's critics have generally agreed that his narratives rely heavily on improbabilities, that his characters are not clearly delineated, and that his plots border on the chaotic. For some, these qualities have represented aesthetic flaws; for others, they have been signposts of the ambiguities and uncertainties of the human mind and the human heart, examples of style conforming to substance. Whatever the justice of these competing views of him, scholarly interest in Brown has never been greater than at present.

*Reception of Wieland* When it was initially published, many critics dismissed *Wieland* as a flawed novel that demonstrated Brown's lack of writing skill. The work was seen as inconsistent, ambiguous, confusing, and overly dependent on Gothic romantic conventions. Some critics did note, however, that Brown had created a compelling and imaginative tale. As one anonymous reviewer noted, "The author has certainly contrived a narration deeply interesting; and whatever may be its faults ... *Wieland*, as a work of imagination, may be ranked high among the productions of the age."

However, *Wieland* has recently been reevaluated by modern scholars. Some critics began praising the novel for the very ambiguities that others had seen as a flaw, remarking that this was part of a deliberate strategy employed by Brown. As James R. Russo wrote, "*Wieland* is told by a confessed madwoman, Clara Wieland, and her narrative seems incoherent at times because she is confused, not because Brown is." Other contemporary commentators consider *Wieland* an indictment of American ideology. As Roberta F. Weldon writes,

By focusing on the error of the Wieland family, the novel examines the flawed design underlying the American ideal. The Wielands believe with Emerson that 'the individual is the world' but experience the danger of self-absorption and are destroyed by it. What emerges from this critical reevaluation of *Wieland* is that Brown may have been a more skilled and complex writer than his contemporaries believed.

## Responses to Literature

1. Early critics accused Brown of a lack of writing skill because his novels were ambiguous and often confusing, while later commentators have considered these features of Brown's writings as strengths that anticipated future developments in American literature. Which of these evaluations of Brown has more merit? Do his novels deserve to be seen as ambiguous and confusing, and in what ways might these features serve to enhance Brown's messages rather than detract from them?

2. One of Brown's literary goals was to help develop a national literature for the United States. In what ways did his novels contribute to this development? In what ways did his other writings contribute? Was his impact on this development greater as a novelist, as a magazine writer, or as a publisher?

3. Brown often wrote magazine essays assessing the current state of American literature at the time. Write an essay that assesses the current state of American literature today. Be sure to note any recent trends you can identify and attempt to discuss where American literature seems to be going.

4. Brown often included supernatural elements in his stories, yet he always resolved the apparent mystery with a rational, scientific explanation. Write a story that includes a mysterious element that appears supernatural at first but which can later be given a rational explanation.

BIBLIOGRAPHY
### Books

Allen, Paul. *The Life of Charles Brockden Brown: A Facsimile Reproduction*. Delmar, N.Y.: Scholars' Facsimiles and Reprints, 1975.

Axelrod, Alan. *Charles Brockden Brown*. Austin, Tex.: University of Texas Press, 1983.

Clark, David Lee. *Charles Brockden Brown, Pioneer Voice of America*. Durham, N.C.: Duke University Press, 1952.

Grabo, Norman S. *The Coincidental Art of Charles Brockden Brown*. Chapel Hill, N.C.: University of North Carolina Press, 1981.

Kimball, Arthur G. *Rational Fictions: A Study of Charles Brockden Brown*. McMinnville, Ore.: Linfield Research Institute, 1968.

Parker, Patricia. *Charles Brockden Brown: A Reference Guide*. Boston: G. K. Hall, 1980.

Petter, Henri. *The Early American Novel*. Columbus, Ohio: Ohio State University Press, 1971.

Ringe, Donald A. *Charles Brockden Brown*. New York: Twayne, 1966.

Rosenthal, Bernard, ed.. *Critical Essays on Charles Brockden Brown*. Boston: G. K. Hall, 1981.

Unger, Leonard. *American Writers: A Collection of Literary Biographies*. New York: Scribners, 1979.

Warfel, Harry R. *Charles Brockden Brown, American Gothic Novelist*. Gainesville, Fla.: University of Florida Press, 1949.

**Periodicals**

Blake, Warren Barton. "Title: Brockden Brown and the Novel." *The Sewanee Review* (Autumn 1910): 431–443.

"Review of 'Wieland; Or, the Transformation'." *The American Review, and Literary Journal* (January-March 1802): 28–38.

Dan Brown   *Brown, Dan, photograph. AP Images.*

# ❀ Dan Brown

BORN:   *1964, Exeter, New Hampshire*

NATIONALITY:   *American*

GENRE:   *Fiction*

MAJOR WORKS:

*Angels & Demons* (2000)

*The Da Vinci Code* (2003)

## Overview

Brown is most known for being the author of the best-selling novel, *The Da Vinci Code*, which sparked controversy because of its representations of the history of the Catholic Church. He combines intricate, fast-paced plotting with extensively-researched conspiracy theories to produce extremely popular mystery-thriller novels.

## Works in Biographical and Historical Context

*An Influential Upbringing*   Brown was born June 22, 1964, in Exeter, New Hampshire into an environment filled with the academic and the artistic: his mother was a musician, as Brown himself would later be, and his father was a math professor, foreshadowing Brown's own later interest in number puzzles and codes. Brown's interest in secret societies, an important component of his work, stems from his New England childhood, where he was surrounded by the secret societies of Ivy League schools and the elite private clubs and lodges, such as the Masonic Lodge. Cracking codes, which is central to Brown's storylines, began at an early age. His parents would leave clues for the children to guide them on treasure hunts as a stimulating form of entertainment.

Brown attended Phillips Exeter Academy, a private school located in his hometown. The environment at Exeter was strongly Christian, and Brown sang in the church choir, went to Sunday school, and attended church summer camp, all of which sparked an interest in religious history that would later influence his choice of subject matter for his novels. He graduated with a B.A. from Amherst College in 1986; during his junior year, he studied art history at the University of Seville in Spain. It was there that he first began studying the works of Leonardo da Vinci, an interest that would serve him in his later writing, particularly in the best-selling *The Da Vinci Code*.

*From Music to Writing*   Before turning to writing, Brown attempted a musical career. He self-produced an album for children entitled *SynthAnimals* and an adult CD entitled *Perspective*. He then moved to Los Angeles to pursue a career as a singer-songwriter, where he taught classes at Beverly Hills Preparatory School to support himself. He also met Blythe Newlon, the National Academy of

# LITERARY AND HISTORICAL CONTEMPORARIES

Brown's famous contemporaries include:

**Barack Obama** (1961–): Obama is an American politician who in 2009 became the 44th President of the United States and the first African American to assume that position.

**Bret Easton Ellis** (1964–): Ellis is an American novelist who is part of the literary Brat Pack that emerged in the 1980s.

**Courtney Love** (1964–): Love is an American musician who was married to Kurt Cobain of Nirvana and who served as the lead singer of her own band, Hole.

**Chris Rock** (1965–): Rock is an American actor and comedian, famous for his time as a performer on *Saturday Night Live*, as well as for his work in films such as *Osmosis Jones* (2001) and *Madagascar* (2005).

**J. K. Rowling** (1965–): Rowling is a British author of the best-selling Harry Potter fantasy novels, which concern a boy and his experiences while attending a school for wizards.

Songwriters' Director of Artistic Development. In 1993, Brown released the self-titled CD *Dan Brown*, but soon afterwards he moved back to New Hampshire to begin teaching English at his alma mater, Phillips Exeter Academy. Newlon went with him, and they were married four years later, in 1997. The previous year, Brown had quit teaching to pursue writing full-time.

It was during his time at Exeter that Brown got the idea for his first novel, *Digital Fortress* (1998). One of his students had been tracked down and briefly detained by the U.S. Secret Service agency, who somehow knew that the teenager had made hostile political comments via e-mail to a friend. This incident inspired Brown to further research government computer intelligence, which became the subject of *Digital Fortress*. This was soon followed by *Angels & Demons* (2000), *Deception Point* (2001), and *The Da Vinci Code* (2003), which spent months at the top of best-seller lists. Following the success of *The Da Vinci Code*, Brown's previous books also became best-sellers.

## Works in Literary Context

Brown is one of a growing number of best-selling mystery-thriller novelists, but his subject matter and approach set him apart from others. He deals primarily with high-level conspiracies and religious history, and his plots are driven by deciphering symbols, cracking codes, and following leads that come from secret information. In other ways, his writing is typical of best-selling thrillers, with undeveloped characters, action-packed chase scenes, and relatively unsophisticated dialogue.

***Doing His Research*** The hallmark of Brown's writing is the use of science and religion within the context of the action-oriented thriller novel. Brown researches his works thoroughly and heavily sprinkles his novels with history and other pertinent background information. As Nancy Pearl noted about *Angels & Demons*, Brown's novel is "both literate and extremely well researched, mixing physics with religion." This mixture has drawn praise from various reviewers and brought Brown a wider audience than is often found in his genre. As Andy Plonka noted of *Angels & Demons*, "The thriller devotees will be pleased, the information junkies content, the intricate puzzle enthusiasts satisfied, and the historical buffs appeased with a bit of church history and art history to contain their appetites." His other novels have been given similar praise. Jeff Zaleski wrote about *Deception Pass* that Brown has "done his research, folding in sophisticated scientific and military details that make his plot far more fulfilling than the norm."

***Secret Societies*** Brown's novels all prominently feature secret societies, either ancient or modern. In both *Digital Fortress* and *Deception Point*, highly secretive government agencies play a central role in both keeping and uncovering hidden information. Brown draws on religious history and conspiracies within Christianity for his other two novels. In *Angels & Demons*, the main character is drawn into an ancient struggle between a secret society and the Catholic Church, while *The Da Vinci Code* presents a controversial treatment of a secret Catholic society dedicated to suppressing certain facts about Jesus's life. These secret societies are driving forces in Brown's plots, not mere thriller window-dressing.

## Works in Critical Context

Brown has been widely praised for his ability to write novels with intricate plots that are fast-paced, suspenseful and entertaining, right up to their conclusions. Some reviewers fault Brown for relying on implausible premises and over-the-top conspiracies, but many find the narrative circumstances of his novels compelling and believable. Other critics have claimed that Brown's writing skills are lacking, that his characters are one-dimensional and his dialogue excruciating, but popular opinion suggests that for most readers, his books are difficult to put down.

***Critical Reception of Digital Fortress*** Brown's first novel, *Digital Fortress* (1998), was well received, and critics were pleased to note the skill and inventiveness of this new entry into the thriller genre. Sybil Steinberg of *Publisher's Weekly* called *Digital Fortress* an "inventive debut thriller." Reviewers noted elements that would be echoed by others writing about Brown's later books, particularly his ability to keep readers fascinated right up to the end. Gilbert Taylor wrote that Brown's skill at hiding his characters' deceits "will rivet cyber-minded readers." Steinberg noted that "Brown's tale is laced with twists and shocks that keep the reader wired right up to the last minute."

### *The Da Vinci Code: Praise and Controversy*

Although Brown's first three novels were well received and sold well, it was not until *The Da Vinci Code* that Brown achieved the popularity and critical attention that he is now known for. As with his other novels, reviewers described *The Da Vinci Code* as a "brainy" thriller, and they were impressed with Brown's ability to combine factual research with compelling intrigue and an entertaining storyline. One critic described *The Da Vinci Code* as "an ingenious mixture of paranoid thriller, art history lesson, chase story, religious symbology lecture and anticlerical screed." Annie C. Bond noted that

> Brown demonstrates not only knowledge of art, art history, and architecture but also a talent at weaving it all together into such an intricate tapestry that it becomes difficult to determine what is his imagination at work and what is actually a mini-lesson in history.

*The Da Vinci Code* was immediately surrounded by controversy, particularly because of Brown's claims about the accuracy of the book's art history and its representations of early Christian history. Critics hotly debated these claims, and while some commented on Brown's impressive research, others noted the implausible historical claims, factual inaccuracies, and distorted representations of the Catholic Church. Maurice Timothy Reidy described *The Da Vinci Code* as "an incredibly simplistic reading of both history and theology." Cynthia Grenier asserted that *The Da Vinci Code* shows "disregard for historical accuracy and a marked hostility to the Catholic Church." However, even hostile reviewers did agree that the book was highly entertaining. As Patrick McCormick, reviewing *The Da Vinci Code* in *The U.S. Catholic*, noted, "Brown's novel is a vastly entertaining read that mixes the thrill of a high-speed chase with the magical pleasures of a quest through an enchanted forest of art, literature, and history."

### Responses to Literature

1. Brown has been praised for the intellectual content of his novels but criticized for employing over-the-top action sequences and implausible premises. In what ways do the action sequences in his books detract from the intellectual content of the books and in what ways do they enhance them? In what ways are his premises implausible, and how does this impact the intellectual nature of his works?

2. Commentators have noted that Brown successfully mixes science with religion and history. In what ways does this mixture set his novels apart from other best-selling mystery-thrillers? Is Brown in a category

---

## COMMON HUMAN EXPERIENCE

Brown's novels are premised on conspiracy theories that present the reader with twists and turns. Here are some other novels that make use of conspiracy theories to generate their plots:

*The Crying of Lot 49* (1966), a novel by Thomas Pynchon. This novel follows the adventures of a woman unraveling a centuries-old underground battle among competing postal services.

*The Illuminatus! Trilogy* (1975), a series of novels by Robert Anton Wilson. These novels weave imaginary and historical conspiracies to explore a wide variety of themes, from numerology to counterculture lifestyles.

*Foucault's Pendulum* (1988), a novel by Umberto Eco. This novel includes a wide variety of esoteric references to topics such as alchemy and Kabbalah while weaving a complex plot around a satirical intellectual game that involves inventing conspiracy theories.

---

all by himself within this genre, or are there other novels and writers that employ a similar mixture with the same results?

3. Brown has been criticized for the historical inaccuracy and simplicity in his novels, particularly *The Da Vinci Code*. Write an argumentative essay that takes a position on the question of how important historical accuracy is for mystery-thriller novels. Use other novels not written by Brown to support your position.

4. Various reviewers and commentators have debated the feminist aspects of the underlying premise of *The Da Vinci Code*. Write an essay that explores the feminist themes in this novel and that takes a position on the message that Brown appears to be sending.

BIBLIOGRAPHY

**Books**

Eder, Doris L. "The Formula: The Novels of Dan Brown." Contemporary Literary Criticism. Farmington Hills, MI: Thomson Gale, 2005.

**Periodicals**

Abbott, Charlotte. "Code Word: Breakout." *Publishers Weekly* (January 27, 2003).

Ayers, Jeff. "Brown, Dan. *The Da Vinci Code*." *Library Journal* (February 1, 2003).

Bond, Annie C. "Review of *The Da Vinci Code*, by Dan Brown." *Phi Kappa Phi Forum* (Fall 2003): 42–43.

"Decoding *The Da Vinci Code*." *Newsweek* (December 8, 2003).

Grenier, Cynthia. "Novel Gods." *Weekly Standard* (September 22, 2003): 32–34.

Heydron, Jo Ann. "Literary Art." *Sojourners* (July-August 2003).

Lawson, Mark. "Signs for the Times." *Guardian* (July 26, 2003).

Lazarus, David. "*Da Vinci Code* a Heart-Racing Thriller." *San Francisco Chronicle* (April 6, 2003).

McCormick, Patrick. "*The Da Vinci Code.*" *U.S. Catholic* (November 2003).

Pearl, Nancy. "Cheap Thrills: Novels of Suspense." *Library Journal.* (November 15, 2000).

Reidy, Maurice. "Breaking the Code." *Commonweal* (September 12, 2003): 46.

"Review of *The Da Vinci Code.*" *Publishers Weekly* (February 3, 2003).

Sennett, Frank. "*The Da Vinci Code.*" *Booklist* (March 1, 2003).

Steinberg, Sybil. "Review of *Digital Fortress.*" *Publishers Weekly* (December 22, 1997).

Taylor, Gilbert. "Review of *Digital Fortress.*" *Booklist* (January 1, 1998): 780.

# Dee Brown

BORN: *1908, Alberta, Louisiana*

DIED: *2002, Little Rock, Arkansas*

NATIONALITY: *American*

GENRE: *Fiction, nonfiction*

MAJOR WORKS:

*Bury My Heart at Wounded Knee: An Indian History of the American West* (1970)

## Overview

Historian and novelist Dee Brown examined the history of westward expansion. His works not only present the hardships and challenges involved in this history, but also draw attention to the impact on Native Americans and chronicle the destruction of their ancient cultures.

## Works in Biographical and Historical Context

*Childhood Interest in Native Americans* Dee Brown was born in a logging camp in Alberta, Louisiana, on February 28, 1908. His father, Daniel Alexander Brown, died when Dee was five years old. Soon afterward, Brown moved with his mother and siblings to Stephens, Arkansas, where his mother became the postmaster of the town. The family lived with Brown's maternal grandmother, whose father had known Davy Crockett. She told stories to her grandson about the famous frontiersman and how her family survived the Civil War.

Brown's interest in Native Americans stemmed from these stories, as well as a childhood in Arkansas, where he

Dee Brown    *Photo courtesy of Charles G. Ellis*

met many Native Americans. Noticing that they bore little resemblance to the villainous stereotypes then prevalent in movies, Brown began to read everything he could about their history and culture.

*Becoming a Librarian and Historian* Following his graduation from Arkansas State Teachers College in 1931, Brown studied library science at George Washington University in Washington, D.C., where he earned a B.L.S. in 1937. Jobs were scarce because of the Great Depression, but Brown managed to find a job at the U.S. Department of Agriculture library. His experience as a librarian greatly influenced his later writing: with such a wealth of reference materials at his disposal, Brown relied heavily on historical documents such as diaries, letters, and official government papers to bolster the authenticity of his nonfiction works. Brown also applied this same level of scrupulous research to his fictional works, many of which were based on actual historical events or people.

Brown's first book, a novel satirizing New Deal bureaucracy under President Franklin D. Roosevelt, who was still in office at the time, was accepted by McCrae-Smith publishers, but the Japanese bombed Pearl Harbor before its publication, and publication was aborted because the publishers considered the novel too unpatriotic. During the months before being drafted into the Army, Brown wrote his first published book, *Wave High the Banner, a Novel Based on the Life of Davy Crockett* (1942). This novel was inspired by stories he had heard his grandmother tell when he was a child.

Brown did not serve overseas during World War II, and during his time in the Army, he had access to the National Archives, where he conducted research that led to his first volumes of history. After World War II, Brown took a job as the librarian of agriculture at the University of Illinois at Urbana-Champaign, where he worked until 1975 as both a librarian and a professor of library science.

*An Ambitious History*   In the late 1960s, after writing numerous books about the American West, including histories, novels and books for young adults, Brown embarked upon his most ambitious and successful historical work, *Bury My Heart at Wounded Knee* (1970), a book that chronicles the settling of the West based on eyewitness reports from the Native Americans who lived there. Brown's reason for writing the book, explained Peter Farb of the *New York Review of Books*, was reflected in his belief that "whites have for long had the exclusive use of history and that it is now time to present, with sympathy rather than critically, the red side of the story."

Brown continued writing at a strenuous pace even as *Bury My Heart at Wounded Knee* was receiving critical acclaim and selling millions of copies. He wrote over a dozen more books during the next thirty years. His last book, a novel for young adults titled *The Way to Bright Star* (1998), was published when he was ninety years old. Brown died on December 12, 2002, at the age of ninety-four at his home in Little Rock.

## Works in Literary Context

As an historian and novelist, Brown has focused almost exclusively on the American West of the nineteenth century. During a career that included over thirty books, Brown has examined nearly every phase of the history of westward movement, and his novels dramatize events and characters in that history. Brown's accounts of Native Americans in both his histories and novels has been pivotal in changing attitudes towards the treatment of the Native Americans and the dominant legends of the West.

*New Perspectives on the Old West*   Brown's work challenged conventional ideas on various historical topics, and his works of fiction, which feature stories set amid the actual conditions of the nineteenth-century West, dramatize many of the themes present in his histories. *Bury My Heart at Wounded Knee* (1970), for example, brought a new perspective to the historical perception of the American frontier and changed the attitude of scholars toward the history of the West. Focusing on racism, deception, and carelessness, *Bury My Heart at Wounded Knee* highlighted the mistreatment of Native Americans between 1860 and 1890. According to C. Fred Williams, a professor at the University of Arkansas at Little Rock, "The effect of *Bury My Heart* was essentially to give voice to the American Indians. They were always an important part of the American West, usually as the indirect object. Dee Brown [made] them the direct object."

Brown's subsequent historical works also diverged from traditional approaches. In *Hear That Lonesome Whistle Blow: Railroads in the West* (1977), Brown wrote about the construction of the Western railroads by exposing the underhanded dealings of the railroad companies. Brown's efforts on that book led the Union Pacific railroad to deny him access to its corporate library. Oddly, Brown's *Wondrous Times on the Frontier* (1993), a collection of stories covering the social and cultural history of the Old West, took a lighter approach to frontier life than other recent histories. As Paula Mitchel Marks of *Washington Post Book World* wrote, "Brown's key word is 'merriment'—there are 'merry' frontier courtrooms and military expeditions, merry cowboys and gold stampeders and gamblers." In general, though, Brown's histories of the settling of the West focused on the hardships and negative effects rather than the standard catalogue of triumphs.

## Works in Critical Context

Critics have mostly praised Brown for the shift in perspective he brought to the history of the West. Donna Seaman wrote that Brown "reminds us that myths are based on actual events, people, places and concepts, and encourages us to learn the 'true' history of the West 'so we can recognize a myth when we see one.'" *Los Angeles Times Book Review* contributor Larry Watson noted Brown's achievement in documenting the "astonishing swiftness" with which Native American customs and cultures were transformed: "Brown documents these losses,

# COMMON HUMAN EXPERIENCE

Brown's works cover the history of the American West during the 1800s with an emphasis on the Native American perspective. Here are some other historical works that cover the same times and places from a similar perspective:

*Trail of Tears: The Rise and Fall of the Cherokee Nation* (1989), a nonfiction book by John Ehle. This book about the removal of the Cherokee tribe to the West also provides a portrayal of the Cherokee nation itself, including Native American legend, lore, and religion.

*Native American Testimony: A Chronicle of Indian-White Relations from Prophecy to the Present, 1942–2000* (1999), a nonfiction book by Peter Nabokov. This book presents a history of relations between Native Americans and European Americans through Native American eyes and with Native American voices.

*A People's History of the United States* (1995), a non-fiction work by Howard Zinn. This book covers American history after Columbus's arrival in the New World to the present by presenting the voices of women, African Americans, Native Americans, war resisters, and poor laborers of all nationalities.

until, finally, the American West feels more like an elegy than history."

Not all reviewers were satisfied with Brown's range or perspective. Elliot West of the *Washington Post Book World* criticized Brown for leaving out many important aspects of the frontier experience. West wrote, "Mountain men and traders, the Mexican War, the Mormons, Lewis and Clark, missionaries and buffalo hunters are only the merest flickerings in the narrative." However, like many others, West praised Brown's storytelling abilities and the strength brought to his work by including the perspectives of ordinary men and women.

**Bury My Heart at Wounded Knee** *Bury My Heart at Wounded Knee* has sold more than five million copies since its initial publication and has been translated into fifteen languages. This was not only Brown's best-selling book, but also his most important contribution to the field of history, a fact noted by several critics. Cecil Eby of *Book World* wrote that *Bury My Heart at Wounded Knee* "will undoubtedly chart the course of other 'revisionist' historical books dealing with the Old West." Helen McNeil of the *New Statesman* called the book "a deliberately revisionist history [that tells] the story of the Plains Indians from an amalgamated Indian viewpoint, so that the westward march of the civilized men ... appears as a barbaric rout of established Indian culture." Peter Farb of the *New York Review of Books* wrote that

Brown "dispels any illusions that may still exist that the Indian wars were civilization's mission or manifest destiny."

One of the most frequently cited strengths of the book was the way that Brown achieved a uniquely Native American viewpoint. In order to do this, Brown not only based his work on eyewitness accounts by Native Americans, but also made extensive use of these eyewitnesses' own words. He also employed the Native American names for the white figures of the period, such as General Custer, who was called "Hard Backsides" by the Native Americans. "When the names are 'consistently used,'" wrote R.A. Mohl in *Best Sellers*, "these become creative and effective literary devices which force the reader, almost without his knowing it, into the position of the defeated, retreating Indian."

## Responses to Literature

1. Brown's novels draw on true events and real characters from history. How do Brown's depictions of such real persons as Custer compare with others' treatment of these same persons? Does Brown's status as an historian give more credence to his fictionalized versions of these characters? Why or why not?

2. Before Brown's ground-breaking *Bury My Heart at Wounded Knee*, most histories of the American West all but ignored the perspective of the Native Americans. To what extent has that oversight been corrected in recent decades? In what ways do present-day history textbooks present the perspectives of Native Americans? Is this presentation adequate to give a sense of the Native American experience?

3. Brown's histories often took a different perspective than that of conventional history books. Choose a conventional history book that covers the same period as one of Brown's books and write an essay comparing it to Brown's treatment. Be sure to note not only differences in style and emphasis, but places where facts and events covered in one book are ignored in the other.

4. Much of Brown's fiction was based on real events and characters from American history. Write a story that dramatizes a historical event in which you are interested or presents a real historical figure participating in an imagined situation.

BIBLIOGRAPHY

**Books**

*Contemporary Authors Autobiography Series*, Volume 6. Detroit, Mich.: Thomson Gale, 1988.
*Contemporary Southern Writers*. Detroit, Mich.: St. James Press, 1999.
Jackson, Kenneth T., Karen Markoe, and Arnold Markoe, eds. *The Scribner Encyclopedia of American Lives*. New York: Charles Scribner's Sons, 2004.

Snodgrass, Mary Ellen. *Encyclopedia of Frontier Literature.* Santa Barbara, Calif.: ABC-CLIO (1997).

**Periodicals**

Courtemanche-Ellis, Anne. "Meet Dee Brown: Author, Teacher, Librarian." *Wilson Library Bulletin* (March 1978): 552–561.

Marks, Paula Mitchell. "Review of *Wondrous Times on the Frontier.*" *Washington Post Book World* (January 5, 1992): 6.

Momaday, M. Scott. "Review of *Bury My Heart at Wounded Knee.*" *New York Times Book Review* (March 7, 1971): 46.

Razer, Bob. "Dee Brown, 1908–2002: Arkansan, Librarian, Historian." *Arkansas Libraries* (February 2003): 1, 7–11.

"Review of *Bury My Heart at Wounded Knee.*" *Library Journal* (December 15, 1970): 42, 57.

# ✸ Rosellen Brown

BORN: *1939, Philadelphia, Pennsylvania*

NATIONALITY: *American*

GENRE: *Fiction, poetry*

MAJOR WORKS:

*The Autobiography of My Mother* (1976)

*Tender Mercies* (1978)

*Before and After* (1992)

Rosellen Brown    *Brown, Rosellen, photograph. © Jerry Bauer. Reproduced by permission.*

## Overview

Rosellen Brown is a well-respected, best-selling novelist and poet whose works are noted for their intensity of metaphor and imagery. Brown's primary focus is on family relations, and her works explore such issues as loyalty, self-preservation and self-fulfillment, and the individual's relationship with the local community.

## Works in Biographical and Historical Context

*A Childhood of Movement*    Brown was born in Philadelphia on May 12, 1939. Because her father was a salesman, Brown's family moved several times during her childhood. Brown often felt alienated at school, and she used writing to fill her free time. In high school she turned to journalism. Because of her writing, she received a scholarship to attend Barnard College, an all-women's college in New York City. After receiving her degree from Barnard in 1960, she went on to graduate studies at Brandeis University, graduating with an MA in 1962. She married the following year.

*Location Influences*    Brown has moved throughout her adulthood, just as she did during her childhood, and the various places she has lived have figured prominently in her writing. In 1965, Brown took a position at Tou-

galoo College in Mississippi, where she witnessed the upheavals of the Civil Rights Movement. During this time, there was a high-profile showdown between the federal government and the Southern states over questions of desegregation and equal access to public facilities. Seeing this showdown firsthand influenced he first collection of poetry, *Some Deaths in the Delta and Other Poems* (1970). Questions of race relations were also important in her later works, particularly in *Civil Wars* (1984).

After leaving Mississippi, Brown and her husband moved to Brooklyn, New York, which became the setting of her second published work, *Street Games: A Neighborhood* (1974). She then lived in New Hampshire, where her poetry collection *Cora Fry* (1977) was set.

Brown continued to move frequently, taking teaching positions at Goddard College in Vermont, Boston University, University of Houston, and Northwestern University and the School of Art Institute in Chicago. Her works continue to draw on her personal experiences moving around the country, though they have also come to focus on questions of family relations. Her latest work, *Half a Heart* (2000), includes many of the themes evident throughout her works, including racial issues, the Civil Rights Movement, and family relationships.

# LITERARY AND HISTORICAL CONTEMPORARIES

Rosellen Brown's famous contemporaries include:

**Richard Brautigan** (1935–1984): Brautigan is an American author who is considered one of the links between the Beat Generation and the counterculture generation.

**Patricia Grace** (1937–): Grace is considered New Zealand's foremost Maori woman writer.

**Margaret Atwood** (1939–): Atwood is a Canadian writer who is one of the most award-winning authors of the late twentieth and early twenty-first century.

**Anne Rice** (1941–): Rice is an American novelist best known for writing popular vampire tales and other Gothic-style novels.

# COMMON HUMAN EXPERIENCE

Brown frequently uses multiple narrative voices to present the perspective of different characters in her stories. Here are some other works that employ a similar narrative technique:

*Talking It Over* (1991), a novel by Julian Barnes. This novel explores the different views and feelings of the three people involved in a love triangle, two of whom are best friends from school days and the third is the wife of one of the two men.

*Q* (1999), a novel by Luther Blissett. This novel, written by four different authors all using the pen name "Luther Blissett," chronicles several Protestant reformation movements in the sixteenth century as told by multiple narrators each participating in a different aspect of the story.

*Innocent Traitor* (2006), a novel by Alison Weir. This novel tells the story of Lady Jane Grey, a real historical figure, from the viewpoint of many of the characters involved in her life, shortly after the death of King Henry VIII.

*Rashomon* (1950), a film by Akira Kurosawa. In this Academy Award-winning film, several witnesses—including, with the help of a medium, a dead man—each recount their own version of a tragic incident in the woods involving a bandit, a samurai, and his wife.

## Works in Literary Context

***Using Dual Perspectives*** Brown frequently employs dual narrative voices to portray her main characters' different perspectives. Her first collection of poetry, *Some*

*Deaths in the Delta*, and her first two novels, *The Autobiography of My Mother* (1976) and *Tender Mercies* (1978), all employed two distinct narrative voices for the main characters. In the novels, Brown showed the different views of the two main characters on the family relationships explored in the story. In *Tender Mercies*, not only are there two different perspectives, Brown employs two distinct styles for her narrators: the husband's voice is straightforward prose while the wife's voice is stream-of-consciousness and often poetic. Brown returned to this technique in *Half a Heart*, exploring a mother-daughter relationship through a narrative that gives the mother and daughter separate voices and styles.

***Fusing Prose and Poetry*** Brown is a poet as well as a novelist, and she is noted for fusing poetry and prose in her novels. She often includes vivid imagery and lyrical writing in her prose, and she employs poetic language to provide distinct voices for different characters in her dual-narrative novels. She explicitly blends poetry and prose in *Cora Fry's Pillow Book* (1994), which is a sequel to her poetry collection *Cora Fry* (1977) that includes the original story continued through a series of poetic verses.

## Works in Critical Context

Brown has been praised for her lyrical prose and skillful use of different narrative styles as well as her evocative and precise descriptions. However, some reviewers have noted that her characters are difficult to empathize with, partly because of her superficial character depictions and fragmented, incomplete details that leave too many questions unanswered. Other reviewers, however, have claimed that she is able to develop her characters through stray details and sporadic background information. In general, though, critics praise Brown's ability to depict families under stress in a realistic and compelling manner, and a number of reviewers have given her major works impressive reviews.

***Tender Mercies*** Brown has often been noted for her ability to take on difficult issues in familial relations with insight and skill. Her second novel, *Tender Mercies*, was called an "intense and challenging" book by a *Chicago Tribune* critic and the monologues that make up some of the book were considered "uncanny, sometimes brilliant" by a reviewer for the *Washington Post Book World*. Joyce Carol Oates states that *Tender Mercies* is "a haunting novel" which "contains prose as masterful, and as moving, as any being written today."

***Before and After*** Brown's 1992 novel, *Before and After*, received more mixed reviews. While a *Washington Post Book World* reviewer called *Before and After* "a superior novel" and, "for all its pain and sadness, ... [Brown's] most affirmative book," a reviewer for the *Nation* "closed this novel unsatisfied." A *Contemporary Novelist* reviewer praised the book for its strong character depictions and challenging themes but concluded that "Reading Rosellen Brown is a highly personal experience; hers isn't the angst for everybody."

## Responses to Literature

1. Brown often explores relationships in families that are under stress or facing a crisis of some kind. In what ways do these works reveal something about the dynamics in families under more normal circumstances? What kinds of things would Brown have to say about a more typical family living a relatively peaceful life?

2. Many of Brown's stories take place in locations where she has personally lived. In what ways do her personal experiences in these locations enhance her writing about the characters living there? Does she make adequate use of her personal knowledge to transport the reader to that location?

3. Brown employs a dual-perspective narrative in her novels in order to present the story from the point of view of two major characters. Write a story that employs the dual-narrative technique, using a different perspective as well as a different style of voice for each character.

4. Some of Brown's novels explore familial relationships. Write an essay the identifies one or two recurring messages that Brown is attempting to send about the nature of the modern family and that assesses the validity of her conclusions about the modern family.

BIBLIOGRAPHY

**Books**

Bonetti, Kay, ed. *Conversations with American Novelists: The Best Interviews from The Missouri Review and the American Audio Prose Library.* Columbia, Mo.: University of Missouri Press, 1997.

*Contemporary Novelists,* sixth edition. Detroit: St. James, 1996.

*Contemporary Literary Criticism,* Volume 32. Detroit: Gale, 1985.

**Periodicals**

Brown, Rosellen and Judith Pierce Rosenberg. "*PW* Interviews: Rosellen Brown." *Publishers Weekly* (August 31, 1992): 54–55.

Brown, Rosellen and Melissa Walker. "An Interview with Rosellen Brown." *Contemporary Literature* (Summer 1986): 144–159.

Dunford, Judith. "Realms of Wrong and Right." *Chicago Tribune Books* (September 6, 1992): 1, 6.

Lee, Don. "About Rosellen Brown." *Ploughshares* (Fall 1994): 235–240.

# ◉ Joseph Bruchac

BORN: *1942, Saratoga Springs, New York*

NATIONALITY: *American*

GENRE: *Fiction*

MAJOR WORKS:
*Keepers of the Earth* (1988)
*Turtle Meat and Other Stories* (1992)
*The Boy Who Lived with the Bears and Other Iroquois Stories* (1995)

## Overview

Joseph Bruchac is the author of more than thirty books of poetry, fiction, and Native American folktales and legends. Throughout his works, Bruchac explores such subjects as spirituality, the sacredness of the natural world, and Native American history, culture, and literature.

## Works in Biographical and Historical Context

***Native American Storyteller*** Born in 1942 near upstate New York's Adirondack mountains, Bruchac is of Slovak, English, and Abenaki heritage. He was raised by his grandparents, and while he was very close to his Abenaki grandfather, Bruchac notes that the older man "would never speak of the Indian blood which showed so strongly in him." It was during his teenage years that Bruchac began to meet other Native Americans and learn both about his Abenaki heritage and other Indian cultures.

Bruchac began writing at an early age, and even after being beaten up by another student after his second-grade teacher read one of his poems in class, he continued writing. He was also a voracious reader, particularly of children's stories about animals. He would later write in this genre himself.

***Becoming a Teacher*** Bruchac earned his bachelor's degree from Cornell University in 1965 and, in order to pursue a career as an educator, he attended Syracuse University, where he earned a master of arts. From 1966 to 1969 he taught English and literature in Ghana, West Africa. Of this experience, he says,

> It showed me many things. How much we have as Americans and take for granted. How much our eyes refuse to see because they are blinded to everything in a man's face except his color. And, most importantly, how human people are everywhere—which may be the one grace that can save us all.

When Bruchac returned to the United States, he began teaching African and black literature and creative writing at Skidmore College in Saratoga Springs. While teaching, he completed his PhD at Union Graduate School. During this time, he also taught creative writing in prisons around the U.S., where he established writing

## LITERARY AND HISTORICAL CONTEMPORARIES

Bruchac's famous contemporaries include:

**Judy Blume** (1938–): Blume is an American author who has achieved widespread popularity; her childrens' and young adults' books frequently tackle difficult and controversial issues.

**Robert Olen Butler** (1945–): Butler is an American author best known for his Vietnam War novels and stories, which include the perspective of the Vietnamese.

**Leonard Peltier** (1944–): Peltier is an American Indian rights activist and member of the American Indian Movement; he was imprisoned after a 1975 shootout between Native Americans and FBI agents on the Pine Ridge Reservation in South Dakota.

**Octavia E. Butler** (1947–2006): Butler is an African American author known for exploring themes of racial and sexual identity within science-fiction settings.

**Louise Erdrich** (1958–): Erdrich is a Native American author and poet of Chippewa descent whose works include *The Beet Queen* (1986) and *The Antelope Wife* (1999), winner of the World Fantasy Award for Best Novel.

workshops to provide encouragement to prisoners who wanted to become writers.

**Preserving Native Culture**   In 1970, Bruchac and his wife Carol founded the Greenfield Review Press to provide an outlet for poetry and short fiction for writers from various cultures. Soon afterwards, he published his first volume of poetry, *Indian Mountain and Other Poems* (1971). In 1984, he compiled *Breaking Silence: An Anthology of Contemporary Asian American Poets*, which won the American Book Award from the Before Columbus Foundation.

Bruchac then returned to exploring his Native American heritage through stories he was telling to his young sons. He wrote down and compiled some of these stories to produce his first collection, *Turkey Brother and Other Tales* (1976). This was soon followed by another collection, *Stone Giants and Flying Heads: Adventure Stories of the Iroquois* (1978). He was soon in demand as a speaker at elementary schools, and he began weaving his Native American traditions into activity books for children, resulting in the best-selling books *Keepers of the Earth* (1988) and *Keeper of the Animals* (1991).

Bruchac also began writing his own stories that were similar to but not copies of Native American legends. *Turtle Meat and Other Stories* (1992) was his first collection of original stories, followed soon after by his first

novel, *Dawn Land* (1993). He has since written, collaborated on, and edited several dozen books for various audiences.

Bruchac now lives with his wife in the house where he grew up. He and others in his family work on projects to preserve the Abenaki culture and language as well as traditional Native American skills.

## Works in Literary Context

Bruchac is best known for his children's books depicting Native American tales and legends, but his literary output also includes poetry, short story collections, and novels, and he has written for a diverse audience, from children to academics. Bruchac's creative works are quite diverse within themselves as well, incorporating various styles, devices, and voices. For example, in *Turtle Meat and Other Stories* he includes such literary forms as adventure tales, childhood reminiscences, and adaptations of the traditional Native American trickster myth.

In addition to his creative works, Bruchac has also edited or co-edited numerous anthologies of Native American folklore and Asian American poetry. His *Breaking Silence: An Anthology of Contemporary Asian American Poets* won an American Book Award in 1984. He is also the founding editor of the Greenfield Review Press, a respected publisher of Native American literature, and is on the editorial board of the journal *Studies in American Indian Literatures*. Through these literary and editorial activities, Bruchac works to preserve and transmit Native culture.

**Writing Down an Oral Tradition**   Many of Bruchac's works exist in the potentially paradoxical position of recording in writing an essentially oral tradition. As Patricia Craig points out, "Native American storytelling was a means of transmitting the history of the group from generation to generation. The storyteller formed the link between the traditions of the past and those of the present." Bruchac is able to transmit this history successfully through the printed work. As a *Publisher's Weekly* reviewer noted, "Even on the printed page, Bruchac's tales ring of the oral tradition he helps preserve."

**Reflecting Native Concerns**   Much of Bruchac's work is an attempt to preserve Abenaki culture and transmit Native American values. He has been very successful at doing this through his collections of stories for children, particularly his best-selling series of children's books, *Keepers of the Earth* (1988) and *Keeper of the Animals* (1991). These are two of his many works that use authentic Native American tales translated by Bruchac himself. These particular books illustrate lessons in natural history and ecology that reflect the environmental concerns of Bruchac's Native American heritage. The *Keepers* books are highly popular with schools, museums, and nature centers. Bruchac's other works that translate or retell Native American tales are similarly oriented around reflecting the Native American respect for the natural world.

## Works in Critical Context

Bruchac's collections of Native American stories and folktales in particular have been highly praised for their incorporation of numerous personas, viewpoints, narrative techniques, and dialects. Critics have also lavishly praised Bruchac's diverse storytelling abilities. Carl L. Bankston III wrote,

> Some writers have a single story they tell over and over again, in the same voice, renaming the characters and rearranging the events. ... Others, the true storytellers, change constantly, adopting a new tone for each tale, submerging themselves in their characters, producing the unexpected in each new narrative. Joseph Bruchac is one of the true storytellers.

*Turtle Meat and Other Stories*   Bruchac's first collection of stories, *Turtle Meat and Other Stories* (1992) was well received by reviewers, who noted his strong storytelling abilities. *Publisher's Weekly* called it "highly entertaining," and Bankston compared Bruchac to "a storyteller seated before a campfire." Bruchac has also been commended for the quality of his writing. Bankston asserts that Bruchac "can express himself in startling imagery." A *Kirkus Reviews* critic noted, "Much of the charm here is in the writing and in the slyly laconic, self-aware humor of Indian conversation. Style, humor, and grace enliven familiar themes; atypical for folkloric writing, most characters emerge three-dimensional and real."

*The Keepers Books*   Bruchac is well known for *Keepers of the Earth* (1988) and *Keeper of the Animals* (1991), his best-selling collections of stories designed to inspire elementary-school children to understand their connections to the natural world. Reviewers have generally praised these books for providing an exciting and compelling introduction to ecology and environmental issues and for giving teachers and children interesting activities to help them learn about nature. However, some reviewers in the educational press have noted that they have a limited role in teaching young readers. Peter Croskery notes about *Keepers of the Animals* that the "biological sections of the book are not well done" and that it needed "better technical editing." Anne Fuller writes in *Science Books & Films*, "I recommend this book as spice for a science program, but it cannot stand alone as a complete ecology curriculum."

## Responses to Literature

1. Bruchac has a diverse ethnic background, and he has worked with writers from many different cultures. In what ways are the influences of cultures other than the Native American evident in his own writings?

---

# COMMON HUMAN EXPERIENCE

Many of Bruchac's works include Native American stories and folktales. Here are some other works that are based on Native American tales:

*Old Indian Legends, Retold by Zitkala-Sa* (1901), stories by Gertrude Bonnin. This collection is based on stories told to the author by her mother and other Yankton Indians she met while living on a reservation.

*Tales of the North American Indians* (1929), an anthology edited by Stith Thompson. The stories in this anthology were collected by the author from government reports, folklore journals, and publications of learned societies.

*Haboo: Native American Stories from Puget Sound* (1985), a collection edited by Vi Hilbert. This book collects thirty-four short, illustrated versions of legends of the Coast Salish and Skagit Indians.

---

2. Many of Bruchac's Native American legends are written for an elementary-school audience. In what ways are these tales capable of being appreciated by people older than this audience? In what ways do the stories take on different meanings for teenagers than they do for younger children?

3. Bruchac has written both translations and retellings of Native American legends as well as created his own legends based on Native American values and ideas. Write your own story based on one of Bruchac's translations of a Native American legend, adding your own original take on the story and infusing it with the values of your own culture.

4. Commentators have noted that environmental awareness is one of the Native American values that is directly apparent in many of Bruchac's writings. Write an essay discussing the other Native American values that underlie the stories Bruchac tells.

BIBLIOGRAPHY

**Periodicals**

Alderdice, Kit. "Joseph Bruchac: Sharing a Native-American Heritage." *Publishers Weekly* (February 19, 1996): 191–192.

Bankston, Carl L., III. "Telling the Truth in Tales." *San Francisco Review of Books* (May–June 1993): 8–9.

———. "Testimonies of Native American Life." *Bloomsbury Review* (May–June 1993): 5.

Bodin, Madeline. "Keeping Tradition Alive." *Publishers Weekly* (December 14, 1992): 23.

Craig, Patricia. "Sage Spirit: Abenaki Storyteller Joseph
Bruchac Tells Tales." *Library of Congress
Information Bulletin* (November 28, 1994): 448.

Di Spoldo, Nick. "Writers in Prison." *America* (January
22, 1983): 50–53.

Frey, Yvonne. "Review of *Turtle Meat and Other Stories.*"
*School Library Journal* (December 1992): 137.

"A review of *Turtle Meat and Other Stories.*" *Kirkus
Reviews* (October 1, 1992): 1201.

"A review of *Turtle Meat and Other Stories.*" *Publishers
Weekly,* (October 19, 1992): 73.

# ⊛ William Cullen Bryant

BORN: *1794, Cummington, Massachusetts*

DIED: *1878, New York, New York*

NATIONALITY: *American*

GENRE: *Nonfiction, poetry*

MAJOR WORKS:

*Poems* (1821)

*The Fountain and Other Poems* (1846)

*Letters of a Traveller* (1859)

*Thirty Poems* (1864)

William Cullen Bryant    *Bryant, William Cullen, illustration. The Library
of Congress.*

## Overview

Considered the most accomplished poet of his time in the
United States, William Cullen Bryant was the first American poet to receive substantial international acclaim. He
was also an influential journalist and liberal editor who
campaigned vigorously for free trade, free speech, and an
end to slavery.

## Works in Biographical and Historical
Context

*An Early Talent*  Bryant was born in Cummington,
Massachusetts, and grew up under the conflicting influences of his father, a liberal Unitarian physician, and his
maternal grandfather, a conservative Calvinist farmer. As
a boy, Bryant read the Bible, eighteenth-century English
literature, and the English Romantic writers, particularly
William Wordsworth. In addition, he studied and was
influenced by the writings of William Shakespeare, John
Milton, Sir Walter Scott, and the Scottish associationist
philosophers Thomas Reid and Dugald Stewart. These
philosophers supported the notion that the world should
be viewed through the lens of common sense as opposed
to abstract ideas about what is real.

His talent asserted itself quite early. He wrote and
was published while still a child; under his father's tutelage, he had learned to write carefully and to revise well.
With the publication of *The Embargo; or, Sketches of the
Times; A Satire; by a Youth of Thirteen* (1808) William
Cullen Bryant began his remarkable career as an important figure in American politics, literature, and journal-

ism. The poem drew much attention from critics who
doubted it had actually been written by one so young.
Bryant's first writing captured the nation's imagination,
and American readers continued to view Bryant as a
political commentator for the rest of his life.

*Lawyer, Poet, Journalist*  In 1810, Bryant studied at
Williams College, but he returned home because of financial difficulties. In 1811 he wrote his first major work of
poetry, "Thanatopsis," which was eventually published in
1817. Poetry was Bryant's first choice for a career, but he
knew that the vocation as a poet would not support him.
In 1815 he was admitted to the bar and started his law
practice in Plainfield, Massachusetts. He married Frances
Fairchild in 1821 and continued to practice law and
publish poetry until 1825.

Feeling encouraged by some of his earlier literary
successes, Bryant abandoned his law practice in 1825
and traveled to New York to try to build a literary career.
He succeeded instead in becoming one of the era's most
influential journalists and editors. He co-founded the *New
York Review and Atheneum Magazine* and became associated with the Knickerbocker group that included such
authors as Washington Irving, Fitz-Greene Halleck, James
Fenimore Cooper, and Gulian Verplanck, in addition to the

artists Asher Durant and Thomas Cole. In 1829 Bryant became the editor-in-chief of the *New York Evening Post*, a position he held for the rest of his life—a period of nearly fifty years. Under Bryant's leadership, the *Post* became a leading liberal newspaper. Bryant's support for such causes as free speech, workers' rights, abolitionism, and the Union cause during the American Civil War made him a prominent and controversial public figure.

***The Issue of Slavery*** Bryant's political development in the 1840s and 1850s came to hinge, as did national politics, on the overriding issue of slavery. The evolution of the *Post*'s position can be said to parallel that of advanced Northern opinion from tacit coexistence with slavery to, ultimately, the realization that it had to be extinguished. After breaking with the Democratic Party over support for the Free Soilers in 1848, Bryant became one of the founders of the American Republican party. Still, it took years more for him to break definitively with the Democrats. In 1852 the *Post* supported the Democratic candidate, Franklin Pierce, but in 1856 it vigorously championed John C. Frémont, the first Republican candidate for president, instead.

As the slavery crisis deepened in the late 1850s, Bryant's position on slavery grew ever firmer. The Supreme Court's decision in the *Dred Scott* case in March 1857, which ruled that slaves could not enjoy the rights of citizens anywhere in the United States, brought forth eight straight days of editorials on that topic. In 1860, Bryant endorsed the nomination of Abraham Lincoln for the presidency, but two years later denounced him for timidity in prosecuting the war. Although Bryant did not label himself an abolitionist at the time, he criticized the president for a lack of zeal for the cause of abolition.

***An Elder Statesman*** Bryant remained politically active throughout his life and struggled to encourage liberal political causes, but he began to withdraw from active participation in the business of the *Post* shortly after the end of the Civil War. His withdrawal was hastened when, after a long, painful illness, his wife died in July 1866. Although still enjoying his own scrupulously preserved good health, he absented himself from daily operations of the *Post* to devote his time to a translation of Homer, the ancient Greek epic poet.

Despite his retirement from the *Post*, Bryant was considered an elder statesman for the rest of his life. Until his death on June 12, 1878, Bryant was regarded as one of the nation's wise men. As a poet, politician, journalist, and grand old man of letters he strove to create an original identity for his maturing nation.

## Works in Literary Context

Bryant's historic importance as a poet rests chiefly on the fact that he was the first American poet to gain international notoriety. Shortly after reaching adulthood he gained a reputation as the best poet in America when his authorship of "Thanatopsis" became known. This

---

## LITERARY AND HISTORICAL CONTEMPORARIES

William Cullen Bryant's famous contemporaries include:

**James Buchanan** (1791–1868): Buchanan was an American politician who was president of the United States from 1857 until 1861, immediately before the Civil War.

**Percy Bysshe Shelley** (1792–1822): Shelley was an English poet associated with the Romantic movement; he is widely considered one of the greatest of all English-language poets.

**John Keats** (1795–1821): Keats was an English poet and prominent member of the Romantic movement in poetry.

**John Brown** (1800–1859): Brown was an American abolitionist who, before the beginning of the American Civil War, launched a raid on the U.S. Army arsenal at Harper's Ferry in an abortive attempt to trigger a slave uprising.

**Alexandre Dumas** (1802–1870): Dumas was a French writer who specialized in historically inspired action stories. He is best known for *The Count of Monte Cristo* (1844–1846) and *The Three Musketeers* (1844).

**Nathaniel Hawthorne** (1804–1864): Hawthorne was an American writer famous for works such as *The Scarlet Letter* (1850) and *The House of the Seven Gables* (1851).

---

judgment was subsequently affirmed when, in 1821, he issued the first of many collected editions of his slim body of verse. Washington Irving secured publication of his work in England, and the critics there as well as those at home recognized his considerable talent. Bryant devoted most of his life to making a living, first as a lawyer and then as an editor. Consequently, he did not complete the ambitious kinds of projects which might have brought him enduring fame as a poet of the first rank. Nevertheless, he became a popular writer in his own day, and he produced a handful of poems of lasting significance.

Bryant's poems express ideas derived from the Enlightenment, from English Romanticism, and from his study of German, Spanish, and Portuguese poetry. The recurring themes of these poems include mutability, loneliness, and the passing of innocence, and both Bryant's prose writings and his poetry attest to his interest in politics, folk themes, the American landscape and history. Commentators on Bryant's poetry have singled out simplicity, instructional purpose, idealism, and a conscious concern for craftsmanship as the most prominent features of Bryant's poetic style.

***Romanticism*** Bryant's chief stylistic hallmark is his treatment of nature, especially his belief that it consoles as well as provides lessons about history and divine

## COMMON HUMAN EXPERIENCE

Bryant's poetry extolled the virtues of nature and expressed his belief that nature comforts and instructs. Here are some other works that exalt contact with nature:

*Nature* (1836), nonfiction by Ralph Waldo Emerson. This short book consists of an essay that argues for a transcendental appreciation of nature that sees God in all things around us.

*Walden* (1854), nonfiction by Henry David Thoreau. This book describes two years in the author's life when he lived in isolation in a cabin near Walden Pond in rural Massachusetts.

*New Hampshire* (1923), poetry by Robert Frost. This collection of poems, which won the Pulitzer Prize, depicts an idyllic life in a rural setting.

purpose. His poetry embodies an acceptance of the cycles of change in nature and in life and a belief that change is providential because it leads to an individual's spiritual progress and moral improvement. His poetic treatment of the themes of nature and mutability identifies him as one of the earliest figures in the Romantic movement in American literature.

***Journalistic Crusading*** Bryant's journalistic career was fully as important as his work as a poet. At a time when most editors of the political press backed candidates because of their party labels alone, Bryant let principle determine to whom he would give his support. Bryant brought to journalism not only the argumentative and rhetorical skills of the lawyer but the sensibility of the poet, and his journalism possessed a civility and literary quality that was generally lacking in the newspaper writing of his contemporaries. He left the imprint of a liberal and humanitarian on nearly every major national issue of his time, and he is remembered as a liberal editor whose campaigns for free trade, free speech, and free men started early and continued throughout his tenure as editor of the *New York Evening Post.*

### Works in Critical Context

Bryant's critical reputation has varied over the course of the nineteenth and twentieth centuries. In fact, Bryant's place as the most eminent American poet was generally unquestioned until the middle of the nineteenth century. Though most critics agree that Bryant's earliest poems are his best work, there has been some variation in critical opinion about his work in general. Edgar Allan Poe, Edmund Clarence Stedman, and Gay Wilson Allen have praised Bryant's skillful and often innovative handling of prosody.

Other critics single out Bryant's sincerity and simplicity of tone as his best trait, while Walt Whitman valued Bryant's high moral tone above all of his other qualities. James Russell Lowell and Henry B. Sedgwick, Jr., however, perceived a lack of passion in Bryant's poems. He has also frequently been criticized for the lack of flexibility and depth in his poetic subjects and themes, as well as for his over-reliance on didactic endings—lessons or instructional messages directed at the reader. The question of whether Bryant's sensibility is more Puritan or Romantic is often debated. Norman Foerster and Fred Lewis Pattee assert that Bryant's Puritan traits dominate his style, whereas Tremaine McDowell and Albert F. McLean, Jr. emphasize Bryant's Romantic characteristics. Stedman praised Bryant's journalistic prose, as did Vernon Louis Parrington, who proposed that Bryant's editorial contributions are equal in importance to his poetry.

Several critics, Charles Leonard Moore and Stedman among them, consider Bryant second only to Poe in literary importance during the pre-Civil War period in America. He is recognized as one of the first poets in the United States to challenge the dominance of traditional eighteenth-century poetic styles. His development of lofty philosophic themes, his editorial contributions, and his verse experiments with iambic rhythm make Bryant an important, if somewhat forgotten, figure in American literature.

***"Thanatopsis"*** "Thanatopsis," which means "a view of death," was Bryant's most famous poem. Composed in 1811, it was not published until 1817. After the *North American Review* published "Thanatopsis," the magazine discontinued its verse department, fearing that the standard Bryant's poems had set was so high that no other contributors could equal it. "Thanatopsis" did not assume its final form until its appearance in Bryant's volume *Poems* (1821), however, and the differences in the versions has led commentators to note an evolution toward a view of death in which man becomes one with all the processes of nature. As E. Miller Burdick put it in 1976, Bryant "chose to cut himself loose from the ego-sustaining nurture of the Romantic universe and to flounder, at least momentarily, in an unsafe agnosticism."

### Responses to Literature

1. Bryant's political positions were not consistent with any particular political party. What kinds of principles underlay Bryant's positions? Based on these principles, what kinds of stances might he take on important issues of our own day?

2. During his lifetime, Bryant's reputation as a newspaper editor overshadowed his poetic career. In retrospect, which of these vocations does Bryant deserve a better reputation for—poet or editor? Explain your choice.

3. Much of Bryant's poetry explored the lessons that nature could teach human beings. Write a poem that draws a life lesson out of some aspect of nature.

4. The bulk of Bryant's output consisted of newspaper editorials commenting on all of the important issues of his day. Write an editorial about an important issue of today using a similar rhetorical and argumentative style.

## BIBLIOGRAPHY

### Books

Bigelow, John. *William Cullen Bryant.* Boston and New York: Houghton Mifflin, 1890.

Bradley, William A. *William Cullen Bryant.* New York: Macmillan, 1905.

Brown, Charles H. *William Cullen Bryant.* New York: Scribners, 1971.

Curtis, George W. *The Life, Character, and Writings of William Cullen Bryant.* New York: Scribners, 1879.

Godwin, Parke. *A Biography of William Cullen Bryant, with Extracts from His Private Correspondence.* New York: Appleton, 1883.

Johnson, Curtiss S. *Politics and a Belly-Full: The Journalistic Career of William Cullen Bryant.* New York: Vantage Press, 1962.

McLean, Albert F., Jr. *William Cullen Bryant.* New York: Twayne, 1964.

Nevins, Allan. *The Evening Post: A Century of Journalism.* New York: Boni & Liveright, 1922.

Peckham, Henry Houston. *Gotham Yankee.* New York: Vantage Press, 1950.

Wilson, James Grant. *Bryant and His Friends: Some Reminiscences of Knickerbocker Writers.* New York: Fords, Howard & Halbert, 1886.

# ⊛ Pearl S. Buck

BORN: *1892, Hillsboro, West Virginia*

DIED: *1973, Danby, Vermont*

NATIONALITY: *American*

GENRE: *Fiction*

MAJOR WORKS:

*The Good Earth* (1931)

*The Exile* (1936)

*Fighting Angel* (1936)

*The Living Reed* (1963)

## Overview

Buck was a prolific author who wrote over one hundred works during her lifetime and enjoyed great popularity with readers. The winner of the 1938 Nobel Prize in Literature, Buck helped to introduce American readers to Asian culture.

Pearl S. Buck    *Buck, Pearl S., 1939, photograph. AP Images.*

## Works in Biographical and Historical Context

***Living in China***    Pearl S. Buck was born in 1892 in Hillsboro, West Virginia, but she was raised by missionary parents in Chinkiang, China. She was privately educated and learned to speak Chinese before English. In 1900, the family fled to Shanghai during the Boxer Rebellion, an uprising of Chinese peasants who believed that foreigners were taking advantage of their country. The family returned to Chinkiang two years later, and Buck attended boarding school in Shanghai from 1907 to 1909. At the age of seventeen, she traveled to the United States in order to attend Randolph-Macon Woman's College in Lynchburg, Virginia, and returned to Chinkiang upon graduation in 1914.

In 1917, she married John Lossing Buck, an agricultural economist who had come to China to work on methods of applying statistical analysis to improve Chinese farming. The couple settled first in Nanhsuchou and then moved to Nanking in 1919 when Lossing Buck was offered a position at Nanking University. Beginning in 1921, Buck taught English literature at the University of Nanking.

***Unhappiness in Personal Life***    On March 4, 1920, Buck gave birth to a daughter, Caroline Grace, who

## LITERARY AND HISTORICAL CONTEMPORARIES

Buck's famous contemporaries include:

**Sinclair Lewis** (1885–1951): Lewis was an American author who, in 1930, became the first American to win the Nobel Prize in Literature.

**Ivo Andric** (1892–1975): Andric was a Yugoslavian author who won the Nobel Prize in Literature in 1961.

**Mao Zedong** (1893–1976): Mao was the leader of the Chinese Communist Revolution and ruler of China from 1949 until his death.

**J. Edgar Hoover** (1895–1972): Hoover was an American law-enforcement agent who helped found, and was the first Director of, the F.B.I.

**William Faulkner** (1897–1962): Faulkner was an American author who is widely considered one of the most important writers of the twentieth century; he was awarded the Nobel Prize in Literature in 1949.

suffered from the metabolic disease phenylketonuria (PKU), which had not at that time been diagnosed and which profoundly affected her mental development. Her daughter's condition was a lifelong source of grief, shame, and guilt for Buck. In addition, the discovery and removal of a uterine tumor in July 1920 necessitated a hysterectomy. Buck was also unhappy that Lossing Buck was absorbed in his work and distanced himself emotionally from her and from Carol, in a way that echoed her father's treatment of her mother. The marriage, which seemed to begin happily, soon disintegrated, though it ultimately lasted for seventeen years.

Buck's mother died in 1921. To comfort herself, Buck began writing her mother's biography as a private memorial to be shared with family members. Years later, this book became *The Exile*, which was one of Buck's most successful books. In 1924 the Bucks returned to America so that both of them could enter graduate school at Cornell University and so that they could have Carol's mental disability properly assessed. At Christmastime they adopted a baby girl, Janice.

***Tumult and Success in China*** Buck shortly resumed her life in Nanking, but the political situation in China was extremely unstable. In March 1927, the Nanking Incident, a violent two days of bloodshed and looting aimed particularly at foreigners, forced the Bucks and other family members to flee Nanking after a terrifying day of hiding in the home of one of their servants. They retreated to the Japanese town of Unzen with little more than their lives and some clothing; the losses included the manuscript of Buck's first novel, though Lossing Buck managed

to save the survey manuscript on which he was working. They were able to return to China in October 1927, settling in Shanghai; Lossing Buck then returned to Nanking, and Buck and the children joined him in July 1928.

During that time, Buck began her writing career. After her story "A Chinese Woman Speaks" appeared in two installments in *Asia* in 1926, she began work on a novel. Her first novel, *East Wind: West Wind*, was issued in the United States in 1930. Her second novel, *The Good Earth*, was awarded the 1932 Pulitzer Prize for Fiction as the best novel of the year. Her first collection of short stories, *The First Wife, and Other Stories*, was published in 1933.

Buck's father died in 1931, and since he could no longer be harmed by the unflattering portrait of him in the work, Buck decided she could publish her biography of her mother. *The Exile* was released in 1936 and was such a success that she quickly produced the sequel, *Fighting Angel*, in which Buck depicts her father's religious zeal, which caused him to neglect his wife and family, and his misogyny; she also chronicles the loneliness and disillusionment of her mother, who was isolated from everything familiar and suffered the losses of her children, her own illnesses, and her husband's disdain.

***Movement Away from Fiction*** Buck moved to Pennsylvania in 1934, beginning permanent residence in the United States. In 1938 she became the first American woman awarded the Nobel Prize in Literature, which was bestowed in honor of her works as a whole—though special mention was made of the biographies of her mother and father. Despite this honor, her literary reputation began slipping steadily in the years and decades that followed.

Buck suspected public interest in stories about China would begin to wane, and she felt she should start writing stories set in America. From the late 1930s, Buck's priorities began to shift away from writing fiction and toward humanitarian and philanthropic activities. Buck's activism was such that the FBI had begun keeping a file on her in 1937, when she expressed her support for the Spanish Loyalists and for the Women's International League for Peace and Freedom. During World War II, her support for racial equality escalated, as did FBI interest in her.

Throughout her life, Buck continued to receive awards and honors, more for her philanthropic work than for her writing. Although her literary reputation waned steadily throughout her later life, she wrote profusely until her death in 1973, sometimes publishing several books in a single year.

## Works in Literary Context

Although Buck is probably best remembered for her fiction, her best work may have been her nonfiction. Peter J. Conn, one of her biographers, asserts that her fiction was hobbled by the way she "used her novels as political and educational instruments, exchanging the challenges of novelistic art for the easier satisfactions of melodrama, propaganda, and protest." Nevertheless, he argues that "her achievements as a writer remain considerable." She was one of the most multicultural and interdisciplinary writers of her generation, and her impact on literature and cultural studies is now being increasingly appreciated.

*Revealing China* Among these achievements, her most noteworthy and best remembered is the contribution she made to the understanding of Asian culture—particularly Chinese life—by the Western world. As Conn writes, "For two generations of Americans, Buck invented China." Critics widely praised Buck's portrayal and interpretation of life in Asia, especially her representation of conflicts arising from oppression, political upheaval, and the shock of Westernization. Some commentators, such as Malcolm Cowley, contend that her greatest skill was the ability to reveal the common bond shared by humanity irrespective of race or culture:

> She has a truly extraordinary gift for presenting the Chinese, not as quaint and illogical, yellow-skinned, exotic devil-dolls, but as human beings merely, animated by motives we can always understand even when the background is strange and topsy-turvy.

*A Controversial Legacy* Buck's literary legacy, much like the 1938 Nobel Prize, is a subject of controversy and disagreement. Detractors suggest that humanistic preoccupations dominated Buck's works as her career progressed, introducing sentimental, didactic, and propagandistic qualities that overshadowed her literary artistry and that her writing was hampered by a dearth of symbolism, myth, and technical experimentation. Others contend that Buck should be remembered as the author of sympathetic yet realistic depictions that relate—in an engaging, story-telling manner—the underlying commonality of human experience and that her critical reputation was most significantly harmed by her prolific output and best-seller status, two characteristics that are often seen as incompatible with literary merit.

## Works in Critical Context

Buck was an immensely popular writer during her lifetime, but she was the subject of much critical derision, and after an early rise, she suffered from a steady decline in her literary reputation. *The Good Earth*, along with the 1936 biographies of her parents, established Buck's early literary reputation and served as the basis of comparison for her later works, which critics viewed as generally unimpressive with a few exceptions such as *The Patriot* (1939), a study that contrasts the national character of the Chinese and Japanese people, and *The Living Reed* (1963), a history of a Korean family.

*The Good Earth* Buck's second novel, *The Good Earth*, was a tremendous success upon its publication. As Buck's biographer, Peter Conn, noted, "Every leading

---

### COMMON HUMAN EXPERIENCE

Buck's novels and biographies depicted ordinary people struggling amid difficult social, political, and economic conditions. Here are some other works that center around similar struggles:

> *Waves* (1985), stories by Bei Dao. This collection of stories explores the various difficulties faced by people living in Communist China during and after the destructive Cultural Revolution.
>
> *Wild Swans* (1991), a novel by Jung Chang. This novel tells the story of three generations of Chinese women surviving the political turmoil of twentieth-century China.
>
> *A Thousand Splendid Suns* (2007), a novel by Khaled Hosseini. This novel tells the story of two women living through the dramatic political changes that took place in Afghanistan during the late twentieth century.

---

newspaper and magazine gave the book a major notice, and almost all the reviews were ecstatic." *The Good Earth* would not only become the best-selling book of both 1931 and 1932, it brought fame and praise to Buck. As one *Bookman* reviewer observed:

> The strange power of a western woman to make an alien civilization seem as casual, as close, as the happenings of the morning is surprising; but it is less amazing than her power to illuminate the destiny of man as it is in all countries and at all times by quietly telling the story of one poor Wang Lung.

Critics have offered several reasons for the tremendous popularity of *The Good Earth*. Buck has been praised frequently for creating recognizable, even familiar characters with universal concerns, despite a setting and race that were previously alien to Western readers. Most Americans in 1931 knew little about China, and what they did know was clouded with clichés of the "heathen Chinese" whose cultural differences were regarded with disdain. Buck's depictions of Chinese life, drawn from her own experiences and observations, presented a vivid and sympathetic portrait. Conn also observes that "Underneath its alien details, the novel is a story of the land, a rather familiar American genre," and Depression-era audiences could especially relate to the struggles of farmers. In addition, the novel, like others of the period, "celebrated the traditional American virtue of simplicity."

*Controversy over the Nobel Prize* When Pearl S. Buck won the Nobel Prize in Literature in 1938, she became only the third American and the first American woman to do so. She also became a figure of controversy. The citation that accompanied the award praised the "rich and generous epic descriptions of Chinese peasant life" in Buck's novels and also singled out *The Exile* (1936) and *Fighting Angel: Portrait of A Soul* (1936) as "masterpieces." Her detractors, however, felt the Swedish Academy had shown poor judgment in selecting Buck over other writers, such as Theodore Dreiser, whose work they considered of superior literary quality. The prevailing attitude in literary circles was one of hostility about the award.

Among the charges leveled at Buck by her detractors was that her prose style was facile, clumsy, and clichéd. Buck's selection tainted the reputation of the prize in some literary circles. Robert Frost was quoted as saying, "If she can get it anybody can." In 1950, William Faulkner wrote in a letter about the possibility of his own nomination: "I dont want it. I had rather be in the same pigeon hole with Dreiser and Sherwood Anderson, than with Sinclair Lewis and Mrs. Chinahand Buck." Others defended her, however, as the anonymous reviewer for *Time* did, stating, "The influence of her writing far transcends its importance as literature."

*Critical Revival* Critical and public interest in Buck's writing has been renewed somewhat by centennial celebrations in 1992, Conn's biography in 1996, and the re-emergence of *The Good Earth* as talk-show host Oprah Winfrey's book club selection for the fall of 2004. Jane M. Rabb, in her analysis of the reasons for Buck's critical neglect among literary and feminist scholars, notes, "The current academic enthusiasm for the multicultural and the interdisciplinary should revive interest in the best works of Buck, who is nothing if not multicultural and interdisciplinary." Conn concludes that Buck's "best work, by and large, was probably her nonfiction." Nevertheless, he argues that "her achievements as a writer remain considerable—surely more notable than her virtually complete neglect by scholars and critics would imply."

## Responses to Literature

1. Buck was one of the first author's to present life in China to a Western readership, which at the time knew little about Chinese culture or society. In what ways has Western knowledge of China expanded since Buck's time, and in what ways is that knowledge still as incomplete as it was in Buck's time?

2. Buck's literary reputation often suffered because she was a very prolific and best-selling author. In what ways is literary merit undermined by these qualities, and in what ways does Buck deserve credit as a literary giant despite her popularity and prodigious output? Should a writer's literary merit in the eyes of scholars be affected his or her popularity? Why or why not?

3. Buck's reputation has revived since her death, particularly since the early 1990s. Many authors who are little regarded while alive undergo a similar transformation. Write an essay describing why Buck was

the type of writer who was likely to be underappreciated in her time but discovered by later generations.

4. Some commentators have charged that *The Good Earth* was considered authentic by readers despite the fact that they had no real knowledge of China to use as a basis of comparison. With greater access to information about the rest of the world, today's readers are in a much better position to assess the authenticity of *The Good Earth*. Write an essay analyzing the authenticity of this novel. Be sure to cite reputable sources for any claims you make about Buck's accuracy or inaccuracy.

BIBLIOGRAPHY

**Books**

Block, Irvin. *The Lives of Pearl Buck: A Tale of China and America*. New York: Crowell, 1973.

Conn, Peter J. *Pearl S. Buck: A Cultural Biography*. New York: Cambridge University Press, 1996.

Doyle, Paul A. *Pearl S. Buck*, revised edition. New York: Twayne, 1980.

Gao, Xiongya. *Pearl Buck's Chinese Women Characters*. Selinsgrove, Pa.: Susquehanna University Press, 2000.

Harris, Theodore F. *Pearl S. Buck: A Biography*, two volumes. New York: John Day, 1969, 1971.

Liao, Kang. *Pearl S. Buck: A Cultural Bridge Across the Pacific*. Westport, Conn.: Greenwood Press, 1997.

Rizzon, Beverly. *Pearl S. Buck: The Final Chapter*. Palm Springs, Calif.: ETC, 1989.

Sherk, Warren. *Pearl S. Buck: Good Earth Mother*. Philomath, Ore.: Drift Creek Press, 1992.

Spencer, Cornelia. *The Exile's Daughter: A Biography of Pearl S. Buck*. New York: Coward-McCann, 1944.

Stirling, Nora. *Pearl Buck: A Woman in Conflict*. Piscataway, N.J.: New Century, 1983.

# ⊛ William F. Buckley

BORN: *1925, New York, New York*

DIED: *2008, Stamford, Connecticut*

NATIONALITY: *American*

GENRE: *Nonfiction*

MAJOR WORKS:

The *National Review* (editor in chief, 1955–1990)
*Up From Liberalism* (1959)

## Overview

As a columnist, lecturer, novelist, essayist, and television host, Buckley was a leading spokesperson for conservatism in the United States during the second half of the twentieth century. While Buckley's outspoken, strongly conservative position on controversial issues has resulted

William F. Buckley, Jr.   *Buckley, Jr., William, photograph. Mario Tama / Getty Images.*

in divided critical opinion, his engaging wit and energetic prose style are widely admired.

## Works in Biographical and Historical Context

*An Influential Father*   William F. Buckley Jr. was born on November 24, 1925, in New York City. William Buckley Sr. was the primary influence on his son's development. The Buckley fortune had arisen from Mexican oil interests, and Mexico was a country where Buckley Sr., known as Will, had great influence until the revolution of the late 1910s. Will joined in counterrevolutionary activities to support the government against the insurgents, and when the government was overthrown, his activities led the new regime to confiscate all of his Mexican holdings in 1922. The lessons imparted by Will infused the intellects of all the children with a fierce family pride, a strong Catholic faith, and a hatred of revolution and communism.

*Educating a Future Conservative*   William F. Buckley was privately tutored and went to school in England and France, an experience that helped to moderate the isolationism so much favored by his father. In 1938 Buckley enrolled at Saint John's Beaumont, an

exclusive Catholic public school in England, on the same day that Neville Chamberlain's agreement with Adolf Hitler at Munich was announced, prompting Buckley to hang an American flag over his bed. Despite the fact that the Buckley children were pulled out of their English schools in 1939 and taken on a tour of fascist Italy, Buckley's time at Saint John's Beaumont was quite influential on his intellectual development. The coming war and his mother's fragile health—she was pregnant—turned him even more toward religion, and he was quite receptive to the instruction by the Jesuits, which cemented his Catholic faith at the same time he began to pursue more secular intellectual interests.

In 1943 Buckley graduated from Millbrook, a small, private, Protestant preparatory school in New York, not far from his family's home in Sharon, Connecticut. During his time at Millbrook from 1940 to 1943, Buckley was fully under the influence of his father's isolationist views and vociferously opposed the United States entering World War II on behalf of Great Britain. Ultimately, Buckley was inducted into the army in June 1944 and barely passed his Officer Candidate School program. He left the army as a second lieutenant. He entered Yale in fall 1946, part of the great influx of former servicemen entering college for the first time. It was at Yale that Buckley came under the influence of Yale professor Wilmoore Kendall. His association with Kendall, a former Trotskyite who had become a fervent anticommunist, was the first example of Buckley's tendency to gravitate toward people who had migrated from the political Left toward the Right. Kendall's political intensity and cultural conservatism attracted Buckley, and he learned much from him.

During his junior year at Yale, Buckley became increasingly involved in the running of the *Yale Daily News*, eventually becoming the editor. Buckley was controversial in this position; he used the editorial columns of the paper to attack the demands on professors to publish at the expense of their teaching and to begin his attack on the idea of academic freedom. He was named student speaker at Alumni Day in 1950. He planned to deliver a scathing speech on the shortcomings of the Yale faculty, but the speech he wrote was opposed by the administration, and he withdrew from the honor. The rejection stung Buckley, and he soon made plans to write a book attacking the anticapitalist and irreligious thought of much of the Yale faculty.

*From Yale to the CIA to Magazine Work*   In April 1951, as he was finishing work on his book, Buckley was accepted into service in the Central Intelligence Agency. After a training period, he and his wife were stationed in Mexico City in September 1951. Buckley's book on his academic travails, *God and Man at Yale: The Superstitions of "Academic Freedom,"* was published by Regnery in October 1951, the 250th anniversary of Yale's founding, and vaulted Buckley into controversy and the national limelight. The book expands the idea he first expounded in the undelivered Alumni Day speech that Yale faculty members—many of them attacked by name in the text—were atheists and socialists and therefore unfit to teach at a university that still claimed a Christian heritage in a capitalist nation.

In March 1952 Buckley went to work for the *American Mercury* as an associate editor. After less than a year Buckley resigned over an editorial disagreement—the magazine refused to print one of his articles. The experience left him more certain of the need for a new conservative magazine.

### Founding of the National Review

The taste of controversy and public success with *God and Man at Yale* and the frustration with his experience at the *American Mercury* had much to do with Buckley's interest in starting the *National Review*. Buckley came to the forefront of the push for a magazine after another controversial book publication. In early 1954 Regnery published *McCarthy and His Enemies: The Record and Its Meaning*, which Buckley wrote with his brother-in-law, Brent Bozell. The book, because of its controversial subject and its even more controversial point of view of supporting McCarthyism, was greeted with silence. It had only one major review outside the conservative press, a negative notice in the *New York Times*. When his book was ignored by the mainstream press, Buckley became more involved in starting a magazine, in the vein of the *New Republic* and the *Nation*, and in which conservative books would be neither ignored nor vilified.

The first weekly issue of the *National Review* appeared on November 14, 1955. Even in the first issue, Buckley—as both publisher and editor in chief—attempted to enliven conservatism with wit and sarcasm instead of relying entirely on the deadly serious moralism so common in other right-wing journals. His own attitude toward conservatism made it easier to adopt such an editorial rationale. Unlike many conservatives and moderates, Buckley saw his political persuasion in full opposition to the status quo.

### Politics and a Broader Media Career

Buckley and the *National Review* spent the next ten years battling what he saw as the liberal status quo. In the aftermath of the 1964 Lyndon Johnson landslide victory over Barry Goldwater, the first truly conservative postwar presidential candidate, Buckley decided to try politics for himself. In 1965 he declared himself a Conservative Party candidate for mayor of New York. His wit and love of controversy found fertile ground in the race against Democrat Abraham Beame and Republican John Lindsay, the eventual winner. Surprising everyone, including himself, Buckley received 13.4 percent of the vote.

His media success in the New York mayoral race led to the beginning of a debate and interview show, *Firing Line*, which was first broadcast on New York station WOR in 1966. Buckley's influence grew beyond the *National Review*, and he soon entered the realm of fiction writing with his successful Blackford Oakes spy novels. The magazine, however, remained influential.

### Buckley and Ronald Reagan

In 1976, Buckley and the *National Review* supported Ronald Reagan in his bid to unseat Gerald Ford as the Republican presidential nominee, a bid that fell short and helped, along with the president's poor campaign, to elect Jimmy Carter. As the 1980 election approached, conservatives once again supported Reagan. But during the debate over the Panama Canal treaties, which Carter had negotiated, Buckley supported Carter and opposed Reagan. Buckley and Reagan went as far as to debate each other in 1978, an event that brought Reagan a national audience. Buckley's stance brought condemnation from many conservatives, but as Buckley noted in his book *Overdrive* (1983), his public support of the treaties and his opposition to Reagan may have ensured the latter's election in 1980.

While he angered many conservatives, he did not endanger his friendship with Reagan, and following Reagan's election the *National Review* reached the pinnacle of its influence on official Washington. A decade later, in 1990, on the thirty-fifth anniversary of the first issue of the *National Review*, Buckley announced that he was stepping down as editor in chief. Buckley still had a nationally syndicated newspaper column and he continued to contribute opinion pieces for the *National Review*. He also lectured and made radio and television appearances and continued to publish books, including ten novels. He died at the age of eighty-two while writing a book about his relationship with Ronald Reagan (published as *The Reagan I Knew* in 2008).

## Works in Literary Context

Although a controversial figure in American politics, Buckley is widely credited with bringing a unique and engaging blend of charm and combativeness to political discourse. As Gene Moore wrote in 1981,

> Buckley's flickering tongue and flashing wit have challenged a generation to remember the old truths while searching for the new, to abhor hypocrisy and to value logic, and to join in the worldwide struggle for human rights and human freedom.

### Conservatism

During Buckley's thirty-five-year editorship of the *National Review*, a magazine he founded in 1955 to present a "responsible dissent from Liberal orthodoxy," the magazine became one of the most influential journals of political opinion in the United States. He himself became one of the most recognizable figures in American journalism in addition to becoming both an inspiration and an icon to several generations of political conservatives. Buckley's career as a magazine editor succeeded far beyond his wildest imaginings or those of his critics. The character of American conservatism, and therefore of contemporary American politics, would be quite different without the influence and the writing of Buckley.

Prior to Buckley's founding of the *National Review*, the conservative movement lacked a mainstream magazine venue in which conservative ideas could affect the national debate on political and social issues. Many in the conservative camp shared this idea, but no one had a firm idea about how to proceed until Buckley came along. During its early years, especially during the 1950s, the *National Review* made few concessions to the reality, and seeming permanence, of the welfare state instituted during the New Deal. Indeed, the magazine seemed to follow the line that it would support most anyone on the Right, regardless of the position expounded, but Buckley's political outlook grew as the magazine began to increase its circulation. Throughout the 1960s and 1970s, the *National Review* began influencing and changing conservatism rather than merely discussing conservative ideas. By the time Ronald Reagan was elected president in 1980, Buckley had helped transform conservative thought into a modern doctrine committed to such ideals as deregulation and individual initiative.

*Espionage*  In addition to his stature as a political and social commentator, Buckley was well regarded as a writer of spy fiction. In such novels as *Saving the Queen* (1976), *Stained Glass* (1978), and *See You Later, Alligator* (1985), among others, Buckley relates the adventures of CIA agent Blackford Oakes. Buckley interweaves his fiction with historical events and figures, particularly those involved in East-West relations in postwar Europe. For example, *See You Later, Alligator* centers around the Cuban Missile Crisis. Critics have commented favorably on these works, praising Buckley's clear prose, fast-paced narratives, and his use of parody, caricature, and other humorous touches to offset the sometimes grim action.

## Works in Critical Context

Buckley's career as editor of the *National Review* made him one of the most recognizable and controversial figures in American journalism. Although dismissed by some critics as a mere gadfly, Buckley's success as an editor, novelist, syndicated newspaper columnist, television host, and sometime politician mark him as more than that. Buckley's sometimes lonely and sometimes strident advocacy of conservative policies was instrumental in laying the foundation for the conservative revival of the 1960s and its triumph in the 1980s.

*Stirring Up Controversy*  Buckley first received national attention with *God and Man at Yale: The Superstitions of "Academic Freedom"*, in which Buckley challenged the "antireligious" stance of some of his professors at Yale University and opposed the use of certain economics textbooks, which, he claimed, favored "collectivism." In a review of this book, Frank D. Ashburn stated that Buckley "distorts some facts, is inaccurate often, sometimes twists conclusions, and does this while assuring the reader that he is being true to a position he repeatedly renounces." On the other hand, Max Eastman

## LITERARY AND HISTORICAL CONTEMPORARIES

William F. Buckley's famous contemporaries include:

**McGeorge Bundy** (1919–1996): Bundy was an American official who served as national security adviser to Presidents Kennedy and Johnson during such events as the Cuban Missile Crisis and the Vietnam War.

**George Wallace** (1919–1998): Wallace was an American politician who served four terms as governor of Alabama; he is best known for battling the federal government over desegregation during the civil rights era.

**Leon Uris** (1924–2003): Uris was an American writer who produced mainly historical fiction and spy novels and is best known for his chronicle of the formation of Israel, *Exodus* (1958).

**Daniel Patrick Moynihan** (1927–2003): Moynihan was an American politician and Democratic leader who served in the U.S. Senate for twenty-four years, starting in 1976.

**George Herbert Walker Bush** (1924–): Bush is an American politician and Republican leader who served as vice president under Ronald Reagan and was elected to a single term as president in 1988.

## COMMON HUMAN EXPERIENCE

Buckley's writings on social and political issues were greatly influential on the conservative movement in the United States. Here are some other works that influenced American conservatism during the twentieth century:

*The Conservative Mind* (1953), a nonfiction book by Russell Kirk. This book traces conservative thought in England and the United States and offers an interpretation of the conservative philosophical tradition.

*Closing of the American Mind* (1987), a nonfiction book by Allan Bloom. In this book, Bloom critiques the liberal, relativist approach taken in modern universities and argues for a more classical, conservative pedagogy.

*The End of History and the Last Man* (1992), a nonfiction book by Francis Fukuyama. In this philosophical work, Fukuyama draws on empirical evidence to argue that history is leading toward a final state where the world will be dominated by democracies that are both secular and capitalist.

applauded *God and Man at Yale* for "its arrant intellectual courage" and called it "brilliant, sincere, well-informed, keenly reasoned, and exciting to read." The furor provoked by this book is typical of the controversy generated by Buckley's later works.

***The National Review*** While often controversial, the *National Review* was recognized by both fans and detractors as a major influence over conservative political thought in the United States and a force for advancing conservatism's appeal, particularly since the 1970s and 1980s. President Ronald Reagan publicly declared that the *National Review* was his favorite magazine and acknowledged its influence in advancing conservative political fortunes. As Morton Kondracke wrote in the *New York Times Book Review*, Buckley

> and his magazine nurtured the [conservative] movement ... and gave it a rallying point and sounding board as it gradually gained the strength and respectability to win the Presidency. Conservatism is not far from the dominant intellectual force in the country today, but neither is liberalism. There is now a balance between the movements, a permanent contest, and Mr. Buckley deserves credit for helping make it so.

## Responses to Literature

1. In addition to being a political writer, Buckley also wrote a number of novels. In what ways do the behavior of the characters in these novels fit in with Buckley's political ideals, and in what ways do the plots of these novels help advance conservative political messages?

2. Buckley's writings were greatly influential among conservatives during the last half of the twentieth century. In what ways does present-day conservatism resemble Buckley's thinking, and in what ways has conservatism developed away from Buckley's vision?

3. Much of Buckley's career was dedicated to writing columns that advanced conservative views on a great variety of political topics of the day. Choose an important political issue of our time and write a political column that either advances a conservative opinion such as Buckley's or criticizes the conservative view on that issue.

4. For much of his life, Buckley was involved in the world of journalism, producing daily or weekly commentary on political life in America. Today, bloggers engage in a similar style of commentary. Write an essay that compares Buckley's journalistic approach to politics with the journalistic and intellectual style favored by conservative bloggers. Be sure to assess how successful bloggers are compared to Buckley at advancing conservative ideas.

### BIBLIOGRAPHY

**Books**

Burner, David, and Thomas R. West, eds. *Column Right: Conservative Journalists in the Service of Nationalism.* New York: New York University Press, 1988.

Cain, Edward R. *They'd Rather Be Right: Youth and the Conservative Movement.* New York: Macmillan, 1963.

Forster, Arnold, and B. R. Epstein. *Danger on the Right.* New York: Random House, 1964.

Judis, John. *William F. Buckley, Jr.: Patron Saint of the Conservatives.* New York: Simon & Schuster, 1988.

Lipset, Seymour Martin, and Earl Raab. *The Politics of Unreason.* 2nd ed. Chicago: University of Chicago Press, 1978.

Lukacs, John. *Outgrowing Democracy: A History of the United States in the Twentieth Century.* Garden City, N.Y.: Doubleday, 1984.

Markmann, Charles L. *The Buckleys: A Family Examined.* New York: Morrow, 1973.

Moore, Gene M. "William F. Buckley, Jr." *DISCovering Authors*, Online ed. Detroit: Gale, 2003.

Nash, George H. *The Conservative Intellectual Movement in America Since 1945.* New York: Basic Books, 1976.

**Periodicals**

Bundy, McGeorge. "The Attack on Yale." *Atlantic Monthly* (November 1951): 51.

# ✺ Thomas Bulfinch

BORN: *1796, Newton, Massachusetts*

DIED: *1867, Boston, Massachusetts*

NATIONALITY: *American*

GENRE: *Fiction*

MAJOR WORKS:
*Bullfinch's Mythology* (1881)

## Overview

Throughout his life, Thomas Bulfinch researched and rewrote classic stories and myths in contemporary literary style, in an attempt to popularize the study of mythology among mainstream readers. Although the compilation of his works, known as *Bulfinch's Mythology* (1881), was popular in its time, his versions have been superseded by retellings that appeal to a more modern taste.

## Works in Biographical and Historical Context

***A Prominent Family*** Thomas Bulfinch was born into a distinguished New England family on July 15, 1796. His father, Charles Bulfinch, was one of the most well-known architects of the time; he designed the Massachusetts State House in Boston and parts of the U.S. Capitol in Washington, D.C. Bulfinch was educated much as other members of the Boston elite were; he attended Boston Latin, Phillips Exeter, and what was then Harvard College.

Despite his family's prominent position and his elite education, Bulfinch displayed no strong sense of career, and after graduating from Harvard in 1814 he drifted from one position to another, briefly teaching at Boston Latin, working at a store owned by one of his brothers, and moving amid businesses in Washington, D.C., and Boston.

*A Lifelong Position*   In 1837, Bulfinch began working as a clerk in Merchants Bank, the largest bank in Boston. He stayed in that position until his death thirty years later, and the job provided him with a stable income and sufficient free time to devote to his studies and writing. He pursued writing as an avocation, using it as a source of relaxation focused on a subject fitting a man of his education and social class. As Bulfinch himself wrote, he hoped "to teach mythology not as a study, but as a relaxation from study; to give our work the charm of a story-book, yet by means of it to impart a knowledge of an important branch of education."

Bulfinch's approach to writing was influenced by his six years of service as the secretary of the Boston Society of Natural History, which was a forum for prominent naturalists. His contact with these scientists made him realize that the expansion of scientific knowledge represented a threat to the classical education that was dominant at the time. Bulfinch wrote *The Age of Fable* (1855) in an attempt to depart from the methodology of rote memorization favored by classicists. Marie Cleary notes that in his writing, Bulfinch "ingeniously copied the naturalists' methods of rearranging and selecting material to find new relationships."

*Victorian-Era Writer*   Bulfinch did not have his first work published until he was fifty-seven years old. This work, *Hebrew Lyrical History* (1853), discussed the Psalms in the context of Jewish history. This was followed by the popular *The Age of Fable* (1855), *The Age of Chivalry* (1858), and *Legends of Charlemagne* (1863). These works, popular on their own, were collected into a single volume in 1881 under the title *Bulfinch's Mythology*. This book has been popular since its original publication, going through many editions despite the fact that Bulfinch's style is notably dated. Writing mostly during the Victorian Era, when it was considered off-limits to discuss such "unpleasant" topics as sex and violence, Bulfinch stripped out anything that might offend the delicate sensibilities of his intended audience.

Bulfinch died on May 27, 1867, in Boston, Massachusetts.

## Works in Literary Context

As a writer, Bulfinch explored a wide range of interests. This is reflected in his published titles, which include *Hebrew Lyrical Poetry* (1853), *The Boy Inventor* (1860),

---

## LITERARY AND HISTORICAL CONTEMPORARIES

Thomas Bulfinch's famous contemporaries include:

**Percy Bysshe Shelley** (1792–1822): An English poet associated with the Romantic movement, Shelley is best known for such long, visionary poems as *Adonaïs* (1821) and *Prometheus Unbound* (1820).

**Mary Shelley** (1797–1851): An important English novelist in her own right, the wife of Percey Bysshe Shelley is best known for writing *Frankenstein* (1818).

**William Cullen Bryant** (1794–1878): An American poet and newspaper editor, Bryant was considered one of the most influential journalists of his time.

**John Keats** (1795–1821): Keats was an English poet who was one of the most prominent members of the Romantic movement in poetry.

**Alexandre Dumas** (1802–1870): A French writer who specialized in historical action stories, Dumas is best known for *The Count of Monte Cristo* (1844–1846) and *The Three Musketeers* (1844).

---

*Shakespeare Adapted for Reading Classes* (1865), and *Oregon and Eldorado* (1866). However, the only works that were popular during his lifetime or that were read by subsequent generations were his retellings of classic stories, fables, and myths.

*Mythology for the Masses*   Bulfinch used his free time from work to become an exhaustive researcher, and he combed through his sources with scholarly thoroughness. The accuracy and solid foundation of his works made his mythologies standard references for many decades. Bulfinch not only retold old myths and legends; he made numerous references to poetry and painting in an attempt to demonstrate the stories' connections to Western culture. As he wrote in the introduction to one of this volumes,

> Our work is not for the learned, nor for the theologian, nor for the philosopher, but for the reader of English literature, of either sex, who wishes to comprehend the allusions so frequently made by public speakers, lecturers, essayists, and poets, and those that occur in polite conversation.

While Bulfinch's mythologies were well-researched, the skillful manner in which the stories are woven together made them popular with a wide audience. Even when replaced with more modern, twentieth-century versions, Bulfinch's work was still read because of the author's remarkable storytelling abilities. Bulfinch did leave out mentions of excessive violence and overt sexuality, but his stories have always been considered especially accessible and consistent, and they provide readers with a solid understanding of timeless stories.

## COMMON HUMAN EXPERIENCE

Among his many retellings, Bulfinch focuses on the stories and fables surrounding King Arthur and the Knights of the Round Table. Here are some other works that retell the King Arthur legend:

*Le Morte d'Arthur* (1485), by Thomas Malory. Malory's version of the Arthurian legend is considered the first major publication of this story, and it has continued to influence later versions up to the present day.

*A Connecticut Yankee in King Arthur's Court* (1889), a novel by Mark Twain. In this humorous take on Arthurian legend, a nineteenth-century American is transported back to sixth-century England, where he uses his scientific knowledge and ingenuity to both positive and negative ends.

*The Once and Future King* (1958), a novel by T. H. White. White's version of the King Arthur story presents a view of the ideal society set amid epic historical events.

*The Mists of Avalon* (1982), a novel by Marion Zimmer Bradley. Bradley retells the adventures of King Arthur from the point of view of the female characters involved in the story.

## Works in Critical Context

***Bulfinch's Mythology*** Although Bulfinch published a variety of works during his lifetime, his renown was entirely based on his mythologies, and it is only for these works that he is remembered into the twenty-first century. Despite more recent and more popular versions of ancient myths, Bulfinch still remains the standard against which others are judged. As Marie Cleary has noted, "*The Age of Fable* formed the image that millions of Americans had of the classical gods and heroes."

Scholars have noted that Bulfinch's versions were written for an audience that might be considered prudish by modern standards. This resulted in the careful omission of many important details from ancient myths. As his obituary noted, the contents of his retellings were "expurgated of all that would be offensive." However, his stories continue to be popular among teachers. As one biography notes, "The Bulfinch myths are an indispensable guide to the cultural values of the American 19th century, yet the Bulfinch version is still the version being taught in many American public schools."

## Responses to Literature

1. What are some of the themes that emerge from Bulfinch's retellings of ancient Greek and Roman myths? Are these themes relevant to a modern audience? Which of these themes are present in more recent versions of these myths, and which are not? What might be some of the reasons for the differences in themes between Bulfinch's versions and more modern versions?

2. Bulfinch's retellings of mythology were influential during the late nineteenth century, but they have since been replaced in most schools by other versions. What are the strengths and weaknesses of Bulfinch's mythological retellings compared to more modern versions? Do Bulfinch's myths deserve a place in modern schools, or are they best viewed as a product of the past?

3. Bulfinch was noted for retelling a wide variety of ancient myths in a manner that readers at the time found accessible. Choose one of the myths that Bulfinch retells and write your own version aimed at present-day readers.

4. *Bulfinch's Mythology* was often used in classrooms during the late nineteenth century and early twentieth century. Write a critical review of this collection intended to be read by present-day teachers who might be considering adopting this book for use in their classroom. Be sure to discuss the relevance of Bulfinch's approach to today's students.

BIBLIOGRAPHY

**Books**

Briggs, Ward W., Jr., ed. *Biographical Dictionary of North American Classicists*. Westport, Conn.: Greenwood Press, 1994.

Cleary, Marie. *Myths for the Millions: Thomas Bulfinch, His America, and His Mythology Book*. New York: Peter Lang, 2007.

**Periodicals**

Cleary, Marie. "A Book of Decided Usefulness: Thomas Bulfinch's 'The Age of Fable.'" *The Classical Journal* (February 1980): 248–249.

Cleary, Marie. "*Bulfinch's Mythology*." *Humanities* (January/February 1987): 12–15.

Cooksey, T. L. and Mary Lefkowitz. "Greek Gods, Human Lives: What We Can Learn from Myths." *Library Journal* (November 1, 2003): 83.

Tucker, Edward L. "Longfellow and Thomas Bulfinch." *ANQ* (Fall 1999): 17.

**Web Sites**

Spiritus-Temporis.com. *Biography of Thomas Bulfinch*. Retrieved October 8, 2008, from http://www.spiritus-temporis.com/thomas-bulfinch/.

The University of Adelaide Library. *Thomas Bulfinch, 1796–1867*. Retrieved October 24, 2008, from http://etext.library.adelaide.edu.au/b/bulfinch/thomas/.

# ✹ Carlos Bulosan

BORN: *1911, Binalonan, Philippines*

DIED: *1956, Seattle, Washington*

NATIONALITY: *American*

GENRE: *Nonfiction, poetry*

MAJOR WORKS:
*The Laughter of My Father* (1944)
*America Is in the Heart: A Personal History* (1946)

## Overview

Challenging racial barriers, Carlos Bulosan rose from an impoverished childhood in the colonial Philippines to become a celebrated author in the United States. Bulosan's education made him the first Asian American immigrant to document his life experiences in the language that could bridge the gap from the Filipino alien to the American mainstream. Because his books and poems bear witness to the racism and hardships Filipinos encountered in their adopted home, Bulosan is looked upon as both a pioneer in Asian American writing and a brave voice of the oppressed.

## Works in Biographical and Historical Context

*A Family's Struggles* Carlos Bulosan was born to a peasant family in Binalonan, a rural area of the Philippines, on November 1911. As a child, he helped his mother sell vegetables at a market and worked as a laborer in the mango fields. In *America Is in the Heart* (1946), Bulosan describes his father's losing battle to keep the small parcel of land that supported their large family. In his vivid portrayal of the setbacks that continually dashed any hopes for improving his family's conditions, Bulosan captures the forces that ultimately drove him—just as it had thousands of others—to seek a better life in America. After saving enough money for his passage, Bulosan boarded a ship bound for Seattle, Washington.

*America: Land of the Unexpected* Filipino immigrants entered America with an undetermined status. Because the Philippines were then a U.S. territory, Filipino immigrants were known as "nationals" and could freely enter America until 1934, when the Tydings-McDuffie Act promised independence to the Philippines in ten years. However, Filipinos were not considered citizens until President Truman signed the Filipino Naturalization Bill granting Filipinos citizenship in 1946.

Bulosan arrived in the United States in July 1930, less than a year after the 1929 stock market crash that devastated the American economy and marked the beginning of the bleak period in American history known as the Great Depression. With unemployment high and competition fierce for the few available jobs, some white Americans, afraid the immigrants would prevent them

from supporting their own families, resented the Filipinos. Immigrants too new to know their rights were often exploited. With no money or family in Seattle, Bulosan worked in the fish canneries of Alaska. After an entire season of hard labor, his earnings—after his bosses had made some questionable deductions—totaled only thirteen dollars. When he left Alaska, Bulosan headed to Los Angeles, finding occasional work as a field hand or crop picker along the Pacific Coast, including the Salinas Valley, the setting for many of John Steinbeck's novels.

Because he was sickly and had difficulty holding jobs, Bulosan lived in Los Angeles with his brother, who helped support him. In Los Angeles, Bulosan witnessed extensive prejudice against Filipinos. At a pool hall there, Bulosan saw two policemen gun down a Filipino. In California, miscegenation laws made it illegal for Filipinos to marry white women, and cars with Filipino men were routinely stopped by police and searched. "I came to know afterward that in many ways it was a crime to be a Filipino in California," Bulosan wrote in his autobiography. "I came to know that the public streets were not free to my people."

*The New Tide of Radical Politics* During the times when he was too ill to work, Bulosan spent his free time in public libraries, reading voraciously. He was fascinated by philosophy and sociology, particularly in the way these disciplines related to the labor movement. He became interested in the communist theorist Karl Marx, often telling friends about the rising power of the working classes and what they would achieve in the coming revolution. Soon, Bulosan became involved in an effort to organize independent unions for Filipinos as a way to fight the arbitrary firings and wage cuts they routinely suffered. The organizing effort led to the formation of a new international union known as UCAPAWA, United Cannery and Packing House Workers of America, representing fish cannery workers in Seattle and packing house workers in Salinas, California, who were often the same workers at different times of the year.

In a time when radical politics were widely discussed in the United States and the labor movement began to emerge as an important force, thousands of small working-class magazines and newspapers were established all over the country. Bulosan took advantage of these avenues to write several political articles that focused on the problems of Filipino workers in America. In 1934, he founded *The New Tide*, a bimonthly radical literary magazine that brought him into contact with some of the great writers of the era, including the poet William Carlos Williams and the novelist Richard Wright.

**Wartime, Racism, and Freedom from Want**
When the United States was drawn into World War II, the Philippines became its ally against the Japanese in the Pacific theater, and attitudes toward Filipinos in the United States improved slightly when President Franklin D. Roosevelt granted enlisted Filipinos U.S. citizenship. During this time, Bulosan began to receive wider acceptance as a writer. In 1943, he published *The Voice of Bataan*, a collection of poems dedicated to the men who died in that crucial battle of the Pacific war. That same year, the *Saturday Evening Post* published articles about the Four Freedoms enunciated by President Roosevelt: freedom of speech, freedom to worship, freedom from want, and freedom from fear. Bulosan was chosen to write the article on freedom from want, a topic he knew well after living in hunger and deprivation for years. The result was a biting essay about the oppression of the working class, the police-state intimidation techniques routinely used against unions, and the rampant racism in America.

In 1944, Bulosan published his first collection of short stories, *The Laughter of My Father*, which was an instant wartime sensation. The book was included in the War Department's arsenal of propaganda, translated into several languages, and transmitted worldwide over wartime radio. In 1946, Bulosan published his most enduring work, the autobiographical *America Is in the Heart*. A merciless critique of a racist society immersed in the Great Depression, the book was a critical success. Although *The Laughter of My Father* and *America Is in the Heart* established Bulosan's reputation as a writer, his fame was not accompanied by fortune.

**Blacklisted into Poverty**  In the conservative postwar climate of the early 1950s, Bulosan fell from favor. His left-wing politics and involvement in union activities were at odds with the fanatical anti-communism of the McCarthy era, a time when Senator Joseph McCarthy led a nationwide hunt for communists and their supporters.

Bulosan was blacklisted—put on a list of allegedly disloyal people whom employers were pressured not to hire. While debate exists about whether he was actually a member of the Communist Party, Bulosan's apparent association with communism negatively affected his reputation not only in the United States, but also in the Philippines, where politically radical writing was denounced. Even Bulosan's friends destroyed letters he had sent them. As he faded into relative obscurity, Bulosan once again fell into poverty, and his health progressively declined. He spent his final years in Seattle and was hospitalized periodically. On September 11, 1956, he died of tuberculosis and malnutrition.

## Works in Literary Context

For nearly twenty years after his death, Bulosan and his works were largely forgotten. However, a generation of Asian Americans rediscovered him when *America Is in the Heart* was reprinted by the University of Washington Press in 1973. It has since become a fixture in Asian American Studies programs across the nation, and Asian American writers and academics such as Jessica Hagedorn and Maxine Hong Kingston have been influenced by Bulosan's exploration of how Filipinos fought for an American identity.

**The Dark Side of the Immigrant Experience**
Today, Bulosan's poetry is widely read and serves a sociopolitical function not only in the creation of an ethnic consciousness among Filipino Americans, but also in the creation of a nondiscriminatory consciousness among all Americans. Capturing the realism of immigrant life, *Letter from America* (1942) includes some of Bulosan's best-known poems. These poems speak of the Depression and lines of unemployed men; the injustice of the jail cell; Nicola Sacco and Bartolomeo Vanzetti, Italian immigrants who were persecuted for their political views; the terror immigrants feel and experience; painful memories of their now-inaccessible homeland; and starving children. The poems are characterized by an uneasiness that is conveyed through repeated images of nightmares, dreams of being hunted down, threats of execution, and planes circling overhead. The poems are ragged, honest, and especially critical of the racism and economic inequality that had once shocked the idealistic young immigrant.

## Works in Critical Context

Carlos Bulosan, one of the first wave of Filipinos to immigrate to the United States during the 1930s, is considered the foremost Filipino expatriate writer. Though his work was very successful and critically acclaimed in the 1930s and 1940s, his reputation was tarnished when he was blacklisted by Senator Joseph McCarthy during the anticommunist movements of the 1950s. Not until *America Is in the Heart* was rediscovered and republished in 1973 was his work placed among classic Asian-American literature.

***America Is in the Heart*** *America Is in the Heart* has been treated by scholars as Marxist, third world, and postcolonial, but it is most often valued by Filipino Americans as simply a narration of racial consciousness, of the way things were. Scholar Roland L. Guyotte comments that *America Is in the Heart* reflects Bulosan's "self-conscious awakening to his Filipino identity, an awakening that occurred in the United States." In that regard, *America Is in the Heart* has become one of the most important works of Asian American literature. Its reach, however, transcends nationality or ethnicity. According to *Saturday Review of Literature* writer Clara Savage Littledale,

> People interested in driving from America the scourge of intolerance should read Mr. Bulosan's autobiography. They should read it that they may draw from it the anger it will arouse in them … the determination to bring an end to the vicious nonsense of racism.

## Responses to Literature

1. *America Is in the Heart* has been criticized for its negative portrayal of Filipinos in America: Drinking, gambling, murder, theft, prostitution. Why would Bulosan show the dark side of Filipino life? By doing so, what point does he make about the lives of these immigrants?

2. Using your library or the Internet, research the Marcos regime that ruled the Philippines from 1965 until 1986. How did the Marcos government and its declaration of martial law in September 1972 contribute to a reawakened interest in Bulosan's work?

3. Even after facing violent discrimination, Bulosan writes with hope, believing that all people will someday be treated equally. What do you think sustained him during difficult times? What other books or movies feature characters who encounter continuous adversity but never give up their hopes and dreams?

4. In *America Is in the Heart*, Bulosan weaves news articles he read and stories that he heard with experiences of his own life to depict the injustices against Filipino immigrants. How does Bulosan's work compare with autobiographies by such other famous Americans as Benjamin Franklin, Henry Adams, or Frederick Douglass?

BIBLIOGRAPHY

**Books**

Bulosan, Carlos. *America Is in the Heart.* Reprinted with an introduction by Carey McWilliams. Seattle, Wash.: University of Washington Press, 1973.

Epifano, San Juan. *Carlos Bulosan and the Imagination of the Class Struggle.* Quezon City, Philippines: University of the Philippines Press, 1972.

Espiritu, Augusto F. *Five Faces of Exile: The Nation and Filipino American Intellectuals.* Stanford, Calif.: Stanford University Press, 2005.

Evangelista, Susan. *Carlos Bulosan and His Poetry: A Biography and Anthology.* Quezon City, Philippines: Ateno University Press, 1985.

Kim, Elaine H., ed. *Asian-American Literature: An Introduction to the Writings and Their Social Context.* Philadelphia.: Temple University Press, 1982.

Morantte, P. C. *Remembering Carlos Bulosan: His Heart Affair with America.* Quezon City, Philippines: New Day, 1984.

**Periodicals**

Feria, Dolores S. "Carlos Bulosan: Gentle Genius." *Comment* 1 (1957).

Guyotte, Roland L. "Generation Gap: Filipinos, Filipino Americans, and Americans, Here and There, Then and Now." *Journal of American Ethnic History* (Fall 1997): 64.

Littledale, Clara Savage. "The Way Father Stretched His Mouth." *The Saturday Review of Literature* (June 3, 1944): 22.

**Web sites**

Mejia-Giudici, Cynthia. *Bulosan, Carlos (1911?–1956).* Retrieved September 12, 2008, from http://www.historylink.org/index.cfm?DisplayPage=output.cfm&File_Id=5202.

---

# COMMON HUMAN EXPERIENCE

In his autobiography *America Is in the Heart*, Bulosan tells of his search for the ideal United States he had learned about in school, as opposed to the real, harsh United States he discovered as an immigrant. Below are other works that feature immigrants who find life in their new homeland difficult and disappointingly less than what they expected:

*The Whirlwind* (2007), young adult fiction by Carol Matas. Fourteen-year-old Ben flees Nazi Germany with his family, finding safety and stability in Seattle, Washington, until Ben's new Japanese American friend is sent to an internment camp.

*Giants in the Earth* (1927), a novel by O. E. Rolvaag. A Norwegian immigrant family making a new life on the Dakota prairie find their dreams challenged by the land and its elements.

*Vita* (2005), fiction by Melania Mazzucco. In this story about two children coming through Ellis Island, Mazzucco describes the poverty, discrimination, and filthy living conditions experienced by immigrants.

# ✺ Edgar Rice Burroughs

BORN: *1875, Chicago, Illinois*

DIED: *1950, Encino, California*

NATIONALITY: *American*

GENRE: *Fiction*

MAJOR WORKS:
*Tarzan of the Apes* (1914)
*A Princess of Mars* (1917)
*At the Earth's Core* (1922)
*Pellucidar* (1923)
*The Land That Time Forgot* (1924)

## Overview

Perhaps best known as the creator of *Tarzan of the Apes*, Edgar Rice Burroughs did much to popularize science fiction and adventure fantasy during the first half of the twentieth century. He created several imaginary societies for his popular adventure series: one in an imaginary version of Africa, one set on Mars, one in the primitive world called Pellucidar located inside the earth, and yet another on Venus. The constant theme running through Burroughs's many books is how alien or primitive societies inspire heroic qualities in his main characters.

Edgar Rice Burroughs    *American Stock / Hulton Archive / Getty Images*

## Biographical and Historical Context

***Predictions of Failure and Expulsion from Yale***
Burroughs was born in Chicago in 1875 and was the youngest of four sons. His father, George Burroughs, had been a captain in the Union army during the Civil War, and his son remembered him as retaining a "very stern and military" aspect. Edgar was an uncomplicated boy, fond of outdoor sports, but a poor student. He was sent to Phillips Academy in Andover, Massachusetts, to prepare for Yale University, but was expelled from the prestigious private school. His father believed his expulsion foreshadowed a life of continuous failure. Indeed, Edgar's life path for the two subsequent decades would be marked mighty effort and few accomplishments.

***An Interest in Paleontology Developed in Military School***    Burroughs continued his schooling at the Michigan Military Academy, where he studied paleontology, a subject that would inform his detailed descriptions of dinosaurs and the process of evolution in later novels such as *The Land That Time Forgot* (1924). Burroughs was certainly not alone in his interest in paleontology; in fact, the United States was seized by something of a dinosaur craze in the late nineteenth and early twentieth centuries. In 1858, American anatomy professor Joseph Leidy had discovered a *Hadrosaurus* skeleton in well-preserved condition. As the United States continued its westward expansion and railroads brought more people to the Great Plains and the western part of the continent,

scientists discovered the Unites States was rich in fossils and prehistoric remains. The discovery of radioactivity in 1896 led to the development and refinement of radiometric dating practices in the first decades of the twentieth century, which meant scientists could accurately assess the age of the dinosaur remains and other fossils they found. The general public was fascinated by these discoveries, and thus very receptive to Burroughs's later fictional tales featuring prehistoric settings.

After completing his schooling at the Michigan Military Academy, Burroughs failed the entrance examination for the United States Military Academy at West Point. He enlisted in the United States Army cavalry, but was soon discharged for having a weak heart.

***Petty Jobs and Ill-Fated Ventures***    During the years from 1897 to 1911, Burroughs engaged in a long succession of mostly petty jobs and ill-fated small business ventures in Idaho and Illinois. He married the daughter of a Chicago hotel owner in 1900, and they headed west to share in the mining ventures of Burroughs's luckless brothers. The couple soon found themselves living in poverty. In 1905 they returned to Chicago and moved back in with George Burroughs while Edgar held down a series of low-paying jobs. Burroughs's military discharge prevented him from serving in World War I, "The Great War," which claimed the lives of more than twenty million people worldwide from 1914 until 1918. The war years, however, saw the blossoming of Burroughs's career as a writer.

### Writing to Cure Boredom Leads to Success

While in Chicago, one of Burroughs's assignments was placing advertisements in pulp magazines, cheap publications featuring adventures stories that enjoyed wide popularity with the general reading public in the first half of the twentieth century. Pulp fiction magazines were an outgrowth of the dime novels of the nineteenth century, which, like the pulp fiction magazines, offered simple adventures stories and stock characters. Burroughs often scoffed that a novice could write as well as any of the top pulp authors; he was soon writing fiction to relieve his boredom. In 1911 Burroughs completed his first novel and sold it to one of the leading fantasy and adventure magazines, *The All-Story*. By the time the novel was published in book form as *A Princess of Mars* (1917), he had nineteen other works in other forms of print, most of them serialized in magazines before book publication. Burroughs is best known for three long series. The Martian novels, beginning with *A Princess of Mars*, concern the conquest of Barsoom (Mars) by "John Carter, gentleman," a Civil War veteran and swordsman from Virginia. In the Pellucidar series, which began in 1922 with *At the Earth's Core*, David Innes, a wealthy Yale graduate, becomes emperor of a prehistoric world deep within the globe. Burroughs's most famous series, Tarzan of the Apes, began with the novel of that title in 1914. In that series, the heir of an aristocratic English family, whose parents were shipwrecked on the African coast, survives their death to grow up in a community of apes and become their leader.

### Marred by Eugenics?

Some critics have argued that the Tarzan novels are marred by their authors' racist interest in eugenics, the study of methods for improving the quality of the human gene pool. Eugenics, in both philosophical and practical form, attracted the interest of many prominent Americans and Europeans in the late nineteenth and early twentieth centuries. U.S. President Woodrow Wilson, inventor Alexander Graham Bell, and health activist Margaret Sanger are just a few examples. Many well-intentioned people interested in eugenics saw it as a way to rid the world of everything from congenital defects to poverty. Edgar Rice Burroughs was also fascinated by the idea of the perfectibility of humankind through selective breeding. With Tarzan, many critics argue, Burroughs appears to be making the argument that a superior human (in this case, one of noble Western European heritage) will rise to the top no matter the circumstances. Others argue that the depiction of a "superior" European who establishes dominion over an uncivilized African jungle is racist. Indeed, most of Burroughs's heroes are gentlemanly whites who come to dominate those around them.

The idea of eugenics was easily molded to suit various political agendas—some purely racist, some ethically questionable. For example, in the United States in the first half of the twentieth century, tens of thousands of mentally ill citizens were forcibly sterilized to prevent them from "passing on" their "defects." In the 1930s and 1940s, when the leadership of the Nazi party used arguments based on eugenics to justify their goal to "purge" what they considered inferior social groups (Jews, homosexuals, the mentally handicapped, and others) by mass murder, the philosophy of eugenics was discredited.

### Filming Tarzan in Hollywood

Burroughs's sudden success enabled him to move to Hollywood, where he could supervise the filming of the immensely popular Tarzan movies. In 1919 he bought an estate near Hollywood, which he named Tarzana. He operated it at a heavy loss. The community that sprang up around the estate adopted the name Tarzana when their town was incorporated in 1928. Burroughs was an enthusiastic stock market gambler, and his bad investments further reduced his fortune. Always pressed for money, he kept up a harried writing pace in hopes of keeping his finances afloat. He averaged three novels a year, producing more than seventy titles in all. A Tarzan comic strip began in 1929 and continued to be published throughout Burroughs's life. Tarzan products, ranging from a brand of gasoline to coloring books, were a part of American culture. A radio serial starring Burroughs's daughter and son-in-law (a former movie Tarzan) enjoyed great popularity. The films were the most successful products of the Tarzan franchise, although Burroughs was pained to see the multilingual aristocrat of his novels reduced to a lumpish commoner grunting in broken English, as depicted by Johnny Weissmuller (a gold-medal-winning Olympic swimmer and actor) who starred in twelve of the films. The character of Tarzan remains a cultural icon and is still popular today.

### Late Life during World War II

While Burroughs's previous military failures prevented him from actively serving in World War II, its outbreak prompted him to become a war correspondent and write a series of morale-boosting pieces for the *Advertiser* of Honolulu, Hawaii, where he was then living. The surprise attack on Pearl Harbor in Honolulu by the Japanese on December 7, 1941, had precipitated the United States's entry into the war. Returning to California in late 1944, Burroughs developed Parkinson's disease and died in 1950 at the age of seventy-four.

## Works in Literary Context

Burroughs was one of the most successful popular novelists America has ever produced. He combined science fiction, fantasy, and romance into a single form with the potential for great flexibility and imaginative exploration. His works may not have been highly philosophical, but they were often more thoughtful and engaged with relevant social themes than they needed to be just to sell

# LITERARY AND HISTORICAL CONTEMPORARIES

Among Edgar Rice Burroughs's famous contemporaries were:

**John Steinbeck** (1902–1968): This American novelist was awarded the Pulitzer Prize in 1940 and the Nobel Prize for Literature in 1962 for his compassionate portrayals of the poor, especially itinerant farm laborers, during the Great Depression and the Dust Bowl years of the 1930s.

**Upton Sinclair** (1878–1968): This Pulitzer Prize–winning American author was famous for such protest novels as *The Jungle* (1906) and *Oil!* (1927).

**Edvard Munch** (1863–1944): Norwegian artist famous for his very familiar painting, "The Scream." As an "Expressionist" painter, Munch's work portrays inner torments, fear, desire, and isolation.

**Mao Zedong** (1893–1976): Leader of the Chinese Communist Party from 1943 until his death. Mao was born to a peasant family and went on to lead a revolution against both the Chinese and Japanese governments, establishing Communism in China.

**George Bernard Shaw** (1856–1950): This prolific writer and social commentator is often seen as the greatest British dramatist since Shakespeare. He explored themes of social equality, women's rights, the class system, and a great many other topics in more than fifty plays and dozens of books over sixty-five years.

copies. Burroughs was influenced by many writers including H. P. Lovecraft, Robert E. Howard, Edmond Hamilton, Leigh Brackett, Ray Bradbury, Gore Vidal, and J. R. R. Tolkien.

***The Melding of Pulp Genres*** While best known for his *Tarzan* series, Burroughs was in fact a very important and popular science-fiction writer. He also wrote a smaller number of westerns, romances, historical novels, and a few unsuccessful attempts at contemporary realism. As a science-fiction writer, Burroughs may be regarded as a descendant of nineteenth-century French writer Jules Verne. Like Verne, Burroughs emphasized strange planets and bizarre creatures in his work. Burroughs did not invent the boy-raised-by-animals novel, the hollow-Earth novel, the interplanetary romance, or any other significant fantasy form; but he did write some of the most successful and completely developed examples of each of these types of fiction.

***Feralism*** Burroughs's *Tarzan* stories and other jungle adventures, while not essentially works of science fiction, contain many elements derived from science fiction and allied forms. After the boy-raised-in-the-wild theme (known as "feralism"), the next most common theme in the books is that of the lost race, tribe, city, or country.

For this Burroughs shows the influence of Sir Henry Rider Haggard (1856–1925), an English author who wrote exotic, mysterious novels often set in Africa. The theme of feralism is itself very old in literature and folklore; it was best known prior to the creation of Tarzan in the character Mowgli from *The Jungle Book* (1894) by Rudyard Kipling.

## Works in Critical Context

Burroughs's writing is often labeled uneven and amateurish. His technique in the *Tarzan* tales of following parallel lines of action through the eyes of various characters has been compared to cinematic cross-cutting, and he often succeeds through a headlong descriptive power. But he often stumbles in characterization and dialogue, sometimes using the crudest stereotypes and stilted language. Critics allow that Burroughs occasionally scores when he writes satire, particularly in *Tarzan and the Ant Men* (1924), which Richard Lupoff, a well-known Burroughs critic, regards as one of the best *Tarzan* novels. But Burroughs's shortcomings as a writer are most apparent in *Beyond Thirty* (published posthumously in novel form in 1957, first published in serial form in 1915), whose theme is the reversion of England and Western Europe to wilderness (a plot subsequently used in a great many science fiction novels). Just when the story gets promising, it grinds to a halt, as though Burroughs's invention had flagged.

***The Tarzan Novels*** The overwhelming commercial success of the *Tarzan* books was somewhat dampened by the critical hostility directed at Burroughs's work in general. Throughout his career, critics were less than kind to Burroughs, labeling his books as little more than crudely written entertainment. Some have even found, just beneath the surface of his fiction, what they considered clear signs of fascism, racism, and anti-intellectualism. However, as author George P. Elliott noted, Burroughs's "prejudices are so gross that no one bothers to analyze them out or to attack them. . . . They were clear-eyed, well-thawed prejudices arrayed only in a loin cloth." Brian Attebury agreed, writing that "Burroughs was neither more nor less than a good storyteller, with as much power—and finesse—as a bulldozer." Writing in *Esquire*, Gore Vidal claimed that, although Burroughs "is innocent of literature," he nonetheless "does have a gift very few writers of any kind possess: he can describe action vividly. . . . Tarzan in action is excellent."

## Responses to Literature

1. Why do you think "feralism" has fascinated writers and audiences for so many years? Using your library and the Internet, research real-life cases of feralism. How do these cases compare to Burroughs's stories?

2. For much of the twentieth century, many Americans' knowledge of Africa was limited to what they saw in

Tarzan movies. What do you think has been the legacy of Tarzan on Africa and Western perceptions of it, even today? Using your library and the Internet, find out more about how Western literature and popular culture portrayed Africa in the nineteenth and twentieth centuries, and analyze whether these portrayals were accurate or not. Pay particular attention to the figure of Tarzan in the Western imagination.

3. Watch different film versions of the Tarzan story from different periods. How do the film versions differ from the original novels? How do they differ from each other? What do you think accounts for these differences?

4. Burroughs wrote several popular science fiction novels set on Venus. To find out more about the real planet Venus, read *Venus Revealed: A New Look Below the Clouds of Our Mysterious Twin Planet* (1998), by David Harry Grinspoon. Grinspoon was the principal scientist attached to the Magellan mission to Venus during the 1990s. The book is a lively, entertaining, informative look at both recent discoveries about Venus and myths surrounding it.

5. Write a paper in which you compare one of Edgar Rice Burrough's novels to a novel by Jules Verne (for example, compare Verne's *Journey to the Center of the Earth* (1864) to Burroughs's *At the Earth's Core*). What part does scientific research play in their stories? How are science and scientists portrayed in each author's works? In what ways does Burroughs differ from Verne?

BIBLIOGRAPHY

**Books**

Brady, Clark A. *The Burroughs Cyclopaedia: Characters, Places, Fauna, Flora, Technologies, Languages, Ideas, and Terminologies Found in the Works of Edgar Rice Burroughs.* Jefferson, N.C.: McFarland, 1996.

Fenton, Robert. *The Big Swingers: A Biography of Edgar Rice Burroughs.* New York: Prentice Hall, 1967.

Fury, David. *Kings of the Jungle: An Illustrated Reference to "Tarzan" on Screen and Television.* Jefferson, NC: McFarland, 1994.

Lupoff, Richard A. *Edgar Rice Burroughs: Master of Adventure.* New York: Canaveral Press, 1965.

Porges, Irwin. *Edgar Rice Burroughs: The Man Who Created Tarzan.* Salt Lake City: Brigham Young University Press, 1975.

Zaidan, Samira H. *A Comparative Study of Haiu Bnu Yakdhan, Mowgli, and Tarzan.* London: Red Squirrel Books, 1998.

Altrocchi, Rudolph. "Ancestors of Tarzan." In *Sleuthing in the Stacks.* Port Washington, NY: Kinnekat Press, 1944.

## COMMON HUMAN EXPERIENCE

A recurring theme running in Burroughs's work is how heroic qualities in people are brought out by encounters with alien or primitive societies. Here are some other works that involve heroic adventurers in strange lands:

*Epic of Gilgamesh* (c. 2000 B.C.E.). This ancient Mesopotamian poem tells of a heroic king who travels the world in search of immortality, battling beasts and experiencing adventures along the way. The best-known version of the poem, written down about three thousand years ago, is one of the oldest pieces of literature known.

*The Odyssey* (c. 720 B.C.E.) by Homer. One of the central works in world literature, this Greek epic recounts the travels of Odysseus and his crew as they sail home to Ithaca after the Trojan War. Through a series of encounters with monsters, gods, giants, sorceresses—and, in the end, men who are out to steal his home and wife—Odysseus comes to embody the full spectrum of heroism.

*The Lost World* (1912), a novel by Sir Arthur Conan Doyle. Doyle, best known as the author of the Sherlock Holmes stories, was also a doctor of medicine who had once been a ship's surgeon on trips to the African Coast. This novel is about an expedition of scientists, hunters, and a journalist that has its own bickering in the Amazon rainforest rudely interrupted by numerous meat-eating dinosaurs.

**Web Sites**

*Edgar Rice Burroughs Inc.* Retrieved March 24, 2008 from http://www.tarzan.org/. Last updated on February 17, 2008.

*ERBzine.* Retrieved March 24, 2008 from http://www.erbzine.com/

*John Carter of Mars.com.* Retrieved March 24, 2008 from http://www.johncarterofmars.com/.

# ⊛ Octavia Butler

BORN: *1947, Pasadena, California*

DIED: *2006, Lake Forest Park, Washington*

NATIONALITY: *American, African American*

GENRE: *Fiction*

MAJOR WORKS:

*Kindred* (1979)

*Bloodchild* (1985)

*Parable of the Sower* (1993)

## Overview

Octavia Butler was the first notable female African American science-fiction writer. Butler's works present familiar

Octavia Butler   *Beth Gwinn / Writer Pictures*

science-fiction topics, such as aliens, psychic powers, genetic engineering, and dystopian futures, in terms of racial and sexual awareness.

## Works in Biographical and Historical Context

*An "Out Kid"*   Octavia Butler was born in 1947 in Pasadena, California, where she grew up in a racially mixed neighborhood. An only child, her father died when she was still a baby, and she was reared by her mother, grandmother, and other relatives in southern California. Her own experience accounts for the positive treatment of such adoptive relationships in all of her novels. She describes herself in childhood as "a perennial 'out kid,'" shy, bookish, and taller than her classmates. Raised by strict Baptists, she was not permitted to dance, or later, to wear makeup. Not feeling accepted by those her own age, she was more comfortable with older people.

Butler's status as a loner child was enhanced by her love of books, which she possessed despite suffering from dyslexia. Always an avid reader, she began writing stories at age ten. Her mother, who had been forced to quit school early in order to work, encouraged her daughter to read and write. As a child, Butler frequented the Pasadena Public Library, but she soon outgrew the children's books, and since she was not allowed in the adult

section, she began browsing the magazines, where she discovered science fiction.

*Contact with Science-Fiction Writers*   As a student at Pasadena City College, and later, California State at Los Angeles, she took courses in English, speech, and social sciences—history and anthropology in particular. Unable to major in creative writing, she quit formal work toward a degree but attended evening writing classes at UCLA while working in a variety of jobs, many described by the female narrator of *Kindred*. Her most useful training as a writer she attributes to work with the Writers Guild of America, West, Inc., an organization that established an "open door" program for aspiring writers in the late 1960s and early 1970s. Through this group she met writers Sid Stebel and Harlan Ellison, who provided the early criticism and encouragement she needed.

It was Ellison who brought Butler to the Clarion Science Fiction Writer's Workshop in the summer of 1970, where she worked under such well-known writers of science fiction as Joanna Russ, Fritz Leiber, Kate Wilhelm, Damon Knight, and Robin Scott Wilson. The six-week session provided nuts-and-bolts advice on writing and publishing science fiction, and she sold her first two stories while a student there. After the Clarion Workshop, she continued her formal training as a science-fiction writer with classes at UCLA given by Ellison and Theodore Sturgeon.

*Influenced by 1970s Social Conditions*   In the early 1970s, Butler went to work on her first series of books, the *Patternist* novels. As she was creating a future world, Butler was influenced by the social turmoil of that time, and her dominant themes were related to the concerns raised by both the feminist movement and the Civil Rights movement. These early novels, which focus on the responsibility of the powerful to the powerless and explore questions about sexual and racial roles, brought contemporary issues into the science-fiction context. However, her writing was not directly influenced by any particular social movement. For feminist critics, her work presented certain problems, particularly since she presents no clear winners or losers in the gender struggle, but indicates where compromises can be made to unify women and men. Similarly, her futuristic settings presented problems for African American literary critics whose attention was largely focused on depictions of the black experience in the past and in the present.

Throughout her career, Butler continued to explore the themes first introduced in her earliest works, even as she branched out from her early *Patternist* novels to write two other series, the *Xenogenesis* trilogy (1987–1989) and the *Parable of the Sower* novels (1993 and 1998), as well as two well-received stand-alone novels, *Kindred* (1979) and *The Fledgling* (2005), which was published shortly before her death at the age of 58.

## Works in Literary Context

Butler's writing explores themes that have generally received cursory treatments in the science-fiction genre, including sexual identity, racial conflict, and contemporary politics. Because of this, Butler's works have been compared to those of authors outside of science fiction, particularly Toni Morrison and Margaret Atwood, and she has earned recognition as a pioneer among women writers.

*The Powerful and the Powerless*  The responsibility of the powerful to the powerless is one of the continuing themes of Butler's writing. Her novels often feature societies in which there is a clear distinction between the powerful and the powerless, and the tensions of this relationship are explored throughout. For example, a class struggle is one of the central concerns of the *Parable of the Sower* novels. Butler's deft handling of this timeless concern has won her work virtually universal acclaim by critics and fans of science fiction and has attracted a wide audience among general readers.

*Sexual and Racial Themes*  Butler's heroines typically are powerful black women who possess large measures of both mental and physical acumen. While they exemplify the traditional female gender roles of nurturer, healer, and conciliator, these women also display courage, independence, and ambition, and embody the belief that hierarchical systems are flawed. They enhance their influence through alliances with or opposition to powerful males. Frances Smith Foster has commented: "Her major characters are black women, and through her characters and through the structure of her imagined social order, Butler consciously explores the impact of race and sex upon future society." The insight displayed in Butler's novels has won her a solid reputation among both readers and critics. One critic noted that her work has a "cult status among many black women readers." She also observed that "Butler's work has a scope that commands a wide audience."

## Works in Critical Context

Most of Butler's novels have enjoyed a favorable critical reception, but it was not until the mid-1980s that she began winning important science-fiction awards. In 1985 she won three of science-fiction's major awards—a Nebula award, a Hugo award, and a Locus award—for her novella *Bloodchild*. She has since won another Hugo Award and another Nebula Award.

*The Patternist Series*  Five of Butler's first six novels (*Kindred* being the exception) were part of the *Patternist* series, and all enjoyed a favorable critical reception. All six of her novels have enjoyed a favorable critical reception, and she was particularly praised for the artistry and power of her most recent works. Feminists and critics of Afro-American literature wrote admiringly of her handling of issues of gender and race, and critics and fans of science

---

### LITERARY AND HISTORICAL CONTEMPORARIES

Butler's famous contemporaries include:

**Judy Blume** (1938–): Blume is an American author who has achieved widespread popularity because of her childrens' and young adult books which frequently tackle difficult and controversial issues.

**Tom Clancy** (1947–): Clancy is an American novelist who writes best-selling spy and military novels.

**Camille Paglia** (1947–): Paglia is an American author and feminist social critic best known for her work *Sexual Personae* (1990).

**Grace Jones** (1948–): Jones is a Jamaican-American actor and singer prominent as a New Wave musician.

---

### COMMON HUMAN EXPERIENCE

Many of Butler's novels are set in dystopian futures where social roles, particularly gender roles, are radically unequal. Here are some other works with a similar setting:

*Consider Her Ways* (1961), a novella by John Wyndham. The story in this novella concerns a future woman-only society in which a caste society modeled on ant colonies has been created by the ruling elites.

*The Handmaid's Tale* (1985), a novel by Margaret Atwood. In this novel, women living in a Christian theocracy society of the near future are subjected to tight social controls and used as surrogate mothers for powerful couples.

*Native Tongue* (1984), a novel by Suzette Haden Elgin. This novel takes place in a future where American women have been stripped of the right to vote and their civil rights.

---

fiction lauded the fully realized worlds of the past and future which spring from her work. An unnamed critic for *Kirkus Reviews* offers a positive review, noting however, that the book is "old-fashioned" in its science-fiction sensibility. A reviewer for *Publishers Weekly* also noted the book's formulaic appeal: "The author carefully spells out the ground rules of her unique world, and the ensuing story of love, chase, and combat is consistently attention-holding."

*Kindred*  Several of Butler's books, particularly *Kindred*, have been recommended by critics as examples of the best that science fiction has to offer. For example, speaking of *Kindred* and *Wild Seed*, John Pfeiffer argued that with these books Butler "produced two novels of such special excellence that critical appreciation of them will take several years to assemble. To miss them will be to miss unique novels in modern fiction." It is the unique combination of elements, particularly in her non-series novels such as *Kindred*, that has captured the attention of readers and reviewers. In her obituary of Butler, Susanna Sturgis wrote that "[t]he mere premise of *Kindred* took my breath away." Similar sentiments were expressed by reviewers when *Kindred* was first released in 1979, not as science fiction, but as mainstream fiction. The novel subsequently became a staple in college classes in both literature and African American studies.

## Responses to Literature

1. Commentators have noted that Butler explores the theme of the responsibility of the powerful to the powerless. What responsibilities do her works indicate that the powerful have? In what ways do her works show that these responsibilities are being met in today's society, and in what ways are they shown as being shirked?

2. Butler is considered a rare science-fiction writer who pursues questions of sexual identity and race relations in her works. In what ways is science fiction not suited for pursuing these questions, and in what ways is science fiction useful for pursuing them? Can science-fiction novels address these kinds of questions more successfully than novels in other genres? Why or why not?

3. Like many science-fiction writers, Butler uses dystopian futures as settings for her stories. Choose one of Butler's novels and a futuristic science-fiction novel by another author and write an essay comparing and contrasting the features of the futures they present. Be sure to discuss the different purposes that each of these authors has for writing their work and analyze how their futuristic settings serve to further those purposes.

4. In *Kindred*, Butler draws on her own work experiences to create the background of her main character. Write a character sketch of a lead character whose background is based on your own experiences.

BIBLIOGRAPHY

**Books**

*Contemporary Novelists.* Detroit: St. James Press, 2001.
"Octavia E(stelle) Butler (1947–)." *Contemporary Literary Criticism.* Edited by Daniel G. Marowski, Roger Matuz, and Jane E. Neidhardt. Vol. 38. Detroit: Gale Research, 1986, pp. 61–66.

Pfeiffer, John R. "Octavia Butler Writes the Bible." In Rusinko, Susan, ed. *Shaw and Other Matters.* Selinsgrove, Pa.: Susquehanna University Press, 1998.
Stevenson, Rosemary. *Black Women in America, An Historical Encyclopedia.* Brooklyn, N.Y.: Carlson Publishing, 1993.

**Periodicals**

Bogstad, Janice. "Octavia E. Butler and Power Relationships." *Janus* (Winter 1978–79): 28–29.
Davidson, Carolyn S. "The Science Fiction of Octavia Butler." *Salaga* (1981): 35.
Elliot, Jeffrey. "Interview with Octavia Butler." *Thrust: SF in Review* (Summer 1979): 19–22.
Foster, Frances Smith. "Octavia Butler's Black Female Future Fiction." *Extrapolation* (Spring 1982): 37–49.
Govan, Sandra Y. "Connections, Links, and Extended Networks: Patterns in Octavia Butler's Science Fiction." *Black American Literature Forum* (1984): 82–87.
Gregg, Sandra. "Writing out of the Box." *Black Issues Book Review* (September, 2000).
Harrison, Rosalie G. "Sci Fi Visions: An Interview with Octavia Butler." *Equal Opportunity Forum Magazine* (1980): 30–34.
Jones, Gerald. "Science Fiction." *New York Times Book Review* (January 3, 1999).
Melzer, Patricia. "'All That You Touch You Change': Utopian Desire and the Concept of Change in Octavia Butler's *Parable of the Sower* and *Parable of the Talents*." *FEMSPEC* (2002).
Mixon, Veronica. "Futurist Woman: Octavia Butler." *Essence* (April 1979): 12–15.
Raffel, Burton. "Genre to the Rear, Race and Gender to the Fore: The Novels of Octavia E. Butler." *Literary Review* (April 1, 1995).
Salvaggio, Ruth. "Octavia Butler and the Black Science-Fiction Heroine." *Black American Literature Forum* (1984): 78–81.
Sturgis, Susanna. "Octavia E. Butler: June 22, 1947–February 24, 2006." *The Women's Review of Books* (May–June 2006): 19.

## Robert Olen Butler

BORN: *1945, Granite City, Illinois*

NATIONALITY: *American*

GENRE: *Fiction*

MAJOR WORKS:
*The Alleys of Eden* (1981)
*Sun Dogs* (1982)
*On Distant Ground* (1985)
*A Good Scent from a Strange Mountain* (1992)

Robert Olen Butler   *Ulf Andersen / Getty Images*

## Overview

Butler is a novelist for whom the Vietnam War was a defining experience, though unlike most Vietnam-oriented authors, he often tells his stories from a Vietnamese point-of-view. Butler's works thus offer Americans a valuable means of understanding the Vietnamese perspective on American involvement in their country.

## Works in Biographical and Historical Context

***Early Theater Training***   Butler was born January 20, 1945, in Granite City, Illinois, a small steel-mill town. An only child, he grew up, as did his parents, in Granite City, in the river bottoms across the Mississippi from Saint Louis and a few miles northwest of Cahokia State Park. His father, Robert Olen Sr., was a retired actor and once served as the chairman of the theater department at Saint Louis University. Speaking of their relationship, Butler said in a 1993 interview: "It was second nature for us to talk late into the night about books, movies, and theater."

Butler was the president of the study body at Granite City High School, and he graduated as class co-valedictorian in 1963. In the 1950s and 1960s, the local steel mills attracted economic exiles from depressed areas of the Midwest and the South, and this led to a collision of cultures that Butler said shaped his personality. During high school and into college, he worked summers at Granite City Steel. He learned to talk Saint Louis Cardinals baseball with coworkers at the blast furnace operation and to discuss aesthetic theory with his father's colleagues.

He attended Northwestern University as a theater major, but shortly before graduating he decided he would "rather write the words than mouth them." Thus, after graduating summa cum laude from Northwestern with a bachelor of science degree in oral interpretation, Butler obtained his M.F.A. in playwriting from the University of Iowa in 1969. Butler married for the first of four times in 1968.

***The Vietnam War***   In the years following World War II, the country of Vietnam, which had for a time been ruled as a colony of France, became an independent nation partitioned into a region under Communist rule (North Vietnam) and a republic (South Vietnam). The two sides were to be united by free election but instead they began battling in a civil war to determine the political and ideological fate of the country. The United States supported the government of South Vietnam and sent nearly three million Americans to the region over the course of the war. During Butler's college and graduate-school years, the Vietnam War was being expanded, and the Army was drafting eligible young men to fight. Butler suspected that after graduate school he would be drafted for military duty in Vietnam, so instead he visited the army recruiter in Granite City and enlisted. He committed to a three-year enlistment to be guaranteed a position in counterintelligence, thinking he would be placed in an American field office doing background checks on U.S. Army personnel applying for security clearances. Instead, he was shipped off to Vietnam after receiving language training.

He was first assigned to a counterintelligence unit. Within six months, he was chosen to be the administrative assistant and interpreter for the American Foreign Service officer advising the mayor of Saigon. In Vietnam, Butler was struck by the starkly different culture, language, and people, and this had a lasting effect upon him. Fluent in Vietnamese, Butler noted the nuances of Vietnamese language and later recreated these subtleties in his writing, making his characters real and multi-dimensional. Butler left Vietnam in December 1971 and the Army one month later.

***Struggling After Vietnam***   Shortly after returning home, Butler divorced his first wife and moved to New York City to became a reporter for *Electronic News*. Shortly thereafter, he married for a second time. Although

## LITERARY AND HISTORICAL CONTEMPORARIES

Butler's famous contemporaries include:

**Oliver Stone** (1946–): Stone is an American film director and screenwriter who came to prominence for his Vietnam film *Platoon* (1986); he has won several Academy Awards for his writing and directing.

**Ron Kovic** (1946–): Kovic is an American anti-war activist, Vietnam veteran, and writer who is best known for his memoir, *Born on the Fourth of July* (1975), which was also made into a popular and award-winning feature-length film in 1989.

**Tom Clancy** (1947–): Clancy is an American novelist who writes best-selling spy and military novels. His work has been used as the basis for several films and video game franchises.

**Al Gore** (1948–): Gore is the former vice president of the United States who is also widely known for his environmental activism and warnings about climate change; he was a recipient of the Nobel Peace Prize in 2007 as well as an Academy Award winner in the same year for his work on the documentary *An Inconvenient Truth* (2006).

**Ian McEwan** (1948–): McEwan is a British novelist and screenplay writer who is widely recognized for the daring originality of his fiction, including the novels *Amsterdam* (1998) and *Atonement* (2001).

**Jim Carroll** (1950–): Carroll is an American writer and musician best known for his autobiographical work *The Basketball Diaries* (1978), which was made into a film in 1995.

he advanced to editor of the journal, he and his second wife decided in mid-1973 to move to Granite City, where he worked as a high-school substitute teacher and freelance writer for a year. Following the birth of a son, Joshua, he rejoined *Electronic News* in Chicago, and after eighteen months, the owner of the paper asked him to return to New York to start a newspaper of his own creating. From 1975 until 1985 he was editor in chief of *Energy User News*, a weekly investigative business newspaper targeted for industrial and commercial consumers and managers of energy.

Butler struggled in the 1970s to think of himself as a writer. He explained to Peter Applebome of *The New York Times* that his early novels were completed "in longhand on legal pads supported by a Masonite lapboard as he commuted on the Long Island Rail Road from his home in Sea Cliff, L.I., to his job in Manhattan." Beginning in 1979 he attended four consecutive semesters of advanced creative-writing courses at the New School for Social Research, and he began working on his first novel, *The Alleys of Eden*.

Vietnam was not a popular subject when Butler started shopping around the manuscript for *The Alleys of Eden*. The book was turned away by a dozen publishers who "admitted every virtue in the book except its marketability," he said. London-based publisher Methuen finally selected the novel for the company's American trade list; however, two months before the novel was published, Methuen notified Butler that it was forgoing the trade-book business. Butler forwarded the manuscript to nine additional publishers before Ben Raeburn, editor of Horizon Press, accepted it in 1980. During the next five years, he wrote three more novels, two of which formed a loose Vietnam trilogy with *The Alleys of Eden*.

*A Successful Writer and Teacher* With the success of his fourth novel, *On Distant Ground* (1985), the third installment of Butler's Vietnam trilogy, his publishing credentials allowed him to change careers. In the summer of 1985, he left *Energy User News* and accepted a position teaching creative writing at McNeese State University in Lake Charles, Louisiana. He has since published six more novels and four collections of short stories, including *A Good Scent from a Strange Mountain* (1992), the collection that earned him the Pulitzer Prize for Fiction in 1993. He has also taught creative writing at several universities around the United States, and he is the judge of an annual short-fiction award, the Robert Olen Butler Prize.

## Works in Literary Context

Butler is a thematically diverse writer, though two of his defining themes are the suffering that results from thwarted desire and the intimacy that characterizes fundamental human relationships. Although most of his novels and many of his stories are somehow related to the Vietnam War or Vietnamese immigrants in the United States, he does not confine his settings or themes exclusively to Vietnam. Butler's short-story collections share few common characteristics: their themes are completely different in each volume; their characters rarely remind the reader of ones in his other collections; their literary techniques are peculiar to each volume; and their tonal range runs the gamut from existential dread to hilarious—even irreverent—parody. To state precisely what Butler's recurring subject matter and themes are is difficult; defining Butlerian "character types" is even more difficult.

*A Unique Perspective on Vietnam* Although one of many Vietnam War authors, Butler is the only major American author who writes about the effects of the war on the Vietnamese people rather than about the American soldier's wartime experience in Vietnam. Many of his protagonists are Vietnamese, and Butler is able to reproduce their intonations and thought patterns with great accuracy. Butler, therefore, presents Americans with a valuable means of understanding the Vietnamese perspective on the presence of the American military force in

Vietnam and the challenge of resettlement to the United States.

*Compelling Voices*  What characterizes Butler's stories most consistently is his ability to tailor his stylistic procedures to the subject matter, but what distinguishes Butler's fiction is his ability to employ a seemingly endless variety of voices. As Richard Eder put it in the *Los Angeles Times Book Review*, one of Butler's "main strengths, is his ability to speak in his characters' voices—an almost perfect English but with odd strains and inflections."

Butler invents his characters by giving them unusual voices rather than through the use of physical description or habitual actions. One of the things that makes Butler an acute listener and observer is his deep knowledge of the Vietnamese language; to be understood properly, the Vietnamese language depends to a great extent on subtle tonal modulations. Butler makes use of this subtlety to produce highly realistic and compelling voices for his varied characters.

## Works in Critical Context

Critical reaction to Butler's works has been generally positive. Besides earning praise for his portrayals of foreign peoples, Butler has been noted for his sensual settings, realistic action, and superb command of characters' voices.

*The Vietnam Trilogy*  Butler has been tagged a Vietnam novelist even though he finds the label disparaging. He told Jon Anderson of the *Chicago Tribune*: "It's like saying Monet was a lily-pad painter; artists get at deeper truths." However, three of his first four books loosely form a Vietnam trilogy, and critics have treated them as such.

Butler's Vietnam novels were critically acclaimed from the outset because, for the first time, the Vietnamese were portrayed with complexity. Many reviewers were as impressed with Butler's style as with his perspective. "It is incredibly exciting to read Butler," stated a *Fort Worth Star-Telegram* review, for Butler shows himself "to be a master stylist. He moves from the most feverish of prose to a flatness and sparseness that is reminiscent of the best of Chandler and Hammett." Tom Clark wrote in the *Los Angeles Times*, "Butler has an ability to catch tiny shifts of feeling, momentary estrangements, sudden dislocations of mood—a tool as valuable to the novelist as a scalpel to the surgeon."

*A Good Scent from a Strange Mountain*  In his Pulitzer Prize-winning collection, *A Good Scent from a Strange Mountain* (1992), Butler continued to narrate from the Vietnamese perspective, concentrating in this collection of fifteen stories on those who had resettled in America. Madison Smartt Bell of the *Chicago Tribune* regards the collection as a "novelistic unit" that maps "a Vietnamese legend onto an American situation," and he believes that "any reader of this book will feel a strange

---

## COMMON HUMAN EXPERIENCE

Butler's Vietnam novels present a rare non-American perspective on the Vietnam War experience. Here are some other works that present a Vietnamese perspective:

*Buffalo Afternoon* (1990), a novel by Susan Fromberg Shaeffer. This novel conveys the emotions and actions of both men in battle and the regular Vietnamese people caught up in the war.

*Paradise of the Blind* (1993), a novel by Duong Thu Huong. This novel depicts daily life in Vietnam during the end of the Vietnam War and during Communist rule in the 1970s.

*The Other Side of Heaven* (1995), edited by Wayne Karlin, Le Minh Khue, and Truong Vu. This collection of stories by Vietnamese and American writers provides various perspectives on the war in Vietnam.

---

and perhaps salutary sense of exposure and be made to wonder just who are the real Americans." Richard Eber says about Butler's subject matter and style that he "writes essentially, and in a bewitching translation of voice and sympathy, about what it means to lose a country, to remember it, and to have the memory begin to grow old. He writes as if it were his loss, too."

Although some critics thought *A Good Scent from a Strange Mountain* to be too melodramatic, they have widely praised the accuracy with which Butler portrayed Vietnamese Americans. Prior to Butler, many Americans viewed the Vietnamese as either sinister or inscrutable or both, but, as George Packer noted in his *New York Times Book Review* article, "*A Good Scent From a Strange Mountain* goes a long way toward making the Vietnamese real." Critics were also impressed with the universal themes that emerged from these stories. As Pat C. Hoy wrote,

> Inside the stories, inside the lives Butler creates, we experience loss and need. We learn about the suffering that comes from desire, and just for an instant we look into things so deep we can't deny them.

## Responses to Literature

1. Butler is often considered a Vietnam writer, but many of his short stories do not concern Vietnam. In what ways are his non-Vietnam stories similar to his tales of Vietnam? In your opinion, are both types of stories equally powerful and compelling? Why or why not?

2. Butler was educated as an actor and a playwright, yet he writes novels and short stories instead of plays.

What is it about his subject matter and dominant themes that makes his writing better suited to prose than to drama? In what ways would his stories be diminished by placing them on a stage? Would they be enhanced in any way if presented to a live audience?

3.  One reviewer noted that although Butler does a very good job presenting the Vietnamese perspective, he is still an outsider and therefore incapable of presenting a truly accurate or authentic perspective. Write an essay that explores the following questions: What would a Vietnamese or Vietnamese-American writer bring to a story that Butler is incapable of presenting? Does Butler's inescapable outsider status make all of his characterizations of the Vietnamese, however accurate seeming to an American audience, suspect? Why or why not?

4.  One of Butler's greatest strengths is his ability to create realistic dialogue that presents a unique and authentic voice for his characters. Write a story that is driven mostly by dialogue in which you attempt to create a unique and authentic voice for each character. Try to use unique speech patterns and word choices as a way of distinguishing between different characters.

BIBLIOGRAPHY

**Books**

Beidler, Philip D. *Re-Writing America: Vietnam Authors in Their Generation.* Athens, Ga.: University of Georgia Press, 1991.

Bonnetti, Kay, ed. "Robert Olen Butler." In *Conversations with American Novelists.* Columbia, Mo.: University of Missouri Press, 1997).

Cash, Erin E. Campbell. "Locating Community in Contemporary Southern Fiction: A Cultural Analysis of Robert Olen Butler's 'A Good Scent from a Strange Mountain.'" In Disheroon, Suzanne, ed. *Songs of the New South: Writing Contemporary Louisiana.* Westport, Conn.: Greenwood Press, 2001.

Nagel, James. "Vietnam Redux: Robert Olen Butler's *A Good Scent from a Strange Mountain.*" In *The Contemporary American Short-Story Cycle.* Baton Rouge, La.: Louisiana State University Press, 2001.

Orlofsky, Michael. "Historiografiction: The Fictionalization of History in the Short Story." In Iftekharrudin, Farhat, ed. *The Postmodern Short Story: Forms and Issues.* Westport, Conn.: Praeger, 2003.

Sartisky, Michael "Robert Olen Butler: A Pulitzer Profile." In Humphries, Jefferson, ed. *The Future of Southern Letters.* New York: Oxford University Press, 1996.

**Periodicals**

Bonetti, Kay. "An Interview with Robert Olen Butler." *Missouri Review* (1994): 85–106.

Eder, Richard. "Seeing the Vietnamese." *Los Angeles Times Book Review* (March 29, 1992): 3, 7.

Hoy, Pat C. "Suffering and Desire." *The Sewanee Review* (Fall 1992): 116–18.

Packer, George. "A Review of *A Good Scent from a Strange Mountain.*" *The New York Times Book Review* (June 7, 1992): 24.

# ❁ William Byrd II

BORN: *1674, Charles City County, Virginia*

DIED: *1744, Charles City County, Virginia*

NATIONALITY: *American*

GENRE: *Nonfiction*

MAJOR WORKS:

*The History of the Dividing Line Betwixt Virginia and North Carolina* (1841)

*The Secret Diaries of William Byrd of Westover* (1941)

William Byrd   *Byrd, William, photograph. The Library of Congress.*

## Overview

William Byrd II was the proprietor of Westover plantation in colonial Virginia during the late seventeenth and early eighteenth centuries. In addition, he left an entertaining and varied body of factual reportage about colonial America. Byrd's diaries, letters, travel narratives, and miscellaneous writings give a revealing picture of the Virginia planter's world.

## Works in Biographical and Historical Context

*Colonial Birth and English Education*  Byrd was born in Virginia on March 28, 1674. His father, William Byrd I, was a London goldsmith who immigrated to Virginia at age eighteen and inherited an estate there from an uncle. He became a wealthy planter and trader with the Indians. When his son reached age seven, he sent him to England under the care of relatives to be given a gentleman's education. Byrd learned Greek and Latin at Felsted Grammar School in Essex. During his stay at Felsted, he witnessed the Glorious Revolution of 1688, a bloodless revolution in England that replaced an absolute monarch with a king supported by parliament.

In 1692, he entered the Middle Temple in London to study law. The Middle Temple, which formed one of the Inns of Court, was a haven for wits and writers during the seventeenth century. It was here that Byrd cultivated lifelong friendships with Sir Robert Southwell, president of the Royal Society, and with Charles Boyle (later the Earl of Orrery). Byrd also formed acquaintances with the dramatists William Congreve, William Wycherley, and Nicholas Rowe. Through the influence of Southwell, Byrd was elected to the Royal Society and kept up an interest in natural science all his life.

*A Political and Aristocratic Career*  In 1696 his father asked him to return to Virginia. Once back in Virginia, Byrd immediately entered the House of Burgesses, Virginia's legislature and the first popularly elected body in the English colonies. Thus began his lifetime of political activity. As a member of the ruling class of planters, Byrd served in a number of high offices and frequently opposed the interests of the English crown in favor of Virginia.

Virginia was a provincial culture of tobacco plantations forming green rectangles along river estuaries. The nearest market town was London, a two months' sail away. Byrd soon found a need to return to England, but he was back in Virginia again in 1705, to take over his inheritance at the death of his father. A year after his father's death he married Lucy Parke, daughter of Daniel Parke, governor of the Leeward Islands. When Daniel Parke died in 1710, Byrd voluntarily assumed some of the Parke family debts in order to acquire a huge Parke landholding in Virginia. The Parke debts turned out to be

more than Byrd expected and for the rest of his life he was often plagued by the need for money.

His wife had died of smallpox in 1716, and Byrd, now in his early forties, wooed in succession three heiresses, failing with each of them. Meanwhile, he conducted business for the colony of Virginia and spent much time gossiping and making contacts at the Virginia Coffeehouse, where the colony's gentry gathered. Finally, in 1724, he married Maria Taylor, who, respectable but without money, ultimately gave him an heir named William. After one last trip to England, Byrd returned to Virginia in 1726 to stay.

*A Diarist of Colonial Life*  During the early years of his first marriage, Byrd settled into the daily routine of an ambitious planter. He kept a diary in cryptic shorthand detailing his daily life. During the last two decades of his life, he wrote the works for which he is best known, four factual narratives of travel through the backcountry. Byrd took up the pen to fill the intellectual vacancies in the routine of a planter's life, a life—busy as it was with overseers, slaves, politics, tobacco, ship movements, and visitors—that could be tedious. The practice of letters was for Byrd an amusement and a refuge. He read and wrote in his library, which at his death contained some 3,600 volumes, making it one of the largest in the Colonies.

When Byrd died in 1744 at seventy years of age, he left an estate of 179,440 acres, complete with an imposing brick house that still stands today, not far from Colonial Williamsburg. He also left an assortment of manuscripts that would be discovered and published centuries after his death.

## COMMON HUMAN EXPERIENCE

Byrd is best known for producing diaries that provide keen insight into life in colonial America. Here are some other diaries that provide similar insights into life in a particular historical period:

*History of Plymouth Plantation* (1856), a diary by William Bradford. This diary, kept by the long-time governor of the Plymouth Colony, chronicled the history of the first thirty years of the Plymouth colony.

*The Diary of Henry Machyn—Citizen and Merchant-Taylor of London (1550–1563)* (1848). This book chronicles a period of rapid political and religious change in England as witnessed and recorded by a citizen of London.

*Reversing the Gaze: Amar Singh's Diary, A Colonial Subject's Narrative of Imperial India* (2002), excerpts from a diary edited by Susanne Hoeber Rudolph, Lloyd I. Rudolph, and Mohan Singh Kanota. These diaries track seven years in the life of an Indian nobleman during the period of British rule.

## Works in Literary Context

Byrd was an urbane, inquisitive, eccentric man who, with sly humor, surveyed life from the heights of colonial aristrocracy. Byrd's eye moved over flora and fauna, landscapes and people. He wrote about American Indians, gentry, women, slaves, medicine, natural history, folklore, diet, religion, and sex. True to the aristocratic tradition, he wrote mainly to amuse his friends in England and America. Although Byrd's major works circulated in manuscript form for many years, none of them was published during his lifetime.

***Observant Travel Writer*** Byrd's first published work and still his best known work, *The History of the Dividing Line Betwixt Virginia and North Carolina* (1841), is an account of his leadership of a Virginia commission charged with settling a boundary dispute between Virginia and North Carolina. His party of surveyors and workmen met up with a similar commission from North Carolina, and they pushed the dividing line between the two states westward from the Atlantic shore. Although the narrative was not published until nearly a century after his death, it has since become known as a classic portrait of backwoods life in the mid-eighteenth century. Byrd had a reporter's eye and a magisterial sense of ridicule, particularly when it came to the North Carolinians.

In 1851 a manuscript by Byrd, titled *The Secret History of the Line* (1929), turned up in Philadelphia. A shorter, alternative version of the *History of the Dividing Line*, *The Secret History of the Line* was probably written first, for a small circle of Virginia friends. In *The Secret History of the Line*, Byrd disguised the names of the party, and for his private audience, Byrd included sexual escapades, including six occasions when members of the Virginia party (but not Byrd himself) assaulted women. Byrd also made no attempt to disguise the personal hatreds that had existed between various members of the group.

***Aristocratic Diarist*** Byrd also chronicled his daily life in a series of diaries, which were also not published until well after his death. *The Secret Diary of William Byrd of Westover, 1709–1712* (1941) contains an amazingly detailed record of the minutiae of life as a Virginia planter. Two other diaries have also been discovered, one covering a period of Byrd's life in London, and the third his later life in Virginia. Byrd's diaries are the fullest set of diaries from the Southern colonies during that period.

## Works in Critical Context

Although Byrd published very little during his own lifetime, the discovery and publication of several of his manuscripts has won him regard as one of the most important American colonial writers. During his lifetime, Byrd was known in London and Virginia for his interest in literature and books, but he was not considered a literary personage himself.

Since the discovery of Byrd's works, critics have focused on two essential elements of Byrd's writing: what they show about life in colonial America and what they reveal about the author himself. His travel narratives and diaries are seen by scholars as important historical records as well as prime examples of the period's best writing. While critics admire Byrd's style, particularly his satirical wit, they also note that his writings reveal a misogynistic and decadent character.

***Byrd's Private History*** Byrd's works were largely circulated among his friends in manuscript form, though he also attempted to prepare some of his works for publication. The various manuscripts that have been found reveal very different public and private personae for Byrd. The private manuscripts were much more revealing and, to modern scholars, valuable for their insight. Pierre Marambaud notes the frequent comparisons between Byrd and a similar English diarist, Samuel Pepys: "Like his famous English counterpart, he had written a day-by-day account of his life that he had really intended to keep secret." Marambaud notes the freedom this gave to Byrd to honestly document his world:

The conviction that his diary would always remain secret led him to record with uninhibited sincerity all sorts of particulars about his daily routine and his main preoccupations; his food and work, his illnesses and remedies, the books he read and the people he met, the pleasures and sorrows he experienced, a complete catalog of his sexual life, and of prayers said or forgotten.

## Responses to Literature

1. During his lifetime, Byrd's writings were mostly read only by his friends. In what ways did this small circle of readers impact the way he constructed his descriptions? What differences can be noted in the works that he intended for a wider audience?

2. Byrd's diaries chronicled life on a colonial plantation, but only from the perspective of the privileged head of that plantation. What kinds of things were left out of Byrd's accounts because of his position? In what ways does the incompleteness of his perspective undermine the use of his diaries as a historical record, and in what ways does this perspective make them uniquely useful?

3. Byrd was noted for the engaging nature of his travel narratives. Choose a more modern travel narrative, such as Jack Kerouac's *On the Road* or Paul Theroux's *Dark Star Safari*, and write an essay that compares the style of writing as well as the nature of the journey in each case.

4. Byrd's personal diaries were written in a code that makes it clear that it was not intended for a wide audience, if for any audience at all. Today, many people keep online diaries in the form of personal blogs. Write an essay comparing the way that Byrd wrote about his life in his private, encoded diary with the way that present-day bloggers write about their lives. Be sure to discuss the style of writing as well as the kinds of observations and ideas contained in these two types of diary.

BIBLIOGRAPHY

**Books**

Adams, Percy G., ed. *William Byrd's Histories of the Dividing Line Betwixt Virginia and North Carolina.* New York: Dover, 1967.

Beatty, Richmond Croom. *William Byrd of Westover.* Boston: Houghton Mifflin, 1932.

Blanton, Wyndham B. *Medicine in Virginia in the Eighteenth Century.* Richmond, Va.: Garret & Massie, 1931.

Bryson, William Hamilton. *Census of Law Books in Colonial Virginia.* Charlottesville, Va.: University Press of Virginia, 1978.

Hatch, Alden. *The Byrds of Virginia.* New York: Holt, Rinehart & Winston, 1969.

Johnson, Herbert A. *Imported Eighteenth-Century Law Treatises on American Libraries, 1700–1799.* Knoxville, Tenn.: University of Tennessee Press, 1978.

Lockridge, Kenneth. *The Diary, and Life, of William Byrd II of Virginia, 1674–1744.* New York: Norton, 1987.

Marambaud, Pierre. *William Byrd of Westover 1674–1744.* Charlottesville, Va.: University Press of Virginia, 1971, pp. 106–116.

Wenger, Mark R. *The English Travels of Sir John Percival and William Byrd II: The Percival Diary of 1701.* Columbia, Mo.: University of Missouri Press, 1989.

Wright, Louis B. *The First Gentlemen of Virginia.* San Marino, Calif.: The Huntington Library, 1940.

**Periodicals**

Wolf, Edwin, II. "Great American Book Collectors to 1800." *Gazette of the Grolier Club* (June 1971): 1–70.

# C

# James Branch Cabell

BORN: *1879, Richmond, Virginia*

DIED: *1958, Richmond, Virginia*

NATIONALITY: *American*

GENRE: *Fiction*

MAJOR WORKS:

*The Biography of the Life of Manuel,* eighteen
volumes (1927–1930)

## Overview

Virginia-born James Branch Cabell was one of the first
voices of a rising chorus of modern southern writers. He
is recognized today as a pioneering novelist and short-story
writer of the southern literary renaissance, and is also
considered an influential early master of the fantasy genre.

## Works in Biographical and Historical Context

*A Venerable Southern Family* James Branch Cabell
was born and raised in Richmond, Virginia, where he lived
out most of his life in a manner typical of a Southern
gentleman of modest means and impeccable pedigree.
Cabell was descended from a venerable Virginia family.
His father, Robert Gamble Cabell II, was the scion of
a long-established Old Dominion family that had produced one governor, Cabell's great-grandfather. Cabell's
mother, Anne Branch Cabell, belonged to a solidly bourgeois family with comfortable fortunes resting on mercantile and banking interests.

In keeping with his family status, Cabell attended
William and Mary College, where his precocious brilliance
was quickly recognized. Because of this, he taught courses
in French and Greek while an undergraduate, and he graduated with high honors.

*Settling Into Domesticity* Following a brief period
of newspaper work in New York City from 1899 to 1901,
Cabell returned to Richmond to pursue his twin interests

of creative writing and genealogy. Between 1901 and
1911 his genealogical researches led to extensive travel
in England and Europe. He wrote steadily, and although
he published several novels and short-story collections
during the first ten years of the 1900s, he remained all
but unnoticed as a writer. In 1911 he decided to try his
hand as a coal-mine operator in the mountains of West
Virginia. He persisted in this experiment until 1913,
when he once again returned to Richmond, where he
was to spend the rest of his life, except for occasional
holidays in the Virginia mountains and in Florida.

In 1913, at age thirty-four, Cabell married a widow
with five children by her previous marriage. This woman,
Rebecca Priscilla Bradley Shepherd, as Cabell called her,
proved an ideal wife for the writer, carefully guarding his
privacy, adroitly managing the practical affairs of the
household, and performing with equal skill the parts of
literary hostess and press agent. Cabell settled into thirty-
five years of contented domesticity.

*Achieving Public Recognition* By 1919, Cabell's
talent was fully mature, and he had published several
more novels and collections. However, his recognition
by the reading public had grown very slowly. The turning
point came in 1919 as a result of his novel *Jurgen: A
Comedy of Justice.* The New York Society for the Preven-
tion of Vice seized the plates and all the copies of *Jurgen*
and charged Guy Holt, Cabell's editor, with violation of
the anti-obscenity provisions of the New York State Penal
Code. In the book, a middle-aged man is given the
chance to be young again, and begins an adventurous
journey across fantastical lands in search of romance.
Along the way, Cabell satirizes many aspects of modern
life, including organized religion, and also offers up passages some readers considered racy. The obscenity trial,
which resulted in a verdict of acquittal, made Cabell a
national celebrity and something of a literary cult figure,
championed by such notables as Burton Rascoe and
H. L. Mencken. He was subsequently surrounded by
admiring fellow writers.

James Branch Cabell   *Cabell, James Branch, photograph. The Library of Congress.*

Yet—except for having to make room for visiting literati and for a growing list of literary intimates, including Sinclair Lewis, Emily Clark, Carl Van Vechten, Hugh Walpole, and his lifelong Richmond friend, Ellen Glasgow—Cabell's life changed surprisingly little in its basic economy and rhythm. He remained in Richmond; the literary world came to him, and Richmond became a literary center during the 1920s, for many embodying the spirit of the Roaring Twenties. There were, to be sure, increased social obligations and a much more extensive correspondence to attend to, but for the most part he continued to divide his time among his writing, his family, and his work as professional genealogist with the Virginia chapter of the Sons of the Revolution and with other historical societies in the state.

Throughout the 1920s, as American prosperity continued to grow and many figured it would last forever, Cabell wrote prodigiously and enjoyed the attention due a major literary figure. Then, with the beginning of the Great Depression, his literary fame was eclipsed almost as suddenly as it bloomed. By 1929, he had completed his monumental, multi-volume work, *The Biography of the Life of Manuel*. The work, influenced largely by his interest in family history and genealogy, depicts several generations of the family of a count from a fictional region in France. Although twenty-five more years of creative work lay ahead

of him, Cabell spent those years unable to escape from the shadow of his own literary monument. From 1932–1935 he joined George Jean Nathan, Theodore Dreiser, Eugene O'Neill, and Sherwood Anderson in editing the *American Spectator* in what turned out to be a futile attempt to carry the spirit of the 1920s into the 1930s.

***Late Life Alienation and Productivity***   After 1935, Cabell suffered repeated attacks of pneumonia, and Priscilla Bradley developed a crippling form of arthritis. These infirmities led to their wintering in the milder climate of Saint Augustine, Florida, and it was there, in 1949, that Priscilla Bradley died of heart failure. Deeply shaken and embittered by the death of his wife, and increasingly alienated from the America of the New Deal, World War II, the atomic age, and the Cold War, Cabell nonetheless continued to write steadily throughout the 1940s and 1950s. In fact, he produced twelve new books, including two memoirs. He died in Richmond, Virginia, in 1958 at the age of seventy-nine.

## Works in Literary Context

Much praised during the height of his career, Cabell is no longer considered one of the major writers of the twentieth century—and indeed he has not been considered such since the end of the 1920s. However, he is viewed as one of the outstanding oddities in American fiction, combining extremes of lavish romance and degraded reality, idealistic fantasy and jaded disillusionment.

***Romantic Vision***   Cabell adhered to a special definition of romance, one that allowed him to portray glorified adventures beyond mundane reality without falsifying what he saw as the harsh truths of existence: the suffering of life, the emptiness of death, and a permanent alienation at the core of even the most intimate human relations. For Cabell the romantic view of life meant following a system of "dynamic illusions," the codes of self-deception—such as reason, religion, or love—by which individuals and societies are sustained.

Cabell's romantic vision is a union of three basic attitudes toward life—the chivalric, the gallant, and the poetic, all of which are attempts to impose arbitrary values on an indifferent universe. This vision is particularly present in *The Biography of the Life of Manuel*. Each work in the *Biography* is designed to dramatize one of these attitudes. The chivalric attitude considers life a trial of the individual: a contest in which certain ideals, including personal honor and public glory, must be valiantly won. The gallant attitude approaches life as a series of pleasures and excitements. More cynical than their chivalric predecessors, the heroes of the gallant novels search for fulfillment of their most extreme desires but end with a disillusioning confrontation with reality. Finally, the poetic attitude perceives life as material for artistic creation. This approach represents yet another scheme for introducing order and perfection into a chaotic world, seeking to harmonize it with human imagination.

*Picaresque Narratives* Many of Cabell's novels can be seen as picaresque tales, a collection of related adventures centered around a main character that are strung together to form a longer story. Cabell had, in fact, begun his career as a short-story writer, and when he turned to novel writing, he did not really abandon the short fiction form. As one commentator noted about many of Cabell's novels, "Upon closer examination they present themselves as loosely constructed romances, highly picaresque in form." A good example of Cabell's use of the picaresque form is *Jurgen*, in which the title character journeys through all of the dream kingdoms on this side and the other side of death in search of justice. Such a narrative framework, which integrated various stories with a common hero, allowed Cabell to continue writing the kind of tales he had begun working on early in his career.

*Archaic Style* Cabell's style is often mannered and, to present-day sensibilities, somewhat labored. Cabell's stylistic aims are exactly opposite Hemingway's. Hemingway strives for the illusion that his prose is a completely transparent medium through which we perceive an immediately present reality. Cabell's prose, by continually calling attention to itself, keeps the reader mindful that all he is witnessing is in fact the creation of a storyteller. Cabell's archaic style was also helpful in circumventing certain taboos of the time period in which he wrote. By couching his descriptions of things likely to be deemed vulgar in a sly if stilted style, Cabell was able to suggest that which he was not permitted to state outright. However, this style was an insecure base for a lasting reputation, as Cabell himself recorded in *Some of Us: An Essay in Epitaphs* (1930). For once the idols have been smashed and the taboos exorcised, the iconoclasm of a particular time and place becomes pointless and ceases to amuse.

## Works in Critical Contexts

Critical reception of Cabell has been unusually polarized. His works have inspired extremes of derogation and praise. Oscar Cargill has called him "the most tedious person who has achieved high repute as a *literatus* in America," while Vernon L. Parrington has stated that "Mr. Cabell is creating great literature." Cabell's work is said to epitomize the sophisticated cynicism of the 1920s, and his popularity was at its height during that era, declining drastically in the 1930s. When he died in 1958, he had been virtually forgotten by the American critical establishment. Since that time, Cabell's works have generated interest only among a select audience of admirers, as is evidenced in the pages of *Kalki* and *The Cabellian*, journals devoted to him. But Cabell's work is rarely anthologized and almost never given a significant place in serious discussions of twentieth-century literature.

*Jurgen* Although most of Cabell's major works have a place within the larger design of *The Biography of the Life of*

# LITERARY AND HISTORICAL CONTEMPORARIES

James Branch Cabell's famous contemporaries include:

**Theodore Dreiser** (1871–1945): Dreiser was an American author noted for his pioneering works in the naturalist school of writing.

**Rainer Maria Rilke** (1875–1926): An Austrian poet, Rilke is widely considered one of the greatest German-language poets of the twentieth century.

**Jack London** (1876–1916): London, an American writer, was a pioneer in commercial magazine fiction. He is best known for his adventure and wilderness stories, particularly *The Call of the Wild* (1903).

**Sherwood Anderson** (1876–1941): An American short-story writer, Anderson was best known for his influential collection, *Winesburg, Ohio* (1919).

**Hermann Hesse** (1877–1962): Hesse was a German-Swiss writer whose best-known works explore the individual search for spirituality; he was granted the 1946 Nobel Prize in Literature.

**Sinclair Lewis** (1885–1951): Lewis was an American author best known for his realism and his stories that were critical of capitalism and American society; in 1930, he became the first American author to win the Nobel Prize in Literature.

**Eugene O'Neill** (1888–1953): An American playwright who pioneered realism in dramatic theater in works such as *Long Day's Journey Into Night* (1956), O'Neill was awarded the Nobel Prize in Literature in 1936.

*Manuel, Jurgen: A Comedy of Justice* stands out on its own. In addition to bringing Cabell fame because of the high-profile obscenity trial associated with this book, *Jurgen* also features a main character who, as Arvin Wells notes, "transcends the role ostensibly assigned him in *The Biography*." The character of Jurgen, Wells goes on to argue, embodies the point of view from which the entire *Biography* was written. Because of the differences in *Jurgen*, a number of critics appeared baffled by its meaning and attributed its notoriety to the obscenity read into it by some. Paul Elmer More wrote, "I cannot help asking myself whether its wider reputation does not depend chiefly on its elusive and cunningly suggestive lubricity." Arthur Hobson Quinn dismissed the importance of *Jurgen*, writing, "[While] the attempt to suppress *Jurgen* was silly, there is an odor of decay about it which is repulsive to any healthy minded reader." Even H.L. Mencken, one of Cabell's strongest supporters in the obscenity trial, wrote about the book that what gave it its reputation "is not anything that Cabell himself put into it."

## COMMON HUMAN EXPERIENCE

Many of Cabell's works were picaresque tales that strung the loosely-related adventures of a main character into a longer story. Here are some other well-known picaresque works:

*Don Quixote* (1605, 1615), a novel in two volumes by Miguel de Cervantes. This novel, which is considered one of the early models of the picaresque form, follows the adventures of a delusional knight-errant and his sidekick Sancho Panza.

*The Life and Adventures of Nicholas Nickleby* (1838–1839), a novel by Charles Dickens. This novel chronicles the adventures of a young man who is attempting to make his way in a complicated world in order to support his mother and sister.

*The Good Soldier Svejk* (1923), a novel by Jaroslav Hasek. This satirical novel follows the adventures of a hapless Czech soldier during the first year of World War I.

*Eva Luna* (1985), a novel by Isabel Allende. This novel follows the title character through several decades, tracing at the same time the history of a fictional Latin American country.

### Responses to Literature

1. Cabell's literary reputation rests largely on the works that were collected into the eighteen-volume work, *The Biography of the Life of Manuel.* In what ways were the themes that were central to this major work consistent with or divergent from the concerns in Cabell's later writings? Did he seem to abandon the main concerns of the *Biography* or continue to explore these concerns in later works?

2. Cabell's popularity was at its height during the 1920s. In what ways did his writings exemplify the tenor of those times? Would the writings that he produced during that decade have been as popular if written in another time? Why or why not?

3. Cabell first came to broad public attention as a result of the obscenity trial for his novel *Jurgen.* Write a statement that either supports the prosecution's case that this work is obscene or supports the defense's case that the novel is not obscene, providing examples from the work to support your statement.

4. Cabell enjoyed great popularity during the 1920s, but critical attention dropped off after 1930, and has remained low ever since. Choose one of his works from the 1920s and one of his works from a later period, and write a critical essay discussing the ways in which Cabell did and did not deserve to lose his reputation.

BIBLIOGRAPHY

**Books**

Brewer, Frances Joan. *James Branch Cabell: A Bibliography of His Writings, Biography and Criticism.* Charlottesville, Va.: University of Virginia Press, 1957.

Davis, Joe Lee. *James Branch Cabell.* New York: Twayne, 1962.

French, Warren, ed. *The Twenties: Fiction, Poetry, Drama.* Deland, Fla.: Everett/Edwards, 1975.

Godshalk, William L. *In Quest of Cabell: Five Exploratory Essays.* New York: Revisionist Press, 1976.

Inge, Thomas and Edgar E. MacDonald, eds. *James Branch Cabell, Centennial Essays.* Baton Rouge, La.: Louisiana State University Press, 1983.

MacDonald, Edgar E. *James Branch Cabell and Richmond-in-Virginia.* Jackson, Miss.: University Press of Mississippi, 1993.

Rubin, Louis D., ed. *The South: Modern Southern Literature and Its Cultural Setting.* Garden City, N.Y.: Doubleday, 1961.

Tarrant, Desmond. *James Branch Cabell: The Dream and the Reality.* Norman, Okla.: University of Oklahoma Press, 1967.

Wagenknecht, Edward. *Cavalcade of the American Novel.* New York: Holt, 1952.

Wells, Arvin R. *Jesting Moses: A Study in Cabellian Comedy.* Gainesville, Fla.: University of Florida Press, 1962.

# ⊛ Truman Capote

BORN: *1924, New Orleans, Louisiana*

DIED: *1984, Los Angeles, California*

NATIONALITY: *American*

GENRE: *Fiction*

MAJOR WORKS:
*Breakfast at Tiffany's* (1958)
*In Cold Blood* (1966)

## Overview

Truman Capote was one the most famous and controversial figures in contemporary American literature. Often known more for his flamboyant lifestyle than for his writings, he produced some memorable works, including the highly influential true-crime classic, *In Cold Blood* (1966).

## Works in Biographical and Historical Context

*A Troubled Childhood* Truman Capote was born in New Orleans on September 30, 1924. He seldom saw his father, Archulus Persons, and his memories of his mother, Lillie Mae Faulk, mainly involved emotional neglect. When he was four years old, his parents divorced, and

Truman Capote  *Capote, Truman, 1966, photograph. Evening Standard / Hulton Archive / Getty Images.*

his mother left her son with various relatives in the South while she began a new life in New York with her second husband, Cuban businessman Joseph Capote. The young Capote lived with elderly relatives in Monroeville, Alabama, and he later recalled the loneliness and boredom he experienced during this time.

His unhappiness was assuaged somewhat by his friendships with his great aunt Sook Faulk, who appears as Cousin Sook in his novellas *A Christmas Memory* (1966) and *The Thanksgiving Visitor* (1967), and Harper Lee, a childhood friend who served as the model for Idabel Thompkins in *Other Voices, Other Rooms* (1948). Lee, in turn, paid tribute to Capote by depicting him as the character Dill Harris in her novel, *To Kill a Mockingbird* (1960).

When Capote was nine years old, his mother, having failed to conceive a child with her second husband, brought her son to live with them in Manhattan, although she still sent him to the South in the summer. Capote did poorly in school, causing his parents and teachers to suspect that he was of subnormal intelligence; a series of psychological tests, however, proved that he possessed an I.Q. well above the genius level. To combat his loneliness and sense of displacement, he developed a flamboyant personality that played a significant role in establishing his celebrity status as an adult.

***Precocious Writer***  Capote had begun secretly to write at an early age, and rather than attend college after completing high school, he pursued a literary apprenticeship that included various positions at the *New Yorker* and led to important social contacts in New York City. Renowned for his cunning wit and penchant for gossip, Capote later became a popular guest on television talk shows as well as the frequent focus of feature articles. He befriended many members of high society and was as well known for his eccentric, sometimes scandalous behavior as he was for his writings.

Capote's first short stories, published in national magazines when he was seventeen, eventually led to a contract to write his first book, *Other Voices, Other Rooms* (1948). Despite occasional critical complaints that the novel lacks reference to the real world, *Other Voices, Other Rooms* achieved immediate notoriety. This success was partly due to its strange, lyrical evocation of life in a small Southern town as well as to the author's frank treatment of his thirteen-year-old protagonist's awakening homosexuality. The book's dust jacket featured a photograph of Capote, who was then twenty-three, reclining on a couch. Many critics and readers found the picture erotically suggestive and inferred that the novel was autobiographical.

Many of Capote's early stories, written when he was in his teens and early twenties, are collected in *A Tree of Night and Other Stories* (1950). The following year, he published his first full-length novel, *The Grass Harp* (1951). In this work, Capote drew on his childhood to create a lyrical, often humorous story focusing on Collin Fenwick, an eleven-year-old boy who is sent to live in a small Southern town with his father's elderly cousins. This novel, which achieved moderate success, is generally considered to offer a broader, less subjective view of society and the outer world than Capote's earlier fiction, and was adapted as a Broadway drama in 1952.

A light and humorous tone is also evident in such works as the novella *Breakfast at Tiffany's* (1958) and the three other stories published in the same volume, "House of Flowers," "A Diamond Guitar," and *A Christmas Memory*. *Breakfast at Tiffany's* features Capote's most famous character, Holly Golightly, a beautiful, waif-like young woman living on the fringes of New York society. Golightly, like the prostitute heroine in "House of Flowers," is a childlike person who desires love and a permanent home. This sentimental yearning for security is also evident in the nostalgic novella *A Christmas Memory*, which, like the later *The Thanksgiving Visitor*, dramatizes the loving companionship the young Capote found with his great-aunt Sook.

***Productivity and Success Followed by Writer's Block and Declining Reputation***  Capote was very productive throughout the 1950s and early 1960s, writing such well-known works as *Breakfast at Tiffany's* and the influential *In Cold Blood*. In late 1959, Capote came upon the idea for *In Cold Blood* when he ran across an article in the *New York Times* about a brutal murder in

# LITERARY AND HISTORICAL CONTEMPORARIES

Capote's famous contemporaries include:

**J. D. Salinger** (1919–): Salinger is an American novelist and short-story writer best known for his best-selling and widely-read novel, *The Catcher in the Rye* (1951).

**Kingsley Amis** (1922–1995): An English author who produced a large body of work; Amis is the father of another well-known English author, Martin Amis.

**Italo Calvino** (1923–1985): Calvino was an Italian author who was popular in Britain and the United States, and he has become the most-translated Italian author of the twentieth century.

**William Buckley** (1925–2008): An American writer, editor, and television host, Buckley was a leading spokesperson for conservatism in the United States during the second half of the twentieth century.

**Harper Lee** (1926–): Lee is an American author and childhood friend of Capote whose only major work, *To Kill a Mockingbird* (1960), won the Pulitzer Prize.

Kansas. For the next six years, Capote wandered the plains of Kansas as he researched the story of the murder of the Clutter family. He became intensely involved in unraveling the whole story, and with extraordinary stamina and patience, he researched, interviewed, collected, and stored information about the murders, the police investigation, the arrest and charges, and the conviction of the men who perpetrated such a seemingly senseless act. The result was a book that blended journalistic style and fictional technique. Anxious to prove that "journalism is the most underestimated, the least explored of literary mediums," Capote hoped that *In Cold Blood* contained "the credibility of fact, the immediacy of film, the depth and freedom of prose and the precision of poetry." From the outset the book was critically acclaimed and highly successful—it was on *The New York Times* bestseller list for more than a year.

In the late 1960s, Capote began to suffer from writer's block, a frustrating condition that severely curtailed his creative output. Throughout this period he claimed to be working on *Answered Prayers*, a gossip-filled chronicle of the Jet Set that he promised would be his masterpiece. He reported that part of his trouble in completing the project was dissatisfaction with his technique and that he spent most of his time revising or discarding work in progress.

During the mid-1970s he attempted to stimulate his creative energies and to belie critics' accusations that he had lost his talent by publishing several chapters of *Answered Prayers* in the magazine *Esquire*. Most critics found the chapters disappointing. More devastating to Capote, however, were the reactions of his society friends,

most of whom felt betrayed by his revelations of the intimate details of their lives and refused to have any more contact with him.

***Gone But Not Forgotten*** Towards the end of his life, Capote succumbed to alcoholism, drug addiction, and poor health, and when he died on August 25, 1984, a month short of his sixtieth birthday, he had few mourners. In a letter to Helen S. Garson after the 1986 publication of Capote's unfinished novel, *Answered Prayers*, Capote's longtime editor, Joe Fox, stated he was happy not to have to work with Capote anymore. Obituaries described bizarre and unattractive aspects of Capote's personality, and pundits predicted that the public had not only seen but also had heard the last of him. Time has proved them wrong. The writer—described mockingly by Capote's lifetime enemy Gore Vidal in his 1996 memoir *Palimpsest* as someone for whom "an interview is his principal art form"—is gone but not forgotten. Revival of interest in Capote led to production of a popular feature film, *Capote* (2005), which chronicles the period in Capote's life when he was writing *In Cold Blood*.

## Works in Literary Context

Originally considered a Southern Gothic writer, Capote was later noted for the humorous and sentimental tone of his works. As Capote matured, his works became less mannered in style, partly as a result of his experiments in nonfiction writing. In his best-known work, *In Cold Blood: A True Account of a Multiple Murder and Its Consequences* (1966), he became a leading practitioner of "New Journalism," popularizing a genre that he called the nonfiction novel.

***Southern Gothic and Humorous Sentiment*** The ornate style and dark psychological themes of Capote's early fiction led him to be categorized as a Southern Gothic writer. The pieces collected in *A Tree of Night and Other Stories* show the influence of writers such as Edgar Allan Poe, Nathaniel Hawthorne, William Faulkner, and Eudora Welty, all of whom are associated to some degree with a Gothic tradition in American literature. Like these authors, as well as the Southern Gothic writers Carson McCullers and Flannery O'Connor, with whom critics most often compare him, Capote filled his stories with grotesque incidents and characters who suffer from mental and physical abnormalities.

Yet Capote did not always use the South as a setting, and the Gothic elements in some of the tales are offset by Capote's humorous tone in others. Critics often place his fiction into two categories: light and sinister. In the former category are narratives that report the amusing activities of eccentric characters. This tone is present in several stories based on his Southern childhood and in the novella *Breakfast at Tiffany's* (1958). More common among Capote's early fiction, however, are the sinister stories, which are heavily symbolic fables that portray characters in nightmarish situations, threatened by evil forces. Frequently in these tales evil is personified as a sinister man.

In other instances evil appears as a weird personage who represents the darker, hidden side of the protagonist. In later years Capote commented that the Gothic eeriness of these stories reflected the anxiety and feelings of insecurity he experienced as a child.

**Combining Fact and Fiction**   In some of his works of the 1950s, Capote abandoned the lush style of his early writings for a more austere approach, turning his attention away from traditional fiction. *Local Color* (1950) is a collection of pieces recounting his impressions and experiences while in Europe, and *The Muses Are Heard: An Account* (1956) contains essays written while traveling in Russia with a touring company of *Porgy and Bess*. From these projects Capote developed the idea of creating a work that would combine fact and fiction. The result was *In Cold Blood*, which, according to Capote himself, was "a serious new art form: the 'nonfiction novel,' as I thought of it."

In writing *In Cold Blood*, Capote avoided conventional forms of journalism and presented facts with an array of literary devices. He told the story chronologically, reconstructing the story in dramatic scenes, thereby achieving a scenic depiction rather than a historical summary. He recorded dialogue in full rather than in the bits and pieces common to reportage and history-writing. He depicted mannerisms, gestures, styles, and manner of dress to portray characters in rich detail. He employed point of view, which new journalism critic John Hollowell writes "generates sympathy for the killers by narrating their stories from the viewpoints of comforting women close to them." Capote extended these techniques to interior monologue by reporting events as his characters were thinking about them. More than one critic said Capote had written a factual story fictionally, apparently meaning that Capote fictionalized some of the facts of the story. The author adamantly denied this, remaining steadfast in his claim to have created a new writing form, a claim that ruffled feathers in the literary community.

## Works in Critical Context

Critical assessment of Capote's career is highly divided, both in terms of individual works and his overall contribution to literature. In an early review Paul Levine described Capote as a "definitely minor figure in contemporary literature whose reputation has been built less on a facility of style than on an excellent advertising campaign." Ihab Hassan, however, claimed that "whatever the faults of Capote may be, it is certain that his work possesses more range and energy than his detractors allow." Although sometimes faulted for precocious, fanciful plots and for overwriting, Capote is widely praised for his storytelling abilities and the quality of his prose.

**Breakfast at Tiffany's**   One of Capote's most lasting successes came with the publication of the novella *Breakfast at Tiffany's*. Many critics felt that Capote had displayed a level of maturity missing in his earlier fiction, and

---

---

that he had finally created characters who were likable, realistic, and fashioned with a humorous pen. Capote had been criticized in earlier works for prose that at times seemed contrived, but for the most part, *Breakfast at Tiffany's* escaped this criticism and had the critic for the *Times Literary Supplement*, as well as others, placing Capote "among the leading American writers of the day." After publication of *Breakfast at Tiffany's*, Norman Mailer wrote that Capote "is the most perfect writer of my generation. He writes the best sentences word for word, rhythm upon rhythm. I would not have changed two words in *Breakfast at Tiffany's*."

**In Cold Blood**   *In Cold Blood*, Capote's best-known and most influential work, was given some of the most extensive critical interest in publishing history. Although several commentators accused Capote of opportunism and of concealing his inability to produce imaginative fiction by working with ready-made material, most responded with overwhelmingly positive reviews. Rebecca West, writing in *Harper's*, called *In Cold Blood* a "formidable statement about reality" and concluded that it was a "grave and reverend book." In the *New York Review of Books*, F. W. Dupee drew comparisons between *In Cold Blood* and works by Cervantes, Hawthorne, and Henry James. The most extended analysis of *In Cold Blood* and its place in Capote's literary career came in George Garrett's *Hollins Critic* essay "Crime and Punishment in Kansas." The comparison invited by the use of Dostoyevsky's title suggested Garrett's high regard for *In Cold Blood*, which he described as "a frank bid for greatness."

There was, however, some negative response. Writing in *The Spectator*, Tony Tanner credited Capote with creating "a stark image of the deep doubleness in American life," yet concluded that *In Cold Blood* suffered by comparison with other works that took their inspiration from reports of actual crimes but developed into true works of the imagination. Diana Trilling treated *In Cold Blood* even more harshly in her *Partisan Review* essay on it. She found Capote's prose "flaccid, often downright inept" and his narrative "overmanipulated." Further, she contended that the objectivity that Capote retained throughout the book served not to produce truth but to protect Capote from the need to take a stand on the issues his work raised.

## Responses to Literature

1. As a literary figure, Capote was generally better known for his persona, as revealed through his interviews, than for his published writing. What themes emerge from each of these presentations Capote made of himself, and which was more compelling? In what ways do his published writings require an understanding of Capote as revealed through his interviews, and in what ways do they stand on their own?

2. Commentators have noted that Capote had two distinct modes of writing: light and sinister. In which of these modes was he most effective, or was he able to be equally effective in both? What aspects of his humorous writing are the most compelling, and what aspects of his Gothic writing are the most compelling?

3. There is a wide range of critical opinion on Capote, from detractors who assert that he was far overrated to supporters who claim that he was one of the best American writers of the twentieth century. Write an argumentative essay that takes a position on Capote's merit as a writer. Be sure to defend your position with an analysis of several of his works.

4. Capote was well known for *In Cold Blood*, which blended fact and fiction to create a nonfiction novel. Using *In Cold Blood* as a model, choose a news story and write a short story that blends fiction with fact in a manner similar to the way Capote did.

BIBLIOGRAPHY

**Books**

Brinnin, John Malcolm. *Dear Heart, Old Buddy.* New York: Delacorte Press/Seymour Lawrence, 1986.

Brinnin, John Malcolm. *Sextet: T. S. Eliot and Truman Capote and Others.* New York: Delacorte Press/Seymour Lawrence, 1981.

Clarke, Gerald. *Truman Capote: A Biography.* New York: Simon & Schuster, 1988.

Dunphy, Jack. *Dear Genius ... A Memoir of My Life with Truman Capote.* New York: McGraw-Hill, 1987.

Garson, Helen S. *Truman Capote: A Study of the Short Fiction.* New York: Twayne, 1992.

Gray, Richard. *The Literature of Memory: Modern Writers of the American South.* Baltimore: Johns Hopkins University Press, 1977.

Grobel, Lawrence. *Conversations with Capote.* New York: New American Library, 1985.

Inge, M. Thomas, ed. *Truman Capote: Conversations.* Jackson, Miss.: University Press of Mississippi, 1987.

Moates, Marianne M. *Truman Capote's Southern Years: Stories from a Monroeville Cousin.* Tuscaloosa, Ala.: University of Alabama Press, 1996.

Nance, William. *The Worlds of Truman Capote.* New York: Stein & Day, 1970.

Reed, Kenneth T. *Truman Capote.* Boston: Twayne, 1981.

Rudisill, Marie and James C. Simmons. *Truman Capote: The Story of His Bizarre and Exotic Boyhood by an Aunt Who Helped Raise Him.* New York: Morrow, 1983.

Windham, Donald. *Lost Friendships: A Memoir of Truman Capote, Tennessee Williams, and Others.* New York: Morrow, 1987.

# ✵ Orson Scott Card

BORN: *1951, Richland, Washington*

NATIONALITY: *American*

GENRE: *Fiction*

MAJOR WORKS:
*Ender's Game* (1985)
*Speaker for the Dead* (1986)
*Red Prophet* (1988)

## Overview

A prolific writer of science fiction and fantasy, Orson Scott Card has the distinction of being the only author to win two sets of Hugo and Nebula awards for consecutive novels in a series. Card stands out in these genres for the moral and philosophical questions he tackles in his works.

## Works in Biographical and Historical Context

*A Start in Theater* Orson Scott Card was born August 24, 1951, in Richland, Washington, into a devout Mormon family. He is related to Charles Ora Card, a son-in-law of early Mormon leader Brigham Young and the founder of the first Mormon settlement in Canada—Cardston, Alberta.

Before science fiction captured the young Card's interest, the theater drew his attention. At age sixteen he entered the Mormon-founded Brigham Young University to study his craft; just a few years later he was penning plays and seeing them produced. Though his education was delayed for a brief time when he served as a Mormon missionary in Brazil during the early 1970s, he founded a theater company upon his return to Utah. Following his graduation with honors in 1975, he accepted a position as an editor for *Ensign* magazine, the official publication of the Mormon religion, and continued working for the BYU Press, a job he had begun while still a student.

Facing a bleak financial situation, he realized he needed to make a vocational change. With his experience as a dramatist, he already possessed some basic techniques of storytelling; moreover, the idea for the story "Ender's Game" as well as notions for other science fiction works had long been brewing in the back of his mind. "All the time that I was a playwright," he told an interviewer, "these science fictional ideas that never showed up in my plays were dancing around in the back of my mind." The genre, he felt, offered him the most expedient way of getting published, since the field thrives on up-and-coming talent and fresh ideas. He also admitted that he chose science fiction because, as he said himself, "I knew the genre. While it was never even half my reading, I had read enough to be aware of the possibilities within it." Card also noted that science fiction was a field in which "high drama" similar to his previous religious works was permissible.

*Breaking Into Science Fiction*    Hoping to break into science fiction, Card sent one of his first short stories to the editor of the leading science fiction magazine *Analog*. The editor rejected the work, but he liked the way Card wrote, so he urged him to submit something that was more in line with the genre. Card next wrote the short story "Ender's Game," which, upon its publication, earned him the World Science Fiction Convention's John W. Campbell Award for best new writer. Though Card was thrilled with his sudden success, he retained his position as editor at *Ensign* and in 1978 began composing audio plays for Living Scriptures. He also continued honing his writing skills. He received mixed reviews for his early works; while commentators criticized his use of violence and standard science-fiction elements, they praised his literary talents and imagination.

*An Established Reputation*    His literary gifts came to fruition with the 1985 publication of the award-winning novel *Ender's Game*, a full-length version of the short story discussed above. The following year, Card released the sequel, *Speaker for the Dead*. Both novels were well-received by science fiction critics and fans, and Card's reputation and literary career were firmly established. Card continued Ender's story five years later in *Xenocide* (1991), and in the early 1990s, Card published the first novel in his "Homecoming" series, *The Memory of Earth*, a volume, according to one reviewer, that "expertly weaves Biblical imagery, modern science, philosophy, and emotion in a tale of a young man ... growing and maturing." Card also created the successful *Tales of Alvin Maker* fantasy series, beginning with *Seventh Son* (1987),

set in a an alternative version of early America and heavily inspired by Mormon tradition and myth.

Since his success of the mid- and late-1980s, Card has written many books in a variety of genres, often under different pen names. He has won several other important awards in the science fiction and fantasy genres, and he has an avid readership.

## Works in Literary Context

*Exploring Moral and Philosophical Questions*    Card acknowledged that his Mormon beliefs inform all of his works, but his writing is not overtly religious or moralistic. His stories do, however, feature characters, usually young people, who are struggling with moral, political, and philosophical problems. In many of his books, Card focuses on the moral development of his young protagonists, whose abilities to act maturely and decisively while in challenging situations often determine the future of their communities. This kind of concern with moral and philosophical questions is an important theme throughout Card's work. In interviews, Card has stated that he is deeply concerned with his own unresolved moral and philosophical questions as well, and he maintains that science fiction affords him the benefit of exploring these issues against a futuristic and imaginative backdrop.

*The Individual in Society*    Card's writing often explores the role of the individual in society. This is illustrated

# COMMON HUMAN EXPERIENCE

Many of Card's works center around characters struggling with personal questions of a moral and philosophical nature. Here are some other works centered around characters facing similar struggles:

*Hamlet* (1601), a play by William Shakespeare. In this classic tragedy, the title character, a prince of Denmark, struggles with himself over the best way to avenge his murdered father.

*Crime and Punishment* (1866), a novel by Fyodor Dostoyevsky. This novel explores the doubts, anguish, and moral uncertainties of a man who has committed a murder.

*The Last Temptation of Christ* (1951), a novel by Nikos Kazantzakis. This novel explores the psychology of Jesus Christ as he faces human temptations and failings, such as doubt, depression, fear, and lust.

"The Ones Who Walk Away from Omelas," (1974), a short story by Ursula K. Le Guin. In this tale, the utopian society of Omelas pays a price for its perfection: a single child must be imprisoned in darkness and squalor so that others may live prosperously.

*Cloudsplitter* (1998), a novel by Russell Banks. In this historical novel, the narrator, the son of famous abolitionist John Brown, explores the religious beliefs and inner tensions that drove his father to undertake drastic actions for the abolitionist cause.

by the importance of individuals such as Ender Wiggins and Alvin Maker, whose abilities have a direct effect on the greater world. Again, Card's Mormon beliefs inform his writing, though more as a thematic inspiration than as a source of answers. He credits his solid religious background with instilling in him both a strong sense of community and an affinity for storytelling. "I don't want to write about individuals in isolation," he once told interviewers. "What I want to write about is people who are committed members of the community and therefore have a network of relationships that define who they are."

## Works in Critical Context

Since publishing the story that evolved into his award-winning novel *Ender's Game*, Card has remained an important writer in the science fiction and fantasy fields, and he has generally received strong reviews in both the genre press and mainstream newspapers and magazines.

*Ender's Game*   Although some critics found the plot of *Ender's Game* formulaic and of the conventional "superhero saves world" variety, most commended Card for his ability to create a character who generates sympathy

from readers even though he commits almost total genocide. Dan K. Moran wrote in the *West Coast Review of Books* that "Ender Wiggin is a unique creation. Orson Scott Card has created a character who deserves to be remembered with the likes of Huckleberry Finn. *Ender's Game* is *that* good." Gerald Jonas observed in the *New York Times Book Review*, "Card has shaped this unpromising material into an affecting novel full of surprises that seem inevitable once they are explained." Commentators also pointed out that *Ender's Game* rises above standard science fiction fare since it ponders moral questions regarding the manipulation of children as well as the significance of compassion.

*Speaker for the Dead*   With the publication of *Speaker for the Dead*, Card became the first writer to win the genre's top awards, the Nebula and the Hugo, for consecutive novels in a continuing series. *Speaker for the Dead* generally met with an enthusiastic reception; many critics considered the work proof of Card's maturing literary strength and praised the author for crafting compelling characters who face issues of acceptance, guilt, fear, empathy, and redemption. As Michael R. Collings wrote in *Fantasy Review*, "*Speaker* not only completes *Ender's Game* but transcends it. ... Read in conjunction with *Ender's Game*, *Speaker* demonstrates Card's mastery of character, plot, style, theme, and development." In *Science Fiction Review*, editor Richard E. Geis notes that Card "has woven a constantly escalating storyline which deals with religion, alien/human viewpoints and perspectives on instinctual and cultural levels, the fate of three alien species.., and quite possibly the fate of mankind itself." Critics also noted the moral and psychological complexity of Card's work. Michael Collings asserts that the *Ender* novels "succeed equally as straightforward SF adventure and as allegorical, analogical disquisitions on humanity, morality, salvation, and redemption."

## Responses to Literature

1. Card has been noted for writing works that explore moral and philosophical questions without being overly moralistic. What are the main moral messages that emerge from Card's works? In what ways are they obviously informed by Mormon belief, and in what ways do these messages transcend a particular religion?

2. Several of Card's heroes are extremely gifted young people who are put in the position of having to make very difficult decisions. In what ways are the struggles of these characters universal human problems, and not merely the problems faced by heroic and gifted individuals? What can people who are not as gifted as these heroes learn from their choices?

3. Card often writes stories that put the main characters through challenging moral and philosophical dilemmas. Choose one of Card's novels or stories and

write an essay that identifies the main dilemma and discusses how Card has the character attempt to solve this dilemma.

4. Card has been noted for writing adventure stories that are really philosophical investigations of difficult questions. Write an adventure story that features a character facing the kind of philosophical problems found in Card's writings.

BIBLIOGRAPHY

**Books**

Collings, Michael R. and Boden Clarke. *The Work of Orson Scott Card*. San Bernadino, Calif.: Borgo Press, 1995.

**Periodicals**

Collings, Michael R. Review of *Speaker for the Dead*. *Fantasy Review* (April 1986): 20.

Easton, Tom. Review of *Ender's Game*. *Analog Science Fiction/Science Fact* (July 1985): 180–181.

Frank, Janrae. "Wars of the Worlds." *Washington Post Book World* (February 23, 1986): 10.

Geis, Richard E. "*Speaker for the Dead*." *Science Fiction Review* (February 1986): 15.

Jonas, Gerald. Review of *Ender's Game*. *New York Times Book Review* (June 16, 1985).

Lassell, Michael. Review of *Ender's Game*. *Los Angeles Times Book Review* (February 3, 1985): 11.

Moran, Dan K. Review of *Ender's Game*. *West Coast Review of Books* (July 1986): 20.

Review of *Ender's Game*. *Kirkus Reviews* (November 1, 1984): 1021.

# ✺ Rachel Carson

BORN: *1907, Springfield, Pennsylvania*

DIED: *1964, Silver Spring, Maryland*

NATIONALITY: *American*

GENRE: *Nonfiction*

MAJOR WORKS:

*The Sea Around Us* (1951)

*Silent Spring* (1962)

## Overview

Rachel Carson, considered one of America's premiere writers on science and nature, is often credited with beginning the environmental movement in the United States with the publication of her book *Silent Spring* (1962). Her nonfiction works were timely and provocative, pressing readers to consider the beauties of nature, the interconnectedness of all living creatures, and humanity's impact on natural systems.

Rachel Carson    *The Library of Congress.*

## Works in Biographical and Historical Context

***An Important Bond*** Carson was born in 1907 in Springdale, Pennsylvania, a town near Pittsburgh, in the valley of the Allegheny River. The family lived on a farm, but Carson's father, Robert Warden Carson, made his living as an electrician and an insurance agent. He also speculated, without much success, in real estate, subdividing the family's land into building lots, most of which went unsold. Her mother, Maria McLean Carson, is generally credited as one of the most important influences on Carson. Although Carson was the youngest of three siblings, she eventually assumed responsibility for her ailing mother and for her older sister's daughters and grandson as well.

Carson was a bright student in elementary and high school, though she was often absent because of illness and her mother's concern about contagious diseases in the schools. Carson was a solitary child who spent much of her time outdoors, but her frequent school absences helped her develop a firm bond with her mother, who often walked with her around the family's farmland, providing natural-history instruction for her daughter.

***Working in the Natural Sciences*** Carson wanted to be a writer from an early age. She began publishing at the age of thirteen with a series of short stories in

## LITERARY AND HISTORICAL CONTEMPORARIES

Carson's famous contemporaries include:

**John Steinbeck** (1902–1968): Steinbeck was an American writer widely credited with being one of the best-known and widely read writers of the twentieth century; he was granted the Nobel Prize in Literature in 1962.

**Karl Popper** (1902–1994): Popper was an Austrian and British philosopher widely considered one of the most influential philosophers of science during the twentieth century.

**Pablo Neruda** (1904–1973): Neruda was a Chilean writer and politician associated with the international communist movement; he was awarded the Nobel Prize in Literature in 1971.

**Jean-Paul Sartre** (1905–1980): Sartre was a French philosopher and author who was a leading figure in the Existentialist movement.

**W. H. Auden** (1907–1973): Auden was an Anglo-American poet, widely regarded as one of the greatest writers of the twentieth century because of his stylistic and technical achievements along with his engagement with moral and political issues.

**Simone de Beauvoir** (1908–1986): De Beauvoir was a French novelist and philosopher best known for her pioneering work in feminism, *The Second Sex* (1949).

*St. Nicholas*, a magazine that had built a reputation for discovering adolescent authors, among them William Faulkner and F. Scott Fitzgerald. Although Carson had intended to study English at the Pennsylvania College for Women, her interest in the natural sciences led her to change her major to biology despite her advisor's warning that writing afforded women greater opportunities.

After graduating in 1929, Carson briefly worked at the Woods Hole Marine Biological Laboratory in Massachusetts, and in 1932, earned an M.A. from Johns Hopkins University. She was subsequently hired by the United States Bureau of Fisheries, where she wrote and edited pamphlets, booklets, and radio scripts and eventually, in 1949, became the editor in chief of publications for the Fish and Wildlife Service. During her tenure with the government, Carson began publishing articles as a freelance writer to supplement her income. The success of "Undersea," a short piece which appeared in the *Atlantic* in 1937, prompted her to write her first book, *Under the Sea-Wind: A Naturalist's Picture of Ocean Life* (1941). In 1952, after writing five more books, including the National Book Award-winning *The Sea Around Us*, Carson left the Fish and Wildlife Service to devote herself full time to her own writing.

*A Pioneer of Environmentalism* Although Carson was only able to publish two more books before her death in 1964, she produced, during this time, her most famous work, *Silent Spring*. The book was an immediate sensation that brought both critical praise and attacks from the chemical industry; it focuses on the harmful effects of pesticides, used frequently in agriculture, on both wildlife and humans. This book has since been widely acknowledged as one of the most important founding works of the modern environmental movement, and in 1980, President Jimmy Carter recognized Carson's contributions to the environmental movement by posthumously awarding her the Presidential Medal of Freedom. Many of Carson's books remain in print, and she continues to receive critical and scholarly attention.

## Works in Literary Context

An influential figure in the environmental movement, Carson is best known as the author of *Silent Spring*, a controversial study of pesticide misuse, and as a crusader in the fight for conservation and ecological awareness. A marine biologist and conservationist who emphasized the interconnectedness of all creation in her writings, Carson attempted to educate readers by instilling in them her own love of nature. Although primarily recognized for the scientific accuracy of her nonfiction, Carson also employed such literary devices as metaphor and allusion in her work, leading some critics to classify her as a participant in the naturalist school of literature.

*Literary Technique in Scientific Works* Carson has been noted for using imaginative techniques to bring her scientific works to life. Her first book, *Under the Sea-Wind*, which focused on the dynamics of the marine world as experienced by a salmon, a migratory waterfowl, and an eel, employed creative anthropomorphism that enabled Carson to create an emotional bond between readers and her wildlife protagonists. Another of her works on sea life, *The Sea Around Us*, which won the National Book Award for nonfiction and became the basis for an Academy Award-winning documentary, made use of literary allusions, analogies, and occasionally a first-person plural point of view to ease readers into what was, for many, unfamiliar material. The National Book Award judges called *The Sea Around Us* "a work of scientific accuracy presented with poetic imagination and such clarity of style and originality of approach as to win and hold every reader's attention." Likening her descriptions of the sea to those of Joseph Conrad and Herman Melville, reviewers asserted that Carson's use of color, sound, and an objective tone convincingly evinced the sights, rhythms, and cycles of the underwater world. Her best known work, *Silent Spring*, also made use of literary technique, opening with a fable and taking its title from a poem by John Keats.

*Influence on Environmentalism* Carson is often credited with playing a seminal role in the formation of the modern environmental movement. One commentator notes that *Silent Spring* "may have changed the course of history," a declaration echoed by the Internet site of the United States Environmental Protection Agency. The book is regularly included at or near the top of lists of the most influential environmental texts of the twentieth century. This influence was recognized at the time of publication, not only in the positive public reaction to the book but also in the extraordinary efforts of the chemical industry to discredit it. The regard in which *Silent Spring* and its author are held has not diminished in the years since her death. Craig Waddell, in the introduction to his critical anthology *And No Birds Sing: Rhetorical Analyses of Silent Spring* (2000), assembles an impressive list of testimonies to the importance of *Silent Spring* as the seminal text of modern environmentalism.

## Works in Critical Context

Carson has generally been praised by reviewers and scholars for both the solid factual basis of her works and the literary merit of her writing. Many of her works sparked controversy, which is evident in the diverse reactions to the messages of her books. However, critics tended to accept that Carson's writings were both provocative and timely.

***The Edge of the Sea***  *The Edge of the Sea* (1955), which focused on the tidal zones and shallow waters of the United States' eastern seaboard, was a sequel of sorts to Carson's National Book Award-winner, *The Sea Around Us*. While some critics deemed the book of lesser literary value than its predecessor, others cited Carson's use of imagery, repetition, alliteration, and rhythm as evidence of the work's merit. Carol B. Gartner, who has compared Carson to Henry David Thoreau, noted that the opening passage of the book can be read as a poem: "And so in that enchanted place / on the threshold of the sea / the realities that possessed my mind / were far from those of the land world / I had left an hour before." Like Carson's other books, *The Edge of the Sea* emphasizes the interdependence and sanctity of all forms of life; Charles J. Rojo observed: "To Miss Carson, the edge of the sea conveys a haunting sense of communicating some universal truth as yet beyond our grasp; a sense that through this region, in which Life began, we can approach the ultimate mystery of Life itself."

***Silent Spring***  Carson is best known for *Silent Spring*, the last of her books to be published in her lifetime. *Silent Spring*, an exposé of the dangers of pesticides, has been compared to such works of social consciousness as Harriet Beecher Stowe's *Uncle Tom's Cabin* (1852) and Sinclair Lewis's *The Jungle* (1906). The book's greatest achievement, however, was in alerting international audiences to the dangers of pollution. Loren Eiseley called *Silent Spring* "a devastating, heavily documented, relentless attack upon human carelessness, greed, and irresponsibility—an irresponsibility that has let loose upon man and the countryside a flood of dangerous chemicals in a situation which,

---

## COMMON HUMAN EXPERIENCE

Carson employed literary devices to make her science and nature books accessible to a popular audience. Here are some other scientific works that were aimed at a popular audience:

*A Brief History of Time* (1988), nonfiction book by Stephen Hawking. This book covers difficult-to-understand topics in physics, such as the Big Bang Theory and black holes in a way that allows general readers to understand recent advances in cosmology.

*The Three-Pound Universe* (1991), nonfiction book by Judith Hooper. This book discusses advances in brain science in a manner that is accessible to general readers.

*Dinosaur in a Haystack* (1995), a collection of essays by Stephen Jay Gould. This collection of essays from the author's column in *Natural History* magazine deals with various topics in evolutionary theory.

---

as Miss Carson states, is without parallel." Representatives of pesticide companies and other industry-related interest groups denounced *Silent Spring* and questioned Carson's credibility, but Carson's findings were substantiated by other scientists, including the Science Advisory Committee appointed by President John F. Kennedy.

## Responses to Literature

1. Carson is noted for using literary devices in her scientific works. Which of these devices work best to reinforce the messages she is trying to convey? Do any of these devices distract the reader from the material? In what ways are Carson's writings more or less effective than works produced by other scientific writers at bringing the material to life for general readers?

2. Carson is generally credited with helping to begin the environmental movement in the United States. It has been over forty years since her works were originally published. Have environmentalists discarded any of the concerns initially expressed in Carson's works? What new concerns have environmentalists developed since Carson's time?

3. Carson occasionally anthropomorphized—or assigned human traits to—her wildlife subjects in order to more closely bond readers to her subject matter. Write a story that conveys a real aspect of the natural world through the creation of an anthropomorphized wildlife character.

4. Some modern critics, including author Michael Crichton, have suggested that *Silent Spring*—which led to an eventual ban on DDT, a chemical used to control insects—was largely responsible for subsequent increases in deaths by malaria. Research this subject using your library or the Internet. What are the arguments offered by each side in this debate? Did Carson herself address the subject of banning chemicals versus responsible testing and use in her original work?

BIBLIOGRAPHY

**Books**

Archer, Jules. *To Save the Earth: The American Environmental Movement.* New York: Viking, 1998.

Brooks, Paul. *The House of Life: Rachel Carson at Work.* Boston: Houghton Mifflin, 1972.

Gartner, Carol B. *Rachel Carson.* New York: Ungar, 1983.

Lear, Linda. *Rachel Carson: Witness for Nature.* New York: Holt, 1997.

McKay, Mary A. *Rachel Carson.* Boston: Twayne, 1993.

Ravage, Barbara. *Rachel Carson: Protecting Our Environment.* Austin, Tex.: Raintree Steck-Vaughn, 1997.

Sterling, Philip. *Sea and Earth: The Life of Rachel Carson.* New York: Crowell, 1970.

Waddell, Craig, ed. *And No Birds Sing: Rhetorical Analyses of Silent Spring.* Carbondale, Ill.: Southern Illinois University Press, 2000.

**Periodicals**

Brooks, Paul. "The Courage of Rachel Carson." *Audubon 89* (January 1987): 14–15.

Wareham, Wendy. "Rachel Carson's Early Years." *Carnegie* (November/December 1986): 20–34.

**Web sites**

Graham, Frank, Jr. *Rachel Carson.* Retrieved October 14, 2008, from http://www.epa.gov/history/topics/perspect/carson.htm.

# ✸ Raymond Carver

BORN: *1938, Clatskanie, Oregon*

DIED: *1988, Port Angeles, Washington*

NATIONALITY: *American*

GENRE: *Fiction*

MAJOR WORKS:

*What We Talk about When We Talk about Love* (1981)

*Cathedral* (1984)

*Where I'm Calling From* (1988)

Raymond Carver    *Carver, Raymond, photograph. © Jerry Bauer. Reproduced by permission.*

## Overview

Raymond Carver's literary career helped shape the direction of contemporary American short fiction. His stark, terse narratives of understated despair have been influential in reviving interest in the short story. His obsessions (Carver disapproved of the word "themes") included male-female relationships, confronting loss, and survival.

## Works in Biographical and Historical Context

*An Average Childhood*    Born in Clatskanie, Oregon, on May 25, 1938, Raymond Carver was three when his parents moved with him to Yakima, Washington, a working-class town in the eastern part of the state, where his father worked in a sawmill. Carver often described his childhood and adolescence as average. His father was a storyteller, embellishing tales about the Civil War and about riding the rails west. Occasionally, Carver would happen upon his father reading works by Zane Grey. Apart from serialized westerns, the young Carver read books by Edgar Rice Burroughs and magazines such as *Outdoor Life* and *Sports Afield*. He associated the act of reading with his father and was drawn to that introspective stance; he also associated alcohol with his father, who often would spend his weekend nights away from home with friends from the mill.

***Various Jobs and Schools*** Married in 1957 and the father of two children before he reached the age of twenty, Carver worked sundry menial jobs and frequently moved with his wife and children between small towns in the Pacific Northwest. In 1958, Carver located in Paradise, California, where he attended Chico State College while working at night. The following year he began studying creative writing under John Gardner—a then unknown novelist—who taught Carver the importance of craft and integrity in writing. At Chico State, Carver founded the literary magazine *Selection*, in which he published his first short story, "The Furious Seasons," a Faulknerian tale written in a stream-of-consciousness style unlike any of his subsequent writings.

In 1960, Carver moved to Arcata, California, and began attending classes at Humboldt State College, where he published stories in the school literary magazine, *Toyon*. He received his bachelor's degree in 1963, and later that year accepted a grant to study at the University of Iowa Writer's Workshop; however, he wrote very little there and failed to complete the graduate program. He returned to California, working at various jobs and publishing only one story between 1965 and 1970, "Will You Please Be Quiet, Please?" which was selected for *Best American Short Stories* in 1967. That same year, Carver secured a white-collar job at a textbook publishing company, a position from which he was fired in 1970 after a company reorganization. Unemployment proved beneficial to Carver as he subsequently received income through severance pay and unemployment benefits, and was afforded sufficient time to write.

***Success as a Short-Story Writer*** In 1976, Carver published his first collection of short stories, *Will You Please Be Quiet, Please?*, which was nominated for a National Book Award. Despite Carver's growing popular and critical success in the 1970s, his personal life was in turmoil due to his alcoholism and martial difficulties. In 1977, Carver stopped drinking and, in the same year, met poet and short story writer Tess Gallagher, with whom he began living after separating from his wife and who significantly influenced his later writings.

During the late 1970s and throughout the 1980s, Carver revised earlier stories and wrote new pieces for such collections as *What We Talk about When We Talk about Love* (1981) and *Cathedral* (1984). He received several awards and grants, including the prestigious Mildred and Harold Strauss Living award in 1983, which stipulated that he write full-time and give up his teaching post at Syracuse University in order to earn a tax-exempt salary for five years. In 1987, Carver was diagnosed with lung cancer. During his last year he continued writing and published the collection *Where I'm Calling From*. He died from lung cancer in 1988.

## LITERARY AND HISTORICAL CONTEMPORARIES

Carver's famous contemporaries include:

**Harlan Ellison** (1934–): Ellison is an American fiction and television writer best known for his work on *Star Trek* and *Outer Limits*.

**Richard Brautigan** (1935–1984): Brautigan is an American author who is considered one of the links between the Beat Generation and the counterculture generation.

**Don DeLillo** (1936–): DeLillo is an American novelist prominent as one of the pioneers of postmodern fiction.

**Peter Jennings** (1938–2005): Jennings was a Canadian-born television news journalist best known for anchoring ABC's national nightly news.

**Judy Blume** (1938–): Blume is an American author who has achieved widespread popularity because of her childrens' and young adult books which frequently tackle difficult and controversial issues.

**Margaret Atwood** (1939–): Atwood is a Canadian writer who is one of the most award-winning authors of the late twentieth century and early twenty-first century.

## Works in Literary Context

Carver is widely recognized as an important influence in contemporary American short fiction. His stories, often set in blue-collar communities of the Pacific Northwest, portray characters on the edge of bankruptcy, both emotionally and financially, and are distinguished by an unadorned, controlled style. While Carver is frequently aligned with minimalist writers, a classification largely based on the truncated prose and elliptical delineation of characters and events in his collection *What We Talk about When We Talk about Love*, many of his short stories in such later collections as *Cathedral* and *Where I'm Calling From* are praised for their expansive treatment of character and the detailed realism of their depictions of everyday life.

***Minimalism*** Carver has been noted for employing a minimalist style in his short stories. His first collection, *Will You Please Be Quiet, Please?*, conspicuously displays an affinity with the works of American realist writer Ernest Hemingway in its terse, economical prose style. Like Hemingway, Carver created tension in his short stories through omission and understatement, thereby forcing conclusions about a story's meaning upon the reader. Critics observe that abrupt endings of such stories as "Neighbors"—the protagonists cling to one another in the hallway of their apartment in unspoken terror—leave the reader wondering what will happen next. Ann Beattie commented on the tableau effect of the ending of a Carver story, stating that "his language freezes moments in time with a clarity and

## COMMON HUMAN EXPERIENCE

Carver's short stories are noted for providing insightful portraits of contemporary life in late twentieth-century America by depicting ordinary people coping with the difficulties of their everyday lives. Here are some other short-story collections that depict characters in a similar manner:

> *Trailerpark* (1981), short stories by Russell Banks. The stories in this collection depict the lives of the various people who live in a trailer park in New Hampshire.
> *The Safety of Objects* (1991), short stories by A. M. Homes. The stories in this collection explore various characters in a familiar yet sometimes surreal suburban setting as they wrestle with their relationship to the American dream.
> *Cold Snap* (1995), short stories by Thom Jones. The stories in this collection explore the reactions, often extreme, of characters to the everyday tragedies of life in contemporary America.

complexity that allows us all the advantages his doomed characters are denied."

The stories in Carver's best-known collection, *What We Talk about When We Talk about Love*, reach extremes of stark understatement. These stories have been called minimalist masterpieces by some critics and laconic, empty failures by others. Shortly before *What We Talk about When We Talk about Love* was published, Carver expressed his literary stance in his essay "A Storyteller's Shoptalk" (later published as "On Writing"): "Get in, get out. Don't linger. Go on." While "in" the story, Carver chose exact details to amplify the underlying terror of seemingly banal events.

**Depicting Despair**   Carver has been deemed a spokesperson for blue-collar despair, and many critics have noted the often grim nature of his stories, observing that the characters have no control over the circumstances of their lives and that they are subject to random, unsettling losses. Since his earliest collections, he has written about the difficulties, both emotional and financial, of contemporary life. The majority of stories in *Will You Please Be Quiet, Please?* depict jobless, melancholy protagonists whose unremarkable lives reflect emptiness and despair. The stories in his next collection, *Furious Seasons* (1977), again portray ordinary, often unhappily married characters and convey a sense of unease. In *What We Talk about When We Talk about Love*, Carver explores his characters' feelings of dislocation and lost identity as well as their awareness of random, uncontrollable changes in their lives.

## Works in Critical Context

Carver has been credited by a number of reviewers with reviving interest in what was once thought of as a dying literary form, the short story. Although reviewers often disagree about the merit of individual stories or the direction of Carver's artistic development, he is widely accepted as one of the most important American authors of the twentieth century.

**What We Talk about When We Talk about Love**   Carver's best-known collection, *What We Talk about When We Talk about Love*, was widely praised and helped catapult Carver to wide renown as America's foremost contemporary short-story writer. One reviewer wrote, "The characters are not impoverished, except in spirit, or uneducated. They just seem squalid. And Carver celebrates that squalor, makes poetic that squalor in a way nobody else has tried to do." The most quoted assessment of *What We Talk about When We Talk about Love* belongs to Donald Newlove: "Seventeen tales of Hopelessville, its marriages and alcoholic wreckage, told in a prose as sparingly clear as a fifth of iced Smirnoff."

Though *What We Talk about When We Talk about Love* is credited for being part of the rejuvenation of the American short story, the book has its detractors. In a review for *Atlantic* James Atlas stigmatized Carver's technique by calling it "severe to the point of anorexia." Others have labeled the book as "K-mart Realism," "Lo-Cal Literature," "Freeze-Dried Fiction," and "Post-alcoholic Blue-Collar Minimalist Hyperrealism." Most often, Carver is accused of writing over his characters' heads, suggesting he condescends to their inadequacies. For critic Michael Gorra, the stories are "entirely without the mingled sense of inevitability that seems to me essential for short fiction—the sense that out of all the things that could happen, this one has."

**Cathedral**   After *What We Talk about When We Talk about Love*, Carver was frequently aligned with minimalist writers, but many of his stories in such later collections as *Cathedral* and *Where I'm Calling From* were praised for their expansive treatment of character and the detailed realism of their depictions of everyday life. In *Cathedral*, Carver rewrote the ending of one of his most acclaimed stories from *What We Talk about When We Talk about Love*. In the original story, entitled "The Bath," a boy is hit by a car on his birthday, preventing his mother from picking up his birthday cake at the bakery, while the baker badgers the family with telephone calls demanding his money. At the end of the original story, Carver leaves the boy's ultimate fate unknown, but in *Cathedral*, he reveals that the boy has in fact died. The parents now answer the telephone and tell the baker their story, to which he replies with his own story of loneliness and despair while comforting them with fresh coffee and warm rolls and telling them that "eating is a small, good thing in a time like this." The change in this story has been remarked by critics as a change in Carver's thematic approach to contemporary life. One reviewer has asserted that while "'The Bath' is a good short story," the newer version, entitled "A Small, Good Thing," "comes breathtakingly close to perfection." A *Washington Post Book World* critic wrote,

> The first version is beautifully crafted and admirably concise, but lacking in genuine compassion; the mysterious caller is not so much a human being as a mere voice, malign and characterless. But in the second version that voice becomes a person, one whose own losses are, in different ways, as crippling and heartbreaking as the one suffered by the grieving parents.

The publication of *Cathedral*, which received both National Book Critics and Pulitzer Prize nominations, was able to catapult Carver beyond the "minimalist" stereotype to which he had been confined. Reviewers and critics differ in their assessments, but they agreed that *Cathedral* marks a transition in Carver's career. Although some critics find his later stories sentimental, most consider that they represent a significant departure toward more insightful portraits of contemporary life and demonstrate his continued artistic development.

## Responses to Literature

1. Carver has been noted for his minimalist style, and commentators assert that this style helps conveys the message of alienation contained in many of his stories. What other purposes might this minimalist style serve, and does this style enhance or detract from the messages Carver is trying to display? Does Carver succeed at engaging his readers' imaginations or does he disappoint by leaving them with too little to go on to understand his characters' lives?

2. Many of Carver's characters were depicted as isolated from each other and unable to communicate their circumstances to others. Carver was writing in a time when modern communication methods such as cell phones, email, text-messaging, and blogging were not yet available. In what ways might these methods have changed the way Carver's characters related to each other, and in what ways would more access to communication not have helped them overcome the difficulties they faced? Would a writer today, setting stories in the present time, be likely to present characters with these kinds of communication difficulties, or are such concerns a relic of the past?

3. Carver frequently wrote about ordinary people facing the difficult circumstances of their everyday lives. Write a story modeled on Carver's minimalist style that puts an ordinary person in a difficult, everyday situation.

4. In two of his later collections, Carver rewrote some of his earlier stories. Choose one or two of these rewrites and write an essay comparing the later version(s) to the original. Be sure to discuss the type of artistic development displayed by the change in the story's style and plot.

BIBLIOGRAPHY

**Books**

Gentry, Marshall Bruce and William L. Stull, eds. *Conversations with Raymond Carver.* Jackson, Miss.: University Press of Mississippi, 1990.

Campbell, Ewing. *Raymond Carver: A Study of the Short Fiction.* New York: Twayne, 1992.

Halpert, Sam. *Raymond Carver: An Oral Biography.* Iowa City, Iowa: University of Iowa Press, 1995.

Meyer, Adam. *Raymond Carver.* New York: Twayne, 1994.

Nesset, Kirk. *The Stories of Raymond Carver: A Critical Study.* Athens, Ohio: Ohio University Press, 1995.

Runyon, Randolph. *Reading Raymond Carver.* Syracuse, N.Y.: Syracuse University Press, 1992.

Saltzman, Arthur M. *Understanding Raymond Carver.* Columbia, S.C.: University of South Carolina Press, 1988.

Stull, William and Maureen P. Carroll, eds. *Remembering Ray: A Composite Biography of Raymond Carver.* Santa Barbara, Calif.: Capra, 1993.

**Periodicals**

Cochrane, Hamilton E. "Taking the Cure: Alcoholism and Recovery in the Fiction of Raymond Carver." *Dayton Review* (Summer 1989): 79–88.

Gorra, Michael. "Laughter and Bloodshed." *Hudson Review* (Spring 1984): 151–164.

Kaufmann, David. "Yuppie Postmodernism." *Arizona Quarterly* (Summer 1991): 93–116.

Meyer, Adam. "Now You See Him, Now You Don't, Now You Do Again: The Evolution of Raymond Carver's Minimalism." *Critique* (Summer 1989): 239–251.

# Ana Castillo

BORN: *1953, Chicago, Illinois*

NATIONALITY: *American, Latino-American*

GENRE: *Fiction, nonfiction, poetry*

MAJOR WORKS:
*The Mixquiahuala Letters* (1986)
*Sapogonia* (1990)
*So Far From God* (1993)

## Overview

Ana Castillo is a prominent and prolific Chicana poet, novelist, editor, and translator whose work has been widely anthologized in the United States, Mexico, and Europe. From her earliest writing she has tried to unite those segments of the American population often separated by class, economics, gender, and sexual orientation.

## Works in Biographical and Historical Context

*A Heritage of Struggles and Storytelling*   Castillo was born in Chicago on June 15, 1953, to Raymond Castillo and Raquel Rocha Castillo, struggling working-class people. She attended public schools in Chicago, and she became involved with the Chicano movement in high school when she was seventeen. Her family's working-class status set the stage for a developing writer who, throughout her literary career, has examined pervasive social and economic inequities that affect women and Latinos in the United States. She also credits her Mexican heritage with providing a rich background of storytelling.

*Education and the Development of a Poetic Voice*
After attending Chicago City College for two years, she transferred to Northeastern Illinois University, where she majored in secondary education, planning to teach art. She received her B.A. in 1975. Castillo's experience as a student at Northeastern Illinois was largely negative, due to what she has described as pervasive racism and sexism. As a result of these experiences, Castillo stopped painting. During her third year of college, however, she resumed writing poetry.

Castillo's literary career began before she finished college. At twenty she gave her first poetry reading at Northeastern Illinois University, and in 1975 *Revista Chicano-Riqueña* published two of her poems. That same year another one of her poems was included in the anthology *Zero Makes Me Hungry* (1975), and the following year the *Revista Chicano-Riqueña* published a second group of her poems about racial injustice, particularly the fate of indigenous peoples in America. Despite her uncertainty about the value of her poems, Castillo continued to write and develop her poetic voice. Caught up in the political fervor of the 1970s, she thought of herself as a political poet committed to talking about the economic inequality of Latino people in the United States.

In 1975, Castillo moved to Sonoma County, California, where she taught ethnic studies for a year at Santa Rosa Junior College. Returning to Chicago in 1976, she pursued a master's degree in Latin American and Caribbean studies in 1978 and 1979. In 1977, she published a chapbook, *Otro Canto* (Other Song), in which she collected her earlier political poems. From 1977 to 1979, she was writer in residence for the Illinois Arts Council, and in 1979 she published her second chapbook, *The Invitation*, a collection that exhibits for the first time Castillo's interest in sexuality and the oppression of women, especially Latinas. She also received her M.A. degree in 1979 from the University of Chicago and between 1980 and 1981, was poet in residence of the Urban Gateways of Chicago. A son, Marcel Ramón Herrera, was born in 1983. In 1984, Arte Público Press published *Women Are Not Roses*, a collection of poems that includes some poems from her chapbooks.

*Beginning to Write Prose*   By 1985 Castillo was once again in California, teaching at San Francisco State University, becoming more and more involved as an editor for Third Woman Press. She began to receive wider notice as a writer when she published her first novel, *The Mixquiahuala Letters* (1986), which she had begun writing in 1979. The book consists of letters written between two female friends—both resembling the author in some ways, but both vastly different in personality and outlook—over the course of ten years. After the novel received the Before Columbus Foundation's American Book Award in 1987, Castillo was further honored by the Women's Foundation of San Francisco in 1988 with the Women of Words Award for "pioneering excellence in literature." Still needing money and finding it difficult to raise her son alone, she taught various courses at universities in California until 1989, when she received a California Arts Council Fellowship for Fiction. The following year, she received a National Endowment for the Arts Fellowship.

Castillo then had her second novel published, *Sapogonia: An Anti-Romance in 3/8 Meter* (1990), which had been written in Chicago in 1984 and 1985 while she was teaching English as a second language and taking care of her new baby. She received her Ph.D. in American studies from the University of Bremen in 1991 with a dissertation on Xicanisma, or Chicana feminism, subsequently published as *Massacre of the Dreamers: Essays on Xicanisma* (1994).

In August 1990, before completing her Ph.D., Castillo moved to New Mexico, where she began to write her third novel, *So Far from God* (1993), which is her best-known work to date. Since the publication of *So Far from God*, Castillo has published four more novels, a short-story collection, and two collections of poetry. She has also spent her time teaching a wide range of subjects, including creative writing, U.S. and Mexican history, the history of pre-Columbian civilizations, Chicano literature, and women's studies.

## Works in Literary Context

Ana Castillo is one of a few Mexican American writers who have attracted the attention of the mainstream reading public. Her novels, short stories, and poetry all emerge from a working-class, Latina sensibility; yet, her work has crossed social and ethnic lines to examine issues common to all people regardless of their cultural backgrounds or ethnicity. Her detailed descriptions of a specifically Latino culture are the backdrop for a body of literature that speaks to people of all cultures.

*A Voice for Women*   Castillo's poetic voice speaks for all women who have at one time or another felt the unfairness of female existence in a world primarily designed by men and for men. Her first collection of poems, *Women Are Not Roses* (1984), examines the themes of sadness and loneliness in the female experience, particularly for Latin women. Castillo pointed out in a 1991 interview that throughout *The Mixquiahuala Letters*, she deals with "a very real, painful reality for Mexicanas, brown women who don't fit into the aesthetic" of what is considered beautiful in North America. According to Castillo, Teresa's letters address "the fact that in patriarchy, all women are possessions, but the highest possession, ... is the white woman."

**Economic and Racial Oppression**  Although Castillo's works center around the problems faced by women, she presents these problems in a broader socio-economic context. Yvonne Yarbro-Bejarano asserts that Castillo needs to be read with an awareness of "the realization that the Chicana's experience as a woman is inextricable from her experience as a member of an oppressed working-class racial minority and a culture which is not the dominant culture."

## Works in Critical Context

Castillo's first three novels were given an enthusiastic critical reception and much scholarly attention, and she won several awards based on this early success. However, she has not since received the critical notice that she did during the late 1980s and early 1990s, though she does continue to be noted for exploring the difficult themes of identity, racism, and classism.

**The Mixquiahuala Letters**  *The Mixquiahuala Letters*, an epistolary novel based on forty letters written by the character Teresa to her friend Alicia, is a provocative examination of the relationship between the sexes. A far-ranging social and cultural exposé, the novel examines Hispanic forms of love and gender conflict. Anne Bower claims that *The Mixquiahuala Letters* "is very much a quest novel ... with form and explanation taking us into the women's emotional and artistic searches," while Erlinda Gonzales-Berry argues that in Castillo's "letter writing project, the letter simultaneously functions as a bridge and as a boundary between subject and object." Gonzales-Berry believes that the letter "verbally links the receiver, (Other), to the sender, (Self), but it also posits the other as the impenetrable mirror that reflects the specular image of the speaking-writing subject." Norma Alarcón suggests a connection between Castillo's earlier poetry and her first novel in that "both reveal the intimate events in the life of the speaker, combined with the speaker's emotional response to them, thus exploring the personal states of mind at the moment of the event or with respect to it." Alarcón sees the epistolary novel as "Castillo's experimentations with shifting pronouns and appropriative techniques for the purpose of exploring the romantic/erotic" and suggests that the female narrator "is betrayed by a cultural fabric that presses its images of her upon her, and her response is to give them back to us, albeit sardonically."

**Sapogonia**  With *Sapogonia*, critics felt that Castillo had hit her full-fledged and sophisticated stride with an intricately woven tale of the destructive powers of male-

female relationships. Told from the viewpoint of the male narrator, whom critic Rudolfo Anaya has described as "an anti-hero who relishes his inheritance as Conquistador while he agonizes over his legacy as the Conquered," the novel traces the obsessive relationship between the narrator and the woman he is unable to conquer. On the back page of the original Bilingual Press edition of 1990, Rudolfo A. Anaya calls *Sapogonia* "a literary triumph." Yvonne Yarbro-Bejarano states that *Sapogonia* "explores male fantasy, its potential for violence against women and the female subject's struggle to interpret herself both within and outside of this discourse on femininity."

**So Far from God**  Considered by critics to be her best novel, *So Far from God* distinguishes itself through Castillo's use of the New Mexicans' English sprinkled with Spanish, Reading *So Far from God* prompted Sandra Cisneros to exult on the jacket of Castillo's book, "Ana Castillo has gone and done what I always wanted to do—written a Chicana *telenovela*—a novel roaring down Interstate 25 at one hundred and fifteen miles an hour with an almanac of Chicanismo." Other Latino critics also praised the Spanish feeling of the novel, and Jaime Armín Mejía called the novel a "contagiously fast-moving, silly, irreverent, yet wise series of tales from Nuevo Méjico." Mejía pointed out that the narrator's Latin voice provides "readers a not always reliable but certainly a culturally rich understanding of the *nueva mexicana* community" where the novel is set.

### LITERARY AND HISTORICAL CONTEMPORARIES

Castillo's famous contemporaries include:

**Jim Carroll** (1950–): Carroll is an American writer and musician best known for his autobiographical work *The Basketball Diaries* (1978), which was made into a film in 1995.
**Sandra Cisneros** (1954–): Like Castillo, Cisneros is a Chicana author born in Chicago; her critically acclaimed works include the novel *The House on Mango Street* (1984).
**Alaa Al Aswany** (1957–): Aswany is a contemporary Egyptian writer whose best-selling books use social realism to take an unflinching look at the problems of modern Egypt.
**Tama Janowitz** (1957–): Janowitz is an American writer considered a member of the American "literary brat pack" that came to prominence in the 1980s.
**Cherríe Moraga** (1952–): A Chicana writer and playwright born in California, Moraga's works explore culture, gender, and sexual orientation.

## COMMON HUMAN EXPERIENCE

Castillo often writes of the difficulties faced by people of Latin American origins living within the dominant white culture of the United States. Here are some other works that explore similar issues:

*How the García Girls Lost Their Accents* (1991), a novel by Julia Alvarez. This novel explores the issues faced by first-generation immigrants from the Dominican Republic attempting to navigate the difficult path between acculturation in the United States and maintaining the customs and traditions of the old country.

*When I Was Puerto Rican* (1994), a memoir by Esmeralda Santiago. This memoir tells the story of a young girl uprooted from her home in Puerto Rico and sent to live with her grandmother in New York, where she must learn to survive in an alien world.

*Drown* (1996), short stories by Junot Diaz. The stories in this collection explore the emotional lives of Dominican teenage boys living in New York and New Jersey as they struggle to cope with the erosion of their families and blossoming adolescent sexuality.

### Responses to Literature

1. In *The Mixquiahuala Letters*, Castillo uses letters from one character to another to tell her story. In what ways does this approach make her story more compelling, and in what ways does this approach limit her ability to tell the story? Would this novel work as well if written as a series of emails or blogs written from various Internet cafes, or would these more modern forms of communication be inappropriate for Castillo's purposes?

2. Commentators note that Castillo's works speak powerfully to women who have felt the unfairness of women's lives in a male-dominated world. In what ways, if any, do Castillo's works speak to men? What can both women and men learn about the world by reading Castillo's works, and are the lessons there primarily useful for women only?

3. Castillo has been praised for attempting to unite segments of the American population that are divided by such factors as ethnicity, gender, sexual orientation, and socio-economic class. Write an analytical essay that discusses the aspects of Castillo's writing that work towards a unification of these different groups.

4. Castillo explores the problems faced by women who are working-class and racial minorities. Write an essay that discusses the nature of these problems as presented by Castillo and assesses how well she conveys these problems to her readers.

### BIBLIOGRAPHY

**Books**

Binder, Wolfgang, ed. *Partial Autobiographies* Erlangen, Germany: Verlag Palm & Enke Erlangen, 1985.

Hererra-Sobek, Maria and Helena Maria Viramontes, eds. *Chicana Creativity and Criticism: Charting New Frontiers in American Literature*. Houston, Tex.: Arte Publico Press, 1988.

Pérez-Torres, Rafael. *Movements in Chicano Poetry*. Cambridge, England: Cambridge University Press, 1995.

Telgen, Dian and Kim Kamp, eds. *LATINAS Women of Achievement*. Detroit: Visible Ink, 1996.

**Periodicals**

Bennet, Tanya Long. "No Country to Call Home: A Study of Castillo's *Mixquiahuala Letters*." *Style* (Fall 1996): 462–478.

Birnbaum, Robert. "Ana Castillo." *Stuff* (June 1993): 53–56.

Delgadillo, Theresa. "Forms of Chicana Feminist Resistance: Hybrid Spirituality in Ana Castillo's *So Far from God*." *MFS: Modern Fiction Studies* (Winter 1998): 888–916.

Dubrava, Patricia. "Ana Castillo: Impressions of a Xicana Dreamer." *Bloomsbury Review* (November–December 1995): 5, 13.

Morrow, Colette. "Queering Chicano/a Narratives: Lesbian as Healer, Saint, and Warrior in Ana Castillo's *So Far from God*." *MMLA* (Spring 1997): 63–80.

Sánchez, Alberto Sandoval. "Breaking the Silence, Dismantling Taboos: Latino Novels on AIDS." *Journal of Homosexuality* (March 1998): 155–175.

Sánchez, Rosaura. "Reconstructing Chicana Gender Identity." *American Literary History* (1997): 350–363.

Walter, Roland. "The Cultural Politics of Dislocation and Relocation in the Novels of Ana Castillo." *MELUS* (Spring 1998): 81–97.

Yarbro-Bejarano, Yvonne. "The Multiple Subject in the Writing of Ana Castillo." *Americas Review* (Spring 1992): 65–72.

## ⚘ Willa Cather

BORN: *1873, Back Creek Valley, Virginia*

DIED: *1947, New York, New York*

NATIONALITY: *American*

GENRE: *Fiction*

MAJOR WORKS:

*O Pioneers!* (1913)

*My Antonia* (1918)

*One of Ours* (1922)

*Death Comes for the Archbishop* (1927)

Willa Cather    *Cather, Willa, photograph by Carl Van Vechten. Reproduced by permission of the Carl Van Vechten Trust.*

## Overview

Cather was an important American author of the early twentieth century. She is best known for novels that present evocative, realistic portrayals of pioneer life and that celebrate the courageous endurance of the early Midwestern settlers and the natural beauty of the prairie landscape. Her works often focus on sensitive, alienated individuals and examine their varying degrees of success in resolving conflict.

## Works in Biographical and Historical Context

***Settling in the Midwest***    Cather was born in Virginia in 1873, and she spent the first decade of her life on her family's farm in Back Creek Valley. In 1884, the Cathers moved to the Great Plains, joining the ethnically diverse group of settlers in Webster County, Nebraska. The family settled in Red Cloud, where Cather began to attend school on a regular basis.

Red Cloud was a farm-to-market town of twenty-five hundred people and a division point on the Burlington Railroad. Although it was a raw, new town, there was a good deal of intellectual nourishment there. The Weiner couple around the corner were educated Europeans who spoke French and German, and encouraged Cather to read in their well-stocked library. Cather also studied

Latin and Greek with William Drucker, an Englishman who clerked in his brother's store. Another neighbor was Julia Miner, who had been born in Oslo, the daughter of an oboist in the Royal Norwegian Symphony. She played the piano expertly to her young neighbor's perennial delight. Cather also took part in amateur theatricals and attended performances of road companies that played in the Red Cloud opera house.

The time she spent living in Nebraska would be a profound influence on her writing. Nebraska would be a dominant subject in her writing and the setting for all or significant parts of six of her twelve novels and many of her short stories.

***Working as a Journalist***    At the age of sixteen-and-a-half, Cather finished high school along with two other students in the second class to graduate. After delivering a commencement oration on "Superstition versus Investigation," a ringing defense of experimental science, she left for Lincoln and the University of Nebraska, where she excelled in studies of language and literature. During her junior year, she assumed the editorship of the college literary journal, in which she published many of her own short stories; by the time she was graduated from the university, she was working as a full-time reporter and critic for the *Nebraska State Journal*. Shortly after graduation, she moved to Pittsburgh to serve as editor of a short-lived women's magazine called the *Home Monthly*. Cather published her first book, *April Twilights*, an undistinguished volume of poetry, in 1903. While she continued to write and publish short stories, she made her living as a journalist and teacher until she moved to New York City in 1906 to assume the managing editorship of the influential *McClure's* magazine.

Cather's affiliation with *McClure's* proved to be pivotal in her life and career: her work for the magazine brought her national recognition, and it was S. S. McClure, the publisher of *McClure's*, who arranged for the release of *The Troll Garden* (1905), her first volume of short stories.

***Devoted to Fiction***    While on assignment in Boston in 1908, Cather met Sarah Orne Jewett, an author whose work she greatly admired; after reading Cather's fiction, Jewett encouraged her to abandon journalism. "I cannot help saying what I think," Jewett wrote to Cather, "about your writing and its being hindered by such incessant, important, responsible work as you have in your hands now." Jewett further advised Cather to "find [her] own quiet centre of life, and write from that to the world." Cather was profoundly influenced by these admonitions, and shortly afterward she relinquished her responsibilities at *McClure's* in order to devote all of her time to writing fiction.

When Cather left *McClure's* in the fall of 1911, she and her Pittsburgh friend Isabelle McClung rented a house in Cherry Valley, New York. The quiet and seclusion produced a great burst of creative energy, one result of which was a story called "Alexandra," which later became

# LITERARY AND HISTORICAL CONTEMPORARIES

Willa Cather's famous contemporaries include:

**Theodore Dreiser** (1871–1945): Dreiser was an American author noted for his pioneering works in the naturalist school of writing.

**Sherwood Anderson** (1876–1941): Anderson was an American short-story writer best known for his influential collection, *Winesburg, Ohio* (1919).

**Gertrude Bonnin** (1876–1938): Bonnin, also known as Zitkala-Sa (Red Bird), was a Native American writer best known for her collections of traditional tribal stories.

**Jack London** (1876–1916): London was an American who was a pioneer in commercial magazine fiction; he is best known for his adventure and wilderness stories, particularly *The Call of the Wild*.

**Stanley Vestal** (1877–1957): Vestal was an American author and historian whose works focused on the Old West.

part of *O Pioneers!* (1913), her first successful novel. Cather had found her "quiet centre of life" in childhood memories of the Nebraska prairie, using them and other incidents from her life to create a series of remarkably successful novels.

Until her death in 1947, Cather maintained residences in New York City but frequently traveled to the American West and to Europe, developing a deep emotional attachment to France. From her years at *McClure's* until her death at age seventy-three, she lived with her close friend Edith Lewis.

## Works in Literary Context

Cather stressed the importance of creativity, imagination, and the many forms of love in transcending adversity. As such, her vision has been described as romantic, yet her unadorned and vivid prose style reflects the influence of nineteenth-century realist author Gustave Flaubert. Another strong influence was Henry James, whom Cather considered "the perfect writer." Cather displayed a passionate idealism and a disdain for materialistic aspirations.

*A Sense of Place* Cather was a writer whose work was deeply rooted in a sense of place and at the same time universal in its treatment of theme and character. The corner of earth that she is best known for depicting is the Nebraska where she lived as an adolescent and where she was educated. Cather combined a regional knowledge of Nebraska with an artistic expertise reminiscent of the nineteenth-century literary masters to portray the lives of Old World immigrants on the American Midwestern frontier in a manner that was at once realistic and nobly

heroic. For her, the homesteading German, Danish, Bohemian, and Scandinavian settlers of that region were the embodiment of the artistic and cultural tradition she cherished. In her Nebraskan novels, courage and idealism are juxtaposed with modern materialistic values.

Cather's work is not confined to Nebraska, however. Another large area of her interest is the Southwest, which she discovered and fell in love with when she was thirty-eight and used as the setting for *Death Comes for the Archbishop* (1927), the novel she thought her best, and significant parts of two other novels. Her interest in the Southwest, which includes the people and their culture as well as the land, turned her attention to the history of that region and to history in general. As a result, three of her last four novels are historical reconstructions of the Southwest, Quebec, and Virginia (her native state), and she was at work on a fourth historical novel to be set in medieval France when she died in 1947.

*Disillusionment and Longing for the Past* Like many artists after World War I, Cather was disillusioned by the social and political order of the world. With the publication of *One of Ours* (1922), for which she won the Pulitzer Prize, an underlying mood of hopelessness entered into her novels, as well as a motif stressing the need to escape from contemporary life. Granville Hicks stated that "once [Cather] had created symbols of triumph . . ., but now she concerned herself with symbols of defeat." This pattern appears in such novels as *A Lost Lady* (1923), which chronicles the gradual process of moral degradation in the protagonist Marian Forrester as well as the social decline in America following World War I, and *The Professor's House* (1925), which contrasts the disillusionment of Professor Godfrey St. Peter over his family's materialism with his reminiscences about an idealistic former student who had died in the war.

A despairing tone is absent in *Death Comes for the Archbishop*—an episodic novel fictionalizing the life and achievements of Archbishop Lamy in mid-nineteenth-century New Mexico—and *Shadows on the Rock* (1931)—a tale set in seventeenth-century Quebec—partly because Cather's desire to retreat from the modern world led her, late in her career, to write novels about historic figures to whom she could once again attribute heroic virtues. While some critics have condemned Cather's retreat into the past, others have praised her insight and rejection of what she perceived as a materialistic society. Edward and Lillian Bloom have asserted that "looking backward to the fixed values of a satisfying past, [Cather] reaffirmed the moral standards she cherished, thus ultimately denying they could be destroyed by temporary upheavals."

## Works in Critical Context

Although she began as a short-story writer, critics have long acknowledged that it is Cather's novels that constitute her major contribution to literature. *Alexander's Bridge* (1912), her first novel, was criticized as highly derivative, both in its form and its sophisticated subject matter, due to the author's desire to write in the manner of Henry James. In subsequent works, however, she began to win praise from critics as she returned to the Nebraska background that had provided her with the settings and characters for many of her early stories.

Her critical reputation began to slip later in her life, but she has survived a long period of relative critical neglect by academics. Her fiction has now assured her a place in the American canon as a major novelist unqualified by such tags as "female," "Western," or even "twentieth-century." Some recent commentators have detected political overtones in much of the negative criticism that accompanied the appearance of Cather's last novels. They argue that Cather's blunt condemnation of materialism in such works as *A Lost Lady* (1923) and *The Professor's House* (1925) was interpreted as an endorsement of socialism in the politically sensitive decades of the 1930s and 1940s. For this reason they believe that these books may not have been assessed fairly by critics at the time of their publication, and they are now beginning to reexamine them. Cather's willingness to experiment with new forms, her technical mastery, and the superb prose style evident in these works have generally led recent critics to take a more positive view of them than that held by Cather's contemporaries. Thus, Cather's unique stylistic and thematic contribution to American letters and her importance as an early modernist writer are now widely recognized.

**O Pioneers!** Cather's second novel, *O Pioneers!* (1913), established her reputation as a major novelist. The reviewer for the *Nation* wrote effusively about *O Pioneers!*, "Few American novels of recent years have impressed us so strongly as this." Other reviewers praised her for her skilled treatment of epic themes. Ferris Greenslet, Cather's editor at Houghton Mifflin, appeared to be right when he had told his colleagues that the novel "ought to ... definitely establish the author as a novelist of the first rank."

**One of Ours** Cather's novel about World War I, *One of Ours*, was based on the life of her cousin who was killed in France in 1918 during the Argonne Forest offensive. When this novel, which took Cather four years to write, appeared in 1922, the critical reception was mixed. H. L. Mencken, who had been a great admirer of Cather's earlier novels, wrote that the appearance of John Dos Passos's *Three Soldiers* the year before had changed forever the war novel and, at one blast, had "disposed of oceans of romance and blather." Any subsequent war novel would inevitably be compared to it, and in this comparison he found Cather's novel wanting. By the time *One of Ours* came out, postwar disillusionment had already set in, and any subsequent war novel in which the protagonist dies believing he is saving the world for democracy was doomed to critical disapprobation. Despite some critics considering *One of Ours* a disappointment, the novel was a best-seller and also won the Pulitzer Prize.

---

## COMMON HUMAN EXPERIENCE

Many of Cather's works depict the heroic struggles of immigrants who pioneered the frontier of the Midwest during the nineteenth century. Here are some other works that depict the struggles of pioneers during the same period:

> *Little House on the Prairie* (1935), a novel by Laura Ingalls Wilder. This novel tells the story of a family that moved from the woods of Wisconsin to the plains of Kansas in the years after the Civil War.
> *Centennial* (1975), a novel by James Michener. This historical novel is an epic tale of the land, people, and history of Colorado which centers around the diverse inhabitants of a fictional town called Centennial.
> *Lonesome Dove* (1985), a novel by Larry McMurtry. This novel paints a realistic picture of life on the frontier by chronicling a cattle drive from Texas to Montana.

## Responses to Literature

1. Commentators have noted that although many of Cather's novels and stories are set in Nebraska, they convey universal themes. What are some of the universal themes elicited by Cather in these novels and stories, and in what ways is she able to use the Nebraska setting to highlight these themes and give them broader applicability? Does this specific setting impose any limitations on the themes Cather explores?

2. Cather has been noted for her disapproval of the materialism she saw around her. Has the materialism in American society increased or decreased since Cather's time? In what ways are her writings still applicable as a critique of materialism in America?

3. Cather was highly praised for her early novels but criticized for her later ones. Write a critical essay discussing whether or not Cather deserved this shift in her reputation. Be sure to site specific works.

4. Many of Cather's stories were set in Nebraska, a location she was familiar with from her childhood. Write a story set in a location familiar to you, using the kinds of details and descriptions that Cather used in her stories and novels.

BIBLIOGRAPHY

**Books**

Bennett, Mildred R. *The World of Willa Cather*, revised edition. Lincoln, Nebr.: University of Nebraska Press, 1970.

Bloom, Edward and Lillian. *Willa Cather's Gift of Sympathy*. Carbondale, Ill.: Southern Illinois University Press, 1962.

Brown, E. K. and Leon Edel. *Willa Cather: A Critical Biography.* New York: Knopf, 1953.

Lewis, Edith. *Willa Cather Living.* Lincoln, Nebr.: University of Nebraska Press, 2000.

Shepley, Elizabeth Sergeant. *Willa Cather: A Memoir.* Philadelphia, Pa.: Lippincott, 1953.

O'Brien, Sharon. *Willa Cather: The Emerging Voice.* New York: Oxford University Press, 1987.

Woodress, James. *Willa Cather: A Literary Life.* Lincoln, Nebr.: University of Nebraska Press, 1987.

Lee, Hermione. *Willa Cather: Double Lives.* New York: Pantheon, 1990.

Gerber, Philip L. *Willa Cather.* Boston: Twayne, 1975.

Stouck, David. *Willa Cather's Imagination.* Lincoln, Nebr.: University of Nebraska Press, 1975.

# ✸ Lorna Dee Cervantes

BORN: *1954, San Francisco, California*

NATIONALITY: *American, Latino-American*

GENRE: *Poetry*

MAJOR WORKS:

*Emplumada* (1981)

*From the Cables of Genocide* (1991)

## Overview

Lorna Dee Cervantes is a Chicana—or female Mexican American—poet whose works are characterized by simplicity of language and boldness of imagery. Her poetry offers commentary on class and sex roles and evokes the cultural clashes faced by many Mexican Americans.

## Works in Biographical and Historical Context

*An Early Start in Poetry* Lorna Dee Cervantes was born into an economically deprived family of Mexican and American heritage on August 6, 1954, in the Mission District of San Francisco. Her parents separated when she was five, and she moved with her mother and brother to San Jose to live with her grandmother. As a child, she discovered the world of books in the houses which her mother cleaned. First she read Shakespeare, then the English Romantic poets. By the time she was twelve, she was reading Byron, Keats, and Shelley over and over aloud, getting a feel for the cadence of the English language.

At home her fascination with the rhythmic possibilities of language were further enhanced through the music of her brother, Steve Cervantes, who later became

Lorna Dee Cervantes  *Francisco J. Dominguez, copyright 2007*

a professional musician. She began writing poetry when she was eight years old. She published some of her earliest poems in her high school's newspaper; these poems were eventually published in a magazine after Cervantes had established her career as a writer.

*Achieving Recognition* In 1974, Cervantes gave her first poetry reading at the Quinto Festival de los Teatros Chicanos in Mexico City, Mexico. The poem she read that day, "Barco de refugiados" ("Refugee Ship"), was published in *El Heraldo*, a Mexico City newspaper. The following year, several of her poems appeared in the *Revista Chicano-Riqueña*, and she began contributing verse to other periodicals as well.

That same year, Cervantes began to devote her full attention to writing and to helping other writers. She learned the trade of printing and, with her savings, bought herself an offset printing press. One of her projects was *Mango*, a literary review which she edited. Through her association with the Centro Cultural de la Gente (People's Cultural Center) of San Jose and through Mango Publications she soon began to publish chapbooks of the work of Chicano writers. By 1978, she was beginning to gain national recognition. That year she received a grant from the National Endowment for the Arts. The following year she spent nine months at the Fine Arts Workshop in Provincetown, Massachusetts, where she completed the manuscript for *Emplumada* (1981).

*Life Changes* Since the publication of *Emplumada*, Cervantes has undergone major transformations in her life. In 1982, her mother was brutally killed in San Jose. In a 1986 interview she said, "I had no more poetry left. I thought I had given it up forever." However, after a long period of grief and introspection, she resumed control of her life. She finished her B.A. from California State University at San Jose in 1984, and in 1990, she finished a Ph.D. at the University of California, Santa Cruz, where she studied philosophy and aesthetics. She then went on to teach creative writing at the University of Colorado in Denver and to edit *Red Dirt*, a magazine of multicultural literature. Although she remains active as an editor and mentor for other writers, she has published only one other collection, *From the Cables of Genocide* (1991).

## Works in Literary Context

Cervantes has the distinction of being one of only a few Mexican-American poets to have been published by a major publishing company. The predominant themes in her poetry include cultural and social conflict, oppression of women and minorities, and alienation from one's roots. Cervantes's poetry is well crafted and has the distinction of using highly lyrical language while at the same time being direct and powerful.

*Alienation and Social Conflict* Cervantes' work, according to Marta Ester Sánchez in *Contemporary Chicana*

*Poetry: A Critical Approach to an Emerging Literature*, is characterized by "two conflicting but central positions." In Cervantes's poetry, the critic finds both a "desire for an idealized, utopian world" and "a realistic perspective that sees a world fraught with social problems." The tension created between these two perspectives is a central element in understanding Cervantes's work.

Some commentators note that the alienation Cervantes feels as a Chicana in an Anglo society is evident in pieces such as "Poem for the Young White Man Who Asked Me How I, An Intelligent Well-Read Person, Could Believe in the War Between Races" and "Visions of Mexico While at a Writing Symposium in Port Townsend, Washington." Marta Ester Sánchez notes that in the first poem, Cervantes explains her feelings at having a "subordinate place in society as Chicana, as woman, and as poet." In the second, which deals with the theme of migration and opposing societal values, Roberta Fernandez concludes in the *Dictionary of Literary Biography* that Cervantes "comes to terms with herself, finding resolution for the many conflicts in her life and in her role as poet."

*Lyrical Language* Marta Ester Sánchez asserts that Cervantes writes in two different modes: "the narrative, discursive, 'hard' mode to communicate the real, divisive world she knows as a Chicana; the lyrical, imagistic, 'soft' mode to evoke contemplative and meditative moods." Critics have noted that she is able to combine these two

# COMMON HUMAN EXPERIENCE

Cervantes often writes of the difficulties faced by Mexican-American women facing sexism and oppression both from within and from outside their culture. Here are some other works that explore similar problems:

*The Mixquiahuala Letters* (1986), a novel by Ana Castillo. This novel, written in the form of letters from one woman to another, explores the painful realities of life for a Mexican-American woman.

*When I Was Puerto Rican* (1994), a memoir by Esmeralda Santiago. This memoir tells the story of a young girl uprooted from her home in Puerto Rico and sent to live with her grandmother in New York, where she must learn to survive in an alien world.

*The Last of the Menu Girls* (2004), short stories by Denise Chavez. This collection of stories is unified around a single character, who focuses on an exploration of Hispanic culture and inter-cultural relations in modern New Mexico.

modes, using lyrical language to communicate such real-world difficulties as poverty, sexism, and cultural conflict. As one commentator notes, "Cervantes's poetry is very well crafted and has the distinction of using highly lyrical language while at the same time being direct and powerful."

## Works in Critical Context

Cervantes has produced two well-received collections of poetry, and she is considered by some to be Mexico's premier poet. Critics applaud her emotionally-charged and evocative verse as well as her support for women and minorities. She has been recognized for her contribution to Mexican-American poetry by the Lila-Wallace Reader's Digest Foundation Writer's Award for outstanding Chicana literature.

*Emplumada*   Most of the commentary on Cervantes's work focuses on her first collection, *Emplumada* (1981), the best-selling title in the University of Pittsburgh's prestigious poetry series. This work established her as an up-and-coming poet whose power could be found in a combination of energy and intelligence. As Frances Whyatt writes, "when she's at her best the poems give off an infectious energy remarkably free from artifice and intellectuality, and yet deceptively intelligent."

In discussing the poems in this collection, Cordelia Candelaria points out that Cervantes uses a distinctive narrator in her poems to achieve "the intimacy reminiscent of Confessional Poetry," a movement originating in the 1950s in which poets revealed difficulties from their own lives. As Whyatt puts it, Cervantes views "her own life as a

journalist might, as a base from which to record nature and events in a particular landscape." Patricia Wallace emphasizes the importance for Cervantes of witnessing "the pressures of particular, historical reality." The work of a poet like Cervantes, Wallace writes, "cannot be separated from the conditions of race, sex and class" which inform all of her writings. Marta Ester Sánchez emphasizes the importance of Cervantes's ethnic background, arguing that as a poet, Cervantes acts "as a mediator between the Chicano community and the larger English-speaking audience."

## Responses to Literature

1. Cervantes is noted for exploring themes of cultural and social conflict. What are some of the specific conflicts that she explores? What kinds of direction does she indicate, if any, for resolving these conflicts?

2. Cervantes has spent much of her career editing and promoting the writings of poets from a number of different cultural and ethnic backgrounds. Are the influences of other cultures besides Mexico and America evident in her poetry? In what ways can she be seen not simply as a Mexican-American poet but as a multicultural writer?

3. Commentators note that Cervantes often writes in the confessional mode. Write an essay that defines confessionalism and explores the strengths and weaknesses of this mode for the kind of socially-conscious poetry that Cervantes produces.

4. Cervantes often writes about specific social problems that she has witnessed or experienced. Using her poetry as a model, write a poem or poems about a social problem about which you are particularly concerned, either because of your personal experience or as a result of issues you have come to be aware of.

BIBLIOGRAPHY

**Books**

Buck, Claire, ed. *The Bloomsbury Guide to Women's Literature*. New York: Prentice Hall, 1992.

Candelaria, Cordelia. *Chicano Poetry: A Critical Introduction*. Westport, Conn.: Greenwood Press, 1986.

Ikas, Karin. *Chicana Ways: Conversations with Ten Chicana Writers*. Reno, Nev.: University of Nevada Press, 2002.

Madsen, Deborah L. *Understanding Contemporary Chicana Literature*. Columbia, S.C.: University of South Carolina Press, 2000.

Sánchez, Marta Ester. *Contemporary Chicana Poetry*. Berkeley, Calif.: University of California Press, 1985.

**Periodicals**

Brinson-Curiel, Barbara. "Our Own Words: *Emplumada*." *Tecolote* (December 1982): 8.

"Cervantes, Lorna Dee (1954–)." *DISCovering Multicultural America*. Detroit: Gale, 2003.

"Freeway 280." *EXPLORING Poetry*. Detroit: Gale, 2003.

Gonzalez, Ray. "I Trust Only What I Have Built with My Own Hands: An Interview with Lorna Dee Cervantes." *Bloomsbury Review* (Sept–Oct 1997): 3, 8.

Monda, Bernadette. "Interview with Lorna Dee Cervantes." *Third Woman* (1984): 103–107.

Rodriguez y Gibson, Eliza. "Love, Hunger, and Grace: Loss and Belonging in the Poetry of Lorna Dee Cervantes and Joy Harjo." *Legacy: A Journal of American Women Writers* (2002): 106–114.

Seator, Lynette. "*Emplumada*: Chicana Rites-of-Passages." *MELUS* (Summer 1984): 23–38.

Wallace, Patricia. "Divided Loyalties: Literal and Literary in the Poetry of Lorna Dee Cervantes, Cathy Song and Rita Dove." *MELUS* (Fall 1993): 3–19.

Whyatt, Frances. "A review of *Emplumada*." *American Book Review* (July/August 1982): 11–12.

# ✸ Michael Chabon

BORN: *1963, Washington, D.C.*

NATIONALITY: *American*

GENRE: *Fiction*

MAJOR WORKS:

*Wonder Boys* (1995)

*The Amazing Adventures of Kavalier and Clay* (2000)

*The Yiddish Policemen's Union* (2007)

Michael Chabon   *Ulf Andersen / Getty Images*

## Overview

Michael Chabon is a highly accomplished novelist, short-story writer, children's fantasy novelist, and screenwriter. Chabon, who consistently exalts the imagination in creating worlds that nourish the spiritual lives of human beings, explores a diversity of recurring themes, including coming of age, nostalgia and memory, family conflicts, love, the growth of the artist, friendship, Edenic happiness, and wasteland desolation.

## Works in Biographical and Historical Context

*A Stellar Start*   Chabon was born in Washington, D.C., on May 24, 1963. His father, Robert, is a physician, lawyer, and hospital administrator; his mother, Sharon, is a retired lawyer. Chabon graduated from the University of Pittsburgh with a B.A. in English in 1984 and earned an M.F.A. at the University of California, Irvine, in 1987, where he worked with novelist and critic Donald Heiney (who wrote fiction under the name MacDonald Harris). He also married poet Lollie Groth in 1987.

After he won a short-story contest with *Mademoiselle* in that same year, he wrote his master's thesis, *The Mysteries of Pittsburgh* (1988); his advisor, Heiney, was so impressed that he sent the manuscript to Mary Evans, a literary agent at the Virginia Barber Agency in New York City. Evans sold the book to William Morrow Publishers for $155,000 at a private auction—one of the highest figures ever paid for a first novel by a virtually unknown author.

*The Mysteries of Pittsburgh* made Chabon instantly famous in the highly competitive world of New York publishing. It became a commercial best-seller praised by most members of the critical and academic establishments. Chabon followed his debut novel with a collection of short stories, *A Model World and Other Stories* (1991). These stories were written and published between 1987 and 1990, mostly in *The New Yorker* but also in *Gentleman's Quarterly* and *Mademoiselle*. Because of the phenomenal success of both his novel and the new collection, Chabon received a substantial advance from his publisher to work on his next novel, tentatively titled "Fountain City." By the time he received the advance, he had been working on "Fountain City" for two years, but the project seemed to be going nowhere. His domestic life was in

# LITERARY AND HISTORICAL CONTEMPORARIES

Chabon's famous contemporaries include:

**Rick Bragg** (1959–): Bragg is an American journalist and memoir-writer who won the Pulitzer Prize for Feature Writing in 1996.

**Barack Obama** (1961–): Obama is an American politician who in 2008 became the first African American to be elected as president of the United States.

**A. M. Homes** (1961–): Homes is an American novelist and short-story writer noted for writing controversial and unusual tales about seemingly ordinary people.

**Bret Easton Ellis** (1964–): Ellis is an American author who is often referred to as a member of the literary Brat Pack that came of age in the 1980s.

**J. K. Rowling** (1965–): Rowling is a British children's writer best known for creating the Harry Potter series of fantasy books.

upheaval; he was divorced in 1991, lived with another woman, and met and married Ayelet Waldman, a lawyer, in 1993. He also moved six times. After five years and an endlessly elaborating plot, he began to see that his book had no center and no direction. His editor at Morrow kept encouraging him, until Chabon had written 1500 pages yet still did not have a publishable manuscript.

*Turning Things Around*   Chabon threw away "Fountain City" and drew on his experiences to write his second novel, *Wonder Boys*, a story about a writer's inability to come up with a worthy successor to his early hit, which many consider a thinly veiled autobiography. With the publication of *Wonder Boys*, Chabon was able to settle into writing again. He has since written several more novels, including a Pulitzer Prize winner, along with several collections of short stories. He now lives with his second wife and their four children in Berkeley, California.

## Works in Literary Context

Few contemporary American fiction writers begin their literary careers with such public notoriety as Michael Chabon gained with his best-selling first novel, *The Mysteries of Pittsburgh*, which made him wildly successful at the age of twenty-four. Though he has been grouped with other popular young authors in their twenties, such as Bret Easton Ellis, Tama Janowitz, and Jay McInerney, Chabon's work could never be mistaken for their consciously minimalistic style, dark subject matter, and social criticism, or their pessimistic view of the materialistic downside of the American Dream. Chabon himself feels he shares little with the so-called literary Brat Pack: "I never thought I had any connection with 'the usual suspects' .... I was

23. I thought in terms of what I had in common with Cheever, Nabokov or Flaubert when they were 23. I had high aims."

*Tackling Serious Themes*   Even as early as his first novel, written in his early twenties, Chabon examined some of the most serious themes of contemporary American literature: how people, consciously or unconsciously, assume fictive roles they then live in; the importance of sexual identity in discovering the heart's true desire; that genuine spiritual transformation always involves pain and suffering; and that an honest life consists of a continuous process of identifying and exposing one's most confounding mysteries. In his next two novels, Chabon explored other serious themes, such as the power of the imagination to produce art and to create ways of escape from both physical and spiritual death, and the fall from innocence to experience.

*Mythologizing the Commonplace*   All of Chabon's novels can be viewed as psychological, spiritual, and mythic journeys that seek to create meaning and significance in an existentially empty world. What unites all of them is that Chabon frequently uses Cheever's favorite fictional technique, "mythologizing the commonplace." His ability to mythologize the activities of seemingly ordinary people is most apparent in his young adult novel, *Summerland* (2002), which has many of the characteristics of what mythologist Joseph Campbell calls the mythological journey of the hero: the call to adventure, the road of trials and dangers, the search for the father, and the hero's attempt to save the world from imminent collapse into a wasteland condition.

## Works in Critical Context

Before the publication of his Pulitzer Prize-winning third novel, *The Amazing Adventures of Kavalier and Clay* (2000), Chabon had won over critics and the reading public with his well-paced plots, charming characters, and inventive prose, but it was with *Kavalier and Clay* that Chabon was hailed as a major voice in contemporary American fiction. *Commentary* reviewer John Podhoretz termed Chabon "an uncommonly good writer, perhaps the best prose stylist of his generation." Many critics have characterized Chabon's writing as elegant, vividly descriptive, polished, and sophisticatedly fluid, likening his work to that of writers such as John Updike, John Cheever, or even F. Scott Fitzgerald.

*The Mysteries of Pittsburgh*   Chabon had come to the attention of critics with the publication of his first novel, *The Mysteries of Pittsburgh*. This debut garnered approving reviews for Chabon, and the book remained on the *Publisher's Weekly* best-seller list for many weeks. Chabon was particularly praised for the book's humor and breezy style. A *Time* magazine review calls it a "bright, funny, mannered first novel," a book whose "pages bounce along amusingly," while the *Pittsburgh Press* review calls it a "very funny and very eloquent book—a book that both earns and wears easily such adjectives as 'brilliant'." A *Cosmopolitan* magazine reviewer writes, "A very daring, vivid and exciting book."

### The Amazing Adventures of Kavalier and Clay

The publication of *The Amazing Adventures of Kavalier and Clay*, Chabon's third novel, elevated his literary reputation into the most prestigious ranks of contemporary American novelists primarily because it won him a Pulitzer Prize in 2001. Critics were, for the most part, ecstatic in their praise of its thematic range and depth. James Sullivan declares in *Book*, "Once again Chabon proves himself a master stylist, capable of capturing an entire epoch in a few microscopic observations," while Troy Patterson of *Entertainment Weekly* writes, "Chabon's got an eye for the spine-tingling image and a near-perfect ear." Sarah Coleman of the *San Francisco Chronicle* sums up critical opinion when she writes that "every risk Chabon takes pays off." Chabon was particularly praised for his ability to capture the detail of 1940s New York. Ken Kalfus of the *New York Times* writes, "In Chabon's telling, pre-war New York, freeing itself from the shackles of the Depression, abounds with raw, confident energy."

### Responses to Literature

1. Chabon's second novel, *Wonder Boys*, was partly based on his own experiences as a successful writer struggling to produce a new book. In what ways does this book provide answers for other writers about how to avoid this problem, and is Chabon's guidance here useful for other writers?

2. Critics have noted that one of Chabon's recurring themes is the power of art and the imagination to help people transcend everyday experience. In what ways does Chabon demonstrate this power? What types of transcendence do his books demonstrate and promise? In what ways, if any, can the lessons from his works be put into practice in real life?

3. Some commentators have remarked that *Kavalier and Clay*, based on the life of two comic-book writers, could have been a comic book series itself. Write the outline and dialogue for a comic book based on a sequence from that novel.

4. Chabon has said that he attempts to mythologize the commonplace. Choose one of his novels or short stories and write an analytical essay discussing the mythological nature of the work. Be sure to compare the elements of Chabon's mythologized version to some familiar myths or legends.

BIBLIOGRAPHY

**Periodicals**

Coleman, Sarah. "More Powerful Than a Locomotive, Michael Chabon's Ambitious New Novel Is Inspired by the True Story of Two Teenagers Who Created Superman." *San Francisco Chronicle* (October 1, 2000): RV1.

Fowler, Douglas. "The Short Fiction of Michael Chabon: Nostalgia in the Very Young." *Studies in Short Fiction* (Winter 1995): 75–83.

Gorra, Michael. "Youth and Consequences." *New Republic* (June 26, 1995): 40–41.

Hearon, Shelby. "Novel Complications: Michael Chabon's 'Wildly Funny' Tale of a Problem-Plagued Writer's Final Fling." *Chicago Tribune Books* (April 2, 1995): 5.

Levi, Jonathan. "Hope Against Hope." *Los Angeles Times Book Review* (October 8, 2000): 2.

See, Lisa. "Michael Chabon: Wonder Boy in Transition." *Publishers Weekly* (April 10, 1995): 44–45.

Tallent, Elizabeth. "The Pleasure of His Company." *Los Angeles Times Book Review* (June 9, 1991): 3, 8.

Ybarra, Michael. "The Novelist as Wonder Boy." *Los Angeles Times* (October 9, 2000): E1, E4.

## ✺ Raymond Chandler

BORN: *1886, Chicago, Illinois*

DIED: *1959, La Jolla, California*

NATIONALITY: *American*

GENRE: *Fiction*

MAJOR WORKS:

*The Big Sleep* (1939)
*Farewell, My Lovely* (1940)
*The Long Goodbye* (1953)

---

### COMMON HUMAN EXPERIENCE

Chabon's first novel, *The Mysteries of Pittsburgh*, was hailed as one of the best coming-of-age tales ever written. Here are some other highly regarded coming-of-age novels:

*This Side of Paradise* (1920), a novel by F. Scott Fitzgerald. This novel tells the story of a young man living a frivolous and disillusioning life in post-World War I America.
*The Catcher in the Rye* (1951), a novel by J. D. Salinger. This novel follows the hapless adventures of Holden Caulfield in the days following his expulsion from another in a long string of exclusive private schools.
*Bright Lights, Big City* (1984), a novel by Jay McInerney. This novel chronicles the adventures and escapism of a young literary hopeful caught up in the fast lane of the mid-1980s.

Raymond Chandler  *Ralph Crane / Time Life Pictures / Getty Images*

## Overview

Raymond Chandler has been placed at the forefront of American crime novelists, mainly because of his novels about the fictional detective Philip Marlowe. He took up the tradition of the hard-boiled detective story from Dashiell Hammett and carried it further, adding a distinctive style, a biting wit, and a concern for descriptive detail that enabled his writing to transcend the formulaic constraints of the detective genre to leave a lasting legacy to American literature.

## Works in Biographical and Historical Context

*A European Education*   Chandler was born in Chicago on July 23, 1888. When he was seven years old, his parents divorced and he was taken by his mother to his grandmother and an unmarried aunt in South London. He attended Dulwich College, acquiring a thorough classical education and taking a particular interest in languages. Among those he studied were Latin, French, German, Armenian, and Hungarian.

In 1905, at the age of seventeen, Chandler left Dulwich to study modern languages on the European mainland. He spent six months in Paris, taking classes in commercial French at a business college, then moved on to Munich, Germany, where he worked with a private tutor. When he returned to England in 1907, he became a naturalized British subject, passed the civil service examination, and

took a clerkship in the supply and accounting departments of the Admiralty. Chandler had literary ambitions, and he hoped that the easy hours in the civil service would allow him time to write on the side. He detested the bureaucratic atmosphere, however, and resigned after six months.

*Back to the United States*   For the next three years, Chandler tried unsuccessfully to make a career as a London man of letters. He worked briefly as a reporter for the *Daily Express*, from which he was fired, then wrote as a freelancer for the *Westminster Gazette*, contributing poems, satirical sketches, and short articles on European affairs. In 1911, he began contributing essays and reviews to *The Academy*, a London literary weekly, but in 1912, he decided he had no future as a London writer.

Chandler next moved to Los Angeles, where he worked odd jobs, including stringing tennis rackets and picking apricots. In 1913, he enrolled in a night-school bookkeeping course and got a job as an accountant. When the United States declared war on Germany in 1917, Chandler enlisted with the Canadian, not the U.S., army. He was sent to the front lines in France, but only a few months later, he was transferred to the Royal Air Force (RAF) for training as a pilot. He remained in England for the rest of the war, which ended before he completed flight school. Following his discharge in 1919, Chandler returned to the U.S. again and spent some time in the Pacific Northwest, where he made another abortive attempt at a writing career. He worked briefly for a British bank in San Francisco and then returned to Los Angeles.

There, Chandler became involved in an affair with Cissy Pascal, the wife of a friend, and by July she had filed for a divorce from her husband. She was forty-eight and Chandler was only thirty-one. In the early 1920s, Chandler took a job as a bookkeeper for the Dabney Oil Syndicate, which was thriving in the midst of the Los Angeles oil boom. He did well with the company, being promoted to auditor and then vice president. A month after the death of his mother from cancer in January 1924, Chandler married Cissy. He continued in his business career, earning $1,000 a month—the equivalent of a modern salary of more than $100,000 a year. He also began drinking heavily, behaving erratically, and having affairs with the younger women who worked in his office. In 1932, after receiving warnings and reprimands, he was fired from his job.

*Another Attempt at a Literary Career*   Chandler turned to fiction writing to earn a living, choosing the detective pulp market, in part because he could get paid while learning his craft, and in part because he thought the form had potential for forceful and honest writing. He used the Los Angeles area, with which he had grown familiar, as the setting for most of his works. His first short story, "Blackmailers Don't Shoot" (1933), was published by *Black Mask*, the most prestigious of the detective pulps. He spent the next six years writing for *Black Mask* and other detective magazines.

In the spring of 1938, Chandler began working on his first novel, *The Big Sleep*, which introduced the detective and narrator Philip Marlowe. The story is drawn from two of his *Black Mask* novelettes, "Killer in the Rain" and "The Curtain," along with a small portion of a story called "Finger Man"—a process he called "cannibalization." Chandler did not cut and paste passages but rather rewrote entire scenes, in the process tightening his prose and enriching his descriptions. The novel took only three months to complete, and it was published by Alfred A. Knopf in February 1939.

**Critical and Commercial Success** By the time Chandler had published his third novel in 1942, he had established himself as one of the leading American detective novelists, but the 1940s mystery market was commercially limited. Detective writers depended primarily upon hardback sales for their income, and sales of a mystery novel seldom topped ten thousand copies. The paperback industry was still in its infancy, and it would not become an important market until after the war ended. At age fifty-five, Chandler had been writing professionally for ten years and was at the top of his form, yet his income was only a few thousand dollars a year.

Because of this, Chandler, like many other novelists during the 1930s and 1940s—including F. Scott Fitzgerald and William Faulkner—turned to Hollywood screenwriting to earn the income his books could not produce. Chandler's career as a screenwriter was a mixture of success and frustration. Chandler recognized the artistic potential of movies and applied himself to learning the craft, but he chafed against the structure of the studio system and the superficiality of movie people. He despised actors, agents, and money men and considered many of the industry's business practices to be dishonest and corrupt. Most of all, he disliked the limits on his independence as a writer. Chandler desired freedom from deadlines and a chance to work with the few directors and producers whom he respected.

**Breaking with Hollywood** By the late 1940s, Chandler was easing himself out of the screenwriting business. His break from Hollywood was made possible, in part, by the development of the American paperback publishing industry, which was flourishing in the postwar book market. Although Chandler published no new fiction during his screenwriting years, his first four novels were all widely reprinted in paperback editions in both England and the United States. Chandler began earning additional royalties on past work when Avon brought out three paperback collections of his pulp stories.

During these years Chandler resumed drinking heavily. He was becoming increasingly aware of his own aging—his wife was now in her seventies—and reacted with periods of melancholy and womanizing. In 1946, Chandler and his wife moved to La Jolla. Their life there was quiet, almost reclusive; they had few friends and seldom made social engagements. Because of his growing commercial success,

Chandler found himself devoting more and more time to business matters—keeping tax records, negotiating the sale of translation or reprint rights, arranging for a Philip Marlowe radio and television series–and was often distracted from his writing. He did eventually produce his sixth novel, *The Long Goodbye* (1953), which is widely considered his best work. The book deals, in part, with Marlowe watching over an alcoholic, suicidal writer whose drinking binges interfere with his completion of a book promised to his publisher—an ominous parallel to events in Chandler's life.

**Declining Productivity and Health** Soon after the publication of *The Long Goodbye*, Cissy Chandler's health worsened. She had been ill with heart and respiratory trouble for some time and spent much of the summer of 1954 in the hospital, where she was diagnosed with fibrosis of the lungs and confined to an oxygen tent. She died on December 12. Chandler was devastated by her death. He began drinking heavily, and in February of 1955 attempted suicide. He was put in the county hospital initially and then spent six days in a private sanatorium. After his release, Chandler decided to leave California. He went briefly to New York, and then sailed for England. During the last four years of his life Chandler divided his time between England and the United States. In London he was treated as a celebrity and established a circle of acquaintances that included writers, artists, and critics. He also suffered from depression and continued his excessive drinking, which on several occasions resulted in his being hospitalized. Despite this, Chandler still completed another Marlowe novel, *Playback* (1958).

During the last year of his life Chandler struggled with alcoholism and poor health, spending a large amount of time in hospitals and clinics. Chandler became involved in the personal affairs of his Australian-born secretary, who was in the process of divorcing her husband; the situation sapped his money and his spirits. The matter led to conflicts with several of his friends, including his agent Helga Greene, and a dispute over who would be named the beneficiary of his will. In February 1959, Chandler was hospitalized in La Jolla, and while recuperating, proposed marriage to Helga Greene. She accepted. They planned to move back to London, but Chandler's health did not permit it. He made a brief trip to New York to accept the presidency of the Mystery Writers of America—an honorary post—then returned to La Jolla and became ill with pneumonia. He died in the Scripps Clinic on March 26, 1959. He left an unfinished Marlowe novel, known as "The Poodle Springs Story," which was posthumously completed by mystery writer Robert Parker and published thirty years after Chandler's death, in 1989.

## Works in Literary Context

Upon the publication of his first novel, *The Big Sleep* (1939), Raymond Chandler was hailed as one of the

## LITERARY AND HISTORICAL CONTEMPORARIES

Raymond Chandler's famous contemporaries include:

**Franz Kafka** (1882–1924): Kafka was a Jewish writer born in Prague whose stories and novels depict a nightmarish world of bureaucracy and alienation.

**James Joyce** (1882–1941): Joyce was an Irish writer known for groundbreaking works such as *Ulysses* (1922) and *Finnegans Wake* (1939).

**Sinclair Lewis** (1885–1951): Lewis was an American author best known for his realism and his stories that were critical of capitalism and American society; in 1930, he became the first American author to win the Nobel Prize in Literature.

**Eugene O'Neill** (1888–1953): O'Neill was an American playwright who pioneered realism in dramatic theater; he was awarded the Nobel Prize in Literature in 1936.

**Dashiell Hammett** (1894–1961): Hammett was an American author who wrote detective stories; he is best known as the creator of the character Sam Spade.

leading practitioners of the American hard-boiled detective novel, but he received virtually no recognition as a writer of serious literature. During the course of his career his reputation slowly grew, first in England and then in the United States. He did not begin to receive academic attention until after his death, but today his books are studied in classrooms not only as premier examples of the detective novel but also as important works of twentieth-century American literature.

Few of Chandler's critics have connected his work with that of modernist writers such as Ernest Hemingway, F. Scott Fitzgerald, E. E. Cummings, and Ezra Pound, perhaps because Chandler did not publish his first novel until 1939, long after the modernist movement had crested. He was, nevertheless, of the same generation as most of the Paris expatriates and other experimental writers of the 1920s. He shared the same upbringing in a culture of strict Victorian morality, witnessed trench warfare firsthand, and was greatly disillusioned after World War I was over. His writing explores some of the same themes as his fellow modernists: the corruption of society, a search for moral standards and codes of conduct, and the need to find order amid chaos.

*Literary Mysteries* Raymond Chandler elevated the genre known as the hard-boiled detective story into an American art form. Throughout his career, Chandler attempted to remove his writings from the formulaic suspense of detective fiction, to the extent that he is often considered an excellent novelist but a rather lame mystery writer. This estimate of Chandler's literary value is per-

haps best expressed by W. H. Auden, himself a devotee of mysteries, who maintained that Chandler's books should be evaluated "as works of art."

Chandler's novels describe luridly realistic action in a sophisticated literary style uncommon to pulp mystery fiction. He wanted to treat genuine mysteries which do not lend themselves to the solutions of deductive reasoning, and added an element of fantasy to his work in order to suggest, as he put it, "the country behind the hill." At the same time, his detective hero Philip Marlowe operates in a world of banal corruption and commercialized living. For many readers Chandler's books represent the essence of southern California: the superficialities of Hollywood, crime and vice glossed over with wealth, the cult of glamour, and a certain enduring mystery which eludes precise definition.

*Self-Aware Tough Guys* One of Chandler's hallmarks was his incorporation of wit and irony into his writing. The detective-narrators of Chandler's stories use wit to shield themselves against excessive emotion and sentimentality, responding with a wisecrack rather than revealing how they genuinely feel. Much of the heroes' toughness, furthermore, is a product, not of physical action, but of dialogue. They engage in sarcastic banter with criminals and cops, using humor to show resolve or to refuse to divulge important information. Chandler's detectives are self-aware, realizing that their hard-boiled exterior is merely a pose—a carryover from the author's own self-awareness: Chandler knew that his stories walked a fine line between believability and cliché. He had a tendency to burlesque the hard-boiled conventions even while conforming to them, and this tension—between the tough-guy persona and ironic self-awareness—forms the foundation of his narrative style.

## Works in Critical Context

Chandler was initially confined by reviewers to the detective genre, but starting in the mid-1940s, some influential British journalists and intellectuals, including Leonard Russell, Elizabeth Bowen, W. H. Auden, Alistair Cooke, and J. B. Priestley, had discovered Chandler's novels and began arguing for his literary value. By the mid-1950s, their arguments were widely accepted in England, and Chandler was being read and discussed, not as a detective writer, but as an important literary novelist. This view has since come to dominant commentary on Chandler, who is considered one of America's great authors, not merely one of its great detective writers.

*The Big Sleep* Chandler's first novel, *The Big Sleep*, in which he introduces the detective and narrator Philip Marlowe, was a commercial success by the standards of the detective genre. The book was widely reviewed, but it was segregated to columns dedicated to mystery fiction, and the reviews focused not on the literary merits of the novel, but rather on the toughness of its tone and material. Isaac Anderson of *The New York Times* notes, "Most of the characters in this story are tough, many of them are nasty and some of them are both .... As a study in depravity, the story is excellent, with Marlowe standing out as almost the only fundamentally decent person in it." The anonymous mystery critic for *Time* reviewed the entire novel in a single sentence: "Detective Marlowe is plunged into a mess of murderers, thugs and psychopaths who make the characters of Dashiell Hammett and James Cain look like something out of Godey's Lady's Book."

Reviewers in Britain, where Chandler first gained respect as a literary writer, were equally dismissive. Nicholas Blake of *The Spectator* wrote that *The Big Sleep* "is American and very, very tough after the *Thin Man* fashion. Almost everyone in the book is wonderfully decadent, and the author spares us no blushes to point out just how decadent they are." These notices are less indicative of the reaction to Chandler than they are of the reviewers' attitudes toward detective fiction, which was considered an escapist form not worthy of serious critical attention. It would be another decade before Chandler began receiving recognition as a writer of serious literature.

***The Long Goodbye*** Chandler's last major work, *The Long Goodbye*, was an occasion for the author to extend the possibilities of the mystery genre, developing its capacity for social and psychological analysis, and expanding the role of the detective. The British response to *The Long Goodbye* was even more enthusiastic than to his previous books and showed that Chandler had developed a considerable literary reputation in England. J. Maclaren Ross of the *London Sunday Times* comments in his review,

> Mr. Raymond Chandler, whose early work belonged superficially to the *genre* popularised by Dashiell Hammett, has become, during recent years, the object of an ecstatic cult among intellectuals in both hemispheres. From the basic pattern of the American crime story outlined by his predecessors, he has evolved a highly personal vision of a jungle world ruled by racketeers and rich megalomaniacs.

The American reception of *The Long Goodbye* was less warm. Though it was given an Edgar Award from the Mystery Writers of America, the reviews of the novel were mixed. Anthony Boucher of *The New York Times Book Review* praised the story, writing, "Perhaps the longest private-eye novel ever written (over 125,000 words!), it is also one of the best—and may well attract readers who normally shun even the leaders in the field." The reviewer for *The New Yorker* found fault, arguing that "Mr. Chandler has practically abandoned anything resembling a coherent plot to devote himself to an exhaustive study of manners and mores in California ... the story ... hardly seems worth all the bother."

## Responses to Literature

1. Commentators have noted that Philip Marlowe underwent a psychological development throughout Chandler's seven Marlowe novels. What changes

---

### COMMON HUMAN EXPERIENCE

Chandler was one of the most influential mystery novelists of all time, transforming the mold of the detective story by introducing new conventions and narrative styles. Here are some other detective novels that have been similarly influential:

*The Maltese Falcon* (1930), a novel by Dashiell Hammett. This novel features Sam Spade, a hard-boiled detective whose detachment can be seen in future detective-hero characters.

*The Talented Mr. Ripley* (1955), a novel by Patricia Highsmith. This novel introduces the shifting and mysterious character of Tom Ripley, who assumes another man's identity in order to improve his fortunes.

*The Grifters* (1963), a novel by Jim Thompson. This novel was one of the pioneering works in the con-artist genre, combining elements of the film-noir style of hard-boiled detective with intricate plot twists and unpredictable mystery.

---

characterize this development, and in what ways do these changes reflect a maturity in Chandler's writing style?

2. During his lifetime, Chandler was both relegated to the status of genre-writer and elevated to the status of a literary author. He has since been hailed as a literary writer by most critics and commentators. In what ways does Chandler deserve this reputation, and in what ways does he still deserve to be thought of as an author belonging to the narrower detective genre?

3. Several of Chandler's novels were adapted into feature-length films. Choose one of these adaptations and write a review of the film version that compares and contrasts the film with the book.

4. Chandler was heavily influenced by the writing of Dashiell Hammett, particularly by Hammett's detective character Sam Spade. Write an essay that compares and contrasts Sam Spade and Philip Marlowe. Pay particular attention to the ways that Chandler followed Hammett's lead but went further in the same direction.

BIBLIOGRAPHY

**Books**

Clark, Al. *Raymond Chandler in Hollywood*. New York: Proteus, 1982.

Durham, Philip. *Down These Mean Streets a Man Must Go: Raymond Chandler's Knight*. Chapel Hill, N.C.: University of North Carolina Press, 1963.

Gross, Miriam, ed. *The World of Raymond Chandler*. London: Weidenfeld & Nicolson, 1977.

Hiney, Tom. *Raymond Chandler: A Biography*. New York: Atlantic Monthly Press, 1997.

Luhr, William. *Raymond Chandler and Film*. New York: Ungar, 1982.

MacShane, Frank. *The Life of Raymond Chandler*. New York: Dutton, 1976.

Marling, William. *Raymond Chandler*. Boston: Twayne, 1986.

Speir, Jerry. *Raymond Chandler*. New York: Ungar, 1981.

Van Dover, J. K., ed. *The Critical Responses to Raymond Chandler*. Westport, Conn.: Greenwood Press, 1995.

Wolfe, Peter. *Something More Than Night: The Case of Raymond Chandler*. Bowling Green, Ohio: Bowling Green University Popular Press, 1985.

# ⊛ Diana Chang

BORN: *1934, New York, New York*

NATIONALITY: *American*

GENRE: *Fiction, poetry*

MAJOR WORKS:

*The Frontiers of Love* (1956)

*Eye to Eye* (1974)

*What Matisse Is After: Poems and Drawings* (1984)

*The Mind's Amazement: Poems Inspired by Paintings, Poetry, Music, Dance* (1998)

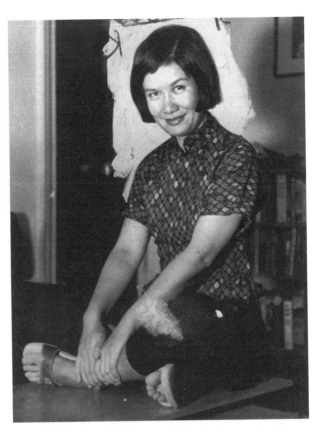

Diana Chang    *The Library of Congress.*

## Overview

Novelist, poet, and painter Diana Chang is recognized as the first American-born Chinese writer to publish a novel in the United States. Although she spent most of her childhood in China, the United States proved to be the setting for Chang's formative years as a writer. Chang is best known for her novel *The Frontiers of Love* (1956), a compelling exploration of ethnic identity in a multiracial environment; however, her writing is not limited to issues of culture or ethnicity. Over the course of her career, Chang has received many awards and honors, testaments to her place in American literature.

## Works in Biographical and Historical Context

Born in New York City to a Eurasian mother and Chinese father, Chang spent her early years in China, primarily Beijing and Shanghai, where her father was an architect. Chang attended an American school in Shanghai's International Sector. After World War II, China descended into civil war. The Communist Party forces won, and Mao Zedong proclaimed the People's Republic of China in 1949. Chang's family fled the country and resettled in New York, where Change attended high school.

*First Publishings* After high school, Chang attended Barnard College, where she studied philosophy, English, and creative writing. She has acknowledged the importance of this education to her writing, especially the influence of philosophers such as Søren Kierkegaard. During her time at Barnard College, two of her poems were published in the prestigious *Poetry* magazine. She began her career as a junior editor in book publishing before devoting herself to writing full-time. At the age of twenty-two, Chang published her first novel, *The Frontiers of Love*, which has become a classic of the Asian American literary canon.

*The Painting Professor* In 1979 Chang returned to Barnard College as an adjunct associate professor, teaching creative writing for ten years in the English department and an interdisciplinary art course called "Imagery and Form in the Arts." She has also worked as a literary editor and, for more than six years, she edited *The American Pen*, a quarterly published by the American Center of PEN in New York. Beyond her literary endeavors, Chang is also an artist who has premiered several solo exhibitions, and her artwork has been used to illustrate one of her chapbooks, *What Matisse Is After: Poems and Drawings* (1984).

**Awards and Publishings** Chang has won several awards for her creative work, including a John Hay Whitney Opportunity Fellowship, a Fulbright Scholarship, and a New York State Council on the Arts Award to adapt her short story "Falling Free" into a radio play that was aired in thirty-five cities in the United States. Her work has appeared in many magazines, including *American Scholar*, *Nation*, *New York Quarterly*, and *Virginia Quarterly Review*.

## Works in Literary Context

*Escaping Ethnic Restrictions* For some writers, understanding the origin and impact of their familial roots is essential to their identity. Chang, however, does not always depend on her ethnic background for subject material; in fact, the experience of being of mixed ancestry and the identity crisis that often results is actually the subject of very little of Chang's work. She has commonly acknowledged the wide-ranging focus of her works, remarking that while some of her writings draw on her Chinese-American heritage, many others could have been written by anyone of any nationality. Because Chang's work is not restricted by ethnicity, scholar Wei-hsiung Wu says, "Chang succeeds in dramatizing a contemporary angst and in demonstrating that life is a constant improvisation." For Chang, the purpose of writing is to explore life's universal truths, to find selfhood as a human, not as a particular race.

*A Creative Nature* Although she is not known primarily for her verse, Chang's various poetry collections have been well received because they are, says Wu, "rich in startling imagery, concise in language, and often cryptic in meaning, ... [issuing] invitations to perceive freshly and to rediscover reality through feeling and form." Without a doubt, all of Chang's volumes of poetry are characterized by both artistic and literary creativity, and nature is a common theme in most of her poems. For instance, "Most Satisfied by Snow," a brief, powerful poem that first appeared in 1974's *Asian-American Heritage: An Anthology of Prose and Poetry*, shows Chang's gift for writing quiet, yet emotionally vivid lyric poetry. The poem, much like her artwork, displays delicately crafted images that are enhanced by the use of metaphor, simile, and personification to convey meaning. Poems such as "Most Satisfied by Snow" demonstrate not only Chang's economy and precision of language, but also, perhaps most importantly, a preoccupation with how nature can lead to self-development and self-awareness.

## Works in Critical Context

*The Frontiers of Love* With its complex and sophisticated portrayal of Eurasian life in Shanghai, the novel *The Frontiers of Love* has prompted academics to recognize Chang as a pioneer in Chinese American literature. Contrary to what some critics have suggested, Chang's

---

## LITERARY AND HISTORICAL CONTEMPORARIES

Chang's famous contemporaries include:

**Maxine Kumin** (1925–): Though praised for her fiction and children's books, Kumin is best known for poetry that is often elegiac and pastoral.

**Audre Lorde** (1934–1992): Much of Lorde's work focuses on racism in the women's movement, as well as sexism in black communities.

**Seamus Heaney** (1939–): In addition to exploring Ireland's mythic and historical past, Heaney's poetry exalts everyday miracles with lyrical beauty.

**Gustavo Alvarez Gardeazábal** (1945–): Gardeazábal's fiction is centered around Colombian political issues, including the effects of the drug trade on society.

**Susan Sontag** (1933–2004): In a collection titled *Against Interpretation* (1966), Sontag argues for less analysis of works of art and more attention to the sensory pleasures they evoke.

**Roland Giguére** (1929–2003): Giguére was a Canadian painter, poet, engraver, and typographer who was greatly influenced by the French surrealists.

---

reputation as an accomplished writer is also strengthened by her concern with issues beyond ethnicity. According to scholar Amy Ling, "In Chang's novels, the questions of stereotypes, ethnicity, duality, and the forging of a new identity fall under a larger existentialist theme. In most of the works of the Asian American writers ... authorial identity is indistinguishable from the author's ethnic identity, but Chang is a protean author, a master of disguises whose authorial identity cannot be fixed by ethnicity."

Chang's approach—or lack of—to cultural identity is a source of critical contention. Critics such as Wu acknowledge that "although Chang has a remarkable understanding of the Chinese way of life, neither her fiction nor her poetry conveys a Chinese sensibility." Chang has frequently attracted criticism from Asian American authors and scholars for writing about non-Asian American themes and characters. Since *The Frontiers of Love* and, to a lesser extent, *The Only Game in Town* are Chang's only novels with Asian American themes, critics accuse Chang of sacrificing her heritage because, says Ling, she "wants to fit in" and is too preoccupied with the "theme of being in the world" in all of its manifestations. Other commentators have been much harsher. For example, the Chinese American writer and critic Frank Chin, notorious for his hostile stance toward Asian American writers he believes have ignored essential Asian American themes, has repeatedly criticized Chang in scathing reviews.

## COMMON HUMAN EXPERIENCE

Though Chang considers herself an author who writes from a human point of view rather than a solely Chinese American perspective, Chang drew upon her experience of growing up in Shanghai and her identity as a young Eurasian woman for her first novel, *The Frontiers of Love*. Here are some other works that explore issues of conflicting racial and cultural identity:

*Black Ice* (1991), a memoir by Lorene Cary. The first African American female to attend the prestigious Saint Paul's School in New Hampshire, Cary writes of feeling like an outsider.

*Clay Walls* (1987), a novel by Kim Ronyoung. This novel depicts two generations of Korean Americans who must find their place in American society after World War II.

*Jasmine* (1989), a novel by Bharati Mukherjee. Born in a village in India, Jasmine migrates to the United States, entering the country as Jyoti Vijh, working as a nanny named Jace, and finally becoming Jane, the wife of an Iowa banker.

**Poetry** Scholars who approach Chang's work from an angle other than ethnicity note the positive influence Chang's visual talent as an artist has on her writing. Academic Dexter Fisher, for instance, says, "As an artist, [Chang] has a visual commitment to imagery that she succeeds in translating into verbal form. ... Her use of understatement lends an element of surprise to her poetry as well as a resonance that goes beyond the subject." In the introduction to *Chinese American Poetry: An Anthology*, editors L. Ling-chi Wang and Henry Yiheng Zhao also compliment Chang's imagistic style, saying, "It seems that, to her, language can go on by itself without referents, just as in paintings, where colors and figures can be significant in their own dynamics without depicting any objects. This ideal state is not as easy to achieve in poetry as in painting. Yet Diana Chang proves that it is still a possibility worth striving for." Certainly, these comments are applicable to "Most Satisfied by Snow," in which a few carefully created images are used to celebrate a speaker's gaining insight into her own process of discovering who she is.

### Responses to Literature

1. In "Most Satisfied by Snow," the speaker of the poem reflects upon the qualities of fog and snow. While she appreciates both of these elements of nature, her preference is for snow. What truths about both universal existence and her own life does snow bring? Why do you think snow is what prompts these feelings? What element of nature or natural occurrence can evoke such a personal response or reaction in you?

2. Do you believe that writers of a certain race or gender or from a certain ethnic background have an obligation to be the voice of their people? Do you think it is acceptable for a writer to create characters whose ethnicity or culture they do not share?

3. A painter as well as a writer, Chang has illustrated a volume of her poetry. Research other authors who have illustrated their own works (examples include William Blake, Beatrix Potter, Shel Silverstein, and Kahlil Gibran). Prepare a PowerPoint presentation that provides information about at least five of these writers along with examples of their illustrations. At the end of your presentation, explain why you think the writers chose to illustrate their works; include a discussion of what you believe the visual effects contribute to the overall presentation and meaning of the works.

4. Do you believe a person of one ethnicity can write an unbiased, authentic novel that features characters of another ethnicity? What if the author is writing a nonfiction book instead of a novel?

BIBLIOGRAPHY

**Books**

Fisher, Dexter, ed. *The Third Woman: Minority Women Writers of the United States*. Boston: Houghton Mifflin, 1980.

Ling, Amy. *Between Worlds: Women Writers of Chinese Ancestry*. New York: Pergamon, 1990.

Nelson, Emmanuel S. *Asian American Novelists: A Bio-Bibliographical Critical Sourcebook*. Westport, Conn.: Greenwood Press, 2000.

Wang, L. Ling-chi, and Henry Yiheng Zhao, eds. *Chinese American Poetry: An Anthology*. Seattle: University of Washington Press, 1991.

Wu, Wei-hsiung. *Oxford Companion to Women's Writing in the United States*. Edited by Cathy N. Davidson and Linda Wagner-Martin. New York: Oxford University Press, 1995.

## ❂ Paddy Chayefsky

BORN: *1923, New York, New York*

DIED: *1981, New York, New York*

NATIONALITY: *American*

GENRE: *Drama, fiction*

MAJOR WORKS:

*Marty* (1953)

*The Tenth Man* (1959)

*Network* (1976)

*Altered States* (1978)

Paddy Chayefsky    *AP Images.*

## Overview

With the birth of television in the late 1940s came a new medium through which writers could reach varied audiences. Recognizing its potential, Paddy Chayefsky produced many remarkable television plays, including *Marty* and *Middle of the Night* (1959). His experience in television led to several motion-picture opportunities, in which his active involvement as a producer and writer was also notable. In addition, Chayefsky's expertise touched the theater; the themes in his works ranged from spiritual concerns to man's obsession with materialism. Few artists have enjoyed success in three different media, but due to his flexibility and talent, Chayefsky excelled on the stage, in television, and in film.

## Works in Biographical and Historical Context

***Influenced by Yiddish Theater***    Born in 1923 to Russian immigrants, Sidney Chayefsky was raised in a traditional Jewish home in the Bronx. Early on, his father exposed him to the Yiddish theater and cultivated in him a respect for education and a love for performing arts. The Yiddish theater would later play an especially large role in Chayefsky's scripts for television, stage, and movies.

***The Birth of Paddy***    Chayefsky graduated from New York's City College with a BS in social science in 1943

and enlisted in the Army that same year. During his two-year stint as a machine gunner, Chayefsky was nicknamed "Paddy" because, although he was Jewish, he opted to attend Catholic mass rather than serve kitchen duty. ("Paddy" is a somewhat offensive slang term used to referred to people of Irish descent in the United States, most of whom are Catholic.) Believing it distinctive, he kept the name professionally. Injured when he stepped on a German landmine, Chayefsky received a Purple Heart and was sent to London. During his recovery there, he penned his first musical, *No T.O. for Love* (1945), in which he performed the starring role during a Special Services tour.

***Hollywood Career***    After the war, Chayefsky became an apprentice in his uncle's New York print shop, at the same time pursuing his writing for the stage. He was paid five hundred dollars for a full-length play that was never produced; however, the work did attract the attention of two Hollywood producers who gave Chayefsky a junior writer's contract in Hollywood. Although he found the woman he would marry while in Hollywood, Chayefsky was not able to find permanent employment, so he returned to New York, where he wrote jokes for a comedian while seeking backers for the plays he was also writing.

***Marty and an Academy Award***    In the early 1950s, Chayefsky began adapting scripts for radio shows, documentary dramas, and television shows. Such work led to his producing original pieces for weekly broadcasts on the *Philco-Goodyear Playhouse* television program. The peak of Chayefsky's television career came in 1953 when *Marty*, one of the most acclaimed of all live television dramas, first aired. Two years later, the television play was developed into a full-length film and took the nation by storm, not only becoming a box office hit, but also earning Academy Awards for best picture, best director, and best actor. Chayefsky won an Academy Award for best screenplay for the movie.

***Burnout and Broadway***    Several more television-to-movie projects followed *Marty*, each one expanding popular drama beyond the restrictive time and set constraints of television, thereby allowing Chayefsky's characters and their conflicts to be more deeply explored. However, Chayefsky's films after *Marty* were not commercially successful. In response, Chayefsky moved on to new territory and larger themes on the Broadway stage with satirical plays that included *The Tenth Man* which draws upon his traditional Jewish background.

***Satirical Screenplays***    When Chayefsky returned to writing screenplays, he enjoyed renewed financial and critical success with the satire genre as he attacked the military, health care, and television networks. He won his second screenwriting Academy Award for 1971's *The Hospital*. In 1976, Chayefsky unleashed his most furious satire, *Network*, for which he won his third Academy Award for screenwriting.

# LITERARY AND HISTORICAL CONTEMPORARIES

Chayefsky's famous contemporaries include:

**V. S. Naipaul** (1932–): Naipaul is a Nobel-prize winning author. He was born to a Hindu family in Trinidad. Naipaul has since settled in London, where he has written novels with themes of political violence and the dehumanization of contemporary society.

**Rod Serling** (1924–1975): Serling, creator of television's *Twilight Zone*, is praised for pointed dialogue filled with penetrating truths about the psychology and motivation of mankind.

**Harold Pinter** (1930–2008): Pinter was a British actor and a writer for television early in his career. Pinter went on to craft staged drama characterized by realistic conversation that explores the layers of meaning in language.

**Roy Lichtenstein** (1923–1997): One of the innovators of America's Pop Art movement, Lichtenstein parodied American popular culture in giant comic book panels.

**Ronald Reagan** (1911–2004): Before becoming the fortieth United States president, Reagan was president of the Screen Actors Guild, and he served as a television host and spokesperson against communism in the film industry.

**Arthur C. Clarke** (1917–2008): Clarke was a renowned science fiction writer and was well known for his work on the film *2001: A Space Odyssey*. With technological details that often seemed to predict new advances in science, Clarke explored the search for humankind's place in the universe.

***Altered Film*** Based on the only novel he ever wrote, Chayefsky's last film was *Altered States*, a satire of the scientific research community, in which a scientist seeks to discover the secrets of the inner self and human evolution through experiments with drug-induced states of sensory deprivation. Production disagreements drove Chayefsky to withdraw his name from the movie's credits in protest. Instead of being a satire as Chayefsky intended, the film version became, in many ways, a straightforward horror movie. Chayefsky was disappointed in the final result. *Altered States* was Chayefsky's last work. He died of cancer in 1981.

## Works in Literary Context

Though Chayefsky's output was not prolific, he influenced every medium of entertainment he touched. One of only a handful of American screenwriters who first achieved fame during the golden age of television, he has inspired many in the screenwriting industry. Mostly set in post-war urban society, Chayefsky's early works take a positive approach to the internal turmoil of the ordinary man. In later plays and screenplays, however, his characters express their anger and disillusionment with a society that impersonally overwhelms their attempts to bring meaning into their lives.

***The Everyman*** Typically middle-class men, Chayefsky's characters embody common human struggles with both real and spiritual existence. Based on people in his New York surroundings, the characters in his plays are not unrealistic and larger-than-life; rather, they *are* people whose problems are universal. In *Marty*, for example, the homely, lonesome protagonist finds meaning in his life by pursuing a relationship with another solitary soul, despite the objections of his mother and friends. Amidst an intensely emotional world of relationships, economics, and love, Marty, as do Chayefsky's other characters, seeks self-preservation as he tries to survive the frenetic pace of contemporary society. Because Marty's plight is familiar to everyone, the play resounds with intimacy and human truth for audiences.

***Satire*** Chayefsky is a master of satire (writing that exposes human or institutional vices with the purpose of effecting a change) and the whole of his work is characterized by his concern with the dehumanizing effects of modern civilization. Chayefsky has been compared to English satirist Jonathan Swift, who, responding to the belief of Whig economists that people are the real wealth of a nation, shocked readers with *A Modest Proposal* (1729), a bitter and ironical pamphlet suggesting that the poor in Ireland should raise children to be sold for food. Though not so extreme as *A Modest Proposal*, *Network* is Chayefsky's most furious satire. A stinging indictment of a powerful element in American society, *Network* won Chayefsky an Academy Award for its portrayal of television executives who will stop at nothing—including murder—to ensure high ratings for their shows. In *Network*, Chayefsky launches an all-out assault on the single-minded quest for high ratings and bigger corporate dividends that sacrifices people's humanity. Chayefsky targets the most common subjects of satire—hypocrisy, ambition, greed, pride, materialism, and pretension—by satirizing the television industry.

## Works in Critical Context

Critics readily agree that Chayefsky brought a sense of contemporary realism to much of his work, reflecting changing society through satire. He has been compared to Clifford Odets, who revolutionized the theater with his satiric, politically heightened sensibilities a generation before Chayefsky. Critics also concur that Chayefsky's strength as a dramatist and screenwriter revolves around his ability to recreate believable and revealing dialogue, which in turn makes his characters more believable.

***Marty*** Perhaps the most representative of Chayefsky's early work is also one of his most popular and critically acclaimed. According to scholar John M. Clum, *Marty* is "one of the classics of both television and the American film because it captures vividly and touchingly a number of aspects of the American experience."

While praise for *Marty* was widespread, it was not unanimous. One detractor is Edouard L. de Laurot, who writes that *Marty*:

> betrays reality rather than reveals it. ... [The hero] discovers no new values and remains essentially an apology for the status quo. His falling in love cannot be considered a dramatic change—it brings him no fresh insights, he is merely carried away passively from his bachelor loneliness to the marital felicity he has always sought. There is no sign that he has found a way to combat the essential desolation of his life.

To Clum, however, the success of *Marty* is "attributable to Chayefsky's fortunate reluctance to resolve all the conflicts he has developed at the end of the play." Clum continues that the play and film are not "not the first ... to treat urban life in a vivid, realistic fashion ... but [*Marty*] . . . managed to celebrate the possibility of beauty in even the homeliest circumstances. The Bronx shown in Marty is a neighborhood of lonely, unhappy people; but the love we see develop during the weekend that the film shows us negates any sense of inevitable entrapment." Clum's conclusion is that "the unique formula that made Marty such an important cinematic event was an effective blend of a romance with a happy ending that was presented within the framework of a naturalistically conceived setting and characters."

## Responses to Literature

1. Watch the film version of *Marty*. Why do you think audiences identified so strongly with the title character at the time? Do you identify with him? Why or why not?

2. Television and electronic media in general have changed a lot since the release of *Network*. In a short paper, compare *Network* to more recent satires of American culture and media such as *Idiocracy* (2006) and television's *The Colbert Report*. Is Chayefsky's critique of American culture still current, or is it dated when compared to more recent satires?

3. Chayefsky once said, "Television is democracy at its ugliest." What is your interpretation of the meaning of his words? Do you agree with him? Why or why not?

BIBLIOGRAPHY

**Books**

Brady, John. *The Craft of the Screenwriter*. New York: Touchstone Press, 1981.
Clum, John M. *Paddy Chayefsky*. Boston: Twayne, 1976.
Considine, Shaun. *Mad as Hell: the Life and Work of Paddy Chayefsky*. New York: Random House, 1994.
Vinson, James, ed. *Contemporary Dramatists*. New York: St. Martin's Press, 1973.

---

## COMMON HUMAN EXPERIENCE

Chayefsky's *Altered States* features a professor of psychology who experiments with sensory deprivation spiral out of control and jeopardize his life. Other works about the devastating effects of man's attempts to transcend human limits in a quest to know the meaning of life and existence include the following:

*Frankenstein; or, The Modern Prometheus* (1817), a novel by Mary Shelley. Obsessed with discovering the secret of life, Victor Frankenstein creates a monstrosity out of old body parts.

*Into Thin Air: A Personal Account of the Mount Everest Disaster.* (1997), a nonfiction work by John Krakauer. In this firsthand account of an expedition up Mount Everest during which eight people died, Krakauer muses that perhaps people should accept the fact that human existence is filled with impenetrable mysteries.

*The Strange Case of Dr. Jekyll and Mr. Hyde* (1886), a novel by Robert Louis Stevenson. By drinking a potion he has concocted, Dr. Jekyll is able to separate the primitive, evil side of himself from that of his restrained, civilized self—until the medicine runs out.

---

**Periodicals**

de Laurot, Edouard L. "All About 'Marty.'" *Film Culture* (Summer 1955): vol. 1, no. 4, pp. 6–9.

**Web sites**

American Theater Guide. *[Sidney] Paddy Chayefsky*. Retrieved September 3, 2008, from http://www.answers.com/topic/paddy-chayefsky.
BrainyQuote. *Paddy Chayefsky Quotes*. Retrieved September 3, 2008, from http://www.brainyquote.com/quotes/authors/p/paddy_chayefsky.html.

## ❀ John Cheever

BORN: *1912, Quincy, Massachusetts*

DIED: *1982, Ossining, New York*

NATIONALITY: *American*

GENRE: *Fiction*

MAJOR WORKS:

*The Enormous Radio and Other Stories* (1953)

*The Wapshot Chronicle* (1957)

"The Swimmer" (1964)

*Falconer* (1977)

John Cheever    *Cheever, John, photograph. The Library of Congress.*

## Overview

Few American writers have been so attentive to detail and so careful with their recurrent subject matter and themes as John Cheever. Finding the extraordinary in the ordinary, Cheever is known for his shrewd, often critical view of middle-class America. With both dismay and compassion, he transforms the commonplace events of daily life into some of the wittiest and most profoundly moving stories in modern American literature.

## Works in Biographical and Historical Context

***Parental Character Types*** John Cheever was born into a middle-class New England family on May 27, 1912, in Quincy, Massachusetts, a seaside community a few miles south of Boston. His mother, an English-born woman named Mary Devereaux Liley, was ten years younger than his father, Frederick Lincoln Cheever. Both of his parents appear throughout his fiction as character types: the hard-drinking, charming father figure in conflict with the hard-working, emotionally reserved mother figure. In Cheever's stories, the mother, never the cause of the family's disintegration, is usually the one who saves the family, paralleling Mary Cheever's role in sustaining the Cheever family by establishing her own businesses

after her husband lost both his job and then their home during the Great Depression.

***Story Beginnings*** Cheever attended Thayer Academy, a preparatory school in Massachusetts, but he was expelled at age seventeen for smoking. The short story he wrote about the experience, "Expelled," published in 1930 in *The New Republic*, marked the beginning of Cheever's literary career. The theme of this piece, the conflict between one's need for order and propriety and one's desire for adventure and pleasure, recurs throughout Cheever's work. Recognizing the young author's talent, Malcolm Cowley, editor of *The New Republic*, arranged for Cheever to spend time at Yaddo, a writers' colony in Saratoga to which he would often return.

During the next several years, Cheever lived primarily in New York City, supporting himself with odd jobs, including a stint writing book synopses for the Metro-Goldwyn-Mayer film studio, while pursuing his literary aspirations. In the 1930s, his short stories appeared in such distinguished magazines as *The Atlantic*, *The Yale Review*, and *The New Yorker*. Cheever's connection with *The New Yorker* began in 1935 and lasted his entire life; well over one hundred of his stories were originally published in that magazine.

***War and Pieces*** In 1939, Cheever met Mary Winternitz, a writer and teacher who worked with his agent. Soon after Cheever and Winternitz married in March 1941, Cheever joined the Army. He was serving in the Army during World War II when his first collection, *The Way Some People Live*, was published in 1943. War and the Great Depression serve as the backdrop for these stories, which deal with Cheever's lifelong subject: how people live in suburbia, the idealized community form that exists between the urban and the rural. After the war, Cheever settled in Scarborough, New York, and wrote television scripts for such programs as *Life with Father*.

Keeping his professional life separate from his home life, Cheever did much of his fiction writing in a rented room at the train station in Scarborough. Instead of seclusion, he relied on being close to the actual pulse of everyday life for productivity. In 1951, Cheever received a generous Guggenheim Fellowship in 1951, which freed him from the financial burdens of supporting a family. In 1953, his next collection of short stories was published under the title *The Enormous Radio and Other Stories*, a work that many critics would later call his greatest single collection.

***Rise and Fall*** In the fall of 1954, Cheever accepted a position at Barnard College to teach creative writing; he also began work on a novel as a way to help support his family. According to biographer Scott Donaldson, Cheever was a superb and inspiring teacher. He encouraged students to write about their own lives—much as he himself did—and to construct a mythology out of the common world. During this time, Harper and Brothers offered to buy out Cheever's contract with Random House and gave him a substantial advance on his novel-in-progress, as well as five years in which to finish it. Cheever decided to call his work *The Wapshot Chronicle*.

At the height of his success, Cheever developed alcoholism, a problem he did not fully admit to until his family placed him in a rehabilitation center in 1975. Earlier, in 1972, he had suffered a massive heart attack. After a long period of recovery, he wrote *Falconer*, a dark novel that introduces several changes into his fiction: a sordid, violent prison setting; extensive Christian symbolism; and coarse language.

*Later Years* From 1977 until his death in June 1982, Cheever's reputation soared as he garnered many awards and prizes for his writing. In 1979, he received the Pulitzer Prize and the National Book Critics Circle Award for *The Stories of John Cheever* (1978). Unfortunately, Cheever would write only one more work, published shortly before his death: *Oh What a Paradise It Seems* (1982), a novella, though he had intended it to be much longer. Cheever, who had been diagnosed with cancer, died on June 18, 1982.

## Works in Literary Context

Cheever's talent for mythologizing his family's background became an integral part of his storytelling reputation throughout his life. Certainly, Cheever's autobiographical approach to his fiction does more than merely record what those experiences meant to him, and it gives credibility to the worlds he creates. Influenced by American author William Faulkner, Cheever likewise demonstrates his ability to invent believable mythic worlds. Faulkner's Yoknapatawpha County is instantaneously recognizable, and so, too, is Cheever's imagined world of St. Botolphs.

*Suburban Satire* Cheever's voice is one of suburban angst; his fictional world commonly portrays individuals in conflict with their communities and often with themselves. The typical Cheever protagonist is an affluent, socially prominent, and emotionally troubled upper-middle-class WASP (White Anglo-Saxon Protestant) who commutes to his professional job in the city from his home in suburbia. Into each picture of his idyllic community, Cheever injects an element of emotional tension arising from the gap between the supposed serenity of suburban life and a person's individual passion and discontent. Cheever's characters are often ambivalent in their desires, so the stories themselves are ambiguous, presenting no clear resolution.

While such ambivalence may take many forms, the most common manifestation in a Cheever story revolves around marital conflict. Adultery, real or fantasized, is a recurring motif in Cheever's works, as his characters struggle with their desires for emotional fulfillment in contrast with both domestic and societal expectations of order.

A typical example of Cheever's critical view of suburban life can be found in his short story "The Swimmer." In the tale, a man at a suburban cocktail party strikes upon the idea that he can traverse the entire neighborhood—all the way back to his house—by swimming the length of each of his neighbors's pools. What begins as a light-hearted, invigorating stunt in the mind of the man soon

proves to be a desperate attempt to recapture all the things he has lost, but has somehow forgotten he has lost: his youth, his wealth, his home, and even his family.

## Works in Critical Context

At the time Cheever was writing, many book reviewers belonged to the New York intellectual elite, a group that tended to look upon Cheever's stories in *The New Yorker* as elitist indulgence that unemotionally chronicled the shallow manners and morals of the upper middle class. Other critics considered his work too depressing because some of the stories dealt with shabby lives mired in urban hopelessness. More recent criticism, however, recognizes Cheever's skill as a storyteller and sharp social commentator. The publication of *The Stories of John Cheever* in 1978—which received the Pulitzer Prize, the National Book Award, and the National Book Critics Circle Award—prompted serious scholars to reappraise his works. Along with noting Cheever's thematic interest in human morality and spirituality, modern critics praise his compassion and abiding belief in the redemptive power of love.

*The Wapshot Books* Critics were divided over the merits of Cheever's first novel, *The Wapshot Chronicle* (1957). Some found fault with its episodic structure; the novel is not built on the kind of linear framework that conservative critics prefer. Still others were put off by its dark vision. In an article appearing in *Critical Essays on John Cheever*, writer and scholar Joan Didion praises it highly, evaluating

## COMMON HUMAN EXPERIENCE

Mostly set in New York City, the pieces in *The Enormous Radio and Other Stories* usually depict optimistic but naïve individuals who experience culture shock after moving to the city. The much-anthologized title story exemplifies one of Cheever's predominant themes: that social proprieties and conventions cannot subdue emotional conflicts. Here are other works that explore the delicate lives of people entangled in social conventions:

*The Great Gatsby* (1925), a novel by F. Scott Fitzgerald. In this bitter attack on the morally barren, affluent society of America's Jazz Age, Gatsby, born to a poor Midwestern family, has gained wealth through unscrupulous means in order to be the kind of man he thinks will win back the woman he loves.

*Pygmalion* (1913), a drama by George Bernard Shaw. Inspiring the highly successful musical comedy *My Fair Lady* (1956), *Pygmalion* satirizes the boundaries of human relations and social distinctions.

*Vile Bodies* (1930), a novel by Evelyn Waugh. Characteristic of Waugh's work, which ridicules fashionable London society and the English upper class, this novel offers a derisive look at how the decadence of London society between World Wars I and II affects the characters' internal and external worlds.

it in the context of novelistic tradition: "It was a novel more like *Tom Jones* than *Madame Bovary*, more like *Tristram Shandy* than *Pride and Prejudice*."

Even though the tone of the *The Wapshot Scandal* differs greatly from *The Wapshot Chronicle*, the critical response to this follow-up novel was generally favorable. In *Critical Essays on John Cheever*, George Garrett best describes the major differences between the two novels: "The sins of *Chronicle* are original sin. *Scandal* moves inexorably toward the end of the world." Friend and editor Malcolm Cowley was alarmed by the anger evidenced in Cheever's world in *The Wapshot Scandal*, calling it, says Donaldson, one of "emotional squalor and incongruity." Hilary Corke, discussing both books in *The New Republic*, notes that although Cheever is "one of the best living short-story writers in the language," his *Wapshot* novels are "fatally flawed" because his view of the society he depicts "gets over-simple, over-stressed, over-ripe—and, finally and disastrously, self-indulgent."

### Responses to Literature

1. In the *Wapshot* novels, Cheever creates the fictional town of St. Botolphs. What other writers can you find who introduce fictional towns in their works? From a literary perspective, what advantages do authors who create their own towns have over authors writing about real places?

2. Research the social and political climate of America in the 1960s. Compare this to the picture of American life presented in "The Swimmer." Next, compare the story to Homer's *Odyssey*. Would you consider Neddy Merrill to be more representative of a mythic hero or of an ordinary man? Why?

3. Do you think Cheever was his generation's voice of American suburbia? What authors, artists, or filmmakers today do you consider to be portrayers of suburban life? Are their depictions accurate?

4. Write a descriptive sketch of a fictional place based on a real city or community in which you have lived. What elements did you change, and what elements remained the same? Do you think other people would be able to recognize the "real" that served as your inspiration? Why or why not?

BIBLIOGRAPHY

**Books**

Bosha, Francis, ed. *The Critical Response to John Cheever*. Westport, Conn.: Greenwood Press, 1994.

Cheever, Susan. *Home before Dark*. New York: Bantam Books, 1991.

Coale, Samuel. *John Cheever*. New York: Unger, 1977.

Collins, R. G., ed. *Critical Essays on John Cheever*. Boston: G. K. Hall, 1982.

Donaldson, Scott. *John Cheever: A Biography*. New York: Random House, 1988.

Donaldson, Scott, ed. *Conversations with John Cheever*. Jackson, Miss: University Press of Mississippi, 1987.

Hunt, George. *John Cheever: The Hobgoblin Company of Love*. Grand Rapids, Mich.: Eerdmans, 1983.

"John Cheever (1912)." *Contemporary Literary Criticism*. Edited by Carolyn Riley. Vol. 3. Detroit: Gale Research, 1975, pp. 105–109

Meanor, Patrick. *John Cheever Revisited*. Boston: Twayne, 1995.

O'Hara, James. *John Cheever: A Story of the Short Fiction*. Boston: Twayne, 1989.

Wadeland, L. *John Cheever*. Boston: G. K. Hall, 1979.

## ◉ Mary Chesnut

BORN: *1823, Stateburg, South Carolina*

DIED: *1886, Camden, South Carolina*

NATIONALITY: *American*

GENRE: *Nonfiction*

MAJOR WORKS:
*A Diary from Dixie* (1905)

# Overview

Mary Chesnut's Civil War diary is one of the most insightful accounts of the war, as well as one of the most fascinating portrayals of life in the Confederacy. Often within the context of women's issues, Chesnut blends fiction and memoir with an intellectual deftness that transforms simple personal recollection into conscientious literary anecdote. In her journal and its revisions, Chesnut creates a powerful literary work with enduring historical, political, and social implications.

# Works in Biographical and Historical Context

*A Political Upbringing*  Born March 31, 1823, in Stateburg, South Carolina, Mary Boykin Miller was the oldest of four children born to Mary Boykin and Stephen Decatur Miller. A lawyer and politician who served as a state senator, the governor of South Carolina, and a United States senator, Miller was a significant influence on his daughter's political development.

Because her father's various positions required the family to move often, Chesnut was educated at home before attending a day school in Camden, South Carolina, beginning in 1833. In 1835, Chesnut was enrolled in Madame Talvande's French School for Young Ladies in Charleston, South Carolina, where she excelled in her general studies. Along with becoming fluent in French and learning to read German, Chesnut developed a love of literature and honed her skills as a witty conversationalist, a talent that would serve her well in political circles. During her time in Charleston, Chesnut met her future husband, James Chesnut, a Princeton graduate who was immediately attracted to her intelligence and energy.

*Plantation Life*  After Chesnut married in April 1840, she and James moved to Mulberry Plantation, the Chesnut family estate, located three miles south of Camden, South Carolina. Quiet, provincial plantation life proved tiresome for Chesnut, a vivacious woman with literary interests and a need for interaction beyond the boundaries of the plantation. Her frustration increased when it became clear that she and her husband were unable to conceive children. In addition to feeling, as a diary entry reveals, that she had failed to fulfill her role as a wife, mother, and hostess, Chesnut had no outlet for her energy and creativity.

*Politics and War*  James became involved in state politics, and by 1854 the Chesnuts had moved to an elegant new home in Camden, a place well-suited to entertaining. When James was elected to the United States Senate in 1858, Chesnut accompanied him to Washington, D.C., enthusiastically entering the social scene there. Although the Chesnuts never defended slavery, James was a proponent of states' rights, a platform that led to his resigning from the Senate in 1860 after the election of Abraham Lincoln. Fearing that Civil War was imminent, Chesnut

began the diary that she would continue until the summer of 1865.

Chesnut wrote her diary from many locations as she and her husband traveled throughout the South in support of the right of southern states to secede. In early 1861, Chesnut was in Montgomery, Alabama, while James attended the constitutional convention that formed the Confederacy. Next, she went to Charleston, where James was involved in negotiations over Fort Sumter. A witness to the first battle of the war in April 1861, Chesnut viewed the shelling of Fort Sumter from a rooftop. After the Battle of Manassas in July 1861, Chesnut visited the sick and wounded, facing, for the first time, the grim reality of her compatriots' deaths.

*Diary Difficulties*  Following an illness in 1862, Chesnut went to Richmond, Virginia, the Confederate capital, with her husband, who had attained the rank of colonel and was appointed as an aide to Jefferson Davis, President of the Confederate States of America. Chesnut's diary reveals that her spirits improved as she renewed her acquaintance with Varina Davis, a friend of many years. Unfortunately, the longer the war went on, Chesnut could not always find paper, and she wrote part of her diary on the back of a recipe book and on whatever scraps of cheap paper she came across. When Union troops advanced on Richmond in 1863, Chesnut burned her papers and letters, including parts of her diary, because she feared her candid discussions about the condition of the Confederacy could be used to the North's advantage.

*After the War*  At the end of the war, the Chesnuts, without resources, moved back to Camden. Northern forces had burned one hundred bales of cotton and damaged mills and gins at Mulberry Plantation, making the years following the war financially difficult. With the death of James's father in 1866, James inherited the Mulberry and Sandy Hill plantations, but the properties brought with them heavy debt. By 1868, Chesnut's husband had returned to politics, and she had taken over the management of their business interests. Although still in debt, the Chesnuts, following a strict budget and selling family heirlooms, were able to build a new house in Camden in 1873. There, Chesnut renewed her interest in her wartime diary. She attempted to write about her life and war experiences in three unpublished novels but eventually realized that a modified diary would best tell her story.

*Diary Work*  In 1875, Chesnut worked to revise her diary; however, her husband and another reader of the manuscript suggested that the content would be offensive to some influential people. Plagued by poor health, Chesnut put the diary aside until 1881. For the next three and a half years, she continued her revising—a process that included omissions, fictional additions, and stylistic improvements while retaining the form and immediacy of a diary. During this period, Chesnut published "The Arrest of a Spy," an expanded piece from her diary, in the *Charleston Weekly*

## LITERARY AND HISTORICAL CONTEMPORARIES

Chesnut's famous contemporaries include:

**Fanny Kemble** (1806–1893): Kemble was a British actress whose American husband inherited a plantation. She detailed the injustices of slavery in a journal she published in response to England's hostility toward Lincoln's Emancipation Proclamation.

**Henry David Thoreau** (1817–1862): Thoreau was an American writer famous for his work *Walden, or a Life in the Woods*. In addition to being a naturalist, Thoreau condemned materialistic values, industrialism, slavery, and a government that would allow the institution of slavery to exist.

**Mary Todd Lincoln** (1818–1882): Lincoln was the wife of President Abraham Lincoln. She was accused of disloyalty to the Union cause when she initiated costly repairs to the White House in 1861.

**Queen Victoria** (1819–1901): Queen Victoria was queen of Great Britain and Ireland from 1837 to 1901. Her name is used to describe the literature, characteristics, and attitudes of the period of her reign.

**Harriet Beecher Stowe** (1811–1896): Stowe was an American abolitionist and writer. She attacked the cruelty of slavery in the influential novel *Uncle Tom's Cabin* (1852).

*News and Courier* series entitled "Our Women in the War." She received ten dollars for the piece, her only published item during her lifetime.

***Later Years*** Chesnut's health began to decline, and she had little opportunity to continue working on her diary. In January 1885, James suffered a stroke and died in early February. Five days after his death, Chesnut's mother died. These stresses added to Chesnut's own deteriorating condition. Upon James's death, the indebted family plantations, in accordance with his father's will, were to pass to a male heir with the Chesnut name. Because she and James had no children, Chesnut was left with only her Camden home and an income slightly over one hundred dollars a year. By selling butter and eggs, she was able to earn an additional twelve dollars a month. Chesnut attempted another expansion of an excerpt from her diary, this time focusing on conditions in Richmond in 1864, but the piece was never published during her lifetime. A heart attack ended Chesnut's life on November 22, 1886.

## Works in Literary Context

Chesnut's diary records her involvement in the war, her attitudes against slavery, and the limited role of women in society. No other civilian diary presents such a comprehensive insider's view of the Civil War from a southern perspective. Without the diary and its revisions, Chesnut might have remained a mere social footnote to her husband's career. With her diary, however, Chesnut has given generations a work of enduring literary significance, one that provides a clearer understanding of the Civil War and its tragic human consequences.

***Southern Women*** The writings of Mary Chesnut reveal that she, the wife of a southern senator who defended states' rights and was the first to resign from the United States Senate, was an abolitionist who celebrated the end of slavery. Chesnut directly connected the structure of a slave society with the inferior political and social status of women. A married woman, she believed, was a slave, as was an unmarried woman who lived in her father's house. The celebrated stereotype of southern women—their soft voices, genteel manners, and gracious accommodation of men—was evidence of their enslaved position. Her diary portrays a southern patriarchy—or society ruled by men—riddled with moral corruption, a reality plainly evident to Chesnut through the example of her father-in-law's union with a slave woman. In her view, many southern women secretly favored the abolitionist cause in reaction to the corruptions of the patriarchal system.

## Works in Critical Context

One problem for modern scholars is determining how much of the original diary Chesnut still possessed when she began revising it for publication. In all, about one hundred thousand words of the original diary have survived, but Chesnut may have had double that number when she rewrote the diary. This problem is difficult to resolve because Chesnut sometimes wrote diary entries on scraps of paper, and the revisions were also written on various kinds of paper and in notebooks. Not only did she burn some entries in 1863, but the entries for 1864 have also been lost, either by Chesnut or by her editors. Nevertheless, according to biographer Elisabeth Muhlenfeld, Chesnut's diary is, "Of all the books to come directly out of the Civil War, one of the most remarkable," providing "an important literary portrait of the Confederacy."

***Editorial Interpretations*** The liberties taken by various editors altered Chesnut's work, sometimes significantly, resulting in early editions that are faulty and incomplete, even though they have been praised for their candor. Chesnut left her manuscripts to longtime friend Isabella Martin, who, together with Myrta Lockett Avary, edited the revised version of the diary for publication by Appleton. Martin and Avary's edition omits approximately one-third of the work and contains reworded passages and changed dates. Martin excluded or altered entries that she considered critical of the antebellum South or portrayed Chesnut as anything other than a "Southern lady." For example, where Chesnut included in her revised work an account from her original diary of slaves murdering one of her cousins, Martin changed the account to read that "family troubles" killed Chesnut's cousin. Serialized in *The Saturday Evening Post* from January 28 through February 22, 1905, the first edition of Chesnut's diary was immediately successful and praised as an original document of the Civil War. Still, the persona, descriptions, characters, and dialogues that earned this early acclaim were not the spontaneous recordings of Chesnut but a painstakingly and consciously produced literary effort that had been shaped by editors.

A 1981 edition of Chesnut's diary, edited by historian C. Vann Woodward and titled *Mary Chestnut's Civil War*, won the 1982 Pulitzer Prize in History.

## Responses to Literature

1. Why is it important to study history from a first-person account? What can you learn about life during the Civil War years from Chesnut's text? Do you believe that *A Diary from Dixie* is unique for its time period?

2. When revising her diary for publication, Chesnut added dialogue, characterization, and background, at the same time deleted personal information about family problems. Because of her extensive revisions and her creation of anonymous female speakers, some scholars regard the revised diary as a fictional autobiography or a journal-novel. Do elements of fiction present in Chesnut's work make the diary less believable as a record of the Civil War? What criteria would you use to define the diary genre?

3. Create a table of contents for an anthology of American literature written from 1800 to 1900. Would Chesnut be an appropriate choice for such an anthology?

4. To what extent did Chesnut believe that the Civil War was fought over the institution of slavery? Did she understand the economic issues of that time period? If you were a political leader during that time period, what solutions would you have suggested to prevent a war?

BIBLIOGRAPHY

**Books**

Muhlenfeld, Elisabeth. *Mary Boykin Chesnut: A Biography.* Baton Rouge, La.: Louisiana State University Press, 1981.

**Periodicals**

Flynn, James. "Mary Chesnut's Reconstruction: The Literary Imagination of a Diarist." *Kentucky Philological Association Bulletin* (1983): 63–72.

Hayhoe, George F. "Mary Boykin Chesnut: The Making of a Reputation." *Mississippi Quarterly* 35, no. 1 (1983): 60–72.

## COMMON HUMAN EXPERIENCE

Some scholars refer to Chesnut's diary as a fictional autobiography or a journal-novel because of her revisions after the Civil War ended. While the revised work retains many elements of history and autobiography, the revised and original diaries are two different works with different narrators. In her revision, for instance, Chesnut has become a fictionalized persona who acts as a witness and reporter of the events around her.

Many other writers have successfully fused fiction and actuality in diary form. Listed below are some of these works:

*Race for the Sky: The Kitty Hawk Diaries of Johnny Moore* (2003), fiction by Dan Gutman. Written from the point of view of a real person who witnessed the Wright Brothers' first flight, this fictionalized diary includes quotations from Orville and Wilbur Wright, as well as real photographs and newspaper articles.

*These Is My Words: The Diary of Sarah Agnes Prine, 1881–1901* (2003), a novel by Nancy E. Turner. Based on actual events in the life of the author's great-grandmother, this fictionalized journal tells the story of a woman's experiences in frontier Arizona at the end of the nineteenth century.

*A Journal of the Plague Year* (1722), historical fiction by Daniel Defoe. In this chronicle by a fictional resident in London during the Great Plague, Defoe presents authentic information from several sources, including official documents.

Mentzer, Melissa A. "Rewriting Herself: Mary Chesnut's Narrative Strategies." *Connecticut Review* 14 (Spring 1992): 49–55.

Woodward, C. Vann. "Mary Chesnut in Search of Her Genre." *Yale Review* 72, no. 2 (1984): 199–209.

## ✵ Alice Childress

BORN: *1916, Charleston, South Carolina*

DIED: *1994, New York, New York*

NATIONALITY: *American*

GENRE: *Fiction, drama*

MAJOR WORKS:

*Florence* (1949)

*Wedding Band: A Love/Hate Story in Black and White* (1966)

*A Hero Ain't Nothin' but a Sandwich* (1973)

*Those Other People* (1989)

Alice Childress   *AP Images*

## Overview

A noted dramatist of adult works that deal with a variety of racial and social issues, Alice Childress is also the author of acclaimed young adult fiction and plays. Like her writings for adults, her young adult works are recognized for vivid characterizations and dialogue that depict the harsh effects of racial prejudice, sexism, and abuse.

## Works in Biographical and Historical Context

*Raised by Her Grandmother in Harlem*   Although the year of her birth is widely recorded as 1920, Alice Childress was born on October 12, 1916, in Charleston, South Carolina. After her parents separated, Childress moved to Harlem to live with her maternal grandmother, Eliza, the child of a slave. Eliza taught her granddaughter to appreciate life itself as education, and she made certain that Childress had a wide range of experiences. As she took Childress on walking tours to different neighborhoods throughout the city, to art galleries, and to the churches of Harlem, she encouraged her granddaughter to reflect on what they observed by writing about it.

*After Death of Grandmother and Mother, a Career in Theater*   Childress quickly discovered that she could turn the stories she had written with her grandmother into books, and she became an avid reader of plays, short stories, novels and screenplays. In school, Childress enjoyed acting, but her public school education abruptly ended in the early 1930s when both her grandmother and her mother died. On her own, Childress left high school and began working to support herself. Shortly thereafter, she met her first husband, Alvin Childress, who had moved from Mississippi to New York in search of a career in the theater. In 1935, Childress's only child was born, and although her personal circumstances had changed markedly, her interest in writing and acting did not diminish. Childress began her career in the theater, initially as an actress and later as a director and playwright. In the late 1930s, she and her husband wrote at least one play together, and by 1941, both were members of the American Negro Theatre (ANT).

*Amos 'n' Andy*   Though tens of thousands of African Americans served their country bravely in World War II, they returned home to find they were still second-class citizens, legally deprived of equal rights with whites. Though President Harry Truman officially ended racial segregation in the armed forces with an executive order in 1948, segregation in civilian life was still the rule. Though many in the black community had actively pushed for equal rights for decades, the post-war experience of black veterans spurred the more widespread civil rights movement of the 1950s and 1960s.

By the late 1940s, Childress's marriage was shaky, in part due to her husband's role in one of the most controversial television shows of the era. Alice lived in New York and was actively involved in the ANT, where she acted, directed, sold tickets, and built sets. At the same time, Alvin lived on the West Coast, preparing for his role as Amos in *Amos 'n' Andy*, the first situation comedy on television to have an all-black cast. *Amos 'n' Andy*, a show conceived and directed by two white men, proved to be the subject of tremendous discord in the black community because of its stereotypical portrayals of blacks. The show's actors, Alvin Childress included, did not see the show as presenting a detrimental view of African Americans. Alice, however, did.

Even though *Amos 'n' Andy* contributed to the failure of Childress's marriage, the show and the issues it raised helped shape her career as a playwright. Both the radio and television versions of *Amos 'n' Andy* focused primarily on African Americans from the rural South, generally portraying them as naïve, unsophisticated, and lacking in dignity and integrity. Such prejudiced misrepresentation clearly rankled Childress, who challenged that stereotype with her first performed play, *Florence*. In this drama, the main character is a smart African American woman from the rural South who assures her daughter that she has the right to be whatever she wants to be, even if the white community tells her she cannot. Childress's message is clear: if stereotypes of African Americans are to be successfully eliminated, then African Americans themselves must demonstrate self-determination.

*Multiple Talents*  In 1957, Childress married musician Nathan Woodard. She spent the 1960s primarily writing dramas; in the second half of the decade alone, Childress finished six different plays during her appointment as a visiting scholar at the Radcliffe Institute for Independent Study in Cambridge, Massachusetts. Her work during these years reflects her continued dedication to the need for black self-determination and definition, and she redoubled her efforts to champion ordinary black women.

During the 1970s, Childress produced her greatest range of work: a one-act play, a musical, two children's plays, and two novels. One of these novels was Childress's landmark young adult work, *A Hero Ain't Nothin' but a Sandwich*, which caused a sensation with its realistic description of the life of a thirteen-year-old heroin addict. *Let's Hear It for the Queen* (1976), a musical children's play written for Childress's granddaughter, and *Sea Island Song*, a musical sponsored by the South Carolina Arts Commission in 1977 in celebration of Alice Childress Week in Columbia and Charleston, were collaborations with Woodard.

*Lifetime Achievement and Dedication to Realism* During the 1990s Alice Childress continued to receive accolades for her work, notably 1993's Lifetime Career Achievement Award from the Association for Theatre in Higher Education, while her plays continued to be produced throughout the country. At the time of her death from cancer on August 14, 1994, she was at work on a book about her grandmother and great-grandmother. Going so far as to research the names of the streets in nineteenth-century downtown Charleston, Childress demonstrated in this, her final project, an unwavering dedication both to realism and to the extraordinary lives of ordinary African Americans—women in particular—who, despite nearly overwhelming obstacles, persevere in creating lives of dignity.

## Works in Literary Context

Encouraged to write early in life, Childress credits her grandmother with helping her develop not only creativity, but also instinct and independence as a writer. Undoubtedly, Childress was a unique, important voice in the development of drama. Her 1952 play, *Gold through the Trees*, became the first play by a black woman ever to be produced professionally on an American stage, and her 1955 drama, *Trouble in the Mind*, received an Obie Award as the best original Off-Broadway play. Despite feeling alone in her ideas challenging racism in the literary world, Childress broke barriers in African-American literature of all genres.

## LITERARY AND HISTORICAL CONTEMPORARIES

Childress's famous contemporaries include:

**Aimé Césaire** (1913–2008): In addition to coining the term "negritude," a movement upholding traditional African culture and its values, this author from Martinique is considered by many scholars to be a foremost surrealist poet.

**Walker Evans** (1903–1975): An American photographer, Evans is known for his moving depictions of rural poverty in American during the 1930s.

**Rosa Parks** (1913–2005): Often called the mother of the modern civil rights movement, Parks, an African-American, sparked the Montgomery Bus Boycott of 1955 when she refused to give up her seat on a public bus in Montgomery, Alabama, to a white passenger.

**Herman Wouk** (1915–): Much of this American novelist's work examines the importance of religious heritage in the lives of American Jews.

**Lyndon Baines Johnson** (1908–1973): President of the United States from 1963 to 1969, Johnson's programs in the areas of civil rights and social welfare were overshadowed by America's involvement in the Vietnam War.

*Characterization*  A predominant feature that runs throughout all of Childress's writings is her focus on portraying the lives of "ordinary" people. In *Black Women Writers*, Childress describes how this is a major thematic concern in her writing: "I continue to write about those who come in second, or not at all. ... My writing attempts to interpret the 'ordinary' because they are not ordinary. Each human is uniquely different. Like snowflakes, the human pattern is never cast twice. We are uncommonly and marvelously intricate in thought and action, our problems are most complex and, too often, silently borne." As a result, her characters are believable and memorable.

In several novels aimed at a young adult audience, Childress displays her ability to create authentic characters. In *A Hero Ain't Nothin' but a Sandwich*, for instance, Childress's approach to the narrative structure of the story strengthens her characterization. Told from a variety of perspectives—not only from the boy's point of view, but also that of friends and family—the book gives insight into the various influences on the boy's life. As she does in her plays for adults, Childress develops powerful characters with gripping dialogue in *A Hero Ain't Nothin' but a Sandwich*. In fact, so realistic are her characters, the vivid details about their lives and their frank language, that the book has been banned from some school libraries. It was

## COMMON HUMAN EXPERIENCE

Childress deals with mature, often controversial subjects in her novels for young adults. A common theme in these works is that of being an outsider. The characters in *Those Other People*, for example, are all outcasts of society in some way: a homosexual, a wealthy black sister and brother in a mostly-white school, a teacher who has molested one of his students, and a psychiatric patient who was sexually abused as a girl. Despite their disparate situations, these characters discover that they share more in common than they ever thought possible. Listed below are other works about children who experience the devastations of being outsiders in their worlds:

> *Night Kites* (1986), a novel by M. E. Kerr. A boy learns about outcasts when his extroverted older brother returns home dying from AIDS.
>
> *Harriet the Spy* (1964), fiction by Louise Fitzhugh. When classmates find the diary in which Harriet has chronicled her fractured home and social life, the twelve-year-old aspiring writer faces painful lessons about honesty, family, and friendship.
>
> *The Meantime* (1984), a novel by Bernie MacKinnon. In this work, Luke, an African American teenager, is drawn into his school's racial conflict even though he wants to be left alone.

also one of nine books included in a book-banning case that reached the U.S. Supreme Court.

## Works in Critical Context

Childress's work is praised for its unflinching treatment of racial issues, its compassionate yet discerning characterization, and its universal appeal. Although her young adult novels have been protested by groups that criticize her language and subject matter, the books are also widely praised for their sensitive, challenging portrayal of the problems facing urban teenagers. As Geraldine L. Wilson remarks, "The themes are painful, but Childress handles them well, resolving the difficult conflicts in realistic, sensitive, direct fashion and in ways that seem consistent with the characters." Despite inciting controversy with her works, Childress successfully relates the story of a significant and underrepresented part of America's population.

*Trouble in Mind*  Staged in 1955, *Trouble in Mind* was one of the first plays in dramatic history to deal with African American themes. As such, it "prompts one's troubled mind to consider how many racial stereotypes persist today," writes reviewer Mike Guiliano. He continues: "The play was written at a time when Jim Crow laws were being judicially exorcised, but condescending social attitudes remained in every stage of American life, even among

well-intentioned white liberals." Expressed with dynamic dialogue that is at once sad and humorous, the issues presented in *Trouble in Mind* continue to be pertinent in today's society.

As in her novels, Childress is direct and unapologetic in *Trouble in Mind* as she writes about African American issues in the theater. *Trouble in Mind* is a play within a play that focuses on a troupe of black actors and their anger and frustration at being cast as stereotypes in a play written, produced, and directed by whites, a situation similar to that of Childress's first husband in *Amos 'n' Andy*. Critic Arthur Gelb comments that in *Trouble in Mind*, Childress "has some witty and penetrating things to say about the dearth of roles for [black] actors in the contemporary theatre, the cutthroat competition for these parts and the fact that [black] actors often find themselves playing stereotyped roles in which they cannot bring themselves to believe." Even though they resent what they have to do in order to appear on stage, the African American actors in *Trouble in Mind* "generally go along with it because, well, work is work," says Giuliano. He further praises Childress's "fine job of elucidating the vary degrees to which they acquiesce to theatrical reinforcement of the social oppression they know so well."

## Responses to Literature

1. Benjie, the main character in *A Hero Ain't Nothin' but a Sandwich*, blames his former best friend for his drug problems. Why do you think he blames other people for his heroin addiction? To what extent do you believe people are responsible for their own actions? What accountability do people have in regard to their lives in general?

2. Do you believe that the kind of drug one is addicted to has anything to do with his or her social class? How do economic circumstances play into drug addiction?

3. Throughout her body of work, Childress refers to various African American leaders in history, including Frederick Douglass, Malcolm X, and Paul Laurence Dunbar, to name a few. Choose one of these people and research his or her life. What contributions did the person make to history? What obstacles did he or she have to overcome in order to reach his or her goals? In what ways do you think this person could be a role model for your own life?

4. In *A Hero Ain't Nothin' but a Sandwich*, Mr. Cohen says, "You can be somebody if you want to." Benjie's response is defensive: "How does he know I'm not somebody right now?" Explain what each character's statement reveals about his approach to life. If you were writing the book, what would you choose to have Mr. Cohen say in response to Benjie? How else could Benjie have responded?

BIBLIOGRAPHY

**Books**

Abramson, Doris E. *Negro Playwrights in the American Theatre, 1925–1959.* New York: Columbia University Press, 1969.

Childress, Alice. "A Candle in a Gale Wind," *Black Women Writers (1950–1980): A Critical Evaluation.* Edited by Mari Evans. New York: Doubleday-Anchor Books, 1984.

Donelson, Kenneth L., and Alleen Pace Nilsen. *Literature for Today's Young Adults.* Glenview, Ill.: Scott, Foresman, 1980.

Evans, Mari, ed. *Black Women Writers (1950–1980).* New York: Doubleday-Anchor, 1984.

Hatch, James V. *Black Theater, U.S.A.: Forty-five Plays by Black Americans.* New York: Free Press, 1974.

Schlueter, June, ed. *A Modern American Drama: The Female Canon.* Madison, N.J.: Fairleigh Dickinson University Press, 1990.

**Periodicals**

Barnes, Clive. "'Wedding Band;' Childress Play Opens at Public Theater." *New York Times* (October 27, 1972): 30.

Gelb, Arthur. "1973: A Selection of Noteworthy Titles." *New York Times* (December 2, 1973): 525.

Giuliano, Mike. "Review of *Trouble in Mind.*" *Daily Variety* (February 15, 2007): vol. 294, no. 35, p. 8.

Wilson, Geraldine. "Review of *Rainbow Jordan.*" *Interracial Books for Children Bulletin* (1981): vol. 12, no. 7–8, pp. 24–25.

# ✸ Frank Chin

BORN: *1940, Berkeley, California*

NATIONALITY: *American*

GENRE: *Drama, fiction, nonfiction*

MAJOR WORKS:

*The Chickencoop Chinaman* (1972)

*The Year of the Dragon* (1974)

*The Chinaman Pacific and Frisco R. R. Co.* (1988)

*Donald Duk* (1991)

## Overview

Frank Chin was a leader in the group of Asian-American writers that emerged on the literary scene during the 1960s, attacking and dispelling Asian-American myths and stereotypes. An unapologetically defiant voice from the margins of American culture, Chin has helped shape modern Asian-American literature, while encouraging new Asian-American authors in their endeavors. Best known for his plays *The Chickencoop Chinaman* and *The Year of the Dragon*, Chin has also written short stories,

novels, and caustic essays that illustrate what it is like to be Chinese and living in America.

## Works in Biographical and Historical Context

*Hidden Away* Frank Chin was born on February 25, 1940, in Berkeley, California, to a Chinese immigrant father and a fourth-generation Chinese American mother. During the middle of the nineteenth century, tens of thousands of Chinese American immigrants came to the United States to work as laborers, first in the mining camps during the Gold Rush, and later on the quickly expanding American railways. Between 1885 and 1943, a ban was placed on Chinese immigration; Chinese Americans already in the United States, largely excluded from mainstream culture, formed communities within the larger cities along the West Coast, primarily Northern California.

As a young child, Chin lived near an abandoned gold mine in California with an elderly white couple. His father was hiding him from his maternal grandmother, who disapproved of her fifteen-year-old daughter's involvement with Chin's father, an older man. At the age of six, Chin went to live with his parents and spent the remainder of his youth in the Chinatowns of Oakland and San Francisco.

From 1958 to 1961, Chin attended the University of California at Berkeley, where he began contributing pieces to the *California Pelican*, the university's humor magazine. As a writer and then editor for the publication, Chin revealed early traces of the abrasive humor and ethnic proclivity that have become trademarks of his work. In 1961, he won a scholarship to attend the prestigious Writer's Workshop at the University of Iowa. Two years later he received his bachelor's degree in English at the University of California at Santa Barbara in 1965.

*Theatrical Success and Literary Obstacles* After graduation, Chin took a job as a clerk with the Southern Pacific Railroad; in 1966, he became the first Chinese American brakeman in the company's history. From there he moved to Seattle, Washington, and spent three years writing for KING-TV until returning to California and teaching Asian Studies at San Francisco State University and the University of California at Davis. As an organizer of the Combined Asian-American Resources Project (CARP), Chin worked with other Asian writers and scholars, including Jeff Chan, Lawson Inada, and Shawn Wong.

Chin began his career in drama in the early 1970s, founding the Asian-American Theater Workshop in San Francisco; he remained its director until 1977. In 1972, he premiered his first play, *The Chickencoop Chinaman*, followed by *The Year of the Dragon* two years later. Both plays were produced off-Broadway by the American Place Theatre, making Chin the first Asian American to have a work presented on a mainstream New York stage.

Although Chin's first novel, *A Chinese Lady Dies*, won the distinguished Joseph Henry Jackson Award for promising young writers of California, it was never

## LITERARY AND HISTORICAL CONTEMPORARIES

Chin's famous contemporaries include:

**Maxine Hong Kingston** (1940–): A first-generation Chinese American, Kingston won the National Book Critics Award for General Nonfiction for *The Woman Warrior: Memoirs of a Girlhood among Ghosts* (1976), which combines cultural criticism with personal history.

**Frank Xaver Kroetz** (1946–): A great deal of this German dramatist's work depicts characters marginalized and damaged by society.

**Alice Walker** (1944–): Walker is an African American novelist best known for her Pulitzer Prize-winning work *The Color Purple* (1982).

**Bo Xilai** (1949–): China's Minister of Commerce until 2007, Xilai, who has a degree in journalism, is known for his articulate speech and charisma when dealing with the media.

**Gao Xingjian** (1940–): Winner of the 2000 Nobel Prize in Literature, this exiled novelist and playwright living in France has established new precedents for the Chinese novel and drama.

**Gus Lee** (1946–): Lee is an American novelist whose *China Boy*, about a Chinese American boy growing up in a San Francisco slum, is loosely based on his own experiences.

published. His second novel, *Charlie Chan on Maui*, was rejected by publishers when the owners of the Charlie Chan copyright threatened legal action. Because of these two failed attempts at publishing his novels, Chin was told by editors that his work was commercially unfeasible. Only after the success of his short-story collection, *The Chinaman Pacific and Frisco R. R. Co.* (1988), did Chin publish his first novel, *Donald Duk* (1991).

*Scholarly Pursuits* Since the 1980s, Chin has had little involvement with the theater, preferring to write fiction and essays about Chinese and Japanese history, culture, and literature. Throughout his literary career, he has explored his feelings toward Chinatown and its inhabitants in his work. He has taught various Asian-American courses at San Francisco State University, the University of California at Berkeley, Davis, and Santa Barbara, and at the University of Oklahoma at Norman. He has also received a number of awards and fellowships during the course of his career.

### Works in Literary Context

The ethnic awareness Chin has developed through both his literary production and his critique of late-modern and contemporary Asian-American literature is reflected in many younger writers, including Chinese American

Mei Ng and Filipino Americans Jessica Hagedorn and Peter Bacho. Chin's efforts to push the boundaries of acceptable ethnic identities—and, some would say, the standards of good taste—have been alternately viewed as both provocative and offensively chauvinistic.

*Cultural Identity* Identity is a major theme in Chin's writing. His works attack stereotypes that erode individual worth and steal cultural identity. Rather than simply blame Anglo-Americans for these stereotypes, Chin argues that everyone in America is responsible for them, including Chinese Americans. *The Chickencoop Chinaman*, for example, illustrates the difference between one's assimilating into American culture and one's rejecting the history of Chinese America in an attempt to become an "honorary white." Chin's works stress the need for Chinese Americans to learn the true history of their people, not the myths and stereotypes that he maintains are taught in school.

In Chin's novel *Donald Duk*, the young protagonist's history teacher tells his class, "The Chinese in America were made passive and nonassertive by centuries of Confucian thought and Zen mysticism. They were totally unprepared for the violently individualistic and democratic Americans." Because of his teacher's words, Donald is ashamed of his Chinese-American heritage until he begins to have dreams about working on the Central Pacific Railroad in 1869. In his dreams he sees incredible feats performed by his ancestors. Armed with newfound pride, Donald goes back to his history class to set the record straight.

### Works in Critical Context

Although some contemporary Asian-American literary studies attempt to marginalize Chin's work, he is still a notable presence in American literature. In general, critics praise Chin's ability to bring characters and their predicaments alive, as well as his ability to paint vivid portrayals and infuse his argumentative and satiric works with humor. Frank Abe, for example, contends that Chin has succeeded in "developing a stream-of-consciousness language crammed with goofy wordplay, unexpected imagery, and exhilarating, liberating hyperbole," all elements that make his work worth reading. Other scholars, however, criticize Chin's use of surreal dream sequences, flashbacks, and other forms of experimentation, complaining that such aspects, along with overall plots that detract from narrative effectiveness, result in works that are vague and difficult to comprehend.

*Donald Duk* Reviewers have responded to Chin's fiction with mixed reactions to his unconventional, complex, and often satiric prose style, as well as his self-indulgent, combative themes. *Donald Duk* is no exception. While many find the humor in the novel to be unrelenting, some academics have difficulty locating any humor in Chin's work. Elaine H. Kim asserts, "One is never quite sure whether or not to laugh at Chin's 'comic manifestations of Asian-American manhood.'" In addition, Kim is bothered by the jarring metaphors, devastating stereotypes, and feelings of distress within the author's work. Even critics who praise Chin's biting humor and his skill as a storyteller question his angry, sometimes hateful perspectives. Remarks scholar Douglas Sun, "Chin's rhetoric is often sharp and funny, but he also rides the high horse of racial bitterness for more than it's worth."

*The Chickencoop Chinaman*   Although he has removed himself from active participation in the theater, Chin remains recognized as an important voice in Asian-American drama. As a result of his withdrawal, some reviewers are less forgiving of the bitterness characteristic of his dramas. Critic Anthony Graham-White, for instance, comments on the fury and alienation in Chin's work for the stage, *The Chickencoop Chinaman* in particular: "We are meant to recognize the truth of the central character's ... attacks upon society, while in the course of the play he himself is presented in such a way as to lose our sympathy." Other commentators interpret Chin's ambivalence toward the theater as a reflection of his own internal conflicts and believe that the opposing character viewpoints in *The Chickencoop Chinaman* represent Chin's own Chinese and American identities in conflict.

## Responses to Literature

1. How have Asian Americans been represented in U.S. popular culture? Find three examples from popular media such as television, films, music, or video games. In your opinion, are any of these representations biased or stereotypical? If so, how?

2. What do you think are the reasons for the characters in *Chickencoop Chinaman* to identify themselves as Asian, American, neither, or both? Are there differences in the ways in which females or males define themselves as Asian American?

3. Is being an "American ethnic" writer different from being an "American" writer? Do you think writers from strong ethnic or cultural backgrounds tend to be viewed differently than other writers by critics, readers, and scholars? If so, in what ways?

4. *Donald Duk* tells the tale of a Chinese American boy coming of age in San Francisco. In what ways are the issues faced by Donald unique to his status as a Chinese American, and in what ways are they universal concerns faced by every person while growing up?

BIBLIOGRAPHY

**Books**

Chin, Frank. *Donald Duk*. Minneapolis, Minn.: Coffee House Press, 1991.
Gish, Robert. "Reperceiving Ethnicity in Western American Literature," in *Updating the Literary West* edited by Thomas J. Lyon. Fort Worth, Tex.: Texas Christian University Press, 1997, pp. 35–43.
Goshert, John. *Frank Chin*. Boise, Idaho: Boise State University Western Writers Series, 2002.
Graham-White, Anthony. "Frank Chin," in *Contemporary Dramatists* edited by Kate Berney. Detroit, Mich.: St. James Press, 1993.
Hagedorn, Jessica, ed. *Charlie Chan Is Dead*. New York: Penguin, 1993.
Lee, Rachel. *The Americas of Asian- American Literature*. Princeton, N.J.: Princeton University Press, 1999.
Li, David Leiwei. *Imagining the Nation: Asian-American Literature and Cultural Consent*. Stanford, Calif.: Stanford University Press, 1998.

**Periodicals**

Abe, Frank. "Frank Chin: His Own Voice." *Bloomsbury Review* (September 1991): vol. II, no. 6, pp. 3–4.
Kim, Elaine H. "Frank Chin: The Chinatown Cowboy and His Backtalk." *Midwest Quarterly* (Autumn 1978): vol. XX, no. 1, pp. 78–91.
Sun, Douglas. "Memories of a Chinese-American Boyhood." *Los Angeles Times Book Review* (January 1, 1989): 6.

---

# COMMON HUMAN EXPERIENCE

Chin's works explore issues of Asian-American identity, history, and culture. Many of Chin's coming-of-age stories reflect the author's own experiences and questions of cultural and ethnic identity. Listed below are examples of other works that illustrate such conflict between one's cultural identity and American society:

*Typical American* (1992), fiction by Gish Jen. Following the life of Ralph Chang, this novel tells the story of a Chinese immigrant in search of the American dream.

*Arabian Jazz* (1993), a novel by Diana Abu-Jaber. This work of fiction depicts the experiences of an immigrant Jordanian family as its members undergo integration into American society.

*How the García Girls Lost Their Accents* (1992), a novel by Julia Alvarez. In this work, four sisters find that adjusting to life in America after fleeing from the Dominican Republic is both difficult and embarrassing.

*My Country and My People* (1935), nonfiction by Lin Yutang. In an attempt to explain China to the West, Yutang's first English work offers an intimate portrayal of the Chinese mindset.

*Fifth Chinese Daughter* (1950), an autobiography by Jade Snow Wong. Wong recounts her struggle with the clash between American individualism and traditional Chinese values during her childhood in San Francisco's Chinatown.

# ✸ Marilyn Chin

BORN: *1955, Hong Kong, China*

NATIONALITY: *American*

GENRE: *Poetry*

MAJOR WORKS:

*Dwarf Bamboo* (1987)

*The Phoenix Gone, the Terrace Empty* (1994)

*Rhapsody in Plain Yellow* (2002)

## Overview

Marilyn Chin is recognized as a contemporary Asian-American poet whose work refutes stereotypical and static images of Chinese Americans, often by providing diverse and dynamic portrayals of Asian-American characters. She addresses the topic of cultural assimilation by attacking the assumption that every Asian American, regardless of specific ethnicity, place of birth, and social status, wants to share a collective identity and political agenda.

## Works in Biographical and Historical Context

***Folk Songs, Opera, and Immigration*** Marilyn Chin was born on January 14, 1955, in Hong Kong. Her early childhood was filled with music. Chin's grandmother

Marilyn Chin  *Chin, Marilyn, photograph. Photo by Niki Berg.*

used to carry her on her back while singing folk songs and chanting poetry. Additionally, Chin's mother was a fan of Cantonese opera and took her first daughter to live performances. Chin memorized the songs she heard there and at home, where her mother played opera recordings. However, Chin immigrated in 1962 with her mother, paternal grandmother, and younger sister Jane to Portland, Oregon, where they joined her father and paternal grandfather and where she forgot all of the Chinese songs she had learned. Chin's father worked as a chef in various Chinese restaurants and even jointly owned some, but his business dealings were unsuccessful. By the late 1960s, Chin's father moved out of the family home, while Chin, her siblings, and her mother continued to live with and be supported by her father's parents. Though Chin's father never legally divorced her mother, he remained estranged from the family.

***Reclaiming the Lost Songs*** In 1977, Chin graduated cum laude from the University of Massachusetts Amherst, with a BA in Chinese language and literature, part of a lifelong process of reclaiming the childhood songs she had lost after emigration. Chin went on to receive an MFA in 1981 in English/Creative Writing from the University of Iowa, where she taught in the comparative literature department and also served as a translator for the International Writing Program. Between 1980 and 1985, Chin spent considerable energy on her interest in language, translating or editing three volumes of world literature. She also worked in 1983 as a bilingual counselor and adult–education instructor at Crestwood Hospital in Vallejo, California.

***Writing about Sociopolitical Change*** After receiving a series of fellowships between 1983 and 1987, including a National Endowment for the Arts Grant in 1985, Chin published her first volume of poetry, *Dwarf Bamboo*. In this collection, Chin self-consciously and critically explores the crossroads she encountered as a child and young adult. She recalls her Chinese immigrant family's experiences and anticipates a future that might faithfully address the bicultural social consciousness that she developed during her coming-of-age in the United States.

In 1989, Chin joined the faculty of San Diego State University as an assistant professor. That year she also received a Gjerassi Foundation Fellowship, and her second National Endowment for the Arts Grant followed in 1991. In 1994 *The Phoenix Gone, the Terrace Empty* was published. In this collection, Chin depends upon and reveals her personal life and political commitments to provide emotional momentum. In an interview with Bill Moyers in *The Language of Life: A Festival of Poets* (1995), Chin discussed the pain of her father's leaving the family and disclosed that "How I Got That Name" and many other poems in the collection function on a personal and familial level.

***Views on Assimilation*** The poem entitled "How I Got That Name," epitomizes Chin's view toward her resistant stance regarding cultural assimilation and romanticizing the Chinese American culture. She critically recounts her father changing her name from "Mei Ling" to "Marilyn," after movie icon Marilyn Monroe; she places this alteration of her name within the context of immigration to the United States and her father's infatuation with a movie star and American culture. Chin makes clear that she views assimilation as a loss of identity, a loss of culture, language, and religion.

In *The Phoenix Gone, the Terrace Empty*, Chin also expresses her dedication to feminist issues. She returns for inspiration to an early feminist influence in "Song of the Sad Guitar," which she dedicates to writer Maxine Hong Kingston. The poem echoes the conclusion of Kingston's book *The Woman Warrior: Memoirs of a Girlhood among Ghosts* (1976), when the narrator finishes a story begun by her mother about the translation of songs across cultural borders. Chin folds together allusions to cultural and feminist ancestors and shared songs, a technique that allows her to juxtapose two cultural views.

*Songs of Loss*  In 1996, Chin became a full professor in the Department of English and Comparative Literature at San Diego State University, teaching courses in poetry in the MFA program and literature classes. In 1999, Chin was awarded a Senior Fulbright Fellowship in Taiwan. When Chin published her third book of poetry, *Rhapsody in Plain Yellow* (2002), the overall tone was different from her first two volumes. Many of the poems in the collection focus on love, relationships, and death, perhaps because they were written during a period in which Chin's mother, grandmother, and lover all passed away. Indeed, the volume is dedicated to Chin's mother, who died in 1994, and her grandmother, who died in 1996. The elegies to Chin's mother and poems that explore mother-daughter relationships are particularly poignant. Unlike in Chin's previous books, this collection is not divided into titled sections. Beyond a recurring melancholy, what connects the poems are the various song forms that Chin adapts and collects, including the blues; Chinese folk songs and ghost stories; Persian *ghazals*, a "Broken Chord Sequence;" an aria; a sonatina, or short sonata; and the emotional and improvisational rhapsody.

Currently, Chin co-directs the MFA program at San Diego State University.

## Works in Literary Context

All three of Chin's published collections of poetry address such themes as the limitations of the American Dream for immigrants, Asian American unity, Chinese cultural traditions, and the function of poetry in Western culture. Exploring a dynamic notion of poetry as a cultural expression of identity—when identity is defined as multiple, contextual, and changing—is one of Chin's significant contributions to contemporary poetry in the United States. However, unlike many activist poets of the late 1960s and 1970s who sought unity through cultural expression and

worked collectively to demand changes in the United States, Chin's poetry focuses on the concept of assimilation.

*Blending Eastern and Western Style*  In order to achieve her distinct poetic voice, Chin boldly blends elements from a range of different cultures and historical periods with a contemporary form and content more familiar to American readers. The cross-cultural exchange and blending of poetic influences parallels the dialogue that Chin often sets up between different speakers or personae within poems as much as it echoes the dynamic and fluid process of Chin's own Asian American identity formation.

By melding different poetic forms, Chin is able to meld her East-West identity. Chin comments: "Once I blended the epigrams of Horace with the haiku of Basho and came up with a strange brew of didacticism and pure image that made a powerful political statement." In *Dwarf Bamboo*, Chin seems to make extensive use of the theme of *sabi* (loneliness) through explicit references to Matsuo Basho, the seventeenth-century Japanese poet known for developing the concept. Chin also seems to reference Basho through unmarked allusions, such as the use of images to evoke emotions, the use of *haikai renku*, or unorthodox linked verse, where poems continue the mood or tone of a poem written by a literary predecessor.

Most provocative perhaps is the overlap among the traditions and historical contexts that Chin highlights. Throughout *Dwarf Bamboo*, but particularly in "We Are Americans Now, We Live in the Tundra," Chin uses *sabi* to

### LITERARY AND HISTORICAL CONTEMPORARIES

Chin's famous contemporaries include:

**Stephen King** (1947–): The master of horror fiction and contemporary thrillers, American novelist King is noted for his writing style that blends traditional gothic tales with modern psychology and science fiction.

**Maxine Hong Kingston** (1940–): One of the most influential Asian American author of the twentieth century, Kingston's memoir, *The Woman Warrior: Memoirs of a Girlhood among Ghosts* (1976) was an immediate literary success.

**Maya Ling Yin** (1959–): This American architect is known for her design of the Vietnam Veterans' Memorial in Washington, D.C., a project she completed her senior year at Yale University. She also designed the Civil Rights Memorial in Montgomery, Alabama.

**Bill Gates** (1955–): American entrepreneur who co-founded Microsoft Corporation. The young Gates vowed to put a computer into every American home.

# COMMON HUMAN EXPERIENCE

Chin's work expresses mixed feeling toward her bicultural identity. Here are some other works that involve struggles with assimilation and cultural identity:

*Nisei Daughter* (1953), a memoir by Monica Sone. This autobiography recounts the story of how Sone, a Japanese-American who grew up in Seattle, was confined to an interment camp during World War II. Sone vividly describes her feelings of confusion about the experience.

*The Circuit* (1997), a short story collection by Francisco Jiménez. This collection of short stories provide a glimpse into Jiménez's life as a young migrant worker. The stories emphasize cultural differences and the hardships of surviving in a foreign country.

*The Line of the Sun* (1989), a novel by Judith Ortiz Cofer. Cofer, a poet, essayist, and novelist, wrote her first book about a family who moves from Puerto Rico to New Jersey. She contrasts the village life with the new world filled with different customs and values. Cofer often writes about her attempts to reconcile her family's traditional values with her experience growing up the United States.

*The Chosen* (1967), a novel by Chaim Potok. Potok, like many American Jewish novelists, questions whether immigrants should sacrifice their culture and religion by joining mainstream America. His first novel, *The Chosen* examines contemporary Jewish-American identity, presenting characters who are drawn to the outside world. Their conflict lies between choosing between Orthodox Judaism and the secular world.

connect thematically the historically distant Chinese context of Western and Japanese imperialism, a more recent revolutionary communist China, and a contemporary Chinese American postcolonial longing for a lost homeland and culture. Few poems include notes that translate or define non-English words, identify Chinese literary and historical figures, or explain cultural references; in most poems, readers are left to their own devices and experiences to make meaning of Chin's impressive synthesis.

## Works in Critical Context

Reviewers of Chin's work find it difficult to characterize her work as specifically Asian American. Scholars insist that considerable attention must be made in how to read the cultural and social context of her work. Several critics have suggested that while readers should heed cultural context, the danger of ethnocentric readings is that they can lead to exclusive attention to the poet's ethnicity. As Xiaojing Zhou writes, this kind of focus feeds "a misconception that a pure and fixed Chinese culture has been inherited" by Chinese American poets and that their poems somehow automatically and clearly reproduce it, expressing one side, the "exotic" or "foreign" side, of an

irrevocably split Chinese American identity. Hence, many scholars prefer to emphasize the eclectic variety of poetic influences evident in Chin's work.

*The Phoenix Gone, the Terrace Empty*  In *The Phoenix Gone, the Terrace Empty*, Chin combines feminism with old stories and American idioms. She juxtaposes images of Chinese culture with her American rearing. One of Chin's most distinctive marks as a poet is her skilled play with language. Anne-Elizabeth Green notes in *Contemporary Women Poets* that Chin "is not afraid of mixing tones and styles within the same poem, evoking radically variant moods and creating strange juxtapositions with differing literary voices. These juxtapositions may be playful, or may shock in the sudden aggressiveness of her shift in tone." In *The Progressive*, critic Matthew Rothschild comments that Chin "has a voice all her own—witty, epigraphic, idiomatic, elegiac, earthy. . . . She covers the canvas of cultural assimilation with an intensely personal brush." Some verses explore the difficulties faced by women immigrants, other verses warn about the dangers of stereotyping.

*Rhapsody in Plain Yellow*  Although many of the poems in this collection are melancholy, the volume also features poems written in a confrontational style that continue Chin's poetic efforts against cultural assimilation and racial injustice. For example, in "Millennium, Six Songs," the speaker insists that "We've arrived shoeless, crutchless, tousle-haired, swollen bellied / We shall inherit this earth's meek glory, as foretold." There are also poems that are explicitly feminist. Donna Seaman of *Booklist* describes the tone of collection: "Chin paces the line demarcated by the words Chinese American like a caged tiger, jury just barely held in check."

## Responses to Literature

1. Read Chin's poem, "How I Got That Name." Bill Moyers has described the poem as "elegiac," meaning it mourns for the loss of someone or something. Do you agree? What, specifically, does the poet mourn for?

2. Read several poems from *Dwarf Bamboo*. Write an evaluation of the collection by highlighting three poems that represent the speaker' experience in America.

3. In a short essay, compare Chin's poetry to poetry by other feminist poets, such as Adrianne Rich or Sylvia Plath. How are the poems similar in tone, imagery, and theme? How are they different?

4. Discuss difficulties first generation immigrants face in America. Use Chin's poems to support your position on this topic.

BIBLIOGRAPHY

**Books**

Lim, Shirley Geok-lin. *Reading the Literatures of Asian America*. Philadelphia: Temple University Press, 1992.
Moyers, Bill. *The Language of Life: A Festival of Poets*. New York: Doubleday, 1995.

**Periodicals**

Chang, Juliana. "Reading Asian American Poetry." *MELUS* 21 (Spring 1996): 81–98.

Gery, John. "'Mocking My Own Ripeness': Authenticity, Heritage, and Self-Erasure in the Poetry of Marilyn Chin." *LIT: Literature Interpretation Theory* 12 (2001): 25–45.

Green, Anne-Elizabeth. "Marilyn Chin." *Contemporary Women Poets* (1998): 61–63.

McCormick, Adrienne. "Being Without: Marilyn Chin's Poems as Feminist Acts of Theorizing." *Hitting Critical Mass* 6 (Spring 2000): 37–58.

Slowik, Mary. "Beyond Lot's Wife: The Immigration Poems of Marilyn Chin, Garrett Hongo, Li-Young Lee, and David Mura." *MELUS* 25 (Fall/Winter 2000): 221–242.

# ✺ Kate Chopin

BORN: *1851, St. Louis, Missouri*

DIED: *1904, St. Louis, Missouri*

NATIONALITY: *American*

GENRE: *Fiction, poetry*

MAJOR WORKS:

"The Story of an Hour" (1894)

*The Awakening* (1899)

## Overview

Once considered merely an author of local color fiction, Kate Chopin is recognized today for the originality of a point of view that defies a conventional American male perspective. In a way that her contemporaries could—or would—not, Chopin unabashedly addresses the complex conflicts between female sexuality and social expectations. While Chopin's psychological examinations of female protagonists are formative works in the historical development of feminist literature, they also provide insight into a society that oftentimes denied the value of female independence.

## Works in Biographical and Historical Context

***A Creole Girl in St. Louis Society*** Chopin, originally Kate O'Flaherty, was born in 1851 to a prominent St. Louis family. Her father died in a train accident when Chopin was four years old, and her childhood was most profoundly influenced by her mother and great-grandmother, who were descendents of French-Creole pioneers. Chopin's great-grandmother cultivated in the young girl a love for storytelling, an interest in the intimate details about such historical figures as the earliest settlers of the Louisiana Territory, and, most importantly, a nonjudgmental intellectual curiosity about life. Chopin also spent a great deal of time with her

Kate Chopin    *The Library of Congress.*

family's Creole and mixed-race slaves, familiarizing herself with their unique dialects. After a nondescript education at a convent school, she graduated at age seventeen and spent two years as a belle of fashionable St. Louis society. Even as she reveled in the St. Louis social scene, Chopin became increasingly aware of the superficialities of high society. In 1870, she married Oscar Chopin, a wealthy Creole businessman.

***Gathering Material from Her Life*** For the next decade, Chopin lived according to the demanding social and domestic schedule of a Southern aristocrat and mother of six, her recollections of which would later serve as material for her short stories. In 1880, financial difficulties forced Chopin's family to move to Natchitoches Parish, located in Louisiana's Red River bayou region. There, as her husband oversaw his father's plantations, Chopin became involved with the Creole community. Even though they were a people who considered themselves different from Anglo-Americans and maintained cultural traditions passed down from their French and Spanish ancestors, Creole society accepted Chopin, admiring her friendly nature and intellect. During her years in Natchitoches Parish, Chopin noted the role of women in Creole society. Men dominated the households and expected their women to provide them with well-kept homes and many children to carry on the family name. While the Creole men caroused, their women pursued music, art,

# LITERARY AND HISTORICAL CONTEMPORARIES

Chopin's famous contemporaries include:

**Anthony Comstock** (1844–1915): Comstock successfully lobbied Congress to enact the Comstock Law of 1873, which outlawed the selling or distribution of materials that could be used for contraception.

**Sarah Orne Jewett** (1849–1909): Jewett's familiarity with the Maine countryside led to her successful local-color writing, such as the well-known short story "The White Heron" (1886)

**Belva Lockwood** (1830–1917): In addition to being the first woman to run for President of the United States, Lockwood was also the first female lawyer admitted to practice before the Supreme Court.

**Mary Cassatt** (1844–1926): Cassatt, one of America's few female Impressionist painters, was commissioned to paint a large mural entitled *Modern Woman* for the Women's Building at 1893's Columbian Exposition in Chicago.

**John Lomax** (1867–1948): This American folklorist collected thousands of folk songs, which he published in numerous books and which became an important part of the Archive of Folk Culture at the Library of Congress.

and conversation. Such refined women enhanced their husbands' social status. These observations would prove to be of monumental importance to Chopin when writing *The Awakening*.

After her husband's death in 1883, Chopin sold most of her property and left Louisiana to live with her mother in St. Louis. At this time of transition, Chopin began reading the works of Charles Darwin and Thomas Huxley in order to keep abreast of trends in scientific thinking, ideas that led her to question ethical restraints and socially imposed mores. Inspired by these thinkers and encouraged to write professionally by family and friends who found her letters entertaining, Chopin began composing short stories. Though her first piece, a poem entitled "If It Might Be" (1889), was published immediately, Chopin then endured a long period of routine rejections when submitting short fiction to various publications. Eventually, though, Chopin's stories were seen in many popular American periodicals, including *Vogue* and *The Atlantic*. When these stories were collected in *Bayou Folk* (1894) and *A Night in Acadie* (1897), Chopin began to receive national attention as a local color writer. Financially independent and encouraged by her success, Chopin turned to longer works.

*The Women's Movement* The 1800s saw a change in the status of women in the United States. As early as 1848, women gathered in New York State to address issues of equality, thereby laying the groundwork for the women's rights movement. During Chopin's lifetime, women's groups continued to organize to educate women about social and political issues and to allow a forum for women's discussions. While women did not gain the right to vote until 1920, these pioneering efforts created a voice in society that would not be quieted. Despite these changes, however, Chopin's next efforts, a novel and a short story collection, were rejected by publishers on moral grounds because the stories promoted female self-assertion and sexual liberation.

Undaunted, Chopin completed *The Awakening* (1899), the story of a conventional wife and mother who, after gaining spiritual freedom through an extramarital affair, commits suicide when she realizes that she cannot reconcile her newfound self to society's moral restrictions. In *The Awakening*, Edna Pontellier, realizing that her life could consist of more than living in her husband's shadow and stifling her own desires and dreams, embodies the need for independence that women during the 1800s began recognizing in themselves. Without a doubt, Edna's actions reflect not only the times, but also the emotions felt by many women who sought personal freedom, including Chopin herself.

*A Backlash Awakened* Now regarded as Chopin's masterpiece, *The Awakening* provoked outrage among critics and readers upon publication. The novel was banned in St. Louis and elsewhere, and Chopin was excluded from local literary groups. As a result of the hostile reception to the novel and difficulties with publishers, Chopin wrote very little at the end of her life. Five years after the publication of *The Awakening*, Chopin died of a stroke in St. Louis on August 22, 1904.

## Works in Literary Context

While her early works especially show the influence of her favorite authors, French writers Guy de Maupassant, Alphonse Daudet, and Molière, Chopin soon found a voice of her own, one shaped by a time in history when women's roles were changing. Set in Louisiana, most of Chopin's fiction focuses on the themes of class relations, relationships between men and women, and feminine sexuality. Her stories portray characters as diverse as Southern belles, Arcadians and Creoles, mulattos and blacks. Even when audiences attempted to censure her work, Chopin challenged the confining boundaries on women set by society, inspiring generations of female writers who followed her.

*Symbolic Awakening* In Chopin's best works, she transcends simple regionalism and portrays women who seek spiritual and sexual freedom amid the restrictive mores of nineteenth-century Southern society. By examining such issues as female sexuality, personal identity, and social propriety, Chopin allows women to awaken to life and, ultimately, to themselves. Scholar Bert Bender observes that Chopin's protagonists "transcend their socially limited selves by awakening to and affirming impulses that are unacceptable by convention. Unburdened of restricting social conventions ... [they] experience the suffering and loneliness, as well as the joy, of their freedom." Though Chopin's characters undergo a figurative awakening, its effects literally change their lives.

Obvious from its title, *The Awakening* unequivocally addresses psychological growth. The theme of awakening is evident in the life of Edna Pontellier, a conventional wife and mother who experiences a spiritual epiphany and an awakened sense of independence that alters her course of life forever. Passionate arousal—whether physical, intellectual or emotional—and the consequences one must face to attain it is supported by sensual imagery that acquires symbolic meanings as the story progresses. This symbolism emphasizes the conflict within Edna, who realizes that she can neither exercise her new-found sense of independence nor return to life as it was before her spiritual awakening. The sea, the novel's central symbol, provides the framework for the narrative's main action, as it is the site of both Edna's awakening and suicide.

## Works in Critical Context

Though Chopin's editors tolerated her daring themes and characters' actions, audiences in the late nineteenth and early twentieth centuries condemned Chopin's frank treatment of such subjects as female sexuality, adultery, and miscegenation (sexual relations between people of different races); consequently, her work fell into neglect. Around the middle of the twentieth century, however, scholars began to take note of Chopin's forthright depictions of race, class, gender, and regional identity. A great deal of critical attention has focused on Chopin's pioneering use of psychological realism, symbolic imagery, and sensual themes, and in more recent years, Chopin and her work have become favored subjects among women critics. No matter the critical perspective from which it is examined, Chopin's work, like that of any great writer, transcends specifics of time and place and holds relevance for readers regardless of gender or nationality.

*The Awakening*    When *The Awakening* appeared in 1899, the literary world was not ready for the realism of Chopin's novel. It was received with indignation, resulting in an overwhelmingly negative dismissal of the novel. Most critics deemed Chopin a pornographer and proclaimed *The Awakening* to be immoral and perverse, going so far as to say they were satisfied by the headstrong protagonist's suicide. American novelist Willa Cather was among the legion of readers who denounced *The Awakening*, complaining that Chopin had wasted herself on a "trite and sordid" theme.

Of course, *The Awakening* was not entirely without supporters. A few reviewers in 1899 praised Chopin's skill in exploring her subject, while others felt sympathy for Edna instead of contempt. Ignored for more decades, *The Awakening* was rediscovered in the 1950s, when it became celebrated for its open treatment of a woman's search for self-knowledge. By 1952, literary historian Van

---

## COMMON HUMAN EXPERIENCE

Chopin's stories detail the subtleties of Louisiana's Cajun and Creole cultures in the late nineteenth century. Works by other writers who are known for their regionalism, or local-color writing, include the following:

*The Adventures of Huckleberry Finn* (1884), a novel by Mark Twain. *The Adventures of Huckleberry Finn* is highly treasured for its colorful description of people and places along the Mississippi River, as well as its use of several different regional dialects in the speech patterns of its characters.

*Balcony Stories* (1914), a collection of short stories by Grace Elizabeth King. Concerned with the challenges Southern women faced after the Civil War, these stories depict the social customs of women in New Orleans.

*A New England Nun and Other Stories* (1891), short fiction by Mary E. Wilkins. Written by a New England regionalist, this work realistically portrays frustrated lives in New England hill towns.

---

Wyck Brooks had acknowledged *The Awakening* as an undeservedly slighted work. He called the book "one novel of the nineties in the South that should have been remembered, one small perfect book that mattered more than the whole life of many a prolific writer," and he commended the novel for its "naturalness and grace." Critics Robert Cantwell and Kenneth Eble echoed Brooks's comments in the mid-1950s, proclaiming *The Awakening* insightful as well as evocative, uninhibited as well as beautifully written. In 1969, Chopin biographer Per Seyersted asserted that in *The Awakening*, Chopin "was the first woman writer in America to accept sex with its profound repercussions as a legitimate subject of serious fiction," an opinion shared by Chopin scholars today.

## Responses to Literature

1. Some critics contend that Edna's suicide in *The Awakening* shows her inability to defy society. Others view her suicide as a final awakening, a decision showing a strength and independence defying social expectation. Which interpretation do you support? Explain your answer.

2. Write an alternative ending to *The Awakening* in which Edna does not commit suicide. Does your new ending ring true to the author's themes in the rest of the book?

3. How does Chopin's exploration of female sexuality compare to poet Walt Whitman's treatment of male

---

sexuality? How do they both emphasize the importance of both body and spirit?

4. Research the history of the women's rights movement beginning with the first political convention held in 1848 at Seneca Falls, New York, and ending with the present. Create a timeline from 1848 to 2000 that shows significant events in the women's movement along with other historical events.

BIBLIOGRAPHY

**Books**

Brooks, Van Wyck. *The Confident Years, 1885–1915.* New York: Dutton, 1952.

Cather, Willa. *The World and the Parish, Volume II: Willa Cather's Articles and Reviews, 1893–1902.* Edited by William M. Curtin. Lincoln, Neb.: University of Nebraska Press, 1970.

Diamond, Arlyn, and Lee R. Edwards. *The Authority of Experience: Essays in Feminist Criticism.* Amherst, Mass.: University of Massachusetts Press, 1988.

Jones, Anne Goodwyn. *Tomorrow Is Another Day: The Woman Writer in the South, 1859–1936.* Baton Rouge, La.: Louisiana State University Press, 1982.

Rankin, Daniel. *Kate Chopin and Her Creole Stories.* Philadelphia.: University of Pennsylvania Press, 1932.

Seyersted, Per. *Kate Chopin: A Critical Biography.* Baton Rouge, La.: Louisiana State University Press, 1969.

Skaggs, Peggy. *Kate Chopin.* Boston: Twayne Publishers, 1985.

**Periodicals**

Bender, Bart. "Kate Chopin's Lyrical Short Stories." *Studies in Short Fiction* (Summer 1974): vol. XI, no. 3, pp. 257–266.

Cantwell, Robert. "*The Awakening* by Kate Chopin." *The Georgia Review* (1956): 489–494.

Eble, Kenneth. "A Forgotten Novel: Kate Chopin's *The Awakening.*" *Western Humanities Review* 10 (1956): 261–269.

**Web sites**

KateChopin.org. *Kate Chopin International Society.* Retrieved September 18, 2008, from http://www.katechopin.org.

# ✿ Sandra Cisneros

BORN: *1954, Chicago, Illinois*

NATIONALITY: *Mexican American*

GENRE: *Fiction, poetry*

MAJOR WORKS:

*The House on Mango Street* (1984)

*Woman Hollering Creek and Other Stories* (1991)

*Caramelo* (2002)

Sandra Cisneros   *Cisneros, Sandra, 1991, photograph. AP Images.*

## Overview

Novelist and short story writer Sandra Cisneros draws upon her childhood experiences and ethnic heritage in her work, and confronts large issues like poverty, self-identity, and gender roles. Most of her characters are of Latin American heritage, and Cisneros depicts their social and cultural alienation through dialogue and sensory imagery rather than conventional narrative structures. Cisneros is best known for *The House on Mango Street* (1984), a volume of vignettes described as both a short story collection and a series of prose poems.

## Biographical and Historical Context

*The Only Daughter, Moving Across Borders*   Cisneros was the only daughter in a family with seven children. With six domineering brothers, Cisneros learned at an early age to speak out. In a January 1993 interview, she said, "You had to be fast and you had to be funny—you had to be a storyteller." Cisneros did not remain in one place for long as a child since her family moved back and forth between the United States and Mexico. In the late 1960s, her parents bought the tiny two-story bungalow in Chicago's North Side that would one day inspire her successful novel, *The House on Mango Street.*

Although Cisneros wrote poetry and prose during her childhood years, she did not realize her potential as a writer until she attended the University of Iowa's Writers Workshop in the late 1970s. Her lack of a stable home life made Cisneros a shy child with few friends. Her mother passed along a love for reading, and Cisneros used the world of books as an escape, often imagining herself the main character in a story controlled by an omniscient narrator.

***Student, Teacher, Lecturer*** Once at Loyola University, as the only Hispanic English major, she began to discover her cultural roots. There, she joined the Chicago poetry scene and found great enthusiasm for her work. She began to write in earnest as a student in the creative-writing program, then applied, and was accepted, to the prestigious Iowa Writers' Workshop. The years she spent at Iowa influenced the trajectory of Cisneros's life and writing. Many of her professors were difficult and intimidating, yet Cisneros built a support system of those who encouraged her as she tried to find her voice. For example, at Iowa, she made friends with Joy Harjo, a Native American writer, who also felt alienated by the challenges of the Iowa workshop. Cisneros's master's thesis, a collection of poems titled *My Wicked, Wicked Ways*, predicted themes that would repeat in her career: self-identity, love relationships, and friendship. Revised, the thesis was published in 1987.

Cisneros taught at Latino Youth Alternative High School in Chicago from July 1978 to December 1980. During this time, she wrote, but never had enough time or energy to finish any of her projects. She became a public speaker/reader after one of her poems was chosen for an ad campaign on the Chicago area public buses, and she enjoyed the adulation of audiences. But soon she missed her writing and decided to focus on completing a book. Cisneros published *Bad Boys* in 1980, an autobiographical poetry collection that portrayed her life in the Mexican ghetto in Chicago.

***From Europe to Mango Street*** During the spring of 1983, Cisneros was artist in residence at the Fondation Michael Karolyi in Vence, France. Earlier, in 1982, she received a National Endowment for the Arts grant, which she used to travel through Europe. During that time she began work on a series of poems that appeared in *My Wicked, Wicked Ways*, a collection that some say broke gender stereotypes by dealing with "bad girl sexual politics." But *The House on Mango Street* (1984) was Cisneros's largest success. Like her previous book of poetry, the novel uses her autobiographical experiences to draw a narrative of an adolescent girl coming of age in the urban ghetto. Cisneros wanted to write through what she called an "anti–academic voice—a child's voice, a girl's voice, a poor girl's voice, a spoken voice, the voice of an American-Mexican."

## LITERARY AND HISTORICAL CONTEMPORARIES

Cisneros's famous contemporaries include:

**Gloria Anzaldua** (1942–2004): Mexican American Anzaldua was a lesbian feminist writer, poet, activist, and scholar.

**Ana Castillo** (1953–): Called "one of the finest Chicana novelists," Castillo is also a critically acclaimed poet, short story writer, and essayist.

**Lorna Dee Cervantes** (1954–): Prolific poet Cervantes won an American Book Award for the collection *Emplumada* (1981).

**Cherrie Moraga** (1952–): Moraga is a poet, playwright, and essayist, as well as the co-editor of *This Bridge Called My Back: Writings by Radical Women of Color* (1984).

***Teaching, Hollering, and Caramelo*** In the late 1980s, Cisneros completed a Paisano Dobie Fellowship in Austin, Texas, and won awards for her short stories in the Segundo Concurso Nacional del Cuento Chicano, sponsored by the University of Arizona. Cisneros also began teaching in 1987 when she joined the faculty of California State University, and has held other visiting professorships at a variety of universities ever since. Her career has flourished in the last two decades, with the critically acclaimed prose collection *Woman Hollering Creek and Other Stories* (1991), books of poetry that include *Loose Woman* (1994), and her most recent novel, *Caramelo* (2002). With *Woman Hollering Creek and Other Stories*, Cisneros became the first Chicana (Mexican American woman) to receive a major publishing contract for a work about Chicanas. *Caramelo* was honored as book of the year by *The New York Times*, *The Los Angeles Times*, and the *Chicago Tribune*. The novel was also nominated for the Orange Prize in England and other prestigious awards.

## Works in Literary Context

Much of Cisneros's work reflects upon the connections between identity, culture, and a strong sense of place. *The House on Mango Street* is narrated by Esperanza Cordero as she comes of age in a poor Hispanic urban ghetto. Cisneros's third book of poetry, *My Wicked, Wicked Ways*, written with financial support from a 1982 National Endowment for the Arts grant, includes autobiographical poems about Cisneros's travels through Europe and the guilt associated with a Mexican and Catholic upbringing. In her short story collection, *Woman Hollering Creek and Other Stories* (1991), Cisneros draws Mexican American characters near San Antonio, Texas, and addresses social

## COMMON HUMAN EXPERIENCE

Cisneros often writes of characters on literal and figurative borderlands. Other books that use borderlands as a theme include:

*La Frontera/Borderlands* (1999), a book of prose-poetry by Gloria Anzaldua. Anzaldua uses a hybrid form of prose and poetry to lyrically imagine the tenuous existence of those living on the borderland between cultures and identities.

*Writing on the Edge: A Borderlands Reader* (2003), an anthology edited by Tom Miller. This collection, which includes works by authors like Carlos Fuentes and Allen Ginsberg, crosses genres to provide readers a new perspective on the U.S./Mexico border.

*The Namesake* (2005), a novel by Jhumpa Lahiri. At the heart of this novel, the protagonist and his family struggle with their transnational identities, trying to hold onto Indian customs while embracing what America has to offer.

*The New World Border: Prophecies, Poems, and Loqueras for the End of the Century* (1996), a collection by Guillermo Gmez-Pea. An American Book Award winner, this collection of essays, poems, performance texts, photographs, and "prophesies" suggests that only when we, as world citizens, see unity in our hybridity, will we grow as a global community.

and economic issues associated with stereotypical roles, minority status, and cultural conflicts.

***Symbolism of the House on Mango Street*** Cisneros, in an essay collection called *From a Writer's Notebook*, writes that not until her experience at the Iowa Writers Workshop did she realize that her childhood home would make a good subject for a book. After reading Gaston Bachelard's *The Poetics of Space* written in the 1950s, "the metaphor of a house" made an impact. Cisneros revised Bachelard's male-oriented perspective and creates a personal reality "about third-floor flats, and fear of rats, and drunk husbands sending rocks through windows, anything as far from the poetic as possible. And this is when I discovered the voice I'd been suppressing all along without realizing it." Scholar Julian Olivares writes, "Mango Street is a street sign, a marker, that circumscribes the neighborhood to its Latino population of Puerto Ricans, Chicanos and Mexican immigrants. This house is not the young protagonist's dream house; it is only a temporary house."

***Cisneros's Feminist Messages*** Feminist messages strongly resound throughout Cisneros's body of work. As she addresses issues of cross-cultural identity and confronts the traditional patriarchal values (those defined historically by men) of Mexican and American heritage, she expresses the idea that "[we women have] got to define what we think is fine for ourselves instead of what our culture says." Jean Wyatt notes Cisneros's engagement with the ways in which a woman's identity is oppressed by her culture and how she focuses specifically on the female protagonists of the short stories "Woman Hollering Creek" and "Never Marry a Mexican," who struggle to relate to conventional Mexican symbols of sexuality and motherhood. These "role models" include: "Guadalupe, the virgin mother," "la Chingada (Malinche), the raped mother," and "la Llorona, the mother who seeks her lost children."

## Works in Critical Context

Cisneros experiments with genre, language, and form throughout her work. Exemplified in *The House on Mango Street*, her style is a marriage of prose and poetry, magic and realism, American culture and Hispanic heritage. Cisneros' unique narrative voice has earned her consistent praise from critics and readers alike.

***Woman Hollering Creek and Other Stories*** Readers and reviewers alike have praised Cisneros's rich characterization and distinctive voice in *Woman Hollering Creek and Other Stories*. They suggest her skills as a poet add depth to her prose and often echo author and *Los Angeles Book Review* writer Barbara Kingsolver: "Cisneros has added length and dialogue and a hint of plot to her poems and published them in a stunning collection." Kingsolver also proclaimed that "nearly every sentence contains an explosive sensory image." Similarly, Bebe Moore Campbell in the *New York Times Book Review* suggested that Cisneros "seduces with precise, spare prose and creates unforgettable characters we want to lift off the page and hang out with for a little while."

***Caramelo*** *Publishers Weekly* called *Caramelo*, written nine years after *The House on Mango Street*, a "major literary event." Critics of the novel praised Cisneros's imagery and realistic bilingual dialogue. Scholar Carol Cujec writes, "Sandra Cisneros bathes our senses in Latino culture as we accompany her characters walking the scorched sands of Acapulco, buying shoes at Chicago's Maxwell Street flea market, … and eventually finding their destinies and their destinations." Cujec concludes her review of the novel by saying, "All in all, this is a stunning, creative novel that shows sparks of genius in its use of language: poetic, authentic, and deliciously spiced with Spanish." Reviewer Toni Fitzgerald agrees, evoking classic comparisons:

> It's impossible not to compare Cisneros' multigenerational tale to *The House of the Spirits* or *One Hundred Years of Solitude*, but unlike Isabel Allende or Gabriel García Márquez, Cisneros's magic comes from actual realism. Each word is a brushstroke.

## Responses to Literature

1. In *The House on Mango Street*, Esperanza says, "In English my name means hope. In Spanish it means

too many letters. It means sadness, it means waiting." Write a short essay on why this brief statement shows Esperanza trapped between cultural "borders." Use other examples from the text to support your opinion.

2. Cisneros often writes about borders and identity. Write a personal essay about the invisible lines drawn in your own life. What do these borders look and feel like? Do these borders hold you back from accomplishing certain things? Or, do these borders challenge you?

3. Family history anchors the novel *Caramelo*. Write a personal prose-poem describing how your family history has shaped your identity.

4. In *Caramelo*, the characters frequently comment on the Mexican people and culture. For example, Zoila asserts that "all people from Mexico City are liars." With a group of your classmates, discuss how you view this type of commentary. Focus on certain scenes in the novel and talk about what inspires different characters to make these remarks.

BIBLIOGRAPHY

**Books**

Duarte-Valverde, Gloria. "Cisneros, Sandra." *Notable Latino Writers*. Vol. 1. Pasadena, CA: Salem Press, 2006.

Herrera-Sobek, Maria and Helena Maria Viramontes Gloria, eds. *Chicana Creativity and Criticism*. Houston, TX: Arte Publico, 1988.

*Modern American Literature*. Eds. Joann Cerrito and Laurie DiMauro. Vol. 1. 5th ed. Farmington Hills, MI: St. James Press, 1999.

**Periodicals**

Aranda, Pilar. "On the Solitary Fate of Being Mexican, Female, Wicked, and Thirty-three: An Interview with Writer Sandra Cisneros." *Americas Review* 18 (Spring 1990): 64–80.

Cujec, Carol. "Caramel–coated Truths and Telenovela Lives: Sandra Cisneros Returns with an Ambitious Novel about the Latino Community." *World and I* 18:3 (March 2003): 228.

Mullen, Harryette. "A Silence Between Us Like a Language: The Untranslatability of Experience in sandra Cisneros' *Woman Hollering Creek*." *MELUS* 21 (Summer 1996): 3–20.

Wyatt, Jean. "On Not Being La Malinche: Border Negotiations of Gender in Sandra Cisneros' 'Never Marry a Mexican' and 'Woman Hollering Creek.'" *Tulsa Studies in Women's Literature*. 14:2 (Fall 1995): 243–272.

**Web sites**

Fitzgerald, Toni. "Caramelo." *Book Reporter*. Retrieved October 4, 2008, from http://www.BookReporter.com/.

Juffer, Jane. "Sandra Cisneros' Career." *Modern American Poetry*. Retrieved October 4, 2008 from http:// http://www.english.uiuc.edu/maps/poets/a_f/cisneros/career.htm/.

# ⊛ Tom Clancy

BORN: *1947, Baltimore, Maryland*

NATIONALITY: *American*

GENRE: *Fiction, nonfiction*

MAJOR WORKS:

*The Hunt for Red October* (1984)
*Patriot Games* (1987)
*Clear and Present Danger* (1989)
*Rainbow Six* (1998)
*The Teeth of the Tiger* (2003)

## Overview

Tom Clancy's novels of adventure and espionage in the international military industrial complex earned him enormous popularity in the 1980s as a creator of the "techno-thriller" genre. Clancy uses highly detailed descriptions of military technology and modern weaponry to create

Tom Clancy *1992, photograph. AP Images.*

dramatic tension. His novels top many best seller lists, and several titles have been franchised into movies and computer games, making Clancy and his thrillers popular worldwide.

## Works in Biographical and Historical Context

### Interest in Military Leads to Research and First Novel
Tom Clancy was born in Baltimore, Maryland, on December 4, 1947, the son of a mail carrier and a credit employee. After graduating from Loyola College in Baltimore in 1969, Clancy married Wanda Thomas, an insurance agency manager, and became an insurance agent in Baltimore and later in Hartford, Connecticut. In 1973, he joined the O. F. Bowen Agency in Owings, Maryland, becoming an owner there in 1980. Though Clancy had hoped for a military career, his poor eyesight made him ineligible. However, Clancy maintained an interest in the military and researched various aspects of the armed forces and military technology.

While conducting his research in the late 1970s, Clancy developed the ideas for several novels and the main characters he wrote about in the 1980s. During this time, Clancy wrote in his spare time while working and raising a family, and in 1984 his first novel, *The Hunt for Red October*, was published by The Naval Institute Press, a noncommercial publisher in Annapolis. The story is about a Soviet submarine commander who defects with his state-of-the art submarine to the United States. Naturally, the novel captured the spirit of the Cold War politics typical of the administration of President Ronald Reagan. Reagan laid enormous stress on the military capability of the Soviet Union and dramatically increased U.S. military spending to meet and surpass the perceived Soviet challenge.

### Praise by a President
President Reagan publicly praised *The Hunt for Red October*, boosting the novel to bestseller lists. Casper Weinberger, Reagan's Secretary of Defense, reviewed the book for *The Times Literary Supplement*, calling it "a splendid and riveting story" and praising the technical descriptions as "vast and accurate." *The Hunt for Red October* was Clancy's first book to be made into a movie.

Clancy's most famous character is Jack Ryan, who takes the lead in eight of Clancy's books. Each novel in the Ryan series provides more background on this "everyman" hero. From his humble beginnings as a history professor at the U.S. Naval Academy, Ryan eventually joins the CIA as a consultant. He permanently joins the CIA as an analyst to track down terrorists and through his daring and intelligence, becomes the Deputy Director at the CIA. From there, Ryan advances as the National Security Advisor to the President, the Vice President, and eventually becomes President of the United States.

### Success after the Fall of the Soviet Union
Clancy's subsequent novels continued to feature plots based upon critical world political issues from the perspective of military or CIA personnel. The primary theme focused on the conflict between the United States and the Soviet Union. However, in 1991, the Soviet Union collapsed, disintegrating into fifteen separate countries. Clancy had to find a new theme for his novels. He turned his focus to stories about the international drug trade and terrorism.

### The Cold War, Drug Wars, and the War on Terror
When the arms race was escalating in the 1980s, Clancy's novels *The Hunt for Red October*, *Red Storm Rising* (1986), and *The Cardinal of the Kremlin* (1988) used different aspects of the Soviet-American conflict for story lines. In the post-Cold War era, Clancy turned to the South American drug trade in *Clear and Present Danger* (1989). The United States declared a War on Drugs, intending to reduce the supply and demand for illegal drugs. During the 1980s, the United States focused on the Columbian drug cartels who were trafficking cocaine into the United States. Instead of Soviets, Clancy focused on a new enemy in *Patriot Games* (1987): IRA terrorists. Terrorists also threaten Middle East peace by threatening to use a nuclear bomb in *The Sum of All Fears* (1991).

### Novels, Movies, and Computer Games
Today, Clancy continues to write successful novels as well as nonfiction works. Several of his books have been adapted as popular films, including *The Hunt for Red October*, *Patriot Games* (1987), and *Clear and Present Danger* (1989).

In addition to writing a string of best sellers, Clancy has also created and marketed multimedia computer games, many of which are based on his novels. His newest game release, *EndWar*, deals with Russia starting World War III. A new movie, *Without Remorse*, is set to release in 2008, though it is based on a novel Clancy wrote in 1993. Clancy introduced John Ryan, Jack Ryan's son, in *The Teeth of the Tiger* (2003).

## Works in Literary Context

Clancy's novels feature international foes, such as the Soviets and terrorists, who try to overcome superior American military technology and intelligence operations. He is often called the king of techno-thrillers. His use of highly involved technical detail incorporated into complex, suspenseful plots has made him the most successful practitioner of the genre. Clancy adds a new level of military realism and sophistication to the traditional adventure novel. His books take their plots from the most pressing international concerns of our times.

### Realistic Fiction and Heroes
In order to create a realistic feel to his novels, Clancy reviews declassified documents and tours vessels and military bases. For someone who is outside the establishment, his accuracy of military-industrial technology is remarkable. Some military officials find his work too close to top-secret reality, revealing too much about classified warfare.

### Spy Fiction
Since the early nineteenth century, spy fiction has been popular, from James Fenimore Cooper's

1821 novel, *The Spy*, to the outrageous James Bond novels by Ian Fleming to Robert Ludlum's *The Bourne Identity* (1980).

Spy novels typically include a hero or government agent who takes extreme action against a rival government. Techno-thrillers use the same structure, however technology is essential to the plot, either creating or ending the conflict. Heroes and villains are easily identifiable.

Clancy uses the techno-thriller structure, using characters from various levels of the military establishment: elite soldiers, crewmen, commanders, generals, espionage operatives, and government officials. Their goals and motives are clearly good or evil, and while later novels feature some ambivalence or introspection in lead characters, most of the moral choices that his characters face are straightforward questions of right and wrong.

In order to draw his characters accurately, Clancy conducts interviews with armed forces personnel. His most notable character is hero Jack Ryan, a sometime CIA agent who epitomizes integrity, bravery, and ingenuity in a changing, high stakes world. Whether he is assigned to resolve a crisis, or stumbles accidently into an international incident and becomes a target for revenge, Ryan is adept at using available technology to achieve his mission.

## Works in Critical Context

Appreciation of Clancy's technological details varies among critics; some find the insider's glimpse of weaponry and tactics presented with clarity, accuracy, and interest, while others, perhaps more knowledgeable about the technology described, find Clancy's renderings inaccurate and implausible. Critics are almost unanimous in their negative reaction to Clancy's skills at characterization, finding them underdeveloped, and the hero Jack Ryan too flawless and unbelievably virtuous. Clancy responded to criticism about Ryan by giving him some vices in later novels, a change some critics found unbelievable.

*The Hunt for Red October* Ronald Reagan called *The Hunt for Red October* "the perfect yarn." According to *Washington Post Book World* critic Reid Beddow, it is "a tremendously enjoyable and gripping novel of naval derring-do." The details in the book about military hardware are hauntingly accurate, and they were based on books and naval documents Clancy studied. He also interviewed submariners and then made his own educated guesses when writing the book. Because the descriptions of high-tech military hardware are so advanced that former Navy Secretary John Lehman, jokingly stated in *Time*, that he "would have had [Clancy] court-martialed: the book revealed much that had been classified about antisubmarine warfare. Of course, nobody for a moment suspected him of getting access to classified information." Richard Setlowe in the *Los Angeles Times Book Review* expressed his opinion: "At his best, Clancy has a terrific talent for taking the arcana of U.S. and Soviet submarine warfare, the

---

# LITERARY AND HISTORICAL CONTEMPORARIES

Clancy's famous contemporaries include:

**Tom Wolfe** (1931–): This American essayist and novelist is credited with developing New Journalism, a form of expository writing that mixes nonfiction techniques, such as interviews and reports with fiction techniques, such as shifting points of view, dialogue, character description, and detailed scene-setting. He is famous for his novels *The Right Stuff* (1979) and *The Bonfire of the Vanities* (1987).

**Ronald Reagan** (1911–2004): The fortieth President of the United States, Reagan served two terms as president, from 1981 to 1989. In 1987, Reagan gave a speech at the Berlin Wall, challenging Soviet leader Gorbachev to tear down the Berlin Wall. Many credit Reagan with initiating the end of the Cold War.

**John Grisham** (1955–2004): An American novelist whose bestselling books, such as *A Time to Kill* (1989) and *The Client* (1993) have captivated readers with intriguing legal predicaments, high tension, and unexpected plot twists.

**Robert Ludlum** (1927–2001): Ludlum was one of America's most prolific authors of best-selling spy and suspense novels. His thrillers were noted for their complicated plots and accurate details. His popular Bourne novels, *The Bourne Identity* (1980), *The Bourne Supremacy* (1986), and *The Bourne Ultimatum* (1990) center around international terrorism.

**John Le Carré** (1931–2004): This British writer depicts the clandestine world of Cold War espionage. He attracted world-wide acclaim with his novels such as *The Spy Who Came in from the Cold* (1963) and *Tinker, Tailor, Soldier, Spy* (1974).

---

subtleties of sonar and the techno-babble of nuclear power plants and transforming them into taut drama."

*Clear and Present Danger* *Clear and Present Danger*, written after the fall of the Soviet empire, highlights the South American drug cartels and America's war on drugs. Former Assistant Secretary of State Elliott Abrams reviewed the novel in the *Wall Street Journal*, claiming, "What helps to make *Clear and Present Danger* such compelling reading is a fairly sophisticated view of Latin politics combined with Mr. Clancy's patented, tautly shaped scenes, fleshed out with colorful technical data and tough talk." Abrams praised Clancy's treatment of the ethical dilemmas that complicate such covert military operations. Still, some reviewers criticized Clancy's characterizations and prose, noting his focus on technology. Yet, Evan Thomas noted in *Newsweek*, "It doesn't really matter if his

## COMMON HUMAN EXPERIENCE

A recurring theme running in Clancy's work is how the United States military addresses Cold War espionage. Here are some other works that deal with spy plots against the United States:

*The Manchurian Candidate* (1959), a novel by Richard Condon. Condon tells the story about an American prisoner of war who is brainwashed by his Chinese captures. He returns to the United States programmed to be an assassin. The novel, banned in Soviet countries, has been adapted for film twice.

*Six Days of the Condor* (1974), a novel by James Grady. The novel features a mild-mannered CIA agent who returns from lunch one day to find that all his coworkers have been murdered. As he tries to report the event to his superiors, he discovers a world of deceit, deception, and betrayal. Made into a motion picture directed by Sydney Pollack, *Three Days of the Condor* tapped into the public's fear that no one can be trusted.

*Invasion of the Body Snatchers* (1956), a film directed by Don Siegel The 1956 film, based on the novel, *The Body Snatchers* (1955) by Jack Finney, is a science fiction allegory that addresses the theme of communist infiltration during the Cold War and fear of nuclear annihilation.

*The Looking Glass War* (1965), a novel by John Le Carré. This novel concerns an obsolete branch of the British Secret Service, whose chief tries to revitalize his department by sending an agent into East Germany to investigate a rumor regarding Soviet missiles placed near the German border.

*The Afghan* (2006), a novel by Frederick Forsyth. This spy thriller tackles present-day fears regarding Al Qaeda terrorists who plan to attack the West. American and British agents work together to uncover the plot.

characters are two dimensional and his machines are too perfect. He whirls them through a half dozen converging subplots until they collide in a satisfyingly slam-bang finale." Thomas called the book "Clancy's best thriller since his first," and "a surprisingly successful cautionary tale."

### Responses to Literature

1. Choose one of Clancy's novels that focus on the conflict between the United States and the Soviets during the Cold War. Create a chart that highlights how Clancy portrays the differences between the two governments. In a group discussion, describe how the two countries are similar and different in their approach to loyalty, nationalism, diplomacy, and politics.

2. Using your library and the Internet, find out more about the spy fiction and techno-thriller genres. Analyze how spy fiction and techno-thrillers are different.

3. Write a paper in which you analyze the character Jack Ryan. Use the novel *Patriot Games* as a source for your analysis. In your paper, discuss whether you think Ryan's character is too one-dimensional. Use text examples to support your position.

4. In addition to writing bestsellers, Clancy started a multimedia entertainment company, Red Storm Entertainment. Clancy's games and film adaptations for his books are just as successful as his novels. Why do you think his books, games, and movies about terrorism are so appealing to the public? What role do stories and games such as Clancy's play in society?

BIBLIOGRAPHY

**Books**

Clancy, Tom, Martin Harry Greenberg, and Roland J. Green, editors. *The Tom Clancy Companion.* New York: Berkeley Books, 1992.

Garson, Helen S., *Tom Clancy: A Critical Companion.* Westport, Conn.: Greenwood Press, 1996.

**Periodicals**

Abrams, Eliot. "Review of *Clear and Present Danger.*" *Wall Street Journal.* (October 22, 1984; August 16, 1989).

Balz, Douglas. "Review of *Red Storm Rising.*" *Chicago Tribune Book World.* (September 7, 1986).

Grigg, William Norman. "*Sum* Doesn't Add Up." *New American.* (July 1, 2002): pp 28–30.

"Eerie Parallels: Clancy Novel Anticipated Kamikaze Attack with a Commercial Airliner." *Barron's.* (September 17, 2001): p. 28.

*Magazine of Fantasy and Science Fiction.* (December, 1991): p. 73.

**Web sites**

"Becoming Tom Clancy: Letters from Tom." Retrieved September 2, 2008, from http://www.geocities.com/everwild7/clancy.html. Last updated on November 12, 2005.

"Tom Clancy." *Penguin Putnam Web site* Retrieved September 2, 2008, from http://us.penguingroup.com/static/html/author/tomclancy.html.

# ✹ Mary Higgins Clark

BORN: *1929, New York, New York*

NATIONALITY: *American*

GENRE: *Fiction*

MAJOR WORKS:

*Where Are the Children?* (1975)

*A Stranger Is Watching* (1978)

*The Cradle Will Fall* (1980)

*A Cry in the Night* (1982)

*On the Street Where You Live* (2001)

Mary Higgins Clark  *Amy Sussman / Getty Images*

## Overview

Novelist Mary Higgins Clark has written more than twenty best-selling suspense novels. Critics have likened her novels to the works of Alfred Hitchcock, citing her talent for weaving stories around people in highly intense and terrifying situations. Like Hitchcock, Clark's books lack graphic violence and sordid details; the violence is implied. Her signature trait is writing suspenseful stories that take place in tight time frames with clear distinctions between good and evil.

## Works in Biographical and Historical Context

*Escaping Poverty through Reading*  Clark was born on December 24, 1929, in New York City to Joseph Higgins and Nora C. Durkin. Mary attended St. Francis Xavier School, a Catholic school. As a child, Mary enjoyed writing poems and skits. Her three brothers were often coerced into performing them with her. The Higgins family struggled during the Great Depression. Joseph Higgins worked long hours. Perhaps as an escape from hardship, Mary loved to read, at first taking great delight in fairy tales and later graduating to mystery stories and

Nancy Drew novels. She sent her first story out for publication when she was sixteen, but it was rejected because the editor found her characters too "upscale": a defining attribute of her later novels that has not hindered their popularity.

*Gaining Strength of Character from Tragedy*  In 1939 Mary experienced a grave loss when her father died unexpectedly of a heart attack, and her mother struggled to support her family. The Higgins took in boarders, and Mary took a job while she was still a student to help make ends meet. Just prior to her graduation from Villa Maria Academy, a Roman Catholic high school, Mary experienced a second loss when her older brother, Joe, a new naval recruit, died of spinal meningitis. Her brother's death spurred her to choose secretarial school rather than college so that she could provide her family with immediate income.

Forgoing a college scholarship, Mary went to Ward Secretarial School and on to a job as an advertising assistant at Remington Rand, working to help support her family. After being fascinated by the tales of a flight attendant friend, Mary decided to see the world. She immediately changed careers, put off marriage, and went to work for Pan American Airlines. She flew for a year, then married Warren Clark, an airline executive and long-time friend of the family.

*Writing about Experience*  Clark gave birth to five children in the first eight years of her marriage and then pursued her interest in writing. She started taking creative writing courses at New York University, writing romance fiction about flight attendants for the next few years. Her stories took place in settings with which she was familiar, and her characters were modeled on people she knew or observed.

Clark kept a disciplined schedule for her writing, rising at 5:00 A.M. and writing until 7:00 A.M., when her children woke up. She published a few short stories and continued to write stories resolutely until two events occurred: first, the short-story market faltered, and then, when she was thirty, Warren Clark learned that he was suffering from severe arteriosclerosis and was not expected to live much longer.

*History Repeats Itself*  In 1964, after five children and fifteen years of marriage, Clark's husband died of a heart attack, leaving her to care for her children alone—the same situation her mother had faced. Clark turned to her natural talent for writing to support her family and went to work for Robert G. Jennings as a radio scriptwriter. She learned to write concisely for radio, building the action quickly and catching and holding the audience's attention. During the early and middle 1960s, it was still considered unusual for a woman to seek a career, and it would have been more traditional for Clark to pursue remarriage rather than work to support herself and her children. However, the social climate would soon change.

# LITERARY AND HISTORICAL CONTEMPORARIES

Clark's famous contemporaries include:

**Agatha Christie** (1880–1976): This British suspense novelist is famous for writing the classic British detective story. Her novels are frequently set in the English countryside and usually focus on a group of upper-middle-class British characters and a detective who reveals the murderer at a final gathering of the suspects.

**Alfred Hitchcock** (1899–1980): Master of cinematic suspense, this English screen director and filmmaker is associated with groundbreaking psychological thrillers and horror movies. He continues to fascinate the public years after his death with classics such as *Psycho* (1960) and *The Birds* (1963).

**Truman Capote** (1924–1984): American novelist, short story, and nonfiction writer, Capote wrote with an ornate style, which many categorized as Southern Gothic. Two of his most famous works include the novella *Breakfast at Tiffany's* (1958) and his controversial nonfiction novel, *In Cold Blood* (1966).

**Geraldine Ferraro** (1935–): This American teacher, lawyer, and politician made history when she became the first female vice presidential candidate representing a major American political party. Walter Mondale, the presidential candidate for the Democrats, selected Ferraro as his running mate in the 1984 presidential elections. Clark modeled her heroine in *Stillwatch* (1984) after Ferraro.

By the late 1960s, and especially in the 1970s, an organized women's rights movement in North America pressed for equal professional opportunities with men and made great inroads into areas that had always been dominated by men.

***A Turning Point and Financial Security*** Clark's first attempt at writing a book-length work, a biography of George Washington called *Aspire to the Heavens* (1968) was a commercial failure. However, she took it in stride and decided to write what she liked to read, which was mystery and suspense novels. Clark's agent sent her first fiction manuscript, *Where Are the Children?* (1975), to Simon & Schuster. Upon finishing a first reading of the book, editor Phyllis Grann called Clark's agent and said, "Don't show Mary Higgins Clark's book to anyone else. I want it." The deal was sealed in May 1974, and Simon & Schuster has published every Clark novel since.

Clark's novel *Where Are the Children?* was an immediate success and became a best seller, earning over one hundred thousand dollars in paperback royalties. The money provided Clark with the opportunity to attend college, and she pursued a degree at Fordham University where she began work on her second novel, *A Stranger Is Watching* (1978). Inspired by news reports, this thriller earned more than one million dollars in paperback rights and was made into a motion picture in 1982. Clark's economic troubles subsided. She now had the security to write full-time.

***Queen of Suspense*** Clark's popularity was not short-lived. Presently, the author of twenty-eight best sellers, Clark shows no signs of quitting. She has received many awards, including the Horatio Alger Award and the Grand Prix de Literature of France. She has received thirteen honorary doctorates, from such universities as Villanova, Fordham, and Seton Hall. Clark has passed on her passion for storytelling to her children as well. She has co-authored several suspense novels with her daughter Carol.

## Works in Literary Context

Clark is one of the most successful suspense novelists today. She likes to weave a plot around ordinary places and people who are suddenly plunged into terrifying situations. She often uses news stories as her inspiration and spends times in courtrooms, observing people and listening to the details of real murder cases.

***Fast-Paced Action*** A signature element of Clark's novels is the fast-paced action. In some works, the action begins immediately, however, the time span of the action may vary. *The Cradle Will Fall* (1980) takes place over the space of a week; the action of *A Stranger Is Watching* covers three days; and *Where Are the Children?* spans a single day. Clark is a master at relating relevant facts or historical information needed for the story through dialogue or through such conventions as a story within a story and conveying simultaneous episodes, all without breaking the pace.

***Heroines and Evildoers*** One of Clark's first novels to feature the opulence and high society that characterize her later works is *Stillwatch*. Her own experience with a break-in was the impetus for *Stillwatch*, a political thriller with two strong female protagonists, each successful and each haunted by her past. By seeing the main characters' points of view and knowing what they are thinking, the reader gets to know them quickly and becomes deeply involved in the story. In addition to constructing a believable and sympathetic heroine, Clark creates a realistic and menacing, oftentimes deranged, killer. In most of her stories, the "whodunit" is revealed as the story unfolds, and the perpetrator's motivation and possible future misdeeds provide the suspense, a technique that has been criticized as a weakness by reviewers looking for a serious mystery.

***Formulaic Suspense Plots*** Many of Clark's novels are all so unmistakably "Clark" as to be almost formulaic. Most are set in New York City with a more affluent cast of characters and a more sophisticated, but still sensitive and strong, heroine than had been the case in her first four novels. The similarity in the pattern of her works may occur because she always follows what has proven to be a rewarding method for her writing: "At my first writing class, I was told to think of a true situation and then ask myself, 'Suppose' and 'What if?' To that I have added a third question, 'Why?'—there must be motivation. Those rules have made it easy for me," Clark relates in *The Writer*.

In spite of writing specifically for a popular audience and keeping to her winning formula, Clark includes profound psychological and philosophical elements in her novels. Many, especially the earlier ones, are concerned with the heroine confronting an often ominous past. Most of the works address parent-child relationships, whether thriving or corrupt, and the heroine's realization of her individual strength and courage in a kind of trial-by-fire approach. Clark's later novels, while more glamorous in setting than the earlier ones, deal with such issues as the nature of beauty, artificial insemination, the death penalty, and child abuse, while practically all of them at some level raise the issue of justice and portray the struggle between good and evil. Clark suffers no ambiguity in her characters; the readers are supposed to identify with the heroines just as they are meant to vilify the murderers.

## Works in Critical Context

***The Master of Technique*** Many reviewers have criticized Clark's work for a lack of character development, calling her personalities flat and wooden, as well as accusing her of being too formulaic. Yet, the critics admit, the formula works. Carolyn Banks from the *Washington Post* notes that there is a kind of "Mary Higgins Clark formula" that readers both expect and enjoy: "There are no ambiguities in any Clark book. We know whom and what to root for, and we do. Similarly, we boo and hiss or gasp when the author wants us to. Clark is a master manipulator."

While some critics commend Clark for handling compact time frames in her novels, others, such as Clarence Petersen, have observed that Clark's fast-paced excitement comes at the expense of detail and human insight. Yet in his review of *Weep No More, My Lady*, Petersen writes that the emotional basis of the story "draws you into sympathy with the heroine ... until nothing can make you close the book." It is Clark's ability to engross readers in frenetic plots that garners her critical and popular attention.

***All Around the Town*** Critics are most impressed with Clark's ability to increase suspense and keep readers turning the page, as in *All Around the Town* (1992). Susan Toepfer of *People* magazine remarked, "There are mystery writers who concoct more sophisticated plots, more realistic settings, more profound characters. But for sheer storytelling power—and breathtaking pace—Clark is without peer." The *New York Times* was also impressed with this novel, claiming "Clark pushes buttons we never dreamed we had." However, not all reviewers were pleased. Though *Kirkus Reviews* states that "Clark returns

---

# COMMON HUMAN EXPERIENCE

Clark writes suspense novels, stories that highlight the dangerous side of experience. Rather than explore solving the crime, she describes how crime affects the victims. Other works that probe the psychological aspects of crime include:

*Strangers on a Train* (1950), a novel by Patricia Highsmith. This well-known novel, made into a movie by Alfred Hitchcock, weaves a sinister tale of murder and betrayal, providing a psychological glimpse into the criminal mind.

*Rebecca* (1940), a film directed by Alfred Hitchcock. Based on the novel by Daphne Du Maurier by the same title, this novel is both a thriller and a romance.

*A Judgment in Stone* (1977), a novel by Ruth Rendell. This psychological thriller explores why a housekeeper murders an entire family.

*Stone Angel* (1997), by Carol O'Connell. This mystery tracks the story of a New York policewoman who returns to her hometown to determine who killed her mother seventeen years ago, and why.

---

to what she does best: using a threatened child to grab you by the throat and shake well," the reviewer also notes that Clark's "heart's not in it: broad hints from the outset will tip off all but the most witless readers. No whodunit, then—but Clark's legion of fans, enthralled by her undeniable skill in pushing their buttons, won't even notice."

## Responses to Literature

1. As Clark was writing *A Cry in the Night*, she used the novels *Rebecca* and *Psycho* as models. Discuss how Clark's book is similar to and different from these two the novels. What is your opinion about authors who use famous novels written by other authors to enhance their own works?

2. As a writer, Clark likes to think about an ordinary situation and ask, "Suppose," "What if?" and "Why?" Find a news article and create an outline for a suspense story using these questions.

3. Clark uses strong female protagonists. Though she does include a touch of romance in her books, the heroines take care of themselves and do not depend on male support. Write a report in which you express your opinion about Clark's protagonists. State whether you think the approach is realistic. Use excerpts from Clark's to support your view.

4. Read Clark's first novel, *Where Are the Children?* Write a critical review of the book, analyzing plot structure, character development, and suspenseful twists. Share your reviews with a group.

BIBLIOGRAPHY

**Books**

Clark, Mary Higgins. *Kitchen Privileges.* New York: Simon & Schuster, 2002.

Pelzer, Linda Claycomb. *Mary Higgins Clark: A Critical Companion.* Westport, Conn.: Greenwood Press, 1995.

Swanson, Jean, and Dean James. "Clark, Mary Higgins." *By a Woman's Hand: A Guide to Mystery Fiction by Women* (1994): 45–46.

Whissen, Thomas. "Mary Higgins Clark." *In Great Women Mystery Writers: Classic to Contemporary.* Westport, Conn.: Greenwood Press.

**Periodicals**

Evans, Paul. "Unsolved Mystery." *Book* (January–February, 2003): 72.

Rozen, Leah. "A Perfect Matchup for a Mystery Queen." *Good Housekeeping* (November 1996): 23–24.

**Web sites**

*Mary Higgins Clark.* Retrieved September 11, 2008, from http://www.maryhigginsclark.com. Last updated in 2008.

*Mary Higgins Clark.* Simon & Schuster Web site. Retrieved September 11, 2008, from http://www.simonsays.com/mhclark. Last updated on June 8, 2007.

# ✹ Beverly Cleary

BORN: *1916, McMinville, Oregon*

NATIONALITY: *American*

GENRE: *Fiction, nonfiction*

MAJOR WORKS:

*Henry Huggins* (1950)

*Beezus and Ramona* (1955)

*The Mouse and the Motorcycle* (1965)

*Dear Mr. Henshaw* (1983)

*A Girl from Yamhill: A Memoir* (1988)

## Overview

Beverly Cleary's humorous, realistic depictions of American children have made her one of the most beloved writers of children's literature for more than fifty years. Throughout this time, she has retained her popularity, critical acclaim, and relevance. A prolific writer with a wide range of interests, Cleary appeals to grade schoolers

Beverly Cleary   *Terry Smith / / Time Life Pictures / Getty Images.*

because of her ability to portray children and their language on a level readers can understand.

## Works in Biographical and Historical Context

*A Safe and Beautiful Farm Town*   The only child of Lloyd and Mabel Atlee Bunn, Cleary was born in McMinnville, Oregon and grew up on an eighty-acre farm in Yamhill, Oregon, where her uncle was mayor and her father was on the town council. In her autobiography *A Girl from Yamhill: A Memoir* (1988), Cleary wrote that living there taught her "that the world was a safe and beautiful place, where children were treated with kindness, patience, and tolerance." All of these qualities would be apparent in her books.

*The Power of Books*   From an early age, Cleary was taught that books had power. In addition to introducing her daughter to such authors as Charles Dickens and Geoffrey Chaucer, Mabel Bunn told the girl stories from her own childhood, as well as folk and fairy tales. Because Yamhill did not have a library, Mabel arranged for the State Library to send books to Yamhill, and she created a small lending area in a room over the town's bank. Amazed by the variety of books available to children, Cleary learned to love books there.

When she was six, Cleary's family moved to Portland, Oregon. Although she was excited by the big city and by the immense children's section of the Portland Library, Cleary felt out of place in school, particularly after an extended illness left her behind the other students in first grade. By the time she returned to school, the class had been divided into three reading groups according to their abilities, and Cleary was in the bottom group. Bored and discouraged, she decided that reading and school were miserable experiences, and she developed an aversion to reading outside of school. When she was eight years old, however, she finally found a book that aroused her interest, *The Dutch Twins* by Lucy Fitch Perkins. In this story about two ordinary children and their adventures, Cleary found release and happiness. Soon, she was reading all the children's books in the library; however, she rarely came across what she wanted to read most of all: funny stories about boys and girls who lived in the same kind of neighborhood and went to the same kind of school that she did.

***Immersed in Books***   When Cleary was in seventh grade, a teacher suggested that she write books for children. This idea had immediate appeal, and Cleary vowed to write the type of book she herself wanted to read. When her mother reminded her that she would need a steady job as well, Cleary decided to become a librarian and focused on literature and journalism during her high school years. Upon graduation, she attended Chaffey Junior College in Ontario, California, and was a substitute librarian at the Ontario Public Library before transferring to the University of California at Berkeley. After graduating with a BA in English in 1938 and a second BA in librarianship from the University of Washington in 1939, she worked as a children's librarian in Yakima, Washington. In 1940, she married Clarence Cleary and moved to San Francisco. During World War II, Cleary served as post librarian at the Oakland Army Hospital.

***Henry Opens Doors***   After the war, she worked in the children's department of a Berkeley bookstore, a job that allowed her the opportunity to review popular children's books, which she found inadequate. Her answer to such substandard children's literature was to write her own, and she began writing on January 2, 1948. Since then, she has begun all her books on the second of January. Published in 1950, *Henry Huggins* was different from many other books of the time, which either presented an idealized version of well-behaved children or told unrealistic stories of children who solved crimes or found long-lost wealthy relatives.

In addition to five more volumes about Henry, Cleary has written other works about children who live in or near Henry's neighborhood. The most notable of

## LITERARY AND HISTORICAL CONTEMPORARIES

Beverly Cleary's famous contemporaries include:

**Roald Dahl** (1916–1990): With works for both adults and children, Dahl, best known for *Charlie and the Chocolate Factory* (1964), became one of the world's best-selling authors.

**P. L. Travers** (1899–1969): This Australian writer is known for her *Mary Poppins* series, which chronicles the adventures of a magical nanny.

**Robert E. Smith** (1917–1998): With the cowboy puppet Howdy Doody on his knee, Smith entranced children nationwide on *The Howdy Doody Show* (1947–1960).

**Philip Larkin** (1922–1985): An American poet, Larkin worked for several years as a librarian at the University of Hull, in England.

**Louis Darling** (1916–1970): As the illustrator of Cleary's early series, Darling gave life to the characters' personalities, capturing the humor of the situations characters faced.

these is a series about the Quimby family, which began with the publication of *Beezus and Ramona* in 1955, the same year Cleary gave birth to twins. Several of her subsequent books reflected the interests and experiences of her children, including the popular Ralph S. Mouse fantasy series, which she wrote when her son showed a fascination with motorcycles and a difficulty in learning to read. During the 1950s, Cleary also wrote several novels for and about teenage girls whose searches for identity involve confusing relationships with the opposite sex, as well as with their families. In doing so, Cleary was able to fill a void in the young-adult fiction market.

***A Kinship with Children***   Prolific over the course of her long career, Cleary has spoken at many schools, interacting with students whose requests she takes to heart. She has conscientiously corresponded with thousands of readers, and wrote *Dear Mr. Henshaw* (1983), a book about a child who exchanges letters with a children's author, in response to requests she received for a book about a child of divorced parents. Cleary's unique talent to invent tales about ordinary children has won her prestigious national and regional literary awards, as well as more than twenty-five child-selected awards.

## Works in Literary Context

While Cleary has referred to many places, people, and incidents from her own experiences for her works, her stories are neither memoirs nor autobiographical fiction. *Twentieth-Century Children's Writers* records that in discussing her motivation as an author, Cleary says, "The

# COMMON HUMAN EXPERIENCE

Cleary transforms everyday occurrences into hilarious incidents. Other works of children's literature that humorously portray grade-school children struggling with the difficulties of everyday life include the following:

*Junie B. Jones and the Stupid Smelly Bus* (1992), fiction by Barbara Park. Premiering the spirited Junie B. Jones, this book comically describes many aspects of childhood.

*Horrible Harry in Room 2B* (1997), fiction by Suzy Cline. In this humorous school adventure, Doug, the narrator, finds that being best friends with Harry, a rowdy boy who enjoys doing horrible things in their classroom, is often difficult.

*Tales of a Fourth Grade Nothing* (1972), a novel by Judy Blume. In this work, which inspired other amusing Fudge books, Peter must deal with the antics of his wild—yet adorable—little brother, Fudge.

stories I write are the stories I wanted to read as a child, and the experience I hope to share with children is the discovery that reading is one of the pleasures of life." In her quest, Cleary has written picture books, realistic fiction, historical fiction, fantasy, and nonfiction for audiences ranging from preschoolers to young adults. As a result, she has inspired generations of readers to view reading as a joy, not just something they have to do at school.

***Childhood Realism*** Because she has an uncanny understanding of her audience, Cleary accurately depicts the world of children with humor, honesty, and compassion. Typically, Cleary's characters are ordinary youngsters with faults, and the small problems they face seem big to them. The difficulties and fears they encounter both at school and at home reflect those generally faced by many children: losing a pet, being bullied at school, sibling rivalry. Cleary's works show that making mistakes is normal and that everyone feels helpless, guilty, misunderstood, or left out at one time or another. Many of her works focus on children who struggle to learn in school, as she herself did, or have difficulty in conforming to adults' expectations. Possibly the most popular of such characters is Ramona Quimby, a mischievous, annoying little sister who eventually attempts to grow up gracefully without losing her feisty personality.

Cleary has explored the experiences and emotions of only children and is one of the first American authors to address the effects of divorce on children. Although she writes about children's problems, however, she does not dwell on the difficulties; rather, she highlights the pleasures of childhood. Perhaps most importantly, Cleary gives her readers a sense of hope. By avoiding endings with moralistic preaching or magical solutions, Cleary assures her readers that her protagonists will handle their situations with courage and common sense. In doing so, Cleary teaches young readers that they can be in control of their own actions when dealing with life's frustrations.

## Works in Critical Context

Most critics embrace Cleary's spirited depiction of children and childhood, praising her books for being empathetic and simply written, but not condescending. They also applaud her gentle humor, memorable characters, and age-appropriate plots. Reviewer Joanne Kelly writes that Cleary's "sharp recollections of the complex feelings of childhood and her ability to relate those feelings in a way that is both humorous and comforting to the reader make her work ever popular with children and adults." In addition, critics commend Cleary's ability to write on several levels at once—for the younger child who identifies with the pesky Ramona, for the older child who sympathizes with being an older sibling, and for the adult who appreciates the books' word play and nostalgic appeal. Because of her unique gift for understanding the fears and joys—as well as the struggles and victories—of childhood and adolescence, Cleary's books have remained relevant for decades of readers.

Negative criticism of Cleary's work has appeared as American society has evolved. For example, critics have noticed the lack of minority and ethnic characters in her books, which almost exclusively feature white, middle-class children and their families. Other critics have charged that Cleary perpetuates stereotypes, such as mothers who are homemakers and do not work outside the home. In recent years, Cleary's works have been criticized because they fail to address contemporary problems or social ills. For the overwhelming majority of critics, however, Cleary is regarded as one of the most innovative and influential children's writers, a natural storyteller who makes reading a pleasure.

***Ramona and Her Father*** Reviewers agree that the conflicts in 1977's *Ramona and Her Father* are credible, as Mr. Quimby loses his job and begins to smoke too much. Once referred to by critic Ellen Lewis Buell as a "most exasperating little sister," a more mature Ramona spearheads an anti-smoking campaign in order to save her father's life—despite her tendency to make things worse before she makes them better. About *Ramona and Her Father*, reviewer Betsy Hearne writes:

> With her uncanny gift for pinpointing the thoughts and feelings of children right down to their own phraseology—while honoring the boundaries of clean, simple writing—the author catches a family

situation that puts strain on each of its members, despite their intrinsic strength and invincible humor. . . . [The story is] true, warm-hearted, and funny.

As in Cleary's previous works, *Ramona and Her Father* illustrates that "the author delineates the contemporary family with compassion and humor, unerringly suggests the nuances of suburban conversation, and develops as memorable a cast of characters as can be found in children's literature," lauds critic Mary M. Burns.

## Responses to Literature

1. In an interview with Miriam Drennan, Cleary said, "I feel sometimes that [in children's books] there are more and more grim problems, but I don't know that I want to burden third- and fourth-graders with them. I feel it's important to get [children] to enjoy reading." Do you think writers of children's fiction are obligated to explore society's controversial issues, or do you think children's authors should write to entertain?

2. Pretend your public library has no books by Cleary in its collection. Prepare a presentation for your town council requesting that three specific Cleary novels be added to the library's collection. Choose which three books you want to add, be knowledgeable about those books, and be able to justify your choices.

3. In addition to responding to thousands of fan letters during her career, Cleary begins *Dear Mr. Henshaw* as a series of letters from a boy to his favorite writer. Choose your favorite author and write a letter to that person expressing your appreciation for his or her work and what it means to you.

4. Research sibling rivalry, theories on birth order, and the ways in which they affect family dynamics. What factors contribute to sibling rivalry? Do you believe one's birth order is significant throughout his or her life? What advantages and disadvantages do children without siblings have?

BIBLIOGRAPHY

**Books**

Berg, Julie. *Beverly Cleary: The Young at Heart*. Edina, Minn.: Abdo & Daughters, 1993.

Berger, Laura Standley, ed. *Twentieth-Century Children's Writers*. Detroit, Mich.: St. James Press, 1998.

Cleary, Beverly. *A Girl from Yamhill: A Memoir*. New York: Morrow, 1974.

Kelly, Joanne. *The Beverly Cleary Handbook*. Englewood, Colo.: Teacher Ideas Press, 1996.

Pfliger, Pat. *Beverly Cleary*. Boston: Twayne, 1991.

**Periodicals**

Buell, Ellen Lewis. "Review of *Beezus and Ramona*." *New York Times Book Review* (September 25, 1955): 34.

Burns, Mary M. "Review of *Ramona and Her Father*." *The Horn Book Magazine* (December 1977): 660.

Davis, Mary Gould. "Review of *Henry Huggins*." *Saturday Review* (November 11, 1950): 48.

Hearne, Betsy. "Review of *Ramona and Her Father*." *Booklist* (October 1, 1977): 285–286.

**Web sites**

Drennan, Miriam. *I Can See Cleary Now*. Retrieved September 24, 2008, from http://www.bookpage.com/9908bp/beverly_cleary.html

# ■ Samuel Clemens

SEE *Mark Twain*

# ◉ Lucille Clifton

BORN: *1936, Depew, New York*

NATIONALITY: *American*

GENRE: *Poetry, nonfiction, fiction*

MAJOR WORKS:

*Good Times: Poems* (1969)

*Good News about the Earth: New Poems* (1972)

*An Ordinary Woman* (1974)

*Generations: A Memoir* (1976)

*Two-Headed Woman* (1980)

## Overview

Highly praised for her strong affirmation of African American culture, Lucille Clifton is a prolific poet whose work conveys concern for the welfare of African American families and youth. Through her work, Clifton evokes a sense of strength and celebration in the face of adversity. She is noted for writing in a simple, unadorned style using free verse and imagery drawn from the ordinary details of life.

## Works in Biographical and Historical Context

***Inspired by Family Love of Literature, Heroic Forebears*** Clifton was born in Depew, New York, on June 27, 1936, to Samuel and Thelma Moore Sayles. Her father worked in the steel mills, and her mother worked in a laundry. Although neither of her parents were educated beyond elementary school, they shared their appreciation for literature with their family. According to Clifton, her mother wrote poems, which she read to her four children. Her father was a storyteller, sharing the oral history of his ancestors, particularly his grandmother,

Lucille Clifton   *Clifton, Lucille, 2000, photograph. AP Images.*

the volume, Clifton seems to make conscious efforts to combat the negative images associated with inner city life by reminding readers that whatever the strictly socioeconomic characteristics of the community, home is what it is called by those who live there.

Clifton's early success came at the height of the civil rights movement in America, a time when both black and white activists worked together to push for social justice for African Americans. The civil rights movement had been dealt several blows in the mid- to late-1960s, and the nation was in turmoil—both over the question of equal rights for blacks and dissatisfaction with the U.S. government's conduct of the Vietnam War. The controversial African American civil rights leader Malcolm X, known for his forceful critiques of the U.S. government and white society, was assassinated in 1965. Martin Luther King Jr., a civil rights leader known for his moving oratory and nonviolent demonstrations, was assassinated in 1968. Presidential candidate Robert F. Kennedy, vocal in his opposition to the Vietnam War and staunch in his support of the civil rights movement, was assassinated just weeks after King. Despite so many reasons for sadness and anger in the black community, Clifton's work remained positive and hopeful.

***Celebrations of Ancestry and Culture***   *Good Times: Poems* was cited by the *New York Times* as one of the best books of the year, subsequently launching Clifton's career. Though she advanced her career as a professor, teaching literature and creative writing at several universities, Clifton has also continued her career as a productive poet. Her second volume of poems, *Good News about the Earth* (1972), was published, reflecting many political ideas of the 1960s and 1970s. The collection suggests that "we as [American] people have never hated one another." Several poems are dedicated to African American leaders, such as Malcolm X, Eldridge Cleaver, and Angela Davis.

In Clifton's third collection, *An Ordinary Woman* (1974), she abandons many of the broad racial issues examined in the two preceding books. Instead, the poems take as their theme a historical, social, and spiritual assessment of the current generation in the genealogical line of Caroline Donald, the poet's great-great-grandmother. Born in Africa in 1822, Caroline was a remarkable woman who, along with her mother, sister, and brother, had been kidnapped from her home in Dahomey, West Africa. Anything but ordinary, the Dahomean woman endured. Caroline not only survived this difficult and harsh introduction to America but managed to instill in members of her family, and the local black community at large, important and lasting principles of faith, dignity, intelligence, and integrity. Clifton shares the full story of Caroline and her descendants in her 1976 memoir, *Generations.*

Caroline, who was abducted from her home in the Dahomey Republic of West Africa and brought to New Orleans, Louisiana, as a slave. In Clifton's prose autobiography, *Generations: A Memoir* (1976), "Ca'line" appears as a woman of almost mythical endurance and courage, reflecting Clifton's characteristic portrayal of women as both strong and deeply nurturing.

In 1953 Clifton attended Howard University in Washington, DC, where she associated with writers LeRoi Jones (Amiri Baraka), A. B. Spellman, Owen Dodson, and Sterling Brown. After two years, she left Howard and attended Fredonia State Teachers College, where she often gave readings, performed in plays, and developed her voice as a writer, using sparse punctuation and a lyricism reflecting spoken words. When poet Robert Hayden entered her poems for the YW-YMHA Poetry Center Discovery Award in 1969, Clifton not only won the award, she also saw the publication of her first poetry collection, *Good Times: Poems* (1969). These early poems reflect the hardships her family endured and the successes they achieved while living in the inner city. Throughout

***Family, Faith, and Hope*** Clifton often explores her African American experience by examining familial relationships and religious themes. In *Two-Headed Woman* (1980), Clifton provides another tribute to the memory of her mother and includes a rather complicated poem in which she explores her feelings toward her father. As with many of her poems, Clifton provides an optimistic view, a testament of the strong faith she has in the power of human will.

In addition to several collections of poetry and an autobiography, Clifton has published more than twenty award-winning books for young readers. The children's books emphasize the importance of staying connected with the past and are characterized by a positive view of the African American culture. Clifton credits her six children with inspiring many of her stories. One of her most durable characters is little Everett Anderson, a young black boy whose realistic life experiences give the character vitality. In order to survive, for example, Everett must understand and accept the death of his father (*Everett Anderson's Goodbye*, 1983) and the remarriage of his mother (*Everett Anderson's 1-2-3*, published in 1977).

## Works in Literary Context

***A Simple Style*** Clifton's poems are known for their straightforward style that often echoes black speech and music. She writes in free verse, often using short lines, slant rhyme, and little punctuation. The simple words evoke strong imagery and big ideas. Clifton has said, "I am interested in trying to render big ideas in a simple way."

***A Political Voice?*** Some critics associate Clifton with the Black Arts Movement of the 1960s and 1970s, which promoted African American arts as tools to overcome racial oppression. Many of Clifton's poems criticize racist attitudes. Clifton's poetry, as well as her young-adult literature, is recognized for its cultivation of black identity and pride through awareness of black history. Yet, while she is concerned with the importance of racial memory and history, most of her themes are traditional. She celebrates the ordinary life of the African American family. She celebrates the importance of communities and everyday heroes, people who manage to lead lives worthy of emulation despite the most trying conditions.

## Works in Critical Context

Because of the deceptive simplicity of Clifton's work—a function of its conciseness, compression, and reliance on an oral tradition—her poetry is undervalued. When written about, her poems are described and praised but rarely given a reading that grants their depth and complexity. Others critics have a different opinion. Writing in Mari Evans's *Black Women Writers (1950–1980): A Critical*

*Evaluation*, Haki Madhubuti states: "She is a writer of complexity, and she makes her readers work and think. ... At the base of her work is concern for the Black family, especially the destruction of its youth."

***Few Words; Big Voice*** Clifton's poems are structurally tight, using few words to relay a powerful song. In a *Christian Century* review of Clifton's work, Peggy Rosenthal noted, "The first thing that strikes us about Lucille Clifton's poetry is what is missing: capitalization, punctuation, long and plentiful lines. We see a poetry so pared down that its spaces take on substance, become a shaping presence as much as the words themselves."

***Good Times: Poems*** Clifton's first collection of poetry was a literary success praised by critics. The poems paint both an optimistic and tragic portrait of life in the inner city. Ronald Baughman in a *Dictionary of Literary Biography* notes that "these poems attain power not only through their subject matter but also through ... the precise evocative images that give substance to

## COMMON HUMAN EXPERIENCE

Clifton was one of many African Americans to seek a greater understanding of her African preslavery ancestors. Other works that feature the search for African heritage include:

*Roots: The Saga of an American Family* (1976), a novel by Alex Haley. This blockbuster novel was based on genealogical research Haley did on his own family, tracing his lineage back to a West African boy caught by slave traders in 1767. The book became an extremely successful television miniseries in 1977.

*The Autobiography of Malcolm X* (1965), a nonfiction work by Malcolm X with Alex Haley. Haley and Malcolm X collaborated on this book, which is considered one of the most important nonfiction texts of the twentieth century. Malcolm X did not pursue knowledge of his African past through genealogy but through his conversion to the Muslim faith and his subsequent travels to Africa

*The Souls of Black Folk* (1903), a nonfiction and fiction collection by W. E. B. DuBois. Sociologist, historian, and civil rights leader DuBois's masterful, multidisciplinary approach to the history of black America is unrivaled. In one essay in this collection he traces African American spirituals to their African roots, using the evolution of black music to help describe the experiences of blacks in America.

*Daughters of the Dust* (1991), a film directed by Julie Dash. This critically acclaimed film is set at the turn of the twentieth century on one of the Sea Islands off the coast of Georgia and South Carolina, home to the Gullah people. Because of their isolation from the mainland, the African slaves of the Sea Islands were able to preserve more of their heritage than slaves elsewhere in the United States. The film's dialogue is in Geechee, which is mostly English but with many West African linguistic patterns and words.

her rhetorical statements and a frequent duality of vision that lends complexity to her portraits of place and character." He calls the title of the collection "ironic," claiming that "Although the urban ghetto can ... create figures who are tough enough to survive and triumph, the overriding concern of this book is with the horrors of the location." Madhubuti thinks that Clifton's first book of poetry "cannot be looked upon as simply a 'first effort.' The work is unusually compacted and memory-evoking." Johari Amini adds in *Black World*, "The poetry is filled with the sensations of coming up black with the kind of love that keeps you from dying in desperation."

## Responses to Literature

1. Choose three poems from *Good Times: Poems*. Discuss the themes of each poem, its meaning, and the effect of the imagery. How do these poems connect with present day?

2. Using the Internet and your library, research the Native American leader Crazy Horse. Read Clifton's poem "the message of crazy horse" from *Next*. What point of view toward history does Clifton take? Why do you think she admired Crazy Horse?

3. Write a short essay in which you discuss the effectiveness of Clifton's concise writing style. How does her technique affect the message? Does it enhance or belittle the difficult and meaningful topics? In your essay, choose one of Clifton's poems to support your thesis.

BIBLIOGRAPHY

**Books**

Evans, Mari, ed. *Black Women Writers 1950–1980: A Critical Evaluation.* New York: Doubleday-Anchor, 1984.

Madhubuti, Haki. "Lucille Clifton: Warm Water, Greased Legs, and Dangerous Poetry." *Black Women Writers (1950–1980); A Critical Evaluation* (1984): 150–160.

**Periodicals**

Hank, Lazer. "Blackness Blessed: The Writings of Lucille Clifton." *Southern Review* 25, no. 3 (July 1989): 760–770.

Johnson, Joyce. "The Theme of Celebration in Lucille Clifton's Poetry." *Pacific Coast Philology* 18 (November 1983): 70–76.

Ostriker, Alicia. "Kine and Kin: The Poetry of Lucille Clifton." *American Poetry Review* 22.6 (November–December 1993): 41–48.

**Web sites**

*Poetry Breaks: Lucille Clifton.* Retrieved September 2007, from http://openvault.wgbh.org/ntw/MLA000296/index.html

## ✹ Judith Ortiz Cofer

BORN: *1952, Hormigueros, Puerto Rico*

NATIONALITY: *American*

GENRE: *Poetry, fiction*

MAJOR WORKS:

*The Line of the Sun* (1989)

*Silent Dancing: A Partial Remembrance of a Puerto Rican Childhood* (1990)

Judith Ortiz Cofer    *Photo by Sortino*

*The Latin Deli: Prose and Poetry* (1993)

*An Island Like You: Stories of the Barrio* (1995)

*The Meaning of Consuelo* (2003)

## Overview

Judith Ortiz Cofer is best known for poetry and novels that explore the meaning of dual culturalism—the influence of two cultures on people, families, situations, or societies. Because she primarily focuses on her personal experience of being a Puerto Rican in the United States, her prose and poetry is both autobiographical and confessional.

## Works in Biographical and Historical Context

*A Tale of Two Cultures*   Judith Ortiz Cofer was born February 24, 1952, in Hormigueros, Puerto Rico. Her father, Jesús Ortiz, believed that his joining the U.S. Navy would help provide for his family; so began a life of different assignments around the world. When Judith was young, her father was assigned to Brooklyn Navy Yard, and the family was relocated to Paterson, New Jersey. Whenever Judith's father was deployed overseas, her mother would pack up the family and return to Puerto Rico, where the family would stay at her grandmother's home. In Puerto Rico, Judith spoke Spanish, listened to Spanish music, and ate Spanish foods. In New Jersey,

Judith had to learn English and adapt to a new culture. The frequent moves between urban life in Paterson and rural life in Puerto Rico made a lasting impression on the young Judith.

Growing up between two disparate places was not easy on Cofer as a child or as a teen. The frequent migrations were a disruption to her school life, her friendships, and her sense of self. Each location had different customs and rules of conduct, especially for young women. In the middle of this confusion, Cofer found a refuge in stories. Whether she was listening to her grandmother's folktales or reading books in the Paterson Public Library, Cofer learned early the importance of words and language. In *The Global Education Project*, Cofer claims that language and its art form was her bridge between both cultures.

*Mastering English*   In 1968, the family moved to Augusta, Georgia. Two year later, Cofer attended Augusta College, where she studied to become a teacher. She met John Cofer, was married, and had a child. She continued her studies and graduated with a degree in English. Cofer and her new family moved to Florida, where she enrolled in the graduate program at Florida Atlantic University. From there she obtained a master's degree in English and continued to teach.

During her graduate years, Cofer focused her writing on Latina women and her immigrant experience. These ideas formed the basis of her first poems, which were published in literary periodicals and collections by small presses. Three chapbooks, or pamphlets, featuring her poems were published in the early 1980s: *Latin Women Pray*, *The Native Dancer*, and *Among the Ancestors*.

*A Latina in Georgia*   In 1984, Cofer and her family moved to Athens, Georgia, where she became an instructor at the University of Georgia. In the following years, Cofer branched out from poetry and wrote her first novel, *The Line of the Sun* (1989), a story about finding balance between living life as a Puerto Rican and an American. The novel was nominated for a Pulitzer Prize. In 1990, Cofer published a collection of poetry and personal essays titled *Silent Dancing*. It, too, deals with her early years of moving back and forth between Puerto Rico and Paterson. Cofer's second novel, *The Meaning of Consuelo* (2003), focuses on a young Puerto Rican girl whose parents are fighting and whose sister suffers from schizophrenia.

Cofer continues to write while teaching full time at the University of Georgia. She is the recipient of numerous awards and grants, including the National Endowment for the Arts fellowship in Poetry, the O. Henry Prize for a short story, and Best Books of the Year citation. Her most recent work is a novel for young adults, *Call Me Maria* (2006).

# LITERARY AND HISTORICAL CONTEMPORARIES

Cofer's famous contemporaries include:

**Alice Walker** (1944–): Walker is an African- American writer who is noted for her works about the civil rights movement. Her novel *The Color Purple* (1982) won the Pulitzer Prize for fiction and the film version won several Academy Awards.

**Tim O'Brien** (1946–): O'Brien is an American writer known for his books about American soldiers in the Vietnam war, including *Going after Cacciato* (1978).

**Fidel Castro** (1926–): Castro was the leader of the first communist nation in the Western Hemisphere. In 1959, Castro led the overthrow of Batista to become Cuba's dictator. He relinquished power to his brother, Raúl, in 2008.

**Neil Simon** (1927–): An American playwright and screenwriter. Simon, who began his career writing for television, is most noted for his plays, such as *The Odd Couple* (1966), *The Sunshine Boys* (1973), and *Biloxi Blues* (1986).

**Enrique A. Laguerre Velez** (1905–2005): Velez was a Puerto Rican writer, poet, teacher and critic. His most famous works include *Solar Montoya* (1966), *Los Amos Benévolos* (1976), and *Los Gemelos* (1992). He was nominated for the Nobel Prize for Literature in 1999.

## Works in Literary Context

Cofer is one of the many notable contemporary Puerto Rican and Latina writers to be recognized in the United States. She writes at length about her bilingual and bicultural experience, in part because she believes the perspective is one that can be shared by many readers. She views her personal experiences as a universal journey in which many have found their identities and sense of self, home, and culture.

*Autobiographical Fiction* Though Cofer writes poetry and fiction, her work is primarily autobiographical. She changes some of the places and people, but the theme that runs through all her work is identity formation—what it means to be a Puerto Rican living in America. She explores the challenge of living between cultures and not being fully comfortable in either. But rather than choosing one culture over the other, Cofer keeps both cultures alive in her work. Though her books are written in English, they are filled with Spanish, the two languages melding together as one. She is committed to her complete herit-

age, filling her works with allusions to Spanish history and culture as well as the sights and sounds of Paterson, New Jersey.

*Female Narratives* In *The Line of the Sun* and *Silent Dancing*, Cofer uses a young female narrator to pass on the stories of women from the past. The stories of the older women, told in the oral tradition, are often humorous, and filled with subtle lessons on how to be strong and independent without letting men know. Cofer's grandmother was indeed one of these powerful storytellers and exerted a strong influence on Cofer. However, unlike her grandmother's stories, Cofer's narratives describe the frustration of living with two cultures and the urge to adopt the one that allows the most freedom.

## Works in Critical Context

Most critics find Cofer's Latina or minority literature exotic, but mainstream enough that readers can enjoy it. While her narratives offer views about universal friendships, hopes, pain, and angst, they also have a distinctive Latina flavor that keep her tales unique and fresh.

*The Line of the Sun* *The Line of the Sun* is a story about three generations of a family told in two parts. In the first part, the female narrator describes the Vivente clan of Salud, a Puerto Rican village. The second half is set in Paterson, New Jersey. Most critics lauded Cofer's first novel for its poetic qualities. In the *New York Times Book Review*, contributor Roberto Marquez hailed it for the "vigorous elegance" of its language. He called Cofer "a prose writer of evocatively lyrical authority, a novelist of historical compass and sensitivity." Though Marquez criticized parts of the plot as contrived, he proclaimed Cofer as "a writer of authentic gifts, with a genuine and important story to tell." In the *Los Angeles Times Book Review*, Sonja Bolle remarked on the beauty of Cofer's passages, stating "her eye for detail brings alive the stifling and magical world of village life."

*Silent Dancing* In *Silent Dancing*, Cofer offers a more personal view of her constant migrations between Paterson and Puerto Rico. Geta LeSeur, a reviewer from MELUS, the Society for the Study of the Multi-Ethnic Literature of the United States, finds the book more instructive than autobiographical: "The reader gets a feel for the dual-culture conflict of America's immigrants; for ethnic prejudices; for the problems of acculturation; ... for Puerto Rican women's culture, for the 'Quincenera' ... for language, for religion, and other concerns of gender, race, and class." Mary Margaret Benson of *Library Journal* reinforces this view, stating that these "eminently readable memoirs are a delightful introduction to Puerto Rican culture."

## Responses to Literature

1. Why do you think so many immigrant authors write about racial and cultural identity? How does Cofer's work in particular appeal to a broader audience? Find examples from *Silent Dancing* to support your position.

2. Write an essay about your own cultural heritage. Talk to family members about places your ancestors lived and what professions they held. In your essay, discuss how your background affects your identity.

3. Discuss how Cofer treats gender roles in *The Meaning of Consuelo*. How might you react if you were suddenly forced to live in a place with different gender expectations?

4. Judith Ortiz Cofer's works are considered ethnic American literature. Using your library and the Internet, research the criteria for labeling literature in this vein. Choose two authors with whom you are familiar who write multiethnic literature, and describe their works. Compare their themes with those of Cofer's works.

BIBLIOGRAPHY

**Books**

*Authors and Artists for Young Adults.* Volume 30, Detroit: Gale, 1999.

*Contemporary Hispanic Biography.* Volume 3, Detroit: Gale, 2003.

Cofer, Judith Ortiz. *Silent Dancing: A Partial Rembrance of a Puerto Rican Childhood.* Houston, Tex.: Arte Público Press, 1990.

**Periodicals**

Acosta-Belen, Edna. "Judith Ortiz Cofer: Poetry and Poetics." *MELUS* (Fall 1993).

Fabre, Genevieve. "Liminality, In-Betweeness and Indeterminacy: Notes toward an Anthropological Reading of Judith Ortiz Cofer's *The Line of the Sun.*" *Acraa* 18 (1993).

Gregory, Lucille H. "The Puerto Rican 'Rainbow': Distortions vs. Complexities." *Children's Literature Association Quarterly* (Spring 1993).

Kallet, Marilyn. "The Art of Not Forgetting: An Interview with Judith Ortiz Cofer." *Prairie Schooner* (Winter 1994).

LeSeur, Geta. "Silent Dancing: A Partial Remembrance of a Puertro Rican Childhood." *MELUS* (Summer 1993).

Novoa, Juan Bruce. "Judith Ortiz Cofer's Rituals of Movement." *Americas Review* (Winter 1991).

Ocasio, Rafael. "An Interview with Judith Ortiz Cofer." *Americas Review* (Fall-Winter 1994): pp. 84–90.

——— "The Infinite Variety of the Puerto Rican Reality: An Interview with Judith Ortiz Cofer." *Callaloo* (Summer 1994).

## COMMON HUMAN EXPERIENCE

A recurring theme in Cofer's work is the conflict immigrants have with assimilating into American culture. Here are some other works that focus on cultural identity:

*How the García Girls Lost Their Accents* (1991), by Julia Alvarez. This novel recounts the story of four sisters who must learn to adapt to the American culture of the 1960s when they leave the Dominican Republic for political reasons.

*The Joy Luck Club* (1989), by Amy Tan. The book comprises sixteen stories told by four Chinese immigrant women and their American-born daughters. The title refers to a club formed in China by one of the mothers to sustain its members' spirits during the communist revolution. Tan uses the novel to explore the emotional conflict between Chinese-American mothers and daughters separated by generational and cultural differences.

*Family Installments: Memories of Growing Up Hispanic* (1982), by Edward Rivera. This semi-fictional autobiography describes how the author and his Puerto Rican family deal with moving to New York City and their struggles to find an identity in America.

*Down These Mean Streets* (1976), by Piri Thomas. Thomas, born in New York to a Puerto Rican mother and a Cuban father, is the first Latino to write about growing up in Spanish Harlem. This harsh but honest autobiography is a coming-of-age story that reveals the difficulties Thomas had trying to find his place in society while growing up in Harlem.

## ✹ Robert P. Tristram Coffin

BORN: *1892, Brunswick, Maine*

DIED: *1955, Portland, Maine*

NATIONALITY: *American*

GENRE: *Poetry, fiction, nonfiction*

MAJOR WORKS:
*Christchurch* (1924)
*Portrait of an American* (1931)
*Ballads of Square-toed Americans* (1933)
*Strange Holiness* (1935)
*Saltwater Farm* (1937)

### Overview

Robert P. Tristram Coffin was one of America's most famous regionalist poets from the 1930s through the 1950s. A talented teacher and artist who often illustrated

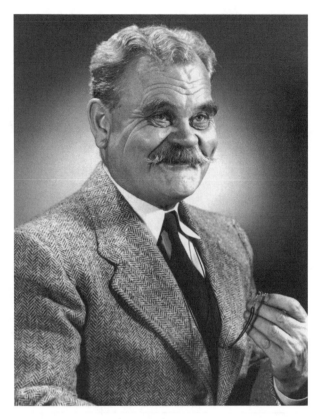

Robert P. Tristram Coffin    *Coffin, Robert Tristram, photo by Mel Jenkins. Bowdoin College. Reproduced by permission of Central Missouri State University.*

his works, Coffin wrote more than forty books, including novels, essays, and a biography. But he is most noted for his poetry that concerns the old American traditions of Puritan New England—simple values and self-reliance.

## Works in Biographical and Historical Context

**Born to be a Man of Letters**    Robert Peter Coffin was born on March 18, 1892, in Brunswick, Maine. He grew up in a house near Bowdoin College, an institution with which he would have a relationship with for the rest of his life. His mother, Alice Mary Coombs Coffin, was the second wife of James William Coffin, a Union Army veteran and widower. James Coffin, who raised two families, was a jack-of-all-trades who worked all kinds of jobs. When he died in 1908, he left a skill and a house to each of the ten children from his second marriage.

Coffin's early years were spent on farms far to the south of town. He was educated at home by his parents. Coffin enjoyed listening to his father's songs and stories, and began writing at an early age. His father knew Coffin would be a man of letters, as did poet and neighbor Sarah Orne Jewett, who predicted that Coffin would be a great poet. Coffin unquestioningly accepted this direction, and assumed as his own poetic mark a family name, Tristram.

When he was about thirteen years old, Coffin was sent to school in Brunswick, and according to his father's wishes, entered Bowdoin College in 1911. Coffin was an excellent student and graduated summa cum laude in 1915. The following year, he took his master's degree in English at Princeton on a graduate scholarship. When he was awarded a Rhodes scholarship, he left the United States to study poetry at Trinity College, Oxford. His schooling there was interrupted when America was drawn into World War I and Coffin enlisted as an artillery officer. Like many Americans, his plans were put on hold until after the war. When he was discharged from the army, he returned to Maine and married Ruth Neal Phillip on June 22, 1918.

**Bringing Oxford to Maine**    In just a few years, Coffin returned to Oxford where he was awarded two more degrees in 1920. A year later, he returned to the United States and took a teaching job in Wells College, New York. During his tenure at Wells, Coffin introduced Oxford's teaching style, implementing lectures and private lessons. While teaching, Coffin wrote poems and published his first collection, *Christchurch*, in 1924. These poems share the tales from the religious background of Coffin's New England ancestors, and are regarded as a testament to his Puritan faith.

Coffin continued to publish more poetry, refining his style with each new work. In 1931, he published a biography of his father *Portrait of an American* in which he shares his father's personal experiences, opinions, and spirituality. The respect he had for his father and family continued in his next collection of poetry, *Ballads of Square-toed Americans* (1933). In this book, he presents his father as Beowulf (a classic literary hero), and also recasts the *Aeneid*, the epic poem by Virgil, as an American adventure story in which he takes a panoramic look at America from "John Brown" to the "Mormons" and "Henry Hudson."

In 1934, Coffin left Wells to teach at Bowdoin College, his alma mater. He was named Outstanding Poet of the Nation at the Ninth Annual Poetry Week observances in 1935, and given a gold medal in recognition of his achievement. His next book, *Strange Holiness* (1935) won the Pulitzer Prize for poetry in 1936, and Robert Frost spoke for him at the presentation ceremonies.

**A Poet's Patriotism**    Coffin continued to write verse in a unique manner that was classically New England. Despite his apolitical nature, in the 1930s he unexpectedly found himself hailed as a Republican poet in a country swept by the New Deal. Unfortunately, the few Republicans with whom he was associated were largely people concerned with appearances, and he had very little in common with them. Coffin found the association troubling, as he preferred to remain apolitical.

At the start of World War II, Coffin decided to visit and teach at Indiana University. There Coffin was excited to find himself in the heartland of America, with people he believed had similar values, thoughts, and experiences as he did. A surge of patriotism poured out in his *Primer for America* (1943), in which he presented the "first lessons in the first principles of being American; the primary stages of the American myth."

***Fading Into Obscurity***   Coffin's family survived World War II intact, and his joy spilled over in his mythically titled *People Behave like Ballads* (1946). Some of these poems are hauntingly poignant, while others roar with a hearty humor. However, Coffin's Puritan patriotism, which featured an increasingly unpopular sense of isolationism, was not well received by many of his colleagues at Bowdoin. His contemporaries considered his ideas outdated, and Coffin began to spend more time lecturing off campus.

At one of these lectures, Coffin was stricken suddenly with a heart attack just before he was scheduled to speak in the chapel of Westbrook Junior College in Portland, Maine. He died in 1955 at the age of sixty three. As proof of how unsympathetic Bowdoin College had become to Coffin's ideas, the Coffin Room in the college union was dismantled shortly after his death. In addition, the Pierce Chair that he held was filled by someone with markedly different tastes. Macmillan, the publisher that held copyrights on most of his works, did little more than see through the production of *Selected Poems* (1955), the verse that had been most popular with his audiences. The rest fell into a sudden silence. Though Coffin was immensely popular during his lifetime, his name and works fell into obscurity after his death.

## Works in Literary Context

***Epic Puritan Poems***   All Coffin's work—poetry, essays, fiction, criticism, history, biography, lectures, and drawings—reflects his Puritan perspective. Everything he wrote celebrates life from the biblical creation to the apocalypse.

Coffin is best known for his narratives that celebrate the life of his family and Puritans. He wrote what he saw, learning to use common speech, ordinary people, and usual sights in his verse as did Robert Frost. Coffin captured the essence of New England life and speech very eloquently. He was a learned, authoritative, and consummate assimilator, enriching his own work with refractions of the past. His true role was that of the traditional epic poet who gives living voice to the past in the context of the immediate present.

## Works in Critical Context

Coffin was named Outstanding Poet of the Nation in 1935, won a Pulitzer Prize for Poetry in 1936, and received the Golden Rose of the New England Poetry Society that same year. He enjoyed fame and popularity during his lifetime. His works appeared in magazines and journals, and he often shared his works at readings.

---

## LITERARY AND HISTORICAL CONTEMPORARIES

Robert Coffin's famous contemporaries include:

**Robert Frost** (1874–1963): Frost was a major American poet and essayist who explored the meaning of life through his images of nature in rural New England. He won the Pulitzer Prize four times and participated in the inauguration of President John F. Kennedy in January, 1961.

**Alfred Kinsey** (1894–1956): This American zoologist was Coffin's roommate at Bowdoin. Kinsey founded the Institute for Sex Research at Indiana University. His explorations in human sexuality broke new ground in the field of sex research.

**Edna St. Vincent Millay** (1892–1950): Millay was an American poet popular with the rebellious post-World War I youth. She is remembered for her poetry, which boldly asserted an independent, nonconformist perspective toward contemporary life rarely expressed by women authors of her time.

**Salvador Dali** (1904–1989): This Spanish artist, famous for his paintings of hallucinatory, disturbingly incongruous dreamscapes, made a dramatic impact on modern art.

**Henry Ford** (1863–1947): American industrialist and inventor known for building the Model T automobile. Ford introduced the first assembly line in 1913, and thus revolutionized automobile manufacturing.

---

Coffin drew on his broad literary education to create a style of classical poetry filled with contemporary themes. He refined his own style of verse that blended history with a modern vision of America. Not all critics embraced his style, however. Many complained his verse was too parochial and homespun. On the other hand, writers such as William Rose Benét called Coffin "our most pictorial poet."

### There Will Be Bread and Love

Mary M. Colum in her *New York Times* review of *There Will Be Bread and Love* (1942) recognized in Coffin the "breath of the divine afflatus that gives him the rare power of revelation. . . . More than anyone except de la Mare, Coffin can touch people and things with mystery and strangeness." She sensed, too, his orphic vitalizing capacity: "his animals are always alive." He was also revered by a more famous poet, Robert Frost, who once said of Coffin, "He may, in time to come, since he will probably outlive me, stand a head taller than I in the world of poetry."

## Responses to Literature

1. Though Coffin was a popular writer and speaker in his time, he is hardly read today. After reading several of Coffin's poems, discuss why they may have been

BIBLIOGRAPHY

**Books**

*Dictionary of Literary Biography, Volume 45: American Poets, 1880-1945.* Farmington Hills, Mich.: Gale, 1986.

*Oxford Companion to American Literature.* London: Oxford University Press, 1965.

Swain, Raymond Charles. *A Breath of Maine: Portrait of Robert P. Tristram Coffin.* Boston: Branden Press, 1967.

**Web sites**

Robert Peter Tristram Coffin Collection. *George J. Mitchell Department of Special Collections & Archives, Bowdoin College Library.* Retrieved September 15, 2008, from http://library.bowdoin.edu/arch/mss/rptcg.shtml. Last updated on 2004.

"Robert P(eter) Tristram Coffin" *Contemporary Authors Online*, Gale, 2003. Retrieved September 15, 2008 from http://infotrac.galegroup.com/itw/infomark/

## COMMON HUMAN EXPERIENCE

Many poets, including Coffin, have used the long narrative poem known as the epic. Here are a few famous epic poems:

*The Odyssey* (c. 720 B.C.E.), by Homer. This Greek epic recounts the travels of Odysseus as ten years after the Trojan war, he struggles to sail back to his home of Ithaca.

*Cantar de mio Cid (El Cid)* (c. 1207), author unknown. This Spanish epic poem—the oldest one in Spanish history—is based on the heroic deeds of Rodrigo Díaz de Vivar. Exiled, the Cid wins favor with the king by taking back territory occupied by the Moors in southern Spain.

*Paradise Lost* (1667), by John Milton. Milton's epic poem is considered one of the greatest poems in English. *Paradise Lost* is an elaborate and detailed account of creation and the fall of man as told in Genesis.

*Hiawatha* (1855), by Henry Wadsworth Longfellow. This epic is about the son of the west wind, Hiawatha, who has supernatural powers. Based on selected tribal myths and legends of the North American Indians, the narrative poem recounts the adventures of Hiawatha and how he becomes the leader of his people. Eventually famine and fever kill many of his people. Before Hiawatha heads west, into the sunset, he teaches his people about the white man and his new religion.

lost in obscurity. Do you think his themes are outdated? Support your position using evidence from the texts you have read.

2. Coffin was fond of writing about his relationship with his father. Read "Portrait of an American," the biography of his father that won him an honorary life membership in the National Arts Club. Write a short essay in which you explain why you think Coffin revered his father, and what he hoped Americans would take away from his biography.

3. In common with many other poets from Maine, Coffin wrote about his state's people and character. Using resources in your library and on the Internet, research other Maine poets such as Henry Wadsworth Longfellow, Edwin Arlington Robinson, Edna St. Vincent Millay and Robert Frost (though Frost was not born in Maine). Choose two or three and analyze how their poems are similar and different in terms of theme, imagery, and tone.

4. Read several poems from *Strange Holiness*. Why do you think this collection won the Pulitzer Prize for Poetry? What sets the poems in this collection apart from Coffin's other works?

## ❀ Eugenia Collier

BORN: *1928, Baltimore, Maryland*

NATIONALITY: *American*

GENRE: *Fiction, drama, nonfiction*

MAJOR WORKS:

"Marigolds" (1969)
*Breeder and Other Stories* (1993)

### Overview

Eugenia Collier is an African American writer and educator best known for her frequently anthologized short story "Marigolds" (1969). Reflecting on her career as an author and critic, she has commented,

> The fact of my blackness is the core and center of my creativity. After a conventional Western-type education, I discovered the richness, the diversity, the beauty of my black heritage. This discovery has meant a coalescence of personal and professional goals. It has also meant a lifetime commitment.

### Works in Biographical and Historical Context

***Depression-era Childhood*** Eugenia Collier was born on April 6, 1928, in Baltimore, Maryland. She is the daughter of Harry Maceo Williams, a physician, and Eugenia Jackson Williams, an educator. The year after Collier was born, the American stock market crashed and sent the country into the Great Depression. Economic hardship was felt across the country and created particular difficulty for already low-income African American neighborhoods such as Collier's. Collier would later use her childhood experiences in the Depression to create the setting for her most famous story, "Marigolds."

***Public Service and Activism*** Because of racial segregation and unequal rights for women, girls—especially black girls—were rarely given the opportunity for an education. But Collier, a precocious child, was encouraged by both her mother and father to obtain a university education and pursue a professional career. She graduated magna cum laude from Howard University in 1948, and then received a master's degree from Columbia University in 1950. After receiving her degree at Columbia, Collier became a case worker at the Baltimore Department of Public Welfare, where she tended to the needs of the urban poor of all ages. Collier would draw many of her future stories from her five years in this job and emerged from the experience dedicated to improving social and economic conditions for black Americans. In particular, her story "Ricky," which she would adapt to a stage play in 1973 and appeared in the 1993 collection *Breeder and Other Stories*, captures the experiences of troubled African American youths in the inner city as they deal with a bureaucratic and insensitive social justice system.

***"Marigolds" and the Civil-Rights Movement*** Collier became an assistant instructor at Morgan State College in Baltimore in 1955, and continued to work on her fiction while she taught and worked toward the PhD she would receive from the University of Maryland in 1976. She also became an activist in the civil rights movement of the 1960s and 1970s, when Martin Luther King Jr. and others spoke out for for the social and political changes that would ultimately inspire racial equality and end segregation. In 1969, at the height of the movement, Collier published her best-known short story, "Marigolds," in which she described the experiences of a girl moving from innocence to adolescence during her Depression-era childhood. For this story she won the Gwendolyn Brooks Award for Fiction.

"Marigolds" has been repeatedly anthologized and was also included in Collier's 1993 collection *Breeder and Other Stories*. Aside from fiction, Collier has written or contributed to various collections of academic nonfiction, including *Impressions in Asphalt: Images of Urban America* (1999) and *Langston Hughes: Black Genius* (1991). She has also written for a wide variety of periodicals and has held teaching posts at the University of Maryland, Howard University, and Southern Illinois University. Since retiring in 1996, she has dedicated herself to writing and spending time with her family. She lives in Baltimore.

## Works in Literary Context

Like her contemporaries Alice Walker, Toni Morrison, Nikki Giovanni, and Maya Angelou, Collier focuses her work on the experiences of African American women.

---

# LITERARY AND HISTORICAL CONTEMPORARIES

Collier's famous contemporaries include:

**Alice Walker** (1944–): Walker is an African American writer and feminist who won the Pulitzer Prize and the National Book Award for her novel *The Color Purple* (1982).

**Toni Morrison** (1931–): Morrison is an American writer. Her most famous works include the novels *Beloved* (1988) and *Song of Solomon* (1977). She was the first black American woman to win the Nobel Prize.

**Oprah Winfrey** (1954–): Winfrey is an American talk-show host, actress, and philanthropist. Winfrey has contributed to the popularity of women's writing through her "Oprah's Book Club."

**Bill Clinton** (1946–): Clinton, the forty-second President of the United States, is known for advocating policies aimed toward racial equality.

**Martin Luther King, Jr.** (1929–1968): King was a leader of the American civil rights movement. He was known for many inspiring and moving speeches, including his 1963 "I Have a Dream" speech.

**James Baldwin** (1924–1987): An African American novelist and activist. Baldwin is best known for his treatment of racial and sexual prejudice in *Go Tell It on the Mountain* (1953).

---

She is also known for her emphasis on children and adolescents—particularly their experiences with often hostile justice systems in urban environments.

***The Urban Black Experience*** Drawing from her background as a social worker in inner-city Baltimore, Collier dedicates much of her fiction to recreating the city environments affecting African American women and children. Often, the characters of Collier's stories are lost—both on the streets and within the system—and must depend on familial or bureaucratic systems that ultimately fail them. For example, the second tale of the collection *Breeder and Other Stories*, entitled "Ricky," features an eleven-year-old boy left orphaned and homeless by the disappearance of his father and the psychological deterioration of his mother. His elderly great aunt, Vi, takes him in but soon finds that even her love cannot undo the damage the child has endured from domestic and institutional neglect. Incompetent parenting and the insensitivity of courts, schools, and child welfare agencies have left the child violent and unmanageable. Similarly, the last story of the collection, "Dead Man Running" tells the story of a teenager caught in a drug deal that ultimately ends in a murder. In both of these tales, Collier uses a grim realism to depict lives significantly compromised by the demands of modern urban life.

Eugenia Collier

# COMMON HUMAN EXPERIENCE

"Marigolds" is the story of Lizabeth, a fourteen-year-old African-American girl being raised in a family facing the hardship of the Great Depression. Here are some other works that have captured the experience of black women facing economic difficulty and racial inequality:

*Incidents in the Life of a Slave Girl* (1861), a nonfiction book by Harriet Jacobs. In this narrative Jacobs describes the experiences and humiliations suffered by female slaves in the South prior to the Civil War. The book has become a core component in the genres of African-American and feminist literatures.

*Their Eyes Were Watching God* (1937), a novel by Zora Neale Hurston. This seminal work of African-American feminist literature chronicles the life of Janie Crawford, a woman who lives in Eatonville, Florida, America's first all-black community of the early twentieth century. Both Alice Walker and Toni Morrison have cited Hurston's book as a primary influence on their work.

*I Know Why the Caged Bird Sings* (1969), an autobiography by Maya Angelou. Angelou's memoir of her childhood in Depression-era Stamps, Arkansas, explores her development as an black female artist. It also includes a highly controversial scene in which Angelou describes being raped by one of her mother's boyfriends at the age of thirteen.

*The Color Purple* (1982), a novel by Alice Walker. This novel describes the lives of women living in the rural South in the 1920s and 1930s. The protagonist, Celie, is abused by her father and husband, but finds hope in her friendship with another woman, Shug, and in the hope of being reunited with her long-lost sister.

*Beloved* (1987), a novel by Toni Morrison. Morrison's novel explores slavery and the trauma it causes. The book won the Pulitzer Prize in 1987 and is considered one of the most important novels ever written by a black American author.

***Feminism*** Almost all of the stories in Collier's collection *Breeder* are told from a female point of view. In many of these narratives, women face difficult decisions brought on by the demands of parenting in a hostile society. In "Rachel's Children," for example, a lonely college professor confronts the ghost of a slave mother seeking beyond the grave for her children. In "Journey," the character Azuree takes her own child's life as a protective measure. Though these stories vividly portray the difficulties black women face, they also often cast these women as the linchpins of their families and communities.

***Coming of Age*** Collier's stories also tend to feature child protagonists. Indeed, "Marigolds" has become one

of the classic coming-of-age stories in American literature. Lizabeth, the fourteen-year-old narrator, destroys the beautiful marigolds in old Miss Lottie's yard in a fit of misguided rage. She describes the moment after her destructive act, when she looks up into the "sad, weary eyes" of Miss Lottie, as "the end of innocence." She states that "innocence involves an unseeing acceptance of things at face value, an ignorance of the area below the surface. In that humiliating moment I looked beyond myself into the depths of another person. This was the beginning of compassion, and one cannot have both compassion and innocence."

## Works in Critical Context

Though Eugenia Collier is recognized for her academic and theoretical work, she is best-known for her collection *Breeder and Other Stories* and, in particular, "Marigolds" which it includes.

***Breeder and Other Stories*** Upon its publication in 1993, critics praised the feminist point of view taken by Collier in *Breeder and Other Stories* and argued for its sophistication. Critic T. Jasmine Dawson stated, "the title alone suggests that Collier was thinking beyond black and female as she repeatedly raised the notion that women indelibly hold families together by embracing the spoils of community despite repeated pitfalls." In addition, many reviewers commented on Collier's ability to weave seamlessly the past and the present. For example, Opal J. Moore, in *Black Issues in Higher Education*, commented that "Far from indulging in self-pity, these stories should engage our understanding and questioning of our revulsion of the past, as well as our self-protective embracing of it." Moore also examined the overall theme of the collection, finding that "each of the stories in *Breeder and Other Stories* describes a condition of profound loss—not the loss of love itself, its pulse or impulse, but of its embrace. They tell of a loss of orderliness, of any of the traditional illusions of safety, of the pure luxury of expectancy."

## Responses to Literature

1. In "Marigolds," the fourteen-year-old narrator Lizabeth describes her coming-of-age moment as the point where she no longer saw the world at face value, and instead "looked beyond myself into the depths of another person. This was the beginning of compassion, and one cannot have both compassion and innocence." What do you think Collier means by this comment? Do you believe it is impossible to have both compassion and innocence? Why or why not? Write an essay in which you clarify Collier's meaning and whether you agree with her.

2. Examine Collier's depictions of civic institutions throughout her stories—particularly courts, schools, and child welfare agencies. How are they described, and what arguments are made in these descriptions?

Write an essay in which you discuss Collier's representation of and attitude toward bureaucracy. Do the stories offer alternatives to these institutions, or suggestions for their reform?

3. Motherhood plays a vital role in the works contained in *Breeder and Other Stories*. Compare and contrast Collier's vision of modern motherhood with those of motherhood in past historical periods (for example in "Marigolds" and "Rachel's Children"). What are the similarities and differences? Why, in your opinion, does Collier make these comparisons with the past?

BIBLIOGRAPHY

**Books**

Peterson, Bernard L., Jr. *Contemporary Black American Playwrights and Their Plays.* New York: Greenwood Press, 1988.

Williams, Ora. *American Black Women in the Arts and Social Sciences: A Bibliographic Survey.* Lanham, Md.: Scarecrow, 1973.

**Periodicals**

Dawson, T. Jasmine. "Eugenia W. Collier" In *The Encyclopedia of African American Writers.* New York: Greenwood Publishing Group, 2007: 103–105.

Moore, Opal J. "The Bill of Wrongs: Stories for the Children" *Black Issues in Higher Education* 14.2 (March 20, 1997): 34.

Kaganoff, Peggy. "Forecasts: Paperbacks." *Publishers Weekly 241*(January 17, 1994): 427.

# ✵ Billy Collins

BORN: *1941, New York, New York*

NATIONALITY: *American*

GENRE: *Poetry*

MAJOR WORKS:

*Pokerface* (1977)

*Picnic, Lightning* (1998)

*Sailing Alone Around the Room: New and Selected Poems* (2001)

## Overview

When poet Billy Collins received a call from Librarian of Congress James Billington offering him the post of United States poet laureate, it never occurred to Collins that he could decline the offer. "I just assumed I was being called up, as though I'd been sitting on the bench of poetry all my life and the coach says, 'Get in there, Collins'," he told *Newsweek*. Collins is the author of several books of poetry, including *Questions about Angels* (1991) and *Sailing Alone Around the Room* (2001). "Billy Collins' poetry is widely accessible," Billington told

Billy Collins   *Collins, Billy, photograph. AP Images.*

CNN.com. "He writes in an original way about all manner of ordinary things and situations with both humor and a surprising contemplative twist."

## Works in Biographical and Historical Context

*Collins's Awkward Phase*   Collins was born in 1941 in French Hospital in Manhattan, where famed American poet William Carlos Williams, who was also a medical doctor, once served. Both Collins's father, an electrician from a large Irish-Catholic family, and his mother, a nurse, were in their forties when they had Collins, their only child. Collins was raised in Queens until he was in junior high school, and his father, switching careers, became a prosperous insurance broker. The family then moved to affluent Westchester County, New York and joined a country club.

Collins produced his first poem when he was twelve years old, and wrote for his high school's literary magazine. Inspired by the issues of the journal *Poetry* his encouraging father brought home to him, Collins's fascination with poetry intensified. Following high school, he attended Holy Cross College, where he earned his bachelor's degree in 1963. He then went on to obtain his

# LITERARY AND HISTORICAL CONTEMPORARIES

Collins's famous contemporaries include:

**Robert Hayden** (1913–1980): Detroit-born poet Hayden was the U.S. poet laureate when Collins published his first poetry collection, *Pokerface*. Hayden's fascination with African American history was deeply influential on his work.

**Stanley Kunitz** (1905–2006): Massachusetts-born poet Kunitz was the Consultant in Poetry to the Library of Congress from 1974–1976. The position was an early version of the current U.S. poet laureate, the post that Kunitz held immediately before the appointment of Collins.

**George W. Bush** (1946–): The forty-third president of the United States, Bush was sworn into office in 2001—the same year that Collins was appointed U.S. poet laureate. The two-term Republican president is the son of George Herbert Walker Bush, the forty-first president of the United States.

**Garrison Keillor** (1942–): American writer and radio personality Keillor is famed for his folksy, Minnesota-based radio program *A Prairie Home Companion*.

**Robert Peters** (1924–): Poet, critic, playwright, actor, and teacher Robert Peters began his long and impressive career with the publication of *Songs for a Son* (1967), a book of poetry inspired by the unexpected death of his son.

PhD in romantic poetry at the University of California, Riverside. Collins remained on the West Coast to be a "proto-beatnik and to write bad Ferlinghetti," as he told Linton Weeks of *The Washington Post*. Still far from developing his own style, he continued, "I took a little bit of everything." Like many poets, Collins began by thinking there was no room for humor in poetry. "My bad poems were bad in the beginning because they were emotionally heavy, brooding, then profound and ponderous" he told *Newsweek*.

*A Poet Matures* Despite the awkwardness of his early work, Collins's passion for poetry was undeterred and he eventually sold several short poems, inspired by the marijuana culture of the time, to *Rolling Stone* for thirty-five dollars each. Subsequently, he began perfecting a more distinctive and personal style of writing, far lighter in tone than the plodding work of his twenties. Having taken on a teaching position at Lehman College in the Bronx in 1970, Collins's work benefited from the clearer mind that came with maturity. In 1977, his life stabilized further when he married Diane Olbright, then of ABC's *Wide World of Sports* and now an architect. Collins and his wife moved to a restored 1860s Colonial home with a few acres of land in Somers, New York, about forty minutes from the Bronx. That year, he published his first collection, *Pokerface* (1977).

Entering his forties in the early 1980s, Collins finally began to explore lighter themes in his work, and developed the unique voice that would bring him to prominence in the world of poetry. That voice was mildly whimsical and welcoming. His chief goal was to make poetry pleasurable, not ponderous. As he would tell a writer for Powell's Books, "My poetry is suburban, it's domestic, it's middle class, and it's sort of unashamedly that." He writes about life's small things, "the mysterious notes one finds in the margins of used books, lingerie catalogues, houseplants, nursery rhyme characters, music."

*The Poet Laureate* In 2001, Collins was rewarded for his fresh, accessible body of work when he was named Poet Laureate of the United States. The honor of poet laureate is bestowed on the most distinguished and representative poet of his or her country, and Collins was eager to take the position. However, he continued to maintain his position at Lehman College. Like the laureates before him, who included Robert Hass, Robert Pinsky, and Rita Dove, Collins's aim was to use the poet laureate position to boost awareness of poetry. "Poetry is a neglected species," he told a reporter for *Newsweek*. Though there are more poetry readings and about two hundred graduate-level programs now—compared to only two when Collins was in college—the laureate planned to travel, "trying to make connections with readers," he told *Newsweek*.

Collins held his title as poet laureate until 2003, and was further honored on his home turf the following year when he was named New York State Poet of 2004. Collins continues to work and reside in New York. His latest work, *Ballistics: Poems*, was released in 2008.

## Works in Literary Context

*Satire* Satire is an approach to any literary, graphic, or performing art that intends to ridicule humanity's follies, vices, and shortcomings. Satire is distinguished by a humorous, ironic, satiric tone. The term was first applied to a collection of poetry by the ancient Roman poet Quintus Ennius (239–c. 169 B.C.E.) that ridiculed his fellow poet Accius. Humorous poet Collins has classified some of his own work as satire, directing his pen at the excesses and pretensions of colleagues, as he did with "Irish Poetry," a satire of Irish poet Seamus Heaney.

## Works in Critical Context

*Sailing Alone Around the Room: New and Selected Poems* Collins has long enjoyed enthusiastic appreciation from both critics and the public for his unpretentious, humorous, and deeply human poetry. His collection of old favorites and recent triumphs titled *Sailing Alone Around the Room* was widely appreciated for its simplicity and accessibility. In an extensive study of the collection in the *Yale Review of Books*, reviewer Allie Stielau took note of the collection's preoccupation with romance, describing him as

> a man who finds poetry in catalogues and calendars and boring Tuesday mornings, who sees sonnets in postcards and can describe a favorite haiku in ten different ways. Indeed, what better advocate of poetry could America have than a poet who sees himself as a lovestruck student, his poems as the paper airplanes that boy folds and flies at his darling, hoping to make a direct hit?

***The Best Cigarette*** Upon its first release, Collins's audio book of poetry *The Best Cigarette* (1997) enjoyed the same praise that the vast majority of his contemporary work has received throughout the literary community. Ira Glass of the National Public Radio program *This American Life* succinctly praised the audio book for being "unpretentious, funny, and good." However, a reviewer for *The New York Times* recognized that Collins was also capable of taking the listener to more solemn territory when it noted how, with his penchant for "[l]uring his readers into the poem with humor, Mr. Collins leads them unwittingly into deeper, more serious places, a kind of journey from the familiar or quirky to unexpected territory, sometimes tender, often profound."

## Responses to Literature

1. Although Collins has professed his appreciation of Irish poet Seamus Heaney, he has also admitted that his own poem "Irish Poetry" was intended as a satire of Heaney's style. Read Collins's "Irish Poetry" and two poems by Seamus Heaney. Explain how Collins's poem is a satire of Heaney's work. Do you think his satire is successful? Why or why not?

2. Collins's work has often been described as "accessible." Read two of Collins's poems. Then explain what you think critics mean when they use the word "accessible" to describe his poetry. Do you agree with this description? Use examples from his work to support your statement.

3. The Creative Commons organization helps writers, artists, musicians, and photographers to make their work available to the public for free. In 2005, Collins released his audio book *The Best Cigarette* under a Creative Commons agreement. How does this relate to the kind of poetry he writes, and to his reputation as an "accessible" writer?

BIBLIOGRAPHY

**Periodicals**

"Pushing Poetry to Lighten Up—and Brighten Up." *Newsweek* (July 9, 2001).

Weber, Bruce. "On Literary Bridge, Poet Hits a Roadblock." *New York Times* (December 19, 1999).

---

## COMMON HUMAN EXPERIENCE

In his poem "Nightclub" (2000), Collins explores his theories of love and beauty while listening to jazz singer Johnny Hartman. "Nightclub" is part of a long tradition of poems influenced by the stirring, improvisational, and technically demanding music of jazz. Other works of poetry inspired by jazz include:

"Jazz Fantasia" (1919), a poem by Carl Sandburg. In this poem, Sandburg compares the fast-paced, fierce sounds of a jazz band to "a racing car slipping away from a motorcycle cop" and a fist fight in a stairwell, drawing attention to the underlying violence in the band's chaotic music.

"Cabaret" (1927), a poem by Sterling Allen Brown. Brown's "Cabaret" captures the wildly improvisational spirit of jazz in both its unusual composition, which at time mimics jazz lyrics and the sounds of blaring trumpets, and in its description of a hot night of music at a jazz cabaret in New Orleans.

"Song" (1932), a poem by Gwendolyn Bennett. Bennet's "Song" focuses on the sensual, seductive side of jazz. Her poem likens the banjo music to which she is listening to "moist, dark lips" and describes the movements of a dancing girl in terms that also conjure exciting music.

"Dream Boogie" (1951), a poem by Langston Hughes. One of the most enduring works by beloved poet Hughes, "Dream Boogie" is a jolly celebration of boogie-woogie, a particularly fast, danceable form of jazz. With its sparse, joyful stanzas, "Dream Boogie" leaps right to the heart of the essence of jazz.

Weeks, Linton. "The Bard of Simple Things: For Poet Laureate Billy Collins, Writing Verse Is a Lot Like Breathing." *Washington Post* (November 28, 2001): C1

Wetzel, Cynthia Magriel. "With Humour, Poet lures Fans to the Serious." *New York Times* (November 30, 1997).

**Web Sites**

*Billy Collins: Complete resource for Billy Collins poems, books, recordings.* Accessed November 13, 2008, from http://www.billy-collins.com/.

*Billy Collins Interview Excerpts.* The Cortland Review: An Online Literary Magazine in RealAudio. Accessed November 30, 2008, from http://www.cortland review.com/features/05/spring/billy_collins.html.

CNN.com Entertainment. *New U.S. Poet Laureate Named.* Accessed November 29, 2008, from http://archives.cnn.com/2001/SHOWBIZ/books/06/21/us.poet.laureate/index.html.

*Guernica / A Magazine of Art & Politics. A Brisk Walk: An Interview with Billy Collins.* Accessed November 29, 2008, from http://www.guernicamag.com/interviews/185/a_brisk_walk/.

*The Poetry Archive. Billy Collins.* Accessed November 13, 2008, from http://www.poetryarchive.org/poetryarchive/singlePoet.do?poetId=6478.

*Online NewsHour with Jim Lehrer. Interview with Billy Collins* (transcript). Accessed November 29, 2008, from http://www.pbs.org/newshour/bb/entertainment/july-dec01/collins_12-10.html.

Weich, Dave. "Billy Collins, Bringing Poetry to the Public." *Powell's Books.* Accessed November 13, 2008, from http://www.powells.com/authors/collins.html.

# ☸ Richard Connell

BORN: *1893, Poughkeepsie, New York*

DIED: *1949, Beverly Hills, California*

NATIONALITY: *American*

GENRE: *Fiction*

MAJOR WORKS:

"A Friend of Napoleon" (1923)

"The Most Dangerous Game" (1924)

## Overview

Richard Connell is an author whose reputation rests largely upon a single short story, "The Most Dangerous Game." However, during his life, his many short stories, novels, and writings for the screen enjoyed great popularity with audiences, and some of his works were also praised by critics.

## Works in Biographical and Historical Context

***Bred for Journalism*** Connell was born on October 17, 1893, in Poughkeepsie, New York. His father, Richard Edward Connell Sr., worked as a reporter and editor for a local newspaper called the *Poughkeepsie News-Press* for twenty-three years before becoming Poughkeepsie police commissioner and redirecting his interests to politics. The younger Richard was more than happy to keep the Connell name prominent in the world of journalism. He began covering baseball games at the age of ten and earned ten cents per story. While in high school, Connell took a position at the *Poughkeepsie News-Press* where he worked as a reporter.

Following high school graduation, Connell attended Georgetown College (now Georgetown University) for a year. His time at Georgetown was cut short when his father was elected to the U.S. House of Representatives. Connell left college to work as his father's secretary in Washington, D.C., in 1910. Unfortunately, Connell's job

and personal life were disrupted in 1912, when his father died at the age of fifty-five. In 1915, Connell decided it was time to continue his studies, and he enrolled in Harvard University. His time at Harvard reignited Connell's love of writing. He became editor of the daily newspaper *The Harvard Crimson* and the university's humor publication, *The Harvard Lampoon*. While managing *The Harvard Crimson*, Connell wrote an article attacking a New York newspaper editor. The editor was so irate that he sued the paper for libel. Ironically, Connell later worked for that editor, after he graduated from Harvard.

Connell continued to maintain his focus on journalism until he was offered a position as an advertising copywriter while he was working as a reporter for the *New York American*. Once again, Connell's professional life was shaken—this time by the onslaught of World War I, a global war that would disturb countless of lives. Connell eagerly enlisted in the U.S. Army in 1917. Forever the devoted journalist, Connell took this opportunity to work as the editor of *Gas Attack*, the newspaper of his camp. In addition to providing Connell with additional journalistic experience, the war also provided travel opportunities: Collins spent a year in France with his unit, the twenty seventh New York Division.

***From Fact to Fiction*** When the war ended in 1918, Connell returned to his job writing advertising copy. A year later he married fellow writer and editor Louise Herrick Fox. More good news arrived that same year, when he published his first short story. Thus officially began his tremendously prolific career as a short-story writer. Connell began publishing stories at a steady rate in such major periodicals as *Collier's* and *The Saturday Evening Post*. His story "A Friend of Napoleon" won him a second-prize O. Henry Award in 1923. By this time, Connell and his wife had been living in Paris, France, for three years, but the couple regularly returned to the United States for visits. A 1924 trip to California inspired the couple to take up permanent residence there. Connell was attracted by the plentiful opportunities for gardening and fishing that the state afforded. He also took an interest in California's budding film industry. Further expanding his already vast repertoire, Connell tried his hand at screenwriting. He began working on silent movies with the established screenwriter Paul Schofield, who helped Connell bring his story "Tropic of Capricorn" to the screen as *East of Broadway* (both 1924).

His cinematic debut notwithstanding, Connell's greatest achievement in 1924 came in the form of a terrifying tale that would become one of the most anthologized short stories of all time. Published on January 19, 1924, in *Collier's*, "The Most Dangerous Game" (also known as "The Hounds of Zaroff") finds New York big-game hunter Sanger Rainsford shipwrecked on a Caribbean island. There Rainsford encounters the Russian aristocrat General Zaroff, an insidious character with a yen for hunting human beings. The adventure story not only won

Connell his second O. Henry Award; it also secured his position as a writer for many years to come. The story was adapted for radio and the cinema several times, often under such alternative titles as *A Game of Death* (1945), *Run for the Sun* (1955), and *The Woman Hunt* (1973).

*Connell's Legacy* The world would most remember Connell for "The Most Dangerous Game," but he had many more stories to tell, and a number of them would be anthologized in the collections *The Sins of Monsieur Petipon* (1922), *Apes and Angels* (1924), *Variety* (1925), and *Ironies* (1930). Not all of these collections were well-received upon publication, but Connell refused to be hindered by mixed responses from critics and continued to produce work at an impressive pace. Much of that work was ultimately brought to the screen. His 1924 serial "A Little Bit of Broadway" was made into a motion picture the following year as *Bright Lights*. In 1927, he published his first full-length novel, *The Mad Lover*, about a millionaire reformed by his love for a poor girl. Two years later, he published *Murder at Sea* (1929), a mystery novel featuring the detective Matthew Keaton.

Connell would go on to write two more novels, *Playboy* (1936) and *What Ho!* (1937). The vast majority of his many stories are now forgotten, although some survive thanks to memorable film adaptations. These include the gangster story *Brother Orchid* (1940), which starred two of the leading big-screen tough guys of the 1940s, Humphrey Bogart and Edward G. Robinson. He also cowrote the original story treatment for the Frank Capra film *Meet John Doe* (1941), for which he won an Academy Award. Connell's long and intriguing career was brought to an end when he suffered a heart attack in 1949. There is no denying that Connell achieved much during his lifetime, but he remains most remembered for that one unforgettable tale, "The Most Dangerous Game."

## Works in Literary Context

*Revenge* The theme of revenge appears toward the end of "The Most Dangerous Game" when Rainsford turns the tables on his hunter, Zaroff. In this way the reader is left with the lingering question of whether or not Rainsford has become a figure just as murderous as Zaroff. Despite winning Zaroff's game by using his wits to survive, he is overcome by the primal desire for revenge and kills Zaroff at the story's conclusion. Since Rainsford has already won the most dangerous game, the act cannot be justified as self-defense, and his apparent satisfaction in killing Zaroff reveals a darkness stirred within Rainsford while engaging in the game.

*Bigotry* In "The Most Dangerous Game," General Zaroff makes racist comments that reflect the attitudes of anti-immigrant Americans during the 1920s. When he explains his nefarious hobby to Rainsford, he makes the revealing statement, "I hunt the scum of the earth—sailors from tramp ships—Lascars, blacks, Chinese, whites,

## LITERARY AND HISTORICAL CONTEMPORARIES

Connell's famous contemporaries include:

**Theodore Roosevelt** (1858–1919): The twenty-sixth president of the United States, Roosevelt is most remembered for his large personality and penchant for adventurous pursuits like hunting and exploring. Roosevelt lived close to Richard Connell's New York birthplace.

**Inez Haynes Irwin** (1873–1970): The Brazilian-born writer Irwin was a journalist who worked as a magazine correspondent during World War I and was the author of several novels and short stories. Her story "The Spring Flight" took the top O. Henry Award in 1924, the same year Richard Connell won his Best Short Story award for "The Most Dangerous Game."

**Ernest B. Schoedsack** (1893–1979): The Iowa-born film director Schoedsack for codirecting the classic monster movie *King Kong* with Merian C. Cooper in 1933. *King Kong* recycled many sets and cast members from the 1932 film version of "The Most Dangerous Game," which Schoedsack co-directed with Irving Pichel.

**Frank Capra** (1897–1991): Considered one of the most important American film directors of the twentieth century, Capra was a master of reproducing small-town life and values on the big screen. He is best known for such cinema favorites as *Mr. Smith Goes to Washington* (1939) and *It's a Wonderful Life* (1946), as well as the Richard Connell-penned *Meet John Doe* (1941).

**Orson Welles** (1915–1985): A tremendously influential actor, writer, director, and radio personality Orson Welles co-wrote, directed, and starred in the 1941 film *Citizen Kane*, often ranked as the greatest movie ever made.

mongrels—a thoroughbred horse or hound is worth more than a score of them." "The Most Dangerous Game" was published only a few decades after an influx of immigrants landed on American shores, which caused many Americans to fear that jobs would become scarce and their standard of living would drop. Such hateful attitudes grew so prevalent that Congress set about restricting the number of African, Asian, and Latino immigrants. By placing the vitriolic sentiments of anti-immigration Americans in the mouth of the villainous Zaroff, Connell's story can be read as a powerful criticism of such attitudes.

## Works in Critical Context

Connell's work was often more popular with readers and filmmakers than it was with critics, but early works like "A Friend of Napoleon" and "The Most Dangerous

# COMMON HUMAN EXPERIENCE

"The Most Dangerous Game" is undoubtedly one of the most well-known tales in which a human is hunted like an animal, but it was certainly not the last. Other works in which humans are hunted include:

*Lord of the Flies* (1954), a novel by William Golding. Golding's classic novel finds a group of English school-boys dividing into warring tribes and resorting to primitive violence after being stranded on a deserted island. The final sequence of this allegorical tale of civilization versus savagery finds two of the boys embarking on a hunt for another boy in the rival tribe.

"The Racer" (1956), a short story by Ib Melchior. Melchior's short story "The Racer" is a grim, futuristic tale in which America's most popular sport is a race in which the drivers earn points by pursuing pedestrians and running them down with their race cars.

"Prey" (1969), a short story by Richard Matheson. A classic terror yarn, "Prey" features a woman named Amelia scrambling for her life after receiving a mysterious Zuni fetish doll. The doll, imbued with the spirit of a Zuni hunter, comes to life and hunts Amelia in the confines of her own apartment.

*The Running Man* (1982), a novel by Richard Bachman. This popular science fiction novel—written under pseudonym by Stephen King—focuses on a popular game called *The Running Man* in which human beings must outrun hunters in order to win a one-billion-dollar prize.

Game" were quite well received, both of the aforementioned stories winning O. Henry Awards. Among Connell's more than three hundred stories, "The Most Dangerous Game" has survived particularly well.

***"The Most Dangerous Game"*** In a detailed 1997 study of "The Most Dangerous Game," Rena Korb deems the story "spare" but not "simplistic." "Connell's careful work turns a plot that could be deemed unrealistic into a story that compels the reader to breathlessly share Rainsford's life-or-death struggle," Korb writes. Scholar David Kippen explains that while most of Connell's work has disappeared due to his underdeveloped characters, "The Most Dangerous Game" has survived because of two important characteristics: "The story is an extremely successful example of the adventure genre, and the stereotypes Connell uses evoke allegories that remain relevant today."

***Variety*** Incorporating several of Connell's most famous stories, including the award-winning tales "A Friend of Napoleon" and "The Most Dangerous Game," the anthology *Variety* (1925) was not impervious to critics. Although a reviewer for *The Saturday Review of Literature* offers a positive assessment of the book, deeming its stories "easy to read, [with] all displaying facility and versatility," other publications were not as kind. A dismissive notice in *The New York Times* states that the collection "ranks, though high, in the great army of the second-rate." For this reason, perhaps, "The Most Dangerous Game" remains his only literary work currently in print.

## Responses to Literature

1. Filmmakers often take liberties with a literary work when adapting it for the cinema. This can be said of the 1932 film version of Richard Connell's short story "The Most Dangerous Game," which differed from Richard Connell's original short story in several significant ways. Read the story and view the film, then write an essay describing the ways they differ. Is the film generally an improvement over the story, or is the story superior? Why?

2. In "The Most Dangerous Game," Rainsford, the hero of the story, appears to undergo a significant change by the story's conclusion. In an essay, explain this transformation. What do you think Connell is attempting to say about human nature?

3. The conclusion of "The Most Dangerous Game" is somewhat open-ended. Rainsford does not immediately free Zaroff's other "prey" as soon as he kills the general, but instead he goes to sleep in the general's bed. Explain what you think Rainsford will do next, using details from the story to support your prediction.

BIBLIOGRAPHY

**Periodicals**

Hall, Mordaunt. "East of Broadway (1924)." *The New York Times* (November 12, 1924).

———. "The Most Dangerous Game (1932)." *The New York Times* (November 21, 1923).

Lansu, Helvi. "The Shape of Literature." *English Journal* (1965): 520–524

Review of *Variety*. *The New York Times* (March 29, 1925): 8.

Review of *Variety*. *The Saturday Review of Literature* (August 8, 1925).

Thompson, Terry W. "The Most Dangerous Game." *The Explicator* (2002): 86–88.

Welsh, Jim. "Hollywood Plays the Most Dangerous Game." *Literature-Film Quarterly* (1982): 134–136.

**Web Sites**

Book Rags. "*The Most Dangerous Game* Study Guide." Accessed November 14, 2008, from http://www.bookrags.com/studyguide-mostdangerous game/bio.html.

The Nostalgia League. *The Most Dangerous Game.* Accessed November 14, 2008, from http://theno stalgialeague.com/olmag/connell-most-dangerous-game.html.

# Pat Conroy

BORN: *1945, Atlanta, Georgia*

NATIONALITY: *American*

GENRE: *Fiction*

MAJOR WORKS:

*The Great Santini* (1976)

*The Lords of Discipline* (1980)

*The Prince of Tides* (1986)

## Overview

Pat Conroy is known primarily for his three best-selling novels, *The Great Santini* (1976), *The Lords of Discipline* (1980), and *The Prince of Tides* (1986), all of which were made into big-budget Hollywood films. Conroy's writing blends fiction, myth, and personal revelation, drawing heavily upon his experiences growing up in a military family in South Carolina. Issues of loyalty to family and friends, the male psyche, and the relationship between love and violence are recurrent themes in his popular books.

Pat Conroy  *Conroy, Pat, photograph. © Jerry Bauer. Reproduced by permission.*

## Works in Biographical and Historical Context

*Youth as a Military Brat*  Donald Patrick Conroy was born in Atlanta, Georgia, on October 26, 1945, the oldest son of seven children. His early years were spent as a military "brat" living short tours in "some of the more notable swamplands of the East Coast"; he claims to have lived in more than twenty locations before reaching age eighteen. Conroy's father, Donald Conroy, was a fighter pilot in the Marines, a gruff man whose methods of parental discipline sometimes veered into physical and emotional abuse. Various fictionalized portraits of his parents, and the harsh dynamics of his upbringing, appear in Conroy's fiction.

*The Citadel and "The Boo"*  Conroy spent part of his high school years in Beaufort, South Carolina, adjacent to a Marine base. The beauty of Beaufort's antebellum mansions and stately trees affected him deeply, and his writing remains highly identified with the South. According to his father's wishes, Conroy attended The Citadel, South Carolina's venerable all-male military academy. In the military academy, Conroy recognized the authoritarian attitudes he had witnessed in his father's behavior. He excelled at the academy, even editing its literary magazine, but he acquired some emotional distance from its rigid codes. His experiences there furnished material for his novel *The Lords of Discipline*.

Conroy's most memorable teacher at The Citadel was Lieutenant Colonel Thomas Nugent Courvoisie, Assistant Commandant of Cadets, also known as "the Boo." Courvoisie became the subject of *The Boo* (1970), Conroy's first novel, a romanticized account of his cadet years.

After graduating from The Citadel in 1967, Conroy taught English at several area high schools. He returned to Beaufort, to the high school from which he had graduated only four years before. In that time, the student body had been integrated, although the faculty was still white. Witnessing firsthand the damage caused by racial prejudice, Conroy became determined to help provide equal educational opportunities for black children. In 1969, he accepted a position teaching disadvantaged black children on Daufuskie Island off the Carolina coast.

*From Teaching to Writing*  Conroy was not prepared for his new students, who were nearly all illiterate. They did not know the name of their country, or that they lived on the Atlantic Ocean, although they did know how to skin muskrats and plant okra. Conroy enjoyed his work, but his unorthodox teaching methods, his unwillingness to allow corporal punishment of his students, and battles with school administrators resulted in his dismissal. In his fury, Conroy wrote *The Water is Wide* (1972), a caustic account of his experiences. The work was adapted for film in 1974

# LITERARY AND HISTORICAL CONTEMPORARIES

Conroy's famous contemporaries include:

**Cormac McCarthy** (1933–): McCarthy is a best-selling American novelist. His novel *Blood Meridian* (1985) is among the most critically acclaimed novels of the past twenty-five years.

**Tom Robbins** (1936–): Robbins is an American novelist whose novels include *Another Roadside Attraction* (1971), *Even Cowgirls Get the Blues* (1976), and *Skinny Legs and All* (1990).

**Anne Tyler** (1941–): Tyler is an American novelist whose popular novels include *The Accidental Tourist* (1985) and *Breathing Lessons* (1988).

**Bill Clinton** (1946–): Clinton was President of the United States from 1993–2001.

under the title *Conrack* starring Jon Voight. After this successful publication, Conroy returned to Atlanta and began writing full time.

Although Conroy's next book, *The Great Santini* (1976), is a novel, it draws heavily on his family background and faithfully renders the dynamics of military family life. "The Great Santini" is the nickname Bull Meecham, colonel in the U.S. Marine Corps, calls himself in his most authoritative roles. Meecham is mostly unable to distinguish his family role from his military role, and he treats his family members like fellow Marines. His eldest son, Ben, a high school basketball player, clearly suffers from his father's domination. Bull intensely desires for his son to succeed, but his efforts are totally misguided and cause conflict each step of the way.

Colonel Donald Conroy was at first taken aback by his son's fictional treatment of his family. However, the movie adaptation, with a memorable performance by Robert Duvall as Bull, helped change the colonel's attitude, and later in life, Donald Conroy took to referring to himself as "the Great Santini."

***The Lords of Discipline*** For his next work, Conroy returned again to the theme of military academies, creating the fictional Carolina Military Institute. In *The Lords of Discipline* (1980), Conroy explores the power struggles and viciousness often associated with military life. Will McLean, the narrator and a senior cadet, is assigned to protect the Institute's first black student from hostile, segregationist forces within the student body. To carry out this assignment, Will must confront many of his fellow cadets, and his conflicting impulses between group loyalty and personal integrity are a source of the novel's dramatic

tension. The novel offended many of Conroy's fellow graduates of The Citadel, although the author claimed he was not basing his depiction solely on his alma mater.

Conroy followed up this major success with his most popular book, *The Prince of Tides* (1986). It follows Tom Wingo, an unemployed high school English teacher and football coach, on a trip from coastal South Carolina to New York City, where he helps his twin sister Savannah recover from a nervous breakdown and suicide attempt. At the request of Savannah's psychiatrist, Tom relates the Wingo family's bizarre history. Despite the horrors the Wingos have suffered, including several rapes, the death of their brother, and a brutish father, the novel retains a sense of optimism due to the love that the Wingo children have for each other. Again, parts of the story were autobiographical: Conroy told the *Toronto Globe and Mail*, "Yes, my sister is also a poet in New York who has also had serious breakdowns." The film adaptation, directed by and starring Barbra Streisand, was a box office hit.

***Carolina Cuisine*** Conroy continued to mine his personal experience in his next work of fiction, *Beach Music* (1995). With its winding, complicated plot, *Beach Music* was not as successful as his prior best sellers. His latest autobiographical work, *My Losing Season* (2002), concerns his years playing college basketball.

Conroy now lives on Fripp Island off the South Carolina coast. The heritage and culture of the Carolinas are an underlying presence in all his fiction. In 1999, Conroy published *The Pat Conroy Cookbook*, which contains recipes and autobiographical anecdotes.

## Works in Literary Context

Conroy cites his mother, Frances "Peggy" Peek Conroy, as the source of his interest in literature and storytelling. He also had an influential high school English teacher, Eugene Norris. Norris introduced him to Thomas Wolfe's coming-of-age novel, *Look Homeward, Angel* (1929), and even brought Conroy to visit Wolfe's childhood home in Asheville, North Carolina. Conroy sought to emulate Wolfe's lyrical, self-revelatory style.

***Bildungsroman*** Most of Conroy's writings follow the time-tested pattern of the coming-of-age story, or bildungsroman. His heroes are typically young men whose hardships, either in family trauma or struggles with authority, ultimately bring them to emotional maturity, freedom, and self-knowledge. Conroy thus fits into one of the dominant traditions of narrative, including the initiation stories of mythology.

***Violence and the Male Ego*** Conroy has said that his father's violent and tyrannical nature is the central fact of his life and of his art. Much of his work is concerned with male psychology and machismo. The codes of honor in *The Lords of Discipline*, for example, reflect the ways young men live with and care for one another in an all-male, homophobic environment. Similarly, Bull Meecham tends to express affection for his son in rough fashion. In the climactic scene of *The Great Santini*, Bull and Ben play an intense game of one-on-one basketball. Ben wins the game (the first time he has ever bested his father in any activity) and Bull responds by bouncing the ball off his son's head, repeatedly. Bull is in a dangerous rage, but he is also forced to acknowledge that his son is becoming a man. Ben, for his part, cannot bring himself to reject his father entirely. Ambivalent, love-hate relationships such as theirs are pervasive in Conroy's books.

## Works in Critical Context

With a string of strong-selling titles, Conroy is among the most commercially successful contemporary American authors. Although some critics find his fictional works implausible and melodramatic, others admire him as a courageous, imaginative, and ironically humorous writer on sensitive cultural topics. His rhetorical style, befitting a Southern raconteur, can strike critics as alternately lyrical and overblown.

*The Great Santini*  Some scholars, notably in the South, have taken an interest in the structure of Conroy's narratives, noting his penchant for coming-of-age stories. In his analysis of *The Great Santini*, Robert Burkholder identifies myths that "seem to consume the characters, functioning as ways of perceiving the world and as cushions against the reality that myths seem to ignore." James Hutchins also notes Conroy's theme, and concludes, "*The Great Santini* is a fine, sensitive novel that deserves to be read by all servicemen with families." Although critics have been quick to praise the emotional impact of the book and the genuineness of its characters, Conroy's writing style has been the focus of some complaint. A reviewer in *The Virginia Quarterly* labeled the writing in *The Great Santini* "somewhat juvenile."

## Responses to Literature

1. In what way to southern settings, particular South Carolina, play a role in Conroy's work? Would they be different if they were set somewhere else? Could they be set somewhere else?

2. In an essay, compare the way Conroy depicts male/female relationships to his treatment of relationships between men. Do you think he finds the same difficulties in all relationships, or are there particular difficulties for each type of relationship?

3. Some critics have remarked that Conroy specializes in stories of initiation, or rites of passage. Citing two or more of his novels, analyze the process of initiation as he perceives it. What challenges must a young protagonist face on his way to maturation?

---

## COMMON HUMAN EXPERIENCE

Conroy's *The Great Santini* portrays a young man resisting domination by an authoritarian father. The works below, all loosely or formally autobiographical, also contain fearsome father figures:

*Go Tell it On the Mountain* (1953), by James Baldwin. A landmark American novel about race relations, religion, moral hypocrisy, and father-son animosity.

*Affliction* (1989), by Russell Banks. In this novel, a policeman is haunted by his relationship with his violent father.

*The Squid and the Whale* (2005), a film written and directed by Noah Baumbach. Two children take sides in their parents' divorce, but the older son begins to question his allegiance to his father.

*A Wolf at the Table* (2008), a memoir by Augusten Burroughs. From the author of the darkly comic *Running with Scissors* (2002) comes another memoir, this one more serious, about life with an angry, alcoholic father.

---

4. In *The Water is Wide*, Conroy mockingly refers to his own youthful idealism, or "do-gooderism." Citing this or other Conroy novels, evaluate the author's attitude toward these idealistic impulses.

BIBLIOGRAPHY

**Books**

Burns, Landon C. *Pat Conroy: A Critical Companion.* Westport, Conn.: Greenwood Press, 1996.

**Periodicals**

Berendt, John. "The Conroy Saga," *Vanity Fair.* (July 1995).

Burkolder, Robert E. "The Uses of Myth in Pat Conroy's *The Great Santini*," *Critique: Studies in Modern Fiction.* 21 (1979): 31–37.

Hamblin, Robert. "Sports Imagery in Pat Conroy's Novels," *Aethlon: The Journal of Sport Literature.* 11 (1993): 49–59.

Hutchins, James N. Review of *The Great Santini*, *Bestsellers*, 36:6 (1976): 180.

Idol, John. "(Un)Blest Be the Ties that Bind: The Dysfunctional Family in *Look Homeward, Angel* and *The Great Santini*," *North Carolina Literary Review.* 9 (2000): 142–150.

Malphrus, P. Ellen. "*The Prince of Tides* as Archetypal Hero Quest," *The Southern Literary Journal.* 39 (Spring 2007).

Review of *The Great Santini*, *Virginia Quarterly Review.* 52:4 (Spring 1976): 134.

Toolan, David. "The Unfinished Boy and His Pain: Rescuing the Young Hero with Pat Conroy," *Commonweal*. 118 (February 1991): 127–31.

York, Lamar. "Pat Conroy's Portrait of the Artist as a Young Southerner," *Southern Literary Journal*. 19 (1987): 34–46.

**Web Sites**

Hamblin, Robert W. "Pat Conroy." *The New Georgia Encyclopedia*. Retrieved September 9, 2008, from http://www.georgiaencyclopedia.org.

# ❈ James Fenimore Cooper

BORN: *1789, Burlington, New Jersey*

DIED: *1851, Cooperstown, New York*

NATIONALITY: *American*

GENRE: *Fiction, nonfiction*

MAJOR WORKS:

*The Pioneers* (1823)

*The Last of the Mohicans* (1826)

*The American Democrat* (1838)

James Fenimore Cooper    *Cooper, James Fenimore, drawing by C. L. Elliot. Source unknown.*

## Overview

The first popularly successful novelist of America, James Fenimore Cooper contributed greatly to the nation's literary and cultural life. His five Leather-Stocking Tales, which included his two great novels, *The Pioneers* (1823) and *The Last of the Mohicans* (1826), led the way to a specifically American form of literature. In romances of forest and sea, tales of colonial and revolutionary history, novels of politics and society, and provocative essays, Cooper helped give the young country its own literary identity.

## Works in Biographical and Historical Context

*Son of a Pioneer* On September 15, 1789, five months after George Washington's inauguration as the first president of the United States, James Cooper was born in Burlington, New Jersey. (He later added Fenimore, his mother's maiden name, to his own name.) As an infant he was carried from his birthplace through the woods of New York State, where his father, William, was making the wilds habitable for settlers. William Cooper founded the village of Cooperstown, on the edge of Ostego Lake, where James spent much of his youth, at play in the woods and on the water. William Cooper became a major figure in the early history of New York: a judge, congressman, and prosperous landlord. He was also a very demanding father.

Cooper was tutored at home and sent to private schools in Burlington and Albany. In 1803, before his fourteenth birthday, he was enrolled in Yale College.

Two years later, after pulling numerous pranks, he was expelled. In 1806, Cooper went to sea aboard a commercial ship. His experiences on the Atlantic served him later when he wrote nautical novels. More immediately, they qualified him to join the U.S. Navy as a midshipman at the beginning of 1808. He saw no active duty at sea, however, and left the service in 1810, after his father's death. He received a substantial inheritance, and in 1811 married Susan Augusta DeLancey, daughter of another wealthy New York Federalist. They had seven children, of whom four daughters and one son survived to adulthood.

In the 1810s, Cooper lived the life of the rural gentry in Scarsdale, New York. However, between his meager talent for business and his brothers' prodigal spending habits, much of the family fortune had been squandered by the end of the decade. At the age of thirty, he made a surprising and impromptu decision that altered the course of his life. One day, he was reading a current British novel aloud to his wife, and found the book so bad that he threw it down, declaring that he could write a better one himself. He took his wife's laughter as a challenge, and sat down immediately to compose a tale. He stuck with it, and by late 1820, he had completed *Precaution*, a novel of manners in the style of Jane Austen, set in England. He published the book anonymously that year.

*First Professional American Writer*  For his second effort, he turned to the manlier model of historical romance popularized by Sir Walter Scott. *The Spy* (1821) is not only set in America but also is about a patriot during the Revolutionary War. Giving his readers the formal elements they expected from British fiction, and a story they could be proud of as Americans, was a brilliant strategy. The public bought the book eagerly.

Now Cooper's career was firmly established. At age thirty-two, he became a man of letters, the first professional novelist in the United States. He moved to New York City in 1821 and stepped directly into the role of celebrity. The next book he wrote was among his most autobiographical, and by scholarly consensus, his greatest work. *The Pioneers* (1823) is based fairly closely on his memories of the village he grew up in. It is the richest account in existence of the infancy of an American frontier community.

*The Pioneers* recreates the founding of Cooperstown, with Judge Marmaduke Temple as a surrogate for William Cooper. At the novel's center is a profound ambivalence toward both the figure of the father and the enterprise of civilizing the continent. In their haste to acquire the forms of civilization, the settlers strip the mountains of their trees, the lake of its fish, and the forest of its animals—not to mention the land of its aboriginal inhabitants. The tone remains respectful toward Judge Temple and what his settlers achieve, but the reader is given more and more reasons to wonder.

*Natty Bumppo Heads for the Sunset*  This ambivalence is brought into focus by the one white character who is in alignment with nature, a character with no precedent in European fiction. He is Natty Bumppo, the Leather-Stocking. Living alone in a hut across the lake from the village, he embodies in his own person the spirit of the frontier; and Natty is not pleased with the way the settlers are driving the game from the woods he has lived in for forty years. Natty's presence grows steadily throughout the novel, and at the end, he leaves the settlement, becoming the first fictional American hero to disappear in the direction of the sunset.

The character of Natty appealed powerfully to contemporary readers. He is featured again, under the name Hawkeye, in Cooper's next Leather-Stocking Tale, *The Last of the Mohicans* (1826). At the start of this melodramatic adventure novel, set during the French and Indian War, two half-sisters, Cora and Alice, stray into the wilderness in an ill-advised attempt to join their father. The woods are full of hostile Indians. Twice the women are captured by the fierce Magua and have to be rescued by Hawkeye, accompanied by the Mohican chief Chingachgook and his son, Uncas. Cora and Uncas develop a quiet attraction, but the prospect of intermarriage is forbidden. Consequently, the only possible resolution to all the passions the novel stirs up is violence: first a massacre of

---

## LITERARY AND HISTORICAL CONTEMPORARIES

Cooper's famous contemporaries include:

**Sir Walter Scott** (1771–1832): The Scottish novelist and poet who achieved singular international popularity for works such as *Ivanhoe* (1819) and *Rob Roy* (1817).

**Lord Byron** (1788–1824): Byron was a noted British poet associated with the Romantic movement.

**Washinton Irving** (1783–1859): An American author known for the stories "Rip Van Winkle" (1819) and "The Legend of Sleepy Hollow" (1820).

**Alexis de Tocqueville** (1805–1859): The French magistrate and author whose essays on *Democracy in America* (1835) still provide insight into the American character.

**Edgar Allan Poe** (1809–1849): Known for his mastery of the macabre, Poe was a prominent American poet and short-story writer.

**Martin Van Buren** (1782–1862): The eighth president of the United States (1837–1841), and, before that, a political boss in New York state

---

whites at Fort William Henry, and finally the slaughter of Indians at a Mingo village in the woods. The title makes clear from the start that the story can only end with a funeral, not a wedding.

*The Last of the Mohicans* was among the nineteenth century's most popular novels; its breathless combination of sex and violence, capture and pursuit, enthralled audiences worldwide. But it satisfied white American readers in a specific way. In 1826, when the novel was published, most of the relocations and wars that came close to destroying Native American culture were still in the future. The novel, though, treats the extinction of "the red man" as an accomplished fact of the distant past, one that white readers could simultaneously mourn and celebrate.

*European Interlude*  Cooper wrote three more Leather-Stocking Tales, including *The Prairie* (1827). He launched another sensation with *The Pilot* (1823), his first sea novel, an adventure full of accurate details garnered from his experiences with the Navy and at sea. He wrote two more nautical novels in the 1820s. By the end of the decade, he ranked only behind Walter Scott in worldwide popularity.

In 1826, Cooper and his family left New York to spend seven years in Europe, where he also had a large following. He befriended the Marquis de Lafayette, the hero of the American Revolution, and grew interested in writing about political questions. In *Notions of the Americans* (1828), Cooper intended to answer conservative European attacks on American democracy. He also

## COMMON HUMAN EXPERIENCE

The conflict between civilization and the wilderness is a central concern of James Fenimore Cooper's masterpiece, *The Pioneers*. Some other notable works of literature call the human relationship with nature into question.

> *Walden* (1854), by Henry David Thoreau. This work, depicting life of simplicity in the woods by Walden Pond, is one of the most widely read American nonfiction books.
> *The Lost Steps* (1953), by Alejo Carpentier. In this landmark Latin American novel, an educated urban musician embarks on an anthropological mission into the Amazon and finds happiness outside of civilization.
> *The Monkey Wrench Gang* (1975), by Edward Abbey. A notorious novel partially responsible for radical environmental "monkey-wrenching," or sabotage.
> *The Practice of the Wild* (1990), by Gary Snyder. In this series of essays on place, nature, and the human condition, Snyder challenges the reader to break down the barrier between the natural world and the human world.

penned his "European trilogy": three romance novels set in Europe and subtly critiquing aristocratic society. From Cooper's perspective, he was fulfilling his vision as an American novelist, but while he put the accent on "American," his readers expected it to fall on "novelist." They wanted adventure, not serious fiction. From this point forward, Cooper fell increasingly out of step with his audience.

*A Quarrel with His Country* Cooper returned home, to the mansion his father built in Cooperstown. He lived there for the rest of his life, and was something of a recluse. In *A Letter to His Countrymen* (1834), Cooper laments that Americans are too culturally enslaved to foreign ideas to support a literature of their own. He published no fiction for the next four years but did produce five travel books and a broader political tract, *The American Democrat* (1838). His return to fiction, in *Homeward Bound* and *Home as Found* (both 1838), used narrative as a vehicle to expand on his social critique about the excesses of democracy. The argument resembled that of French political scientist and historian Alexis de Tocqueville (1805–59), who had also, in his travels to the United States, observed a dangerous "tyranny of the majority" during the days of Andrew Jackson's presidency.

Late in his career, Cooper told others that the only motive he still had for writing was financial, yet the 1840s were the most prolific period of his career. He composed

sea yarns, romances, several novels with religious themes, and the final two Leather-Stocking Tales, which brought Natty back to life as a young man. He also wrote three polemical novels, the *Littlepage Manuscripts* (1845–46), to defend land owners, or "patroons," against insurgent tenants in the anti-rent battles of New York state. Cooper died of dropsy in 1851, a day before his sixty-second birthday.

## Works in Literary Context

Cooper said that his mother, Elizabeth, imbued him with a taste for fiction that led to his eventual choice of a literary career. When he began to write, he made explicit use of British models: first, Jane Austen, whose *Persuasion* became a blueprint for Cooper's *Precaution*, and then, Sir Walter Scott, master of the historical romance. There was a reason for these choices. At the time Cooper took up the pen, America was still suffering from the cultural inferiority complex that was a legacy of its colonial dependency on England. Soon enough, Cooper was being identified as "the American Scott." His aim was not merely to emulate British models, however, but to surpass them.

*American Mythology* In his Leather-Stocking Tales and other works, Cooper created American myths of the frontier, the lone pioneer, and the Indian that remain part of the national consciousness. In some ways, Cooper's portrayal of Native Americans is complex; he differentiates between good Indians (heroic, dignified, and noble) and bad Indians (ferocious and dangerous). This decision was very popular with the majority of readers, but it has also contributed to cultural stereotypes that have proven hard to dispel. Ultimately, Native Americans are a lesser people than whites in his books, although some whites are portrayed as cruel, as well.

*Ideals in Tension* The power of Cooper's best writing, especially in *The Pioneers* and *The Last of the Mohicans*, stems from its ambivalence, its refusal to resolve the contradictions upon which American society rests. The claims of the wilderness versus the pursuit of progress, the freedom of the individual versus the obligations that come from membership in society—these are cultural issues that remain alive to this day. *The Last of the Mohicans* can be read as justifying the conquest of the West, but it is also mindful of its darker consequences. These ambiguities are embodied in the character of Natty Bumppo, which the author himself acknowledged as his greatest literary accomplishment. Natty represents the unspoiled wilderness, a place outside the conventional social order—a world that, in reality, neither he nor anyone else has ever lived in. Of course, the Leather-Stocking was not the first American to escape the evils of society by fleeing to the innocent world of nature; he was later joined there in spirit by such significant figures as Henry David Thoreau and the fictional Huckleberry Finn.

**The Pioneer** In these respects, James Fenimore Cooper was himself a literary pioneer. He established some of the central images, themes, and ideas in American literature. Countless writers have followed in his footsteps by imitating, elaborating, or countering his creations. He is credited as a progenitor of that hardy American literary species, the western, as well as the genre of nautical fiction, in which the sea serves as a primeval setting not unlike the frontier. Cooper set American letters on a path which has never ended.

## Works in Critical Context

James Fenimore Cooper achieved a remarkable degree of fame early in his career. Looking forward to the latest work by the author of *The Spy*, Americans bought 3,500 copies of *The Pioneers* on the morning of its publication, an extraordinary number for the time. The nation's first celebrity novelist, Cooper was also the first to become trapped inside the literary image he himself had created, the expectations he had fostered in his readers. He never quite got over the commercial failure of his European trilogy. Some of his later, politically motivated work was attacked by reviewers with a vehemence that was unprecedented in American literary culture. Although his prestige was somewhat tarnished, and the rupture with his readership never quite mended, Cooper remained the foremost American novelist at his death in 1851.

Cooper's seminal writing garnered critical attention for generations after his death. An outrageously funny and notoriously unfair essay by Samuel Clemens (Mark Twain), titled "Fenimore Cooper's Literary Offenses" (1895), helped to damage Cooper's artistic reputation. The Leather-Stocking Tales remain the principal focus of critical interest. Beginning with D. H. Lawrence's provocative discussion of them in *Studies in Classic American Literature* (1923), scholars have found that the tales dramatize the ideological forces surrounding the nineteenth-century American settlement (or conquest) of the continent. Cooper's prose style and narrative approach have not aged well; his writing never seems "modern," compared with authors such as Edgar Allan Poe, Walt Whitman, and Emily Dickinson. However, his body of work will continue to command attention due to its prominent place in American cultural history.

## Responses to Literature

1. Compare one of Cooper's novels, such as *The Pioneers*, with one of his later ones, such as *The Little-page Manuscripts*. Do their conflicting perspectives strike you as an evolution or a contradiction?

2. Can you detect the influence of Natty Bumppo on any contemporary heroes of popular literature or film?

3. In what ways do *The Pioneers* or *The Last of the Mohicans* embody, or differ from, the qualities of the classic Western?

4. Reading Cooper's political nonfiction, how would you describe his most important ideas about American society? Explore the reasons why you agree or disagree with his point of view.

BIBLIOGRAPHY

**Books**

Adams, Charles Hansford. *The Guardian of the Law: Authority and Identity in James Fenimore Cooper*. University Park. Pa.: Pennsylvania State University Press, 1990.

Clavel, Marcel, ed. *Fenimore Cooper and His Critics: American, British and French Criticisms of the Novelist's Early Work*. Aix-en-Provence: Imprimerie Universitaire de Provence, 1938.

Dekker, George. *James Fenimore Cooper the Novelist*. London: Routledge and Kegan Paul, 1967.

House, Kay, *Cooper's Americans*. Columbus, Ohio: Ohio State University Press, 1966.

Lawrence, D. H. *Studies in Classic American Literature*. New York: Seltzer, 1923.

McWilliams, John. *Political Justice in a Republic: James Fenimore Cooper's America*. Berkeley, Calif.: University of California Press, 1972.

Motley, Warren. *The American Abraham: James Fenimore Cooper and the Frontier Patriarch*. New York: Cambridge University Press, 1987.

Peck, H. Daniel. *New Essays on The Last of the Mohicans*. Cambridge: Cambridge University Press, 1992.

Philbrick, Thomas. *James Fenimore Cooper and the Development of American Sea Fiction*. Cambridge, Mass.: Harvard University Press, 1961.

Phillips, Mary E. *James Fenimore Cooper*. New York: John Lane, 1913.

Railton, Stephen. *Fenimore Cooper: A Study of His Life and Imagination*. Princeton, N. J.: Princeton University Press, 1978.

Spiller, Robert E., *Fenimore Cooper: Critic of His Times*. New York: Minton, Balch, 1931.

Walker, Warren S. *James Fenimore Cooper: An Introduction and Interpretation*. New York: Barnes & Noble, 1962.

**Periodicals**

Clemens, Samuel Langhorne (Mark Twain). "Fenimore Cooper's Literary Offenses." *North American Review* 161 (July 1895): 1–12.

## ❀ Robert Cormier

BORN: *1925, Leominster, Massachusetts*

DIED: *2000, Boston, Massachusetts*

NATIONALITY: *American*

GENRE: *Fiction*

MAJOR WORKS:

*The Chocolate War* (1974)

*I Am the Cheese* (1977)

Robert Cormier   *RICK CINCLAIR / Boston Globe / Landov*

*After the First Death* (1979)
*Fade* (1988)
*We All Fall Down* (1991)

## Overview

Best known for his novel *The Chocolate War* (1974), Robert Cormier is a distinguished writer of fiction for young adults. Tackling themes that are sometimes considered too dark for his readers, he has brought controversy and, simultaneously, a new dimension to the field of young-adult literature. He has earned the respect of readers of all ages because of his refusal to compromise the truth as he sees it. He forces his readers to think with suspenseful narratives and sophisticated literary techniques.

## Works in Biographical and Historical Context

*A Writer in His Soul* Robert Edmund Cormier was born on January 17, 1925, in the French-Canadian neighborhood of Leominster, Massachusetts, about fifty miles west of Boston. His father, originally from Quebec, supported his family by working in factories. His mother, of Irish ancestry, created a warm and loving home. Cormier was one of eight children, but when he was five,

his three-year-old brother died. He decided on a literary career early in life. After a seventh grade teacher at his Catholic school praised a poem he had written, he told an interviewer, he always felt like "a writer in my soul."

Cormier attended Fitchburg State College, where an art teacher took an interest in his writing and actually sold one of his stories to a national Catholic magazine for him—his first publication. He dropped out of college and went to work writing commercials for a radio station, then got a reporting job with a local newspaper. A good reporter and wire editor, Cormier excelled when it came to human-interest stories. He won the Associated Press Award for Best New England News Story of 1959 for his article about a child severely burned in an automobile accident. He received the same award in 1973, this time for a story written from the perspective of mentally retarded people.

A reporter and columnist for thirty years, Cormier wrote fiction in his spare time, publishing numerous stories in magazines such as *Redbook* and the *Saturday Evening Post*. He also published three novels for adult readers in the early 1960s, including *Now and At the Hour* (1960), about a factory worker dying of cancer. These books received positive reviews, but sold very few copies.

*Asking "What If?"* Cormier found literary inspiration in an incident that happened to his teenage son, who was asked to raise funds for his school by selling chocolates, and refused. "He was the only kid in the place who didn't sell the chocolates," Cormier said in a taped interview for Random House/Miller Brody. "Nothing happened to him, but something happened to me. I used the thing all writers use: 'What if?'" Imagining a nightmare scenario of pressure from peers and school authorities, Cormier concocted *The Chocolate War*.

After reading the first forty pages of the manuscript, Cormier's agent suggested that the story might succeed with a young-adult audience. Cormier had not written for children before, but he did not change any aspect of his writing; he even refused to change the downbeat ending, which caused several publishers to reject the book before it was accepted by Pantheon. His decision not to "talk down" to younger readers was probably a key to his success. *The Chocolate War* launched him to prominence as a young-adult writer.

The novel tells the story of Jerry Renault; however, Cormier introduces a host of other students and faculty of Trinity High School, where abuse of power runs rampant among children and adults alike. The metaphorical language suggests broader implications: Trinity is a microcosm of the world. Jerry is forced to stand alone for his beliefs, against overwhelming odds, and he does not win. By closing the book on a pessimistic note, Cormier was breaking an unstated rule of children's fiction that there must be some hope, something positive for teenagers to assimilate. However, despite Jerry's defeat, his fight provides an inspiration or a warning that more people need to take a stand.

*I Am the Cheese*  Cormier went deeper into society's darker properties in his second young-adult novel, *I Am the Cheese* (1977). The full impact of this book only hits the reader in the final pages, due to its original structure. Half is narrated by the protagonist Adam Farmer, the son of a murdered government witness, and half is the "transcript" of conversations between Adam and his psychiatrist. The two narrative threads merge in stunning fashion at the novel's conclusion. This chilling account of government corruption challenges young readers' assumption that adults are always looking out for their best interest.

The success of *I Am the Cheese*, like that of *The Chocolate War*, reflects cultural changes affecting America in the 1970s. The counterculture and youth movements that had begun in the 1960s, the drawn-out military engagement in Vietnam, and the disgrace and resignation of President Richard Nixon, all fed into a pervasive skepticism toward government and other symbols of authority. Cormier tapped into that skepticism with his efforts to expose sordid depths beneath the shiny surfaces of American life, and young readers responded.

*Chilling Subject Matter*  His next publication, *After the First Death* (1979), also aimed to shatter the reader's complacency. Depicting a terrorist hijacking of a busload of schoolchildren, the novel focuses on the inner thoughts of its three teenage protagonists: Miro, one of the hijack-

---

## LITERARY AND HISTORICAL CONTEMPORARIES

Robert Cormier's famous contemporaries include:

**Roald Dahl** (1916–1990): British author of children's and adult works, including *Charlie and the Chocolate Factory* (1964).

**Kurt Vonnegut** (1922–2007): American novelist and essayist, author of such works as *Slaughterhouse-Five* (1969) and *Breakfast of Champions* (1973).

**Joseph Heller** (1923–1999): American novelist and satirist; author of the classic black comedy *Catch-22* (1961).

**Judy Blume** (1938–): American novelist whose frank work on controversial topics influenced adolescent literature.

**S. E. Hinton** (1948–): American young-adult novelist, author of *The Outsiders* (1967).

---

ers; Kate, the driver of the bus; and Ben, son of an Army general in negotiation with the terrorists. All three are traumatized by the personal and political manipulations of the adults they trust. Again, Cormier whips up a series of shocks for the reader in the concluding chapters.

Having established his unique approach to young adult fiction, Cormier continued to produce thematically challenging, structurally complex novels. Among his most notable titles are *Fade* (1988), a supernatural horror story reminiscent of Stephen King; *We All Fall Down* (1991), the complex plot of which concerns vandalism, romance, guilt, and vengeance; *In the Middle of the Night* (1995), based on a true event in which 500 people died in a fire in an overcrowded nightclub; and *Tenderness* (1997), about a charismatic, psychopathic, teenage serial killer. *The Rag and Bone Shop* (2001) was published posthumously in 2000.

## Works in Literary Context

Robert Cormier's literary influences include the American novelist Thomas Wolfe, whose novel *The Web and the Rock* (1939), about a young boy living in a small town, struck a responsive chord in him. He also admired Ernest Hemingway and William Saroyan, and took after them by developing a terse, fast-paced writing style. No doubt the discipline of compressing ideas and information into radio commercials also contributed to the lean economy of his prose. A lover of mystery and suspense, Cormier recognizes the reader's desire for action; he uses dialogue, vivid metaphors, and imagery, rather than lengthy description.

*No Easy Way Out*  Cormier's writing for young adults is driven by the common themes of the genre: the search for identity, the development of character through ethical choices, and initiation into adulthood. But his bracingly realistic work also examines such issues as the nature and abuse of power, personal and political corruption, the consequences of fanatical patriotism, and the victimization

## COMMON HUMAN EXPERIENCE

Realistic fiction such as Robert Cormier's books can help young people comprehend and cope with death, war, and other traumas of life. The following are among the most acclaimed books for young readers that grapple with dark subjects.

*The Diary of Anne Frank* (1947), by Anne Frank. The world-famous diary of a young Jewish girl who hid from the Gestapo in an Amsterdam attic.

*Sadako and the Thousand Paper Cranes* (1977), a novel by Eleanor Coerr. This novel is based on a true story of a dying girl after the atomic bombing of Hiroshima during World War II.

*Tiger Eyes* (1981), a novel by Judy Blume. A young adult novel about a teenage girl's struggle to cope with her father's murder.

*Number the Stars* (1989), a novel by Lois Lowry. In this children's novel, ten-year-old Annemarie Johansen and her family bravely try to save their Jewish friends during the Nazi Holocaust.

*Soldier's Heart* (1998), a novel by Gary Paulsen. In this historical novel, a fifteen-year-old boy's life is scarred after he fights in the Civil War.

of the innocent. Both *The Chocolate War* and *I Am the Cheese* illustrate the powerlessness of the individual to stand alone against a corrupt society. Cormier steadfastly refuses to allow his readers an easy way out; there are no sentimental endings in his stories. Uncompromising in his pursuit of truth, Cormier has explained that he sees his novels as an antidote to the artificial realism of television, where one need not doubt that the hero will survive to appear next week. *The Chocolate War* deliberately violates the cultural expectation, fed by television and Hollywood movies, that brave, solitary heroes will eventually prevail.

***Still Ahead of the Curve*** The bold, bleak realism of Robert Cormier's stories, and the risks he took in overturning narrative conventions, made a profound impact on the genre of young-adult literature. He paved the way for other authors to explore tragic personal and historical events, subjects previously considered inappropriate for young readers. However, few authors of juvenile literature have truly followed his lead. The vast majority continue to temper their realism with a spoonful of sentimentality.

## Works in Critical Context

Beginning with his first novel, *Now and At the Hour*, Cormier's fiction has received tremendous critical acclaim. For example, *The Chocolate War*, *I Am the Cheese*, and *After the First Death* were all included on the American Library Association's Best of the Best list for 1970–1982.

***The Chocolate War*** However, Cormier's work has stirred up more than its share of controversy. *The Chocolate War*'s brutal depiction of violence and corruption in a high school, and the utter bleakness of its ending, drew a negative reaction from numerous educators and parents. Norma Bagnall, for example, objected that the book lacked positive role models and presented only the ugly side of life. Cormier's subsequent works have also provoked the reaction that their stark depiction of violence and sexuality, and their unvarnished pessimism, make them unsuitable reading material for children. Three Cormier titles are among the 100 Most Frequently Challenged Books of the 1990s, according to the American Library Association, with *The Chocolate War* listed at #4.

On the other hand, Cormier's many supporters defend not only his artistic license and right to free expression, but the appropriateness of his objectives. In "Realism in Adolescent Fiction: In Defense of *The Chocolate War*," Betty Carter and Karen Harris argue that "The unpleasant should not be confused with the unsuitable. Cormier's responsibility to his craft requires him to present characters and images, not as one would like them to be, but as they must be in order to make the novel and its message credible." Educator Kara Keeling urges readers to interpret *The Chocolate War* through the literary conventions of tragedy, and claims that young readers are perfectly capable of handling tragic messages, and even benefiting from them. Cormier's young readers would seem to agree; unlike some of their grown-up counterparts, they understand and appreciate the author's unflinching honesty.

## Responses to Literature

1. Do you think Robert Cormier's dark, tragic stories are appropriate reading for children? Why or why not?

2. Analyze the narrative structure of a Cormier novel, and how it helps strengthen the impact of the plot or message.

3. Use your library and the Internet to research various definitions of "tragedy." Write a paper in which you compare *The Chocolate War* to one of William Shakespeare's tragedies, arguing whether or not you feel Cormier follows the conventions of Shakespearean tragedy.

4. Write an essay on the theme of loyalty and betrayal in the novels of Robert Cormier, citing two or more examples of his work.

BIBLIOGRAPHY

**Books**

Campbell, Patricia J. *Presenting Robert Cormier*. Boston: G. K. Hall, 1985.

**Periodicals**

Bagnall, Norma. "Realism: How Realistic Is It? A Look at *The Chocolate War*." *Top of the News*. 36 (Winter 1980): 214–217.

Carter, Betty, and Karen Harris. "Realism in Adolescent Fiction: In Defense of *The Chocolate War*." *Top of the News*. 36 (Spring 1980): 283–285.

Davis, William A. "Tough Tales for Teenagers." *Boston Globe Magazine*. (November 16, 1980).

DeLuca, Geraldine, and Roni Natov. "An Interview with Robert Cormier." *The Lion and the Unicorn*. 2 (Fall 1978): 109–135.

Grove, Lee. "Robert Cormier Comes of Age." *Boston Magazine*. (December 1980).

Iskander, Sylvia Patterson. "Readers, Realism, and Robert Cormier." *Childre's Literature Journal*. 15 (1987): 7–18.

Keeling, Kara. "'The Misfortune of a Man Like Ourselves': Robert Cormier's *The Chocolate War* as Aristotelian Tragedy." *The ALAN Review* 26 (1999): 9–12.

MacLeod, Anne Scott. "Robert Cormier and the Adolescent Novel." *Children's Literature in Education*. 12 (Summer 1981): 74–81.

Myszor, Frank. "The See-Saw and the Bridge in Robert Cormier's *After the First Death*." *Children's Literature Journal*. 16 (1988): 77–90.

Veglahn, Nancy. "The Bland Face of Evil in the Novels of Robert Cormier." *The Lion and the Unicorn*. 12 (June 1988): 12–18.

# ⚙ Hart Crane

BORN: *1899, Garrettsville, Ohio*

DIED: *1932, Gulf of Mexico*

NATIONALITY: *American*

GENRE: *Poetry*

MAJOR WORKS:
*White Buildings* (1926)
*The Bridge* (1930)

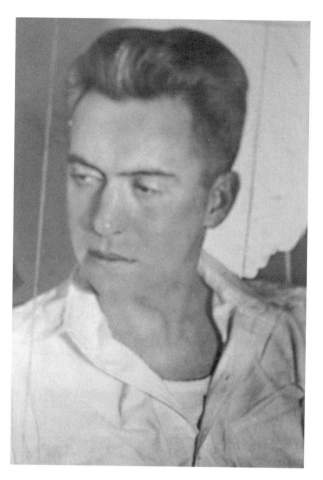

Hart Crane   *Crane, Hart, photograph by Walker Evans. The Library of Congress.*

## Overview

Hart Crane is a legendary figure among American poets. He lacked self-esteem, was prone to depression and alcohol abuse, and committed suicide at the age of 32. His art, however, was boldly ambitious and optimistic. His longest work, *The Bridge*, retains its character as a monumental experiment, and as such stands as a landmark in twentieth-century American poetry. His work has had many detractors over the years, but he has acquired an iconic stature as the quintessential Romantic poet.

## Works in Biographical and Historical Context

***From an Ivory Tower to New York***   Harold Hart Crane was born on July 21, 1899 in Garrettsville, Ohio. His family was upper-middle-class; his father, Clarence A. Crane, built a fortune as a chocolate candy manufacturer.

His mother, Grace Hart Crane, was famously beautiful and profoundly neurotic. Their marriage was stormy and as their only child, Hart Crane was often the victim of their antagonism. His mother smothered him with affection, turned him against his father, and ensnared him in an unhealthy, stifling bond from which he could never free himself. Biographers attribute Crane's unstable, excitable personality to the effects of these early traumas.

When Grace Crane suffered a nervous breakdown in 1908, Hart moved to his grandmother's house in Cleveland. It was a big, three-story frame house with a pair of turrets on the front. There Crane created his own private "ivory tower" with many books, a phonograph, and a typewriter. His grandmother's library was extensive, featuring editions of complete works by poets such as Ralph Waldo Emerson and Walt Whitman, both of whom became major influences on his writing. His aunt recalled that Crane announced at the age of ten his desire to make poetry his vocation. He stuck single-mindedly to this ambition throughout his life.

Crane enrolled in one of Cleveland's finest secondary schools, but his education was undermined by family

## LITERARY AND HISTORICAL CONTEMPORARIES

Crane's famous contemporaries include:

**James Joyce** (1882–1941): Irish author; his novels *Ulysses* (1922) and *Finnegans Wake* (1939) are considered among the finest literary works written in English.

**T. S. Eliot** (1888–1965): Anglo-American poet, author of *The Waste Land* (1922).

**E. E. Cummings** (1894–1962): Popular American modernist poet.

**F. Scott Fitzgerald** (1896–1940): American novelist of the Jazz Age, author of *The Great Gatsby* (1925).

**Langston Hughes** (1902–1967): American poet, a leader of the African-American artistic boom known as the Harlem Renaissance.

**Charles Chaplin** (1889–1977): British comedian and filmmaker, the world-famous creator of the "Little Tramp" character.

problems that led to prolonged absences. He never graduated, and instead taught himself, haunting bookstores and reading literary magazines. Finally, in 1916, after his parents separated, Crane left Cleveland and set off for New York. He hoped to pass Columbia University's entrance examination, but that plan never materialized. He was too eager to become a successful poet right away to be willing to spend four more years in school. He immersed himself in New York's literary scene, and wrote diligently, managing to publish some early pieces in a Greenwich Village journal, *Pagan.*

Struggling financially, Crane sold magazine advertising to supplement the financial support he received from his parents, who were divorced in 1917. Hart sided totally with his mother in the divorce disputes, but as a result her emotional demands on him were still greater. Grace Crane, along with her mother, came to live with Hart in his one-bedroom Manhattan apartment, and demanded his near-constant attention. His father then demanded that Crane get a steady job. America had entered the World War I, and Crane attempted to enlist, but was rejected because he was still under age. He then returned to Cleveland and worked in a munitions plant for the duration of the war.

***Jazz Age Poetry*** When the war ended, Crane took a job reporting for the *Cleveland Plain Dealer.* He briefly worked in his father's company, then worked in advertising firms in Cleveland and, again, New York. Because of his restless nature, and because he always saw himself as a poet first, he never held a job for long. His romantic life was similarly scattered. Hart Crane was homosexual and promiscuous; he had a zeal for sailors, who were always on the move, and he suffered from many unrequited infatuations.

In the early 1920s, Crane hit his stride as a poet; Among the most important of his poems from this period is "Chaplinesque," which he produced after viewing the great comic Charlie Chaplin's film *The Kid.* Crane saw in Chaplin the archetype of the poet in the modern world—a combination of clown, Everyman, and holy fool. The idea of the poet as wry comedian was in keeping with the sensibility of America in the Jazz Age. Similar ideas appear in the work of Wallace Stevens, and in T. S. Eliot's "Love Song of J. Alfred Prufrock" (1917). Crane's poem "For the Marriage of Faustus and Helen" (1923) places mythic characters in a contemporary urban setting: Helen, the embodiment of ideal beauty, appears as a flapper in a jazz club.

Crane's passionate affair with a seaman named Emil Opffer inspired him to write a suite of love poems, called "Voyages," in the fall of 1924. The series contains some of Crane's finest lyrical passages, using the sea as a metaphor for the beauty, power, and danger of human love. Crane included "Voyages" in his first published volume, *White Buildings* (1926).

***The Bridge*** By the time he finished "Voyages" in 1924, Crane had already commenced the first drafts of his ambitious poem *The Bridge* (1930). In composing *The Bridge*, Crane had in mind a response to T. S. Eliot's erudite masterwork, *The Waste Land* (1922)—but he intended it to be an uplifting affirmation, not a bleak negation, of modernity.

As he worked on *The Bridge* its scope and length expanded, until it comprised fifteen sections. With this long poem, Crane sought to create a panorama of the American experience. The Brooklyn Bridge serves as the work's sustaining metaphor: a work of functional art, a product of modern technology, and a symbol of America's idealistic aspirations for unity and social progress. The Brooklyn Bridge, opened for use in 1883, was and is a marvel of engineering. When it was completed, it was by far the longest suspension bridge in the world. It became an official National Historic Landmark in 1964. Crane invokes various American icons, from Christopher Columbus to Rip Van Winkle to the Wright Brothers, to celebrate the visionary element of American life.

Crane poured his heart and soul into *The Bridge.* The generally hostile, bewildered, and indifferent reception his poem received was devastating to him. After his father's death in 1930, he plunged into a depression from which he never recovered. With the money he inherited, Crane traveled to Paris, where he associated with prominent figures in the city's American expatriate community. He wrote little in Europe, indulging instead in alcohol and carousing. He wallowed further in these behaviors when he returned to the United States. He sensed the decline in his literary skills. In 1931, he traveled to Mexico, where he had periods of hopefulness about his writing, followed by moments of despair. The despair won out, for on April 27, 1932, during a cruise on the Gulf of Mexico, Hart Crane leapt overboard to his death.

## Works in Literary Context

Crane's self-directed education led him to absorb many literary influences, starting from Ralph Waldo Emerson and Walt Whitman, whom he read as a child. In his teens, his reading broadened to include such writers as Plato, Honoré de Balzac, Percy Bysshe Shelley, and Algernon Swinburne. His earliest poems were long rhapsodies in the manner of Swinburne, full of gods and goddesses.

*Modernism and "Young America"* In New York, Crane came under the influence of two very different, but perhaps complementary, spheres of literary activity. One was that of the journal *Little Review*, which published the work of modernists such as Eliot, W. B. Yeats, and James Joyce. The other sphere of influence centered on the journal *Seven Arts*, whose contributors called themselves "Young America" and were intent upon revitalizing American civilization through the arts; their guiding spirit was Whitman.

Crane moved freely between these two circles and drew upon them both. The synthesis Crane achieved between these very dissimilar sources is an important part of his contribution to American literature. The spirit of Young America led Crane to endeavor a creative answer to the pessimism of Eliot's *The Waste Land*, one that would echo Eliot's modernist techniques, but apply them in service of more spiritual values. *The Bridge* sought to unite the style of modernism with the spirit of American romanticism.

*Logic and Metaphor* Crane's poetry is often difficult to comprehend, primarily because of the author's poetic theory. According to Crane, logic should not be allowed to strip the complexity from real experience. His poems are often guided by what he called a "logic of metaphor," filled with private symbolism and emotions inspired by the sounds of words. He was more concerned with the spontaneous associations aroused by words than with their definitions, which he understood as a way of limiting perception. Crane sometimes sought spontaneity of expression by writing while drinking and listening to jazz.

*Romantic Visionary* Although he left only a small body of work, Crane is important as a lyric poet in the tradition of the romantic visionary. As such, his work is often compared to that of William Blake and Charles Baudelaire. Crane exuded the expansive optimism of modern America; despite his unhappy life, he was not the type of poet whose perspective stems from alienation from society. It was Crane's ambition to build upon the emotional illuminations of his private life and extend them into a broad vision of all America. Crane's world view had a significant influence on later poets such as Charles Olson and Robert Creeley, as well as the prominent literary critic Harold Bloom.

## Works in Critical Context

Crane's collection *White Buildings* earned him critical respect, but its highly original style prompted speculation

---

# COMMON HUMAN EXPERIENCE

On the day the Brooklyn Bridge opened to traffic, May 24, 1883, circus master P. T. Barnum led twenty-one elephants across the East River. Hart Crane was not the only author to recognize the enormous potential of the great bridge as a symbol of America; it has served in these other works of literature as well:

"Brooklyn Bridge" (1925), a poem by Vladimir Mayakovsky. A Russian poet rhapsodizes: "Yonder paw of steel/ once joined the seas and the prairies;/ from this spot,/ Europe rushed to the west,/ scattering to the wind Indian feathers."

"The Brooklyn Bridge" (1931), a poem by Lewis Mumford. In a popular magazine essay, America's greatest architecture critic analyzes the bridge as "both a fulfillment and a prophecy"—a meeting of the architectural past and the architectural future.

*Tropic of Capricorn* (1939), a novel by Henry Miller. Miller refused to celebrate the bridge, characterizing it instead at "the dead center" of the brutal America he later termed "the air-conditioned nightmare."

*Bridge to Brooklyn* (1944), a novel by Albert Idell. This is the second book in a popular trilogy of historical novels about the struggle for democracy and social justice in the Gilded Age.

*The Great Bridge* (1972), a nonfiction work by David McCullough. A landmark work of American history, chronicling the period of the bridge's construction in New York.

---

that Crane was an imprecise and confused artist who sometimes settled for sound instead of sense. These doubts contributed to the disappointing reception accorded *The Bridge*. Some influential critics found his effort worthy, but lacking in overall unity and coherence. Even some of Crane's greatest admirers panned the poem in print. Lacking in detachment from his work, Crane took the criticism to heart.

*Crane and the New Criticism* Hart Crane's opposition to the modernist ethos expressed by T. S. Eliot was deep-rooted. Eliot, that most intellectual of poets, distrusted the emotions and rejected the romantic visionary imagination. Eliot was a major literary critic himself, and his viewpoint heavily influenced a generation of critics who were essentially hostile to Crane's poetry. Some proponents of the so-called New Criticism took the entire romantic tradition as their target; Crane was the unfortunate example of that tradition. The report of his suicide, which fueled the legend of Hart Crane as the tragic romantic poet-hero, also prevented an objective evaluation of his body of work.

***Reassessment*** Since the 1960s, as the influence of the New Criticism has waned, Crane has earned recognition as an accomplished poet, albeit one whose goals exceeded his capabilities. Later critics have reassessed *The Bridge*: they still believe the poem fails as an epic encapsulation of the American experience, but they contend that it succeeds admirably as the portrayal of a quest for a new mythic vision. Works of scholarship, most notably those by L. S. Dembo and R. W. B. Lewis, have clarified many of his poems' obscurities. Crane is now perceived as an important, even a pivotal figure in American literature.

## Responses to Literature

1. Write about the influence of Walt Whitman on the poetry of Hart Crane, with particular attention to *The Bridge*.

2. How did Hart Crane unite the romantic and modernist poetic traditions?

3. Read one or two Crane poems closely, and write about how the poet uses the sounds of words to create an emotional effect.

4. Explore the theme of suffering and redemption in the poetry of Hart Crane.

BIBLIOGRAPHY

**Books**

Butterfield, R. W. *The Broken Arch: A Study of Hart Crane*. Edinburgh: Oliver and Boyd, 1969.

Clark, David R., ed. *Critical Essays on Hart Crane*. Boston: G. K. Hall, 1982.

Combs, Robert. *Vision of the Voyage: Hart Crane and the Psychology of Romanticism*. Memphis, Tenn.: Memphis State University Press, 1978.

Cowley, Malcolm. *Exile's Return: A Literary Odyssey of the 1920s*. New York: Viking, 1951.

Dembo, L.S. *Hart Crane's Sanskrit Charge: A Study of The Bridge*. Ithaca, N.Y.: Cornell University Press, 1960.

Hazo, Samuel. *Hart Crane: An Introduction and Interpretation*. New York: Barnes and Noble, 1963.

Leibowitz, Herbert A. *Hart Crane: An Introduction to the Poetry*. New York: Columbia University Press, 1968.

Lewis, R. W. B. *The Poetry of Hart Crane: A Critical Study*. Princeton, N.J.: Princeton University Press, 1967.

Unterecker, John, *Voyager: A Life of Hart Crane*. New York: Farrar, Strauss, 1969.

Weber, Brom. *Hart Crane: A Biographical and Critical Study*. New York: Bodley Press, 1948.

Wilson, Edmund. *The Shores of Light: A Literary Chronicle of the Twenties and Thirties*. New York: Farrar, Straus, 1952.

**Periodicals**

Arpad, Joseph J. "Hart Crane's Platonic Myth: The Brooklyn Bridge." *American Literature* 39 (March 1967): 75–86.

Frank, Waldo. "The Poetry of Hart Crane." *New Republic* 50 (March 16, 1927): 116–117.

Metzger, Deena Posy. "Hart Crane's Bridge: The Myth Active." *Arizona Quarterly* 20 (Spring 1964): 36–46.

Tate, Allen. "The Self-made Angel." *New Republic* 129 (August 31, 1953): 17–21.

## ✸ Stephen Crane

BORN: *1871, Newark, New Jersey*

DIED: *1900, Badenweiler, Germany*

NATIONALITY: *American*

GENRE: *Fiction, poetry*

MAJOR WORKS:

*Maggie: A Girl of the Streets* (1893)

*The Red Badge of Courage* (1895)

*The Open Boat, and Other Tales of Adventure* (1898)

Stephen Crane   *Crane, Stephen, photograph. The Library of Congress.*

## Overview

Stephen Crane was one of the most gifted and influential writers of the late nineteenth century, noted for his innovative style, ironic sense of life, and penetrating psychological realism. He wrote his first novel, *Maggie: A Girl of the Streets* (1893), when he was only twenty-one and had his masterpiece, *The Red Badge of Courage* (1895), published before he was twenty-four. When he died in 1900 at the age of twenty-eight, he had written six novels, over a hundred short stories, two books of poems, and voluminous journalism and war correspondence. His works have been credited with marking the beginning of literary naturalism in America.

## Works in Biographical and Historical Context

*Youngest Child in a Large, Religious Family* Crane was born on November 1, 1871, in Newark, New Jersey, the last of fourteen children. His father, the Rev. Jonathan Townley Crane, was a well-known Methodist clergyman; his mother, Mary Helen Peck Crane, was active in church and reform groups, such as the Women's Christian Temperance Union. Both his parents wrote religious articles, and his brother Townley was a journalist who operated a news agency for the *New York Tribune*. In the summers Stephen helped gather news and gossip from the Jersey shore for Townley's column.

*Maggie: A Girl of the Streets* An indifferent student, Crane had one unsuccessful year of higher education before deciding that "humanity was a more interesting study" than the college curriculum. He began to work full-time as a reporter and writer. Crane met the writer Hamlin Garland in 1891, and followed his advice to immerse himself in the social problems of the city. He began to frequent the Bowery section of New York City and acquire a firsthand view of its bohemian life. He would shape this material into his first novel.

His first published fiction, however, depicted life in rural upstate New York. These stories, first collected and published in 1949 as *The Sullivan County Sketches of Stephen Crane*, develop a metaphor of man at war against nature. Crane's irony is directed at the pomposity of his unnamed protagonist, the "little man" who conjures demons in the landscape as he assaults caves, forests, and mountains.

In 1893 Crane privately published *Maggie: A Girl of the Streets* under a pseudonym after several publishers rejected the work on the grounds that his description of slum realities would shock readers. While Crane appropriated much of the novel from popular reports of slum life, his presentation of the depravities of poverty was brutally straightforward. Crane was certainly not alone in calling attention to the plight of the urban poor, however. The Progressive Era in American politics, usually dated from 1890–1920, was dominated by outspoken social activists, writers, and artists committed to promoting workers' rights and helping the poor. One of these activists was reporter Jacob Riis, who had shocked New York high society with his groundbreaking work of photojournalism *How the Other Half Lives* (1890), which offered heartbreaking pictures of tenement life. Other notable Progressives included Jane Addams, who founded Chicago's Hull House in 1889, offering educational and social services to the poor, and Upton Sinclair, author of *The Jungle* (1906) and many other novels critical of what he considered the worst social problems in the United States. The first edition of *Maggie: A Girl of the Streets* won Crane the support of such literary figures as Garland and William Dean Howells, but the book was not widely read until 1896, when Crane tempered the story in a second edition.

*War Novel Brings Renown* Crane began a second novel of the slums, a satire eventually published as *George's Mother* (1896), but he set it aside to finish a Civil War story he had begun. Again, the story line arose from conventional sources; Crane had no personal experience with warfare. Nevertheless, the work he fashioned, *The Red Badge of Courage* (1895), achieved a narrative vividness and sense of immediacy matched by few American novels. This short, essentially plotless novel consists of a series of memorable episodes in which a young soldier, Henry Fleming, confronts a gamut of emotions in his attempt to understand his battlefield experiences. The book quickly won its author international fame.

While writing *The Red Badge of Courage*, Crane was also finishing his first book of poems, *The Black Riders* (1895). Although not widely known, this volume of free verse foreshadowed the work of the Imagist poets with its concise, vivid images. More than half of the poems in this volume concern religious questions, reflecting Crane's uncertainty about the nature of God and man's relation to him. This religious impulse is also present in Crane's war novel; from the beginning, Henry Fleming is thinking about how he measures up to nature, and by extension, to God. Crane deleted religious imagery from the novel's concluding chapters, suggesting continued ambivalence.

During this time, Crane continued to work as a journalist. In 1895, a newspaper publisher sent him on a journalistic mission through the American West to Mexico. His dispatches ironically note the disparity between the romantic legends of the West and the reality of its modern cities, a theme that would appear in several of his later works of fiction. Returning to New York later that year, Crane wrote *The Third Violet* (1897), a bohemian comedy considered among his poorest works.

*Wars and Stories* Crane continued to write war stories, with some reluctance, because editors demanded them. He itched for the chance to be a war correspondent and set off at the end of 1896 to cover an insurrection in Cuba. The Cubans were struggling to free themselves from Spanish control; two years later, the United States' insistence that Spain relinquish control of Cuba helped to

## LITERARY AND HISTORICAL CONTEMPORARIES

Stephen Crane's famous contemporaries include:

**H. G. Wells** (1866–1946): British author celebrated for such science–fiction stories as *The Time Machine* (1895).

**Ruben Dario** (1867–1916): A Nicaraguan poet who invigorated modern Spanish literature.

**Frank Norris** (1870–1902): An American novelist of the naturalist genre.

**Marcel Proust** (1871–1922): The French modernist author of the classic *Remembrance of Things Past* (1922–1931).

**Willa Cather** (1873–1947): An American novelist of the frontier and the Great Plains.

**Sigmund Freud** (1856–1939): The Austrian psychologist who revolutionized Western thought by studying the unconscious mind.

spark the Spanish American War. While he was on his way to Cuba, Crane's ship sank near Daytona Beach, Florida. Crane survived the disaster and wrote about it in the *New York Press* and, later, in one of his best short stories, "The Open Boat" (1897).

During his travels in 1896, Stephen Crane met Cora Taylor, the proprietress of a discreet brothel named the Hotel de Dream. In April 1897 she accompanied Crane to Greece, where she covered the Greco-Turkish conflict as the first female war correspondent. Together as common-law husband and wife they moved to England, where Crane formed literary friendships with authors such as Joseph Conrad and H. G. Wells and wrote stories at a great clip. Along with "The Open Boat," two of his most celebrated stories are "The Bride Comes to Yellow Sky" (written in 1897) and "The Blue Hotel" (written in 1898). Both are Westerns that parody conventional preconceptions of the Wild West with great psychological insight.

Although his health was poor, the outbreak of the Spanish-American war fired his imagination, and he sailed from England to Cuba in 1898. He exposed himself needlessly to Spanish fire at Guantanamo and San Juan, but won the admiration of senior war reporters for his work. Afterwards, he busied himself in Havana writing stories and completing another unsuccessful novel, *Active Service* (1899). Crane continued writing fiction when he returned to England, to satisfy his artistic needs and to earn money. But by 1900, his health had rapidly deteriorated due to general disregard for his physical well-being. Crane died of tuberculosis at the age of 28.

## Works in Literary Context

Stephen Crane developed his powerful writing style from numerous influences, including the theories of realism advanced by Hamlin Garland and William Dean Howells, the ideas expressed by the realist painter-hero of Rudyard Kipling's novel *The Light That Failed*, and the ironic voice and psychological realism of Leo Tolstoy's *Sebastopol*. Crane adapted all these ideas and methods to serve his own vision and purposes. He downplayed the importance of plot, shifting the focus from the drama of external events and situations to the drama of thoughts and feelings in the psychological life of his subjects. By the age of twenty-one, when he was writing *The Red Badge of Courage*, Crane already commanded formidable literary resources: a journalist's training in keen observation and concise expression; an attitude toward conventional material shaped by theories of realism; a character developed in his Sullivan County studies of the "little man"; and, a vivid impressionistic style.

***Realism and Naturalism*** Crane wrote that his first novel, *Maggie: A Girl of the Streets*, "tries to show that environment is a tremendous thing in the world and frequently shapes lives regardless." Some critics call *Maggie: A Girl of the Streets* the first American naturalist novel. Literary naturalism derived from Charles Darwin's theory of natural selection, viewing character and behavior as a product of a perso's surroundings. Naturalist literature shares with realist literature a focus on everyday settings characters and careful representation of natural speech. Naturalism can be seen as a somewhat more pessimistic form of realism in that naturalist literature often features characters that are trapped or destroyed by their environments.

Critics have long debated the literary movement under which to classify Crane's masterwork *The Red Badge of Courage*; realists, naturalists, symbolists, and impressionists have all claimed the novel as their own, each with some justification. While it can be broadly classed as a work of realism, Crane's book is marked by an almost painterly style in some sections, and Crane's skillful use of complex symbolism has been the subject of much critical attention.

***Irony and Perception*** Crane was a master of irony, employing a technique that reveals the gap between an individual's perception of reality and reality as it actually exists. Some of his characters, like the Swede in "The Blue Hotel," are done in by their preconceived notions, suggesting humanity's radical alienation in a problematic world. Others are more conscious and introspective, like the correspondent in "The Open Boat," who realizes that the sea, like nature, appears sometimes cruel and deadly, sometimes beautiful and picturesque, and other times stolidly indifferent. All these characteristics are simply projections of the narrator's own shifting inner state.

***Pioneering Modernist*** A relativist, ironist, and impressionist, Stephen Crane anticipated the modernism of Ernest Hemingway, F. Scott Fitzgerald, and William Faulkner by thirty years. Like Hemingway, he was preoccupied with violence, finding in the reaction of his hero under extreme duress the mystery of the hero's character and fate. Like

Fitzgerald and Faulkner, he dramatized the power of illusion to shape events and destinies. He seems closer to these writers in manner and spirit than to the writers of his own day. His novels, stories, and poems all left a lasting mark on the development of twentieth-century literature.

## Works in Critical Context

***The Red Badge of Courage*** *The Red Badge of Courage* became an international sensation in 1895 and made its young author a famous man. Critic Bernard Weisberger said that the novel "paints the experience of all young men who go into battle, familiar with fright but strangers to themselves." Interestingly, most of the early praise for Crane came from English, not American, critics who stressed the realism of the novel and often incorrectly assumed that Crane was a Civil War veteran writing from personal experience (many actual veterans who read the novel made the same assumption). By the mid-twentieth century, critics such as R. W. Stallman were taking a new approach to *The Red Badge of Courage*, emphasizing its imagist and symbolist elements. Stallman's focus on the Christian subtext behind Crane's descritipion of a setting sun as a "communion wafer" sparked ongoing controversy. Still, whatever their interpretations, critics have been nearly unanimous in hailing the work as one of the greatest war novels of all time. As Eric Solomon wrote: "Stephen Crane's novel is the first work in English fiction of any length purely dedicated to an artistic reproduction of war, and it has rarely been approached in scope or intensity."

***Rediscovery in the 1920s*** Crane remained well–known and widely admired until his untimely death. His reputation was greatly diminished for the next twenty years, but he was rediscovered in the 1920s by poets and novelists such as Willa Cather and Sherwood Anderson, who recognized in his experiments with new themes and subject matter something of the spirit of their own literary aims. As scholarship on Crane's work has proliferated, his reputation has swelled. Contemporary critics generally agree that Crane was at his best in short works of fiction, and that his bold imagery and frankness advanced a robust, modern form of literary realism.

## Responses to Literature

1. Write a paper discussing the use of irony in Crane's "The Blue Hotel."

2. Crane worked as a journalist throughout his short life. Can you identify journalistic elements in his fiction, and if so, how do they strengthen (or weaken) its impact?

3. Reading Crane's *Maggie: A Girl of the Streets*, do you find that it confirms the naturalistic premise that the forces of environment and heredity determine human actions? Why or why not?

---

## COMMON HUMAN EXPERIENCE

*The Red Badge of Courage* set a high standard for Civil War fiction. No novelist has surpassed Crane's achievement in recounting the visceral experience of that war. However, the following works, some of them also American classics, tackle other aspects of the War Between the States:

*The General* (1926), a film directed by and starring Buster Keaton. Keaton's masterpiece, one of the most acclaimed films of all time, is a hilarious but taut drama of a Confederate railroad engineer behind Union lines.

*Gone With the Wind* (1936), a novel by Margaret Mitchell. The story of Scarlett O'Hara of Georgia is one of the best-loved works of American literature, not to mention the source of one of Hollywood's greatest triumphs.

*Andersonville* (1955), a novel by MacKinley Kantor. This novel, which won the Pulitzer Prize, combines the stories of real and fictional characters inside a Confederate prison camp.

*Lincoln* (1984), a novel by Gore Vidal. This historical novel imagines the inner workings of the Lincoln administration, from the point of view of cabinet members, Lincoln's family, John Wilkes Booth, and others.

*Cold Mountain* (1997), a novel by Charles Frazier. The Odyssey-like journey of a Confederate deserter and the woman who awaits him, was adapted from the page to the screen in 2003.

---

4. Crane's fiction includes powerful descriptions of nature: the blizzard in "The Blue Hotel," the sea in "The Open Boat," the forest in *The Red Badge of Courage*. Select two or three of Crane's works and highlight his descriptions of nature. Compare them. Do you think Crane used "nature" consistently in his works? How does he portray natural forces? How do his characters interact with nature?

BIBLIOGRAPHY

**Books**

Baum, Joan H. *Stephen Crane*. New York: Columbia University Libraries, 1956.

Bergon, Frank. *Stephen Crane's Artistry*. New York: Columbia University Press, 1975.8

Berryman, John. *Stephen Crane*. New York: Sloane, 1950.

Bruccoli, Matthew J. *Stephen Crane 1871–1971*. Columbia, S.C.: Department of English, University of South Carolina, 1971.

Cady, Edwin H. *Stephen Crane*. Boston: Twayne, 1980.

Holton, Milne. *Cylinder of Vision: The Fiction and Journalistic Writing of Stephen Crane*. Baton Rouge, La.: Louisiana State University Press, 1972.

Robertson, Michael. *Stephen Crane: Journalism and the Making of Modern American Literature*. New York: Columbia University Press, 1997.

Solomon, Eric. *Stephen Crane: From Parody to Realism*. Cambridge, Mass.: Harvard University Press, 1966.

Stallman, R. W. *Stephen Crane: A Biography*. New York: Brazillier, 1968.

"Stephen Crane (1871–1900)." *Twentieth-Century Literary Criticism*. Ed. Paula Kepos. Vol. 32. Detroit: Gale Research, 1989. 132–190.

Weatherford, R. M., ed. *Stephen Crane, The Critical Heritage*. London: Routledge and Kegan Paul, 1973.

# ⬢ Robert Creeley

BORN: *1926, Arlington, Massachusetts*

DIED: *2005, Odessa, Texas*

NATIONALITY: *American*

GENRE: *Poetry, nonfiction*

MAJOR WORKS:

*The Black Mountain Review* (1954–57)

*For Love: Poems, 1950–1960* (1962)

*Words* (1965)

*The Gold Diggers and Other Stories* (1965)

*On Earth: Last Poems and An Essay* (2006)

Robert Creeley    © *Christopher Felver / Corbis*

## Overview

Most known for his participation in the "Black Mountain" school of poetry, Robert Creeley produced volumes of poetry, fiction and drama throughout the second half of the twentieth century. His writing is marked by an almost spontaneous feeling, and it captures natural speech patterns and sparse emotion rather than adhering to standard poetic forms. Creeley participated in the major poetic movements of the second half of the twentieth century, maintained friendships with numerous influential poets and writers, and received numerous awards for his work.

## Works in Biographical and Historical Context

*Farm Life to Harvard*    Robert White Creeley was born in Arlington, Massachusetts, and after the death of his father, he moved at the age of four with his mother and sister to nearby West Acton. His childhood was spent in this rural neighborhood, and at fourteen he entered Holderness School in Plymouth, New Hampshire, where he was a scholarship student and contributed to school publications. After three years at Holderness, Creeley entered Harvard in the fall of 1943, leaving after one year to drive an ambulance in the India-Burma theatre of World War II. He married Ann McKinnon in 1946, commuted to Harvard for a while before dropping out

for good, and started a close and fruitful friendship with Cid Corman, who conducted a Boston radio program called "This is Poetry."

Having recently survived the Great Depression of the 1930s, in which jobs and housing were scarce, financial stability was always a concern in Creeley's family, as well as in the nation more generally. Establishing a livable income would drive Creeley's choices throughout much of his early career.

*Writing Influenced by Relationships with Other Writers*    During this postwar period, Creeley had been strongly swayed by the ideas in *The Wedge* (1944) by William Carlos Williams and *Make It New* (1934) by Ezra Pound, both celebrated modernist poets. Modernist poetry, popular especially in the first half of the twentieth century, questions ideas of progress and religion and finds transcendence in art itself.

In 1951, with children to support, the Creeleys moved to France, hoping to survive more economically on Ann Creeley's income. Because of the inflation in France the Creeley family moved to Majorca, Spain. On Majorca Creeley and his wife started the Divers Press, an independent press that focused on publishing experimental writers. Creeley's stimulating relationship with writer Charles Olson, began in 1950, led to Creeley's association with Black Mountain College in North Carolina when Olson recommended he edit the *Black Mountain*

*Review.* Creeley taught at Black Mountain College through his divorce from Ann, and eventually earned a bachelor's degree in 1955. Creeley's time at the college created his most influential work, becoming known as the Black Mountain School of Poetry.

Creeley left Black Mountain in 1956 and went to San Francisco, where he met Jack Kerouac, Allen Ginsberg, Kenneth Rexroth, and Gary Snyder, the giants of the group of emerging experimental writers known as the Beat Generation. These writers were part of the radical movements in the 1960s that questioned traditional social, racial, and gender roles. By the time Creeley received his MA degree from the University of New Mexico in 1960, he had seven books of poems to his credit. The year 1960 was to be of considerable importance for him. In May 1960 *Poetry* magazine published ten new poems by Creeley and awarded him its Levinson Prize. Donald Allen's significant collection, *The New American Poetry: 1945-1960*, published in the same month, included a number of Creeley's poems. In 1961–1962 Creeley taught at the University of New Mexico, and he became affiliated with universities for the rest of his life, becoming in 1978 Gray Professor of Poetry and Letters at the State University of New York at Buffalo.

*Later Career* Creeley attained and accepted the status of an elder statesman of poetry in his later years. Some of his most notable later literary accomplishments include his autobiography, the occasional prose essay, interviews, orally presented poetry, and lectures. Aside from teaching he made literary tours of the United States and the world. His works have been translated and published in the Netherlands, Germany, Austria, Spain, Mexico, Italy, Denmark, Norway, Czechoslovakia, and France, among other countries. Perhaps most significantly Creeley enjoyed the distinction of having been elected to the American Academy of Arts and Letters. He died during an artist's residence in Texas, in 2005.

## Works in Literary Context

*The Black Mountain School and Projectivist Poetry* Black Mountain College focused on the performing and traditional arts as well as literature, and produced many students who became influential in the avant-garde movement of the 1960s. Creeley's poetry is most closely associated with Projectivism, an outgrowth of the Black Mountain School of poetry. Writer Charles Olson, and friend of Creeley, helped establish this style of poetry which breaks down the expectation of a poem to follow any established form apart from the particular piece. Emphasizing the immediacy of the specific poem, Creeley famously established projectivism's style by stating, "form is never more than an extension of content." Under this progressive approach, the creative process is as important as the finished product, the writing of the poem as crucial

## LITERARY AND HISTORICAL CONTEMPORARIES

Robert Creeley's famous contemporaries include:

**Ezra Pound** (1885–1972): This American Modernist poet and critic helped establish the literary style popular after World War I and spanning much of the twentieth century.

**William Carlos Williams** (1883–1963): This American poet's concentration on everyday life in his writing, as opposed to the Modernist focus on elaborate imagery, deeply influenced the writers of the Black Mountain School of poetry.

**Denise Levertov** (1923–1997): A British poet who moved to America in the 1940s, Levertov became influenced by and then a member of the Black Mountain School of poetry.

**Allen Ginsberg** (1926–1997): One of the founders of the American Beat poetry movement of the 1960s, Allen Ginsberg is best known for his poem "Howl". Creeley and Ginsberg met and became friends in 1956.

**Jack Kerouac** (1922–1969): Inspiring the Beat Generation of poets as well as writers and musicians throughout the 1960s and 1970s, Kerouac's most famous book is *On the Road* (1957).

as the poem itself. Like the Beat poets, projectivist poets focus on the poetic experience rather than more traditional measures of poetry like stanza and measured meter. The Black Mountain poets included Charles Olson, Robert Duncan, and Denise Levertov, whose styles, like Creeley's, were highly experimental. Their work reflected a new path, away from the formal approach of the New Critical literary tradition of the 1950s, favoring more loosely constructed poetry and prose.

*Beat Poets* Creeley spent significant time in contact with the Beat poets in San Francisco. The Beats produced experimental writing that placed high value on stream-of-consciousness and performance elements, and Creeley established a lasting connection between them and the Black Mountain poets. The widespread financial insecurity caused by the Depression of the 1930s, together with the huge number of deaths caused by the holocaust and World War II, were defining elements of this generation of writers. This produced what Creeley called "a sort of terrifying need to demonstrate the valuelessness of one's own life." Creeley, with the Beat poets, challenged the formal nature of poetry that dictated the structure of a poem. Like the many political upheavals occurring in the 1960s, including the Civil Rights movement advancing the rights of black Americans, and the social revolution promoting sexual freedom and recreational drug use,

## COMMON HUMAN EXPERIENCE

Creeley's correspondence with Charles Olson lasted much of his life, and produced a creative collaboration. Other famous correspondence includes:

*My Dearest Friend: Letters of Abigail and John Adams* (1876), a series of letters from the late eighteenth century. For much of their deeply compatible marriage, Founding Father John Adams and his wife, Abigail, corresponded about topics both personal and romantic and political and quarrelsome.

*Open Me Carefully: Emily Dickinson's Intimate Letters to Susan Huntington Dickinson* (1998), a series of letters from the mid-nineteenth century. Over thirty years of correspondence between the famous and mysterious American poet and her sister-in-law reveal a deep relationship between the two women.

*De Profundis* (1905), a letter by Oscar Wilde. Written during his imprisonment for charges relating to homosexuality, this letter to his lover addresses themes of loneliness and affection.

*Letters to a Young Poet* (1934), a series of letters written by Rainer Maria Rilke. In these ten letters, Rilke gives advice to a young poet, encouraging him in the many areas of the artistic life.

*Door Wide Open: A Beat Love Affair in Letters 1957–1958* (2000), a series of letters between Jack Kerouac and Joyce Johnson. Both active writers during the emerging Beat Generation, Kerouac and Johnson write letters that reveal both their deepening relationship and their creative process.

Creeley and the Beat poets did not look to the past for traditional inspiration. Instead they challenged old patterns by writing poetry that existed in the moment.

### Works in Critical Context

With the release of his 1991 *Selected Poems*, a compilation of over forty years of work, most critics acknowledged Creeley as a major influence on younger writers and an influential voice in American literature.

***For Love: Poems 1950–1960*** *For Love* was widely reviewed and generally praised and earned a nomination for a National Book Award in 1962. Its sales, as of 1978, were over 47,000 volumes, making it Creeley's most successful book commercially. *For Love* is a considerable achievement, and one of the most celebrated collections of American poetry in its decade. The collection presents many of Creeley's characteristic concerns, including language and human relationships. The poet, writes Peter Davison in *Atlantic*, "has a subtle, almost feminine sensibility, and the best of his poems are those dealing with the

intricacies that exist between men and women." Creeley, Frederick Eckman writes, is "the most *conserving* poet I know; he wastes nothing—in fact, at times, rather too little. Creeley's poems are characterized by constriction, the partially revealed vision, economy of utterance ..."

### Responses to Literature

1. Creeley's poetry uses fairly simple language but arresting line breaks. Choose a poem and rearrange the lines: make one complete sentence, for instance, or condense four lines into two. How do these changes influence how the poem sounds, and what it means? Reread the poem in its original form, and assess again why Creeley may have chosen the line breaks he did.

2. Creeley writes about darkness and doors frequently. Find at least two examples of these themes in his poetry, and try to determine what they might represent for this writer. Do any other images accompany references to darkness and doors? What do these images mean in Creeley's poetry?

3. Creeley spent years corresponding with fellow writer Charles Olson, discussing their theories of poetry. Find a partner, and share a piece of writing. Ask for specific comments about what you would like to accomplish with your writing, and name areas with which you are having difficulty. Using the commentary, revise your writing and consider how another reader can help improve your writing.

4. Research two other writers who are considered Black Mountain poets. Make lists of each writer's poetic style and basic themes. Consider how such different writers can be considered part of the same poetic movement. What specific connections can you draw between these writers?

BIBLIOGRAPHY

**Books**

Allen, Donald M. *Robert Creeley, Contexts of Poetry: Interviews, 1961–1971.* San Francisco: Four Seasons Foundation, 1973.

Butterick, George F. *Charles Olson and Robert Creeley: The Complete Correspondence.* Santa Rosa, Calif.: Black Sparrow Press, 1980.

Clark, Tom. *Robert Creeley and the Genius of the American Common Place: Together with the Poet's Own Autobiography.* New York: New Directions, 1993.

Eckman, Frederick. *Over the West: Selected Writings of Frederick Eckman, with Commentaries and Appreciations.* Linda Wagner-Martin, ed. Orono, Maine: National Poetry Foundation, 1999.

Edelberg, Cynthia Dubin. *Robert Creeley's Poetry: A Critical Introduction.* Albuquerque, N.M.: University of New Mexico Press, 1978.

Fass, Ekbert and Maria Trombaco. *Robert Creeley: A Biography.* Hanover, N.H.: University Press of New England, 2001.

Novick, Mary. *Robert Creeley: An Inventory.* Kent, Ohio: Kent State University Press, 1973.

Sheffler, Ronald Anthony. *The Development of Robert Creeley's Poetry.* Amherst, Mass: University of Massachusetts Press, 1971.

Terrell, Carroll F. *Robert Creeley: The Poet's Workshop.* Orono, Maine: University of Maine Press, 1984.

Wilson, John, editor. *Robert Creeley's Life and Work: A Sense of Increment.* Ann Arbor, Mich.: University of Michigan Press, 1987.

**Periodicals**

Davison, Peter. "New Poetry: The Generation of the Twenties." *Atlantic Monthly* (Feb 1968): 141.

**Web sites**

*Robert Creeley at American Academy of Poets.* Retrieved September 7, 2008 from http://www.poets.org/poet.php/prmPID/184/.

*Robert Creeley Author Homepage.* Retrieved September 7, 2008 from http://epc.buffalo.edu/authors/creeley//.

# ✸ J. Hector St. John de Crèvecoeur

BORN: *1735, Caen, France*

DIED: *1813, Sarcelles, France*

NATIONALITY: *French, American*

GENRE: *Fiction, nonfiction*

MAJOR WORKS:

*Letters from an American Farmer: Describing Certain Provincial Situations, Manners, and Customs, Not Generally Known; and Conveying Some Idea of the Late and Present Interior Circumstances of the British Colonies of North America. Written For the Information of a Friend in England, by J. Hector St. John, A Farmer in Pennsylvania* (1782)

## Overview

Michel-Guillaume Jean de Crevecoeur's reputation rests on his first major publication, *Letters from an American Farmer* (1782), a unified series of narratives and the earliest fiction in American literature to express how America differs culturally from Europe. Its chapter "What Is an American?" has been considered the classic statement of American identity.

## Works in Biographical and Historical Context

**The Frenchmen Travels to North America** Born in Caen, France in 1735, Crèvecoeur received his education at the Jesuit college in that Norman city. His father was a respected member of the region's minor nobility, and his

J. Hector St. John de Crevecoeur *author of "Letters of an American Farmer," 1782, photograph.* © *Bettmann / Corbis.*

mother was a banker's daughter with a better education than most women had in her day. Crèvecoeur left Normandy when he was nineteen, going first to England to live with distant relatives; then immigrating, at age twenty, to French North America. In Canada, his knowledge of mathematics and draftsmanship enabled him to make his living as a surveyor and cartographer for the colonial militia. He saw service in the wilderness campaigns of the war then being fought in North America between France and Great Britain, and in 1757, was present at the surrender of the fort on Lake George, where he witnessed the slaughter of its disarmed British garrison by Indian allies of the French. In 1758, through the influence of noblemen friendly to his father, he was commissioned a lieutenant in a regiment of the regular army of France. The following year, shortly after the battle at Quebec, an action in which he was wounded, he resigned his commission and left Canada to live in the British colonies.

**Living in the British Colonies until the Revolution** During the next decade (between ages twenty five and thirty five), he appears to have traveled through New York, the Ohio region, and Vermont as a surveyor. In 1769, he married Mehitable Tippet, a New York lady

## LITERARY AND HISTORICAL CONTEMPORARIES

Crèvecoeur's famous contemporaries include:

**Benjamin Franklin** (1706–1790): One of the Founding Fathers of the United States, Franklin not only helped in the formation of American independence by participating in the Continental Congress, but he also contributed to the new nation in numerous ways. Not only a writer, scientist, and inventor, Franklin is also credited with such wide accomplishments as creating bifocals and the lightening rod, as well as founding the first library and the University of Pennsylvania.

**Mary Wollstonecraft** (1759–1797): British writer of *A Vindication of the Rights of Women* (1792), Wollstonecraft became an early feminist voice, calling for equal access to education for women at a time when men's education was primary.

**Thomas Paine** (1737–1809): Paine became famous for writing pamphlets encouraging American independence from Great Britain. His most famous work is *Common Sense* (1776).

**Wolfgang Amadeus Mozart** (1756–1791): A musical prodigy, Mozart was an Austrian musician and composer who could play music at age five. Along with Ludwig van Beethoven, Mozart is the most well-known classical composer, and is remembered for his operas and symphonies, including *The Magic Flute* (1791).

from a well-to-do Westchester family, and bought land some thirty miles west of West Point, New York, in Orange County. The American Revolutionary War began six years later, a war fought to end Britain's control over the North American colonies and to create an independent United States, lasting through 1783. At the outbreak of war, Crèvecoeur was the father of a daughter and two sons, an established farmer, and the author of some unpublished manuscripts in English. His attempt to remain neutral during the war caused both the Americans and the British to suspect him of spying, and the British imprisoned him for three months.

***Publishing about America while Living in Europe*** In September 1780 he left New York for Europe, taking with him his older son, age eight, while his American wife stayed to care for their farm and the two younger children. Seven months after arriving in Great Britain, he sold *Letters from an American Farmer* to a London publisher and in August 1781 he returned to France, which he had left in 1754. *Letters from an American Farmer* consists of twelve fictional letters organized into a well-defined beginning, middle, and end of nearly equal lengths. Direct reference to the American Revolution occurs only at the end of the work, which criticizes the war indirectly by dramatizing the culture it interrupted.

In the form this fiction takes, James's first three letters, the initial part of his narrative about his American life, are supposedly datable from their internal historical references as communications written between the spring and winter of 1775. Far from expressing concern about the battles in Canada and New England that were fought in these months between American and British forces, these letters tell the history of the American farmer and of the peacefulness that have characterized life in America in comparison to Europe's long history of poverty and strife. He does indicate that slavery and war are present in America as well, though, and thus America is no utopia. During the Revolutionary War period, slavery was well-established in the colonies, both north and south. Plantation slavery, however, would come to be the dominating use of American slaves, with northern states ending slavery in the late eighteenth century.

During Crèvecoeur's two years of asylum in France, while waiting for the end of the revolution in America so he could rejoin his wife and younger children, he became the protégé of Madame d'Houdetot and the Marquis de Turgot at the French court. In these years, he wrote *Lettres d'un Cultivateur Américain* (1784), which is not at all the simple translation of *Letters from an American Farmer* that its title page and introduction suggest, but a new composition in French, adapting and incorporating the English materials of Crèvecoeur's first book. *Lettres d'un Cultivateur Américain* is a loose collection of sixty-four letters, sketches, and "anecdotes" (as they are called) instead of a dramatic progression of twelve letters; its time span is eleven instead of three years; and the new recipient of James's correspondence is an American instead of an Englishman. The main intention in this much longer, less structured account of America is to display a large amount of information rather than to create an emotionally coherent ideological fiction.

***Return to America Short-lived*** When Crèvecoeur returned to America in the autumn of 1783, it was in the important capacity of French consul to New Jersey, Connecticut, and New York. He discovered that his farm, Pine Hill, had been burned during the closing months of the Revolution, that his wife was dead, and that no one knew what had become of his two children (though they were eventually located in Boston). A successful consul, Crèvecoeur supervised the first regular packet service between France and America, promoted an exchange of agricultural products and information between the two former wartime allies, and appreciably increased the existing goodwill between them. During these years, he wrote an additional volume for *Lettres d'un Cultivateur Américain*, enlarging it by half its original length (1787). His active service as consul ended in 1790 with a furlough to France, and he never returned to America. His remaining years were passed almost entirely in France.

In his mid-sixties he wrote and published yet another book about America, *Voyage dans la Haute Pensylvanie et dans l'état de New-York* (1801), which pretends to be a translation into French of fragments of an English-language manuscript by S. J. D. C., "an adopted member of the Oneida Indians." It describes a trip through the northern and middle parts of the United States in the years following the American Revolution and contains much actual information about postwar economic and political developments in the nascent democracy, word pictures of American landscapes, and depictions of American Indians. This final book of his career is a reaffirmation of belief in America's promise. It praises Americans for having avoided, in the aftermath of their revolution, "the bloody fury of anarchy."

Crèvecoeur died twenty-three years after his last residence in America. An American who had crossed the Atlantic with him in 1787 recalled of his character: "The milk of human kindness circulated in every vein. Mild, unassuming, prompt to serve, slow to censure, extremely intelligent and universally respected and beloved, his society on shipboard could not but be a treasure."

## Works in Literary Context

***Revolutionary Literature*** From *The Federalist Papers* to the pamphlets of Thomas Paine, the era approaching the Revolutionary War generated much writing about the American identity. As the British colonies considered independence from Great Britain, there was much discussion about the new identity the colonies had developed apart from British rule. Crèvecoeur's work, especially *Letters from an American Farmer*, considered this new identity and articulated it in a bold and positive way. Its chapter, "What Is an American?", has been considered the classic statement of American identity, and Crèvecoeur suggests that, uncoerced in America by institutionalized pressures to conform to received beliefs and habits, these former Europeans and their descendants moved about freely, married whom they chose, thought their own thoughts, spoke as they wished, and worshiped as they believed fitting. He concludes, "Here individuals of all nations are melted into a new race of men, whose labours and posterity will one day cause great changes in the world."

***Epistolary Novels*** British writer Samuel Richardson's *Clarissa* (1747) helped make epistolary novels popular in the eighteenth century. The effect of a narrative told through letters is to produce a realistic appearance, creating a believable narrative voice within a recognizable and common form of communication. All of Crèvecoeur's novels are in the eighteenth-century epistolary tradition. His reputation rests on *Letters from an American Farmer*, a unified series of expository narratives and the earliest fiction in American literature to express how America differs culturally from Europe. Crèvecoeur's narrative exposition of ideas is so skillful that many literary historians and critics have mistaken it for an autobiography.

---

## COMMON HUMAN EXPERIENCE

Crèvecoeur describes a new, foreign land in his writing. Other works that narrate experiences attached to a specific place include:

*The Journal of Christopher Columbus* (1492), a nonfiction account by Christopher Columbus. Recovered through biographer Bartolome de las Casas, Columbus's journal describes what he found when he landed in the Bahamas after intending to sail to Asia. He writes about the climate and vegetation in the new land, as well as the native people he encounters.

*Notes on the State of Virginia* (1784), a nonfiction work by Thomas Jefferson. Authored by one of the Founding Fathers and the third president of the United States, this work describes Virginia in great detail, from weather and crop conditions to descriptions of the politics of slavery.

*The Interesting Narrative of the Life of Olaudah Equiano, or Gustavus Vassa, the African* (1789), an autobiographical work by Olaudah Equiano. An early slave narrative, Equiano details his capture into slavery, his voyage on the slave ship, his labor and mistreatment, and his subsequent life as a freed slave in England. His narrative was a bestseller upon its publication.

*Let Us Now Praise Famous Men* (1941), a nonfiction book written by James Agee and with photographs by Walker Evans. This book details the harsh lives of Southern sharecroppers in the 1930s, through powerful language and equally powerful, stark photographs.

---

## Works in Critical Context

Like Henry David Thoreau, Crèvecoeur published only a few works. But his one book in English, like Thoreau's *Walden*, is a classic representation of American faith in the possibility of renewal, though he doubted that mankind could attain a completely new moral life. Also like Thoreau, he rejected wars, political parties, and governments as instruments of human progress. Perhaps because of its pacifist criticism of the American Revolution, *Letters from an American Farmer* was not republished in the United States until 1904, after its first appearance in 1793. Naturally this circumstance hindered Crèvecoeur's reputation. Recognition of his abilities as a creative writer has also been lacking because his success in projecting a living narrator in *Letters from an American Farmer* misled too many readers into considering it an autobiography. This mistake was easy to make since in America, he sometimes used the surname St. John, though he was never known to have used James or Hector, the first and the middle names of his fictional American farmer.

***Letters from an American Farmer*** Critics have re-examined Crèvecoeur's major work in order to illustrate more problematic aspects of American culture that the writer presents. Myra Jehlen, for instance, examines the apparent contradiction between Crèvecoeur's loyalty to America and his opposition to the Revolutionary War. An independent nation would mean less freedom to Crèvecoeur, Jehlen writes, "because he could see in the accommodations of majority rule no advantages but only a loss of freedom for each individual." James E. Bishop further discusses Crèvecoeur's writing by studying masculinity in *Letters From an American Farmer*. He states that the work can be viewed "as a book that reveals the deep ambivalence that American men felt about the burgeoning American nation, about their identities as men, and about the natural environment." Jeff Osborne focuses on Crèvecoeur's discussions of slavery in his work, and claims that the positive portrait of a new country with new ideas about equality are actually undermined; "these principles themselves," Osborne writes, "are effects of social arrangements built on violence and suffering."

## Responses to Literature

1. How is the America described in *Letters from an American Farmer* similar to America today? How is it different? Do Americans still place value on the same ideals?

2. Write your own short essay that answers the question, "What is an American?" Use examples from your own life as well as examples from current events to define an American in your time period.

3. you think it is easier for an outsider to objectively describe a culture than it is for a person who has lived within the culture since birth? Or do you think an outsider, having been raised elsewhere, is less likely to fully understand a foreign culture?

BIBLIOGRAPHY

**Books**

Adams, Percy G. *Crèvecoeur's Eighteenth-Century Travels in Pennsylvania & New York*. Lexington, Ky.: University of Kentucky Press, 1961.

Emerson, Everett. "Hector St. John de Crèvecoeur and the Promise of America" in *Forms and Functions of History in American Literature: Essays in Honor of Ursula Brumm*. Berlin: Schmidt, 1981.

Philbrick, Thomas. *St. John Crèvecoeur*. New York: Twayne, 1970.

**Periodicals**

Bishop, James E. "A feeling farmer: masculinity, nationalism, and nature in Crèvecoeur's Letters." *Early American Literature* 43.2 (2008): 361–377.

Jehlen, Myra. "J. Hector St. John Crèvecoeur: A Monarcho-Anarchist." *American Quarterly* 31.2 (1979): 204–222.

Osborne, Jeff. "American Antipathy and the Cruelties of Citizenship in Crèvecoeur's *Letter From an American Farmer* (J. Hector St. John De Crèvecoeur)." *Early American Literature* 42.3 (2007): 529–553.

# ✸ Michael Crichton

BORN: *1942, Chicago, Illinois*

DIED: *2008, Los Angeles, California*

NATIONALITY: *American*

GENRE: *Fiction*

MAJOR WORKS:
*The Andromeda Strain* (1969)
*The Great Train Robbery* (1975)
*Jurassic Park* (1990)
*State of Fear* (2004)
*Next* (2006)

## Overview

Michael Crichton is best known as a novelist of popular fiction whose stories explore the clash between traditional social and moral values and the demands of the new technological age. *Jurassic Park* (1990), his most successful novel about re-creating living dinosaurs from ancient DNA, examines what can go wrong when greedy people

Michael Crichton *AP Images*

misuse the power of new and untested technologies. Although some critics fault Crichton for stereotypical characterizations and old-fashioned plotlines, many have praised his taut, suspenseful, and fast-paced stories, entertaining narrative style, and his ability to impart specialized technical information to the uninitiated reader.

## Works in Biographical and Historical Context

*From Doctor to Writer* Crichton was born in Chicago and raised on Long Island. At fourteen years of age, he wrote and sold articles to the *New York Times* travel section, and, in 1964, earned a BA in anthropology from Harvard University. The following year, while on a European travel fellowship in anthropology and ethnology, he met and married Joan Radam; they eventually divorced, in 1970. Returning to Harvard University in 1965, Crichton entered medical school, where he began to write novels under the pseudonym John Lange in order to support his medical studies. While doing postdoctoral work at the Salk Institute for Biological Studies in La Jolla, California, Crichton published *The Andromeda Strain* (1969), a technological thriller that garnered literary acclaim and national prominence for the author. Upon completing his medical training, Crichton began a full-time writing career.

*Technological Thrillers Gain Popularity* Crichton's stories generally take place in contemporary settings and focus on technological themes, although his earliest works were traditional mystery novels. Writing under the pseudonym John Lange, Crichton published a mystery novel entitled *Odds On* (1966), followed by *A Case of Need* (1968), written under the pseudonym Jeffrey Hudson. *A Case of Need* received favorable reviews and the 1968 Edgar Allan Poe Award of Mystery Writers of America. In 1969, Crichton published *The Andromeda Strain*, a novel that, Crichton acknowledges, was influenced by Len Deighton's *The Ipcress File* (1962) and H. G. Wells's *The War of The Worlds*. *The Andromeda Strain* is a technological thriller about a seemingly unstoppable plague brought to earth from outer space; it became a Book of the Month Club selection and a 1971 motion picture, directed by Robert Wise and starring Arthur Hill.

The 1970s and 1980s were times of vast technological changes, from the advent of the computer age to medical advances such as the first successful *in vitro* fertilization, or, test tube baby, in 1978 and artificial heart replacements in the eighties. With these changes in a human's ability to manipulate nature, Crichton's work reflects the social discussion about the dangers of taking on god-like abilities. Cloning, which began in earnest in the seventies leading to serious breakthroughs in the nineties, especially incited fears of what destruction might arise from human beings weilding too much power over life and death.

*A Detour into Historical Fiction on the Way to Jurassic Park* While Crichton's *The Great Train Robbery* (1975) recalls the history of an actual train robbery in

---

# LITERARY AND HISTORICAL CONTEMPORARIES

Crichton's famous contemporaries include:

**Tom Clancy** (1947–): Author of numerous novels that have been made into successful movies, Clancy writes action/adventure stories that lean heavily toward government and military plotlines. His most famous books feature tortured hero Jack Ryan and include *The Hunt for Red October* (1984), *Patriot Games* (1987), and *Clear and Present Danger* (1989).

**Stephen King** (1947–): King is a bestselling writer of horror fiction and other genres, including such popular titles as *Carrie* (1974), *The Shining* (1977), and *Firestarter* (1980). Many of King's novels have been made into successful films.

**Steven Spielberg** (1946–): Known for directing such blockbuster movies as *E.T.* (1982), *Schindler's List* (1993), and *Saving Private Ryan* (1998).

**Al Gore** (1948–): Vice president of the United States from 1993 to 2001, Al Gore received a Nobel Prize in 2007 for his work in raising international awareness of the potential dangers of climate change.

---

Victorian England, and *Eaters of the Dead* (1976) is set among tenth-century Vikings, and is supposedly the retelling of the *Beowulf* myth, *Congo* (1980) marks Crichton's thematic return to the dangers of technology, greed, and power. An encounter with alien life forms and alien technology in the ocean is the focus of Crichton's next novel, *Sphere* (1987).

In 1990, Crichton published his nationally acclaimed best-seller, *Jurassic Park*, which recounts the now-classic tale of greed and a genetic experiment gone awry. A wealthy entrepreneur and his scientists lose control of their experiment to re-create living dinosaurs for a wild-animal park on a deserted island off the Costa Rican coast. Steven Spielberg's 1994 Academy award-winning film *Jurassic Park* also helped to ensure the world-wide popularity and success of the novel. Crichton returned to the theme of genetic engineering in *The Lost World* (1995) and *Next* (2006).

Crichton's cautionary tales about genetic engineering grew out of increased scientific breakthroughs in the late twentieth century. The manipulation of DNA, human genetic material, began in earnest in the 1970s, first with successfully cloned mice and culminating with Dolly the sheep's cloning in 1996. The Human Genome Project, an unprecedented international effort established in 1990 to map the entire human genetic code, brought both the possibility of eliminating genetic disease and the fear of abusive control over human identity.

*The Climate Change Controversy* In 2004, Crichton made headlines with his controversial novel *State of Fear*, which presents a controversial perspective on global climate change. The story challenges scientific data claiming that global warming is a real threat, instead positing

## COMMON HUMAN EXPERIENCE

Crichton considers the dangers of technology in many of his books. Other stories that consider how technology affects humanity include:

*Frankenstein* (1818), a novel by Mary Shelley. When a scientist discovers how to create another human being through artificial means, he suffers the consequences of interfering with human identity and natural processes.

*Brave New World* (1931), a novel by Aldous Huxley. This science fiction story presents the dangers of a society driven by comfort and perfection rather than human interaction.

*Nineteen Eighty-Four* (1949), a novel by George Orwell. This cautionary novel looks ahead thirty-five years from its publication and imagines the horrors that can arise from a totalitarian government knowing too much about its citizens' lives. Big Brother, as the surveillance group is called, investigates and controls every aspect of society.

*Minority Report* (2002), a film directed by Steven Spielberg. This movie explores the ethical implications of a futuristic world where crimes can be anticipated and prevented through mind control. One man must fight back against the entire system in order to prove his innocence when he is falsely accused of murder.

that political and financial aspirations have influenced scientific findings. With efforts like the Kyoto Protocol, a 1997 international agreement to significantly reduce greenhouse gases around the world by 2012, Crichton's premise was felt to undermine positive progress towards curbing the negative impacts of climate change.

Crichton's mass appeal continued to rise as most of his novels drew multi-million dollar film deals soon after their publication. Between his page-turning action and his detailed technical and scientific elements, Crichton's stories energize audiences and draw them both to bookstores and movie theaters. Despite their sometimes over-moralizing qualities, Crichton's thrillers both entertain audiences and cause them to question some of the main technological advances of the twentieth and twenty-first centuries.

Crichton died in Los Angeles in 2008 after a battle with cancer.

## Works in Literary Context

Crichton's books have come to be classified as techno-thrillers for their combination of high-action plotlines and detailed technical elements. But his writing is also an outgrowth of more traditional genres developed by writers such as George Orwell and Wells.

*Science Fiction and Science-Based Storytelling* Science fiction presents fantastic events that have not or do not occur in regular life, but these elements are usually presented in a believable way. Crichton's novels do not invent entirely new worlds but instead build on a basically realistic environment to present an extraordinary occurrence. Like other science fiction novelists, Crichton relies on scientific principles in his stories, offering detailed and compelling evidence for the extraordinary events he presents. Often, the futuristic science and technology in these stories leads to destruction rather than human improvement. *Jurassic Park*, for instance, follows as regenerated dinosaurs attack and murder humans; the dinosaurs' existence seems possible because of elaborate descriptions of genetic preservation through prehistoric fossilization.

*Science-Based Entertainment* Crichton's work fits into a larger, and popular, body of work in which late twentieth- and early-twenty-first century storytellers present detailed scientific knowledge to audiences for entertainment purposes. Other well-received examples of using science in stories include Tom Clancy novels and *CSI: Crime Scene Investigation* television shows. Crichton himself pioneered this kind of television show with his work on *ER*, a medical television drama, portraying the lives of emergency room doctors in great detail. Audiences respond to in-depth explanations of military, medical, and scientific phenomenon when they are combined with heightened drama, and Crichton has based his career on that exact mixture.

## Works in Critical Context

Crichton's works have received mixed reviews. While most critics applaud his ability to make technological information understandable and engaging, some fault his traditional and predictable plotlines and shallow characterization.

*Jurassic Park* As G. Thomas Goodnight notes, Crichton is "famous for doing his homework, for introducing popular audiences to complex concepts. ... His character Ian Malcolm presents us with Chaos Theory, often taken for granted, and this view represents the postmodernist, skeptical view of life as we know it." Other critics see Crichton's main theme as one of techno-dystopia, a warning against technology out of control. Some reviewers claim that the scientist character, Hammond's "re-creation" of dinosaurs is not reality; it is a new reality with an unknown outcome, and scientists in their greed for fame and fortune fail to recognize this unpredictability. Evan Watkins views *Jurassic Park* as a retelling of the creation story, with Hammond as God of a creation that fails to behave as he wants—and in which the tenets of Chaos Theory interfere. Whether Crichton imbues his scientific characters with a God complex or some other motivation, critics recognize Crichton's tendency to portray scientists with flaws: overwhelming pride, greed, and lust for control.

## Responses to Literature

1. Crichton's stories either look forward or back, portraying a futuristic world or one set in the historical past. Examining one of each kind of story, consider how Crichton conceives of the past, present, and future.

Does he make any significant distinctions between life a hundred years ago versus today or the future? What benefits do current technologies afford Crichton's characters, and what drawbacks do they present?

2. Several of Crichton's stories involve the controversy of genetic engineering. From his novels, what are the serious dangers of manipulating human genetic material? What are some of the potential advancements that humans may achieve with the help of genetic science? What kinds of safeguards could protect against the serious threats of genetic engineering?

3. Crichton's novel *State of Fear* caused a controversy with its anti-environmentalist stance on the issue of climate change. Using your library and the Internet, find out more about climate change. Be very careful to evaluate the sources of your information, and avoid biased material. Is there any consensus in the scientific community about whether climate change is happening? Do scientists agree on whether climate change is caused by humans? What is the position of the governments of the world's leading nations on this issue? Write a paper summarizing your finding.

4. Writers have considered the dangers of technology in every generation. Read at least one other anti-utopian novel in which a potentially-perfect society ends in destruction, such as *We* (1921) or *Farenheit 451* (1953). What themes and fears do these kinds of books have in common, despite different time periods? What themes and fears change depending on the historical context of the story?

BIBLIOGRAPHY

**Bibliography**

**Books**

Aaseng, Nathan. *Michael Crichton*. San Diego: Lucent Books, 2002.

Grazier, Kevin Robert. *The Science of Michael Crichton: An Unauthorized Exploration into the Real Science Behind the Fictional Worlds of Michael Crichton*. Dallas: BenBella Books, 2008.

Trembley, Elizabeth A. *Michael Crichton: A Critical Companion*. Westport, Conn.: Greenwood Press, 1996.

**Periodicals**

Benford, Gregroy and Martin Hoffert. "Fear of Reason: Michael Crichton's *State of Fear*" *New York Review of Science Fiction*. 17.8 (2005): 15–16.

Blanch, Robert. "Medieval Fictional Odysseys: Better Time Travel Through Hallucinogens, Nets, and Quantum Foam" *Extrapolation: A Journal of Science Fiction and Fantasy*. 45.3 (2004): 305–17.

Goodnight, G. Thomas. "The Firm, the Park and the University: Fear and Trembling on the Postmodern Trail" *Quarterly Journal of Speech* 81.3 (1995): 267–90.

Hahn, Torsten. "Risk Communication and Paranoid Hermeneutics: Towards a Distinction Between 'Medical Thrillers' and 'Mind-Control Thrillers' in Narrations on Biocontrol" *New Literary History: A Journal of Theory and Interpretation*. 6.2 (2005): 178–204.

Watkins, Evan. "The Dinosaurics of Size: Economic Narrative and Postmodern Culture." *Centennial Review* 39.2 (1995): 189–211.

**Web sites**

*Michael Crichton: The Official Site*. Retrieved September 6, 2008, from http://www.crichton-official.com/.

*The Michael Crichton Homepage*. Retrieved September 6, 2008, from http://www.randomhouse.com/features/crichton/.

# ✺ Mark Crilley

BORN: *1966, Hartford City, Indiana*

NATIONALITY: *American*

GENRE: *Fiction, graphic novel*

MAJOR WORKS:

*Akiko on the Planet Smoo* (2000)

*Billy Clikk: Creath Battler* (2004)

Mark Crilley  *Crilley, Mark, photograph by Mary Moylan. Reproduced by permission of Mark Crilley.*

# LITERARY AND HISTORICAL CONTEMPORARIES

Crilley's famous contemporaries include:

**Ann Brashares** (1967–): American author of *The Sisterhood of the Traveling Pants* novels, Brashares writes about four friends who are continually united in their adventures by a pair of seemingly magical blue jeans.

**Christopher Paolini** (1983–): This American author gained media attention for writing his first book while still a home-schooled teenager. The *Eragon* stories follow a young farm boy as he seeks to save a kingdom with the help of his newfound best friend, a magical female dragon named Saphira.

**J. K. Rowling** (1965–): Amassing a fortune that has been said to rival the Queen of England's, British writer J. K. Rowling has created a series of seven stories about a young wizard named Harry Potter. Movies and merchandising surrounded her fiction, making Harry Potter globally popular.

**Bono** (1960–): Lead singer and front man for Irish rock band U2, Bono became a world presence at the turn of the twenty-first century with his pioneering work to engage Western countries in the global effort against extreme poverty and AIDS in Africa.

**Apolo Anton Ohno** (1982–): Olympic gold-medalist for the non-traditional sport, short-track speed skating, Ohno is a Japanese-American athlete who has garnered widespread popularity among American youth.

## Overview

Mark Crilley never intended to write young adult novels. Instead, he considered himself much more of an artist and illustrator than a writer. Still, after his first comic book gained popularity and a publisher encouraged him, Crilley launched his highly successful graphic novel series about the adventures of a strong young girl named Akiko.

## Works in Biographical and Historical Context

*Education and Plans for an Art Career* Crilley was born in 1966 into a family that always encouraged his art. Raised in Indiana, he spent his teenage years sketching and becoming well-known in his high school for his considerable drawing talent. Not only did he hone his artwork skills; he also spent time in the drama department, developing a stage presence that has helped him pursue a substantial speaking career as an adult. It was not until he was in college, however, that he truly considered art as an occupation. Under the mentorship of writer/illustrator David Small at Kalamazoo College, he refined his skills and began considering publishing as a career.

After graduating from college, though, Crilley spent five years teaching English in Taiwan and Japan. While there, he developed the character of Akiko, a fourth-grade girl who embarks on a series of adventures on a planet named Smoo. Once Crilley was back in the U.S., the comic book was picked up by Sirius Comics and published in 1995. It eventually found its way to Random House Children's Books, where editor Lawrence David encouraged Crilley to expand his narrative. Working together, they developed the Akiko storyline into a larger series of young adult graphic novels, published in 2000. The stories gained a popular audience, earning an impressive twelve Eisner awards, the highest award given out by the comic book industry.

Crilley's work came out as a genre of Japanese comics called "manga" was finding popular success in the West. By the time the *Akiko* series debuted, the distinct style of manga (and the animated version, called "anime") were recognizable to and adored by American youth culture. Crilley's work also appealed to the growing trend of strong female characters in young adult fiction, showing girl characters as strong, independent, and capable of having their own adventures.

## Works in Literary Context

*Unlikely Heroes* Young adult literature often features a seemingly unexceptional child who turns out to possess extraordinary gifts and heroic potential. Often the main character is orphaned or otherwise without regular parental guidance and is somehow different from his or her peers. The character is often an unlikely hero, overlooked by the crowd as not having any enviable qualities. Akiko, a Japanese-American ten-year-old in the first novel, follows this pattern by being taken from Earth because King Froptoppit believes she has special powers to save his son. Although shy and reluctant to be any kind of leader, Akiko sets out on a series of adventures and finds she has more strength than she imagines. Along the way, she meets several unusual characters who join her in her quest, among them Mr. Beeba, Poog, and Spuckler.

*Manga and Graphic Novels* The Akiko stories have grown out of the popular Japanese manga genre. While comics in the United States are generally viewed as children's literature, the Japanese tradition is broader. Offering comic books and their extended version, the graphic novel, for readers of all ages, manga is often divided into stories meant for boys (called *shonen*) and those aimed at girls (called *shojo*). Crilley's work focuses on a girl hero and could be loosely considered *shojo*. Crilley's Akiko character exhibits standard features of this genre, including special powers and striking, unique fashion statements. Crilley's illustrations also incorporate the large-eyed characters most often associated with manga characters. The Akiko adventures take the main character away from everything familiar and place her in unlikely scenarios where her strength and loyalty are tested.

## Works in Critical Context

*The Akiko Series* Crilley's work has been well-received from its initial publication. From an underground following of his comic book to a legitimate reading audience, Crilley's books use adventure and unexpected twists to entertain. Critics praise his Akiko series for its avoidance of violence or adult humor, instead crediting Crilley with creating interesting characters and a charming story. Diane Roback and Jennifer M. Brown at *Publishers Weekly* say that Akiko has a "global flair," and Chris Sherman at *Booklist* credits Crilley with writing a "fast-paced" story that keeps readers "wondering what will come next." The Akiko books are also recommended for children who might not otherwise read. Shelle Rosenfeld of *Booklist* says Crilley is a good choice for "reluctant readers or children making a transition from comics to novels."

## Responses to Literature

1. Consider how the Crilley's images influence the story of Akiko. How would reading the adventures of Akiko be different without the illustrations? Which illustrations reflect how you imagine the story? Which illustrations create a different image than you imagined?

2. Akiko is the hero of Crilley's stories. What are her main strengths? How does she compare to other story heroes you know? What makes her succeed in her adventures? Does she have help? How would the stories be different if the main character were a boy?

3. Read a manga comic or graphic novel meant specifically for boys. List specific differences between the Akiko series, potentially more popular with female audiences, and stories meant for boys. What do the writers assume about the preferences of girl and boy readers?

4. Research the many genres of Japanese manga and anime, including those meant for adults. Why do Western adult audiences respond less enthusiastically to animated stories? Consider some popular Western children's stories who have developed an adult audience, such as the *Harry Potter* stories. Why are some children-based stories more acceptable than others?

BIBLIOGRAPHY

**Periodicals**

Abbot, Alana. "Miki Fallas: Winter" (Book review) **School Library Journal**. 54.7 (2008): 119.

"Akiko and the Journey to Toog" (Book review) **Publishers Weekly**. 250.39 (2003): 67.

"Akiko on the Planet Smoo; Akiko in the Sprubly Islands" (Book review) *Publishers Weekly*. 248.25 (2001): 83.

Goldsmith, Francisca. "Akiko and the Alpha Centauri 5000" (Book review) *Booklist*. 99.18 (2003): 1660.

---

### COMMON HUMAN EXPERIENCE

Crilley chooses a young girl as the heroine in many of his adventure stories. Other works that focus on young female heroines who have extraordinary experiences include:

*His Dark Materials Trilogy* (2000), three novels by Philip Pullman. This trilogy follows a young girl who not only stumbles on an alternative world, but learns she holds special powers to influence the future.

*Matilda* (1988), a children's book written by Roald Dahl and illustrated by Quentin Blake. When young Matilda becomes overwhelmed with the angry and incompetant adults in her life, she learns that she has special powers to make things right.

*The Lion, the Witch and the Wardrobe* (1950), a novel by C.S. Lewis. This first book in the *Chronicles of Narnia* series, the story follows four children who find a magical world, led by the faith of the youngest girl, Lucy.

*The Royal Diaries* (1999–2005), a series of young adult historical fiction. This series of Canadian books tells the stories of young girls who become famous world leaders throughout history.

*The King's Equal* (1992), a fairy tale by Katherine Paterson and illustrated by Vladimir Vagin. This story, in which a prince cannot become king until he finds an equal partner for marriage, shows how the young Rosamund discovers how her own wisdom and magical abilities surpass even the prince's.

---

"Mark Crilley: Cult Cartoonist" *Entertainment Weekly*. 438–9 (1998):90.

**Web sites**

Akiko's Homepage. *Random House Kids Website*. Retrieved September 7, 2008, from http://www.randomhouse.com/kids/akiko/.

The Official Website of Author/Illustrator Mark Crilley. *Mark Crilley.com.*. Retrieved September 7, 2008, from http://www.markcrilley.com/.

## ✹ Davy Crockett

BORN: *1786, Green County, Tennessee*

DIED: *1836, San Antonio, Texas*

NATIONALITY: *American*

GENRE: *Autobiography, fiction*

MAJOR WORKS:

*A Narrative of the Life of David Crockett, of the State of Tennessee.* (1834)

Davy Crockett    *Crockett, Davy, circa 1820, photograph. Hulton Archive /
Getty Images.*

## Overview

American frontiersman and politician, David "Davy"
Crockett became during his own lifetime a celebrity and
folk hero, particularly to Americans living in the newly
settled midwestern regions of the country. Although he is
known chiefly for his exploits as a hunter and soldier,
Crockett's major contributions included political efforts
to get free land for frontier settlers, relief for debtors, and
an expanded state banking system for Tennessee.

## Works in Biographical and Historical Context

### *Poverty and Lack of Education in the Early Years*
Davy Crockett, the son of John and Rebecca Crockett,
was born on August 17, 1786, in Hawkings County, East
Tennessee. John Crockett failed as a farmer, mill operator, and storekeeper. Because of continuing poverty,
Davy's father put him to work driving cattle to Virginia
when he was twelve years old. Returning to Tennessee in
the winter of 1798, Davy spent five days in school. After a
fight there, he played hooky until his father found out
and then, to escape punishment, ran away.

Crockett worked and traveled throughout Virginia
and did not return home for nearly three years. After
deciding that his lack of education limited his marriage
possibilities, he arranged to work six months for a nearby

Quaker teacher. In return Crockett received four days a
week of instruction. He learned to read, to write a little,
and to "cypher some in the first three rules of figures."

In 1806 Crockett married Mary Finely. Frontier
farming proved difficult and unrewarding to Crockett,
who enjoyed hunting more than work. After five years
he decided to move farther west. By 1813 he had relocated his family to Franklin County, Tennessee.

### *Frontier Life*
Shortly after this move, the so-called
Creek War began. During the summer of 1813 a party of
frontiersmen ambushed a band of Creek Indian warriors
in southern Alabama. Settlers in the area gathered at a
stockade called Fort Mims. The Native Americans
attacked on August 30, 1813, found the garrison unde-
fended, and killed over five hundred people. Within two
weeks frontier militia units gathered for revenge, and
Crockett volunteered for three months' duty that year.
In September and October he served as a scout. During
the famous mutiny against Andrew Jackson in December,
Crockett was on leave, and reports that he deserted the
militia during the Creek War are unfounded. He served
again from September 1814 to February 1815. During
this campaign Crockett was a mounted scout and hunter;
apparently his unit encountered little fighting.

In 1815 Mary Crockett died. Within a year Crockett
remarried. While traveling with neighbors in Alabama to
examine the newly opened Creek lands during 1816, he
contracted malaria and was left along the road to die. But
he recovered and returned to Tennessee, pale and sickly,
much to the surprise of his family and neighbors who
thought he was dead. He has been quoted as remarking
about his reported death, "I know'd this was a whopper
of a lie, as soon as I heard it."

### *A Rising Political Star*
Davy Crockett had grown
to manhood in a backwoods area. He experienced the
crudeness and poverty of the frontier squatter and later
used this knowledge in his political campaigns. A master
storyteller, the semiliterate Crockett proved a formidable
political campaigner, as well as the personification of the
characters in the frontiersmen's "tall tales" of that day.
Emerging primarily from American frontier life, tall tales
have become foundational elements of American folklore,
emphasizing both the humor and strength needed in an
individual who would survive difficult wilderness living.

In 1817 Crockett was a justice of the peace and the
next year was serving also as a county court referee. In
1818 his neighbors elected him lieutenant colonel of the
local militia regiment, and that same year he became one
of the Lawrenceburg town commissioners. He held this
position until 1821, when he resigned to campaign for a
seat in the state legislature. During the campaign Crockett first displayed his shrewd ability to judge the needs of
the frontiersmen. He realized that their isolation and
need for recreation outweighed other desires. Therefore,
he gave short speeches laced with stories, followed by a
trip to the ever-present liquor stand—a tactic well

received by his audience, who elected him. Having grown to manhood among debt-ridden squatters, Crockett proposed bills to reduce taxes, to settle land claim disputes, and in general to protect the economic interests of the western settlers. Settling the American West was a large concern of the nineteenth century, with many settlers venturing west under the allure of land ownership. Life was extremely difficult under frontier circumstances, but it produced romantic and exaggerated images of adventure and independence.

When the legislative session ended in 1821, Davy went west again, this time to Gibson County, Tennessee, where he built a cabin near the Obion River. Two years later he was elected to the Tennessee Legislature. This victory demonstrates his improved campaign techniques and his realization that anti-aristocratic rhetoric was popular. Again he worked for debtor relief and equitable land laws.

***Crockett in Washington***   During 1825 Crockett ran for Congress; he campaigned as an anti-tariff man, however, and the incumbent easily defeated him. Two years later Crockett won the election. Throughout his congressional terms he worked for the Tennessee Vacant Land Bill, which he introduced during his first term. This proposal would have offered free land to frontier settlers in return for the increase in value which they would bring about because of their improvements.

In 1829, although he opposed several of President Andrew Jackson's measures, Crockett's campaign for reelection as a Jacksonian was successful. But during his second term in Congress, Crockett grew increasingly hostile to Jackson. He opposed the president on issues such as land policy and the Second National Bank. Crockett especially opposed Jackson's Indian removal policies, the movement in the nineteenth century to purchase land from Native American tribes in the American Southeast under questionable circumstances, and he would become well-known for his congressional debates on this issue. Crockett was defeated in the election of 1831. Two years later he regained his congressional seat by a narrow margin. By 1834 he had become such an outspoken critic of Jackson that Whig Party leaders used Crockett as a popular symbol in their anti-Jackson campaigns.

In 1835 Crockett co-authored, along with Thomas Chilton, his autobiographical *Narrative of the Life of David Crockett, of the State of Tennessee*. At around the same time, several other purported biographies and autobiographies of Crockett appeared. Their purpose was to popularize him and to show that not all frontiersmen supported the Jackson administration. These literary efforts failed to sway most of the voters, and Crockett was defeated in 1835, ending his congressional career.

During his three terms in Washington, Crockett tried to represent the interests of his frontier district. In doing so, he became enmeshed in a dispute with the Tennessee Jackson forces. The continuing fight with this group not

## LITERARY AND HISTORICAL CONTEMPORARIES

Davy Crockett's famous contemporaries include:

**Daniel Boone** (1734–1820): An American folk hero, Daniel Boone was a hunter and frontiersman who explored and settled in Kentucky. Like Crockett, his adventures became legendary and inspired tall tales for generations after his death.

**Andrew Jackson** (1767–1845): The seventh president of the United States, Jackson oversaw massive removal of land from indigenous Native American tribes and signed the Indian Removal Act in 1830.

**James Fenimore Cooper** (1789–1851): A popular American writer in the nineteenth century, Cooper wrote stories about the frontier. His most famous novel is *The Last of the Mohicans* (1826).

only prevented him from making any lasting legislative contributions but also ended his political career.

***Death at the Alamo***   In 1835 Crockett and four neighbors headed into Texas looking for new land. By January 1836 he had joined the Texas Volunteers and within a month he reached San Antonio. In the first week of March, he and the other defenders of the Alamo died during the siege and capture of that fort. The Battle of the Alamo was part of the war for Texas independence, and although leader Sam Houston ordered Colonel William Travis to surrender the mission to the Mexicans, Houston instead enacted the famous standoff between the Texans and Santa Anna's Mexican troops. No Texas soldier survived the thirteen-day siege, and the fight led to the famous battle cry "Remember the Alamo." Popular tradition places Crockett as one of the last defenders who died protecting the bedridden Travis during the final assault. However, Crockett was in fact one of the first defenders to die, alone and unarmed.

## Works in Literary Context

Davy Crockett's adventures gave him a legendary status during his lifetime and beyond. From real-life exploits to exaggerated tales, Crockett stories have circulated throughout American culture.

***Contemporary Stories and Tall Tales***   Crockett was known as the "coonskin congressman" because of his many stories about hunting raccoons and bears. He loved to tell tall tales that showed him as stronger, smarter, braver, and a better shot than anyone else in the land. The stories grew more fantastic after his death, thanks largely to a series of adventure books featuring Crockett as the hero. In these tales, he climbed Niagara Falls on an

## COMMON HUMAN EXPERIENCE

Davy Crockett legends are abundant. Stories that describe other characters whose deeds became legend include:

The *Odyssey* (c. 720 BCE), an epic poem by Homer. One of the central works in world literature, this Greek epic recounts the travels of Odysseus and his crew as they sail home to Ithaca after the Trojan War. Through a series of encounters with monsters, gods, giants, sorceresses—and, in the end, men who are out to steal his home and wife—Odysseus comes to embody the full spectrum of heroism.

The *Narrative of the Life of Frederick Douglass, Written By Himself* (1845), an autobiography by Frederick Douglass. Written by a runaway slave turned famous abolitionist orator, this slave narrative details the specific horrors slaves endured in the American South. Used as an abolitionist text to protest the institution of slavery before the Civil War, Douglass's narrative describes his extraordinary escape from slavery and continues to be the primary text of the slave narrative genre.

The *Once and Future King* (1958), a novel by T. H. White. This novel, originally broken into four parts, tells the legendary story of King Arthur's Court. From Arthur's enchanted childhood in which he pulls the sword Excalibur from a stone to his famous Round Table of knights and epic battles, Arthur fulfills his destiny by fighting for good above all else.

*Elizabeth* (1998), a film by Shekhar Kapur. Starring Cate Blanchett and Geoffrey Rush, this historical film follows Elizabeth I's rule over England in the sixteenth century, while battling the strict gender expectations of her time.

alligator's back, drank the entire Gulf of Mexico, twisted the tail off a comet, and outsmarted a businessman. He also traveled the world performing marvelous feats of daring and skill. In many ways, Davy Crockett is America's own celebrated hero, whose deeds and adventures compare to those of legendary ancient warriors such as Achilles and Beowulf.

*Modern Tales*   Stories about Davy Crockett have continued throughout the twentieth century. Television shows like the 1950s' ABC series *Davy Crockett, Indian Fighter* and the 1988 *The New Adventures of Davy Crockett* appeared, as well as movies like Walt Disney's *Davy Crockett, King of the Wild Frontier*. These media representations not only encouraged a generation of children to start wearing coonskin caps, but they also captured the larger-than-life American figure Crockett embodies. Crockett's legendary status continues to help define the myth of American rugged individualism.

## Works in Critical Context

*A Narrative of the Life of David Crockett, of the State of Tennessee.*   The only work critics agree that Crockett himself authored, with the help of Thomas Chilton, emphasizes humorous, folksy stories over serious, accurate historical accounts. Historian Vernon Louis Parrington wrote in 1927 that Crockett's work "is the great classic of the southern frontier" and it "exhibits the honesty, the wit, the resourcefulness, the manly independence of a coonskin hero." While many readers use Crockett's narrative as an accurate accounting of his life and experiences, Joseph J. Arpad chooses to read the text as a piece of literature. Arpad suggests that although the writing "may appear credible and real" it is really "an imaginative story told by Crockett to satisfy America's desire for a romantic frontier hero." Richard Boyd Hauck agrees, claiming that Crockett used the right amount of literary style to make his readers believe him, with his "genius" being his "clear understanding of how best to evoke his audience's sense of values."

## Responses to Literature

1. Crockett's adventures have been greatly exaggerated, making him a mythical American icon. What American ideals does Davy Crockett represent? How are Crockett's strengths important to the image of America as an independent nation? Are Crockett's virtues still considered positive American values today?

2. Are there tall tales in your family? Write down one extraordinary story that you know from your family history, or ask other family members if they know of any such stories. What are the key elements of that story? What parts do you think are exaggerated or not true? What does the story say about your family?

3. Name another character from a book or movie whose strength is exaggerated beyond realistic human ability. How would the story be different if it did not contain extraordinary elements? List as many stories as you can that focus on everyday characters who do not possess heroic qualities. Can "normal" people be heroes even if they do not possess legendary strength?

BIBLIOGRAPHY

**Books**

Arpad, Joseph J. "Introduction." *A Narrative of the Life of David Crockett of the State of Tennessee.* Edited by Joseph J. Arpad. Lanham, MD: Rowman & Littlefield, 1972, pp. 7–37.

Burke, James W. *David Crockett, the Man Behind the Myth.* Facsimile ed. Austin, Tex.: Eakin Press, 1984.

Cobia, Manley F., Jr. *Journey into the Land of Trials: The Story of Davy Crockett's Expedition to the Alamo.* Franklin, Tenn.: Hillsboro Press, 2003.

Derr, Mark. *The Frontiersman: The Real Life and Many Legends of Davy Crockett.* New York: William Morrow, 1993.

Hauck, Richard Boyd. *Crockett: A Bio-Bibliography.* Westport, Conn.: Greenwood Press, 1982.

Lofaro, Michael A. *The Man, the Legend, the Legacy, 1786–1986.* Knoxville: University of Tennessee Press, 1985.

Lofaro, Michael A., and Joe Cummings, eds. *Crockett at Two Hundred: New Perspectives on the Man and the Myth.* Knoxville: University of Tennessee Press, 1989.

Parrington, Vernon Louis. *Main Currents in American Thought, Vol. 2.* New York: Harcourt Brace Jovanovich, 1927.

**Periodicals**

Heale, M. J. "The Role of the Frontier in Jacksonian Politics: David Crockett and the Myth of the Self-Made Man." *Western Historical Quarterly* 4 (1973): 405–423.

Stiffler, Stuart A. "Davy Crockett: The Genesis of Heroic Myth." *Tennessee Historical Quarterly* 16 (1957): 134–140.

**Web sites**

Biographical Directory of the United States Congress. *David Crockett.* Retrieved September 15, 2008, from http://bioguide.congress.gov/scripts/biodisplay.pl?index=C000918.

The Handbook of Texas Online. *Davy Crockett.* Retrieved September 15, 2008, from http://www.tshaonline.org/handbook/online/articles/CC/fcr24.html.

# ⚫ Victor Hernández Cruz

BORN: *1949, Aguas Buenas, Puerto Rico*

NATIONALITY: *American, Puerto Rican*

GENRE: *Poetry*

MAJOR WORKS:
*Panoramas* (1966)
*Snaps: Poems* (1969)
*Red Beans* (1991)

## Overview

Considered one of the leaders of the Nuyorican movement—a branch of Hispanic literature derived from Puerto Rican culture and language—Victor Hernández Cruz is known for his collections of poetry and prose that examine the status of Puerto Ricans in America and the reality of life in Spanish Harlem. He imbues his work with a combination of Spanish and English ("Spanglish") diction and syntax, nature imagery, historical references, and the rhythm of Latin American popular music.

Victor Hernández Cruz    photograph by Nestor Bareto. Courtesy of Victor Hernandez Cruz.

## Works in Biographical and Historical Context

***Writing during the Emerging Nuyorican Movement***
Cruz was born in Aguas Buenas, Puerto Rico, on February 6, 1949, to Severo and Rosa Cruz. Because of the difficult economic conditions in Puerto Rico, his family migrated to New York City in 1955 and settled on the Lower East Side of Manhattan, in one of the areas designated as "el barrio," or Spanish Harlem. Following the divorce of his parents soon after the move, Cruz's mother worked to support the family. When he was about fourteen years old, Cruz began to write verse, and at seventeen he composed his first collection of poetry titled *Papo Got His Gun! and Other Poems* (1966). Cruz's career got an early boost when an avant-garde New York magazine, the *Evergreen Review*, featured several poems from the collection. Six months before he was to have graduated high school in 1967, Cruz quit school. The following year, he cofounded the East Harlem Gut Theater, a Puerto Rican collective of actors, musicians, and writers that closed after a year. Cruz joined *Umbra* magazine in 1967 as an editor.

Cruz began writing within a growing and active group of Puerto Rican Americans that is often referred to as Nuyoricans. Combining "New York" and "Puerto

# LITERARY AND HISTORICAL CONTEMPORARIES

Victor Hernández Cruz's famous contemporaries include:

**Miguel Algarín** (1941–): New York-based poet of Puerto Rican descent who cofounded the Nuyorican Poets Café.

**José Rivera** (1955–): Obie Award–winning playwright and screenwriter whose screenplay for *The Motorcycle Diaries* (2004) made him the first writer of Puerto Rican descent to earn an Academy Award nomination.

**Stephen Morse** (1945–): A poet originally from Oakland, California, and heavily influenced by the Beat Generation, Morse later founded the influential poetry magazine *Juice*.

**Andy Warhol** (1928–1987): Beginning his career as a commercial illustrator, Warhol later became famous for contributions to the pop art movement in 1960s New York. He is widely recognized for his paintings of Campbell's soup cans.

**Gloria Steinem** (1934–): Steinem has been a leading feminist voice throughout the twentieth and twenty-first centuries. She advocates for women's rights and calls herself a radical feminist.

Rican," the term Nuyorican refers generally to second- and third-generation Puerto Rican artists, with a concentrated population in the Northeast United States, especially Spanish Harlem. Cruz's work helped establish the Nuyorican identity.

***Teaching and Writing in California*** Cruz moved to California in 1968, where he soon made contact with other authors. He accepted a job teaching a group of junior high school boys in a Berkeley experimental public school that same year and began work on his first major work, *Snaps* (1969). He was in California at the same time the influential Beat movement was transforming into the countercultural hippie movement, and the larger American anti–Vietnam War movement was growing. The Beat poets produced experimental writing that placed high value on stream of consciousness and performance elements and was led by poet Allen Ginsberg. Cruz remained in the California area through the end of the decade, taught a poetry workshop at the University of California at Berkeley in 1972, and served as an instructor of ethnic studies at San Francisco State College. He received a Creative Artists Program Service (CAPS) grant in 1974, through which he composed his third volume of poetry.

In 1975 Cruz married Elisa Ivette, and the couple had a son, Vitin Ajani, later that year. He became a contributing editor for *Revista Chicano Riqueña* in 1976. That same year he began an association with the San Francisco Neighborhood Arts Program, working with schools, senior citizen centers, prisons, and city festivals. The job supported him while he completed his third book, *Tropicalization* (1976). In 1979 Cruz took part in the One World Poetry Festival in Amsterdam. Cruz's second child, Rosa, was born in 1980, and in 1982 he published a collection of prose and poetry titled *By Lingual Wholes*. That same year, Cruz's first novel was published and, since the early 1980s, he has concentrated on fiction more than poetry. Drawing from a wide range of historical events and characters to explore his Puerto Rican heritage, Cruz incorporates African, Native American, and Spanish cultural motifs in both of these works.

## Works in Literary Context

***Nuyorican Poets*** More than anything else, the first generation of Nuyorican writers was one that was dominated by poets, many of whom had come out of an oral tradition and had honed their art through public readings; thus the creation of the Nuyorican Poets' Café was a natural outcome of the need to create a specific space for the performance of poetry. Among the consummate performers of Nuyorican poetry were Cruz, Tato Laviera, Miguel Piñero, and Miguel Algarín. Like his fellow poets, Cruz's initiation into poetry was through popular music and street culture; his first poems have often been considered to be jazz poetry in a bilingual mode, except that English dominated in the bilingualism and thus opened the way for his first book to be published by a mainstream publishing house, *Snaps: Poems*.

***Musical Style and Spanglish*** In *Snaps* were the themes and styles that would dominate and flourish in Cruz's subsequent books; in all of his poetry sound, music, and performance are central. He also experiments with bilingualism as oral poetry and written symbols of oral speech and he searches for identity through these sounds and symbols. His next two books were odysseys that take the reader back to Puerto Rico and primordial Indian and African music and poetry (*Mainland*, 1973) and across the United States and back to New York, where the poet finds the city transformed by its Caribbean peoples into their very own cultural home (*Tropicalization*, 1976). *By Lingual Wholes* (1982) is a consuming and total exploration of the various linguistic possibilities in the repertoire of a bilingual poet.

Like Beat poetry, Cruz's writing focuses on the oral quality of a poem, often including musical elements or switching between English and Spanish languages. He also emphasizes speech patterns by altering grammar and syntax. *Tropicalization*, for instance, uses humor and energetic language as well as more experimental structures in order to capture the spiritual side of barrio life, and *By Lingual Wholes* and *Red Beans* combine Spanish and English diction and syntax to create Spanglish, a language that also relies on the rhythm of Latin American music.

## Works in Critical Context

Critics have acknowledged Cruz's growth as a poet from *Snaps* to *Red Beans*, lauding the increasing depth of his language, humor, and imagery. His early work, and especially the snapshot technique used in *Snaps*, was derided by most reviewers as monotonous and derivative, though some approved of its unconventional form and realistic portrayals of street life. Regarding his later verse, commentators have praised both the wider thematic scope and increased stylistic experimentation, particularly Cruz's use of Spanglish, popular Latin American musical rhythms, and his handling of nature imagery and wit. Cruz's nonfiction has also been lauded for its reflections on the author's Hispanic heritage. Nonetheless, some commentators argue that Cruz's nonfiction overlooks the concerns of Hispanic women.

*Red Beans* *Publishers Weekly* called Cruz's collection of poetry a "successful expansion of a perspective born in the Caribbean into a worldview of striking vitality and importance." Anne C. Bromley at *American Book Review* says that Cruz's poems serve "public functions," explaining that "his are poems that remember, poems that declaim, poems that celebrate language as a pathway into and out of dreams." And Nicolás Kanellos faults *Red Beans* for being sometimes confusing from "a lack of deft bilingual editing and proofing" but still a "celebration" of the "blending of European, African, and American cultures that have made up the New World experience."

## Responses to Literature

1. Cruz uses a combination of Spanish and English in his poems, a language that has become known as Spanglish. Choose one poem and rewrite it entirely in English. How does the meaning and rhythm of the poem change? What is the point of incorporating two different languages in Cruz's poetry?

2. Cruz writes about different places in his work. Using his poetry, describe three different places that are significant to the writer. Does any one place become his home? Which places are positively described and which are negatively described? What role does place play in the writer's identity?

3. Write your own poem of identity. Choose two different places that are significant to you and describe them in detail, using as many senses as you can. What colors, sounds, and smells are associated with those places? How do they help contribute to your personal identity?

BIBLIOGRAPHY

**Books**

Dick, Bruce Allen. *A Poet's Truth: Conversations with Latino/Latina Poets*. Tucson: University of Arizona Press, 2003.

---

### COMMON HUMAN EXPERIENCE

Cruz focuses on personal identity specifically as related to ethnicity in America. Other texts that examine ethnicity include:

*The Autobiography of Malcolm X* (1965), a biography by Alex Haley. Haley compiled this narrative after a series of conversations with American political activist and Nation of Islam leader Malcolm X. Malcolm X espoused aggressive political action to restore rights to African Americans in the civil rights movement of the 1960s.
*The House on Mango Street* (1984), a novel by Sandra Cisneros. Mexican American writer Cisneros tells the story of a girl named Esperanza (Spanish for "hope") who lives in a poor section of Chicago.
*Woman Warrior: Memoirs of a Girlhood Among Ghosts* (1976), a memoir by Maxine Hong Kingston. Author Kingston explores her identity as a Chinese American woman through many different narrative styles, including autobiography, folklore, and imaginative storytelling.
*The Bluest Eye* (1970), a novel by Toni Morrison. This novel, Morrison's first, tells the tale of Pecola, a poor black girl growing up in the Depression-era Midwest.

---

Ickstadt, Heinz, ed. *Crossing Borders: Inter- and Intra-Cultural Exchanges in a Multicultural Society*. Berlin: Peter Lang, 1997.

Sheppard, Walt. "An Interview with Clarence Major and Victor Hernández Cruz." In *New Black Voices*. Edited by Abraham Chapman. New York: New American Library, 1972, pp. 545–552.

**Periodicals**

"A Review of *Red Beans*." *Publishers Weekly* 238, no. 40 (1991): 99.

Aparicio, Frances R. "Salsa, Maracas, and Baile: Latin Popular Music in the Poetry of Victor Hernández Cruz." *MELUS* 16, no. 1 (1989–1990): 43–58.

Bromely, Anne C. "The Poetics of Migration." *American Book Review* 13, no. 6 (1992): 26–27.

Eserrich, Carmelo. "Home and the Ruins of Language: Victor Hernández Cruz and Miguel Algarín's Nuyorican Poetry." *MELUS* 23, no. 3 (1998): 43–56.

Kanellos, Nicolás. "A Review of *Red Beans*." *Americas Review* 20, no. 1 (1992): 87.

Rosa, Victor. "Interview with Victor Hernández Cruz." *Bilingual Review* 2 (1975): 281–87.

Wallenstein, Barry. "The Poet in New York: Victor Hernández Cruz." *Bilingual Review* 1 (1974): 312–319.

**Web sites**

Poets.org site. *Victor Hernández Cruz.* Retrieved September 15, 2008, from http:www.poets.org/ poet.php/prmPID/681.

# ⊛ Countee Cullen

BORN: *1903, Louisville, Kentucky*

DIED: *1946, New York, New York*

NATIONALITY: *American*

GENRE: *Poetry*

MAJOR WORKS:

*Color* (1925)

*Copper Sun* (1927)

*The Ballad of the Brown Girl* (1927)

*The Black Christ and Other Poems* (1929)

*One Way to Heaven* (1932)

## Overview

Countee Cullen was one of the foremost poets of the Harlem Renaissance, a cultural movement of unprecedented creative achievement among black American writers, musicians, and artists centered in the Harlem section of New York City during the 1920s. While Cullen strove to establish himself as the author of romantic poetry on such universal topics as love and death, he also wrote numerous poems treating contemporary racial issues, and it is for these that he is best remembered.

## Works in Biographical and Historical Context

***Adoption and Introduction to American Racial Politics*** Countee LeRoy Cullen was born on May 30, 1903. Little is known about Cullen before his adoption in 1918. Even his place of birth is uncertain, though it is generally considered to be Louisville, Kentucky. The boy's mother, Elizabeth Lucas, named him Countee LeRoy Porter and then passed him over to his grandmother, who looked after him until her death. The fifteen-year-old Countee Porter was then adopted by a minister and his wife, Frederick and Carolyn Cullen of the Salem Methodist Episcopal Church in Harlem.

In his adopted father's home, Cullen came under the influences that would shape his poetry, for the Salem Methodist Episcopal Church was a nerve center of local action. Here he heard discussions about racial injustice and the many other problems concerning the black community. His adopted father, Reverend Cullen, was an active member of the Harlem chapter of the National Association for the Advancement of Colored People (NAACP) and later served as its chapter president.

***Writing during the Harlem Renaissance*** Already writing some poetry before being adopted, Cullen was

Countee Cullen   *Cullen, Countee, photograph by Carl Van Vechten. Reproduced by permission of the Carl Van Vechten Trust.*

encouraged to develop his talent. At the largely white De Witt Clinton High School in New York he joined the local poetry group. He also edited the school magazine, which in 1921 published his poem "I Have a Rendezvous with Life." He graduated from high school in 1922.

Cullen won writing prizes during college years, including awards for his 1923 *Ballad of the Brown Girl*. He graduated with a BA from New York University, was accepted to a master's degree program at Harvard, and had his first book of poems, *Color*, published by the well-known trade publisher Harper & Row. Many of Cullen's best-known poems appeared in *Color*. The book collects seventy-three poems arranged in three sections—"Color," "Epitaphs," and "Varia"—and it deals with the major themes that were to dominate his work. The theme of racial injustice is movingly expressed in such poems as "Incident" and "Atlantic City Waiter." "Atlantic City Waiter" also emphasized African origins and a romantic nostalgia for the old days in Africa, a theme repeated in "Heritage" and many other poems in *Color*. Cullen enjoyed great success with *Color*, which received excellent reviews and was awarded the Harmon Foundation's first gold medal for literature two years later.

After completing his master's degree from Harvard in 1926, Cullen worked as assistant editor at *Opportunity* magazine, for which he wrote a column called "The Dark Tower." In 1928 he won a Guggenheim Fellowship, allowing him to travel, and he spent much of the next six years in France. Prior to leaving, he married Nina Du Bois, the daughter of W. E. B. Du Bois, a well-known leader of the African American intellectual community. The wedding was Harlem's social event of the year, though the marriage failed almost immediately. Cullen had a happier second marriage, in 1940, to Ida Robertson.

By the end of the 1920s, Cullen published three more poetry collections, *The Ballad of the Brown Girl* (1927), *Copper Sun* (1927), and *The Black Christ and Other Poems* (1929). Although he later published several more collections, Cullen is remembered for these earlier works.

Cullen's writing emerged during the Harlem Renaissance, a period that grew out of the frustrated expectations the black community experienced following World War I. World War I (1914–1918) produced over forty million casualties during trench warfare mostly occurring in Europe and resulted in large-scale disillusionment with technology and the idea of progress. Black soldiers who had risked their lives in the war could not even find jobs when they returned home. They thronged the cities looking for work, and the injustice was expressed by the intellectuals, many of whom voiced their protest through their art. This came hand in hand with the expansion of middle-class black communities in the northern part of the country, especially in New York City. This led to the development of music, literature, dance, and art that arose from distinctly African-American roots. Notable figures of the Harlem Renaissance include activist Du Bois, author Zora Neale Hurston, musician Duke Ellington, and singer Billie Holiday. The artistic achievements of members of the Harlem Renaissance extended far beyond their own neighborhood, shaping the development of literature and music in mainstream American culture throughout much of the twentieth century.

***Writing for Children and Early Death*** In 1932 Cullen published his only novel, *One Way to Heaven*, but he was more successful with his stories for children. After returning from France in 1934, he taught at Frederick Douglass Junior High School in New York, and to help inspire sound values in young people he wrote two collections of stories: *The Lost Zoo* (1940) and *My Lives and How I Lost Them* (1942). Cullen had also been trying his hand at writing for the theater; his most noted effort being the musical "St. Louis Woman," based on fellow writer Arna Bontemps's first novel. Objections raised about the work being demeaning to blacks delayed the show's production, and Cullen never lived to see it staged. He died of uremic poisoning in New York on January 9, 1946, three months before the show opened in New York.

---

## LITERARY AND HISTORICAL CONTEMPORARIES

Countee Cullen's famous contemporaries include:

**Jessie Redmon Fauset** (1882–1961): One of the most prominent artists during the Harlem Renaissance, Fauset was a novelist, poet, and editor. She edited the NAACP's influential magazine, the *Crisis*.

**Langston Hughes** (1902–1967): A Harlem Renaissance poet, novelist, playwright, and essayist, Hughes is best known for poems like "A Dream Deferred" (1951).

**Marcus Garvey** (1887–1940): Garvey was a popular African American leader who encouraged African Americans to return to Africa.

**F. Scott Fitzgerald** (1896–1940): Fitzgerald was an American novelist who personified the post–World War I "Lost Generation." His most famous work is *The Great Gatsby* (1925).

**Pablo Picasso** (1881–1973): A Spanish artist known for his experimental style, Picasso was influential in non-representational art such as the cubist movement.

---

## Works in Literary Context

Cullen produced most of his writing during a time when many African-American artists were considering how race should or should not influence art. Cullen's work both participated in a new racial artistic identity and at the same time challenged it by following traditional literary forms.

***Race Writing and the Harlem Renaissance*** Believing that good literature transcends race, Cullen stated that he wanted to be recognized as a poet, not a "Negro poet." Nevertheless, critics have asserted that he often seemed uncertain about the purpose of his poetry. As Alan R. Shucard has suggested, Cullen often appeared "to vacillate between playing the pure aesthete and the racial spokesman." Cullen himself reflected in an interview,

> In spite of myself ... I find that I am actuated by a strong sense of race consciousness. This grows upon me, I find, as I grow older, and although I struggle against it, it colors my writing, I fear, in spite of everything I can do. His success in a largely white culture at school and university made him resent being later classified by color. This was his theme in his well-known poem "Yet Do I Marvel": "Yet do I marvel at this curious thing / To make a poet black, and bid him sing!"

***Traditional Forms of Poetry*** Cullen believed that poetry consisted of "lofty thoughts beautifully expressed," and he preferred poetic forms characterized by dignity and control. He wrote a number of sonnets and used quatrains, couplets, and conventional rhyme, frequently incorporating religious

## COMMON HUMAN EXPERIENCE

Cullen focuses on ways in which racial identity affects, or does not affect, an individual's life. Other texts that consider racial identity are:

*Incidents in the Life of a Slave Girl* (1861), a memoir by Harriet Jacobs. Written under the pseudonym Linda Brent, this is the most studied American female slave narrative.

*The Heart of Darkness* (1902), a novella by Joseph Conrad. This canonized story describes a boat voyage into the Congo and is highly symbolic of European colonizing and stereotypical attitudes toward Africa.

*Black Like Me* (1961), a nonfiction work by John Howard Griffin. Journalist Griffin documents the sharp contrast between how he is treated as a white man and how he is treated as a black man (attained through artificial skin darkening), in communities throughout the American South in the early years of civil rights movement.

*Beloved* (1987), a novel by Toni Morrison. This Pulitzer Prize–winning work recounts the difficult choice an ex-slave mother faces when her children might be recaptured into bondage.

imagery and classical allusions. While some critics have praised his skill at traditional versification, others suggest that Cullen's style was not suited to the treatment of contemporary racial issues and that his adherence to conventional forms resulted in poems that are insincere and unconvincing. Despite the controversy surrounding his traditional poetic style and his ambivalence toward racial subject matter in art, Cullen remains an important figure in black American literature.

Because Cullen was determined to bridge the gap between black and white writers, he did not find it inconsistent to take the English poet John Keats as his model. The "Epitaphs" section of *Color* contains poems on Keats as well as on the nineteenth-century African American writer Paul Laurence Dunbar, while the "Varia" section includes the well-known poem "To John Keats, Poet. At Springtime."

### Works in Critical Context

Not until Houston A. Baker Jr.'s short book on Cullen's work, *A Many-Colored Coat of Dreams: The Poetry of Countee Cullen* (1974), was there really a sustained and sound study of the body of Cullen's poetry. In the 1920s, black and white critics alike had tended to heap uncritical praise on him, though there had been a growing admission, as his collections came out over time, that he was not growing as a poet. If the early critics were too gentle with Cullen for nonpoetic reasons, for nonpoetic reasons, too, the African American critics of the 1960s were too harsh with him. Creating the militant new black aesthetic of the 1960s, and conditioned by it, Don

Lee (Haki Madhubuti) and others overlooked the exploration of the racial theme in Cullen, overlooked the protest and the pain. Looking for a direct political message in Cullen but not finding it, they condemned Cullen as a sort of racial pacifist. Lee even referred to him as "a well-known poet of the Harlem Renaissance period [who] refused to acknowledge that he was a 'negro' or Black poet."

*"The Black Christ"* While most critics prefer Cullen's more praised poems like "Heritage," Quiana Whitted gives a sustained reading of "The Black Christ" saying that Cullen "modernizes Christ's resurrection" within the context of a lynching. She writes,

Of ultimate importance to Cullen, and arguably to the legions of black American writers and artists who take up the black Christ metaphor, is the *affect* of terror and the way in which black communities of faith negotiate the questions of moral evil and diving justice that are central to the Book of Job.

*Color* Cullen's first collection of poems, *Color*, was extremely well received by contemporary critics and remained one of his greatest artistic achievements. Prominent Harlem Renaissance voice Alain Locke in 1926 called Cullen "a genius," stating that the collection comes out of the "intimate emotional experience of race" but at the same time transcends race by appealing to "the universally human moods of life." In 1963, Beulah Reimherr argues that race is actually quite central to Cullen's work, stating that *Color* is "impregnated with race consciousness" and that fully one-third of the poems address racial issues directly. Michael Lomax, in 1987, proposes a kind of middle ground regarding race and Cullen's work; he contends that Cullen's poetry deals with race in a similarly divided fashion as Cullen did in his own life. Lomax writes that "the volume as a whole and several poems in particular are haunted by the unresolved conflict of Cullen's perception of himself as simultaneously a black man and a culturally assimilated ... Westerner."

### Responses to Literature

1. How does Cullen perceive racial identity? What is its influence on the voices in his poems? How are his views similar to or different from current perspectives on race?

2. Read a poem from two other Harlem Renaissance writers, such as Langston Hughes, Claude McKay, or Jessie Redmon Fauset. Compare the form and content of those poems to one of Cullen's poems. How are the poems similar or different? How does each writer think of issues like art and race?

3. Cullen did not wish to be remembered as a black poet but rather as simply a poet. For a time, this seems to have negatively influenced his legacy among African Americans, who saw him as denying his racial identity. In your opinion, should writers strive to embrace their ethnic or cultural identity or should they instead concentrate on universal themes that extend beyond race or culture? What are the inherent risks with each approach?

BIBLIOGRAPHY

**Books**

Baker, Houston A., Jr. *A Many-Colored Coat of Dreams: The Poetry of Countee Cullen*. Detroit: Broadside Press, 1974.

Ferguson, Blanche E. *Countee Cullen and the Negro Renaissance*. New York: Dodd, 1966.

Hutchinson, George, ed. *The Cambridge Companion to the Harlem Renaissance*. Cambridge: Cambridge University Press, 2007.

Lomax, Michael. "Countee Cullen: A Key to the Puzzle." In *The Harlem Renaissance Re-examined*. New York: AMS Press, 1987.

Shucard, Alan. *Countee Cullen*. Boston: Twayne, 1984.

Tarver, Australia, and Paula C. Barnes, eds. *New Voices on the Harlem Renaissance: Essays on Race, Gender, and Literary Discourse*. Madison, N.J.: Fairleigh Dickinson University Press, 2005.

Turner, Darwin T. *In a Minor Chord: Three Afro-American Writers and Their Search for Identity*. Carbondale: Southern Illinois University Press, 1971.

**Periodicals**

Dorsey, David F. "Countee Cullen's Use of Greek Mythology." *College Language Association Journal* 13 (1970): 68–77.

Kuenz, Jane. "Modernism, Mass Culture, and the Harlem Renaissance: The Case of Countee Cullen." *Modernism/Modernity* 14, no. 3 (2007): 507–515.

Locke, Alain. "*Color*: A Review." *Opportunity* 4, no. 37 (January 1926): 14–15.

Reimherr, Beulah. "Race Consciousness in Countee Cullen's Poetry." *Susquehanna University Studies* 7, no. 2 (1963): 65–82.

Whitted, Quiana. "In My Flesh Shall I See God: Ritual Violence and Racial Redemption in 'The Black Christ.'" *African American Review* 38, no. 3 (2004): 379–393.

**Web sites**

Poets.org site. *Countee Cullen*. Retrieved September 15, 2008, from http://www.poets.org/poet.php/prmPID/55.

# ✹ E. E. Cummings

BORN: *1894, Cambridge, Massachusetts*

DIED: *1962, North Conway, New Hampshire*

NATIONALITY: *American*

GENRE: *Poetry, nonfiction*

MAJOR WORKS:

*The Enormous Room* (1922)

*Tulips and Chimneys* (1923)

E. E. cummings  *1938, photograph. AP Images.*

## Overview

E. E. (Edward Estlin) Cummings is a poet known to many readers as e. e. cummings, and is remembered for his innovative, playful spirit, his celebration of love and nature, his focus on the primacy of the individual and freedom of expression, and for his treatment of the themes, in his own words, of "ecstasy and anguish, being and becoming; the immortality of the creative imagination and the indomitability of the human spirit."

## Works in Biographical and Historical Context

*Artistic Youth and Harvard Education*  Cummings grew up in Cambridge, Massachusetts, where his father was a sociology professor at Harvard and a noted Unitarian clergyman. Demonstrating a strong interest in poetry and art from an early age, Cummings enjoyed the full support and encouragement of his parents. He attended Harvard from 1911 to 1915, studying literature and writing. He eventually joined the editorial board of the *Harvard Monthly*, a college literary magazine, where he worked with his close friends S. Foster Damon and John Dos Passos. In his senior year he became fascinated by avant-garde art, modernism, and cubism, an interest reflected in his graduation dissertation, "The New Art." In this paper, Cummings extolled modernism as practiced by Gertrude Stein, Ezra Pound, Amy Lowell, and Pablo Picasso. He also began incorporating elements of these styles into his own poetry and paintings. His first published poems appeared in the anthology *Eight Harvard Poets* in 1917. These pieces feature experimental verse forms and the lower-case personal pronoun "i"—symbolizing both the humbleness and the uniqueness of the individual— that became his trademark. The copyeditor of the book, however, mistook Cummings's intentions as typographical errors and made "corrections."

### World War I Service

In 1917, Cummings moved to New York, was employed very briefly at a mail-order book company, and soon began working full-time on his poetry and art. With World War I raging in Europe, he volunteered for the French-based Norton-Harjes Ambulance Service. World War I produced over forty million casualties during trench-warfare mostly occurring in Europe, and resulted in large-scale disillusionment with technology and the idea of progress. Cummings spent time in Paris upon his arrival and was completely charmed by the city's bohemian atmosphere and abundance of art and artists. He was particularly impressed by the sketches of Pablo Picasso, whose cubist techniques later helped shape much of his own work.

Because of a misunderstanding involving his disregard of regulations and his attempts to outwit the wartime censors in his letters home, Cummings spent four months in an internment camp in Normandy on suspicion of treason, an experience documented in his prose work *The Enormous Room* (1922). Making use of his contacts in government, Cummings's father was able to secure his son's release. Cummings was drafted shortly after he returned to New York in 1918 and spent about a year at Camp Danvers, Massachusetts. Beginning around this time, Cummings, with the knowledge and approval of his friend Schofield Thayer, had an affair with Schofield's wife Elaine. Cummings's daughter Nancy was born in 1919, but she was given Thayer's name. Cummings and Elaine Thayer married in 1924, at which time Cummings legally adopted Nancy. The marriage ended in divorce shortly thereafter.

### European Travels and Growing Fame

During the 1920s and 1930s, he traveled widely in Europe, alternately living in Paris and New York, and developed parallel careers as a poet and painter. Politically liberal and with leftist leanings, Cummings visited the Soviet Union in 1931 to find out how the system of government subsidy for art functioned there. *Eimi* (1933), an expanded version of his travel diary, expresses his profound disappointment in its indictment of the regimentation and lack of personal and artistic freedom he encountered. From that time, Cummings abandoned his liberal political views and social circle and became an embittered, reactionary conservative on social and political issues. He continued to write prolifically and reached the height of his popularity during the 1940s and 1950s, giving poetry readings to college audiences across the United States until his death in 1962.

### Unique Technique

Cummings's innovative and controversial verse places him among the most popular and widely anthologized poets of the twentieth century. While linked early in his career with the Modernist movement, he wrote poems with themes that more closely resemble the works of the New England Transcendentalists and English Romantics. Rejecting what he perceived as the small-mindedness of "mostpeople," Cummings's work celebrates the individual, as well as erotic and familial love. Conformity, mass psychology, and snobbery were frequent targets of his humorous and sometimes scathing satires.

Cummings was also a painter and a student of such modernist art forms as cubism, an early twentieth-century avant-garde art form that depicts images angularly and from multiple perspectives. Pablo Picasso was an innovator of cubism, and he greatly influenced Cummings's work. Cummings's knowledge of the visual arts led him to experiment with punctuation, idiomatic speech, compressed words, dislocated syntax, unusual typography, line division, and capitalization to capture the particulars of a single movement or moment in time. Discussing Cummings's technique, critic Randall Jarrell explained:

> Cummings is a very great expert in all these, so to speak, illegal syntactical devices: his misuse of parts of speech, his use of negative prefixes, his word-coining, his systematic relation of words that grammar and syntax don't permit us to relate—all this makes him a magical bootlegger or moonshiner of language, one who intoxicates us on a clear liquor no government has legalized with its stamp.

## Works in Literary Context

### Modernism

Modernist art and writing became popular in Europe and America between 1910 and 1920. Concerned with the individual's role within a society that was increasingly technological and often destructive, modernist writers included T. S. Eliot and Ezra Pound. Like other modernist poets, Cummings was well-schooled in traditional verse but then chose to experiment with nontraditional styles. Although more playful in his language than many other modernists, Cummings was one of the earliest modern poets to introduce typographical eccentricities into writing. His linguistic experimentation was in fact painstakingly measured to control sound—pacing, syllable stress, juncture—and sight.

The strong visual character of Cummings's writing owes much to his parallel development as a painter. Indeed, his alteration of syntax derived from the advances in contemporary European visual art, particularly cubism. M. L. Rosenthal wrote in *The Modern Poets: A Critical Introduction*: "The chief effect of Cummings' jugglery with syntax, grammar, and diction was to blow open otherwise trite and bathetic motifs. ... He succeeded masterfully in splitting the atom of the cute commonplace."

### Individualism and Romanticism

The American Romantic period occurred during the nineteenth century and involved writers such as Ralph Waldo Emerson and Nathaniel Hawthorne. To many Romantic writers, all truth, beauty, and transcendence are attached to the individual rather than an institution, such as a government or a church. However modern the stimulus for and the superficial appearance of his writing may have been, much of Cummings's work arises from this nineteenth-century romantic reverence for natural order over man-made order, for intuition and imagination over routine-grounded perception. He echoes these romantic ideals in his poems as his attacks on concepts like the mass mind, conventional patterns of thought, and society's restrictions on free expression, were born of his strong commitment to the individual. In the "nonlectures" he delivered at Harvard University Cummings explained his position: "So far as I am concerned, poetry and every other art was, is, and forever will be strictly and distinctly a question of individuality."

"Cummings' lifelong belief," Bernard Dekle stated in *Profiles of Modern American Authors*, "was a simple faith in the miracle of man's individuality. Much of his literary effort was directed against what he considered the principal enemies of this individuality—mass thought, group conformity, and commercialism." For this reason, Cummings satirized what he called "mostpeople"—that is, the herd mentality found in modern society.

## Works in Critical Context

Critical opinion of Cummings's poems is markedly divided. Beginning with *Tulips and Chimneys*, reviewers described Cummings's style as eccentric and self-indulgent, designed to call attention to itself rather than to elucidate themes. Some critics also objected to Cummings's explicit treatment of sexuality, while others labeled his depictions of society's hypocrisy and banality elitist. When his *Collected Poems* were published in 1938, Cummings's sharp satires caused some reviewers to call him a misanthrope. His later, more conservative poetry came under attack for anti-Semitism, a charge that is still debated.

Critics have noted, too, that Cummings's style did not change or develop much throughout his career. Some commentators speculate that Cummings found a style early on that suited him and simply continued with it; others, however, have faulted the author for insufficient artistic growth. For example, many critics censured *50 Poems*, accusing Cummings of relying too much on formulaic writing and habitual stylistic mannerisms. A group of scholars posited that Cummings's verbal experimentation and idiosyncratic arrangement of text actually draw readers' attention from the poetry itself.

Despite these negative assessments, Cummings remains an extremely popular poet, and his poems are widely anthologized. By the time of his death in 1962, Cummings held a prominent position in twentieth-century poetry. John Logan in *Modern American Poetry: Essays in Criticism* (1970) called him "one of the greatest lyric poets in our language." Stanley Edgar Hyman wrote in *Standards: A Chronicle of Books for Our Time* (1966): "Cummings has written at least a dozen poems that seem to me matchless.

## LITERARY AND HISTORICAL CONTEMPORARIES

E. E. Cummings' famous contemporaries include:

**Jeannette Rankin** (1880–1973): In 1916, Rankin became the first woman elected to the U.S. Congress, serving as the representative from Montana. She was a leading peace activist and suffragist and helped pass the Nineteenth Amendment, securing women's right to vote, in 1920.

**Pablo Picasso** (1881–1973): A Spanish artist known for his experimental style, Picasso was influential in non-representational art such as the Cubist movement.

**Ernest Hemingway** (1899–1961): A member of the "Lost Generation," Hemingway was a writer known for his sparse language and masculine subject-matter. He is best remembered for novels like *The Sun Also Rises* (1926) and *For Whom the Bell Tolls* (1940).

**Gertrude Stein** (1874–1946): An expatriate in Paris, Stein was an American writer and supporter of the arts who was part of the avant-garde community. She hosted an artistic "salon," attended by visual and literary artists, and influenced modernist writing.

**John Dos Passos** (1896–1970): Friends with Cummings, Dos Passos was an experimental American novelist and playwright. He lived in France for a time, served in World War I, and is known for his novel *Manhattan Transfer* (1925).

Three are among the great love poems of our time or any time."

*"anyone lived in a pretty how town"* Cummings's famous poem details the generic lives of people in a generic town, using the progress of the seasons to represent the passage of time. Cummings writes: "Women and men (both little and small) / cared for anyone not at all / they sowed their isn't they reaped their same / sun moon stars rain." B. J. Hunt explains that, although the rhythm of the poem is light, the subject matter is considerably darker. He writes:

> On one hand, the playful rhythm and sound complement nature's sequences where life cycles rotate throughout the nine stanzas like a merry-go-round, life on a proverbial fast-paced playground. Masked, however, is life's monotony and death's certainty as the four-line stanzas, mostly tetrameters that mirror the four seasons, lead, perhaps, to an immutable certainty: everyone dies.

## Responses to Literature

1. Read two E. E. Cummings poems silently. Then read them aloud. What differences in meaning do you

## COMMON HUMAN EXPERIENCE

Cummings is known for his unusual use of syntax and positioning of words on the page. Here are some other works that use similar techniques:

*Alice's Adventures in Wonderland* (1865), a children's book by Lewis Carroll. In this classic tale, Carroll uses wordplay, creative typography, and puzzles to tell the story of a little girl and her curious journey down a rabbit-hole.

*Winnie-the-Pooh* (1926), a story collection by A. A. Milne. The book that launched one of the most beloved literary characters of all time, *Winnie-the-Pooh* features not only iconic illustrations by Ernest H. Shepard but also words that move across the page as a reflection of the whimsical tales.

*Montage of a Dream Deferred* (1951), a poetry collection by Langston Hughes. In this collection, Hughes uses the rhythms and sounds of jazz to shape his short, thematically linked poems about life in Harlem.

"I Have No Mouth, and I Must Scream" (1967), a short story by Harlan Ellison. In this Hugo Award-winning story, Ellison uses not only unusual text formations but also machine code to convey the frightening tale of the last five human survivors of a worldwide war, who find themselves at the mercy of a powerful, sentient computer that tortures them psychologically for its own enjoyment.

notice? How did hearing the rhythm of the poem add to its meaning?

2. Choose two Cummings poems about love. Compare them to another, more traditional love poem, such as a Shakespeare sonnet or one from Elizabeth Barrett Browning's "Sonnets from the Portuguese." Find similarities in both the poems' theme and style. How does Cummings's style influence the idea of romantic love?

3. With one other person, choose a Cummings poem and draw a picture of the images in the poem. Compare the two drawings. What different items does each drawing emphasize? What visual aspects are present in the poem? How did Cummings's interest in art influence his poem?

### BIBLIOGRAPHY

**Books**

Dekle, Bernard. *Profiles of Modern American Authors.* Rutland, Vt.: Chas. E. Tuttle, 1969.

Hyman, Stanley Edgar. *Standards: A Chronicle of Books for Our Time.* New York: Horizon, 1966.

Jarrell, Randall. *The Third Book of Criticism.* New York: Farrar, Straus & Giroux, 1969.

Kennedy, Richard S. *Dreams in the Mirror: A Biography of E. E. Cummings.* New York: Liveright, 1980.

———. *E. E. Cummings Revisited.* New York: Twayne, 1994.

Mattson, Francis O. *E. E. Cummings @ 100: With a Checklist of the Exhibition.* New York: New York Public Library, 1994.

Mazzaro, Jerome. *Modern American Poetry: Essays in Criticism.* New York: McKay, 1970.

Rosenthal, M. L. *The Modern Poets: A Critical Introduction.* New York: Oxford University Press, 1960.

**Periodicals**

Friedman, Norman. "E. E. Cummings and the Modernist Tradition." *Forum (Houston)* 3, no.10 (1962): 39–46.

Hunt, B. J. "Cumming's 'Anyone Lived in a Pretty How Town'." *Explicator* 64, no. 4 (2006): 226–228.

## ✺ Michael Cunningham

BORN: *1952, Cincinnati, Ohio*

NATIONALITY: *American*

GENRE: *Fiction*

MAJOR WORKS:
*A Home at the End of the World* (1990)
*The Hours* (1998)

### Overview

Michael Cunningham is an author whose work portrays the struggles of family life, and who is best known for his Pulitzer Prize–winning novel *The Hours*, a unique reimagining of Virginia Woolf's 1925 novel *Mrs. Dalloway* featuring the author herself as one of the main characters.

### Works in Biographical and Historical Context

***From Painting to Writing*** Cunningham was born on November 6, 1952, in Cincinnati, Ohio, to Don and Dorothy Cunningham. Don Cunningham's advertising career led the family to make several moves, including a four-year residence in Germany, before they ultimately settled in Pasadena, California, when Cunningham was ten. In his teenage years Cunningham began to develop an interest in serious literature, reading works by Virginia Woolf and T. S. Eliot. In 1972 he entered Stanford University, intending to study painting but eventually focusing on literature courses. He graduated from Stanford in 1976 with a degree in English. Two years later he

Michael Cunningham    *Cunningham, Michael, photograph. AP Images.*

entered the University of Iowa Writer's Workshop, graduating with a master of fine arts degree in 1980. At the University of Iowa, Cunningham was able to study with talented writers and teachers, including novelist Hilma Wolitzer, and to work at refining his style. While in the program, he began to submit stories and quickly had several accepted for publication in periodicals such as *Atlantic Monthly*, *Paris Review*, and *Redbook*.

After leaving the University of Iowa in 1980, Cunningham accepted a one-year residency at the Province-town Fine Arts Work Center; after this residency he began working in New York City for the Carnegie Corporation, where he wrote annual reports and press releases. During the early 1980s he became frustrated because his initial success had not endured, and finding publishers for his material was no longer as easy as it had been a few years before. Intent upon finishing a novel before he reached the age of thirty, Cunningham wrote his first novel, *Golden States* (1984), a work that he has referred to as "a journeyman effort."

### Novels about Family Establish a Literary Reputation

Cunningham's writing focuses on the family unit, from traditional to radical, and includes deaths, divorces,

homosexuality, adultery, and suicide. The beginnings of Cunningham's central literary concerns can be seen in his early stories. His first published story, "Cleaving" (1981), tells the story of Bobby, a gay man who has just ended one relationship and unsuccessfully attempts to begin a new one with a son he has never met. In "Bedrock" (1981), a recently divorced man retreats to his parents' house to heal, only to be encouraged to reengage in life again. In each of these early stories the importance of family to individuals serves as the focal point.

*Golden States* is a coming-of-age story about a young boy who feels it is his duty to protect his mother and sisters after the family has been abandoned by father-figures. Published in 1990, *A Home at the End of the World* chronicles several decades and various incarnations of family life, this time focusing on two friends and the life they create together.

As Cunningham moved on to his third novel, he imagined a trajectory of a broadening scope in the progression of his works. He explained in an interview with Philip Gambone that he views *Golden States* as the story of a single character, while *A Home at the End of the World* is "a big step ... in terms of scale" because it is "about more lives. It's a bigger picture." He called his third novel, *Flesh and Blood* (1995), "another step forward along those lines" because of its magnitude. Certainly, in its attempt to chronicle three generations of a single Greek American family over a hundred-year period, *Flesh and Blood* became Cunningham's most ambitious work and perhaps his most extensive examination of the essence of American families.

Seeming to depart from the subject matter of his first three novels, Cunningham turned to one of his literary heroes, Woolf, for his next work. Cunningham's lifelong fascination with Woolf began as teenage admiration but eventually developed into a careful study of her work. At one point he planned to write a biography of the author, and he has written an introduction to a 2000 edition of her first novel, *The Voyage Out* (1915). His admiration most clearly reveals itself, however, in his novel *The Hours*, which was Woolf's initial title for her novel *Mrs. Dalloway*. Cunningham's novel serves as an homage to Woolf and her famous work but also as a larger meditation on suicide and living. The narrative follows three women through a single day of their lives. One of these characters is Woolf herself, depicted in the prologue to the novel on the 1941 day when she filled her pockets with stones and walked into a river, ending her life out of the fear of both artistic failure and madness. Response to *The Hours* was enthusiastic. It was awarded the Pulitzer Prize and the PEN/Faulkner Award in 1999 and became an Oscar-winning Hollywood film in 2002.

### Gay Activism and Literary Reputation

Throughout the 1980s and most of the 1990s, Cunningham was involved in gay activist politics ranging from publishing confrontational pieces in *The New York Times* and *Mother*

# LITERARY AND HISTORICAL CONTEMPORARIES

Cunningham's famous contemporaries include:

**William Jefferson Clinton** (1946–): The forty-second president of the United States, Bill Clinton served two terms highlighted by a balanced federal budget and the creation of the Digital Millennium Copyright Act.

**Edmund White** (1940–): Professor, critic, and novelist, White is known for writing *A Boy's Own Story* (1982), one of the first American "coming out" stories in which he describes how his main character comes to terms with his own homosexuality.

**Pat Conroy** (1945–): Conroy is one of the most successful contemporary Southern writers, best known for his novels *The Prince of Tides* (1986) and *The Great Santini* (1976).

**Erica Jong** (1942–): Author of the feminist landmark novel *Fear of Flying* (1973), Jong has been an outspoken member of second and third wave women's liberation movements.

**Stephen Colbert** (1964–): South Carolina native known for his satirical news television show *The Colbert Report*.

*Jones* to participating in radical political demonstrations arguing for more government funding for AIDS research. He chained himself to a White House gate and later was arrested for interrupting a speech by President George H. W. Bush. He helped to engineer an on-air disturbance of the *MacNeil/Lehrer News Hour* in 1991. Both the gay content of his work and his personal activism overshadowed Cunningham's early work, and he rarely transcended this designation as a gay writer.

However, during the mid 1990s Cunningham's reception began to change. For example, Richard Eder in the *Los Angeles Times* called Cunningham "perhaps the most brilliant of the many novelists who have dealt with gay themes over the past dozen years, and one of our very best writers, in any case, on any theme." Cunningham won the 1999 Pulitzer Prize in fiction for *The Hours*. He has taught creative writing at Brooklyn College and continues to write in his studio in Greenwich Village.

## Works in Literary Context

*The Meaning of Family*  Many writers challenge the ideals that have come to define America—ideals such as equal opportunity for all and unlimited potential for wealth. At the heart of the American persona is the image of a nuclear family, consisting of two heterosexual, middle class, Caucasian parents living with their children in a suburban environment. In this portrait, the mother generally stays home to raise the children while the father goes out to work. This "perfect" family has been taken apart by many artists in order to show that no family is perfect, and that families can appear in many different forms. Cunningham's novels present many different kinds of alternative families, from those without fathers, to those with members dying of AIDS, to those without any members actually related to each other. For instance, *A Home at the End of the World* follows two boyhood friends as they create various types of families amidst homosexual and heterosexual relationships, AIDS, childbirth, and abandonment. *Flesh and Blood* further questions the family structure as the Stassos family is an all-American family in appearance only. In reality the husband's selfishness slowly tears the family apart, leaving the children to find lives separate from each other. In the end, Cunningham's writing focuses on the love and support a family unit can offer its members despite the always tenuous nature of relationships.

*Homosexuality in Fiction and Coming Out Stories*  While homosexual relationships have been portrayed in literature since the earliest Greek texts, the late twentieth-century fight for gay rights in the U.S. has created many more fictional representations of homosexuality. The term "coming out" refers to the process by which a gay individual comes to recognize his or her difference and then expresses that homosexual identity to family and community. Cunningham's novels portray a variety of coming out stories, some more primary to the main plotline than others. Critic Tim Gauthier mentions that in general, Cunningham tackles different—and controversial—topics powerfully, and "the manner in which Cunningham subtly inserts the many references to homosexuality has an effortless, natural quality." He continues, "This is no longer the 'fearful closet' novel of the 1960s nor the 'defiant ghetto' writing of the 1970s, rather it is fiction that treats homosexuality ... as just one subject among many." Gauthier also noted that Cunningham's characters are not just mere representations in a story; they are also very powerful ones. They have a "nagging suspicion that they are not living the lives they should be, that they are engaged in acts of 'impersonation' that belittle their true selfhood."

## Works in Critical Context

Cunningham's writing received considerable critical recognition before he achieved popular success. His early works were praised for their careful writing style and fully developed characters, and Cunningham rarely received many negative reviews despite slow sales. About his second book, *A Home at the End of the World*, for instance, *Nation*'s David Kaufman noted the author's "exquisite way with words" and declared, "This is quite simply one of those rare novels imbued with graceful insights on every page." A review of *Flesh and Blood* by Paul Burston included the claim that "Michael Cunningham is one of the most gifted writers around."

***The Hours*** Cunningham's deep connection to Virginia Woolf's novel *Mrs. Dalloway* and Woolf's tragic life led to the author's most successful work to date. Robert Plunket of the *Advocate* wrote, "*The Hours* is one of the best books I've read in years, profoundly sad, perhaps, but always exhilarating." Plunket went on to write, "And best of all, it's a real book. It could never, ever be a movie." Plunket's declaration notwithstanding, the novel, which won the Pulitzer Prize for Fiction in 1999, was adapted to film in 2002 by Stephen Daldry and earned actress Nicole Kidman an Academy Award for her portrayal of Virginia Woolf.

## Responses to Literature

1. Cunningham's novels portray some characters who are infected with AIDS. Research the AIDS epidemic in the U.S. using your library and the Internet. How does Cunningham represent society's reaction to AIDS? How do his characters care for each other through the disease?

2. What is Cunningham's definition of a healthy family? Look at two different family units in his books, and describe how they work. Who makes up the family? What roles do the members play? What is the purpose of a family, according to Cunningham?

3. Draw your family tree through at least your grandparents. What are the stories your family tells? In a novel about your family, who would be the main character? What would the main plotline be? Do you see any connections between your family's story and any of the families Cunningham represents in his books?

BIBLIOGRAPHY

**Books**

Gambone, Philip. "Michael Cunningham." In *Something Inside: Conversations with Gay Fiction Writers*. Madison: University of Wisconsin Press, 1999.

**Periodicals**

Donahue, Deidre. "*Specimen* is Much More Than Its Parts." *USA Today* (June 9, 2005): D5.
Eder, Richard. "The Greater Risk" (Book Review). *Los Angeles Times* (Apr 9, 1995).
Kauffman, David. Book Review. *Nation* (July 1, 1991): 21–24.
Plunkett, Robert. Book Review. *Advocate* (Dec 8, 1998): 87.

**Web sites**

Gauthier, Tim. *Michael Cunningham Biography*. Retrieved September 21, 2008, from http://biography.jrank. org/pages/4244/Cunningham-Michael.html.
Literati.net. *Michael Cunningham*. Retrieved September 15, 2008, from http://literati.net/Cunningham.
*The Official Website of Michael Cunningham*. Retrieved September 15, 2008, from http://www.micha elcunninghamwriter.com.
*Guardian Unlimited*. "Paul Burston's Favorite Gay Fiction." Retrieved September 20, 2008, from http://books.guardian.co.uk/top10s/top10/ 0,6109,523071,00.html.

## COMMON HUMAN EXPERIENCE

Cunningham often investigates family life and homosexuality in an overwhelmingly heterosexual world. Other texts that explore this topic include:

*And the Band Played On: Politics, People and the AIDS Epidemic* (1987), a nonfiction work by Randy Shilts. This best-seller gives an in-depth analysis of how AIDS became a world-wide epidemic. Shilts faults governments, medical professionals, and community leaders for ignoring the crisis and allowing it to grow out of control. The book was adapted into a television movie in 1993.

*Philadelphia* (1993), a film by Jonathan Demme. This Academy Award-winning film about homophobia and AIDS stars Tom Hanks and Denzel Washington. Inspired by a true story, the movie depicts a lawyer's legal case against his employer for unjustifiably firing him due to his HIV status.

*The Color Purple* (1982), a novel by Alice Walker. Celie is a poor girl in 1930s Georgia, trying to survive after numerous episodes of abuse and injustice. Along her journey, she learns about family, support, and the love between women. The novel has been made into a film and a musical, and received the 1983 Pulitzer Prize for fiction.

*The Picture of Dorian Gray* (1891), a novel by Oscar Wilde. A classic novel about beauty, hedonism, and death, this book tells the tale of a painter who becomes obsessed with a portrait he has painted.

# D-E

## Richard Henry Dana, Jr.,

BORN: *1815, Cambridge, Massachusetts*

DIED: *1882, Rome, Italy*

NATIONALITY: *American*

GENRE: *Nonfiction*

MAJOR WORKS:

*Two Years Before the Mast* (1840)

### Overview

American author and lawyer Richard Henry Dana, Jr., wrote one of the most persistently popular nonfiction narratives in American letters, *Two Years before the Mast*. He was also an adviser in the formation and direction of the Free Soil party.

### Works in Biographical and Historical Context

*Son of a Poet Writes a Bestseller* Son of Richard Henry Dana, Sr., the Massachusetts poet and editor, the younger Dana distinguished himself in 1834 when he abruptly left the security of Harvard undergraduate life and shipped round Cape Horn to California on a tiny hide-trading sea vessel. He returned two years later, completed his studies, and in 1840 was admitted to the bar. In the same year *Two Years before the Mast* was published by Harper and Brothers, and though the publisher had deftly lifted the copyright (paying Dana just $250), the author hoped that the book would at least bring him some law practice.

Dana's hopes were realized—indeed his office filled with sailors and he became known as the "Seaman's Champion"—and he eventually shaped an impressive legal career. Still, the fact that his publisher realized $50,000 from the book did at times move Dana to complaint. He comforted himself with the knowledge that if he had lost money he had gained fame. The book was embraced by all factions—reformers, temperance crusaders, and romantic lovers of the sea, who saw the oceans as at least comparable to the prairies when it came to charting a frontier to explore. Since the day of its publication the book has never been out of print.

Years later, however, Dana wrote to his son: "My life has been a failure compared with what I might and ought to have done. My great success—my book—was a boy's work, done before I came to the Bar." There were other books: *The Seaman's Friend* (1841), a manual and handbook for sailors; and *To Cuba and Back* (1859), an interesting account of a vacation voyage.

*Practicing Law and Politics* Dana's real commitments were not to literature but to the law, where he finally prospered, and to politics, where he ultimately failed. Celebrated as the legal champion of fugitive black slaves, whose legal status was debated throughout the nineteenth century, Dana unsuccessfully tried to parlay his involvement in politics into a career move.

Slavery was a hotly debated issue in the U.S. for the entire life of the young republic. As slaves consistently tried to escape from Southern states into the free Northern states, the early nineteenth-century government grappled with how to handle the ex-slaves once they achieved freedom. The Compromise of 1850, also known as the Fugitive Slave Act, stated that the escaped slaves must be returned to their owners in the South. Enormous protest followed the passage of this law, and the abolitionist movement gained popularity as the Civil War, fought primarily over the financial and ethical questions regarding slavery and states rights, approached.

Despite his legal work regarding slavery, Dana consistently missed opportunities for high public office, even within the Free Soil party he had helped create. Active in the 1848 and 1852 presidential elections, the Free Soil party opposed legislation to extend slavery into new territories in the West, thus calling for all newly acquired "soil" to be free soil. In 1878, Dana finally packed up and

# LITERARY AND HISTORICAL CONTEMPORARIES

Dana's famous contemporaries include:

**Frederick Douglass** (1818–1895): An escaped slave turned abolitionist orator, writer, and leader, Frederick Douglass was one of the most influential figures in African American history. He details the horrors of slavery in several texts, most popularly *Narrative of the Life of Frederick Douglass, an American Slave* (1845), and he became famous for his passionate and eloquent appeals to end human bondage.

**William Lloyd Garrison** (1805–1879): Garrison was a leading abolitionist in the nineteenth century, advocating for the immediate freeing of American slaves. He led, lectured, and wrote in support of abolitionist causes, edited the abolitionist newspaper *The Liberator*, and founded the American Anti-Slavery Society.

**Ralph Waldo Emerson** (1803–1882): Emerson was a prominent thinker, speaker, poet, and essayist throughout the nineteenth century. He founded the Transcendentalist movement, a philosophical group who believed in the spiritual unity of all nature as experienced through the individual.

**William Wordsworth** (1770–1850): Wordsworth, with fellow writer Samuel Taylor Coleridge, led the literary period of English Romanticism. His publication of *Lyrical Ballads* (1798) helped change the focus of poetry from reason to artful emotion, from classical forms to the experience of the sublime.

**Elizabeth Cady Stanton** (1815–1902): A founder of the women's rights movement, Stanton was a leader at the Seneca Falls Convention in 1848 which sparked a charge for women's suffrage throughout the nineteenth century. She also supported broad women's rights, abolition, and temperance.

left for Europe, furious that his potential appointment as minister to England had failed approval in the Senate.

In Europe Dana joined some of the brilliant expatriate circles then dominating Rome and seemed to find some peace. He called it "a dream of life." He died in January 1882, and he was buried in the same Italian graveyard that contained the remains of British writers John Keats and Percy Bysshe Shelley.

## Works in Literary Context

*Realism* Dana's narrative claims to depict "the life of a common sailor at sea as it really is," meaning he did not intend to embellish or romanticize life at sea. While the writing process necessarily adds an element of artfulness, Dana's narrative nevertheless uses a semirealistic approach that became popular in American literature towards the second half of the nineteenth century. His writing predates the literary movement of Realism by between twenty and fifty years, as the movement became popular after the American Civil War. Partly in reaction to the devastation of the war, writers who espoused realism not only used a simple writing style but also maintained that humans were not in control of their destiny. Outside forces were as powerful in determining an individual's fate as that individual's choices. Romantic writers, by contrast, believed that the individual was the wellspring of opportunity and destiny. Dana shows signs of realistic elements in his text, from his unembellished language to the harsh conditions the sailors faced. The success of the realistic approach Dana used in *Two Years Before the Mast* is attested to by the public interest the book sparked in the daily life of common seamen and the Spanish colony of California.

In subject matter and theme, *Two Years Before the Mast* is an important forerunner of the early novels of Herman Melville, and its balanced structure, which grows organically from the facts of Dana's voyage, prefigures the structure used by Henry David Thoreau, one of Dana's Harvard classmates, in *Walden*. *The Seaman's Friend*, which was also prompted by Dana's experiences aboard ship, was intended by Dana to be a handbook for the common sailor, including descriptions of ship construction and a glossary of nautical terms, a section describing duties aboard ship, and a practical guide to maritime law. As such, *The Seaman's Friend* is a detailed glimpse of nineteenth-century sailing life for the reader of today.

*Seafaring Stories* Part adventure novel, part exploration story, and part travel narrative, the seafaring narrative has been a popular form of literature for centuries. From pirate stories to slave narratives, most seafaring tales share the same basic elements. Generally, a seafaring story provides a restricted location—a single ship—and thus a heightened dramatic element for its plotline. Crew politics usually become crucial to the storyline as sailors must jockey to maintain their position or achieve more power. Masculinity often plays a central role as well, as the sailors tend to be all male characters. *Two Years Before the Mast* contains each of these elements, taking place on a two-year voyage including a trip around Cape Horn. Dana describes the brutal ship conditions for sailors, the dangerous storms at sea, and the economic considerations of the ship's trade. Although Dana's narrative has fallen out of popularity, its prominence as the most widely-read seafaring novel of its time cannot be understated. Even Dana's friend, Herman Melville, author of the now-classic sea novel *Moby-Dick* (1851), praised Dana's work for its dramatic impact on readers.

## Works in Critical Context

Dana's literary reputation rests solely upon *Two Years Before the Mast*, even though that book was hurriedly written and full of stylistic errors. But, rhetorical problems do not detract from the central interests of the story, an initiation narrative in diary form that follows Dana from boyhood to manhood and also seeks to introduce the reader to the truth about life at sea and in California in the 1830s. Even with its stylistic problems, the book still became an instant best-seller after its publication, and readers continued to praise the book for much of the nineteenth century. Prominent writers like Ralph Waldo Emerson and Herman Melville praised the book for its realistic portrayal of life at sea and for its indictment of oppressive working conditions for sailors. Robert F. Lucid writes, "The success of the book was instantaneous ... critics found *Two Years* to be thrilling, sometimes lyrically beautiful, always classically simple in style; but, most consistently, they found it to be a social documentary of devastating power." In his later life Dana considered *Two Years Before the Mast* a book for boys written by a boy. He intended his reputation to rest on his legal writing. To that end, Dana planned to write his masterpiece on international law during his final visit to Europe, but that study and other projected works were left incomplete at his death.

***Two Years Before the Mast*** John Gatta links Dana's writing to many other nineteenth-century narratives in his inclusion of realistic as well as romantic elements, and also in his depictions of lower class characters. He writes, "Unlike the many romanticized tales of seafaring available by the early nineteenth century, *Two Years Before the Mast* claims to tell it as it is. For the most part Dana's transparently informative prose style does precisely that." However, it also contains artistic elements that Gatta links to Dana's own political leanings:

> By the time Dana concludes *Two Years Before the Mast*, he has extended the truth-claims of his narrative well beyond factually accurate reportage toward morally charged testimony. His personal narrative assumes features of a social exposé. Dana would later become an attorney who defended seamen as well as fugitive slaves. Accordingly, the concluding chapter of his narrative shades into an advocate's brief on behalf of that seafaring underclass whose condition Dana has witnessed but no longer shares.

## Responses to Literature

1. Research sailing conditions in the nineteenth century using the library and the Internet. What elements of Dana's story seem accurate, and what elements seem exaggerated or misrepresented? What were the main dangers of the seafaring life?

---

# COMMON HUMAN EXPERIENCE

Dana's writing uses the ocean as the background for his stories. Other narratives about sea voyages include:

*The Odyssey* (c. 720 B.C.E.), an epic poem by Homer. One of the central works in world literature, this Greek epic recounts the travels of Odysseus and his crew as they sail home to Ithaca after the Trojan War. Through a series of encounters with monsters, gods, giants, sorceresses—and, in the end, men who are out to steal his home and wife—Odysseus comes to embody the full spectrum of heroism.

*Robinson Crusoe* (1719), a novel by Daniel Defoe. This fictional narrative details the title character's adventures as he is shipwrecked and then forced to live on a deserted island for nearly thirty years.

*Moby-Dick* (1851), a novel by Herman Melville. A classic American novel about Captain Ahab's obsessive hunt for the giant white whale, Moby Dick, that attacked him and took his leg. The story illustrates the various politics of seafaring life, and begins with the famous opening line, "Call me Ishmael."

"The Old Man and the Sea" (1952), a novella by Ernest Hemingway. Hemingway wrote this tale about a Cuban fisherman trying to catch a marlin while living in Cuba. In the story, the old fisherman finally lands the enormous fish only to have it eaten by sharks on the dangerous ride home.

*Middle Passage* (1990), a novel by Charles Johnson. This novel takes place on the horrific sea voyage that stolen Africans endured to become slaves in the West, also known as the Middle Passage. Johnson details the barbaric conditions on the slave ship, where one character infiltrates the crew and helps the slaves revolt. The novel won the National Book Award.

---

2. Research the working conditions of paid sailors in the nineteenth century. Dana joined a ship's crew by choice, after voluntarily leaving college. How might his own choice to work as a sailor—with the knowledge that he could leave at any time—influence his perspective in the narrative?

3. Watch your favorite movie that takes place on a ship, such as *Moby Dick* (1956) or *Pirates of the Caribbean* (2003). What elements of life at sea are similarly portrayed between the movie and Dana's narrative? What parts of seafaring life do we find entertaining? Why is the subject of life at sea equally entertaining now as it was two hundred years ago?

BIBLIOGRAPHY

**Books**

Adams, Charles Francis. *Richard Henry Dana: A Biography (2 vols.).* Boston: Houghton Mifflin, 1890.

Gale, Robert L. *Richard Henry Dana, Jr.* New York: Twayne, 1969.

Shapiro, Samuel. *Richard Henry Dana, Jr.: 1815–1882.* East Lansing, Mich.: Michigan State University Press, 1961.

**Periodicals**

Egan, Hugh. "'One of them': The Voyage of Style in Dana's *Two Years Before the Mast.*" *American Transcendental Quarterly* 2.3 (1988): 177–90.

Gatta, John. "The Elusive Truths of Literary Narrative." *Sewanee Review* 115.1 (2007): 131–36.

Hill, Douglas B., Jr. "Richard Henry Dana, Jr., and *Two Years Before the Mast.*" *Criticism* 9 (1967): 312–25.

Lucid, Robert F. "*Two Years Before the Mast* as Propaganda." *American Quarterly* 12.3 (1960): 392–403.

**Web sites**

San Diego Historical Society. *San Diego Biographies: Richard Henry Dana.* Retrieved September 15, 2008, from http://www.sandiegohistory.org/bio/dana/dana.htm.

## ✸ Edwidge Danticat

BORN: *1969, Port-au-Prince, Haiti*

NATIONALITY: *American*

GENRE: *Fiction*

MAJOR WORKS:
*Breath, Eyes, Memory* (1994)
*Krik? Krak!* (1995)
*The Farming of Bones* (1998)
*Behind the Mountains* (2002)
*The Dew Breaker* (2004)

### Overview

Winner of a Pushcart Short Story Prize and a finalist for a National Book Award in 1995, Edwidge Danticat is a Hatian-American writer whose work has received positive critical attention. Her first novel, *Breath, Eyes, Memory* (1994), was selected for Oprah Winfrey's Book Club.

### Works in Biographical and Historical Context

***Immigration from Haiti*** Fiction writer Danticat was born in Haiti and lived there the first twelve years

of her life. In 1981, she came to the United States, joining her parents who had already begun to build a life for themselves in New York City. When she started attending junior high school in Brooklyn, she had difficulty fitting in with her classmates because of her Haitian accent, clothing, and hairstyle. Danticat recalled for Garry Pierre-Pierre in the *New York Times* that she took refuge from the isolation she felt by writing about her native land. As an adolescent, she began what would evolve into her first novel, 1994's highly acclaimed *Breath, Eyes, Memory*. Danticat followed her debut with a 1995 collection of short stories, *Krik? Krak!*—a volume that became a finalist for that year's National Book Award. According to Pierre-Pierre, the young author has been heralded as "'the voice' of Haitian-Americans," but Danticat told him: "I think I have been assigned that role, but I don't really see myself as the voice for the Haitian-American experience. There are many. I'm just one."

***Publishing in New York City*** Danticat's parents wanted her to pursue a career in medicine, and with the goal of becoming a nurse, she attended a specialized high school in New York City. However, she abandoned this aim to devote herself to her writing. An earlier version of *Breath, Eyes, Memory* served as her master of fine arts thesis at Brown University, and the finished version was published shortly thereafter. Like Danticat herself, Sophie Caco, the novel's protagonist, spent her first twelve years in Haiti, several of them in the care of an aunt, before coming wide-eyed to the United States. There the similarities end. Sophie is the child of a single mother, conceived by rape. Though she rejoins her mother in the United States, it is too late to save the still-traumatized older woman from self-destruction. Yet, women's ties to women are celebrated in the novel, and Sophie draws strength from her mother, her aunt, and herself in order to escape her mother's fate.

***Haitian Politics Influence Writing*** Haiti's difficult history influences much of Danticat's work. Father and son dictators, Francois and Jean-Claude Duvalier, brutally ruled Haiti from the 1950s through the 1980s with the help of a vicious army called the Tonton Macoutes. When the younger Duvalier was overthrown in 1986, Haitians were overjoyed and full of hope for a democratic country. Former members of the Tonton Macoutes took power, however, and circumstances did not improve much until 1990, when former Roman Catholic priest Jean-Bertrand Aristide was elected president. Political violence and persistent poverty have remained central features of Haitian society. The Tonton Macoutes are the subject of Danticat's novel *The Dew Breaker* (2004).

Danticat continues to write about the dual experience of life in Haiti and America throughout her fiction.

Edwidge Danticat    *Danticat, Edwidge, 1998, photograph. AP Images.*

matter which mirrors the nation's brutal political climate; she often depicts violent death, incest, rape, and extreme poverty. Danticat fills her stories with characters who exist within a painful external world. Like Haitian writers who have come before her, Danticat battles against the despair of the past and the pain of exile while also describing a culture in which people learn, love, and laugh. Despite growing up in a society which often seeks to silence women, Danticat has found her voice. She has found a way to tell the stories of her country's men and women in a modern voice that brings attention to the problems of the past.

*Oral Narrative*    Oral narrative is the method that many cultures have used to maintain their family histories; a mother tells stories to her daughter, for instance, as a way of keeping the family identity alive. A strong part of Haitian culture is its tradition of storytelling. The title of Danticat's second book, *Krik? Krak!*, a collection of short stories, bears witness to her rich heritage of storytelling and is explained in the epigram: "We tell the stories so that the young ones will know what came before them. They say Krik? We say Krak! Our stories are kept in our hearts." *Krik? Krak!* takes its title from the practice of Haitian storytellers. Danticat told Deborah Gregory of *Essence* magazine that storytelling is a favorite entertainment in Haiti. A storyteller inquires of his or her audience, "Krik?" to ask if they are ready to listen; the group then replies with an enthusiastic, "Krak!" The tales in this collection include one about a man attempting to flee Haiti in a leaky boat, another about a prostitute who tells her son that the reason she dresses up every night is that she is expecting an angel to descend upon their house, and yet another is exploring the feelings of a childless housekeeper in a loveless marriage who finds an abandoned baby in the streets. *Ms.*'s Jordana Hart felt that the tales in *Krik? Krak!* "are textured and deeply personal, as if the twenty-six-year-old Haitian-American author had spilled her own tears over each."

She won the National Book Award in 1999 for her book *The Farming of Bones* (1998), a historical novel centering on the massacre of thousands of Haitians living near the Dominican border in 1937. Danticat lives, writes, and teaches in New York City.

## Works in Literary Context

*Haitian-American Novel*    Danticat focuses on Haitian culture and tradition in her writing. *Breath, Eyes, Memory*, told through the eyes of Sophie Caco, details the lives of four generations of Haitian women as they struggle against poverty, violence, and prejudice in Haiti and the United States. Encompassing contemporary Haitian history, the novel portrays the country's recent upheavals at the hands of the Duvalier regime and its brutal secret police, the Tonton Macoutes. While the stories in *Krik? Krak!*—the title refers to a Haitian storytelling game in which one person's story is exchanged for another—employ a wide range of plot types and characters, each story is part of the larger tale of Haiti. Some of the power of Danticat's fiction lies in its shocking subject

## Works in Critical Context

Most commentators have found Danticat's works to be powerful fiction, conveyed with sure-handed style. *Breath, Eyes, Memory* has been praised by many critics for its lyric language, which provides a counterpoint to the novel's occasionally dire subject matter. Some reviewers suggested that Danticat did not display complete control of her material in this book, lavishing detailed descriptive passages on things and events that did not warrant them. Most point out that this is a flaw common to many first novels. Critics have lauded *Krik? Krak!* for the diversity of narrative voices and literary styles presented in the stories. Danticat is again praised for making potentially downbeat material readable and

# LITERARY AND HISTORICAL CONTEMPORARIES

Danticat's famous contemporaries include:

**Jamaica Kincaid** (1949–) Kincaid's writing often focuses on the British colonial background of her childhood life in Antigua, as she learned British traditions despite the larger Caribbean culture. Her books include *Annie John* (1986) and *The Autobiography of My Mother* (1996).

**Julia Alvarez** (1950–) Alvarez's family fled from the Trujillo dictatorship and the Dominican Republic. Alvarez, like Danticat, revisits her homeland in her work and describes the horrors of living under a regime of terror. She is known for *How the Garcia Girls Lost Their Accents* (1991).

**Madison Smartt Bell** (1957–): Bell is an American novelist who tells the story of Toussaint L'Ouverture and the Haitian revolution in his novel *All Souls Rising* (1995).

**Colson Whitehead** (1969–): Whitehead is an African-American novelist and essayist, who broke through with *The Intuitionist* (1999), a hard-boiled novel about elevator repairmen.

**Uzodinma Iweala** (1982–): Iweala is a Nigerian-American author of *Beasts of No Nation* (2005), a novel about a child soldier in an unnamed African nation.

**Wyclef Jean** (1972–): Jean is an Haitian-American musician, actor, and philanthropist, and former member of the hip-hop band The Fugees.

# COMMON HUMAN EXPERIENCE

Danticat writes about characters who find themselves in new and challenging cultural environments. Other novels about fitting in include:

*White Teeth* (2000), a novel by Zadie Smith. This novel by young British author Smith follows several different characters, Indian and British, from teenagers to middle-aged men, as they navigate life in the culturally diverse atmosphere of modern London.

*Black Boy* (1945), an autobiographical novel by Richard Wright. This autobiography details Wright's coming of age in the racist South of the early twentieth century.

*The Secret Life of Bees* (2002), a novel by Sue Monk Kidd. A young white girl in the 1960s South, dealing with an abusive father and a family tragedy which she believes she caused, goes to live with some old friends of her mother, three African American sisters who tend bees for a living.

*The Kite Runner* (2003), a novel by Khaled Hosseini. This novel takes place in Afghanistan under the brutal rule of the Taliban. The main character returns to his home country after becoming successful in America, in order to save a friend and right a past wrong.

enjoyable through her skillful, lyrical use of language. Critics have noted that some of the stories reveal a too self-conscious manipulation of form and structure, a false note of "preciousness" that detracts from their realism. Most critics agree with Richard Eder, however, that the "best of [the stories], using the island tradition of a semi-magical folktale, or the witty, between-two-worlds voices of modern urban immigrants, are pure beguiling transformation."

**Breath, Eyes, Memory** *Breath, Eyes, Memory* caused some controversy in the Haitian-American community. Some of Danticat's fellow Haitians felt that some of the practices she documented portrayed them as primitive and abusive. American critics, however, widely lauded *Breath, Eyes, Memory*. Joan Philpott in *Ms.* hailed the book as "intensely lyrical." Garry Pierre-Pierre in the *New York Times*, reported that reviewers "have praised Ms. Danticat's vivid sense of place and her images of fear and pain." Jim Gladstone concluded in the *New York Times Book Review* that the novel "achieves an emotional complexity that lifts it out of the realm of the potboiler and into that of poetry." Bob Shacochis, in his *Washington Post Book World* review, called the work "a novel that rewards a reader again and again with small but exquisite and unforgettable epiphanies." Shacochis added, "You can actually see Danticat grow and mature, come into her own strength as a writer, throughout the course of this quiet, soul-penetrating story about four generations of women trying to hold on to one another in the Haitian diaspora."

## Responses to Literature

1. Describe at least two different significant female characters in Danticat's writing, listing specific personality traits. How might Danticat's stories be different if they were told by, and about, men?

2. Research the recent history of Haiti by reading a book such as Jean-Bertrand Aristide's *In the Parish of the Poor: Writings from Haiti* (1990). How does Danticat's work reflect this conflicted history?

3. Write your family's story, following the model of Danticat's *Breath, Eyes, Memory*. How would your story be different from another member of your family's? What elements would you emphasize? What elements would you leave out?

4. Danticat felt out of place as a young Haitian girl in an American school. Investigate current children's books, magazine ads, and television shows for contemporary cultural norms. Who "fits in" according to these models? Who is an outsider?

### BIBLIOGRAPHY

**Periodicals**

Eder, Richard. "A Haitian Fantasy and Exile." *Newsday* (March 30, 1995): B2, B25.

Epstein, Grace A. *Antioch Review* (1990): 106.

Farley, Christopher John. *Time* (Sept. 7, 1998): 78.

Gladstone, Jim. Review of *Breath, Eyes, Memory*. *New York Times Book Review* (July 10, 1994): 24.

Gregory, Deborah. "Edwidge Danticat: Dreaming of Haiti" (interview). *Essence* (April 1995): 56.

Hart, Jordana. Review of *Krik? Krak!*. *Ms.* (March-April 1995): 75.

Philpott, Joan. "Two Tales of Haiti" (review of *Breath, Eyes, Memory*). *Ms.* (Mar-Apr 1994): 77–78.

Pierre-Pierre, Garry. "Haitian Tales, Flatbush Scenes." *New York Times* (Jan. 26, 1995): C1, C8.

Shacochis, Bob. "Island in the Dark." *Washington Post Book World* (Apr 3, 1994): 6.

**Web sites**

Edwidge, Danticat. *Voices from the Gap*. Retrieved September 29, 2008, from http://voices.cla.umn.edu/vg/Bios/entries/danticat_edwidge.html.

# ✸ Rebecca Harding Davis

BORN: *1831, Washington, Pennsylvania*

DIED: *1910, Mount Kisko, New York*

NATIONALITY: *American*

GENRE: *Fiction, journalism*

MAJOR WORKS:

"Life in the Iron-Mills" (1861)

*Margret Howth* (1862)

*Waiting for the Verdict* (1868)

*Silhouettes of an American Life* (1892)

*Bits of Gossip* (1904)

## Overview

"Life in the Iron-Mills" launched Rebecca Harding Davis's fifty-year career, during which she wrote some five hundred published works, including short stories, novellas, novels, sketches, and social commentary. She was one of the first writers to portray the American Civil War impartially, to expose political corruption in the North, and to unmask bias in legal constraints on women.

## Works in Biographical and Historical Context

*Early Experiences Lead to Working Class Sympathy* Born in Pennsylvania in 1831, Rebecca Blaine Harding spent her first five years in Alabama. Her mother came from a prominent Washington, Pennsylvania, family; her father was an English immigrant. In 1837 Richard and Rachel Harding took the nearly six-year-old Rebecca and her one-year-old brother, Wilson, to live in Wheeling, in the western part of Virginia that later became West Virginia. With her imagination and creative expression nurtured by her mother's linguistic virtuosity and her father's storytelling and love of classic literature, young Rebecca Harding was an avid reader and often climbed into the backyard tree house to read books. She was most influenced by nineteenth-century American romantic writer Nathaniel Hawthorne, to whom she attributed her choice of commonplace subject matter in her writing.

Schooled at home by her mother and various tutors until she was fourteen, Harding entered Washington Female Seminary in 1845. After graduating in 1848 as valedictorian, the seventeen-year-old returned home to help her mother manage a bustling household of seven. Twelve years elapsed between graduation and her first published literary work. During this time Harding honed her writing skills by working occasionally for the *Wheeling Intelligence*. She was transformed from obscure spinster to renowned writer when James T. Fields, editor of *The Atlantic Monthly*, accepted "Life in the Iron-Mills" for his prestigious journal. According to literary critic Sharon M. Harris, that initial publication was so compelling and daring that when it appeared in April 1861, it shook the eastern intellectual community to its foundations, launching Harding's social reform efforts not only for the working class, but eventually for blacks, women, and others she believed to be essentially powerless.

*Politics and the Civil War Influence Writing* The nineteenth century brought vast changes for black, female, and working Americans. Slavery was hotly debated all across the United States, as abolitionists protested human bondage until civil war broke out in 1861. Nearly splitting the young United States in half over states rights, specifically the right to own slaves, the American Civil War ended in 1865, after the southern states were defeated and President Abraham Lincoln freed the slaves through the Emancipation Proclamation (1863). Women's roles were also controversial as a large movement arose in the mid-century to give women the right to vote; that privilege did not come until 1920, although black American men were given the right to vote in 1870. Industrialization also began in the nineteenth century, with the construction of national railroads and the new factory model of work. With mass labor came poor working conditions, however, and Davis, like British writer Charles Dickens, helped expose the difficulties of living a working-class life.

As a result of "Life in the Iron-Mills", Davis was offered an advance to write another story. At this point she was still living in Virginia, a border state that was put under martial law during the Civil War. Not only was Wheeling a crossroads for the Underground Railroad, but Federal troops had recently set up headquarters across the street from her home. Davis became one of the few writers of her era to depict the national catastrophe realistically.

During this time of national and local crisis, the fledgling writer was working on a second work of fiction. Her novel *Margret Howth: A Story of To-Day* was serialized and then published as a book in 1862. The novel, about American industrialism, is considered less artful than it could have been because Davis succumbed to her editor's substantial changes, making the story much more sentimental than it was originally. The profession of authorship in nineteenth-century America was increasingly subject to the restraints of polite society, but for writers who attempted to create accurate portraits of crushing social conditions, their efforts were especially constrained.

*The Atlantic Monthly* then published four of Harding's stories about slavery in 1862 and 1863. In these stories she treated the personalities and experiences of blacks as complex rather than one-dimensional, as in most renderings of her era. The stories also take issue with the tacit approval of the war by mainstream Southern churches, while also revealing her disgust of the institution of slavery and suggesting that women's inferior position in American life allowed them a better understanding of the suffering of slaves. Davis's frank portrayal of racial privilege and animosity was unusual for that period. She offered a female perspective on suffering without employing Christian language to gloss over abject degradation and dehumanization.

She married editor Clarke Davis in 1863 and moved into the home of his widowed sister and her children in Philadelphia. Living with her husband's relatives at the same time she was adjusting to marriage was trying for her physically and emotionally. Her plans to write at the Philadelphia Library went awry. Soon after the wedding, Davis was faced with nursing her sick husband and his sister. About the time they recovered, Davis herself became ill and then learned she was pregnant. The illness was not named, but was considered to be a disease of the "nerves," which required her to cease all reading or writing. Her severe depression lasted until the spring of 1864, when she gave birth to a son. Soon the new family moved into their own home, and they began associating with nationally prominent figures, remaining in those circles for the rest of their lives.

### Successful Career Championing the Oppressed
In 1866, she gave birth to her second son. In February 1867, nearly two years after the assassination of President Lincoln, Davis's ambitious Civil War novel, *Waiting for the Verdict*, began to appear serially, and then in book form in 1868. The central issue in *Waiting for the Verdict* was a major question of the Reconstruction era: How would the nation integrate the freed slaves into the mainstream of American life? Davis believed that Americans needed to redefine what they meant by humanity and democracy. *Waiting for the Verdict* suggests that dehumanizing some of the members of the human family finally brutalizes the whole.

After years of publishing short stories in various literary journals during the 1870s, Davis expanded her range to include juvenile literature, the political novel, and journalism, the form best suited to her feminist leanings and social conscience. She gave birth to a daughter in 1872. Davis's most impressive writing of the 1870s was her journalism, as she carried through the social protest she had voiced in her fiction. From this time forward, Davis was a full-fledged journalist.

Racial issues continued to dominate Davis's writing throughout the 1880s and 1890s, as she directed her readers' attention to poverty-stricken blacks, entering a national conversation led by pragmatic thinker Booker T. Washington and intellectual W.E.B. DuBois. Throughout her writings on the subject, Davis consistently stressed the connections between racism and economic struggle.

### A Prominent Family
By the mid-1890s, both Davis's sons, Richard and Charles, had become writers. During the 1890s the Davis family became one of the most prominent families in America, frequent companions of two U.S. presidents. In 1904 Houghton, Mifflin published Davis's memoir *Bits of Gossip*, a book far more substantive than its title implies. The compelling human story of Davis's time, *Bits of Gossip* is a significant book, helpful for understanding the nineteenth-century American society.

Following her husband's death in 1904, Davis continued writing, publishing seventeen more pieces, including social commentaries and two works of fiction. In 1910 Davis suffered a stroke while visiting her son in New York. She died there of heart failure on September 29, at the age of seventy-nine.

## Works in Literary Context

### Realism and Naturalism
Partly in reaction to the devastation of the American Civil War, nineteenth century writers began popularly espousing realism, using not only a simple writing style but also maintaining that humans were not in control of their destiny. Outside forces were as powerful in determining an individual's fate as that individual's choices. Naturalism specifically focuses on this fatalistic approach to human life. Romantic writers believed that the individual was the wellspring of opportunity and destiny. "Life in the Iron-Mills" is one of the first detailed and realistic pictures of the factory in American fiction. The characters in "Life in the Iron-Mills" speak in authentic vernacular and varying dialects. The story announces its commonplace perspective, not only in its realistic language, but also in the narrator's vow to be honest, to make real the lives of the working class. The main character's consuming hunger, which could have been satisfied by education and

opportunity, instead brutally determines his descent and ultimate death. Thus, he is one of the first naturalistic portraits in American literature.

*Writing and the Woman Question* The question of women's roles in society was constantly debated throughout the nineteenth century. From the movement to give women the right to vote, to the revitalization of domestic image of women, writers continually presented arguments about how women should behave in the home and in public. Davis's artistic achievement is distinguished not only by the aesthetic of realism but also by the essentially female perspective infusing her writing. Though she affirmed women's traditional roles, she exposed suffocating attitudes or conditions that disrupted women's professional pursuits, and she strategically challenged the ideology of domesticity.

Like the adverse effect of industrialism on American life, and the class distinctions that undermined Americans' concept of democracy, the problems of the woman artist were an inspiration for her fiction. "The Wife's Story" (1864), for instance, explores Davis's feelings about the effect of marriage on the woman artist's struggle for creative expression and autonomy. Prior to her wedding, Davis had worried that familial and domestic duties would interfere with her literary work. This story introduces a motif that recurs frequently in Davis's writing: the woman writer's conscious and constant mediation of the public and private spheres. Davis can be considered a conservative feminist because, throughout her life, she insisted that a woman needed both personal fulfillment as wife and mother and professional fulfillment through meaningful work.

## Works in Critical Context

Davis's writing, particularly "Life in the Iron-Mills," caught the attention of such well-known figures as Ralph Waldo Emerson, Louisa May Alcott, and Nathaniel Hawthorne. Her work was influential in its stark depiction of the struggling working class. Critical assessment of Davis's work increased significantly in the late twentieth century. Her primary contribution was to the development of literary realism, and her steadfast employment of subject matter previously considered unsuitable for literature, provoked criticism of her fiction from her contemporaries—on the same grounds for which twentieth-century readers and scholars praised her work, that is, for her realistic portrayal of oppressed working class characters.

*"Life in the Iron-Mills"* Davis's writing, while popular during her lifetime, was often criticized for awkwardness. As it turns out, this may have been as a result of her editor's changes to original stories. Her work has been re-examined, however, by late twentieth- and early twenty-first century feminist critics. Jean Fagan Yellin, for instance, importantly sketches the changes Davis was compelled to make to her writings by her editor, softening the harsh social criticisms in favor of mild storylines.

Yellin states that although "Rebecca Harding Davis was to produce steadily for the commercial press for more than forty years," her editor's influence meant that "rarely would she again attempt to treat overtly themes like those that had ignited her early writings of social protest." Janice Milner Lasseter further claims that the original text of "Life in the Iron-Mills," before the editor's changes, "is stylistically superior—more poetic, more technically accurate, and less effusive and declamatory" than the published version. Critics have recovered Davis's original texts in order to reclaim and reassert her artistic ability and skill.

## Responses to Literature

1. Davis writes about characters whose choices are often limited due to lack of education and money. Research the working poor and the minimum wage today. A country like the U.S. claims to offer equal

opportunity and education to each citizen. Find examples in which this dream is realized, and examples where it falls short for working people.

2. A central issue in women's lives has been the balance between home and work. Davis juggled being a mother and a successful writer, often writing about how family life can take time away from career. Ask several women you know about this balance in their lives. What choices do they have to make? What are their priorities?

3. Using the library and the Internet, research labor unions. What advances have they made for basic workers' rights? Are they still effective and/or necessary today?

BIBLIOGRAPHY

**Books**

Harris, Sharon M. *Rebecca Harding Davis and American Realism*. Philadelphia: University of Pennsylvania Press, 1991.

Olsen, Tillie. "A Biographical Interpretation," in *Life in the Iron-Mills and Other Stories*. Edited by Olsen.

Old Westbury, New York: Feminist Press, 1985, pp. 69–174.

Rose, Jane Atteridge. *Rebecca Harding Davis*. New York: Twayne, 1993.

**Periodicals**

Harris, Sharon M. "Rebecca Harding Davis: From Romanticism to Realism." *American Literary Realism* 21 (1989): 4–20.

Lasseter, Janice Milner. "The Censored and Uncensored Literary Lives of Life in the Iron-Mills." *Legacy: A Journal of American Women Writers* 20.1–2 (2003): 175–190.

Pfaelzer, Jean. "Legacy Profile: Rebecca Harding Davis." *Legacy: A Journal of American Women Writers* 7 (1990): 39–45.

Yellin, Jean Fagan. "The 'Feminization' of Rebecca Harding Davis." *American Literary History* 2.2 (1990): 203–219.

**Web sites**

"Rebecca Harding Davis." Textbook site for *The Heath Anthology of American Literature*. Retrieved September 28, 2008, from http://college.cengage.com/english/lauter/heath/4e/students/author_pages/early_nineteenth/davis_re.html.

# ✸ Borden Deal

BORN: *1922, Pontotoc, Mississippi*

DIED: *1985, Sarasota, Florida*

NATIONALITY: *American*

GENRE: *Fiction*

MAJOR WORKS:
*Dunbar's Cove* (1958)
*The Insolent Breed* (1959)
*Dragon's Wine* (1960)
*The Other Room* (1974)

## Overview

Although Borden Deal's novels are invariably set in the South, they have gained far more than regional acceptance. His work has been adapted for the screen, the stage, radio, and television. *The Insolent Breed* (1959) was the basis for the Broadway musical *A Joyful Noise* (1966). *Dunbar's Cove* (1958) was combined with William Bradford Huie's novel *Mud on the Stars* (1942) to form the movie *Wild River* (1960), directed by Elia Kazan. Deal's works have been translated into more than twenty languages.

## Works in Biographical and Historical Context

*A Youth of the Depression* Bordean Deal was born Loyse Youth Deal in Pontotoc, Mississippi, and raised in

Borden Deal   *AP Images*

Union County, near New Albany. The economic struggles of his family during the Depression years made an indelible impression on him and later provided abundant material for his fiction. His father, like many other farmers, lost his land when the price of cotton dropped disastrously. Aided by Roosevelt's rehabilitation program, the family procured two mules and traveled to a communal, government-sponsored farming project in Enterprise, Mississippi. This small community of renters was depicted years later as Bugscuffle Bottoms in the novel *The Least One* (1967). The Darden community, the site of a later family farming venture, became Hell Creek Bottom in *The Other Room* (1974).

Deal left home in 1938, the year of his father's death in a truck accident. Over the next few years he went through a variety of occupations, including hauling sawdust for a lumber mill, working on a showboat, battling forest fires with the Civilian Conservation Corps, and following the wheat harvest with other migrant workers by freight train. His pursuits would soon swing from the physically demanding to the intellectual.

***The Literary and the Mystical*** Borden Deal's first publication occurred in 1948 when he was in college. His short story "Exodus" won first prize in a national contest and was reprinted in *Best American Short Stories of 1949*. Deal received his BA from the University of Alabama in

# LITERARY AND HISTORICAL CONTEMPORARIES

Deal's famous contemporaries include:

**Herbert Hoover** (1874–1964): The thirty-first president of the United States, Hoover served from 1929 until 1933. During his first year as president, the United States economy began its slide toward the economic crisis known as the Great Depression.

**Dorothea Lange** (1895–1965): Photographer and photojournalist Dorothea Lange was famous for capturing troubling, troubled, and inspiring images of humanity during the Great Depression. Like Borden Deal, she is remembered as an artist who helped define that very difficult period of American history.

**Walt Disney** (1901–1966): A major figure in both the artistic and commercial development of animated films, Walt Disney was the creative force behind such cinematic classics as *Snow White and the Seven Dwarves* (1937) and *Fantasia* (1940).

**George Orwell** (1903–1950): The British novelist George Orwell is most famous for using fables and science-fiction tales as social and political allegories. Just as Borden Deal had been in the United States, Orwell was inspired by the devastating effects of the Great Depression when he wrote his book *The Road to Wigan Pier* (1937).

**Elia Kazan** (1909–2003): The Greek-American filmmaker Elia Kazan created powerful classics like *A Streetcar Named Desire* (1951) and *On the Waterfront* (1954). Kazan also directed the film *Wild River* (1960), which was partially based on Borden Deal's novel *Dunbar's Cove*.

**William Bradford Huie** (1910–1986): Alabama-born journalist, novelist, and publisher William Bradford Huie is the author of *Mud on the Stars*. Along with Borden Deal's *Dunbar's Cove*, *Mud on the Stars* would be adapted into the feature film *Wild River*.

1949 and in 1950 was a graduate student in Mexico City. In 1954, Deal resolved to devote himself to writing full-time. So began the flood of novels and short stories he would continue to publish for the duration of his life.

By 1957 Deal had achieved national recognition with his first novel, *Walk Through the Valley* (1956), which received an honorable mention in the American Library Association Liberty and Justice Awards. A major theme in the Deal canon—and perhaps that for which he received the most critical attention—is humankind's mystical attachment to the earth itself. *Walk Through the Valley* distinguished him as a novelist who writes with the authority of experience of farming and the rhythms of the seasons. This tale is about a dream-seeking pilgrim named Fate Laird who leaves the sterile land of his father's Texas farm in search of a more fertile and prosperous country. Central to this novel is the romantic kinship Fate feels with the forces of nature and with the land he works. Deal's characters are typically honest and uncomplicated people who are motivated by the basic drives of human nature: family pride, the desire for independence, and the longing for land that will yield security and those material comforts that tell a man he is progressing toward a better, gentler life.

There is perhaps no Deal novel in which the land itself looms as a more important element than in *Dunbar's Cove* (1958). This story revolves around two men with conflicting dreams: Matthew Dunbar, farmer and ordained guardian of his ancestral property, who vehemently fights against the massive dam-building project of the Tennessee Valley Authority—a government-created corporation designed to create jobs during the Depression through public works programs—and the young and idealistic engineer Crawford Gates, who represents the federal government. Although his land is destined to be flooded, Dunbar refuses to sell to the TVA because he feels a mystical pact with the ancestral defenders of the cove—an obligation to preserve it as a sanctuary for any Dunbar who should ever want to return.

Deal's next novel, *Dragon's Wine* (1960), represents a deeper and perhaps darker side of Deal's creative character. The novel is a dark and bloody tale that treats the outbreak of greed and demonic ambition in the human personality. The novel revolves around Homer and Kate Greaves, two larger-than-life characters who dominate the sawmill manor where they are tenants. Quite a shift from the focus on adult passions in *Dragon's Wine*, *A Long Way to Go* (1965) is a treatment of the ritual of initiation. Three precocious children embark on a six-hundred-mile journey to their home after being mysteriously abandoned by their parents. The book is a sensitive account of how innocent children, suddenly severed from family dependency, adjust to the not-so-innocent world.

Also appearing in 1965 was *The Tobacco Men*, a fictional account of the Kentucky tobacco wars of the early 1900s and J. B. Duke's American Tobacco Company in the last decade of the nineteenth century. Deal based the novel on notes by Theodore Dreiser and Hollywood writer Hy Kraft. He obtained the notes on the condition that he would be allowed complete artistic freedom in writing the book. The novel is about a shrewd robber baron named Oren Knox, patterned after J. B. Duke, and the stormy expansion of his tobacco empire. Knox is opposed by Amos Haines, a selfless country doctor.

*The Least One* and its sequel *The Other Room* are Deal's semi-autobiographical stories of the Sword family's search for the elusive land of promise. Central to the novels is the idea that a person's values and identity are generated by certain vital experiences. In *The Least One*, Lee Sword leaves his son, simply called Boy, the task of naming himself. Deal reflects upon the biblical creation story in which Adam, through naming the living creatures and by exercising his will, shaped the world to some degree into a creation of his own making.

*A Product of His Past*   In all his work, Deal was, first of all, a product of his region and past. Like many of his Southern contemporaries, his writing shows a strong sense of place and time. Undoubtedly, his family's perseverance in the Depression years accounts greatly for the pervasive themes of land quest and personal ambition as well as the host of stubborn dreamers in his books. There is, however, much in Deal's work that transcends its regional flavor. A universal quality in his writing stems, in part, from his preoccupation with the timeless ritual of self-discovery. Deal believed that his novels were "given" to him by the historically consequential times in which he lived. Deal continued publishing his spiritually searching works right up until his death from a heart attack in 1985.

## Works in Literary Context

*Man's Relationship to the Land*   A theme that arises throughout much of Deal's work is the relationship between man and the land he works. The relationship is often depicted as a complex one, as the land can either be a fruitful provider of food and financial stability or a barren, stubborn hindrance. In *Walk Through the Valley*, the symbolically named Fate Laird finds his own fate at the whim of the sterile land on his father's Texas farm. In this case, the land provides Fate with an opportunity to leave the security of his home and explore the world in search of prosperity. Conversely, *The Tobacco Men* features a ruthless industrialist bent on controlling the land in order to expand his tobacco empire.

*Pulp Fiction*   Although the majority of Borden Deal's work can be categorized as southern literary fiction, Deal also experimented with the genre of crime fiction often referred to as pulp with his novels *The Killer in the House* (1957) and *The Devil's Whisper* (1961). Pulp fiction is defined by its luridness, which is often reflected in the shadowy violent images on pulp book covers that generally depicted men with guns and women in distress. Pulp fiction originally gained popularity during the 1920s and 1930s when magazines like *Startling Stories* and *Black Mask* collected violent stories of crime and adventure. The magazines were nicknamed pulps because of the cheap wood pulp paper on which they were printed. By the 1950s, the kinds of stories that were originally published in pulp magazines appeared in mass-market paperback books also referred to as pulps. Some of the leading authors of their generations, such as Isaac Asimov, Upton Sinclair, William S. Burroughs, and Joseph Conrad, wrote for pulp magazines.

## Works in Critical Context

*Dunbar's Cove*   One of Deal's most famous novels, *Dunbar's Cove* is also one his novels that has left the

---

# COMMON HUMAN EXPERIENCE

Deal was one of the many Americans affected by the economic crisis known as the Great Depression. Other works inspired by the Great Depression include:

*Tobacco Road* (1932), a novel by Erskine Caldwell. Set in Georgia during the Great Depression, Caldwell's novel follows the Lesters, a family of farmers who refuse to be put out of work by the burgeoning industrialization of farming.

*U.S.A.* (1938), a novel trilogy by John Dos Passos. The three distinctive works that comprise the trilogy (*The 42nd Parallel*, *1919*, and *The Big Money*) form an experimental, sardonic critique of the mindless pursuit of wealth that served as a grim, cynical reflection of the country's economic woes during the Depression.

*The Grapes of Wrath* (1939), a novel by John Steinbeck. Widely considered one of the great American novels of the twentieth century, *The Grapes of Wrath* tells the story of the Joads, a sharecropping family suffering through the Great Depression. The Joads experience a drought that forces them to leave their farm and sets them on a search for work and hope in California's Central Valley.

*Let Us Now Praise Famous Men* (1941), a book by James Agee with photographs by Walker Evans. Agee's book is an exploration of southern poverty during the Great Depression. Although journalistic in intent, Agee's prose is poetic and artistically supported by the stark, powerful black and white images that Evans provided.

---

longest lasting impression on critics. This may be in part due to its well-received big screen adaptation by influential filmmaker Elia Kazan, *Wild River*. In his 1960 review of the film, A. H. Weiler of *The New York Times* remarks that it was blessed with "an embarrassment of riches" in its source material. In 1981, James B. Lloyd provided a more detailed appraisal of the book, describing it as "an emotional statement, in terms of characters and drama and conflict, about an experienced event, a balancing and a molding of fact and fiction into a truth greater than either alone."

*The Insolent Breed*   Along with *Dunbar's Cove*, *The Insolent Breed* is generally regarded as Deal's most essential work. Precious few original critical assessments of the novel survive, but Deal's obituary in *The New York Times* includes a revealing quote from the *Times*' original review of the novel, in which critic Orville Prescott classifies Deal as "a novelist who actually enjoys amusing his readers and who doesn't think it beneath him to hold their attention." The popularity of the novel would eventually result in its adaptation into the Tony Award-nominated Broadway musical *A Joyful Noise*.

---

## Responses to Literature

1. One of the defining qualities of Deal's work is the way he portrays the southern United States. Read one of Deal's novels and explain what devices he uses to create a vivid portrait of the South. Support your response with details from the novel.

2. Deal followed up his novel *The Least One* with a sequel called *The Other Room*, both novels tracking the development of a character simply named Boy. Read both novels and describe how Boy is portrayed in each one. Does he change significantly from *The Least One* to *The Other Room*? If so, in what ways does Boy change?

3. Just seven years after its publication in 1959, Deal's novel *The Insolent Breed* was brought to the stage as the musical *A Joyful Noise*. Read *The Insolent Breed*. Which qualities of the novel do you think made the producer's of *A Joyful Noise* believe it could be successfully adapted into a stage musical? Write your response in an essay, making sure to support your response with details from the novel.

BIBLIOGRAPHY

**Books**

Dollarhide, Louis. "November 10, 1957 . . . a new novel by a Mississippian," in *Of Arts and Artists: Selected Reviews of the Arts in Mississippi, 1955–1975.* Jackson, Miss.: University of Georgia, 1980, pp. 8–9.

Lloyd, James B. *Lives of Mississippi Authors, 1817–1967.* Jackson, Miss.: University Press of Mississippi, 1981: 125–127

McCarthy, Kevin M. *The Book Lover's Guide to Florida.* Atlanta, Ga.: University of Georgia, 1980, 69–72.

**Periodicals**

"Borden Deal, 62, a Novelist, Who Wrote 'Insolent Breed.'" *The New York Times* (January 25, 1985).

Weiler, A. H. *The New York Times* (May 27, 1960).

**Web Sites**

*Mississippi Writers & Musicians.* "Borden Deal." Accessed November 17, 2008, from http://www.mswritersandmusicians.com/writers/borden-deal.html.

*Murder with Southern Hospitality: An Exhibition of Mississippi Mysteries.* "Borden Deal." Accessed November 17, 2008, from http://hermes.lib.olemiss.edu/mystery/exhibit.asp?display=10&section=3.

*This Goodly Land: Alabama's Literary Landscape.* "Borden Deal." Accessed November 30, 2008, from http://www.alabamaliterarymap.org/author.cfm?AuthorID=99. Last updated May 30, 2008.

# ⚙ Don DeLillo

BORN: *1936, New York, New York*

NATIONALITY: *American*

GENRE: *Fiction, drama*

MAJOR WORKS:
*White Noise* (1985)
*Libra* (1988)
*Mao II* (1991)
*Underworld* (1997)

## Overview

Don DeLillo has established himself as one of the most important contemporary American novelists. His works probe the postmodern American consciousness in all its neurotic permutations, offering a compelling and disturbing portrait of the contemporary American experience.

## Works in Biographical and Historical Context

*Catholic Upbringing and Rituals of the Church*
DeLillo was born on November 20, 1936, in New York

Don DeLillo *AP Images*

City, the son of Italian immigrants. He grew up in the predominantly Italian American Fordham section of the Bronx, and he apparently led a typical boyhood centered around family and sports. Reared a Catholic, DeLillo was exposed early on to the mysteries and rituals of the church, and these had a major influence on his work. He has attributed the sense of mystery that permeates his fiction to his Catholic upbringing, as well as his fiction's concern with various forms of discipline, ritual, and spectacle.

### An Avid Learner with an Aversion to School

DeLillo attended Cardinal Hayes High School in New York, which he despised, and then Fordham University, which he also found less than inspiring. He has cited his aversion to school as the reason he now refuses to give academic lectures or to teach. This antipathy toward formal schooling, however, should not be equated with an indifference to learning, as the massive research projects he undertook in preparation for *Ratner's Star* (1976) and *Libra* (1988) would indicate.

### Writing to Make a Living

After graduating from Fordham, DeLillo began a "short, uninteresting" career at the advertising agency of Ogilvie and Mather. He wrote fiction in his spare time, publishing his first short story, "The River Jordan," in *Epoch* in 1960. Throughout the decade, he would publish a handful of other stories in *Epoch*, *Kenyon Review*, and *Carolina Quarterly*. DeLillo quit his job at Ogilvie and Mather in 1964 and began working as a freelance writer in nonfiction. He wrote pieces on such diverse topics as furniture and computers, and lived on approximately $2,000 a year.

### Techniques Refined in Early Novels

DeLillo began his first novel, *Americana* (1971), in 1966. *Americana* is a sprawling, free-form novel. Such a project possesses an affinity with the Beat aesthetic, and in many ways *Americana* emulates, even satirizes, the "road" novels of writers such as Jack Kerouac. Along with Allen Ginsberg, William S. Burrough, and others, Kerouac belonged to The Beat Generation, a label referring to a group of writers who published works in the late 1950s and early 1960s. These "beatniks," as they are sometimes called, inspired a cultural phenomenon that emphasized spontaneity, emotional engagement with life's difficulties, and spiritual yearning. Although they were characterized by some as bohemian hedonists, their artistic efforts served to liberalize restrictions on published works in the United States.

After *Americana*, DeLillo devoted himself full-time to writing fiction, abandoning all freelance work. He began his second novel, *End Zone* (1972), within weeks of completing *Americana* and in a burst of creative energy finished it within a year. *End Zone* is a more tautly structured and cohesive novel than *Americana*, perhaps an indication that DeLillo learned quite a bit about the craft of novel writing during the four-year ordeal of *Americana*. DeLillo also shifted his thematic focus with his

new novel. Whereas *Americana* was primarily concerned with the influence of the media image on identity in America, *End Zone* explores the importance of language in defining reality.

DeLillo continued the sports theme of *End Zone* shortly after its publication with another contribution to *Sports Illustrated* (November 27, 1972): "Total Loss Weekend," a story about a compulsive gambler who bets on every possible sporting event. But his third novel, *Great Jones Street* (1973), which also appeared within the year, moved into new territory. Having tackled the American pop phenomena of television, film, and football in his first two novels, DeLillo took on a third in *Great Jones Street*: rock and roll. The 1950s and 1960s had seen the rise of the rock star as a pop culture phenomenon. Artists like Elvis Presley and bands like the Beatles were hugely popular. The rock stars of the 1970s, however, became famous as much for their music as for their notoriously wild lifestyles. Stories of promiscuous partying and drug use by rock bands such as Led Zeppelin and the Rolling Stones made headlines in the early 1970s. In *Great Jones Street*, as in his preceding works, DeLillo chose a protagonist and narrator who is an inside player—in this case Bucky Wunderlick, a rock star—who becomes alienated and attempts to withdraw from society. Critics have speculated that DeLillo based his character in part on Bob Dylan, a prolific and influential musician known for his sometimes erratic behavior.

### Searching for a Fresh World View

In contrast to the rapid production of *End Zone* and *Great Jones Street*, DeLillo's fourth novel, *Ratner's Star* (1976), took three years to complete. DeLillo conducted an enormous amount of research in the field of mathematics in preparation, a project he undertook because he "wanted a fresh view of the world." *Ratner's Star* is a long, abstruse novel whose primary subject matter is math and logic. In it, DeLillo abandoned the first-person narration he had used in his first three novels but continued his exploration of human ordering structures, their limitations, and their distortions. He also took on yet another literary genre: science fiction. In addition, in 1975 DeLillo married and moved to a suburb of New York City.

*Ratner's Star* was followed by the shorter, more quickly written novel *Players* (1977). Once again, DeLillo grappled with another phenomenon of the contemporary landscape, terrorism, and appropriated another literary genre as his vehicle, the spy thriller. Yet, despite the different subject matter and form, DeLillo continued to explore his themes of the emptiness and alienation of modern life and the effect of the media upon it. DeLillo's subsequent novel, *Running Dog* (1978), is another spy thriller. Like *Players*, it too examines the dynamics and appeal of conspiracy, as well as exploring DeLillo's recurrent themes of the power of images, commodification, and human organizing structures.

# LITERARY AND HISTORICAL CONTEMPORARIES

DeLillo's famous contemporaries include:

**John F. Kennedy** (1917–1963): The thirty-fifth President of the United States who served from 1961 until his assassination in 1963; his administration was marked by the Civil Rights Movement, the Space Race, and the early years of the Vietnam War.

**Salman Rushdie** (1947–): Indian-British novelist who wrote *Midnight's Children* (1981), which was awarded the Booker Prize, and *The Satanic Verses* (1988), the latter of which prompted Ayatollah Khomeini to issue a fatwa—a religious edict—calling for the author's death.

**Jack Kerouac** (1922–1969): American author, best known as a member of the Beat Generation; his most famous works include *On the Road* and *Dharma Bums*.

**Ayatollah Khomeini** (1902–1989): Political leader of the 1979 Iranian revolution which overthrew Mohammad Reza Pahlavi, the last Shah of Persia; after the revolution, Khomeini ruled Iran until his death in 1989.

**Jean-Luc Godard** (1930–): Franco-Swiss film-maker and founding member of the French New Wave—an informal movement marked by a rejection of classic cinema in favor of youthful iconoclasm.

In the years immediately following, DeLillo wrote a two-act play, *The Engineer of Moonlight* (1979), which has yet to be performed, and lived in Greece for three years researching and writing his seventh major novel, *The Names* (1982). Another examination of the American condition, *The Names* is a postmodern expatriate novel in which DeLillo moves his characters and concerns onto the international scene. It explores American attitudes toward, and interactions with, foreigners and vice versa, focusing on language as the structural underpinning of their divergent conceptions. *The Names* was widely regarded as a departure for DeLillo, a movement away from the fantastic of his previous fiction and toward realism—the depiction of life as it occurs without interpretation.

***Literary Breakthrough*** After completing *The Names*, DeLillo began work on what would become his breakthrough novel, *White Noise* (1985). In 1983, however, he took time off from its composition to research and write an essay on the assassination of President John Kennedy, "American Blood: A Journey through the Labyrinth of Dallas and JFK," which was published in *Rolling Stone* in December of that year. President John Kennedy was shot dead while riding in an open car in Dallas, Texas, on November 22, 1963, an event that profoundly shocked and saddened the country.

***Fictionalizing the Kennedy Assassination*** DeLillo's two-act play, *The Day Room*, premiered at the American Repertory Theater in April 1986, then was performed at the Manhattan Theater Club in New York City and published in 1987. During this time, DeLillo was working on his ninth novel, *Libra*, a fictionalized account of the Kennedy assassination that he began in the fall of 1984 before *White Noise* was even published. The Kennedy assassination was a pivotal event for DeLillo's generation and for modern America in general, a watershed that he has repeatedly acknowledged as a major literary influence and to which he had alluded in many of his previous novels. *Libra* would prove to be DeLillo's most artistically successful work to date.

***Defending Artistic Freedom*** DeLillo began his tenth novel, *Mao II* (1991), in March 1989, shortly after the Ayatollah Khomeini—at that time the leader of the Islamic government of Iran—issued a death sentence for British author Salman Rushdie for "blaspheming" Islam in his novel *The Satanic Verses* (1989). DeLillo viewed this event as a threat to artistic freedom everywhere, and it strongly affected his new novel. DeLillo, along with several other writers, read from Rushdie's work at the Columns in New York City in a show of support for Rushdie and freedom of speech that was organized by the Author's Guild, PEN American Center, and Article 19. DeLillo worked on *Mao II* for the next two years, during which time (April 1990) his short play *The Rapture of the Athlete Assumed into Heaven* (1990) was performed by the American Repertory Theater.

***Unique Views of History*** DeLillo's most recent works of fiction include *Underworld* (1997), which traces the journeys of a baseball and remains one of his better-known works, *The Body Artist* (2001), an unusually philosophical novel for DeLillo, *Cosmopolis* (2003), set in a billionaire's limousine moving across Manhattan, and *Falling Man* (2007), the story of a survivor of the September 11, 2001, terrorist attacks on the United States.

## Works in Literary Context

Widely regarded as a preeminent satirist of modern culture, DeLillo depicts American society as rampant with paranoia and malaise and on the brink of chaos. His fiction displays a preoccupation with the overwhelming influence of the American media and the ritualistic qualities of language, the latter of which he considers the only human means capable of imposing order on random events. DeLillo's work is often compared to that of Thomas Pynchon and Kurt Vonnegut for its black humor and apocalyptic vision. Although he credits writers such as Gertrude Stein, Ezra Pound, and, later, Pynchon and William Gaddis for awakening him to the possibilities of writing, it was the European films (particularly those of Franco-Swiss film-maker Jean-Luc Godard), jazz, and Abstract Expressionism to which he was exposed in New

York that he acknowledges as primary influences. DeLillo has suggested that the assassination of President John F. Kennedy had a bigger impact on his writing than any of his literary predecessors.

### The White Noise of the Post-modern Experience

A darkly comic novel, *White Noise* focuses on a single American family in another attempt to probe the post-modern American experience. White noise—the sound of all audible radio frequencies heard simultaneously—is the central metaphor of the novel, linking its major themes. As information without meaning, white noise suggests, on one level, the media bombardment designed not to inform the public but to sell commercial products to it. One consequence of the mediated existence, of life removed from the direct apprehension of experience, is that life and death become abstractions. The novel's protagonists, the Gladneys, are fascinated by "media disaster," the floods, earthquakes, and accidents that make up the television news, but are nonplussed when they find themselves in the midst of one during the Airborne Toxic Event.

DeLillo's work has influenced numerous contemporary authors including, but not limited to, Bret Easton Ellis, David Foster Wallace, and Jonathan Franzen.

## Works in Critical Context

DeLillo's early works were not widely reviewed and critiques of *Americana*, *End Zone*, *Great Jones Street*, *Ratner's Star*, *Running Dog*, and *The Names* ranged from qualified praise to descriptions of the author's many limitations. It was with the publication of *White Noise*, in 1985, that DeLillo achieved wide-spread critical acclaim. Since then, his works have become increasingly popular, establishing him firmly as an important contemporary American author.

### White Noise

*White Noise* was highly acclaimed and won the 1985 American Book Award for fiction. Richard Eder in the *Los Angeles Times Book Review* (January 13, 1985) called *White Noise* a "stunning book" that adroitly captured the contemporary American mood. The novel, he declared, was "a moving picture of a disquiet we seem to share more and more." Eder waxed poetic about DeLillo's talent: "The author is Charon as a master mariner; his flame, like Quevedo's, knows how to swim the icy water. He brings us across the Styx in a lilting maneuver that is so adept that we can't help laughing as we go." Jayne Anne Phillips in *The New York Times Book Review* (January 13, 1985) also praised DeLillo's insight into the American psyche, calling *White Noise* "timely and frightening ... because of its totally American concerns, its rendering of a particularly American numbness." She found Jack Gladney's narrative voice "one of the most ironic, intelligent, grimly funny voices yet to comment on life in present-day America." Diane Johnson in the *New York Review of Books* (March 14, 1985) agreed, citing Jack's "eloquence" as mitigating what might otherwise have been an overly "exacting and despairing view of

---

## COMMON HUMAN EXPERIENCE

Foremost among the themes in DeLillo's *White Noise* is the fear of death. In particular, this novel shows various attempts people make in modern life to avoid confronting this fear. Other works that negotiate death include the following:

> *The Waste Land* (1922), a poem by T. S. Eliot. Frequently regarded as one of the seminal works of modernist literature, this complex work draws on many different religious and mythological traditions—as well as historical moments—in offering an extended meditation on death.
>
> *As I Lay Dying* (1930), a novel by William Faulkner. The multiple narrators showcase a variety of responses to death, specifically that of Addie Bundren.
>
> *The Denial of Death* (1973), a nonfiction book by Ernest Becker. This work, winner of the 1974 Pulitzer Prize, builds on a philosophical foundation containing ideas from Søren Kierkegaard, Sigmund Freud, and Otto Rank; and argues that human civilization is a defense against our knowledge of mortality.

---

civilization." Like many reviewers, Walter Clemons in *Newsweek* (January 21, 1985) predicted that *White Noise* would gain DeLillo "wide recognition ... as one of the best American novelists."

In stark contrast to his earlier works, the novels that followed *White Noise* were widely reviewed and positively received. *Libra* became a best-seller and a critical success. It won the Irish Times-Aer Lingus International Fiction Prize and was nominated for the American Book Award. *Mao II* won the PEN/Faulkner Award.

## Responses to Literature

1. Analyze the Gladney's reaction to the Airborne Toxic Event in *White Noise*. Why do they react the way they do? What can their reaction tell us about Don DeLillo's perspective on media in society?

2. Why is Murrey pleased that "No one sees the [most photographed] barn" in *White Noise*?

3. Throughout *White Noise*, Jack's fear of death is revealed. By the end of the novel, does he overcome this fear?

4. What role does the supermarket play in *White Noise*?

BIBLIOGRAPHY

**Books**

Duvall, John. *Don DeLillo's Underworld: A Reader's Guide*. New York: Continuum International Publishing Group, 2002.

Kavadlo, Jesse. *Don DeLillo: Balance at the Edge of Belief.* New York: Peter Lang Publishing, 2004.

Keesey, Douglas. *Don DeLillo.* New York: Twayne, 1993.

Lentricchia, Frank (ed.). *New Essays on White Noise.* New York: Cambridge University Press, 1991.

Ruppersburg, Hugh (ed.), Engles, Tim (ed.). *Critical Essays on Don DeLillo.* New York: G.K. Hall, 2000.

**Periodicals**

Bryant, Paula. "Don DeLillo: An Annotated Biographical and Critical Secondary Bibliography, 1977–1986." *Bulletin of Bibliography* 45 (September 1988): 208–212.

DeCurtis, Anthony. "'An Outsider in This Society': An Interview with Don DeLillo." *South Atlantic Quarterly* 89 (Spring 1990): 281–304.

# ✿ Kate DiCamillo

BORN: *1964, Philadelphia, Pennsylvania*

NATIONALITY: *American*

GENRE: *Fiction*

MAJOR WORKS:

*Because of Winn-Dixie* (2000)

*The Tale of Despereaux* (2004)

Kate DiCamillo  *DiCamillo, Kate, photograph. Reproduced by permission of Kate DiCamillo.*

## Overview

From adverse conditions, talented writers often emerge. Beloved children's author Kate DiCamillo is a testament to this. As a young child, she suffered from pneumonia five years in a row. As an adult, she is delighting children all over the world with such whimsical tales as *Because of Winn-Dixie* (2000) and *The Tale of Despereaux* (2004).

## Works in Biographical and Historical Context

*A Troubled Childhood* DiCamillo was born on March 25, 1964, in Philadelphia, Pennsylvania. Her earliest years were her most difficult. When she was five years old her father left her and her mother. The years prior to his disappearance were no easier, as she suffered from severe pneumonia. A doctor recommended a warmer climate for the DiCamillos for the sake of Kate's health, so her family moved to central Florida. While still a girl, DiCamillo developed a love of literature that inspired her to try her hand at composing stories of her own, and she soon discovered that she had considerable talent.

*In Pursuit of a Dream* Success was not instantaneous, and DiCamillo supported herself with a number of odd jobs, including, in her words, "selling tickets at Circus World, planting philodendrons in a greenhouse, calling bingo at a campground, running rides at an amusement park." As she bounced from job to job, she continued to write, composing at least two pages each day. The result of this approach was her first short story, although she admits, "It was a very bad short story." However, she revised the piece and felt comfortable enough with the results to submit it to a magazine. Although the magazine rejected it, DiCamillo had developed a taste for writing and became more keenly focused on her dream than ever.

Having moved from Florida to Minnesota in 1994, DiCamillo took a job with a book wholesaler where she filled book orders. This job left her with the time to read some of the books that surrounded her. As it so happened, she worked on the floor of the office building where the children's books were stored. So, between taking care of orders from bookstores and libraries, DiCamillo became acquainted with a variety of children's books. As she relates:

> I read picture books and poetry books and board books and one day, I picked up a novel written for children called *The Watsons Go to Birmingham, 1963.* Christopher Paul Curtis's book changed my life. I read it and decided I wanted to try to write a novel for kids.

*Capturing the Dream* DiCamillo devoted herself to working on her first children's novel. *Because of Winn-Dixie* reflects DiCamillo's interests at the time she wrote it. Opal, the novel's main character, is a girl who has just moved (although she has moved to Florida instead of away from it) and makes her first friend: a dog she meets at the Winn-Dixie supermarket. While writing the book, dog-lover DiCamillo was also suffering because she lived in an apartment building in which dogs were not allowed, "and suffering mightily from a disease I refer to as 'dog withdrawal,'" she says in her autobiography. Opal is also similar to DiCamillo in her love of stories. As the ten year old continues to make friends throughout the summer, she avidly collects their own personal stories.

*Because of Winn-Dixie* was published in 2000. The book is not only an entertaining and enjoyable tale for kids; it is also a poignant exploration of loss. (Like DiCamillo's real-life father, Opal's mother is absent in the novel.) The complexity of the book was not lost on critics, who praised it as a poignant and humorous coming-of-age story. The novel also earned DiCamillo several awards, including the Josette Frank Award and the Newbery Honor, and appeared on many "best book of the year" lists. More importantly, it served as a signpost that DiCamillo had finally achieved her long-sought dream.

DiCamillo followed her debut novel with *The Tiger Rising* (2001), the story of a young boy named Rob Horton who makes a strange and wonderful discovery when he finds a caged tiger in the woods by his Florida home. Three years later, she published *The Tale of Despereaux*. "My best friend's son asked if I would write a story for him," she told About.com. "'It's about an unlikely hero,' he said, 'with exceptionally large ears.'" After asking the boy, "What happened to the hero," he replied, "I don't know. That's why I want you to write this story, so we can find out." Again, DiCamillo wowed readers and critics alike. *The Tale of Despereaux* won her another Newbery award. Her fourth novel, *The Miraculous Journey of Edward Tulane*, followed in 2006, to more acclaim.

*Exploring New Territory* While still maintaining her focus on young people, DiCamillo has diversified her writing. She has written several chapter books— books aimed at intermediate readers—featuring a pig named Mercy Watson. The pig gets into various adventures, whether she is attempting to rescue a mysteriously sinking bed in *Mercy Watson to the Rescue* (2005) or tumbling into Halloween-related high jinks in *Mercy Watson Princess in Disguise* (2007). "Mercy Watson had been in my head for a long time," DiCamillo explains on her Web site, "but I couldn't figure out how to tell her story." A discussion with one of her friends "about the many virtues of toast" suddenly triggered inspiration, and the toast-loving Mercy came into focus. According to DiCamillo, "Sometimes you don't truly understand a character until you know what she loves above all else." DiCamillo has also written two picture books: *Great Joy* (2007) and *Louise, the Adventures of a Chicken* (2008).

In 2005, DiCamillo's work branched out further when *Because of Winn-Dixie* was adapted into a major motion picture starring Jeff Daniels and Cicely Tyson and directed by Wayne Wang. An animated film version of

*The Tale of Despereaux*, with Matthew Broderick providing the voice of the title character, was released in 2008.

DiCamillo continues to live in Minnesota and publish regularly. She is the owner of a pup named Henry, who brings her as much pleasure as the crowd and critic-pleasing stories she conjures. As she says on her web site, "I think of myself as an enormously lucky person: I get to tell stories for a living."

## Works in Literary Context

*The Fairy Tale* Fairy tales, sometimes called fairy stories, are fictional yarns that often include such outlandish elements as talking animals, bizarre creatures, and magic. Fairy tales may have existed for as long as stories have been told, the originals being passed along in the oral tradition. The most well-known and influential collection of fairy tales was published in 1812 by the German brothers Wilhelm and Jacob Grimm. *Children's and Household Tales* would expose the world at large to such

# COMMON HUMAN EXPERIENCE

In her novel *Because of Winn-Dixie*, DiCamillo explores the friendship between a girl and her dog. The theme of human relationships with animals is a common one in children's literature. Other children's books that focus on human/animal relationships include:

*The Story of Doctor Dolittle* (1920), a book by Hugh Lofting. *The Story of Doctor Dolittle* marks the first appearance of the extraordinary Dr. Dolittle, a medical doctor with the uncanny ability to communicate with animals.

*The Black Stallion* (1941), a book by Walter Farley. The first in a series of books following the friendship between a horse and its young companion Alec Ramsay, *The Black Stallion* finds Alec and the Black stranded on a desert island together. A close bond forms between the boy and the horse as they rely on each other to survive.

*Old Yeller* (1956), a novel by Fred Gipson. *Old Yeller* is a moving story of friendship and responsibility focusing on young Travis Coates and his dog.

*Gentle Ben* (1965), a book by Walt Morey. A captive bear is visited by a boy named Mark, and a close friendship develops between the unlikely pair. This much-loved children's book was turned into a television series that aired for two years in the late 1960s.

famous stories as "Snow White" and "Hansel and Gretel" and provide the backbone of the fairy tale tradition that continues to the modern age with contemporary fairy tales like DiCamillo's *The Tale of Despereaux*.

***Magical Realism*** The artistic genre called magical realism is defined by the appearance of magical elements in an otherwise realistic setting. The term was first coined by the German art critic Franz Roh to apply to the visual arts in an essay titled "After Expressionism: Magical Realism" published in 1925. The term as used in the visual arts implied a very realistic representation of reality. In the 1960s, the term was used to describe literature that combined fantasy and naturalistic reality in a seamless manner. This method of storytelling was particularly favored by Latin American writers like Carlos Fuentes and Gabriel García Márquez. While the works of Fuentes and Márquez are decidedly adult, the term magic realism has also been applied to writers like DiCamillo, who blends the real and the unreal in novels like *The Tale of Despereaux* and *The Miraculous Journey of Edward Tulane*.

## Works in Critical Context

***Because of Winn-Dixie*** DiCamillo's debut novel won over critics as soon as it was published. Critics took special note of the novel's structure, with a reviewer for *Publishers Weekly* commenting, "In this exquisitely crafted first novel [a Newbery Honor book], each chapter possesses an arc of its own and reads almost like a short story in its completeness." However, the qualities that most moved critics were the novel's warm tone and poignant vision of a girl's maturity. Betsy Groban, in her review for *The New York Times Book Review*, calls it "a poignant and delicately told story of a dog as a child's much-needed best friend." Christine M. Heppermann, in her review for *Horn Book Magazine*, concedes that the book "teeters on the edge of sentimentality and sometimes topples right in," but concludes, "All in all, this is a gentle book about good people coming together to combat loneliness and heartache—with a little canine assistance." The novel's enthusiastic response was further emphasized by its winning of several major literary awards, including a 2001 Newbery Award.

***The Tale of Despereaux*** DiCamillo's third novel, *The Tale of Despereaux*, proved to be another in her impressive string of critical successes. More of a fairy tale than her previous work, *The Tale of Despereaux* was intended for a younger audience, but critics still appreciated it for its whimsy and engrossing characters and action. Miriam Lang Budin, in a review for *School Library Journal*, calls the book "entertaining, heartening, and, above all, great fun." In her review for *Bulletin of the Center for Children's Book*, Janice M. Del Negro writes, "There is a classic charm to this picaresque tale ... that and a pace that lends itself to reading aloud will make this novel a favorite among those ready for some gentle questing." Once again, DiCamillo was honored for her book with a Newbery Award.

## Responses to Literature

1. When the film version of *Because of Winn-Dixie* was released in 2005, some critics did not respond favorably. Research and read three negative reviews of the *Because of Winn-Dixie* film. Then read the novel on which the film was based. Do the negative comments made by film critics apply to the book? Why or why not? Write your response as a short essay.

2. DiCamillo has written a variety of children's literature, including picture books for young children like *Louise, the Adventures of a Chicken* and novels for older kids like *Because of Winn-Dixie*. Read one of DiCamillo's books intended for young children, and one intended for older readers. Do you notice any similarities between the two books that define DiCamillo as an author? How does her writing differ? Write your response in an essay, using examples from her work to illustrate your points.

3. *The Tale of Despereaux* has been described as a contemporary fairy tale. Read the novel, and then write

an essay explaining which qualities of *The Tale of Despereaux* make it part of the fairy tale tradition. Support your response with details from the novel.

## BIBLIOGRAPHY

**Periodicals**

Blais, Jacqueline. "Author Newbery is No Small Thrill." *USA Today* (January 14, 2004).

Budin, Miriam Lang. Review of *The Tale of Despereaux*. *School Library Journal* 49, no. 8 (August 2003): 126.

Del Negro, Janice M. Review of *The Tale of Despereaux*. *Bulletin of the Center for Children's Books* 57, no. 3 (November 2003): 99.

Groban, Betsy. Review of *Because of Winn-Dixie*. *The New York Times Book Review* (May 14, 2000): 26.

Heppermann, Christine M. Review of *Because of Winn-Dixie*. *Horn Book Magazine* 76, no. 4 (July–August 2000): 455–456.

Margolies, Jane. "Pleasantly Stunned, a Star Children's Author Hits the Tour Trail Again." *The New York Times* (February 21, 2006).

**Web Sites**

About.com. *Newbery Medal Winner Kate Dicamillo.* Accessed November 18, 2008, from http://childrensbooks.about.com/cs/authorsillustrato/a/katedicamillo.htm.

Book Browse. *Kate DiCamillo—Biography.* Accessed November 18, 2008, from http://www.bookbrowse.com/biographies/index.cfm?author_number=573.

Candlewick Press. *Kate DiCamillo.* Accessed November 18, 2008, from http://www.candlewick.com/authill.asp?b=Author&m=bio&id=1989&pix=y.

Kate DiCamillo.com. *About Kate.* Accessed November 18, 2008, from http://www.katedicamillo.com/about.html.

Wilson Biographies.com. *Kate DiCamillo: Autobiographical Statement.* Accessed November 18, 2008, from http://wilsonbiographies.com/print/jrauthorbk_9th_dicamillo.htm.

# ⊛ Philip K. Dick

BORN: *1928, Chicago, Illinois*

DIED: *1982, Santa Ana, California*

NATIONALITY: *American*

GENRE: *Fiction*

MAJOR WORKS:
*The Man in the High Castle* (1962)
*Do Androids Dream of Electric Sheep?* (1968)
*Ubik* (1969)
*Flow My Tears, the Policeman Said* (1970)
*A Scanner Darkly* (1973)

Philip K. Dick   *Photo courtesy of Anne Dick / Courtesy of the Philip K. Dick Trust*

## Overview

Philip K. Dick has been hailed as one of the most original and thought-provoking writers of science fiction. Often addressing the delicate balance between illusion and reality, Dick used the standard fare of this genre—robots, space ships, and alternative universes—to explore the complexities of human nature. He published more than thirty novels and one hundred short stories during his lifetime, but only after his death did his fame spread from science-fiction fans to mainstream audiences.

## Works in Biographical and Historical Context

*Love for Music* Philip Kindred Dick was born in Chicago in 1928, but he lived most of his life in California in the San Francisco Bay area. A longtime music lover, he worked while still in his teens as an announcer for a classical-music program on station KSMO in 1947; he also operated a record store from 1948 to 1952. He attended the University of California at Berkeley in 1950, but dropped out because the required R.O.T.C. (Reserve Officer Training Corps) component of the curriculum conflicted with his antiwar convictions.

*Abandoning Short Stories for the Novel* From Dick's first sale of a story entitled "Roog" to Anthony Boucher of the *Magazine of Fantasy and Science Fiction* in 1952 and his first published story, "Beyond Lies the

Wub" in *Planet Stories* (the same year), his publishing career has followed a curious course. Of his some 110 short stories, 28 were published in 1953 and another 28 in 1954, but beginning with the appearance of *Solar Lottery* in 1955 he turned primarily to the novel.

***Literary Output Peaks*** Dick's early works, including *Eye in the Sky* (1957) and *Time Out of Joint* (1959), reflect his curiosity about the nature of reality as well as a fear of omnipotent authority and political oligarchies. These subjects are particularly evident in his Hugo Award-winning novel *The Man in the High Castle* (1962). In this work, Dick envisioned a world in which Germany and Japan have divided the United States between them after winning World War II. Through this scenario Dick examined an America willing to give up its own culture under occupation and whose racial fears and prejudices are compatible with Nazism. Although *The Man in the High Castle* was published in 1962, his novel-writing peak was perhaps from 1964 to 1969, when sixteen volumes were published.

In *Dr. Futurity* (1960) a physician named Jim Parsons finds himself in the remote future, among tribesmen who force him to play a role in which he must tamper with destiny. This novel was followed by *The Man in the High Castle*; *The Game-Players of Titan* (1963), a further development of game theory and other standard Dick themes; *Clans of the Alphane Moon* (1964); and *The Penultimate Truth* (1964). The last, another story of rulers and the ruled, is further evidence of Dick's concern with fascism and oppression of any kind. In *The Penultimate Truth*, set in 2025 C.E., most people live in underground factories to construct robots that are being used in World War III.

***A Religious Vision*** In 1975, Dick won the John W. Campbell Memorial Award for *Flow My Tears, The Policeman Said* (1970). In this novel, Dick uses the recurring subjects of a stifling bureaucracy and synthetic organisms to explore such philosophical queries as the nature of identity and the definition of morality. Dick is also concerned with the existence of God, a matter that became increasingly important to him. In 1974, Dick claimed to have had a religious vision, and he spent the remainder of his life working on an "exegesis" to come to terms with this revelation. Dick's preoccupation with theological issues in his later years is apparent in his last novels, *VALIS* (1981), *The Divine Invasion* (1981), and *The Transmigration of Timothy Archer* (1982).

***Public Speaking and Other Interests*** In his later years, he lectured on college campuses. In early 1975, he was also invited to participate in a series of lectures at the Institute of Contemporary Arts in London, in a series organized by anthropologist Ted Polhemus. However, Dick was unable to attend because of illness; his contribution, "Man, Android and Machine," was printed in *Science Fiction at Large* (1976).

Evidence of his varied interests was shown by his memberships in organizations ranging from the Animal Protection Institute to the Science Fiction Writers of America, by his authorship of radio scripts for the Mutual Broadcasting System, by his work in antiabortion efforts and drug rehabilitation, and by his discussions about religion with the late Bishop James A. Pike. These interests were in part summarized in 1975 by Dick: "My major preoccupation is the question, 'What is reality?' Many of my stories and novels deal with psychotic states or drug-induced states by which I can present the concept of a multiverse rather than a universe. Music and sociology are themes in my novels, also radical political trends; in particular I've written about fascism and my fear of it."

***Fixation on Drug Abuse*** Proof of the depth of his concern with drug abuse is his dedication of *A Scanner Darkly* (1973) to some fifteen "comrades" who are either deceased or permanently damaged as a result of drug abuse. In *A Scanner Darkly*, Dick arrives at what one reviewer has called his "enigmatic best." A detailed account of a future drug culture, it weaves a plot in which Fred, an undercover narcotics agent, and Robert Arctor, a user, are one and the same more-or-less human being until the irreversible brain damage caused by "Substance D" leaves only a lesser being called Bruce. The central enigma of the novel is Dick's insistence that "There is no moral to this novel," when the book so obviously attacks the drug culture; and the answer to this enigma sums up much of what Dick's work has been all about.

On occasion, Dick published stories under the pseudonym Richard Phillips, and in addition to his vast science-fiction canon he wrote a mainstream novel, *Confessions of a Crap Artist* (1975). Dick died of a massive stroke in 1982.

***Film Adaptations Prove Successful*** Since his death, at least nine of Dick's works were adapted for film including the novel *Do Androids Dream of Electric Sheep?* (1968) as *Blade Runner* (1982), the short story "We Can Remember It for You Wholesale" (1966) as *Total Recall* (1990), *Minority Report* (2002), based on Dick's story by the same name, and *A Scanner Darkly*, its name unchanged, premiered in 2006. The films brought Dick's name to the attention of a much wider audience than his novels had enjoyed during his lifetime. His literary reputation has also risen dramatically in the years since his passing. In 2007 and 2008, nine of his novels were published in two volumes by the Library of America. They were the first science fiction works included in that prestigious series of literary classics.

## Works in Literary Context

Dick's work was influenced by numerous authors, including Gustave Flaubert, Honoré de Balzac, Immanuel Kant, Marcel Proust, Carl Jung, Samuel Beckett, Fyodor

Dostoyevsky, Nathanael West, Jorge Luis Borges, and the satirical science-fiction writer John Sladek. Dick often portrayed bleak futuristic landscapes, oppressive government bureaucracies, and the destructive potential of advanced technology, especially mechanical or electronic simulations of organic life. Two basic narratives recur in his work. One favorite plot device is that of alternative universes or parallel worlds, of which *The Man in the High Castle* is a prime example.

*Simulacra*  The other favorite plot device involves what Dick characteristically calls "simulacra," devices ranging from merely complex mechanical and electronic technology to humanlike androids, and the paradoxes created by their relationships to organic life, especially human beings. Typical examples are *The Simulacra* (1964), *We Can Build You* (1972), and the better-known *Do Androids Dream of Electric Sheep?* (1968). In *The Simulacra*, as the title indicates, Dick emphasizes mechanical, electronic, or other simulations of organic life.

As with so many of Dick's books, *Now Wait for Last Year* (1966) is an extended meditation on the nature of reality and on the necessary distinctions between the real and the merely simulated. Yet there is always ambivalence embedded within Dick's treatment of simulacra, as is seen in the sympathetic treatment of the persecuted androids in *Do Androids Dream of Electric Sheep?* In this novel, nominated for the Nebula Award in 1968, androids originally used in the colony worlds develop increasingly human traits; some escape to Earth and pose as human beings, although they are subject to destruction by bounty hunters. What, the book asks, is the real meaning of humanity?

Dick's works have been highly praised by such fellow science-fiction writers as Anthony Boucher, Harlan Ellison, Michael Moorcock, and Robert Silverberg. John Brunner, himself a master of parallel universes, has repeatedly called Dick "the most consistently brilliant science fiction writer in the world." According to some scholars his work has influenced novelists such as Jonathan Lethem, Roberto Bolaño, and Rodrigo Fresán; philosophers such as Jean Baudrillard, Frederick Jameson, and Slavoj Zizek; and filmmakers such as David Cronenberg, Richard Linklater, and the Wachowski brothers.

## Works in Critical Context

For the most part critics have greeted Dick's work with high regard. Although he is occasionally faulted for an awkward prose style and hackneyed dialogue, he is commended for creating sympathetic protagonists who, while not heroic, attempt to carry on with their lives under difficult circumstances. Dick's proponents have asserted that his complex narrative structures provide the framework for the equally complex philosophical questions that he asks of his readers. While often impugning the validity of American social and political institutions, Dick expresses confidence in a fundamental

## LITERARY AND HISTORICAL CONTEMPORARIES

Dick's famous contemporaries include:

**Alvin Toffler** (1928–): The American author, futurist, and former editor of *Fortune* magazine; his works deal with the digital and communications revolution.

**Anne Sexton** (1928–1974): The confessional work of American poet Sexton is often unfairly overshadowed by the controversy surrounding her mental health.

**Paul Johnson** (1928–): A British journalist, speech writer, historian, and author of more than forty books whose work has grown increasingly conservative throughout his career.

**Andy Warhol** (1928–1987): Warhol was an author, artist, and public figure most famous for his success as a commercial illustrator and central figure of the pop-art movement.

**Ursula K. Le Guin** (1929–): American author of "thought experiments" in the science fiction and fantasy genres, as well as children's books.

human capacity for compassion and tenderness. Following Dick's death, Norman Spinrad commented that Dick possessed a "clear and genuine metaphysical insight and loving warmth that made him the great writer that he was."

*High Praise for Flow My Tears, the Policeman Said*  Dick received the John W. Campbell Memorial Award for *Flow My Tears, the Policeman Said*, a novel of the near future in which popular television talk-show host Jason Taverner wakes up one morning in a world where he is unknown. "Dick skillfully explores the psychological ramifications of this nightmare," Gerald Jonas commented in the *New York Times Book Review*, "but he is even more interested in the reaction of a ruthlessly efficient and computerized police state to the existence of a man, who, according to the computers, should not exist." Similar praise came from critic Richard Hammersley of *Infinity Plus*, "One of the best of Dick's plots ... Dick throws out ideas for the future here, there and everywhere that a lesser writer would hoard for other books. ... The book remains one of the best novels by someone with a literally amazing imagination, which is rarer in [science fiction] than you might think."

Dick is generally regarded as one of the finest science fiction writers of his time. Peter Nicholls of the *Science Fiction Review* considered him "one of the greatest science fiction writers in history, and one of this century's most important writers in any field." Offering more reserved praise, John Clute of the *Times Literary Supplement* holds that Dick was the "greatest of science fiction

## COMMON HUMAN EXPERIENCE

Central to Dick's work is the question, "What does it mean to be human?" Other works that explore this theme include the following:

*The Human Condition* (1958), a nonfiction book by Hannah Arendt. This philosophical text explores human history from the ancient Greeks to modern Europe, ultimately suggesting possibilities for the modern world.

*What Does it Mean to Be Human?* (2001), a nonfiction book by Frederick Franck, Janis Roze, and Richard Connolly. This inspirational work combines a diverse set of meditations on the human condition.

*The Monkey in the Mirror* (2002), an essay collection by Ian Tattersall. This work contains essays on the science of what makes us human.

writers—though he's by no means the best writer of science fiction." In her evaluation of Dick's work, Ursula K. Le Guin, writing for the *New Republic*, stresses that it is easy to misinterpret Dick. A reader "may put the book down believing that he's read a clever sci-fi thriller and nothing more," Le Guin writes. "The fact that what Dick is entertaining us about is reality and madness, time and death, sin and salvation—this has escaped most readers and critics."

### Responses to Literature

1. Why do you think Dick chose to phrase the title of his novel *Do Androids Dream of Electric Sheep?* as a question?

2. How does Dick satirize the function of technology in modern society?

3. Why do you think Dick's fiction is so appealing to Hollywood film makers?

4. Dick's work challenges readers to ask themselves such questions as, "What does it mean to be human?" and "What is real?" Drawing from Dick's fiction, pose and try to answer such a question for yourself, noting any difficulties you encounter as you go along.

BIBLIOGRAPHY

**Books**

Moskowitz, Sam. *Seekers of Tomorrow.* New York: Ballantine, 1967.

Taylor, Angus. *Philip K. Dick & The Umbrella of Light.* Baltimore: T-K Graphics, 1975.

Warrick, Patricia S. and Martin Harry Greenberg. *Robots, Androids, and Mechanical Oddities: The Science Fiction of Philip K. Dick.* Carbondale, Ill.: Southern Illinois University Press, 1984.

**Periodicals**

Aldiss, Brian W. "Dick's Maledictory Web: About and Around *Martian Time-Slip.*" *Science-Fiction Studies* 2 (March 1975): 42–47.

Bray, Mary Kay. "Mandalic Activism: An Approach to Structure, Theme, and Tone in Four Novels by Philip K. Dick." *Extrapolation* 21 (Summer 1980): 146–157.

Green, Terence M. "Philip K. Dick: A Parallax View." *Science Fiction Review* 5 (1976): 12–15.

Le Guin, Ursula K. "Science Fiction as Prophesy: Philip K. Dick." *New Republic* 175 (October 30, 1976): 33–34.

Lem, Stanislaw. "Philip K. Dick: A Visionary Among the Charlatans." *Science-Fiction Studies* 2 (March 1975): 54–67.

Mullen, R. D. and Darko Suvin, eds. "The Science Fiction of Philip K. Dick." *Science-Fiction Studies* 2 (March 1975): 3–75.

Suvin, Darko. "P. K. Dick's Opus: Artifice as Refuge and World View (Introductory Reflections)." *Science-Fiction Studies* 2 (March 1975): 8–22.

## James Dickey

BORN: *1923, Buckhead, Georgia*

DIED: *1997, Columbia, South Carolina*

NATIONALITY: *American*

GENRE: *Poetry, fiction, nonfiction*

MAJOR WORKS:

*Buckdancer's Choice* (1965)

*Deliverance* (1970)

*The Strength of Fields* (1979)

*Alnilam* (1987)

*To the White Sea* (1993)

### Overview

A prominent figure in contemporary American literature, James Dickey is best known for his intense exploration of the primal, irrational, creative, and ordering forces in life. Often classified as a visionary Romantic in the tradition of Walt Whitman, Dylan Thomas, and Theodore Roethke, Dickey emphasizes the primacy of imagination and examines the relationship between humanity and nature.

### Works in Biographical and Historical Context

***Early Awareness of Death*** Born in Buckhead, Georgia, an affluent community then on the outskirts of Atlanta, on February 2, 1923, James Lafayette Dickey, the second son of lawyer Eugene Dickey and Maibelle Swift Dickey, grew up with the knowledge that he was a "replacement child" for Eugene Jr., a brother who had

James Dickey    *1990, photograph. AP Images.*

died of meningitis. This early awareness of the relationship between death and life, reinforced by his combat experiences in early adulthood, contributed to his later poetic theme of living the energized life.

***From Athletics to Academics***  Dickey's high-school interests centered on athletics, particularly football and track. After graduating from North Fulton High in 1941, he attended Darlington School in Rome, Georgia, from 1941 to 1942. While he was there, in December 1941, the United States entered World War II. In the fall of 1942, he entered Clemson A&M (now Clemson University) where he played tailback on the freshman football squad, but at the end of his first semester he joined the U.S. Army Air Corps. From 1943 to 1945, he participated in approximately one hundred combat missions as a member of the 418th Night Fighter Squadron in the South Pacific.

After the war, Dickey enrolled at Vanderbilt University. This change in schools marked his shift in interest from athletics to academics. At Vanderbilt, Dickey soon came to the attention of English professor Monroe Spears, who recognized his student's literary talent and guided him to major in English and philosophy and minor in astronomy. On November 4, 1948 Dickey married Maxine Syerson, with whom he would have two sons, Christopher and Kevin. In 1949, Dickey earned a

BA degree in English, graduating magna cum laude. Then, in 1950, he received his MA. His thesis for the latter was titled "Symbol and Image in the Short Poems of Herman Melville."

Dickey began his teaching career at Rice Institute in September 1950, but four months later he was recalled to active military duty, in the training command of the U.S. Air Force during the Korean War. After completing his military obligations, he returned to Rice and began making journal entries toward a novel that thirty-six years later he would publish as *Alnilam* (1987).

***Advertising Career and Poetry Accolades***  In 1954, Dickey received a *Sewanee Review* Fellowship, with which he traveled to Europe and concentrated on writing poetry. A year later, he moved to the University of Florida where, with the help of novelist and historian Andrew Lytle, he had obtained a teaching appointment. He resigned this position, however, in the spring of 1956, following a controversy arising from his reading of his poem "The Father's Body." Dickey then left Florida for New York; there he established himself in a successful advertising career, first as a copywriter and later as an executive with McCann-Erickson. During the next three years, Dickey was associated with a series of advertising agencies. He eventually returned to Atlanta where he created advertisements for such companies as Coca-Cola and Delta Air Lines.

While writing ad copy, Dickey also added to his growing list of poetry publications and awards. In 1958, he received the Union League's Civic and Arts Foundation Prize from the Union League Club of Chicago for poems published in *Poetry: A Magazine of Verse*. A year later, he won the Vachel Lindsay Prize and the Longview Foundation Award. A collection of his poetry was published as *Into the Stone and Other Poems* with work by Jon Swan and Paris Leary in *Poets of Today VII* (1960), and the following year he permanently abandoned his career in advertising. During 1961–1962 a Guggenheim Fellowship allowed Dickey to travel to Positano, Italy, where he composed *Drowning with Others* (1962).

***Poet-in-Residence***  Dickey returned to the United States in 1962 and spent the next four years as a poet-in-residence at such schools as Reed College (1963–1964), San Fernando Valley State College (1964–1965), and the University of Wisconsin-Madison (1966). His collection *Helmets* appeared in 1964, and his recognition as a poet was heightened when he received the 1966 National Book Award for *Buckdancer's Choice* (1965), the Melville Cane Award from the Poetry Society of America, and a National Institute of Arts and Letters Award. Between 1966 and 1968 Dickey served as consultant in poetry for the Library of Congress. During that time his *Poems 1957-1967* (1967) and his collection of reviews and essays *Babel to Byzantium: Poets and Poetry Now* (1968) were published. In 1968, he was appointed poet-in-residence at the University of South Carolina, but because of

## LITERARY AND HISTORICAL CONTEMPORARIES

James Dickey's famous contemporaries include:

**Jimmy Carter (1924– ):** The thirty-ninth President of the United States who served from 1977–1981; he was awarded the 2002 Nobel Peace Prize for his work in international diplomacy through the Carter Center, a non-profit organization.

**Anthony Hecht (1923–2004):** Hecht was a notable American poet whose work often includes the horrors of the Second World War and the Holocaust.

**Joseph Heller (1923–1999):** The preeminent American novelist, short story writer, and playwright who wrote the influential novel *Catch-22* (1961), a black comedy about Americans who served during World War II.

**Yves Bonnefoy (1923– ):** Bonnefoy, a French poet and essayist, was awarded the Franz Kafka Prize in 2007.

**Wislawa Syzmborska (1923– ):** The Polish poet, essayist, and translator who was awarded the 1996 Nobel Prize in Literature.

contractual requirements with the Library of Congress, he did not begin his teaching position until the fall of 1969. In 1970, he was named First Carolina Professor of English at the University of South Carolina.

Dickey lived in Columbia, South Carolina, and taught at the University of South Carolina from 1969 to 1997. In this setting he produced many of his major works, including his popularly and critically acclaimed first novel, *Deliverance.* In this harrowing novel, four middle-aged city-dwellers take a weekend canoe trip that turns into a transforming encounter with violence. Dickey also wrote the screenplay, suggested the musical theme "Duellin' Banjos," and acted the role of Sheriff Bullard in the Academy Award-nominated 1972 Warner Brothers movie based on his novel. Other major Dickey works appearing during the early to mid-1970s were a poetry collection, *The Eye-Beaters, Blood, Victory, Madness, Buckhead and Mercy* (1970); two books on writing and the creative process, *Self-Interviews* (1970) and *Sorties* (1971); and a long poem, *The Zodiac* (1976).

***Writing for Jimmy Carter*** Dickey's first wife, Maxine, died in 1976, and that same year he married Deborah Dodson, with whom he had a daughter, Bronwen. Jimmy Carter invited Dickey to write and read a poem for the 1977 inaugural celebration in Washington, D.C. "The Strength of Fields," the poem Dickey wrote for that occasion, served as the title poem of his 1979 collection. *The Strength of Fields* was followed in 1982 by *Puella*, one of Dickey's most experimental poetry volumes, and in 1987 by *Alnilam*, his most ambitious novel. On May 18, 1988

Dickey was inducted into the fifty-member American Academy of Arts and Letters, and in 1989 he was selected a judge for the Yale Series of Younger Poets, a clear indication of his continuing importance to and influence on American writers.

***An Energetic Writer*** In his seventies, Dickey remained a prolific, energetic writer: he produced his final collection of poetry, *The Eagle's Mile* (1990), and his third novel, *To the White Sea* (1993). From November 1994 to his death in early 1997, Dickey endured serious health problems but continued writing and conducting classes at the University of South Carolina. He taught his last class on January 14 and on the following day was hospitalized for the last time. At the time of his death he was at work on *Crux*, a novel set during World War II, and was overseeing preliminary work on a movie adaptation of his novel *To the White Sea*.

### Works in Literary Context

James Dickey frequently describes confrontations in war, sports, and nature as means for probing violence, mortality, creativity, and social values. In his poetry, Dickey rejects formalism, artifice, and confession, and instead favors a narrative mode that features energetic rhythms and charged emotions. Dickey has stated that in his poetry he attempts to achieve "a kind of plain-speaking line in which astonishing things can be said without rhetorical emphasis." In addition to his verse, Dickey has authored the acclaimed novels *Deliverance* (1970) and *Alnilam* (1987), symbolic works that explore extremes of human behavior. His works show the influence of Theodore Roethke, Dylan Thomas, James Agee, and the Fugitive Agrarians, a Southern literary group centered around Vanderbilt University.

***The Horrors of War*** Dickey's war poetry, also introduced in his first three collections, further expands his complex relationship to the dead, particularly as a combat survivor. He senses that he has been given a second opportunity for life, that he has been singled out for a special purpose, but that he cannot fully escape the immersion in death to which war has subjected him. The stages in the process of moving from painful memories to a renewal of life are constant in Dickey's war poetry. His speakers first manifest self-lacerating anguish brought on by the harrowing combat deaths they have witnessed. They confront the horrors of war through detailed re-creations of combat memories: "The Performance" in *Into the Stone* and "Between Two Prisoners" in *Drowning with Others* are two well-known early examples of the dramatically re-created scene. Finally, Dickey's speakers come to terms with their experiences with death, as in "The Firebombing," collected in *Two Poems of the Air* (1964), and *Buckdancer's Choice*. This process of experiencing anguish, conjuring up the horrors that have produced this anguish, and reordering their understanding of their war experiences becomes the basis for his protagonists' renewal to life.

Throughout his career as poet and novelist, Dickey drove himself to fulfill Ezra Pound's dictum to "make it new." Because his works are not only "new" but also compelling and engaging, James Dickey will be remembered as one of the most important literary voices in America.

## Works in Critical Context

James Dickey was widely regarded as a major American poet because of what critics and readers identified as his unique vision and style. "It is clear," said Joyce Carol Oates in her *New Heaven, New Earth: The Visionary Experience in Literature* (1978), "that Dickey desires to take on 'his' own personal history as an analogue to or a microscopic exploration of twentieth-century American history, which is one of the reasons he is so important a poet." Critical attention to Dickey increased steadily following his receipt of the National Book Award for *Buckdancer's Choice*, in 1965, and peaked with the publication of *Deliverance* in 1970. His later works received less critical attention.

*Deliverance: A Monument to Tall Tales*  In Dickey's internationally bestselling novel *Deliverance*, critics generally saw a thematic continuity with his poetry. A novel about how decent men kill, it is also about the bringing forth, through confrontation, of those qualities in a man that usually lie buried. "In writing *Deliverance*," said the *New York Times*'s Christopher Lehmann-Haupt, "Dickey obviously made up his mind to tell a story, and on the theory that a story is an entertaining lie, he has produced a double-clutching whopper … Best of all, he has made a monument to tall stories." Though Christopher Ricks, critiquing the novel in the *New York Review of Books*, believed *Deliverance* was "too patently the concoction of a situation in which it will be morally permissible—nay, essential—to kill men with a bow and arrow," Charles Thomas Samuels pointed out in the *New Republic* that Dickey "himself seems aware of the harshness of his substructure and the absurdity of some of his details" and overcomes these deficiencies through his stylistic maneuvers: "Such is Dickey's linguistic virtuosity that he totally realizes an improbable plot. How a man acts when shot by an arrow, what it feels like to scale a cliff or to capsize, the ironic psychology of fear: these things are conveyed with remarkable descriptive writing. His publishers are right to call *Deliverance* a tour de force."

## Responses to Literature

1. Discuss the tone of "The Performance." How does it relate to Dickey's experiences in war? Describe your emotional reaction to the text.

2. How does the rhythm of "Falling" impact the action within the poem?

---

### COMMON HUMAN EXPERIENCE

Dickey's experiences in World War II heavily influenced his work. Other important works concerning the combat experiences of soldiers in World War II include the following:

*The Naked and the Dead* (1948), a novel by Norman Mailer. Based on the author's experiences of intense combat during World War II, this work concerns the reconnaissance mission faced by a platoon of rifleman on an island in the South Pacific.
*The Young Lions* (1949), a novel by Irwin Shaw. This story follows the experiences of three ordinary soldiers (a German officer, an American-Jewish GI, and a cowardly draftee) as they try to endure the futility of war.
*The Thin Red Line* (1962), a novel by James Jones. This work is a fictional account of the author's firsthand experiences in the Guadalcanal campaign of World War II, the first major offensive the Allied forces made against the Japanese.

---

3. Some critics have stated that *To the White Sea* contains a more truthful account of Dickey's wartime experiences than previous novels. Do you find the writing in *To the White Sea* believable? Why or why not?

4. Compare the journey undertaken in *Deliverance* with that of Dante's *Inferno*. With this comparison in mind, interpret the meaning of the title "Deliverance."

BIBLIOGRAPHY

**Books**

Baughman, Ronald. *Understanding James Dickey.* Columbia, S.C.: University of South Carolina Press, 1985.

Baughman, Ronald, ed. *The Voiced Connections of James Dickey: Interviews and Conversations.* Columbia, S.C.: University of South Carolina Press, 1989.

Bloom, Harold, ed. *James Dickey: Modern Critical Views.* New York: Chelsea House, 1987.

Calhoun, Richard J. *James Dickey: The Expansive Imagination: A Collection of Critical Essays.* DeLand, Fla.: Everett/Edwards, 1973.

Calhoun, Richard J. and Robert W. *James Dickey.* Boston: Twayne, 1983.

Kirschten, Robert. *"Struggling for Wings": The Art of James Dickey.* Columbia, S.C.: University of South Carolina Press, 1997.

Kirschten, Robert, ed. *Critical Essays on James Dickey.* New York: G. K. Hall, 1994.

Van Ness, Arthur Gordan. *Outbelieving Existence: The Measured Motion of James Dickey.* Columbia, S.C.: Camden House, 1992.

Weigl, Bruce and T. R. Hummer, eds. *The Imagination as Glory: The Poetry of James Dickey.* Urbana, Ill.: University of Illinois Press, 1984.

**Periodicals**

Oates, Joyce Carol. "Out of Stone, Into Flesh: The Imagination of James Dickey." *Modern Poetry Studies* 5 (Autumn 1974): 97–144.

Smith, Dave. "The Strength of James Dickey." *Poetry* 137 (March 1981): 349–358.

*The Texas Review, Special Issue: The Fiction of James Dickey* 17 (Fall/Winter 1996/1997).

Weatherby, H. L. "The Way of Exchange in James Dickey's Poetry." *Sewanee Review* 74 (July–September 1966): 669–680.

# ✹ Emily Dickinson

BORN: *1830, Amherst, Massachusetts*

DIED: *1886, Amherst, Massachusetts*

NATIONALITY: *American*

GENRE: *Fiction, poetry*

MAJOR WORKS:

*Poems of Emily Dickinson* (1890, posthumous)

*The Poems of Emily Dickinson* (1955, posthumous)

Emily Dickinson    *Dickinson, Emily, photograph. The Library of Congress.*

## Overview

Emily Dickinson is regarded by many as one of the greatest American poets. Although very few of her poems were published during her lifetime and her work drew harsh criticism when it first appeared, many of her short lyrics on the subjects of nature, love, death, and immortality are now considered among the most emotionally and intellectually profound in the English language.

## Works in Biographical and Historical Context

***Puritanism Fails to Provoke Religious Awakening*** Dickinson was born in Amherst, Massachusetts, where she lived her entire life. Dickinson's father, Edward Dickinson, was a prosperous lawyer who served as treasurer of Amherst College and also held various political offices. Her mother, Emily Norcross Dickinson, has been described as a quiet and frail woman, though her disposition is a subject of debate amongst scholars. Dickinson's formal education began in 1835, with four years of primary school. She then attended Amherst Academy from 1840 to 1847 before spending a year at Mount Holyoke Female Seminary. Her studies, which included courses in

the sciences, literature, history, and philosophy, were largely informed by New England Puritanism, with its doctrines of a sovereign God, predestination, and the necessity for personal salvation. Dickinson, however, was unable to accept even the fairly liberal teachings of the Unitarian church attended by her family and, despite her desire to experience a religious awakening, remained agnostic throughout her life.

***Withdrawal from Society*** Following the completion of her education, Dickinson lived in the family home with her parents and younger sister, Lavinia, while her older brother, Austin, and his wife, Susan, lived next door. Although some details of her life are unclear, scholars believe that Dickinson first began writing poetry seriously in the early 1850s. Her otherwise quiet life was punctuated by brief visits to Boston, Washington, D.C., and Philadelphia in the years from 1851 to 1855. Biographers speculate that during one stay in Philadelphia Dickinson fell in love with a married minister, the Reverend Charles Wadsworth, and that her disappointment in love and the lack of a married life triggered her subsequent withdrawal from society. While this and other suggestions of tragic romantic attachments are largely conjecture, it is known that Dickinson became increasingly reclusive in the following years, spending her time primarily engaged in domestic routine—which she despised—and long solitary walks.

***Emotional Crisis Catalyzes Literary Productivity*** Biographers generally agree that Dickinson experienced an emotional crisis of an undetermined nature in the early 1860s. Her traumatized state of mind is believed to have inspired her to write prolifically: in 1862 alone she is thought to have composed more than three hundred poems. In the same year, Dickinson initiated a correspondence with Tomas Wentworth Higginson, the literary editor of the *Atlantic Monthly*. During the course of their lengthy exchange, Dickinson sent nearly one hundred of her poems for his criticism. While Higginson had little influence on her writing, he was important to her as a sympathetic adviser and confidant. Dickinson's reclusiveness intensified during 1869, and her refusal to leave her home or to meet visitors, her enigmatic remarks, and her habit of always wearing white garments earned her a reputation for eccentricity among her neighbors. Her isolation further increased when her father died unexpectedly in 1874 and she was left with the care of her invalid mother. The death of her mother in 1882, followed two years later by the death of Judge Otis P. Lord, a close family friend and Dickinson's most satisfying romantic attachment, contributed to the onset of what Dickinson described as an "attack of nerves." Later, in 1886, she was diagnosed as having Bright's disease, a kidney dysfunction that resulted in her death in May of that year.

***Posthumous Discovery of Dickinson's Poetry*** Only seven of Dickinson's poems were published during her lifetime, all anonymously and some apparently without her consent. The editors of the periodicals in which her lyrics appeared made significant alterations to them in an attempt to regularize the meter and grammar, thereby discouraging Dickinson from seeking further publication of her verse. Subsequently, her poems found only a private audience among her correspondents, family, and old school friends. Her family, however, was unaware of the enormous quantity of verse that she composed. After Dickinson's death, her sister Lavinia was astounded to discover hundreds of poems among her possessions. Many were copied into "fascicles," booklets formed from sheets of paper stitched together, but a large number of the poems appeared to be mere jottings recorded on scraps of paper. In many instances Dickinson abandoned poems in an unfinished state, leaving no indication of her final choice between alternative words, phrases, or forms.

***Publication Efforts Slowed by Family Disputes*** Despite the disordered state of the manuscripts, Lavinia Dickinson resolved to publish her sister's poetry and turned to Higginson and Mabel Loomis Todd, a friend of the Dickinson family, for assistance. In 1890, *Poems of Emily Dickinson* appeared and, even though most initial reviews were highly unfavorable, the work went through

## LITERARY AND HISTORICAL CONTEMPORARIES

Emily Dickinson's famous contemporaries include:

**Paul Johann Ludwig von Heyse** (1830–1914): The German author who was awarded the Nobel Prize in Literature in 1910 for his work "as a tribute to the consummate artistry, permeated with idealism, which he has demonstrated during his long productive career as a lyric poet, dramatist, novelist and writer of world-renowned short stories."

**Christina Rossetti** (1830–1894): Rossetti, an English poet, is best known for her poem *Goblin Market* (1862), which tells the story of two sisters who are lured by goblins to buy mysterious fruit.

**Frédéric Bartholdi** (1834–1904): Most famous for his work Liberty Enlightening the World (the Statue of Liberty), this French sculptor was partially inspired by the Suez Canal project in Egypt.

**Emily Davies** (1830–1921): The English suffragist who authored *The Higher Education of Women* (1886); she helped found Girton College—the first British college for women—in 1869.

**Lucy Delaney** (1830–1890): Delaney was the African American author of *From the Darkness Cometh Light, or, Struggles for Freedom* (1892), a memoir of her experiences as a slave.

**Louisa May Alcott** (1832–1888): Massachusetts author Alcott was principally known for the novel *Little Women* (1868).

**Mark Twain** (1835–1910): The American novelist, essayist, short-story writer, and literary celebrity; the author of *Adventures of Huckleberry Finn* (1884), sometimes claimed as the greatest American novel.

eleven editions in two years. Encouraged by the popular acceptance of *Poems*, Todd edited and published two subsequent collections of Dickinson's verse in the 1890s as well as a two-volume selection of her letters. Family disputes over possession of manuscripts hindered the publication of further materials, yet over the next fifty years, previously unprinted poems were introduced to the public in new collections. It was not until 1955, with the appearance of Thomas H. Johnson's edition of her verse, that Dickinson's complete poems were collected and published together by the Harvard University Press, in an authoritative text.

## Works in Literary Context

Drawing on imagery from biblical sources, particularly from the Book of Revelation, and from the works of William Shakespeare, John Keats, and Elizabeth Barrett Browning, Dickinson developed a highly personal system

# COMMON HUMAN EXPERIENCE

One of the reoccurring themes that is present throughout Dickinson's poetry is a skepticism toward religion, particularly with regard to an afterlife. Other works that explore the possibility of life after death include the following:

*Aeneid* (late first century B.C.E.): a Latin epic by Virgil. In this work Aeneas, a Trojan prince, visits the underworld—a place of transition where, according to Greek mythology, most souls reside after death.

*Theologus Autodidactus* (1213–1288): a novel by Ibn-al-Nafis. This coming-of-age story—written to explain Islamic religious teachings—is often regarded as one of the first science-fiction novels and explores questions of the end of the world, resurrection, and the afterlife.

*The Book of the Dead* (1842): an ancient Egyptian funerary text translated and compiled by Karl Richard Lepsius. This work describes the afterlife as it was conceived by ancient Egyptians; it contains hymns, spells, and instructions that are thought to aid the deceased in navigating the afterlife.

of symbol and allusion, assigning complex meanings to colors, places, times, and seasons. Her tone in the poems ranges widely, from wry, laconic humor to anguished self-examination, and from flirtatious riddling to childlike naiveté. Dickinson's diction is similarly diverse, incorporating New England vernacular, theological and scientific terminology, and archaisms. The meters of her poems are characteristically adapted from the rhythms of English hymns or nursery rhymes. Dickinson's stylistic experimentation, with techniques such as assonance (repetition of vowel sounds), consonance (repetition of consonant sounds), and half rhyme, defied the poetic conventions of her day. So did her idiosyncratic capitalization and punctuation, especially her use of dashes for emphasis or in place of commas. The terse, elliptical aspects of Dickinson's style further distinguish her poetry from the mainstream of nineteenth-century American verse.

***Love, Nature, Time, and Eternity*** Nearly eighteen hundred poems by Dickinson are known to exist, all of them in the form of brief lyrics (often of only one or two quatrains), and few of them titled. In her verse, Dickinson explores various subjects: nature, her preoccupation with death, her skepticism about immortality, her experience of love and loss, the importance of poetic vocation, and her attitude toward fame. Dickinson's forthright examination of her philosophical and religious skepticism, her unorthodox attitude toward her gender, and her distinctive style—characterized by elliptical, compressed expression, striking imagery, and innovative

poetic structure—have earned widespread acclaim, and, in addition, her poems have become some of the best loved in American literature.

Although Dickinson engendered no particular school of poetry, poets as diverse as Amy Lowell, Hart Crane, and Adrienne Rich have acknowledged her verse as an influence on their writings. Dickinson has continued to elicit fascination for both readers and scholars. For her originality, range, and emotional depth, Dickinson is now among the most universally admired and extensively studied figures in English literature. As Joyce Carol Oates has written, "Here is an American artist of words as inexhaustible as Shakespeare, as vigorously skillful in her craft as Yeats, a poet whom we can set with confidence beside the greatest poets of modern times."

## Works in Critical Context

Most nineteenth-century critics viewed Dickinson's poetry with a combination of disapproval and bewilderment, objecting to her disregard for conventional meter and rhyme, her unusual imagery, and her apparent grammatical errors. One of the exceptions to the harsh criticism voiced during her lifetime was Thomas Wentworth Higginson, her mentor. Commenting on the value of her work he writes, "the main quality of [her] poems is that of extraordinary grasp and insight, uttered with an uneven vigor, sometimes exasperating, seemingly wayward, but really unsought and inevitable." By the turn of the century, Dickinson had acquired an enthusiastic popular following, but she was still regarded as a sentimental poet of minor importance. Interest in her eccentric lifestyle and alleged love affairs was the main focus of Dickinson scholarship over the next several decades, but there were also some serious critical assessments, especially by the New Critics, who concentrated on the technical aspects of her poetry.

The single most important development in Dickinsonian scholarship was Johnson's 1955 edition of the complete poems. Numerous studies of her works have followed, utilizing linguistic, psychological, philosophical, historical, and feminist approaches. Studies of Dickinson's language and style often center on the complex interplay of her diction and imagery with her innovative meter and rhyme. Her adept use of images drawn from nature and literature has also been widely examined. Dickinson's unorthodox religious beliefs, her relation to the Romantic and Transcendental movements, and her personal philosophy of skepticism as expressed in her poems have been the main concerns of other research. In the 1970s and 1980s, feminist critics have explored such issues as the difficulties Dickinson encountered as a woman poet, the significance of her decision to withdraw from society, her use of language as a means of rebellion, and her importance to contemporary women writers.

***Mixed Reaction to "Because I Could Not Stop for Death"*** "Because I Could Not Stop for Death" is the most famous of Dickinson's many works concerning the subject of death and immortality. It has also been printed under the title "The Chariot." Renowned American literary critic Allen Tate, writing in his book *On the Limits of Poetry: Selected Essays, 1928–1948* (1948), praises the poem as "one of the greatest in the English language." Other critics disagree. Yvor Winters, writing in his *In Defense of Reason* (1947), disagrees that the work is one of Dickinson's best, judging it to be unconvincing and "fraudulent." In response to the praise offered by Allen Tate, Winters comments that Tate "appears to praise [the poem] for its defects."

Today an ample and increasing number of studies from diverse critical viewpoints are devoted to her life and works, thus securing Dickinson's status as a major poet.

## Responses to Literature

1. Discuss the different views of death in the following poems: "Because I could not stop for Death"; "I heard a Fly buzz"; "I felt a Funeral, in my Brain"; "My life had stood,"; and "My life closed twice before its close—."

2. Identify the unusual poetic devises employed by Dickinson in her poetry and explain their effect.

3. Characterize Dickinson's approach to nature in her poetry. Are there any images of nature that reoccur in her work? In what ways is the appearance of nature in her poetry connected with questions of religion, love, or death?

4. Identify the experience in "After great pain" that is described as "a formal feeling." Is this pain physical, psychological, or both? What kinds of crucifixion are present? Explicate the meaning of the poem in a short essay.

BIBLIOGRAPHY

**Books**

Cody, John. *After Great Pain: The Inner Life of Emily Dickinson.* Cambridge, Mass.: Harvard University Press, 1971.

Habegger, Alfred. *My Wars are Laid Away in Books: The Life of Emily Dickinson.* New York: Random House, 2001.

Johnson, Thomas H. *Emily Dickinson: An Interpretive Biography.* Cambridge, Mass.: Harvard University Press, 1955.

Leyda, Jay. *The Years and Hours of Emily Dickinson.* (2 volumes.) New Haven, Conn.: Yale University Press, 1960.

Loving, Jerome. *Emily Dickinson: The Poet on the Second Story.* Cambridge: Cambridge University Press, 1986.

Mossberg, Barbara. *Emily Dickinson: When a Writer is a Daughter.* Bloomington, Ind.: Indiana University Press, 1982.

Sewall, Richard B. *The Life of Emily Dickinson.* (2 volumes.) New York: Farrar, Straus & Giroux, 1974.

Whicher, George. *This Was a Poet: A Critical Biography of Emily Dickinson.* New York: Scribner's, 1938.

Wolff, Cynthia Griffin. *Emily Dickinson.* New York: Knopf, 1986.

## ✸ Joan Didion

BORN: *1934, Sacramento, California*

NATIONALITY: *American*

GENRE: *Fiction, nonfiction*

MAJOR WORKS:
*Slouching Towards Bethlehem* (1968)
*Play It as It Lays* (1970)
*The White Album* (1979)
*Salvador* (1983)
*The Year of Magical Thinking* (2005)

### Overview

Joan Didion is a distinguished figure in American letters, respected both as a novelist, screenwriter, and as a writer of personalized, journalistic essays. The disintegration of American morals and the cultural chaos upon which her essays comment are explored more fully in her novels, where the overriding theme is individual and societal fragmentation. Consequently, a sense of anxiety or dread permeates much of her work, and her novels have a reputation for being depressing and even morbid.

Joan Didion    *Didion, Joan, photograph. © Jerry Bauer. Reproduced by permission.*

## Works in Biographical and Historical Context

*Embracing Wagon Train Morality* The daughter of Frank Reese and Eduene Jerrett Didion, Joan Didion was born in Sacramento on December 5, 1934. She comes from a family that has been rooted in northern California since 1848. Some of her best writing is about the pioneer legacies left to her native state, where the past coexists with the present. Her great-great-great-grandmother came to California with the ill-fated Donner-Reed party—a group of several dozen American settlers led by George Donner and his brother James F. Reed—but left the group before it became stranded in the Sierra Nevada winter and resorted to cannibalism. Didion insists on "wagon train morality," a code that values survival and responsibility over utopian ideals. For Didion, the Donner Pass always lies just ahead.

Didion was raised in Sacramento, which was closer in resemblance to a farm town than the buzzing state capital it is today. In her essay "On Going Home" in *Slouching Towards Bethlehem* (1968), she describes her family as "difficult, oblique, deliberately inarticulate," while sharing a love of nature, independence, and community. However, during her childhood, "some nameless anxiety colored the emotional charges" between Didion and the place she came from.

*Launch of Writing Career and Married Life* Didion received her undergraduate degree in English from the University of California, Berkeley in 1956, then moved to New York after winning both a literary prize, the Prix de Paris, and a job at *Vogue* magazine. In 1963, she left *Vogue* and married *Time* magazine editor John Gregory Dunne, with whom she moved to Los Angeles in 1964. Didion and Dunne collaborated on screenplays, columns, and other projects until Dunne's death in 2003. In 1966, they adopted a daughter, Quintana Roo, who died recently in 2005.

Didion's first novel, *Run River* (1963), is the story of two proud families, the McClellans and the Knights, who live in the Sacramento Valley of Didion's childhood. The novel explores the changes brought about by World War II, its aftermath, and how those changes affected people who live out the mythologies and illusions of their pioneer ancestors.

Didion narrows the epic vastness of this changing California landscape in *Slouching Towards Bethlehem* (1968), an admired collection of twenty reports and essays, many of them previously published in the *Saturday Evening Post*. The book contains a preface followed by three sections. "Life Styles in the Golden Land" contains eight stories dealing with western figures; five "Personals" are more intimate reflections; and "Seven Places of the Mind" unifies the external and interior landscapes of the two previous sections.

*Reputation Solidifies with Backing from Tom Wolfe* After spending time in San Francisco's Haight-Ashbury, Didion was less than taken with the 1960s youth counterculture. She found that for the first time she had "dealt directly and flatly with the evidence of atomization, the proof that things fall apart." (The phrase "things fall apart," and the title *Slouching Towards Bethlehem*, both refer to the famous poem "The Second Coming" by W. B. Yeats.) Best-selling American author and journalist Tom Wolfe, who had written his own critical profile of the counterculture, *The Electric Kool-Aid Acid Test* (1968), included Didion's essay "Some Dreamers of the Golden Dream" in his anthology *The New Journalism* (1973). Following this inclusion, Didion came to be regarded as a preeminent literary journalist as well as a novelist.

Didion's most successful novel, *Play It as It Lays* (1970), became a best-seller and was nominated for a National Book Award. In it Maria Wyeth, an actress separated from her husband, a self-absorbed film director, seeks a traditional family but is unable to find meaning or security in the moral vacuum of the cinema capital, Hollywood.

*A Book of Common Prayer* (1977) is the story of Charlotte Douglas, a mysterious socialite who becomes involved in the political life of an imaginary Central American country while seeking her eighteen-year-old daughter. All the characters in the novel are in some way touched by political violence, which seems the end product of the chaos of the 1960s—a decade marked by social and political upheaval both in the United States and abroad. In a world devoid of apparent meaning, it is only by choosing to love one another that life becomes redemptive. *A Book of Common Prayer* is the most existentially powerful of Didion's novels.

*Telling Stories* (1978) contains an essay and also three short stories Didion wrote in 1964. Also in 1978, Didion and Dunne moved to Brentwood Park in Los Angeles, where she completed *The White Album* (1979), Didion's lament for the late 1960s and early 1970s. The book is organized in five sections containing a total of twenty magazine stories, most of which appeared in *Esquire* between 1968 and 1978.

*The White Album* begins with Didion in confusion and despair. In 1968, she had been described in a psychiatric report, which she includes in the preface, as alienated, pessimistic, and depressed. Didion's state of mind seems appropriate to the events she writes about. Didion meets Linda Kasabian, a participant in the Charles Manson trial, and other cultural icons such as The Doors, Janis Joplin, and Eldridge Cleaver. Through these encounters and interviews she further beholds the disorder she began to document in *Slouching Towards Bethlehem*. Issues no longer matter. She finds only disorder for the sake of disorder. For Didion the 1960s came to an end in 1971 when she moved to Trancas, a coastal town near Los Angeles. Her new house, like Didion, seemed haunted with memories of the previous decade.

***Critique of Women's Movement Stirs Controversy***
Didion's critical essay on the women's movement, which generated controversy when it first appeared in the *New York Times Book Review* in 1972, attempts to separate the movement's political, social, historical, and moral dimensions and is followed by profiles of Doris Lessing and Georgia O'Keeffe. Whereas what is known as the "first wave" of the women's movement was centered around giving women the right to vote at the end of the nineteenth and beginning of the twentieth century, the "second wave" of the movement—the one to which Didion is responding in her essay—lasted from the early 1960s through the late 1980s. Participants of the second wave movement sought an end to the discrimination women faced in all aspects of their lives.

*Salvador* (1983), Didion's most successful work of journalism, was originally published as two articles in the *New York Review of Books* in October 1982 and was nominated for a Pulitzer Prize. Ostensibly a report on the war in El Salvador, based on a two-week visit with Dunne to the embattled republic in June 1982, *Salvador* reprises Joseph Conrad's *Heart of Darkness* (1902). *Salvador* contemplates the meaning of existence when one confronts absolute evil.

Didion's 1984 novel *Democracy* is the story of Inez Christian Victor, the wife of a United States senator with presidential ambitions. *Miami* (1987), a work of reportage less absorbing than *Salvador*, attempts to unravel the complex political structure of the Florida city, which received much media attention during the 1980s. *After Henry* (1992) is a collection of essays, most of which first appeared in *The New Yorker* and the *New York Review of Books*. In the title essay Didion pays homage to her late editor, Henry Robbins, a literary craftsman who nurtured Didion and left her with the knowledge that she could carry on without him. *After Henry* ends with Didion's return to New York, where she took up residence in 1988. The final essay, an astute blend of journalism, literary and cultural criticism, and rhetorical analysis, examines an assault on a jogger in Central Park.

In 2001, Didion published *Political Fictions*, a collection of essays that had first appeared in the *New York Review of Books*. Issues and personalities covered in the essays included The religious right, Newt Gingrich, and the Reagan administration. *Where I Was From* (2003), a memoir, explores the mythologies of California, and the author's relationship to her birthplace and to her mother. Indirectly, it also examines the American frontier myth and the culture that we see today in California as a direct consequence of a population of survivalists who made it "through the Sierra," Didion finally poses the question, "at what cost progress?"

***Coping with Grief*** Didion's *The Year of Magical Thinking* (2005) was awarded the National Book Award

## LITERARY AND HISTORICAL CONTEMPORARIES

Didion's famous contemporaries include:

**Tom Wolfe** (1931–): Wolfe is the American author whose literary nonfiction helped establish the "New Journalism" movement; author of *The Right Stuff* (1979) and the novel "*The Bonfire of the Vanities*" (1987).

**Yoko Ono Lennon** (1933–): The Japanese artist and musician known for her avant-garde work and marriage with John Lennon.

**Eddie Adams** (1933–2004): Adams, an American photographer and photojournalist whose work covered thirteen wars, was awarded the Pulitzer Prize for Spot News Photography in 1969 for his piece entitled 'General Nguyen Ngoc Loan executing a Viet Cong prisoner in Saigon'.

**Sonia Sanchez** (1934–): An African-American poet who advanced both the civil rights movement and the Black Arts movement.

**Wole Soyinka** (1934–): The Nigerian author, poet, and playwright who was awarded the Nobel Prize for Literature in 1986, making him the first African to receive the award.

**Ken Kesey** (1935–2001): Kesey, a major figure of America's 1960s counterculture, is best known for his novel *One Flew Over the Cuckoo's Nest* (1962).

for nonfiction. This long essay chronicles the year after her husband's death, while their daughter remained seriously ill. The book explores the grieving process and offers a vivid account of Didion's experience with losing her partner of forty years. Quintana died of complications from acute pancreatitis on August 26, 2005. Didion did not adapt her already published work to reflect her daughter's death. She did, however, adapt the memoir into a one-woman play, which premiered on Broadway in 2007 to mixed reviews.

In 2007, Didion received the National Book Foundation's annual Medal for Distinguished Contribution to American Letters for "her distinctive blend of spare, elegant prose and fierce intelligence" and the Evelyn F. Burkey Award from the Writers Guild of America. She currently resides in New York City.

## Works in Literary Context

An elegant prose stylist and celebrated journalist, Joan Didion possesses a distinct literary voice, widely praised for its precision and control. She began, by her own admission, as a nonintellectual writer, more concerned with images than ideas and renowned for her use of telling details. For years, Didion's favorite subject was her

## COMMON HUMAN EXPERIENCE

Among Didion's themes is the rise and fall of cultural cohesion in the United States. Other works that explore the loss of community in society include the following:

*Bowling Alone: The Collapse and Revival of American Community* (2000), a nonfiction book by Robert D. Putnam. In this work, Putnam tracks the decline of the necessary "social capital" in the United States and discusses the implications of public disengagement.

*The Careless Society: Community and Its Counterfeits* (1996), a nonfiction book by John McKnight. This work examines the failures of professional services intended to address social ills and presents alternative means of community repair.

"The Community Question Re-Evaluated" (1988), an essay by Barry Wellman. This work, published in *Power, Community, and the City* places questions of the rise and fall of community in society in its historical context.

*The Pursuit of Loneliness* (1970), a nonfiction book by Philip Slater. This witty, penetrating work of 1960s social criticism links the American infatuations with technology and individualism, creating a sociological portrait of a society purposely unraveling its social bonds.

native California, a state that seemed to supply ample evidence of the disorder in society. She has broadened her perspective in more recent years, turning her attention toward the troubled countries of Central America and Southeast Asia for new material; her most recent work, *The Year of Magical Thinking*, explores her experiences dealing with loss and grief. Didion has acknowledged the influence of writers including Henry James, Ernest Hemingway, Evelyn Waugh, William Faulkner, and F. Scott Fitzgerald amongst many others.

***Despair and Moral Emptiness*** For Didion, what ails American society is a growing loss of community caused by materialism, media, militarism, self-indulgence, the loss of heroes, and the absence of belief. As the culture disintegrates, subcultures arise in an attempt to restore community. A troubling sign of the social discord is the corruption of language, creating "an army of children waiting to be given the words," as she writes in *Slouching Towards Bethlehem*.

Hillel Italie of the Associated Press, reporting on Didion's National Book Award, notes the significance of Didion's recent work on American literature. She writes, *The Year of Magical Thinking* "is quickly becoming a classic portrait of grief." Didion's contribution to literature has been recognized with numerous awards including, in 2005, the Gold Medal for Belles Lettres from the

American Academy of Arts and Letters, which is given every six years. Likewise, Didion was awarded the Robert Kirsch Award for lifetime achievement at the 2006 *Los Angeles Times* book awards.

## Works in Critical Context

Despite a rough start to her career as a freelance essayist, Didion succeeded in carving out a niche for herself, and eventually drew significant critical attention to all of her work. She is most highly regarded for her work as an essayist, although she draws positive reviews of her fiction, screenwriting, and memoir. "Didion is one of the most interesting writers in America," writes Vivian Gornick in *Women's Review of Books*, "a writer whose prose continues to lure readers high and low with its powerful suggestiveness."

Critics generally liked *Slouching Towards Bethlehem*, but the book had its detractors as well. In *The Christian Science Monitor* (May 16, 1968) Melvin Maddocks, while praising Didion's originality, saw her insistence on converting themes into myths, dreams, and symbols as a journalistic conceit. In the *National Review* (June 4, 1968) C. H. Simonds attributed to Didion "a perfect eye for detail and an unfoolable ear," while T. J. O'Hara complained in *Best Sellers* (June 1, 1968) that most of the essays "suffer from a lack of relevance or depth when they are not smothering under the heavy hand of irony." Dan Wakefield, in the *New York Times Book Review* (July 21, 1968), found the book "a rich display of some of the best prose written in this country."

While contemporary critics differ in their opinions of her work, most agree that Didion is a significant figure in modern literature, a perceptive chronicler of the tumult of culture and consciousness.

## Responses to Literature

1. Explain what Joa Didion means when she writes "We interpret what we see, select the most workable of the choices. We live entirely, especially if we are writers, by the imposition of a narrative line upon disparate images, by the 'ideas' with which we have learned to freeze the shifting phantasmagoria which is our actual experience" in *The White Album*. Why does she then retreat from this statement when she continues, "Or at least we do for a while"?

2. In her essay "The White Album," Didion mentions her experience being diagnosed with multiple sclerosis. Why does she include this information? What impact does it have on your reading of the text?

3. To what extent is Didion presenting herself as an objective observer in her essay "The Women's Movement?" What does she mean when she says that "nobody forces women to buy the package"?

4. Do you notice any discrepancies between the male and female characters in Didion's fiction?

BIBLIOGRAPHY

**Books**

Connery, Thomas B., ed. *A Sourcebook of American Literary Journalism: Representative Writers in an Emerging Genre*. New York: Greenwood Press, 1992.

Henderson, Katherine Usher. *Joan Didion*. New York: Ungar, 1981.

Loris, Michelle Carbone. *Innocence, Loss and Recovery in the Art of Joan Didion*. New York: Peter Lang, 1989.

Winchell, Mark Royden. *Joan Didion*. Boston: G. K. Hall, 1989.

**Periodicals**

Davidson, Sara. "A Visit with Joan Didion." *New York Times Book Review* (April 3, 1977): 1, 35–38.

Harrison, Barbara Grizzuti. "Joan Didion: The Courage of Her Afflictions," *The Nation* 229 (September 26, 1979): 277–286.

Kazin, Alfred. "Joan Didion: Portrait of a Professional." *Harper's* 243 (December 1971): 112–122.

# ✳ Annie Dillard

BORN: *1945, Pittsburgh, Pennsylvania*

NATIONALITY: *American*

GENRE: *Fiction, poetry, nonfiction*

MAJOR WORKS:

*Pilgrim at Tinker Creek* (1974)

*Holy the Firm* (1977)

*Teaching a Stone to Talk: Expeditions and Encounters* (1982)

*An American Childhood* (1987)

*For the Time Being* (1999)

## Overview

An essayist, poet, and fiction writer, Annie Dillard is best known for her nonfiction narrative, *Pilgrim at Tinker Creek* (1974), which was awarded the 1975 Pulitzer Prize for General Nonfiction when she was twenty-nine. Dillard has served as contributing editor for *Harper's* since 1974 and has written many essays, short stories, and poems.

## Works in Biographical and Historical Context

***Combining Scientific Knowledge with Literary Grace*** Born to Frank and Pam Doak in Pittsburgh, Pennsylvania, Annie Dillard grew up in an affluent world of country clubs and private girls' schools, where she began writing poetry and fiction in high school. She was born in 1945, the same year that Japan surrendered to the Allied powers, and thus ended World War II. By the

Annie Dillard *Dillard, Annie, photograph. © Jerry Bauer. Reproduced by permission.*

war's end, the United States led the world in industrial output, while elsewhere the war-torn nations of Europe and Asia struggled to regain their pre-war productivity. Growing up in affluence, Dillard was largely sheltered from the aftermath of the war. While economic recovery was swift in many parts of the world, the economic ruin in England—where Dillard spent time as an adult—only worsened in the decade following the war's end.

Eventually, Dillard enrolled in the writing program at Hollins College in Roanoke, Virginia, where she was elected to Phi Beta Kappa and received a BA (1967) and an MA (1968), both in English. In 1964, while still a student at Hollins, she married writer R. H. W. Dillard, her teacher. She read widely in such diverse fields as theology, philosophy, physical sciences, anthropology, and literature; critics have praised the accuracy of her scientific knowledge, especially as it is revealed in *Pilgrim at Tinker Creek*. During her formative years, the United States was engaged in two international conflicts, first with the Korean War from 1950 to 1953 and then with the Vietnam War, which lasted from 1959 until 1975.

***Longing for a Hidden God*** Dillard's first book, *Tickets for a Prayer Wheel* (1974), collected some previously unpublished poems along with many that had appeared earlier in magazines. The poems portray human

## LITERARY AND HISTORICAL CONTEMPORARIES

Annie Dillard's famous contemporaries include:

**Dean Koontz** (1945–): An American author best known for his suspense thrillers, several of which have appeared on the *New York Times* Best-seller List.

**Richard Ford** (1944–): Ford is an American novelist and short story writer who was awarded both the PEN/Faulkner Award and the Pulitzer Prize for Fiction for his book *Independence Day* (1995).

**Alice Walker** (1944–): The African-American feminist author who wrote the Pulitzer Prize-winning novel, *The Color Purple* (1983).

**Andrea Dworkin** (1946–2005): An American radical feminist and antiwar activist who is most famous for arguing that pornography is directly linked to violence against women.

**Gerd Brantenberg** (1941–): A Norwegian feminist writer and educator who wrote *The Daughters of Egalia* (1977).

characters and explore themes of human love and desire; however, the main impetus behind the poems is strongly religious. Dillard writes of the intricacy and detail of nature, the changing lights of consciousness, the mystery of time's relation to eternity, the futility of asking questions about God, and ultimately, through all the poems, the poet's urgent longing for a God who is hidden. Finally, according to the poet, the union of a human with God depends as much on God's action as on the human's, and when the divine presence acts upon her, the poet says, "I rang a hundred prayers of praise." The final poem, "Tickets for a Prayer Wheel," is considered by Dillard to be her best; it contains the refrain to be heard later in *Holy the Firm* (1977): "who will teach us to pray?"

### Dillard Wins the Pulitzer Prize for Nonfiction

Dillard herself was surprised by the publishing world's overwhelming recognition of *Pilgrim at Tinker Creek*. The book grew out of notes she wrote during 1972 while living on Tinker Creek, in the Roanoke Valley of Virginia. For a year, she says, she read voraciously as she gathered material, took walks, and "did nothing." But those daily walks and her reading of naturalists, anthropologists, physicists, and biologists were recorded in detail. When she did begin to write, she worked for eight months, seven days a week, up to fifteen and sixteen hours a day in a library carrel, recording her insights and observations from 1,103 index cards. *Pilgrim at Tinker Creek* weaves together Dillard's meticulous observations of the physical world with moments of metaphysical illumination. She sent the first chapter to a New York agent who successfully placed it with *Harper's* magazine.

Almost immediately the chapters of *Pilgrim at Tinker Creek* were snapped up by *Harper's* and other magazines; the completed book was a Book-of-the-Month Club main selection, and in October 1973, Dillard was invited to become a contributing editor of *Harper's*.

When *Pilgrim at Tinker Creek* won the Pulitzer Prize and became a best-seller, Dillard's success brought her many offers to make appearances, give readings, and even write film scripts, but she declined most offers in an effort to maintain the privacy and energy necessary for serious writing. During one summer she traveled to the Galapagos Islands for *Harper's*, where she wrote a long essay discussing the interplay between freedom and evolutionary necessity. For this essay, "Innocence in the Galapagos," she won the New York Presswomen's Award for Excellence in 1975. She also traveled and wrote several columns for the journal of the Wilderness Society, the *Living Wilderness*, between 1974 and 1976.

### A Move to the Pacific Northwest

When her marriage of nine years ended in 1974, Annie Dillard moved to the Pacific Northwest to become scholar-in-residence at Western Washington University at Bellingham. There she taught creative writing and poetry, and began work on *Holy the Firm*, published in 1977. In this work, Dillard again struggles with the problem of pain, but she is more explicitly concerned with the metaphysical aspects of pain than she was in *Pilgrim at Tinker Creek*. She is also more concerned with philosophical discussions about time, reality, and the will of God. Although the book is only seventy-five pages long and covers the events of only three days, it took her fifteen months to write. Its language is highly condensed and poetic, and its narrative framework is built from a complex set of internal elements that interrelate and recur in the reflexive manner of a complicated poem. Some critics argue that the book is more self-consciously artistic than *Pilgrim at Tinker Creek*. Although *Holy the Firm* was highly praised by reviewers, some considered it less penetrable than its predecessor. It has been widely reprinted and a dramatic version has been performed by Atlanta's Imaginary Theatre.

Her long piece of fiction, "The Living," which appeared in *Harper's* (1978), deals with human consciousness and awareness of time and death. Set in 1905, the story concerns Clare, an easygoing and unreflective man who teaches high-school shop near Northern Puget Sound. When one of his ex-students announces that he plans someday to kill him, Clare becomes intensely conscious for the first time of his own mortality. Dillard traces the changes in Clare's life and his consciousness with great psychological acuity, as the story builds to his final realization of his place in time and his unity with the eternal.

Dillard is professor emeritus at Wesleyan University in Connecticut and during the summer of 1981, the Centennial of the Boston Symphony Orchestra, the orchestra performed *The Tree With Lights In It*, a symphony by Sir Arthur Tippett based on *Pilgrim at Tinker Creek*.

During the 1990s Dillard published three major works: a novel entitled *The Living* (1992), a poetry collection entitled *Mornings Like This* (1995), and a nonfiction narrative entitled *For the Time Being* (1999). All three works have been recognized with awards for literary excellence. Her latest work of fiction, *The Maytrees* (2007), a short novel, is set in Cape Cod at an artist community and focuses on a marriage on the rocks. *The Maytrees* was honored as a finalist for the prestigious PEN/Faulkner Award in 2008.

## Works in Literary Context

Annie Dillard has carved a unique niche for herself in the world of American letters. Over the course of her career, Dillard has written essays, a memoir, poetry, literary criticism—even a western novel. In whatever genre she works, Dillard distinguishes herself with her carefully wrought language, keen observations, and original metaphysical insights. Dillard's many essays and poems describe her essentially spiritual vision. Her subjects include the role of the artist, the artistic process, evolution, and wildlife—all discussed in the larger context of her philosophical concerns. Influences on her work include Emily Dickinson, Ralph Waldo Emerson, and Henry David Thoreau, about whom she wrote her master's thesis.

*Scrutiny of Minutiae* Dillard is esteemed as an inspirational author of fiction and nonfiction that explores religion, philosophy, natural phenomena, the role of the artist in society, and the creative process. Commended for her startling imagery and precise prose, Dillard characteristically focuses on minute details in art or wildlife, investing her observations with scientific facts and obscure allusions gathered from her broad reading in science and literature. From this scrutiny of minutiae, she investigates wider philosophical implications; for example, in one episode of *Pilgrim at Tinker Creek*, Dillard reflects on nature's intricacy as she describes the 228 muscles in the head of a caterpillar. In her subsequent works, Dillard examines theology, literary theory, and her own childhood, offering personal revelations on artistic pursuit and the meaning of existence.

Annie Dillard has been acclaimed not only as an inspiring writer but also as a stimulating intellectual. She questions boldly as she ponders the role of the artist in the modern world; her works continue to reflect humanity's concern with the eternal.

## Works in Critical Context

Dillard entered the literary scene with what was categorized at the time as a Thoreauvian natural history, *Pilgrim at Tinker Creek*. Dillard's broad interests are reflected in the praise she received for the accuracy of her scientific observations. Readers relish Dillard's minute observations of nature, her lush and lyrical prose, and her high-spirited humor that only places in higher relief her serious metaphysical quest.

## COMMON HUMAN EXPERIENCE

Among the recurring themes in Dillard's work is the intricacy of natural phenomena. Other works that explore nature in great detail include the following:

*Philosophiae Naturalis Principia Mathematica* (1687), three nonfiction books by Isaac Newton. Holding an important place in the realm of scientific letters, this work traces the path from Newton's astute observations of nature to his ground-breaking laws of motion, law of universal gravitation, and Kepler's law, which accounts for the motion of planets.

*Nature* (1936), an essay and short book by Ralph Waldo Emerson. In this famous work, Emerson lays out the tenants of transcendentalism—a belief system that regards nature as divine.

*On the Origin of Species* (1859), a nonfiction book by Charles Darwin. This book, the seminal work of evolutionary biology, presents evidence for his theory of natural selection—a process in which populations evolve over time.

*Silent Spring* (1962), by Rachel Carson. An argument for limitations on the use of pesticides such as DDT, this book is credited as one of the inspirations for the modern environmental movement.

*Pilgrim at Tinker Creek Immediately Popular*
*Pilgrim at Tinker Creek*, Dillard's second book, met with immediate popular and critical success. "One of the most pleasing traits of the book is the graceful harmony between scrutiny of real phenomena and the reflections to which that gives rise," noted a *Commentary* reviewer. "Anecdotes of animal behavior become so effortlessly enlarged into symbols by the deepened insight of meditation. Like a true transcendentalist, Miss Dillard understands her task to be that of full alertness." Other critics found fault with Dillard's work, however, calling it self-absorbed or overwritten. Charles Deemer of the *New Leader*, for example, claimed that "if Annie Dillard had not spelled out what she was up to in this book, I don't think I would have guessed. ... Her observations are typically described in overstatement reaching toward hysteria." A more charitable assessment came from Muriel Haynes of *Ms.* While finding Dillard to be "susceptible to fits of rapture," Haynes asserted that the author's "imaginative flights have the special beauty of surprise."

*Contemporary Approaches to Dillard* The major shift in critical appreciation of Dillard's work took place during the 1990s when scholars and critics shifted away from noting Dillard's kinship with the nineteenth-century transcendentalists to appreciating her differences from them. Readers have gone from linking Dillard to Thoreau to finding her affinity with Nathaniel Hawthorne and Herman Melville as well.

## Responses to Literature

1. Pick a particular passage in *An American Childhood* and write in detail about your own response to it. Does it resonate with your own experience of childhood? Why or why not?

2. *Pilgrim at Tinker Creek* is filled with minute details. Discuss the advantages and disadvantages of a heavy emphasis on detail. What use does Dillard make of them?

3. Has *Pilgrim at Tinker Creek* shifted your perspective on the world around you? In what ways? Are there any portions of this work that seem particularly accessible to you as a reader?

4. Why are scenes of death included alongside scenes of procreation in *Pilgrim at Tinker Creek*? What impact does this have on your overall reading of the text?

BIBLIOGRAPHY

**Books**

Johnson, Sandra Humble. *The Space Between: Literary Epiphany in the Work of Annie Dillard*. Kent, Ohio: Kent State University Press, 1992.

Slovic, Scott. *Seeking Awareness in American Nature Writing: Henry Thoreau, Annie Dillard, Edward Abbey, Wendell Berry, Barry Lopez*. Salt Lake City: University of Utah Press, 1992.

Smith, Linda. *Annie Dillard*. New York: Twayne, 1991.

**Periodicals**

Major, Mike. "Annie Dillard, Pilgrim of the Absolute," *America* 128 (May 6, 1978): 363–364.

Smith, Pamela A. "The Ecotheology of Annie Dillard: A Study in Ambivalence," *Cross Currents: The Journal of the Association for Religion and Intellectual Life* 45 (Fall 1995): 341–358.

**Web sites**

Dillard, Annie. *Annie Dillard—Official Website*. Retrieved September 4, 2008, from http://www.anniedillard.com. Last updated on May 17, 2007.

# ✸ Chitra Banerjee Divakaruni

BORN: *1956, Calcutta, India*

NATIONALITY: *American, Indian*

GENRE: *Fiction, poetry, nonfiction*

MAJOR WORKS:

*Arranged Marriage* (1995)

*Leaving Yuba City: New and Selected Poems* (1997)

*Mistress of Spices* (1997)

*Sister of My Heart* (1999)

*The Vine of Desire* (2002)

## Overview

Chitra Banerjee Divakaruni is a versatile Indian-American author of fiction, poetry, children's stories, and nonfiction essays—whose work brings to life the realities of living as an immigrant in America.

## Works in Biographical and Historical Context

*Growing Up Middle-Class in India*   Chitra Banerjee was born in Calcutta on July 29, 1956, and spent the first nineteen years of her life in India. Her father, Rajendra Kumar Banerjee, an accountant by profession, and her mother, Tatini Banerjee, a schoolteacher, brought up their four children in modest middle-class ambience. As the second-born child and only girl among three brothers, Partha, Dhruva, and Surya, Chitra spent her childhood days in sibling rivalry and camaraderie. She studied at Loreto House, a convent school run by Irish nuns, and graduated in 1971. In 1976, she earned her bachelor's degree in English from Presidency College, University of Calcutta.

*Move to the United States*   At the age of nineteen Divakaruni moved to the United States to continue her studies as an English major and got her master's degree from Wright State University in Dayton, Ohio, in 1978. Working under Stephen Greenblatt on the topic "For Danger Is in Words: A Study of Language in Marlowe's Plays," she received her Ph.D. in English from the University of California at Berkeley in 1984. She held different kinds of jobs to pay for her education, including babysitting, selling merchandise in an Indian boutique, slicing bread at a bakery, and washing instruments at a science lab. She did not begin to write fiction until after she graduated from Berkeley, when she came to realize that she loved teaching but did not want to do academic writing: "It didn't have enough heart in it. I wanted to write something more immediate." In 1979, she married Murthy Divakaruni, an engineer by profession. Her two sons, Anand and Abhay, were born in 1991 and 1994.

*Reaching Out to Women in Need*   Divakaruni and her husband moved to Sunnyvale, California in 1989. For several years she was interested in issues involving women and worked with Afghani women refugees and women from dysfunctional families, as well as in shelters for battered women. In 1991, she became founder-member and president of Maitri, an organization in the San Francisco area that works for South Asian women in abusive situations. She also associated herself with Asians against Domestic Abuse, an organization in Houston. Her interest in these women grew when she realized that there was no mainstream shelter for immigrant women in distress—a place where people would understand their cultural needs and problems—in the United States. Because of the experience she gathered from counseling sessions, the lives of Asian women opened up to her, revealing unimaginable crises.

### Exploring Cultural Differences through Poetry

For all of the years that Divakaruni lived in the Bay Area, she taught at Foothill College in Los Altos Hills. She turned to writing as a means of exploring the cultural differences she encountered as a newcomer to the United States. Initially, she started writing for herself, and during the mid 1980s she joined a writer's group at Berkeley University. She wrote poems during that time, and, as she told Roxane Farmanfarmaian in *Publishers Weekly*, her venture into serious poetry writing began after she received the news of her grandfather's death in her ancestral village in India: "Poetry focuses on the moment, on the image, and relies on image to express meaning. That was very important to me, that kind of crystallization, that kind of intensity in a small space."

As he has been with the publications of many Indian writers in English, Professor P. Lal of the Writers Workshop in Calcutta was instrumental in publishing Divakaruni's first book of poetry, *Dark Like the River* (1987). She had already established herself as a poet by the time she published *The Reason for Nasturtiums* (1990), her first verse collection published in the United States. The subtitle of the volume explains her primary interest and indicates that her main focus is the immigrant experience and South Asian women. She shows the experiences and struggles involved in Asian women's attempts to find their own identities.

As the title suggests, Divakaruni's volume of poems *Leaving Yuba City: New and Selected Poems* (1997) includes new poems as well as ones from *Dark Like the River*, *The Reason for Nasturtiums*, and *Black Candle: Poems about Women from India, Pakistan, and Bangladesh* (1991). These poems draw on similar subject matter to her fiction: womanhood, family life, exile, alienation, exoticism, ethnicity, domesticity, love, and romance. *Leaving Yuba City* won a Pushcart Prize, an Allen Ginsberg Prize, and a Gerbode Foundation Award.

### Career as a Fiction Writer Begins

After three books of poetry, Divakaruni realized that there were things she wanted to say that would be better expressed in prose. In 1992, she enrolled in an evening fiction-writing class at Foothill College, where she had started teaching twentieth-century multicultural literature the year before. Divakaruni's first volume of short stories, *Arranged Marriage* (1995), explores the cross-cultural experiences of womanhood through a feminist perspective, a theme that continues to inform her work.

Divakaruni's first novel, *The Mistress of Spices* (1997), is distinct in that it blends prose and poetry, successfully employing magic realist techniques. The novel was named one of the best books of 1997 by the *Los Angeles Times* and one of the best books of the twentieth century by the *San Francisco Chronicle*, and was nominated for the Orange Prize in England in 1998.

---

## LITERARY AND HISTORICAL CONTEMPORARIES

Divakaruni's famous contemporaries include:

**Arundhati Roy** (1961–): Roy is an Indian author of *The God of Small Things* (1997), winner of the 1997 Booker Prize. Her activism against globalization, neo-imperialism, and foreign policy of the United States have earned her many awards, including the 2002 Lannan Cultural Freedom Prize.

**Medha Patkar** (1954–): Patkar is an Indian social activist who started a twenty-day hunger strike in protest of the Narmada Dam project. She has received numerous humanitarian awards for her advocacy and political activism.

**Madonna** (1958–): Madonna is an American singer, actress, and entertainer. She was inducted into the Rock and Roll Hall of Fame in March of 2008.

**Rita Dove** (1952–): Dove is an African American author considered one of the leading poets of her generation. She is best known for *Thomas and Beulah* (1986), which received the 1987 Pulitzer Prize in poetry.

**Oprah Winfrey** (1954–): Winfrey is an American television host of the internationally syndicated *Oprah Winfrey Show*, which has been awarded multiple Emmy Awards.

---

### Non-fiction Work Confronts Old Traditions

Apart from her poems and fictional writing, Divakaruni has also established a reputation for herself with her non-fiction pieces. In "Foreign Affairs: Uncertain Objects of Desire," which appeared in the March 2000 issue of *Atlantic Monthly*, she sifts through several hundred carefully categorized matrimonial advertisements in *The Times of India*, surmising that in India, a country that straddles the old and the new, they are a good place to look for signs of shifting values.

The female protagonists of eight of the nine stories in Divakaruni's sensuously evocative collection *The Unknown Errors of Our Lives* (2001) are caught between the beliefs and traditions of their Indian heritage and those of their, or their children's, new homeland, the United States.

### Artistic Versatility

Divakaruni's versatility as a writer was confirmed by her first children's book, *Neela: Victory Song* (2002). Part of the "Girls of Many Lands" series, featuring books and dolls based on young girls from various historical periods and cultural traditions, it is the story of a twelve-year-old girl caught up in the Indian Independence movement. Published in September 2003 and chosen as one of the best books of the year by *Publishers Weekly*, Divakaruni's second book for children, *The Conch*

# COMMON HUMAN EXPERIENCE

Cross-cultural experiences of womanhood, as seen from a feminist perspective, feature prominently in Divakaruni's writing. Other works that explore this theme include:

"Can the Subaltern Speak?" (1988), an essay by Gayatri Spivak. This controversial piece exposes the way in which colonial dynamics legitimate themselves as systems wherein "white men are protecting brown women from brown men."

*Indian Women Novelists* (1995), an eighteen-volume set of collected essays edited by R. K. Dhawan. This work combines feminist perspectives of many female Indian authors who address the issues of gender and culture in their historical context.

*The God of Small Things* (1997), a novel by Arundhati Roy. In this work, womanhood in India—particularly in the context of social class—is juxtaposed against the experiences of women in England and the United States, including Indian women who have moved abroad.

*Bearer*, blends action, adventure, and magic in a kind of quest fantasy.

Divakaruni's sixth novel, *Queen of Dreams* (2004), again utilizes the magic realist mode and details one woman's experience living in the United States as an Indian. Since the release of *Queen of Dreams*, Divakaruni has published two more works of fiction: *The Mirror of Fire and Dreaming* (2005)—a sequel to *The Conch Bearer* and *The Palace of Illusions: A Novel* (2008).

## Works in Literary Context

Belonging to the group of young Indian writers that emerged on the literary scene after Salman Rushdie, Chitra Banerjee Divakaruni's position as a South Asian writer in English is distinct and well established. As someone who has spent more time outside India than in it, she has been accepted as an Asian American writer, living with a hybrid identity and writing partially autobiographical work. Most of her stories, set in the Bay Area of California, deal with the experience of immigrants to the United States, whose voice is rarely heard in other writings of Indian writers in English. They are informed by her personal experience with immigration and working with other Indian women who are struggling to adjust to life in America.

*Old Beliefs and New Desires* One common theme that runs through all the stories is that Indian-born women living new lives in the United States find independence a mixed blessing that involves walking a tightrope between old beliefs and newfound desires. Though the characters vary, the themes of the short stories are essentially the same—exploration of the nature of arranged marriages as well as the experience of affirmation and rebellion against social traditions.

*Cross-cultural Experiences of Prejudice* Many of Divakaruni's writings deal with the difficulties that come with cross-cultural experiences. For example, in her novel *Queen of Dreams*, Rakhi, who as a young artist and divorced mother living in Berkeley, California, is struggling to keep her footing with her family and with a world in alarming transition. As Rakhi attempts to divine her identity, knowing little of India but drawn inexorably into a sometimes painful history she is only just discovering, her life is shaken by new horrors. In the wake of the terrorist attacks of September 11, 2001, she and her friends must deal with dark new complexities about their acculturation. The ugly violence visited upon them forces the reader to view those terrible days from the point of view of immigrants and Indian Americans whose only crime was the color of their skin or the fact that they wore a turban.

## Works in Critical Context

The critical acclaim and increasing recognition that Chitra Banerjee Divakaruni has received has established her as a promising writer interested in the immigrant experience as a whole, not simply that of those who move from East to West. It is a cross-cultural scenario where, through her writings, the diversity of Indian writing in English is revealed.

*Leaving Yuba City* The power of Divakaruni's poetry is evidenced by its emotional impact on readers. Author Meena Alexander writes, "Chitra Divakaruni's *Leaving Yuba City* draws us into a realm of the senses, intense, chaotic, site of our pleasure and pain. These are moving lyrics of lives at the edge of the world." Scholar Neila C. Seshachari of the Weber State English department offers praise for the emotional complexity of the work:

Those who read Divakaruni's poems for the first time may be astonished at how the poet writes with such sensitivity and poetic sensibility on issues like abandoned babies on hospital steps, a daughter recollecting her nights spent with her prostitute mother, young Hindu girls growing up in the care of Catholic convent sisters who despise their religion and traditions. It is not surprising, then, that with this work Divakaruni drew the respect of her contemporaries. Author Quincy Troupe writes, "The poetry of Chitra Divakaruni carries a wisdom rarely seen in contemporary poetry, runs through the reader like a cool drink of water on a hot day." This work, he concludes, "is a magical, beautiful book of poetry, strong, passionate, and lyrical."

## Responses to Literature

1. How does Divakaruni's novel *The Conch Bearer* resemble traditional fantasy as you understand it? How is it different? Do you think the portrayal of a culture unknown to the reader is harmful or beneficial to the fantastical nature of the tale?

2. How do characters in *The Unknown Error of Our Lives* have difficulty communicating? What causes the breakdown of communication?

3. What do the fantasies in *The Unknown Error of Our Lives* tell us about reality for each character?

4. Explain the meaning of the title *The Unknown Error of Our Lives.*

BIBLIOGRAPHY

**Books**

Banerjee, Debjani. "'Home and Us': Re-defining Identity in the South Asian Diaspora through the Writings of Chitra Banerjee Divakaruni and Meena Alexander." In *The Diasporic Imagination: Asian American Writing*, volume 2, edited by Somdatta Mandal. New Delhi: Prestige, 2000.

Barat, Urbashi. "Sisters of the Heart: Female Bonding in the Fiction of Chitra Banerjee Divakaruni." In *The Diasporic Imagination: Asian American Writing*, volume 2, edited by Mandal. New Delhi: Prestige, 2000, 44–60.

**Periodicals**

Pais, Arthur J. "Spice Girl has a Fresh Recipe for Women." *India Today* (January 25, 1999): 73.

Softky, Elizabeth. "Cross-Cultural Understanding Spiced with the Indian Diaspora." *Black Issues in Higher Education* 18 (September 1997): 26.

**Web sites**

*Chitra Banerjee Divakaruni.* Retrieved September 20, 2008, from http://www.chitradivakaruni.com.

## ✺ Chuck Dixon

BORN: *1954, Philadelphia, Pennsylvania*

NATIONALITY: *American*

GENRE: *Fiction*

MAJOR WORKS:

*Moon Knight* (1989)

*Robin* (1991)

*Batman: Knightfall* (1993)

*Batman: No Man's Land* (1994)

## Overview

Chuck Dixon is renowned in the comic-book world for his work with such eternally popular characters as Bat-man, Robin, the Green Lantern, and the Punisher. Over the course of his constantly evolving career he has written hundreds of comics and created a number of crowd-pleasing new titles of his own.

## Works in Biographical and Historical Context

*A Boy and His Comics*   Dixon was born on April 14, 1954, in Philadelphia. On his web site, Dixonverse.com, he describes his earliest years as "unremarkable" and "full of movies and TV and pick-up softball and backyard shoot-em-ups." What distinguished his childhood most was his voracious love of comic books. "I honestly can't remember a time when I wasn't interested in comics," he explained in an interview with Web site Geek in the City. "I seemed to be drawing my own comics before I could talk and going through piles of them long before I could read." On his web site, he further explains, "I amassed a huge collection by haunting garage sales and paper pulpers and buying out neighborhood kids' collections for pennies-a-comic. See, they outgrew them but I knew I never would." Making his own comics, his focus shifted from drawing to writing. As he states, "By thirteen I realized I would never be a comic artist like my idol, Steve Ditko. So I began to turn more toward writing comics."

Although he loved reading all genres of comics, his particular fondness for Steve Ditko, the artist and writer who cocreated the superheroes Spider-Man and Doctor Strange for Marvel comics, was telling. Dixon would eventually make his name in the kind of superhero comics he loved as a child, but the first character he created was quite different from the likes of Spider-Man.

*The Early Creations*   Dixon's first creation, *Evangeline*, was quite a shift from the characters he fell in love with as a boy. The title character was not only "a sexy killer vigilante nun" but also a feminist, an unusual creation for the politically conservative Dixon. Dixon's wife at the time, Judith Hunt, provided the rich pen and ink illustrations that adorned its pages, as well as the hand-painted images featured in the comic's first few issues published by Comico Comics in 1984.

Never having achieved more than a cult following with *Evangeline*, Dixon still sought to make a bigger splash in the world of comics. He got his chance to work for the publisher of so many of the comics he adored as a child in 1985. That year he was hired to write backup stories for a comic called *The Savage Sword of Conan* for famed Marvel Comics. Dixon expanded his enterprise the following year, when he took a job at Eclipse Comics, where he wrote for a horror comic anthology series called *Tales of Terror*. That same year he began writing for the long-running series of aviator adventures entitled *Airboy*. By 1987, Dixon now found himself to be one of the hottest comic writers in the industry. Along with his continued work on *Tales of Terror* and *Airboy*, he wrote for the *Alien Legion* series on the Marvel imprint Epic Comics and collaborated with artist Paul Gulacy on a new series called *Valkyrie* for Eclipse. By the end of the 1980s, he could also add a comic adaptation of J. R. R. Tolkein's fantasy classic *The Hobbit* and work on *Marc Spector: Moon Knight* to his resume. However, it was his work in the 1990s that would transform Dixon into a star.

***Years of Fame and Hard Work***  Dixon first worked on the tremendously popular *Punisher* Marvel Comic series in 1990. The comics follow the title vigilante anti-hero as he uses such extreme techniques as kidnapping, torture, extortion, and murder in the pursuit of his concept of justice. The dark, sometimes brutal *Punisher* comics propelled Dixon to his greatest success yet and caught the attention of an editor from that other giant of American comics, DC Comics, publisher of such perennial favorites as *Superman*, *Wonder Woman*, and *Batman*. Editor Denny O'Neil approached Dixon to write a *Batman* spin-off series focusing on the Caped Crusader's Boy-Wonder sidekick, Robin. Dixon jumped at the opportunity. The *Robin* miniseries became such a success that Dixon began work on two more Batman-related titles: *The Joker's Wild* in 1991 and *Cry of the Huntress* the following year. He also launched a triad of other *Bat-*

*man* offshoots—*Robin*, *Nightwing*, and *Batgirl*—and regularly wrote for *Catwoman*.

Dixon's work was not limited to tales set in Batman's Gotham City, though. He also created the superhero teams *Birds of Prey* for DC and *Team 7* for WildStorm/Image and launched a series titled *Prophet* for Extreme Studios.

***The Writer Today***  After several years working on projects for other studios, Dixon found himself back at the DC offices. There he worked on titles like *Richard Dragon* and *Green Arrow* and a number of comic adaptations of popular films like *Nightmare on Elm Street* and *Snakes on a Plane*. He also returned to the Batman universe with work on *Robin* and *Batman and the Outsiders*.

In June of 2008, Dixon's long-running relationship with DC came to a sudden end. The huge western fan has since taken on work from publisher Dynamite Entertainment, where he will be writing a series based on the character known as The Man with No Name, famously portrayed by Clint Eastwood in a trilogy of films directed by Sergio Leone. He is also slotted to write a series based on the long-running *G.I. Joe* comics for IDW Publishing.

## Works in Literary Context

***Superheroes***  Much of Dixon's career has been spent writing about superheroes. A longtime staple of comic books, the superhero can be traced back to 1938 when the most famous such character debuted in the first issue of DC Comics' *Action Comics*. Superman embodied many of the traits that would come to be associated with superheroes. He possessed a number of superhuman abilities, defended "Freedom, justice, and the American way," concealed his powers by adopting a "secret identity," and dressed in an outlandish costume. Not all superheroes would possess all of these traits. Batman, Bob Kane's character that debuted a year after Superman's first appearance, did not have any superhuman abilities. Instead, his chief gimmick was the many gadgets in his arsenal, which he designed himself and funded with his immense fortune. While the superhero's origin lies firmly in the realm of comic books, superheroes have since become staples on television and in the movies as well.

***Horror Comics***  Perhaps the most controversial genre in comic-book history, horror comics, first became popular in the early 1950s after William Gaines inherited Educational Comics from his father and changed the focus from education to entertainment. He commenced publishing a line of comics including *Tales From the Crypt* and *The Vault of Horror*, each of which contained gruesome yet moralistic stories. The success of Gaines's horror comics was short-lived; a 1954 book titled *Seduction of the Innocent* by Fredric Wertham accused horror comics of inspiring a rise in juvenile delinquency. The book led to a trial in which the horror comic industry was persecuted. Gaines's career publishing horror comics was ruined by the trial, but the genre has proven to be a most enduring and influential one, spawning modern comics like *Tales of Terror*, a series for which Dixon wrote during its 1985–1987 run.

## Works in Critical Context

*Robin* Comic fans have long responded enthusiastically to Dixon's writing. One of his first major series was the *Batman* spin-off titled *Robin*, which Web site Pop Culture Shock.com deems is "one of his most memorable." Web site IGN.com was especially enthusiastic about Dixon's *Robin*, declaring this in its review of the series' final issue:

> I know I sound like a broken record pointing this out in nearly all of my reviews of Dixon's but when it's firing on all cylinders, his run on the title can feel like the best of Spiderman, with a teenage hero wisecracking his way through dangerous situations and common adolescent experiences alike.

*Batman and the Outsiders* Dixon's work on the *Batman and the Outsiders* series is among his most well-known. In a review on IGN.com, the series is said to have taken some time to develop a distinctive personality amongst the myriad Batman comic series, but the site declares that by its seventh issue it is "at last developing into an exciting cloak and dagger series that sees Batman's operatives thrown into one stickier situation after another." Still, the series was not above some criticism. IGN goes on to note, "For the entire series so far, Batman and his Outsiders have been up against a rather lifeless evil corporation, a device that has been far too common in DC comics these days."

## Responses to Literature

1. Although Dixon is famous for the *Batman* stories he has written, he is not the first writer to contribute to the popular comic-book series. Read a *Batman* comic written by Chuck Dixon and one written by another writer. How do the two writers differ in their approaches to the Batman character and his world? Use examples from both comics to support your response.

2. While Dixon writes the stories and dialogue in his comic books, his creative process is very much a collaborative one. Choose one of his comics, and explain how Dixon's words and the artist's illustrations work together to tell a complete story. Write your response as a brief essay.

3. Dixon's career has been a long and varied one. Read one of his *Evangeline* comics from the mid-1980s and one his more recent *Robin* from the late 2000s. Has Dixon's writing style changed in some notable way over the years? If it has changed, how has it changed?

---

# COMMON HUMAN EXPERIENCE

In his first comic series, Dixon created a strong, confident, and memorable female character named Evangeline. Other works that feature strong female heroes include:

*Wonder Woman* (1941–), a comic-book series by William Moulton Marston. Wonder Woman is a member of a fictional Amazonian tribe who is sent to what is referred to as "man's world" to serve as an ambassador. She possesses superhuman strength, but also employs her bullet-deflecting wristbands and invisible jet to combat crime and injustice.

*Aeon Flux* (1991–1995), a television series by Peter Chung. This surreal animated series made its debut on the MTV (Music Television) Network in 1991 as a recurring feature on its animation anthology show *Liquid Television*. The series is set in a strange vision of the future ruled by an oppressive government. The character Aeon Flux is a wily, acrobatic female assassin intent on overthrowing the corrupt government. In 1995, the character became the subject of her own series. A live-action film adaptation followed a decade later.

*Buffy the Vampire Slayer* (1997–2003), a television series created by Joss Whedon. This cult favorite series features Buffy Summers, a seemingly normal high school girl who learns that she has the superhuman ability to kill vampires—and that her hometown is an entranceway for evil creatures such as these.

*Elektra Saga* (1983), a comic book created by Frank Miller. The character Elektra first appeared in Marvel Comics' *Daredevil* series in 1981, but was eventually featured in a series of her own in 1983. The character is a female Greek assassin whose trademark weapons are a pair of Japanese blades called sai.

BIBLIOGRAPHY

**Web sites**

Comic Book DB.com: The Comic Book Database. *Charles 'Chuck' Dixon.* Accessed November 19, 2008, from http://www.comicbookdb.com/creator.php?ID=747.

Comic Book Resources. *Chuck Dixon to Write G.I. Joe For IDW.* Posted September 8, 2008, from http://www.comicbookresources.com/?page=article&id= 17962.

The Official Home Page of Chuck Dixon. Accessed November 19, 2008, from http://dixonverse.net.

Geek in the City.com. *Talking with Chuck Dixon!* Accessed November 30, 2008, from http://www.geekinthecity.com/comics/talking_with_ch.php.

IGN.com. *Batman and the Outsiders #7 Review.* Accessed November 30, 2008, from http://comics.ign.com/articles/875/875923p1.html.

IGN.com *Robin #174 Review.* Accessed November 30, 2008, from http://comics.ign.com/articles/875/875922p1.html.

Mr. Media.com. *Chuck Dixon, "The Simpsons" comic book writer: Mr. Media Interview.* Accessed November 30, 2008, from http://www.mrmedia.com/2007/07/chuck-dixon-simpsons-comic-book-writer_05.html.

Newsarama. *Chuck Dixon to Write the Man With No Name.* Accessed November 30, 2008, from http://www.newsarama.com/comics/080820-Dixon MWNN.html.

Popular Culture Shock.com. *Chuck Dixon Returning to Robin.* Accessed November 30, 2008, from http://www.popcultureshock.com/blogs/chuck-dixon-returning-to-robin/.

TransFans. *Chuck Dixon Interview.* Accessed November 30, 2008, from http://transfans.net/interviews_dixon.php.

# ⊛ Gregory Djanikian

BORN: *1949, Alexandria, Egypt*

NATIONALITY: *American*

GENRE: *Poetry*

MAJOR WORKS:

*The Man in the Middle* (1984)
*Falling Deeply into America* (1989)
*Years Later* (2000)
*So I Will Till the Ground* (2007)

Gregory Djanikian    *Courtesy of Gregory Djanikian*

## Overview

Gregory Djanikian is a nationally renowned poet of Armenian heritage who immigrated to the United States as a child. He has won numerous awards and pleased countless critics and readers with his thematically varied, but consistently lyrical, work. Djanikian has published at least five collections of his work, including *The Man in the Middle* (1984) and *So I Will Till the Ground* (2007). He currently lives in Narbeth, Pennsylvania.

## Works in Biographical and Historical Context

*A Multicultural Boyhood*  Gregory Djanikian was born on August 15, 1949, in Alexandria, Egypt. At the age of eight, he and his family traversed the Atlantic Ocean to settle in Williamsport, Pennsylvania, in the United States. He quickly acclimated to American life, stating in a public television interview that "my acculturation to this country occurred in some ways on the baseball fields of that town." Although Djanikian was open to Americanization to a degree, he never lost sight of his Armenian heritage.

As a boy, Djanikian's interests were not limited to the baseball field. In a 2007 interview with the *Armenian Reporter*, he explained,

> My mother had gone to both French and British schools in Alexandria, and when my sister and I were children, she recited to us both French and British poetry ... and we were encouraged to memorize poems and recite them at family gatherings ... [even] words I didn't really know the meaning of, though I liked the sound of them.

That childlike appreciation for the sheer sounds of poetic language would become well apparent in the work he would compose as an adult.

*From Architecture to Poetry*  Djanikian did not attempt original composition until his fascination with poetry was reignited while attending the University of Pennsylvania. Although enrolled as an architecture major, he had his most profound experience in a freshman English class in 1968. Deeply affected by the violent era—one marked by the war in Vietnam and the assassinations of the social and political leaders Martin Luther King Jr. and Robert Kennedy—Djanikian began wondering if there was more to his future than designing buildings. He told the *Armenian Reporter*, "I brashly changed my major to English soon after, went to my professor and asked him if he would be kind enough to mentor me, which he generously did."

Djanikian's personal relationship with poetry developed rapidly and intensely. "I feel that poetry is a communication between people on the most intense level, even if it's only between two people, writer and reader," he told the Pennsylvania Center for the Book. "This relationship may be one of the most intimate we might experience, when one intuitively and deeply speaks to another."

After receiving his undergraduate degree in English at the University of Pennsylvania, Djanikian continued his studies at Syracuse University in New York State, where his newfound love of poetry inspired him to focus on creative writing. Following graduation he remained in New York for some time, working as both a public school English teacher and a lecturer at his alma mater in Syracuse. He also brought his lecturing skills to the University of Michigan in Ann Arbor.

*Rising to Prominence in the World of Poetry* In 1983 Djanikian decided to return to his home state. He took a position at the University of Pennsylvania as an English professor and director of the creative writing department. The following year Carnegie Mellon University Press published his debut poetry collection. *The Man in the Middle* opened the door to an influential and artistically satisfying side career as a poet. His work would cover the breadth of the poet's obsessions, including romantic love and his childhood in Alexandria. Combining the personal with the socio-political, he has written of the horrific Armenian genocide of 1915, in which the Ottoman government schemed to reduce its Armenian population by way of slaughter.

Djanikian has also written of his adopted home, saying of his poem "Immigrant Picnic," published in *Poetry* magazine in 1999, that it

> describes a July 4th get-together of my immigrant family, who ... contribute to that great melting pot that is the English language, that, for many of us who have come from different countries, our difficulties with American idioms often lead to unexpected syntactic constructions and surprising turns of phrase which enrich the language and by which we all are enriched.

Regardless of his subject matter, Djanikian's work consistently displays the fascination with language he mentions in this quote and a facility for vivid, descriptive imagery.

Djanikian has placed his work regularly with various poetry magazines and journals like the *Nation, Three Rivers Poetry Journal,* and the *American Scholar.* He has also published an additional four collections of his poems: *Falling Deeply into America* (1989), *About Distance* (1995), *Years Later* (2000), and most recently, *So I Will Till the Ground* (2007). Djanikian's work has been greeted with fervent praise from the poetry community. He is the recipient of several prizes, including a 2002 Friends of Literature Award, a 2004 Anahid Literary Award from the Armenian Center of Columbia University, and a National Endowment for the Arts fellowship. Djanikian continues to reside in the state in which he grew up with his wife and two children, still teaching creative writing at the University of Pennsylvania.

## LITERARY AND HISTORICAL CONTEMPORARIES

Djanikian's famous contemporaries include:

**Stephen Dunn** (1939–): American poet Dunn has penned fourteen collections of his work. In 2001, Dunn received the Pulitzer Prize for Poetry for his book *Different Hours* (2000).

**Tomaz Salamun** (1941–): Slovenian avant-garde poet Salamun had some of his work banned by his country's communist government in the 1960s.

**Robert Hass** (1941–): American poet Hass won the 2008 Pulitzer Prize for Poetry for his collection *Time and Materials* (2007).

**Garrison Keillor** (1942–): American writer and radio personality Keillor is famed for his folksy Minnesota-based radio program *A Prairie Home Companion.* Djanikian is a contributor to Keillor's radio program *The Writer's Almanac.*

**Orhan Pamuk** (1952–): Turkish novelist Pamuk was awarded the 2006 Nobel Prize in Literature; his citation proclaimed that his work "discovered new symbols for the clash and interlacing of cultures."

**Marine Dilanyan** (1957–): Dilanyan is an internationally exhibited, award-winning artist. Her work is on prominent display at the Modern Art Museum in her hometown of Yerevan, Armenia.

**Alvin Ayler** (1936–1970): American jazz tenor saxophonist associated with the "free jazz" movement, a form of jazz distinguished by its wild, chaotic, improvisational style. Gregory Djanikian has acknowledged that Ayler's music was influential on his poetry.

## Works in Literary Context

*Free Verse* Free verse is a form of poetry composed without strict meter, rhyme, or rhythm. The cadence of common speech is often used in place of a traditional rhythmic pattern. The term "free verse" was first coined by late-nineteenth-century poets, such as Jules Laforgue and Arthur Rimbaud. These poets sought to "free" poetry from the traditional metric strictures. In the twentieth century, poets such as T.S. Eliot, William Carlos Williams, and Ezra Pound became prominent users of the free verse style, and Djanikian has followed in this modernist tradition.

*Love Poetry* The theme of romantic love has long inspired poetry. In the Middle Ages, lyric poetry often dealt with the theme of courtly love, an idealized but illicit code of romantic behavior. In the late sixteenth and early seventeenth centuries, William Shakespeare composed his sonnets, which are among the most famous

## COMMON HUMAN EXPERIENCE

Themes of his Armenian heritage pervade the poetry of Gregory Djanikian, particularly in his most recent collection *So I Will Till the Ground*. Other literary works inspired by the writer's Armenian heritage include:

*The Fool* (1881), a novel by Raffi. The essential novel by famed Armenian writer Raffi is a patriotic work intended to rile his fellow Armenians after they lost their independence to the Ottoman Turks at the close of the fourteenth century. The novel, originally serialized in an Armenian journal called *Mshak*, was considered essential reading for all Armenian revolutionaries.

*Rainbow* (1907), a poetry collection by Misak Metsarents. This collection of poems by the prominent Armenian poet Metsarents gathers romantically composed but harrowing verses focused on the plight of the Armenian people under the control of the tyrannical sultan Abd al-Hamid II during the late nineteenth century.

"Martial Call" (1941), a poem by Avetik Isahakian. Composed during World War II by a former political prisoner, "Martial Call" is an impassioned poem of patriotism, steeped in deep pride in the Armenian heritage

*Khodenan* (1950), a novel by Khachik Dashtents. This tragic story tells of the horrid Armenian genocide perpetrated by the Ottomans during World War I.

and influential love poems in history. Throughout the years, love poetry has never diminished in popularity, notably having a sweeping influence on popular song lyrics. Gregory Djanikian's 2000 collection *Years Later* found the poet shifting from his usual themes of heritage, family, and culture to romantic love poetry.

## Works in Critical Context

**Falling Deeply into America** Gregory Djanikian has long enjoyed favorable responses to his poetry, winning numerous awards for his work. From his earliest works, he has been considered an important and approachable poet. His second collection, *Falling Deeply into America*, received high praise from the respected newspaper the *Washington Post*. In the *Post*'s review, Howard Frank Mosher wrote that the book is "one of the most lyrical, and readily accessible, books of poetry I've read in years."

**So I Will Till the Ground** For the majority of Gregory Djanikian's books of poetry, critical reviews, positive or negative, are not as plentiful as the praise of

his colleagues. Fellow poet Stephen Dunn has been particularly vocal about his adoration of Djanikian's work. Upon the publication of the collection *So I Will Till the Ground*, Dunn deemed the title poem "marvelous" and said of the volume as a whole, "This is Djanikian's book of history and of memory, no holds barred, his most urgent to date."

## Responses to Literature

1. Because poems are often expressed with subtle imagery rather than direct statements, they often require careful thought on the part of the reader to determine their meanings. Read the poem "Mind/Body" by Gregory Djanikian. Then compose an essay explaining what you think the poem means. Be sure to use details from the poem to support your analysis.

2. Poems about love are common, but they can be approached in many different ways. Read William Shakespeare's "Sonnet 18" and "Years Later" by Gregory Djanikian. How does each poet deal with love? Are the poems noticeably different from each other? Explain.

3. Although Gregory Djanikian is a man of Armenian heritage who was born in Egypt, he has been living in America since he was a young boy. Djanikian addresses his varied cultural background in the poem "Immigrant Picnic." Read the poem and explain what you think Djanikian is trying to convey about his culture in an essay. Support your response with details from the poem.

4. Research the genocide perpetrated on the Armenian people in 1915. How does this historical experience shape Djanikian's expression of his heritage?

BIBLIOGRAPHY

**Periodicals**

Kitchen, Judith. "In Pursuit of Elegance." *Georgia Review* 54 (2000): 763–780.

Mosher, Howard Frank. "Good Times and Verse." *Washington Post* (August 6, 1989).

Sternstein, Aliya. "'Penn'ing Great Poetry." *Daily Pennsylvanian* (October 26, 2000).

Straus, Robert. "Ode to Joi(sey)." *New York Times* (April 27, 2003).

"Words in Exotic Flavors." *Armenian Reporter Arts & Culture* (September 8, 2007): C27–C29.

**Web sites**

"Gregory Djanikian." *The Cortland Review*. Accessed November 20, 2008, from http://www.cortlandreview.com/issuethree/greg3.htm.

"Poems by Gregory Djanikian." *The Writer's Almanac with Garrison Keillor*. Accessed November 20, 2008, from http://writersalmanac.publicradio.org/author.php?auth_id=1210.

"Poet Celebrates Family Picnics and 'Great Melting Pot' of Language." PBS.org. Accessed November 20, 2008, from http://www.pbs.org/newshour/bb/entertainment/july-dec07/picnic_07-04.html.

"Radio Times with Marty Moss-Coane" (audio interview). Center for Programs in Contemporary Writing, University of Pennsylvania. Accessed November 20, 2008, from http://writing.upenn.edu/pennsound/x/Djanikian.html.

# ✸ E. L. Doctorow

BORN: *1931, New York, New York*

NATIONALITY: *American*

GENRE: *Fiction, nonfiction, drama*

MAJOR WORKS:
*The Book of Daniel* (1971)
*Ragtime* (1975)
*World's Fair* (1986)
*Billy Bathgate* (1989)
*The March* (2005)

## Overview

A major contemporary fiction writer, E. L. Doctorow achieved widespread recognition with the overwhelming

E. L. Doctorow  *1994, photograph. AP Images.*

critical and commercial success of *Ragtime* (1975), a novel that vividly recreates the turbulent years of pre-World War I America.

## Works in Biographical and Historical Context

***Growing up Middle Class in The Bronx***  The son of David Richard and Rose Levine Doctorow, Edgar Lawrence Doctorow was born in New York City to a family with a strong radical bias. He characterizes the setting as "a lower-middle-class environment of generally enlightened, socialist sensibility." The family resided in the then-middle-class borough of the Bronx. After graduating from the Bronx High School of Science in 1948, Doctorow entered Kenyon College in Ohio. He had chosen Kenyon because he wanted to study with the poet and essayist John Crowe Ransom.

Doctorow majored in philosophy, not English, and he acted in campus dramatic productions instead of pursuing a literary apprenticeship and an academic career. After earning an AB degree with honors in 1952, he studied English drama and directing at Columbia University (1952–1953) and then served from 1953 to 1955 with the U.S. Army in Germany. He married Helen Setzer on August 20, 1954.

***Editing, with a Side of Writing***  Instead of going back to graduate school after leaving the Army, Doctorow struck out on his own, earning a living as an expert reader for film and television production companies in New York. It was exhausting piecework but a wonderful education. He read a book a day, seven days a week, and wrote a twelve-hundred-word synopsis-critique of each book, evaluating its potential for the visual media. An informal evaluation of a novel for Victor Weybright, the editor in chief of the New American Library, led Weybright to hire Doctorow as an associate editor in 1959.

Doctorow's vision of "what the West must really have been like," *Welcome to Hard Times* (1960), not only attracted excellent reviews but was also adapted as a Hollywood movie in 1967. The novel is the story of a western massacre, the shaping of a "family" from the survivors of that massacre, and the creation of a tiny parody of a village from the ashes. Of all Doctorow's novels to date *Welcome to Hard Times* has excited the longest loyalties and the least dissent.

By 1964, he was a senior editor, and that same year he was hired as editor in chief at Dial Press, where he became a vice president and remained until 1969. Doctorow's next novel, an attempt at science fiction called *Big as Life*, was not published until 1966. "Unquestionably, it's the worst I've done," Doctorow later told one interviewer.

***Writer-In-Residence***  After leaving Dial Press, he became a writer in residence, or member of the faculty, at the University of California at Irvine (1969–1970).

# LITERARY AND HISTORICAL CONTEMPORARIES

Doctorow's famous contemporaries include:

**Toni Morrison** (1931–): An American author who was awarded the 1988 Pulitzer Prize for her novel *Beloved* (1987) and the 1993 Nobel Prize in Literature.

**Sylvia Plath** (1932–1963): An American poet, novelist, and short story writer famous for her confessional poetry, her semi-autobiographical novel *The Bell Jar* (1963), and her suicide.

**Jacques Derrida** (1930–2004): An Algerian-born French author whose philosophy of deconstruction influenced both literary theory and continental philosophy.

**Shel Silverstein** (1930–1999): An American self-taught poet, children's author, cartoonist, composer, and screenwriter most famous for his poetry collection *Where the Sidewalk Ends* (1974).

**Gary Snyder** (1930–): An American poet and environmental activist often associated with the Beat Generation, Snyder's poetry collection *Turtle Island* (1974) was awarded the Pulitzer Prize in Poetry in 1974.

With his next novel, *The Book of Daniel* (1971), Doctorow tried yet another narrative form: the historical novel, using the spy trial and executions of Julius and Ethel Rosenberg in the early 1950s as the animating energy at the core of his tale. Daniel's voice is also the voice of a generation that seems characterized everywhere by slogans and symbols of upheaval, by its frank, jovial, self-congratulatory rejection of every sort of established authority. *The Book of Daniel* demands that the reader respond to it as a political tract as well as a private description of experience. Some critics argue that the novel is unabashedly a work of leftist propaganda and highly charged with moral outrage.

***Ragtime: Retelling History*** Doctorow next published his most famous book, *Ragtime* (1975), delighting and puzzling readers at the same time. In contrast to *The Book of Daniel*, *Ragtime* took more liberties with history and identity. In this novel, Harry Houdini, Henry Ford, J. P. Morgan, Emma Goldman, and a half-dozen other real people speak, think, and interact in ways that cannot be verified historically.

Doctorow followed *Ragtime* with a play, *Drinks before Dinner* (1978), and a novel *Loon Lake* (1980), an audacious book in style and construction. Doctorow returned to more traditional tones and narrative procedures for his next two books, *Lives of the Poets* and *World's Fair* (1985). Doctorow won an American Book Award for *World's Fair*. The fact that *World's Fair* is most centrally concerned with Doctorow's family relationships

is of foremost importance in examining the book as an autobiography. *World's Fair* is his tribute to family life itself, "life as it is lived," a family memoir more than a private memoir, created with neither propaganda nor sentimentality nor condescension. Doctorow won an American Book Award for *World's Fair*, a blend of memoir and fiction. In the book, Doctorow's life and this life of his protagonist (also names Edgar) converge and diverge against the backdrop of the 1939–1940 World's Fair in New York City, which both the real Doctorow and his fictional counterpart attended. The World's Fair setting gives Doctorow the ability to present a slice of world history itself (including the Great Depression andthe beginnings of World War II) side by side with the lives of his own family members.

***Ongoing Publications and Accolades*** Doctorow's subsequent work includes the National Book Critics Circle Award winner *Billy Bathgate* (1989). The "disreputable genre materials" that inspired *Billy Bathgate* (1989) may have been the comic book and the Depression-era pulp thriller. Doctorow seems to have tried to give his novel the joyful velocity and preposterousness of what the literary establishment calls "subliterature."

After *Billy Bathgate*, Doctorow published a novel, *The March* (2005), two volumes of short fiction, *Lives of the Poets I* (1984), and *Sweetland Stories* (2004), and two volumes of essays. Of these, *The March* was most successful, winning the PEN/Faulkner Award for Fiction, the National Book Critics Circle fiction award, and a nomination for the Pulitzer Prize.

In 2007, Doctorow was awarded the Chicago Tribune Literary Awards' Literary Prize for lifetime achievement.

## Works in Literary Context

Doctorow is known for his use of historical (and quasi-historical) figures and events in his work. His writing is influenced by the literary, political, and intellectual discussions he was immersed in while growing up, his family's Jewish heritage, his experience working as an "expert reader" for Columbia Pictures, and authors, including the German playwright Heinrich Von Kleist.

***The American Dream*** In *Ragtime*, as in much of his fiction, Doctorow presents a multilayered narrative and historical settings and personages while exploring issues important to contemporary society. Central to Doctorow's work is his portrayal of characters who search for the material prosperity and social equality promised by the "American Dream" yet become victims of the oppressiveness of class division and capitalism. For Doctorow, history is a cyclical process in which his characters fall prey to a future over which they have no control.

In addition to his contributions to American letters, Doctorow remains active in the literary community and is involved in political activism. Doctorow encourages his peers to speak out on issues that extend beyond the literary world. For example, in 2004, Doctorow criticized President George W. Bush during a commencement address he gave at Hofstra University. His voice continues to be influential in a variety of communities.

## Works in Critical Context

Although Doctorow received little critical attention for his early novels, he was praised for his inventive approaches to the genres of the Western and science fiction as well as for his exploration of the relationship between good and evil. *The Book of Daniel* is considered by many to be a poignant critique of the anti-Communist climate during the McCarthy era.

*Ragtime*    *Ragtime* received high praise from critics and other reviewers. For example, George Stade of *The New York Times Book Review* claimed that Doctorow had achieved an impressive breakthrough in his invention of a technique that could capture "the fictions and the realities of the era of ragtime." Eliot Fremont-Smith, writing for the *Village Voice*, said that Doctorow's novel was "simply splendid" on one level and yet also "complicatedly splendid" in its deeper levels of meaning, implication, and irony, "a bag of riches, totally lucid and accessible, full of surprises, epiphanies, little time-bombs that alter one's view of things." Yet, the novelist's meddling with objective historical facts made several reviewers uneasy. For example, Hilton Kramer distrusted the message he felt was concealed beneath the novel's surface charm:

> The stern realities of Mr. Doctorow's political romance—its sweeping indictment of American life, and its celebration of a radical alternative—are all refracted, as it were, in the quaint, chromatic glow of a Tiffany lamp, and are thus softened and made more decorative in the process.

Martin Green leveled a similar charge, accusing Doctorow of taking "gross liberties with history in the name of art" and of encouraging the reader to indulge himself in a radical chic daydream, "to give ourselves the airs of revolutionaries, in purely fantasy and wish-fulfillment conditions."

## Responses to Literature

1. Who is the narrator of *Ragtime*? Why do you think Doctorow chose this narrative style for the novel?

2. What elements of *Ragtime* could be considered allegorical?

3. How is technology presented in *Ragtime*? How does Doctorow seem to view the increase in industrial production during the Progressive Era?

4. How are the characters in *Ragtime* each constrained, or imprisoned? How does Doctorow show these constraints to readers?

---

## COMMON HUMAN EXPERIENCE

One of the key themes in Doctorow's fiction is the pursuit of the American dream. Other works that explore this theme include the following:

*Epic of America* (1931), a nonfiction work by James Truslow Adams. This book tells a story about American heritage and introduces the term "The American Dream" into the American lexicon.

*The American Dream* (1965), a sermon given by Martin Luther King, Jr. In this speech, King talks about the universality of the American dream intended by the founders of the United States and argues that in order for the American dream to become a reality, all races must be treated equally.

*The American Dream: A Short History of an Idea that Shaped a Nation* (2003), a nonfiction work by Jim Cullen. This book explores the meaning of the American dream at various points in the history of the United States.

---

BIBLIOGRAPHY

**Books**

Brienza, Susan D. "Writing as Witnessing: The Many Voices of E. L. Doctorow." *Traditions, Voices and Dreams: The American Novel since the 1960s*, edited by Melvin J. Friedman and Ben Siegel. Newark, DE.: University of Delaware Press, 1995, pp. 168–195.

Budick, Emily Miller. *Fiction and Historical Consciousness: The American Romance Tradition*. New Haven, Conn.: Yale University Press, 1989, pp. 185–215.

Claridge, Henry. "Writing in the Margin: E. L. Doctorow and American History." *The New American Writing: Essays on American History*, edited by Graham Clarke. New York: St. Martin's Press, 1990, pp. 9–28.

Fowler, Douglas. *Understanding E. L. Doctorow*. Columbia: University of South Carolina Press, 1992.

Harter, Carol C. and James R. Thompson. *E. L. Doctorow*. Boston: Twayne, 1990.

Levine, Paul. *E. L. Doctorow*. New York: Methuen, 1985.

Morris, Christopher D. *Models of Misrepresentation: On the Fiction of E. L. Doctorow*. Jackson: University of Mississippi, 1991.

Parks, John G. *E. L. Doctorow*. New York: Continuum, 1991.

Siegel, Ben. *Critical Essays on E. L. Doctorow*. New York: G. K. Hall & Company, 2000.

Williams, John. *Fiction as False Document: The Reception of E. L. Doctorow in the Postmodern Age*. Columbia, S.C.: Camden House, 1996.

**Periodicals**

Cooper, Barbara. "The Artist as Historian in the Novels of E. L. Doctorow." *Emporia State Research Studies* 29 (Fall 1980): 5–44.

Emblidge, David. "Marching Backward into the Future: Progress as Illusion in Doctorow's Novels." *Southwest Review* 62 (Autumn 1977): 397–409.

Hague, Angela. "*Ragtime* and the Movies." *North Dakota Quarterly* 50, no. 3 (1983): 101–112.

Harpham, Geoffrey Galt. "E. L. Doctorow and the Technology of Narrative." *PMLA* 100, no. 1 (1985): 81–95.

Parks, John G. "The Politics of Polyphony: The Fiction of E. L. Doctorow." *Twentieth Century Literature* 37 (Winter 1991): 454–488.

Persell, Michelle. "The Jews, *Ragtime,* and the Politics of Silence." *Literature and Psychology* 42 (Fall 1996): 1–15.

Weber, Bruce. "The Myth Maker: The Creative Mind of Novelist E. L. Doctorow." *New York Times Magazine* (October 21, 1985): 25–31.

# ✹ Hilda Doolittle

BORN: *1886, Bethlehem, Pennsylvania*

DIED: *1961, Zurich, Switzerland*

NATIONALITY: *American*

GENRE: *Poetry*

MAJOR WORKS:
*Collected Poems* (1925)
*Trilogy* (1944–1946)
*Tribute to Freud* (1956)
*Bid Me to Live* (1960)
*Helen in Egypt* (1961)

## Overview

Hilda Doolittle (often referred to simply as H. D.) is often called "the perfect imagist," and her early free verse poetry is credited with inspiring Ezra Pound's formulation of Imagism. Doolittle's later poetry transcended the principles of this school of verse to include mythology, occult and religious themes, psychoanalytic concepts, and symbolism. Her work retains interest for its role in establishing the tenets of imagism, and because much of it reflects Doolittle's association with some prominent figures in English and American intellectual life in the early twentieth century, including Ezra Pound, Richard Aldington, D. H. Lawrence, and Sigmund Freud.

## Works in Biographical and Historical Context

***Engagement to Ezra Pound*** Doolittle was born in Bethlehem, Pennsylvania on September 10, 1886, and

Hilda Doolittle    *Doolittle, Hilda, photograph. The Library of Congress.*

for two years attended Bryn Mawr College, where the poet Marianne Moore was also a student. In the early 1900s, Doolittle, Moore, Pound, and William Carlos Williams were friends, and studied and wrote together. Doolittle and Pound were briefly engaged, but her family forbade the marriage, and some biographers theorize that she traveled to England in 1911 to rejoin him.

***Pound Arranges for Publication of Doolittle's Work*** From London Pound arranged for the publication of several of Doolittle's poems in Harriet Monroe's *Poetry* magazine in January 1913. Submitted under the name "H. D. Imagiste," the poems "Hermes of the Ways," "Priapus," and "Epigram" embodied Pound's concept of imagism, which includes the use of concrete, sensual images, common speech, conciseness, a wide range of subject matter, and the creation of new rhythms, intended to produce, according to the credo published in the 1915 imagist anthology, "poetry that is hard and clear, never blurred nor indefinite."

***Life in Literary London*** Doolittle's participation in the social and intellectual life of literary London, on the eve of the First World War, included association with D. H. Lawrence, May Sinclair, W. B. Yeats, and Richard Aldington, whom she married in 1913. Together Aldington and Doolittle edited the *Egoist*, a literary forum for imagist writers, and both were major contributors to *Some Imagist Poets: An Anthology*, a collection of imagist poetry edited by Pound and published in 1914. When

Pound abandoned imagism following the publication of this volume, Doolittle and Aldington, in conjunction with Amy Lowell, led and further developed the movement; they were instrumental, for example, in arranging for the publication of three succeeding imagist anthologies. Doolittle's first volume of poems, *Sea Garden*, was published in 1916.

*Adverse Events Lead to Divorce*    Following a series of stressful events, including Aldington's absence while in military service during World War I, the deaths of Doolittle's brother and father, and the miscarriage of her first pregnancy, she and Aldington separated in 1918. For many years thereafter she lived with the novelist Winifred Ellerman, who took the pen name of Bryher. The two women traveled extensively after the birth of Doolittle's daughter in 1919, eventually settling in Switzerland. Two subsequent volumes of poetry, *Hymen* (1921) and *Heliodora and Other Poems* (1924), established Doolittle as one of the most important free verse writers in English.

*Experimenting Genre and Technique*    After her first three volumes of poetry were gathered as *Collected Poems* in 1925, she began to experiment more widely with different genres and techniques. In ensuing works of poetry, she expanded the technical innovations of imagist verse, and ultimately departed altogether from the tenets of imagism. She also wrote drama and fiction, including two experimental works, *Palimpsest* (1926) and *Hedylus* (1928), which are nominally considered novels, although they defy easy categorization and are primarily commended for their poetic prose. Critics have acknowledged the complexities of these prose works; Babette Deutsch, for example, termed *Palimpsest* a book "for poets and patient intellectuals."

*Undergoing Psychoanalysis with Freud*    In 1933 and 1934, Doolittle underwent psychoanalysis with Sigmund Freud in Vienna, and later published her recollections of the experience in *Tribute to Freud* (1956), a book of prose characterized by her biographer Vincent Quinn as essentially "a self-portrait brought into focus by her confrontation with Freud."

*War-torn London Inspires War Trilogy*    Doolittle returned to England during the Second World War and subsequently wrote her "war trilogy," comprising *The Walls Do Not Fall* (1944), *Tribute to the Angels* (1945), and *The Flowering of the Rod* (1946), works inspired by the realities of living in war-torn London that make greater use of religious imagery than her previous poetry. After the war she returned to Switzerland, where she wrote her third major work of fiction, *Bid Me to Live* (1960), a semiautobiographical account of her life in London in the 1920s. Doolittle's last major poetic work, *Helen in Egypt* (1961), is a book-length mixture of poetry and prose in three parts that retells the Helen of Troy legend. In 1960, she became the first woman to receive the Award of

## LITERARY AND HISTORICAL CONTEMPORARIES

Hilda Doolittle's famous contemporaries include:

**Ezra Pound** (1885–1972): The American poet, critic, intellectual, and major figure of the modernist movement of the twentieth century.

**D. H. Lawrence** (1885–1930): A prolific English writer whose work responds to the dehumanizing impact of modernity and industrialization; his works—particularly those dealing with human sexuality—generated much controversy, which resulted in his voluntary exile during the second half of his life.

**Richard Aldington** (1892–1962): An English author most famous for his World War I poetry, novel *Death of a Hero* (1929), and controversial biography *Lawrence of Arabia* (1955).

**Adolf Hitler** (1889–1945): The Leader of the National Socialist German Worker's (or "Nazi") Party, Hitler was an Austrian-born German political leader who is best known for precipitating World War II and the genocide of approximately six million Jews during the Holocaust.

**Sigmund Freud** (1856–1939): A neurologist, medical scientist, biologist, and writer, this Austrian is widely regarded as the father of psychoanalysis; Hilda Doolittle was amongst his many patients.

Merit Medal from the American Academy of Arts and Letters. She died in 1961 after suffering a major stroke.

## Works in Literary Context

Doolittle is best remembered as an exemplar of imagism, the first important movement in twentieth-century poetry and a precursor of literary modernism, and thus remains of primary interest as an important influence on modern poetry. The development of Doolittle's increasingly complex and resonant texts is best understood when placed in the context of other important modernists, many of whom she knew intimately and all of whom she read avidly—especially poets such as Ezra Pound, T. S. Eliot, William Butler Yeats, William Carlos Williams, Marianne Moore, and Wallace Stevens, and novelists such as D. H. Lawrence, Dorothy Richardson, Virginia Woolf, James Joyce, Gertrude Stein, Colette, May Sinclair, Djuna Barnes, and William Faulkner. Within this modernist tradition, Doolittle's particular emphasis grew out of her perspective as a woman regarding the intersections of public events and private lives in the aftermath of World War I and in the increasingly ominous period culminating in the Atomic Age. Love and war, birth and death are the central concerns of her work. In her search for the underlying patterns ordering and

## COMMON HUMAN EXPERIENCE

In her later work, Doolittle returns to a key moment in Western culture's idea of itself: the Trojan War. Other works that recast significant moments in cultural history in a new perspective include the following:

*Antony and Cleopatra* (1623), a tragedy by William Shakespeare. Based on the Thomas North translation of Plutarch's *Life of Markus Antonius* (1579), this story follows the relationship between Mark Antony and Cleopatra from the Parthian war until Cleopatra commits suicide.

*Ulysses*, (1922) a novel by James Joyce. Drawing many parallels with Homer's *Odyssey*, this story follows its protagonist, Leopold Bloom, during an ordinary day in Dublin.

*Absalom, Absalom!* (1936), a gothic novel by William Faulkner. Set before, during, and after the Civil War, this work tells the story of three families in the American South.

uniting consciousness and culture, she examined, questioned, and reconstituted gender, language, and myth.

***Imagism*** Examination of her own career reveals that Doolittle continued to experiment with different poetic techniques after writing the works that established the essential principles of imagism. Poetry written after the publication of the *Collected Poems* in 1925, for example, employs increasingly complex rhymes and rhythms. Doolittle ultimately moved away from the predominantly visual imagery characteristic of imagist verse, instead relying on phonetic and rhythmic effects to recreate moods and objects. Many commentators contend that the works that follow the *Collected Poems* are her best, although a few maintain that she broadened her range at the expense of the clarity and conciseness that had been her trademark as the quintessential imagist poet. Still, her technical achievements, her poignant portrayals of her personal struggles, and the beauty of her work have all earned a significant amount of praise. As C. H. Sisson pointed out, the prospective reader of Doolittle might be a little surprised to find that "[Doolittle] offers more than the formal virtues which are usually allowed to her work, and that ... work abundantly repays the not very strenuous labor of reading it."

To many, Doolittle will be remembered as "a poets' poet." "To be such," wrote Horace Gregory, "has few tangible rewards, for this means that the poet who holds that title must often wait upon the future for true recognition." Hyatt H. Waggoner asserted that "the notes she made in her journey, in her poems, compose one of the really distinguished bodies of work of this century."

## Works in Critical Context

Critical assessments of Doolittle's poetry have exhibited the kind of shifts that demonstrate the relative nature of all literary criticism and epitomize the problems many women writers have faced in gaining admission to the established canons of literature. On the whole, Doolittle's work in the 1910s and 1920s was highly praised and widely anthologized. But beginning with the publication of *Red Roses for Bronze* (1931), reviews tended to be mixed. The publication of *Trilogy* during the war led to some enthusiastic reviews, some complaints about her abandonment of imagism, and some negative reviews, with Randall Jarrell's brief and disparaging review of *Tribute to the Angels* being the most damaging. Ignoring the later development of Doolittle's fellow imagists, Jarrell argued that "imagism was a *reductio ad absurdum* upon which it is hard to base a later style."

***Critical Reaction to Helen in Egypt*** When compared with her earlier work, Doolittle's final work, *Helen in Egypt* received scant critical attention. When it was first published, it received only five reviews. However, since its initial appearance, the work has been praised by scholars as a bold epic, told from a distinctly feminine perspective. Kathryn Gibbs Gibbons writes, "H. D.'s last book, *Helen in Egypt*, is a long psychological meditative lyric which represents the height of her art. ... It is the culmination of long years of poetic experimentation and refinement. As we would have expected, the writing does not lack depth or intricacy in its examination of the relation of the personal problem of guilt to the social problem of war." Likewise, Albert Gelpi considered it "the most ambitious and successful long poem ever written by a woman poet, certainly in English."

***Revival of Critical Attention*** Critical attention to Doolittle dwindled in the decade following her death, until 1969, when a special issue of *Contemporary Literature* devoted to her work appeared. The volume includes some two hundred pages of previously unpublished poetry. Stimulated by this publication of Doolittle's unavailable work, scholars covering the spectrum of critical perspectives and methodologies began writing about Doolittle. While the Doolittle revival has gathered great momentum, the reassessment of her work is still in the process of change. Some critics, such as Hugh Kenner and Alfred Kazin, still consider Doolittle a minor chapter in literary history, notable largely for her contributions to imagism. But a growing chorus of critics—including, for example, Louis Martz, Sandra Gilbert, Albert Gelpi, Susan Gubar, Denis Donoghue, Susan Stanford Friedman, Rachel Blau DuPlessis, Alicia Ostriker, Adalaide Morris, Sherman Paul, Carroll Terrell, Cyrena Pondrom, Diana Collecut, and Paul Smith—consider Doolittle a major poet belonging both to the modernist mainstream and the tradition of women's writing.

## Responses to Literature

1. Choose one of Doolittle's early imagist poems and explain its meaning. What literary devices does she use, and why?

2. How does Doolittle regard the natural world? Is her approach similar to other poets you have read?

3. Compare Doolittle's early poetry with that of Ezra Pound. Explain any differences you notice.

4. How do being a woman and being a poet influence Doolittle's experience as a patient of Sigmund Freud, as expressed in her *Tribute to Freud*?

5. Doolittle has drawn recent attention from feminist scholars. Explain the difficulties Doolittle would have had to overcome as a female poet writing in the early twentieth century. Do any of her texts strike you as "feminist?"

BIBLIOGRAPHY

**Books**

Chisholm, Dianne. *H. D.'s Freudian Poetics: Psychoanalysis in Translation*. Ithaca, N.Y.: Cornell University Press, 1992.

DuPlessis, Rachel Blau. *H. D.: The Career of That Struggle*. Bloomington, Ind.: Indiana University Press, 1986.

Friedman, Susan Stanford. *Psyche Reborn: The Emergence of H. D.* Bloomington, Ind.: Indiana University Press, 1981.

Gregory, Eileen. *H. D. and Hellenism: Classic Lines*. Cambridge: Cambridge University Press, 1997.

Laity, Cassandra. *H. D. and the Victorian Fin de Siècle: Gender, Modernism, Decadence*. Cambridge: Cambridge University Press, 1996.

Ostriker, Alicia Suskin. *Stealing the Language: The Emergence of Women's Poetry in America*. Boston: Beacon, 1986.

Sword, Helen. *Engendering Inspiration: Visionary Strategies in Rilke, Lawrence, and H. D.* Ann Arbor, Mich.: University of Michigan Press, 1995.

**Periodicals**

Gubar, Susan. "The Echoing Spell of H. D.'s *Trilogy*." *Contemporary Literature* 19 (Spring 1978): 196–218.

Morris, Adalaide. "Signaling: Feminism, Politics, and Mysticism in H. D.'s War Trilogy." *Sagetrieb* 9 (Winter 1990): 121–33.

**Web sites**

*The H. D. Home Page*. Retrieved September 14, 2008, from http://www.imagists.org.

# ❀ Michael Dorris

**BORN:** *1945, Louisville, Kentucky*

**DIED:** *1997, Concord, New Hampshire*

**NATIONALITY:** *American*

**GENRE:** *Fiction, poetry, nonfiction*

**MAJOR WORKS:**

*A Yellow Raft in Blue Water* (1987)

*The Broken Cord* (1989)

*The Crown of Columbus* (with Louise Erdrich) (1992)

## Overview

An author of a diverse body of work in different genres, Michael Dorris is praised for his sensitive and intelligent treatment of Native American concerns. He is best known for his novels, short stories, essays, and his collaborations with his much-acclaimed wife, the writer Louise Erdrich.

## Works in Biographical and Historical Context

*Growing Up with Strong Women* Born in Louisville, Kentucky, on January 30, 1945, Michael Anthony Dorris is of Irish and French descent on his mother's side

Michael Dorris *Dorris, Michael, 1989, photograph. AP Images.*

and reported Native American descent—Modoc—on his father's. When Dorris was two years old, his father, Jim, an army lieutenant, was killed in a vehicle accident near Passau, Germany. Shortly thereafter, Mary Besy Burkhardt Dorris and her son returned from Germany to Louisville. She never remarried, and Dorris was raised as an only child in a house full of strong and loving women. "My role models," he says in *The Broken Cord* (1989), "were strong, capable mothers, aunts, and grandmothers."

### Building a Family and a Career

In 1967, Dorris graduated cum laude and Phi Beta Kappa with a B.A. in English and the classics from Georgetown University. After a year in the graduate program of the department of history of the theater at Yale University, he switched to anthropology, receiving an M.Phil. from Yale in 1970. He was an assistant professor at the University of Redlands in California in 1970 and at Franconia College in New Hampshire in 1971–1972. In 1971, the unmarried Dorris adopted a three-year-old Sioux boy whom he named Reynold Abel. The next year, he accepted a position at Dartmouth College in Hanover, New Hampshire. In 1974, he adopted another son, also a Sioux, whom he named Jeffrey Sava after a deceased Native Alaskan friend; in 1976 he adopted a Sioux daughter, Madeline Hannah. Later, in 1979, he became a full professor and chair of the Native American studies department. Dartmouth graduate Erdrich returned to the campus as a writer in residence in 1981, and on October 10 of that year she and Dorris were married. Together they have three daughters: Persia Andromeda, Pallas Antigone, and Aza Marion.

### A Call to Consider Historical Context of Native Literatures

As an anthropologist, Dorris conducted field-work in Alaska, New Zealand, Montana, New Hampshire, and South Dakota. He published the nonfiction works *Native Americans: Five Hundred Years After* (1975) and, with Arlene B. Hirschfelder and Mary Gloyne Byler, *A Guide to Research on North American Indians* (1983). Among his academic articles, "Native American Literature in an Ethnohistorical Context" (1979) is notable for its call for Native literatures to be considered in their cultural and historical contexts rather than interpreted from a supposedly "objective" New Critical—that is, European American—perspective that conflates hundreds of tribal literatures into the monolithic category of American Indian literature. Notable also are his many essays and interviews, often addressed to educators, which challenge stereotypical representations of Native Americans.

### Work Brings Respect and Accolades

From 1977 to 1979 Dorris served on the editorial board of *MELUS: The Journal of the Society of Multiethnic Literatures in the United States*; he also served in the same capacity for the *American Indian Culture and Research Journal* starting in 1974. During his career as an academic and writer, Dorris was the recipient of numerous financial awards and literary honors. In 1989, Dorris stepped down from his academic position to devote more time to his writing.

### Collaborative Partnership with Louise Erdrich

Dorris's writing career began in earnest after his marriage to Erdrich. They published several short stories jointly under the pseudonym Milou North—the first name combines parts of their first names; the last refers to the part of the country in which they were living. The Dorris-Erdrich collaboration has been the topic of considerable curiosity; although they generally published a book under the name of whichever of them was the primary author, they collaborated on every piece. They insisted that their collaboration enhanced, rather than limited, their individual creativity, and that it kept them from suffering from writer's block.

### Invoking Modernist Techniques

Although his poetry has been published in such journals as *Sun Tracks*, *Akwesasne Notes*, *Wassaja*, and *Ploughshares*, Dorris is best known for his prose. His first novel, *A Yellow Raft in Blue Water* (1987), has received critical praise and is examined in literature courses at colleges and universities throughout the United States. In this novel, Dorris presents the interrelated but distinct narratives of three generations of women. In a typical modernist technique, each of the novel's three sections is narrated by a different character: the story begins with the fifteen-year-old, part-Indian Rayona; continues with her mother, Christine; and concludes with Rayona's "grandmother," Ida, who prefers, for reasons that are surprising and dramatic when they are finally revealed, to be called "Aunt Ida." Each of the narrators is convincing, even when she contradicts or quibbles with what the others have said.

### Disappointment with The Crown of Columbus

His second novel, *The Crown of Columbus* (1991), carries both Dorris and Erdrich's names on the title page. They planned the novel during a 1988 automobile trip across Saskatchewan; the publisher, HarperCollins, gave them a $1.5 million advance for the book on the basis of a brief outline. Inspired, they told Moyers, by a "translation of Bartolomé de Las Casas's sixteenth-century edition of Columbus's diary" and by the quincentennial of Christopher Columbus's arrival in America, they planned to take the almost unimaginable leap—for Native American authors—of writing the novel from Columbus's point of view. Instead, some critics argue that the book turned out to be an Indian version of American history, an ironic counterpoint to Columbus's "discovery" of the so-called New World, and a satire of academia. As a result, it drew mixed reviews.

*Working Men* (1993) is a collection of fourteen short stories, ten of which were published previously. The stories are narrated by diverse voices—American Indian and non-Indian, young and old, gay and straight, male and female—and are set in locales as various as Washington, Montana, New Jersey, New Hampshire, Kentucky, and Alaska. Most of the characters are going about their jobs as flight attendants, pharmaceutical salesmen, disc jockeys, pond designers, or snowplow drivers when something happens to trigger a self-revelatory moment.

In his award-winning novel *Morning Girl* (1992), aimed at young adult readers, Dorris imagines life among the pre-Columbian Taino Indians. Chapters are narrated alternately by twelve-year-old Morning Girl and her ten-year-old brother, Star Boy. Opposites in every way, Morning Girl and Star Boy at first antagonize each other as only siblings can. But their relationship grows into friendship, and Star Boy gives his sister a new name: The One Who Stands Beside.

As in *Morning Girl*, in *Guests* (1994), another novel for young adults, Dorris offers a new perspective on a familiar American theme—in this case a Native American boy's view of Thanksgiving. Also like *Morning Girl*, *Guests* is both a children's coming-of-age story and a contact narrative, or the story of the meeting between two cultures.

### Dealing with Personal Strife through Writing

Dorris's *The Broken Cord* is the story of Abel, Dorris's adopted son—called Adam in the book—who was diagnosed as suffering from fetal alcohol syndrome. In his essay collection *Paper Trail* (1994) Dorris writes that after twenty years of wavering between hope and despair, denial and acceptance, anger and understanding, he came to the conclusion that he "could not affect Abel's life, but [he could] document it"; so he wrote *The Broken Cord*. Reynold Abel Dorris was hit by a car—a direct consequence of the diminished capacities produced by fetal alcohol syndrome—and died two years after *The Broken Cord* was published.

Because of *The Broken Cord*, Dorris was often invited to serve on national and international committees and boards devoted to children's health and welfare. He was a member of the board of directors of the Save the Children Foundation in 1991–1992 and served as an advisory board member; he became a member of the U.S. Advisory Committee on Infant Mortality in 1992. As a part of his work for the Save the Children Foundation, Dorris visited drought-ridden Zimbabwe, where thousands of men, women, and children die from lack of water, food, and medicine. To publicize the situation in Zimbabwe, Dorris wrote *Rooms in the House of Stone* (1993). The essays in the book address the burnout of donors, the alternation of the press from sensationalism to silence, and the needs of those who are still alive in Zimbabwe.

### A Decade of Suffering

The 1990s proved to be rough for Dorris and his family. Jeffery, their adopted son, was institutionalized for problems connected with a milder form of Fetal Alcohol Syndrome and served time

---

## LITERARY AND HISTORICAL CONTEMPORARIES

Michael Dorris's famous contemporaries include:

**Annie Dillard** (1945–): American author best known for her Pulitzer Prize-winning book *Pilgrim at Tinker Creek* (1974), a work of narrative nonfiction.

**Alice Walker** (1944–): African-American feminist author who wrote the Pulitzer Prize winning novel, *The Color Purple* (1983).

**Louise Erdrich** (1954–): Native American author, member of the Chippewa nation, and often associated with the Native American Renaissance; she married and collaborated with Michael Dorris.

**Salman Rushdie** (1947–): Indian-British author whose novel *Midnight's Children* (1981) won the Booker Prize and, more recently, was voted the best book to have won the Booker by a public vote.

**Richard Russo** (1949–): American author whose novel *Empire Falls* (2001) was awarded the Pulitzer Prize in 2002; in addition to novels, Russo writes screenplays and short stories.

---

in jail. In addition, he demanded that his parents pay him $15,000 in addition to publishing a manuscript he had written and, when they refused, he threatened physical violence. Later, Erdrich and Dorris separated—an event that exacerbated a bout of depression that Dorris reported began during their marriage. In 1997, reports surfaced alleging that Dorris was under investigation for sexually abusing his daughters. After one unsuccessful suicide attempt, he was hospitalized and sent to a rehabilitation center. Not long after his release, on April 10, 1997, Dorris killed himself at a motor inn in New Hampshire.

## Works in Literary Context

In his fiction, scholarly and popular nonfiction, and poetry, Michael Dorris repeatedly returns to a few major themes: the centrality of family relationships, the reconstruction of American history from Native American perspectives, and the necessity for mixed-blood individuals to search for their identities, and to situate themselves in relation to Indian and non-Indian communities. He acknowledged diverse influences on his writing, from family storytelling and Native American oral traditions to the highly literary work of Albert Camus, Sinclair Lewis, Toni Morrison, Gloria Naylor, Barbara Pym, Paul Theroux, John Updike, Laura Ingalls Wilder, and Tennessee Williams; but he insisted that the single most important influence on his writing was his wife. In intimate collaboration with Erdrich, Dorris combined

## COMMON HUMAN EXPERIENCE

Mixed-blood identity is a prominent theme in Dorris's writing. Other works that explore this theme include the following:

*Cogewea, the Half Blood: A Depiction of the Great Montana Cattle Range* (1927), a novel by Mourning Dove. This work tells the story of a woman, Cogewea, who lives on the Flathead Indian Reservation.

*Mixed Blood: Intermarriage and Ethnic Identity in Twentieth-Century America*, (1989), a nonfiction book by Paul Spikard. This book focuses on patterns of intermarriage between African Americans, Japanese Americans, white Christian Americans, and American Jews.

*The Magazine Novels* (1901–1903), three serially published novels by Pauline Hopkins. Through the lens of a mystery, these works—particularly *Of One Blood; Or, the Hidden Self*—examine the social treatment and self-perceptions of Americans of African descent, especially those of mixed blood.

everyday words into simple sentences that evoke a sense of the extraordinary, juxtapose simplicity and surprise with a sense of the mysterious, and seduce readers into fresh ways of perceiving the world.

*Mixed-Blood Identity*  Although mixed-blood identity is a common theme in twentieth-century Native American literature, Dorris was the first writer to present a mixed-blood character who is part Native American and part African American, as he does in *A Yellow Raft in Blue Water*. In this work, the protagonist, Rayona, describes herself as "too big, too smart, not Black, not Indian, not friendly." With Rayona, Dorris complicates the generic plot of a mixed-blood protagonist torn between two worlds. In an interview, Dorris explains that "Rayona grows up very much an urban, black, Indian kid in a northwest city." When she ends up on the reservation, she is "inappropriate in every respect": wrong color, wrong background, wrong language. Nonetheless, Rayona's search, like the quests of so many other characters in Native American novels, is, as William Bevis has noted, a search for a home. Although the plot sounds like a romantic search for a lost past, Dorris resists easy answers: going home does not guarantee a warm welcome or a gift-wrapped Indian identity.

The influence of Dorris's work extends beyond the realm of Native American literature. Despite mixed critical reaction to *The Broken Cord*, Dorris's nonfiction work about Fetal Alcohol Syndrome, it is credited with persuading Congress to vote for legislation requiring alcoholic beverages to display warning labels about the dangers of drinking alcohol while pregnant.

## Works in Critical Context

Dorris received sparse critical attention for his early academic work. After he began collaborating with Louise Erdrich, his work began to attract critical acclaim. Scholars and academics praised his modernist poetry and commented frequently on his sensitive portrayal of women, particularly in his novel *A Yellow Raft in Blue Water*. Beginning with *The Crown of Columbus*, reviews were increasingly mixed. Dorris and Erdrich were harshly criticized for what many perceived to be catering to a white perspective. Dorris recovered his critical reputation somewhat with *Working Men, Morning Girl*, and *Guests*, only to be once again attacked for *The Broken Cord*.

*The Broken Cord*  As would be expected with such a painful and controversial topic, not all reviewers agreed with Dorris's condemnation of pregnant women who drink in *The Broken Cord*. Katha Pollitt, for example, accuses him of blaming women—especially single mothers—who were themselves victims of oppressive social and economic conditions and the consequent lack of medical care. In a similar vein, Margit Stange claims that "the strain of antidisease logic" displayed in writing about fetal alcohol syndrome and alcoholism generally "enables a healing discourse to become an antiwoman discourse." In his book *Manifest Manners*, academic scholar Gerald Vizenor criticized Dorris and his recommendation that alcoholic Native American mothers be incarcerated. Vizenor categorized the views espoused by Dorris as catering to a white stereotype of Native American alcoholism. Despite the criticisms, his work continues to be praised for raising concern about Native American issues.

## Responses to Literature

1. Analyze the narrative style of the three women in *A Yellow Raft in Blue Water*. Are they each unique and believable, as Native Americans and as women? Why or why not?

2. Discuss the claim made by some scholars that Dorris caters to a white perspective. To what extent to you agree or disagree? In your opinion, who is the intended audience for Dorris's fiction?

3. Analyze the critical reaction to *The Broken Cord*. Is there anything about his writing that makes him more vulnerable to the attacks he received from critics?

4. Dorris's final years were clouded with controversy, culminating in his suicide. Do you think the events of a writer's personal life should affect how they are viewed by critics, readers, and literary scholars? Why or why not?

BIBLIOGRAPHY

**Books**

Buelens, Gert and Ernst Rudin, eds. *Deferring a Dream: Literary Sub-versions of American Columbiad.* Boston: Birkhauser Verlag, 1994: 99–119.

Erdrich, Louise. *Conversations with Louise Erdrich and Michael Dorris.* Jackson, Miss.: University of Mississippi, 1994.

Owens, Louis. *Other Destinies: Understanding the American Indian Novel.* Norman, Okla.: University of Oklahoma Press, 1992.

Weil, Ann. *Michael Dorris.* Austin, Tex.: Raintree Steck-Vaughn, 1997.

**Periodicals**

Matchie, Thomas. "Exploring the Meaning of Discovery in The Crown of Columbus." *North Dakota Quarterly* 69 (Fall 1991): 243–250.

Pollitt, Katha. "'Fetal Rights': A New Assault on Feminism." *Nation* 250 (26 March 1990): 409–418.

# ✿ John Dos Passos

BORN: *1896, Chicago, Illinois*

DIED: *1970, Baltimore, Maryland*

NATIONALITY: *American*

GENRE: *Fiction*

MAJOR WORKS:
*Manhattan Transfer* (1925)
*The 42nd Parallel* (1930)
*1919* (1932)
*The Big Money* (1936)

John Dos Passos    *Dos Passos, John, photograph. The Library of Congress.*

## Overview

Best known for his sociopolitical novels of pre–World War II America, Dos Passos was a master novelist and chronicler of twentieth-century American life. He is considered a writer of the Lost Generation, a loose grouping of creative Americans who lived abroad following World War I and wrote largely about the disillusionment with modern life brought on by the experiences of war.

## Works in Biographical and Historical Context

***Eager Entry into World War I***   Dos Passos was born in Chicago to John Roderigo Dos Passos, a wealthy Portuguese immigrant, and Lucy Addison Sprigg Madison; the two did not wed until their son was fourteen. Dos Passos spent most of his youth traveling in Europe and the United States with his mother. At the age of fifteen, Dos Passos was accepted at Harvard and began classes the following year. As an undergraduate he edited

the *Harvard Monthly* and wrote poetry that was later published in *Eight Harvard Poets* (1917) along with poems by E. E. Cummings and Robert Hillyer. He traveled to Spain upon graduating in 1916 and, eager to participate in World War I, he volunteered for service the following year as an ambulance driver in France. In doing so he joined a host of other volunteers—including Cummings, Hillyer, and Ernest Hemingway—who would all later gain recognition as writers. Dos Passos recorded his wartime experiences in the novel *One Man's Initiation—1917* (1920), an impressionist work that had begun as a collaboration with Hillyer, though the published novel includes only the chapters written by Dos Passos.

***Antiwar Sentiments***   In late 1917, Dos Passos transferred to the American Red Cross Ambulance Corps in Italy, where he was dismissed in 1918 for his antiwar sentiments. Returning to France, he joined the U.S. Army Medical Corps, in which he served until his enlistment expired in 1919. At that time Dos Passos was already at work on his next novel, *Three Soldiers* (1921), which raised him to prominence as a writer and became the first important war novel of World War I. Clearly a condemnation of the social and political mechanisms behind the war, *Three Soldiers* quickly drew critical attention for its frank portrayal of the war's destructive influence on its three protagonists. Despite its romantic tone, the novel marks Dos Passos's departure from his early, impressionistic style and aesthete philosophy to one of anger and rebellion against what he perceived as the power of industrial capitalism to crush individual freedom.

*Leftist Political Views*   Dos Passos traveled throughout Europe and the United States during the 1920s. He also grew increasingly active in leftist political causes and explored various artistic movements. He incorporated such influences as cubism and expressionism into his own works. Dos Passos was both prolific and diverse, publishing novels, dramas, poetry, travel books, and essays. In the late 1920s he joined the New Playwrights Theatre, an experimental left-wing theater group. His dramas—*The Garbage Man* (1926), *Airways, Inc.* (1928), and *Fortune Heights* (1933)—contain strong political themes protesting against the ill effects of American capitalism and democracy. He also wrote for the *New Masses*, a radical periodical he helped found in 1926. His disillusionment over the injustices against the individual in a capitalist society culminated in 1927 when he covered the trial of Nicola Sacco and Bartolomeo Vanzetti, immigrants and anarchists who, Dos Passos firmly believed, had been wrongfully accused of murder. He was arrested and jailed after taking part in demonstrations on behalf of the accused men; in his pamphlet *Facing the Chair: Story of the Americanization of Two Foreignborn Workmen* (1927), he attempted to present evidence of the men's innocence. The eventual execution of Sacco and Vanzetti embittered Dos Passos and strengthened his distrust of the government.

*The Great Depression*   Beginning with the stock market crash of 1929, an event known as Black Tuesday, many countries around the world suffered a large economic depression. This hardship, known as The Great Depression, lasted until World War II. Families in the United States struggled to make ends meet and many people lost their jobs and homes. In response to this crisis, President Franklin D. Roosevelt initiated a series of programs known as the New Deal, which aimed to provide relief to those suffering and reform business practices. It was during this time that Dos Passos composed his most famous works.

*Disillusionment with the Left*   During the late 1920s and early 1930s, Dos Passos continued his involvement with the Left, contributing essays to the *New Masses*, the *New Republic*, and *Common Sense*. Although he never publicly claimed allegiance to the Communist party, his writings and activities, including a visit to the Soviet Union in 1928 and to the coal fields in Harlan, Kentucky in 1931 to assess miners' working conditions,

aligned him with communism. His novels during this time, including *Manhattan Transfer* (1925), *The 42nd Parallel* (1930), *1919* (1932), and *The Big Money* (1936), portray the failure of the American Dream, but, as critics note, do not overtly support any political program or party. (The American Dream is the belief that anyone in the United States who works hard enough can achieve success, often defined in material terms).

Following the completion of the *U.S.A.* trilogy (which is comprised of his novels *The 42nd Parallel*, *1919*, and *The Big Money*), Dos Passos journeyed to Spain in 1937 with Hemingway to report on events of the Spanish Civil War between Marxist-backed Republican and Fascist-backed Falangist groups. There he became disillusioned with the Left when he learned that his friend Jose Robles, a Republican supporter, had been executed by Republican forces, allegedly under Communist orders. When Hemingway refused to question the integrity of the Republican cause, Dos Passos broke off his friendship with him and severed ties with Europe. He returned to the United States with a new-found devotion to his homeland.

*Defending the Individual*   His dissatisfaction with leftist political groups is evident in his next novel, *Adventures of a Young Man* (1939), which delineates an idealistic protagonist who goes to Spain to fight for his vision of individual freedom only to be killed under the order of the political group he had supported. The other two novels, which with *Adventures of a Young Man* form the *District of Columbia* trilogy, are *Number One* (1943) and *The Grand Design* (1949). In these, Dos Passos continues to depict corruption that results from power and the devastating effects exercised by institutions and governments over the individual. *The Grand Design*, generally considered the best work of the trilogy, satirizes Franklin Roosevelt's New Deal policies as an impractical failure of centralized government. However, *District of Columbia* was poorly received, partly because the novels no longer evinced support for leftist causes and also because the narratives were regarded as straightforward and one-dimensional, unlike Dos Passos's accomplishment in *U.S.A.* His nonfiction also markedly shifted from radical-Left beliefs toward those of the conservative Right, generating consternation among many of his former supporters. Nevertheless, Dos Passos maintained that he had not betrayed his former beliefs.

*Devotion to Jeffersonian Democracy*   From the 1940s through the rest of his life, Dos Passos lived mainly at Spence's Point, Virginia, on a farm he had inherited from his father, and in Provincetown, Massachusetts. He developed the reputation of a country squire who was now devoted to the ideals of Jeffersonian democracy and the study of American history and order. In his well-received historical works—which include *The Ground We Stand On* (1941), *The Head and Heart of Thomas Jefferson*

(1954), and *Mr. Wilson's War* (1962)—Dos Passos examines United States history from the roots of American government, with its traditions of self-government and individual freedom, to the era of World War I, when industrial capitalism strongly influenced the government.

***Changing Attitudes Shape Later Fiction*** Dos Passos's later fiction also reveals his changing attitudes. His earlier fiction, noted for its highly objective viewpoint, was replaced by novels evincing personal narratives closely linked to Dos Passos's own life. Several critics maintain that this shift resulted after Dos Passos lost his wife, Katy, in an automobile accident in 1947. *Chosen Country* (1951), a nostalgic novel—or "chronicle" as Dos Passos had begun calling his fictions—offers a sentimental portrait of Lulie, a character based on Katy, and Jay Pignatelli, Dos Passos's own double. His most significant late novel, however, was *Midcentury* (1961), a despairing account of the corruptions of labor unions. In this novel Dos Passos returned to a cross-section narrative reminiscent of *U.S.A.*, and he used the juxtapositions of fiction, biography, news stories, and authorial reflections, to broadly delineate American society. The work was praised for displaying artistic sophistication that many critics had found lacking in Dos Passos's fiction since *U.S.A.*

***A Last Forlorn Chronicle of Despair*** Dos Passos continued to write histories, memoirs, travel essays, and journalistic works through his later years. At the time of his death at age seventy-four, he was at work on the novel *Century's Ebb: The Thirteenth Chronicle* that was published posthumously in 1975. Intended as a record of American lives from the time of the Spanish Civil War to the lunar landing, and described by Dos Passos as his "last forlorn Chronicle of Despair," the work offers both negative views of American society and an underlying sense of hope in the nation's potential for good.

## Works in Literary Context

Dos Passos's reputation rests primarily on his Depression-era works with sociological and political themes. He was influenced by James Joyce, Walt Whitman, Theodore Dreiser, T. S. Eliot, Pío Baroja, Gustave Flaubert, Sergei Eisenstein, Thorstein Veblen, and Randolph Bourne.

***Failure of the American Dream*** Dos Passos's central concerns, which included such social injustices as the exploitation of the working class, the loss of individual freedom, and the harmful emphasis upon materialism in American society, were delineated in *Manhattan Transfer* and the novels of the *U.S.A.* trilogy. In these and other works, Dos Passos presents characters pursuing the American Dream. Because most of these characters are corrupted by their pursuit of material success, the author's moral implications are evident.

***Collage*** In his novels, Dos Passos often presents multiple types of writing juxtaposed with each other so that the difference and similarities between them produced new layers of meaning in his work. This technique is similar to the collage form used by many modernist painters, including Pablo Picasso and Juan Gris. It is also similar to the technique of intercutting in film in which the director cuts between several scenes in order enhance the excitement of the action or to underscores parallels between different plot lines. Dos Passos's writing was influenced both by modern art and film. For example, in *Manhattan Transfer* Dos Passos juxtaposes prose poems with popular songs and various images. This creates a literary collage that presents a unique, modern cross section of New York City.

Dos Passos's writing influenced numerous authors, including Jean-Paul Sartre, Simone de Beauvoir, Alfred Döblin, Camilo José Cela, Norman Mailer, Don DeLillo, and E. L. Doctorow.

## Works in Critical Context

While Dos Passos produced an extensive body of work, critical attention has focused predominantly upon *Manhattan Transfer* and the *U.S.A.* trilogy. These strongly political works, rooted in the left-wing revolutionary philosophy Dos Passos held during the 1920s and 1930s, were widely praised. In 1938, Jean-Paul Sartre lauded Dos Passos as "the greatest writer of our time"; however,

## COMMON HUMAN EXPERIENCE

Much of Dos Passos's work concerns the Great Depression. Other works that explore this period include:

*Migrant Mother* (1936), a photograph by Dorothea Lange. This depiction of a migrant worker and her children became a symbol of the Great Depression. It is now housed at the Library of Congress under the title *Destitute Pea Pickers in California*.

*The Grapes of Wrath* (1939), a novel by John Steinbeck. Awarded both the Pulitzer Prize and the Nobel Prize, this story concerns changes that occurred in the agricultural industry during the Great Depression.

*Let Us Now Praise Famous Men* (1941), a nonfiction work by James Agee with photographs by Walker Evans. Agee and Evans spent eight weeks in 1936 producing a startling record of the lives of sharecroppers in the poorest parts of the American South.

*The Blind Assassin* (2000), a novel by Margaret Atwood. In this work the protagonist, Iris Chase, reflects on her youth in Canada during the Great Depression.

Dos Passos did not achieve such recognition for his later writings.

Much of the critical condemnation of Dos Passos's later works was based upon the perception that he had abandoned his political and social beliefs and had failed to maintain the artistic and innovative standards that *Manhattan Transfer* and *U.S.A.* had established. Critics also fault much of Dos Passos's later fiction for his characters' lack of psychological depth, though others maintain that Dos Passos's strength was in writing collective novels in which he delineated a wide range of character types, and that he deliberately did not explore the inner lives of his characters. While several commentators have admonished Dos Passos for portraying an overly grim and pessimistic vision of American society, many assert that he still held an intrinsic belief in the good of the individual.

Although Dos Passos' reputation declined in the 1940s and 1950s, scholars in more recent years have reaffirmed the artistic merit of his innovative methods and consider him a significant voice in twentieth-century literature. Dos Passos is now recognized as a major chronicler of American life and as an important literary innovator for his imaginative experiments in narrative.

***The U.S.A. Trilogy*** Reviews of his earlier works reflect the expectations that Dos Passos raised in the literary world. Sinclair Lewis heralded *Manhattan Transfer* a work that anticipates the *U.S.A.* trilogy, as "a novel of the very first importance; a book which the idle reader can devour yet which the literary analyst must take as possibly inaugurating, at long last, the vast and blazing dawn we have awaited." Mary Ross wrote of *1919*: "Mr. Dos Passos's writing ... has a directness, independence and poignancy of thought and emotion that seems to me unexcelled in current fiction ... *1919* will disturb or offend some of its readers." After the completion of the *U.S.A.* trilogy, Theodore Spencer declared: "He writes from a wise and comprehending point of view; his construction is firm; his narrative is swift, realistic, and interesting." However, Alfred Kazin noted that while *U.S.A.* became an epic, "it is a history of defeat. ... It is one of the saddest books ever written by an American." Even so, Kazin added, "what Waldo Frank said of Mencken is particularly relevant to Dos Passos: he brings energy to despair."

## Responses to Literature

1. Some of the literary techniques employed by Dos Passos (inserting news items into his fiction, etc.) were considered experimental and innovative in his day. Discuss your opinion of these techniques and their ability to engage modern readers.

2. How is Dos Passos's perspective on the American Dream expressed in his works? How does this view compare to your own view on this subject?

3. Some critics fault Dos Passos for portraying a grim vision of American society, while others insist that such simplistic descriptions of his work miss his belief in the good of the individual. To what extent do you agree with these views? Provide examples from his work to support your view.

4. To what extent do you think Jimmy Herf in *Manhattan Transfer* is an alter ego for John Dos Passos? What parallels do you see between them?

BIBLIOGRAPHY

**Books**

Carr, Virginia Spencer. *Dos Passos: A Life*. Garden City, N.Y.: Doubleday, 1984.

Belkind, Allen, ed. *Dos Passos, the Critics, and the Writer's Intention*. Carbondale, Ill.: Southern Illinois University Press, 1971.

Brantley, John D. *The Fiction of John Dos Passos*. The Hague: Mouton, 1968.

Clark, Michael. *Dos Passos's Early Fiction, 1912–1938*. Selinsgrove, Penn.: Susquehanna University Press, 1987.

Colley, Iain. *Dos Passos and the Fiction of Despair*. London: Macmillan, 1978.

Cowley, Malcolm. *Exile's Return*. New York: Viking, 1951.

Freudenberg, Anne and Elizabeth Fake. *John Dos Passos: Writer and Artist 1896–1970 A Guide to the Exhibition at the University of Virginia Library*. Charlottesville, Va.: University of Virginia Library, 1975.

Landsberg, Melvin. *Dos Passos' Path to U.S.A.: A Political Biography 1912–1936.* Boulder, Colo.: Colorado Associated University Press, 1972.

Ludington, Townsend. *John Dos Passos: A Twentieth Century Odyssey.* New York: Dutton, 1980.

Maine, Barry. *Dos Passos, the Critical Heritage.* London: Routledge, 1988.

Pizer, Donald. *Dos Passos's U.S.A: A Critical Study.* Charlottesville, Va.: University Press of Virginia, 1988.

Rohrkemper, John. *John Dos Passos, A Reference Guide.* Boston: G. K. Hall, 1980.

Rosen, Robert C. *John Dos Passos, Politics and the Writer.* Lincoln, Nebr.: University of Nebraska Press, 1981.

Wrenn, John H. *John Dos Passos.* New York: Twayne, 1961.

# ✺ Frederick Douglass

BORN: *c. 1817, Tuckahoe, Maryland*

DIED: *1895, Washington, D.C.*

NATIONALITY: *American*

GENRE: *Nonfiction*

MAJOR WORKS:

*Narrative of the Life of Frederick Douglass, An American Slave, Written by Himself* (1845)

*My Bondage and My Freedom* (1855)

*Life and Times of Frederick Douglass, Written by Himself* (1881)

Frederick Douglass   *Douglass, Frederick, photograph. The Library of Congress.*

## Overview

Promoting the theme of racial equality in stirring orations and newspaper editorials in the mid-1800s, Frederick Douglass was recognized by his contemporaries as a foremost abolitionist of his era. Douglass's status as a powerful and effective prose writer is based primarily on his 1845 autobiography, *Narrative of the Life of Frederick Douglass, an American Slave, Written by Himself*, a work that remains a premier example of the slave narrative, a significant genre in American literature, and places Douglass among other authors who stress the importance of individual experience and moral conviction. Regarded as one of the most compelling documents produced by a fugitive slave, the *Narrative* has transcended its immediate historical significance and is now regarded as a landmark American autobiography.

## Works in Biographical and Historical Context

***An Avenue to Freedom*** Frederick Douglass, born a slave in Tuckahoe, Maryland, around 1817, often lamented the fact that he did not know the exact date of his birth. Although the common assumption was that he was the son of his master, Captain Aaron Anthony, Douglass never knew for certain the identity of his father. Separated from his mother as an infant, he was raised by his maternal grandmother on Anthony's estate and enjoyed a relatively happy childhood until he was transferred to the plantation of Anthony's employer. At the age of eight, he was again transferred, this time to the Baltimore household of Hugh Auld, where he served as a houseboy. His time with the Aulds proved to be invaluable, as his mistress began teaching him to read until her husband insisted that she stop. Overhearing Auld rebuke his wife for educating a slave, Douglass realized that literacy could be an avenue to freedom, and he secretly continued learning to read on his own.

At the age of thirteen, Douglass obtained a copy of *The Columbian Orator*, a collection of essays and speeches about human freedom. While the book would prove to have a lasting impact on the young man, its immediate effect was to increase Douglass's desire to experience the freedom he could only read about. In 1835, while rented out to a farmer, Douglass began clandestinely teaching other slaves, as well as free African Americans, to read. He also planned to escape with five other slaves by stealing a boat and sailing up the Chesapeake Bay before heading on foot to Philadelphia. Before they could act, however, their plan was discovered, and they were all jailed. Douglass was returned to Auld and then sent to work in the Baltimore shipyards. In 1838, Douglass disguised himself in sailor's clothing and escaped to New York.

# LITERARY AND HISTORICAL CONTEMPORARIES

Douglass's famous contemporaries include:

**Harriet Beecher Stowe** (1811–1896): Stowe wrote *Uncle Tom's Cabin* (1852), which contributed to the abolitionist movement with its depiction of a slave's suffering and lack of human dignity.

**Stephen A. Douglas** (1813–1861): This politician, famous for being a participant in the Lincoln-Douglas Debates, lost the support of Southern Democrats when he opposed a proslavery constitution for Kansas.

**Susan B. Anthony** (1820–1906): A pioneer of the women's movement in America, Anthony was an active abolitionist who supported suffrage for African Americans as well as women.

**Harriet Tubman** (1826–1913): An escaped slave, Tubman was an important leader in the underground railroad, a secret system for transporting slaves to freedom.

**Clara Barton** (1821–1912): In addition to founding the American Red Cross in 1881, Barton became an activist for African American rights.

***Narrative Gifts*** Once free, Douglass became a prominent figure in the abolitionist movement. After speaking about his life as a slave at a meeting in 1841, Douglass embarked on a career as a lecturer for the Massachusetts Antislavery Society, becoming the most prominent African American figure in America. Ironically, his exceptional public speaking abilities led many of his white audiences to question his slave upbringing and the truth of his stories. In response, Douglass published *Narrative of the Life of Frederick Douglass, An American Slave, Written by Himself* (1845), one of the few slave narratives that was not produced by a ghostwriter. At the same time the book explained his early life and how he gained his knowledge and oratory skills, it also revealed his whereabouts to his master.

***The Costs of Slavery*** Concerned that he could be returned to captivity under the fugitive slave laws, Douglass traveled to England and Ireland, where he was well received by social reformers. With funds he received from sympathetic abolitionists, Douglass returned to the United Sates in 1847 and bought his permanent freedom from his last owner. With his remaining money, he established *The North Star*, a weekly abolitionist paper. Although devoted mainly to antislavery, the paper also supported the causes of African American education and women's suffrage. While many members of the American Anti-Slavery Society believed that moral arguments were the best way to end slavery, Douglass championed direct political action and even encouraged violence by slaves.

***Revision and Rebellion*** During the 1850s and 1860s, Douglass continued his activities as a journalist and abolitionist speaker. In 1855, he published *My Bondage and My Freedom*, a revision of his autobiography. The following year, he began meeting with the fiery abolitionist John Brown. Though Douglass agreed with Brown's idea of a slave rebellion, he did not support Brown's plan to seize the federal arsenal at Harpers Ferry, Virginia, in October 1859. Nevertheless, after Brown's raid failed, Douglass feared he might be arrested as an accomplice, so he fled to Canada before traveling back to England, where he lectured for six months.

***Civil War and Reconstruction*** After the American Civil War began in 1861, Douglass openly criticized President Abraham Lincoln when he did not immediately name ending slavery as the main goal of the war. Lincoln, however, recognized the importance of Douglass's input and twice summoned him to the White House for conferences. Throughout the war, Douglass supported the use of African American troops to help the Union cause. When two African American Massachusetts regiments were finally created in 1863, two of Douglass's sons were among the first recruits.

During the years of Reconstruction that followed the end of the Civil War, Douglass pushed for civil and voting rights for African Americans. In 1868, he saw Congress pass the Fourteenth Amendment, recognizing the citizenship of all people born in America. Two years later, Congress ratified the Fifteenth Amendment, which extended voting rights to all black males. Many women criticized Douglass for supporting this amendment, as it did not give women the right to vote as well.

***Always an Activist*** Douglass spent his last years in civil service positions. In addition to serving as the U.S. Marshal for the District of Columbia, he was assigned consul-general to the Republic of Haiti. In 1881, he published the final version of his autobiography, *The Life and Times of Frederick Douglass*. For the rest of his life, he continued speaking out on black civil rights and other issues of inequality. In 1884, two years after his first wife's death, he married Helen Pitts, his white secretary who was twenty years his junior, a move that drew severe criticism from people of both races. Douglass died in Washington, D.C., of a heart attack on February 25, 1895, having just returned from a women's suffrage convention.

## Works in Literary Context

Of the approximately six thousand documented slave narratives, Douglass's *Narrative of the Life of Frederick Douglass, An American Slave, Written by Himself* is the most remarkable. Regarded as a classic in African American autobiography, it was one of the most influential works of the nineteenth century. Five thousand copies were sold in four months, and more than thirty thousand copies were sold domestically and internationally during the first five years the book was in print.

*Slave Narratives* One of the most influential genres in African American literature, the slave narrative generally refers to a first-person account by a slave or former slave describing how slavery shaped his or her life. The earliest form of African American prose, as well as the earliest form of African American autobiography, the most famous slave narratives were published between 1830 and 1860 when the abolitionist movement in the United States increased demand for eyewitness accounts of slavery. Because they circulated information not only about slavery, but also about Southern life, slave narratives were a vital part of the abolitionist movement.

Slave narratives are also important in African American history because they are a declaration of African American humanity and a testament to the relationship between literacy and freedom. Specifically in the case of Douglass's narrative, abolitionists pointed to the quality of its writing to demonstrate the intellect of an author who, once considered property, was to be recognized as a rational human. Nonetheless, Douglass's skillful writing led some to doubt the authenticity of the *Narrative of the Life of Frederick Douglass, An American Slave, Written by Himself*, arguing that a former slave lacked the literacy to produce such a work. Some Southerners were eager to prove that Douglass's accounts of brutality were lies, even though the *Narrative of the Life of Frederick Douglass, An American Slave, Written by Himself* is filled with specific names and places, a daring level of realism in writing for one who was legally still a runaway slave. Valued by historians as a detailed, credible account of slave life, the *Narrative of the Life of Frederick Douglass, An American Slave, Written by Himself* is also widely acclaimed as an extraordinarily expressive story of self-discovery and self-liberation.

## Works in Critical Context

Some of Douglass's contemporaries questioned the veracity of his works. Other critics viewed his works as simply antislavery propaganda. This view persisted until the 1930s, when scholars called attention to the intrinsic merit of Douglass's writing, acknowledging him as the most important figure in nineteenth-century African American literature. Appealing to the various political, sociological, and aesthetic interests of generations of critics, Douglass has maintained an enviable reputation as a speaker and writer. In the 1940s and 1950s, academics, such as Alain Locke, deemed Douglass's autobiographies to be classic works symbolizing the African American role of protest, struggle, and aspiration in American life. In recent years, Douglass's critics have become far more exacting, analyzing, for example, the specific narrative strategies that Douglass employs to establish a distinctly individual black identity.

### *Narrative of the Life of Frederick Douglass* Of the many slave narratives produced in the nineteenth century, the *Narrative of the Life of Frederick Douglass, An*

---

# COMMON HUMAN EXPERIENCE

Once he escaped slavery, Douglass did not limit his fight to the inequalities of African Americans; rather, he objected to all forms of discrimination—social, racial, and sexual. Listed below are other works by authors who stress the importance of civil rights and moral convictions:

"Civil Disobedience" (1849), an essay by Henry David Thoreau. A classic work of social and political activism, this influential essay presents Thoreau's argument for not paying a poll tax to a government that tolerates slavery.

*Native Son* (1940), a novel by Richard Wright. This novel challenges both whites and African Americans to face the reality of racial issues in the United States.

"I Have a Dream" (1963), a speech by Martin Luther King, Jr. In this speech, the great civil rights leader shares his vision for an America that lives up to the ideals that inspired its creation.

---

*American Slave, Written by Himself* has received the most critical attention and is widely regarded as the best. Scholar David W. Blight claims that "what sets Douglass's work apart in the genre ... is that he interrogated the moral conscience of his readers, at the same time that he transplanted them into his story, as few other fugitive slave writers did." Nevertheless, the *Narrative of the Life of Frederick Douglass, An American Slave, Written by Himself* remained out of print from the 1850s until 1960, primarily because its was recognized for its prominence in the slave narrative genre, not for its value as literature. Not until critic H. Bruce Franklin called attention to the *Narrative of the Life of Frederick Douglass, An American Slave, Written by Himself* in the 1970s was it approached as a literary work.

Since then, the text has received scrutiny from a wide variety of perspectives. Scholar Kelly Rothenberg, for instance, discusses Douglass's use of elements from African American folklore. John Carlos Rowe examines Douglass's text in economic and political terms, asserting that the author "was clearly developing his own understanding of the complicity of Northern capitalism and Southern slave-holding in the 1845 *Narrative of the Life of Frederick Douglass, An American Slave, Written by Himself*." Academic A. James Wohlpart has explored Douglass's work in the context of religion. According to Wohlpart, Douglass, attempting to reconcile the institution of slavery with the institution of the Christian Church that supported slavery, operated "within the discourse of white Christianity at the same time he challenged it." Still other critics have examined the politics of language in the *Narrative of the Life of Frederick Douglass, An American Slave, Written by Himself*, with Lisa

Yun Lee noting that in the first half of the narrative, Douglass is silent and powerless, but as he acquires the ability to speak within the "dominant discourse," he becomes increasingly powerful.

## Responses to Literature

1. How is Douglass able to maintain his religious faith when his owners use religion to justify their treatment of slaves? What other examples can you think of that involve the oppression of a group based on another group's religious or cultural beliefs? Is such suppression ever justifiable?

2. One of the most prominent themes in the *Narrative of the Life of Frederick Douglass, An American Slave, Written by Himself* involves the association of literacy with freedom. Douglass describes knowledge as "valuable bread" and literature as his "meat and drink." In what ways does literature sustain him? How was literacy a curse as well as a blessing for Douglass?

3. Douglass says that he is troubled by not knowing when he was born. Why is this fact so important to him? Why do you think slave owners purposely kept slaves ignorant about their birth and parentage? How would not knowing when you were born affect your life?

4. Compare Douglass's portrayal of the struggle of African Americans in white America with the narratives of Alex Haley, Alice Walker, and Maya Angelou. How has the *Narrative of the Life of Frederick Douglass, An American Slave, Written by Himself* influenced the works of other African Americans?

BIBLIOGRAPHY

**Books**

Baker, Houston. *The Journey Back: Issues in Black Literature and Criticism*. Chicago: University of Chicago Press, 1980.

Blight, David W. *Frederick Douglass' Civil War: Keeping Faith in Jubilee*. Baton Rouge: Louisiana State University Press, 1989.

Couser, G. Thomas. *American Autobiography: The Prophetic Mode*. Amherst: University of Massachusetts Press, 1979.

Locke, Alain. *The New Negro*. New York: Atheneum, 1977.

Rowe, John Carlos. "Between Politics and Poetics: Frederick Douglass and Postmodernity." In *Reconstructing American Literary and Historical Studies*, ed. by Günter H. Lenz, Hartmut Keil, and Sabine Bröck-Sallah. Frankfurt, Germany: Campus Verlag, 1990.

Stepto, Robert B. *From Behind the Veil: A Study of Afro-American Narrative*. Urbana: University of Illinois Press, 1979.

**Periodicals**

Franklin, H. Bruce. "Animal Farm Unbound Or, What the *Narrative of the Life of Frederick Douglass, An American Slave* Reveals about American Literature." *New Letters* 43 (Spring 1977): 25–46.

Lee, Lisa Yun. "The Politics of Language in Frederick Douglass's *Narrative of the Life of an American Slave*." *MELUS* 17 (Summer 1991–1992): 51–59.

Stone, Albert E. "Identity and Art in Frederick Douglass's *Narrative*." *College Language Association Journal* 17 (1973): 192–213.

Wohlpart, A. James. "Privatized Sentiment and the Institution of Christianity: Douglass's Ethical Stance in the *Narrative*." *American Transcendental Quarterly* 9 (September 1995): 181–194.

# ✺ Rita Dove

BORN: *1952, Akron, Ohio*

NATIONALITY: *American*

GENRE: *Fiction, poetry*

MAJOR WORKS:

*The Yellow House on the Corner* (1980)

*Thomas and Beulah* (1986)

*Grace Notes* (1989)

Rita Dove    Dove, Rita, photograph. AP Images.

## Overview

Best known for *Thomas and Beulah*, which received the 1987 Pulitzer Prize for Poetry, Dove is considered one of the leading poets of her generation. She was the second African American to win a Pulitzer Prize for Poetry, the first being Gwendolyn Brooks in 1950. In addition to her many honors, Dove served as poet laureate of the United States for two years from 1993 to 1995.

## Works in Biographical and Historical Context

### Early Recognition for Superior Academic Record

Dove was born in Akron, Ohio, into a highly educated family. An excellent student, Dove was a Presidential Scholar, ranking nationally among the best high school students of the graduating class of 1970. She traveled to Washington, DC, to receive the award during a time when many were protesting the Vietnam War at the nation's capital. After obtaining a bachelor's degree in English from Miami University of Ohio in 1973 and then studying in Germany, Dove enrolled at the Iowa Writers' Workshop. She graduated with an MFA from the University of Iowa in 1977 and published her first full-length collection of poetry and autobiographical work, *The Yellow House on the Corner*, shortly after in 1980. Dove taught creative writing at Arizona State University from 1981 to 1989. During her time teaching, Dove continued to publish her work. After releasing a chapbook (a pocket-sized booklet) for publication, she authored *Museum* (1983), and in 1986 her crowning work, *Thomas and Beulah*, appeared.

### Writing about the Nobodies of History

Similar to her previous work, *Thomas and Beulah* combines racial concerns with historical and personal elements. Loosely based on the lives of Dove's maternal grandparents, *Thomas and Beulah* is divided into two sections. "Mandolin," the opening sequence of poems, is written from the viewpoint of Thomas, a former musician haunted since his youth by the death of a friend. "Canary in Bloom," the other sequence, portrays the placid domestic existence of Thomas's wife, Beulah, from childhood to marriage and widowhood. Through allusions to events outside the lives of Thomas and Beulah—including the Great Depression, the black migration from the rural South to the industrial North, the civil rights marches of the 1960s, and the assassination of President John F. Kennedy—Dove emphasizes the couple's place in and interconnectedness with history. Dove remarked: "I was interested in the thoughts, the things which were concerning these small people, these nobodies in the course of history." For her efforts, *Thomas and Beulah* won the Pulitzer Prize for Poetry.

Dove's next work, *Grace Notes* (1989), contains autobiographical poems that delineate Dove's role as mother, wife, daughter, sister, and poet. "Pastoral," for instance,

describes Dove's observations and feelings while nursing her daughter, and "Poem in Which I Refuse Contemplation" relates a letter from her mother that Dove received while in Germany. Like her previous works, *Grace Notes* has been favorably reviewed by critics. Sidney Burris observed that *Grace Notes* "might well be [Dove's] watershed because it shows her blithely equal to the ordeal of Life-After-A-Major-Prize: she has survived her fame."

### First Novel Explores Black Identity

Dove's first novel, *Through the Ivory Gate* (1992), incorporates elements often considered typical of her poetry. The story of a young black artist named Virginia King, *Through the Ivory Gate* has been praised for its unique structure, which relies heavily on the characters' memories and storytelling abilities. Documenting the protagonist's acceptance of her black identity in a society that devalues her heritage, the novel relates Virginia's attempts to reconcile herself to events and prejudices experienced and learned in her childhood, adolescence, and early adulthood.

Upon leaving her position at the University of Arizona in 1989, Dove joined the faculty at the University of Virginia in Charlottesville; she was promoted in 1993 and currently holds the chair as Commonwealth Professor of English. Also in 1993, Dove read her poem *Lady Freedom among Us* (1994) at a ceremony celebrating the two-hundredth anniversary of the U.S. Capitol. It was later published in a limited edition.

### Service as U.S. Poet Laureate

Dove holds the distinction of being the first African American—as well as the youngest individual—to hold the post of United

States poet laureate. She served in this role for two years from 1993 until 1995 while President Bill Clinton was serving his first term in office. In awarding Dove the U.S. poet laureateship in 1993, James H. Billington praised her as "an accomplished and already widely recognized poet in mid-career whose work gives special promise to explore and enrich contemporary American poetry."

## Works in Literary Context

In her work, Dove draws on personal perception and emotion while integrating an awareness of history and social issues. These qualities are best evidenced in *Thomas and Beulah*, which commemorates the lives of her grandparents and offers a chronicle of the collective experience of African Americans during the twentieth century. Dove's poetry is akin to that of such other modern American poets as Robert Frost, Langston Hughes, and Gwendolyn Brooks, especially as to rhetorical structure. Dove's readers learn that she often melds several time-tested devices to shape an original idiom. Like Alice Walker in *Good Night, Willie Lee, I'll See You in the Morning* (1979), and like Zora Neale Hurston in virtually all of her fiction, Dove bridges the gap between oral communication and written text. Among the authors emulated by Dove are William Shakespeare, Melvin B. Tolson, Derek Walcott, Lucille Clifton, Langston Hughes, Don L. Lee, Amiri Baraka, and Anne Spencer.

*Confronting Prejudice and Oppression* Dove's poetry is characterized by a tight control of words and structure, an innovative use of color imagery, and a tone that combines objectivity and personal concern. Although many of her poems incorporate black history and directly address racial themes, they present issues, such as prejudice and oppression, that transcend racial boundaries. Dove has explained: "Obviously, as a black woman, I am concerned with race. . . . But certainly not every poem of mine mentions the fact of being black. They are poems about humanity, and sometimes humanity happens to be black." In *The Yellow House on the Corner*, for example, a section is devoted to poems about slavery and freedom. "Parsley," a poem published in *Museum*, recounts the massacre of thousands of Haitian blacks because they allegedly could not pronounce the letter "r" in *perejil*, the Spanish word for "parsley."

## Works in Critical Context

Rita Dove's body of work was a success from the beginning. Her dedication to the writing process is evidenced in the overwhelming positive reception her poetry continues to receive. Donna M. Williams writes in *Ms.* magazine, "The power of Dove's poetry lies in her ability to wrest beauty from the most ordinary of life's moments: leafing through *Jet* magazine, eating figs, unpacking a bottle of Heinz ketchup." Similarly, critic Peter Stitt calls attention to the sensitivity of Dove's writing in the *Georgia Review*: "The very absence of high drama may be what makes the poems so touching—these are ordinary people with ordinary struggles, successes, and failures." He concludes, "Rita Dove has taken a significant step forward in each of her three books of poems; she must be recognized as among the best young poets in the country today."

*Thomas and Beulah* Critics praised *Thomas and Beulah* and its author. Helen Vendler, in the *New York Review of Books*, described Dove as one who has "planed away unnecessary matter: pure shapes, her poems exhibit the thrift that Yeats called the sign of a perfected manner." Few, if any, of Dove's numerous reviewers gave this volume a negative notice, and many were lavish in their praise. Emily Grosholz, in the *Hudson Review* (1987), wrote that "Rita Dove . . . understands the long-term intricacies of marriage, as the protagonists of her wonderful chronicle . . . testify." Critics have also described this work as wise and affectionate. Dove succeeds in treating two sides of her subject, and she informs her reader, at the bottom of the book's dedicatory page, that these poems "tell two sides of a story and are meant to be read in sequence." Dove emphasizes the separateness and the individuality of her grandparents, who dealt with hostilities and the loss of love, as well as grief at the loss of life. But through good times and bad, this ancestral pair never fell out of love, maintaining their devotedness to the other. All critics of the book, in their own ways, have celebrated this melding of biography and lyric, one of Dove's trademarks.

## Responses to Literature

1. To whom is Dove speaking in *Lady Freedom Among Us?*

2. Describe your emotional response to "Augusta the Winged Man and Rasha the Black Dove." Explain Dove's choice of subject matter.

3. What significance do the lives of ordinary individuals seem to have for Dove?

4. After analyzing Dove's poetry, do you consider her a feminist? Why or why not?

BIBLIOGRAPHY

**Books**

Righelato, Pat. *Understanding Rita Dove.* Columbia: University of South Carolina Press, 2006.

Steffen, Therese. *Crossing Color: Transcultural Space and Place in Rita Dove's Poetry, Fiction, and Drama.* New York: Oxford University Press, 2001.

**Periodicals**

McDowell, Robert. "The Assembling Vision of Rita Dove." *Callaloo* 25 (Winter 1985): 61–70.

Rampersad, Arnold. "The Poems of Rita Dove." *Callaloo* 26 (Winter 1986): 52–60.

Steinman, Lisa M. "Dialogues Between History and Dream." *Michigan Quarterly Review* 26 (Spring 1987): 428–438.

Stitt, Peter. "Coherence Through Place in Contemporary American Poetry." *Georgia Review* 40 (1986): 1021–1033.

**Web sites**

University of Virginia Web site. *Comprehensive Biography of Rita Dove.* Retrieved September 15, 2008, from http://people.virginia.edu/~rfd4b/compbio.html.

## ✿ Theodore Dreiser

BORN: *1871, Terre Haute, Indiana*

DIED: *1945, Los Angeles, California*

NATIONALITY: *American*

GENRE: *Fiction, poetry, nonfiction*

MAJOR WORKS:

*Sister Carrie* (1900)

*An American Tragedy* (1925)

## Overview

One of the most prominent naturalistic authors in the United States during the early twentieth century, Theodore Dreiser was an instrumental figure in promoting a

Theodore Dreiser   *Dreiser, Theodore, photograph by Pirie MacDonald. The Library of Congress.*

realistic portrayal of life in America. He is best known for his novels *Sister Carrie* (1900) and *An American Tragedy* (1925), both of which paint unflattering portraits of American culture before and after the turn of the twentieth century.

## Works in Biographical and Historical Context

*Career in Journalism* Dreiser was born in Terre Haute, Indiana; he was the twelfth of thirteen children. His father, a German immigrant, had been a successful businessman, but a series of reversals left the family in poverty by the time of Dreiser's birth, and the family members were often separated as they sought work in different cities. While Dreiser did not excel as a student, he did receive encouragement from a high school teacher who paid Dreiser's tuition when he entered the University of Indiana in 1889. Dreiser was acutely self-conscious about differences between himself and wealthier, better-looking classmates, and he attended the university for only one year. On leaving, he worked at a variety of jobs, including a part-time position in the offices of the *Chicago Herald* that kindled in him an interest in journalism, and in April 1891 he obtained a post with the *Chicago Globe*. After several years as a reporter in Chicago, Dreiser pursued a career as a newspaper and magazine writer in St. Louis, Pittsburgh, and New York. Commentators maintain that his years as a journalist were instrumental in developing the exhaustively detailed literary style that is the hallmark of his fiction.

In New York, Dreiser supported himself—and, after 1898, his wife—with freelance magazine writing and editing while he worked on the manuscript of *Sister Carrie* (1900), a story about a woman who moves to Chicago, becomes a prostitute, and eventually achieves success as an actress. The novel was not promoted by the publisher, and it sold poorly. Marital difficulties and failing health further contributed to Dreiser's suffering from severe depression. After not working for several years, he was aided by an older brother, who had become a successful music-hall performer and songwriter under the name Paul Dresser. Dresser arranged for his brother to recuperate at a health resort and then helped him find work. Dreiser later credited several years of light manual labor with restoring his mental as well as physical health.

In 1905, Dreiser resumed freelance magazine writing and editing, and over the next two years he rose to the editorship of three prominent women's magazines. He lost this position in 1907 because of a scandal involving his romantic pursuit of a coworker's teenage daughter; that same year *Sister Carrie*, which had been received favorably in England, was reissued to positive reviews and good sales in the United States.

### The Trilogy of Desire

Over the next eighteen years, Dreiser published a succession of novels to widely varied but rarely indifferent critical notice. His next novel was *The Financier* (1912), the first in the Cowperwood series, or Trilogy of Desire. It described the life and career of businessman Frank Algernon Cowperwood. Both *The Financier* and *The Titan* (1914), the second volume of the trilogy, utilized imagery based on Darwinian evolutionary theory and offered somewhat didactic presentations of Dreiser's deterministic philosophy. Influenced by Charles Darwin, the economic determinism of Karl Marx and Friedrich Engels, and the forerunners of literary naturalism—Hippolyte Taine, Edmond and Jules Goncourt, and Emile Zola—these novels outline Dreiser's "chemicomechanistic" concept of life as little more than a series of "chemisms," or chemical reactions. Cowperwood's rise, fall, and second triumph in the world of high finance are recounted with a journalistic attention to detail that some commentators contend becomes an overly extensive listing of discrete facts. The third volume of the trilogy, *The Stoic* (1947), is considered vastly inferior to its predecessors. It concludes with the death of Cowperwood and the dispersal of his fortune and ends on an incongruous note of Eastern mysticism, which was an interest of Dreiser's second wife.

### Attempts at Suppression

Dreiser's fifth novel, *The "Genius"* (1915), was controversial for its portrayal of the artist as a person who is beyond conventional moral codes. Commentators maintain that this semiautobiographical work is Dreiser's thinly veiled self-justification of his own behavior and view some unflatteringly portrayed characters as Dreiser's revenge upon those who, he believed, had mistreated or misunderstood him. Sales of *The "Genius"* were initially good and early reviews largely favorable; however, in the year following its publication *The "Genius"* came to the attention of the New York Society for the Suppression of Vice, which labeled the book immoral and sought to block its distribution. Like other Americans of German descent, Dreiser was castigated and labeled "unpatriotic" during World War I (1914–1918). H. L. Mencken, who disapproved of the book on artistic grounds, nevertheless circulated a protest against the suppression of *The "Genius"*. The protest was signed by hundreds of prominent American and British authors, including Robert Frost, Sinclair Lewis, Ezra Pound, and H. G. Wells.

### A Career as Novelist Leads to Activism

The publication of *An American Tragedy* (1925) established Dreiser as among the country's foremost novelists then living. In this story the protagonist, Clyde Griffiths, leaves his religious upbringing in Kansas City behind and travels to New York, where he is ruined by the American system. The book was inspired by and closely modeled on the real-life murder of Grace Brown by Chester Gillette in 1906. Dreiser had studied the case for years, and he was interested not only in the scandalous details of the murder but also in the social-class inequalities that drove the ambitious Gillette to kill his girlfriend. The book was a popular success and brought Dreiser financial security until the Great Depression, which began with the stock market crash of October 1929. Following *An American Tragedy*, Dreiser became involved in social and political affairs. He went to Russia in 1927 to observe the results of the Communist Revolution, and he published his findings in *Dreiser Looks at Russia* (1928). He also joined investigations of labor conditions in Kentucky coal mines in 1931.

### Ideological Reversal and Activism

In his final novel, *The Bulwark* (1946), Dreiser seemingly repudiated both naturalism and the pessimistic determinism that informs his earlier novels. In *The Bulwark* the moral scruples of a Quaker businessman, Solon Barnes, conflict with the reality of American business dealings. In a reversal for Dreiser, Barnes, who upholds traditional mores and values, is portrayed sympathetically.

Dreiser published four autobiographical works, *A Traveler at Forty* (1913), *A Hoosier Holiday* (1916), *A Book about Myself* (1922), and *Dawn* (1931), as well as volumes of poetry, short stories, sketches, and essays, many of the latter pertaining to his social and political activism. Attention to this aspect of Dreiser's life exceeded the critical attention given his literary works during the 1930s and 1940s. At the time of his death on December 28, 1945, Dreiser was better known as a social and political activist than as a novelist. He had not published a novel in twenty years, and his career as a novelist was considered by many to have ended with *An American Tragedy*.

## Works in Literary Context

As one of the principal American exponents of literary naturalism at the turn of the century, Dreiser led the way for a generation of writers seeking to present a detailed and realistic portrait of American life. The philosophy of Herbert Spencer and the realism of Honoré de Balzac influenced Dreiser's beliefs and written work.

*Naturalism and Biological Determinism* Naturalism was a movement in literature that sought to portray events and characters as realistically as possible. Another important element of naturalism is the idea that a story's characters should be primarily affected by their environmental, social, and genetic circumstances. In such novels as *Sister Carrie* and *An American Tragedy*, Dreiser departs from traditional plots in which hard work and perseverance inevitably yield success and happiness. Instead, he depicts the world as an arena of largely random occurrences. For example, *Sister Carrie* differs markedly from the gentility and timidity that characterized much realistic fiction during the nineteenth century. Dreiser uncompromisingly detailed the events that led his protagonist first into prostitution and then, as if the author were pointedly avoiding a moral, to the attainment of success and financial security as an actress. The novel illustrates Dreiser's interpretation of complex human relationships as purely biological functions: Carrie exhibits what has been called "neo-Darwinian adaptability," surviving and prospering because she is able to adjust to whatever advantageous situations develop.

*Critique of the American Dream* *An American Tragedy* is considered Dreiser's most important work. Although some critics deplored Dreiser's stylistic and grammatical flaws—Mencken labeled his lack "of what may be called literary tact"—they considered *An American Tragedy* a powerful indictment of the gulf between American ideals of wealth and influence, and the opportunities available for their realization. The entire American system is blamed for the destruction of Clyde Griffiths, a weak-willed individual who aspires to the American dream of success.

Many commentators contend that Dreiser's chief importance is one of influence. His sprawling, flawed, but powerful novels helped to establish the conventions of modern naturalism.

---

## LITERARY AND HISTORICAL CONTEMPORARIES

Dreiser's famous contemporaries include:

**Marcel Proust** (1871–1922): The French author most famous for writing *In Search of Lost Time*, also known as *Remembrance of Things Past* (1913–1927).

**Colette** (1873–1954): Colette was most famous for her novel *Gigi* (1944).

**W. E. B. Du Bois** (1868–1963): The American author who helped define black social and political causes in the United States; he is widely remembered for his conflict with Booker T. Washington over the role to be played by blacks in American society—an issue that he treated at length in his famous *The Souls of Black Folk* (1903).

**Maxim Gorky** (1868–1936): This Russian writer is recognized as one of the earliest and foremost exponents of socialist realism in literature.

**Herbert Hoover** (1874–1964): President of the United States during the stock market crash of 1929. He was subsequently blamed by many for failing to provide adequate relief for the unemployed.

---

## Works in Critical Context

Many conservative critics, who favored the gentility and Puritan moralism characteristic of most writing at the time, attacked Dreiser's works for their awkward prose style, inadequately conveyed philosophy, and excessive length and detail. Nevertheless, he won the regard of other commentators for his powerful characterizations and strong ideological convictions in novels considered among the most notable achievements of twentieth-century literature. During his lifetime, the closest Dreiser got to winning a major literary award was when he was the runner-up for the 1930 Nobel Prize in Literature. The award went instead to Sinclair Lewis, who acknowledged Dreiser in his acceptance speech.

*An American Tragedy* Reaction to *An American Tragedy* was generally positive. In a *New Republic* article, Irving Howe called the novel "a masterpiece, nothing less," observing that in this work the author "mines his talent to its very depth." Joseph Warren Beach, author of *The Twentieth Century Novel: Studies in Technique* (1932), asserted that *An American Tragedy* "is doubtless the most neatly constructed of all Dreiser's novels, as well as the best written." Still, a number of reviewers found flaws in the book, most of which concerned problems that a number of critics found in all of Dreiser's books. For example, Arnold Bennett, author of *The Savour of Life: Essays in Gusto* (1928) withheld his recommendation of *An American Tragedy* because it "is written abominably, by a man who evidently despises style, elegance, clarity,

---

## COMMON HUMAN EXPERIENCE

Much of Dreiser's fiction concerns the unsuccessful struggle human beings wage against their fate, which, in his view, was predetermined by external factors. Other works that explore this theme include the following:

*On the Nature of Things* (first century B.C.E.), a book-length poem by the Roman author Lucretius. In this work, the author explains Epicurean philosophy and the principles of atomism, asserting that the universe is ruled by chance.

*Communist Manifesto* (1848), a political treatise by Karl Marx and Friedrich Engels. This work articulates a materialist conception of history, which regards the economics of society as the determining factor in human behavior.

*Beyond Freedom and Dignity* (1971), a nonfiction book by B. F. Skinner. In this work, Skinner argues against views of human behavior that value free will and the moral autonomy of individuals. Rather, Skinner asserts that human behavior is largely the result of environmental factors.

*Tess of the d'Urbervilles* (1891), a novel by Thomas Hardy. Hardy here presents the beautiful English peasant girl Tess who seeks only respect and happiness, but is destroyed by the cruel whims of fate, the hypocritical rules of society, and the selfishness of men.

even grammar. Dreiser simply does not know how to write, never did know, never wanted to know." *The Shape of Books to Come* (1944) author, J. Donald Adams, added that "Dreiser's thinking was never more confused and never more sentimental than it was in the writing of *An American Tragedy.*"

Reevaluation of Dreiser's literary reputation began with the posthumous publication of *The Bulwark* (1946) and *The Stoic* (1947). Widely varied critical opinions still stand regarding the merit of Dreiser's individual novels, with the exception of *An American Tragedy*, which is almost uniformly regarded a masterpiece of American literature.

### Responses to Literature

1. Discuss the moral implications of Hurstwood's failure and Carrie's success in *Sister Carrie*.

2. To what extent is Clyde Griffiths responsible for his fate and, alternatively, how much is he the victim of circumstances beyond his control in *An American Tragedy*?

3. *An American Tragedy* has been filmed twice—first in 1931 and again in 1951 under the title *A Place in the Sun*. Compare either filmed version to the original

book. In what ways to the two differ? Do Dreiser's most important themes come through in the film version?

4. After reading examples of Theodore Dreiser's fiction, explain what you think the author believes about the human condition. Articulate your understanding of his worldview using examples from his work.

BIBLIOGRAPHY

**Books**

Bloom, Harold, ed. *Twentieth Century American Literature*, Volume 2. New York: Chelsea House, 1986, pp. 1124–1154.

Dudley, Dorothy. *Dreiser and the Land of the Free*. New York: Beechhurst, 1946.

Elias, Robert H. *Theodore Dreiser: Apostle of Nature*. Ithaca, N.Y.: Cornell University Press, 1970.

Hakutani, Yoshinobu. *Young Dreiser: A Critical Study*. Cranbury, N.J.: Associated University Presses, 1980.

Moers, Ellen. *Two Dreisers*. New York: Viking, 1969.

Swanberg, William Andrew. *Dreiser*. New York: Scribner's, 1965.

**Periodicals**

Hakutani, Yoshinobu. "Theodore Dreiser's Editorial and Free-Lance Writing." *Library Chronicle* 37 (Winter 1971): 70–85.

Katz, Joseph. "Theodore Dreiser. *Ev'ry Month.*" *Library Chronicle* 38 (Winter 1972): 44–66.

**Web sites**

Pizer, Donald, Richard W. Dowell, and Frederic E. Rusch. *Theodore Dreiser Bibliography*. Retrieved October 23, 2008, from http://sceti.library. upenn.edu/dreiser/bibliography.pdf.

# ⊛ W. E. B. Du Bois

BORN: *1868, Great Barrington, Massachusetts*

DIED: *1963, Accra, Ghana*

NATIONALITY: *American, Ghanaian*

GENRE: *Nonfiction, fiction*

MAJOR WORKS:

*The Philadelphia Negro* (1899)

*The Souls of Black Folk* (1903)

*Dusk of Dawn: An Essay toward an Autobiography of a Race Concept* (1940)

*The Autobiography of W. E. B. Du Bois: A Soliloquy on Viewing My Life from the Last Decade of Its First Century* (1968)

## Overview

Any history of W. E. B. Du Bois must also be, to some extent, a history of the late nineteenth through the mid-twentieth century. Du Bois was involved in nearly every

W. E. B. Du Bois    *photograph. The Library of Congress.*

a youth of exceptional intelligence and ability, and when his mother died soon after his high school graduation some residents gave Du Bois a scholarship on condition that he attend Fisk University. Fisk was a southern school founded expressly for the children of emancipated slaves, and Du Bois rebelled against the implicit racism of this apparent generosity; he had always dreamed of attending Harvard University. The townspeople offering the scholarship were insistent, however, and in 1885 Du Bois traveled to Fisk in Nashville, Tennessee—his first journey to the southern United States.

***A Young Black Northerner in the Post-Reconstruction South*** Du Bois arrived, with little preparation, to witness the drama that had ensued with the end of "Reconstruction" in the South. Reconstruction (1863–77) had been a period during which southern society was restructured, in the wake of the Civil War (1861–65) and the freeing of the slaves (1863), with a particular emphasis on ensuring democracy and at least a measure of racial equality. During the post-Reconstruction period, however, white supremacists regained power throughout the South, deliberately disenfranchising both black and poor voters and introducing "Jim Crow" laws that imposed segregation in public facilities and transportation. Du Bois later wrote in the last of his three memoirs, his posthumously published *Autobiography* (1968), "No one but a Negro going into the South without previous experience of color caste can have any conception of its barbarism."

Yet Du Bois was also, as he described it, "deliriously happy" at Fisk, where he met other young intellectuals of his own race. There he excelled at studies and during summers taught the young blacks who lived in destitute rural areas of Tennessee. After graduating with honors from Fisk in only three years, Du Bois entered Harvard in 1888—to receive a second bachelor's degree and eventually his doctorate. Although many fellow students greeted him with animosity—demonstrating that the liberal North wasn't nearly as free from racism as some liked to think—Du Bois found at Harvard professors who would provide lifelong inspiration: Josiah Royce, George Santayana, Albert Bushnell Hart, and William James, who became a mentor and also a friend.

***Scholarly Prowess Meets Institutional Racism*** Needing only to complete a dissertation to receive his doctorate in history, Du Bois enrolled at the University of Berlin in Germany. There, in Europe (considered a racial paradise of sorts by many African Americans, both then and on through the mid-twentieth century) he studied philosophy, sociology, and history for two years. Upon return to the United States in 1894, however, he promptly rediscovered what he described as "'nigger'-hating America," where the chances of a black history instructor finding a teaching position were slim.

In 1895, Du Bois completed his dissertation, *The Suppression of the African Slave-Trade to the United States of America, 1638–1870*. The work became the first

social movement of significance during this period: Reconstruction and ongoing efforts thereafter to develop civil rights in America, campaigns for U.S. involvement in World War I, the Harlem Renaissance, American communism (and even Stalinist philosophy), the McCarthyism of the Cold War era, anti-colonial movements and more. Throughout the many domestic and world crises of his ninety-five years of life, Du Bois maintained an attitude of "noble critique," an unabashed readiness to see both the good and the ill in the world around him. For this, he became one of the most influential writers of his time, alternately damned and praised by a long succession of friends and enemies.

## Works in Biographical and Historical Context

***A Stable Childhood in Sleepy Great Barrington*** Born in 1868, William Edward Burghardt (W. E. B.) Du Bois had a childhood less marked by outright racism than those of many African Americans of his generation. Coming of age in the small town of Great Barrington, Massachusetts, he was a member of a stable community in which his family had long resided. Born with what he described as "a flood of Negro blood, a strain of French, a bit of Dutch, but, thank God! no 'Anglo-Saxon,'" Du Bois lived, with his mother, Mary Burghardt Du Bois, a somewhat meager existence (his father, Alfred Du Bois, had left his mother around the time W. E. B. was born). But, to his good fortune, the town recognized Du Bois as volume of the Harvard Historical Studies series, and Du Bois became the first black American to receive his doctorate from Harvard. Two years later, in 1897, he began what would become a thirteen-year tenure as a professor of sociology and economics at Atlanta University. In 1899 Du Bois published the sociological study *The Philadelphia Negro*, the product of interviews with five thousand black persons living in the "dirt, drunkenness, poverty, and crime" of Philadelphia. The work, commissioned by the University of Pennsylvania, pioneered the scholarly study of black Americans. Yet the university itself would not give Du Bois a position on its faculty. Du Bois found this to be typical; despite his advanced degrees and important published works, time and again he was denied teaching positions at historically white institutions on the basis of the color of his skin.

### *"Accommodationism" versus Civil Rights Consciousness*

In his time, Du Bois came to be one of the most outspoken public intellectuals in the United States. Equally, he came to be one of the African-American community's strongest voices. At the advent of the twentieth century, however, the best-known champion of black Americans was still Booker T. Washington, then the principal of Tuskegee Institute in Alabama and a powerful advocate of long-term, incremental change. In the preface to his *W. E. B. Du Bois: Negro Leader in a Time of Crisis*, Francis L. Broderick describes Washington's "accommodationist" tactics as "speaking soft words to white men and careful words to colored men." Washington laid the blame for blacks' social position on their inferior economic positions—and their "unreadiness" to contribute to an economy more advanced than that which had previously relied on their labor as slaves.

As a spokesman for his race, Washington was prepared to let black Americans be disenfranchised until they contributed to the economy by learning trades in agriculture and industry. Du Bois, however, could not abide by this stance. Broderick writes of Du Bois, "Long restive under Washington's acquiescence in second-class citizenship, Du Bois ordered the Negro to be a man and demanded that white America recognize him as such." Though Du Bois often claimed to see himself as basically in agreement with Washington, the two men were diametrically opposed in their views toward education in particular, and each found supporters—what ensued was a historic conflict over "racial uplift," the process whereby black Americans were to pull themselves up out of the mud into which slavery and ongoing prejudice had stamped them. In 1903 Du Bois published his best-known work, a collection of essays entitled *The Souls of Black Folk*. Du Bois's critique of *Up from Slavery*, Washington's autobiography, was one of the essays in *Souls*, and with the work's publication Du Bois became inextricably involved in the fight for equality for blacks.

In 1905 Du Bois formed the Niagara Movement, the first black protest movement of the twentieth century. Twenty-nine black men met on the Canadian side of Niagara Falls and set out a plan for dismantling segregation and discrimination, and for generally opposing the politics of racism to which they felt Washington fell prey. Du Bois helped institute a more lasting movement still, in 1909, when he became the only black founding member of the National Association for the Advancement of Colored People (NAACP). The NAACP had, in fact, been founded by a group of white writers and social workers as a response to the 1908 race riots in Springfield, Illinois. These riots, sparked by the lynching of two blacks, resulted in the deaths of four more people and the injury of over seventy more. Du Bois, who for many years was the organization's only prominent black member, also founded and edited *Crisis*, the official publication of the NAACP. Under his editorial hand, it was the most important magazine directed at a black audience of its time, and served in part to initiate what would grow over time to be a massive civil rights movement.

### *From Editing Crisis to Living through Crises*

In *Crisis*, Du Bois wrote editorials condemning lynching and disenfranchisement, and his discussion of arts and letters there is still considered to have been a catalyst for the Harlem Renaissance (a New York-centered, African-American literary and artistic movement—the first of its kind in the United States). Du Bois determined from the very beginning to make the *Crisis* not only a national black magazine, but also his magazine. Since the NAACP had originally underwritten the magazine as a house organ for its own publicity and not a vehicle for the opinions of its editor, confusion and friction attended its early years. In fact, debate between Oswald Garrison Villard, the chairman of the NAACP, and Du Bois over the magazine threatened to destroy the organization itself. Eventually Du Bois's uncompromising energy won out; Villard resigned his position, and his successor, Joel Spingarn, gave Du Bois control over the magazine so long as he reported organization business and refrained in his editorials from "petty irritations, insulting personalities, and vulgar recriminations." The magazine's generally accepted high quality, however, stood as testament to Du Bois's integrity as an editor, and was fully self-supporting after its first two years—an impressive feat for what was essentially a protest magazine.

But in 1914, Du Bois lost credibility with many when he urged black support for American involvement in World War I, in the editorial "Close Ranks"; later, he would discover widespread racism in the U.S. armed forces in Europe and speak out on that issue. At this time, though, many black Americans turned away from Du Bois's leadership. As an intellectual and member of the middle class, he seemed at a great distance from many African Americans; some thought him simply anti-populist. For instance, Du Bois was bewildered at the widespread popular appeal accorded to Marcus Garvey, Jamaican leader of the Universal Negro Improvement Association and "back-to-Africa" movement. His conflict with Garvey, whom he eventually called "the most dangerous enemy of the Negro race in America and the world," indicated his alienation from a large part of the black population in America.

Such conflict was a hallmark of Du Bois's long, outspoken career. Du Bois lived through several eras of great change—from Reconstruction and post-Reconstruction to World War I and World War II—and maintained throughout his long life a vigorous critique of racism and other forms of oppression. After several more years as a professor at Atlanta University (1934–1944), where he founded the long-influential journal *Phylon*, he returned to the NAACP, now as Director of Special Research. But there his positions on politics, inflected by Marxism and the brand of communism espoused by Soviet leader Joseph Stalin, brought him into conflict with the organization's more conservative executive director, Walter White. Du Bois was forced to resign after only four years, to which he responded by turning to more radical politics. In the ensuing years, Du Bois was no friend of the U.S. government, which was dominated by the paranoia of Senator Joseph McCarthy and the perceived need to respond to the threat of global communism, a reaction also known as the Red Scare. Writing of one particularly trying experience—his indictment and trial as a subversive—in 1951, during the infamous McCarthy era, Du Bois revealed his attitude toward the numerous crises of his long life: "It was a bitter experience and I bowed before the storm. But I did not break."

### Anti-imperialism, Communism, and Death in Ghana

Despite having been found innocent of any crime or treason, Du Bois lost his passport for several years. This was part of the U.S. government's policy of preventing influential black and politically radical citizens from traveling abroad. Nonetheless, Du Bois continued to fight for basic freedoms and equality for all people, remaining involved with both the international peace movement that had led to his indictment and the Pan-African movement that had begun to link anti-colonial struggles around Africa and the world. Blacklisted by the NAACP, prevented from traveling by the U.S. government, and struggling still under the weight of injustice and inequality in America, Du Bois found great common ground with the communist movement, paying tribute in *In Battle for Peace* (1952) to "the communists of the world for their help in my defense."

Indeed, "the communists of the world" became Du Bois's ardent supporters and, with progressives in America, his constituency. The organs of the more conservative black press closed to him, he wrote widely for such left-wing periodicals as the *National Guardian*. Between 1958 and

## LITERARY AND HISTORICAL CONTEMPORARIES

W. E. B. Du Bois's famous contemporaries include:

**Frank Lloyd Wright** (1867–1959): Wright was a famed American architect, whose efforts to make the built human environment better reflect and integrate the natural world have since inspired millions.

**Joseph Stalin** (1878–1953): A Soviet Russian revolutionary and leader whose interpretation of Karl Marx's ideas about socialism and ultimate role as longtime Soviet dictator have been widely criticized.

**Claude McKay** (1889–1948): McKay, a Jamaican writer and poet who emigrated to the United States, became an influential member of the Harlem Renaissance.

**Booker T. Washington** (1856–1915): A black American leader, whose stance on segregation was very popular with whites and brought him into increasing disfavor with progressive blacks.

**Richard Wright** (1908–1960): An African-American novelist and nonfiction-writer whose work drew heavily on Du Bois's notion of the "double consciousness" implicit in the black American experience.

**Pauline Hopkins** (1859–1930): Hopkins was an American novelist and playwright of African descent. Her work ranged from a dramatic treatment of escape from slavery to meditations on the nature and value of race consciousness.

1959, his passport, after court action, was finally released by the government, and he traveled extensively throughout Eastern Europe and Asia. He received an honorary degree from Prague University and had audiences with the leaders of the Soviet Union and the People's Republic of China. In 1961, at the age of ninety-three, he officially joined the Communist Party of the United States.

Later, during the same year, he accepted an invitation from Prime Minister Nkrumah to visit Ghana and became a resident of that African nation. Shortly before his death in 1963, he renounced his American citizenship altogether, dying in Accra as a citizen of Ghana. Du Bois died the day before the March on Washington (a key moment in the civil rights movement, with over three hundred thousand protesters marching on the capitol) and Martin Luther King, Jr.'s "I Have a Dream" speech. Though the America he had hoped and worked for did not come into being during his lifetime—and still has not—strides were being made. The March, like Du Bois's struggles throughout his life, is credited with having helped extend a true franchise to African Americans: the Civil Rights Act (1964) and the National Voting Rights Act (1965) began the long, still-ongoing process of consolidating the gains for which the civil rights movement had fought.

# COMMON HUMAN EXPERIENCE

In *The Souls of Black Folk* and elsewhere, Du Bois outlines the idea of "double consciousness" in the life of African Americans, suggesting that black people in the United States suffer under the demands of a split identity: African, on the one hand, and American, on the other. This is, however, part of a long tradition of exploring the splitting of human psyches. Here are some other pieces that examine the ways in which we humans are inevitably both more and less than just ourselves:

> "The Transcendentalist" (1843), an essay by Ralph Waldo Emerson. Here, Emerson uses the term "double consciousness" to describe the difficulty of remaining aware of both a transcendental, spiritual truth and the everyday, secular world.
>
> "The Hidden Self" (1890), an essay by William James. In this article for *Scribner's*, Du Bois's mentor considers the mystical, the occult, and the parts of ourselves that we hide from ourselves.
>
> *Psychopathology of Everyday Life* (1901), a psychological treatise by Sigmund Freud. In this classic work, Freud explores the meaning and manifestations of the human unconscious, that part of us that we are unaware of but that contains some of the most powerful impulses and desires that shape our conscious experience.
>
> *The Psychic Life of Power* (1997), a philosophical text by Judith Butler. Butler looks at the way human beings come into "subjectivity" or "selfhood" in relationships of inequality, and at our passionate attachment to the inequalities that then become part of who we are.

## Works in Literary Context

Though Du Bois published both fiction and nonfiction during his long career, he is most enduringly known for the sociological and autobiographical essays contained in *The Souls of Black Folk*. There as elsewhere, his writing picks up on the tradition of independent thought exemplified in earlier American letters by Walt Whitman and Henry David Thoreau, and is often both lyrical and stirring. Likewise, Du Bois's way of thinking and writing recalls the thorough, careful honesty of his mentor William James and the social conscience of his predecessor and sometime adversary Booker T. Washington. Du Bois has influenced each generation of writers to succeed him, from the black authors of the Harlem Renaissance in the 1920s and early 1930s, to mid-century authors of protest novels such as Richard Wright and James Baldwin, to present-day writers such as Sherman Alexie (whose *Reservation Blues* ends each chapter with a line of music—the way *The Souls of Black Folk* begins each chapter).

*Civil Rights Consciousness* *The Souls of Black Folk* was not well received when it first came out, however. Prior to this, Du Bois's work had been of a self-consciously academic—even conservative—nature. This, though, was both rigorously academic and deeply activist. Houston A. Baker, Jr. explains in *Black Literature in America* that white Americans were not "ready to respond favorably to Du Bois's scrupulously accurate portrayal of the hypocrisy, hostility, and brutality of white America toward black America." Many blacks were also shocked by the book, for in it Du Bois announced his opposition to the conciliatory policy of Booker T. Washington and his followers, who argued for the gradual development of the Negro race through vocational training.

Du Bois himself declared: "So far as Mr. Washington apologizes for injustice, North or South, does not rightly value the privilege and duty of voting, belittles the emasculating effects of caste distinctions, and opposes the higher training and ambition of our brighter minds—so far as he, the South, or the Nation, does this—we must unceasingly and firmly oppose him. By every civilized and peaceful method we must strive for the rights which the world accords to men." These words were, in many ways, the beginning of civil rights consciousness on a large scale in America. That is, prior to Du Bois, any number of people had argued for some measure of equality, but his was one of the most forceful, compelling, and well-respected voices to make the case for true civil rights, for genuine equality for all. In many ways, the civil rights movement of the 1950s, 1960s, and 1970s traced its roots back to Du Bois's call to consciousness and action in this early piece.

## Works in Critical Context

*The Souls of Black Folk* Though its initial appearance prompted resentment in many readers, in retrospect, scholars have pointed to *The Souls of Black Folk* as a prophetic work. Harold W. Cruse and Carolyn Gipson note in the *New York Review of Books* that "nowhere else was Du Bois's description of the Negro's experience in American Society to be given more succinct expression.... *Souls* is probably his greatest achievement as a writer." Poet Langston Hughes has underscored the power of Du Bois's writing in recalling, "My earliest memories of written words are those of Du Bois and the Bible." Likewise, literary critics Henry Louis Gates, Jr. and Terri Oliver have argued that Du Bois "provides a social gospel based on history, sociology, and personal experience." Although, as literary critic Arnold Rampersand puts it, he was "unable to fashion an autobiography to match Washington's, young Du Bois nevertheless infused a powerful autobiographical spirit and presence into his essays." Over the course of time, however, he would also produce two more complete autobiographies: *Dusk of Dawn* (1940), and the posthumously published *The Autobiography of W. E. B. Du Bois* (1968).

*The Autobiography of W. E. B. Du Bois* Edward Blum has suggested that Du Bois's autobiographical efforts ought not be read as simple expressions of self, nor as simple expressions of a particularly white narrative tradition. Rather, he writes, "By presenting a black mythology of self, Du Bois participated in and built on a long tradition of African-American autobiographizing." In a similar vein, Vanessa Dickerson argues that though "Du Bois's regard for Europe's cultural capital would never wane," he nonetheless came in his autobiographical writing to "the recognition of how England and Europe were implicated in the problem of the color line." These autobiographies were, in the end, not only about communicating the experiences of a lifetime, but also about developing a picture of the world that could make sense of racism, progress, world wars, capitalism, oppression, scholarship, activism and the personal experience of journeying through it all.

## Responses to Literature

1. Consider the structure and content of *The Souls of Black Folk*. To what genre would you say this book belongs? Explain your position with close analysis of the text itself.

2. What do you see as the purpose and significance of the snatches of song at the beginning of each chapter of *The Souls of Black Folk*? What effect(s) do they have on you as a reader?

3. Identify one or two trends (connections between essays, repetitions of structure or content, etc.) that most strike you in *The Autobiography of W. E. B. Du Bois*? How do these trends relate to the overall "self" Du Bois has fashioned in this autobiography?

4. How does Du Bois conceive of racial consciousness? Explain your understanding with detailed reference to one or more of the essays in *The Souls of Black Folk*. What aspects of Du Bois's understanding of racial consciousness seem like they would be difficult for today's readers to understand or accept? Does Du Bois challenge you to see the world differently in some ways? If so, how?

BIBLIOGRAPHY

**Books**

Blum, Edward J. *W. E. B. Du Bois: American Prophet.* Philadelphia: University of Pennsylvania Press, 2007.

Dickerson, Vanessa D. *Dark Victorians.* Champaign, Ill.: University of Illinois Press, 2008.

Gates, Jr., Henry Louis, and Terri Hume Oliver, eds. *The Souls of Black Folk: W. E. B. Du Bois.* New York: Norton Critical Editions, 1999.

McKay, Nellie. "W. E. B. Du Bois: The Black Women in His Writings—Selected Fictional and Autobiographical Portraits" in *Critical Essays on W. E. B. Du Bois*, William L. Andrews, ed. Boston: G. K. Hall, 1985.

**Periodicals**

Dickson, Jr., Bruce D. "W. E. B. Du Bois and the Idea of Double Consciousness." *American Literature: A Journal of Literary History, Criticism, and Bibliography* 64 (2): 299–309.

**Web sites**

*W. E. B. Du Bois.* Retrieved October 5, 2008, from http://www.naacp.org.

## ✸ Andre Dubus

BORN: *1936, Lake Charles, Louisiana*

DIED: *1999, Haverhill, Massachusetts*

NATIONALITY: *American*

GENRE: *Fiction*

MAJOR WORKS:
*Adultery and Other Choices* (1977)
*The Last Worthless Evening* (1986)
*Dancing after Hours* (1996)

Andre Dubus  *AP Images.*

# COMMON HUMAN EXPERIENCE

Adultery is a common theme in the work of Andre Dubus. Other works that focus on this topic include the following:

*The Tragedy of Othello* (1623), a play by William Shakespeare. In this story, Othello—a general in the Venetian army—is manipulated into believing his wife, Desdemona, is having an affair.

*The Scarlet Letter* (1850), a novel by Nathaniel Hawthorne. Hester Prynne, who lives in a Puritan community, wears a red letter "A" as a symbol of the adultery she committed while her husband was in Europe.

*The Unbearable Lightness of Being* (1982), a novel by Milan Kundera. This story concerns the lives of Tomas, a womanizer, his wife, Tereza, his mistress, Sabina, and Sabina's lover Franz.

## Overview

Characterized as a Southerner who seldom writes about the South, Andre Dubus is known for his realistic fiction, which explores the desires, disillusionment, and moral dilemmas of contemporary American society. He is also noted for his deft creation of believable characters in everyday circumstances. Critics particularly acknowledge Dubus's realistic portrayal of the thoughts and emotions of his female protagonists.

## Works in Biographical and Historical Context

*Growing Up in Bayou Country*   Andre Dubus (the family pronounces the name "Duh-buse") was born on August 11, 1936, in Lake Charles, Louisiana, of Cajun Irish stock. The son of his namesake, Andre Dubus Sr., a civil engineer who loved golf and smoked a great deal, and Katherine Burke Dubus, who listened to broadcasts of the Metropolitan Opera on winter Saturday afternoons, Andre grew up with his two sisters in the bayou country around Baton Rouge and Lafayette. His childhood was spent in lower-middle-class circumstances. He attended the Christian Brothers' Cathedral High School and, upon graduation in 1954, he enrolled at McNeese State College, earning his BA in English in 1958.

In 1958, having married Patricia Lowe in February, he accepted a second lieutenant's commission in the marines. This same year saw the birth of his first child, Suzanne, and in each of the next three succeeding years another child was born: Andre, Jeb, and Nicole. Abroad, political violence in South Vietnam was escalating and would soon lead to an increased presence of U.S. armed forces in the area.

*Breaking into the Literary Arena*   In 1963, the same year his father died of cancer at age fifty-nine, Dubus, now a captain, resigned his military commission to take his family to the University of Iowa, where he studied writing. This career change occurred just as U.S. involvement in Vietnam was escalating. Dubus had been writing stories since he was nineteen, and in 1963 he succeeded at breaking into print in the *Sewanee Review* with "The Intruder."

With an MFA from the Iowa Writers' Workshop, he headed with his family back to Louisiana for a year's teaching in Thibodaux before going north to Bradford College in Massachusetts. Until 1984, Dubus taught writing and literature at Bradford College. During this time his first marriage ended, and he would marry twice more, first, to Tommie Gail Cotter in June 1975, a marriage that ended childless three years later, and then in 1979 to a woman many years his junior, Peggy Rambach, who gave birth to two children, Cadence in 1982 and Madeleine in 1987, the final year of their marriage. While at Bradford College, Dubus published his only novel, *The Lieutenant* (1967), and several stories in prestigious quarterlies.

*Confronting Catholic Traditions*   Five years after Martha Foley chose the Dubus story "If They Knew Yvonne" for inclusion in *Best American Short Stories 1970*, Dubus published *Separate Flights* (1975), his first collection of stories. "If They Knew Yvonne" is a retrospective first-person narration that also draws on Dubus's youth. Writing during a period when the Catholic Church in America was beginning to loosen its authoritarian strictures as a result of the Second Vatican Council, the story ends hopefully with a whispered hymn of praise to human vitality and common sense. In addition to exposing what he perceived as Catholicism's bias against women, the story reflects the moral dilemma Dubus confronted in deciding to abandon church teaching and to use birth control.

In addition to the title story and "If They Knew Yvonne," this volume includes the novella "We Don't Live Here Anymore," which, together with the novellas "Adultery" (1977) and "Finding a Girl in America" (1980) was to become the tripartite saga of Terry and Jack Linhart and Edith and Hank Allison—two married couples employed in academia whose circumstances resemble closely those of the Dubus family—in the 1984 collection *We Don't Live Here Anymore.*

*Success as an Author*   In 1977, Dubus was the recipient of a Guggenheim Fellowship and he published the well-received *Adultery and Other Choices* (1977), a collection of nine short stories, and the novella "Adultery." Of the stories, "The Fat Girl" has subsequently achieved the most prominence in anthologies. The following year, Dubus received a National Endowment for the Arts grant and in 1979 he saw his story "The Pitcher" placed in *Prize Stories: The O. Henry Awards.*

On the whole, reviews of Dubus's work were largely favorable in the 1970s, and his reputation in the 1980s continued to grow as writers such as John Updike and Joyce Carol Oates brought him to the attention of a growing readership. *The Last Worthless Evening* (1986) and *Selected Stories* (1988) led to Dubus's introduction into college literature classes and have stirred critical interest.

In 1984, Dubus published *Voices from the Moon*, a novella that later was collected in *We Don't Live Here Anymore* and *Selected Stories: Voices from the Moon*. It is told in the third person but in the limited-omniscient mode so that different sections of the story reveal the minds of different members of the Stowe family, who have been dispersed through marriage and divorce. Although the complications of the story transcend the ordinary turmoil of middle-class divorce in America, they still reflect society's mores in a general way just as they must mirror Dubus's own problems: he was married at the time to a wife the age of his own children.

*The Accident*   Early on the morning of July 23, 1986, Dubus was struck by a car near Wilmington, Massachusetts, where he was assisting a distressed motorist on Interstate 93. Accounts of this accident, which resulted in injuries that caused him to lose a leg and require a wheelchair, appear in his well-received volume of personal essays *Broken Vessels*. Four months after the accident his wife left him, and five days after that she "came with a court order and a kind young Haverhill police officer and took Cadence and Madeleine away." After that he suffered writing blocks but continued to work and to lecture, often in pain. A show of support, both moral and financial, by such disparate American writers as Ann Beattie, E. L. Doctorow, Kurt Vonnegut, John Irving, Gail Godwin, and Richard Yates proved enormously gratifying to the dispirited Dubus, as did a MacArthur Fellowship he received when his morale had reached a particularly low point. In the years after the shaking events of 1986, he came to view the accident as a transcendent experience that allowed him to understand more deeply the nature of human suffering, forgiveness, and love. He remained a practicing and believing Catholic, although he had to modify for himself a few of the church's strictures.

In April 1996 Andre Dubus won the Rea Award for the Short Story, recognizing his career achievement. That same year, he published *Dancing after Hours*—a *New York Times* Notable Book of the Year—and, then, in 1998, *Meditations from a Moveable Chair*. In 1999, Dubus died from a heart attack at the age of sixty-two. His son, Andre Dubus III, is also an author.

## Works in Literary Context

Like his contemporaries Russell Banks and Raymond Carver, Andre Dubus is often perceived as a "son of Ernest Hemingway," a judgment that would likely please neither Hemingway nor Dubus but one that serves as a rough frame of reference nonetheless. He often writes in a prose style made familiar by Hemingway—a style that might be called nonexperimental, plain American style.

## LITERARY AND HISTORICAL CONTEMPORARIES

Andre Dubus's famous contemporaries include:

**E. L. Doctorow** (1931–): A major American contemporary fiction writer, Doctorow achieved widespread recognition with the overwhelming critical and commercial success of *Ragtime* (1975), a novel that vividly re-creates the turbulent years of pre–World War I America.

**Don DeLillo** (1936–): An American author who has established himself as an important contemporary American novelist with works such as *White Noise* (1985) and *Underworld* (1997).

**Tom Robbins** (1936–): American author most famous for his satirical novels, including *Even Cowgirls Get the Blues* (1976).

**Judy Blume** (1938–): American author of best-selling stories for children and young adults including *Are You There, God? It's Me Margaret.* (1970).

**Raymond Carver** (1938–1988): American short story writer who contributed to the reemergence of the short story in the 1980s.

Dubus's work was influenced by the cultural climate of the 1970s and 1980s, his debilitating accident, and the difficulties he faced in his personal relationships.

*Compassion for Ordinary People*   In depicting ordinary people—single mothers, divorced husbands, and victims of failing marriages—Dubus treats in a freshly original manner a host of problems that occupied American minds in the 1970s and 1980s. But merely to list the issues raised in his stories runs the danger of making Dubus's writing sound trendy, slick, or superficial—all qualities he avoided. Abortion, drugs, child and wife abuse, racism, rape, anorexia, divorce, birth control, exercise and body building, and the aftermath of Vietnam find expression in his stories.

*Postwar America*   Andre Dubus writes of an America of vanishing expectations, a country slipping from postwar confidence, with eroded small cities where jobs are hard to find and pay is minimum wage. In his works, the middle class has lost direction as marriages and the church begin to fail. In stories such as "Falling in Love" and "The Veteran," his main characters have returned from war and find themselves in what they see as less than ideal relationships—not because of war, but because of life after the war.

## Works in Critical Context

Dubus has received generally favorable critical attention throughout his career. His ability to explore the ethical contradictions of society through the perspective of ordinary people whose everyday lives are laced with ambivalence and moral conflict has been particularly noted. Although some critics have found Dubus's work powerful and relevant but "depressing to read," as Charles Deemer remarked, or his characters "resolutely ungiving and uncharming," as Joyce Carol Oates asserted, Dubus's sensitive portrayal of the inner lives of both men and women in his fiction and his craftsmanship of style and technique have merited critical praise. Many reviewers have remarked on the impact of Dubus's accident on his writing, praising the wisdom and grace with which he recovered from and managed the devastating changes it brought to his life.

*Selected Stories* *Selected Stories* was greeted with enthusiastic reviews in the *New Republic* and the *New York Times Book Review*, as well as receiving favorable notices in the *Times Literary Supplement* and *New Statesman*. Writing for the *New Republic*, Anne Tyler praised Dubus for truly understanding his characters, saying that "he feels morally responsible for his characters, and it's this sense of responsibility that gives his work its backbone." Tyler felt that Ray Yarborough of "A Pretty Girl" becomes "even likable," despite his myriad moral failings—an opinion that demonstrates the sorcery Dubus can work. In the *New Statesman*, Kirsty Milne reminded readers of Dubus's "eloquence," a quality undervalued by critics more likely to talk of his "voice" or "moral vision" or "unabashed humanism."

## Responses to Literature

1. How would you characterize the style of Dubus's writing? What literary techniques seem most important to his work?

2. Discuss any differences you notice between the story "The Intruder" and Dubus's later work. What do you think would explain these differences?

3. Some critics argue that the women in Dubus's short stories are distinctly "other"—meaning they are often enigmatic, dangerous, or in need of male protection. Do you agree? Find an example of a female character from his work to support your opinion.

4. How does Dubus's Catholic background influence his work? Do you see evidence of Dubus's religious or spiritual views in his story collection *Dancing after Hours*?

BIBLIOGRAPHY

**Books**

Kennedy, Thomas E. *Andre Dubus: A Study of Short Fiction*. Boston: Twayne, 1988.

Wolff, Tobias. *Introduction to Dubus's* Broken Vessels. Boston: Godine, 1991.

**Periodicals**

Breslin, John B. "Playing Out the Patterns of Sin and Grace: The Catholic Imagination of Andre Dubus." *Commonweal* 115 (December 2, 1988): 652–656.

Dahlin, Robert. "Andre Dubus." *Publishers Weekly* 226 (October 12, 1984): 56–57.

Doten, Patti. "Andre Dubus: Pain Yes, Rage No." *Boston Globe* (August 19, 1991): 33, 36.

Hathaway, Dev. "A Conversation with Andre Dubus." *Black Warrior Review* 9 (Spring 1983): 86–103.

Kornbluth, Jesse. "The Outrageous Andre Dubus." *Horizon* 28 (April 1985): 16–20.

Nathan, Robert. "Interview with Andre Dubus." *Bookletter* 3 (February 14, 1987): 14–15.

# ⊛ Andre Dubus III

BORN: *1959, Oceanside, California*

NATIONALITY: *American*

GENRE: *Fiction*

MAJOR WORKS:

*The Cage Keeper and Other Stories* (1989)

*Bluesman* (1993)

*House of Sand and Fog* (1999)

Andre Dubus III   *AP Images*

## Overview

Andre Dubus III resisted the idea of being an author for many years because his father, Andre Dubus, who died in 1999, continues to be well recognized as one of America's best short-fiction writers, and the younger Dubus simply wanted to do something different. The younger Dubus has held a variety of jobs—bounty hunter, private investigator, carpenter, bartender, actor, and, finally, teacher—but, as he told Oprah Winfrey in a 2001 television interview, "Growing up, I never wanted to be a writer. I found that when I did start writing, I felt more like myself than I've ever felt. I had to write to be me." The Dubus stock has had a significant impact upon the writing of the late twentieth and early twenty-first centuries.

## Works in Biographical and Historical Context

*In and Out of Literature* Andre Dubus III (the family pronounces the name "Duh-buse") was born on September 11, 1959, in Oceanside, California, to Andre Dubus Jr. and his wife, social worker Patricia Lowe. Dubus's parents divorced when he was eleven years old, but he maintained a strong relationship with his father. As a result of his parents' divorce, however, the family lived in poverty for many years. After high school Dubus attended Bradford College in Massachusetts and earned an associate of arts degree in 1979, and then continued his studies at the University of Texas at Austin, drawn there by its progressive curriculum and atmosphere. In 1981 he earned his B.A. in sociology and political science. Shortly thereafter, he returned to Massachusetts for a year to, as he says in an interview with Robert Birnbaum, "get out of the books a bit."

In Massachusetts he worked in construction and boxed at the Lynn Boys Club. At the time, he was dating one of his father's students. When she told Dubus that she had a crush on a classmate because she was impressed by his writing, Dubus read the classmate's manuscript and became inspired to write. He began writing a short story to impress the girlfriend, but he ended up enjoying writing so much that he continued for his own sake.

Dubus initially planned to earn a Ph.D. in Marxist social science at the University of Wisconsin and then to attend law school. He went to Wisconsin but stayed just four days, quickly realizing that he did not want to be a sociologist. He then returned to Texas briefly and then went to Colorado for a year, where he worked at a prison while he continued writing. His first published story, "Forky," appeared in *Playboy* in 1984 and won the National Magazine Award a year later.

*Life into Fiction* In 1989 Dubus married Fontaine Dollas, a dancer and choreographer. In 1989 he also published his first book, a collection of short fiction called *The Cage Keeper and Other Stories*. In it Dubus draws extensively on his life experience, from working in a Colorado corrections facility in the early 1980s to grow-

ing up during the Vietnam War in the 1960s and 1970s. The Vietnam War was a deeply unpopular conflict in which American forces battled on the side of the South Vietnamese against the communist North Vietnamese in order to prevent the spread of communism in Asia. The volume includes the prize-winning "Forky," which chronicles the experiences of an inmate as he moves from prison to civilian life and goes on a date with a woman. Other stories involve a troubled Vietnam veteran's ill-fated relationship with a younger lover and a camping trip undertaken by two children and their stepfather, newly estranged from their mother. Dubus's first book delves into many troubling sides of contemporary society: urban violence, decaying relationships, loss of community and family, loss of identity, and unfulfilled dreams.

Like his first book, Dubus's second work, *Bluesman*, which appeared in 1993, garnered little public or critical attention. This introspective novel differs from his first collection, however, which was filled with much more action. *Bluesman* is a coming-of-age story in which sixteen-year-old Leo Sutherland learns about life, the blues, and Marxism during the late 1960s and early

# COMMON HUMAN EXPERIENCE

A central theme of *House of Sand and Fog* is the immigrant experience and the conflict that often arises between cultures and neighbors, and among families. Here are some other works that explore the immigrant experience in America:

*Interpreter of Maladies* (1999), a short story collection by Jhumpa Lahiri. This collection of stories by Indian-American author Lahiri portrays the experiences—often difficult—of Indian immigrants trying to balance the culture in which they were raised with that of their adopted homeland. The book, Lahiri's first, won the Pulitzer Prize for fiction.

*Bread Givers* (1925), a novel by Anzia Yezierska. Yezierska's novel is set in the immigrant neighborhoods of New York, where hundreds of thousands of Jews from Eastern Europe had flocked by the first decades of the twentieth century. The novel's protagonist yearns to experience the many things that life in America has to offer but constantly struggles against a father who clings desperately to his old-world values.

*Zoot Suit* (1981), a film directed by Luis Valdez. Based on the Broadway play of the same name, *Zoot Suit* tells the story of the wrongful conviction for murder of a group of Mexican–Americans, and of the trial's aftermath: the so-called "Zoot Suit riots." The film and play are based on actual events that took place in Los Angeles in the early 1940s.

1970s. For many young people in this era, life in America demanded soul-searching. The Civil Rights movement, the war in Vietnam and the anti-war movement, and the counterculture of drugs, music, and free love all caused young Americans to question their own values and decide upon their own identity. Never before had widespread social movements caused such a generational rift between old and young. The resulting shift in values and norms has made a huge impact on twentieth-century literature as well as on Dubus's writing.

***Oprah, the Movies, and Success at Last*** *House of Sand and Fog*, Dubus's third work, took him four years to write and was turned down by more than twenty publishers before it was finally accepted and published in 1999. The novel concerns a tragic conflict between a mentally unstable American woman and an Iranian immigrant who buys her house after it is seized for nonpayment of taxes. Dubus's inspiration for the novel came from his experiences with the Iranian family of a woman he had dated for several years while pursuing his undergraduate degree and from a newspaper clipping that detailed the story of an older woman who was wrongly evicted from her home for not paying taxes (which she in fact did not owe). The man who bought her house at auction was named

Mohammed, which sparked Dubus's interest in incorporating the Iranian expatriate element into the novel.

Although the novel did well after publication, moving to the top of the *New York Times* bestseller list, it became a publishing phenomenon after being chosen by talk show personality Oprah Winfrey as an Oprah Book Club selection in 2000. Sales of the novel went from 165,000 copies to more than 1,700,000. In 2003, *House of Sand and Fog* was made into a feature film directed by Vadim Perelman and starring Oscar-winning actors Jennifer Connelly and Ben Kingsley.

***Inside the Mind of a Terrorist*** Dubus followed up *House of Sand and Fog* with the 2008 novel *The Garden of Last Days* a novel set in 2001 and inspired by reports that one of the terrorist hijackers responsible for the September 11, 2001, attacks on the United States visited a Florida strip club while in the state taking flying lessons. The novel, like *House of Sand and Fog*, is a tragedy that springs from chance interactions and seemingly banal coincidences.

Dubus lives with his family in Newbury, Massachusetts, and is an adjunct faculty member at the University of Massachusetts, Lowell.

## Works in Literary Context

***Realism*** Dubus's work belongs to the tradition of American literary realism, a style that formed in the nineteenth century with writers like Mark Twain and Henry James and persisted alongside the many stylistic movements that changed the face of American literature, from Modernism to postmodernism. At its origins, American literary realism aimed at an honest representation of life as it was lived by Americans at all levels of society, with whatever grit, suffering, and struggle made that representation accurate. While the movement's philosophical edge might have been dulled by the end of the nineteenth century, writers have continued to portray life as it is actually lived, by real people. From writers like Ernest Hemingway, F. Scott Fitzgerald, and Katherine Anne Porter, through Philip Roth, Norman Mailer, and J. D. Salinger, to John Updike, Andre Dubus (Dubus III's father), and Joyce Carol Oates, the practice of representing life's powerful stories in plain, direct language has remained a powerful literary presence. Dubus's novels and stories carry on this tradition, turning features of everyday life into the driving themes of the works themselves.

## Works in Critical Context

***The Cage Keeper and Other Stories*** Dubus's first published book, *The Cage Keeper and Other Stories*, received few reviews. Starr E. Smith of the *Library Journal* gave the collection an A grade, while the *New York Times Book Review* critic Deborah Solomon stated that it was an average book. A review in the the *Los Angeles Times* described the collection as "Darkly powerful stories of the American underclass: drifters, bikers, ex-cons and drop-outs." Another reviewer from the *Los Angeles Times*, asserted that Dubus "crafts powerful stories about people struggling to find something to affirm in the weary souls and bleak surroundings." Given Dubus's popularity following his novel *House of Sand and Fog* (1999), these stories may receive more critical attention in the future.

***Bluesman*** *Bluesman*, Dubus's second published book, earned praise from some critics for its portrayal of the Vietnam War and war era: a *Publishers Weekly* review commented that "Dubus . . . understands the rhythms of hard labor and the needs of the people who do it; the sensitivity and decency of his working-class heroes make them genuinely compelling and likeable." Patrick Samway, in his review for *America*, asserted: "Dubus deftly explores what he seems to know best: family life, music and searching for love." With the publication of the Vintage Contemporary edition, one reviewer from the *TLS: The Times Literary Supplement* stated that the novel is "written with a thoughtful eye that marks the casual detail of important events, although it often misses the mark in its assessments of what distance to keep in relation to adolescent preoccupations."

***House of Sand and Fog*** Dubus received high praise for *House of Sand and Fog*. Even before the fanfare that comes with being named an Oprah book, critics had already heralded the novel. Larry Weissman asserted in *Bold Type Magazine* that "Though their decisions are often infuriating, these characters are as real and involving as any in contemporary literature. Told with generous empathy, *House of Sand and Fog* is a powerful modern-day Greek tragedy that marks the arrival of a true literary star." Richard Eder called the novel "fine and prophetic" in his review in *Newsday*, yet he noticed two elements with which he takes issue: the "code switching" of Colonel Behrani from Persian language to English, and the "madness and violence" to which the book descends at the end. Ultimately, however, Eder praised the novel for its originality and integrity. Reba Leiding of *Library Journal* felt that the novel conveyed "a hard-edged, cinematic quality, but unlike many movies, its outcome is unexpected." Few if any critics wrote negative reviews of the novel, and *House of Sand and Fog* was a finalist for the 1999 National Book Award in fiction.

## Responses to Literature

1. *House of Sand and Fog* paints a very dark portrait of life in America for Iranian immigrants. Firoozeh Dumas's collection of essays, *Funny in Farsi: A Memoir of Growing Up Iranian in America* (2003) shows the lighter side of the immigrant experience. Read both books, and contemplate the contrast. Is there something essential about the experience that manages to come through?

2. *The Garden of Last Days* explores the mind of the terrorist Bassam before he commits his crime. Use your library and the internet to research the activities of the real-life 9/11 terrorists, and write a paper comparing the fictional version with reality.

3. Popular culture is filled with films about the Vietnam War, as diverse as *Good Morning, Vietnam* (1987) and *Apocalypse Now* (1987). View a film about the war and discuss its point of view. Does it comment on the war's impact on society? Are there any heroes?

4. *House of Sand and Fog* got great reviews as a book, and was then made into a successful film that nevertheless got mixed reviews. Write a paper in which you ponder the transformation from page to screen. You might focus on the aspects of the story that translate well to a visual medium, or you could comment on the director's interpretive choices in making that translation. How do the two versions differ? Would you have done anything differently?

BIBLIOGRAPHY

**Periodicals**

Eder, Richard. "Strangers in a Strange Land." *Newsday*, February 22, 1999.

Kramer, Jerome V. "Double Dubus." *Book*, March/April 1999.

Macgowan, James. "Oprah Helps a Son Come into His Own" *Ottawa Citizen*, May 13, 2001.

Markovits, Benjamin. "Going to Truth City." *TLS: The Times Literary Supplement*, September 21, 2001.

Raksin, Alex. "Fiction in Brief." *The Los Angeles Times*, March 5, 1989.

Smith, Starr E. Review of *The Cage Keeper and Other Stories. Library Journal* January 1, 1989.

Solomon, Charles. Review of *The Cage Keeper and Other Stories. The Los Angeles Times*, February 11, 1990.

Solomon, Deborah. "In Short; Fiction". *The New York Times Book Review*, February 5, 1989.

**Web Sites**

Birnbaum, Robert. "Interview: Andre Dubus III." *Identity Theory/The Narrative Thread*. Accessed September 23, 2008. http://www.identitytheory. com/people/birnbaum3.html

Weissman, Larry. "A Conversation with Andre Dubus III." *Bold Type*. Accessed September 23, 2008. http://www.randomhouse.com/boldtype/0300/ dubus/interview.html

# ✸ Firoozeh Dumas

BORN: *1966, Abadan, Iran*

NATIONALITY: *American*

GENRE: *Memoir*

MAJOR WORKS:

*Funny in Farsi: A Memoir of Growing Up Iranian in America* (2003)

*Laughing Without an Accent: Adventures of an Iranian-American, at Home and Abroad* (2008)

# LITERARY AND HISTORICAL CONTEMPORARIES

Dumas's famous contemporaries include:

**Jhumpa Lahiri** (1967–): London-born American writer of Indian origin. Jhumpa Lahiri's first book, the story collection *Interpreter of Maladies* (1999) won the Pulitzer Prize for fiction. These stories, as well as those of her subsequent works of fiction, deal intimately with the struggles of immigrants to assimilate into American society.

**Marjane Satrapi** (1969–): Iranian-born graphic novelist. Marjane Satrapi is an Iranian-born writer and illustrator whose comic book series *Persepolis* is a memoir of growing up during the Islamic Revolution and the Iran-Iraq war. *Persepolis*, originally written in French, has been translated into numerous languages and has recently been made into an Oscar-nominated animated feature film, released in 2007.

**Mahmoud Ahmadinejad** (1956–): President of Iran since 2005. Mahmoud Ahmadinejad spent his early career in academia (he holds a PhD and taught civil engineering) before becoming involved in politics. He was elected to the highest office in Iran on a populist platform, aiming to share oil profits with the Iranian citizenry. He has been an outspoken opponent of the United States and takes a radical anti-Israel stance.

**David Sedaris** (1957–): American essayist. Like Dumas, David Sedaris has mastered the art of turning the woes of childhood and family life into engaging, humorous stories that, quirky as they are, have a universal appeal. His humorous essays on growing up eccentric in an eccentric family are collected in such acclaimed volumes as *Holidays on Ice* (1997), *Me Talk Pretty One Day* (2000), and *Dress Your Family in Corduroy and Denim* (2004).

## Overview

With no background as a writer whatsoever, Firoozeh Dumas sat down to record the funny stories from her childhood for the benefit of her two daughters. Dumas's tales of her Iranian-American childhood in the shadow of the Iranian Revolution wound up striking a universally human note. Her first book, *Funny in Farsi: A Memoir of Growing Up Iranian in America* (2003) has been embraced by communities around the country and even in Iran.

## Works in Biographical and Historical Context

*Growing Up in America During the Iranian Revolution* Firoozeh Dumas (born Firoozeh Jazayeri) was seven years old in 1972 when her father, an Iranian petroleum engineer, brought her family to America. They lived for two years in the town of Whittier, California, a suburb of Los Angeles, before heading back to Tehran, Iran, where the family stayed for another two years. They returned permanently to Southern California, first settling in Whittier and then Newport Beach, and began a long process of assimilation that taught Dumas a great deal about the American character as well as her own place in the world as an Iranian-American.

Dumas's family left Iran during the oppressive regime of the U.S.-backed dictator Shah Muhammed Reza Pahlavi, when corruption, inflation, and shortages often made for a tough life. Life in California was, by contrast, full of freedom, abundance, and opportunity. The family watched from afar as the Iranian Revolution took hold in 1979, overthrowing the shah's monarchy and instituting an Islamic republic under the control of Muslim cleric Ayatollah Khomeini in its place. Unfortunately for Iranians living in America, the revolutionaries were hostile to the influence of the West in their country. In the United States, the public was appalled by what they saw as an extremist, ultra-religious uprising against a pro-U.S. government. Public opinion turned sharply against Iran when a group of militant students stormed the U.S. Embassy in Tehran and took 52 American diplomats hostage for 444 days, provoking an international crisis. Iranians who managed to emigrate at this time, including some of Dumas's relatives, were received coldly, if not with hostility, by Americans.

*College and Beyond* When Dumas headed north for college, to attend the University of California, Berkeley, she entered a university still humming with the spirit of the student protests of the late 1960s. Berkeley had been famed for its student activism since the free-speech movement of 1964 and the clash between the students and the university in 1969 over a plot of land known as People's Park. Dumas was prepared for the politicized atmosphere of Berkeley college life; what she was not prepared for was all the partying and binge drinking. As a non-drinker, Dumas had to find other ways to socialize, which produced its share of comedy: she once joined a church group, thinking it might provide some nonalcoholic fun. As she writes in *Laughing Without an Accent: Adventures of an Iranian-American, at Home and Abroad* (2008), her second book, "They probably would have been fun if there had been more than six of them and if I had not mentioned that I was Muslim."

Dumas met her husband at college and refers to him as "the Frenchman." The relationship meant yet another encounter with culture shock, but they formed what Dumas refers to as a one-couple melting pot. Dumas and her family currently live in Palo Alto, California, with Dumas traveling regularly to speaking engagements across the country. She also performs *Laughing Without an Accent* as a one-woman show.

## Works in Literary Context

*The Immigrant Experience* Dumas's books carry on a powerful tradition of documenting the immigrant experience in America, and are at home with such works as Amy Tan's *The Joy Luck Club* (1989), Jhumpa Lahiri's *Interpreter of Maladies* (1999), and Junot Diaz's *Drown* (1996). Dumas's first book, *Funny in Farsi* is a quintessential immigrant story, complete with the tug-of-war between cultures, the shedding of old skin and fitting uneasily into the new. Dumas makes her points about assimilation and cultural displacement without underlining them with a heavy hand, but takes care to show her readers the prejudices and cultural ignorance her family had to deal with. Dumas writes about her relatives who immigrated after the Iranian Revolution of 1979: "The Americans they met rarely invited them to their houses. These Americans felt that they knew all about Iran and its people, and they had no questions, just opinions."

Dumas's second book, *Laughing Without an Accent* continues in the same vein as *Funny in Farsi*, this time going deeper into the experience of culture shock that extended into her college years, but also presenting stories of life back in Iran. Both books are part humor, part memoir, and as such, they belong to the traditions of both literary genres. It is rare, however, to find the same book acclaimed as humor and as non-fiction: *Funny in Farsi* was a finalist for both the PEN/USA Award and the Thurber Prize for American Humor.

## Works in Critical Context

*Funny in Farsi* Both of Dumas's literary efforts have been received warmly immediately upon their release. According to Kristine Huntley in *Booklist*, *Funny in Farsi* provides "a unique perspective on American culture." The book has sold very well among Iranian-Americans but has also found a mainstream audience of readers seeking to learn more about the immigrant experience. *A Kirkus Reviews* critic described the work as "light-as-air essays" that are "warm and engaging." *Library Journal* correspondent Debra Moore dubbed the book "a valuable glimpse into the immigrant experiences of one very entertaining family." Susan H. Woodcock in *School Library Journal* felt that Dumas's humor "allows natives and non-natives alike to look at America with new insight."

*Laughing Without an Accent* As for Dumas's follow-up collection, Lee Thomas, in *The San Francisco Chronicle*, writes that in *Laughing Without an Accent* Dumas "exudes undeniable charm" even if "the stories can seem a bit rambling at times, a bit unevenly paced, as if the reader were tagging along to a friend's family reunion." Dumas was interviewed about the book on NPR on June 21, 2008, and has spent the past five years traveling the country, speaking at graduation ceremonies, libraries, churches, synagogues, and mosques.

### COMMON HUMAN EXPERIENCE

Here are some other works whose creators found, like Dumas, that growing up, however painful, can be seriously funny:

*Running With Scissors: A Memoir* (2002), a memoir by Augusten Burroughs. Burroughs no doubt wins the prize for most eccentric cast of characters in a memoir, though the frequent laughs Burroughs's writing elicits do very little to obscure the suffering and heartbreak of growing up the way he did.

*Dress Your Family in Corduroy and Denim* (2004), essays by David Sedaris. While most of David Sedaris's books deal with his upbringing in a very eccentric family, *Dress Your Family in Corduroy and Denim* describes his family in hilarious detail that has been softened by time and by love.

*Radio Days* (1987), a film by Woody Allen. *Radio Days* is Woody Allen's look back on childhood in the 1940s, the golden age of the radio, amid the chaos of an extended family living together in Queens, New York.

*The Wonder Years* (1988–1993), a television "dramedy" created by Carol Black and Neal Marlens. *The Wonder Years* traces the awkward teenage years of Kevin Arnold from 1968 to 1973 as he confronts the standard bugbears of adolescence, from girls and bullies to a strict father, as well as the major changes going on in the world around him.

## Responses to Literature

1. Find out more about the roots of current tensions between the governments of the United States and Iran by reading *All the Shah's Men: An American Coup and the Roots of Middle East Terror* (2005) by Stephen Kinzer. Kinzer, a veteran foreign correspondent, focuses on American involvement in the 1953 overthrow of Iran's elected leader Mohammad Mossadegh.

2. Firoozeh Dumas's essays describe a foreign family trying to fit into American culture, as do many memoirs, essays, and stories written by and about immigrants. Read one of Dumas's works and write a paper in which you compare her struggles with those of average Americans.

3. Relations between the governments of Iran and the United States have ranged from tense to outright hostile for a generation. The actions of a government, however, do not necessarily reflect the sum total of a nation's culture. In Iran, modern popular culture flourishes, from rock bands to cinema. Using the Internet and your library, find out about modern Iranian culture, choosing an art form or a social movement to focus on, and write a report summing up your findings.

4. Get in touch with somebody who is new to the United States, through your school or church, and conduct an interview of that person. Ask her to tell you her story. What was life like before she emigrated? What was the journey and transition like? How has she managed with a new language and new customs? Bring a tape recorder or, if you do not have access to one, make sure to type up your notes afterward while they're still fresh in your mind.

BIBLIOGRAPHY

**Periodicals**

Huntley, Kristine. Review of *Funny in Farsi: A Memoir of Growing Up Iranian in America*. *Booklist*, June 1, 2003.

Review of *Funny in Farsi: A Memoir of Growing Up Iranian in America*. *Kirkus Reviews*, May 1, 2003.

Moore, Debra. Review of *Funny in Farsi: A Memoir of Growing Up Iranian in America*. *Library Journal*, April 1, 2003.

Saidi, Janet. "Comedy of Growing Up Unveiled". *Christian Science Monitor*, July 10, 2003.

Silverstone, Mina. "Funny in Farsi: Author in LA." *Salam Worldwide*, July 2, 2003.

"This American Life." *LA Weekly*, July 31, 2003.

Thomas, Lee. "Memoir Review: *Laughing Without an Accent*". *San Francisco Chronicle*, May 28, 2008.

Toosi, Nahal. "Memoir Shows Culture Shock Can Be a Laughing Matter." *Milwaukee Journal Sentinel*, June 28, 2003.

Woodcock, Susan H. Review of *Funny in Farsi: A Memoir of Growing Up Iranian in America*. *School Library Journal*, November, 2003.

**Web Sites**

Dumas, Firoozeh. http://www.firoozehdumas.com.

## ⚘ Paul Laurence Dunbar

BORN: *1872, Dayton, Ohio*

DIED: *1906, Dayton, Ohio*

NATIONALITY: *American*

GENRE: *Poetry, fiction*

MAJOR WORKS:

*Oak and Ivy* (1892)

*Lyrics of Lowly Life* (1897)

*The Uncalled: A Novel* (1899)

*The Strength of Gideon and Other Stories* (1900)

*Lyrics of Sunshine and Shadow* (1905)

### Overview

Paul Laurence Dunbar was the first black American to achieve national renown as a writer. A prolific writer in both prose and verse, he has in recent years received

Paul Laurence Dunbar    *Dunbar, Paul Laurence, photograph. The Library of Congress.*

increasing recognition for his novels and short stories, but it was as a poet that he won his fame and continues to be best remembered. Dunbar was the first black writer to have his work published by major American magazines and publishing houses, which guided the literary tastes of an almost entirely white audience. Like many artists who died young, Dunbar was remarkably prolific right up to the end.

### Works in Biographical and Historical Context

*The Child of Slaves*    Paul Laurence Dunbar was born on June 27, 1872, in Dayton, Ohio, the child of freed slaves who had made their way north from Kentucky. His parents, who divorced in 1876, told Dunbar stories of their experience as slaves, and he would later draw on these tales in writing many of his dialect poems and plantation stories. Dunbar's childhood and schooling in Dayton were happy, fulfilling, and almost untouched by racial prejudice. He began writing poetry in earnest at age twelve, publishing his first three poems in the *Dayton Herald* when he was fourteen.

After graduation Dunbar took a job as an elevator boy in an office building, finding himself shut out of Dayton's business and professional worlds. But he kept writing and publishing poems, articles, and stories, and passed time in the elevator reading and rereading his favorite poets, including William Shakespeare, Edgar Allan Poe, Tennyson, and—perhaps most important of all—James Whitcomb Riley, at that time probably the most popular and widely read poet in America. Riley's use of dialect and humor were to be especially influential on Dunbar's later work. Dunbar's short story, "One Man's Fortunes," written later in his career, reflects this period of his life.

In the summer of 1892 the Western Association of Writers met in Dayton, where one of Dunbar's former high-school teachers arranged for him to read his work at a meeting. His listeners were impressed enough to ask Dunbar to join their association, and one even wrote a piece about him that was reprinted in newspapers across the Midwest. It caught the attention of James Whitcomb Riley, who sent Dunbar a letter of encouragement. Dunbar decided to publish a collection of poems, *Oak and Ivy* at his own expense, paying the printer by installments from the proceeds of sales of the book to subscribers and audiences at his readings.

**The World Beyond Ohio**   In June 1893 Dunbar determined to try his luck in the big city and made his way to Chicago, where he hoped to find work in the World's Columbian Exposition, the first world's fair. There he made the acquaintance of Frederick Douglass, the foremost black abolitionist leader in nineteenth-century America, who arranged for Dunbar to read a selection of his poems at the Colored American Day celebrations at the Exposition. Through Douglass, Dunbar also met a number of young black writers and performers, including the composer Will Marion Cook, with whom he would later collaborate writing musicals for black theaters.

After the stimulating experience of Chicago, Dunbar returned to Dayton to work on his next collection. His work had continued to be accepted in local newspapers and in 1895 it began to appear in major newspapers such as the *New York Times* and in popular and national magazines such as the *Independent* and the *Century* magazine. With the financial assistance of his friends and patrons, Dunbar published his second book, *Majors and Minors* (1895). The book shows the influence of a burgeoning civil rights movement in the African American community that began to coalesce in response to the passage of numerous so-called Jim Crow laws—laws designed to keep black Americans from exercising their voting right and segregate them from white society. Such laws received support at the highest levels of the U.S. government; for example, the Supreme Court decision *Plessy v. Ferguson* (1896) maintained that African Americans could legally be separated from white Americans in the public school system. Coupled with the increase in laws discriminating against blacks was a dramatic surge in violence against blacks, especially in the South. Lynchings by such hate groups as the Ku Klux Klan had been common in the period immediately following the Amer-

ican Civil War (1861–1865), but had diminished for some years before spiking again in the 1890s. In 1892 alone, 161 African Americans were killed by mobs. In all, more than 700 African Americans were lynched in the 1890s.

A copy of *Majors and Minors* eventually reached the hands of William Dean Howells, the most influential literary critic in America. His review of Dunbar's volume of poems was life-changing. (See "Works in Critical Context" for more on Howells's review.) In 1896 Dunbar was invited to New York, where he met Howells and Major James B. Pond, a well-known entrepreneur of the literary-lecture circuit. Dunbar, who was already an accomplished reader of his own work, gave a number of readings in the New York area and became a new kind of celebrity, attracting offers from publishers. The best offer, from Dodd, Mead, including an advance payment of $400 for Dunbar's next book, *Lyrics of Lowly Life*, which included an introduction by Howells. Only 11 of the 105 poems in this volume were new, and none of this new material was particularly significant, but the volume was the most important Dunbar ever produced because it introduced his work to a nationwide audience.

**Marriage, and Making It as a Writer**   In 1896 and 1897 Dunbar also met many important people, notably two of the major black leaders of the time, Booker T. Washington and W. E. B. DuBois, with whom he often appeared on public platforms, reciting his own work in support of various black causes. Dunbar's deepest feelings on racial matters were expressed in a number of newspaper articles, published between 1898 and 1903, which reflect his hatred of oppression of African Americans as practiced in the South and often condoned in the North.

In February 1897 Dunbar met Alice Moore, whom he married in 1898. The two settled in Washington, where Dunbar's career entered its most buoyant and productive phase. His work was sought eagerly and accepted readily. In 1899, Dodd, Mead published *Lyrics of the Hearthside*.

While his career boomed, Dunbar's relationship with his wife was deteriorating. They separated permanently in 1902. Dunbar went on to collaborate on various theatrical ventures, from 1898 onward, with Will Marion Cook; the shows were considered by some to be racially degrading. Dunbar contributed the lyrics to some productions, including *Clorindy* (1898), *Uncle Eph's Christmas* (1899), *Jes Lak White Fo'ks* (1900), and *In Dahomey* (1902). *In Dahomey* became the first all-black show staged in the heart of New York's theater district; after a successful run there it was taken to London and achieved even greater success, including a command performance at Buckingham Palace. The shows were highly successful, yet the price of his success became apparent when one of the reviews of *Uncle Eph's Christmas* referred to Dunbar as the "prince of the coon song writers."

## LITERARY AND HISTORICAL CONTEMPORARIES

Paul Laurence Dunbar's famous contemporaries include:

**Wilbur and Orville Wright** (1867–1912 and 1871–1948, respectively): Aviation pioneers associated with the birth of the airplane not because they were the first humans to fly, but for their invention of the fixed-wing aircraft. Long before they flew it, however, they embarked on a short-lived printing venture with a teenaged Paul Laurence Dunbar, their schoolfellow in Dayton, Ohio.

**Theodore Dreiser** (1871–1945): American author of such novels as *Sister Carrie* (1900) and *An American Tragedy* (1925).

**Will Marion Cook** (1869–1944): African American musician and composer. A collaborator of Paul Laurence Dunbar's, Cook was one of the most famous composers of his day.

**Booker T. Washington** (1856–1915): African American author, orator, and political leader. Born into slavery, Washington rose to become first an educator, then an advocate for education for African Americans, and ultimately the most influential black American in the country.

***Decline, but No Fall*** Dunbar's health began to decline in 1899 following a bout with pneumonia that brought on latent tuberculosis. However, he continued give readings, and the four years following the onset of his illness were astonishingly prolific. His last years were troubled and unhappy, and not only because of the certainty of an early death and the failure of his marriage; he also felt that he had compromised his artistic talent for the sake of commercial success. Dunbar died in Dayton on February 9, 1906.

### Works in Literary Context

By the early stages of his short career Dunbar was remarkably well-read in the classic English and American poets. The stanza forms and formal diction of John Milton, John Dryden, Thomas Gray, and William Cowper, as well as established nineteenth-century American standards, are discernible in all his work.

***African-American Dialect Works and Racial Stereotypes*** Despite his grounding in the classics of Western literature, Dunbar is mostly remembered for his "dialect" poems—poems that represent the speech and culture of African American living in the late nineteenth century. Of the fifty-seven poems in *Oak and Ivy*, only six are in dialect. This ratio would change dramatically as Dunbar realized how popular his dialect works were. Afri-

can American dialect as a poetic voice was a natural and significant choice for Dunbar. It was a well-established mode in poetry and song for both black and white writers by the 1870s, and it had a tendency to present stereotypical and offensive portraits of black Americans. The two African American dialect pieces in *Oak and Ivy*, "A Banjo Song" and "Goin' Back," avoid the more grotesque exaggeration of comic verse by writers such as Thomas Nelson Page (author of romanticized stories of Southern slave life, such as those in *In Ole Virginia*, 1887), but they match very closely the characterization and sentiment of Page's stories about plantation blacks. They are the first intimation of what was to become Dunbar's heavy dependence, in verse and prose, on the largely degrading stereotypes of black character and language developed in the plantation tales and minstrel shows which had gained increasing popularity since the 1830s.

Dunbar's endeavors to express the life and soul of his race in poetry had not been simple or uncomplicated for him. There was immense difficulty in finding appropriate language and style, since there was no real precedent for Dunbar apart from minstrel shows (popular entertainments in the nineteenth century that offered up buffoonish and insulting versions of black characters for comic purposes) and the humor of a few dialect poets. But Dunbar also aspired to be more than a poet of racial themes. The larger proportion of his work in verse was without any racial connotation in style or subject. Yet his simple love poems, pastorals, meditative reflections, and poems of homespun philosophy are competent but usually unremarkable expressions in the mainstream verse tradition established principally by Longfellow, with an admixture of influence from Alfred Tennyson, John Keats, and such Americans as Bayard Taylor and Thomas Bailey Aldrich. The love poems are the strongest of these nonracial poems.

### Works in Critical Context

Dunbar achieved national fame almost overnight, when his book *Majors and Minors* was reviewed by William Dean Howells. Howells, a fellow Ohioan, had in the past introduced many other young writers to a wider public. His lengthy and reflective review of the book in *Harper's Weekly* for June 27, 1896, brought the young poet's name to the attention of readers throughout America, but it set a direction of criticism of Dunbar's work that persisted throughout his career and, as Dunbar himself came to feel, limited the development of his talent.

***Majors and Minors*** Howells rightly assumed that the "Majors" were poems in standard English and the "Minors" (about a quarter of the total and at the end of the book) were poems in dialect, but he declared that there was nothing in the standard-English poems that "except for the Negro face of the author" one could find especially notable. "It is when we come to Mr. Dunbar's Minors that we feel ourselves in the presence of a man with a direct and a fresh authority to do the kind of thing he is doing." He found some poems that "recall the too easy pathos of the pseudo-negro poetry of the minstrel show" but singled out "When Malindy Sings" for special praise as "purely and intensely black" and responded to "the strong full pulse of the music in all these things." He remarked that Dunbar was "the first man of his color to study his race objectively, to analyze it to himself, and then to represent it in art as he felt it and found it to be; to represent it humorously, yet tenderly, and above all so faithfully that we know the portrait to be undeniably like."

Dunbar well merited the accolade, first bestowed by Booker T. Washington and later repeated by critics and admirers of both races, of "Poet Laureate of the Negro Race." At his death and long afterward, his position as the first black writer in America to achieve national acclaim by his expression of the thoughts and feelings of his race was accepted without demur, but in the 1940s and 1950s a sharp reaction, typified by Victor Lawson's markedly hostile critical study, sought to emphasize Dunbar's concessions to the detrimental stereotyping of black life imposed by the demands of white publishers and editors. In recent years a critical reappraisal has begun, assisted by the publication of much previously uncollected work in *The Paul Laurence Dunbar Reader* (1975) and by the new historical awareness engendered by the development of black studies, which has made it possible to see Dunbar in the context of his own times. This reappraisal has so far gained most strength from study of the novels and stories, but there is a growing understanding of the particular merits of the poetry and an increased realization that the dialect poems are, in poet Nikki Giovanni's words, "the best examples of our plantation speech," that at their best they transcend the degrading tradition from which they appear to spring.

## Responses to Literature

1. Paul Laurence Dunbar earned an income and became famous doing readings of his own work. Attend an author's reading at a local bookstore—or locate a book on tape that is read by its author—and take notes on how the author reads his or her own work. Does the author seem to "perform" it, and to know the material by heart? How do the words sound coming out of the author's mouth? Write a paper in which you evaluate the reading, comparing it, if you can, to the plain words on the page.

2. Famous though he was, Paul Laurence Dunbar was not the first African American writer to come to public attention. Using your library and the internet, research other black poets and writers of the eighteenth and nineteenth centuries. Choose one that interests you, and write a paper that explores the triumphs and/or difficulties of writing as an African American in the early days of the country.

---

### COMMON HUMAN EXPERIENCE

Paul Laurence Dunbar's most celebrated mode of expression was the use of dialect in his poetry. Literature is filled with wonderful examples of the use of vernacular, or popular speech. Here are some other works whose characters or narrators express themselves in dialect:

*Adventures of Huckleberry Finn* (1885), a novel by Mark Twain. Considered by many critics to be the best American novel ever written, *Huckleberry Finn* makes masterful and careful use of various dialects common in Missouri in the 1830s. The book is the story of a pair of runaways: an adult slave named Jim and his uneducated, but wily, young friend Huck.

*Their Eyes Were Watching God* (1937), a novel by Zora Neale Hurston. Hurston's novel, set among the all-black towns of Florida in the early twentieth century, tells the story of Janie Crawford's awakening as she makes her way from innocent young girl to strong, self-sufficient woman.

*Jude the Obscure* (1895), a novel by Thomas Hardy. Like most of Thomas Hardy's novels, *Jude the Obscure* is set in the fictional region of Wessex, England, and many of its characters communicate in a dialect Hardy took from observations of real life.

*Trainspotting* (1993), a novel by Irvine Welsh. Welsh's disturbing and darkly comic novel about a group of friends and their various addictions is written in Scottish vernacular.

---

3. Using your library and the Internet, research nineteenth-century minstrelsy in America. Write a paper describing this tradition in American entertainment, tracing its roots and noting ways in which the tradition survives today.

BIBLIOGRAPHY

**Books**

Brawley, Benjamin. *Paul Laurence Dunbar: Poet of His People.* Chapel Hill: University of North Carolina Press, 1936.

Cunningham, Virginia. *Paul Laurence Dunbar and His Song.* New York: Dodd, Mead, 1947.

Gayle, Addison, Jr. *Oak and Ivy: A Biography of Paul Laurence Dunbar.* Garden City, N.J.: Doubleday, 1971.

Lawson, Victor. *Dunbar Critically Examined.* Washington, D.C.: Associated Publishers, 1941.

Martin, Jay, Ed. *A Singer in the Dawn: Reinterpretations of Paul Laurence Dunbar.* New York: Dodd, Mead, 1975.

Metcalf, E. W., Jr. *Paul Laurence Dunbar: A Bibliography.* Metuchen, N.J.: Scarecrow Press, 1975.

Redding, J. Saunders. *To Make a Poet Black*. Chapel Hill: University of North Carolina Press, 1939.

Wagner, Jean. *Black Poets of the United States: From Paul Laurence Dunbar to Langston Hughes*. Trans. Kenneth Douglas. Urbana: University of Illinois Press, 1973.

Alexander, Eleanor. *Lyrics of Sunshine and Shadow: The Tragic Courtship and Marriage of Paul Laurence Dunbar and Alice Ruth Moore: A History of Love and Violence Among the African American Elite*. New York: New York University Press, 2002.

Revell, Peter. *Paul Laurence Dunbar*. Boston: Twayne, 1979.

# ✸ Lois Duncan

BORN: *1934, Philadelphia, Pennsylvania*

NATIONALITY: *American*

GENRE: *Fiction, nonfiction*

MAJOR WORKS:

*Ransom* (1966)

*Hotel for Dogs* (1971)

*I Know What You Did Last Summer* (1973)

*Daughters of Eve* (1979)

Lois Duncan    *Duncan, Lois, photograph. Courtesy of Lois Duncan.*

## Overview

Award-winning writer Lois Duncan's young adult novels of suspense and the supernatural have made her a favorite of adult critics and young readers alike. According to reviewer Jennifer Moody, Duncan is "popular ... not only with the soft underbelly of the literary world, the children's book reviewers, but with its most hardened carapace, the teenage library book borrower."

## Works in Biographical and Historical Context

*A Young Creative Writer*    Lois Duncan Steinmetz was born in Philadelphia, Pennsylvania in 1934, and was raised in Sarasota, Florida. Duncan grew up in a creative family where her early efforts at writing were encouraged by her parents, noted photographers Joseph and Lois Steinmetz. She started writing stories for magazines as a preteen and progressed to book-length manuscripts as she matured. She enrolled in Duke University in 1952, but found it a difficult adjustment after the relaxed, creative environment in which she had been raised. She also grew frustrated with the lack of privacy in dormitory life, and left after one year to get married.

One of her first serious efforts at publication was a love story for teens, *Debutante Hill* (1958). The young homemaker and mother of three wrote this piece as a way of passing the lonely hours while her first husband served in the U.S. Air Force and then enrolled in law school.

When her first marriage ended in divorce, Duncan returned to magazine writing to support her family. In 1962 she relocated to Albuquerque, New Mexico, accepted a teaching job in the University of New Mexico's journalism department, and eventually earned her bachelor's degree. In 1965 she married engineer Don Arquette, with whom she had two more children. These changes inspired her to begin writing fiction again. In this period, she wrote *Ransom* (1966), a suspense novel that set the tone for the rest of her lucrative career in young adult fiction. While teaching, studying, and raising her five children, Duncan continued to publish young adult suspense novels along the lines of *Ransom*, including *I Know What You Did Last Summer* (1973), *Down a Dark Hall* (1974), and *Summer of Fear* (1976).

*A Real-Life Murder*    In 1989 Duncan's youngest daughter, Kaitlyn, was murdered in an incident that paralleled the plot of *Don't Look behind You*, a novel Duncan had published just a month before the crime took place. In the novel, the character April—who was based on Kaitlyn—is run down and killed by a hitman in a Camaro. In real life, Kaitlyn was chased down and shot to death by someone driving the same type of automobile. The similarities between the fictional crime and the real one were unmistakable. Furthermore, the brutal crime ultimately involved Duncan and her family in a police investigation similar to that described in *Killing Mr. Griffin* (1978).

It also featured their use of a psychic similar to the one described in Duncan's novel *The Third Eye* (1984). Although three men were arrested in connection with the murder of Duncan's daughter, none were ever charged.

Duncan shared her tragic experience with readers in *Who Killed My Daughter?* (1992), in the hope that it might be read by someone with information regarding the chilling event. Through private investigators hired by the family, she learned that her daughter's boyfriend had been involved in an insurance fraud scam, and Duncan came to suspect that Kaitlyn had learned of the scam and was planning to break up with him. As the facts became known, Duncan realized that other circumstances surrounding her daughter's murder paralleled her fiction. The murder of Kaitlyn Duncan remains unsolved, however.

*A New Focus*  For the next few years Duncan focused on editing collections of suspenseful short fiction and penning books for younger readers, such as *The Circus Comes Home: When the Greatest Show on Earth Rode the Rails* (1993), about the Ringling Brothers-Barnum & Bailey circus that wintered near Duncan's childhood home in Florida. She also produced *The Magic of Spider Woman* (1996), a retelling of a Navajo myth. However, with *Gallows Hill* (1997), Duncan returned to her characteristic suspense format.

Several of Duncan's books have found their way onto television and movie screens, including *I Know What You Did Last Summer*. A movie version of *Hotel for Dogs* was in production as of 2008.

## Works in Literary Context

As a prolific writer of primarily young adult fiction, Duncan benefited from a shift in cultural mores as society loosened up in the 1960s. When she began writing her first suspense novel, *Ransom* (1966), Duncan found she was no longer constricted by many of the taboos of the 1950s. When Duncan's publisher refused to handle the book because it deviated from her former style, Doubleday took it on, and *Ransom* became a runner-up for the prestigious Edgar Allan Poe Award. Duncan's story of five teenagers kidnapped by a school-bus driver also received a healthy dose of critical praise, with reviewer Dorothy M. Broderick commenting in the *New York Times Book Review* that the character of Glenn Kirtland, whose consistently selfish behavior endangers the whole group, "sets the book apart and makes it something more than another good mystery." *Ransom* firmly established Duncan in a genre she would master to great success.

Duncan's writing style remained consistent and simple. As a writer for *Twentieth-Century Children's Writers* once observed, Duncan "places an individual or a group of normal, believable young people in what appears to be a prosaic setting, such as a suburban neighborhood or an American high school. On the surface everything is as it should be, until Duncan introduces an element of sur-

prise that gives the story an entirely new twist." These surprise elements often feature the supernatural. In *Summer of Fear*, for example, a young witch charms herself into an unsuspecting family, while *Down a Dark Hall* involves a girls' boarding school whose students are endangered by the malevolent ghosts of dead artists and writers. With its deployment of supernatural elements, Duncan's novels merge young adult fiction with fantasy, separating them from other popular young adult novels such as those by Judy Blume, but linking them to a long tradition of popular fiction that goes back to the gothic novels of the early nineteenth century.

## Works in Critical Context

Ever since her earliest successes with young adult fiction, critics have appreciated the extent to which Duncan takes adolescence seriously. As critic Sarah Hayes has observed in the *Times Literary Supplement,* "Duncan understands the teenage world and its passionate concerns with matters as

Duncan's famous contemporaries include:

**Joan Didion** (1934–): Like Duncan, American author Joan Didion's writing spanned many genres—novel, nonfiction, and journalism, to name a few. For books like *Slouching Toward Bethlehem* (1968) and *Salvador* (1983), Didion has earned high praise for her highly polished style, keen intelligence, and provocative social commentary.

**Judy Blume** (1938–): The author of more than twenty books for children and young adults, Judy Blume became the humorous voice of both the thrill and the awkwardness of adolescence. Her novels *Are You There God? It's Me, Margaret* (1970) and *Blubber* (1974), among many others, have become classics for their frank and sometimes explicit handling of childhood and teenage experience.

**Stephen King** (1947–): American author Stephen King has been famous for his frightening tales ever since the success of his first novel, *Carrie* (1974), about an outcast high-school girl with telekinetic powers. King's powerful gift for storytelling has meant that many of his novels—not all of them belonging to the horror genre—have been made into films.

**Gloria Steinem** (1934–): Steinem is an American journalist and women's-rights activist. As cofounder of the National Women's Political Caucus and founder of the feminist magazine *Ms.* in 1972, Gloria Steinem remains a chief icon for her foundational writings on women's issues and her ongoing political activism.

# COMMON HUMAN EXPERIENCE

One of Lois Duncan's plot standbys is the plan that goes wrong, an experience many readers can identify with. Plans gone wrong allow for characters' true colors to come out, and for tension and suspense to begin in earnest. Here are some other works that take advantage of this device:

*Crime and Punishment* (1866), a novel by Fyodor Dostoevsky. The hero of this classic Russian novel, young Raskolnikov, carefully plans the murder of an old woman. He is unprepared, however, for the psychological torments and the cat-and-mouse game that follow his deed.

*Macbeth* (1606) a play by William Shakespeare. One of Shakespeare's greatest tragedies, *Macbeth* is based on actual historical events. Macbeth and his wife scheme to kill their king and take control of Scotland, where Macbeth is a nobleman. What they fail to understand, however, is the force of the prophecies that predict their fatal mistakes, and the plan results in tragedy.

*Raising Arizona* (1987), a film by Ethan and Joel Coen. In this comedy, an infertile couple, one of them a petty career criminal, decides to kidnap one of a set of quintuplets to raise as their own. They make off with the baby, but are soon beset by crime buddies, counter-kidnappers, and blackmailers who want the baby for themselves.

diverse as dress, death, romance, school, self-image, sex and problem parents." While other young adult writers tend to show teenage life in a humorous, optimistic light, Hayes notes that "Duncan suggests that life is neither as prosaic nor as straightforward as it seems at first."

Duncan's use of evil and the supernatural in her plots has also been praised. "It is a mark of Duncan's ability as a writer that the evils she describes are perfectly plausible and believable," notes an essayist in *St. James Guide to Young Adult Writers*. "As in her use of the occult, her use of warped human nature as a tool to move the plot along briskly never seems contrived or used solely for shock effect; it is integral to the story." An example of this is found in *Stranger with My Face* (1981), which details a young girl's struggle to avoid being possessed by her twin sister, who uses astral projection to take over the bodies of others. While in another author's hands the novel's premise might be difficult to accept, "Duncan makes it possible and palatable by a deft twining of fantasy and reality, by giving depth to characters and relationships, and by writing with perception and vitality," writes Zena Sutherland in the *Bulletin of the Center*

*for Children's Books.* This depth is typical of all of Duncan's mystic novels, and a main reason for her success. As the writer for *Twentieth-Century Children's Writers* commented, "an element of the occult is an integral part of [Duncan's] fast-moving plot, but it is always believable because Duncan never carries her depiction of the supernatural into the sometimes goofy realms that a writer such as Stephen King does. Character and plot are always predominant; the books are first and foremost good mysteries made even more interesting for young readers by some aspect of the unusual."

*Who Killed My Daughter?*, Duncan's first work of nonfiction, was praised by numerous reviewers and was nominated for teen reading awards in nine states. According to *Kliatt* contributor Claire Rosser, readers "will find this tragedy all the more poignant simply because it is horrifyingly true." While Mary Jane Santos notes in her appraisal for *Voice of Youth Advocates* that readers might "get lost in the myriad of minutia" that Duncan marshals in her effort to solve her daughter's murder—numerous transcripts and other factual evidence is presented in the book—the critic ultimately concludes that "the strength and tenacity of Duncan is admirable." Critics were less unified when it came to Duncan's other non-fiction effort, however. *School Library Journal* contributor Cathy Chauvette found *Psychic Connections* (1995), a nonfiction work that explains to teens various types of psychic phenomenon such as ghosts, telepathy, and psychic healing, "compelling," while Nancy Glass Wright deemed the work in *Voice of Youth Advocates* "a comprehensive overview" that is only "sometimes riveting." *Bulletin for the Center of Children's Books* critic Deborah Stevenson was not impressed at all with *Psychic Connections*, calling it "successful neither as a collection of true mysterious tales nor as a science-based defense of a controversial subject."

## Responses to Literature

1. Lois Duncan has been praised for realistically portraying unrealistic stories, such as those that feature the supernatural. Discuss one of Duncan's books in which you think she successfully brought realism to a supernatural plots. What did you find believable about the story? What details add credibility to it? Does being able to believe it make the story better, in your opinion? Why or why not?

2. The Anglo-Irish writer Oscar Wilde once said, "Life imitates art far more than art imitates life." Write an essay on how this quote applies to the murder of Duncan's daughter, Kaitlyn, which eerily paralleled the plots of Duncan's novels. Be specific about which details, characters, and plot elements of Duncan's books were reflected in her daughter's murder.

3. Duncan's 1973 book, *I Know What You Did Last Summer*, was in 1997 made into a movie directed by Jim Gillespie. Read the book and then watch the

film, and compare and contrast their similarities and differences. What liberties did Gillespie take with Duncan's story? What similarities exist between the two versions? Make sure your answer contains specific details and references to both the book and the film.

BIBLIOGRAPHY

**Books**

Chevalier, Tracy, Ed. *Twentieth-Century Children's Writers*, 3rd edition. Detroit: St. James Press, 1989.

Duncan, Lois. *Chapters: My Growth as a Writer*. Boston: Little, Brown, 1982.

*St. James Guide to Young Adult Writers*, 2nd edition. Detroit: St. James Press, 1999.

**Periodicals**

Chauvette, Cathy. Review of *Psychic Connections. School Library Journal* (May 1997).

Hayes, Sarah. "Fatal Flaws". *Times Literary Supplement* (January 29–February 4, 1988).

Rosser, Claire. Review of *Who Killed My Daughter? Kliatt* (May 1994).

Santos, Mary Jane. Review of *Who Killed My Daughter? Voice of Youth Advocates* (December 1992).

Stevenson, Deborah. Review of *Psychic Connections. Bulletin of the Center for Children's Books* (September 1995).

Sutherland, Zena. Review of *Stranger with My Face* . *Bulletin of the Center for Children's Books* (April 1982).

Wright, Nancy Glass. Review of *Psychic Connections. Voice of Youth Advocates* (August 1995).

# ✸ Jonathan Edwards

BORN: *1703, East Windsor, Connecticut*

DIED: *1758, Princeton, New Jersey*

NATIONALITY: *American*

GENRE: *Nonfiction*

MAJOR WORKS:

*God Glorified in the Work of Redemption* (1731)

*A Faithful Narrative of the Surprising Work of God in the Conversion of Many Hundred Souls* (1736)

*Sinners in the Hands of an Angry God* (1741)

*A Farewell Sermon* (1751)

*The Great Christian Doctrine of Original Sin Defended* (1758)

## Overview

Philosopher, theologian, preacher, historian, and scientist, Jonathan Edwards was the most prolific writer of the American colonial period and one of the most prolific

Jonathan Edwards    *Edwards, Jonathan, photograph. The Library of Congress.*

authors in American history. Edwards is most remembered as the harsh dogmatist who terrified his listeners with his fire-and-brimstone sermon, *Sinners in the Hands of an Angry God* (1741). He was eventually rejected by his own congregation and sent into exile in the wilderness. But in reality, Edwards was a subtle, original metaphysician and ethicist whose ideas were right in line with the science and philosophy of his day.

## Works in Biographical and Historical Context

***An Early Education in the Life of the Mind***
Born in East Windsor, Connecticut, on October 5, 1703, Edwards was the fifth of eleven children and the only son of the Reverend Timothy Edwards and Esther Stoddard Edwards. His maternal grandfather was the Reverend Solomon Stoddard, a prominent preacher in the town of Northampton, Massachusetts. The family was connected to some of the most prominent figures in early America. Stoddard was the grand-nephew of John Winthrop, the first governor of Massachusetts, and took over as pastor for the brother of Increase Mather, the Puritan minister who was notoriously involved in the Salem Witch Trials. It was this powerful and prestigious line of ministers from which Edwards emerged.

Edwards's elementary education was provided by his father. Even as a child he brought a naturalist's eye to the world. At thirteen he matriculated at what eventually became Yale University, where he was influenced by the works of the British philosopher John Locke and the mathematician and physicist Sir Isaac Newton. During this time, he wrote notes for treatises that were titled "Of Being," "The Mind," and "Of Atoms", which were not published until after his death. The treatises discussed very weighty ideas for such a young thinker, indicating the young theologian's intelligence and sensitivity to some of the most challenging ideas of his time. In "Of Being," for example, Edwards argues that nonbeing or nothingness is inconceivable and hence cannot exist; being therefore exists necessarily, eternally, and everywhere.

### The Call of Church and Family

After graduating in 1720, Edwards remained at Yale for two years to study theology. During this time he overcame his intellectual objections to the Calvinist doctrine of predestination, which says that people are either saved or damned from all eternity regardless of their actions during their time on Earth. Early in 1721, he underwent a conversion experience, which led him to see predestination as beautiful and just. He preached these convictions in a Presbyterian church in New York City from August 1722 through March 1723. He received his M.A. in 1723 and tutored at Yale from 1724 until he became seriously ill in September 1725.

In August 1726, Edwards was asked to preach at the Northampton church of his grandfather Stoddard. That November he was invited to "settle" with the congregation and became his grandfather's assistant. He was ordained in February 1727, and that summer he married seventeen-year-old Sarah Pierrepont, the daughter of one of the founders of Yale. Stoddard died the following February, and Edwards succeeded him as pastor at Northampton. Like his own parents, Edwards and his wife had ten daughters and a son. Though infant mortality was high at the time, all eleven children survived infancy. Edwards tutored his daughters at home, and sent his son, Jonathan Jr., to school.

### Success at the Pulpit and Beyond

In July 1731, Edwards gave a public lecture in Boston that became the basis of his first published book, also published that year. *God Glorified in the Work of Redemption, by the Greatness of Man's Dependence upon Him in the Whole of It* holds that only God's grace, not human free will, can overcome the effects of original sin and result in salvation. With sermons delivered in 1734—published that same year as *A Divine and Supernatural Light, Immediately Imparted to the Soul by the Spirit of God*—Edwards sparked a revival movement in New England that resulted in the conversion of at least three hundred people. He documented the movement in *A Faithful Narrative of the Surprising Work of God in the Conversion of Many Hundred Souls* (1736). Edwards explains these conversions in detail, recording observations about the behavior of individuals before and after the conversion experience. The book went through three editions and twenty printings by 1740, and remained the standard guide for church revivals for the next hundred years.

Between 1740 and 1742, a wider revival movement, known as the Great Awakening, swept through the colonies. Edwards played a role in that movement with sermons such as *Sinners in the Hands of an Angry God* (1741). Edwards, whose prior sermons had been rational,

unemotional, and delivered without the arm-waving histrionics employed by many evangelists, began to change his style. In *Sinners in the Hands of an Angry God,* for example, he warned his audience:

> O sinner! Consider the fearful danger you are in: it is a great furnace of wrath, a wide and bottomless pit, full of the fire of wrath, that you are held over in the hand of that God, whose wrath is provoked and incensed as much against you, as against many of the damned in hell. You hang by a slender thread, with the flames of divine wrath flashing about it, and ready every moment to singe it, and burn it asunder; and you have no interest in any Mediator, and nothing to lay hold of to save yourself, nothing to keep off the flames of wrath, nothing of your own, nothing that you ever have done, nothing that you can do, to induce God to spare you one moment.

In his writings of this period, Edwards defends these spirited revivals against those who doubted their authenticity or whose theological perspective was contrary to the Calvinist view. He takes great pains to show that these revival experiences are consistent with his famous grandfather Stoddard's sermons from 1679, as well as with New Testament descriptions of conversion experiences.

### Trouble Brews

During this time, the churches of New England were increasingly discussing who should hold power in their organizations: the pastors, or their congregations. This debate soon began to hit home for Edwards, as tensions had been rising between Edwards and his congregation since 1734. The congregation thought that Edwards and his family did not live as frugally as a pastor should. Furthermore, Edwards was an intellectual, and many of his sermons were not understood by his parishioners. Lastly, although he was always ready to comfort the sick and afflicted, Edwards did not observe the custom of paying regular visits to parishioners' homes.

The breaking point came in 1749, when Edwards discontinued the time-honored practice of allowing church members to partake in the Eucharist, even if they had not undergone a conversion experience. Edwards thought that in order for churchgoers to take Communion, they had to publicly profess such a conversion—he wanted to see an "experience of the heart." Parishioners became disillusioned with Edwards, and one of them, a man whose father had committed suicide during the first of Edwards's revivals, led a movement that resulted in Edwards's dismissal in June, 1750.

After being dismissed from Northampton, Edwards received offers from several churches across America and in Scotland, but ultimately accepted one close to home, in Stockbridge, Massachusetts. Here he served as a missionary to Native Americans who barely understood his language, let alone his message. During this period the Edwardses became intimately involved in the French and

Indian War (1754–1763). The local Native Americans took the side of the French when the war broke out, while the Edwardses sided with the British. A fort was quickly built around the Edwards' home, where area residents and even some soldiers took shelter.

Edwards's last call was to serve as president of the College of New Jersey (which later became Princeton University) following the death of the former president, Edwards's son-in-law Aaron Burr, in September 1757. Edwards was inaugurated on February 16, 1758, but died of fever in March, a month after receiving a smallpox vaccine that was supposed to save his life.

## Works in Literary Context

*The Psychology of Religion*   Though Edwards was not the first American to pioneer the study of the psychology of religion—that honor belongs to American philosopher William James, who wrote, *The Varieties of Religious Experience: A Study in Human Nature* (1902)—Edwards's *A Faithful Narrative of the Surprising Work of God in the Conversion of Many Hundred Souls* (1736) is an important forerunner of the genre. Both Edwards and James deal with the essence of religious experiences. They seek to understand the changes they produce in the persons involved and make the experiences of individuals central. In fact, James cites Edwards extensively in *The Varieties of Religious Experience* when discussing the relationship of internal experience to outward behavior.

*The Jeremiad*   While Jonathan Edwards was a significant intellectual and the first comprehensive American philosopher, he saw his role primarily as that of a theologian. In his many published works, he devoted his intellectual energies to interpreting scripture and trying to make sense of what it means for regular people as they try to live their lives in accordance with it. As such, he was part of a tradition of reformed theologians that extends from John Calvin through John Witherspoon during the American Revolution, and Lyman Beecher during the early republic. As a composer of sermons, and the author of *Sinners in the Hands of an Angry God* (1741) in particular, Edwards mastered the sermon form known as the jeremiad, so-called because its approach originated with the biblical prophet Jeremiah. This type of sermon arose out of the tensions between secular and sacred fulfillment that characterized much of New England life in the last decades of the seventeenth century. Edwards's aim was to bring about a conversion, and he often did.

## Works in Critical Context

*Sinners in the Hands of an Angry God*   Though not a poet or writer of creative works, Jonathan Edwards nevertheless wrote with an imaginative and illuminating prose style. His sermons show a conscious commitment to imagery, an attempt to show that God may be com-

## LITERARY AND HISTORICAL CONTEMPORARIES

Jonathan Edwards's famous contemporaries include:

**George Whitefield** (1714–1770): English Methodist preacher. As a leader of the Methodist movement within the Church of England, George Whitefield traveled to America and led the Great Awakening, in which masses of people discovered a more personal approach to religious awareness.

**Benjamin Franklin** (1706–1790): American diplomat, inventor, politician, political theorist, and printer. As one of the Founding Fathers, Benjamin Franklin left his mark on the major events of early American history, from producing texts that define the American character, to securing the aid of the French in the Revolutionary War.

**Cotton Mather** (1663–1728): American Puritan minister. Cotton Mather, the son of Increase Mather, another prominent preacher, was a prolific writer on religious matters. He became one of the most influential spiritual leaders in America. He and his father are linked to the Salem Witch Trials of the 1690s, during which Cotton spoke out in support of the judges.

**David Hume** (1711–1776): Scottish philosopher. As one of the leading thinkers of the Enlightenment, David Hume espoused ideas almost directly contrary to the Puritan revivalists. Hume was a staunch critic of religion, placing value on the power of human reason rather than divine authority.

municated through the senses as well as through the language of scripture. It is not accidental, therefore, that Edwards is best remembered in the popular imagination for a single sermon, *Sinners in the Hands of an Angry God*. It was so successful that Edwards delivered it a second time. Today, it is the work by Edwards most often included in anthologies of American literature.

Most readers today find *Sinners in the Hands of an Angry God* as exciting as Edwards's eighteenth century listeners did, if not as frightening. Thomas J. Steele writes that the sermon is "a virtuoso performance upon the keyboard of the tactile sense, where his carefully contrived imagery evokes a remarkably profound response." Other present-day scholars recognize yet another aspect of Edwards's famous sermon: its ability to give comfort. As scholar Robert Lee Stuart writes, "Edwards wanted to frighten those who were complacent about the state of their souls. But fright was only the means to an end far more compassionate and human than most critics have recognized." In other words, critics now recognize the tough love behind Edwards's fire and brimstone imagery.

## COMMON HUMAN EXPERIENCE

Jonathan Edwards was fascinated by the conversion experience, a phenomenon he helped bring about in his parishioners. As a result, he wrote about these experiences at length. Here are some other works which focus on the conversion experience:

*The Apostle* (1997), a film written and directed by Robert Duvall. Emphasizing the power of personal faith and redemption, *The Apostle* tells the story of a present-day Evangelical preacher who falls from grace but manages to redeem himself and be born again.

*Wise Blood* (1952), a novel by Flannery O'Connor. Hazel Motes, the anti-hero of Flannery O'Connor's novel, has rejected the religion in which he was raised so intently. He sets out to preach the "Church without Christ". Events soon bring him so low that he winds up seeking redemption in the most extreme of ways.

*The Mission* (1986), a film directed by Roland Joffé. Set in South America in the eighteenth century, *The Mission* tells the story of a mercenary who has been enslaving the native people. When he undergoes a conversion of the soul, he joins forces with a Jesuit priest to attempt to save them. The film stars Robert De Niro and Jeremy Irons.

*The Autobiography of Malcolm X* (1965), as told to Alex Haley. *The Autobiography of Malcolm X* follows the life of the charismatic Malcolm Little, from his gambling and crime-ridden youth, to his conversion to Islam while in prison, to his rise as a leader of the controversial Nation of Islam and eventual assassination.

### Responses to Literature

1. *Sinners in the Hands of an Angry God* is famous for its powerful imagery, much of it frightening. Using your library and the Internet, locate some modern-day sermons. Compare the imagery used today with Edwards's language. Are there similarities and/or differences? What kinds of images do you think are most effective in reaching listeners in today's congregations?

2. While Edwards is most often remembered for one very memorable sermon, he published stacks of other powerful writing. Dig deeper into Edwards's other writings by searching out one or two of his other works. How do these "read" from a twenty-first century perspective? Do any of Edwards's ideas appeal to you? Do any of them offend you? Include pieces of the texts you have read in your answer.

3. Edwards was one of the most important figures of the Great Awakening, but the movement was far from a one-man show. Research another figure from the Great Awakening and write a paper in which you examine that figure's impact, writings, and effectiveness in bringing about the new religious consciousness.

BIBLIOGRAPHY

**Books**

Brand, David C. *Profile of the Last Puritan: Jonathan Edwards, Self–Love, and the Dawn of the Beatific.* Atlanta: Scholars Press, 1991.

Cherry, Conrad. *The Theology of Jonathan Edwards: A Reappraisal.* Garden City, N.Y.: Anchor, 1966; revised edition, Bloomington: Indiana University Press, 1990.

Elwood, Douglas J. *The Philosophical Theology of Jonathan Edwards.* New York: Columbia University Press, 1960.

Fiering, Norman. *Jonathan Edwards's Moral Thought and Its British Context.* Chapel Hill: University of North Carolina Press, 1981.

Jenson, Robert W. *America's Theologian: A Recommendation of Jonathan Edwards.* New York: Oxford University Press, 1988.

Smith, John E. *Jonathan Edwards: Puritan, Preacher, Philosopher.* Notre Dame, Ind.: University of Notre Dame Press, 1992.

Winslow, Ola Elizabeth. *Jonathan Edwards, 1703–1758: A Biography.* New York: Octagon, 1973.

**Periodicals**

Faust, Clarence H. "Jonathan Edwards as a Scientist," *American Literature* 1 (1930): 393–404.

Steele, Thomas J., S.J. and Eugene R. Delay. "Vertigo in History: The Threatening Tactility of 'Sinners in the Hands.'" *Early American Literature.* 1983–1984 Winter; 18 (3): 242–256.

Stuart, Robert Lee. "Jonathan Edwards at Enfield: 'And Oh the Cheerfulness and Pleasantness ... '" *American Literature: A Journal of Literary History, Criticism, and Bibliography* . 1976 Mar; 48 (1): 46–59.

## ❊ Dave Eggers

BORN: *1970, Boston, Massachusetts*

NATIONALITY: *American*

GENRE: *Fiction, nonfiction*

MAJOR WORKS:

*A Heartbreaking Work of Staggering Genius* (2000)

*You Shall Know Our Velocity* (2002)

*What Is the What: The Autobiography of Valentino Achak Deng* (2006)

## Overview

Dave Eggers has been widely recognized for his best-selling novelistic memoir, *A Heartbreaking Work of Staggering Genius* (2000), which recounts his experiences raising his eight-year-old brother while the author was in his early twenties. As the founder and editor of two humor and literary magazines, *Might* and *McSweeney's*, Eggers has made a name for himself as the voice of his generation, espousing an irreverent brand of ironic, self-conscious, postmodern humor that speaks to the twenty-something youth culture of the 1990s.

## Works in Biographical and Historical Context

*A Life-Changing Event*   Dave Eggers grew up in Lake Forest, Illinois, a well-to-do suburb not far from Chicago. His life changed dramatically during his senior year of college: he had been living at home to care for his mother, who was dying of stomach cancer, when his father suddenly and unexpectedly died of lung cancer. Less than five weeks later, his mother passed away. These deaths left Eggers and his three siblings orphans. Only one sibling, eight-year-old Christopher (nicknamed "Toph"), was still underage, and with the older brother and sister busy with their lives, Eggers took on the role of surrogate parent. Eggers's older sister Beth later noted in interviews that Eggers's book about these experiences downplays her role in helping to raise Christopher in order to exaggerate his responsibility as sole caretaker of their brother. She later recanted these claims.

In 1993, Eggers moved with Christopher from the family home in Illinois to San Francisco and Berkeley, California, where he pursued a career as a writer and editor and struggled through the daily challenges of parenting. Eggers held various odd jobs, including one for a geological-surveying company and another in the graphic-design department of the *San Francisco Chronicle*. He also created the satirical magazine *Might*, serving as the periodical's editor until it went out of business. Eggers then went on to work as an editor for *Esquire* magazine, but soon quit out of a distaste for the commercial publishing industry. In 1998 he founded *McSweeney's*, a quarterly print and online literary journal devoted to literature, culture, and politics. Eggers was twenty-nine when *A Heartbreaking Work of Staggering Genius*, his first book, was published in 2000. It catapulted him to the status of a nationally recognized young writer whom critic William Georgiades referred to as the year's "wonder boy of American letters."

*Branching Out as a Writer and an Activist*
Eggers again experienced family tragedy in 2001, when his sister Beth committed suicide with an overdose of antidepressants. Despite the emotional setback, Eggers published in the following year the novel *You Shall Know Our Velocity*, which follows two childhood friends as they

## LITERARY AND HISTORICAL CONTEMPORARIES

Eggers's famous contemporaries include:

**David Foster Wallace** (1962–2008): As author of the massive postmodern novel *Infinite Jest* (1996) and other books, American writer David Foster Wallace became known for sardonic humor and a complicated style that have led to him being cited as the late twentieth-century's first avant-garde literary hero.

**Michael Chabon** (1963–): Regarded as a skilled storyteller, American novelist Michael Chabon writes of adolescence, broken families, and unrequited love. He is best known for his *Wonder Boys* (1995), which was adapted into a critically acclaimed film in 1999, and *The Amazing Adventures of Kavalier & Clay* (2000), winner of the 2001 Pulitzer Prize for fiction.

**Vince Vaughn** (1970–): A school classmate of Dave Eggers, American actor Vince Vaughn became a movie star for Generation X, starring in films like *Swingers* (1996), which documented the single life in Los Angeles, and comedies like *Wedding Crashers* (2005), which represents the current generation of buddy flick.

**Jon Stewart** (1962–): As host of Comedy Central's *The Daily Show* since 1999, American comedian Jon Stewart has left little of American culture unsatirized. With an audience of about 1.5 million viewers nightly, *The Daily Show* focuses on culture and politics but frequently features literary and popular guests.

crisscross the world trying to get rid of $80,000. The book was published by McSweeney's Books and made available for purchase only in independent bookstores and online via the *McSweeney's* Web site. This work, bound in plain cardboard, displays the opening sentences of its story on the front cover, and demonstrates Eggers's iconoclastic attitude toward publishing. In 2002 he also began editing an annual series entitled *The Best American Nonrequired Reading*, which collects notable short fiction, nonfiction, comics, screenplays, and other literary pieces. That same year, he founded 826 Valencia, a charity learning center for underprivileged youth located in a working-class Hispanic neighborhood of San Francisco called the Mission. Named for its street address, 826 Valencia provides reading tutors, SAT test-preparation courses, writing workshops, and college scholarships. It also houses *McSweeney's* and the publishing company McSweeney's Books. Since its founding, 826 Valencia has spawned a number of affiliated organizations, as well as other branches in cities across the United States.

In 2006 Eggers combined social activism with fiction writing in *What Is the What: The Autobiography of Valentino*

## COMMON HUMAN EXPERIENCE

The experience of losing both his parents—and the aftermath—kick-started Dave Eggers's career as a writer. Here are some other works that explore the experience of being orphaned:

*Bleak House* (1852–53), a novel by Charles Dickens, is full of orphans, including one of the narrators, Esther Summerson, and the two wards of court, Richard and Ada, and Jo the crossing sweeper, a boy who can only fend for himself. The novel's main characters, from all walks of life, show us both the perils and the freedoms of life without parents.

*Housekeeping* (1981), a novel by Marilynne Robinson. Robinson's first novel follows the lives of two young girls after their mother commits suicide. They are looked after by a series of female relatives, none of whom proves to be up to their own or the community's standards of good parenting. The idea of "housekeeping" becomes a metaphor for nurture in this prize-winning novel.

*You Can Count on Me* (2000), a film written and directed by Kenneth Lonergan. *You Can Count on Me* focuses on the troubled but loving relationship between two adult siblings, a brother and sister, whose parents were killed in a car crash when they were children, and who learn that they need each other in unpredictable ways.

*Oedipus Rex* (fifth century B.C.E.), a play by Sophocles. Sophocles' powerful drama about fate tells the story of Oedipus, whose royal parents leave him to die as an infant after it is prophesied that he will one day murder his father. The baby survives, ignorant of his parentage, only to ultimately encounter and kill his father.

*Achak Deng.* The real-life hero of the novel, whose story Eggers recasts as a novel, is a refugee from the Sudan, one of the "Lost Boys" who made their way from refugee camps to the United States in the 1990s and early 2000s. During the Sudanese Civil War, which raged for most of the 1980s and 1990s, young boys were separated from their families, many of whom were killed, when opposing factions systematically massacred entire villages. Thousands of young boys managed to escape and travel to neighboring Ethiopia and Kenya; many of them were rescued from refugee camps and resettled in cities across the United States. Eggers's retelling of Valentino's story brought the Sudanese Civil War to the public consciousness in a different way, while detailing the often difficult and bewildering experience of the Lost Boys in their new homeland.

Eggers has been married to the novelist and editor Vendela Vida (born 1971) since the early 2000s. They have a daughter, October, born in 2005, and live in San Francisco, where both are involved with 826 Valencia and continue to write.

## Works in Literary Context

*Creative Nonfiction*  Much of Eggers's work sits on a blurry line between fiction and nonfiction. After the initial publication of his first book, the memoir *A Heartbreaking Work of Staggering Genius*, Eggers admitted that he altered events to streamline the narrative. His third book, *What Is the What*, is part biography, part novel. Writing that is ostensibly nonfiction yet exhibits many self-consciously novelistic elements is often classified as creative nonfiction, a term that could be used to describe classic works such as *The Autobiography of Benjamin Franklin*, as well as modern classics like Truman Capote's *In Cold Blood*. Although these works are based on real-life events, they are often constructed like works of fiction.

*Postmodernism*  Literary writing that acknowledges and often mocks its own conventions is often described as "postmodern." On the first page of *A Heartbreaking Work of Staggering Genius*, Eggers advises readers who are short on time to skip the table of contents and even to skip whole chapters. After a certain point, Eggers says, the book "is kind of uneven." Often conflated with irony, postmodernism is distinguished by a mistrust of grandiose claims of truth in religion, politics, and science. Indeed, in philosophy, the "postmodern condition" is a term often used to describe a sort of contemporary nihilism or relativism. Eggers's generation is not the first to be labeled "postmodern." The term has also been used to characterize such older writers as Don Delillo, Thomas Pynchon, and Kurt Vonnegut.

## Works in Critical Context

*A Heartbreaking Work of Staggering Genius*  Critical response to *A Heartbreaking Work of Staggering Genius* (2000) generally hinges on whether or not a given reviewer acknowledges genuine emotion at the heart of Eggers's story. Reviewers who found his ironic tone distancing and his overall narrative lacking in candid emotional expression offered negative assessments. Alexander Star, for example, observed that "there is something disingenuous" about Eggers's narrative voice, commenting, "Eggers's monologues are more like performance art than the dramatization of inner conflict." Star added, "The book displays a great deal of self-consciousness and very little self-reflection." On the other hand, those who felt that Eggers succeeded in conveying honest feelings in the book offered high praise. Nicholas Confessore asserted that the work is not, as some critics argued, an expression of detached cynicism. "On the contrary," he stated, "it is imbued with an almost desperate longing ... to find some kind of irreducible truth in it all." Other reviewers have remarked on the depth of humor in Eggers's memoir, and have contended that the author's greatest achievement lies in his ability to describe the emotional tenor of specific moments in his life, characterizing his debut work as an examination of empathy and grief. As commentator Marta Salij stated, Eggers "knows where the heart of his story is," adding, "When he hits, as in the first passages on his mother's death, he is sharp, strong, true and, yes, heartbreaking."

**You Shall Know Our Velocity and Later Works**
*You Shall Know Our Velocity* (2003) was greeted with mixed commentary. As with *A Heartbreaking Work of Staggering Genius*, critical discussion of *You Shall Know Our Velocity* has centered around questions of sincerity and irony, with scholars opining on the degree to which Eggers moved beyond the hip, irreverent tone of his memoir. Commentator Benjamin Markovits observed that *You Shall Know Our Velocity*, like Eggers's first book, "deals in the current generational anxieties of the American middle class." Correspondingly, the book has been compared to the coming-of-age novel *The Catcher in the Rye*, by J. D. Salinger, and the cross-country odyssey *On the Road*, by Jack Kerouac, both of which were hailed as works expressing the anxieties of discontented middle-class youth. Lorraine Adams described Eggers's second book as "[a]n *On the Road* for the millennial generation," while John de Falbe concluded that the characters in Eggers's novel "have neither the charm nor the subtlety of Holden Caulfield, and the road is not as interesting as Kerouac's."

Reviewers have favorably compared *What Is the What* (2006) to Mark Twain's *Huckleberry Finn*, and have highlighted its epic scope and thought-provoking emotional resonance. They have also lauded the short-story collection *How We Are Hungry*, regarding it as a showcase for Eggers's literary talents, which in this work, according to critic John Green, extend beyond "the charming, smirky, self-conscious narrative voice that helped make *A Heartbreaking Work of Staggering Genius* so popular."

## Responses to Literature

1. Dave Eggers worked as a graphic designer before starting to write books, and his works continue to have a strong visual identity. Read a McSweeney's publication, and think about how the design of the object interacts with the contents. Does the creative presentation enhance the content? If so, in what way?

2. The protagonist of *What Is the What* fled the Sudanese Civil War, a topic to which the world is still attuned: an extremely bloody conflict persists in the Darfur region of the Sudan. Research the various activist groups attempting to do something about the conflict, and write a report based on your findings. What are their proposed solutions, or plans of action? What have they accomplished?

3. The well-rendered memoir has good reason to be considered a literary art form. To deepen your sense of what the genre is all about, read a celebrated memoir such as Vladimir Nabokov's *Speak, Memory* (1951) or Joan Didion's *The Year of Magical Thinking* (2005), and reflect on the ways a good writer turns his or her experiences into art.

BIBLIOGRAPHY

**Periodicals**

Adams, Lorraine. "The Write Stuff: From Cult to Culture, Dave Eggers and Co. Are Taking Their Idealism to the Streets." *American Prospect* (February 2003).

Confessore, Nicholas. "Finite Jest." *American Prospect* (June-July 2000).

De Falbe, John. "Round-the-World Spending Spree." *The Spectator* (October 19, 2002).

DeMott, Benjamin. "Notes of a Son and Brother." *New York Review of Books* (September 21, 2000).

Georgiades, William. "Ego Trip." *New Statesman* (July 17, 2000).

Green, John. Review of *How We Are Hungry*, by Dave Eggers. *Booklist* (December 15, 2004).

Markovits, Benjamin. "Novel of the Week." *New Statesman* (February 24, 2003).

Mattson, Kevin. "Is Dave Eggers a Genius?: Rebelling and Writing in an Age of Postmodern Mass Culture." *Radical Society* (October 2002).

Smith, Sidonie, and Julia Watson. "The Rumpled Bed of Autobiography: Extravagant Lives, Extravagant Questions." *Biography* (Winter 2001).

Star, Alexander. "Being and Knowingness." *The New Republic* (August 14, 2000).

# ⊛ Barbara Ehrenreich

BORN: *1941, Butte, Montana*

NATIONALITY: *American*

GENRE: *Nonfiction*

MAJOR WORKS:

*The Hearts of Men: American Dreams and the Flight from Commitment* (1983)

*Re-making Love: The Feminization of Sex* (1986)

*Fear of Falling: The Inner Life of the Middle Class* (1989)

*Nickel and Dimed: On (Not) Getting by in America* (2001)

*Bait and Switch: The (Futile) Pursuit of the American Dream* (2005)

## Overview

An outspoken feminist, journalist, and socialist-party leader, Barbara Ehrenreich crusades for social justice in her books. Although many of her early works were shaped by her formal scientific training—she holds a PhD in biology—her later works have moved beyond

Barbara Ehrenreich  *Ehrenreich, Barbara, photograph. AP Images.*

health-care concerns to the plight of women and the poor. In addition to her numerous nonfiction books, Ehrenreich is widely known for her weekly columns in *Time* and the *Guardian*.

## Works in Biographical and Historical Context

***From Science to Social Justice***  Barbara Ehrenreich (née Barbara Alexander) was born August 26, 1941, in Butte, Montana, to a working-class atheist family with a longstanding ethic of independent thinking. Her first marriage, to John Ehrenreich in 1966, produced two children, Rosa and Benjamin, and ended in divorce. She married her second husband, Gary Stevenson, in 1983.

Ehrenreich's education prepared her for a career in the sciences: she received a BA in chemical physics from Reed College in Portland, Oregon, in 1964, and in 1968 she completed a PhD in cell biology at Rockefeller University in New York City. During her time at Rockefeller, in the middle of the tumultuous 1960s, Ehrenreich became involved in Vietnam War protests and the civil rights movement. Subsequent to finishing school, Ehrenreich's career choices gradually led her into a life of social activism: she worked at the Health Policy Advisory Cen-

ter in New York, taught health sciences at the State University of New York College at Old Westbury, was a fellow at the New York Institute for the Humanities and then the Institute for Policy Studies, and by the early 1980s was co-chair of the Democratic Socialists of America.

Ehrenreich's first book, cowritten with her then-husband John Ehrenreich, was published in 1969. Called *Long March, Short Spring: The Student Uprising at Home and Abroad*, it inaugurated Ehrenreich's forty-year writing career devoted to social justice and feminism. While still working for the Health Policy Advisory Center, Ehrenreich published a scathing critique of the American health "empire," exposing its inefficiency, inhumanity, and self-serving policies. Then, turning from the population in general to women in particular, Ehrenreich, with coauthor Deirdre English, unveiled the male domination of the female health care system in *Complaints and Disorders: The Sexual Politics of Sickness* (1973) and *For Her Own Good: One Hundred Fifty Years of the Experts' Advice to Women* (1978).

***Becoming a Famous and Controversial Writer***  Ehrenreich first made an impact with her controversial book *The Hearts of Men: American Dreams and the Flight from Commitment* (1983), a full-fledged leap into feminist polemic. Describing *The Hearts of Men* as a study of "the ideology that shaped the breadwinner ethic," Ehrenreich surveys the three decades between the 1950s and the 1980s, arguing that male commitment to home and family collapsed. Rather than feminism being the cause of the disintegration of the family, she writes, it can be blamed on men's abdication of their traditional role as breadwinner while still insisting that women maintain their role as submissive nurturer. *The Hearts of Men* led Ehrenreich to further topics concerning women and feminism. She followed it in 1986 with *Re-making Love: The Feminization of Sex*, coauthored with Elizabeth Hess and Gloria Jacobs, in which the authors report on and applaud the freer attitudes towards sex that women adopted in the 1970s and 1980s.

Soon Ehrenreich shifted her focus to class issues—which are often intimately tied to women's issues—where it has more or less remained. Her next work to attract critical notice, *Fear of Falling: The Inner Life of the Middle Class* (1989), examines the American middle class and its attitudes towards people of the working and poorer classes at a time when the disparity in income between classes had reached its greatest point since World War II. She continued her exploration of 1980s cultural malaise in *The Worst Years of Our Lives: Irreverent Notes from a Decade of Greed*, a series of reprinted articles about what some consider to be one of the most self-involved and consumeristic decades in American history.

In June 1998 Ehrenreich embarked on what was to become perhaps her best-known project. "I leave behind everything that normally soothes the ego and sustains the body—home, career, companion, reputation, ATM card—," as she explained in a 1999 *Harper's* article, "and plunge into the low-wage workforce." To do this, the author created a new persona—Barbara Ehrenreich, divorced homemaker with some housekeeping experience—and set off on a tour of the country in an attempt to sustain herself working in entry-level jobs, in the the way that millions of other Americans are forced to. In Ehrenreich's case, this meant waiting tables and cleaning hotel rooms in Key West, Florida; working at a nursing home in Portland, Maine; and becoming a Wal-Mart "associate" in Minneapolis. In all, Ehrenreich spent two years living the life of the American working class, and what she discovered was turned into the best-selling 2001 exposé, *Nickel and Dimed: On (Not) Getting by in America.*

With women and work being two of Ehrenreich's major themes, she turned her focus to the often-overlooked intersection of the two: the plight of working immigrant women. *Global Woman: Nannies, Maids, and Sex Workers in the New Economy* (2003), which she coedited with Arlie Russell Hochschild, is a collection of fifteen essays that examine the impact that globalization has had on millions of women from third-world countries as they leave the poverty of their homelands to undertake jobs as domestic servants in first-world nations.

With *Bait and Switch: The (Futile) Pursuit of the American Dream* (2005), Ehrenreich took the next logical step from *Nickel and Dimed* by looking at the reality facing the unemployed white-collar professional. With the corporate world scourged by the effects of downsizing and outsourcing, she found that the prospects for white-collar job seekers were bleaker than ever. Forging yet another new identity, Ehrenreich presented herself as a former homemaker seeking to reenter the workplace. Her goal was a job paying somewhere near $50,000 per year, with benefits. Her search netted her few responses and fewer job offers. Instead, she discovered an extensive but parasitical network of career coaches, networking professionals, image renovators, and others whose stated goal is to help people find jobs, but who deliver few results. The book ends up being a critique of these side-industries as much as an analysis of the problems facing the white-collar workforce.

Ehrenreich currently writes for a broad array of newspapers and magazines; many of her pieces from the last several years appear in *This Land Is Their Land: Reports from a Divided Nation* (2008), which picks up the thread of *The Worst Years of Our Lives* and *Nickel and Dimed* in exploring the ever-growing gap between rich and poor, and what that means for American culture.

## Works in Literary Context

### Literary Journalism and the New Journalism
Literary journalism (literature that is both factual but presented with the storytelling skill of a literary artist) has a long history in the United States; it goes back at

## LITERARY AND HISTORICAL CONTEMPORARIES

Ehrenreich's famous contemporaries include:

**Cesar Chavez** (1923–1993): A Mexican-American labor leader and civil rights activists who cofounded the National Farm Workers Association.

**Geoffrey Nunberg** (1945–): As a professor and writer, linguist Geoffrey Nunberg writes for both academic and popular audiences, presenting his ideas about language through media outlets such as National Public Radio and in books such as *Talking Right* (2006), an examination of the language of politics.

**Alan Dershowitz** (1938–): As an attorney, Alan Dershowitz has been involved with many of the most high-profile criminal cases of the twentieth century—from Patricia Hearst to Jim Bakker to O. J. Simpson. As the author of numerous nonfiction books, Dershowitz brings his jurist background to bear on the more pressing issues in world affairs, from the Israel-Palestine conflict to the use of torture.

**Ralph Nader** (1934–): With the publication of *Unsafe at Any Speed* in 1965, social activist Ralph Nader changed the way Americans—including politicians—thought about automobiles and the rights of the consumers who drive them. Though never far from the public eye, Nader became famous again for his 2000 presidential run, which altered the outcome in a way that few third-party candidates have been able to do.

**Gloria Steinem** (1934–): A prominent American journalist and women's rights activist. As cofounder of the National Women's Political Caucus and founder of the feminist magazine *Ms.* in 1972, Gloria Steinem remains a feminist icon for her foundational writings on women's issues and her ongoing political activism.

least to the war reporting of Stephen Crane and the journalism of Jack London over a hundred years ago. Another early name in the genre is John Reed, an American journalist who wrote a vivid eye-witness account of the Bolshevik Revolution in Russia, *Ten Days that Shook the World* (1919), which became a classic of its kind. In the 1930s and 1940s, John Dos Passos and James Agee wrote notable literary journalism, especially Agee's *Let Us Now Praise Famous Men* (1941), which reported on the eight weeks he spent living among sharecroppers in Alabama.

Literary journalism took a new turn in the 1960s, when many journalists began experimenting with viewpoints and storytelling techniques deemed "nonconventional" by the mainstream press. Writers of "New Journalism"—as literary journalism would later be labeled—often wrote in the first person, including their

# COMMON HUMAN EXPERIENCE

Barbara Ehrenreich became famous for her investigation of the lives of the working poor. Here are some other works from various time periods that show how hard it can be to get by:

*The Road to Wigan Pier* (1937), a nonfiction work by George Orwell. This book investigates how the poor lived in the economically depressed regions of northern England. The book was based on Orwell's own visits to Wigan and other northern cities, where for several months he lived and mingled with the poor.

*The Jungle* (1906), a novel by Upton Sinclair. Set in the meatpacking industry of the turn of the twentieth century, and inspired by his experiences in Chicago, Upton Sinclair's novel shed light on the harsh, often brutally unfair working conditions facing factory laborers, and the corruption that reigned among those with the power to improve them.

*Hard Times* (1854), a novel by Charles Dickens, is a critique of the utilitarian philosophy that was popular at the time. It shows how such a philosophy guided the Industrial Revolution but wrecked the lives of the workers who made it run.

*Roger & Me* (1989), a documentary film directed by Michael Moore, shows the devastation of the town of Flint, Michigan, after General Motors closed some of its plants there and left tens of thousands of workers out of a job.

own opinions and experiences in their reporting. For this reason such work was also sometimes referred to as "personal journalism." Norman Mailer, Hunter S. Thompson, and Truman Capote were early pioneers of the genre, which also includes Tom Wolfe and Gay Talese. Ehrenreich's name is not always included in this list, because her work is often more politically committed than that of other New Journalists. Ehrenreich, unlike many New Journalists, is interested in specific issues such as feminism, the minimum wage, and health care, whereas New Journalists are often more interested in storytelling as an art. Nevertheless, her use of literary techniques and unconventional reporting methods, and her willingness to stand in the shoes of those she is reporting on, are common elements of this movement.

## Works in Critical Context

**The Hearts of Men** Widely reviewed in both magazines and newspapers, *The Hearts of Men* was hailed for its provocative insights, even as individual sections of the study were soundly criticized. In her *Village Voice* review, for example, Judith Levine wrote: "Barbara Ehrenreich—

one of the finest feminist-socialist writers around—has written a witty, intelligent book based on intriguing source material. *The Hearts of Men* says something that needs saying: men have not simply reacted to feminism—skulking away from women and children, hurt, humiliated, feeling cheated of their legal and emotional rights. Men, as Ehrenreich observes, have, as always, done what they want to do." But at the same time, Levine judged the central thesis of the book as "wrong": "When she claims that the glue of families is male volition and the breadwinner ideology—and that a change in that ideology caused the breakup of the family—I am doubtful," commented the critic. "The ideology supporting men's abdication of family commitment is not new. It has coexisted belligerently with the breadwinner ethic throughout American history."

**Nickel and Dimed** The critical reaction to *Nickel and Dimed* ranged from skeptical to admiring. In the former camp was Julia Klein, whose question in *American Prospect* was: "In the end, what has [Ehrenreich] accomplished? It's no shock that the dollars don't add up; that affordable housing is hard, if not impossible, to find; and that taking a second job is a virtual necessity for many of the working poor." After labeling the author "a prickly, self-confident woman and the possessor of a righteous, ideologically informed outrage at America's class system that can turn patronizing at times," Klein went on to acknowledge that *Nickel and Dimed* is still "a compelling and timely book whose insights sometimes do transcend the obvious." Similarly, *Humanist* contributor Joni Scott mentioned her early reluctance to read the memoirs of an affluent person living temporarily as poor, but found that Ehrenreich's work is "an important literary contribution and a call to action that I hope is answered. I believe this book should be required reading for corporate executives and politicians," Scott concluded. In the view of Bob Hulteen of *Sojourners*, "Definitional books come around about once a decade. Such books so describe the reality of the age in simple terms that the impact is felt from after-dinner conversations to federal policy discussions." *Nickel and Dimed*, he added, "will likely join this pantheon."

## Responses to Literature

1. Read more about the history of the working poor. Some titles you might pick up: Bruce Watson's *Bread & Roses: Mills, Migrants, and the Struggle for the American Dream* (2005), which looks at the history of immigrant labor in early twentieth-century America, or Henry Mayhew's *London Labour and the London Poor* (1851), which for its time was a groundbreaking study of contemporary urban poverty.

2. When Barbara Ehrenreich writes about class issues, she is often writing about women's issues, too.

Read one of her books about class and/or working, and reflect on the intersection of these two issues in a short essay. How are women affected by working-class conditions in America? What is Ehrenreich's opinion about it? Do you agree?

3. Read *Nickel and Dimed* and then start a discussion about what is to be done about improving the lives of the working class. To do this, you will need to conduct some research into the history of the minimum wage, the arguments for and against raising it, and the causes of unemployment and job scarcity.

BIBLIOGRAPHY

**Periodicals**

Altschuler, Glenn C. Review of *Bait and Switch*. *Philadelphia Inquirer* (November 16, 2005).

Beck, Joan. Review of *Re-making Love: The Feminization of Sex*. *Chicago Tribune* (September 25, 1986).

Helwig, Maggie. Review of *Fear of Falling: The Inner Life of the Middle Class*. *Globe and Mail* (August 26, 1989).

Hulteen, Bob. Review of *Nickel and Dimed*. *Sojourners* (January-February 2002).

Klein, Julia. Review of *Nickel and Dimed*. *American Prospect* (July 30, 2001).

Levine, Judith. Review of *The Hearts of Men*. *Village Voice* (August 23, 1983).

Mitgang, Herbert. Review of *The Worst Years of Our Lives: Irreverent Notes from a Decade of Greed*. *New York Times* (May 16, 1990).

Newman, Katherine. "Desperate Hours." *Washington Post* (June 10, 2001).

Scott, Joni. Review of *Nickel and Dimed*. *Humanist* (September 2001).

Ulin, David. "Life at the Bottom of the Food Chain." *Los Angeles Times* (June 15, 2001).

# ❂ Will Eisner

BORN: *1917, Brooklyn, New York*

DIED: *2005, Lauderdale Lakes, Florida*

NATIONALITY: *American*

GENRE: *Fiction*

MAJOR WORKS:

*The Spirit* (1940–1952)

*PS Magazine* (1950–1952)

*A Contract with God and Other Tenement Stories* (1978)

*Will Eisner's The Dreamer* (1986)

*Fagin the Jew* (2003)

## Overview

Will Eisner is regarded as a pioneer of the comic book art form and is credited with coining the term *graphic novel* in reference to his hallmark semiautobiographical work *A Contract with God and Other Tenement Stories* (1978), which is cited as one of the primary influences on the graphic novel format. Widely recognized for writing and illustrating the weekly feature *The Spirit*, a detective adventure comic that ran from 1940 to 1952, Eisner is also known for *PS Magazine* (1950–1972), an educational comic that he produced for the U.S. Army. In a career spanning six decades, Eisner helped to establish comic books as something more than entertainment for kids.

## Works in Biographical and Historical Context

*An Early Calling to the Funny Pages* Eisner was born in 1917 in Brooklyn, New York, the son of Jewish immigrants. He attended DeWitt Clinton High School in the Bronx, where his first published comic strip appeared in the school paper. He studied briefly at the New York Art Student's League, but he left for a position in advertising at the *New York American* in 1935. From there he got his first comics job, writing and drawing for *Wow, What a Magazine!*, edited by Jerry Iger. When the magazine went bankrupt after a few issues, Eisner and Iger formed their own syndicate, producing comics to sell to magazines and newspapers. The Eisner-Iger studio employed such future comic book innovators as Jack Kirby (creator of the X-Men and the Hulk, among other characters) and Bob Kane (creator of Batman) before closing in 1939. Eisner then became art director and editor of several titles issued by Quality Comics. In 1940 he began producing a sixteen-page color insert for Sunday newspapers that included an episode of *The Spirit* as its lead feature.

Employing cinematic angles, dramatic lighting, and expressionist tones in his drawings, Eisner pushed the boundaries of the comic book genre with *The Spirit*. In this long-running series, which reflected the noir sensibility of film and literature of the 1940s, Eisner presented a realistic crime fighter, equipped with a secret identity but devoid of superhuman powers. This hero, Denny Colt, is a former private investigator who, after mistakenly being pronounced dead, transforms himself into the mysterious Spirit, wearing a business suit, fedora, and mask as he battles inner-city ills. Through the framework of the adventure comic, Eisner developed an enduring hero—a righteously indignant yet vulnerable crime fighter who eradicates societal evils while uncovering the city's most captivating stories. In addition to its overwhelming popularity and influential style, *The Spirit* is notable for its inclusion of Ebony, the first African American character to appear on a recurring basis in American comics. Eisner officially retired *The Spirit* in 1952, and the comic is regarded today as a classic of its form. The title has been reissued in a variety of formats for more

Will Eisner   © *Alberto Estevez / epa / Corbis*

than sixty years, in everything from hardbound, full-color volumes to periodical reprints.

Eisner was drafted into the army in 1942 and served until 1945, during which time he worked on comics and illustrations for troop education and instruction. *PS Magazine*—the instruction manual that Eisner developed for soldiers during World War II—employs direct language and comic book–style illustrations to replace the unwieldy technical manuals formerly used by military trainers. After the war, Eisner continued to produce *The Spirit* but eventually shifted his focus to his new business, American Visuals Corporation, which became a successful producer of educational and corporate comics for the next twenty-five years. In 1967 the U.S. Department of Labor asked Eisner to create a comic book that would appeal to potential high school dropouts. The result was a series of booklets titled *Job Scene*, which advised young people to seek higher education.

In the mid-1970s Eisner began working on *A Contract with God and Other Tenement Stories*, which came out in 1978. This book, along with Eisner's subsequent graphic novels, changed the landscape of the comic book industry, inspiring a generation of young comic artists to view their medium as a legitimate form of literature. Set in the Bronx during the Great Depression, which began after the stock market crash of 1929 and made for a hardscrabble adolescence for most people of Eisner's age, *A Contract with God and Other Tenement Stories* relies on black-and-white artwork to emphasize the stark realism of the book. The book is made up of four stories: a Jewish father mourning the death of his young daughter, a singer's dalliance with an aged diva, a building superintendent with an eye for young girls, and a group of vacationers dealing with class differences in the Catskills. All four draw from Eisner's experiences growing up in New York City. Described by Eisner as "sequential art," *A Contract with God and Other Tenement Stories* dramatically changed the comic book medium, influencing fellow artists and becoming the first successful graphic novel.

*Pioneering a New Genre*  Eisner went on to produce a number of other successful graphic novels, the form he innovated. *Will Eisner's The Dreamer* (1986) tells the semiautobiographical story of a young man in the 1930s who dreams of working in comic books, while *The Building* (1987) chronicles the experiences of people connected by a city building that is being torn down. *A Life Force* (1988), like *A Contract with God and Other Tenement Stories*, is set during the Great Depression and examines the lives and dreams of Jewish Americans coming of age in a world threatened by the looming shadow of Nazi Germany and World War II. *Dropsie Avenue* (1995) surveys the history of the South Bronx neighborhood in which *A Contract with God and Other Tenement Stories* and *A Life Force* take place. These three graphic novels are collected in *The Contract with God Trilogy* (2006). *A Family Matter* (1998) reveals dark secrets and resentment among family members as they gather for their patriarch's ninetieth birthday, and *Minor Miracles* (2000) continues the saga of Dropsie Avenue with four more tales of tenement life. A study of Charles Dickens's famous character from *Oliver Twist* (1838), Eisner's *Fagin the Jew* (2003) exposes the prejudices often found in classic literature. *The Name of the Game* (2001) is an ambitious, multigenerational tale of immigration focused on the business dealings of an affluent Jewish American family. One of Eisner's last works, *The Plot* (2005), recounts the history of *The Protocols of the Elders of Zion* (1964), an infamous piece of anti-Semitic propaganda.

His first book on technique, *Comics and Sequential Art*, appeared in 1985, and his second, *Graphic Storytelling*, was published in 1996; both books provide an inside look at the technical aspects of Eisner's meticulous approach to comic book art. Eisner also taught at New York's School of Visual Arts from 1972 to 1993. The National Cartoonists Society presented Eisner with the Milton Caniff Lifetime Achievement Award in 1995 and the Reuben Award for Outstanding Cartoonist of the Year in 1998. The Will Eisner Comic Industry Awards were established in his honor in 1988. Eisner's work was featured in an exhibition at the Whitney Museum of American Art in 1996. He died in Florida on January 3, 2005, of complications following open-heart surgery.

## Works in Literary Context

*The Graphic Novel*  Though Will Eisner's early career was steeped in the superhero-comic tradition, he eventually came to pioneer a new use for the art form: the graphic novel. Other comic book artists younger than he had begun, in the 1960s, to make comics that could be described as anti-superhero, either chronicling the bizarreness to be found in ordinary life, like R. Crumb's *Zap Comix*, or parodying the superhero comic, such as Gilbert Shelton's *Wonder Wart-Hog* stories. The success of these underground comics inspired Eisner to begin

## LITERARY AND HISTORICAL CONTEMPORARIES

Will Eisner's famous contemporaries include:

**Mickey Spillane** (1918–2006): American writer Spillane began his career writing comic books and then turned to a genre of crime fiction called "hard-boiled." Spillane's recurring character was a detective named Mike Hammer who lived and worked on the margins of mainstream respectability. Like Eisner, Spillane helped win critical acclaim for a popular genre that many considered "low-brow."

**Edward R. Murrow** (1908–1965): American radio and TV journalist. As a correspondent in Europe for CBS during World War II, Murrow brought home the realities of the war in a way that was revolutionary for the time period. While most broadcasters read from a script in a studio, Murrow reported live from the field. Later, during the 1950s, Murrow confronted Senator Joseph McCarthy during the Red Scare, an episode that was portrayed in the 2005 film *Good Night, and Good Luck*.

**Kirk Douglas** (1916–): American actor known for his gravelly voice, cleft chin, and tough-guy persona, Douglas is an icon of American cinema. Douglas often played characters with a strong moral compass but who clashed with the norms of society. Among his most famous films are *Spartacus* (1960), *Gunfight at the O.K. Corral* (1957), and *Paths of Glory* (1957).

**Benny Goodman** (1909–1986): American jazz musician and band leader, Goodman, who grew up in an impoverished Jewish neighborhood in Chicago, had become known as "the King of Swing" by the 1930s. An accomplished clarinetist in addition to a popular bandleader, Goodman influenced some of the biggest names in jazz. He was also an early promoter of racial integration, casting musicians of all colors in his bands.

work on his first graphic novel (a term he is credited with coining), *A Contract with God and Other Tenement Stories* (1978), which fused the visual vocabulary of the comic book with long-form narrative. The graphic novel as a genre has since taken off and is used to powerful effect as a vehicle for personal stories of great social significance. Standouts in the genre include Art Spiegelman's *Maus: A Survivor's Tale* (1991), a story of Nazi Germany and Holocaust survival, and Marjane Satrapi's *Persepolis* (2003), about the author's childhood in Iran after the 1979 revolution.

## Works in Critical Context

*A Contract with God and Other Tenement Stories and Other Works*  Eisner is renowned among critics and fans as a titan of the comic book industry, and his work continues to be a source of inspiration for many contemporary comic artists, including Frank Miller and Neil Gaiman. Critics have lauded the emotional impact of the illustrations in Eisner's graphic novels and have considered his work in *PS Magazine* further evidence of his aptitude for concise visual storytelling, albeit in an instructional vein. Commentators have valued his candid depiction of the daily lives of Jewish immigrants for adding much-needed social relevance to the comic book genre. Furthermore, critics have praised the frank representation of sexuality in *A Contract with God and Other Tenement Stories* for its authenticity. According to scholar David A. Beronä, "Eisner's skillful approach to the sexual themes in [*A Contract with God and Other Tenement Stories*] was another progressive step in further opening the doors of pictorial realism to an adult audience." Although some reviewers have faulted Eisner for relying too heavily on expository dialogue and have condemned his portrayal of Ebony in *The Spirit* as racially insensitive, Eisner has remained a beloved figure in the comics industry, prompting critic Mike Benton to label him "[t]he most influential person in American comics."

## Responses to Literature

1. Explore the dueling comic traditions of the 1960s in a research paper comparing mainstream superhero comics to underground comics. What do the two traditions have in common? What kinds of themes appear in both? How do they speak to what was going on culturally in the 1960s?

2. Like film, the graphic novel has two components: images and words. Read at least two of Will Eisner's graphic novels and write a short essay in which you discuss the interaction of word and image. How does each element contribute to the story? What tools or devices best bring out the author's meaning?

3. The graphic novel lends itself well to personal narrative. Read Eisner's *A Contract with God and Other Tenement Stories* and another personal graphic novel, such as Art Spiegelman's *Maus* or Marjane Satrapi's *Persepolis*, and start a discussion about the authors' visual rendering of people and places they knew well. What are the techniques they use to bring people and places to life?

4. Will Eisner wanted comics to be more than just kid stuff. Visit a comic book store and browse the shelves. Who seems to be the audience for comics today? What age groups are various comics pitched to, and what do readers' interests seem to be? You might also take note of the store's other customers.

BIBLIOGRAPHY

**Books**

Benton, Mike. "Will Eisner." In *Masters of Imagination: The Comic Book Artists Hall of Fame*. Dallas: Taylor, 1994.

Couch, N. C. Christopher, and Stephen Weiner. *The Will Eisner Companion: The Pioneering Spirit of the Father of the Graphic Novel*. New York: DC Comics, 2004.

Eisner, Will, and Frank Miller. *Eisner/Miller: A One-on-One Interview Conducted by Charles Brownstein*. Milwaukie, Oreg.: Dark Horse Books, 2005.

Wiater, Stanley, and Stephen R. Bissette. *Comic Book Rebels: Conversations with the Creators of the New Comics*. New York: Donald I. Fine, 1993.

**Periodicals**

Benson, John. "Will Eisner: Before the Comics, an Oral Reminiscence Recorded by John Benson." *Comics Journal* (April/May 2005).

Beronä, David A. "Breaking Taboos: Sexuality in the Work of Will Eisner and the Early Wordless Novels." *International Journal of Comic Art* (Spring/ Summer 1999).

Grant, Steven. "The Spirit of Will Eisner." *Comics Journal* (April/May 2005).

Harvey, R. C. "Will Eisner and the Arts and Industry of Cartooning: Part 1." *Cartoonist Profiles* (September 2001).

Medoff, Rafael. "Will Eisner: A Cartoonist Who Fought Antisemitism." *Midstream* (January/February 2006).

Raiteri, Steve. "Graphic Novels." *Library Journal* (March 15, 2005).

# ✸ Bret Easton Ellis

BORN: *1964, Los Angeles, California*

NATIONALITY: *American*

GENRE: *Fiction*

MAJOR WORKS:

*Less Than Zero* (1985)

*The Rules of Attraction* (1987)

*American Psycho* (1991)

*Lunar Park* (2005)

## Overview

The novels of Bret Easton Ellis portray a violent subculture of white youths who live promiscuous lives desensitized by drugs and the video revolution. Their depravity reflects the moral and spiritual deterioration of American society. Reviewers have praised Ellis's novels as incisive social commentary. Ellis's third novel, *American Psycho* (1991), solidified his reputation as an author of shockingly graphic fiction.

Brett Easton Ellis    *Brad Barket / WireImage / Getty Images*

## Works in Biographical and Historical Context

*Privileged Upbringing and Posh Education*    Bret Easton Ellis was born on March 7, 1964, in Los Angeles. As a young man, he attended a prestigious college preparatory school called the Buckley School. After graduation, he earned his Bachelor of Arts degree at Bennington College in Vermont, a private and very expensive school that inspired the fictional Camden Arts College, a setting in his novel *The Rules of Attraction* (1987), among other books.

In the 1980s, before pursuing a serious career as an author, Ellis played keyboard in various bands. However, just before he graduated from Bennington, he wrote and published *Less Than Zero* (1985), a story of wealthy, disconnected teens in Los Angeles who obsess over drugs, sex, and money. Critics praised the novel, even going so far as to compare it to the classic novel of teenage disillusionment *The Catcher in the Rye* (1951) by J. D. Salinger.

*Bret in the Brat Pack*    In 1987 Ellis moved to New York City for the publication of his second novel, *Rules of Attraction*, which contained themes and characters similar to his first novel. At the time, other authors such as Tama Janowitz and Jay McInerney were also focusing on the ennui of passive, detached characters and, with Ellis, became what critics called a literary Brat Pack. The popular *Village Voice* named the Brat Pack's writing style "socialite realism." During the age of MTV and framed by President Ronald Reagan's doctrine of progress and prosperity, novels about the spiritual bankruptcy and moral downfall of privileged teenagers exposed the negative effects of excess and decadence that many social critics believe typified the 1980s.

*Cult Status*    Ellis generated further buzz with the books that followed *Rules of Attraction* and *Less Than Zero*. Simon & Schuster pulled out of publishing *American Psycho* (1991), a first-person narrative of a high-class Manhattan serial killer, calling it too violent and disturbing. The novel was eventually printed by Vintage Books, a division of Random House. Many critics blasted *American Psycho* for its scenes of extreme violence against women. On the other hand, others labeled its raw style groundbreaking. In either case, the book inspired discussions about censorship, artistic freedoms, and literary standards. Today, *American Psycho*, a book Ellis calls a "black comedy," has reached cult status.

After *American Psycho*, Ellis returned to his Los Angeles setting for his collection of short stories about vampires, called *The Informers* (1994), as well as his violent themes in *Glamorama* (1998), a novel dealing with high fashion, politics, and terrorism. The novel also gives major roles to characters from *Rules of Attraction*, Lauren Hynde and Bertrand Ripleis.

# COMMON HUMAN EXPERIENCE

In many of his novels, Ellis captures the angst and apathy of youth during the Reagan era. His bored, wealthy characters have meaningless sex, lose themselves in drugs, and seek out violence as a form of entertainment. Similar works from this period include:

> *Slaves of New York* (1991), a short story collection by Tama Janowitz. This short story collection deals with New York City artists and grad students, junkies and collectors in the mid-1980s.
>
> *Bright Lights, Big City* (1984), a novel by Jay McInerney. The novel focuses on a character trapped in the fast lane of New York City in the 1980s. The unnamed main protagonist works as a fact checker for a literary magazine by day and, by night, is a cocaine addict.
>
> *From Rockaway* (1987), a novel by Jill Eisenstadt. This coming-of-age tale follows four teenagers from Rockaway Beach in Queens.

# LITERARY AND HISTORICAL CONTEMPORARIES

Ellis's famous contemporaries include:

**Nicolas Cage** (1964–): This Academy Award–winning American actor is known for his leading roles *Leaving Las Vegas* (1995), *Adaptation* (2002), and *National Treasure* (2004).

**Stephen Colbert** (1964–): This American comedian is recognized for his ironic wit and satire. He drew a wide following from his role on the news-parody program *The Daily Show*, which led to his own show, *The Colbert Report*.

**Dmitry Medvedev** (1965–): Medvedev was inaugurated as the president of Russia in 2008. He won the election with nearly 70 percent of the vote.

**Patrick Roy** (1965–): Now retired, Roy was an ice hockey goaltender for the Colorado Avalanche and Montreal Canadiens. As a member of those teams, he won two Stanley Cups and earned the title of "greatest goaltender in NHL history" by forty-one writers and a fan vote. Roy was born in Quebec.

**Ann Scott** (1965–): In France, Scott is part of the "socialite realist" movement. Her second novel, *Superstars* (2000), much like Ellis's *American Psycho*, has garnered cult status for its portrayal of apathetic youth.

**Self and Other** In 2005 Ellis departed from the novel genre to write a hybrid work (part autobiography, part horror) called *Lunar Park*. Ellis fictionalizes himself and his career, framing the story around the time of *Glamorama*'s publication. The tale focuses on the haunting of the house Ellis shares with his wife and son in a suburb outside New York City. Ellis has said the book was partly an homage to horror novel writer Stephen King.

Ellis's most recent project is a television series written for Showtime. Created in true Ellis fashion, the series, called *The Canyons*, is a dark drama about twenty- and thirty-somethings who find themselves in violent and unusual circumstances that may or may not be real.

## Works in Literary Context

*Moralism* In an article for the *Taipei Times*, Ellis called himself a "moralist," as his characters are sinners who often must find redemption or do penance. He often frames his discussion about the conditions of the American dystopia—violence, oppression, disease, excess, greed, and inhumanity—in the lives of characters who are consumed by materialism and could care less about the world around them. In this respect, Ellis takes part in the tradition of such Progressive Era–authors as Upton Sinclair (author of *The Jungle*, 1906) and John Dos Passos (author of *Manhattan Transfer*, 1925), who, along with other authors like them, pointedly criticized American consumerism.

*Socialite Realism* Ellis's work contributed to a literary movement called "socialite realism." While the realist novels of the nineteenth century focused mainly on offering unvarnished depictions of the working class and poor, these novels focused on the excessive, glittery, empty worlds of the rich and privileged. Tama Janowitz was also part of this movement, and Ian McMechan's characterization of Janowitz fits Ellis as well: "Few can match Tama Janowitz's commentaries on the race of fakes, freaks, and flakes who inhabit the sprawling metropolis of social non-achievement." These works differ from the novels of such writers as Evelyn Waugh and Aldous Huxley, both of whom gained fame for their sharp satires of the urban elite during the 1920s, in that they offer little direct criticism of their characters.

## Works in Critical Context

Criticism on Ellis varies widely. Some align Ellis with twentieth-century writers like Ernest Hemingway and F. Scott Fitzgerald because of Ellis's ability to depict a particular era, place, and attitude. Ellis captures the youth culture of the 1980s, revealing its moral and ethical decay. His language is uncomplicated and stunning. Other critics consider Ellis's work nothing more than shallow "yuppie lit." In the early days of Ellis's career, he was seen by critics as a reflection of his work: a jaded man of privilege looking at the world with indifference.

*Less Than Zero* The novel tells the morality tale of privileged youth in Los Angeles. These young people are made numb by American consumerism and try to cure their boredom by drug addiction, sexual promiscuity, and violence. In the end, they are driven to gang-raping a twelve-year-old girl. Critics lauded the cool, distant tone of Ellis's prose; the voice keenly demonstrates the narrator, Clay, as affectless and self-absorbed. Overall, they noted that Ellis's representation of youth begins with language, specifically the tired and inarticulate speech of these "lost" teenagers. For example, in terms of style, John Rechy of the *Los Angeles Times Book Review* wrote: "Expertly, Ellis captures the banality in the speech of his teenagers."

In the novel, as horrifying incidents pile atop each other, the tone and affectation of Ellis's characters push the reader to grow accustomed to the atrocities. Some critics insist this technique was carefully engineered by Ellis to emphasize the inertia experienced by Clay and his jaded companions.

*American Psycho* The protagonist of *American Psycho* is Patrick Bateman, a young, successful investment banker. He uses a flat, dispassionate tone to discuss his materialistic lifestyle, his obsession with his appearance, and the series of brutal murders he has committed. Many critics see Bateman as a symbol of the greed and inhumanity associated with the American upper class, while his victims represent voiceless and disadvantaged groups of society. British novelist Fay Weldon observed: "Those who are killed don't rate—they are the powerless, the poor, the wretched, the sick in mind, the sellers of flesh for money: their own and other people's."

But some critics view this novel as having all the artistic worth of a low-budget horror movie. At the time of its publication, the novel's violence toward women prompted one chapter of the National Organization for Women to boycott not only the book itself but all books by its publisher, Vintage, and its parent company, Random House.

The book has continued to receive critical attention since its publication, most of it positive. Jonathan Keats in an article for *Salon* comments that Ellis "has advanced beyond the workaday concerns of character and plot and found truth and beauty, the bookends between which our classics stand." Keats suggests that Ellis's work has earned a place in the literary canon, arguing, essentially, that "it misbehaves so severely by existing standards that it demands a scale of its own—one on which future works, previously unimaginable, can at last be built."

## Responses to Literature

1. With a group of your classmates, address the different critical perspectives on Ellis's work. Where do you each of you stand? Do you see Ellis's work as exposing the seedy realities of wealthy youth? Do you think Ellis speaks to the morality of American culture, or, in contrast, do you see Ellis's work as shallow? Discuss specific examples from an Ellis text to defend your opinions.

2. Watch the movie version of *Less Than Zero*, then read the book. Discuss how the novel was translated onto the screen: What are the similarities? What are the differences? Does the film capture the tone and message of the book?

3. About *Less Than Zero*, John Rechy of the *Los Angeles Times Book Review* wrote: "Expertly, Ellis captures the banality in the speech of his teenagers." Write a two- to three-page paper supporting Rechy's opinion. Use examples from the text to illustrate your points.

4. Controversy surrounded the publication of *American Psycho*, particularly because of its supposed misogyny. Write an essay in first-person point of view that discusses whether or not you find the novel misogynistic. Give specific examples from the text to support your argument.

BIBLIOGRAPHY

**Web sites**

Bottoms, Greg. "The Strange Fame of Bret Easton Ellis." January 1999. *Gadfly Online*. Retrieved August 24, 2008, from http://www.gadflyonline.com/archive/January99/archive-ellis.html.

Keats, Jonathan. "Great American Novelist." January 22, 1999. *Salon* . Retrieved August 24, 2008, from http://archive.salon.com/books/feature/1999/01/cov_22feature2.html.

*Tama Janowitz Biography*. Biography.jrank.org. Retrieved August 24, 2008, from http:// biography.jrank.org/pages/4464/Janowitz-Tama.html.

Vane, Sharyn. "Bret Easton Ellis Loses a Few Marbles in 'Lunar Park.'" August 21, 2005. *Taipei Times*. Retrieved August 24, 2008, from http://www.taipeitimes.com/News/feat/archives/2005/08/21/2003268662.

# ✸ Ralph Ellison

BORN: *March 1, 1914*

DIED: *April 16, 1994*

NATIONALITY: *American*

GENRE: *Fiction*

MAJOR WORKS:

*Invisible Man* (1952)

*Shadow and Act* (1964)

*Going to the Territory* (1986)

Ralph Ellison    *Ellison, Ralph, photograph. Ben Martin / Time and Life Pictures / Getty Images.*

## Overview

Although he was a Renaissance man who took on many roles including jazz trumpeter, editor, freelance photographer, and furniture maker, Ralph Waldo Ellison is best known as an award-winning novelist. His novel *Invisible Man* plays upon themes common to most of Ellison's work: invisibility, blindness, betrayal, initiation, and violence; yet, ultimately, Ellison emphasizes that the individual must assume responsibility for shaping his own identity. At the time of their publication, his novels were instrumental in portraying the experiences of an African-American male as oppressed by white society but who was, at the same time, presented with ample opportunities to succeed.

## Biographical and Historical Context

***From Tuskegee to Harlem***    Ralph Ellison was born in Oklahoma City on March 1, 1914. Ellison's father died when Ralph was three. As a young man, Ellison learned that his father had named him after the American poet-philosopher Ralph Waldo Emerson in hopes that his son would one day become a poet. Ellison's mother raised him, along with his brother Herbert.

Ellison was awarded a scholarship by the state of Oklahoma in 1933 to attend Booker T. Washington's prestigious Tuskegee Institute, a college attended predominantly by African Americans, in Alabama. Ellison did not see the scholarship as completely positive, however, because he suspected the funding to send him to an all-black school was motivated by a desire to keep him (and other black students) out of Oklahoma's state universities. The Tuskegee Institute offered teacher training and instruction in practical skills, such as carpentry.

Booker T. Washington, born a slave in 1856, was a famous African American educational leader, but his efforts at the Tuskegee institute were not without detractors. Washington founded the school at a time when African Americans had few options in higher education. Washington sought to create more opportunity by working with wealthy white patrons who helped fund his projects. His critics, among them social scientist W. E. B. Du Bois, labeled Washington an "accommodationist" because he did not push his white supporters forcefully to give blacks equal educational opportunities with whites. Ellison's experience at Tuskegee would shape his future work. A fictionalized version of Tuskegee Institute served as a setting in *Invisible Man*.

Although Ellison had an interest in music and studied the subject at Tuskegee, he never graduated. Instead, he went to New York City in 1936, where he met two influential men: Alain Locke and Langston Hughes, both leading figures in the Harlem Renaissance, an artistic flowering in the mostly black New York neighborhood of Harlem that began in the 1920s.

***Writing in New York City***    In New York City, Ellison sought to parlay his interest in the arts into employment. With the encouragement of Richard Wright (author of *Native Son*, 1940), Ellison wrote book reviews, articles, and short stories. In 1938, he became involved with the Federal Writers' Project (FWP), a New Deal program created by President Franklin Delano Roosevelt under the Works Progress Administration. The FWP provided jobs for unemployed writers, editors, and scholars during the Great Depression by assigning them to record local and oral histories, spearhead ethnographical projects, and write essays on various cultural subjects. The program helped move Ellison's writing career forward.

***World War II and Invisible Man***    During World War II, Ellison served as a cook for the Merchant Marines from 1943 to 1945 and began to gather ideas for what was to become *Invisible Man*. Eventually, the story grew into a rich narrative about a nameless African-American man who is losing both his sense of identity and his faith in people. Ellison married Fanny McConnell in 1946 and spent several years, both in Vermont and New York City, working on the novel. When *Invisible Man* was published in 1952, segregationist laws were still in full force in many

American states. The Supreme Court decision *Brown vs. Topeka Board of Education*, which overturned an earlier court decision declaring "separate but equal" public schools for black and white children legal, was not given until 1954. The Montgomery Bus Boycott, considered the spark that started the Civil Rights movement, did not happen until 1955. The book's frank treatment of racism was shocking to many readers, but critics considered the novel a key work in defining race relations in America, especially from a black perspective. It won numerous honors, including the National Book Award.

***Honors, Awards, Teaching, and Fire*** For over a decade following the publication of *Invisible Man*, Ellison continued to write and was awarded honorary degrees and fellowships from several universities, including Harvard and Tuskegee. But, twelve years passed after the release of his popular novel before he published a collection of essays and interviews called *Shadow and Act*. During this interim, Ellison turned to teaching. In 1954, as recipient of the Rockefeller Foundation Award, he lectured at the Salzburg Seminar, taught Russian and American literature at Bard College between 1958 and 1961, and served as a visiting professor at the University of Chicago and Rutgers University. In 1964, Ellison was given a visiting fellowship in American studies at Yale University. He also began work on a second novel; however, in 1967, a fire at Ellison's home destroyed nearly 350 pages of the manuscript. Pieces of the novel have been printed in various literary journals, but the book as a whole was lost. Years later, John F. Callahan, an English professor at Lewis and Clark College in Oregon, took on the daunting challenge of reconstructing the unfinished book. Using drafts and other notes, Callahan published *Juneteenth* in May 1999, to mixed reviews.

In 1969, Ellison received the Medal of Freedom, America's highest civilian honor, from President Lyndon B. Johnson. Throughout the 1970s, Ellison wrote and taught, and in 1986 he released *Going to the Territory*, a collection of previously published essays, including those that gave new insight into the lives of William Faulkner and Richard Wright, as well as other culturally important African Americans. In 1994, Ellison died of pancreatic cancer.

## Works in Literary Context

An avid reader, Ellison as a young man gravitated toward work by modernists, including Ezra Pound, Gertrude Stein, and F. Scott Fitzgerald. But in writing his novels, Ellison looked to the democratic principles and moral resolve of such nineteenth-century writers as Herman Melville and Henry James. Ellison also admired their depiction of American slavery as well as their portrayal of African Americans.

***Beyond the Protest Novel*** Although the protest genre is loosely defined and includes vastly different works such as Steinbeck's novel *The Grapes of Wrath* and Richard

---

## LITERARY AND HISTORICAL CONTEMPORARIES

Ellison's famous contemporaries include:

**Rosa Parks** (1913–2005): Called the "mother" of the Civil Rights movement in America, Parks sparked the Montgomery Bus Boycott in 1955 when she refused to give up her seat in a public bus in Montgomery, Alabama, to a white man.

**Octavio Paz** (1914–1998): Paz, a Mexican writer, poet, and diplomat, won the 1990 Nobel Prize in Literature.

**Lyndon B. Johnson** (1908–1973): President of the United States from 1963 to 1969. Johnson's administration is remembered both for its support of the Civil Rights movement and for its escalation of the U.S. military commitment in the Vietnam War.

**Joe Louis** (1914–1981): An American heavyweight boxer, Louis was nicknamed the Brown Bomber and was considered to be one of the greatest champions in boxing history.

**Dylan Thomas** (1914–1953): This Welsh poet also wrote short stories and scripts for film and radio. He is best known for his poem "Do not go gentle into that good night."

---

Wright's *Black Boy*, Ellison's novel does not squarely fit in that category. Specifically in terms of the African American novel, the protest novel genre, for the most part, sought to expose socio-political injustices and "culturally sponsored ignorances," in the words of critic Maryemma Graham. In 1949, James Baldwin attacked the genre in "Everybody's Protest Novel," suggesting that the genre trapped African Americans in certain roles and tied them to particular destinies. Along similar lines, with *Invisible Man*, Ellison sought to capture more than the struggle of the African American. In fact, when he accepted his National Book Award for the novel, he admitted that he did not envision an inherently black book, but rather "dream[ed] of a prose which was flexible, and swift as American change is swift, confronting the inequalities and brutalities of our society forthrightly, but yet thrusting forth its images of hope, human fraternity, and individual self-realization."

***The Ideals of the Frontier*** Ellison spent his childhood in Oklahoma when the state was just a territory, and the symbolism of the frontier underscores the thematic nature of *Invisible Man*, despite the fact the novel is set in Harlem. The book's narrative deals with the tension against personal and physical boundaries and the struggle for freedom, often illustrated in American literature through the conflict between "east" and "west." *Invisible Man* encapsulates Ellison's personal realization

# COMMON HUMAN EXPERIENCE

*Invisible Man* offered a frank assessment of the black experience in America during the first part of the twentieth century. Other works that examine the lives of African Americans at different points in American history include:

*Native Son* (1940), by Richard Wright. This novel confronts systemic racial inequality and social injustices through the story of twenty-year-old Bigger Thomas, an impoverished African-American living in 1930s Chicago. Bigger accidentally kills a white woman and runs from the police but eventually is caught and tried.

*Their Eyes Were Watching God* (1937), by Zora Neale Hurston. In the novel, the protagonist, Janie, represents a new generation of black women in the years long after slavery.

*Adventures of Huckleberry Finn* (1885), by Mark Twain. This novel challenged racist attitudes through the journey of the young, uneducated adventurer Huck and his friend Jim, a runaway slave. The literary image of the two friends drifting down the Mississippi River on their raft has endured as an American symbol of escape and freedom and reappears throughout literature.

*Uncle Tom's Cabin* (1885), by Harriet Beecher Stowe. Subtitled "Life Among the Lowly," this sentimental novel, written by abolitionist Stowe, portrays the cruelties of slavery alongside the Christian theme of love conquering all.

*Malcolm X* (1992), a movie by Spike Lee. Based on *The Autobiography of Malcolm X*, this film tells the story of African American Civil Rights activist and political leader Malcolm X, played by Denzel Washington.

that the frontier spirit had limitations, particularly in the South, at least for the African American adult. In the novel, the narrator's belief in freedom and possibility slowly decays in the presence of a restrictive social and political reality. Ellison makes his character aware that he has a "personal moral responsibility to participate in and contribute to democracy," a message that reverberates throughout much of Ellison's work.

## Works in Critical Context

Although the reception of *Invisible Man* was overwhelmingly positive, earning Ellison numerous honors, critics have disagreed about how Ellison's work fits into African-American cultural politics. Many black nationalists, or those who contributed to a political movement that fought in the name of black pride, as well as black economic and socio-political independence from mainstream society, railed against the novel for its lack of militancy toward civil rights issues, yet no one could deny the

novel's deft construction, inherent symbolism, and masterful language.

*Invisible Man* Many critics have viewed the novel as a chronicle of African-American history. The book marks the Reconstruction legacy left by the narrator's grandfather, the narrator's own experience at a Southern college for blacks, the emotional and social effects of World War I on black veterans, the Great Migration of blacks from South to North, and the difficulties of gaining employment in a discriminatory and exploitive capitalistic economy. In this way, some critics note, Ellison presents a history common to both his protagonist and African Americans in general.

Stewart Lillard suggests, "As a novelist, Ellison seems to have engaged his literary talents in a conscious effort of recording a century of Negro culture in *Invisible Man*. He records speech habits and musical lyrics of an oral tradition before they are lost to future ages."

Some readers see *Invisible Man* as going beyond the specific boundaries of African American history to tell a more universally American story. Ellison himself recognized *Invisible Man* as the tale of an American individual, a man who struggles to define his values and his identity despite his transience. Jonathan Baumbach joins this opinion in noting that, "Ellison's world is at once surreal and real, comic and tragic, grotesque and normal—our world viewed in its essentials rather than its externals. Though the protagonist of *Invisible Man* is a southern Negro, he is, in Ellison's rendering, profoundly all of us."

## Responses to Literature

1. Think about an instance in your life where you have felt "invisible." Write an essay using first-person point of view to describe this incident. Use examples from Ellison's *Invisible Man* to compare, contrast, and frame your story.

2. Regarding *Invisible Man*, Barbara Wachal wrote, "The appeal of Ellison's narration lies in the fact that the hopes, disappointments, fears, frustrations, and viewpoints that he expresses resonate as strongly with the experience of any alienated group in the United States today—and those who would alienate them—as they did when Ellison published his only novel." Discuss whether you agree or disagree with Wachal's observation. Use examples from the text and from your personal experiences to support your opinions.

3. Many of Ellison's short stories contain a lesson or moral message. Find a scene or passage in *Invisible Man* that you think employs this same strategy. Write a brief essay that summarizes the passage and explains what message or lesson you believe Ellison is trying to convey.

BIBLIOGRAPHY

**Books**

Graham, Maryemma. *Cambridge Companion to the African American Novel.* Cambridge: Cambridge University Press, 2004.

Ellison, Ralph. *The Collected Essays of Ralph Ellison.* Ed. John F. Callahan. New York: Random House, 1995.

Rampersad, Arnold. *Ralph Ellison: A Biography.* New York: Knopf, 2007.

Warren, Kenneth W. *So Black and Blue: Ralph Ellison and the Occasion of Criticism.* Chicago: University of Chicago Press, 2003.

Wright, John Samuel. *Shadowing Ralph Ellison.* Jackson: University Press of Mississippi, 2006.

**Periodicals**

Allen, Brooke. "The Visible Ralph Ellison." *New Criterion.* (May 2007): 24–9.

Stewart, Lillard. "Ellison's Ambitious Scope in *Invisible Man.*" *English Journal,* 58:6 (September 1969).

# ✳ Ralph Waldo Emerson

BORN: *1803, Boston, Massachusetts*

DIED: *1882, Concord, Massachusetts*

NATIONALITY: *American*

GENRE: *Nonfiction, poetry*

MAJOR WORKS:
*Nature* (1836)
*The American Scholar* (1837)
*Essays* (1841)

## Overview

Ralph Waldo Emerson is known as a founder of the Transcendentalist movement. He espoused what would become a distinctly American philosophy, one that emphasized optimism and individuality in addition to mysticism. Raised to be a minister in nineteenth-century New England, Emerson stressed the recognition of "God Immanent," or the presence of ongoing creation by a god apparent in all things. Emerson also believed in an Eastern concept that seeks to unify all thoughts, persons, and things in a divine whole. In general, Emerson focused on the individual and his quest to forego the trappings of the illusory world and discover the godliness of the inner self.

## Biographical and Historical Context

*The Young Minister* Emerson was born in Boston, Massachusetts on May 25, 1803, and grew up as the sheltered son of a Unitarian pastor. The latest in a long line of ministers, he was tagged a 'rather dull scholar' by his father, who died when Emerson was eight. Emerson

Ralph Waldo Emerson   *Mansell / Time Life Pictures / Getty Images*

attended Boston Latin School and Harvard College, and after graduation he became a schoolmaster at the school for young ladies that his brother had established. From there, Emerson went to Harvard Divinity School, where he studied to become a minister and discussed controversial translations of Hindu and Buddhist poetry. These nontraditional influences, among many others, would have a significant impact on Emerson's thinking: by the time he was twenty-six, when he became the pastor of a Boston church, he was questioning the Christian belief system with which he'd been raised. Also during this period Emerson married his first wife, Ellen, who died of tuberculosis two years later.

*European Travels and Naturalism* In 1832, Emerson resigned from the church and spent the next few years writing and studying his way across Europe. During these wandering years, he encountered other famous writers, including Samuel Taylor Coleridge, William Wordsworth, and Thomas Carlyle. He decided to become a "naturalist." The Naturalist movement, led by French novelist Emile Zola, promoted writing, particularly fiction, that presented human life through the objective lens of scientific inquiry. Naturalists believed human beings fell into two categories: they were either products of "biological determinism," ruled by instinct and a need for survival or products of "socioeconomic determinism," ruled by social and economic forces that they could not

# LITERARY AND HISTORICAL CONTEMPORARIES

Emerson's famous contemporaries include:

**Prosper Mérimée** (1803–1870): Mérimée was a French dramatist, historian, and short-story writer who is best known for his novella *Carmen* (1845), which was adapted by Georges Bizet into the opera of the same name.

**Jim Bridger** (1804–1881): Bridger was a mountain man who explored the United States frontier between 1820 and 1840 and told tall tales of his experiences.

**Franklin Pierce** (1804–1869): Pierce was a Democrat and served as the fourteenth president of the United States, from 1853 to 1857.

**George Sand** (1804–1876): Amandine Aurore Lucile Dupin, Baroness Dudevant, used the pseudonym George Sand to build her career as a French novelist and feminist.

**Nathaniel Hawthorne** (1804–1864): Hawthorne was an American novelist and short-story writer who featured heavy moral allegory in his works and was inspired by Puritanism. Two of his most well-known works are *The Scarlet Letter* (1850) and *The House of the Seven Gables* (1851).

control. Emerson later wrote of his travels in *English Traits* (1856).

**A Lecture Tour and Controversy** During the late 1830s and early 1840s, upon returning to the United States, Emerson began a speaking career. He lectured as a part of the new lyceum movement; writers, politicians, philosophers, and historians traveled across the United States on "tours" of lectures, debates, and dramatic performances. Emerson presented his most idealistic work, which included the essay "Nature" (1836), a pamphlet denouncing materialism and conventional religion and identifying nature as the divine example for inspiration as well as the source of boundless possibilities for humanity's fulfillment. Emerson delivered an address titled "The American Scholar" to Harvard's Phi Beta Kappa Society in 1837; the speech criticized American dependence on European ideology and urged the creation of a new literary heritage. A year later, Emerson spoke again at Harvard, and his "Divinity School Address" caused a huge stir. In the speech, he dismissed the tenets of historical Christianity and defined Transcendentalist philosophy in terms of the "impersoneity" of God.

**Well-Known Doctrines of Transcendentalism** Emerson enhanced and expanded the Transcendentalist ideas in "Nature," "The American Scholar," and the "Divinity School Address," publishing revised versions of these essays in *Essays* and *Essays: Second Series* (1844). Emerson's Transcendentalist philosophy espoused a unity in all creation and touted Nature as a symbol of spiritual truth. Essentially, it said that one must cultivate a connection to nature in order to understand spirituality. Additionally, Transcendentalism promoted emancipation from stagnant traditions and conventions and consequently inspired progressive social movements, such as the abolition of slavery and education reform.

Emerson became the spokesperson for Transcendentalism in the 1840s and headed the quarterly periodical *The Dial*. This publication was considered a "a medium for the freest expression of thought on the questions which interest earnest minds in every community," but it had only a small readership. However, the journal did publish work by women's rights activist Margaret Fuller and Naturalist philosopher Henry David Thoreau, as well as Emerson's first poems.

Around this time, Emerson associated with a tight-knit group of original and liberal thinkers who eventually became the Transcendental Club. Every major Transcendentalist (including Bronson Alcott, Henry David Thoreau, Margaret Fuller, and Elizabeth Peabody) came to these gatherings; however, conflict over the group's mission, the definition of Transcendentalism, and the "nature of intuitive knowledge" eventually dissolved the circle.

**Emerson the Poet and Personal Matters** In *Essays: Second Series*, Emerson published "The Poet," a tribute to the creative imagination. Emerson suggests that a poet articulates the meaning of the universe and that poetry reflects the truth and symbolism of nature. Though some critics accused Emerson of not having the "soul of a poet," he worked hard at his verse, as evidenced by the collections *Poems* (1847) and *May-Day and Other Pieces* (1867). Readers best know Emerson for the poem the "Concord Hymn," which celebrates "the shot heard round the world" that started the Battle of Concord, at the onset of the American Revolution.

Emerson married second wife Lydia in 1835. They had four children together. Some say his once-radical Transcendentalist beliefs became more conservative, or more stoic, after his first child, five-year old Waldo, died of scarlet fever. Emerson himself died on April 27, 1882, and was buried in Sleepy Hollow Cemetery in Concord, Massachusetts.

## Works in Literary Context

While contemporaries had varying opinions of Emerson's work and philosophy, there is no doubt today that Emerson had a profound impact on the course of American literature. It was Emerson who insisted that American writers break free of old European literary models and look to the American experience—the American landscape in particular—for inspiration. Emerson actively sought out and championed writers (such as Thoreau,

Herman Melville, and Walt Whitman) whom he believed could offer such purely American literature. His oft-anthologized essays encapsulate what many Americans have come to believe about their culture: that the United States is a country of vast size and potential peopled by rugged individualists who pursue their dreams no matter the consequences.

***Lessons in Living*** "How shall I live?"—the implicit question in Emerson's "Self-Reliance"—is the central question of *The Conduct of Life*, which is Emerson's clearest philosophical statement. According to Emerson, a person seeks self-understanding and self-actualization. Emerson stressed that staying true to one's purpose in the face of societal censure takes courage, but that truly great people can muster this courage. Because of his insistence on nonconformity, Emerson became a hero of the countercultural movement of the 1960s and 1970s.

***Nature*** Emerson's essay "Nature" epitomizes the Romantic idea of nature as holy, almost a deity itself. In "Nature," Emerson declares that through humankind's connection to nature, people will "enjoy an original relation to the universe." "Nature" inspired Henry David Thoreau's famous *Walden; or a Life in the Woods*, a book Thoreau wrote while living in a cabin on land owned by Emerson. "Concord Hymn," while popular for its patriotic sentiment, also reflects Emerson's ideology of man connecting with nature. Emerson's ideas about nature influenced many future American writers, including American essayist and conservationist John Burroughs and Scottish-born American naturalist and writer John Muir.

## Works in Critical Context

In the past, although critics could not deny the impact Emerson's work had on other writers and literary movements, let alone social, political, and cultural philosophies, they could not clearly categorize Emerson's influence. His writings imparted proverbial wisdom that was rooted itself in American culture, yet his poetry and philosophy did inspire the future work of Whitman and Dickinson. Ultimately, however, critics have embraced Emerson's body of writing as individualistic, yet as unified as his natural doctrines themselves.

***"Nature"*** As noted by Joel Myerson, recent commentators have tended to emphasize Emerson's historical significance, his affinities with modern intellectual trends like symbolic philosophy and existentialism, and his achievement as a writer. The apparent murkiness of his essays has been explained as the expression of a conscious aesthetic within the tradition of the Romantic movement and the major Victorian prose writers. One of the foremost historians of literary criticism, René Wellek, called Emerson "the outstanding representative of romantic symbolism in the English-speaking world." Viewing Emerson's work in a sociopolitical context, other modern criticism has emphasized the significance of his philo-

---

## COMMON HUMAN EXPERIENCE

Emerson is known for his essay "Self-Reliance," in which he championed principled nonconformity and brave adherence to one's personal calling in life. Other works that trumpet the virtues of nonconformity include:

*Walden; or a Life in the Woods* (1854), a nonfiction book by Henry David Thoreau. In this work, Thoreau reflects upon his experiences during his two-year stay at a cabin near Walden Pond, an experience that demonstrated his commitment to self-reliance and living simply. In his conclusion to that work, he writes, "If a man does not keep pace with his companions, perhaps it is because he hears a different drummer. Let him step to the music which he hears, however measured or far away."

*Adventures of Huckleberry Finn* (1885), a novel by Mark Twain. This novel, considered by many literary critics to be the greatest work of American literature yet written, features a decidedly strong-willed young hero named Huck Finn, who avoids "civilization" as often as possible.

*Pippi Longstocking* (1945), a novel by Astrid Lindgren. The beloved heroine of several children's novels, Pippi is introduced in this book as a wild, oddly dressed girl who lives on her own, with her monkey and her horse, in a large house in a small Swedish village.

*Harold and Maude* (1971), a film directed by Hal Ashby. This cult classic of the counterculture revolves around a lonely, morbid young man named Harold who finds joy in his unusual relationship with an old woman named Maude.

---

sophical contributions. Rhetorician Kenneth Burke wrote that Emerson "struggles to see high moral principles behind men's economic acts. And he places modern inventions in this pattern of an idealized utility." Ultimately, Burke concluded, "In Emerson secular agency is a function of divine purpose." Similarly, Joyce Warren wrote, "Emerson's first published work, 'Nature,' established his concern with the self. He begins with an appreciation of nature, but it soon becomes apparent that his essay is not a hymn to the glories of the natural world in the tradition of the nineteenth-century nature worshippers but rather a glorification of the individual man."

***"Ponderous" Essays*** At the time of publication of *Essays*, *The Daily Advertiser* in Boston printed a rather negative review, calling the work "tough, distorted, ponderous, and labored." At the same time, the work was received remarkably well: the 1,500 copies of the first American edition sold out. Emerson printed the book in England at the same time, and that printing sold out as well. *Essays* consisted of twelve pieces on moral, religious, and intellectual complimentary themes, for example, Love and Friendship, and Prudence and Heroism. The guiding message in one of the essays, "Self-Reliance," was particularly controversial: it stated that people must rely on their own instincts of what is right and who they are, lest they commit moral suicide.

*"Concord Hymn" and Other Poetry* Early critiques of Emerson focused largely on the artistic merits of his work. Matthew Arnold, a British poet and critic, judged Emerson's poetry to be bland, lacking energy and passion. In 1884, however, Arnold made an exception to his general sentiments in an essay later published in his *Discourses on America*, in which he singles out "Concord Hymn" as deserving of praise: "Such good work as the noble lines on the Concord Monument is the exception." Similarly, in an 1880 essay, Walt Whitman criticized Emerson's artistic choices and thematic content, stating that he found Emersonrsquo;s verse cold and artificial. Whitman's words were cutting: "It has been doubtful to me if Emerson really knows or feels what Poetry is." Despite his views on the quality of the latter's verse, Whitman did think Emerson's spirit to be "exactly what America needs," because Emerson advocated for a cultural identity distinct from that of America's European roots.

## Responses to Literature

1. With a classmate, define "Transcendentalism." Then together, using resources from your school library or on the Internet, find examples of Transcendentalism in everyday pop culture—for example: television shows, music, commercials, and comic strips. Create a fifteen-minute report that you both will share with the rest of your class.

2. With a group of your classmates, discuss the role nature plays in your life. For instance, how are your moods affected by the weather? Do you see nature as something spiritual? If so, how? How does nature represent freedom, individuality, community? Use examples from Emerson's *Nature* to guide your conversation.

3. Emerson wrote, "Nature magically suits a man to his fortunes, by making them the fruit of his character." Explain in a short, first-person essay what you think Emerson means by this. You may use examples from Emerson's other work to support your ideas, if needed.

BIBLIOGRAPHY

**Books**

Cayton, Mary Kupiec. *Emerson's Emergence: Self and Society in the Transformation of New England, 1800–1845.* Chapel Hill: University of North Carolina Press, 1989.

Hodder, Alan D. *Emerson's Rhetoric of Revelation: Nature, the Reader, and the Apocalypse Within.* University Park: Pennsylvania State University Press, 1989.

Holmes, Oliver Wendell. *Ralph Waldo Emerson.* Boston: Houghton, Mifflin, 1885.

Myerson, Joel, ed. *A Historical Guide to Ralph Waldo Emerson.* New York: Oxford University Press, 2000.

Paul, Sherman. *Emerson's Angle of Vision: Man and Nature in the American Experience.* Cambridge, Mass.: Harvard University Press, 1952.

Porte, Joel. *Emerson and Thoreau: Transcendentalists in Conflict.* Middletown, Conn.: Wesleyan University Press, 1966.

Porter, David. *Emerson and Literary Change.* Cambridge, Mass.: Harvard University Press, 1978.

Robertson, Susan L. *Emerson in His Sermons: A Man-Made Self.* Columbia: University of Missouri Press, 1995.

Yannella, Donald. *Ralph Waldo Emerson.* Boston: Twayne, 1982.

Zwarg, Christina. *Feminist Conversations: Fuller, Emerson, and the Play of Reading.* Ithaca, N.Y.: Cornell University Press, 1995.

# ❀ Eve Ensler

BORN: *1953, New York, New York*

NATIONALITY: *American*

GENRE: *Drama*

MAJOR WORKS:
*The Vagina Monologues* (1996)
*Necessary Targets* (1996)
*The Good Body* (2004)

## Overview

Playwright Eve Ensler shot into the international spotlight because of her role as a feminist activist and creator of *The Vagina Monologues*. Honored with the prestigious Obie Award, the play came from Ensler's interviews with 200 women and was viewed as a proclamation about what it means to be a woman at the turn of the twenty-first century. The play has been performed and adapted worldwide. Since *The Vagina Monologues*, Ensler has written and produced other plays using the same personal interview process.

## Works in Biographical and Historical Context

*The Facts Outside of Monologues* Eve Ensler was born in New York City on May 25, 1953. She received her bachelor's degree from Vermont's Middlebury College in 1975, where she joined the feminist movement. After graduation, she lacked real purpose and slipped into

Eve Ensler    *Ensler, Eve, photograph. AP Images.*

masturbation, from rape to giving birth—that are intimately connected to the most intimate part of the female body. The play gave Ensler the nickname "The Vagina Lady," as well as plenty of worldwide attention. Ensler used the play's popularity to showcase women's causes internationally by producing benefit performances of the play featuring celebrities like Glenn Close and Whoopi Goldberg. These benefits, under the name V-Day, have raised millions for women's organizations. V-Day was incorporated in 1998 as a non-profit international organization advocating for an end to violence against women.

***Giving the Public More Necessary Targets***    After the successful *Vagina Monologues,* Ensler told another empowering story that targeted women's issues: *Necessary Targets* (1996). This play follows two American women, a Park Avenue psychiatrist and a human rights worker, who go to Bosnia to help women confront their memories of a war that raged there from 1992 to 1995. Directed by Ensler, the play debuted at the famous Helen Hayes Theatre in New York City as a benefit performance and starred Meryl Streep and Anjelica Huston.

Like *The Vagina Monologues,* *The Good Body* (2004) confronted women's body image. The play discusses how women feel bound to society's standard of beauty. Ensler traveled the globe for four months to conduct personal interviews, yet also connected inspiration for the play to the larger issues surrounding the war in Iraq, which started in 2003 when the administration of President George W. Bush claimed that Iraq held weapons of mass destruction. In the preface to the play, Ensler acknowledges the oddity in writing a play about body image while the world is in turmoil, but then counters: "Maybe because I see how my stomach has come to occupy my attention, I see how other women's stomachs or butts or thighs or hair or skin have come to occupy their attention, so that we have very little left for the war in Iraq—or much else, for that matter."

In 2006, Ensler addressed the Iraq War in another play, *The Treatment.* This play is told through a man's voice; the protagonist, Man, who served in Iraq, struggles with PTSD (Post-Traumatic Stress Disorder) after he spent time as a soldier torturing detainees. Woman, dressed as a uniformed medic, appears to be his psychiatrist, but symbolizes the American system. The play becomes a treatise on how society defines brutality, torture, humanity, and war.

***2006: Year of the Inspirational Summit and Memoir***    Along with her on-stage activism, Ensler has also participated in a variety of public events to raise awareness about important women's issues. In 2006, with Madame Jeanette Kagame, First Lady of Rwanda, global humanitarian Zainab Salbi, and noted Christian AIDS advocate Mrs. Kay Warren, Ensler contributed to the CNN Inspire Summit. The Summit honored women who inspired others to get involved in political and humanitarian activism. Ensler was part of a program that

abusive relationships with men, drugs, and alcohol. When she hit bottom, she met Richard McDermott, who took her in. They married in 1978 and divorced ten years later. Ensler adopted McDermott's son, actor Dylan McDermott, when he was eighteen and she was twenty-six. Her career was jumpstarted in 1996 with *The Vagina Monologues,* though she was an active writer and theatrical performer prior to the success of that play. For instance, in 1983, Ensler wrote a series of pamphlets called "Acting You," which offers pedagogical strategy for teachers and students to access emotions and resolve conflict using theatre techniques.

***Advocating for Women Through Monologues***
The idea for *The Vagina Monologues* came from Ensler's abusive childhood. Her father, a food industry executive, abused her physically, often assaulting her with a belt or mistreating her sexually from the time she was five years old until she was about ten. Ensler began writing at a young age to deal with her pain, confusion, anger, and emotional shock.

Ensler interviewed 200 women for *The Vagina Monologues.* The monologues call attention to the variety of experiences in women's lives—from menstruation to addressed religious- and government-sanctioned violence against women and the AIDS epidemic, among other key areas of international concern.

In the same year, Ensler wrote *Insecure at Last: Losing It in Our Security-Obsessed World*. The book used America's quest for national security in the wake of 9/11 to frame experiences from Ensler's own life, her own quest for security. At the same time, Ensler juxtaposed her story with interviews with women in Afghanistan, Indonesia, and Mexico, as well as with American antiwar activist Cindy Sheehan.

***Political Essayist and Blogger*** In the last few years, Ensler has blogged political commentaries for *The Huffington Post*, a liberal news website founded in 2005 by Greek-born syndicated columnist Arianna Huffington. Ensler's blog subjects include the vice presidential nomination of Alaska governor Sarah Palin, Condoleeza Rice's "bad theatre," and Ensler's own V-Day monologues.

## Works in Literary Context

***The Personal is Political*** In an interview with Eve Ensler, Wendy Weiner declares that "[t]he inseparability of Ensler's art and activism are evident." Though she refers specifically to Ensler's play, *Necessary Targets*, the statement describes most, if not all, of Ensler's work. From *The Vagina Monologues* to *The Treatment*, Ensler confronts important women's issues, like sexual abuse, body image, and the violence of war within a framework of personal experiences. Ensler herself has made a purposeful decision to express her politics through her art: "For a long time," she said in an article written with Andrea Lewis, "I really struggled with those two forces in my life. Fortunately, I bless the great goddesses that it's come together and I've found a way to manifest both those things at the same time." Critic F. Kathleen Foley remarked that *The Vagina Monologues*, "is not just a play anymore. It's a social movement."

***Body and Theatre*** Much of Ensler's work deals with the relationship between a woman's body and the larger world, as well as how that relationship can be portrayed on stage. In an interview with Jim Mirrione, Eve Ensler pronounced:

> I am really interested in the theatre of the body and discovering just what the relationship is of the body to theatre—and of the body to everything. I think one of the reasons that feminism has not been successful yet is that it hasn't translated into the body—it's just in the head. I believe when the translation actually happens, so that women actually love their bodies, feel safe in their bodies, feel empowered in their bodies, then the world will change. And theatre has the capacity to do that—to really let things enter the body, and I continue to be interested in that.

## Works in Critical Context

Ensler's drama exposed international and personal issues through the specific experience of the individual. Critics praised Ensler for her directness, especially in the way she uses and reclaims language usually whispered, denounced, or hidden. For many women, *The Vagina Monologues* brought a newfound awareness of and pride in the female body.

***Mixed Reviews about Female Sexuality*** In her review of *The Vagina Monologues* in the feminist publication *Off Our Backs*, Roxanne Friedenfels suggests the play "serves as a vehicle for continuing discussions about female sexual experience. It also, however, shows how in a sex-saturated society we are only slouching slowly toward honest recognition of how women attain sexual pleasure." Some feminists also critiqued Ensler for aligning a woman's empowerment with sexuality rather than intellect by making the vagina a symbol of power, and thereby perpetuating the very gender inequity that Ensler was trying to protest. But most critics fully embraced the frank conversation started by *The Vagina Monologues*. For many, Ensler cut through the shame associated with the word "vagina" and encouraged a sense of ownership in women's sexuality. In the *Los Angeles Times*, F. Kathleen Foley wrote, "As dramatic literature, *The Vagina Monologues* is rough-hewn, ranging from the soaringly poetic to the uncomfortably pornographic. As a neo-feminist celebration, however, it is an occasion for rejoicing."

***"Navel-gazing"*** In reviewing Ensler's *The Good Body*, Nirmala Nataraj writes: "Navel-gazing is an allegation that Ensler has often been hit with, and her brand of 'radical activism' has been attacked as retrograde theater, naive and sentimental ruminations that trivialize women's issues." Others find Ensler's "navel-gazing" as, in fact, an inward exploration fanning outward. For them, Ensler's technique of using interviews as a basis for her dramatic topics and language takes the intimacy and privacy of the personal and makes it public and universal, essentially sharing the experience of Everywoman.

## Responses to Literature

1. With a group of your classmates, discuss the multitude of ways in which you see the female body portrayed in the media. Then, using resources on the Internet (film clips, advertising, music), create an audiovisual presentation that expresses your vision of how women are portrayed in today's society.

2. Ensler's "outing" of the vagina in her play has changed public perception and reception of the word and the body part. Write a short essay, using first person point of view, discussing how you feel about the word becoming mainstream. Do you use the word often? Do members of your family or your friends? What connotation does the word

have? Do you use other words in place of the word, and if so, why?

3. With a group of your classmates, write your own skit using *The Good Body* or *The Vagina Monologues* as inspiration. Perform the skit for your class. Afterward, discuss the play with the class and explain why you made certain choices in plot, tone, and characterization. Talk about whether and why you think your play could be considered controversial or activist.

BIBLIOGRAPHY

**Periodicals**

Ensler, Eve and Andrea Lewis. "All about Eve." *The Progressive* 65 (March 2001).

Ensler, Eve and Jim Mirrione. "Eve Ensler: Body Trouble." *American Theatre* 20 (December 2003).

Foley, F. Kathleen. "*Monologues*: Harrowing, Candid and Often Hilarious." *Los Angeles Times* (Oct. 16, 2000).

Friedenfels, Roxanne. "*The Vagina Monologues*: Not So Radical After All?" *off our backs* (May-June 2002).

Nataraj, Nirmala. "More Body, Less Vagina." *SFSTATION* (Aug. 18, 2004).

# ⊛ Olaudah Equiano

BORN:  *c. 1745, Nigeria*

DIED:  *March 1797, London, England*

NATIONALITY:  *American*

GENRE:  *Nonfiction*

MAJOR WORKS:

*The Interesting Narrative of the Life of Olaudah Equiano, or Gustavus Vassa the African, Written by Himself* (1789)

## Overview

Olaudah Equiano's autobiography, *The Interesting Narrative of the Life of Olaudah Equiano, or Gustavus Vassa the African, Written by Himself* (1789), represents an important artifact and notable example of the slave-narrative genre, which was not yet a recognized literary form at the time of Equiano's writing. The autobiography also serves as an early record of the black African diaspora during slavery. Equiano's story is filled with personal struggle and triumph. He was kidnapped, sold into slavery, and shipped to America, but eventually earned his freedom, traveled the world, and became an abolitionist in England.

## Works in Biographical and Historical Context

***Taken for a Slave*** Equiano was born in the interior of Nigeria, in or about 1745. At the age of eleven, he was kidnapped with his sister by a band of African raiders. Equiano was sold to British slave traders bound for

Olaudah Equiano   *Vassa, Gustavus (Olaudah Equiano), holding book in right hand, engraving. New York Historical Society.*

America. In his autobiography, he describes life in his tribe prior to his enslavement, as well as his experience on the slave ship heading to the New World:

> The closeness of the space, and the heat of the climate added to the number in the ship which was so crowded that each had scarcely room to turn himself, almost suffocating us. This produced copious perspiration, so that the air soon became unfit for respiration, from a variety of loathsome smells, and brought on a sickness among the slaves, of which many died, thus falling victims to the improvident avarice ... of their purchasers.

Equiano also described the brutal treatment of the slaves:

> a load of heavy iron hooks hung about their necks. Indeed, on the most trifling occasions, they were loaded with chains; and often instruments of torture were added. ... I have seen a Negro beaten till some of his bones were broken, for only letting a pot boil over.

***New Name, New Place, New Face***   After the deplorable conditions of the voyage, Equiano was taken to Virginia. He became the property of "one Mr. Campbell," who assigned him to field work for only "weeding grass, and gathering stones in a plantation." This stint of manual labor did not last long, however. After just a few

weeks, Campbell sold Equiano to Michael Henry Pascal, a former lieutenant in the Royal Navy and the commander of a merchant ship. Pascal became fond of Equiano and bought him as "a present to some friends in England." Pascal also renamed Equiano Gustavus Vassa, after the sixteenth-century Swedish king. When Equiano resisted the name, he was physically punished.

While working for Pascal on his ship, Equiano became friends with Richard (Dick) Baker, a teenaged American sailor who helped Equiano learn about Western culture. He also helped Equiano become fluent in English. This relationship paved the way for Equiano's writing. In his narrative, Equiano writes,

> I had often seen my master and Dick employed in reading, and I had a great curiosity to talk to the books as I thought they did, and so to learn how all things had a beginning: for that purpose I have often taken up a book and have talked to it and then put my ears to it, when in hopes it would answer me; and I have been very much concerned when I found it remained silent.

Once in England, Equiano was treated well compared with other slaves in his position. When Pascal took Equiano to Falmouth, Equiano served as a member of the family. Not long after, Pascal sent him to live in another kind, even respectful, household. Living in white households caused Equiano to become confused about his identity. He was subservient to the others in his house, yet also lived among them. He recalls trying to change his appearance by scrubbing his face until his cheeks turned rosy like the white children with whom he lived.

***Education at School and at Sea***   Equiano was eventually given to Pascal's cousins, the Guerin sisters, who sent him to school for a formal education. Also concerned for his spiritual development, the sisters also had him baptized. Pascal soon brought Equiano back to sea again, to help him serve in the Seven Years' War, a conflict that officially began between France and England in 1756.

This conflict erupted over the issue of control of various colonies and "commodities," including African slaves. Equiano wrote about his role in the war to show his readers that by participating in it, he reclaimed the very humanity that had been taken from him when he was kidnapped and sold into slavery and also gained a new level of respect and honor. Equiano wrote about the war with the precise tone of a correspondent. He offered crisp, vivid details of the sea battles between the British and the French. For example, Equiano keenly portrayed his own active role in one such engagement: "My station during the engagement was on the middle deck, where I was quartered with another boy, to bring powder to the aftermost gun ... Happily I escaped unhurt, though the shots and splinters flew thick about me during the whole fight."

*Opportunity in Enslavement* After the war, Pascal sold Equiano to a captain, who in turn sold the young man to Robert King, a Philadelphia merchant who operated in the West Indies. Seeing potential in Equiano, King gave him a respectable position as shipping and receiving clerk, as well as his personal barber, currier of his horses, and even the manager of his ships. Equiano also helped Thomas Farmer, a captain who shipped cargo for King throughout the West Indies and the southern American colonies. In this position, Equiano had considerable responsibility and traveled for four years, and beheld sights many other slaves could not. However, he never stopped yearning for his freedom. Finally, in 1765 King struck a deal with Equiano—he would allow him to buy his freedom for forty pounds, the price King had paid for him. Equiano saved money from side trading that King allowed him to do, and, when he was in his early twenties, accumulated enough to purchase his freedom.

*Free Man* As a free man, Equiano traveled throughout the West Indies and America and eventually returned to England. There, he decided to improve himself through education. He indulged both practical and eclectic interests and learned arithmetic, hairdressing, and how to play the French horn. More than anything, Equiano wanted to increase his income and achieve the status of a "cultured gentleman." To this end, he got a job working for Dr. Charles Irving, a well-known scientist who experimented with the purification of salt water. Equiano also traveled through Europe and the Mediterranean, where he experienced grand opera, studied architecture, and savored gourmet food and wine. In 1773 Equiano joined Dr. Irving on an expedition to the Arctic to search for a passage to India. Equiano eventually returned to America where he became involved in the study of different religions and in the abolition movement.

*Later Years in London* In later years, Equiano went back to London and was appointed commissary for Stores for the Black Poor, an emigrationist group whose goal was to return blacks to Africa. Equiano publicly challenged the mismanagement of funds and supplies he had witnessed during his own emigration experience and worked to expose the inhumane treatment of slaves. In 1788, Equiano even petitioned the Queen of England on behalf of his enslaved fellow Africans. Equiano married Susanna Cullen in April 1792 and had two daughters, Ann Maria and Johanna. He died just five years later, on March 31, 1797.

## Works in Literary Context

Equiano is justly considered a pioneer in the slave-narrative genre. His writing is one of the earliest written accounts of the African-American experience. Scholars appreciate Equiano's autobiography for introducing the themes of the quest, redemption, alienation, and exile that resonate through later African-American writings.

## LITERARY AND HISTORICAL CONTEMPORARIES

Equiano's famous contemporaries include:

**Jonathan Edwards Jr.** (1745–1801) Edwards was a Congregationalist minister who wrote one of the earliest anti-slavery publications in the Library of Congress collections.

**Hannah More** (1745–1833): The social reformer Hannah More was known for her writings on abolition and her contribution to the Society for Effecting the Abolition of the African Slave Trade.

**Elizabeth Freeman** (1742–1829): After experiencing physical abuse as a slave, Freeman (also known as Mum Bett), with the help of a lawyer, launched the case *Brom and Bett v. Ashley* against her owners. This set a precedent for the abolition of slavery in Massachusetts.

**Thomas Jefferson** (1743–1826): The principal author of the Declaration of Independence, Jefferson was a slave owner who eventually came to believe that slavery was immoral and should be abolished.

*Pioneer of the Slave Narrative* The slave narrative emerged in the early seventeenth century and was founded on personal accounts written in a variety of forms by enslaved Africans. Despite its early roots, the genre did not become popular until the mid-nineteenth century with Frederick Douglass's *Narrative of the Life of Frederick Douglass, An American Slave* (1845) and Booker T. Washington's *Up From Slavery; An Autobiography* (1901). But, Equiano's *The Interesting Narrative of the Life of Olaudah Equiano, or Gustavus Vassa, the African*, notes critic Paul Edwards, is "the most remarkable of the 18th century." Equiano once said he wanted to be "an instrument of [his] suffering countrymen." Wilfred D. Samuels suggests that "Equiano's narrative must, to a great degree, be perceived as the mold from which much early black fiction was first cast, particularly since it is apparently one of the first records to shape the experiences of the black African diaspora during slavery." At a time when slavery was not often discussed publicly, Equiano championed the issue through his own story and by criticizing proslavery rhetoric.

*Religion in The Interesting Narrative of the Life of Olaudah Equiano* Critics say one reason that Equiano's narrative became popular was its spiritual references. In a way, they argue, the heart of his story grows from his religious freedom more than from his physical freedom. Even in his portrait, printed in the book, he holds a Bible showing Acts 4:12, which states: "For there is no other name under heaven by which we must be saved." For Equiano's readership, this reference showed

# COMMON HUMAN EXPERIENCE

*The Interesting Narrative of the Life of Olaudah Equiano* was one of the first books to document the personal experience of an early African American and to give displaced people a voice. Other slave narratives that capture the African American experience include:

*Incidents in the Life of a Slave Girl* (1861), a memoir by Harriet Jacobs. This autobiographical slave narrative follows Jacobs' courageous story as she chooses to hide out in a crawl space for years, all in her quest for freedom.

*The American Slave: A Composite Autobiography* (1972–1979), edited by George P. Rawick. This collection of narratives from over 2,300 former slaves was gathered from 1936 to 1938 through the Works Progress Administration.

*Narrative of Sojourner Truth* (1850), a memoir by Sojourner Truth. Dictated to Olive Gilbert, the narrative chronicles Truth's life as a slave in rural New York, her separation from her family, her religious conversion, and her life as a traveling preacher.

*The Confessions of Nat Turner* (1831), as recorded by Thomas R. Gray. Gray, Turner's lawyer, published the book about Turner's participation in a brutal slave revolt after Turner's trial and execution.

Equiano looking only to Jesus for salvation. Additionally, when he writes of his early childhood in Nigeria, Equiano uses many religious and cultural analogies to show commonality between his Ibo people and the Jews, a nation with their own historical trials and persecution, and truly believed "that the one people had sprung from the other."

Not only was religion featured in Equiano's book, but it and other narratives like it helped pair religion and the abolitionist movement. Espousing the message that all souls are equal, Equiano's helped strengthen opposition to slavery and earned the attention and support of evangelists like John Wesley, the abolitionist founder of Methodism. Sermons took on a new antislavery message, and by the 1780s, Baptist and Methodist groups were encouraging their followers to free their slaves as proof of their faith in God.

## Works in Critical Context

***The Interesting Narrative of the Life*** With its vivid portrayal of the African-American experience, *The Interesting Narrative of the Life of Olaudah Equiano* changed the face of autobiographical writing at a time when African Americans were little more than commodity. Equiano's narrative made details of enslavement public and, in its authenticity, forced readers to realize the injustice, violence, and reality of slavery.

Equiano's memoir was received positively response by readers and was reviewed in leading journals. Interestingly, many did not believe Equiano, or any black man, could write a story that well. *The Monthly Review* critic wrote: "We entertain no doubt of the general authenticity of this very intelligent African's interesting story; though it is not improbable that some English writer has assisted him in the compilement, or, at least, the correction of his book: for it is sufficiently well written."

## Responses to Literature

4. In a sense, Equiano's narrative represents a series of personal voyages. Write an essay comparing the voyage that the captive Equiano makes to America with the voyage that the "free" Equiano makes years later aboard various trading vessels. Use examples from his narrative to compare, contrast, and frame your essay.

5. Equiano's narrative strongly convinced John Wesley and other religious evangelists to oppose slavery. Discuss what parts of Equiano's narrative you think might have persuaded Wesley and others to publicly promote the notion that all people are the same, and should be treated as such, in the eyes of God.

6. Some critics have called Equiano's narrative a book about spiritual transformation. Write a short essay in which you agree or disagree with that classification, using examples from the narrative to support your ideas.

BIBLIOGRAPHY

**Books**

*African American Autobiography: A Collection of Critical Essays.* Ed. William L. Andrews. Englewood Cliffs, N.J.: Prentice-Hall, 1993.

Baker, Houston. *The Journey Back.* Chicago: University of Chicago Press, 1981.

Blassingame, John. *The Slave Community.* New York: Oxford University Press, 1972.

Bontemps, Arna, ed. *Great Slave Narratives.* Boston: Beacon Press, 1969.

Brawley, Benjamin. *Early Negro American Writers.* Chapel Hill, N.C.: University of North Carolina Press, 1953.

Butterfield, Stephen. *Black Autobiography in America.* Amherst, Mass.: University of Massachusetts Press, 1974.

Curtin, Philip. *Africa Remembered.* Madison, Wis.: University of Wisconsin Press, 1967.

Samuels, Wilfred D. "Olaudah Equiano." in Harris, Trudier, ed. *Dictionary of Literary Biography, Volume 50: Afro-American Writers Before the Harlem Renaissance.* Detroit: Gale, 1986.

# ✸ Louise Erdrich

BORN: *1954*

NATIONALITY: *American*

GENRE: *Poetry, fiction*

MAJOR WORKS:

*Love Medicine* (1984, 1993)

*The Beet Queen* (1986)

*Tracks* (1988)

*Baptism of Desire* (1989)

*The Antelope Wife* (1998)

*A Plague of Doves* (2008)

## Overview

The strength and endurance of the Chippewa people inspire Louise Erdrich's work. The notion of survival drives her storytelling no matter what genre she chooses. Whether she writes about Native Americans or people outside that community, Erdrich plays with the theme of human transcendence. In both her poetry and her fiction, she demonstrates that tribal culture endures in new forms, even as Native American life seems relegated

Louise Erdrich  *AP Images.*

to the margins of society. Erdrich's characters are comic and eccentric, yet fall into a mythic category as they try to overcome feelings of alienation, abandonment, and exploitation.

## Biographical and Historical Context

***Growing Up On Turtle Mountain***  Karen Louise Erdrich was born in Little Falls, Minnesota, but spent her childhood near or on the Turtle Mountain Chippewa reservation in North Dakota. Her maternal grandparents lived on the reservation, and her parents—her German–born father and Chippewa mother—worked as teachers for the Bureau of Indian Affairs boarding school. Family members inspired much of her writing. For example, her paternal grandmother, Mary Erdrich Korll, became a character in the novel *The Beet Queen* (1986) as well as in the poetry sequence called "The Butcher's Wife," included in the books *Jacklight* (1984) and *Baptism of Desire* (1989). Erdrich, in an interview for *Reader's Digest* points to her family as the source of her narrative creativity:

> The people in our families made everything into a story. They love to tell a good story. People just sit and the stories start coming, one after another. You just sort of grab the tail of the last person's story: it reminds you of something and you keep going on. I suppose that when you grow up constantly hearing the stories rise, break and fall, it gets into you somehow.

***Turning Reality Into Fiction***  Erdrich was educated, for the most part, in public school, but did attend a parochial school for a few years. Her stint in private school inspired at least one small detail in *The Beet Queen*, in which character Wallace Pfef is described as a supporter of the B# piano club. When Erdrich took piano lessons with Sister Anita at parochial school, she was elected to her own B# piano club. These and other details from her early education informed her experiences and her later writing.

In 1972, Erdrich received scholarships to Dartmouth College as part of its first coeducational class. That same year Michael Dorris, her future husband, was appointed head of the Native American studies department. Over a decade later, they would begin their successful collaboration on "The Broken Cord" (1989), a children's story, which Dorris wrote and Erdrich illustrated. At Dartmouth, Erdrich also published work in university literary magazines, but did not realize her talent until the magazine *Ms.* accepted one of her poems. Shortly thereafter, in 1975, the American Academy of Poets prized her work.

After graduating from Dartmouth with a Bachelor's degree in 1976, Erdrich worked at various minimum-wage jobs, many of which added texture to her fiction. In 1979, Erdrich accepted a fellowship at Johns Hopkins University, where she was able to focus solely on her

## LITERARY AND HISTORICAL CONTEMPORARIES

Louise Erdrich's famous contemporaries include:

**Sherman Alexie** (1966–) Alexie, the son of a Spokane Indian mother and a Coeur d'Alene Indian father, is a poet, novelist, and short story writer.

**Leslie Marmon Silko** (1948–): A novelist and poet, Silko was credited in 1977 as being the first female American Indian novelist.

**Buffy Sainte-Marie** (1941–): Singer, songwriter, activist, and Cree Indian, Sainte-Marie is known for her antiwar song, "Universal Soldier." She won an Oscar for writing the song, "Up Where You Belong," from the film, *Officer and a Gentleman*.

**Robbie Robertson** (1941–): Of Mohawk heritage, Robertson is the guitarist and principal songwriter for Bob Dylan's The Band, but has also composed music for films like *Raging Bull*.

writing. With her master's degree in hand, she became editor of the Boston Indian Council newspaper, *The Circle*. Erdrich also received writing fellowships in 1980 to the MacDowell Colony and in 1981 to the Yaddo Colony.

***Literary Success Across Genres*** Erdrich's literary career officially began in 1984 with a collection of poems, *Jacklight*. The jacklight of the title poem refers to the bright light that hunters use illegally to draw deer from the forest. Throughout the course of her career, Erdrich also collaborated on several works with Michael Dorris. They married in 1981 and had six children together. Their critically-acclaimed, award-winning projects include short stories and Erdrich's first novel, *Love Medicine* (1984), a very popular book which Erdrich revised in 1993. *Love Medicine* was made into a television serial, and movie rights were also optioned. The work was also translated into more than eighteen languages. Dorris and Erdrich also worked together on the novel *The Crown of Columbus* (1991).

After the success of *Love Medicine*, her second novel, *The Beet Queen* (1986), received mixed reviews for not completely focusing on Native American themes. It also incited what some call "the Silko-Erdrich controversy," in which writer Native American writer Leslie Marmon Silko criticized the novel for not exposing enough of the racism running through North Dakota society. Erdrich returned to her Native American roots in her third novel, *Tracks* (1988), a favorite among her readers. A year later, her second book of poetry, *Baptism of Desire* (1989), revisited the themes and personages of *Jacklight*.

In addition to publishing several more novels and poetry collections, Erdrich contributed numerous short stories, essays, and book reviews to periodicals such as the *New Yorker* and *Kenyon Review*. Sadly, the collaborative projects she enjoyed producing with her husband ceased upon his death in 1997. Her most recent book, *The Porcupine Year* (2008), takes place in the nineteenth century and tells the story of an eleven year old girl named Omakayas. The novel follows Omakayas as she and her family journey by canoe from the shores of Lake Superior along the rivers of northern Minnesota in search of a new home.

***Teaching and Honors*** Erdrich has taught poetry with the North Dakota State Arts Council and creative writing at Johns Hopkins University. She also returned to Dartmouth College as a visiting fellow. Her work has earned a Pushcart Prize, an American Book Award, a National Book Critics Circle Award, and a *Los Angeles Times* Book Award, among other honors. Erdrich has also garnered a Guggenheim fellowship and a fellowship from the National Endowment for the Arts. Erdrich now lives with her family in Minnesota.

## Works in Literary Context

***Ethnicity and Humanity: Love Medicine*** Much of Erdrich's work revolves around similar themes, motifs, and conflicts. A recurring theme in Erdrich's work is the conflict between American Indian culture and white culture. For example, in *Love Medicine*, most of her characters are greatly affected by their position as Indians trapped inside white culture. Their narratives show the realities of contemporary reservation life: alcoholism, suicide, abandoned children, as well as the community of extended families, hope for better lives, and a reliance on humor. Though issues of race and ethnicity reside at the core of the book, the novel promotes the idea of being primarily human, rather than being primarily Indian. Racial prejudice in the story goes both ways, and in this novel, blood ultimately means less than love.

***The Voices of Multiple Narrators*** Erdrich often uses multiple narrators to build her stories. She experiments with multiple narrators to give the reader a comprehensive understanding of the world created inside her work, and to foster a sense of community. This collective of voices allows for different perspectives and different realities, as well as presents the opportunity for certain details and events to be better clarified for the reader. The narrators also deepen the complex relationships Erdrich draws in her novels. In *Love Medicine*, for instance, multiple narrators act as storytellers, yet each voice remains distinct. In this way, the solo voices combine to mimic a chorus of tribal storytelling. In *The Beet Queen*, Erdrich also employs several first-person narrators, in addition to a third-person omniscient narrator who summarizes and explains things more thoroughly. Readers have appreciated this aspect of her work. An essayist for *Contemporary Novelists* noted:

Erdrich's accomplishment is that she is weaving a body of work that goes beyond portraying contemporary Native American life as descendants of a politically dominated people to explore the great universal questions—questions of identity, pattern versus randomness, and the meaning of life itself.

## Works in Critical Context

Erdrich has been recognized throughout her career for illuminating the many facets of Native American culture. As critic and scholar Elizabeth Blair wrote: "The painful history of Indian-white relations resonates throughout her work. In her hands we laugh and cry while listening to and absorbing home truths that, taken to heart, have the power to change our world."

*Critical Praise for Love Medicine*    Critics of *Love Medicine* confront the book's thematic elements, narrative strategies, and structural readings of Chippewa culture. The novel received mostly praise from the press, academics, and fellow writers. For example, Native American novelist Louis Owens complimented Erdrich's portrayal of contemporary Native American life in the following way: "The seemingly doomed Indian[s] ... hang on in spite of it all, confront with humor the pain and confusion of identity and, like a storyteller, weave a fabric of meaning and significance out of the remnants." Critic Thomas Matchie called the novel "A Female *Moby Dick*" in an article which referenced the nickname. He also wrote:

> *Love Medicine* is different from so much of Native American literature in that it is not polemic—there is no ax to grind, no major indictment of white society. It is simply a story about Indian life; its politics, humor, emptiness, and occasional triumphs. If Erdrich has a gift, it is the ability to capture the inner life and language of her people.

*Silence and Energy in The Beet Queen*    Although *The Beet Queen* was nominated for the National Book Critics Circle Award, Erdrich was harshly criticized for her work on that book. To many readers, reviewers, and critics, the novel, as suggested by Susan Meisenhelder, "is unusual in Native American literature because of its apparent silence on the issue of race." Leslie Marmon Silko accused the novel of not being Indian enough, but other critics like Meisenhelder and Gerald Vizenor, a Chippewa critic and author, ultimately defended Erdrich's approach. As Dorothy Wickenden observed: "[Erdrich] has conveyed unforgettably the mixture of the prosaic and the uncanny that informs the lives of dreamers and plodders alike. And she has endowed all of her characters with an idiosyncratic trait that both isolates them and allows them to survive: the energy and ingenuity to grapple with the terrors of intimacy."

## Responses to Literature

1. Write a one-page essay detailing what you know about your heritage. Then, using your background

---

## COMMON HUMAN EXPERIENCE

Louise Erdrich closely bases her poetry and fiction on her personal experiences and Native American heritage. Other works inspired by a similar combination of biographical and cultural elements include:

*People of the Whale* (2008), a novel by Linda Hogan. Written by a Native American Pulitzer Prize finalist, this novel is grounded in the world of the fictional A'atsika, a Native people of the American West Coast who find their mythical origins in the whale and the octopus.

*Ceremony* (1986), a novel by Leslie Marmon Silko. This novel follows Tayo, a young Native American, held captive by the Japanese during World War II. His return to the Laguna Pueblo reservation forces him to deal with his feeling of estrangement and alienation.

*Zitkala-sa American Indian Stories, Legends* (2003), a collection by Zitkala-sa. Raised on a Sioux reservation, Zitkala-sa was educated in the late nineteenth century at boarding schools that enforced assimilation. These stories illuminate her personal experience.

*Ten Little Indians* (2003), a short story collection by Sherman Alexie. This critically acclaimed collection offers different stories about Native American characters who stand at personal and cultural crossroads.

---

as inspiration, write a poem or short story that reflects your feelings about where you come from. Look to Erdrich's writing for inspiration.

2. Louis Owens, in writing about *Love Medicine*, said: "The seemingly doomed Indian[s] ... hang on in spite of it all, confront with humor the pain and confusion of identity and, like a storyteller, weave a fabric of meaning and significance out of the remnants." Referencing examples in the novel, discuss whether or not you agree with Owens.

3. Many of Erdrich's stories have more than one narrator. Choose one of Erdrich's novels and write an essay in which you discuss the effect these multiple points of view have on the novel.

BIBLIOGRAPHY

**Books**

Beidler, Peter. "Louise Erdrich" *Dictionary of Literary Biography, Volume 175: Native American Writers of the United States.*. Ed. Kenneth Roemer. Detroit: The Gale Group, 1997.

Rosenberg, Ruth. "Louise Erdrich" *Dictionary of Literary Biography, Volume 152: American Novelists Since World War II*. Ed. James and Wanda Giles. Detroit: The Gale Group, 1995.

Silberman, Robert. "Opening the Text: *Love Medicine* and the Return of the Native American Woman." *Native American Indian Literatures.* Ed. Gerald Vizenor. Albuquerque: University of New Mexico Press, 1989.

Woodward, Pauline Groetz. "Louise Erdrich" *American Writers Supp. 4.* Woodbridge, Conn.: Charles Scribner's Sons, 1996.

**Periodicals**

Matchie, Thomas. "*Love Medicine*: A Female *Moby Dick*" *The Midwest Quarterly.* 30:4 (Summer 1989).

Meisenhelder, Susan. "Race and Gender in Louise Erdrich's *The Beet Queen*" *Ariel.* 25:1 (January 1994).

Smith, Jean. "Transpersonal Selfhood: The Boundaries of Identity in Louise Erdrich's *Love Medicine*." *Studies in American Indian Literatures.* 3 (Winter 1991).

Towery, Margery. "Continuity and Connection: Characters in Louise Erdrich's Fiction." *American Indian Culture and Research Journal.* 16:4 (1992).

Van Dyke, Annette. "Questions of the Spirit: Bloodlines in Louise Erdrich's Chippewa Landscape." *Studies in American Indian Literatures.* 4 (Spring 1992).

# ✸ Martín Espada

BORN: *1957, Brooklyn, New York*

NATIONALITY: *American*

GENRE: *Poetry*

MAJOR WORKS:

*The Immigrant Ice Boy's Bolero* (1982)
*Trumpets from the Islands of Their Eviction* (1987)
*Rebellion Is the Circle of a Lover's Hands* (1990)

## Overview

Throughout his career, poet Martín Espada has been inspired by social and political issues, with emphasis on Hispanic causes. His work reflects the gritty reality of individual resistance and, in portraying this resistance, offers a glimmer of hope for the immigrant and working-class community. In depicting Puerto Ricans and Chicanos adjusting to life in the United States or South American Latinos standing up to their own repressive governments, Espada gives poetic voice to their "otherness," their powerlessness, poverty, and alienation.

Martín Espada    *SUZANNE KREITER / Boston Globe / Landov*

## Works in Biographical and Historical Context

*Childhood Activism*  Espada's interest in social and political activism began at an early age in Brooklyn, New York. His father, Frank Espada, was a longtime leader in the Puerto Rican community and a vocal participant in the civil rights movement. For example, in 1964, Frank was one of eight hundred people arrested at the World's Fair in New York for boycotting the Schaefer Beer Brewery because it did not hire African Americans or Puerto Ricans. After this incident, Martín believed his father was dead since no one had heard from him for five days. When father and son reunited, Frank began to take Martín to rallies and meetings, providing Martín with a hands-on political education. "These were imprints on my imagination," Martín recalls. Frank's dedication to his principles and his similarity to a guerilla teacher in Emiliano Zapata's army (Zapata was a revolutionary in the Mexican army) inspired the title of Martín's book of essays, *Zapata's Disciple* (1998).

*Poetry, History, and Politics*  Espada began writing poetry at age sixteen. In an interview with Elizabeth Gunderson, Espada talks about how writing came from his search for identity:

> I think for the period of three years that I was going to high school on Long Island I heard the word 'spic' more often than I heard my own name. There's one of two ways that you can respond to that pressure. You can either run like crazy from the identity being attacked and say, 'no, I'm not that, I'm not what you're calling me,' or you can confront the hostility directly by asserting your identity. I chose the second path. I did it with poetry.

Espada pursued his creative interest through to college at the University of Maryland, but he left after a year because he could not personally identify with the traditional poets he was required to study. However, through a friend, he discovered the voices of emerging Latin American poets whose work was inspired by their explosive culture and politics. He returned to his postsecondary education at the University of Wisconsin where he eventually received a Bachelor of Arts degree in history from the University of Wisconsin–Madison, as well as a J. D. from Northeastern University. For many years, he worked as a tenant lawyer and a supervisor of a legal services program.

*An Award-winning Poet*  In 1982, Espada published his first book of poetry, *The Immigrant Iceboy's Bolero*, which included photographs taken by his father. But he only started considering himself a true poet when he received a $5,000 grant from the Massachusetts Artists Foundation while attending law school at Northeastern University in Boston. In 1986, he received a $20,000 fellowship from the National Endowment of the Arts. His

second book, *Trumpets from the Islands of Their Eviction*, published in 1987 by Bilingual Press and funded by the Hispanic Research Center of Arizona State University, brought him a bit more attention. But his third book, *Rebellion Is the Circle of a Lover's Hands*, published in 1990, won the PEN/Revson award and the Paterson Poetry Prize. Critics praised the work in the *Boston Globe* and the *New York Times Book Review*. He also landed an interview on National Public Radio.

*Teaching and Honors*  In 1993, Espada joined the English department faculty at the University of Massachusetts, Amherst, where he teaches creative writing workshops and courses in Latino poetry. He actively writes and has published several poetry collections over the last few years. *Imagine the Angels of Bread* (1996) garnered an American Book Award and was a finalist for the National Book Critics' Circle Award.

## Works in Literary Context

Linda Frost in the *Minnesota Review* once described Espada's poetic approach: "Espada uses his characters as excavated archetypes, cultural heroes who give names and faces to the members of this ignored community who have been 'evicted' from their original home of Puerto Rico ... and their not-so-friendly new home in the United States." As Frost suggests, Espada provides an alienated, exiled community with symbols, voices, and

## COMMON HUMAN EXPERIENCE

Martín Espada uses his personal experiences, political conviction, and Puerto Rican heritage to inspire his poetry. Other works inspired by a similar combination of biographical and cultural elements include:

*Caramelo* (2003), a novel by Sandra Cisneros. This novel follows the Reyes family from 1920s Mexico City and Acapulco to 1950s Chicago.

*Infinite Divisions: An Anthology of Chicana Literature* (1993), a collection edited by Tey Diana Rebolledo and Eliana S. Rivero. This anthology includes a century's worth of Chicana writers and explores the Chicana identity, culture, and American experience.

*Poetry Like Bread: Poets of the Political Imagination* (1994), a collection edited by Martín Espada. This anthology includes works by poets throughout North and South America.

*A Simple Plan* (2007), a poetry collection by Gary Soto. In this book, National Book Award finalist Gary Soto confronts his Mexican American heritage, his childhood, and a kinship with the less fortunate.

agency. Thematically and stylistically, Espada draws attention to the presence of peoples and cultures forgotten or ignored.

***Political Imagery*** Politics generate much of the imagery throughout Espada's work. In his poem "Tiburon," he metaphorically links the American assimilation of Puerto Rico to a shark devouring a fisherman, while "From an Island You Cannot Name" tells the story of a Puerto Rican veteran enraged when identified as a Negro by hospital authorities. Even in *City of Coughing and Dead Radiators* (1993), though Espada employs somewhat of a humorous tone, his imagery and narratives still contain a darker edge that cuts across larger issues. For example, the poem "Skull Beneath the Skin" juxtaposes mangoes with the image of piled skulls belonging to victims of El Salvadoran death squads. In an interview with Steven Ratiner, Espada said: "[W]hat I am striving for is to tell the story as a journalist would, and that involves a multiple series of choices including choice of story, choice of sources, choice of images and language."

***The Voices of Hope and Resistance*** Critic David Charlton wrote: "Espada has proven himself a strong adversary for supporters of a status quo that thrives on keeping a class of people as victims." The entwined themes of hope and resistance rise throughout Espada's work, born from the experiences of his American work-ing-class and immigrant subjects. For example, in the poem "Trumpets from the Islands of Their Eviction," a woman protests the squalor in which she must live by sending dead mice from her apartment to her landlord. In "Jorge the Janitor Finally Quits," the title character leaves his menial job after being unappreciated and scolded for his bad attitude. Unfortunately, resistance in Espada's poems is rarely rewarded, even when it is shown as the right thing to do; the woman who sends dead mice to her landlord is evicted, and Jorge imagines that no one will even notice he has left his job.

### Works in Critical Context

Espada been lauded throughout his career for poetically confronting issues important to the working class and the immigrant. But his work has been controversial: for instance, in Espada's essay "All Things Censored," he recounts the story of how, after inviting him to write a poem, National Public Radio refused to air the work because it defended Mumia Abu-Jamal, the African American journalist on death row.

***Rebellion Is the Circle of a Lover's Hands*** In the *Partisan Review*, Roger Gilbert described *Rebellion Is the Circle of a Lover's Hands* (1990) as "continually informed by anger at social and economic injustices. This anger gives the book considerable moral urgency." Also with admiration, Alan Gilbert of the *Boston Review* called "the individuality of Espada's voice ... one to which any attentive reader can respond. These poems deserve an audience." John Bradley also praised the collection in the *Bloomsbury Review*, as did Leslie Ulman in the *Kenyon Review*: "the poems in this collection tell their stories and flesh out their characters deftly, without shrillness or rhetoric, and vividly enough to invite the reader into a shared sense of loss."

***Zapata's Disciple*** With *Zapata's Disciple* (1998), Espada departs in genre but not theme, tapping into the familiar culture of machismo, the resistance against Latino immigrants and the Spanish language, and American colonialism. Rafael Campo in *Progressive* said Espada had courage in writing a collection of essays that "take[s] on the life-and-death issues of American society at large." Campo also suggested "Espada builds his hopes for a better world: one informed by poetry's ability to forge such empathic connections." Rebecca Martin of the *Library Journal* described the work as "passionate yet unsentimental prose."

### Responses to Literature

1. Choose a poem from Espada's second book, *Trumpets from the Island of Their Eviction*. Write a one-page paper describing how the narrative in the poem might be called a story of both resistance and hope.

2. Linda Frost, in writing about *Trumpets from the Island of Their Eviction*, said: "Espada writes to stir

up the blood of those in despair and those in ignorance, and in these goals, he is indeed quite successful." Choose two poems in the collection and write an essay describing how the poems support or contradict Frost's commentary.

3. Choose one of your favorite Espada poems and think about its political and social message. Write an essay in which you discuss how the poem can be classified as "a powerful song we cannot ignore." Use examples from the poem to illustrate your argument.

BIBLIOGRAPHY

**Books**

Espada, Martín, and Steven Ratiner. "Giving Their Word: Conversations with Contemporary Poets." *Giving Their Word: Conversations with Contemporary Poets.* Amherst: University of Massachusetts Press, 2002. Reprinted in *Poetry Criticism.* Vol. 74. Edited by Michelle Lee. Gale, 2006.

**Periodicals**

Browning, Sarah. "Give Politics a Human Face: An Interview with Lawyer-Poet-Professor Martín Espada." *Valley Advocate* (November 18, 1993).

Espada, Martín and Elizabeth Gunderson. "Poets and Writers." *Poets & Writers* 23:2 (March–April 1995). Reprinted in *Poetry Criticism.* Ed. Michelle Lee. Vol. 74. Gale, 2006.

Salgado, Cesar A. "About Martín Espada." *Ploughshares* 31.1 (Spring 2005).

# ✸ Jeffrey Eugenides

BORN: *1960, Detroit, Michigan*

NATIONALITY: *American*

GENRE: *Fiction*

MAJOR WORKS:

*The Virgin Suicides* (1993)

*Middlesex* (2002)

## Overview

Eugenides's critically-acclaimed novels *The Virgin Suicides* (1993) and *Middlesex* (2002) are praised for their inventive point of view and narration. *Middlesex* won a Pulitzer Prize for fiction and was selected by Oprah Winfrey for her Book Club.

## Biographical and Historical Context

***From Grosse Pointe to Calcutta to Gettysburg***
Eugenides was born in 1960 to a Greek-American family in Grosse Pointe, Michigan, where *The Virgin Suicides* is set. He attended Grosse Pointe's University Liggett School, followed by Brown University in 1983. Before

Jeffrey Eugenides    *Eugenides, Jeffrey, photograph. © Jerry Bauer. Reproduced by permission.*

graduating from Brown, however, Eugenides had a variety of jobs, including cab driver in Detroit and volunteer for Mother Teresa in Calcutta, India, at her Home for the Dying. He even entertained the notion of becoming a Trappist monk. He later earned a Master of Arts degree in Creative Writing from Stanford University. In 1988, he published his first short story in the *The Gettysburg Review.*

***Suicides and Coppola***    *The Virgin Suicides* was inspired by his babysitter who had contemplated, along with her sisters at one time or another, committing suicide. The novel gained the interest of the mainstream public when it was adapted into a film by Sofia Coppola, but the novel had gotten its start when the writer George Plimpton published the first chapter in his magazine *The Paris Review.* The excerpt garnered the journal's Aga Khan Prize for Fiction that year. Though the book was unfinished, an agent signed Eugenides, which inspired him to finish the novel. *The Virgin Suicides* sold to the first publisher who read it.

***Marriage and Middlesex***    After *The Virgin Suicides,* Eugenides married and started a family. They traded New York for Berlin, where he finished *Middlesex* (2002), which was inspired by an autobiography written in the

# LITERARY AND HISTORICAL CONTEMPORARIES

Eugenides's famous contemporaries include:

**Kwame Kilpatrick** (1970–): Kilpatrick was the youngest person ever to be elected mayor of Detroit, Michigan—he was thirty-one when he was elected in 2001. Kilpatrick won a second term in 2005, but a series of scandals forced him to resign in 2008.

**David Sedaris** (1956–): Sedaris is an autobiographical humorist, a comedian, and the author of best-selling essays and short stories.

**Arianna Huffington** (1950–): Born in Athens, Huffington writes a syndicated socio-political column and founded *The Huffington Post*, an online liberal news site.

**Phedon Papamichael** (1962–): A Greek American cinematographer and director, Papamichael is known for his cinematography work on films such as *Walk the Line* (2005) and *3:10 to Yuma* (2007).

**Tina Fey** (1970–): Of Greek American heritage, Fey is an award-winning writer, comedienne, actress, and producer.

nineteenth century by Herculine Barbin. Barbin was identified as a female at birth and raised in a Catholic orphanage, but at age twenty-two, became identified as a male during a medical examination. *Middlesex* won a Pulitzer Prize for Fiction in 2003.

*Accolades* Eugenides's work has been published widely, including short stories in *The New Yorker*, *The Paris Review*, *Best American Short Stories*, and *The Gettysburg Review*. He has been honored with fellowships from the Guggenheim Foundation and the National Endowment for the Arts, and the Harold D. Vursell Award from the American Academy of Arts and Letters, among others. In 2008, Eugenides edited the short story collection, *My Mistress's Sparrow is Dead: Great Love Stories, from Chekhov to Munro*. The title of the collection comes from a line created by the Latin poet Catullus, whose pet sparrow was a constant obstacle in his desire for his girlfriend Lesbia.

## Works in Literary Context

Many critics find the most distinctive thing about Eugenides's writing is the point of view. In an interview with *3 A.M. Magazine*, Eugenides acknowledged the unique narrative voices that have made his work popular with readers and well-received by critics:

> I don't know why I seem to like impossible voices. There's something I like about … not being able to know exactly where the voice is coming from. Certainly, that's the case in *The Virgin Suicides*

where you don't know how many boys it is. Is it one, two or a hundred, you don't know. But the voice is compelling and holding your attention and it seems to me that only in novels and in literature can you come up with such voices. So I, at least in these two novels, tried to take advantage of the ability of novels to be told by voices that you don't encounter every day.

*The Voices of Middlesex* In a review of *The Virgin Suicides* in *The Times*, columnist Michael Wright wrote, "Literary novelists are forever experimenting with narrative voices first person ('I') or third person ('she') in the quest to find an authentic and original means of expressing their vision." For Eugenides, authentically capturing the self-conscious voice of the *Middlesex* narrator was difficult: "The voice was one of the big problems, because I wanted to tell his story in the first person—I wanted this intimate portrait of an intersex person written from the inside." The novel also features elements of third-person narration, necessary to convey a story that spans generations. According to Eugenides, "After a while I stopped worrying about the voice from moment to moment, whether it sounded like a woman or a man, I just let the voice be either masculine or hermaphroditic, whatever it was."

*Classical Themes in Middlesex and The Virgin Suicides* Critics find classical allusions running through both of Eugenides's novels. Some see similarities between the boys in *The Virgin Suicides* and a Greek Chorus, but the epic *Middlesex* evokes the most obvious references, particularly since the story deals with three generations of a Greek family. In fact, in a book review for *Daily Press*, Jeff Turrentine wrote, "[Eugenides is] well on his way to becoming a spectacular mythologist." Turrentine describes the "origin" of the protagonist in *Middlesex* as "mythic" and points out that "Odysseys, shape-shifters, incest, Sapphic lust and generation-spanning 'curses' fill the book." Eugenides was inspired by the ancient myth of wise old Greek Tiresias, who had experienced life both as a woman and a man. Calliope, the protagonist, was named for the goddess of epic poetry.

## Works in Critical Context

Critics and scholars find similar themes holding up both of Eugenides's novels. For example, Mark Lawson of *Europe Intelligence Wire* compares the novels, noting that while *The Virgin Suicides* "reflected on connections between sex and death, its successor considers the links between sex, life and inheritance." But, critics do find pointed differences: Keith Gessen of *Nation* believes *Middlesex* is a "politically effective" novel that puts "too much energy" into "the assurance of the author's good intentions" and results in "a measured, highly adequate bloodlessness." Kristin McCloy of the *Los Angeles Times Book Review*, however, said of *The Virgin Suicides*, "Mordant to be sure, and always understated, Eugenides's sense of the absurd is relentless."

***Middlesex*** Most critics of *Middlesex* praise the novel's characterization. Max Watman, in *New Criterion*, commented that Eugenides made normal "the experience of a hermaphrodite and turns Cal into something other than a freak." James Wood, in the *New Republic*, agreed: "Eugenides makes Calliope credible: she is not merely a theme." Joanne Wilkinson for *Booklist* applauds his "affecting characterization of a brave and lonely soul and [his] vivid depiction of exactly what it means to be both male and female."

***The Virgin Suicides*** In his review of *The Virgin Suicides* in *The Times*, Michael Wright noted that "the extent to which text resonates is utterly dependent on . . . the reader's creative participation, on his or her willingness to scratch away at the black waxy surface to reveal the bright colours hidden beneath." Wright also suggests Eugenides "has a macabre imagination, and he paints his weird images with memorable intensity." Similarly, Michiko Kakutani of the *New York Times* described the novel's ending as "lyrical and portentous, ferocious and elegiac." In the same vein, *New York Review of Books* critic Alice Truax wrote, "On [the novel's] first page, he makes it clear that his title means what it says, and that he plans to spin a dreamy, elegiac tale from its terrible promise."

## Responses to Literature

1. In *Middlesex*, Cal speaks of his own conception: "The timing of the thing had to be just so in order for me to become the person I am. Delay the act by an hour and you change the gene selection." Write an essay in which you discuss your own belief in chance, fate, or free will and compare your ideas to those in *Middlesex*. To better illustrate your points, use examples from the novel.

2. With a group of your classmates, discuss why you think Cal in *Middlesex* chooses to live as a man rather than as a woman. Look at specific sections of the novel to support your ideas.

3. Write an essay in which you discuss how *Middlesex* could be considered a novel about America and the American Dream.

4. Eugenides's work is known for its innovative narrative strategy. With a group of your classmates, discuss the collective narrative of *The Virgin Suicides*. What do you see as the effect of more than one narrator?

---

# COMMON HUMAN EXPERIENCE

In *Middlesex*, Eugenides creates an unusual bildungsroman, or coming of age novel. Other bildungsromans include:

*Girl Walking Backwards* (1998), a novel by Bett Williams. This coming-of-age novel focuses on a sixteen-year-old lesbian who lives in California with her mother, who is on the verge of a nervous breakdown.

*A Hero Ain't Nothing But a Sandwich* (1978), a novel by Alice Childress. This novel, set in 1970s Harlem, chronicles the life of a thirteen-year-old heroin addict through multiple points of view.

*The Red Tent* (2005), a novel by Anita Diamant. This novel follows the life and womanhood of the Biblical Dinah, as told through her own voice.

*Black Swan Green* (2006), a novel by David Mitchell. This partial autobiography depicts one year in the life of a thirteen-year-old English boy, Jason Taylor.

BIBLIOGRAPHY

**Books**

"Eugenides, Jeffrey (1960–)." *Major 21st Century Writers*. Edited by Tracey Matthews. Vol. 2. Detroit: Gale, 2005.

"Middlesex." *Novels for Students*. Edited by Ira Milne. Vol. 24. Detroit: Gale, 2007.

**Periodicals**

Kakutani, Michiko. "Review of *The Virgin Suicides*." *New York Times* (March 19, 1993).

Lawson, Mark. "Gender Blender" *Europe Intelligence Wire* (October 6, 2002).

Mesic, Penelope. "Identity Crisis." *Book* (September–October 2002).

Turrentine, Jeff. "She's Come Undone." *Chicago Tribune* (September 1, 2002).

Wright, Michael. "Cosmic Tragedy of Small-town Nymphs; Books." *The Times (London)* (June 10, 1993).

**Web sites**

Moorhem, Bram. "Bram Moorhem Interviews Jeffrey Eugenides, author of *Middlesex* and *The Virgin Suicides*." *3 A.M. Magazine*. Retrieved October 11, 2008, from http://www.3ammagazine.com/litarchives/2003/sep/interview_jeffrey_eugenides.html. Last updated September 2003.

# Glossary of Literary Terms

The glossary contains terms found in various entries throughout the *Gale Contextual Encyclopedia of American Literature*. This glossary includes terms for various literary components or techniques relevant to the work of the authors, terms for important artistic movements or groups discussed in relation to the authors, and terms for social, political, or philosophical ideas that profoundly impacted American literature. Definitions for more basic literary terms, such as "figurative language," have not been included.

**ALLEGORY:** A work in which the entire narrative serves as a symbol for something beyond the surface-level story.

**ANACHRONISM:** A thing or idea mentioned in a work of art that occurs outside its normal place in time. In William Shakespeare's play *Julius Caesar*, for example, the author mentions the striking of a clock to indicate time passing—even though no such clocks existed in ancient Rome, the time period in which the play is set.

**ANTI-HERO:** A main character in a literary work whose actions and ideals would not generally be regarded as heroic, though the character may still be portrayed sympathetically by the author. Holden Caulfield, the protagonist of J. D. Salinger's novel *The Catcher in the Rye* (1951), is an example of an anti-hero.

**AVANT-GARDE:** Meaning "advance guard" in French, a term used to describe artists or artistic works that are considered innovative or nontraditional.

**BALLAD:** A poetic work written in the form of a traditional song that commonly relates a folk tale, myth, or legend. Ballads are often written in four-line stanzas with alternating lines of eight and six syllables, in which the lines with six syllables contain end-rhyme.

**BEAT GENERATION:** A collective term for a group of writers who rose to prominence in the late 1940s and 1950s. Their work and their lifestyles were marked by defiance of legal and cultural authority, experimentation with drugs and unconventional sexual relationships, interest in Eastern religions, and an affinity for improvisational jazz music. Famous Beat writers include: Allen Ginsberg, Jack Kerouac, and William S. Burroughs.

**BILDUNGSROMAN:** Taken from a German term meaning "novel of formation," a novel that documents the maturation of the protagonist. The bildungsroman is also commonly known as a "coming of age" novel.

**BLANK VERSE:** A type of poetry which follows a set pattern of stressed and unstressed syllables in each line, but does not feature consistent rhyme. Poet Robert Frost wrote many of his poems in blank verse.

**CAPTIVITY NARRATIVE:** A first-hand, nonfiction account of the captivity of a white American settler by Native Americans.

**COMEDY:** In classical Greek drama, a play that ends happily for its major characters; many ancient comedies poked fun at political figures or cultural stereotypes, which inspired the laughter modern audiences now associate with the term.

**CONFESSIONAL POETRY:** Confessional poetry is a kind of poetry popularized in the 1950s and 1960s characterized by revelations of extremely intimate, often unflattering details of the poet's private life. Subjects often include sex and drug use. Major confessional poets include Sylvia Plath and Anne Sexton.

**ENJAMBMENT:** In poetry, the splitting of a continuous phrase or sentence into two or more lines. The result is that a single line may appear to express an incomplete thought, though the work as a whole is afforded a more complex rhythm and structure. Poet e. e. cummings made frequent use of enjambment.

**EPIC:** A literary work, originally a work in poetic form, that focuses on large-scale events and themes, and often takes place over a long period of time. *The Odyssey*, an ancient Greek epic by Homer, is one of the earliest examples. The term is now often applied to long works that cover a time span of many years, such as Margaret Mitchell's 1936 novel *Gone With the Wind*.

**EPIGRAM:** A short, clever statement—often in the form of a couplet—intended to impart humor and insight. Dorothy Parker was famous for her witty epigrams.

**EPISTOLARY NOVEL:** A novel in which the story is told through letters written by one or more characters. Samuel Richardson was an early practitioner of the epistolary novel, with works such as *Pamela* (1740) and *Clarissa* (1748). Alice Walker produced a more recent version with her 1982 novel *The Color Purple*.

**EXISTENTIALISM:** A philosophical movement that gained popularity in the first half of the twentieth century, thanks to literary works by Jean-Paul Sartre and Simone de Beauvoir, among others. Existentialism is characterized by the idea that life does not have a greater meaning or purpose beyond that which people choose to create for themselves. Many prominent African American writers have been labeled existentialist, including Ralph Ellison and Richard Wright.

**EXPERIMENTAL NOVEL:** A work which defies the traditional structure or subject matter of a novel, and emphasizes style or technique over content. Thomas Pynchon's 1973 novel *Gravity's Rainbow*, for example, is considered an experimental novel.

**FABLE:** A short tale whose purpose is to impart a message or lesson, usually featuring animals as characters. "The Tortoise and the Hare" is a well-known example of a fable. James Thurber and Joel Chandler Harris are known for their fables.

**FARCE:** A dramatic work characterized by characters being put into comedic situations that are unlikely or improbable, as in Thornton Wilder's *The Matchmaker* (1954).

**FLASH FICTION:** Short fiction, usually under one thousand words, that despite its length contains all the traditional elements of story such as a protagonist and conflict that is somehow resolved. O. Henry and Ray Bradbury are both authors of flash fiction.

**FRAME NARRATIVE:** A literary device in which the main story being told to the reader is presented as a story being told by one of the characters within the work, as in "The Celebrated Jumping Frog of Calaveras County," an 1865 short story by Mark Twain.

**GONZO JOURNALISM:** A subjective style of journalism in which events are described from the reporter's point of view. Gonzo journalism originated with Hunter S. Thompson.

**GOTHIC FICTION:** A literary sub-genre that emerged in the last half of the eighteenth century and was characterized by eerie atmosphere, melodrama, mystery, and romance.

**IMAGISM:** A poetic movement of the early twentieth century that emphasized direct expression through concise imagery and non-standard structure. Ezra Pound was instrumental in the development of the Imagist movement, and poet Amy Lowell was a leading practitioner.

**IMPRESSIONISM:** An artistic movement that emerged during the latter half of the nineteenth century, and focused on artistic impression over realistic representation. In literature, impressionism was characterized by a focus on the depiction of the interior, mental landscapes of characters, and was associated with other literary movements such as Symbolism.

**IRONY:** A literary device in which a character's perception of reality differs from actual reality, or in which a character's words do not express their true feelings. Sarcasm is a well-known form of irony. Dramatic irony occurs when an audience is given information that is not known by one or more characters in the play.

**LIBRETTO:** A text for the vocal portion of an opera or other musical work, often written in verse form. Composers frequently employ well-known writers to write libretti for their works, and writers such as Paul Laurence Dunbar, Langston Hughes, and Gertrude Stein sometimes worked as librettists.

**LOST GENERATION:** A term used to describe a loosely defined group of American writers who spent time in Europe—especially Paris—following World War I. These writers, including Ernest Hemingway, F. Scott Fitzgerald, and Sherwood Anderson, were notable for themes of disillusionment in their works.

**MAGICAL REALISM:** A literary style developed primarily in South America in which fantastic or supernatural elements are woven into otherwise realistic tales. Writers commonly associated with magic realism include Jorge Luis Borges, Alejo Carpentier, Gabriel García Márquez, and Carlos Fuentes; however, the work of some North American writers has been labeled magical realist, including Toni Morrison's 1987 novel *Beloved* and John Cheever's famous 1947 short story "The Enormous Radio."

**MELODRAMA:** A literary work which contains heightened or exaggerated emotions from the characters. The term originally applied to theatrical productions in which music (or melody) was used to accentuate the drama occurring on the stage.

**MODERNISM:** An artistic movement during the early twentieth century influenced by the rapid industrialization, scientific advancements, and devastating warfare of the time. Modernist writers were noted for their radical departure from traditional literary forms, with notable Modernist works including T. S. Eliot's poem "The Waste Land" (1922) and James Joyce's novel *Ulysses* (1922).

**MUCKRAKERS:** A term applied to journalists and fiction writers of the late nineteenth and early twentieth century whose work uncovered corruption in the government and big business. Authors Frank Norris and Upton Sinclair were both considered muckrakers.

**NATURALISM:** A literary movement of the late nineteenth century that focused on realistic portrayals of people and situations, and specifically dealt with the effects of heredity and environment on a characters's personality and development. Stephen Crane is widely regarded as a Naturalist.

**NEOCLASSICISM:** A term describing art that sought inspiration in ancient Greek and Roman forms, with emphasis on rationalism and proportion. Phillis Wheatley is considered a neoclassical poet.

**NEW JOURNALISM:** A style of journalism popularized in the 1960s and 1970s in which the journalist employed such literary techniques as setting scenes, presenting subjects as fleshed out "characters," and offering details of setting and scene.

**NIHILISM:** A philosophical movement that first appeared in the nineteenth century and is characterized by the belief that life has no objective purpose, moral code, or value. Writers associated with nihilism include Ivan Turgenev, whose novel *Fathers and Sons* (1862) described the Russian Nihilist movement and popularized the concept. More recent fiction has also been labeled Nihilist, including Bret Easton Ellis's 1985 novel *Less Than Zero*.

**PARABLE:** A short tale meant to impart a message or lesson to the reader. Parables are similar to fables, but do not include supernatural or fantastic elements such as talking animals.

**PARODY:** A literary work designed to mock or criticize another, usually well-known literary work or genre. An early example is *Shamela* (1741), Henry Fielding's parody of the successful Samuel Richardson novel *Pamela* (1740). Wendy Wasserstein's *Sloth* (2006) is a recent example of a parody.

**PASTORAL:** Literature that depicts rural life, nature, and the people of a rural region in a highly idealized way. The *Eclogues* (c. 40 B.C.E.) by the ancient Roman poet Virgil are among the oldest examples of pastoral poetry. Some works by Willa Cather and Wallace Stegner contain pastoral elements.

**PICARESQUE:** A type of novel first developed in Spain that focuses on the adventures of a rogue, or clever antihero. Among many others, James Branch Cabell's 1919 novel *Jurgen* exhibits the key traits of the picaresque.

**POSTMODERNISM:** A post-World War II literary movement characterized by nonlinearity, or a nonstandard narrative timeline, as well as metafiction, in which the author shows awareness of the story as a work of fiction and may even appear as a character within it.

**PSEUDONYM:** An alternate name used by a writer, often to hide the writer's identity. For example, William Sydney Porter used the pen name O. Henry when writing his celebrated short stories.

**PSYCHOLOGICAL FICTION:** A type of fiction in which a great deal of attention is paid to the thoughts and feelings of the characters, as opposed to external action. Henry James was well known for his psychological fiction.

**REALISM:** An artistic movement characterized by a desire to portray characters and environments as objectively, or as close to reality, as possible. Realism relies heavily upon physical descriptions, and Gustave Flaubert's novel *Madame Bovary* (1856)—with its almost grotesque precision to detail—is considered a landmark work of realism. Prominent American realists include Mark Twain and Edith Wharton.

**ROMAN À CLEF:** A literary work containing fictionalized depictions of real people and events. The work may be autobiographical, as in Sylvia Plath's *The Bell Jar* (1963), or it may refer to thinly disguised versions of well-known people, as in Truman Capote's *Answered Prayers* (1987).

**ROMANTICISM:** An artistic and philosophical movement that developed throughout Europe in the late eighteenth and early nineteenth centuries, and was popular in the United States throughout the nineteenth century (thought it reached its peak near the middle of the century). Romantic literature is notable for its expression of powerful emotions and use of natural settings. The work of Walt Whitman, Ralph Waldo Emerson, and Harriet Beecher Stowe is considered Romantic.

**SATIRE:** A type of literature intended to attack a person, group, institution, or idea through parody or irony. Very often, the satirist exposes the shortcomings of its subject by ironically expressing a position in support or praise of the subject. Benjamin Franklin, Stephen Crane, and Dorothy Parker are a few of the many American writers known for their satires.

**SERIAL PUBLICATION:** The printing of consecutive portions of a novel or other lengthy work of literature in successive issues of a periodical. Some of Mark Twains's works were first printed through serial publication.

**SOCIAL REALISM:** An artistic movement of the nineteenth century defined by sympathetic yet realistic depictions of the working class and the poor conditions in which they lived. Upton Sinclair's 1906 novel *The Jungle* is an example of social realism.

**SONNET (ELIZABETHAN):** A poetic form typically consisting of fourteen ten-syllable lines and an alternating rhyme scheme. William Shakespeare is perhaps the most famous practitioner of English-language sonnets.

**SOUTHERN GOTHIC FICTION:** A type of Gothic fiction (see definition) in which grotesque, supernatural, melodramatic, and mysterious elements are deployed for the sake of exploring the culture of the American South. Prominent authors of Southern Gothic literature include Flannery O'Connor, William Faulkner, Carson McCullers, and Tennessee Williams.

**STREAM OF CONSCIOUSNESS:** A literary technique meant to emulate the flow of thought in a character's mind. This is sometimes expressed through disjointed or run-on sentences, repetitions of words or phrases, or tenuous associations between different subjects. Notable works that use the stream of consciousness technique include *The Sound and the Fury* (1929) by William Faulkner and *On the Road* (1957) by Jack Kerouac.

**SURREALISM:** An artistic movement of the early twentieth century noted for its embrace of the irrational. Surrealist literary works often contained jarring juxtapositions of unrelated things, seemingly random or nonsensical phrases, and dreamlike situations. William Burroughs is considered a surrealist.

**TRAGEDY:** In classical Greek drama, a play that focuses on themes such as love, fate and betrayal, and does not end happily for one or more of the main characters. The play *Antigone* (c. 442 B.C.E.) by Sophocles is a typical Greek tragedy. Eugene O'Neill wrote several famous tragedies that drew heavily on ancient Greek models.

**TRANSCENDENTALISM:** A philosophical movement that originated in New England in the first half of the nineteenth century, Transcendentalism prized individualism and forwarded the idea that each individual has the ability to achieve a transcendent spirituality by communing with nature and remaining true to his or her essential self.

**VERNACULAR:** The casual and natural speech of a group of people or culture. Mark Twain's 1884 novel *Adventures of Huckleberry Finn* makes masterful use of the American vernacular of the 1830s.

# Index

B

**B**

**C**

**D**

**E**

**F**

**G**

**H**

**H**

I-J

**K**

**N**

O

P

**Q-R**

**R**

**S**

**S**

**T**

**U-W**

**W**

Y-Z

# Nationality/Ethnicity Index